# HENRY

T0334944

David Carpenter is professor of medieval history at King's College London. He is the author of numerous books, including the widely acclaimed *Henry III: The Rise to Power and Personal Rule, 1207–1258*, the first volume of this biography, published by Yale, and a new study of the Magna Carta published by Penguin Classics.

# HENRY III

Reform, Rebellion, Civil War, Settlement
1258–1272

David Carpenter

YALE UNIVERSITY PRESS
NEW HAVEN AND LONDON

First published in paperback in 2024

For information about this and other Yale University Press publications, please contact:
U.S. Office:   sales.press@yale.edu   yalebooks.com
Europe Office:   sales@yaleup.co.uk   yalebooks.co.uk

Set in Baskerville by IDSUK (DataConnection) Ltd
Printed in Denmark by Nørhaven

Library of Congress Control Number: 2024933666

ISBN 978-0-300-24805-0 (hbk)
ISBN 978-0-300-27933-7 (pbk)

A catalogue record for this book is available from the British Library.

10 9 8 7 6 5 4 3 2 1

*To Jane, Katie and James,*
*and in memory of my parents*

# CONTENTS

# ILLUSTRATIONS AND MAPS

## PLATES

1. The shield of Simon de Montfort in the choir of Westminster Abbey. © Dean and Chapter of Westminster.
2. The seal of Eleanor de Montfort. © Bibliothèque nationale de France, Département des Manuscrits, Clairambault 1188.
3. Henry III's proclamation announcing the authority of the council in 1258. © Oxfordshire History Centre (OCA4/1/A1/58).
4. Henry bearing the coffin of Louis IX's son in Paris. © Bibliothèque Nationale, Paris, Department of Manuscripts, Clairambault 632.
5. The ruling council's ratification of the peace with France, October 1259. © Archives Nationales de France (J 629 / 10).
6. The battlefield of Lewes. By kind permission of The Sussex Archaeological Society.
7. English Heritage reconstruction drawing of Kenilworth castle. © Historic England Archive (IC053_028).
8. The chapter house of Westminster Abbey. © Dean and Chapter of Westminster.
9. Charter, 1265. © Herefordshire Record Office (BG/11/15/6).
10. Henry III's itinerary before the battle of Evesham. © The National Archives.
11. The mutilation of Simon de Montfort's body at the battle of Evesham. © British Library Board. All Rights Reserved / Bridgeman Images.
12. The Douce Apocalypse. CC by NC 4.0. © Bodleian Libraries, University of Oxford.
13. Vault of Westminster Abbey. © Paul Grover / Alamy.
14. Westminster Abbey's Cosmati pavement. © Dean and Chapter of Westminster.
15. Centre stone of Westminster Abbey's Cosmati pavement. © Dean and Chapter of Westminster.
16. *Coronation of Edward the Confessor*, as copied by Charles Stothard, 1819. Yale Center for British Art, Paul Mellon Collection (B1977.14.22593).
17. Sketch of Henry III's head on memoranda roll of the exchequer, 1266–7. © The National Archives.
18. King Edward, from the sedilia of Westminster Abbey. © Dean and Chapter of Westminster.

19. King Henry, from the sedilia of Westminster Abbey. © Dean and Chapter of Westminster.
20. Shrine of Edward the Confessor and tomb of Henry III. © Greg Funnell 2007. All rights reserved.
21. Engravings of a queen and young woman. © Dean and Chapter of Westminster.
22. Henry III's head from the effigy on his tomb in Westminster Abbey. © Dean and Chapter of Westminster.

## MAPS

# PREFACE

Volume 1 of this biography ended with the parliament of April 1258 when an armed march on Westminster Hall forced Henry III to accept reform of the realm. Volume 2 continues from that point and takes the story to Henry's death in 1272. Although it covers only fourteen years of the reign as opposed to volume 1's over forty, it is much the same length. I am not conscious of writing at any different pace. It is simply that the years from 1258 are the more packed with incident, indeed politically they are amongst the most dramatic and traumatic periods in English history. After the Westminster parliament, a baronial council took control of the country and promulgated reforms far more revolutionary and wide-ranging than those of Magna Carta in 1215. They were known as the Provisions of Oxford. In 1261, Henry recovered power only to lose it in 1263 to a movement pledged to restore the Provisions. It was led by his brother-in-law, Simon de Montfort, earl of Leicester, one of the greatest figures in English history, venerated and vilified in equal measure. On 14 May 1264 Montfort won a miraculous victory at the battle of Lewes, taking prisoner both Henry and his eldest son, Lord Edward. Thereafter Montfort governed England down to his defeat and death (his body gruesomely mutilated) at the battle of Evesham on 4 August 1265. The royalist victory, however, only brought more war. Henry's government attempted to disinherit Montfort's supporters and the result was two further years of strife. The period between 1263 and 1267 saw widespread destruction. There was a massacre of the Jews in London and attacks on them in other towns. Both sides ravaged the estates and seized the possessions of their enemies. The political community was torn apart in a way unseen again until the 1640s. But in the end the policy of disinheritance was reversed, the wounds of the war closed over and Henry's reign ended in peace.

The period of reform and rebellion between 1258 and 1265 has been accorded great social and constitutional significance, rightly so. Hostility to the king's foreign relations and fear of foreign invasion sharpened and defined a sense of English national identity. In 1263, Simon de Montfort even promulgated a 'statute' expelling aliens from the country, 'never to return'. The political community expanded in size and came to embrace knights, townsmen and peasants as well as earls and barons. Knights representing the counties and burgesses the towns were summoned to Simon de Montfort's parliament of 1265, 'the first parliament with a house of commons'. A precedent was set. The parliaments of Henry's last years were very different in terms of structure from those before 1258. These events were inseparable from political ideas and those ideas were inseparable from religion. Leading churchmen deeply influenced the political actors, none more so than Simon de Montfort himself. That is one reason why the reforms, in a unique way, were as much concerned with the malpractices of magnates as with those of the king.

The period created new relationships between England and its neighbours, although they were not to last. The Treaty of Paris in 1259, with Henry resigning his claims to Normandy, Anjou and Poitou, while accepting he held Gascony as a fief from the king of France, reshaped the political structure of Europe and ushered in thirty-five years of Anglo-French peace. The treaty of Montgomery in 1267 set up a new political structure in Wales, with the ruler of Gwynedd, Llywelyn ap Gruffudd, being recognized as its prince. Scotland, meanwhile, was left to itself. King Alexander III, thanks to the good relations fostered by Henry before 1258, behaved very differently from his father in the rebellion against King John. Alexander II had sided with the barons. Alexander III was about to send forces to Henry's aid when forestalled by news of Evesham. There was equally no repeat of the interaction between English and Irish politics seen both under King John and in the crisis of 1233–4.

The political revolution robbing Henry of power means he is less central to volume 2 than to volume 1. In 1258–9 the great reform of the realm, its ambitions, motivations and achievements, holds the stage. Thereafter, the story is increasingly dominated by Simon de Montfort, one of the few medieval nobles whose character and ideas shine forth from abundant source material. Henry also comes to be overshadowed by his eldest son. From 1263, Lord Edward is the essential commander of the royalist cause. The contrast between Henry's inertia and Edward's drive is extreme. Also important was Henry's queen, Eleanor of Provence. Far more steely than her husband, she had much to do with his varying fortunes in 1258, 1261 and 1263. In 1264 she raised an army to invade England after Henry's and Edward's capture at Lewes. Yet, for all the prominence of Simon de Montfort, Lord Edward and the queen, Henry can never be ignored. His will, if exercised spasmodically, often impacted on events. He survived battles and captivity to die peacefully in his bed. By then, he had one great achievement to his credit, the greatest he would have thought of his reign. On 13 October 1269 his new Abbey at Westminster was consecrated and the body of Edward the Confessor translated to its glittering new shrine behind the high altar.

Given their appeal and importance, the years between 1258 and 1267 have been much travelled by historians, far more so than many periods of Henry's personal rule.[1] I could not have written this book without their manifold and great labours. Many have shared with me the fruits of so far

---

[1] A clear and concise account can be found in Adrian Jobson's *The First English Revolution: Simon de Montfort, Henry III and the Barons' War*.

unpublished research. I thank them all in the following pages. If, nonetheless, I have missed or misapplied the work of fellow scholars, I apologize. As I said in the introduction to volume 1, every time I read something new or look again at something old, I find material I wish to include. But that would make a long book even longer. I fear I remain an academic rather than a popular historian, more concerned to delve down into the detail than to think how to get the reader to turn the page. But I trust the uniqueness and drama of the story will carry the reader through, or at least encourage reading a part here, a part there (the chapters are divided into sections), rather as I dip into Jacques Le Goff's 1,000-page biography of Henry's brother-in-law Saint Louis, although that certainly is a very different book.

It is somewhat daunting to realize that forty years have passed since I signed up to write the biography of Henry III in what was then the Methuen English Monarchs series. I do not regret the delay. After all it gives me less time to learn I have got it all wrong! More seriously, had the book come out around 1990, as first intended, it would have been far less rich. That is very much due to the work of so many fellow historians in the intervening years. It is also because I hope I have gained a deeper understanding of the primary sources. These enable the day-to-day politics of the reign to be traced in unprecedented detail, which is fortunate for me as I have always been fascinated by events, by the 'what happened next and why' in history.[2] I think also, over the years, I have gained a greater appreciation of how Henry's story opens a window onto the wider culture of the age. This is why, as well as giving them separate treatment in volume 1, I have tried to graft Henry's piety and artistic patronage into the political narrative throughout, like the shells in a shaft of Purbeck marble. To the narrative in volume 2, I have added two thematic chapters. One, 'Henry and his People', looks at the light shed on his personal rule by all the complaints made against royal and baronial officials in 1258–9. The other, 'Montfort's Kingdom', considers the material and ideological basis for the great earl's revolutionary regime.[3] I have also included a Glossary explaining some of the terms appearing in the book.

[2] It would have been impossible for Jacques Le Goff to have written the same kind of detailed narrative of the reign of Saint Louis, not that he would have wanted to do so anyway.

[3] I salute here the unnamed heroes who produced so much of the source material of the reign, namely the royal clerks who wrote up the rolls of the chancery, the exchequer and the law courts. The chancery rolls alone, recording the king's charters and letters (as published now either in full Latin transcription or in English calendar), run to over 14,500 pages. The translations of the Henry III fine rolls by Paul Dryburgh and Beth Hartland, placed online by the Henry III fine rolls project (www.finerollshenry3.org.uk), run to around two million words. No wonder the clerks occasionally lightened their labours by including marginal drawings, doggerel poems and such remarks as 'every man the first good wine (*omnis homo primum bonum vinum*)', thus adapting Christ's observation that every man serves the best wine first (John 2:10): TNA E 159/31, m. 8d (image 0101). Illustrations of marginalia are brought together in Hershey, *Drawings*.

In the process of seeing the book through to publication, I have incurred many debts. One is to Stephen Church and Michael Prestwich, who read a draft of the book for Yale and made many valuable suggestions.[4] The book has also benefited from being read by Richard Cassidy, Adrian Jobson and my brother, Michael Carpenter. Richard has produced the Index, while Adrian has compiled the Bibliography and put the footnotes into consistent form. As with volume 1, the text has been copy-edited by Richard Mason, its clarity and consistency being much improved by his eagle-eyed expertise.

At Yale I owe a great debt to Heather McCallum, who has kept faith with Henry III over very many years. The two volumes of this biography would not have appeared without her encouragement and support. Her colleagues Rachael Lonsdale, Katie Urquart and Meg Pettit have all worked on the book, while Heather Nathan and James Williams have looked after marketing and publicity. As with volume 1, the proofreader was Chris Shaw and the maps were drawn by Martin Brown. I am grateful to them all.

I thank Matthew Payne, Tony Trowles and Christine Reynolds for all their help in the Library and Muniment Room at Westminster Abbey and Jessica Nelson and Paul Dryburgh for their help at The National Archives. Throughout the years I have been inspired and sustained by the very many undergraduates, MA students and doctoral students who have worked with me on the reign of Henry III. I have been sustained and inspired too by the congenial environment created by my colleagues in the History Department at King's. Daniel Hadas has continued to help me with both Latin translations and questions of theology. Alice Taylor I thank as before. Thanks to Amicie Pélissié du Rausas for locating image 4 of the plate section; additionally map 2 is based on one drawn by Amicie.

The book is dedicated to my wife Jane and my children Katie and James.

As I walk round Westminster Abbey, admire the beauty of the south transept and see the heads of Henry and Eleanor in the muniment room and the sculpture of the smiling craftsman in the triforium, I reflect that my lease on these has now all too short a date. I feel the same when reading through the letters on the chancery rolls, those letters taking us so close to the personality and outlook of the king. But the lease will pass, has passed, on to others. I hope they will have as much fun studying the reign of Henry III as I have done.

David A. Carpenter
King's College London, July 2022

[4] Inspired by Michael's information about the fish (when commenting on volume 1), I have now sampled lampreys. They taste like beef stew and are thus an excellent meat substitute. One can understand why Henry and Eleanor thought other fish 'insipid'. For the recipe (cooked by Claire Gaskell), see https://worldoffinewine.com/2021/10/21/at-the-table-lamproie-a-la-bordelaise. The lampreys came, however, from the Dordogne, not, as with Henry, the Severn.

# A NOTE ON THE TEXT

## MONEY AND ITS VALUE

In the reign of Henry III, save for a brief period in the 1250s when he launched a gold coinage, there was only one coin of the realm, namely the silver penny, or in Latin '*denarius*'. Although amounts of money were frequently expressed in terms of pounds (Latin '*libra*'), shillings (Latin '*solidus*') and pence (hence l. s. d.), pounds and shillings were terms of account. There were no pound or shilling coins. There were 240 pennies in a pound, 12 pennies in a shilling and 20 shillings in a pound. Another term of account was 'mark', worth two-thirds of a pound, so 13s 4d or 160 pennies. Rather than convert all money into pounds, shillings and pence, I have for the most part followed the contemporary sources in using sometimes pounds and sometimes marks, so having 100 marks rather than the cumbersome £66 13s 4d. Unless otherwise stated all money is expressed in terms of these English values.

In Henry's reign a day's wage for a male labourer was 1½d and for a female 1d. When Henry III fed paupers, the cost was usually between 1d and 1½d per head per day. Bread came in half- or quarter-penny loaves. (It was lawful to cut the silver penny into halves and quarters.) The day's wage for a professional knight was 24d or 2s. In 1244 landholders with incomes of £20 a year were obliged to take up knighthood. In 1256 the level was lowered to £15. Many barons had incomes of several hundred pounds a year. The annual income of an earl could be several thousands. After it had recovered from collapse in the 1215–1217 civil war, the ordinary annual income of the crown was around £25,000 a year.[1]

## FOOTNOTES AND BIBLIOGRAPHY

In the footnotes, works by contemporary authors appear for the most part under either the name of the author (so Paris, short for Matthew Paris) or, in the case of chronicles where the author is unknown, under the name of the place where the chronicle was written (so Dunstable). Record sources are cited by an abbreviated form of the published title (so *CR*, with the

---

[1] For standards of living, see C. Dyer, *Standards of Living in the Later Middle Ages: Social Change in England c.1200–1520* (Cambridge, 1989).

relevant dates, for *Close Rolls*). Full references to all these sources may be found in the Bibliography. In references to unprinted sources, BL stands for the British Library, TNA for The National Archives at Kew and WAM for Westminster Abbey Muniments. Other archival references are given in full. Secondary sources are cited by the surname of the author and a short form of the title of the work, italicized in the case of books, within inverted commas in the case of articles and chapters in volumes of essays. Full details may be found in the Bibliography under the name of the author. I have stuck to the division between primary and secondary sources although many printed primary sources have important introductions by their editors.

## PERSONAL NAMES

In the case of toponymic surnames, the modern form of the place has been given preceded by 'of', so Warin of Bassingbourn. The exceptions are where this would overturn established usage, so Gilbert de Clare not Gilbert of Clare. If the place is in France, the modern form is given preceded by 'de', but again exceptions are made where this contradicts established usage, so Robert de Ferrers, not de Ferrières. Where places have not been identified, a common contemporary form is used preceded by 'de'. In general, I have tried to follow the forms found in the translations of the fine rolls: https://finerollshenry3.org.uk/home.html

For the paperback edition I have corrected some mistakes pointed out by kind readers. The only substantial change is to p. 556 where I have re-written a paragraph about the ascent to the Confessor's shrine in Westminster Abbey.

1. Wales in the 1250s and 1260s

Chapter 1

# REVOLUTION AND REFORM
## 1258–1259

In April 1258 a great parliament met at Westminster. Its climax came on 30 April when a group of barons marched into Westminster Hall and confronted King Henry III. Although they left their swords at the entrance to the Hall, they were in full armour. Henry appreciated at once the novelty and menace of this demonstration. 'What is this, my lords, am I, poor wretch, your prisoner?' he cried out. The answer was 'no' but he must now accept a baronially led reform of the realm.[1] The revolution of 1258 had begun.

What had brought to this perilous pass a king famed for his personal piety, a king who had given many years of peace to the country and quite lacked the cruelty and malevolence of his father, King John? It is not difficult to answer the question. Henry's open-handed patronage of his foreign relations, first the Savoyard uncles of his queen, Eleanor of Provence, and then his own Lusignan half-brothers from Poitou, had created factional struggles at court he quite lacked the skill and authority to control.[2] Added to this, there was the failure of Henry's 1257 campaign in Wales and worse, far worse, the folly of his scheme to place his second son, Edmund, on the throne of Sicily. This involved agreeing to pay the pope £90,000 for the offer of the throne and, once this was paid, sending an army to conquer Sicily from its Hohenstaufen ruler. Henry was told, quite rightly, that the terms were utterly impossible and illustrated both his 'simplicity' and his readiness to forge ahead without the realm's counsel and consent. Nonetheless at the Westminster parliament Henry had demanded a gigantic tax to pursue the project, while a papal envoy had threatened the realm with an interdict if it was not conceded.

[1] Volume 1, 696.
[2] The queen's uncles were the brothers of her mother, Beatrice, a daughter of the count of Savoy. Of them, Peter of Savoy became lord of Richmond in Yorkshire and Pevensey in Sussex while Boniface became archbishop of Canterbury. The king's half-brothers were the children of his mother Isabella of Angoulême's second marriage to Hugh, lord of Lusignan in Poitou and count of La Marche. Two of the brothers settled in England, the youngest, Aymer, who became bishop-elect of Winchester, and William de Valence who, besides Hertford castle and other lands, gained, through marriage, Pembroke in Wales. Two other brothers, Guy and Geoffrey de Lusignan, made frequent visits to England and were given wardships and money pensions.

Alongside these problems of patronage and policy, there were other reasons for Henry's isolation. For all his piety, he had alienated the church, most recently by allowing its taxation by the pope in the Sicilian cause. There was also dissatisfaction with the king's rule throughout the counties of England. Unlike his brother-in-law King Louis IX of France, Henry had done little to reform the running of local government. Denied significant taxation from parliament, he had demanded more and more money from his sheriffs and justices, thus making them increasingly unpopular. Equally unpopular were the local officials of leading magnates, both native and foreign, something Henry lamented but did nothing about. Indeed, his protection, or so it was believed, obstructed the bringing of lawsuits against those in his favour. During the Westminster parliament itself, he was accused of refusing justice to the magnate John fitzGeoffrey when John complained about the king's half-brother Aymer de Lusignan, bishop-elect of Winchester. This was one of the triggers of the revolution.[3]

Taking all this together, it was easy by 1258 to think that Henry was incapable of effective rule and had reduced the realm, as the barons put it, to an 'imbecilic state'.

What made this more serious for the king was that criticisms of his rule were expressed and remedies propounded at an institution new both in name and power. This was parliament.[4] Of course kings had always summoned the great and good of the land to give them counsel. Under the Anglo-Saxon kings such assemblies had been called witans, under the Anglo-Norman and Angevin, 'councils' or 'great councils'. The name parliament arrived in the 1230s and stuck. It was more than just a new name for an old institution. It reflected the fact that such assemblies were radically new in terms of their power. This was because the king, for the first time in English history, wished, on a regular basis, to supplement his ordinary revenues with levies of general taxation. Thanks to all the gifts of Henry's predecessors, royal income from land was much diminished. Magna Carta had made it more difficult to exploit other sources of revenue. If Henry was to pursue great projects, if he was to recover his lost continental empire or conquer Sicily, he needed general taxation. But both practical politics and the stipulations of the 1215 Magna Carta meant such taxes required the consent of parliament. In the 1240s and 1250s, Henry had gone again and again to parliament and asked for taxation. Again and again he had been refused save on terms he deemed unacceptable.[5] The great lever of parliamentary power down the ages, control over taxation, thus appeared for the first time in real action. It was the demand for a tax at the Westminster parliament that brought Henry's regime crashing to the ground.

[3] See volume 1, 688; *SERHB*, i, no. 5.
[4] The classic work on parliament is John Maddicott's *The Origins of the English Parliament.*
[5] See volume 1, 758 (the index under parliament).

The final march on the king's hall was almost certainly masterminded by seven magnates who had leagued themselves together earlier in the parliament. They were Richard de Clare, earl of Gloucester and Hertford, Roger Bigod, earl of Norfolk, Simon de Montfort, earl of Leicester, Peter of Savoy, Hugh Bigod (Roger Bigod's brother), John fitzGeoffrey and Peter de Montfort (no relation of Simon, though, as we will see, a close ally).[6] All, save Roger Bigod, had been on the king's council before 1258, so this was very much a revolution within the court of Henry III. The seven were determined to bring down the Lusignans, take over the government of the realm and carry through, to some degree at least, a wider programme of reform. The fact that Queen Eleanor's uncle Peter of Savoy was one of the seven showed that the queen herself sympathized with the revolution. It would, she hoped, lay low her Lusignan enemies and prevent them allying (a particular anxiety) with the heir to the throne, her son Lord Edward.[7]

The ensuing revolution was unprecedented in its scope and scale. The king was stripped of power and a baronial council took over the government of the country. This was far more revolutionary than Magna Carta in 1215, which had placed all kinds of restrictions on King John but left him in control of central government and free to appoint whom he liked as his ministers. The revolution also overhauled the running of local government, with measures focusing on the abuses of magnates as well as those of the king. Here, too, '1258' was very different from '1215'. The intended beneficiaries were knights, free tenants and even peasants. The political community was expanding in size. The foundations were being laid for the summoning of knights and burgesses to parliament. Meanwhile, of the major items on Henry III's agenda before the revolution, the campaign in Wales was abandoned by the barons, while the Sicilian project was effectively terminated by the pope, for all Henry's hopes of its revival. The peace with France, however, went ahead. So, in a watershed moment in European history, Henry abandoned claims to his lost continental empire and did homage to Louis IX for Gascony, his one remaining continental possession.

Given the years 1258–9 are amongst the most charged and complex in English history, I have divided my account between the next three chapters. In this I outline the development of the reforms and consider how the barons were able to achieve so much. In chapter 2 I discuss baronial motives and in particular those of Simon de Montfort. Chapter 3 looks at the place of the king, queen and Lord Edward in the ongoing revolution, while chapter 4 is about the peace with France.

---

[6] Bémont, *Simon de Montfort*, 327. I give the names in the order found in the text of the alliance.

[7] For the style 'Lord Edward', see volume 1, 503 n. 76.

## JUNE 1258: THE OXFORD PARLIAMENT

The Westminster parliament closed in early May. The Oxford parliament, where the reforms were to begin, was due to meet on 9 June. In the interval, Henry went to Winchester, where he celebrated Whitsun, and then to Clarendon and Marlborough. These were the last days of the old court. The king had with him the Poitevins William de Sancta Ermina, Guy de Rochefort, Elyas de Rabayne and, from an older generation, the keeper of the wardrobe, Peter de Rivallis. All were soon to be swept from his side – Sancta Ermina, Rochefort and Rabayne indeed swept from England.

Henry had reason to be apprehensive. At the Westminster parliament, Roger Bigod, earl of Norfolk, had demanded the removal of his Poitevin half-brothers and the surrender of his seal. Henry knew his powers of patronage would be restricted. On 1 June he promised Alice, widow of Edmund de Lacy, the wardship of her late husband's lands on condition the Oxford parliament agreed.[8] Around the same time, the exchequer official John le Francis acknowledged the chancery might not 'dare' issue the letters he sought 'on account of the twenty-four', the twenty-four men, that is, who were to reform the realm.[9] On this point Henry had already given way. Having agreed to reform at the Westminster parliament, he had wanted to carry it through *himself* by Christmas, counselled simply by unspecified 'faithful men' and by a (doubtlessly friendly) papal legate. Instead, he had accepted reform would be the work 'as they see best' of twenty-four men meeting in June at a parliament in Oxford. Of these twenty-four he had chosen twelve, but the other twelve were to be chosen by the opposition barons.[10]

While at Winchester for Whitsun, Henry bestowed gifts on the local friars and the prior of the cathedral. Thinking back to Westminster, he ordered the tomb in the Abbey of his beloved daughter Katherine to be covered with a silken cloth. At the same time, the paintings both in his chamber and that of William de Sancta Ermina were to be cleaned.[11] Was Henry also plotting armed resistance with his Poitevin half-brothers? Certainly Aymer de Lusignan, bishop-elect of Winchester, now asked the Hampshire knight William de Lisle, 'since we have special trust in your fidelity', to join him at Oxford with horses and arms.[12] On 25 May Henry himself ordered eleven Burgundian knights to be given their pay and sent on to the Oxford parliament. At the end of the month, the most famous

---

[8] *CPR 1247–58*, 632. Alice, daughter of the marquis of Saluzzo, was the widow of Edmund de Lacy, heir to the earldom of Lincoln.

[9] TNA SC 1/7/16.

[10] See volume 1, 697.

[11] *CR 1256–9*, 222.

[12] Gonville and Caius College Cambridge, MS 205, fo. 303v; Sayles, *Functions of the Medieval Parliament*, 64.

of Henry's household knights, Nicholas de Molis, he who had won a war in Gascony and marched through the length of Wales, suddenly appeared at court. Already castellan of Dover and sheriff of Kent, he was now made warden of the Cinque Ports. He was ideally placed to bring foreign soldiers into the country. Henry's household knights, combined with the retinues of William de Valence and Lord Edward, might amount to a significant force. There was some overlap between the three groups. Roger of Leybourne, destined to play a vigorous and violent part in events to come, featured in all three.[13]

Henry finally left Marlborough on 7 June. On the eleventh he celebrated the feast of St Barnabas at Abingdon abbey.[14] On the twelfth, three days late, he arrived in Oxford for the opening of the parliament. If he was reluctant to appear, it was no wonder. The atmosphere was fevered. He found the barons gathered in the house of the Dominican friars and already busy drawing up plans for reform.[15] They had come in arms, ostensibly for the campaign in Wales planned to follow the parliament, in reality because they feared the king and his 'Poitevin brothers' were going to resist the reforms and were summoning help from abroad. So much is said by Matthew Paris, the great chronicler at St Albans abbey, now entering the last phase of his career.[16] The fear, as we have seen, had some foundation. Civil war was close. How Henry must have wished his brother, Richard, earl of Cornwall, had been around to exercise his usual skills as a moderator and mediator. But Richard was now king of Germany (or king of the Romans to use his official title) and had been absent from England since 1257. The chronicler Thomas Wykes believed the barons took action in 1258 from fear that king and kingdom would never be guided again by Richard's wise counsels.[17] That may be an exaggeration, but had Richard been present the revolution might have taken a different course.

That the campaign in Wales was merely an excuse for a muster in arms was quickly apparent. As early as 17 June a truce was being arranged with Llywelyn ap Gruffudd, the ruler of Gwynedd, one designed to run all the way through to August 1259.[18] Under its terms, Henry and his men were permitted to 'visit' the castles of Deganwy and Dyserth and send two boats to munition them. If the sea conditions made that impossible, then

---

[13] Around the time of the Westminster parliament, Leybourne received the Easter instalment of the 40-mark annual fee he received from the king: TNA E 403/3114.

R.F. Walker, using the evidence from the liberate rolls, states that in 1257 thirty-nine household knights were in receipt of annual fees: Walker, 'Anglo-Welsh wars', 70.

[14] *Abingdon*, 50.

[15] Nothing now remains of either the house of the Dominicans or the adjoining house of the Franciscans, although foundations, partly excavated, survive under the Westgate shopping centre and adjoining buildings.

[16] Paris, v, 695–6; Burton, 438.

[17] Wykes, 118.

[18] *F*, i, 372 (*CPR 1247–58*, 636).

Llywelyn would allow supplies through from Chester. The truce showed all too clearly that the Four Cantrefs between the Conwy and the Dee, conquered by Henry in the 1240s and then given to Lord Edward, were now almost completely in Llywelyn's hands. The revolutionary regime just let that go. Its priority was reform in England. In Wales, it calculated the marcher barons could look after themselves. The losers from the truce would be the king and Lord Edward.[19] There was no point throwing back Llywelyn in order to strengthen them.

If all those summoned for the Welsh campaign actually appeared, then over 130 tenants-in-chief mustered in Oxford, ranging from earls and barons to men of knightly status.[20] Many more knights must have been present in the retinues of the earls and greater barons. The baronial leaders, therefore, commanded considerable coercive power. The question was whether it would outmatch that being rallied by their enemies. The knights at Oxford were important in another way. Their presence, voicing the discontent in the shires, ensured reform of local government was planned from the start. This was not to be just a court coup and a rearrangement of the king's council. Thus one set of proposals drawn up at Oxford for future legislative reform, although called by historians 'The Petition of the Barons', voiced as well the grievances of local society against the sheriffs and justices in eyre. The Petition also complained that magnates had oppressed lesser men by buying up the debts that the latter owed the Jews.[21]

Another factor affecting the composition of the Oxford parliament gave the barons the freer rein. This was the absence of the bishops. With one exception, that of Fulk Basset of London, they were not prepared to intervene on Henry's side.[22] At the Westminster parliament itself they had withdrawn rather than do anything to prevent the king's coercion. Their abstention was hardly surprising given the church's sufferings during Henry's rule. Apart from the Sicilian taxation, there were resentments over the king's interference with the appointment of bishops, his exploitation of vacant sees during the resulting disputes and his challenge to the church's jurisdictional privileges, all, so it was said, in breach of Magna Carta.[23] The archbishop of Canterbury, meanwhile, the queen's uncle

---

[19] Two marchers on the baronial twelve and council of fifteen, the earl of Hereford and Roger de Mortimer, were not apparently at Oxford. Presumably they were busy in Wales.

[20] Maddicott, *Simon de Montfort*, 157.

[21] *DBM*, no. 3, esp. pp. 86–7, cap. 25.

[22] For a full analysis of why the bishops did not join the revolution, see Ambler, *Bishops in the Political Community*, ch. 5. Ambler (pp. 108–12) argues convincingly that the bishops did not promulgate a sentence of excommunication at Oxford against those who opposed the reforms. Such a sentence was rather promulgated in October 1259 in support of the Provisions of Westminster.

[23] See volume 1, 216, 434–5 (where I discuss how so pious a king could offend the church), and 460–1.

Boniface of Savoy, far from siding with the king, condoned or at least accepted the revolution in the hope of besting his Lusignan enemies.

If, however, the bishops gave no help to the king, only Walter de Cantilupe of Worcester was an out-and-out baronial partisan. When it came to the church's grievances, the bishops had decided to go it alone rather than look to the barons for help. They knew the latter had little sympathy for their jurisdictional claims. After the Westminster parliament Archbishop Boniface had convened a church council to meet at Merton in Surrey on 6 June. It drew up a series of provisions and promulgated numerous sentences of excommunication against those who violated the church's liberties.[24] After the council finished on 8 June, very few of those present seem to have come on to the Oxford parliament. Only the bishops of Worcester and London were certainly there. A memorandum drawn up at the parliament about reforms to be promulgated simply said that the twenty-four would 'amend the state of the church . . . as soon as they can find time'.[25] They never did. This does not mean churchmen were unenthusiastic about the reforms. But, for the moment, they were mostly outside the episcopal bench. Later this was to change. A new group of bishops, appointed in and after 1258, was to give passionate support to Simon de Montfort's cause.

## THE REVIVAL OF THE JUSTICIARSHIP

The first thing done by the Oxford parliament was to appoint a chief justiciar. So at last the office was revived.[26] There had been no justiciar since 1234, in part because the great council at Gloucester, sweeping away the remnants of the regime of Peter des Roches, had not filled the post. The council doubtless remembered the way the justiciar Hubert de Burgh (in charge of government from 1219 to 1232) had dominated the king and made a fortune at his expense. Henry himself saw no reason to revive the office for much the same reason. But gradually, faced with the defects of his rule, the political community coveted a great official who would hear everyone's complaints and give justice to all. Hence the demands at parliament after parliament in the 1240s and 1250s for the office's revival.

The person selected as justiciar was Hugh Bigod, a good choice.[27] Born in or before 1220, Hugh was acceptable to the king, or as acceptable as possible in the circumstances. He was on the council before the revolution

---

[24] C&S, ii, 568–85; Hoskin, 'Natural law, protest and the English episcopate', 86.

[25] DBM, 106–7, cap. 12.

[26] For the office, see volume 1, 453, 459. The documents relating to the provisions drawn up at Oxford and later in 1258 are discussed in Clementi, 'The documentary evidence for the crisis of government in England in 1258', and Valente, 'The Provisions of Oxford'.

[27] For Hugh, see Hershey, 'Success or failure?' Hugh Bigod and judicial reform during the baronial movement'; Hershey's introductions to SESK, xxiii–xxxvii, and SERHB, i, pp. xviii–xxiv; Brand, 'Hugh Bigod'; and Knowles, 'The justiciarship in England'.

and remained on good terms with Henry thereafter. In May, with the king still a free agent, he helped draw up the replies to the pope's Sicilian proposals and was appointed as one of the ambassadors going out to Louis IX. At Oxford itself Henry's half of the twenty-four chose him as one of the electors of the new ruling council. Yet Hugh was absolutely committed to the revolution. He was part of the original confederation of seven magnates formed at the Westminster parliament. He was the brother of Roger Bigod, earl of Norfolk, and the brother-in-law of John fitzGeoffrey. Later he appears as an executor of Earl Richard de Clare's will. His marriage (by February 1244) to Joan de Stuteville, widow of Baldwin Wake, made him powerful in his own right. He enjoyed a life interest in Joan's baronies of Cottingham in Yorkshire and Liddell Strength in Cumberland. He also controlled, until the heir, Baldwin, came of age in 1259, the Wake barony of Bourne in Lincolnshire.[28] From his mother, a daughter of the regent, William Marshal, he had gained Bosham in Sussex. As a member of the king's council before 1258, Hugh knew how law and government worked. He was also a good man of business, having paid off steadily the 10,000-mark fine made by his wife for custody of the lands of her first husband.[29] Matthew Paris applauded Hugh's appointment. He was 'a native of the land of the English' and a famous knight, skilled in the law, who would vigorously execute the office of justiciar and uphold the rights of the realm.[30]

Although Hugh, in the mode of previous justiciars, came to act as the king's chief minister, at Oxford he was given a more specific brief, one reflecting exactly why parliaments had called for the office's revival. Hugh was to remedy the abuses of lesser officials and give justice to everyone. To render him immune from bribes, he was given a salary of 1,000 marks a year. 'It is right that the king should pay his justices . . . sufficiently so that they have no need to accept anything from anyone else', declared the plan of reform.[31] The barons certainly expected Hugh to remedy their own grievances, but at Oxford procedures were also worked out whereby Hugh could address local grievances as well. So four knights were to be appointed in each county to sit in the county court and record all complaints against sheriffs, bailiffs and everyone else. The complaints were to be enrolled

---

[28] Joan was the sole heir of Nicholas II de Stuteville. Baldwin Wake was her heir but, under English custom, Hugh Bigod had a life interest in the baronies, having a child by Joan (the future Roger Bigod, earl of Norfolk). For Joan and the marriage, see Wilkinson, 'Reformers and royalists: aristocratic women in politics', 154–5, 158–9.

[29] Joan's fine for the wardship (and also to marry whom she wished, presumably Hugh) was made in 1242: *CFR 1241–2*, no. 105. The regular payments can be traced in the Yorkshire section of the pipe rolls. Since Hugh's brother, Roger Bigod, was childless after many years of marriage, Hugh was heir to the earldom of Norfolk.

[30] Paris, v, 698.

[31] *DBM*, 102–3, cap. 6; 106–9, caps. 13, 16; *CLR 1251–60*, 446. The king had paid salaries to his senior judges before 1258 and these continued.

hundred by hundred, ready to be heard and determined by Hugh Bigod on his arrival in the county. This was the first reference to procedure by 'complaint', '*querela*'. More than anything else it enabled Hugh Bigod to right the wrongs that people were suffering.

## PLANS TO REFORM THE SHERIFF'S OFFICE

One other local reform planned at Oxford related to the office of sheriff, a vital issue for local society.[32] The sheriff was the king's chief local agent, appointed to run a county or group of counties. Answerable to the exchequer at Westminster, he collected the debts owed the king by individuals and answered every year for a sum of money known as 'the farm', a sum derived largely from the proceeds of pleas in the county and hundreds courts and from various traditional payments like 'sheriff's aid'. The sheriff also arrested criminals, summoned juries and executed judicial verdicts. He employed a large staff of clerks and sergeants and often controlled the county castle.

The king expected the sheriff above all to look after the interests of the crown, especially when it came to raising money. He could also stress (most notably in a speech made in 1250) that the sheriff should treat justly the people in his charge.[33] That of course was very much the view of the people themselves. The problem was how to strike a balance between the two responsibilities. In the reforms of 1236 something like that had been attempted. The sheriffs appointed had been important local knights, just as the counties wanted. They had been given allowances for their expenses and sworn an oath not to accept rewards.[34] But as the king's financial position worsened in the 1240s and 1250s, these standards were not maintained.[35] The sheriffs, or so it was believed, ceased to be 'prudent and knowledgeable knights of their counties' and were instead 'men coming from far away and utter strangers in the counties'.[36] Whether they continued to take the oath of 1236 is unknown.[37] They certainly no longer received expenses, and were made to answer for higher and higher sums – 'increments' – above the traditional county farms.

---

[32] Collingwood, 'Royal finance', ch. 3, has a full discussion of the reform of the shrieval office.

[33] See volume 1, 528–30.

[34] For the reforms of 1236, see volume 1, 191–2.

[35] For discussion of the tensions between the sheriffs' fiscal accountability at the exchequer, on the one hand, and their accountability to local communities, on the other, see Sabapathy, *Officers and Accountability*, 113–20, 132–4.

[36] *DBM*, 274–7, cap.6. This is the allegation in the statement of the baronial case made to Louis IX in 1264.

[37] Matthew Paris says the oath soon lost its force: Paris, *HA*, ii, 389. In 1253 there is a reference to the customary oath taken by the sheriff on entering office but without any indication of its nature: *CR 1251–3*, 385. I owe these references to Richard Cassidy.

The barons at Oxford planned to put this right in ways reminiscent of the reforms of 1236. So the sheriffs were to be 'vavasours' of their shires, that is, major county knights. The increments were to be abolished and once again the sheriffs were to receive allowances for their expenses.[38] As a further bar against corruption, they were to hold office only for a year. Later a new oath of office was devised. None of these proposed reforms should have been anathema to Henry. Indeed, had he possessed more drive and sense, he would have carried them through himself before 1258. It was quite different when it came to the reform of the king's council.

## THE RULING COUNCIL

On 22 June, at Oxford, Henry gave permission for the election of the new council to proceed.[39] Under the agreed procedure, his own twelve chose the Bigod brothers from the twelve of the barons. The baronial twelve chose from the king's twelve the clerk, John Mansel (Henry's most faithful councillor), and John de Plessis, earl of Warwick.[40] These four now chose the new council. For Henry the results were disastrous. Nine of the baronial twelve made the council, where they were joined by the queen's uncles Archbishop Boniface and Peter of Savoy. From Henry's twelve only Mansel and Plessis made the cut.[41] The omission of Fulk Basset, bishop of London, was particularly pointed. 'A noble man of a great family' (in the words of Matthew Paris), Basset was no curial bishop for (with Walter de Cantilupe) he had vigorously opposed taxation of the church for the Sicilian project. He had nonetheless, like Cantilupe, returned to the king's

---

[38] *DBM*, 108–9, cap. 17. As in 1236, this involved the sheriffs accounting for all the revenue they received, the amount over and above the farm being termed 'profit'.

[39] *CPR 1247–58*, 637.

[40] For Mansel and Plessis, see volume 1, 219–21.

[41] The nine were Walter de Cantilupe, bishop of Worcester, Simon de Montfort, Richard de Clare, Roger Bigod, Humphrey de Bohun, Roger de Mortimer, John fitzGeoffrey, Peter de Montfort and Richard de Grey. Only William Bardolph, Hugh Despenser and Hugh Bigod dropped out from the baronial twelve, Hugh Bigod because he was now chief justiciar. The other two members of the council were William de Forz, earl of Aumale, and James of Audley. Both were probably unknown quantities as far as Henry was concerned. Though in receipt of occasional favours (*CR 1256–9*, 5, 59) neither had been much at court before the revolution. Forz (lord of Cockermouth and Holderness) had been sheriff of Cumberland since 1255. He had succeeded his father in 1241 on the payment of a £100 relief in accordance with Magna Carta, of which 100 marks were pardoned: *CFR 1240–1*, no. 751; *CFR 1241–2*, no. 127. For him, see English, *Lords of Holderness*, 49–53, where the degree of grievance over the Chester inheritance may be exaggerated. As English says, perhaps he had a 'docile nature'. Audley, from a knightly family associated with the earls of Chester (see volume 1, 72), succeeded his father, Henry, in 1246. In 1252 he was lord of no fewer than twenty-seven manors in Shropshire and Staffordshire (where Audley itself was), as well as other properties in Wales and Cheshire: *CChR 1226–57*, 409. He was, therefore, a very powerful magnate. In the civil war he was to support the king. For a biography of Audley, see Lloyd, 'James Audley'.

council before the revolution and been prominent at court during the Oxford parliament. He had every right to be on the new council. But, as both Matthew Paris and the Tewkesbury annalist recorded, he had doubts about the revolution so he was out.[42] The reason for his opposition is unknown, but since he was in charge of King Richard's affairs in England, perhaps he argued that nothing should be done without Richard's counsel and consent.[43]

That things went so badly for the king was hardly surprising. Henry's twelve had far less political weight than the baronial twelve, a mark of his isolation. John de Plessis, a Norman by birth, had started his career as a mere household knight and was earl of Warwick simply in right of his wife.[44] Only one fully fledged earl was on Henry's side, John de Warenne of Surrey. He had married Henry's half-sister Alice de Lusignan, and the alliance with the Lusignans had survived Alice's death. That was partly because Warenne was daggers drawn with Peter of Savoy, a man very much 'in' with the revolutionary regime as we will see.[45] Alongside Warenne, Henry had only one English magnate on his side, Fulk Basset himself, who, besides being bishop of London, was head of the High Wycombe branch of the Basset family. The king had too his twenty-three-year-old nephew, Henry, son of King Richard (or Henry of Almain as he was generally called), but, unmarried, he had no resources independent of his absent father. For the rest, the king's twelve included three of his Lusignan half-brothers – Aymer, bishop-elect of Winchester, Guy de Lusignan and William de Valence – and the clerics Richard of Croxley, abbot of Westminster, John Mansel, Henry of Wingham (keeper of the seal), and the king's confessor, John of Darlington.

The baronial twelve had altogether greater weight. They were headed by Walter de Cantilupe, bishop of Worcester, who easily matched Bishop Basset in terms of status and prestige. There were then four English earls – Simon de Montfort, Richard de Clare, Humphrey de Bohun (of Hereford) and Roger Bigod. Next came the great marcher baron Roger de Mortimer, followed by six substantial English magnates – John fitz-Geoffrey, Hugh Bigod, William Bardolph, Richard de Grey, Peter de Montfort and Hugh Despenser, the last three, as we will see, ardent followers of Simon de Montfort.

Making matters worse, Henry's twelve had been weakened by the defection, as he would have seen it, of Richard de Clare. Earl of Gloucester and Hertford, lord of Glamorgan, with great castles at Clare in Suffolk and

---

[42] Paris, v, 705, 747; Tewkesbury, 165. For the differing stances of Cantilupe and Basset, see Ambler, *Bishops in the Political Community*, 118–19. There is a full account of Basset's career in Hoskin, *EEA, London*, xli–li.

[43] *CR 1256–9*, 65. I owe this suggestion to Adrian Jobson.

[44] For the circumstances of his marriage, see volume 1, 265–6.

[45] Warenne's quarrel with Peter is illuminated in Spencer, '"A vineyard without a wall"', 57–64. For a biography, see Waugh, 'John de Warenne'.

Tonbridge in Kent, he was easily the most powerful of the barons at
Oxford. Brought up at court, a leading councillor before the revolution,
and with his son married to a Lusignan, he would surely be on Henry's
side. Henry certainly thought so. As late as 22 June he named Clare as one
of his twelve.[46] He soon found out otherwise. In the surviving lists giving
the names of the twenty-four, Clare appears amongst the baronial twelve
while, doubtless thanks to his defection, Henry's contingent has only eleven
men.[47]

Even before the choice of the new council, the king's supporters were
being edged out from court. At Oxford, royal charters were issued on eight
days between 12 and 21 June. Bishop-elect Aymer, Guy de Lusignan, John
de Warenne and John de Plessis attest none of them. Only on one day
(19 June) do William de Valence and Geoffrey de Lusignan appear.[48] For
the rest, aside from Fulk Basset and John Mansel, the court was dominated
by the members of the baronial twelve who were soon to be on the new
ruling council: Bishop Cantilupe, Montfort, Bigod, Clare, Hugh Bigod,
John fitzGeoffrey, Richard de Grey and Peter de Montfort. Peter of Savoy
was there too, evidently, like the queen, a willing partner to the revolution
and soon to be on the ruling council.[49]

Even worse for Henry than its personnel were the new council's powers.
They amounted to a complete emasculation of royal authority. It was thus
the councillors not the king who were to choose the justiciar, chancellor
and treasurer, the three most senior officials in the kingdom. For the
reformers, control of the chancellor was pivotal because it was through the
charters, letters and writs he issued in the king's name and authenticated
with the great seal that England was governed. A chancellor independent
of the king could act as a brake on the king's irresponsible acts of
patronage. He could also ensure that writs to commence legal actions were
properly issued instead of being denied to those wishing to litigate against
the king's favourites.[50] Ralph de Neville, bishop of Chichester, given the
seal by a great council in 1218 and controlling it for the next twenty years,
was by repute just this type of chancellor. But thereafter the seal had been
held by men, however personally worthy, who had no independent status.
Many were described as king's clerks rather than chancellors. The office
seemed in abeyance. Hence the demand in the 1240s and 1250s that Henry
allow parliament to choose a chancellor was also a demand for the office's
revival. In the event, in 1258 the reformers left Henry's keeper of the seal,

---

[46] *CPR 1247–58*, 637; *DBM*, 100–1, caps. 2–3. It is unclear why Geoffrey de Lusignan was
not one of the king's twelve.

[47] *DBM*, 100–1, cap. 2.

[48] William de Sancta Ermina appeared with them.

[49] *RCWL*, ii, 120–1. Fulk Basset heads the witness lists of all the charters issued between
12 and 20 June.

[50] Both these points were made in a baronial manifesto of 1264: *DBM*, 260–3 cap. 9.

Henry of Wingham, in place, but they made it clear he was now a chancellor responsible to and controlled by the ruling council. Under the oath to be taken, the chancellor was to seal nothing 'on the sole command of the king'. Instead, everything going out under the seal, other than routine writs, would need the council's consent.[51] Another version of the oath required the council's consent to grants of wardships, escheats and money. Henry's distribution of patronage was thus to come specifically under the council's control. Indeed, he could do nothing significant without the council's consent.

How long was this regime to last? The answer, a chilling one for Henry, was a full twelve years.[52] When the council's authority was finally up, Henry would thus be in his sixties, an age reached by only one king (Henry I) since the Norman Conquest. He was quite likely never to rule unfettered again.

## THE PLACE OF PARLIAMENT

The reformers did not envisage ruling alone in oligarchical isolation. For the first time in English history, a defined role was given to parliament.[53] It was to meet three times a year 'to view the state of the realm and deal with the common business of the realm and the king together'. So Henry had now lost the power to convene and dismiss parliament whenever he wished. The fifteen councillors were of course to attend the parliaments. Also to be there were twelve men now chosen by the barons. These were to treat of 'the common business . . . on behalf of the whole community of the land'. (It was to this committee of twelve that Fulk Basset was relegated.)[54] The idea here was to spare the general body of magnates the cost of having to turn up thrice annually, while at the same time ensuring everyone was bound by parliament's decisions. (It was stated specifically that the 'community' was to accept whatever the twelve decided.) This did not mean that parliament would simply consist of the fifteen and the twelve. It was the minimum requirement. Almost certainly, the general body of tenants-in-chief continued to be summoned as before.

---

[51] *DBM*, 102–3, cap. 7; 106–7, cap. 15. Wingham took the oath 'before the barons of England' on 28 June: *CR 1256–9*, 315–16. Before 1258 he had sometimes been called chancellor but was often just styled the king's 'clerk', see volume 1, 616.

For Henry III's chancellors and keepers, see Dibben, 'Chancellor and keeper of the seal', 39–51. An important new study of Henry III's chancery is found in Adam Chambers' doctoral thesis, 'Aspects of chancery procedure in the chancery rolls of Henry III'. Another doctoral thesis by Andrew Kourris is forthcoming.

[52] This is clear from the oath taken by the new castellans mentioned below, 14.

[53] Maddicott, *Origins of the English Parliament*, 238–9.

[54] In another version they are to be chosen by 'the community': *DBM*, 104–5, cap. 10; 110–11, cap. 21. The council's personnel were listed both in the chancery and the exchequer: *CR 1256–9*, 473–4; TNA E 368/35, m. 4d (image 5659).

One striking fact emerges from the parliamentary constitution now envisaged. The barons still thought 'the community' could be represented by twelve magnates chosen by themselves.[55] In this revolutionary period, knights were assigned a major role in the reform of local government, but they were not to attend parliament as representatives of their counties. Here '1258' still looked back to 1215 where Magna Carta's assembly giving consent to taxation was largely baronial in its membership and lacked any representative element.[56]

## CONTROL OF CASTLES AND THE OXFORD OATH

The reformers were concerned with constitutional forms. They were equally concerned with physical power. In 1215 the barons had left King John in command of his castles. The mistake was not repeated in 1258, an indication of how much more complete was the king's collapse.[57] At the parliament, a set of new keepers were appointed who all took an oath not to surrender their castles without the council's consent. (It was this oath which revealed that the council's authority was to last for a full twelve years.)[58] Important castles were entrusted to leading members of the regime – so the Tower went to Hugh Bigod, Dover to Richard de Grey, Bridgnorth to Peter de Montfort, Nottingham to William Bardolph, Northampton to Ralph Basset of Sapcote (a follower of Simon de Montfort) and Winchester to Simon de Montfort himself.[59]

The power and purpose of the new regime was underpinned by an oath taken by all present at the Oxford parliament: 'the oath of the community of England at Oxford', as it was called. The oath bound everyone to help each other against all comers. It also, setting the standards for future conduct, bound everyone to act justly and take nothing that could not be taken without doing wrong. All this was to be saving faith to the king and the crown, an indication, ominous for Henry, that loyalty to the crown (and kingdom) might be separate from that owed to any individual king. The oath was modelled on the one sworn by the seven baronial leaders when they confederated together at the Westminster parliament. But there was one crucial extra clause, designed both to

[55] The twelve consisted of a bishop, Fulk Basset of London (a baron in his own right), an earl, nine magnates and one knight.

[56] In the 1215 Magna Carta only tenants-in-chief were summoned to the assembly with only greater barons (lay and ecclesiastical) receiving a personal summons, the lesser tenants-in-chief being summoned generally through the sheriffs. However, as John Maddicott first showed, many of the lesser tenants-in-chief were of knightly status: Maddicott, ' "An infinite multitude of nobles" '.

[57] For the importance of castles in this period, see Oakes, 'King's men without the king'.

[58] TNA E 159/ 32. m.1 (image 0003), a special schedule attached to the exchequer's memoranda roll; and see *DBM*, 258–9, cap. 2.

[59] *CPR 1247–58*, 637–9, 654; *DBM*, 112–13, cap. 24.

deter opposition and justify, if necessary, the use of brute force. Anyone contravening the oath was to be treated as a mortal enemy. That meant they could be attacked and killed.[60] This went far beyond the oath of 1215. Then 'the commune of all the land' had sworn to support twenty-five barons in enforcing Magna Carta if the king sought to break it. But the methods envisaged had simply been the seizure of his lands and castles. No reference was made to treating opponents as 'mortal enemies'. 'The notion of mortal enmity was pervasive in medieval society.'[61] But it was one thing for it to envenom feuds between individuals, quite another for it to underpin a national political programme. This was sensationally new. The extreme violence now envisaged reflected the extreme importance of the programme and the extreme anxiety about attempts to oppose it. In 1263 the 'mortal enmity' clause in the oath was used to justify the violence beginning the civil war. It was with a shrewd eye that, looking back, the chronicler Thomas Wykes identified 'mortal enmity' as the part of the Provisions that polluted all the rest.[62]

## THE EXPULSION OF THE LUSIGNANS

If things went badly for Henry at Oxford, they went even worse for his Lusignan half-brothers. They were excluded, as we have seen, from the council of fifteen. They were also threatened with material loss. This stemmed from a proposal that the lands and castles Henry had given away should be resumed into his hands. Presented as a way of curing the king's poverty, in reality this was aimed at the Lusignans and in particular at William de Valence. Apart from Henry's brother, the conveniently absent King Richard, William had received far more land from the king than anyone else. Faced with this threat, the half-brothers swore 'by the death and wounds of Christ' to surrender nothing given them by the king. That just raised the stakes. 'Either you surrender your castles or you lose your head,' Simon de Montfort spat at William de Valence.[63] To prove his own virtue, Montfort added that he would return Kenilworth and Odiham castles to the king despite all the money he had spent upon them.

Under this pressure, the Lusignans' nerve broke. Towards the end of June, while breakfast was being prepared, they fled from Oxford to Winchester, where they took refuge in Aymer's castle of Wolvesey. The barons broke up the Oxford parliament and hurried in pursuit, taking the

---

[60] *DBM*, 100–1, cap. 4; Bémont, *Simon de Montfort*, 327–8; Maddicott, *Simon de Montfort*, 153. For the oaths of 1258, see Hey, 'Two oaths of the community'.

[61] Hyams, *Rancor and Reconciliation*, 59, and 253–4 for the role of 'mortal enmity' in the period of reform and rebellion. Ch. 8 as a whole asks 'Was there an enmity culture in thirteenth-century England?', with the conclusion that there was.

[62] Wykes, 119–20.

[63] Paris, v, 697–8.

king with them. They surrounded the castle and demanded that all four brothers leave the kingdom. At this point Henry at last intervened. Hoping they would thereby be allowed to stay, he offered to guarantee his brothers' acceptance of the baronial provisions. The intervention paid more tribute to his heart than his head. It was foolish to link himself to his brothers' hopeless cause. In the event, the barons said Aymer and William (with their larger stake in the country) could stay but only as prisoners until reform was completed. Guy and Geoffrey de Lusignan were still to leave immediately. Not surprisingly, allowed to take some of their wealth, the brothers decided to depart together. Letters giving them a safe conduct were issued on 6 July. On 18 July they crossed to Boulogne. According to Matthew Paris, Louis IX refused to allow them to stay in France, having heard from his queen how they had 'enormously diffamed and slandered' her sister. How Eleanor must have rejoiced at their departure. These events ended any further resistance. John de Warenne had fled with the Lusignans from Oxford. He now submitted. So did Lord Edward.

## EDWARD AND THE REVOLUTION

In the 1320s, the heir to the throne, the future Edward III, was to be the titular leader of the revolt against his father, the hapless Edward II. In 1258, had circumstances been different, Lord Edward might have played a similar if more active role. Later he was indeed to join forces with Simon de Montfort. But Edward, much to his mother's dismay, was now allied with the king's half-brothers, the very men the barons were hunting down. In June 1258 itself he tried to place Gascony and the isle of Oléron under none other than Geoffrey and Guy de Lusignan.[64]

At the time of the revolution, Edward was just short of nineteen years old. Over 6 feet tall, with his blonde hair and big chin, he was a striking figure.[65] Having already shown his martial prowess in tournaments, he was a very different proposition from his pacific father. Potentially too he commanded vast resources. He held Chester, Bristol and numerous English manors. He was the immediate ruler of Gascony and of the king's territories in Wales and Ireland. In the government of Gascony he had already shown a vigour quite foreign to his father.[66] Not surprisingly, therefore, the barons were just as keen to control him as they were the king. Indeed, the council's twelve-year term might well carry its authority into Edward's reign. Back at the Westminster parliament, Edward had

[64] CPR 1247–58, 639, 664; CR 1256–9, 319; Ridgeway, 'The Lord Edward and the Provisions of Oxford', 89.

[65] The big chin appears in several contemporary images of Edward, see Prestwich, Edward I, plates 2, 18, 20.

[66] Billaud, 'Similarities and differences', 96. Edward's resources are fully discussed in Wait, 'Household and resources of the Lord Edward'.

sworn to accept the coming reforms, but as he came to see the implications for himself, he had every reason to change his mind. The baronial failure to do anything about the Welsh conquest of the Four Cantrefs provided another motive for doing so.[67] Yet Edward's own resistance soon fizzled out. On 10 July he issued a letter promising to accept the baronial reforms. The keepers of his lands and castles were now to be chosen by the council of fifteen. His appointment of the Lusignans to run Gascony was cancelled. He was also given four councillors, his chancellor swearing to seal nothing without their agreement.[68] It seemed he was to be just as much controlled by the regime as was his father.

## THE FAILURE OF RESISTANCE

Given these extraordinary changes, so detrimental, so disastrous for the king, his half-brothers and his son, why had they failed to make common cause against them? After all, they had evidently made some preparations to do so. The answer lies in the facts of power. The baronial side was by far the stronger and had evidently mustered at Oxford greatly superior forces. The Lusignans had also to contend with the general hostility to foreigners sweeping through the parliament. The Petition of the Barons, the proposals for reform drawn up at Oxford, thus defined disparagement in marriage as marriage to those 'who are not of the nation of the kingdom of England', an obvious attack on the many marriages to the king's foreign favourites arranged before 1258.[69] The Petition also demanded that royal castles be committed to men 'born of the kingdom of England'. A newsletter, describing events at the parliament, added that nearly all of the castles had previously 'been in the hands of foreigners', an exaggeration but it showed what was thought.[70] Hostility to foreigners was even expressed at the heart of the administration. So the clerk writing up the chancery rolls described Henry's order summoning Burgundian knights to Oxford as 'concerning knights of an alien race (*alieni generis*) coming to England'.[71]

As for any co-operation between Henry and Edward, here there was another problem. Father and son had fallen out. The annals of Winchester

---

[67] The Welsh dimension is stressed in Burt, *Edward I and the Governance of England*, 57–8, 77–8.

[68] Richardson and Sayles, 'The Provisions of Oxford', 320, cap. 26; 321, cap. 30; *DBM*, 94–5. The councillors were John de Balliol, John de Grey, Stephen Longespée and Roger of Mold.

[69] *DBM*, 80–1, caps. 4, 6.

[70] *DBM*, 80–1, cap. 4; 90–1. The Petition added that castles guarding ports should be entrusted to Englishmen given the dangers arising from them being in the hands of 'others': *DBM*, 80–1, cap. 5. The Poitevin, Elyas de Rabayne, was accordingly deprived of Corfe.

[71] *CR 1256–9*, 223–4, 297. The note itself was routine, all chancery letters in the rolls having a marginal note describing their content.

speak of their 'discord' and how they were eventually reconciled in the
Winchester chapter house. Since this was in July, the reconciliation took
place very much under baronial auspices. Quite probably, egged on by the
barons, Henry had resented the way Edward had placed Gascony under
the Lusignans without his assent. His interference in Edward's appanage
had always been a source of friction.[72] The quarrel may also reflect how
Henry was far readier than his son to bow down before the baronial
regime. Events might have been very different had there been real leadership from the top. Nicholas de Molis, head of the household knights in any
resistance, drew his own conclusions. Although removed from Dover
castle, he agreed to become castellan of Rochester.[73]

At Runnymede, in the days leading up to the promulgation of
Magna Carta, King John had bargained hard with the barons and
secured significant concessions.[74] There is no sign Henry did the same at
Oxford. Indeed, until his futile intervention on behalf of the Lusignans,
he gives no sign of activity at all. Perhaps his interventions were just
brushed aside. Or had he simply given up? According to a baronial
letter to the pope, he ignored bishop-elect Aymer's pleas to make a stand.
Henry not merely arrived late for the parliament. He also seems, during
its course, to have retired to Woodstock. The Burton annalist says he
was there when the Petition of the Barons was drawn up. We can think of
him perhaps, brooding in the cloisters beside the pools of Everswell (the
retreat close to Woodstock palace), while his fate was decided ten miles
away in the Dominicans' house in Oxford.[75] The London chronicler
Arnold fitzThedmar has Henry accepting the reforms at Oxford 'unwillingly', surely, in one mood, the case. Yet Matthew Paris thought he went
along 'willingly, *gratanter*'.[76] Perhaps the king was frightened by what might
happen if he resisted. He had after all, confronted by the march on
Westminster Hall, thought for a moment he was a prisoner. Perhaps he
remembered the war which had followed his father's rejection of Magna
Carta. Perhaps he still hoped the reforms would indeed produce the taxation for Sicily vaguely promised by the barons. At Oxford twenty-four men
were 'appointed by the community to treat of a tax for the king'. The

---

[72] Winchester, 97. The friction is a major theme in Studd, 'The Lord Edward and King
Henry III' and see Ridgeway, 'King Henry III's grievances against the council', 240, cap.
20.

[73] *DBM*, 112–13, cap. 24.

[74] Carpenter, *Magna Carta*, 342–3.

[75] Burton, 438. For Henry going to Woodstock, see also Winchester, 97. However, the
chancery remained in Oxford for no royal letters were witnessed at Woodstock.

[76] FitzThedmar, 37 (Stone, FitzThedmar, no. 710); Paris, v, 696, where '*graviter*' in the
printed text is a mistake for '*gratanter*'. In my footnotes, references such as FitzThedmar, 37
(Stone, FitzThedmar, no. 710), refer first to the old Thomas Stapleton edition and second
to Ian Stone's forthcoming new edition of fitzThedmar's book to be published in the
Oxford Medieval Texts series.

reformers were making some effort to reconcile Henry to what had happened.[77]

## THE COURSE OF REFORM, JULY 1258–NOVEMBER 1259

In the year and a half from July 1258 a vigorous and valiant effort was made to implement the local reforms planned at the Oxford parliament. Four knights in each county investigated local abuse. The justiciar, Hugh Bigod, began to hear the resulting cases as well as complaints brought before him by individuals. Sheriffs became county knights, took an oath to behave justly and held office on new financial terms. The baronial leaders accepted that their officials, as much as those of the king, must be subject to reform. Legislation, known to later historians as the Provisions of Westminster, dealt with the malpractices of the sheriffs, the justices in eyre and, going beyond anything contemplated at Oxford, limited the jurisdiction of private baronial courts.[78] Henry's own role in this new dawn is analysed later in chapter 3. Here we outline the reforms themselves.

## THE COUNCIL TAKES CONTROL

Having expelled the Lusignans, the regime moved to secure the allegiance of London. On 23 July a group of councillors, headed by Roger Bigod, Simon de Montfort and John fitzGeoffrey, came to the Guildhall and obtained an oath from the mayor and aldermen to accept the reformers' provisions.[79] By this time, the work of the twenty-four (in reality the baronial twelve with one or two from the king's side) was done. The body ceased to exist. Instead, the council of fifteen moved centre stage. Its authority was explained and affirmed by a great proclamation, witnessed by nearly all the councillors and issued in the king's name at the October parliament of 1258.[80] Henry thus commanded everyone to take an oath to obey the council's 'establishments' and aid each other in so doing against all comers. Anyone acting contrary to the oath was to be treated as a mortal enemy. The threat embodied in the original oath taken by those present at Oxford thus now appeared in an oath to be taken by everyone in the realm.

The proclamation was given maximum publicity. Whereas previous custom was for government documents to be issued in Latin, this one was issued in both French and English as well. The three versions were sent to every county. The English version was a dramatic innovation, being the first royal document to be written in English since soon after the Norman Conquest. The purpose was clear. The regime wished to reach out to the

---

[77] *DBM*, 104–7, cap. 11.
[78] For these courts, see below, 641 (The Glossary, under 'honourial court').
[79] FitzThedmar, 38 (Stone, FitzThedmar, no. 714).
[80] *DBM*, 116–19.

great bulk of the population, reach out to the freemen, peasants and townsmen for whom English was the only language. The French version also had a purpose. The earls, barons and knights of thirteenth-century England were bilingual, trilingual if they had some Latin. English they could use to address the lower orders. It was also gradually intermingling with French as a language they used amongst themselves. But French remained the language of business, culture and conversation, hence it was in French that treatises of estate management were written and unofficial translations of Magna Carta circulated. In 1258 the regime wanted nothing unofficial. It was determined to get its message across and hence provided its own French translation of the Latin text.[81] Its authority was to be known and be upheld by everyone in the realm.

The council did not form a separate executive. Instead, it worked through the king, issuing letters in his name and authenticating them with his seal. All the indications are that, in essentials, it took over the government of the country. In the chancery rolls between July 1258 and October 1259 over 150 letters were issued on the authority of 'the council' or 'the magnates who are of the king's council.' By contrast, between July 1258 and August 1259, the king authorized but two letters on his own, one letter with the justiciar, one with another minister and one with the council.[82] This picture of an emasculated king is confirmed by a newsletter sent out to Provence in 1259. 'The state of England', the writer declared, 'is such that the king has no power of doing anything without the counsel of the twelve barons', meaning here clearly the council of fifteen. 'These take counsel and deliberate without the king on whatever pleases them on affairs either side of the sea, saving however on some great matters where they wish to honour the king or where it is necessary to have the consent of the king and his son, Lord Edward.'[83]

Since the council worked through the king, its members or some of them needed to be at court. This was easier to achieve because Henry's itinerary for much of 1258–9 had the same 'home counties' aspect as before the revolution. Indeed, in 1259, prior to leaving for France in November, he spent 168 days at Westminster. At the time of the parliaments, probably nearly all the fifteen came together. The great proclama-

[81] For bilingualism see Short, 'Bilingualism in Anglo-Norman England', and Crane, 'Social aspects of bilingualism in the thirteenth century'. For the use of French, see Wogan-Browne et al., *Language and Culture in Medieval Britain*; Fenster and Collette, *The French of Medieval England*; Brand, 'The languages of the law in later medieval England'.

[82] The great majority of the letters have no authorization note at all. They were issued on the authority of the chancellor who, as we have seen, was controlled by the regime.

[83] The letter is now preserved in the Archives des Bouches-du-Rhône in Marseilles. It is printed in Villard, 'Autour de Charles d'Anjou', 34–5, no. 5. I am grateful to Nicholas Vincent for drawing the letter to my attention along with other remarkable material in the Marseilles archives. Vincent has also sent me his transcriptions of the originals which correct mistakes and omissions in the versions printed by Villard.

tion of October 1258 was witnessed by fourteen of them, headed by Archbishop Boniface. At parliament too, there is evidence the twelve magnates representing the community were also present.

Alongside the councillors, the effective head of the government soon became Hugh Bigod. Despite absences hearing pleas in the counties, he spent a great deal of time at court, where he dealt with a whole range of business and presided over the court *coram rege*.[84] In the chancery rolls between July 1258 and October 1259 he authorized over ninety royal letters, far more than anyone else, acting occasionally with the council, in the very great majority of cases alone.

At the start of the revolution, the council had secured control over the seal and, through Hugh Bigod, the law courts. In November 1258 it gripped the exchequer, replacing Henry's treasurer, Philip Lovel, with Master John of Crakehall, a man of very different stamp.[85] John had been for many years the steward of Robert Grosseteste, the great scholar bishop of Lincoln, and had responsibility for running the episcopal estates. Present at Grosseteste's death, he had told Matthew Paris all about it. His brief now was to reform the exchequer and help ensure the revenues of the kingdom were paid there, instead of going direct to the king's wardrobe.[86] To ensure his probity, he was given a salary of 100 marks a year, the first treasurer of the exchequer to receive one.[87]

Henry later observed that the kingdom was governed by three things: 'the law of the land, the great seal and the exchequer'.[88] The regime now controlled all three. It also controlled the king's household. On 8 July 1258, at Winchester, 'by provision of the barons', Peter de Rivallis was removed as keeper of the wardrobe. This was a key position since the wardrobe, travelling with the king, provided the money for his food, drink, stables and almsgiving. It also financed both purchases of cloth and precious objects and payment of fees and wages. In time of war it bought munitions and hired soldiers, its expenditure thus vastly increasing. Much of the wardrobe's money (absorbing a large proportion of the crown's annual revenue) came from the exchequer, but the wardrobe also drew directly on local revenues, something the reformers, as mentioned, hoped to stop.[89] Although Peter de Rivallis was replaced by his deputies, the clerks Aubrey de Fécamp and Peter of Winchester, they were now subject to the baronial regime.[90] Whereas, in the past, Henry had been able to use his wardrobe

---

[84] Hershey, 'Success or failure?', 83–4.
[85] *CPR 1247–58*, 1; Paris, v, 719–20. For his career, see Jobson, 'John of Crakehall'.
[86] *DBM*, 107, cap. 14; 260–1, cap. 8, and see below, 36.
[87] *CLR 1251–60*, 475.
[88] *DBM*, 236–9, cap. 28.
[89] The classic study of the wardrobe under Henry III remains that in Tout, *Chapters*, i, ch. vi. Its accounts at the exchequer have now been edited for the Pipe Roll Society by Benjamin Wild: Wild, *WA*.
[90] Wild, *WA*, cxxxi, 87, 102; Tout, *Chapters*, i, 298–9.

money just as he liked, now its expenditure was controllable by the council. Another significant change took place at the level of the stewards, the officials who were at the head of the royal household. Here a completely new man appeared, Giles de Argentan, a knight hitherto quite out of favour.[91] He was to become a staunch Montfortian. The court was also purged of the Poitevin knights Elyas de Rabayne, Guy de Rochefort and William de Sancta Ermina – William who had stood behind Henry at table, towel on arm, and carved his meat. All three were expelled from the kingdom. Together the three exemplified complaints about foreigners receiving too much patronage, holding royal castles, being foisted on heiresses and behaving in an oppressive and lawless fashion.[92]

## THE JUSTICIAR'S EYRE

While it was cleansing court and country of the Poitevins, the regime moved to fulfil the promises of local reform made at Oxford. By the end of July 1258 the four knights who were to investigate the abuses in each county had been chosen and writs went out setting them to work.[93] In the scheme drawn up at Oxford, the knights were to hear 'all complaints' and make a written record ready for Hugh Bigod's arrival. Now, however, there was a significant change of plan. Instead of the knights handing over their records to the justiciar, they were to present them to the council at Westminster on 6 October (the point at which parliament was scheduled to begin). This was sensible. It recognized the justiciar could not possibly hear all the cases by October, and gave the council a view of the grievances in the shires. There was also a change in how the knights were to proceed. Instead of sitting in the county court and hearing individual complaints, they were to carry out their investigations according to a set of questions, most of them drawn from the inquiries of before 1258. The answers were to be given on oath by 'trusted and law-worthy men', knights

---

[91] *DBM*, 104–7, cap. 11; *CR 1256–9*, 243. While the stewards William de Grey and the Savoyard Imbert Pugeys, remained in post after the revolution, Robert Walerand (although still employed by the new regime) was rarely at court. Giles was the son of the distinguished knight Richard de Argentan, sometime steward of the royal household. The family held the manor of Great Wymondley in Hertfordshire by the service of bearing a silver cup at coronations. Three silver cups were proudly displayed on their coat of arms: *Rolls of Arms, Henry III*, 43. Active from the 1230s, Giles failed to follow his father at court. For his grievance over not recovering the manors of Lilley and Willian, next door to Great Wymondley, see *CRR*, xv, no. 1758; *CChR 1226–57*, 276; volume 1, 126, 131; *CIM*, nos. 707, 711. For a biography, see Ridgeway, 'Sir Giles d'Argentine'.

[92] Rabayne had held Corfe and Rochefort, Colchester: Ray, 'Alien courtiers of thirteenth-century England', ch. 8; Ridgeway, 'The politics of the English royal court', 237, 299–300; Ridgeway, 'Dorset in the period of baronial reform', 23; and volume 1, 556–7.

[93] For the argument that the knights were elected locally, hence the delay before they were commissioned, see *SESK*, xxxix–xli (Hershey's introduction).

and others, assembled in juries from the hundreds into which counties were divided.[94] The returns for one hundred (Loes in Suffolk) survive.[95] This change too was sensible. While plaintiffs could bring cases direct to Bigod, as many did, it was above all through the evidence of the hundredal juries, receiving both individual and communal complaints, that the malpractices of officials would be brought to light.

While awaiting the returns of the knights, Bigod decided to show his face in the counties. In late July, leaving the king at Westminster, he journeyed to Northampton, where the sheriffs had earned an evil reputation.[96] Then, in August and September, this time with the king, he travelled as far north as Nottingham and Lincoln. The great majority of the cases coming before him were routine assizes, but he also heard complaints from a wide variety of people.[97] Those accused (not always successfully) included the bishop of London, the sheriffs of Surrey and Lincoln, two sheriffs of Northampton and the bailiffs both of William de Sancta Ermina and the earl of Gloucester.[98] While Bigod and the king were at Nottingham, the poor men of Grimsby complained about the wrongs they had suffered at the hands of richer merchants. The result was the immediate dispatch of Bigod's colleague, the judge Gilbert of Preston, to the town. There he heard the complaints and secured agreement to a series of reforms. In early November these were confirmed by the king and council in a letter authorized by 'Hugh Bigod, justiciar of England'.[99]

At the Westminster parliament in October 1258, knights from at least fifteen counties came with the results of their investigations.[100] By this time there was considerable impatience with the pace of local reform. Had the knights been working on just another inquiry, like so many in the past, from which nothing would come? Was the justiciar ever going to tour the

[94] *DBM*, 114–15. The writ setting up the four knights just said they were to inquire throughout their counties by the oaths of law-worthy men. It is evident from Bigod's rolls that the questions were put to juries from each hundred: *SESK*, p. 1, and no. 54, and *SERHB*, ii, p. 43.

[95] TNA SC 5/9/5/9. The roll, carefully transcribed by E.F. Jacob, is printed in full in his *Studies*, 337–44. I thank Paul Dryburgh for locating the modern reference to the roll at TNA.

[96] In ch. 3 I give a full account of the evidence from the eyres of Hugh Bigod and his colleagues between 1258 and 1260.

[97] Apart from John fitzGeoffrey, the complainants included the abbot of Cerne, the knight Stephen de Chenduit, the bailiffs of Southampton, the men of Walthamstow and Chingford, 'many men of the city of London', a widow from the king's manor of Havering, a London widow, a 'poor' widow from Ketton in Rutland and the villein sokeman on the king's manor of Brill in Buckinghamshire. In Bigod's first roll (no longer complete), recording cases between June and September with some more in late December, he heard 238 civil pleas and 46 complaints: Hershey, 'Success or failure?', 86–7.

[98] *SERHB*, i, nos. 5, 17, 23, 28, 33, 41, 67, 98, 111, 161, 166, 308, 365.

[99] *SERHB*, i, nos. 373–9; *CChR 1257–1300*, 14–16. For the whole episode, see Hershey, 'Baronial reform, the justiciar's court and commercial legislation', and *SERHB*, i, pp. xlix–lvii.

[100] *CR 1256–9*, 332–3; Treharne, *Baronial Plan*, 115–16.

kingdom to hear the cases they had recorded? So far, he had only heard complaints from individuals.[101]

Faced with this discontent, on 18 October the council, in the king's name, issued a great proclamation, one known by historians as the Ordinance of the Sheriffs. Again the letter was written in three languages, Latin, French and English, and was to be read in the county courts. Once again the regime was determined to get its message across. The proclamation announced the king's wish that all wrongs should indeed be reported to the four knights.[102] If they could not be redressed as fast as the king wished, that should cause no surprise (evidently it had). Things had gone wrong for so long that they could not speedily be put right. But there was hope. The justiciar and 'other good men' *would* be coming to give redress.

This time something more was done. In November and December, Hugh Bigod went to Bermondsey to hear pleas for Surrey; in January 1259 he was at Canterbury hearing those for Kent. Although assizes still came before him, they were outnumbered by the cases arising from the testimony of the four knights and the hundredal juries. There were 91 of the former and 117 of the latter. So at last the work of the knights was bearing fruit. At the same time Bigod continued to hear individual complaints. Of these there were 113. In both counties, sheriffs and other royal officials were targeted. Targeted too were the officials of magnates, including those of Aymer, Guy and Geoffrey de Lusignan, Boniface and Peter of Savoy, the earl of Gloucester, William de Say and Richard de Grey. The punishments meted out were severe, indeed too severe in the view of the London alderman and chronicler Arnold fitzThedmar. In Surrey, Bigod 'not only amerced many bailiffs, but imprisoned them, clerk and lay; and from some he exacted fines of 20 marks, from some 40 marks and more, and many for small offences he burdened beyond measure'.[103] There was in all this a striking difference between Bigod's eyre and the visitations before 1258. In Surrey and Kent, officials who had sailed unscathed through the eyre of 1255 were now punished while jurors silent then about abuses now opened their mouths.[104] Above all, for the first time, thanks to the action by *querela*, plaintiffs secured compensation for their sufferings.


## THE ACTION BY *QUERELA*

Fundamental to Hugh Bigod's eyres was the action by complaint, *querela*. It was not new. Complaints are found occasionally in manorial and baro-

---

[101] Paris says, however, that the demands of the harvest reduced the number of complaints: Paris, v, 710.

[102] This suggests the four knights had remained in being and could still carry out inquiries.

[103] FitzThedmar, 39 (Stone, FitzThedmar, no. 717).

[104] For punishments and the opening of mouths, see below, 139, 144.

nial courts as well as in the court *coram rege*, the courts of the exchequer and the justices in eyre.[105] What was completely new was the sheer volume of *querelae* coming before the justiciar. His court had been opened up to complainants in a way not seen before. Whereas before the government had given no encouragement to complaints, now through the inquiries of the knights and Bigod's promised arrival, it was positively inviting them. Why then did people accept the invitation? What explains the utility and popularity of the procedure? The answer lies in four characteristics.

First, the subject matter of the complaint. Here there were restrictions. It was not possible to proceed by *querela* in matters concerning right and possession. These needed to be pleaded by writ according to the forms of the common law.[106] But this did little to detract from the value of the *querela*. The common law assizes worked well, especially novel disseisin with its speedy remedy for those deprived of free tenements 'unjustly and without judgement'. Many such cases came before Hugh Bigod. Complaints, by contrast, were concerned 'with trespasses and injuries, *de transgressionibus et iniuriis*', as it was put during the Oxford parliament.[107] What was meant here is clear from the complaints themselves. They covered such matters as violence to person, false imprisonment and, again and again, seizure of crops and farm animals, often by way of distraint. In many cases such actions were described as taking place 'by force of arms in breach of the king's peace', and these words were to become standard in later actions of trespass. But, a blessing of the eyres, Bigod made no stand on forms and heard many cases where such words were not employed.[108] Indeed, the trespasses and injuries often covered various forms of extortion, or alleged extortion, where no actual violence had taken place.[109]

Second, the targets. From the word go, complaints were expected against the sheriffs and bailiffs of the king. During the course of 1259 the regime made clear that magnates and their officials could be aimed at too. It was local officials, royal and seigneurial, who more than anyone else were guilty of the excesses and injuries outlined above. A speedy and effective means of redress was desperately needed and the action by *querela* provided it.

That was partly, a third point, thanks to the ease of the procedure. Many of the abuses complained about on the eyres could have been

---

[105] For discussion of the origin and processes of procedure by *querela*, see Richardson and Sayles' introduction to *SCWR*; Jacob, *Studies*, 65–70; Hershey, 'Justice and bureaucracy', 843–51, and *SERHB*, i, pp. xxvi–vii. For examples in manorial and honourial courts, see *SPMC*, 7, 21, 53, 56, 65–6.

[106] For the distinction, see *SCWR*, 125; *SERHB*, ii, nos. 508–9.

[107] *DBM*, 98–9, cap. 1; and 160–3, caps. 2, 7.

[108] A point made in Hershey, 'Justice and bureaucracy', 844–5.

[109] The government itself did not stick to '*de transgressionibus et iniuriis*'. It also referred to '*les torz*' (wrongs) and to complaints '*de omnimodis excessibus*' and '*de aliquo gravamine*': *DBM*, 112–15, 118–19, 162–3, cap. 7. Occasionally Bigod allowed property to be recovered as a by-product of a *querela* action, for example, *SCWR*, 127–8.

tackled via actions of trespass commenced by writs. A writ could also be obtained to order the sheriff to return chattels unjustly seized. But here there were problems. One was the bother and expense of going to the chancery, itinerating as it did with the king, to get the writ. Another was the suspicion a writ might be difficult to obtain if aimed at a favourite of the king. With *querelae*, by contrast, there was no need for a writ.[110] Complaints could be made directly to the four knights and the hundredal jurors and also directly to Bigod himself.[111] There is some evidence that complaints were sometimes made through a written 'bill', but many may simply have been oral.[112] There was also, on Bigod's eyre, the intention of settling the cases on the spot, for sufficient knights and law-worthy men were to be there before him to give their verdicts.[113] The complainants had the prospect of immediate redress.

Redress. We now come, fourthly, to a cardinal feature of procedure by *querela*, indeed its chief attraction for plaintiffs. This was the prospect, if the jury came down in their favour, of immediate redress either through the restoration of what had been taken or the payment of damages, or both. The claim for damages had always been integral to trespass procedure, necessarily so when the complaint was about violence to person and property rather than just the seizure of goods. On Bigod's eyre, the juries spent as much time on the assessment of damages as on deciding guilt and innocence. They pulled down exorbitant claims and sometimes estimated in precise detail the value of seized crops and animals.[114] Bigod too was directly involved. On occasion, he both 'taxed' damages personally and took steps to see they were actually paid.

In all this, there was a sharp contrast with common law procedures. There damages could be awarded but they were very often simply given to the judges' clerks. So the plaintiff gained nothing from them. The main point of the procedure was the return of the tenement in question, not the recovery of damages suffered by its detention. With the *querela*, the difference is total. In hardly a single case before Hugh Bigod were the damages given to the clerks. Restoration and damages were the whole point of the procedure.

---

[110] For the problems of proceeding by writ and the advantages of the *querela*, see Hershey, 'Justice and bureaucracy'.

[111] The relationship between individual plaints and the testimony of the hundredal jurors in the great inquiry of 1274/5 is a theme in Scales, 'The Cambridgeshire ragman rolls'.

[112] For procedure by bill, see Hershey, 'The earliest bill in eyre', and his introduction to *SESK*, lxxxii–v. For an inconclusive discussion as to the balance between oral and written plaints, see Richardson and Sayles, *SCWR*, lvii–lxviii. For whether plaintiffs spoke through a lawyer, a '*narrator*', see Hershey, 'Justice and bureaucracy', 845.

[113] *DBM*, 98–9, cap. 1.

[114] For a striking example, *SESK*, no. 103. For the valuation of losses and injuries, with a view to compensation, in the French *enquêtes* procedure, see Dejoux, 'Valeur des choses'. The term 'damages', however, hardly appears.

There was also here a contrast between Hugh Bigod's eyre and the judicial eyres before 1258. On the latter, hundredal jurors answered a whole series of questions about events since the last eyre. Their answers, evidently gathered from individual complainants, sometimes covered the malpractices of officials. But while the culprits might be punished, the victims gained no redress. On the 1255 Surrey eyre, a jury thus accused the bailiff, Henry Gargat, of seizing a quarter of corn worth 6s 6d from one Peter de Bydon. But it was not till Bigod's eyre that Bydon received half a mark in compensation.[115] In another case, before the Sussex eyre of 1255, a hundredal jury accused Peter of Savoy's steward of falsely imprisoning one Geoffrey of Rottingdean. The bailiff was convicted and amerced. But again Geoffrey himself got nothing. It was only post-1258, when he brought a *querela*, that he at last secured compensation. As the judgement stated, while the steward (through the amercement in 1255) had satisfied the king for his trespass, 'to Geoffrey who suffered the trespass, he has made no emends'.[116] The same could be said of nearly all the cases of abuse coming before the eyres before 1258. The contrast with Hugh Bigod's eyre is again total. In *querela* actions in Surrey and Kent alone, he issued over sixty orders for the restoration of property and or the payment of damages. Showing that justice was speedily done, these awards are the best testimony to the utility and success of his eyres.

Why did the reformers open up the *querela* procedure in this novel and dramatic way? They were certainly making a practical response to the trespasses, injuries and extortions suffered at the hands of local officials. They were also influenced by the example of King Louis and the teachings of leading churchmen. Of that more later.[117] Behind the work of the eyres one senses above all the care and zeal of Bigod himself. As well as targeting notorious cases of abuse and punishing severely both royal and baronial officials, he asked probing questions of defendants, taxed personally the damages of even the poorest litigants and swept aside objections to his authority from those, like the Londoners, the abbot of St Albans and Dunstable priory, claiming liberties and exemptions.[118] The justice meted out on the eyre seems even handed, with convictions balancing acquittals. The Poitevin, Elyas de Rabayn, before his expulsion from the kingdom, actually won two cases. The queen's steward, Matthias Bezill, on the other hand, although still constable of Gloucester, was convicted of seizing land

---

[115] TNA JUST 1/872, m. 32 (image 9145); *SESK*, no. 98.

[116] TNA JUST 1/537, m. 1 (image 3146). The case came before Hugh Bigod's successor as justiciar, Hugh Despenser.

[117] See below, 62–3.

[118] His work is anlaysed more fully in ch. 3. For objections, see FitzThedmar, 39–40 (Stone, FitzThedmar, nos. 717–19); Paris's Continuator, 427; Dunstable, 212.

from a peasant (Bezill claimed he was a villein) and sentenced to gaol.[119]
Some of the cases reveal Bigod's humanity. He ordered a man 'monstrously'
tortured by the sheriff of Northampton to be taken to a hospital, there to
be tenderly nursed in the hope of his recovery. He acquitted of theft three
men who had taken bread and cheese in the summer (during the great
famine of 1258) simply to sustain life.[120]

## THE REFORM OF THE SHERIFF'S OFFICE IMPLEMENTED

The Ordinance of the Sheriffs in October 1258 did more than offer reassurance over the four knights and the justiciar's eyre. It also set out a new
oath to be sworn by the sheriffs. This built on an oath introduced in 1236
and was probably far more detailed (it runs to nearly a page in a modern
printed version).[121] In the new oath, the sheriffs were to swear to serve the
king loyally, but for the rest the concern was to ensure the fair treatment
of the people. The sheriffs were thus to give justice to everyone, poor as
well as rich, and be moderate in their acceptance of hospitality. They were
to take no more food and drink than that normally given at table. They
were only to stay with those who had land worth £40 a year (a level
excluding many knights) and then when invited and bringing only five
horses.[122] They were to accept no present worth more than 12d, a sum
equivalent to twelve days' wages for a female labourer. The oath's other
major concern was with the sheriffs' subordinates. His sergeants should be
men of substance, able to answer for their deeds. No more should be
employed than necessary lest the country be burdened with their food and
drink. They were to swear not to take goods or money 'from any man, free
or villein . . . as many have been accustomed to do in the past'. Henry III,
in his speech to the exchequer in 1250, had said sheriffs were only to lease
hundreds at higher rents to those who would treat the people justly. The
final clause of the oath now forbad the letting out of hundreds altogether.
If the oath was obeyed it promised a new era in the relationship between
the sheriff and the county.

Having set out the oath, the Ordinance of the Sheriffs announced two
more reforms. The sheriffs were to stay in office only for a year, so people
would fear them less and be more ready to expose their wrongs. And at
the end of the year, they would receive their expenses from the king so

---

[119] Hershey, 'Success or failure?', 73; *SERHB*, i, nos. 300, 339, 355; *CR 1256–9*, 339, 352.

[120] *SERHB*, i, nos. 161, 171.

[121] We only have Matthew Paris's summary of the 1236 oath: Paris, iii, 363. It bound the
sheriff not to accept gifts by which justice might be corrupted, so nothing in land and only
a moderate amount of food and drink. Paris says it soon had no effect: Paris, *HA*, ii, 389.
For other references to oaths see *CR 1251–3*, 385 (a reference I owe to Richard Cassidy);
and see *CFR 1235–6*, no. 75. For a full discussion of oaths of office in the long thirteenth
century, see Lachaud, *L'éthique du pouvoir au Moyen Âge*, 479–97.

[122] They were only to stay at religious houses with incomes of at least 100 marks a year.

would have no need to take anything from anyone else. At the same time, the council began to fulfil its promise to appoint sheriffs who were substantial local knights. Between 23 October and 3 November 1258 nineteen knights were appointed to twenty-eight counties. In seventeen cases they came from the panels of knights elected in each county to investigate abuses.[123] All of them were made to swear the new oath.[124] The council also abolished the increments above the county farms demanded from the previous sheriffs. Instead, in a return to the arrangements in 1236, the sheriffs were made 'custodians' who provided detailed lists of all the revenue from which had come the farm and the increments. They were now to pay all of this into the exchequer, with the implication that in return they would receive expenses.[125]

## THE MAGNATES BOW TO REFORM

Parliament met again, in accordance with the Provisions, in February 1259. Here another great proclamation was drawn up, this one making absolutely clear that the leaders of the regime were themselves subject to the reforms. Evidently there had been doubts on that score. Known to historians as the 'Ordinances of the Magnates', this remarkable document was issued in the name of both the council of fifteen and the twelve representing the community at parliament. The two groups announced that all the wrongs committed by themselves and their bailiffs were to be redressed by the king or the justiciar. They would hinder no one from bringing complaints. They also promised to obey Magna Carta in their dealings with tenants and neighbours. And they undertook to make their officials swear the same oath to act justly as that taken by the sheriffs. This last stipulation was the reverse of a perfunctory one-liner. The oath, the Ordinances explained, was to be taken in the lord's court at every change of official and in the presence of the four knights elected in each county, presumably the four knights appointed to investigate abuses back in 1258. The Ordinances then rehearsed the oath all over again. The officials were to swear to serve loyally both the king and their lords. They were to give right to all people, take nothing by which justice might be perverted and employ no more subordinates than necessary. The subordinates in their turn were to take nothing of value from 'cleric or layman, house of religion or villein'.[126]

---

[123] Treharne, *Baronial Plan*, 121–2; Ridgeway, 'Mid thirteenth-century reformers and the localities', 67, and between 63 and 71, where there is a full discussion of the new sheriffs.

[124] The swearing of the oath is stated specifically in respect of the new sheriff of Devon: TNA E 159/32, m. 5d (image 0096). The exchequer made a record of the oath: TNA E 159/32, m. 2 (image 0004).

[125] Cassidy, 'Bad sheriffs, custodial sheriffs', 41–9.

[126] *DBM*, 130–7.

In the proclamation, the council and the twelve also looked to the future and promised to accept whatever legislation was promulgated by November 1259 with respect to suit (meaning attendance) at private courts. In the event, this legislation was to form another major plank in the programme of reform. It had begun life with the Petition of the Barons at the Oxford parliament and had then been developed in daily meetings at the New Temple in the summer of 1258. More work was done, with some input from the king's judges, at the parliaments of October 1258 and February 1259. Account was probably taken of the grievances revealed by the inquiry of four knights and the complaints before Hugh Bigod. In March 1259, after the parliament was over, a draft of the legislation (although only a draft) was proclaimed at the New Temple.[127] Running to twenty-five chapters, it sought to remedy the abuses of the sheriffs and the justices in eyre. It also in its first thirteen chapters dealt with the issue of suit of court. Here the main aim was to provide a remedy for tenants who, against previous custom, had been forced to do suit 'by distraint and power of great nobles'.[128]

The leaders of the regime, it seemed, were purging themselves in the fire of reform. Yet some were all too keen to turn down the heat. The legislation, long in gestation, had been proclaimed but only in draft form. It was not yet the law of the land. There was also a delay when it came to publishing the Ordinances of the Magnates. On 22 February, Simon de Montfort and Richard de Clare had sealed them on behalf of the council. But then they had lain hidden. Only on 24 March were they embodied in a royal proclamation and sent round the country with orders they be read in the county and hundred courts.

Resistance was understandable. In hearing cases on his Surrey and Kent eyres against Archbishop Boniface, Peter of Savoy, Richard de Clare and Richard de Grey, Hugh Bigod was allowing attacks on members of the ruling council. All this was a huge contrast to '1215', when the local inquiries commissioned by Magna Carta were concerned simply with the abuses of royal officials. At the February 1259 parliament itself, Peter of Savoy had to call in Domesday Book to prove his peasants at Witley in Surrey were villeins and thus could bring no action against him. What on earth was happening when the queen's uncle, an international statesman, was being put to this trouble by his serfs? Why had Hugh Bigod even agreed to hear such a case? The world was turning upside down.[129] Richard de Clare was especially vulnerable to the ongoing complaints and proposed legislation given his uniquely large network of private courts and

---

[127] *DBM*, 122–31. For the evolution of the legislation, see Brand, *Kings, Barons, and Justices*, 20–33.

[128] *DBM*, 124–5, cap. 4.

[129] *SESK*, no. 105. The complaint was about how Peter had raised the rent.

officials. With Simon de Montfort, he had sealed the Ordinances of the Magnates but then he seems to have had second thoughts.[130]

The evidence here comes from Matthew Paris. According to his account, in the days after the February parliament, Clare was upbraided by Simon de Montfort for weakening in his commitment to reform. With the earl of Hereford and others taking up Montfort's cry, Clare sent his steward (Hervey of Boreham) through his lands to correct what was wrong 'according to the form of the new promise', a reference surely to the Ordinances of the Magnates. It looks as though Clare had been dragging his feet over their publication and implementation. In dispatching his steward to put matters right, he was exploiting the Ordinances' acknowledgement, quite probably of his making, that lords in their own courts could put right the trespasses of their officials, so of course escaping the justiciar's intervention.[131] Were Clare and his allies also responsible for the publication of the Ordinances in French, but not also in English, thus limiting their appeal?

## THE PARLIAMENT OF OCTOBER 1259

By the time parliament met in October, the negotiations for a peace with France had almost reached a conclusion. The summer had also seen Henry's one attempt, as unavailing as it was misconceived, to break free from baronial control.[132] This raised a question addressed at the parliament, namely the need to have councillors permanently at court. It was thus decided that two or three councillors of 'middle rank' should always be in attendance on the king. The full council would review their work at each parliament and also meet itself between parliaments when necessary. Although sometimes interpreted as a hit against the greater barons, this was rather a recognition that the latter could not spend all their time at court.[133]

The parliament had other more resonating business than this tweak to the council's organization. Once again there was frustration at the slow progress of reform, just as there had been at the parliament of a year before. The legislation proclaimed back in March 1259 had not been made official. Hugh Bigod during the spring and summer of 1259, leaving the king behind, had heard pleas at Oxford, Lechlade, Reading, Newport

---

[130] Maddicott, *Simon de Montfort*, 178.

[131] Paris, v, 744–5; Maddicott, *Simon de Montfort*, 180–1; *DBM*, 134–5. On 20 February 1259, Clare had secured a concession protecting the liberties of the jurisdictional area (the 'lowy') around Tonbridge castle: *CPR 1258–66*, 49–50. In the articles of the nationwide eyre commissioned in November 1259, justice was to be done to those complaining of private officials, but only if the lord had failed to mete it out: *DBM*, 162–3, cap. 7. This too sounds like Clare's work. According to the Ordinances of the Magnates, if the lord did redress the grievance in his court, he was entitled to any amercement imposed.

[132] See below, 76.

[133] *DBM*, 150–1, cap. 7.

Pagnell, Huntingdon, Cambridge and Ware.[134] But over half the counties had not seen him at all. At the parliament, therefore, there was a protest. According to the well-informed Burton abbey annalist, a body described as 'the community of the bachelery of England', probably composed of knights at the parliament, complained to Lord Edward, Richard de Clare and other councillors that the barons had so far looked after themselves and done nothing for 'the utility of the republic'.[135] Edward at once declared that, although he had taken his initial oath unwillingly, he would now stand by the community to the death and force the barons to fulfil their promises. Under this pressure, the barons at last promulgated the legislation, published in draft form back in March, dealing with attendance at their courts, as well as the abuses of the sheriffs and the justices in eyre. Perhaps the legislation would have been promulgated anyway, but given all the delays, the community of the bachelery had reason for thinking otherwise.[136]

The Provisions of Westminster, as they are called by historians, were now given great publicity. On 24 October the king had them read in Westminster Hall before earls, barons and 'innumerable people', no quick process as they have twenty-four separate chapters, some lengthy.[137] At last the church too came behind the reforms. The bishops had been conspicuously absent from the 1258 Oxford parliament, and had pronounced no sentence of excommunication against those who opposed the revolutionary reforms. The Provisions of Westminster, provisions the king might have issued anyway of his own volition, were different. After they were proclaimed in Westminster Hall, Archbishop Boniface and the bishops in full pontificals excommunicated all who contravened them.[138]

## THE NEW EYRE

In November 1259, soon after the close of the parliament, Hugh Bigod addressed the problem of his solitary eyre. 'To improve the state of all the kingdom', he now organized a judicial visitation in which panels of judges were to tour all the counties of England.[139] There were to be seven circuits, one under Bigod himself, the others under a member of the council, a member of the parliamentary twelve and a professional judge,

---

[134] No records survive of Bigod, on these visitations, hearing, in any consistent way, the complaints brought to light by the four knights and the hundredal jurors, but it is possible some of his plea rolls are missing. For discussion by Hershey, see *SESK*, xxi–ii; *SERHB*, i, pp. xv, lvii; Jacob, *Studies*, 64–5.

[135] For further discussion of this episode, see below, 48.

[136] For the detail of the legislation, see below, 158–9. It is comprehensively analysed in Paul Brand's *Kings, Barons and Justices*.

[137] Brand, *Kings, Barons and Justices*, 413–27; *DBM*, 136–49.

[138] FitzThedmar, 42 (Stone, FitzThedmar, no. 726).

[139] Bigod, rather than the king, attested the writs setting the eyre up: *CR 1259–61*, 139–40.

the involvement of the councillors and the twelve being an indication of the eyre's importance.[140] There was to be no doubt about the availability of the *querela*. It was to be publicly proclaimed in cities, boroughs and markets that the eyres would hear 'all who shall wish to complain of trespasses committed against them in the last seven years'. Two types of complaint were particularly specified, those made against royal and seigneurial officials acting in breach of their recent oath, and those against violators of Magna Carta, the first time judges had been given a commission to that effect. There was also to be another inquiry in each county by hundredal jurors, while the judges were to have before them the inquiry made by the four knights the year before. Given the judges were also to hear common pleas, this would be the most comprehensive and deep-digging judicial visitation ever to take place in England.[141]

## MORE CHANGES TO THE SHERIFF'S OFFICE

The Westminster parliament saw important changes to the shrieval office. In accordance with the original plan of reform, nearly all the sheriffs were replaced, so they had indeed only held office for a year. The new appointees were once again mostly vavasours, that is, senior knights, of their shires. All again took the oath to act justly devised in October 1258. There was also a scheme to make the office partly elective. The sheriffs this time were chosen by the justiciar, two senior judges and the exchequer, but for the next year the plan was to have four candidates elected in the county court, with the exchequer then selecting one as sheriff.[142] The desire for royal officials to be locally elected was long-standing. In the 1215 Magna Carta, the four knights who were to sit with the king's judges to hear the assizes were to be elected in the county court. So were the twelve knights who were to investigate abuses in each county. From King John's reign counties had occasionally offered money for permission to elect their own sheriffs. Two of the sheriffs of 1258–9 had been elected by the four knights commissioned to hear complaints in their counties. The four knights themselves may well have been elected locally.[143] Making the sheriff's office partly elective was thus a clear move to conciliate the shires.[144]

---

[140] In fact, the involvement of the councillors and the twelve did not work as planned: Crook, *Records of the General Eyre*, 189–91.

[141] *DBM*, 158–65; *CR 1256–9*, 141–4; Jacob, *Studies*, 104–5. The eyre, however, was never completed: Crook, *Records of the General Eyre*, 189–91.

[142] *DBM*, 154–5, cap. 22; *CFR 1257–8*, no. 1178; TNA E 159/33, m. 4d (image 0074), for the oath. For the new sheriffs, see Ridgeway, 'Mid thirteenth-century reformers and the localities', 71–4.

[143] Ridgeway, 'Mid thirteenth-century reformers and the localities', 66–7.

[144] There were also schemes, apparently stillborn, to have a standing committee of four knights in each county to monitor the activities of the sheriff and hear everyone's complaints between eyres.

If the reformers thus fulfilled their pledge to appoint sheriffs who were county knights, they were unforthcoming when it came to conceding them expenses. The granting of expenses or salaries to office-holders had been a key feature of the reforms, one designed to ensure the probity of officials by removing the need to accept bribes and other illicit payments. Both Hugh Bigod and the treasurer of the exchequer, John of Crakehall, had been given salaries, as we have seen. Salaries in place before 1258 had also continued for the king's judges, the justices of the Jews and various household officials.[145] That the sheriffs should receive expenses had been stated specifically in the Ordinance of October 1258. Yet while expenses were ultimately claimed by around half a dozen sheriffs, none were actually conceded during the lifetime of the regime.[146] Here, however, the reformers had some excuse. The new sheriffs had accounted not for fixed increments above the ancient farms, but for all the issues they received, the amount obtained above the farms being described as 'profit'.[147] In the event the profits accounted for in 1258–9 were less than the previous increments to the tune of around £1,500. The new sheriffs were also less successful in actually raising the money.[148] The contrast reflected the burdens imposed on the counties before 1258 and the way they had now been lightened. But the government was entitled to suspect that, in the difference between the old increments and the new profits, there was money the sheriffs were keeping for themselves. They were in effect taking their own expenses.

For the future, the government decided to abandon the idea of expenses altogether and with it the sheriffs accounting for variable profits. Instead, when the new sheriffs were appointed in 1259, the system of farms and fixed increments was reinstated. This was administratively far easier to run.[149] It was also less of a retreat from reform than it might seem, for the new increments were set at a level some £600 lower than those in force before 1258. In Norfolk–Suffolk (a joint sheriffdom), the amount demanded went down from 400 marks to 300; in Yorkshire from 470 marks to 350; in Devonshire from 130 marks to 100. The sheriffs of Lincolnshire and Hampshire were 'given hope' by Hugh Bigod that their increments might be further reduced if they served the king well and could not find the

---

[145] *CLR 1251–60*, 441–6, 457, 461, 465, 478.

[146] For claims, see TNA E 368/35, mm. 18d, 20d–21, 24, 27–9. Eventually, between 1262 and 1273, nine sheriffs did succeed in getting expenses. See Collingwood, 'Royal finance', 127–37, and Cassidy 'Fulk Peyforer's wages'. Richard Cassidy has also sent me a detailed table on the subject.

[147] The issues here were those contributing before to the farm and increment (see below, 642 (the Glossary)). They had nothing to do with private debts.

[148] Cassidy, 'Bad sheriffs, custodial sheriffs', 41.

[149] For the administrative strain of the custodial system, see Barratt, 'Crisis management', 68.

whole amount.[150] The sums demanded were considerably more than those yielded by the profits of 1258–9, yet represented a sensible attempt to reach a modus vivendi with the shires.

## ROYAL FINANCE

The reform of local government, with its smaller harvest of revenue, obviously posed a problem for what had always been proclaimed as a second aim of reform, namely to restore the crown's financial position. The magnates, in a letter to the pope, thus said they were taking measures to see the king 'abounded in riches', the realm having suffered from 'two wounds', the one being the king's injustices, the other his poverty. For both the Lusignans were blamed: they had 'denied justice to subjects and taken away the riches of the prince'.[151]

One immediate measure to improve the king's position and reverse the profligacies of the past came to nothing. There was no general act of resumption. Having been used to intimidate the Lusignans, the idea was quietly dropped. Simon de Montfort never surrendered Kenilworth and Odiham. On the other hand, when it came to the distribution of patronage, the council did set a new course. It had, of course, absolute control since the chancellor could seal no substantial grant of money, land or wardship without its consent.[152] In the whole of 1259, outside a settlement for Simon de Montfort discussed later, the king made only one significant grant of land, that of the manor of Brandeston in Suffolk to Roger Bigod. The concession was witnessed by Hugh Bigod and five councillors.[153] The council also exercised a firm control over the granting of wardships.[154] In 1259 around a dozen of significant size came into the king's hands. In half the cases the council's role in their distribution is specifically mentioned, while in the others it can be suspected.[155] In all but two cases (both showing the influence of Peter of Savoy), the recipients had to offer money, thus fulfilling the plan that wardships should be sold, rather than given away free as so often under Henry. In 1259, Hugh Bigod himself agreed to pay £3,000 at £400 a year for the wardship of the lands and heirs of William of Kyme.[156] Between

---

[150] *CFR 1259–60*, nos. 754–74; TNA E 159/33, m. 5d (image 0075); TNA E 159/38, m. 1 (image 0004); Cassidy, 'Bad sheriffs, custodial sheriffs', 41; Ridgeway, 'Mid thirteenth-century reformers and the localities', 74–5.

[151] Burton, 464–5. This was in the speech prepared for delivery to the pope.

[152] *DBM*, 102–3, cap. 7.

[153] *CChR 1257–1300*, 22; *RCWL*, ii, 125. The manor was said to be an escheat of the lands of the Normans. Bigod did not hold on to it: Morris, *Bigod Earls of Norfolk*, 79 n. 149.

[154] See Collingwood, 'Royal finance', 157–61.

[155] *CFR 1258–9*, nos. 178, 193–4, 299, 551, 635, 655, 673, 890, 906, 912; *CFR 1259–60*, nos. 30, 51, 58; *CPR 1258–66*, 9–10, 12, 15, 21, 29, 32, 35–7, 46, 58, 60; *CR 1259–61*, 225.

[156] *CFR 1259–60*, no. 51; *CPR 1258–66*, 60. Bigod would have wanted the wardship as his custody of the Wake estates ended in 1259.

1256 and 1258 the sums offered for wardships averaged 86 marks a year. Between 1259 and 1261 they averaged 2,425 marks a year.[157]

The government also achieved some success in what was done with the money. At Oxford it was decided that all the crown's revenues should be paid into the exchequer.[158] The aim was to prevent them going directly into the king's wardrobe. Henceforth it was to be funded exclusively by subventions from the exchequer. Henry had bypassed the exchequer before 1258 largely for reasons of convenience. It was often quicker to draw directly on local revenues than wait while those revenues went into the exchequer and out again into the wardrobe. In seeking to end the practice, the reformers were not motivated by distrust of the wardrobe. They controlled it now just as much as they did the exchequer. Rather, the motives were practical. For the old system left the wardrobe living hand to mouth and scraping money together from a multiplicity of sources. Far better for it to be financed in orderly fashion by regular block grants from the exchequer. Indeed, even before the revolution, there had been plans for that to happen.[159] But it could only happen if the exchequer had the money, and for that it needed to receive all the revenues of the kingdom. Hence the reform proposed in 1258.

An attempt was made to make the new system work. Between November 1258 and May 1259 the exchequer supplied the wardrobe with four sums of 1,000 marks and one of £1,000. After that the sums became more irregular, but still in the financial year 1258/9, 75 per cent of wardrobe revenue, £8,638, did come from the exchequer. This compared to 16 per cent between January 1255 and April 1256 and 56 per cent between 1245 and 1252.[160]

The council later claimed that under Hugh Bigod part of the money from wardships was set aside to pay the king's debts and meet the costs of his household.[161] There is no evidence of this happening and indeed a debt of £772 owed to cloth merchants for purchases made in 1257/8 remained outstanding.[162] Yet there was an improvement in the solvency of the wardrobe. In the first wardrobe account after the revolution (covering the period from July 1258 to July 1261) its receipts and expenditure were more or less in balance.[163] The receipts themselves were much the same as

---

[157] Waugh, *Lordship of England*, 256–7. The comparison is subject to all kinds of qualifications and explanations but still makes a point.

[158] *DBM*, 106–7, cap. 14. For reform at the exchequer under John of Crakehall, see Jobson, 'John of Crakehall'.

[159] See volume 1, 664–5.

[160] Wild, *WA*, cxv, cxxix, cxlv, cxlviii; Barratt, 'Crisis management at the exchequer', 64. The very low figure for 1255/6 is partly explained by a large loan contributing to wardrobe receipts.

[161] *DBM*, 150–3, caps. 8, 14; 220–1, cap. 1 [3].

[162] *CR 1264–8*, 421–2.

[163] Wild, *WA*, cxxxiv, cl.

in 1255/6, averaging £247 per week as against £243 (this for the whole period 1258–61 covered by the accounts).[164]

  If the decline in money from the county farms in 1258/9 had been part of an overall collapse in revenue, the reform regime would have been in trouble. But there was no such collapse, as indeed the wardrobe receipts indicate. The total cash received by the exchequer in the financial year 1258/9, at just over £16,000, was actually some £2,660 more than the average for the two previous years, a rise of some 20 per cent.[165] The total revenue revealed by the pipe roll of 1258/9 at around £24,500 was around £2,000 more than that in the roll of the previous year.[166] These figures are, however, subject to a major qualification. Behind the success there was one fruitful windfall. It came from the issues of the bishopric of Winchester, taken into the king's hands on Aymer's expulsion. Between September 1258 and December 1260 these were worth some £10,000 to the crown. In 1259 a total of £3,865 reached the exchequer from both the issues and from Aymer's stored treasure. Before the reforms the money would almost certainly have gone straight to the wardrobe.[167] Another 1,000 marks of Aymer's treasure funded the envoys going to Rome to seek his removal![168] Fundamentally, the Winchester money was keeping the regime afloat, a fair exchange many would have thought for all the trouble caused by the bishop-elect. The money enabled the regime to square the circle, allowing it to alleviate the burden on the shires (at least when it came to the county farms) while at the same time maintaining the king's revenue. Of course, this could only be a short-term fix, but the collapse of the regime in 1260–1 meant it never had to find another solution.[169] That was left to Edward I with the customs on wool exports, the role played by Italian bankers and the granting of taxation by parliament.

[164] Wild, *WA*, cxliii.

[165] For similarly positive figures from the 1259 exchequer receipt rolls and the money the sheriffs brought at the start of the Easter and Michaelmas terms: Whitwell, 'The revenue and expenditure of England under Henry III', 710; Cassidy, 'The English exchequer', table 5; Barratt, 'Crisis management at the exchequer', 66; Cassidy, 'Adventus vicecomitum', 616, 622, 624.

[166] The revenue revealed by the pipe roll includes money paid into the exchequer, money paid into the wardrobe and money spent locally. The financial year covered by the pipe roll ran from Michalemas to Michaelmas (so, for example, from Michaelmas 1258 to Michaelmas 1259), but some cash received and expenditure incurred after the Michaelmas terminal date could be included in the roll. For the figures (subject to many qualifications), see Cassidy, 'The English exchequer', 29, 34. Collingwood, 'Royal finance', 145–6, after various adjustments, gives a higher figure.

[167] For a positive decision by the council it should go to the exchequer: *CLR 1251–60*, 447.

[168] TNA E 401/39 and TNA E 401/40 (figures from Richard Cassidy); Wild, *WA*, 85, 99–101; Howell, *Regalian Right*, 238; Cassidy, 'The English exchequer', table 5. Treharne, *Baronial Plan*, 126–30, has a full summary of what was done with Lusignan money.

[169] For a critical appraisal of the attempts at financial reform, see Barratt, 'Crisis management at the exchequer', with the conclusion at 69–70.

## THE REGIME'S ACHIEVEMENT

In the fifteen months since the revolution of 1258, the achievements of the new regime had been remarkable. It had purged the realm of the Lusignan half-brothers and their satellites. It had gained control of the whole apparatus of central government – council, chancery, household and exchequer. It had gone some way to putting the finances of the exchequer and wardrobe onto a new footing. It had promulgated major legislation, the first since the 1230s, legislation attacking the malpractices of royal officials and limiting the jurisdiction of private courts. It had made the sheriffs local knights, holding office for a year. It had also reduced the financial burden they had to shoulder and thus the pressures placed on those subject to them.[170] Meanwhile, in every shire, panels of knights and hundredal jurors had inquired into local abuses. Hugh Bigod, on his visitations to the shires, had heard some of the resulting cases as well as many individual *querelae*, and now his efforts were to be supplemented by a nationwide eyre. In a great proclamation in French and English as well as Latin, the council had explained its authority and imposed on everyone an oath to obey its commandments. At the same time, again in all three languages, it had set out in detail the oath to be taken by the sheriffs. In another proclamation the councillors and the twelve representing the community at parliament had subjected themselves and their officials to the process of reform. The reforms had been far more radical than in 1215, when Magna Carta had left the king in control of central government. They had also, unlike '1215', addressed the malpractices of magnates and their officials. It was not just the king and his men who were under attack.

Central to this achievement was the way the baronial coalition had held together. A speech prepared for delivery before the pope had spoken of the danger of division. For that reason a legate was requested who might keep the rival factions in check. No legate had been sent and yet the regime had survived, despite the quarrels between Montfort and Richard de Clare. The queen and Peter of Savoy had remained on side. The king's one attempt to break free, as will be seen, had been easily defeated. The threat from Lord Edward had been contained. Indeed, he had supported the Provisions of Westminster.

## THE ABSENCE OF OUTSIDE INTERFERENCE

Important in permitting these successes had been the absence of outside interference. However much King Alexander of Scotland sympathized with the plight of his father-in-law, he made no move to intervene. Indeed, the baronial regime hoped Scotland might prove an ally in any future

---

[170] A table in Collingwood, *Royal Finance*, 100–1, shows the contrast between the annual appointments in 1258 and 1259 and the earlier situation.

crisis. In November 1258 it asked Alexander's councillors, if requested, to give 'counsel and help with all their power within the kingdom of England'.[171] As for King Louis, despite the barons preventing Henry meeting him at Cambrai in November 1258, he continued the peace negotiations and ultimately recognized the council's authority. When it came to the pope, the barons took great pains to justify their conduct both through letters and envoys.[172] In his reply, Pope Alexander warned the barons to show due fealty and reverence to Henry, 'a most Christian prince', but more or less accepted their version of events.[173] If the reforms were indeed for the good of the church and the realm, then he was all for them. At the same time, Alexander turned down the baronial request to send a legate. If some leaders of the regime genuinely hoped a legate might compose their differences, others probably welcomed this escape from papal interference. Alexander had probably sensed as much for he asked whether everyone really did want a legate to be sent. In 1258–9, therefore, no papal thunderbolts crashed down on England to match those sent by Innocent III when he quashed Magna Carta in 1215.[174]

## THE RETURN OF KING RICHARD

The barons were equally successful in warding off the most dangerous outside threat of all, or so at least they thought it – the threat, that is, of King Richard's return in company with the Lusignans. Some such alarm was probably behind the appointment in August 1258 of Roger Bigod, to keep the Norfolk and Suffolk coastline, equipped with an oath of loyalty to be sworn by locals to the regime.[175] Alarm probably explains too the request for help from Scotland and the co-ordinated attack on Guy de Rochefort and Elyas de Rabayne.[176] The fears reached a climax at the end of 1258 when it was clear Richard was returning. His reason (so he said

---

[171] CR 1256–9, 461–2; Paris, v, 739–40; Reid, Alexander III, 153–4. The letter was written in the king's name. It assumed the councillors were in charge of the Scottish government and Alexander's minority was thus still continuing. In fact, the crisis of 1257–8 (see volume 1, 675) had ended with Alexander (seventeen in 1258) effectively in control, having formed a council reconciling competing factions: Reid, Alexander III, 138–40.

[172] See below, 44.

[173] Paris, vi, 410–16 (F, i, 379–80); Treharne, Baronial Plan, 106–7.

[174] F,, i, 379–80; Paris, vi, 410–16. Alexander, anyway short of cardinals, declared that neither the Sicilian affair nor the peace negotiations were in such a state as to require a legate. A newsletter from 1259 speaks of the hostility towards the papacy in England, centring on papal provisions and the payment of the annual tribute: Villard, 'Autour de Charles d'Anjou', 34–5, no. 5. The council had taken good care to repay the loans taken out to pay the tribute: CLR 1251–60, 437, 459; TNA E 403/ 17B, m.1; E 403/ 3115, m.1.

[175] CPR 1247–58, 649; RL, ii, 129; CR 1256–9, 462. For measures taken by the regime to guard the coast, see Jobson, 'The maritime theatre', 220–1. He points out that ten of the twenty-one castles given new castellans at Oxford were coastal.

[176] See Ridgeway, 'The politics of the English royal court', 299–300.

later) was to prevent the barons confiscating his possessions.[177] The barons for their part believed he was planning to restore his half-brothers, destroy the reforms and punish the reformers. A tense stand-off resulted until Richard finally bowed to the baronial terms. He landed at Dover on 27 January 1259 and next day swore the same oath to accept the reforms as everyone else, this with an additional clause binding him never to bring back the Lusignans 'by force' and without the magnates' consent.[178] The oath was sworn in the chapter house at Canterbury cathedral after Richard had been summoned to take it (by Richard de Clare) as earl of Cornwall rather than king of Germany. A newsletter sent to Provence in 1259 relates how Richard had initially resented his brother's treatment but, seeing the barons' united front, he had decided to concentrate on making money for his own affairs.[179] Writing himself on 20 March 1259, Richard said he had reached an agreement with the regime and was sure it would do nothing to his disadvantage. Soon the barons, so Matthew Paris observed, did not bother whether he came or went.[180]

## JUSTIFICATIONS OF THE REVOLUTION

The regime's achievements also depended on the absence of internal protest. Not the least extraordinary feature of '1258' is how calmly everyone seems to have accepted the revolution. There was no upsurge of protest, no challenge to the legitimacy of what had happened. Later, Henry complained that his subjection to the council 'deprived him of all honour and pristine royal dignity'.[181] But if Fulk Basset, bishop of London, thought the same, as opposed just to protesting on King Richard's behalf, his voice was stilled by his death in May 1259. If Henry had advocates in 1258, their views have gone unrecorded. To be sure, the chronicler Thomas Wykes thought the revolution illegitimate, but he was writing in light of the subsequent civil war. Even with hindsight, he gave a far from unsympathetic account of baronial motives. Despairing of King Richard's return with his wise counsels, Henry had been judged by the barons as 'useless and insufficient for disposing of the affairs of the kingdom'. Wykes also saw the Provisions of Oxford as perfectly acceptable, apart from the

---

[177] He states this specifically in a letter of 20 March 1259: Villard, 'Autour de Charles d'Anjou', 30, no. 1. Richard may also have been worried about the way the reforms were impinging on his government of Cornwall: Page, 'Cornwall, Earl Richard and the Barons' War', 27–30.

[178] CPR 1258–66, 10; Paris, v, 735–6; Wykes, 121–2.

[179] Villard, 'Autour de Charles d'Anjou', 34–5, no. 5.

[180] Paris, v, 746. For the letter, see above, n. 177. The letter was written to Laurence de St Martin, bishop of Rochester, who Richard hoped would help promote his cause at the court of Rome.

[181] Ridgeway, 'King Henry III's grievances against the council', 241, cap. 27.

clause about treating opponents as mortal enemies.[182] In London, the alderman Arnold fitzThedmar wrote of the 'insane' parliament at Oxford, but the word 'insane' was written over an erasure after the fall of the Montfortian regime. Writing while the regime was in power (during 1264–5), he actually thought the Oxford parliament had abolished evil customs by which the realm had long been oppressed. That may well have been his view at the time.[183] In fact, no contemporary account of '1258' suggested anything shocking had taken place.

One strand here was the way the revolution seemed to echo ideas of canon lawyers about how a king like Henry should be treated.[184] Whatever was thought of Henry's rule, it was very difficult to portray him personally as a tyrant, a '*rex tyrannus*'. He seemed rather to fit another familiar type of king, namely that of the '*rex inutilis*', 'the useless king'. What was to be done with such a ruler? In discussing this question, canon lawyers made a distinction between the *rex inutilis*, who was stained by personal vice, and the *rex inutilis*, who was personally blameless. The first was liable to deposition, as Pope Zacharias had deposed the last Merovingian king, Chilperic. The second should be given a '*coadjutor*' to take over the administration of the kingdom. These ideas influenced Pope Innocent IV's dealings with King Sancho of Portugal. Sancho, Innocent stressed, had not been a wicked king, but he had been 'negligent', 'idle' and 'foolish'. Accordingly, Innocent, while leaving him as king, had entrusted the government of the realm to his brother Alfonso. For Sancho, then, why not read Henry, and for Alfonso, a baronial council?[185] In fact, in the propaganda of 1258, no worked-out case was made against Henry on such canon law lines. One can see why. The canonists took it for granted that only the pope could remove or restrain such a king and the last thing the barons wanted was to be dependent on any papal say so. They had gone ahead without the pope and merely wanted his ex post facto blessing. Yet there are some hints that ideas about the '*rex inutilis*' did have some purchase. Thomas Wykes, as we have seen, said that the barons in 1258 considered Henry 'useless and insufficient, *inutilem et insufficientem*, for disposing of the affairs of his kingdom'.[186] The great Montfortian tract, *The Song of Lewes*, later justified placing restrictions on a king who was 'foolish, *insipiens*' and 'less wise than he ought to be'.[187] The canonists also thought that 'simplicity', of which

[182] Wykes, 118–19.

[183] FitzThedmar, 37 (Stone, FitzThedmar, no. 710); Stone, 'Book of Arnold fitz Thedmar', 36, 43, 217.

[184] For what follows, see Peters, *Shadow King*, chs. 3 and 4.

[185] Since Innocent dealt with Sancho at the council of Lyon, where an English delegation was headed by Roger Bigod, the episode was presumably known in England. Alfonso had married the heiress of Boulogne in 1238.

[186] Wykes, 118–19. For '*insufficiens*', in the thought of the canonists, being synonymous with '*inutilis*', see Peters, *Shadow King*, 121.

[187] *Song of Lewes*, lines 757–9. For the *Song*, see below, 410–5.

Henry was so often accused, was one reason why a king might be judged *inutilis*. When the barons told the pope that Henry had reduced the kingdom to a '*statum imbecillem*', they were echoing Pope Innocent's statement that King Sancho had been guilty of '*cordis imbecillitatem*'.[188]

If, however, canon law ideas about the *rex inutilis* poured a little oil on the wheels of revolution, that they turned so smoothly was due far more to the course of English politics since Henry's minority. As a result, there seemed nothing very novel in the baronial proposals. Since 1244 a succession of parliaments had wanted to choose the king's leading ministers. Under the never implemented 'Paper Constitution' of that year, the four councillors elected by parliament were to give justice to complainants, control the king's expenditure of money and choose the king's chief ministers. Their powers were very comparable to those of the council of fifteen in 1258. Such demands could claim some precedent. Great councils during the king's minority had sanctioned the appointment of both Ralph de Neville as keeper of the seal in 1218 and Hubert de Burgh as justiciar in 1219. In 1234 they had forced the king to change his ministers and right his wrongs. In 1236, Neville had declared that, appointed by the kingdom, he could only surrender the seal with the kingdom's consent. In fact, the appeal to precedent was pretty spurious. Henry later pointed out that kings of England had always been free to choose their ministers and, save in exceptional circumstances, that had indeed been the case. The baronial demands were in truth revolutionary. And yet one further feature made them seem less so. The barons maintained they had not coerced the king. Rather he had agreed to their demands quite voluntarily in return for the promise of a tax.

Here too there was a pedigree. In 1225, Henry had issued a new version of Magna Carta in return for a tax. In 1237, again in return for a tax, the Charters had been confirmed. The parliaments of the 1240s and 1250s had likewise offered a bargain: 'let us choose your ministers, and we will give you a tax'. Henry had always refused the bargain. Now, in 1258, he had accepted it. That was all that had happened. Henry's proclamation on 2 May 1258 thus explained he was accepting reform in return for a promised tax to further the Sicilian business. In the same vein, both the baronial letter to the pope and a speech drafted for delivery at the papal court had Henry going along willingly with the new regime. Only one chronicle (Tewkesbury's) mentioned how the revolution had begun with an armed march on Westminster Hall and the king's coercion. Matthew Paris's account of the parliament, detailed though it was, simply pictured Henry acknowledging the criticisms and coming to his senses.

The stated purpose of the reforms enhanced the impression of a fruitful co-operation between king and realm. They were promulgated,

---

[188] Peters, *Shadow King*, 138 n. 5.

the king was made to say, 'for the honour of God, and in fealty to us, and for the profit of our realm'.[189] 'In fealty to us', so clearly there was no question of the reforms breaching the loyalty owed the king.[190]

To enhance this impression, the councillors took one final precaution. They concealed the extent of their powers. This was a secret revolution.[191] In the great proclamation of October 1258, Henry thus announced that the council had been chosen 'by us and the community of the realm'. He wished whatever it decided to be 'established in all things forever'. Everyone was to swear to observe its statutes and treat those who contravened them as mortal enemies.[192] Yet, even with the reference to mortal enmity, it could seem the council, with Henry's consent, had merely a temporary commission to issue reforms for the good of king and realm. The proclamation said nothing about the council controlling the king's seal and being, for twelve years, the effective ruler of the country.

What the proclamation did say, however, was quite enough. There could be no doubt that the council, by the king's willing delegation, had the power to right the wrongs from which the realm had suffered. In the process of that righting, the barons drew strength from how they described their enterprise.[193] The 'state of the realm, *status regni*', they said, often using more than one word, was to be subject to 'reform', 'correction' and 'rectification' ('*reformatio, correctio, rectificatio*').[194] Historians, writing about the period between 1258 and 1267, have generally focused here on the word 'reform', hence the titles of E.F. Jacob's *Studies in the Period of Baronial Reform and Rebellion* and R.F. Treharne's *The Baronial Plan of Reform*. This is not illegitimate for 'reform of the realm' appears as a stated objective throughout the period.[195] Used in a political context, as here, the word was strikingly new.[196] Although meaning much the same thing, Magna Carta

---

[189] *DBM*, 116–19.

[190] This point is made in Burton, 'Politics, propaganda and public opinion', 37–8.

[191] For this theme, see Carpenter, 'The secret revolution of 1258'.

[192] *DBM*, 116–19.

[193] Although my emphasis is slightly different, in what follows I have been greatly helped by the discussion of the terminology, and especially the word '*reformatio*', in Power, 'The uncertainties of reformers', and Dejoux, 'À la recherche de la *reformatio regni* dans les royaumes de France et d'Angleterre au XIIIᵉ siècle'. Marie Dejoux kindly sent me a copy of the latter paper, forthcoming in a volume of essays she has edited, *Les mots pour dire la réforme à la fin du Moyen Âge*.

[194] In May 1258 the '*status regni*' was thus to be 'rectified and reformed'. In June 'correction and reform' was to be applied to 'state of Henry, Edward and all England': *DBM*, 74–5, 76–7, 96–9.

[195] In the baronial letter of explanation to the pope in 1258 and the speech prepared for delivery before him (Burton, 457, 464); in the reissues of the Provisions of Westminster in 1263 and 1264 (Brand, *Kings, Barons and Justices*, 430), where linked to '*melioracio*'; in the baronial case made to Louis IX (*DBM*, 256–7), where linked to '*rectificatio*'; and in *Song of Lewes*, lines 211–16, 325–8.

[196] This is shown in Dejoux, 'À la recherche de la *reformatio regni*'.

in 1215 had spoken of '*emendatio*', not '*reformatio*'. The introduction of 'reform' into the political discourse was thanks in part to the Ordinances Louis IX introduced in 1254 'to reform the state of the realm for the better, *ad statum regni reformandum in melius*'.[197] Equally, perhaps more important, was ecclesiastical example. Here 'reform' was used in two senses. One was the general 'reform of the state of the church' as in the Legate Otto's much circulated statutes of 1237.[198] The other was reform of the moral and religious life of individuals, especially clergy, as in the responsibilities assigned to prelates in the decrees of the Fourth Lateran Council.[199] By speaking of reform of the realm, the baronial leaders had found a powerful way of describing their enterprise, one which invested it with considerable spiritual authority. To this point we will return.[200]

The barons were equally successful in showing how necessary reform was, given Henry's misrule. This was done in two great manifestos. One was the letter to the pope, sealed by Hugh Bigod and most of the councillors 'on behalf of all the community'. The modern printed text runs to nearly four pages. The other was the speech prepared for delivery before the pope. Dealing also with the peace with France, it runs to over five pages. Although destined for the papal court, the manifestos were widely circulated in England. The letter to the pope was transcribed in full by Matthew Paris and the Tewkesbury and Burton annalists. The latter also had the text of the speech.[201]

Because a central aim was to persuade the pope to dismiss Aymer de Lusignan as bishop-elect of Winchester, both manifestos concentrated largely on the sins of the Lusignans.[202] They contained nothing about the malpractices of sheriffs and itinerant justices, let alone those of the barons

---

[197] Dejoux, *Les Enquêtes de Saint Louis*, 351. The baronial letter of explanation to the pope in 1258, likewise spoke of the king's wish '*regnum suum . . . in melius reformare*': Burton, 457. And see Burton, 438, for the Burton annalist describing the barons as being engaged in '*reformationem regni in melius*'.

[198] *C&S*, 245.

[199] Power, 'The uncertainties of reformers', 1–2 (Canons of the Fourth Lateran Council, chs. 6 and 7). As Power notes, the word is used in the same way in the letters of Robert Grosseteste and Adam Marsh: *Letters of Grosseteste*, 376; *Letters of Adam Marsh*, i, 206–7, though see also *Letters of Adam Marsh*, i, 82–3, for a more political context. Julia Barrow, in 'The ideas and application of reform', shows the use of the word before the twelfth century in the Pauline sense of seeking conformity with the life of Christ and, less commonly, in a monastic context, in the sense of reform of the church. I am grateful to Julia Barrow for sending me a copy of her paper.

[200] See below, 59–65.

[201] Paris, vi, 400–5; Tewkesbury, 170–4; Burton, 456–66. Treharne, *Baronial Plan*, 104, suggested the speech was delivered by John Clarel, who was the only clerk amongst the four envoys sent to the pope in August 1258. For discussion of both the letter and the speech, see Powicke, *King Henry III*, i, 387–91.

[202] The aim of the speech was also to persuade the pope to send a legate.

and their bailiffs.[203] Nonetheless, the critiques were powerful affairs. Henry had embarked on the Sicilian affair, the pope was told, without the counsel of his magnates. He had become infatuated by the Lusignans, wasting the kingdom's resources on them and placing them above the law. Indeed, 'shameful to say and terrible to hear', if anyone brought a legal action against the half-brothers, instead of being a 'propitious judge', Henry turned against the complainant and became a 'terrible enemy'. It was not just magnates who had suffered. The Lusignans' 'ministers and officials' had despoiled the poor, favoured the impious and rejoiced in oppressing their inferiors. They had made Henry wholly forget that a 'prince ought not to exist for himself but for his subjects', indeed they had 'damnably whispered to him that a prince was not subject to the laws'. Although this stopped short of calling Henry a tyrant, it showed he had been close to fulfilling the criteria to be one.

The manifestos went on to explain how the new councillors, 'nights without sleep', were labouring to put matters right. Addressing the two 'wounds' from which the kingdom had suffered, they were restoring the king's finances and 'teaching' him to do justice. Now at last would be heard the clamour of the poor, the tears of widows, the groans of orphans and the just petitions of everyone else. The regime's proclamations spoke in the same vein. 'We have provided by the counsel of our magnates that all my days full and swift justice shall always be done to all without any kind of reward' the king was made to say in the Ordinance of the Sheriffs. 'We have made our officials swear to do right in common to all people, clerk and lay, freeman and villein, house of religion and village' ran the Ordinances of the Magnates.[204] The judges appointed in November 1259 were instructed to give special attention to offences committed 'since the last parliament at Oxford'.[205] It was to be a new dawn.

What is striking is the extent to which contemporaries accepted this view of the council's work. Amongst the chroniclers there was a chorus of approval. The annals of Waverley described how the barons and prelates, divinely awakened to the depressed state of the kingdom, had set about 'reforming and renewing' old laws and customs. The annals of Burton had the magnates meeting at Oxford to make provision 'for the reformation of the kingdom'. Matthew Paris in 1259, having said the 'magnates of England' no longer worried about King Richard, added that they were now devoting themselves entirely to abolishing 'evil customs, injustices and corrupt practices'. At Barlings abbey in Lincolnshire, 'the new statutes at Oxford' were thought to 'relieve the state of England miserably depressed

---

[203] In that sense, the critique was very different from that drawn up later in the conflict for presentation to Louis IX at Amiens.

[204] Burton, 464–5; *DBM*, 132–5. In both cases, I have run together passages.

[205] *DBM*, 160–3, caps. 2–7.

by justices, sheriffs and other bailiffs'.[206] Most remarkable of all was the praise showered on Hugh Bigod by the St Albans monk who continued Matthew Paris's chronicle after Matthew's death. It conveys, more powerfully than anything else, the excitement created by the movement of reform and the way its moral centre was thought to be the redress of grievances and the giving of justice to all.

'About this time', the chronicler writes, 'Hugh Bigod, a man of great probity, and chief justiciar of all England . . . began to go on circuit through all England, from county to county and liberty to liberty, giving justice to everyone according to desert.' Bigod and his colleagues (the judges Roger of Thirkleby and Gilbert of Preston) 'had sworn that, treating equally rich and poor, serf and free, known and unknown, they would, without receiving gifts . . . give fitting judgements in all and everything'. Having reflected on how, in mixing justice and mercy they were following the example of Christ, the chronicle then described how Bigod and his colleagues 'vigorously and urgently following up the inquiry made by four knights in each county, brought to light and severely punished numerous offences and wrongs, hitherto forgotten . . . They yielded not to promises or entreaties, although they came from powerful people, but sought earnestly for the truth and did their work of retribution with speed.'[207]

Matthew Paris's summary of the year 1258 dwelt gloomily on the great famine. The grave diggers had been overwhelmed and bodies had to be buried in pits. The summary of 1259 by Paris's successor was far more positive. The harvest was better and that was not all. 'For,' he wrote, 'England, so long languid and subject to the power and oppression of diverse people as though they were kings, began in this year, with a new justice arising, and with hoped for remedies, to breath again.'[208]

[206] Waverley, 350; Burton, 438; Paris, v, 746; Barlings, cxiii–iv; Dunstable, 209; and for comment Burton, 'Politics, propaganda and public opinion', 43–4.

[207] Paris's Continuator, 426–7; Jacob, *Studies*, 64.

[208] Paris, v, 725; Paris's Continuator, 439. Paris's Continuator went on to contrast in detail the two harvests.

Chapter 2

# THE MATERIAL AND THE MORAL: SIMON DE MONTFORT AND BARONIAL MOTIVES
## 1258-1259

If many in 1258 thought reform of the realm was a necessary and right-eous enterprise, in truth the forces driving forward the baronial leaders were diverse and conflicted. Some of the leaders were inspired by material concerns and political calculations, others by idealism and religiosity. Some had no view of the kind of world they wished to create, others had a vision of the reforms as helping to create a well-ordered Christian commonwealth.

Several baronial leaders expected the revolution to remedy grievances and provide material gains.[1] John fitzGeoffrey complained about bishop-elect Aymer's lawless conduct. Archbishop Boniface recovered damages for a disseisin suffered at the hands of William de Valence.[2] Roger de Mortimer commenced litigation to recover the rich manor of Lechlade from Richard of Cornwall.[3] Roger Bigod replaced Guy de Rochefort as castellan of Colchester and received custody of a wardship held by William de Sancta Ermina. Peter de Montfort got Sancta Ermina's London houses.[4] Richard de Clare replaced bishop-elect Aymer as lord of Weymouth and the isle of Portland, a stupendous increase in his local power.[5] Nearly all the baronial leaders had clashed, at one time or another, with the Lusignans and were glad to see their backs.[6]

Yet if the baronial leaders gained, they also lost. One of the most striking features of the reforms, as we have seen, is how they attacked the malpractices of magnates and their men. This had not been envisaged at

---

[1] See Ridgeway, 'The politics of the English royal court', 305.

[2] *CR 1256–9*, 276.

[3] Carpenter, 'A noble in politics', 186–200. For the case, see below, 168.

[4] *CPR 1247–58*, 653, 655; *CR 1256–9*, 254; Morris, *Bigod Earls of Norfolk*, 79–80. Bigod also established his right, as marshal, to the custody of prisoners taken on the eyre of the justiciar: Jacob, *Studies*, 58 n. 1.

[5] Ridgeway, 'Dorset in the period of reform and rebellion', 28–9. For Clare vigorously expanding his rights in Weymouth at the abbot of Cerne's expense, see TNA KB 26/166, m. 30d (image 0189).

[6] Carpenter, *Reign of Henry III*, 191–2.

the start. In the Petition of the Barons at Oxford there was but the briefest reference to the issue of attendance at private courts.[7] By October 1259 the subject took up the first part of the Provisions of Westminster. The brief given to the four knights in 1258 spoke vaguely of them inquiring into the abuses of royal officials 'and all other persons'. By November 1259, the justices were quite specifically to hear cases against 'magnates and their bailiffs'. This transformation did not take place without resistance. Richard de Clare probably obstructed the publication of the Ordinances of the Magnates. Similar obstruction may explain the failure to provide Bigod with help until the nationwide circuits of November 1259. Even then the instructions to the judges, as in the Ordinances of the Magnates, allowed magnates to put right the abuses of their officials in their own courts.[8]

## PRESSURE FROM BELOW AND THE NEED FOR SUPPORT

One factor explaining the development of the reforms is pressure from below. The volume of cases against magnates and their men coming before the 1258–60 eyres suggests how strong this was. The complainants ranged from individual peasants and peasant communities up to substantial county knights. The number of knights is particularly striking. The grievances were often over suit of court, distraint out of fee and the '*beaupleder*' fine, the very issues dealt with in the legislation.[9] Knights were already demanding more be done at the October parliament of 1258, if we may judge from the apologetic tone taken by the Ordinance of the Sheriffs. Of the groups of knights supposed to bring their inquiries to the parliament, at least six had done so before the Ordinances were issued.[10] A year later at the Westminster parliament, protest was more vocal and more organized. There is much unknown about 'the community of the bachelery of England'. For a start, was the name bestowed by the Burton annalist or adopted by the group itself? The name suggests a body with a defined membership for many communities were bound together by oath, most notably the 'community of England' formed at the Oxford parliament. That, in 1259, 'the community of England' appears again, this time as a community of its 'bachelery', suggests sufficient numbers were involved to justify such a claim. It also suggests the group was in some ways representative of those with similar interests in the country as a whole, or at least could be thought to be so.

---

[7] *DBM*, 86–7, cap. 24.

[8] *DBM*, 162–3, cap. 7. There was also some watering down of the legislation on suit of court to make it more favourable to lords: Brand, *Kings, Barons, Justices*, 36 and n. 81.

[9] For detailed discussion, see below, 158–9.

[10] *CR 1256–9*, 333.

Who then were these 'bachelors' present at the parliament?[11] The most likely answer is that they were first and foremost knights in the followings of lords. The term is often used in that sense. While some of the bachelors may have been young knights, as the term suggests, they could also be men of substance. In 1267 some twenty men were described as 'bachelors' of Earl Gilbert de Clare (Earl Richard's son), and several had significant landed estates.[12] Two, Simon of Pattishall and Hamo Hauteyn, are found on the panels of knights appointed in 1258 and then as sheriffs of their counties.[13] Quite possibly they were part of the community of the bachelery at the Westminster parliament. Pattishall, himself, on Hugh Bigod's eyre, complained about his sufferings at the hands of the baron William de Beauchamp of Bedford.[14] The 'community of the bachelery of England', therefore, was very capable of voicing the grievances festering in the shires about the pace of reform. One can well believe they demanded the immediate publication of the new legislation.

Even as great a baron as Richard de Clare, if he was to maintain a reputation for good lordship, could not ignore the grievances being expressed by his tenants and neighbours, knightly and otherwise. Significantly the community of the bachelery's appeal was made to Clare as well as Lord Edward. If we know nothing of Clare's reply, earlier in the year, after Montfort's attack, he had sent his steward round his estates to hear complaints. Then, in July 1259, all complaints against himself and his bailiffs in Essex, Norfolk and Suffolk were to be heard by a judge empowered to make amends 'according to the law and custom of the realm'. The sheriffs of the counties concerned were to proclaim that all those wishing to complain should appear.[15] It seems that Clare, at court at this time, was responding to a tide of complaints against his bailiffs. Indeed, the month before, in a case before Hugh Bigod, one of his bailiffs was convicted of forcing a Buckinghamshire knight into performing suit at the earl's court when none was owed, precisely the kind of issue covered in the proposed legislation.[16]

The baronial leaders had, then, powerful prudential reasons for responding to discontents in the shires. However much they pretended otherwise, they were revolutionaries embarked on a difficult and dangerous voyage in uncharted waters. They needed to make their regime popular, they needed all the support they could get. There were plenty of indications (as we will see) that the king's 'serene' face hid his real feelings. If he

[11] In what follows, I am indebted to Jacob, *Studies*, 126–34, but for a different view see Crouch, *The English Aristocracy*, 95–6, 273–4 n. 42 and n. 43.

[12] *CPR 1266–72*, 145–7. Gilbert was securing for his followers remission of the king's anger.

[13] *CPR 1247–58*, 648, 654–5.

[14] For Pattishall, see Brand, 'Simon of Pattishall', and below, 147.

[15] *CPR 1258–66*, 53; *RCWL*, ii, 124–5.

[16] See below, 152.

and, perhaps even more, if Edward recovered power, would they not wreak vengeance on their enemies? Right at the start, fear of reprisals had led Richard de Clare, the Bigods, Fulk Basset, John de Plessis and John Mansel to extract letters from Henry promising that he and his heirs (so Edward) would 'save them harmless' for what they did in the way of reform.[17]

Central to these anxieties early on was the fear that the Lusignans would return helped by King Richard, as we have seen. But even when such fears evaporated, anxiety remained. In May 1259, Richard de Clare's steward, Walter of Scotney, went on trial at Winchester before Hugh Bigod, escorted there by thirteen sergeants on horseback and twenty-five on foot. This was the final stage of a pitiful affair. At Winchester back in July 1258, several nobles had fallen seriously ill. William de Clare, Richard's younger brother, and the abbot of Westminster had both died. Richard himself scarcely escaped, losing his hair, teeth and nails. The rumour soon spread that this was all due to a Poitevin poison plot. And the person blamed for administering the poison, bribed, it was said, by William de Valence, was none other than Walter of Scotney. Had not William de Clare said as much on his deathbed? Scotney protested his innocence, but was convicted by a jury drawn from three counties. He was then dragged by horses through the streets of Winchester and hanged. At least Henry and Hugh Bigod (Henry here making a rare appearance) took pity on his widow. The accusations against Scotney are surely incredible. Later the chronicler Thomas Wykes said they were believed '*a vulgo*'. That they led to Scotney's destruction shows the levels of alarm and suspicion running through England in 1258–9. Indeed, the Waverley annals claimed that the Lusignans planned to poison all the native magnates, replace the king and subject the whole of England to their rule.[18]

Another sign of the tensions in 1259 comes in the alliances being formed by the baronial leaders. A legate had been requested in the hope he would sedate their conflicts, and such conflicts were real, even if they remained, for now, as words rather than deeds. Simon de Montfort and Richard de Clare had clashed over the Ordinances of the Magnates and were to do so again over the peace with France.[19] Both were seeking allies, allies who would help them dominate the ruling council. In March 1259, Clare made an alliance with none other than Lord Edward.[20] Each swore to give aid and counsel to the other and to do the same for each other's

---

[17] *RL*, ii, 127–8; *CPR 1247–58*, 637.

[18] Paris, v, 704–5, 709, 725–6, 737–8, 747–8; Tewkesbury, 167; Winchester, 98; Wykes, 120; Waverley, 349–50; *CR 1256–9*, 447–8; Cassidy, '1259 pipe roll', ii, no. 2250. Unfortunately, the record of the case before Bigod is now lost.

[19] See below, 90.

[20] 'Letter of Richard, earl of Gloucester'. A translation is in Hennings, *England under Henry III*, 93–5, a very useful volume with a wide range of translations.

allies. The latter were listed in the agreement, showing that Clare had put together a powerful party, headed by Hugh Bigod and with the councillors Roger Bigod and William de Forz.[21] Hugh Bigod was described as justiciar of England and the agreement was made saving fealty to the king and the oath to support the Provisions. But Bigod surely demeaned the office he otherwise did so much to promote by appearing as a mere supporter of Richard de Clare. The alliance suggests there was little trust between Clare and Edward, elaborate provisions for arbitration being made in the event of them falling out. Fall out they soon did and in October 1259 it was Simon de Montfort's turn to make an alliance with the heir to the throne. Here the possibility of violence was openly acknowledged. Edward was not to 'make war' on anyone involved in the baronial enterprise but only provided they accepted awards of the king's court.[22]

## THE ROLE OF SIMON DE MONTFORT

Amongst the baronial leaders, there were, then, in 1258–9 material ambitions, prudential considerations and factional conflicts. Yet to reduce the revolution just to that would be grotesque. One cannot read the proclamations and propaganda poured out by the regime without sensing the commitment and the fervour behind its reforms. Nowhere is the presence of both the material and the moral more apparent and more perplexing than in the case of the greatest baronial leader of them all, Simon de Montfort.[23]

In terms of prestige and personality, Montfort stood head and shoulders above the other reformers. The son of an illustrious father who had led the Albigensian crusade and died in its cause, Montfort had come to England as a young man and made good his family claim to the earldom of Leicester. He had then married the king's sister Eleanor, crusaded in the Holy Land and been the king's regent in Gascony. His campaigns there, as well as his work at Kenilworth castle, had furbished and burnished a military fame enjoyed by none of his baronial colleagues. His conduct in Gascony had also shown how easily he provoked opposition and how ready he was to use force to crush it. Intelligent, insistent, inflexible, self-righteous, extreme, both sharp and silver tongued, he was determined with the revolution to improve his material position, yet he was driven also, like his father, by a deep sense of piety and mission.[24] (One aspect of

---

[21] Edward's part in the alliance is discussed below, 81–2.

[22] Carpenter, *Reign of Henry III*, 251.

[23] John Maddicott's classic biography, *Simon de Montfort*, came out in 1994 and has been by my side for much of the work on this book. The same is true of Margaret Howell's equally classic *Eleanor of Provence*, published in 1998.

[24] The influence of his father is a major theme in Sophie Ambler's *Song of Simon de Montfort*; see the index at p. 426 where page references are given.

his piety was hostility to the Jews, whom he expelled from Leicester.)
Montfort's landed estate and resources hardly compared with those of
Richard de Clare, but by 1258 he was one of the richer earls.[25] He had
built up a significant following of midlands knights (particularly from the
areas around Kenilworth and Leicester), some of them his tenants, some
not.[26] His calibre as a leader was recognized internationally. In 1241 'the
barons, knights and citizens' of the kingdom of Jerusalem had asked the
emperor Frederick II to make Montfort their regent until Frederick's own
arrival.[27] In 1253, according to Matthew Paris, the French magnates, with
Louis IX away on crusade, had wished to make him 'steward' of the
kingdom, after the death of the regent, Queen Blanche.[28]

## MONTFORT'S 'FRIENDS'

Montfort's power was enhanced by close allies at the very top of the
regime. Three of his 'friends', as the king angrily called them, sat on the
council of fifteen, namely Walter de Cantilupe, bishop of Worcester, Peter
de Montfort and Richard de Grey.[29] Grey was also castellan of Dover and
warden of the Cinque Ports. All three had been members of the baronial
twelve drawing up the reforms of Oxford. All were men of mature age
and political weight, quite unlike the 'young boys' (as Wykes contemptu-
ously called them) who later flocked to Montfort's standard.

Born around 1195, and bishop of Worcester since 1237, Walter de
Cantilupe was easily the most senior bishop on the episcopal bench. He
came from a high-status family, his father, William de Cantilupe I, having
been a steward of King John and then in charge of the early household
of Henry III. Walter's brother William de Cantilupe II was one of Henry's
stewards from 1239 until his death in 1251. Although the family was
Norman in origin, and only really established in England under King
John, by the 1250s, the Cantilupes were probably regarded as 'coming from
the noble stock of the barons of England'.[30] Despite ups and downs in
their relationship (he opposed the Sicilian taxation), Bishop Cantilupe
worked for Henry as a diplomat and was on the king's council before the
1258 revolution. In 1252, along with Peter de Montfort, he was one of the
few who from the first supported Montfort when on trial for his misconduct
in Gascony.[31] The relationship may well have gone back to the early 1230s
and was strengthened by Montfort's acquisition of Kenilworth castle, for

[25] For Montfort's growing wealth, see Maddicott, *Simon de Montfort*, 44–52.
[26] See below, 362–3.
[27] Maddicott, *Simon de Montfort*, 30.
[28] Paris, v, 366.
[29] *DBM*, 200–3, cap. 16.
[30] This was said about his nephew Thomas de Cantilupe by his successor during
Thomas's canonization proceedings: Carpenter, *Reign of Henry III*, 293.
[31] *Letters of Adam Marsh*, i, 78–9.

that made Cantilupe his diocesan bishop. An important family manor at Aston (now Aston Cantlow), where the Cantilupes built the lovely chancel to the parish church, was only twelve miles from the great fortress.[32]

The Cantilupes were almost certainly responsible for bringing Peter de Montfort into Montfort's circle.[33] Aston Cantlow and Peter's castle at Beaudesert (above Henley in Arden in Warwickshire) were only four miles apart. Peter's mother was the daughter of William de Cantilupe I, and Bishop Cantilupe was thus Peter's uncle. A minor on his father's death, Peter spent many years as William I's ward and later, on his seal, proudly displayed the fleur-de-lys of the Cantilupe arms. In his early fifties by the time of the revolution, Peter had gone out with Montfort to Gascony in 1248. Over the years he attests many of Montfort's charters and in 1259 was charged in Montfort's will within giving advice to the executors. But Peter also forged an independent career with the king and Lord Edward. He served them in Wales, went with Edward to Spain for his marriage, acted as a diplomat and by 1258 was on the king's council. Yet the £50 annual fee he received from the king had never been converted into land. Peter had been eying up Garthorpe manor in Leicestershire, but it went instead to a more favoured courtier, Robert Walerand.[34] The grievance constituted another bond with Montfort whose much larger fee had likewise not been changed into land. Doubtless they moaned together.

Richard de Grey, around sixty in 1258, was one of the few people, active in the period of reform and rebellion, whose career stretched back to John's reign, Bishop Cantilupe being another.[35] The connection with Montfort probably came through tenure and neighbourhood for Grey was lord of Alvington just by Leicester and held land from Montfort around twenty miles south-west of Kenilworth. Grey had a long record of royal service, having been a household knight, sheriff of several counties, keeper of the Channel Islands and briefly seneschal of Gascony. His younger brothers, John and William, were both stewards of the king's household. (They took a very different line in the civil war.) Richard had a considerable landed estate, being lord of Codnor in Derbyshire, Hoo and Aylesford in Kent, and Thurrock Grays in Essex. That, at his considerable age, he came out of semi-retirement and returned to front-line politics shows the strength of both his political opinions and his Montfortian connections.

There was one other magnate who could afford Montfort significant support both nationally and locally. This was Hugh Despenser. He was one of the baronial twelve who drew up the reforms in 1258 and though not

---

[32] Aston had been a gift from King John as was the manor of Eaton Bray in Bedfordshire.

[33] For Peter de Montfort, see Cokayne, *Complete Peerage*, ix, 123–6; Carpenter, 'Peter de Montfort'; and Maddicott, *Simon de Montfort*, 64–6.

[34] *CChR 1257–1300*, 51, 56; *CPR 1247–58*, 215; *CIM*, no. 769.

[35] For Richard de Grey, see Stacey, 'Richard de Grey', and Maddicott, *Simon de Montfort*, 62.

formally on the council was a leading member of the regime.[36] In 1259 he too appears as an advisor in Montfort's will. In 1260 he succeeded Hugh Bigod as justiciar. These four friends, Bishop Cantilupe, Peter de Montfort, Richard de Grey and Hugh Despenser, gave Montfort a unique position at the heart of the baronial regime. No other earl had an equivalent following.

## MONTFORT IN ACTION

With all his personality, power and connections, Montfort was well placed to influence the course of events in 1258. He certainly did so. The fact that he kept in his archives a text of the baronial confederation formed at the Westminster parliament (the only one known) suggests he was its prime mover.[37] In Matthew Paris's chronicle, far more than any other noble, he appears as the driving force behind events. Given Paris's death in 1259, there is here no element of hindsight.[38] Montfort first appears at the Westminster parliament (the only earl named) clashing with William de Valence. At the Oxford parliament he then threatens Valence with decapitation if he does not bow to the reforms and surrender his gains from the king. When the Lusignans depart for France, they are pursued by Henry de Montfort, Montfort's eldest son, keen to avenge their insults to his father. It was at this point that Paris felt moved to insert a glowing passage in Montfort's praise. People abroad, he said, were astonished at the abuse suffered by 'this man, so noble and of such high birth and one pre-eminent amongst all on both sides of the sea'.[39] At the Oxford parliament itself, Montfort's pre-eminence had been signalled in a deeply symbolic way. He was made the keeper of Winchester castle and thus for twelve years would control the king's birthplace and the ancient capital of the kingdom.[40]

Two other pieces of evidence fill out this early picture. Just after the Westminster parliament, Montfort was one of the delegation sent to France to conclude the peace negotiations. It was surely he who ensured that, under the terms now agreed, Henry could only spend the money promised to hire knights with the consent of 'upstanding men of the land elected by the king and by high men of the land', a clear reference to the twenty-four men who were now to reform the realm.[41] Later, in July 1258,

[36] Thus Despenser, with the other councillors, attested the October 1258 proclamation setting out the council's authority.

[37] See Carpenter, *Reign of Henry III*, 241–2, and n. 7. The text only survives in an eighteenth-century copy, with fine drawings of the seals. It is illustrated in Maddicott, *Simon de Montfort*, 153.

[38] Paris, v, 732, 737.

[39] Paris, v, 703. The praise is an insertion over an erasure of what may have been a less complimentary comment.

[40] I owe this point to Adrian Jobson.

[41] *Layettes*, iii, no. 4416; *DD*.

it was Montfort, with the earl of Norfolk and John fitzGeoffrey, who went to the Guildhall to secure the allegiance of the Londoners to the new regime.[42]

Around this time in the summer of 1258, Matthew Paris narrates an atmospheric confrontation between Montfort and Henry himself. One day Henry embarked at Westminster and was rowed downstream for a picnic, only for a thunderstorm to force him in at the bishop of Durham's palace, whose grounds ran down from the Strand to the river.[43] Here Henry was greeted by Simon de Montfort. The scene should have been immortalized in paint by Turner: 'the disembarkation of Henry III at the bishop of Durham's palace: thunder storm coming on'. Montfort sought to reassure the frightened king, only for Henry to burst out 'I fear you more than all the thunder and lightning in the world.' These astonishing words, Paris opined, were produced by Montfort's role, 'vigorous and fervent' in 'exterminating' the half-brothers and compelling the king to obey baronial counsels.[44]

In Paris's narrative, Montfort next appears at the February 1259 parliament. Before that he had been out of England for three months, gravely weakening, Paris believed, the baronial council. 'All England' deplored his absence.[45] Evidently Paris thought Montfort was central to the ongoing reforms and was acting very much in England's interests. It was after the February 1259 parliament, in Paris's account, that Montfort upbraided Richard de Clare for weakening in support of the 'wholesome statutes' being promulgated.[46] Hitherto, Montfort seems chiefly concerned with control of the king and 'exterminating' the Lusignans. Now he appears in quite a different light supporting what were almost certainly the Ordinances of the Magnates. Since on 22 February he had sealed the Ordinances with Clare, Montfort had probably played a large part in their conception. He thus believed the magnates as much as the king should be subject to the process of reform.

In Paris's narrative of the confrontation with Clare, Montfort draws attention to the oath they had all sworn to the reform of the realm. The higher Clare was, the more he should be bound by it. Here is the first sign of a cornerstone of Montfort's conduct in the years to come: his attachment to the oath sworn in 1258 and his contempt for those who contravened it.[47] It was an oath, as we have seen, which involved treating such people as mortal enemies. The requirement was very much in Montfort's spirit and one suspects of his making. It would justify the force he always

---

[42] FitzThedmar, 38 (Stone, FitzThedmar, no. 714).

[43] The site is now marked by Durham House Street.

[44] Paris, v, 706.

[45] Paris, v, 732, 737.

[46] Paris, v, 744–5.

[47] For the various oaths, see Hey, 'Two oaths of the community'.

thought must underpin the baronial enterprise, the kind of force he had used so often in Gascony. Quite probably Montfort had the oath in mind when right at the start of the enterprise he threatened Valence with decapitation if he did not accept the act of resumption.

## MONTFORT'S GRIEVANCES

The record of 1258–9 thus speaks to Montfort's commitment to reform, but without revealing much about his motives. When it comes to the restrictions on the king, there was something very personal. Montfort still resented his sacking as regent of Gascony. His contempt for Henry's 'simplicity' was intense and probably unique. When the baronial letter of explanation to the pope spoke of Henry having reduced the kingdom to an 'imbecilic state', that sounds like Montfort talking. In 1242 had he not said that Henry should be taken and kept apart like the Carolingian king Charles the Simple? Now in effect that had happened. Montfort also, more perhaps than anyone else, expected the new regime to deal with his personal grievances and improve his material position.

One of these grievances concerned the money he was owed by the king. This had been reduced by payments of £600 early in 1258 but still amounted to over £1,000.[48] A second grievance concerned Henry's failure to convert into hereditable land the £400 annually being paid as Eleanor's marriage portion from the revenues of the midland counties. Henry had promised such a conversion, but had done nothing to bring it about. Montfort had looked on enviously as William de Valence's similar fee was steadily changed into land. A final grievance, the most intractable, related to Eleanor's dower as the widow of her first husband, William Marshal, earl of Pembroke. This, the Montforts claimed, had been undervalued to the tune of 1,400 marks a year, leaving them now owed a colossal 36,400 marks.[49] There was here another bone of contention with the Lusignans, for the Montforts claimed that the dower should have come from William de Valence's lordship of Pembroke.

With the revolution, it was vital for Montfort to make the best use of his new position to remedy these grievances, for his material position was

---

[48] *CPR 1247–58*, 609; TNA E 403/15A. I am grateful to Richard Cassidy for a complete schedule of payments to Montfort. See also Barratt, 'Crisis management at the exchequer', 61–2, and Maddicott, *Simon de Montfort*, 136–7. A large part of the debt arose from Henry's obligation to pay Eleanor £400 a year as compensation for the dower she had never received in Ireland and Wales as the widow of William Marshal, earl of Pembroke, who died in 1230. The payment should have been made by the Marshal heirs, who were the gainers from retaining lands otherwise lost to Eleanor as dower. But Henry had foolishly agreed to make the payment himself and then recoup the money from the heirs, something he never managed to do in full measure.

[49] Carpenter, *Reign of Henry III*, 246.

precarious and he had many mouths to feed. Even as undervalued, half his wealth came from Eleanor's dower and he could lose that at any moment if she died.[50] Henry, Montfort's eldest son, named after the king, was nearly of age. Henry's brothers, Simon and Guy, were not much younger. All three were to play major parts in the events to come. Montfort had somehow to find them resources worthy of their status and ambition. Right at the start, on 5 May 1258, Montfort, therefore, extracted a promise that the twenty-four magnates, appointed to reform the realm, should make an award dealing with his complaints. After that, to force a settlement through, the Montforts steadfastly refused to make the concessions demanded by Louis IX from Eleanor, as King John's daughter, thus holding up the peace with France. The blackmail worked. In the first half of 1259, Montfort received the money he was owed. Then, in the summer, the council awarded him a series of royal manors in place of his annual fee. This was the very reverse of the act of resumption with which Montfort had threatened William de Valence.[51]

In all this Montfort seems very much out for himself, and he is open to another criticism. He had hardly put his shoulder consistently to the wheel of reform. He had left England in November 1258 for Cambrai, there to represent the king at a meeting with King Louis. He did not return until February 1259. Then again, having set off for France as one of the king's envoys that March, he remained abroad until October 1259, apart possibly from a brief visit to England in July.[52] The reasons for these absences seem largely personal and material. During the first Montfort secured the county of Bigorre for himself and his heirs.[53] During the second, almost certainly, he explained to Louis Eleanor's grievances and her refusal to make the concessions demanded of her in the peace treaty until they were redressed.[54] If, moreover, Montfort returned to England in October 1259, his aim was not to further reform at the great parliament about to open.

---

[50] A point made in Maddicott, 'Who was Simon de Montfort?', 46–7.

[51] For all this, see below, 90.

[52] In London on 21 July 1259 and again on 13 October, Montfort, with his fellow councillors, addressed letters ratifying the peace with France. The letters also bore his seal: *TR*, nos. 109–10; *Layettes*, iii, no. 4555. This is not, however, conclusive proof of his presence. The 13 October letter also bears the seal of Peter of Savoy, who was certainly absent (*F*, i, 391). Montfort's seal could have been applied later or he could have left his great seal in England (to be used by his agents when so authorized) and taken his small seal to France. The letters he issued in Paris in May 1258, dealing with the peace, are sealed with his small seal, the 13 October letter with his great one. The seals on the July letter, although once there, have now gone. On the other hand, in London on 15 October 1259, Lord Edward ratified his alliance with Montfort and it is hard to see how this could have been arranged without Montfort's presence. A striking exchequer writ in Montfort's favour issued during the Michaelmas term of 1259 may be another sign of his presence: TNA E 159/33, m. 2 (image 0005).

[53] *Layettes*, iii, nos. 4453–5, 4476; Maddicott, *Simon de Montfort*, 172–3.

[54] See below, 91.

Rather it was to make an alliance with Lord Edward, one designed to secure the latter's support for an award over the dower. Hence the way Edward was permitted to make war on anyone who rejected awards of the king's court. Having concluded the alliance and ratified the final text of the French treaty with his fellow councillors, Montfort left immediately for France. Again his motive seems personal, as we will see.[55] At the parliament, the bachelery of England thus complained to Clare and Edward, not to Montfort. When the Provisions of Westminster were finally published in that solemn ceremony in Westminster Hall, he was nowhere to be seen.

Yet we may be sure Montfort would have rejected with contempt the idea that he was acting improperly. As he said later, 'he was doing no wrong if he demanded his rights'.[56] Nor were his absences entirely unrelated to the cause of reform. It is highly likely that in France he spent time explaining the revolution to Louis IX, as he certainly did to John, duke of Brittany. In a way, he was the regime's ambassador at the French court. Quite probably the text of the October 1258 proclamation, now preserved in the French Archives Nationales, was delivered to Louis by Montfort himself.[57] The proclamation, as we have seen, gave a somewhat sanitized version of the council's authority and perhaps reflects how Montfort explained things. As a result, Louis did nothing to help Henry III.

Another insight into Montfort's absences comes from the quarrel with Richard de Clare, as narrated by Matthew Paris. Here Montfort declares 'I do not care to live and hold conversation with men so changeable and treacherous.' Montfort had preached reform and been ignored. Probably Clare and others found his sanctimonious imprecations insufferable. Like the prophet Job, Montfort found himself 'laughed to scorn by men of a younger generation'. (Clare was a dozen years the younger.) Intolerable. Montfort had pointed the way forward. He would lead, but he would not be led. If his counsel went unheeded, he would not stay around to be insulted and over-ruled.[58] At the end of his account of the quarrel, Paris adds one final point. Because of the 'correction' to which Clare eventually submitted, people entertained all the greater hopes of Montfort's return.[59] Exactly. As later events (in 1262–3) showed, Montfort would return when he felt people were worthy of him and when the cause of reform could be upheld. This does not, to be sure, excuse Montfort's absence from the October 1259 parliament. But at least in the alliance concluded on 15

---

[55] See below, 95.

[56] *DBM*, 204–5, cap. 22.

[57] *Layettes*, v, no. 690. I am grateful to Amicie Pélissié du Rausas for bringing this text to my attention. It is in French and has a portion of the king's seal.

[58] In loftier terms (and in more evocative prose), Powicke, *King Henry III*, i, 390–1, is presenting, I think, a similar picture.

[59] Paris, v, 744–5.

October, he bound Lord Edward to maintain with all his power 'the enterprise made by the barons of the land'.[60] Edward's earlier alliance with Richard de Clare had merely said, much more weakly, that it was made to save the oath taken to support the Provisions.

## MONTFORTIAN IDEOLOGY

Montfort's work for reform was thus intermittent, but also in moments intense, like a bonfire dying down and then suddenly, with a gust of wind, flaring into life. To explain the intensity simply in terms of material grievances and a lust for power is to misunderstand the man and the age. With Montfort, more than any other baronial leader, we can sense the wider ideas behind support for reform. Vital here was Montfort's place within the circle of Robert Grosseteste, bishop of Lincoln, and of Adam Marsh, the master of Oxford's Franciscan friars.[61]

Over many years Grosseteste and Marsh had acted as Montfort's spiritual councillors. Physically imposing (his skeleton showed he was over six foot tall), Grosseteste's writings on science and theology had made him the greatest scholar of the age. For ten years between 1225 and 1235 he had taught in Oxford, latterly lecturing to the Franciscan friars established in the town. Then, already in his mid-sixties, he became bishop of Lincoln, ruling the diocese with ferocious energy down to his death in 1253. Adam Marsh became a Franciscan 'for love of most high poverty' and probably got to know Grosseteste in Oxford where Marsh too became a famous lecturer. His extraordinary correspondence, prolix and passionate, irritating and endearing, shows his closeness to Grosseteste and the way Montfort was embraced within their friendship. The circle also included John of Crakehall and Richard of Gravesend. The latter, an Oxford master, dean of Lincoln and archdeacon of Oxford, accompanied Grosseteste to the papal court in 1250. In September 1258, Gravesend became bishop of Lincoln. Next year he is found as another executor of Montfort's will just as he and Crakehall had earlier been of Grosseteste's. Walter de Cantilupe was part of the same milieu. He too was a university master, having probably studied in Oxford. His tract on confession and penance, circulated to his clergy, was based on Grossesteste's *Templum Dei*.[62] In one of his letters to Montfort, Adam Marsh tells him to get advice from Cantilupe and Grosseteste, both bishops being in his company. The

---

[60] Carpenter, *Reign of Henry III*, 251.

[61] For discussion of Montfort and this circle, see Maddicott, *Simon de Montfort*, 79–85, 117–18, 121; Ambler, *Song of Simon de Montfort*, 74–5, 103–4, 114–15, 145, 330; and Jahner, *Literature and Law in the Era of Magna Carta*, 153–61.

[62] Goering and Taylor, 'The "summulae" of bishops Walter de Cantilupe and Peter Quinel'. Grosseteste's influence on Cantilupe, especially when it came to the king's treatment of the church, is explored in Hoskin, 'Cantilupe's crusade?'

two of them, he observed, 'favour you above all men in their special friendship'.[63]

These churchmen all shared an intense concern with 'the cure of souls', the more so since the last days might be near. Putting that cure before all else, Grosseteste, with a fiery extremism much like Montfort's own, clashed with king, pope, fellow bishops and his cathedral chapter.[64] He regarded the king's treatment of the church as a contravention of 'natural law', the over-arching law, coterminous with the will of God, on which the order of nature was based.[65] In his statutes, Grosseteste sought to regulate the lives of his clergy. He also in his letters counselled laymen and laywomen on many aspects of their conduct, for there was little that did not in some way touch on souls and salvation. Whether Grosseteste would have condoned the revolution of 1258 is a moot point, but his ideas may well have shaped Montfort's understanding of Henry's rule.[66]

Thanks to Grosseteste, Montfort was familiar with the distinction between a king and a tyrant, Grosseteste's memorandum on the subject having been sent to him. Drawing on Aristotle's *Nichomachean Ethics*, the memorandum explained how a tyrant was a ruler who consults his own interests, while a king was concerned with the good of his subjects.[67] Another common definition, surely well known to Montfort, was that a tyrant was a ruler who broke the law.[68] Such ideas clearly shaped the great manifestos of 1258 justifying the revolution. The speech to the pope referred directly to Aristotle and went on to allege that the Lusignans, looking only to their private interests, had prevented Henry ruling for the common good, 'although the prince ought not to rule for himself but for his subjects'. They had also whispered to him that he was above the law.[69]

In Grosseteste's view tyranny and finance were closely linked for it was lack of money that turned men into tyrants. Without resources (legitimately gained of course), a ruler would become a '*clerotes*', a Greek term meaning a ruler chosen by lot. Unable to sustain himself, he inevitably oppressed his

[63] *Letters of Adam Marsh*, ii, 338–9, 352–3.

[64] Southern, *Robert Grosseteste*, ch. 10.

[65] For this aspect of Grosseteste's thought, see Hoskin, 'Natural law', 89–91.

[66] For all his opinions on tyrants and '*clerotes*' (for which, see below), Grosseteste believed that kings were ordained by God and were part of the natural order of things. If individual acts of injustice might be resisted, he said nothing to justify the total emasculation of royal power: Ambler, 'On kingship and tyranny', 126.

[67] Gieben, 'Robert Grosseteste', 377–80; *Letters of Adam Marsh*, i, 57. For a full discussion, see Ambler, 'On kingship and tyranny: Grosseteste's memorandum and its place in the baronial reform movement'.

[68] For this aspect of tyranny (and also how a tyrant is only concerned for himself), see John of Salisbury, 25 (Bk III, cap. 15), 28–9 (Bk IV, cap. 1), 190–3 (Bk VIII, cap. 17).

[69] Burton, 463. The speech was stretching a point when it cited Aristotle ('the philosopher') as saying the prince owed everything to God, and much to his country and native countrymen, but nothing to aliens.

people.[70] Here again the speech to the pope echoed Grosseteste's thought for, as we have seen, it saw Henry's injustices and his poverty as the 'two wounds' from which the kingdom suffered. Reforms were thus needed to ensure Henry 'abounded in riches'.[71] Quite probably John of Crakehall at the exchequer thought in those terms. Perhaps it was in such terms too that Montfort justified the act of resumption at the start of the revolution. Of course, as it turned out, the act was simply a way of attacking the Lusignans. Next year, no one did more to undermine the king's solvency and diminish his landed estate than Montfort himself. But Montfort would not have seen the contradiction. The king needed to be wealthy, yes, but, as the speech to the pope indicated, he also needed to fulfil his obligations to those closest to him rather than wasting his resources on aliens.

The ideas of churchmen were at their most crucial when it came to the most original feature of the local reforms, namely the way they tackled the malpractices of magnates and their officials just as much as the malpractices of the king. Some intellectuals put concern for the lower orders who suffered from such malpractices in a wider context. The Oxford Franciscan John of Wales, using 'the well worn physiological simile', popularized by John of Salisbury and echoed in the baronial letter to the pope, likened the state to a human body.[72] Within that body the workers had a place like everyone else. If the 'prince' was the head, the 'labourers' were the feet. Since, moreover, the labourers were of great service to the body, they must be protected and safeguarded. Judges must be particularly careful to give justice to 'the poor'. 'Village bailiffs' must be careful not to abuse their authority. John of Wales also stressed that 'laws should be kept as much by the powerful as by lesser folk'. If not 'they became like a spider's web, which traps the weaker animals, but allows the stronger to pass through'.[73]

Lords expected their local officials to be efficient estate managers. There was nothing new in the idea that they should also, just like the officials of the king, treat fairly the people in their charge.[74] What *was* new in the mid-thirteenth century was the intensity with which this view was urged on lords by reformist churchmen. In the rules drawn up by Grosseteste for the countess of Lincoln, her bailiffs were not to 'molest, hurt or ruin' her 'tenants, rich or poor in any way through tyrannical demands or fear of accusations, or through the receipt of presents or gifts'. In another set of rules for his own bailiffs, Grosseteste said they should

---

[70] For Grosseteste's thought on this matter, see Ambler, 'On kingship and tyranny', 122, and Ambler, *Bishops in the Political Community*, 54–5, 155–6.

[71] Burton, 463.

[72] In talking of the disruption caused by the Lusignans, the letter said there should not be separation between the limbs of one body: Burton, 459.

[73] Swanson, *John of Wales*, 69.

[74] For wider discussion, chronologically and conceptually, see ch. 2 of John Sabapathy's *Officers and Accountability*.

seek to multiply his movable wealth but 'justly and honestly'.[75] Likewise, the friar Walter of Henley, in his book about estate management, while giving detailed advice about how to run manors efficiently, urged lords to 'take not wrongfully from any man'. In their courts they should allow tenants to be amerced by their peers, moderating the amounts if their consciences told them they were too high.[76] One oath of office designed for a bailiff had him swearing both to reclaim his lord's rights and also 'to bear himself honestly towards both rich and poor'.[77]

What made this concern for the good conduct of officials all the more vital was that if officials sinned, the lord did too. As Grosseteste remarked (in a letter to the countess of Winchester) 'the vices of your agents will be considered your sins, and a cloud, exhaling from their foul and wanton behaviour, will dim the light of your own good works'. Likewise the friar Ralph Bocking, in a letter to the countess of Arundel, stressed that she sinned herself if she tolerated the faults of her household.[78] In short, lords needed to ensure the good conduct of their officials in order to save their souls.

If lords and their officials did transgress, then the only remedy was 'fitting reparation' and the return of things 'wrongly acquired'.[79] The statutes drawn up by Bishop Poore for the Salisbury diocese stressed that 'the sin cannot be remitted unless what has been taken is restored'.[80] In Grosseteste's rules for the countess of Lincoln, if bailiffs behaved badly, then the facts were to be ascertained by a formal inquiry so that the grievances could be 'amended and redressed'.[81]

That Simon de Montfort heard counsels along these lines is certain. In one letter, Adam Marsh exhorted him 'your goodness in Christ', to make sure his officials stopped 'slaying souls for whom the Author of life died'. (Montfort was told to write to his steward Richard of Havering specifically on the subject.)[82] Another influence was Louis IX, for Louis too was impregnated by these ideas. When in his *enquêtes* he sought to provide compensation for the abuses of himself and his officials, his aim quite literally was to save his soul.[83] No English noble knew Louis better than

[75] 'Rules of Robert Grosseteste', 390–1, and '*Statuta*', 409.

[76] Walter of Henley, 310–11, with 125–8 (in Dorothea Oschinsky's introduction) for his identity. Walter may have worked as steward of Richard de Clare's son, Gilbert, before becoming a friar in later life which is when he wrote his treatise.

[77] *Court Baron*, 77, quoted by Sabapathy, *Officers and Accountability*, 69. The tract here (late Henry III on the running of courts) stressed (p.70) how righteous conduct (including hearing the complaints of the poor) would bring salvation.

[78] *Letters of Grosseteste*, 70; *Saint Richard of Chichester*, 84, 162.

[79] Goering and Taylor, 'The "summulae" of bishops', 592–4 (a work of Walter de Cantilupe), and Grosseteste, *Templum Dei*, 57.

[80] *C&S*, i, 74, cap. 44.

[81] 'Rules of Robert Grosseteste', 390–1.

[82] *Letters of Adam Marsh*, ii, 350–1.

[83] This is the major theme of Dejoux, *Les Enquêtes de Saint Louis*. For Louis's influence on Montfort, see also Maddicott, *Simon de Montfort*, 166–9.

Simon de Montfort. They had met many times since 1254 while involved in the peace negotiations. In May 1258, Louis had insisted that the 'restitutions and amends' he had ordered should go ahead in the lands to be ceded to Henry under the terms of the coming peace. As one of Henry III's ambassadors in Paris, Simon de Montfort issued the letter giving the requested guarantee.[84]

The impact on Montfort of these ideas can be seen in that most personal of things, his will. This was drawn up in January 1259 while, significantly, Montfort was in France. It was written out by Henry, his eldest son, himself a former Grosseteste pupil. In the will, Montfort asks his executors to provide from his goods for 'the poor people of my land', 'the cultivators', whom he might have oppressed. It was no wonder that Montfort returned to England a passionate advocate of the Ordinances of the Magnates. His concerns were well known. Sometime in the 1250s, Matthew Paris rewrote an old passage about Montfort from the year 1238. It now had him 'in the name of justice' ordering his debts to be paid and everything which his officials had taken from his people to be restored.[85]

A magnate then had responsibility for the evils committed in his name and needed to redress or prevent them to secure his own salvation. The intensity with which Montfort believed this was probably unique, as was his closeness to Grosseteste's circle. No other nobleman features like he does in Grosseteste's and Marsh's correspondence.[86] There was no concern about the oppression of his peasants in the will of Roger Bigod drawn up a few months earlier than Montfort's.[87] Yet it would be wrong to see Montfort as standing quite alone. The ideas of reforming churchmen were part of the air these nobles breathed. John of Wales's works, composed in the 1260s, were intended as preaching aids for friars.[88] The baronial leaders must all have heard sermons along such lines. Peter of Savoy slapped down the peasants of Witley, yet, in a fervent letter from the friar Adam Marsh (admittedly the only one to Peter in the collection), he was urged to act justly in all things and show compassion and generosity to subordinates. He should remember 'the dread sentence of judgement', 'exclude consideration of worldly needs' and direct all his actions 'to that end where God is all in all, eternity is sure and peace is perfect'.[89] Marsh also believed that John Mansel, at some point in the 1250s, 'fired by a new yearning for his salvation' and 'stricken with a fear of divine judgement', had upbraided

---

[84] *Layettes*, iii, no. 4417. This letter was pointed out to me by Amicie Pélissié du Rausas.

[85] Paris, *HA*, ii, 409. One suspects Montfort had spoken to Paris directly about his concerns. For Montfort's relations with St Albans, see Maddicott, *Simon de Montfort*, 103–4.

[86] I owe this point to my old supervisor, John Prestwich.

[87] Morris, *Bigod Earls of Norfolk*, 218–19, and 75–9 for discussion of his role in 1258.

[88] Swanson, *John of Wales*, 3, 66–8, 83–6, 94–5, 98. See also Slater, *Art and Political Thought*, 122–4.

[89] The quotation was from Augustine: *Letters of Adam Marsh*, ii, 360–3; Power, 'The uncertainties of reformers', 15.

the king for his treatment of the church.[90] Above all one suspects the influence of such ideas on Hugh Bigod, given all we have seen about his conduct on his eyres. He was certainly well aware of what was going on in France. It was not just Simon de Montfort who issued the undertaking that Louis IX's reparations should continue in the territories to be ceded under the terms of the peace. The letter was also written in the name of his fellow ambassadors Hugh Bigod and indeed Peter of Savoy.

The ideas of churchmen thus help explain why reparation was so central a feature of the eyres between 1258 and 1260. They explain, too, the Ordinances of the Magnates with their intense concern for the good behaviour of seigneurial officials. Such concern also underlay the legislation on suit of court in the Provisions of Westminster. Before 1258, ideas about the treatment of subordinates could influence how magnates ran their own estates. Now, having taken over central government, they had the authority to enforce good conduct not merely on the king but also on themselves.[91] It is this combination of new authority and new vision that explains the special quality of the English revolution.

The moral reasons for a baron monitoring the conduct of his officials moved within the more general concern for 'reform of the realm', words with a significant religious charge, as we have seen. Hence the way the Waverley annalist in 1258 believed the barons were divinely awakened to the need to 'reform' the laws of England.[92] In the view of Marsh and Grosseteste, the aim of secular as well as religious leaders should be to create a well-ordered Christian community, purifying the lives of the people and ensuring their redemption.[93] They should work together 'to maximise salvation of the population', ensuring the transitory world as far as possible 'reflected the eternal will of God'.[94] Admittedly, in 1258–9, there was no equivalent to King Louis's measures in 1254 against blasphemy and gambling. Yet, if later stories can be believed, with the revolution of 1258, Montfort transformed his religious life. He put on a hair shirt, dressed in plain clothes and stayed up at night in prayer, austerities very much in Louis's spirit.[95] The tone of moral rectitude vibrating through the English reforms was for some very much part of a wider vision where '1258' might mark a new start in the salvation of the English people.

[90] *Letters of Adam Marsh*, i, 184–7.

[91] For the 'authority' behind the reforms, see below, 171–2.

[92] Waverley, 350.

[93] The reforms of Louis IX have thus been described as a work of 'redemptive governance': Jordan, *Men at the Center*, 36, 61, 70, 90, 93, 101, 104; Power, 'The uncertainties of reformers', 18. The interconnection between religious and secular reform is a major theme in Jahner, *Literature and Law in the Era of Magna Carta*, ch. 4, which explores Grosseteste's pastoral model of governance.

[94] Power, 'The uncertainties of reformers', 14, drawing on the *Letters of Adam Marsh*, ii, 578–9, and Southern, 'Robert Grosseteste' (in the *Oxford Dictionary of National Biography*) 10.

[95] Maddicott, *Simon de Montfort*, 88–91.

Adam Marsh, resident in Oxford and soon to be an executor of Montfort's will, was surely present at the Oxford parliament of 1258. He had only to step across the road from the Franciscan friary to arrive at the house of the Dominicans where the barons were meeting.[96] Earlier, during Montfort's tribulations in Gascony, Marsh had advised him to read the scriptures and in particular chapters twenty-nine, thirty and thirty-one of the book of Job.[97] In chapter thirty-one, having reviewed the highs and lows of his life, Job mounts a passionate defence. Has he ever, he asks, rejected the plea of his slave or slave girl, when they asked for justice? Has he ever raised his hand against the innocent knowing his influence over the courts? Has he failed to succour the poor, the widow and the orphan? Has 'his land ever cried in reproach and its furrows joined in weeping'? No, Job's conscience is clear. If his adversaries put down their accusations in a 'book', he will plead the whole course of his life in his defence.[98] Have we not here both the spirit behind Montfort's will and the terms in which he urged reform on his colleagues? If they failed in their great task, where would they be, in Job's words, 'when God rises up and acts as judge'? Reform of the realm was thus a moral crusade, vital for the spiritual health of Montfort himself, the other leaders and the wider realm. On another occasion, Marsh had praised Montfort for supporting Grosseteste in some great enterprise, we do not know exactly what. 'He exalts it, he praises it, and, as it seems to me, embraces it, burning with enthusiasm and ready with grand ideas, prepared according to the counsels of heaven, to gird himself for it with his confederates.' This surely could have been a description of Montfort in 1258 and 1259, at least for some of the time.[99]

[96] Maddicott, *Simon de Montfort*, 93–4, 162.
[97] *Letters of Adam Marsh*, ii, 336–7.
[98] I have adapted these passages from the translation in the New English Bible.
[99] *Letters of Adam Marsh*, i, 58–9.

Chapter 3

# HENRY, QUEEN ELEANOR
# AND LORD EDWARD
## 1258–1259

In 1258, at the time of the political revolution, Henry III was fifty years old. He was in good health and could reasonably expect years more of life. Of his predecessors, William the Conqueror, Henry I, Stephen and Henry II had all lived considerably longer. If William Rufus, Richard the Lionheart and John had died in their forties, only John had perished from natural causes.[1] In the event, Henry was to live for another fourteen years, dying just after his sixty-fifth birthday in 1272. Impulsive and emotional, Henry's will had hitherto been the driving force in government, however much subject to political and financial constraints. Up to the last he had pushed forward the Sicilian project and given munificent rewards to his Poitevin kin. How did he react now to momentous and monstrous changes reducing him to a cipher? The question cannot be given a definitive answer. After the Oxford parliament in June 1258, Henry's seal and chancery were controlled by a baronial council. The great flow of royal letters continues, but they no longer reveal the king's attitudes, aims and actions. We are left with odd glimpses of Henry's words and deeds as they are recounted by chroniclers and newsletters. It is as though Henry, having been the chief actor in the play, is now upstage, reduced to bit parts and speaking the odd line. Even if the reports of Henry's words are accurate, one cannot know how far they represent his real feelings. Matthew Paris felt that much was concealed beneath the king's outwardly placid demeanour.

At times the barons seem to have worried about what Henry might say. In July 1258 they turned down the Londoners' request to speak to him before accepting the new provisions.[2] Later in the year they prevented him going to Cambrai to meet Louis IX. Yet a newsletter, written after the exile of the Lusignans, has him begging that none but Englishmen should stay around him.[3]

---

[1] At the time of their deaths, William I was fifty-nine; Henry I, sixty-seven; Stephen, fifty-seven; and Henry II, fifty-six. William Rufus was forty-four; Richard I, forty-one; and John, forty-nine.

[2] FitzThedmar, 39 (Stone, FitzThedmar, no. 714).

[3] *DBM*, 94–5.

Outwardly there was little to indicate a new regime. Henry, Eleanor and a large body of magnates went to Salisbury at the end of September 1258 for the dedication of the new cathedral by Archbishop Boniface, surely a happy occasion. In November, staying at St Albans (the last visit described by Matthew Paris), Henry had the saint's body carried in procession through the cloister, he and his entourage following and reverently and devoutly making offerings. Hearing of John fitzGeoffrey's death, Henry ordered the convent to celebrate a mass for his soul. He also ordered a cloth of gold to cover John's body on its transit through London. The two seemed to have become reconciled before John's death. In the new year Paris spoke of Henry wearing a 'serene face'.[4]

In the area of Henry's religion, much did continue as normal. In late November 1258 he was able to go on pilgrimage to Bury St Edmunds. (While there a great gale blew down many trees and houses.)[5] On the death of the elephant given him by Louis IX, he gave its bones to Westminster Abbey's sacrist 'to do as the king enjoined him'.[6] Henry was still feeding 100 paupers every day and 150 when the queen was at court. At Easter 1259, as customary, he clothed (and presumably washed the feet of) 171 paupers for the health of the queen, himself and his children. Later in the year, he arranged for the chapel in Scarborough castle to have a chaplain and a lamp burning day and night. Services were to be celebrated daily as in his other castle chapels throughout England.[7] Henry's falconry too continued. In October 1258, at the start of the season, there was the usual gathering of falconers at court.[8]

While major acts of patronage were beyond him, Henry retained some freedom in making gifts of deer and wood from the royal forests. These had always been a significant form of royal patronage and they flowed to religious institutions, churchmen and laymen sometimes daily from Henry's open hand.[9] As the beneficiary saw the king's deer in his parks, ate the king's venison and burnt his firewood, he was all the more encouraged to give good service, or so Henry might hope. While, moreover, venison and firewood were soon consumed, a house or church built with the king's timber were permanent reminders of the generous monarch. In the year after the revolution, Henry was able to make around fifty gifts of deer and wood to friaries and religious houses, actually more than double the number the year before.[10] Henry also seems to have retained some

[4] Paris, v, 724; *CR 1256–9*, 345; *CLR 1251–60*, 451.

[5] Bury St Edmunds, 24.

[6] *CR 1256–9*, 256.

[7] *CLR 1251–60*, 474.

[8] Volume 1, 411.

[9] An analysis is forthcoming by Andy Ford. For a comparison of Henry's gifts with Edward I's, see Spencer, 'Royal patronage and the earls in the reign of Edward I', 26–31.

[10] This is comparing a year after the revolution with a year before it so from July 1258 to June 1259 and from April 1257 to March 1258. The orders for the gifts are in the close rolls.

freedom in his gifts to laymen. Those to Fulk Basset, John de Plessis, the sister of John Mansel, Guy de Rochefort (before his expulsion), Walter of Merton and the chancery clerk Adam of Chesterton, amongst others, were presumably freely made. Members of the regime rewarded included John fitzGeoffrey, Roger Bigod, Hugh Bigod, Humphrey de Bohun, Roger de Mortimer, Peter de Montfort, William Bardolph, Hugh Despenser, Giles de Argentan, Ralph Basset of Sapcote and Ralph Basset of Drayton. Were these gifts made grudgingly under pressure or spontaneously with the hope of winning men to Henry's side? Or were they made with little reference to the king at all? It is impossible to be sure.[11]

Appearances were helped and the king appeased by Hugh Bigod's evident respect. Against cases touching the rights of the crown, he often minuted 'discuss with the king'.[12] Just occasionally Henry seems to be acting as of old. During the Easter term of 1259 he entered the exchequer and respited the debts owed by the executors of his former steward Ralph fitzNicholas.[13] There was one characteristic outburst of anger, although against an old servant, not a member of the new regime. Early in August 1258, Henry had given four deer in Northamptonshire's Whittlewood forest to Philip Lovel, still treasurer of the exchequer despite the revolution. When, however, later in the month, Henry passed by the forest on his way north with Hugh Bigod, he was told Lovel had taken far more deer than entitled to under the gift. In a fury, Henry seized Lovel by the arm and placed him under arrest. As so often, the anger did not last. Lovel, with the king calmed down by his friends, was soon released and escaped further punishment.[14] Contrary to Paris's belief, the episode, in all probability, had nothing to do with Lovel's eventual removal as treasurer in November.[15]

Henry did have two friends on the council of fifteen, the only survivors from his panel of twelve: John de Plessis, earl of Warwick, in right of his wife, and John Mansel. The plausible Plessis was to stand by the king during his recovery of power in 1261, but in this period seems to have been little help. He witnessed both the baronial letter to the pope and the letter

[11] In the year July 1258 to June 1259, Henry made in all around 125 gifts of deer, much the same number as between April 1257 and March 1258. He also made over 90 gifts of wood, around 40 more than in the previous year. Apart from those to religious institutions and individual churchmen, the gifts went as before mostly to councillors, ministers, royal servants and magnates.

[12] For example, SERHB, i, nos. 7, 28, 34, 118, and see no. 161 for Henry giving bail to the constable of Northampton castle. Laurence del Brok, as the king's attorney, continued to prosecute cases about the rights of the crown.

[13] TNA E 159/32, m. 11 (image 0031). The Easter term of 1259.

[14] For the gift of the deer, see CR 1256–9, 251. The only source for the quarrel is Paris, v, 714–15, 731, but see CPR 1247–58, 651. For Lovel's career, see Vincent, 'Philip Lovel', and Barratt, 'Crisis management at the exchequer', 67–8.

[15] Paris, v, 719–20; CPR 1258–66, 1. As Paris noticed, Lovel's dismissal was part of other changes to the exchequer's personnel.

proclaiming the council's authority. Thereafter he was rarely at court.[16] John Mansel was very different. He was prominent at court and handled a wide variety of business.[17] He must have given Henry wise counsel and a sympathetic ear. He managed to avoid witnessing both the letter to the pope and the proclamation of the council's power. Later, in 1261, he was central to Henry's bid for freedom. Yet in 1258–9 Mansel was clearly acceptable to the barons. In November 1258 the council, headed by Montfort and Richard de Clare, allowed him to fortify his house at Sedgwick in Sussex.[18] Knowing the odds, Mansel probably advised Henry to keep calm and wait for better times. Sympathy and sensible advice probably came too from Philip Basset, who replaced John fitzGeoffrey on the council of fifteen.[19] Certainly, like Mansel, he was to play a major part in the king's eventual recovery of power. Fulk Basset himself died in May 1259 and Henry must have welcomed the election of the chancellor, Henry of Wingham, as his successor. If now answerable to the council, he had, after all, been Henry's keeper of the seal before 1258. Fulk's death also strengthened Philip Basset's position since, now head of the family, he gained valuable manors at High Wycombe, Woking, Upavon and elsewhere.

## THE CONTINUATION OF THE ABBEY

In one area of the regime's activity, Henry could find some reassurance. Only rarely was he personally blamed for acts of injustice.[20] This was very different from 1234, after the fall of Peter des Roches, when the king was made to publicly confess his sins. The regime also did one thing close to Henry's heart.[21] This was to continue with the building of Westminster Abbey. The revolution had been a potential danger to the Abbey. By the end of 1258 the radiating chapels, east end (where the new shrine was to be), sanctuary and transepts of Henry's church were more or less complete. They joined on to the choir and nave of the Confessor to the west. So a whole church was in being. The baronial council had thus a perfect excuse for pausing the work. But nothing like that happened. In June 1259, Henry ordered a further section of the Confessor's church to

---

[16] Between November 1258 and October 1259 he witnessed only one charter on the charter roll (in June 1259): *RCWL*, ii, 123–4.

[17] He witnessed royal charters in November 1258 and in January, February, May, July–November 1259. Only one royal charter was enrolled in December 1258 and none in March 1259.

[18] *CPR 1258–66*, 1.

[19] Basset was appointed between April and July 1259: *CR 1256–9*, 474; *TR*, nos. 109–10. Given his closeness to King Richard, the appointment also reflects the regime's rapprochement with Richard.

[20] This is discussed more fully below, 167–8.

[21] For what follows, see Carpenter, 'Westminster Abbey in politics', 49–58.

be cast down.[22] In its place four new bays were to be built, thus providing a new choir for the monks. Throughout the subsequent period of reform, rebellion and civil war, these new bays were rising up at Westminster. They were no pared-down version of the earlier work. Quite the reverse. In what must have been detailed and delightful discussions with his master masons, Henry decided that extra mouldings should be added to the Purbeck marble columns of the main arcade, that the single octofoil windows of the triforium should be replaced by three cinquefoils (not a change I like), and that extra shafts should be added to the vault.[23]

Part of the background to the new work was that Henry felt there was plenty of time to complete it.[24] Back in 1254 he had wanted the Abbey consecrated and presumably the Confessor translated on 13 October 1255, so before he departed on his crusade the following year.[25] With that idea abandoned (alongside the crusade), Henry may next have wondered about a consecration in 1258. The east end and transepts, as we have seen, were more or less ready by then, and the year was especially appropriate since the ecclesiastical calendar was exactly the same as in the year of the Confessor's first translation in 1163. All the movable feasts, controlled as they were by Easter, would thus be on the same dates, and all the feasts, fixed and movable, on the same days of the week: 13 October 1258 thus fell on a Sunday, just like 13 October 1163. In the event, of course, the Sicilian preoccupation and then the revolution ruled out 1258 as the year of consecration, but Henry had another chance. The next possible year, with the wonderful coincidence of calendar, was not so far away. It was 1269. Since the chronicler Thomas Wykes comments on the symmetry between 1269 and 1163, it was obviously well known.[26] Probably, having missed 1258, 1269 was always Henry's target date. He knew he would live that long. It was meant to be.

The crucial order starting the new work was sanctioned by the regime. Hugh Bigod, three councillors and two members of the parliamentary twelve were at court when it was issued. The council itself had already found some of the necessary funds by assigning to the works the £362 a year owed by Alice, widow of Edmund de Lacy, for the wardship of her late husband's lands. Later in 1259 the proceeds of another wardship, worth £100 a year, were assigned in the same way.[27] The regime was trying to conciliate the king. It was also seeking the Confessor's blessing for

---

[22] *CR 1256–9*, 390 (*BA*, 196–7).

[23] After Henry de Reyns' death in 1253, the master masons were John of Gloucester (1253–60) and Robert of Beverley (1260–72).

[24] For what follows about the timescale, see Carpenter, 'Westminster Abbey in politics'.

[25] *RG*, i, no. 2469; *BA*, 194–5 (*CPR 1247–58*, 281, 381).

[26] Wykes, 226.

[27] *CFR 1258–9*, nos. 635, 906, 912; *CPR 1258–66*, 12, 32. Earlier, in August 1258, the council had assigned to the works the 1,100-mark fine made by the convent for the keeping of the Abbey during the abbatial vacancy: *CPR 1247–58*, 650.

the movement of reform, another indication of the religiosity running through so much of what was done. It is no coincidence that the order assigning the Lacy revenues to the Abbey was issued on the same day (22 February 1259) as the Ordinances of the Magnates.

## HENRY'S GRIEVANCES

At the start of the revolution perhaps some councillors, Hugh Bigod in particular, hoped the co-operation seen at the Abbey would prove the rule rather than the exception. As Sir Maurice Powicke put it, 'they had never intended to put the king under constraint, but to help him be a king'.[28] The council's proclamation of its authority could be interpreted in those terms, as we have seen. But it did not work out like that, for all Hugh Bigod's respect and Henry's efforts (if such they were) to win men over with gifts of wood and deer. Henry later spoke of this period with great bitterness.

There was first of all the sheer affront to his whole concept of kingship. Henry had confirmed Magna Carta and accepted he was not above the law. He probably accepted, too, Grosseteste's view that anointing at the coronation conferred no priestly functions. But nonetheless, as Grosseteste had explained in answer to Henry's inquiry, anointing had poured into him all the blessings of the Holy Spirit.[29] In the titles at the start of every document Henry issued he was proclaimed king 'by the grace of God'. Henry never forgot the unique status conferred by his coronation and on his death was buried in coronation robes.[30] In 1259 his new seal made telling reference to the divinely protected nature of kingship, as we will see. In 1264 he argued that the restrictions of 1258 were invalid since they violated his coronation oath to protect the rights of the crown. His subjects had violated their own oath of fealty in forcing such things upon him.[31] For all his superficial acceptance, Henry surely, in some moods, viewed the revolution, as later did Thomas Wykes, in the terms of the second Psalm: the people 'imagining vain things' and 'the princes conspiring together against the Lord and his anointed king'.[32] The whole revolution, as Wykes put it, had changed the natural order of things, with the king being ruled by his subjects rather than ruling over them.[33] How Henry must have hoped those conspiring against him would suffer the fate of the princes in the Psalm: the king 'will break them with a rod of iron and shatter them like a clay pot'!

---

[28] Powicke, *King Henry III*, i, 394.
[29] *Letters of Grosseteste*, 366–9; Paris, v, 377. For Henry's coronation, see volume 1, 45–6.
[30] See below, 618–9.
[31] *DBM*, 256–7.
[32] Psalm 2: 1–2; Wykes, 119. Apart from its place in the liturgical calendar, the psalm featured in the office of the Confessor: *Missale Westmonasteriensis*, iii, col. 1342.
[33] Wykes, 119.

Quite apart from the affront to the status of kingship, the revolution, so Henry believed, also violated established custom. The councillors had chosen his chief ministers when before they had always been chosen by the king himself. There was also the way the councillors had behaved. They had ignored his wishes, controlled his seal and treated him like a ward. They had not asked him to their meetings anymore than they asked 'the humblest subjects in the realm', although he was head of the council. They had deprived him of his 'power, dignity and regality'.[34] Henry was saying all this in 1261, but the picture coincides exactly with that in the Provencal newsletter quoted in chapter 1, as also with the evidence of the authorization notes on the chancery rolls.[35]

Another sign of Henry's eclipse came in the realm of gifts. Throughout his reign these had flowed in from everyone who wanted his favour. Between January 1255 and April 1256 he had received no fewer than 316 precious objects including rings, cups, dishes, silver and gold brooches, two peacocks set with stones and a silver incense boat given by Simon de Montfort. In 1258–9, in a period only three and a half months shorter, the number of gifts he received was down to 72. Henry loved precious objects. He had thus been cut off from one of the great joys of his life.[36] Henry was also cut off from the joy of giving. If he could still make presents from his forests, he no longer controlled the more important gifts of escheats, wardships and money. In September 1259 he had to write a begging letter to Hugh Bigod just to get £100 assigned to the works at the Abbey.[37] Henry must surely have resented those who had brought this about. That many of them had been councillors before 1258 and recipients of favour made the betrayal all the worse. In the year before the revolution Henry had made gifts from the royal forests to Bishop Cantilupe, Roger Bigod, Humphrey de Bohun, John fitzGeoffrey, Hugh Bigod, Roger de Mortimer and Peter de Montfort. Eleanor de Montfort had received a present of six deer and the two sons of Richard de Clare, studying at Oxford, four dead trees for firewood.[38]

A further cross to bear were the changes at court. In had come the uncongenial Giles de Argentan and out had gone William de Valence, Guy and Geoffrey de Lusignan, William de Sancta Ermina, Guy de Rochefort and Elyas de Rabayne. Guy de Lusignan, over the years, had brought to court three jesters and Geoffrey a chaplain described by Matthew Paris as 'jester more than priest'. It was he who had pelted Henry and his courtiers

[34] DBM, 222–7.
[35] See above, 20.
[36] The figures come from my analysis of the wardrobe keepers' 'jewel accounts': Wild, WA, 82–4, 89–90.
[37] CR 1256–9, 441; CLR 1251–60, 478; Carpenter, 'Westminster Abbey in politics', 53–4.
[38] Henry would have been all the more disappointed because he markedly increased his gifts of deer in the years immediately before the revolution: Spencer, 'Royal patronage and the earls', 30.

with apples and squirted the juice of grapes into their eyes while they were relaxing in the garden at St Albans.[39] There was far less fun at court without the Lusignans. There was also far less flattery. 'To his most excellent lord, and dearest brother, beloved above all mortals, ready in all things to do your pleasure, with all kinds of service, reverence and honour' was how Geoffrey de Lusignan wrote to Henry. And it was not just words. The same letters show him very ready to do Henry's bidding.[40]

## THE SICILIAN DISAPPOINTMENT

Adding to these grievances were other vexations. Henry had hoped very much that a papal legate would arrive to monitor the reforms and ensure their acceptability. To win the pope's favour, in one of his last acts before the revolution, he had even borrowed 2,000 marks so as to pay off the arrears of the annual census owed the papacy.[41] But no legate had come either to oversee the reforms or, as Henry also hoped, to revive the Sicilian affair. Henry had bowed to reform thanks to the promised tax to pursue the Sicilian project, or so at least he could claim. But again no tax had been forthcoming. Admittedly, the promise was so qualified as to be pretty worthless, but then Henry was never very grounded in reality. Believing the project might be also helped by the peace with France, he had far from abandoned his Sicilian dreams.

At first the baronial council had at least gone through the motions. It informed the pope of the deal struck back in May 1258: if Henry would reform the realm and the pope modify the conditions, then the council would do its best to secure a tax for the project. At the Oxford parliament, as we have seen, twenty-four magnates were appointed to conduct negotiations about the tax. But Pope Alexander saw the hollowness of these promises and realized there was no more money to be had. In December 1259, 'considering the power of the king' (meaning considering his lack of power), he decided the project could no longer 'usefully' be pursued. He was, he said, now free to offer the kingdom to 'other persons'.[42]

Henry, however, could still hope, for Alexander had left the door a crack ajar. If Henry could fulfil all the conditions of the original grant before another candidate was found, then Edmund, his second son, might still be preferred to anyone else. Henry knew that Louis IX, under the terms of the peace, was supposed to give enough money to hire 500 knights for two years, so here would be a core of a Sicilian army. Indeed, Henry spoke optimistically of 100,000 marks being forthcoming, although admitting

---

[39] *CR 1247–51*, 18, 56; *CR 1253–4*, 264; *CLR 1251–60*, 26; and see volume 1, 552.

[40] *DD*, nos. 325, 354–5, 361.

[41] *CPR 1247–58*, 631. A point I owe to Richard Cassidy.

[42] Paris, vi, 412–13.

that Louis IX was arguing for less.[43] Sicily was indeed discussed at the parliament held in February 1259. The magnates, evidently, now felt absolved from any further need to consider a tax. The pope had not modified the conditions, as they had asked, and anyway he was now considering other candidates. But the parliament came up with a suggestion. Why not ask King Richard to take over the whole business? For the magnates this was just a way of washing their hands of Sicily for good and all. For Henry on the other hand, it seemed a lifeline.

A mild illness had prevented Richard coming to the parliament, so, in early March, the king and the barons went to see him at Wallingford. Richard's objectives at this time were clear: the pope was to crown him as emperor, while rejecting the rival claims of the king of Castile. If the reports of the Sicilian knight Roger de Lentini can be believed, Richard now reacted favourably to the parliament's proposal and took over the affair on his nephew Edmund's behalf. He hoped the pope 'might admit him to the empire and his nephew to the kingdom'. If the pope agreed, Richard would go to the papal court for his coronation and provide 500 knights of his own in the Sicilian cause.[44]

In his naive way, Henry was probably overjoyed, yet nothing altered the basic facts on the ground. The illegitimate son of the Emperor Frederick II, Manfred, crowned in August 1258, was now entrenched in the kingdom of Sicily. It would take a gigantic military effort to oust him. Richard certainly hoped to be crowned emperor and at times Pope Alexander seemed to favour the idea. But Alexander knew the barons had refused a Sicilian tax. They also, thanks to Montfort's doing, might well control the money for the 500 knights.[45] Was Richard's own promise any more than empty rhetoric? He had never yet done any fighting or put an army in the field. Alexander drew the obvious conclusions and never revived Edmund's candidature. Henry was left to complain angrily about the council's broken promises.[46]

## THE NEW GREAT SEAL

The revolution of 1258 had not, as we have seen, stopped Henry's gifts to churchmen and religious institutions, indeed they had increased. He thus

---

[43] This optimistic view (which I surmise came from Henry himself) is found in a report written by the Sicilian knight Roger de Lentini: Villard, 'Autour de Charles d'Anjou', 32–3, no. 3. For Lentini, see the next note

[44] The details in this and the preceding paragraph come from Roger de Lentini's letters in Villard, 'Autour de Charles d'Anjou', 31–2, no. 2; 32–3, no. 3. Roger had acted for Henry at the papal court (*CPR 1247–58*, 629, 639; *CPR 1258–66*, 112). He arrived in England at the time of the February parliament and had then (much complaining about the weather) gone on to Wallingford. (Lentini describes the meeting as taking place at a castle belonging to Richard and the king's itinerary shows him at Wallingford in early March.)

[45] See above, 54.

[46] *DBM*, 212–13, cap. 1 [20]; 230–3, cap. 20 [1].

demonstrated his piety and solicited the prayers of the beneficiaries, prayers, he might hope, for his recovery of power. In the late summer of 1259 he found another way of proclaiming the virtues of his kingship. As the negotiations for the French peace drew to a close, he had to replace the seal used since 1218 with a new one, a seal no longer with the titles duke of Normandy and count of Anjou. Accordingly, on 8 August a writ was issued from Windsor commanding the goldsmith William of Gloucester to make the new seal 'in the fashion enjoined on him and Edward of Westminster, king's clerk'.[47] The writ does not say the injunctions came from Henry personally but almost certainly they did. This was not a matter in which the council interfered. Henry was close to both William of Gloucester and Edward of Westminster. The former had made his gold penny, the latter was his chief agent in all the works at the palace and the Abbey. Indeed, it was Edward who had suggested the lions under the throne in the great hall would be more 'sumptuous' in bronze rather than marble. The new seal was ready by 9 September, when it was used to authenticate a letter about the peace with France.[48]

The reverse of the seal, apart from the new titles, was comparatively unchanged. Henry sits astride a great horse. He is in full armour, his head encased in a crowned helm. He brandishes a sword and holds a shield bearing the leopards of England. The sword arm, however, is flung back further than before, as though to give more heft to the strike, while one of the back legs of the horse now kicks into the very edge of the seal, giving a greater sense of movement. Is there here a warning of what awaits those seeking to confound the king's authority?

The changes to the front of the seal had more obvious meaning. Henry now sat not on a low bench but on a high-backed throne, a throne supported on either side by small standing leopards and surmounted by all manner of crockets, orbs and finials. The majesty of Henry's kingship appears as never before, thus offsetting, or so Henry might hope, his loss of the continental possessions and his humbling in England. The seal also said something about the nature of Henry's rule. Instead of holding a sword, as on his first seal, he now held a rod topped with a dove. This was not because Henry had lost the ducal sword of Normandy, although some took it that way. Rather, it was to demonstrate Henry's devotion to Edward the Confessor, for the Confessor, on his own seal, had sat with a rod surmounted by a large and striking dove.[49] The dove signified that Henry's rule, like the Confessor's, was distinguished by its peace. Just as God,

---

[47] *CLR 1251–60*, 472.

[48] The letter is now in the Archives Nationales in Paris: *Layettes*, v, no. 696.

[49] The image of the Confessor with the bird (some think it is an eagle not a dove) appears on the reverse of what is called his first great seal. What Henry saw may in fact have been a twelfth-century forgery: Harmer, *Anglo Saxon Writs*, 102–3. For Henry's change of seal, see Binski, *Westminster Abbey and the Plantagenets*, 84–5, and Carpenter, *Reign of Henry III*, 439–41.

having chastised the world with the flood, had then sent a dove bearing an olive branch to reveal 'the return of peace to the earth', so Henry's reign had restored peace to England after its sufferings under King John. The seal made one final point.[50] The king, a feature introduced in 1218, sat trampling a lion and a dragon underfoot. The reference was to Psalm 91, the point being the divinely protected nature of kingship: 'There shall no evil befall thee, neither shall any plague come nigh thy dwelling. For he shall give his angels charge over thee, to keep thee in all thy ways. Thou shall tread upon the lion and the adder: the young lion and the dragon shalt thou trample under foot.'[51]

Henry's seal thus radiated eloquent and urgent messages about his kingship. Here was a majestic king, guarded and guided by God and his patron saint, who would give peace to his people. How terribly wrong, therefore, that the barons should deprive such a king of power, how utterly grotesque that they had done so by controlling *his seal*. Before long he would surely spur his horse into action and punish those who had laid him low.

## HENRY'S DEFIANCE OF THE COUNCIL

How far, in fact, those seeing the new seal would imbibe these messages remained to be seen. Initial reaction was not encouraging.[52] Henry, however, was not confined to visual messages. At precisely the time he was conceiving his new seal, he was acting directly against the baronial regime. Unfortunately, the issue over which he chose to make a stand was singularly ill chosen.

The pope had failed to condemn the revolution, and had refused to send a legate, but there was one area where he was ready to intervene. This was over the restoration of Henry's half-brother, bishop-elect Aymer, to his see of Winchester.[53] The baronial leaders themselves were desperate to prevent Aymer's restoration. They wrote to the pope on the subject in the most strident terms. They even persuaded the Winchester monks to elect a new bishop, Andrew their prior, in Aymer's place.[54] Although such an election was completely illegitimate without papal sanction, on 29 July 1259 Henry was made to give his consent. He did so, however, as a cover for his real intentions, for at this very time, helped by chancellor Wingham's absence from court, he managed to take the seal into his chamber and authenticate letters giving the papal envoy, Velascus, safe conduct to enter England. The

---

[50] For what follows, see Slater, *Art and Political Thought*, 76–7.

[51] Psalm 91: 10–13.

[52] See below, 105.

[53] There is a full account of what follows in Treharne, 'An unauthorized use of the great seal', 403–11. The main primary sources are Paris's Continuator, 432–4; *CR 1256–9*, 484–5, 490–2; *CPR 1258–66*, 35, 42.

[54] For a detailed account of efforts to remove Aymer, see Ridgeway, 'The politics of the English royal court', 321–5.

delay in sending the letters earlier, Henry explained, he would 'insinuate' when they met.[55] The reason, of course, was that only now had Henry been able to get control of his seal and thus let Velascus into England, let into England, that is, the very envoy empowered by the pope to effect Aymer's restoration. When Velascus arrived at Dover he was allowed to proceed on his way to court by the castellan, Richard de Grey, the letters of conduct asserting, quite falsely, that this had been agreed by the council.

Now, however, Henry's plot went awry. As soon as Velascus's mission became known there was an explosion of alarm and anger. Richard de Grey, unfairly it seems, was made the fall guy and replaced at Dover by Hugh Bigod. (This was also a hit at Simon de Montfort, given his closeness to Grey.) When Velascus appeared before the king, council and assembled magnates, his demands were rejected out of hand. The 'universitas of the kingdom', an abject and apologetic Henry explained to the pope, would never accept Aymer's restoration. Velascus himself was soon on his way home. Thus ended Henry's one significant attempt to defy the council in 1258–9. It was not well conceived. The idea that the magnates would quail before Velascus's threats of excommunication was fanciful in the extreme. It was also a foolish ground on which to fight, given Aymer was totally persona non grata with the English barons.

Failing any direct challenge to the council's authority, Henry's best hope was that its restrictions would gradually weaken, allowing him more scope for individual action. There are signs, around the time of the October 1259 parliament, that something like this was happening for Henry is found authorizing royal letters in a way not seen since before the revolution. Sometimes he acted with Hugh Bigod or another minister, but quite often alone. So Henry was involved in gifts of robes, payments of fees and debts, and the establishment of the Dominican friars in Dunstable.[56] In one characteristic act, he ordered £100 to be paid for a cameo given to the shrine of the Confessor although he had earlier offered only 100 marks for it.[57] Ultimately, in 1261, Henry would mount a direct challenge to the council, but for the moment such individual acts were the best way forward. He would have far more scope for them once in France for the ratification of the peace, as we will see.

## THE QUEEN AND PETER OF SAVOY

Henry's attempt to bring Aymer back to England had one other grievous consequence. In his folly he had destroyed any immediate chance of an alliance with his queen. According to the well-informed Waverley annals,

---

[55] *CR 1256–9*, 484. The letter is dated 28 July.

[56] *CR 1256–9*, 443, 444, 452; *CR 1259–61*, 6, 15, 138; *CLR 1251–60*, 484, 485; *CPR 1258–66*, 47, 57, 58.

[57] *CLR 1251–60*, 462, 488.

Eleanor had supported the revolution of 1258 because it brought down the Lusignans. Indeed, her uncle Peter of Savoy had been part of the original baronial confederation formed at the Westminster parliament. The Lusignans, so Eleanor thought, had undermined her relationship with Henry, deprived her of patronage and alienated her eldest son, Lord Edward.[58] The last thing she wanted was their restoration. A newsletter of 1259 mentions her displeasure at efforts made on Aymer's behalf.[59] Yet here was Henry trying to bring him back! If Henry wished to recover power, he needed the support of the queen and Peter of Savoy. But he wanted to recover power in part at least so he could restore the Lusignans, and that made any such alliance impossible.

There were certainly strains in the relationship between the queen and the reformers. Eleanor knew that at the Oxford parliament a tide had been running against all foreigners, not just the half-brothers. Imbert Pugeys, who had come with her to England, thus lost the Tower of London and Ebulo of Geneva lost Hadleigh castle. And then, amidst the other reforms, there were plans to restrict the payment of 'queen's gold', a levy of one-tenth paid to the queen on all fines made with the king, a threat to a good slice of her income.[60] After a long and largely happy marriage, Eleanor had every reason to be at one again with her indulgent husband, provided, that is, he was now separated from the Lusignans. Even at the Westminster parliament, Peter of Savoy was trying to build bridges with the king.[61]

There is indeed some evidence of Henry and Eleanor being back on terms. She must have welcomed his promise of the Lacy wardship to her kinswoman Alice, daughter of the marquis of Saluzzo.[62] The only two letters Henry authorized on his own between July 1258 and August 1259 both showed Eleanor's influence. One, in September 1258, made a gift of firewood to the Savoyard castellan of Windsor, Aymon Thurbert. The other letter, in August 1259, granted a valuable wardship, with the marriage of the heiresses, to the Savoyards Peter de Champvent and Imbert de Montferrand.[63]

King and queen were also brought together, as we will see, by the negotiations both for the peace with France and the marriage of their daughter,

---

[58] The *locus classicus* for this is Ridgeway, 'The Lord Edward and the Provisions of Oxford'.

[59] Villard, 'Autour de Charles d'Anjou', 34–5, no. 5.

[60] *DBM*, 78–9; 152–3, cap. 14; Howell, *Eleanor of Provence*, 164, 262–3, 273–4.

[61] While a member of the original baronial confederation, Peter was not one of the baronial twelve. He was absent from the king's twelve as well but was the only member of the confederation to attest (on 2 May 1258) Henry's letter bowing to reform, doing so amongst the members of Henry's twelve.

[62] Alice was the daughter of the marquis of Saluzzo and Beatrice, Eleanor's cousin. Peter of Savoy had arranged her marriage to Edmund de Lacy.

[63] *CR 1256–9*, 271; *CPR 1258–66*, 36, 38. The wardship was also shared with Ingram de Percy. Getting hold of the heiresses proved endlessly difficult.

Beatrice. As a result, Eleanor began to share her husband's hostility to Simon de Montfort who obstructed both. Yet none of this meant that Eleanor was ready to break with the regime. If Imbert Pugeys was deprived of the Tower, he remained as steward (alongside Giles de Argentan) of the king's household. As well as Aymon Thurbert at Windsor, another queen's man, Mathias Bezill, remained as castellan of Gloucester.[64] In the event, nothing was done about queen's gold and Eleanor instructed the exchequer to help her clerk collect it.[65] Above all, Eleanor had her two uncles on the ruling council, Archbishop Boniface and Peter of Savoy. Boniface was rarely at court and took little part in political affairs save for pronouncing, in October 1259, the sentence of excommunication against those who contravened the Provisions of Westminster. Peter of Savoy was different.

In 1258, it was seventeen years since Peter had first swooped, like a great eagle, down from the mountains and lakes of Savoy to the royal palaces of home counties England.[66] Since then he had divided his time between the two, becoming through war and diplomacy the leading force in what is now western Switzerland, while, through his intelligence and savoir faire, remaining always a leading councillor of the king. The dual role had continued after the revolution. In London in May 1259, surrounded by a crowd of Savoyards, Peter had liquidated rival claims to the county of Geneva. Around the same time, he was joining with fellow councillors in the final negotiations for the peace with France.[67]

The precision with which Peter battened down the Geneva surrender was equally seen in the way he defined and defended his rights as lord of Richmond and Pevensey.[68] In Sussex his actions alienated John de Warenne and numerous local knights, but at the national level he succeeded far better than the Lusignans in securing allies, hence his membership of both the baronial confederation and ruling council. Thereafter he was at the heart of the regime. He witnessed both the council's letter to the pope (with its denunciation of Henry and the Lusignans) and the letter proclaiming the council's authority. He was at court in every month from November 1258 to March 1259. He was at court again in May, July, August and September. He was doubtless behind Henry's gift of the Forz wardship to Peter de Champvent and Imbert de Montferrand (they were the first

---

[64] One of the diplomatic letters of 1259 speaks of going to see Henry and Eleanor at Windsor: Villard, 'Autour de Charles d'Anjou', 33–4, no. 4.

[65] TNA E 159/32, m. 7 (image 0018), during the Hilary term of 1259.

[66] There seems no evidence Peter ever visited Richmond in Yorkshire although he was as sharp as steel in maintaining the rights that came with the honour.

[67] Von Wurstemberger, *Peter der Zweite*, iv, nos. 507–9; Cox, *Eagles of Savoy*, 295; Howell, *Eleanor of Provence*, 50–1, 53, 159. Vincent, 'Peter of Savoy', brings out the duality of his career between England and Savoy.

[68] Peter's precision in defining his rights is a major theme in Ridgeway, 'An English cartulary roll of Peter of Savoy'.

witnesses of the Geneva agreement). On the same day as the wardship's concession, Peter, with other councillors, arranged for the 'bishop elected' in Aymer's place to be supported from the Winchester revenues.[69] That showed very clearly where he and Eleanor stood over Aymer's restoration. Earlier (in March 1259), 3,000 marks of Winchester revenues had been used to pay the pensions owed to Peter's brothers Amadeus and Thomas of Savoy. Since both were dead and the money was to be paid to Peter himself, probably he just kept it. In this scheme, he had the support of Richard de Clare, Hugh Bigod, John Mansel and Chancellor Wingham. Simon de Montfort, by contrast, refused to be involved, another indication of his worsening relations with the queen and the Savoyards. Presumably he thought this was an illegitimate use of the money.[70]

In all this, Eleanor was very far from a pale shadow behind Peter's back. Indeed, in November 1259 (in Peter's absence) she was able to secure a valuable wardship for Imbert Pugeys and the promise of another for Matthias Bezill. In the latter case the concession, authorized by Hugh Bigod and John Mansel, was made specifically 'at the instance of the queen'.[71] A newsletter sent to Provence earlier in the year testifies powerfully to her importance and agency. 'Concerning the state of England', the report went, 'you should know that the queen is lady (*'domina'*) as she was, and all things are done with her knowledge and at her will and nearly all the barons are with her save some who have virtually no power.'[72] The contrast with what was being said about Henry could not have been more marked.

## EDWARD'S ROLE

There was then little chance of Henry getting support from the queen in any attempt to break free. On the face of it, a far more likely ally was his son and heir, Lord Edward. Unlike his mother, he was very far from being reconciled to the regime. Indeed, he was doing all he could to break its shackles. In particular, he resented the way the council was trying to appoint the keepers of his lands and castles. In July 1259, headed by Richard de Clare, it had made Robert Walerand constable of Bristol, a principal Edwardian base. Walerand was sworn not to surrender the castle without the council's consent. As soon as he could Edward dismissed him.[73] Apart from some money, the council was also giving him no help in Wales. And it was continuing the negotiations for a peace with France to which he was opposed.

[69] *CPR 1258–66*, 36.

[70] *CPR 1258–66*, 16–17, 30.

[71] *CPR 1258–66*, 62–3. Pugeys had to pay for his wardship.

[72] Villard, 'Autour de Charles d'Anjou', 32–3, no. 3. (from Roger de Lentini). A roll (TNA E 101/349/26, images 0083–124) shows that between 1258 and 1263 the queen made gifts of over 600 rings, one in January 1259 to Hugh Bigod.

[73] Pershore, *Chronicle*, 243–4; *CPR 1258–66*, 29, 32, 63–4. Nonetheless Edward, in his alliance with Clare, did name Walerand as one of his party.

This period was crucial in Edward's political education and helps explain why he became so considerable a king. If only Henry had enjoyed a similar grounding. Up to this point, in England, Edward had earned an evil reputation. Matthew Paris pictures him travelling round with a large entourage seizing what he needed for his food, drink and transport. In one brutal episode, exemplifying his 'tyranny', he had a young man's ear cut off and eye gouged out.[74] Yet this is not the whole story. In his government of Gascony, Edward had been concerned to give justice to the people. Indeed, when he left in October 1255, he commissioned three local men to hear complaints against his bailiffs, complaints about 'the denial of justice, false judgements and oppression'.[75] Of course, Edward's situation in Gascony was delicate and he had every reason to stand forth as a good lord. In England he had far less need to bother. Until, that is, the revolution of 1258. Suddenly he found himself subject to humiliating and debilitating restrictions. For the first time in his life he had to consider the political forces in English society and how to enlist their support.

In 1258–9 the baronial leaders had reached out for the support of local society. Edward did the same. Very much in the spirit of the Ordinances of the Magnates, in August 1259 he instructed his officials in Cheshire to give 'common justice to everyone'. If it was denied, he would 'lose the favour of God and man'.[76] If Edward's concern became well known, it would explain why 'the community of the bachelery' protested to him at the Westminster parliament. The episode certainly shows Edward seeking the support of the knights. Henry himself, of course, is conspicuous by his absence.

Edward also enlisted the support of magnates. In March 1259 there was his alliance with Richard de Clare.[77] Each promised to give aid and counsel to the other and to the other's allies. Clare specifically agreed to help Edward get control of his lands and castles.[78] Edward's list of allies shows he had assembled a powerful party including Henry of Almain, John de Warenne, Philip Basset, the marcher lords Roger of Clifford and Hamo Lestrange, and the knights Roger of Leybourne and Warin of Bassingbourn. The list also showed how far he had moved from the wing of his mother, for Peter of Savoy and other Savoyards were conspicuously absent.[79] The alliance with Clare did not last long, probably thanks to rival

---

[74] Paris, v, 539, 592–4, 646.

[75] Studd, 'Acts of Lord Edward', no. 590; Billaud, 'Similarities and differences', 96. Both this paper and Billaud's 'The Lord Edward and the administration of justice' stress Edward's concern for the good government of his appanage.

[76] Carpenter, *Reign of Henry III*, 250–2, and also Studd, 'Acts of Lord Edward', no. 843; Billaud, 'Similarities and differences', 106.

[77] 'Letter of Richard, earl of Gloucester', 68–9.

[78] It seems probable that Edward had already shaken himself free from the four councillors who were supposed to control his seal, if indeed they ever acted to do so.

[79] For Edward's new followers and the Savoyard eclipse, see Ridgeway, 'The politics of the English royal court', 338–41.

claims to Bristol, which Clare claimed as part of the honour of Gloucester. It was only King John who had taken it away.[80] Clare's role in placing the town under Robert Walerand may have seemed to Edward a first step in making good his claim.

Edward was not friendless for long. He soon replaced his alliance with Clare with one even more striking, as we have seen. In a pact sealed on 15 October 1259, he swore to aid and counsel Simon de Montfort, his heirs and friends in all their needs. We do not know what Montfort swore in return but presumably it was again to help Edward get control of his lands and castles. Edward and Montfort were united by their common hostility to Clare and by their support for local reforms. When Edward, in the pact, swore to maintain the 'enterprise made by the barons of the land', he was probably thinking of these. He was certainly not thinking of the restrictions placed on himself. This was a far solider alliance than that with Richard Clare and was soon to have major political consequences.

Why then could not father and son have made common cause in overthrowing the restrictions from which they both suffered? After all, the two had been reconciled in the chapter house of Winchester back in July 1258. If Henry was still attached to the Lusignans, so was Edward. In 1260, Guy, Geoffrey and William de Valence went out to Gascony on his behalf. Yet there is no sign of father and son standing together in 1259. They were divided by their different views about the peace with France. Perhaps Henry also resented Edward going his own way. The alliance with Clare was acceptable, but that with Montfort absolutely was not. Edward, when he agreed to stand by 'the enterprise made by the barons of the land', must have accepted Montfort's view that this meant maintaining the restrictions on the king. Heedless of the implications for the rights and dignity of the crown, he wanted to free himself from the council's control while leaving his father a subject king.

By the time he was setting off for France in November 1259 for the conclusion of the peace, Henry was becoming alarmed by Edward's activities. With John Mansel, he authorized a writ telling Walerand not to surrender Bristol without his own and the council's consent. Likewise with Mansel, remembering the fiasco over Velascus, and hearing presumably of Edward's intentions, he tried to prevent the Lusignans returning via Bristol to England.[81] Next year, tensions between father and son were to bring the kingdom near to civil war. Those tensions had much to do with differing views about the peace with France, negotiations for which had been running parallel with reform of the realm throughout 1259. To the peace we now turn.

---

[80] Pershore, *Chronicle*, 243–4; *CPR 1258–66*, 29, 32, 63–4.
[81] *CPR 1258–66*, 63–4; *CR 1259–61*, 138. For a biography of Walerand, see Harding, 'Robert Walerand'.

## Chapter 4

# THE TREATY OF PARIS
## 1258-1259

At the Westminster parliament of April 1258, Henry III had taken a deep breath and accepted the peace terms offered by Louis IX. He would surrender for ever Normandy, Anjou and Poitou, the heart of his dynasty's old continental empire.[1] While retaining Gascony, he and his heirs would do liege homage for it to the king of France. As some compensation for his losses, Henry was promised all Louis's rights and possessions (or an appropriate exchange) in the Three Dioceses of Limoges, Cahors and Périgueux. He was also promised the Saintonge if it escheated to the French crown on the death of Alphonse of Poitiers and the Agenais if it escheated on the death of Alphonse's wife, Countess Joan. As the couple had no children, there was a good prospect this would happen.[2] Meanwhile, in respect of the Agenais, Henry was to receive an annual payment equivalent to its value. There was also to be a cash payment equal to the cost of maintaining 500 knights for two years.

Having agreed to King Louis's terms, Henry might have hoped the whole process of treaty making would be over in a few months. Yet it took over a year and a half. For Henry the delay was both humiliating and infuriating: humiliating because it stemmed from the authority of the baronial council, an authority Louis himself came to accept; infuriating because it was caused too by the demands of Simon de Montfort. Montfort's intervention also devalued the money for the knights, money so essential if Henry was to continue with the Sicilian project, the whole point of making peace with France in the first place. While in domestic politics, apart from the Velascus episode, Henry seems a shadowy figure; in the negotiations for the treaty his feelings and actions come more into light. He was very involved too, here working in tandem with the queen,

---

[1] Maine and Touraine were included in the surrender too. The first detailed study of the Treaty of Paris was Michel Gavrilovitch's *Étude sur le traité de Paris de 1259*. In what follows I am much indebted to the comprehensive examination in Amicie Pélissié du Rausas's doctoral thesis 'De guerre, de trêve, de paix: les relations franco-anglaises de la bataille de Taillebourg au traité de Paris', 445–702.

[2] For the considerable value of these territorial concessions on the frontiers of Gascony, see volume I, 682–3.

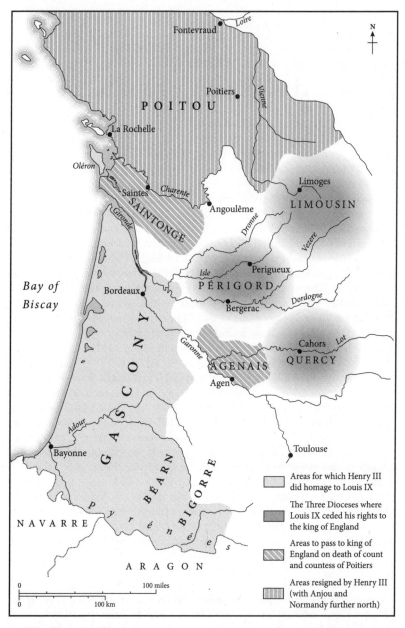

Areas for which Henry III did homage to Louis IX

The Three Dioceses where Louis IX ceded his rights to the king of England

Areas to pass to king of England on death of count and countess of Poitiers

Areas resigned by Henry III (with Anjou and Normandy further north)

2. The Treaty of Paris

in pushing forward, as a subtext to the treaty, the marriage between his daughter Beatrice and the eldest son of the duke of Brittany.

The process leading to the conclusion of the treaty in December 1259 is long and complex. I have told it in detail here both because of the subject's importance, for the treaty changed fundamentally relations between England and France, and also because abundant source material makes it possible to see, in this case, how medieval diplomacy worked. By way of introduction, it may be helpful to summarize the key procedural stages through which negotiations passed.[3] Of these there were no fewer than ten, themselves interrupted by attempts to meet the demands of the Montforts.

*Stage 1 May 1258: the oaths of the proctors swearing to the treaty*
The swearing to the texts of the treaty by the proctors of the two kings in Paris in May 1258.

*Stage 2 November 1258: the failed meeting at Cambrai*
The oaths of the proctors should have been followed by the two kings ratifying the treaty in their own names and then putting it into force. This was scheduled to take place at Cambrai in November 1258. But the meeting was abandoned.

*Stage 3 February 1259: the oaths of the proctors again*
In February 1259, this time in England, a fresh set of proctors, for reasons we will see, swore to the terms of the treaty all over again. Henry and the council also now realized that the renunciation of the ceded territories required in the treaty from Eleanor de Montfort, as King John's daughter, would not be forthcoming until the Montforts' grievances were redressed. A process of arbitration was set in train to settle the matter, but no progress was made. One result was a furious quarrel between Simon de Montfort and Richard de Clare.

*Stage 4 May 1259: Henry's dual ratification of the treaty*
After major concessions to the Montforts, Henry ratified the treaty on 20 May in two alternative sets of letters issued in his own name. One set included the requirement that Eleanor de Montfort renounce her claims, the other set (in case the renunciations were still not made) omitted it.

*Stage 5 June 1259: King Louis insists the English council ratify the treaty*
Having received Henry's ratification, Louis now insisted the council of fifteen ratify the treaty too. He also made clear he wanted the treaty with Eleanor de Montfort's renunciations.

---

[3] What follows is developed from Chaplais, 'Making of the treaty of Paris'.

*Stage 6 July 1259: the English council ratifies the treaty*
On 21 July, Hugh Bigod and all fifteen members of the council issued a
letter ratifying the treaty. (This was the version with the renunciation
clauses.)

*Stage 7 August 1259: King Louis accepts the treaty without the renunciation clauses*
With the renunciations still not made but with Montfort assuring Louis
they would be forthcoming, Louis agreed to accept a version of the treaty
without the renunciation clauses.

*Stage 8 September 1259: Henry's abandoned ratification*
On 3 September, Henry issued a letter once again ratifying the treaty (the
version without the renunciation clauses), but it was never sealed.

*Stage 9 October 1259: the final ratifications of the treaty*
On 13 October at Westminster, both Henry and the council issued their
own letters ratifying the treaty. In the same month in Paris, Louis issued
his parallel letter.

*Stage 10 December 1259: the publication and implementation of the treaty*
Louis IX had always insisted that the treaty could only be published and
implemented once Henry had done him homage. This Henry did in Paris
on 4 December 1259. In the same ceremony, the treaty was read out and
went live. The day before, outside the text of the treaty, Eleanor de
Montfort made her renunciations.

* * *

## STAGE 1 MAY 1258: THE OATHS OF THE PROCTORS
## SWEARING TO THE TREATY

After his decision at the Westminster parliament, Henry despatched proctors to France with full power to swear to the terms of the treaty on his
behalf. They were Simon de Montfort, Peter of Savoy and Hugh Bigod.
In Paris on 28 May they took the required oath while a parallel oath was
sworn by Louis's proctors.[4] The three then hurried back to England in
time for the Oxford parliament. Henry's reaction was surely mixed:
delighted to see the money for the knights was safely in the treaty, dismayed
to find it could only be spent with the consent of the 'upstanding men of
the land elected by the king and by high men of the land'. As we have
seen, this was almost certainly Montfort's doing.[5]

---

[4] *Layettes*, iii, no. 4416; *DD*, no. 299.
[5] See above, 54.

## STAGE 2 NOVEMBER 1258: THE FAILED
## MEETING AT CAMBRAI

The proposal now was that Henry and Louis should meet with King Richard at Cambrai in late November, there to ratify and publish the final treaty. Knowing Henry hoped a legate would be present, Louis asked for one to be sent who 'sincerely loves' the French kingdom.[6] It all came to nothing. The barons would not allow Henry to leave the country, doubtless fearing what he might say to Louis and Richard. In Henry's place, Montfort, Roger Bigod and the bishops of Worcester and Lincoln were chosen to go instead, a delegation very much reflecting Montfort's influence.[7] But since the treaty could only be completed with Henry doing homage to Louis, the meeting became pointless and Louis refused to attend.[8]

## STAGE 3 FEBRUARY 1259: THE OATHS OF
## THE PROCTORS AGAIN

The whole process now hung fire until February 1259 when fresh envoys from Louis arrived in England. The first stage, in which the proctors had sworn to the text of the treaty on behalf of their masters, now needed to be gone through all over again. This was because, under the original oaths, Henry was only bound to make his renunciations if Louis ratified the treaty by 2 February 1259, something he had obviously failed to do.[9] (Probably Louis's proctors had entered a similar reservation about his concessions, although its text does not survive.) Accordingly, on 17 February 1259, the earls of Hereford and Aumale swore on Henry's soul that he would accept the terms of the treaty. So Montfort, who had sworn to the original treaty (with Hugh Bigod and Peter of Savoy) back in May 1258, was now replaced, probably because, embroiled in quarrels with Richard de Clare over the Ordinances of the Magnates, and making demands of his own connected with the treaty, he was no longer acceptable. The earls of Hereford and Aumale were safe, uncontroversial substitutes.[10]

Alongside the oath of his proctors, Henry himself issued a letter acknowledging that he would receive neither land nor money for the knights until he had performed liege homage to Louis. So the two kings would have to meet before the treaty could be implemented. Louis had

---

[6] Delaborde, 'Instructions d'un ambassadeur envoyé par saint Louis à Alexandre IV à l'occasion du traité de Paris', a reference I owe to Amicie Pélissié du Rausas.

[7] For Montfort and the bishops of Worcester and Lincoln, see below, 269–70.

[8] Paris, v, 720–1; Burton, 460–1.

[9] *Layettes*, iii, no. 4420. The editorial change of 'rex Francie' to 'rex Anglie' is a mistake.

[10] *Layettes*, iii, no. 4466. By 24 February, Louis's envoys (Guy, dean of Tours, Odo the treasurer of Bayeux and the knight Nicholas de Meneto), acting as his proctors, had taken a similar oath on Louis's behalf: *F*, i, 380 (*CPR 1258–66*, 14).

insisted on this acknowledgement. After the fiasco at Cambrai, he wanted no misunderstanding on the point. Henry, however, so anxious to expedite matters, especially over the knights, was probably disappointed. At any rate, John Mansel failed to hand the letter over and in March Henry's envoys were still empowered to receive what was due to the king under the treaty.[11] Perhaps hoping it would encourage Louis to change his mind, on 24 February Henry himself renounced all his claims to Normandy, Anjou and Poitou, doing so in the presence of Louis's envoys. Louis, however, stood firm and made no move to anticipate his own concessions.[12]

## THE MONTFORT BLACKMAIL

The next step in the negotiations was for both kings to ratify the texts sworn to by their proctors. But here, by February 1259, another major obstacle hoved into view. It brings us to the thorny issue of the renunciation clauses. The text of the treaty required from King Richard his own 'quittance' of everything Henry was surrendering. The same quittance was required from Henry's sister Eleanor de Montfort and her children. Henry's sons, Edward and Edmund, for their part, were to give letters showing they had sworn to uphold the treaty. Louis was quite clear he would not ratify the treaty until all these letters had been received.

King Richard, very much party to the negotiations, made no difficulty over his quittance. He was hoping that the settlement with France would secure Louis's support for his imperial coronation and indeed might lead to a formal alliance. Accordingly, both in June 1258 and again in February 1259 he issued the required letters.[13] Likewise, in February, a dutiful Edmund announced he had taken his oath to abide by the treaty.[14] Edward was different. As its immediate ruler, he would suffer from the treaty changing Gascony into a fief held from the king of France, whereas previously (or so the English and the Gascons argued) it had not been held from anyone at all.[15] He had also been given by his father all the claims to the lost continental territories, so was the immediate loser from their surrender.[16] When Henry finally ratified the treaty on 20 May, Edward was said to have taken his oath, but in fact it was not till 25 July that he actually issued a letter saying he had done so.[17]

---

[11] CPR 1258–66, 14–15, 18.

[12] F, i, 380 (CPR 1258–66, 14).

[13] Layettes, iii, nos. 4413, 4415 (the proposal for an alliance), 4423, 4426, 4462–3 (the last a parallel letter from Richard's son Henry of Almain); Church, Henry III, 56.

[14] CPR 1258–66, 14.

[15] Canterbury/Dover, 209–10. The statement here about Gascony's status, written soon after the treaty, is the best evidence for the English and the Gascon views of the matter.

[16] F, i, 296 (CPR 1247–58, 271).

[17] Layettes, iii, nos. 4500–1; TR, nos. 104–5. Edward also said he accepted the quitclaims made by his father.

Eventually, then, Edward was reined in. The Montforts proved far less compliant. They absolutely refused any quittance until their grievances were redressed: grievances over the money owed them by the king, the failure to convert Eleanor's marriage portion into land and the way she had been short-changed over her dower.[18] In all this they worked very much as a team. Judging from the way Adam Marsh rebuked her both for anger and extravagance, Eleanor is unlikely to have been a calming influence.[19] When Montfort was out of the country it was she who pressed the demands and turned down the king's proposals.[20] Henry's fury can be seen in the charges he brought in 1260: Montfort had delayed the whole treaty and as the price for the quittance had extracted concessions damaging to the rights of the crown. Blackmail! Montfort, of course, rejected such aspersions. Why should Eleanor surrender her rights when her own grievances had not been redressed?[21]

Henry believed that Montfort himself put into Louis's mind the need for Eleanor's resignation, thus getting the blackmail weapon into the treaty. Montfort denied the charge. And even without his prompting, Louis would surely have demanded quittances from all the surviving children of King John. Yet it seems certain that Montfort rubbed into Louis the need for Eleanor's renunciation. He admitted that at various times he had positively demanded Eleanor's share of King John's overseas territories.[22] The place given Eleanor in the treaty was itself unique. She was required to make her renunciation for 'her heirs and children', something not required of King Richard or, when it came to his daughters, of Henry himself, as indeed Henry pointed out. What is more, Eleanor and her children, alongside Henry himself and Henry's sons, were also bound (unlike King Richard and his children) to take an oath to accept the treaty.[23]

In order to find a way out of the impasse, when Henry's envoys went back to France in early in April 1259, they were empowered to reach a settlement with the Montforts, if necessary by appointing arbitrators. At the same time they took with them the letter containing Henry's renunciations and the text of the treaty as sworn to by the earls of Hereford and Aumale on 17 February. The envoys, headed by Richard de Clare and Montfort himself, were to expedite the peace and (optimistically) receive the things due to be assigned the king under its terms. They could select

---

[18] See above, 56.

[19] *Letters of Adam Marsh*, ii, 378–83, 386–7; Wilkinson, *Eleanor de Montfort*, 12–13. I owe 'unlikely to have been a calming influence' to a letter from my old supervisor, John Prestwich. Louise Wilkinson's fine biography of Eleanor is now central to understanding her career.

[20] *DBM*, 196–9, cap. 10; *CPR 1258–66*, 25.

[21] *DBM*, 194–205, from which much of what follows comes.

[22] *DBM*, 204–5, cap. 22. This was the occasion Montfort remarked that 'he was doing no wrong if he demanded his rights'.

[23] *DBM*, 194–5, cap. 4.

two of their number to act in any process assessing the money due for the knights.[24]

In the event, no progress was made in reaching a settlement with the Montforts and the result out in France was a furious quarrel between Montfort and Clare, one of the last episodes narrated by Matthew Paris. He tells of how, with the peace process impeded by Eleanor refusing to resign her claims to Normandy, Clare (doubtless remembering Montfort's attack over the Ordinances of the Magnates) hurled abuse at Montfort and, with Montfort replying in kind, there was nearly bloodshed. It was doubtless for just such a conflict with Montfort that Clare, before his departure, had concluded his alliance with Lord Edward. The two angry earls were eventually restrained by their friends, but (leaving Montfort in France) Clare and his colleagues returned with nothing achieved. Evidently Louis would not move forward without Eleanor's renunciation.[25]

## THE CONCESSIONS TO THE MONTFORTS: MAY 1259

If the peace was to be concluded, there seemed no alternative but to appease the Montforts, as doubtless his allies at the top of the regime urged. In May, therefore, the council, led by Richard de Clare, authorized full payment of the debts Montfort was owed by the king.[26] The council also persuaded Henry (at last) to convert into land the £400 annual pension Eleanor was receiving (from the revenues of midland counties) as her marriage portion. Henry thus gave the Montforts and their heirs nine manors. If investigation showed these were not part of the royal demesne, then Henry would grant them to the Montforts in hereditary right. If they were royal demesne, then the Montforts would hold them 'on lease' until they could be granted other land in hereditary right from escheats coming into the king's hands.[27]

Henry felt particularly bitter about this transaction. He later accused Montfort of breaking his oath as a councillor not to consent to alienations from the royal demesne (the oath taken at Windsor in 1257). Montfort's reply was that if the manors were royal demesne (as indeed most of them were), then he and Eleanor only held them on lease until granted land elsewhere. Henry was not the only person to feel uneasy. Both Peter of Savoy and John Mansel agreed to the grant saving the oath they had taken

---

[24] *CPR 1258–66*, 18; *CLR 1251–60*, 457; Paris, v, 741. The other envoys were John Mansel, John de Balliol and Robert Walerand. The arbitrators in the Montfort dispute were to be Clare, Mansel and Walerand, or alternatively Clare and Peter of Savoy.

[25] Paris, v, 741, 745.

[26] Testimony to Monfort's influence, the debts only amounted to £236 thanks to £1,400 handed over since Michaelmas 1258: *CLR 1251–60*, 460; TNA E 403/ 17B; E 403/ 3115.

[27] *CChR 1257–1300*, 18, 20; *RCWL*, ii, 123–4. Where the manors were held on an existing lease, the Montforts only received the revenue until the lease ran out.

at Windsor.[28] Henry and the council also moved to deal with the Montforts' final grievance, namely over the dower, hoping again the issue might be settled by arbitration. Here, Henry spoke out loud and clear in his own defence. He insisted the arbitrators investigate whether he had really forced Eleanor into a disadvantageous settlement in the first place. He also revived his old claim (not of much merit) that the pension granted to the Montforts in 1244 had secured release from their claims over the dower.[29]

## STAGE 4 MAY 1259: HENRY'S DUAL RATIFICATION OF THE TREATY

On the same day, 20 May 1259, that the manors were granted to Montfort and arrangements made for the arbitration, Henry at last went ahead and issued his own ratification of the treaty. But, despite all that had been done, doubts remained over whether the Montfortian renunciations would be forthcoming. They had evidently given no cast-iron assurances and probably were waiting to see what the arbitration produced. So Henry ratified the treaty in two alternative forms, one with the renunciation clauses and one without.[30] In the hope that Louis might accept the latter, Henry promised to indemnify him against Eleanor's claims if she refused to renounce them.

## STAGE 5 JUNE 1259: KING LOUIS INSISTS THE ENGLISH COUNCIL RATIFY THE TREATY

In June the king's envoys (Richard de Clare, Peter of Savoy and John Mansel) were back in Paris where they met Louis and Montfort. They were in for a shock. For Louis, now raised another hurdle. He insisted that the whole council of fifteen ratify the treaty. Henry's sole ratification was not enough. This was surely Montfort's work. With the text of its October 1258 proclamation to hand, he had explained to Louis the council's authority.[31] Even if its task was just to help Henry be a king, Louis now saw that without its imprimatur the treaty might not stick. At the same time, Louis reiterated that he would accept no treaty without Eleanor's renunciation. So Montfort still had his weapon and he wielded it to good purpose, forcing the envoys to improve in all kinds of detailed ways the offer over the manors. This steely man was intent on extracting the last ounce out of the situation.[32]

---

[28] *TR*, no. 116.

[29] *F*, i, 383; *CPR 1258–66*, 25–6. This pension was later transformed into the £400 a year secured on the counties: *CChR 1226–57*, 278. See also volume 1, 575–6.

[30] *TR*, no. 103. The renunciation required of Richard was also omitted. Louis had, of course, already received it.

[31] For this text, see above, 58.

[32] BN Clairambault 1188, fos. 10v–11; *TR*, no. 116.

## STAGE 6 JULY 1259: THE ENGLISH COUNCIL
## RATIFIES THE TREATY

When the envoys returned to England, the council complied with Louis's demands. On 21 July all fifteen members, together with Hugh Bigod, undertook 'before the envoys of the king of France sent for this by him' both to observe the treaty (the version with the renunciation clauses) and labour to ensure Henry observed it too. All of them sealed the resulting document.[33] At the same time, the improved offer over the manors was embodied in royal charters attested by Hugh Bigod and the councillors.[34] The issue of the dower, meanwhile, was to be arbitrated by the earl of Norfolk, the earl of Hereford and Philip Basset. The Montforts even agreed, or so it seemed, that once the arbitrators had taken their oath and begun their work, they would make the required renunciations. The councillors for their part swore to accept the forthcoming award. They were also to receive the money due for the 500 knights until Henry did as well.[35] So once again Montfort had obstructed Henry's hold of the money.[36]

By the end of July both king and council, therefore, believed that the obstacles had been overcome and the treaty could go forward. They decided that Henry should leave England at the start of September and meet Louis at Abbeville. That would give plenty of time for the Montfortian quittance to come through. In preparation, a seal with Henry's new titles was ordered and Henry made a pilgrimage to St Albans, one recorded by the able monk who now took over Matthew Paris's chronicle. In the morning, having heard divine service, Henry caused the feretory with St Alban's body to be raised above the High Altar. He then prostrated himself underneath in prayer while the convent sang the martyr's canticle. A monk, in a sermon, explained the reason for Henry's coming. 'The prince and head of the kingdom' was about to cross overseas and was asking for the help of the martyr and the prayers of the convent. Having offered hearty thanks for the convent's support, Henry, 'confirmed in faith', departed happy. However, the chronicler added, news from France soon put a stop to his journey.[37]

---

[33] *TR*, nos. 109–10.

[34] *CChR 1257–1300*, 20; *RCWL*, ii, 124. Apart from Montfort himself, the only member of the council not attesting was John de Plessis.

[35] *TR*, nos. 109–21, 128; *CChR 1257–1300*, 20; *CPR 1258–66*, 34–5; BN Clairambault 1188, fos. 15, 72; *DBM*, 200–1, caps. 13–14.

[36] At this time the council agreed to a deal under which Montfort committed to Henry the county of Bigorre. Given its strategic position to the south-east of Gascony bordering Béarn, Henry's desire to hold Bigorre was understandable, but the money he now owed Montfort added a further tangle to their relationship: *TR*, nos. 122–7; *CR 1256–9*, 456–7; and Maddicott, *Simon de Montfort*, 183–4, for a full account of this complicated transaction.

[37] *CPR 1258–66*, 39; *CLR 1251–60*, 472; Paris's Continuator, 431–2.

## STAGE 7 AUGUST 1259: KING LOUIS ACCEPTS THE TREATY WITHOUT THE RENUNCIATION CLAUSES

It was the Montforts again! They were still refusing the renunciations. Whatever had been agreed, they were unwilling to make them until the arbitrators had actually pronounced their award. So again there was deadlock. It was finally broken by Montfort himself in his one and only concession. Clearly under immense pressure, he now told Louis, both by word of mouth and messengers, that he *was* prepared to make the renunciations whenever Louis wanted.[38] Louis, therefore, no longer needed the section in the treaty requiring Henry to secure Eleanor's quittance. It could be given separately direct to Louis and the treaty could proceed without it. Here Louis was himself making a major concession, one which showed his faith in Montfort and also how much he wanted the treaty to be concluded. Montfort, however, had far from given up the hope of extracting concessions in return for the renunciation, as we will see.

## STAGE 8 SEPTEMBER 1259: HENRY'S ABANDONED RATIFICATION

Henry, overjoyed by Louis's change of heart, pressed on at once with a fresh ratification of the treaty.[39] Technically, he could have used his alternative ratification of 20 May 1259, the one without the renunciation clauses, but that was a clumsy document and Henry's clerks now prepared a new version, as well as re-ordering some of the clauses within the text of the treaty. (It was set out in all the ratifications.) Louis's own eventual ratification followed Henry's text so at least here the English side was influential. Henry's ratification with its new version of the treaty, dated 3 September, was prepared for sealing. But it was never sealed and sent to Louis. A battered relic, it languishes today in The National Archives at Kew.[40] The problem was once again the council. It had ratified the treaty back in July, but with what was now the *wrong* text, the one *with* the renunciation clauses! So it now needed to ratify the treaty in its new form.[41] Although Hugh Bigod and nine councillors were at court in early September, that still left six who were absent. And so it was decided to wait till the October parliament

---

[38] *DBM*, 198–203, caps. 12, 13, 19. I am speculating that it was at this point Montfort made the concession. It was, according to his testimony (I think here believable), before Henry left for France.

[39] *DD*, no. 302.

[40] *DD*, no. 302.

[41] As no longer operative, the text the council subscribed to in July (the one with the renunciation clauses) was returned to England and is now in the British Library. It is marked 'vacat', lines are drawn across it and the seals have been removed from their tags: BL Cotton MS Caligula D III, no. 2: *TR*, no. 110. The text without the clauses does not survive.

where a full or fuller contingent would be present. Henry could have gone ahead and sealed his letter and then waited for that of the council, but it was better for both letters to bear the same date.

Meanwhile, Henry gave an outing to his new seal and new titles, no longer duke of Normandy and count of Anjou. On 9 September he issued a letter acknowledging he would receive no arrears for the period during which the amount of money due to him under the treaty was being assessed. Over this, Henry put up a fight for he drew up another letter adding this would only be true if the valuation took place within three years from the time of his homage. But it was the first letter that was actually sent to Louis.[42]

## STAGE 9 OCTOBER 1259: THE FINAL
## RATIFICATIONS OF THE TREATY

So to the October parliament. On 13 October, the day of its opening, Henry issued his letter ratifying the treaty. It followed exactly the form drafted back in September. In a letter likewise of 13 October, Hugh Bigod and all the councillors recited Henry's ratification and then said that, before the envoys of the king of France, they had sworn to uphold the treaty and to do all they could to ensure Henry upheld it. This letter was duplicated, doubtless at Louis's request. He wanted no doubt about the council's adhesion to the treaty. Both the king's letter and one of those issued by the councillors were written in what looks like a French rather than an English hand, presumably by clerks in the entourage of Louis's envoys. If this was because the chancery at the start of the parliament had much else to do (preparing a final text of the Provisions of Westminster for a start), it also symbolized how Louis was the real gainer from the treaty.

The English ratifications of the treaty, the one issued in Henry's name, the two issued in the names of the councillors, reside in the Archives Nationales in Paris.[43] Beneath the former hangs Henry new seal, beneath the two latter the seals of the councillors.[44] Fittingly, the most spectacular are the seals of Montfort and Clare, the former galloping to the hunt,

---

[42] *DD*, no. 304; *Layettes*, v, no. 692.

[43] Archives Nationales Paris (hereafter AN), J 629/8, is Henry's ratification, while the councillors' letters are AN J 629/10 (in a French hand) and AN J 629/10 bis. They are printed in *Layettes*, iii, nos. 4554–5. I am most grateful to Jean-François Moufflet for allowing me and Elisabeth Lalou to examine together all the documents in the Archives related to the Treaty of Paris.

[44] Neither letter has quite a full complement of seals. AN J 629/10 has James of Audley's twice over, while it lacks the seal of William de Forz, earl of Aumale. AN J 629/10 bis lacks Audley's seal, presumably because it had been used twice on J 629/10. The seal of Richard de Grey is also missing, whether because it was never there or through subsequent loss is unclear. I thank Amicie Pélissié du Rausas for clarifying these points. AN J/ 629 10 is illustrated in plate 5.

blowing his horn and with a greyhound running beneath, the latter in full armour astride a caparisoned war horse, brandishing his sword, with on the reverse, large scale, a shield with the three chevrons of the Clares.[45] Of all the documents produced in the period of revolution and reform, it is these letters in the Archives Nationales that give the most powerful visual testimony to the council's authority. Louis's own ratification of the treaty survives in The National Archives at Kew. It stands alone.[46] Louis needed no councillors to sanction what he was doing.

The unity shown by the councillors, in this moment of time, was illusory. Montfort was already at odds with Richard de Clare and Peter of Savoy. Next year he fell out with Hugh Bigod. In the eventual civil war, Montfort with Bishop Cantilupe, Richard de Grey and Peter de Montfort were to be on one side, and Humphrey de Bohun, Hugh Bigod, Peter of Savoy, Roger de Mortimer, Philip Basset and James of Audley on the other. It was Mortimer who was credited with killing Montfort at the battle of Evesham.

On 13 October, Montfort had been one of the councillors ratifying the treaty. Two days later, in London, his alliance with Lord Edward was concluded. He must then have left at once, or even earlier, for on 19 October he is found with Louis IX at Evreux in Normandy.[47] Having received the news that king and council had ratified the treaty, Louis, once back in Paris, went ahead and issued his own ratification.[48] Montfort, however, was more than just a messenger. He still said he *would* make the renunciations when Louis wanted, but he also stressed he was under no *obligation* to do so since the promises made to him had not been kept.[49] The arbitrators after all had pronounced no award. Louis, therefore, in all justice, should find some way of keeping pressure on Henry. He should also give Eleanor some compensation of his own.

Montfort's complaint over the arbitration was accurate but disingenuous. The arbitrators had indeed pronounced no award. They had until 1 November to do so but probably by this time none was expected. Henry later claimed Montfort himself through his friends on the council had got the award delayed.[50] Montfort did not deny the charge. Presumably he had disliked what was emerging. The demands over Eleanor's dower were gigantic. The Montforts wanted from the king 36,400 marks worth of

---

[45] The reverse of Montfort's seal shows small scale a shield with the Montfort fork-tailed lion. On AN J 629/10, Montfort's seal is in white wax and on AN J 629/10 bis it is green. For the Montfort seals, see Ambler, *Song of Simon de Montfort*, 111–12 and plates 1013.

[46] *DD*, no. 305.

[47] Only Edward's text of the alliance survives, and this is where the 15 October in London date comes from: Carpenter, *Reign of Henry III*, 251.

[48] It bears no date other than October: *DD*, no. 305.

[49] I deduce what follows from *DBM*, 200–3, caps. 12, 13, 19.

[50] *DBM*, 200–3, cap. 16. Henry claimed it was thus ready to be declared before the November deadline.

arrears and an extra 1,400 marks a year for the future.[51] The alternative was for the king to cause the dower to be 'delivered'. The consequences of that would have been explosive, for the numerous Marshal heirs would all have had to surrender land. Three of them, Roger Bigod (one of the arbitrators), Richard de Clare and Roger de Mortimer, were on the council of fifteen.[52] Probably what Montfort wanted now was an award through some fresh process. It was with a view to implementing a settlement on such lines that Edward, in his alliance with Montfort, swore to enforce the 'awards of the king's court'.[53] Such an award would certainly need some enforcing.

## THE BRETON MARRIAGE

Seventeen months had thus elapsed between the proctors swearing to the text of the treaty in May 1258 and the ratifications of the kings in October 1259. Had it not been for the trust between the royal families the whole process might have broken down. Fortunately, that trust, engendered by the meetings in Paris in 1254, was consolidated in 1259 itself by something new, namely a proposal for Henry and Eleanor's daughter Beatrice to marry John, son and heir of John, duke of Brittany. In 1259, Beatrice, 'beautiful' Beatrice as Henry described her when a baby, was aged seventeen. (She had been born in 1242 out in Bordeaux during Henry's disastrous Poitevin campaign.) Whom she should marry must have been increasingly debated by her parents and indeed the wider realm. Preferably it would be to someone who would bring the kingdom 'a great alliance in foreign parts', as it was put during the discussions over the marriage of Henry's sister Eleanor (later Montfort's wife), back in the 1220s.[54]

According to Henry, it was Louis IX's wife, Queen Margaret, who first suggested Beatrice should marry John of Brittany and she was certainly involved throughout in the negotiations.[55] Queen Eleanor was equally involved, and the sister queens drove the marriage forward together in happy co-operation. The fact that Beatrice was named after their mother, Beatrice of Savoy, created another familial strand to their efforts.[56]

In 1259, John of Brittany was twenty years old, so he and Beatrice were of an age. From the English point of view, the marriage certainly brought a great alliance in foreign parts. It was far better than a previously mooted match to the son of the king of Norway.[57] But in the context of 1259 there

[51] *TR*, no. 120; Carpenter, *Reign of Henry III*, 246.
[52] *DBM*, 200–3, no. 16.
[53] Carpenter, *Reign of Henry III*, 244–8. For Montfort's reference to a new arbitration, see *DBM*, 200–3, cap. 16.
[54] *DD*, no. 140.
[55] *DD*, no. 313.
[56] For a study of the involvement of the two queens, see Armstrong, 'Sisters in cahoots'.
[57] *CR 1256–9*, 476–7.

was nothing threatening here to France; Queen Margaret would never have suggested the marriage if there had been. It was thus quite different from the earlier Anglo-Breton alliance back in 1229–34. The aim now was to underpin the peace between England and France through Eleanor's daughter and Margaret's niece marrying the heir to one of the great French principalities. Henry was right in spirit if wrong in detail in saying the marriage had been 'expressly mentioned' in the peace treaty.[58] There was even the possibility that John of Brittany would be endowed with the English lordship of Richmond, thus making him a vassal of both the king of France and England, something impossible in the 1240s when both kings had ruled out any such dual allegiance.

The two queens' commitment to the marriage is shown by the way they both had to overcome obstacles in its path. Margaret needed to persuade her daughter Blanche and Blanche's husband, Theobald II of Champagne and Navarre, to release land in Champagne so it could be used as part of the young couple's endowment.[59] Eleanor's problem concerned Richmond. The honour had often in the past been held by the dukes of Brittany. Indeed, Duke John's father, Peter de Dreux, duke of Brittany in right of his wife, had held it during his alliance with Henry between 1229 and 1234.[60] It was inevitable that Duke John would demand Richmond's return so that it too could form part of his son's endowment. But here came the rub. Richmond was now held in hereditary right, under numerous royal charters, by none other than Eleanor's uncle Peter of Savoy! It seems inconceivable that Eleanor wanted Peter to surrender the honour. Her own position would be immeasurably weaker if he lost his great base in England. She also stood to be the ultimate loser, having been left all Peter's lands under his will of 1255.[61] Probably Henry took the same view. His attempt to restore bishop-elect Aymer had prevented any immediate alliance with Peter and the queen, but he must have hoped for one in the future. A Peter disinherited of Richmond would prevent that and also hinder any bid to recover power. So somehow a way had to be found round the difficulty.

The first sign that proposals for the marriage were in train comes in March 1259 when Richard de Clare and John Mansel were empowered to act as Henry's proctors in the negotiations. In the presence of Queen Margaret and Duke John they seem to have reached some agreement over

---

[58] *CR 1256–9*, 476–7. This is in his letter of apology to the king of Norway.

[59] *DD*, no. 313. John of Brittany's father, Duke John, was married to Theobald II's sister Blanche (John of Brittany's mother). As part of an eventual marriage settlement, he was promised lands in Champagne and the county of Perche, and it was with these he proposed to endow his son.

[60] See volume 1, 40, 62, 87–8.

[61] Andenmatten, 'Contraintes lignagères et parcours individuel', 284–6; Von Wurstemberger, *Peter der Zweite*, iv, no. 407.

the return of Richmond or a substitute for it.[62] The next step came in May
when Henry now gave full power to Queen Margaret, Clare, Mansel and
also Peter of Savoy to settle the terms of the marriage.

We next have a glimpse of Queen Eleanor's role in the affair. In
October 1259 when she herself passed through St Albans, hurrying
(though ill) to Westminster for the feast of the Confessor and the parliament, she was accompanied by John Mansel and the chief Breton nego-
tiator, the bishop of Brienne. At the parliament, it was in her chapel at
Westminster that Duke John's letters about the marriage were handed over
to Mansel for safekeeping in the presence of the king and council.[63] At the
same time, Henry wrote to Duke John explaining the situation over
Richmond. Peter of Savoy had waited a long time for the arrival of John's
envoys, but had now left England. In his absence nothing could be done.
But in December Peter would be with the king in Paris. If Duke John
could be there too the matter might be settled. If Henry could not obtain
the surrender of Richmond, he would give John an exchange either from
the lands Louis was giving him under the treaty or from lands in England.
As Henry had no lands to give in England, the treaty needs must be the
solution.

The negotiations for the Breton marriage had one important side effect.
They brought Henry and Queen Eleanor together on the issue of Simon
de Montfort. One of the newsletters sent out to Provence in 1259 spoke of
Eleanor being on good terms with Montfort, itself an indication of his
importance.[64] They certainly had a common hatred of the Lusignans. But
Eleanor must have shared her husband's dismay at the way Montfort's
demands were delaying the French peace. She must equally have regretted
his interference in the Breton marriage. For here (another sign of his
attachment to the reforms), Montfort had warned Duke John that if the
king gave a gift of land with his daughter it would need the council's
consent. In 1260, Henry angrily recalled this attempt, as he saw it, to upset
the marriage.[65]

## HENRY GOES TO FRANCE: NOVEMBER, DECEMBER 1259

After the October parliament, Henry could at last look forward to his visit
to France. In preparation, the council divided its forces. The home government was left in the hands of Hugh Bigod, supported by Roger de
Mortimer and Philip Basset, while another group, as we will see, went with
Henry to France. On 1 November at Westminster, Henry and Eleanor
celebrated the feast of All Saints, feeding 390 paupers and burning, across

---

[62] *CPR 1258–66*, 18; *F*, i, 391 (*TR*, no. 129).
[63] Paris's Continuator, 435–6; *F*, i, 391.
[64] Villard, 'Autour de Charles d'Anjou', 34–5, no. 5.
[65] *DBM*, 204–5, cap. 23.

the vigil and the feast, 230 pounds of wax for candles in the chapel and the almonry, this against the more normal daily figure of 25 to 30 pounds. Next week they left London and on the tenth announced their arrival at Canterbury by feeding 220 paupers and burning this time 114 pounds of wax.[66] Apart from the wax and almsgiving, the court was entertained in all things by Archbishop Boniface (who was staying in England). Four days later Henry embarked at Dover and crossed over to Wissant.

This time the destination was Paris. Henry could admire again the great buildings of the French capital and bask in the warmth of Louis's and Queen Margaret's welcome. Queen Eleanor, of course, could do the same. The family party of 1254, which had done so much to facilitate the peace, could be renewed. For that to happen was vitally important. The Treaty of Paris was a beginning not an end. The homage Henry now did for Gascony would inaugurate an entirely new relationship between the kings, with many potential points of conflict. The implementation of the treaty, moreover, might take years: the Agenais had to be valued, as had the costs of supporting the 500 knights; Louis's rights in the Three Dioceses had to be determined and handed over; and then ultimately, with the death of the count and countess of Poitiers, the king of England had to take possession of the Saintonge and the Agenais. Co-operation between the royal families was also very necessary for realizing the proposed marriage between Henry's daughter and John of Brittany.

Although Henry was sure of Louis's sympathy and support, he also had a point to prove. He was determined to show his kingship was still intact, despite the restrictions imposed upon him. That was partly a matter of outward show and here through the size of his entourage, the generosity of his gifts, the scale of his almsgiving, the lavishness of his hospitality and the general *débonereté* of his conduct Henry rose to the challenge. It was also a matter of power. At the very least, Henry hoped to make the reforms work as he felt they always should have worked with himself as the respected head of the council.

In realizing these aims, Henry was fortunate in the councillors with him in France: Richard de Clare, William de Forz, Peter of Savoy (who joined in Paris), Richard de Grey and John Mansel. Of these, only Richard de

---

[66] The evidence frequently cited in this chapter and also in ch. 6 for the feeding of paupers, and also for the daily costs of Henry's food and drink, and the amount of wax consumed for candles in the chapel and almonry, comes from the household roll for Henry's forty-fourth regnal year (28 October 1259–27 October 1260), the only one to survive in full for the whole of Henry's reign: TNA E 101/349/27 (images 0126–75). One wonders if the roll survived because it recorded Henry's momentous visit to Paris. The information about the feeding of paupers is calendared in Dixon-Smith, 'Feeding the poor', 272–82. The roll forms the basis for much of what is said in my 'Meetings of kings', where fuller references to some of what follows may be found. The spiritual benefits of feeding paupers are discussed in volume 1, 285–97.

Grey was a Montfort man. Montfort himself, though in France, was not part of Henry's entourage. Absent too was another member of the council, Montfort's great ally Peter de Montfort. He appears only once, as a witness to Henry's eventual homage to Louis, and quite probably remained throughout in Simon's company.[67] Apart from his councillors, the king's entourage included his second son, Edmund, his daughter Beatrice and at least seventy-eight knights, clerks, magnates and ministers. There were also the bishops of Lincoln, Norwich, Carlisle and Ely and the bishop-elect of London, the chancellor, Henry of Wingham. According to Matthew Paris's continuator, those meeting Henry's train across the sea affirmed that so fine a company had never before left England. The number of the king's sumpter horses alone was extraordinary, leaving aside the palfreys of the magnates and noble carriages of the queen and her ladies. The French themselves were impressed. The monk of Saint-Denis, William de Nangis, in his life of Saint Louis, recalled how Henry had come to France with the earl of Gloucester (it's significant he was singled out) and 'many nobles and princes of his kingdom'.

## STAGE 10 DECEMBER 1259: THE PUBLICATION AND IMPLEMENTATION OF THE TREATY

So Henry moved towards Paris. On 21 November he reached Amiens where he could admire again the great cathedral. On 25 November he was welcomed at Saint-Denis by Louis himself, the archbishop of Rouen and a solemn procession of monks.[68] Next day, feted by the citizens, he entered Paris and was received by another procession into the cathedral of Notre-Dame. So Henry was on time. On 26 November he was supposed to be in Paris and on that date he was there, correct etiquette all of a piece with his general deportment during this visit. Initially, Henry stayed at Louis's own palace with its Saint Chapelle in the centre of the city. Then he moved to the great monastery of Saint-Germain-des-Prés just to the west of the city walls. Probably, with his usual tact and understanding, the move was suggested by Louis himself so as to give Henry more independence and more space. In one crucial area Henry was very determined to be independent. According to Nangis, while staying in the royal palace he received from Louis 'choice wines and dishes and large rewards'. But Henry never allowed Louis to take over all his costs. To have done so would have detracted from his kingly dignity. If, moreover, beyond a

---

[67] *Layettes*, iii, no. 4566, a reference I owe to Amicie Pélissié du Rausas. Montfort attested no royal charters while the king was in France.

[68] A subtext to the negotiations for the treaty was Henry's recognition of Saint-Denis's rights over its cell at Deerhurst in Gloucestershire, the original grant dating back to Edward the Confessor. For this, see Jordan, *A Tale of Two Monasteries*, 55–8, in his ch. 3 on the Treaty of Paris.

certain point Henry was reluctant to accept hospitality, he was very keen to offer it. He thus displayed his royal wealth and status, something all the more important given his political situation.

So we come to the celebrations during the week of the Treaty of Paris itself, the week between Sunday 30 November and Saturday 6 December. They were important for both kings had been criticized for concluding the treaty: Henry for having surrendered Normandy, Anjou and Poitou; Louis for having conceded his rights in the Three Dioceses and the reversion of the Agenais and the Saintonge. The date of 30 November itself was a good day to start celebrating the treaty's 'adventus' for it was Advent Sunday, and also a bad one since Louis fasted in Advent in the same way as in Lent.[69] If Henry did the same he did not inflict alimentary austerities on anyone else. On 30 November itself the costs of his household, largely in supplying food and drink, soared to £92, against the £10 to £15 that was normal for a quiet day in England. Four days later, on 4 December, the great ceremony took place. Eudes Rigaud, archbishop of Rouen, 'recited and published' the treaty 'in the orchard of the king of France' and Henry did homage to Louis under its terms. An orchard in winter must have been a cold place for such a ceremony (Henry burnt 19s worth of firewood in his hall and chamber on the day), but the numbers witnessing the event were doubtless too large for any building. Henry certainly contributed his share of the entertainment, for the costs of the household on the day reached £77.

## HENRY'S GREAT FEAST, 6 DECEMBER 1259

On 5 December the royal household's costs fell to £30, so perhaps Henry was Louis's guest. It was very different on the following day. 'We dined with the king of England at Saint-Germain-des-Prés', Archbishop Rigaud recorded. He could have said that again for on this day Henry threw an absolutely gigantic feast. The cost was a stupendous £176 with the kitchen alone supplying food worth £126. Henry also made a special effort for the poor, the costs of the pantry in feeding them rising from around 6s a day to £5 6s. The 150 paupers Henry fed daily in France as in England (when with the queen) would have been very full indeed had they eaten all the resulting bread, enough for 2,544 halfpenny loaves or 5,088 farthing ones. Clearly there was a mass distribution of bread to the poor.

Drawing in part on the descriptions by Matthew Paris and the Burton annalist of the feast Henry threw at the Paris Temple in 1254, we can conjure up this joyful day: the great crowd of Parisians, including the paupers getting their loaves, thronging the buildings of the monastery for no one was denied entry; and in the hall itself, seated according to rank, the knights, barons, earls, dukes, archbishops, bishops, abbots, countesses,

[69] Sundays themselves, however, were not fast days.

queens, and royal princes with at the centre of the high table Henry and
Louis themselves. The feast of 6 December affirmed the family unity at
the heart of the Treaty of Paris and radiated the celebrations through the
differentiated ranks of diners in the hall into the undifferentiated masses
eating outside. I think of the funeral of Diana, princess of Wales, with the
great and good seated according to status in Westminster Abbey and the
masses outside sharing and responding through watching on the great
screens, image here replacing food as the unifying element.

Of course, the funeral of Diana revealed at its heart not family unity
but disunity. It was very different on 6 December 1259. We can imagine
Henry and Louis sitting together now talking quietly about private and
pious things, now joining in the general fun. Had the two kings begun the
proceedings with the same delicate parade of politesse they had exhibited
in 1254? Then, Louis had wanted Henry to sit in the central place only for
Henry to refuse on the grounds that (if there was a peace) Louis would be
his lord. In 1259 did Henry place Louis in the centre and say with a smile,
'well now you really are my lord'? If a great feast worked well, as this one
surely did, it brought the intimate and the inclusive fruitfully together with
those on the High Table, those below it and those outside being mutually
vivified by each other's company; in a sense the opposite of what happened
at Diana's funeral when the good and the great reluctantly joined in as the
applause of the crowd reverberated into the Abbey. Matthew Paris said of
Henry's feast in 1254 that with the variety of the splendid dishes, the abundance of delicious drink, the attentiveness of the servants and the status
of the guests, there had never been such a banquet even in the times of
Assuerus, Arthur and Charlemagne.[70] He would surely have said the same
about the feast celebrated on 6 December 1259.

The only discordant note was struck by the Montforts. Presumably
Montfort himself was somewhere on the high table and his wife, Eleanor,
with the queens and countesses. They had withheld their renunciations
absolutely to the last moment, doubtless hoping to the last to extract some
concession in return. What they did extract was Henry's agreement on
3 December that 15,000 marks due to him under the treaty should be withheld by Louis until his quarrels with the Montforts had been settled. There
was also compensation from Louis himself, if, as seems likely, it was now
that he granted Montfort a rent worth £110 a year. On these terms, on
4 December itself, in the presence of Henry and Louis, Eleanor at last made
her renunciations.[71] The Montforts had not come away empty handed from

---

[70] For Assuerus, who 'reigned from India to Ethiopia over 127 provinces', see ch. 1 of the
Book of Esther, where he throws a gigantic banquet. I owe this reference to Elizabeth Tetlow.
[71] Layettes, iii, nos. 4,564–5; DD, no. 306; CPR 1258–66, 106–7; Maddicott, Simon de
Montfort, 187. Simon himself also surrendered all his claims to the county of Evreux and
his father's Albigensian conquests: BN Clairambault 1188, fo. 14d. He had clearly been
pressing these also. The 15,000 marks were deposited at the Paris Temple.

their blackmail. To Henry's chagrin, they had replaced their money pension with an endowment in land, a big improvement, albeit most of the land was held on lease.[72] But they had made no progress in settling their grievance over the dower. The withholding of the 15,000 marks maintained some pressure on Henry, but a similar offer had been on the table since July.[73] The issue of the dower was to rumble on till the end of Montfort's life.

## THE CONCLUSION OF THE BRETON
## MARRIAGE AGREEMENT

In the days after the publication of the treaty, the negotiations for the Breton marriage also reached a conclusion. The settlement was a triumph for Peter of Savoy and the queen.[74] On 13 December in Paris, John, duke of Brittany, resigned to the king all his claims to the honour of Richmond so Peter's tenure, as the king's tenant, was secure.[75] In return, the compensation mooted back in October was now specified.[76] It was indeed to come from what Louis was promising under the treaty. Duke John was to receive the Agenais, when it became available, and before that the money Louis was to pay in lieu. If valuations showed the Agenais was worth less than Richmond, then Henry would make up the difference. If the Agenais, or the money in lieu, was unavailable within a year of the marriage (the valuation having yet to be made), then Henry would pay the duke in the meantime the value of Richmond.

There was one other stipulation in the agreement, one likely to increase Edward's aggravation, namely that the duke was to receive the Agenais money and ultimately hold the Agenais itself direct from Louis, doing him homage and becoming his 'man'. Louis later indicated this had happened at Henry's request.[77] If so, Henry was surely acting on Duke John's insistence. As overlord of the Agenais, the king of England might be an easier lord than the king of France, but when it came to getting

[72] But in the uprated offer in July, they had received the manor of Gunthorpe (Nottinghamshire), valued at 100 marks a year, in full hereditary right: *CChR 1257–1300*, 20.

[73] *TR*, no. 128, where the council was to retain all the money due for the 500 knights until a settlement was reached.

[74] In November 1259, Peter had taken steps to consolidate his alliance with the queen. In default of a son (unlikely after many years of marriage), he conceded to her, after his death, the honour of Pevensey, detailing its constituent parts and giving her the right to dispose of it as she wished. This was done with the agreement of Henry, King Richard and several councillors. Although, under the will of 1255, Eleanor had been left all his possessions in England, they had been unspecified: TNA CP 25/1/283/15/358, and Ridgeway, 'An English cartulary roll of Peter of Savoy', no. 21.

[75] Von Wurstemberger, *Peter der Zweite*, iv, no. 527, and see also *CChR 1257–1300*, 41. Amicie Pélissié du Rausas drew my attention to this quittance of Duke John. It is also noticed in Ridgeway, 'The politics of the English royal court', 334.

[76] For the documents recording the agreements, see *DD*, nos. 307–8.

[77] *DD*, no. 349.

money there was no contest. The possession of the Agenais itself might be years away. In the event countess Joan lived till 1271. The money, on the other hand, would be due as soon as the Agenais was valued and Louis was likely to be a far more reliable payer than Henry. The proof of that was soon to come, for Henry quite failed to keep up with the payments due while waiting for the valuation to take place.

These then were the terms on which Duke John agreed his son could marry Henry's daughter.[78] It was his son who was to be the immediate beneficiary because on the marriage taking place (in January 1260, as we will see), the duke settled the whole of the exchange for Richmond on John of Brittany and the legitimate heirs by his wife. It was John of Brittany accordingly who eventually did homage to King Louis for the Agenais money.[79]

## THE TREATY OF PARIS: THE BALANCE OF ADVANTAGES

The Treaty of Paris was a triumph for King Louis. By obtaining the final resignation of Normandy, Anjou and Poitou, he had rounded off the work of his predecessors and secured all their conquests. He had also enforced the view that Gascony was a fief held from the French crown, not a province held by the king of England in full sovereignty. There was now no doubt that the French kingdom reached to the Pyrenees.

Louis had been tough and clear-sighted in pursuit of his objectives. He had insisted that Henry could receive nothing under the treaty until he had done homage for Gascony. He had insisted there would no arrears paid for the period between Henry's homage and the point the money owed for the Agenais was assessed. Yet at the same time Louis saw that to bring Henry in, he needed to make concessions, hence his promises of both land and money. In the end he accepted that the Montfort renunciation could be outside the treaty rather than within it. There was more here than material calculations. Louis wished with all his heart for there to be peace between royal families so closely connected. This was recognized in England. The Waverley annalist said that Louis had made concessions 'to preserve in perpetuity the mutual love in Christ' between himself and Henry.[80]

Henry had less reason to be happy, indeed he acknowledged that through the treaty his condition was worsened.[81] This may explain the curious way in which the ratifications by himself and the council were dated 13 October, 'the Monday before the feast of Luke the Evangelist', Luke's feast being on 18 October and the Monday before in 1259 falling on

[78] Very important for Henry and Eleanor, the terms (*DD*, no. 308 [6]) provided Beatrice with an ample dower in case she was widowed. See Armstrong, 'The daughters of Henry III', 141–4.

[79] *DD*, no. 349.

[80] Waverley, 350–1.

[81] *CR 1256–9*, 314–15.

the thirteenth. But 13 October was, of course, the premier day in Henry's religious year, the feast of the translation of Edward the Confessor. So why not use that as the date? The reason surely was to avoid associating the Confessor with the defeat that the treaty represented.

The treaty did not receive a good press. The Canterbury/Dover annalist commented on Gascony's changed status and Edward's consequent displeasure.[82] Others lamented the loss of the old continental possessions, 'ignominious' the Burton annalist called it.[83] Since Henry had to drop the titles duke of Normandy and count of Anjou, there was no concealing what had happened. The first title had been held by kings of England since 1066, the second since 1154. On his new seal Henry tried to compensate by placing himself on a splendid throne rather than the previous bench, but this merely sparked a spiky question from a papal official: why had Henry now a grander seal than before when he was duke of Normandy?![84] On the seal, the king showed himself holding a dove-topped sceptre rather than the previous sword, almost certainly, as we have seen, in imitation of the Confessor.[85] But to many the change merely showed how Merlin's prophecy that the sword, the ducal sword of Normandy, would one day be separated from the kingdom, had come to pass.[86] A lament on the treaty, quoted by the annalist of Bury St Edmunds, summed up the views of many: 'Would that the concord of 1259 had been a happy one; Anjou, Poitou, Normandy have been ceded to you, France, the people of the English having been deserted. The seals are changed, the names removed, the sword flees, the sceptre is displayed.'[87]

There was also a feeling that Henry had squandered his gains under the treaty. Matthew Paris's continuator averred that, under the Breton marriage agreement, Henry had given away the 'opulent lands' he had received from Louis.[88] The Waverley annalist, without mentioning the marriage, said much the same thing, and added that Henry, in agreeing the treaty, had acted 'without the consent of Edward and the magnates in England'.[89] With Edward that was true enough, but the treaty itself and the terms of the Breton marriage, allowing Peter of Savoy to keep Richmond, had been accepted by Henry's councillors.[90]

---

[82] Canterbury/Dover, 209–10.

[83] Burton, 486–7; FitzThedmar, 43 (Stone, FitzThedmar, no. 732); Paris's Continuator, 440–1.

[84] DD, no. 367 (at the end). Henry's envoy to the papal court said he felt ashamed to pass the remark on but dared not keep silent.

[85] Carpenter, Reign of Henry III, 438–42, and above, 75–6.

[86] Burton, 486–7.

[87] Bury St Edmunds, 25. I am putting into prose here four lines of verse.

[88] Paris's Continuator, 440–1. The promise of lands was said to include the reversion of Poitou.

[89] Waverley, 350–1. I owe the significance of this passage to Amicie Pélissié du Rausas.

[90] DD, nos. 307, 308 [1–3, 5–6]. For a different view, see Ridgeway, 'The politics of the royal court', 357, and Howell, Eleanor of Provence, 161–2.

Henry's councillors had also, of course, agreed The Treaty of Paris itself. Indeed, they had sanctioned major concessions to the Montforts to make it possible, admittedly at the king's expense.[91] The treaty did nothing for English barons who had lost ancestral lands in Normandy, yet did not exclude such claims.[92] Perhaps both Richard de Clare and Richard de Grey thought the peace might make their claims easier to pursue, although the attempts made by Grey's wife and Clare's son (in 1279) came to nothing.[93] The treaty was equally silent about the Normans who had lost ancestral lands in England and for that reason did not disturb the many lords who had received such lands from the king. Probably most of the baronial leaders thought the treaty, as far as they were concerned, was unlikely to disturb the tenurial status quo and with that they were content.[94] If, beyond that, they supported the treaty it was because once started the process was hard to stop. They may also have felt a peace with France, given the lost lands seemed unrecoverable, was better for the kingdom than the uncertainties of continued truce.

The treaty achieved none of Henry's original objectives. He had hoped the peace with France would further the Sicilian project, but that proved as chimerical as ever. The money for the knights was never used to fund a Sicilian army, indeed much of it went to combating Simon de Montfort. Yet, for all these disappointments, there was some comfort to be had. The total sum eventually agreed for the knights (in January 1264) was far short of the 100,000 marks – £66,666 – for which Henry had fondly hoped. Yet at some £30,500 it was still substantial, indeed the rough equivalent of a year's annual revenue in the 1250s.[95] From 1260 onwards, moreover, Louis was making payments on account, without any stipulation that the money should be spent with baronial consent. By January 1264, Henry had received some £17,000.[96] His success in recovering power in 1261 owed much to the money for the knights.

Henry might also hope that, held now as a fief from the king of France, Gascony would be far more secure than under a regime of continual truce. There were, too, immediate gains from the territorial concessions Louis made under the treaty. On 16 December his subjects in the dioceses

---

[91] Doubtless also Montfort's allies on the council argued his money fee should have been converted into land long ago,

[92] For what follows, see Power, 'The Treaty of Paris and the aristocracy', especially 152–7.

[93] John de Balliol, very involved in the negotiations, had a particular interest in the peace since he was one of the very few barons to have retained lands in France (in Ponthieu): Beam, *The Balliol Dynasty* (20–4); *CPR 1258–66*, 14, 18, 24–6.

[94] But see the case of Peter de Montfort: Power, 'The Treaty of Paris and the aristocracy', 155; Maddicott, *Simon de Montfort*, 198.

[95] The burden of finding the money and the size of Louis's concession is brought out in Pélissié du Rausas, 'De guerre, de trêve, de paix', 572–5.

[96] *F*, i, 434–5, 440; *CPR 1258–66*, 81, 121, 123, 194, 317, 379; Wild, *WA*, 87.

of Périgueux, Limoges and Cahors were told they should henceforth obey Henry as their lord.[97] The knight Bertram de Cardaillac was immediately appointed as seneschal in the area, having been released from his allegiance to the king of France.[98] There were some advantages in what was done with the Agenais, despite the complaints made at St Albans and Waverley. The Breton marriage could now go forward, without alienating Peter of Savoy. Peter went on to give sterling service during Henry's recovery of power in 1261, while John of Brittany immediately shaped up as a dutiful son-in-law. He remained at Henry's court for some months after his marriage in January 1260 and was knighted with great ceremony at the following feast of the Confessor.[99] In 1261, Duke John said he was happy for his son to obey Henry in all things.[100] Henry placed great store on familial relationships and called young John his 'son', just as he did another son-in-law, King Alexander of Scotland.[101] There also remained the possibility that, after Peter of Savoy's death, Richmond might go to John, in which case Henry and Edward would recover the Agenais.[102]

Of course, on the day Henry performed homage to Louis in the orchard in Paris, how things would work out was unknown. But ultimately the results were very much as Henry must have wished. He did get the money for the knights even if he did not spend it as originally intended. John of Brittany did get Richmond on Peter of Savoy's death. After the deaths of both Alphonse of Poitiers and Countess Joan in 1271, Edward I did eventually secure both the Saintonge and the Agenais, thus gaining considerable revenues and the great town of Saintes from which Henry had fled so ignominiously in 1242.[103] That this happened was because the Treaty of Paris was about more than material things. It was about peace for its own sake.

Henry had not embarked on the negotiations as an out-and-out peacemaker. Indeed, he had wanted peace with France to wage war in Italy. It

---

[97] DD, no. 308 [4].

[98] CPR 1258–66, 109. But for difficulties involved in the transfers, in part from those claiming exemption from being put out of the allegiance of the king of France, see DD, nos. 311–12, 329, 341–2; Pélissié du Rausas, 'De guerre, de trêve, de paix', 676–700.

[99] CR 1259–61, 277.

[100] DD, no. 327.

[101] For Henry and his sons-in-law, see Armstrong, 'The daughters of Henry III', 198–206.

[102] For the possibility of an exchange being given for the Agenais, see DD, no. 307, clarified in CPR 1258–66, 82.

[103] For the revenues, see volume 1, 683. Henry's financial obligations over the marriage also turned out to be less than might have been feared. Although he had failed to set a time limit on the valuation of the Agenais, it was completed by September 1261, so Henry only had to make two years' worth of payments, not that he managed fully to do so: CR 1259–61, 267–8 (DBM, 166–7). The valuation left Henry paying 800 marks a year as the difference between the annual 2,000 marks he had agreed for Richmond and the 1,200 marks a year at which the Agenais was valued.

was Louis who had wished for peace from the start alongside his material objectives. Yet in the end Henry came to share Louis's vision. He would have agreed completely with the sentiments expressed in a speech prepared for delivery to the pope. 'The prince of peace has given peace to our princes . . . Glory be to God in the heavens.' Homicide, rapine, heresy and other plagues, arising from the discord of kings, would be no more, 'for in the peace of princes there is quiet and joy for the peoples'. The dove on his rod symbolized perfectly how Henry, like the Confessor, wished to be a 'rex pacificus'. Without that wish, there would have been no peace of Paris.[104]

Underlying Henry's desire for peace, as underlying Louis's, was the friendship forged by the happy meetings in 1254, a friendship between kings who were brothers-in-law and queens who were sisters. It was right, Louis observed, that there should be love between families so closely related.[105] For Henry the ties were drawn all the closer now Louis was his lord. As he wrote in 1261, 'we trust you above everybody, considering you are our lord and we your kinsman, and we have married sisters, and there is such a great bond between us. And since the taking of our homage, you have helped us liberally and kindly so often in our affairs as a propitious lord.'[106]

Of course, had Henry been a monarch of more martial mien, had he been a Richard the Lionheart or Edward III, he might have forged the continental alliances, galvanized the home support and waged the mighty wars needed to recover some or all of his continental empire. As the events of the next centuries were to show, despite the discrepancies between French and English resources, he might for a while have been successful. But thank God he was not like that, given the sacrifices and sufferings such wars would have brought. To be sure, the Treaty of Paris has been blamed for laying the foundations for the Hundred Years War. Ultimately, both kings of France and kings of England found the relationship it forged incompatible with their ideas of sovereignty. The former wanted to conquer Gascony. The latter wanted to hold it in full sovereignty and not as a fief of the king of France. The Treaty of Paris was seen as a ghastly mistake. But this is but a partial perspective. In its own time the treaty was a brilliant success. The family concord begun in 1254 survived into the next generation just as Louis and Henry hoped it would. It enabled the difficulties arising from the implementation of the treaty to be overcome. The treaty's peace lasted for thirty-four years all the way down to 1294, giving security to Gascony and benefiting both the English and French peoples. The Treaty of Paris was one of the great achievements of Henry's reign.

---

[104] For Powicke's perspective, see *King Henry III*, i, 257–8.

[105] Joinville, cap. 679; Paris, v, 481–2.

[106] *F*, i, 407 (*CPR 1258–66*, 169). Henry was here (in July 1261) appealing to Louis to take action over the value of the Agenais, given Alphonse of Poitiers' refusal to co-operate. The valuation had been done by September: *CPR 1258–66*, 174. For Louis as Henry's lord, kinsman and friend (stated in a letter to Queen Margaret): *CR 1261–4*, 281.

Chapter 5

# HENRY AND HIS PEOPLE

While the peace with France was being concluded and celebrated in Paris, reform of the realm was continuing in England. The new sheriffs, appointed in accordance with the Provisions, were getting into their stride. The judges commissioned to tour the realm and hear everyone's complaints were beginning their work. Those complaints, with the ones heard earlier by Hugh Bigod, throw much light on the condition of England, from the peasantry upwards, during Henry's personal rule. Their testimony lies at the heart of this chapter.[1] I have set it out in detail, rather than providing just a few illustrative examples. That is partly to give a voice to men and women often unheard. It is also because only by appreciating the sheer weight of complaint can one understand the tidal pressure for reform sweeping over England in 1258. To put the grievances against both royal and seigneurial officials into context, the chapter begins with a sketch of secular society, or at least aspects of secular society, in Henry's time.[2]

## EARLS AND BARONS

In terms of wealth, England in the thirteenth century was a very divided society, as, of course, most societies have been before and since. There was a huge gulf between the peasants at the bottom of the scale, even the most prosperous with incomes of around £2 a year, and the earls at the top with incomes of thousands.[3] In his conversation with Matthew Paris in 1257, Henry III remembered the names of 250 English baronies. He was doing better here than the leading modern authority on the subject, who could only find 102 baronies and another 48 'probable baronies' in existence between 1087 and 1327.[4] In 1215, Magna Carta had laid down that 'barons' were to succeed to their 'baronies' on payment of an entry fine of £100 called a 'relief'. As a result, a clear distinction could seemingly be drawn between barons and everyone else. There were, however, many

---

[1] Readers may, of course, move on at once to the next chapter if they prefer to continue with the narrative.

[2] For discussion of towns and the role of women in politics, see below, 378–97.

[3] See Dyer, *Standards of Living in the Later Middle Ages*, with 109–18 for calculations of peasant incomes.

[4] Sanders, *English Baronies*.

families (like the Greys, Despensers and Bassets of High Wycombe) who had estates of baronial proportions, worth hundreds of pounds a year, without actually holding a barony from the crown. Often this was because the estates had been put together, over a course of time, from a series of piecemeal acquisitions, usually by men who were leading servants of the king. Using the term loosely, as perhaps Henry was, such men too might be called 'barons'. 'Magnate', another term in frequent use, helpfully blurred the distinction between the two groups. Above the barons were the earls, never more than a dozen, the most powerful with mighty castles and incomes of thousands of pounds a year. In the survey made after his death in 1262, Richard de Clare, earl of Gloucester and Hertford, is found as lord of around sixty demesne manors and boroughs across fourteen counties, and to that he could add his lordship of Glamorgan and other lands in Wales and Ireland.[5] The earls of Leicester, Gloucester, Norfolk, Hereford and Aumale were all on the ruling council set up by the 1258 revolution.[6] John de Warenne, earl of Surrey, and Robert de Ferrers, earl of Derby (who came of age in 1260), were both to play major parts in the turmoil to come.

Earls and barons held their baronies from the king.[7] The whole entity, made up of demesne manors and tenanted land, was described as the baron's 'honour' or 'fee, *feodum*' (hence 'feudalism'). The heir to a baron, on entering his inheritance, performed homage to the king and paid his relief. If the heir was underage, the king had the wardship of the land till the heir's majority at the age of twenty-one, taking the revenues for himself. The king could also arrange the marriage of the heir and had some say in the remarriage of a baronial widow. In default of a son, a daughter or daughters would be the heirs, their marriages a particular important source of patronage. The king's 'feudal' rights were all subject to regulation in Magna Carta and with some effect. Thereafter, relief was generally the £100 stipulated for an earl and a baron while widows no longer had to pay either to obtain their lands or to remain single, although the king sometimes pressurized them to marry his favourites. Tension also continued over the exploitation of wardships and the marriage of heiresses to the king's foreign kin.

The relationship between the king and the baron was replicated in that between the baron and his tenants. In a large honour (like that of Tutbury held by the Ferrers earls of Derby) there might be forty or fifty of them, many but not all knights. The baron had the same 'feudal' rights as the king and also held a court (the 'honorial court' as it is called by historians),

---

[5] *CIPM*, no. 530. A demesne manor was a manor in the lord's own hands rather than held by a tenant.

[6] Gloucester was also earl of Hertford, and Hereford also earl of Essex.

[7] There was no difference structurally between the barony of an earl and that of a baron. Henceforth I just speak of barons.

which he expected his feudal tenants to attend.[8] That court, together with homage and relief, wardship and marriage, provided barons with money, patronage, authority and social control. The efforts they made to maintain and exploit their 'feudal' rights are very apparent in the cases coming before the eyres between 1258 and 1260.[9]

What kind of men featured in the followings of earls and barons? The question is not easy to unravel for the source material of earlier and later periods is lacking. In the twelfth century the witness lists of charters, issued by great men, throw much light on their entourages. But far fewer charters are extant in the thirteenth century, thanks chiefly to the decline in gifts to religious houses. Only thirteen of Roger Bigod's charters are known, a small harvest for a forty-five-year career.[10] Equally, historians lack the written contracts and pay rolls used to construct the followings of the later medieval nobility.[11] Henry III's chancery rolls show him paying annual fees and making gifts of money, deer, wine and wood to those in his service or his favour. Almost certainly magnates were doing the same but there is little to prove it.[12]

These problems are at their strongest when it comes to divining what might be called the outer circle of followers, those connected to the lord but not regularly in his company. For the inner circle, by contrast, there is usually enough material to come to at least some conclusions. The immediate entourage, even of earls, was thus comparatively small. In the case of Roger Bigod, for example it seems to have been around a dozen knights. The same was true for Simon de Montfort.[13] This does not mean that the earls could only place a military force of that size in the field. In times of emergency, they could look for support from the outer circles of their following or simply recruit *de novo* knights and men at arms in return for pay. At the end of the 1263–7 civil war, Gilbert de Clare, Richard's son, gave his protection to twenty knights described as his 'bachelors', many of them wealthy men and quite able to command retinues of their own.

[8] The court could hear disputes over the tenure of land held feudally from the lord and also disputes over the services due the lord. However, its jurisdiction was restricted by the development of the common law, see below, 142.

[9] For the importance of these 'feudal' structures in the thirteenth century, see Carpenter, 'The second century of English feudalism'. The form of tenure was usually called tenure 'by knight service', but the quotas of knights that a baron owed the king's army, and the numbers owed him by his tenants, were only relevant when it came to the assessment of scutage, the tax in place of military service. Barons usually mustered with far less than their nominal service. See Prestwich, *Armies and Warfare in the Middle Ages*, 68–71, and Sanders, *Feudal Military Service*.

[10] Morris, *Bigod Earls of Norfolk*, 60.

[11] Spencer, *Nobility and Kingship*, 130–1.

[12] For the development of money fees in the thirteenth century, see Waugh, 'Tenure to contract'.

[13] Morris, *Bigod Earls of Norfolk*, 70; Maddicott, *Simon de Montfort*, 69.

At Christmas 1264, Montfort himself was said to have 140 knights in his pay.[14]

When it comes to the inner circle, a significant segment was recruited from knightly tenants, often from families with long traditions of service to the lord. The tenurial bond, and the loyalty pledged in its act of homage, gave a special quality to such relationships. Yet there were also, in all followings, a significant, usually a larger, number of knights who lacked any tenurial connection with the lord, the origin of the relationship often residing in ties of neighbourhood. How far the move away from 'feudal' retinues accelerated during Henry's reign is almost impossible to say. In the case of Roger Bigod, knightly tenants were less prominent in the 1250s and 1260s than they had been early in his career.[15] Yet they were still conspicuous in the followings of both Robert de Ferrers, earl of Derby in the 1260s, and Henry de Lacy, earl of Lincoln in the reign of Edward I.[16] A great deal, of course, depended on the history and geography of an honour. Feudal ties were more likely to subsist where an honour had remained in one family over generations and was geographically compact, or at least had a solid geographical core. (Both were true of the Ferrers earldom of Derby.) Yet however much feudal ties and concepts persisted, one fact is absolutely clear. In the reign of Henry III lords, on a large scale, were looking outside their tenantry for service and support. This takes us on to the role played in this period by the knights.

## THE KNIGHTS

R.F. Treharne, writing about the knights, described the years of reform and rebellion between 1258 and 1267 as 'a critical phase in the rise of a new class', this in the sense that a 'sudden crisis' revealed the results of changes that had been maturing over a long period of time.[17] That the balance of power between barons and knights shifted in favour of the knights during the course of the thirteenth century seems certain. So much is clear when we look at consent to taxation. Magna Carta in 1215 envisaged it coming from a largely baronial assembly without any presence of knights representing the shires. Such assemblies consented to Henry's taxes in 1225, 1232 and 1237.[18] But in the second half of the

---

[14] Jacob, *Studies*, 127–33; Pershore, *Flores*, 504–5. For a discussion of the size of retinues, see Oakes, 'The nature of war and its impact on society during the Barons' Wars', 51–6. He suggests a knight might have a retinue of around half a dozen men.

[15] Morris, *Bigod Earls of Norfolk*, 68, although see the qualification on 71 n. 88.

[16] Spencer, *Nobility and Kingship*, 121; Carpenter, 'The second century of English feudalism', 51–2, behind which is the catalogue of Robert's charters in Golob, 'The Ferrers earls of Derby', ii, nos. 235–321.

[17] Treharne, 'The knights in the period of reform and rebellion', 269.

[18] I suspect, however, that some 'magnates' received personal summonses to these assemblies. John Maddicott has shown how many lesser tenants-in-chief were of knightly or less than knightly status: Maddicott, ' "An infinite multitude of nobles" '.

century, earls and barons no longer felt able to answer for the realm. From 1267 onwards, when taxation was in question, knights representing the counties (as well as burgesses the towns) always came to parliament to give their consent. The rise of the knights in the more general business of the realm can be charted even more narrowly. Parliament as conceived by the Provisions of Oxford in 1258 did not have them. Simon de Montfort's parliaments of 1264 and 1265 did.

The fundamental reason for this change lay in the shifting nature of lordly followings already touched on.[19] Barons no longer, to the extent they once had, commanded the allegiance of a cohesive and coherent body of tenants. Magnates whose estates were composed largely of demesne manors and other properties had few if any knightly tenants at all. England could no longer be seen as a collection of honours, marching to the drum beat of their lords, with the lords for that reason able to answer for the realm.

There were many factors behind this change in perceptions. Knights had gained an independence and a role outside the honour by holding local office under the crown and staffing the multiplying positions spawned by royal government. While in the 1250s knights often secured exemptions from such burdens, many continued to shoulder them. In Northamptonshire, twenty-two of the fifty-eight knights studied in one sample from the 1260s had been in royal or occasionally seigneurial service before 1264. The knights were also prolific litigators in the king's courts, thereby gaining first-hand knowledge of law and legal administration. Of the Northamptonshire knights, twenty-nine were involved in cases on the 1261–2 eyre while fourteen had at some time litigated in the central courts.[20] The whole development of the common law gave knights and free tenants an escape from the jurisdiction of honorial courts.

Another factor undermining allegiance to a tenurial lord was the way knightly families acquired land outside the honour through marriage or purchase. Yet another was the break-up of honours through the failure of male heirs. The social and political structure of the midlands was transformed when the earldom of Chester (with many tenants in the area) was divided after 1237 between the four sisters of the last earl and their husbands.[21] It changed further with the death of the last Newburgh earl of Warwick in 1242 and the passage of the earldom (its resources anyway depleted by dower portions) to his sister and her husband, the king's Norman favourite, John de Plessis, who seems to have made little effort to stamp his authority on the area.[22] The personality of a lord could itself be a factor in weakening tenurial ties. The vacuum of 'feudal' lordship in the

---

[19] But for the importance of ideas about consent, see below, 327.

[20] Fernandes, 'The role of the midlands knights in the period of reform and rebellion', 73–80.

[21] See volume 1, 233.

[22] For the earldom, see Crouch, 'The local influence of the earls of Warwick'.

midlands was increased by the behaviour of Roger de Quincy, earl of Winchester, who shared the honour of Leicester with Simon de Montfort. With estates in Scotland, he played little part in English politics.[23]

One example (amongst many) of a knight who seems free of tenurial ties, at least when it comes to anything like loyalty, is provided by Gilbert of Elsfield, from an old Oxfordshire knightly family. His father, John, had been exempted from sitting on juries, save when ordered to do so by the king whether by word of mouth or letter. The king evidently valued his service for a few years later (in 1251) he was commissioned, with three other knights, to sell the undergrowth from the royal forests in Oxfordshire.[24] Elsfield itself, on a hill a couple of miles north-east of Oxford (it is still a small village), was held from the county's greatest baronial family, the Doillys of Hook Norton.[25] But by Gilbert's time the family had failed of male heirs and ceased to exist.[26] Gilbert held another manor at East Isley in Berkshire from the Somerys of Dudley in Staffordshire. A third manor, Drayton in Berkshire, he held from the now divided honour of Chester, having acquired it through marriage to Juliana, daughter of a former sheriff Alan of Farnham.[27] There is no sign Gilbert had any personal relationship with his tenurial lords.[28] Yet, grievously at odds with William de Valence, as we will see, he badly wanted the protection and patronage that might come from lordship. By 1257 he was in Richard of Cornwall's entourage going out to Germany. (Elsfield is next door to Beckley, a major Richard residence.) The relationship, however, did not prosper and Gilbert is next found in the service of Hugh Despenser. (He too had gone with Richard to Germany.) This time the connection lasted to the end and Gilbert died with Hugh at Evesham.

When, during Montfort's ascendancy, Gilbert was given licence to hunt the hare, fox, badger and cat throughout Oxfordshire's forests, he was described proudly as 'a knight of Hugh Despenser, justiciar of England'.[29] Another factor behind the 'rise of the knights' lay in the transformation of knighthood itself, so that men like Gilbert of Elsfield had become part of a small elite. In King John's reign, it has been estimated there were some 4,500 knights

[23] Quincy in 1258 was placed on the parliamentary twelve and in October witnessed the proclamation setting out the council's authority, but did little else. For him, see Simpson, 'The *familia* of Roger de Quincy', and Cokayne, *Complete Peerage*, xii (2), 751–4.

[24] *CPR 1232–47*, 499; *CFR 1250–1*, nos. 604, 621.

[25] I always remember the view towards Elsfield from John and Menna Prestwich's house in Headington.

[26] *BF*, ii, 826, 838; *RH*, ii, 720; *St Frideswide Cartulary*, ii, 70–6, 82–4; *Victoria County History (hereafter VCH) Oxfordshire*, v, 116–22. The last Doilly lord, himself an incompetent nonentity, died in 1232. The honour then passed to his sister Margaret, who was married to the earl of Warwick. Thereafter it followed the descent of the earldom and so came to John de Plessis. There was a mesne tenant, in 1242 and 1279 William de Strafford, between the Elsfields and the Doilly heirs.

[27] *BF*, ii, 845, 850, 855; *VCH Berkshire*, iv, 341–4.

[28] Roger de Somery was on the king's side in the war.

[29] *CPR 1258–66*, 352.

throughout the counties of England. A few hundred were direct tenants of the crown. The rest held their land from earls and barons, sometimes, as we have said, from more than one of them. A large county, Yorkshire, had around 240 knights, a small one, Surrey, 90. A hundred years later, lists of knights in England have only around 1,250 names. The chronology of this decline is debated, but it certainly took place in Henry's reign. One cause was Henry himself. He was hardly the man to burnish the martial ardour of his subjects. The drive to get men to take up knighthood in 1256 was largely to make money from those buying permission not to do so. Another cause, more significant, was the changing nature of knighthood itself.[30]

The figure of 4,500 knights in John's reign comes largely from those who sat as knights on juries. Whether all or even the majority of such men had actually gone through a formal ceremony and been girded with the sword of knighthood is doubtful. The occasional call for jurors to be 'belted knights' makes the point. In the 1190s the abbot of Crowland complained that the four 'knights' who had testified against him were 'low fellows not of the knightly order nor girt with the sword'. One could not even speak French. Evidently men could be accepted as knights because they vaguely looked the part. By the 1250s this was no longer the case. To be a knight required a formal ceremony. The force behind the change was royal policy and the king's need for money. Increasingly throughout the reign, culminating in the drive of 1256, Henry insisted that men suitably qualified should take up knighthood or buy exemption from it. That clearly meant they must go through a formal ceremony or show they had done so. A dividing line was being drawn as never before between those who were knights and those who were not.

On which side of the line you fell depended above all on money. The initial capital cost of assuming the honour was significant. The prospective knight had to provide himself with arms, armour and horses, and then fund the ceremony where he was girded with the sword of knighthood either by a lord or by the king. There was also an entourage to equip and maintain, at a minimum an esquire and two grooms to look after three horses.[31] The cost of an exemption was usually half a mark of gold, so £3 6s 8d of silver. Evidently the cost of taking up knighthood was greater and would absorb a good part of the annual income of the potential knight, especially of those with only £15 or £20 a year. Hence the desire to avoid or postpone taking up the honour.[32]

---

[30] For the number of knights in John's reign and an analysis of the subsequent decline in numbers, see Faulkner, 'Transformation of knighthood'. For later numbers, see Quick, 'The number and distribution of knights in thirteenth-century England', and Denholm-Young, 'Feudal society in the thirteenth century'. Peter Coss's *The Knight in Medieval England* is a good survey with many illustrations, while his *Lordship, Knighthood and Locality* and *The Origins of the English Gentry* are essential reading.

[31] For such an entourage see Brand 'Oldcotes v. d'Arcy', 91–2.

[32] For the cost, see Coss, *The Knight in Medieval England*, 62–71, with ch. 3 as a whole on the changing nature of knighthood.

The result of all this was a stratification of the early thirteenth-century knightly class. The 4,500 knights at the start of the century covered a broad social spectrum. At the top of the scale were those with several manors and incomes of baronial proportions, in the middle were knights with one or two manors and perhaps incomes of between £15 and £40 a year. At the bottom were knights who held parcels of land and were not lords of manors at all. As new and expensive criteria for being a knight were introduced, it was only the upper echelons of the old knightly class who consistently assumed the honour. Those in the middle group sometimes did and sometimes didn't, depending on inclination and resources, those in the bottom group (the abbot of Crowland's 'low fellows') not at all.

Whether these changes left more than a minority feeling significantly declassed may be doubted. Those who flocked to buy exemptions, or were too poor to be asked to assume knighthood in the first place, were not in most cases being deprived of an honour their ancestors, never belted knights, had ever possessed.[33] Since, moreover, knighthood was not hereditary, no hard and fast line was being drawn between knightly and non-knightly families. Some families moved in and out of knighthood over generations. A key status, moreover, was retained by all those above the bottom level of the old knightly class. They were all lords of manors and as such held their own courts with sway over peasant tenants. The changing nature of knighthood was nonetheless immensely significant. It created within local society a knightly elite, very conscious of its prestige, an elite separated by knighthood from those below them and joined by it to the king, earls and barons above, for whom knighthood had always been a high honour. (Hence the importance given to Henry's knighting by William Marshal at the start of the reign.) By the 1250s, witness lists of local charters were giving knights their titles in a way never done before, thus separating them from the other witnesses. In one case before Hugh Bigod in 1259, special care was taken to assess the damages owed to Eustace de Grenville for a violent assault 'as he was a knight'.[34] Something of the style and bravado of a mid-thirteenth-century knight can be glimpsed in Matthew Paris's picture of Ralph de Chenduit. Built like a bull, he rode around on a valuable horse with a large entourage, hunting in the St Albans abbey's demesnes and maltreating its servants. He laughed at the abbot's sentences of excommunication: they had, he said, made him so fat he could hardly sit in his saddle![35]

---

[33] There were some, however, who could not really afford the honour yet strained to find the funds to obtain it: Brand, 'Oldcotes v. d'Arcy', 64, 69–70, 91–2.

[34] *SERHB*, ii, no. 871.

[35] Paris, *GA*, i, 319–20; Paris, iv, 262; *CRR*, xvi, nos. 1364, 1459. Chenduit may have heard a similar joke in a sermon but, if so, he did not heed the warning, for there the blasphemer was struck down by sudden death, as ultimately was Chenduit himself! See Hill, '*Damnatio*

Empowered by their new status, the knights were to play a crucial role during the period of reform, rebellion and civil war. Providing the great lords with local influence and military might, they were well placed to influence policies at the highest level. They held office as sheriffs and keepers of the peace, mustered in the armies, formed the core of 'the community of the bachelery of England' and ultimately appeared as knights of the shire in parliament.

A couple of other hypotheses have sometimes been canvassed about the 'rise of the knights'. The first is that the mid-thirteenth century was for them a 'golden age' of freedom, between the ties of 'feudalism' on the one hand and the trammels of 'bastard feudalism' on the other. Knights no longer had to follow the lords from whom they held their land. They had not yet been retained and constrained by grants of money-fees and promises of good lordship.[36] The second hypothesis, closely related, is that lords faced a critical situation, a crisis even, as they struggled to keep control of tenants increasingly going their own way. Such hypotheses are attractive but hard to square with the immediate realities of mid-thirteenth-century politics. If, in broad terms, society was becoming more fluid, if there was a shift in the balance of power between lords and knights, the power of lordship, at particular times and places, remained strong. We will see later how Simon de Montfort stepped into the vacuum in the midlands and became there a dominant force.[37] The complaints on the eyres give telling witness to the methods that lords used to affirm and assert their local rule. Lords, moreover, had much to gain from recruiting good men where they found them rather than being confined to some honorial straitjacket. The 'feudal' retinue was weakened from above by the lord's search for good service, just as much as from below by the knight's search for good lordship. The aphorism 'lordship lasted while it was good lordship or until it was ousted by better' cut both ways.[38]

One other hypothesis advanced to explain the prominence of the knights is that they were radicalized by financial difficulties and 'the horrors of debt' owed to the Jews. All this, it is suggested, was part of a broader social and economic crisis endured by the class, one caused both by the rising costs of knighthood and by the failure to adapt sufficiently to

*eternae mortis*', 44. The Chenduit case is discussed in her forthcoming book, *Excommunication in Thirteenth-Century England: Community, Politics and Publicity*. Ralph de Chenduit was also a good man of business and enlarged his holdings within his manor of Cuxham in Oxfordshire. See Harvey, *A Medieval Oxfordshire Village*, 113–15.

[36] For mention of this hypothesis, see Valente, *Theory and Practice of Revolt*, 106.

[37] See below, 363.

[38] For David Crouch's view that lords shifted fairly effortlessly from feudal to non-feudal retinues, see his 'From Stenton to McFarlane', and see also his *The English Aristocracy*, 152–9. For debate about these changes, see Coss, 'Bastard feudalism revised', and Crouch, Carpenter and Coss, 'Debate: bastard feudalism revised'.

the move from rents to demesne farming.[39] This hypothesis has been much debated. It is perfectly true that between Lewes and Evesham the Montfortian regime pardoned in whole or part debts owed by around fifty individuals to the Jews.[40] This was done on a scale seen neither before nor afterwards and was clearly a distinctive form of Montfortian patronage. Yet very few of those favoured appear amongst the groups of county knights active in this period and studied by historians.[41] The most conspicuous beneficiaries were magnates like Ralph de Camoys, Peter de Montfort junior and the northerners John de Eyville, Roger Bertram of Mitford, Thomas of Moulton and Norman Darcy. When it came to owing money to the Jews, there was also little difference between the sides. Such senior royalists as Roger of Leybourne, Roger of Clifford, Alan la Zouche and James of Audley were also heavily in debt.[42] Regional studies, moreover, suggest that knightly families struggling with debt and selling off their property were in a minority. The majority were resilient, able to overcome or avoid difficulties and to retain, develop and sometimes expand their lands. The role of the knights in the period of reform and rebellion seems more due to their material strength than weakness.[43]

However busy as office-holders, jurors and litigators, the knights remained very much a military class. They would never have played the role they did had that not been the case. In Cogenhoe church in Northamptonshire there is the effigy of the knight Nicholas of Cogenhoe. He lies in full armour, with a large shield bearing his coat of arms, one hand drawing his sword, the other holding the scabbard, his head encased in mail.[44] Nicholas's arms and armour, new to the thirteenth century, affordable only by knightly elite, marked his status. They also helped make him a formidable warrior. Nicholas was the reverse of a Montfortian. He was a knight of Lord Edward, his property ravaged in 1264 after the battle

[39] For demesne farming, see below, 642.

[40] The concessions are in the fine rolls: *CFR 1263–4* and *CFR 1264–5*. See Coss, 'Sir Geoffrey de Langley and the crisis of the knightly class', 31–2.

[41] For such county studies, see below, 366–7.

[42] *CFR 1263–4*, no. 228; *CFR 1265–6*, no. 698; *CFR 1266–7*, no. 419.

[43] For this debate, see Coss, 'Sir Geoffrey de Langley and the crisis of the knightly class'; Coss, *Lordship, Knighthood and Locality*, especially chs. 6 and 8; King, 'Large and small landowners in thirteenth-century England'; Carpenter, 'Was there a crisis of the knightly class in the thirteenth century? The Oxfordshire evidence'; and Polden, 'A crisis of the knightly class? Inheritance and office among the gentry of thirteenth-century Buckinghamshire'. The records of Jewish moneylending are studied in Dean Irwin's doctoral thesis, 'Acknowledging debt in medieval England', with 215–24 for cases of borrowing in proportion to means.

[44] Nicholas, who died in 1281, was probably responsible for rebuilding the nave of Cogenhoe church where his arms again appear and alongside those of his associates. See *VCH Northamptonshire*, iv, 236–40, and Coss, 'Knighthood, heraldry and social exclusion', 56–8 (a reference I owe to Nigel Saul). I am grateful to the rector of Cogenhoe, the reverend Eddie Smith, for kindly showing me the church and effigy.

of Lewes as a result. But his arms and armour might have been those of any Montfortian knight.

## FREE TENANTS

A hinge group in English society were the free tenants between the lords of manors and the great run of the peasantry. Hinge because, as many studies have shown, they staffed the juries and inquiries on which law and government depended. The names of jurors from each hundred who gave evidence to Hugh Bigod and his colleagues are lost. But when the personnel of equivalent juries are examined, they include a few lords of manors, knightly and non-knightly at the top of the scale, and a few with holdings of peasant size at the bottom. The great majority of the jurors are men with holdings somewhere in between. The jurors from Blackbourn hundred in Suffolk at the time of a great inquiry in 1279 included those with holdings of 56, 64, 86, 110, 129, 145 and 180 acres. The average holding was 79 acres. Such men often sat on juries over many years and thus had wide experience of the workings of law and local government.[45]

Henry was perfectly familiar with people of this type. While the great majority of them held their land from other lords, some were tenants of the king himself and, on succeeding to their estates, had to come before him to agree their relief and perform homage. Between 1234 and 1258, Henry received the homage of well over 350 individuals, many of them holding fractions of a knight's fee, or lands rated in terms of acres, virgates, bovates and carucates. In one Essex example, a man did homage for 130 acres of land, 5 acres of pasture, 3½ acres of meadow, 2½ acres of woodland, and a half share in a mill.[46] It was such people who often bore the brunt of shrieval oppression and complained about it bitterly when they came before the 1258–60 eyres.

## PEASANTS

Henry could name the number of earldoms and baronies in England. He had some grasp of the pool of potential knights. Between 1256 and 1258 over 460 men came to court to obtain exemptions from the honour. With his usual eye for documentary detail, Henry may well have scanned the

---

[45] Carpenter, *Magna Carta*, 136, and 525 n.; Stevenson, 'From Domesday Book to the hundred rolls', 287–310, for a discussion of hundredal jurors, with 299 for the Blackbourn jurors. Other juries are studied in Asaji, *Angevin Empire*, ch. 7; Boatwright, *1286 Buckinghamshire Eyre*, 40–3; Kosminsky, *Studies in the Agrarian History*, 259–60; Masschaele, *Jury, State and Society*, ch. 5; Scales, 'The Cambridgeshire ragman rolls', 559–62; Stewart, *1263 Surrey Eyre*, ch. 10. For the growing importance of the group, see Forrest, 'Power and the people in thirteenth-century England', although I think such jurors were not predominantly peasants.

[46] *CFR 1248–49*, no. 92.

long lists, sent in by the sheriffs, of those obliged to assume the honour.[47] However, he had no idea of the total population of his kingdom. Historians have achieved little certainty on the subject either. A comparison between Domesday Book in 1087 and the great 'hundred roll' survey of 1279, along with other evidence, shows the population rose markedly in the twelfth and thirteenth centuries. One common estimate gives England around two million people in 1100 and six million in 1300, although the 1300 figure has also been put both higher and lower. Commercial expansion in the thirteenth century had probably increased the number of townspeople faster than the general rise of the population, but even so, by the end of the century they probably accounted for less than 15 per cent of the whole. The overwhelming bulk of England's population in Henry's reign were peasants.

Manorial surveys, mostly in Latin, had many names for a peasant. (The word itself is of late medieval origin.) He might be a 'villein', a 'serf', a 'rustic', a 'bondsman' or a 'cottar'. Such terms usually implied that the peasant was unfree. A 'sokeman', on the other hand, was a peasant of free or freer status. There were also many men, described as free tenants, who held land of similar extent to their unfree neighbours and were in much the same economic condition. By Henry's reign the king's judges had evolved a clear test to decide who was unfree. At its heart was whether the peasant or his ancestors had performed agricultural labour services to the lord. If he had, the peasant was unfree, if not, holding instead for rent, he was free. The consequences of unfreedom we will see in due course. The proportion between free and unfree peasants varied across the country. A study of midland shires suggests that nearly two-thirds were unfree. In East Anglia and the north the proportion of sokemen and other free tenants was much higher.

In many parts of the country the institution governing the lives of the peasant was the manor, although manors varied greatly in shape and size. Sometimes they were coterminous with a village, sometimes villages and their surrounding fields were divided between several manors. Within the manor, the lord retained a large proportion of the land (his 'demesne') in his own hands, making much of his income by selling the produce. To cultivate the demesne, he might use various combinations of both paid labour and the labour services owed by his unfree tenants. Another source of income was the money rent owed by both the free and the unfree. The size of the peasant tenements varied. At the top of the scale, in many manors, were peasants holding whole virgates of land (often the equivalent of twenty-four or thirty acres). A middle group held half virgates, while beneath them might be groups of 'cottars', with holdings of no more than a few acres.

[47] See volume 1, 663.

The running of a manor was controlled by the manorial court, presided over by the lord or his bailiff. It dealt with disputes between the tenants and the lord over services, and between the tenants themselves over the tenure of the land. It could also try minor cases of disorder. A manor of middling size is exemplified by Cuxham in south Oxfordshire.[48] Here the three great fields around the village contained something between 350 and 400 acres. In the survey of 1279 the lord is said to hold about 200 acres in demesne, although that was perhaps an underestimate. There were eight 'serfs', each with 12 acres of land (half virgates) held largely in return for labour services. They had to provide a man to work two days a week on the lord's demesne, with extra help at harvest time. They also owed customary renders including providing the lord with a cock, two hens and two loaves of bread at Christmas although they could give 6d instead. They received no Christmas present from the lord. Below the serfs were thirteen 'cottars', each holding a 'cottage'. In the only instance where the amount of land held is specified (for the first cottar on the list), it is a paltry one and a half acres. Although the cottars were said to hold 'in servile condition', their labour services were much lighter than those of the serfs and they chiefly held by money rents. (These varied between 1s 2d and 4s a year.) Finally, the survey shows there were two free tenants holding from the lord, one with a half virgate and nine acres, another with a little more than three acres.

Between Domesday Book and the survey of 1279, Cuxham's peasant population had more than doubled. In other manors the rise was steeper. The result almost certainly was land shortage with a growing segment of the peasantry living in poverty. Great efforts were made to meet the rising demand for food by bringing new land into cultivation, clearing woods and draining marshes. But in some areas there was limited scope for such expansion. As a result, a growing proportion of the peasant population were smallholders. At Cuxham, between Domesday Book and 1279, while the number of peasants with half a virgate of land increased by one, the number of cottars tripled from four to thirteen. Almost certainly, they could not support themselves from their land alone. They must have had other sources of income, for example from wage labour, using the resulting money to pay their rent and buy their bread. But when prices rose sharply in years of bad harvest, there was no similar rise in their cash income. It was probably such peasant smallholders and altogether landless men who

[48] The Chilterns on the horizon and watered by a stream, the village of Cuxham lies in a small valley with the land sweeping up around. There are several footpaths, and it is easy to make out the three fields of the medieval period (they are still there on the pre-enclosure map of 1767). Alison and Matthew Symonds kindly beat the bounds with us, an excellent way of appreciating the extent of a medium-sized medieval manor. For Cuxham see P.D.A. Harvey's fine book *A Medieval Oxfordshire Village: Cuxham 1240–1400*. In 1268, Ralph de Chenduit's son, Stephen, granted the manor to Walter of Merton, whence it formed part of Merton College's endowment.

perished during the great famine of 1258. The 'unknown' malefactors, accused of committing so much thirteenth-century crime, likewise came from such groups. The chattels of identified criminals were nearly always pathetically small; many had no chattels at all. Very few peasants can have reached Henry III's age at death of sixty-five.[49]

## THE JEWS[50]

In Henry's reign there were probably no more than 5,000 Jews in England, mostly concentrated in major towns. Despite their small numbers they played a vital part in the economic life of the country for they made their living as moneylenders; indeed given the church's ban on Christian usury they were often the main source of credit. The borrowers ranged across society, peasants, free tenants, knights, barons, earls, bishops and religious houses. Some debts could run into thousands of pounds, with such business being conducted by a small number of Jewish plutocrats, whose town houses excited awe and envy. The interest rates could run at one or two pence in the pound per week, so 22 per cent or 44 per cent a year. As customers and neighbours, Christians had close relations with Jews, while at the same time resenting and fearing them. The resentment stemmed from their role as moneylenders, the fear, sharpening in Henry's reign with the teachings of the friars, from the threat they posed to the Christian faith. Henry himself, very much in tune with the new hostility, had issued anti-Jewish legislation and tried to convert Jews to Christianity. He was also the first ruler, during terrible events in Lincoln in 1255, to sanction the libel that the Jews captured and crucified Christian boys in a macabre parody of the crucifixion of Christ. Yet Henry too needed the Jews for they were royal property and a major source of income. He could tax them at will and take into his own hands the debts they were owed, so Christians could end up owing Jewish debts to the king. In the years between 1240 and 1260 the taxation was so heavy it destroyed much of the wealth of the Jews in England.[51]

## THE PLEA ROLLS OF 1258–60

Three rolls survive recording cases heard by Hugh Bigod between June 1258 and July 1259. In the first, running down to December 1258, he heard

---

[49] For some figures bearing on peasant life expectancy, see Carpenter, *Struggle for Mastery*, 57.

[50] For works on the Jews, see Hillaby and Hillaby, *The Palgrave History of Medieval Anglo-Jewish History*; Richardson, *The English Jewry under the Angevin Kings*; Mundill, *England's Jewish Solution*; and Huscroft, *Expulsion*. I am grateful for advance sight of John Tolan's forthcoming book, *England's Jews*.

[51] See Stacey, '1240–60: a watershed in Anglo-Jewish relations?' For Henry and the Jews, see volume 1, 753 (the index).

pleas in London and in twenty-five other locations across fourteen counties. The second roll has pleas for Kent and Surrey, heard respectively in November 1258 and January 1259. In the third roll, covering the period from April to July 1259, there are pleas heard in ten places across ten counties, five of the latter having not seen Bigod before. As for the eyres commissioned in November 1259, rolls (some very incomplete) survive for Bigod himself in Essex and his colleagues in Oxfordshire, Warwickshire and Leicestershire. Later, in 1260, Bigod heard some cases in Yorkshire, while his successor, Hugh Despenser, visited Sussex. The cases themselves were of three types: common law assizes, the majority being of novel disseisin; complaints, *querelae*, prosecuted both by individuals and communities; and cases arising from the inquiries by the hundredal jurors and the four knights of 1258.[52]

Clearly, in geographical terms this evidence is very incomplete. Many shires are not represented at all. Many others were visited by Hugh Bigod very briefly. Only for Surrey, parts of Kent, a hundred in Hampshire and three hundreds in Oxfordshire do testimonies from the hundredal jurors survive and it is such testimonies, more than individual assizes and *querelae*, that really drill down into what was going on.[53] In terms of lordship and topography there were of course major contrasts between counties and indeed within them. In Kent it mattered whether one lived in hundreds controlled by the sheriff, the archbishop or the earl of Gloucester.[54] There were big differences between the north of the county and the wooded low-lying weald in the south. Simon de Montfort himself had a fine view over the weald from his castle at Sutton, where Adam Marsh sometimes stayed.[55]

---

[52] In truly pioneering work, E.F. Jacob was the first to unravel and analyse this material: Jacob, *Studies*, chs. 2 and 3. There is further analysis in Treharne, *Baronial Plan*, 111–14, 196–204. A great debt is owed to Andrew Hershey who has now put Bigod's rolls into print, the Surrey and Kent eyres with the Surrey Record Society, and the other rolls with the Selden Society, the two publications here cited as *SESK* and *SERHB*. Both volumes have a full introduction to the material. The other rolls are: TNA JUST 1/953 (Warwickshire); TNA JUST 1/456 (Leicestershire); TNA JUST 1/713 (Oxfordshire); and TNA JUST 1/911 and TNA JUST 1/537 (Sussex). Some of the cases from the 1260 eyres are printed and translated in *SCWR*, 105–13, 122–34. Hugh Bigod, in the summer of 1260, also heard what were largely assizes in Yorkshire: *Three Yorkshire Assize Rolls*, 88–139. A.J.P. Taylor's autobiography (*A Personal History*) has some attractive glimpses of Jacob as a consensual if impulsive Head of Department at Manchester University. The impulsiveness was shown in the way he appointed Taylor and later Lewis Namier, so it was in a good cause. I saw Jacob once when he gave a talk at my school. Sadly, all I remember is him putting his head in his hands, when trying to remember some detail, and saying 'my mind's like a sieve'.

[53] In Kent, there are returns for only twenty-two of the county's sixty-three hundreds: *SESK*, xlvi.

[54] For Kent, I am indebted to Jeremy Quick's thesis, 'Government and society in Kent, 1232–80'. For a study of the county under Edward I, see Burt, *Edward I and the Governance of England*, ch. 3, and see also Ward, 'The Kent hundred rolls'.

[55] Now Sutton Valence, reflecting its passage to William de Valence after Montfort's death.

The procedures of the eyres were helpful to litigants. In contrast to the inquisitions into heresy in the south of France, the aim was to elicit not confessions but complaints.[56] In the case of the common law assizes, some litigants paid 6s 8d (half a mark) to bring their pleas before Hugh Bigod, but this was a standard amount, not considered exorbitant. In the majority of assizes there is no evidence of payment and probably they came before him via the kind of writs costing a mere 6d that brought actions before the justices in eyre. Those who proceeded by *querela* could make their complaint either direct to the judges or via the inquiries of the four knights and the hundredal jurors. Probably some were by made by means of simple oral plaints, especially when brief, while others came via a written 'bill'.[57] In one or two cases, long schedules of grievance were presented.[58] There were certainly difficulties and dangers in proceeding against the powerful lords and their agents, but many such actions did get through. The regime welcomed all that could be thrown against the Lusignans.

This ease of procedure raises, however, a problem, namely that of the truth of the testimony. Some of the accusations have a formulaic ring. When a raiding band is described as being composed of 200 or 300 men, presumably that just means a large number. The very precise descriptions of goods seized, so many sheep, so many oxen, can also invite suspicion. There is clearly a distinction to be made between individual complaints and complaints that have the imprimatur of the hundredal jurors, as there is also between the complaints themselves and the eventual verdicts of the trial jurors. I have tried to notice that distinction in what follows. But of course juries can be biased and, especially in the circumstances of '1258', sympathetic to litigants. One needs also to remember that all the testimony depends on what the clerks wanted or were told by the judges to record. Such caution and scepticism can, however, be pushed too far. The procedures on the eyres, set by Hugh Bigod himself, seem remarkably even handed. Juries acquitted as well as convicted. Even some of the king's foreign favourites won cases. The evidence, as a whole, is sufficiently ample, wide ranging and balanced to give a good impression of the grievances agitating the localities during Henry III's personal rule.

The plea rolls of the years 1258 to 1260 provide a panorama of English society. Those appearing either as plaintiffs or defendants, sometimes both, range from bishops, religious houses, earls, the king's councillors and his foreign relatives, through barons, knights and substantial freemen,

---

[56] I am grateful to Rebecca Searby for letting me see in advance of publication her 'Rethinking the royal prosecution of c.1234', about testimonies of Jews against the regime of Peter des Roches, where comparisons are drawn with inquisition procedures. For the latter, see John Arnold's *Inquisition and Power: Catharism and the Confessing Subject in Medieval Languedoc*.

[57] See above, 26.

[58] The barriers to litigation by unfree peasants are discussed in the next section.

down to the poorest peasants male and female. In London, we see the chronicler and alderman Arnold fitzThedmar closing a brothel in his ward by removing its doors, the usual practice in the city. In Southampton, the merchant Claremunda had the sails of her ship seized, thus delaying its voyage to Gascony, and causing losses, so she claimed, of £40. (The defence was that she still owed 70 marks for the purchase of the ship.)[59] Some of Hugh Bigod's best work was done in settling the disputes between the greater and lesser townsmen in Grimsby and Scarborough.[60]

The Jews also appear. Several cases between Christians turned on the way that payment of a debt owed a Jew had been secured on a particular piece of land.[61] In another case, to which Hugh Bigod gave close attention, a Christian tried to escape punishment as a clipper of coin by saying he had borrowed the money, all of 2s 6d, from Benedict, a Jew of Stamford, this in return for pledging some cloth and a tunic of perse. The case went to a jury of twelve Christians and six Stamford Jews. The former said Benedict was guilty, the latter innocent. Indeed, at the time he was supposed to have lent the money he was celebrating 'mass' in the synagogue. But under cross examination the Jews began to tell different stories, and Benedict was eventually hanged, despite his wife's desperate efforts to save him. (Looking through a window of Stamford castle where the man caught with the coins was imprisoned, she tried to persuade him to say he had received them from someone else.)[62] A *cause célèbre*, heard by Bigod at the Tower of London, revealed a climactic feud between leading London Jews. Here Cresse, son of Rabbi Moses, accused Elias le Eveske of hiring someone to assault his brother Hagin. The latter had suffered a deep wound in the neck from a pickaxe and fallen to the ground as though dead. The assailant had then fled through St Olave's churchyard to Elias's house where he was sheltered until he got away. In the end, Elias, fearing doubtless the fate suffered by Benedict, resigned all his property to the crown and converted to Christianity. Several of his accomplices had been Christians including the assailant himself and Nicholas de Wauncy, a former sheriff of Surrey. Like much other evidence, including of course that from the lending of money, this reflected how closely Christians and Jews interacted.[63]

[59] *SERHB*, i, no. 104; ii, no. 516. The ship was loaded with merchandise. For a case brought *coram rege* in the Michaelmas term of 1260 by Claremunda's executors about the taking of a chest belonging to her containing gold, jewels and precious silver vases, see TNA KB 26/168, m. 2d (image 0057).

[60] See Hershey, 'Baronial reform, the justiciar's court and commercial legislation'.

[61] *SESK*, nos. 40, 187, 371, 378, 401; *SERHB*, i, nos. 42, 153; ii, nos. 532, 682, 799.

[62] *SERHB*, i, no. 191. At an earlier stage, the Stamford Jews had offered the king half a mark of gold so that the case was not heard 'on their sabbath as it was against the commandment of their laws to plead or answer for any trespass on the sabbath'.

[63] *SERHB*, i, no. 118; Paris, v, 730. For the careers of Elias, Master Moses and Hagin, see Hillaby and Hillaby, *The Palgrave Dictionary of Medieval Anglo-Jewish History*, 242–6, 253–5.

## PEASANTS IN THE PLEA ROLLS OF 1258–60

In the plea rolls of 1258 to 1260 there are over forty cases turning on the relations between peasants and their lords. Some were brought by individual peasants male and female, others, usually the most striking, by peasant communities. The plaintiffs in these cases, whether individual or communal, sought to redress their grievances through one of three procedures mentioned above, that is, through a common law assize (nearly always novel disseisin),[64] through a *querela* direct to the judges or through complaints to the hundredal juries.

In seeking to litigate in one of these ways, peasants faced a fundamental problem. If they were deemed unfree, they had no access to the king's courts in any matter concerning the terms on which they held their land. Those terms were entirely for lords to decide. Lords could thus increase services and indeed disseise unfree peasants as they pleased. It was with clear design that Magna Carta limited protection against unlawful disseisin to those who were free. Lords were not to be deprived of their ultimate disciplinary weapon.[65] Again and again between 1258 and 1260 peasants fell at this first legal hurdle. When Amabilia, widow of Gilbert Thurold, complained of disseisin and sought damages, her lord just said he had no case to answer since she held her land in villeinage. The jury agreed and Amabilia was placed in mercy for a false claim.[66] Likewise when the men of Bampton Doilly in Oxfordshire complained of new tallages, the lord, the knight Roger Doilly, said they were villeins not sokemen and he could tallage them as he pleased. The men had to concede the point and again were placed in mercy for a false claim.[67] Richard Wolf suffered the same fate when complaining of the seizure of grain and bread. The lord, the jury agreed, could seize the chattels 'as his own' since Richard refused to perform his villein services.[68] The case also exemplified the legal rule that lords could sell their unfree tenants 'like oxen and cows'. The abbot of Durford had granted the entire tenement that Richard held in villeinage, 'along with Richard his villein and all his progeny', to a new lord, Simon the Draper.[69]

In these circumstances, how did peasants proceed at all? There were various routes. One obviously was to say they were free and hope the jury would agree. In a case from Godalming in Surrey, the jury, having done

---

[64] The action novel disseisin provided a remedy for those dispossessed (disseised) unlawfully and without judgement of land held freely.

[65] Carpenter, *Magna Carta*, 113–14.

[66] To be 'placed in mercy' means to become liable for a fine (an amercement). *SERHB*, i, no. 166.

[67] *SCWR*, 106. For other cases where peasants lost because they were judged unfree, see *SERHB*, i, nos. 208, 342; ii, nos. 460, 568, 639; *SESK*, nos. 20, 25; TNA JUST 1/953, m. 2 (image 7261).

[68] *SERHB*, ii, no. 504.

[69] *London Eyre of 1244*, no. 346; *SERHB*, ii, no. 504.

just that, convicted the lord of various trespasses.[70] Another route was for peasants to claim they enjoyed 'ancient demesne' status. This was the status possessed by peasants who lived on manors once part of the 'ancient demesne' of the crown, usually defined as a manor held by the king at the time of Domesday Book. Such peasants were entitled to the same customs and services in force while the manor was in royal hands, and could bring legal actions against lords who sought to impose additional burdens. Knowledge of this protection was widespread and it was claimed by men from nine manors on the eyres.[71] Equally in a privileged position were the peasants living on the king's current demesne, for they could litigate over exactions contrary to the custom of their manors. Peasants, whether free or unfree, could also, in legal theory, bring actions in the king's courts complaining of violence done them in breach of the king's peace.[72] 'Be it remembered', declared the judges on the London eyre of 1244, 'that earls, barons, and free tenants, may lawfully put their serfs in the stocks, but not in irons; and . . . they may not kill them, maim them, or wound them because the bodies and members of the serfs belong only to the king.'[73] In one case before Hugh Bigod, the widow Agatha complained of a punch below the ear suffered because she refused to leave Beaumont fields outside Oxford where she was collecting corn. Because this was indeed done in breach of the peace she was awarded damages by Bigod himself.[74]

Exploiting one of these routes, even lone peasants were able to pursue their causes through a variety of courts and procedures. Clement fitzJohn's claim of unjust disseisin by the queen's steward and castellan of Gloucester Matthias Bezill was heard by the court *coram rege*, by a justice of assize and eventually by Hugh Bigod himself. Bezill claimed that fitzJohn was a villein whom he could tallage (and thus disseise) at will, but two juries disagreed and convicted him of disseisn.[75] Clement fitzJohn was litigating over two virgates of land in Sherston (Wiltshire), so probably between forty and fifty acres. His holding, therefore, was considerably larger than that usually held by an unfree peasant. But it was not only peasants with, in peasant terms, largish holdings who were able to litigate. In another case Ralph Stipol sought the return of a messuage and eight acres while Amabilia, widow of Gilbert Thurold, was litigating over one virgate. After

---

[70] *SESK*, no. 103.

[71] Godalming, Witley, Dulwich, Leigham, Walworth, Newington (*SESK*, nos. 103, 105, 167, 168); Mears Ashby, Offord Cluny (*SERHB*, i, no. 129; ii, no. 639); Hardwick (TNA JUST 1/713, m. 1d [image 9783]).

[72] For the whole subject of the villein as litigant, see Hyams, *King, Lords and Peasants*, 125–51. For discussion of pragmatic legal knowledge and participation in the royal courts, see Musson, *Medieval Law in Context*, chs. 3 and 4.

[73] *London Eyre of 1244*, no. 346; *Bracton*, ii, 34, 438.

[74] *SERHB*, i, no. 349.

[75] *SERHB*, i, no. 339.

she had lost, like some other peasant litigants, she was pardoned her amercement because she was 'poor'.[76]

Although single peasants could pursue cases, it was obviously better to do so as part of a group. Here there could be considerable organization. The men of Somerton, Bampton Doilly and Hardwick all drew up 'articles' setting out their grievances.[77] At Brill on its hill above the Oxfordshire and Buckinghamshire plain, the villagers combined to bring forward a series of individual complaints. There were seventeen of them including several from four women. At Coleby in Lincolnshire, seven peasants clubbed together to pay 20s for an assize of novel disseisin to be heard by Bigod.[78] The case was against the king's household knight Bartholomew Peche. Some of the peasants involved had very small holdings (rated in terms of tofts and crofts), but the majority had more substantial holdings of around thirty acres.

Communal cases could have a long history. The men of Mears Ashby in Northamptonshire struggled for the best part of a decade to prove they were sokemen and not villeins tallageable at their lord's will, their opponents being Robert de Mears (hence the village's name), a much-favoured king's knight, and then his widow, Sibilla. The case came before the court *coram rege* during the Oxford and Winchester parliaments of June and July 1258, thus plunging the men into the midst of the political revolution. There were subsequent proceedings before Hugh Bigod, his successor, Hugh Despenser, the judge Gilbert of Preston and the justices of the bench. Eventually, in June 1261, before the itinerant justices at Northampton, Sibilla and the men set out their differences in comprehensive detail, and Sibilla at last backed down. In return for a payment of 4½ marks she agreed that the men could hold by the customs and services they acknowledged until her son came of age. The men seem to have maintained their victory for a survey of Ashby, on her son's death in 1282, described the twelve virgates she had claimed to be villeinage as 'held in free socage'.[79]

At the centre of many grievances was the seizure of chattels. In a Godalming case the lord, the jury agreed, had taken from his victim four quarters of rye, one bushel of beans and one cartload of hay. He had also pastured his beasts on seven acres of sown oats.[80] Such seizures were often accompanied by physical maltreatment. In a Derbyshire case, Alan Kuc suffered the loss of an ox, ten sheep, four lambs, a cow and a mare. He

---

[76] The Stipol case came before the 1257 Norfolk eyre: TNA Just 1/567, m. 29 (image 7888).

[77] The men of Somerton (in Somerset) were litigating in 1258 in the court *coram rege* against the bailiff who held the manor from the king at farm, see TNA KB 26/ 158, m.4 (image 0012). Hardwick, like Bampton Doilly, was in Oxfordshire.

[78] *CFR 1257–8*, no. 1032.

[79] Carpenter, *Reign of Henry III*, 325–6, where full references are given.

[80] *SESK*, no. 103, and Hershey's comment at lxxiii–iv.

was also arrested and placed in the stocks, languishing there from matins until the ninth hour.[81] Richard Wolf, for his part, alleged that his lord and seven named men had broken the doors and windows of his house, wounded his wife, and taken away grain and bread worth 37s. They had then pursued him with bows and arrows to the church, forcing him to take refuge there for eight days. A little later they came again, this time knocking down Richard's buildings and carrying away thirty-four beehives and the grain grown on fourteen acres of land.[82]

Such treatment was rarely an end in itself. Rather it was designed, as in the Godalming, Kuc and Wolf cases, to force the victim to acknowledge his villein status. At Coleby, Bartholomew Peche 'took and imprisoned' one of his tenants 'and so flagellated him that by compulsion he recognised that he held his tenement in villeinage'. The evils flowing from villeinage, in such cases, were occasionally connected with labour services, but more often they were about having to pay higher rents or being tallaged at the lord's will. The men of Witley in Surrey complained that under Peter of Savoy their annual rent had been raised by £18. Ralph Stipol was disseised by the king's knight Peter Braunche because he refused to be tallaged. The men of Weybridge, Byfleet and Ruxley said they were being 'wholly destroyed' by new tallages, the men of Bampton Doilly that the tallages were so heavy they could not 'support their service', probably meaning they could not pay their rent.[83] Other issues were the payment of merchet and having to act as the lord's reeve, the official charged with running the manor.[84] At his manor of Warehorne in Kent, the knight Alfred de Dene took money from three men since they did not wish to act as reeve.[85] At Birling in the same county, the bailiff, William de la Green, appointed fourteen reeves in four years and made them all 'borrow' money from the men of the manor for the benefit of his lord, the baron William de Say. Green also heavily amerced the men for small offences.[86]

The most detailed insight into events within manors is provided by the articles of complaint drawn up by the men of Hardwick and Brill. Those at Hardwick covered twelve separate issues, including appointment of the reeve, exactions at the view of frankpledge, having to reap till night without food and being made to stack corn at Standlake when only obliged to do so at Hardwick. On one occasion when the lord's meadow had been mowed perfectly well, the bailiff nonetheless made a 'great

---

[81] *SERHB*, i, no. 256. The lord, Henry of Ashbourne, admitted the charges but said he had acted within his rights since Kuc was his villein. No conclusion was reached in the case.
[82] *SERHB*, ii, no. 504.
[83] *SESK*, nos. 105, 146; *SCWR*, 106.
[84] Merchet was a payment to the lord on marriage.
[85] *SESK*, no. 354. Alfred had acted as under-sheriff (no. 337).
[86] *SESK*, nos. 312, 314.

complaint' and forced the men to give him 2s. The first complaint on the list was being tallaged 'against all justice and usage'. In order to enforce one payment the bailiffs seized 19 oxen, 7 cows, 7 bullocks, 4 horses and 126 sheep. An order from the king for their return was obstructed by the animals being driven from Hardwick to Cogges, another manor of the lord Walter de Grey.[87]

At Brill, the grievances of the sokemen were about not rents and services, but other forms of extortion, often connected in some way with the running of the manorial court. The culprits were William fitz Simon and his colleagues, the bailiffs who held the manor at farm from the king.[88] Thus three of the sokemen, having paid money so as not to attend the court, were then amerced for default. Another paid 6d for a court record of a land transfer and then was ejected from the land. Four women made complaints, one unmarried. The latter, Christiana le Rus, said that though very poor with goods not worth 5s, she was amerced 19d for once brewing against the regulations. The bailiffs had broken into her house while she was away, taken a brass pot worth 20d and sold it as they wished.[89] Such complaints are sometimes dismissed by historians as 'petty'. They were not petty for the people involved. The indignation is reflected in the statement of William Sqwake. Having accidently blinded a horse by striking it in the eye, he was made to attend the court and pay nearly 4s. 'He says the horse with both eyes was not worth more than 2s'![90] 'By these wrongs, extortions and pillages', the men concluded, 'they have been so harmed and impoverished . . . that there hardly remains anyone who is able to answer to the king for the farm owed for their land.'

If there was indignation at Brill, at Woodstock near Oxford there was anger. Here two shocking charges were laid against the bailiff, William of Rushton.[91] He had so 'flagellated with various torments' William le Blund that William had been taken up dead from the prison at Woodstock. Sarah of Islip, arrested with various cloths in her possession, had been hanged when she was pregnant, 'with a live infant', although she was prepared to show she had obtained the cloths honestly. More of this tragic case later.

At the eyres it was perfectly possible for peasants to bring cases against well-connected knights and indeed barons. But there were no complaints about customs and services from the manors of Richard of Cornwall and Richard de Clare. With such great men, the difficulties and dangers of

---

[87] TNA JUST 1/713, m. 1d (image 9783), and see *CFR 1259–60*, nos. 196, 264.

[88] *SERHB*, i, no. 89. See Jacob, *Studies*, 44–7, for an analysis of the complaints with the text between 344 and 349.

[89] Another of the women was amerced for a brewing offence.

[90] Jacob, *Studies*, 345.

[91] *SERHB*, i, no. 126. The entry is under a heading 'pleas of the crown', this while Hugh Bigod was hearing pleas at Woodstock in August 1258. It begins 'William of Rushton is accused . . .'. Presumably the accusation came from a local jury. Rushton too was answering for a farm.

complaining were multiplied many times over. That is seen in one case which did make it before Hugh Bigod. Here the villein, John le Rok, complained of being arrested in the cemetery of All Saints Wallingford by the earl of Cornwall's bailiff, Peter of Ashridge. He was then taken to Wallingford castle, placed in irons and held for five weeks, the first three days without food and drink. This was not a 'manorial' case for Ashridge explained (and the jury agreed) he was arresting le Rok for theft, but clearly a spell in one of King Richard's castles, at the very least, might be the fate of anyone disputing their customs and services.[92] Ashridge was not a man to be trifled with. In one of his letters, Adam Marsh decried his 'many forms of violence'. He was 'the hammer of the whole country, made abominable, as everyone says, to God and man by his shameful misdeeds and crimes'.[93]

Another warning was issued by Richard de Clare's steward, Quintin of Winchester. When the reeve of the earl's manor of Yalding in Kent, Richard of Selling, got into debt on his account, he was arrested and taken off to Tonbridge castle. There he was held in chains and tortured until he granted Quintin ten acres of land. When he subsequently tried to recover the land before the justices of the bench at Westminster, he found himself carted off to Newgate prison, where he remained for around a year.[94] This was on the pretext he had burnt down Quintin's house.[95] Richard de Clare gave full backing to his man, and brought an action in the court *coram rege* against Selling and his wife for the arson.[96] The villagers of Birling were in a similar predicament. When their oppressive bailiff, William de la Green, was attacked and his sword seized, the lord William de Say brought an action *coram rege* against the assailants.[97]

Given the limited geographical coverage of the material, the cases we have seen were almost certainly part of a much wider groundswell of discontent. That view is reinforced by the evident sympathy the jurors felt for the complainants, not surprising since most were freemen, who would have lacked villein tenants, and were not so far removed in terms of wealth from their more prosperous villein neighbours, or neighbours whom lords alleged were villeins. Many of the accusations came up through the hundredal juries and were then confirmed in whole or part by jury verdicts at trial. Trial juries thus upheld at least some of the complaints made by the

---

[92] *SERHB*, ii, no. 469. John le Rok's villein status can be deduced from his being in a tithing. The tithing's refusal to go bail for him was part of Ashridge's defence.

[93] *Letters of Adam Marsh*, ii, 298–9. Marsh was also worried about the earl of Cornwall's intervention on Ashridge's behalf. For Ashridge's alleged malpractices when Richard's sheriff in Rutland, see TNA JUST 1/721, mm.8, 8d (images 0348, 0373–4).

[94] For the case before the bench in 1250, see *CRR*, xix, no. 1595, where Richard Atteham is clearly the same person as Richard of Selling.

[95] *SESK*, no. 340. The verdict of the jury and Selling's own testimony largely coincided.

[96] TNA KB 26/147A, m. 3 (image 0003) (Trinity term of 1252).

[97] TNA KB 26/147A, m. 7 (image 0007).

men of Mears Ashby and Hardwick. A jury agreed that Agatha, collecting corn in Beaumont fields, had been punched, although this had not caused her to lose the sight of an eye. (That had come from the fumes of her brewing.)[98] In other cases the jurors were full square behind the plaintiffs. Two juries braved Matthias Bezill and said Clement fitzJohn was free.[99] At Brill, they detailed a series of additional misdemeanours. The bailiffs had summoned all the tenants to attend the manorial court on one day, only not to turn up themselves. They had then held the court on another day without any summons and amerced the tenants for failing to appear. They had also taken money to bribe the exchequer and secure a delay in paying the farm, only to exact the farm and keep it for themselves. At Woodstock, the original verdict of the manorial court was reviewed by thirty men drawn from five neighbouring villages. They agreed absolutely with the first verdict. William le Blund had died in prison 'flagellated by diverse torments'. Sarah of Islip had never admitted to theft and had been pregnant. Indeed, having been sentenced to hang, 'she asked for the infant to be cut from her womb', a pathetic detail reflecting the jury's indignation at her fate. Something of the same tone was sounded at Writtle in Essex, where a jury convicted the bailiff of so harrying the villagers that they hardly 'dared stay in their own homes'. A woman was imprisoned for two days 'in the lord's manor' simply because, having found the hood of the prior of Blackmore, she had reported it not to the bailiff but to the parish chaplain. The result was that the woman's baby 'remaining at home had died for lack of its mother's care'.[100]

A similar sense of outrage is seen in the verdicts against William de Bussey, the chief steward of the Lusignans. In Surrey he had increased so much the tallages at Weybridge, Byfleet and Bisley that 'the tenants were wholly destroyed'.[101] In Cambridgeshire, jurors told of how a man at Trumpington had died as a result of 'the cruel punishment and most harsh imprisonment' inflicted by Bussey's agents. Although not convicted of any felony, they had then 'hanged him up dead'. When the jurors were asked whether all this had taken place on Bussey's order, they replied 'yes'. The episode had become scandalous long before it was reported on the eyre of 1261. It was recorded in detail by Matthew Paris shortly before his death in 1259.[102]

The level of discontent can also be inferred from Hugh Bigod's own responses. He evidently felt there was something very wrong in the way

---

[98] *SERHB*, i, no. 349.

[99] But for mutual interests between lords and jurors see Forrest, 'Power and the people in thirteenth-century England', 24–7. See also his 'Transformation of visitation', 29–38.

[100] *SERHB*, ii, no. 883. The lord was Robert de Bruce, grandfather of the future king of Scotland.

[101] *SESK*, nos. 146, 182. For earlier 'terrifying' threats against the reeve of his manor of Chadstone in Northamptonshire: TNA JUST 1/615, m. 12 (image 0923).

[102] TNA JUST 1/82, mm. 24d (image 0560); Paris, v, 739. For Bussey, see Hershey, 'The rise and fall of William de Bussey'.

lords were treating their men. It was surely with his encouragement that so many details, sometimes heinous, sometimes pathetic, were recorded by the clerks.[103] That Bigod was prepared to hear the men of Witley's case against Peter of Savoy and the villein John le Rok's against Peter of Ashridge tells a great deal about his attitude. He was quite ready to intervene directly in cases even for the poorest in the land. In that of Agatha, punched in Beaumont fields, Bigod himself, as we have seen, 'taxed' her damages.[104] They were all of 2s. In the Coleby case, although the men had yet to win their action completely, Bigod nonetheless had the damages assessed.[105] He was very prepared to question juries. He asked whether so many reeves had been appointed at Birling on the orders of the lord, William de Say, or out of the 'malice' of the bailiff. The jury said the latter.[106] At Woodstock, Bigod asked whether Sarah of Islip had admitted her theft and been hanged by judgement of the court, as William of Rushton claimed. The answer was absolutely not. Indeed, the members of the court had left rather than be involved.[107]

The sentences suffered by those convicted is another indication of Bigod's attitude and the scale of the problem. At Birling, Brill, Woodstock and Writtle, the bailiffs were gaoled and amerced.[108] By the time Matthew Paris wrote about the Trumpington case, William de Bussey too was in prison, indeed in the Tower, 'accused of various trespasses'. Paris liked to think he was seized not by the straps of his coif but by the throat, this to the cry 'If I do you wrong, who will do you justice?', an ironic echo of Bussey's taunting question to his own victims.[109] Bigod's desire to redress the grievances of even the humblest litigants stands out in case after case. He absolutely deserved the encomium penned by Matthew Paris's successor at St Albans.[110]

---

[103] The clerks were, of course, translating the French or English of the litigants into the Latin of the record. There must have been a great deal of editing, with some cases set out in detail, others very briefly. For filtering and consolidation in the French *enquêtes* and the 1274–5 inquiry, see Dejoux, 'Des juges au travail: les enquêteurs réparateurs de Louis IX', 233–5, 241–2, and Scales, 'The Cambridgeshire Ragman Rolls', 564, 571, 573.

[104] *SERHB*, i, no. 349.

[105] *SERHB*, i, no. 272. It was, however, quite common for damages to be assessed prior to any judgement.

[106] *SESK*, no. 314.

[107] He also asked questions in the Richard of Selling v. Quintin of Winchester case: *SESK*, no. 340.

[108] *SERHB*, i, nos. 126, 136; Cassidy, '1259 pipe roll', ii, no. 605; *CFR 1258–9*, nos. 431–2; *SERHB*, ii, no. 883.

[109] Paris, v, 726, 738–9; *CR 1256–9*, 342; *CR 1259–61*, 17, 98; *CR 1261–4*, 483; *CLR 1260–7*, 11; *CFR 1258–9*, no. 804; *CFR 1259–60*, no. 486; *CFR 1260–1*, nos. 818–19, 831–2. There appears to be no record of any trial. He was released and recovered his lands on William de Valence's return in 1261.

[110] See above, 46. For the judge, Bracton, influencing the content of his rolls, see McSweeney, *Priests of the Law*, 210–39.

## THE SHERIFFS AND THEIR BAILIFFS

Manors were situated within the wider framework of royal administra-tion.[111] England was divided into thirty-two counties, each under a sheriff appointed by the king.[112] The counties themselves were divided into units called hundreds or wapentakes, some 628 in all.[113] They varied greatly in size and number. Surrey had 14 hundreds, Leicestershire only 4. Of the hundreds some 270 were royal and subject directly to the authority of the sheriff and his bailiffs.[114] That left 358 hundreds subject, in some degree, to the authority of a lord. Within counties, the balance between royal and private hundreds again varied. In some it was roughly even, in others either royal or private hundreds preponderated. Fortunately, the surviving eyre material has a good offering of both. There was also a variation in the authority wielded by the lord. Some of the greatest lords, ecclesiastical and secular, had the 'franchise of return of writs' and were entitled to exclude the sheriff from the hundred altogether. In other cases, king and lord might share authority, dividing, for example, the revenues of the hundred court, and with the sheriff, along with the lord's bailiff, presiding at its principal sessions.[115] Even top of the range private hundreds were part of the king's government of the country. The 'writs' delivered or 'returned' to the lord's bailiffs were orders from the king, ones commanding the levying of debts, the summoning of juries and the implementation of verdicts. If they were not obeyed, the sheriff might be ordered to enter the hundred to see they were. In the last resort the hundred might be taken into the king's hands. The process, however, was rarely smooth. As the numerous orders from judges and the exchequer show, private hundreds frequently obstructed the judicial and financial administration of the country.

Between 1258 and 1260 virtually the whole range of shrieval activity was a subject of complaint: the running of the hundred and county courts, the implementation of writs, the summoning of juries, the collection of debts and the seizure of prises.[116] The sheriffs were accused of making false accusations, torturing prisoners and imposing arbitrary amerce-

[111] The best survey remains Helen Cam's classic *The Hundred and the Hundred Rolls*. For the county court, see Robert Palmer's *The County Courts of Medieval England*.

[112] It was customary for some adjoining counties to be placed under the same sheriff, examples being Warwickshire and Leicestershire, Norfolk and Suffolk, and Surrey and Sussex.

[113] In the four northernmost counties the divisions were called wards.

[114] From now onwards, I include wapentakes under the term hundred. For a compre-hensive survey of the lordship of hundreds in 1274, see Cam, *The Hundred and the Hundred Rolls*, 259–85.

[115] Cam, *The Hundred and the Hundred Rolls*, 137–9; see also Clanchy, 'Franchise of return of writs'.

[116] The king's right of prise was the right to purchase goods, often at a low price. The bills were often left unpaid.

ments. They enforced their will above all by distraint, the seizure of crops, household goods and, most often, again and again, animals – cows, oxen, sheep and horses. The impression given by the plea rolls is of roads clogged by herds of animals driven off under armed guard to wherever the sheriff wished to park them (often a meadow below the county castle). Not surprisingly, efforts were often made to prevent the seizures in the first place or 'rescue' the animals once taken, all the more so since the legal means for their recovery could lead nowhere.[117] The whole procedure was a recipe for violence. The sheriff had formidable coercive power, at least against ordinary people. He could muster posses of considerable size while at his back was the county castle, his administrative base and also a place of imprisonment and torture. In the 1258–60 material, Gloucester, Winchester, Rochester and Dover castles all feature.

Sometimes grievances on the 1258–60 eyres were ventilated by the whole county or a whole hundred. In other cases, individuals gave long narratives of their sufferings. Some sheriffs had just to face one or two accusations. Others, particularly where there is testimony from the hundredal jurors, left a trail of protest in their wake. In a few instances, that testimony, as if opening a can of worms, reveals the squirming mass of subordinate bailiffs making life a misery within a single hundred.

In Surrey, the entire county, village by village, accused the sheriff, John of Gaddesden (1227–31 and 1236–40), of establishing a second annual tourn at the hundred court where previously there had only been one. Since far more people had to attend the tourn than the court's ordinary three weekly sessions, this either doubled the vexation of turning up or doubled the amercement for failing to do so, the latter being probably the real purpose of the exercise. These innovations had been continued by subsequent sheriffs.[118] In Kent, all the hundreds complained that the sheriff, John de Wadeton, had increased the exactions at the tourn. Here again the new impositions had become customary. At the time of a subsequent inquiry in 1274–5, Wadeton was still remembered 'for a certain extortion called the tourn of the sheriff'.[119] A similar pattern is found in Oxfordshire. In Ploughley hundred, the individual villages detailed the rising exactions at the tourn and view of frankpledge: from 2s to 8s, 1s to 4s and so on.[120] The tourn and the view were indeed issues throughout the

---

[117] For distraint and the means of recovery, see Cam, *The Hundred and the Hundred Rolls*, 82–5; Brand, *Kings, Barons and Justices*, 94–8.

[118] *SESK*, nos. 80, 152. There is a biography of John of Gaddesden in Meekings and Crook, *Surrey Eyre*, i, 196–7.

[119] *SESK*, nos. 295–6; see also no. 379; *RH*, i, 223. Wadeton (his name is spelt in many ways) was the under-sheriff of the household knight and later steward of the household Bertram de Criel, sheriff for much of the 1230s and 1240s.

[120] TNA JUST 1/713, m. 3 (image 9777–8). For Ploughley, see *VCH Oxfordshire*, vi, 1–6. The view of frankpledge was the annual check (at the Michaelmas tourn) as to whether the unfree peasant population were arrayed in tithings, the groups of adult males sworn to

kingdom. In Northumberland, an inquiry found that, whereas there had once been no tourns in the county, the sheriff William Heron (1246–58) 'distrained all the freeholders of the county to come to two tourns yearly, and if they did not come they were amerced heavily by his own will. This was extortion since he was acting without warrant from the king or his council.'[121]

When it came to complaints about the running of the shire court, the whole county of Surrey complained of the way, 'to its great damage', the location had been moved from Leatherhead to Guildford.[122] In Kent, nearly every hundred lamented the way Reginald of Cobham (sheriff 1249–57) would hear no testimony in the county court about death and misadventure until an arbitrary fine had been made with him to escape penalization. This fine, known as '*beaupleder*', made so as to escape penalties for mistakes in giving evidence, was a burning issue elsewhere.[123] In Oxfordshire, the men of Ploughley hundred refused to give it. The men of Bloxham hundred coughed up 46s 8d, but complained bitterly of the exaction. An example of the practice that the fine was designed to escape was revealed on the Herefordshire eyre back in 1255. Here the sheriff was accused of handing 'diverse chapters' with questions to those attending the tourn. If they did not reply to them all word for word, he amerced them 'at his will'.[124]

Alongside communal allegations, the royal officials faced complaints from individuals. They were brought against the sheriffs of Gloucestershire (William of Lashborough), Lincolnshire (John of Cockerington), Cambridgeshire (William of Stow), Hampshire (James Savage) and two sheriffs of Northamptonshire, William de Lisle and Hugh de Manneby.[125] Lashborough admitted that, to enforce the payment of debt owed by Henry of Maisemore, he had seized Henry's sister's cow, kept it for a year and used it to draw his plough. When at last he released the cow, having initially refused to obey orders from the king to do so, he extorted money for its upkeep and kept its calf. His men were accused of breaking into Henry of Maisemore's house, beating his wife and taking his son off to imprisonment in Gloucester castle. Although William de Lisle was actually acquitted of the charge brought against him, there must have been

---

keep the peace and ensure the good conduct of their fellows. There were many ways the sheriff or the hundred bailiff could make money out of the view, hence the regulations in Magna Carta 1217 (cap. 42).

[121] *CIM*, no. 364. The inquiry was in 1268. For Heron, see Cassidy, 'William Heron'.

[122] *SESK*, nos. 59, 75.

[123] For the fine, see Brand, *Kings, Barons and Justices*, 87–90.

[124] TNA JUST 1/300C, m. 21 (image 8020). The sheriff was John le Breton (1254–7). For complaints about the running of the forest in Surrey see *SESK*, p. 1 (Hershey's introduction), and nos. 74, 76, and see *DBM*, 80–1, cap. 7. Had more evidence survived we would probably find such complaints echoed in other counties where the forest was a major issue.

[125] *SERHB*, i, no. 308; ii, nos. 524, 685; Cam, *Liberties and Communities*, 39.

many more (an indication of missing material) for he was fined the very large sum of 100 marks for 'his many trespasses'.[126] Six complaints apiece were brought against two sheriffs of Warwickshire–Leicestershire, William Mansel and Alan of Swinford.[127] In Mansel's case, ten men from Clawson in Leicestershire alleged that he had taken a horse from each of them, this because men from the village had been hanged at the last eyre, so this was a way of seizing their chattels, or rather the equivalent in horses. But the jury agreed that the chattels had been in the hands not of the villagers but of Mansel's bailiffs all along.[128]

It is when we have testimony from the hundredal juries that most light is thrown on the local situation. In Ploughley hundred, there were a dozen charges against the sheriff, Nicholas of Hendred (1254–8). In one case he had extracted half a mark from the village of Bainton because some boys, finding their mother's door shut, had undone the bolt, entered the house and taken some bread.[129] In Surrey, around a dozen allegations, from five separate hundreds, were made against the sheriff, Gerard of Evington (1257–8).[130] In Wotton hundred, on becoming sheriff, he had held the tourn when his predecessor had already done so. In the county court he had encouraged approvers to accuse men unjustly and then taken money for their release.[131] He had himself accused Alice de Aula of homicide and taken £5 from her. He routinely took payments to release people on pledge till the eyre's arrival; indeed he claimed all his predecessors had done so.[132] Ordered to raise the money to pay a debt at the exchequer he had seized two horses, refused to allow the owner to buy them back and then sold them (presumably to friends) at far less than their real value.[133]

It was the sheriff of Northamptonshire, the clerk Hugh de Manneby, who faced the accusation that seems most to have appalled the eyre. Its treatment testifies powerfully to Hugh Bigod's determination to expose shrieval malpractice even when the victim was at the very bottom of society, in this case an outlaw, Richard de Glaston.[134] Arriving in Northampton in August 1258, Bigod encouraged Glaston to tell his story

[126] *SERHB*, i, no. 365. Perhaps one complaint related to the case which had brought about Lisle's fall in 1256 as narrated in Paris, v, 577–81. Both Lisle and his successor, Hugh de Manneby, were investigated at the exchequer for their unjust exactions: Cassidy, 'Bad sheriffs, custodial sheriffs', 40.

[127] Mansel was sheriff in 1252–6 and again in 1257–8 with Swinford the interim sheriff.

[128] TNA JUST 1/456, m. 11d (image 4766).

[129] TNA Just 1/ 713, m. 4 (image 9780).

[130] *SESK*, nos. 54, 55, 69, 95, 106, 108–9, 154, 160–1.

[131] This is a very common accusation in the 1274 inquiry.

[132] This was a common accusation on the 1255 Herefordshire eyre: TNA Just 1/ 300C, mm. 21d, 22d, 23, 23d, 26, 27d.

[133] *SESK*, no. 160.

[134] *SERHB*, i, no. 161.

in all its harrowing detail.[135] Accused of theft, Glaston had taken sanctuary and then abjured the realm. On his way to the nearest port, he had been on the road between Northampton and Newport Pagnell when he was assaulted by Manneby's men. While he clung to a cartwheel, they beat him so severely with bows and clubs that the flesh of his arms and back had putrefied. Having been dragged back to prison at Northampton, he was so cruelly tortured his life was despaired of. The only explanation Manneby offered for such conduct was that Glaston had been arrested for straying from the road, as outlaws were absolutely forbidden to do. This cut no ice with the jurors. They convicted him and added more details, giving the names of Glaston's assaulters (he did not know them), and saying directly, in answer to Bigod's question, that the attack had been on Manneby's orders. To avoid being seized Glaston had not only gripped the cartwheel but bit the earth with his teeth. Back in Northampton, his place of torture had been a cellar beneath the chamber in Manneby's house. Bigod's judgement, hearing all this, was that Manneby should be sent to gaol, since 'that trespass has been committed so manifestly and enormously against the peace of the king and the law and custom of the kingdom'. Glaston, meanwhile, was to be taken to the hospital of St John in Northampton, there to be tenderly nursed and looked after. If, however, he did recover, he was to set off once more out of the kingdom.

Beneath the sheriffs were an array of under-sheriffs and hundredal bailiffs. Sometimes the clerks, perhaps overwhelmed by the material, simply noted that such men had been amerced 'for many trespasses' without going into details.[136] In other cases there are details a plenty. In Kent, Guy de Norton was convicted of breaking into houses, stealing their contents and imprisoning a man unjustly in Dover castle. There had been complaints against him on the 1255 Kentish eyre, but it was only now he was brought to book. He was sentenced to gaol and eventually fined £5 for all his trespasses while a bailiff of the king.[137] Bigod was equally determined in dealing with a Surrey bailiff, Henry Gargat. His evil reputation went back to the eyre of 1235 when he was accused of carrying out one rape and commanding two of his men to commit another.[138] On the eyre of 1255 he was had up for taking money and goods from men imprisoned in Guildford castle although they had been allowed to go free by the king's judges.[139] Again it was only on Hugh Bigod's eyre that Gargat was properly punished. Convicted of unjust seizures, false accusations and false imprisonments, with the usual payments from the victims to

---

[135] The case arose because Bigod decided to try the cases of those, like Glaston, imprisoned in Northampton gaol.

[136] *SESK*, nos. 90–1, 310, 315.

[137] *SESK*, no. 299.

[138] Meekings and Crook, *Surrey Eyre*, ii, no. 453 and n. (p. 540), for the Gargat family.

[139] TNA JUST 1/872, m. 32 (images 9145).

secure release, he was sentenced to gaol and was fined £2 for 'his many trespasses'.[140]

In some cases, the sheer number of bailiffs working below the sheriff is revealed. In Hinckford hundred in Essex, the jurors named twenty men, 'once under-sheriffs, bailiffs and under-bailiffs' guilty of abuse. They had placed 'many men' on juries and then taken money to allow some to go home. They had also committed numerous unspecified trespasses, inflicting so much damage on the country that the jurors could not value it.[141] Similar numbers were indicted in Milton hundred in Kent.[142] On the 1255 eyre its officials had felt not a breath of criticism. It was very different in 1258. The jurors first reported a long-standing breach of 'gavelkind', the custom by which much land in Kent was held. Under gavelkind, they explained, the guardianship of an underage heir and his lands belonged to the mother or nearest relation to the mother. The heir, moreover, should succeed on simply paying a reasonable relief according to the custom of the hundred. But now, over many years, the bailiffs had allowed neither the guardians nor the heirs to have possession until they paid a heavy fine, sometimes of 20 marks, sometimes more, sometimes less.[143] Alongside this general complaint, there were others against around twenty individual bailiffs.[144] Sometimes their crimes went unspecified. Hamo Chut, for example, like several others, was simply said to have exacted money unjustly from numerous people. Simon Kokel, on the other hand, as well as extracting 38s 6d via unspecified extortions, faced seven individual charges. His most common method of attack was to take money for remitting false accusations, accusations of being a thief, harbouring thieves and brewing against the assize of measures (one woman accused had never brewed at all).[145]

In the cases before the eyres, the victims were often, indeed generally, men and women of small account, so much being clear from the paucity of what was taken. By contrast, there were no complaints from men of baronial status. The sheriffs preyed on the first group but left the second alone. The power of the sheriffs, however, was quite able to stretch to

---

[140] *SESK*, nos. 79, 81, 83–6, 98, 100; Cassidy, '1259 pipe roll', ii, no. 4390. Thomas Albelyn was another bailiff with a wide range of activity: *SESK*, nos. 364, 383, 401, 424, 428.

[141] *SERHB*, ii, nos. 854, 857, 865.

[142] Beyond the North Downs and bordering the isle of Sheppey, the hundred centred on the royal manor of Milton and included eighteen other villages, one of them Sittingbourne. Milton Regis itself sits on a small hill and retains a fine high street with several old buildings, including an early fifteenth-century court hall with its own lock-ups. In 1264 (information from Henry Summerson) those awaiting trial were imprisoned in a mill.

[143] *SESK*, no. 392, and p. liii n. 32, for a succinct summary of gavelkind with full references.

[144] *SESK*, nos. 393–427. The situation in Milton hundred did not improve: see *RH*, i, 215–16, for the inquiry of 1275.

[145] For the bailiff of Marden, a hundred attached to Milton, being brought to book, see *SESK*, nos. 429, 431, 433–5; Cassidy, '1259 pipe roll', ii, no. 2186.

members of the knightly class. In Oxfordshire, the county coroner, Ralph de Aundely, charged the sheriff Nicholas of Hendred with extorting 20s because Aundely's miller took a toll (although it was customary) and another 4s because his men had allegedly committed the 'crime' of making charcoal at Brackley.[146] Hendred was convicted on both counts. In Warwickshire, the knight Bardolph of Chastleton accused a hundredal bailiff of seizing 60s worth of chattels from one of his villeins. The knight, Thomas de Clinton (in Gascony with the king in 1253), complained that although he and his opponent gave the sheriff, William Mansel, money to suspend the hearing of a case, it went ahead anyway, thus causing him damage of 40s.[147] Most striking of all was the conflict between Mansel and Robert Wandard, the lord of Shotteswell.[148] Wandard complained of being unjustly imprisoned until 'by force' he gave Mansel 6 marks. Wandard was also penalized to the tune of 20s for refusing to feed a boy Mansel had sent to his house. He put his total damages at 10 marks. Mansel's explanation links to the policies of the king and the attempt (in 1256) to make everyone with incomes of over £15 a year take up knighthood. Mansel had tried to force Wandard to assume the honour, but had then accepted 20s to treat him leniently and relax the distraint.[149] Wandard nonetheless had still to give the king half a mark of gold (5 marks of silver) to be exempted from knighthood, so he lost out on two counts.[150]

The jurors of Milton hundred, having listed the extortions of the bailiff, Nigel the clerk, added that 'in all other matters pertaining to his bailiwick, he behaved faithfully and well'![151] Not one of the other twenty or so bailiffs received such a testimonial, but there must surely have been sheriffs and bailiffs who, for the most part, did behave 'faithfully and well'. By its very nature, they do not appear in the record, although perhaps deductions can be made from the silence. The sheriffs and bailiffs who do appear, moreover, were sometimes acquitted of malpractice. William of Swinford, in not executing a judgement, had been following instructions from the judge himself; Gerard of Evington had not forced approvers to accuse men of theft, they had done so willingly.[152] Against the totals of

[146] In 1256, Aundely had given half a mark for an inquiry into the value of his lands to see if he was liable for knighthood: *CFR 1256-7*, no. 35. An exchequer plea roll (*SCEP*, 39–40) has the knight and former sheriff, John de Turbervill, complaining against Hendred.

[147] TNA JUST 1/953, m. 1d (image 7278); *CPR 1247-58*, 292, 298. Presumably Clinton was amerced for his non-appearance. Later he was a rebel: *CR Supp*, no. 438.

[148] For the Wandards, see Coss, *Lordship, Knighthood and Locality*, 230, 235, 260, 262–3, 299–300.

[149] TNA JUST 1/953, m. 6d (image 7287). The jury convicted Mansel on all counts and added further information about Wandard's grievances.

[150] *CFR 1255-6*, no. 945; *CPR 1247-58*, 523. Wandard seems, however, to have remained loyal during the war: *CIM*, no. 836.

[151] *SESK*, no. 415.

[152] TNA JUST 1/456, m. 9 (image 4734); *SESK*, nos. 54, 108.

men and women with whom they had to deal, the number of accusations made against all these sheriffs was small.

Yet had more material survived the catalogue of malpractice would clearly have been much greater. The types of abuse revealed by the 1258–60 eyres have many parallels before 1258 and are confirmed in over-whelming detail by the great Edwardian inquiry launched in 1274.[153] Although, moreover, officials were sometimes acquitted, they often were not. As the Glaston case shows, jurors could be just as appalled by the conduct of sheriffs as they were by that of manorial officials. When, moreover, there were convictions, Hugh Bigod saw both to reparation and to punishment. Lisle, as we have seen, was amerced to the tune of 100 marks, John of Gaddesden gave 50 marks 'for his many trespasses and the raising of new customs'.[154] Evington too was amerced.[155] Manneby was sent to gaol before claiming benefit of clergy.[156] Lashborough, Stow, Mansel and Swinford were all sentenced to gaol and amerced.[157] At a lower level, the same fate was suffered by the bailiffs of Framelund hundred in Leicestershire, Kingston and Guildford in Surrey, and Southwark and Marden hundred in Kent. In Milton hundred, fifteen bail-iffs were gaoled and or amerced.[158]

Matthew Paris only narrated in detail the crime of one sheriff, William de Lisle, but he saw this as part of a general pattern. 'In these times', he wrote (in 1256), 'nearly every sheriff in England' was worse than his pre-decessor, so that those whom the predecessor had 'flayed', the successor 'mercilessly eviscerated'.[159] There must have been many in Henry's reign who would have agreed with Nicholas Franciscus, a man with no land and chattels worth a bare 10s in Westerham in Kent. He declared in 1265 that the king's bailiffs 'deserved to be hanged for they never did good when they could do ill'.[160] Many too would have joined in heartily with the contemporary *Song of the Sheriffs*:

> Who can tell truly
> How cruel sheriffs are?

---

[153] The latter forms the basis for Cam's *The Hundred and the Hundred Rolls*.

[154] In what follows 'amercement' covers fines made in place of amercements.

[155] Cassidy, '1259 pipe roll', ii, nos. 4382, 4387.

[156] *CR 1256–9*, 262; Paris, v, 715–16. Here and in what follows one does not know whether the gaol order was actually carried out.

[157] *SERHB*, ii, nos. 438, 685; Cassidy, '1259 pipe roll', ii, no. 3316; TNA JUST 1/456, mm. 1d, 6–6d, 15d.

[158] TNA JUST 1/456, m. 15d (image 4770); *SCWR*, 110; *SESK*, nos. 79, 81, 396, 400, 408, 435; Cassidy, '1259 pipe roll', ii, nos. 2186–8, 4381, 4390, 4392.

[159] Paris, v, 576–7.

[160] *CIM*, no. 760. The occasion was when the bailiffs summoned the men of the hundred to come before the king's judges for the September 1265 inquiry into who had joined the rebellion.

Of their hardness to poor people
No tale can go too far,
If a man cannot pay,
They drag him here and there,
They put him on assizes,
The juror's oath to swear.
He dares not breathe a murmur,
Or he has to pay again,
And the saltness of the sea
Is less bitter than his pain.[161]

## MAGNATES AND THEIR MEN

Alongside the king's officials, many cases on the eyres were brought against magnates and their men. These go far beyond the treatment of the peasantry explored earlier and testify to the wide range of magnate power and rule. The plea rolls show how keen lords were to monitor events in their honours. They sought to prevent land transfers without their consent, keep control of relief, wardships, marriages and escheats, and get tenants to pay both scutage (the last for Henry's Welsh campaign of 1257) and occasional 'aids' (like that taken by Richard de Clare for the marriage of his daughter). At the heart of their power were private courts. Around twenty-five of them feature in the 1258–60 material. Although a good deal of overlap, there were three main types, that of the manor, the honour and, as a 'liberty' held from the crown, the private hundred.[162]

The business of these courts was limited by the jurisdiction of the crown. They had nothing to do with 'the pleas of the crown', the serious crimes which had to come before the king's judges. Equally, their hearing of civil pleas over land and rights had been much reduced by the development of the common law. No one was obliged to defend an action over right to a free tenement in a private court unless it had been commenced by the king's writ.[163] Having made that point two defendants, in a case before Richard de Clare's court at Thrapston in Northamptonshire, promptly got up and left.[164] Not surprisingly, many plaintiffs preferred to litigate from the start before the king's justices. But all this still left private courts with a good deal of business, as the 1258–60 plea rolls show. They could hear complaints about the seizure of goods and violence to persons. They could record transfers of property and, where the defendants

---

[161] Translated by Helen Cam from BL Harley MS 913 in her *The Hundred and the Hundred Rolls*, 106. For comment in the same vein, see Robert of Gloucester, ii, lines 11,146–62

[162] For these courts, see below 640–1.

[163] A free tenement meant land or rights held freely so not by villein tenure.

[164] *SERHB*, i, no. 363; Brand, *Kings, Barons and Justices*, 100.

agreed, hear cases over lands and rights.[165] Where possessed, the liberty of 'infangenthief' meant lords could try and hang thieves taken red-handed within the bounds of the manor or hundred.

The plea rolls of 1258–60 have numerous complaints about the functioning of private courts: complaints about being forced to attend either on a regular basis or for a particular case; complaints about the manipulation of procedures and the denial of justice, despite sometimes paying for it. The running of private hundreds gave rise to much the same grievances as when they were in the hands of the king: grievances over exactions at the tourn and the failure to pay debts into the exchequer; over false accusations and taking money for release on bail. In Roger Bigod's hundred of Loes in Suffolk, thirteen villages complained about the exaction of the *beaupleder* fine at the view of frankpledge.[166] The great weapon of enforcement, as with the king, was distraint. The roads of England seemed as clogged by animals driven away by baronial as by royal bailiffs. The beasts seized might not be returned even after successive orders from the king. Judging by the numbers of bailiffs and under-bailiffs involved, the size of the baronial posses easily rivalled the sheriff's. While bailiffs sometimes admitted they were acting on their own initiative, behind them was always the authority of their lord. One bailiff declared he had 'power through the powerful men (*potestates*) of England and through royal power', thus putting the first quite on a par with the second.[167]

## THE LUSIGNANS

The determination to exploit rights, or what were claimed as rights, is very clear in the case of William de Valence. One victim was the knight, Gilbert of Elsfield, whom we have already met. Elsfield complained of being ejected (in 1256) from his manor at Drayton in Berkshire by Valence's bailiff and 500 armed men. The doors and windows of the manor house had been broken in to effect entry, goods had been seized and fish taken from the fish pond. Elsfield put the damage at £100. The reason for this assault was the belief that the manor had escheated to Valence on the death of its lord, Alan of Farnham. Elsfield, on the other hand, claimed the manor as the inheritance of his wife, Juliana, Alan's daughter. The issue of title was not decided on the eyre but the bailiff was gaoled for breaking into the house.[168] Two other knights who fell foul of

[165] For example, *SERHB*, ii, no. 730, and see no. 422.

[166] Jacob, *Studies*, 34–5, 341–2. This is from the inquiry of the four knights in 1258.

[167] TNA JUST 1/713, m. 5 (image 9781).

[168] *SERHB*, ii, no. 477. For Drayton, see *VCH Berkshire*, iv, 241–4. The basis of Valence's claim is unclear. He did not retain the manor: *CIM*, no. 625. The bailiff was gaoled for breaking into the manor house when only told to take possession of the manor. However, the jury said the goods seized had been Alan of Farnham's not Elsfield's and his executors had been satisfied for their value.

Valence and his men, this time in Buckinghamshire, were Thomas de
St Andrew and Eustace de Grenville. The former said that bailiffs on
Valence's orders had extorted from him 17 marks and done £5 worth of
other damages. The latter complained of seizure of his cattle and damages
worth 13 marks. The cause of the quarrels is unstated but perhaps lay in
demands the two men attend Valence's court at Ashendon where or near
where they were his tenants.[169]

The running of Valence's hundred court at Bampton in Oxfordshire
certainly caused discontent. Under clever new rules introduced by his
bailiff, the inevitable William de Bussey, it became impossible to make the
excuses previously allowed for non-attendance and men unable to come
were heavily amerced for default. In addition, instead of the customary
payments of 6d and 12d before and after judgement (in effect a *beaupleder*
fine), Bussey had taken from some half a mark, from others 10s.[170]

Valence's ruthlessness is seen in another case. In 1257, on the strength of
a very conditional promise from the king, he took possession of the small
manor in Hallingbury in Essex on the death of the king's tailor, Robert de
Ros, thus disseising Ros's sister, Thomasia. Although Thomasia was present
'outside the gate' at both his coming and going, asking him to reverse the
disseisin, Valence refused to do so. When Bigod heard pleas at Stratford
in August 1258, she brought an assize of novel disseisin against Valence
and won her case.[171] The statement that Thomasia was present outside the
gate comes from the verdict of the jurors. It reflects their hostility to the
Lusignans and, in its inclusion, that of the enrolling clerk as well. Equally
indicative is the description, in another case, of William de Bussey as a
'Poitevin'. Since he was English, this was just a term of abuse.[172] The feelings of hostility to the Lusignans as Poitevin foreigners were made even
plainer by the jurors of Brixton hundred in Surrey. Silent on the eyre of
1255, they now recorded in detail the attack on Lambeth palace in 1252 by
a 'multitude of armed Poitevins' from the households of Aymer, bishop-
elect of Winchester, William de Valence and their brothers.[173]

A series of cases show how keen Aymer's officials, notably Nicholas
Achard and the unpleasantly named Gerard la Grue (the Crane), were to
defend and expand his rights and monitor events in his honour.[174] In the

---

[169] *SERHB*, ii, nos. 593–4; *RH*, i, 23, 42; Boatwright, *1286 Buckinghamshire Eyre*, 472; *VCH
Buckinghamshire*, iv, 3–7, 130–4.

[170] TNA JUST 1/713, m. 1d (images 9783–4).

[171] *SERHB*, i, no. 10; *CR 1256–9*, 89–90; *CPR 1247–58*, 577, 625; *CChR 1226–57*, 255, 366,
and see *CChR 1257–1300*, 44, 84. For the history of this part of Great Hallingbury
(Hallingbury La Walle), see *VCH Essex*, viii, 113–24.

[172] *SERHB*, i, no. 325. The description was first commented on in Hershey, 'The rise and
fall of William de Bussey', 114.

[173] *SESK*, no. 163.

[174] For an unflattering drawing of a woman, Philippa de Peauton, as a crane in the
chancery rolls of King John, see Vincent, 'King John's lost language of cranes'. However,

process they offended amongst others the Surrey knight Ralph of Imworth and the men of Southampton.[175] One of Aymer's major tenants, William de Coleville, because he refused to sell his land to the bishop-elect, was subjected to a long course of persecution. Whereas, Coleville claimed, he was merely obliged to attend fortnightly the bishop-elect's court at Winchester, he found himself compelled by heavy and frequent distraints to attend the court at Farnham in Surrey as well. Since he was given the same day for both and was prevented (despite the king's orders) from appointing attorneys, he inevitably defaulted at one or the other![176] Over the course of one year, 45 marks were extorted from him in resulting amercements. On one occasion, Coleville added, Nicholas Achard, here called the marshal of the bishop-elect's fees, had seized three of his ploughs, each joined to eight oxen and three horses, and driven them to Winchester. They were never returned. The end result was that Coleville's land had lain uncultivated for six years. His damages he put at £300. Gerard la Grue and Achard denied the charges, but the record ends abruptly before their defence was set out. At the eyre Achard was, however, amerced 10 marks for his many trespasses, another indication of missing material.[177]

## OTHER LORDS AND COURTS

It was not merely the Lusignans whose local activities created friction, however much they had a special notoriety. Conflict over attendance and procedures at private courts was widespread. At his hundred of Godley in Surrey the abbot of Chertsey's steward forced many free men to attend the court every three weeks, whereas previously they had only come once a year.[178] In Kent, the Cobhams likewise distrained men to attend the two law-days at Shamwell hundred, even when they were entirely non-resident.[179] It was the same in the north. In Yorkshire, Adam of Jesmond forced the abbot of Rievaulx to attend the court at Bingley every three weeks.[180] In Lincolnshire, when a tenant failed to appear at Philip de

---

some consider cranes very gainly birds. For Gerard la Grue, see Ridgeway, 'Ecclesiastical career of Aymer de Lusignan', 164.

[175] *SESK*, no. 147; *SERHB*, ii, no. 534. For other cases, *SESK*, no. 147; *SERHB*, ii, nos. 488, 500, 529, 534; TNA JUST 1/778, m. 13d (image 7958). For his earlier clashes with Roger Bigod, earl of Norfolk, and Robert Walerand, see Carpenter, *Reign of Henry III*, 192; Morris, *Bigod Earls of Norfolk*, 52.

[176] He was also given the same day to attend the ecclesiastical court, where Aymer was bringing a case against him.

[177] *SERHB*, ii, no. 542; Cassidy, '1259 pipe roll', ii, no. 238. Coleville's manor was at Itchel. Aymer had helped with his debts to the Jews and hence perhaps hoped to buy his land: *CFR 1242–3*, no. 608; *CR 1256–9*, 24.

[178] *SESK*, no. 117. He was convicted of this by a jury.

[179] *SESK*, no. 331; *DBM*, 140–3, cap. 4. A law-day was an especially well-attended session of the court akin to the tourn.

[180] TNA JUST 1/1049, m. 2 (image 2129).

Arcy's court of Stallingborough, he was amerced 'by judgement of the court' and then forced by the seizure of a horse to pay the amercement. A further default was followed by a further amercement and seizure. The tenant acknowledged he owed suit but denied absenteeism. Indeed, he had appeared, ready to rebut accusations of trespass against Philip, only for the bailiff to rise up and leave the court, thus stopping the case.[181] Whatever the provocation it was wise to hold one's tongue. When John of Dunwich insulted the earl of Oxford in his court at Colne in Essex, he was attacked by the earl's bailiff and a posse a dozen strong. They threw him from his horse, tied him to its tail and dragged him through a fish pond before depositing him on a dunghill![182]

With some lords, only one action was brought against them at the eyre. Others faced many accusers, a striking example being the Beauchamp lords of the barony of Bedford. After the great siege of 1224, the Beauchamps had recovered the ruins of Bedford castle but had never rebuilt it, having just a house in the inner bailey. They remained, however, major barons with many tenants in the county.[183] In 1257 a chancery clerk described William de Beauchamp as 'the count, li conte' of the county of Bedford'.[184] On Hugh Bigod's eyres of 1258–9 seven individuals brought cases, sometimes more than one case, against William, his wife, Ida, and their son, another William, the three usually appearing together.[185] Ida was there because of her high birth and the feisty part she played in family affairs.[186] William junior appeared because in 1257 the barony had been passed to him by his ageing father.[187] The plaintiffs in the cases included the clerk of the king's wardrobe, Aubrey de Fécamp, the county knight Simon of Pattishall (appointed sheriff of Bedfordshire–Buckinghamshire in 1258) and, in a long-running dispute, the abbot of Warden.[188] Much of the conflict arose from the Beauchamps' attempts to maintain authority over their honour. So they are found seeking arrears of scutage from the Welsh campaign of 1257, obstructing provision for a tenant's younger son, taking possession of a wardship and enforcing attendance at their court of Stagsden. The jurors agreed that one tenant was distrained so grievously, he was unable to cultivate his land or take any profit from it for three

---

[181] SERHB, i, no. 314. Before Hugh Bigod, both men placed themselves on the 'record of the court', and a jury was summoned, but its verdict is not given.

[182] SERHB, ii, no. 786.

[183] BF, ii, 885–8, for the fees of the barony.

[184] CR 1256–9, 79.

[185] SERHB, i, nos. 35, 147; ii, nos. 603, 610, 622–3, 625, 627, 630, 634, 636, 641, 652–3, 745.

[186] Ida was the daughter of William Longespée and Ela, in her own right countess of Salisbury.

[187] CPR 1247–58, 553; CR 1256–9, 51. William de Beauchamp junior offered the king 500 marks for the concession.

[188] For the abbot and the Beauchamps, see CR 1254–6, 153–5.

years.[189] Simon of Pattishall (a major tenant) complained of being unable to recover the animals taken despite orders from the king. As befitted a grandson of the great judge, Martin of Pattishall, he appealed to the 'law of the kingdom' and said the Beauchamps had acted 'in contempt of the king and to the injury of king's crown'.[190]

The Beauchamps were able to put significant forces in the field. In one case they were accused of mustering 300 armed men to prevent the complainant, William Pasket, taking possession of land granted him by the king's treasurer, Philip Lovel. In response, Hugh Bigod ordered the sheriff to take 'the posse of the county' and put Pasket in seisin. But, after less than a month, the Beauchamps came 'with a great multitude' to thresh the corn in the land and take it away.[191] As for Simon of Pattishall, Ida herself took revenge for all the trouble he had caused. While he was away at the exchequer, accounting as sheriff, she broke into his manor house at Little Crawley with a gang of fifteen men. According to Pattishall, they opened his chests, and seized all the sheriff's rolls and tallies as well as money collected for the king. The gang itself had a different story. They had merely come to the manor at Ida's invitation to have a good meal! The jury dismissed this laughable defence and agreed they had broken in. They had, however, taken some of Pattishall's armour, not the sheriff's rolls, tallies and money. Perhaps Pattishall had added them in to make the offence seem like one against the king as well as himself.[192]

## RICHARD OF CORNWALL

The power of the Beauchamps was as nothing compared to Richard of Cornwall's. The evil reputation of Richard's steward, Peter of Ashridge, has already been noted. In one case, he took 6 marks from someone accused of receiving a stolen piglet, when in fact the piglet had been bought quite legally from a pig-man, and anyway only cost 2d. This at any rate was the accusation. The sheriff was ordered to produce Ashridge before Hugh Bigod to answer the charge and quite failed to do so. He had, he said, passed the order on to the honour of Wallingford's bailiffs and they had done nothing about it. This was hardly surprising since Ashridge was their boss! His main job was to run the honour with its many fees across Wiltshire, Berkshire and Oxfordshire, all of them in practice

---

[189] *SERHB*, ii, no. 641. The distraint was for arrears of rent.

[190] *SERHB*, ii, no. 630; *BF*, ii, 885–7; see also *CFR 1260–1*, no. 360. For a biography of Simon, see Brand, 'Simon of Pattishall'.

[191] *SERHB*, i, no. 35; ii, nos. 603, 623; *CR 1256–9*, 299.

[192] TNA KB 26/167, m. 13 (image 0034); TNA KB 26/167, m. 2d (image 0083); Jacob, *Studies*, 223 n. 2. Ida's attack on Little Crawley was sufficiently notorious to be mentioned in the Dunstable annals. She is said there to have pulled down houses and set fire to trees: Dunstable, 215.

exempt from shrieval interference.[193] Even the limited information available (for little survives from these counties) shows Ashridge and his colleagues acting with a will. In Oxfordshire's Ploughley hundred, in the villages held from the honour, they imposed heavier burdens at the view of frankpledge.[194] Coming up against one of the honour's major knightly tenants, Sampson Foliot (a later sheriff), they took peat from his woods and pastured King Richard's animals in his fields and meadow.[195]

Most striking of all were the events at Chesterton, also in Ploughley hundred, as revealed by the complaints of the coroner, again Ralph de Aundely.[196] Here (in 1254) when a thief took sanctuary in the village church, Aundely and the king's bailiff in the hundred, Thomas the Beadle, summoned men from the four nearest villages to witness the thief abjuring the realm. Since Chesterton itself was held from the honour of Wallingford, they also summoned men from villages belonging to the honour. Then all hell broke loose. Peter of Ashridge was furious they had acted 'without the bailiff of the honour and against its liberties'. He got the sheriff to seize Aundely and 'whatever he had in the world' and eventually extorted 10 marks from him for 'exercising his office within the boundaries of the honour'. Aundely considered all this as done 'against the crown and dignity of the king'. He did not suffer alone. Thomas the Beadle was also arrested, threatened with imprisonment in Wallingford castle and accused of acting 'in contempt' of the earl. In the end, by Ashridge's will, without any judicial procedure, Thomas was made to pay 20s. Surely, as he said, this was to the shame of the king whose minister he was.[197] If all this was designed to teach a lesson it worked. On the 1261 Oxfordshire eyre the jurors reported that Ralph de Aundely did not dare hold an inquest on another dead body, remembering the 10 marks Ashridge had extorted from him earlier.[198]

The earl of Cornwall's officials were equally active in protecting or expanding the liberties of another honour, that of St Valery. According to a case from the 1255 Hampshire eyre, *'per vim and potestatem suam'*, they forced all the tenants to attend its court (probably held at Beckley in Oxfordshire), with the result they no longer attended the courts of the hundred.[199] The tenants did not themselves complain. Their plight, if

---

[193] For the honour, see Tilley, 'The honour of Wallingford 1066–1300'.

[194] TNA JUST 1/713, mm. 3d–4 (images 9777–9).

[195] TNA JUST 1/713, m. 3 (image 9778).

[196] For what follows, see *SCWR*, 107–8; for Chesterton, see *VCH Oxfordshire*, vi, 92–103.

[197] Ashridge rejected the charges and called Richard of Cornwall to warrant. There was no verdict in the case. Another complaint of multiple persecution was made by the rector of the church where the thief fled: *SCWR*, 106–7.

[198] Jobson, '1261 Oxfordshire Eyre', ii, no. 505.

[199] TNA JUST 1/778, m. 11 (image 7822). For the earl's liberty of Eye 'which no sheriff dare enter', see *CRR*, xix, no. 1503.

such it was, emerged in the course of another lawsuit.[200] They were wise to keep silent given that behind the officials was Earl Richard himself. The Chesterton affair took place in 1253–4 while he was regent of the kingdom. Indeed, Richard himself, according to Ashridge, had instructed the sheriff of Oxfordshire to seize Ralph de Aundely's goods.

## ARCHBISHOP BONIFACE IN KENT

In the case of Earl Richard, or King Richard as he was by 1258, there are only occasional glimpses of his local power. A more concentrated picture comes from Kent and concerns the officials of Boniface of Savoy, no fewer than fifteen of them appearing in the record.[201] They were involved in running Boniface's private hundreds, administering his manors and exercising the rights over his tenants. The accusations against them will be familiar: false accusations, harsh imprisonment, failure to pay debts into the exchequer, unjust disseisin and distraint. In one case, the jurors stated that the bailiffs had come with 300 armed men to seize an individual's plough, ox and cow. This had been done to raise money owed the king but was 'not in the manner in which a king's bailiff ought to make distraint'. Asked by Hugh Bigod whether the village had previously impeded the raising of a debt, the jurors answered 'no'! There were also accusations of increased burdens at the hundred courts and attempts to overturn the rights of those holding in gavelkind. The truth of the latter allegation was to be investigated by knights from the five lathes into which the Kentish hundreds were divided.[202]

Two earlier cases before the Kentish eyre of 1255 show the invocation of spiritual penalties to support the archbishop's rights. When the men of Faversham judged and hanged a thief, despite the archbishop's bailiffs claiming he was the archbishop's man, they were excommunicated till they paid a fine of £100. The bailiffs then dug up the body and buried it at the archiepiscopal manor of Teynham.[203] The other case concerned events in Maidstone hundred, an archiepiscopal hundred but one where the king retained some rights. The trouble arose when the king's bailiff distrained one John de Brok for a debt owed the king and began to drive the animals seized towards Rochester castle. When, however, the bailiff broke his journey overnight, the next morning a posse, sent by the archbishop's

---

[200] The lord of this private hundred demanded various individuals to attend its court. They then explained why they no longer did so.

[201] For the cases involving Boniface and his bailiffs, see *SESK*, nos. 217, 278, 292, 333, 335, 338, 346, 350, 359, 370–1, 374, 377, 379, 383–6, 390. For the archbishop's hundreds in Kent, see Cam, *The Hundred and the Hundred Rolls*, 270–2. On the eyre there were verdicts for four of them and another four held jointly with the king.

[202] *SESK*, nos. 335, 374, 384–5. The verdict is not recorded. For the issue, see Du Boulay, *The Lordship of Canterbury*, 144–5.

[203] TNA JUST 1/361, m. 50 (image 3340).

steward, Richard of Shearsted, both recovered the cattle and took the bailiff's men off to imprisonment at Maidstone. The bailiff himself had his plough and oxen seized and then, excommunicated, was whipped round Maidstone church on three successive Sundays. Both cases demonstrate, in the digging up of the body and the whipping, how very publicly the archbishop's rights were vindicated.[204]

## RICHARD DE CLARE

There was one other great baronial player in Kent, of course, Richard de Clare, earl of Hertford and Gloucester. The gigantic gatehouse that Clare built at Tonbridge castle remains, a stunning combination of military might and decorative finesse, the most imposing demonstration of baronial power to survive in England from the thirteenth century. On the outside, the gateway reaches high under layered arches, surrounded on either side by great drum towers. On the side facing the inner bailey, flanking towers contain spiral staircases, while the main room is lit by two windows composed of trefoiled lancets and roundels, the framing arch above being supported by grimacing heads, while 'even the arrow loops are externally ornamented with delicate mouldings'.[205] The overall structure was probably influenced by Henry III's new gateway at the Tower of London. In its sophistication as well as its might, the gatehouse makes all the more understandable Clare's desire to play a part on both the national and international stage.

In Kent, Clare had many knightly tenants while Tonbridge castle was surrounded by the 'lowy' of Tonbridge, an extensive jurisdictional area from which the sheriff was excluded.[206] In Surrey, too, there were many tenants and a great base, around twenty miles from Tonbridge, at Bletchingley where there was a borough and another castle.[207] On Bigod's eyre a jury convicted Clare's steward of seizing eight cows, eight oxen and seven heifers from Denise de Munchesney's manor at Nutfield and driving them to Bletchingley. The reason was not stated but, as the jury said, this was 'distraint out of fee' since Nutfield belonged not to a Clare honour but to that of Boulogne. Perhaps the fact that Bletchingley and Nutfield are only two miles apart was a cause of friction. Denise was a very different proposition from the reeve of Yalding imprisoned in Tonbridge castle by the odious Quintin. She was the widow of the great baron Warin de

---

[204] TNA JUST 1/361, m. 42d (image 3467). The jurors made the point that the distraint took place outside the archbishop's liberty.

[205] Goodall, *The English Castle*, 191.

[206] See Hasted, *History of Kent*, v, 173–6. I recommend Deborah Cole's *The Tonbridge Knights Walk*, on sale at the castle. It has fourteen walks around the perimeter of the lowy as perambulated by a panel of knights in 1279. For a settlement of disputes between Richard de Clare and Archbishop Boniface, see Du Boulay, *The Lordship of Canterbury*, 85–7 and 295–6.

[207] For the Kent and Surrey fees, *BF*, ii, 671–2, 684–5.

Munchesney and an heiress (Nutfield was part of her inheritance). On Warin's death she had rejected the prospective husband chosen for her by the king (the Poitevin Guy de Rochefort) and married someone else, paying 200 marks for permission to do so.[208] It says something that Clare's men thought nothing of taking on this distinguished and wealthy woman.

The steward involved in the Nutfield case, Roger de Scaccario, was active elsewhere.[209] Indeed, the complaints on the eyres reveal the geographical range of Clare's power. Apart from Kent and Surrey, they came from Oxfordshire, Gloucestershire, Hampshire, Buckinghamshire, Huntingdonshire, Essex and Northamptonshire. The officials committed the usual abuses within private hundreds,[210] seized wardships into Clare's hands, monitored land transactions and asserted that no one had the right to take a toll within the honour of Gloucester without the lord's permission.[211] The numbers of named bailiffs rivalled those of the archbishop in Kent. Clare's courts feature again and again. Indeed, of the twenty-five or so private courts mentioned in the eyres around half were his.

Most striking of all is the role of the court held at Clare in Suffolk for the tenants of the honour, or allegedly of the honour, many of them living distances away. 'All splendour' has now departed wrote R.A. Brown about the site of the castle, but from the top of the motte, 260 metres in circumference at the base and 30 metres high, one can still make out the castle's great extent.[212] Three Essex landowners and one from Buckinghamshire won cases complaining of distraint out of fee, distraint made to compel attendance at the court, in the Essex cases to answer individual charges, in the Buckinghamshire one to do regular suit there.[213] One of the Essex victims was the knight Hugh of Culworth, whose father had been, at various times sheriff of both Northamptonshire (where Culworth was) and Essex–Hertfordshire. Here, Hugh Bigod sentenced the bailiff responsible for the distraints to gaol and took considerable pains to see the damages awarded (over £10) were paid.[214] On one occasion the steward of the Clare

---

[208] *SESK*, nos. 68, 73; *CPR 1247–58*, 420, 543; *VCH Surrey*, iii, 222–9; Cokayne, *Complete Peerage*, ix, 421–2. The husband was Robert (or Richard) Butler. For her, see Clanchy, *From Memory to Written Record*, 198; Cokayne, *Complete Peerage*, ix, 424. Her son William became a leading supporter of Simon de Montfort.

[209] Roger de Scaccario is sometimes described as the earl's former steward, though whether he had been dismissed for malpractice we do not know. He appears in a different light as one of the founders of the Austin friary at Clare: *Clare Cartulary*, 3 and nos. 14–17.

[210] For Clare's hundred at Chadlington in Oxfordshire, see Jobson, '1261 Oxfordshire Eyre', ii, no. 664.

[211] For this last episode (and the resulting conflict with the burgesses of Southampton), see *SERHB*, i, no. 17.

[212] Brown, *Castles from the Air*, 90.

[213] *SERHB*, ii, nos. 588, 802, 805, 858.

[214] *SERHB*, ii, nos. 800–1, 805, 899, 967. There is much about the Culworths in the usual printed sources. Hugh was bringing the case with his mother, Philippa, herself an heiress.

honour, Roger de Scaccario again, was acquitted of commanding a distraint. Indeed, at the earl of Oxford's instance, he had ordered the animals seized to be returned. But in another case, the jury, having come down against him, added that 'he made many such kinds of distraints outside the fee of his lord'.

The most detailed account of Scaccario at work comes from a Buckinghamshire case. Here he ordered his under-bailiff to distrain Robert de Cauceys to perform suit at the court of Clare on the grounds that Cauceys held his manor of Caldecote from the honour. The distraint was severe. Cauceys, so he said, was unable to cultivate his land and had to offer several marks to get his animals back. In the end, since Clare was some sixty miles from Caldecote, he offered money to be allowed to attend the earl's court at Stewkley, half a dozen miles away, instead. There he did suit once every three weeks, something he had never done before. What made this all the more illegitimate was that, as the jury said, Cauceys held neither from the honour of Clare nor from the fee of Stewkley, and should have attended neither court. He did hold from Richard de Clare, but from the honour of Giffard.[215] Cauceys had not the status of Denise de Munchesney but he was still a man of some account. After the civil war he was appointed to collect the revenues from the lands of rebels within Moulsoe hundred where his lands lay.[216]

There were also complaints about procedures within the earl's courts. Alice, daughter of Nicholas, alleged that she had given Scaccario 10s, for the earl's use, to bring a case in the court of Stambourne. It was about a trespass done her by one of the earl's tenants. She had attended several courts, only to find Scaccario unwilling to give her justice. The jury agreed and Scaccario was ordered to return the money.[217] In the court of Thrapston in Northamptonshire, although the defendants had refused to answer without a writ of the king, and indeed had left the court, the bailiff went ahead anyway and gave the plaintiffs possession of the disputed land.[218] At Fairford in Gloucestershire likewise litigants were cheated out of land through court procedures to which they had not agreed, this time the beneficiary being the earl's bailiff.[219] At Clare itself, in a dispute over land outside the earl's fee, a man was forced by distraint to answer in the court and was imprisoned when he got there until 2½ marks were given to the earl's bailiffs for the earl's use.[220] The knight Eustace de Grenville did rather better in the same court. He complained of an

---

[215] *SEHRB*, ii, no. 588.
[216] *VCH Buckinghamshire*, iv, 289–93; *CIM*, no. 632. 'Cauceys' is spelt in many different ways, often without a 'de'. I have used the spelling in the plea roll. He had a second manor at Bow Brickhill alongside Caldecote (both quite small).
[217] *SERHB*, ii, no. 839.
[218] *SERHB*, i, no. 363.
[219] *SERHB*, ii, nos. 421–2, but *SERHB*, ii, no. 730; *PQW*, 278.
[220] *SERHB*, ii, no. 964.

assault: he had been thrown from his palfrey, trampled underfoot and given three great wounds on his head with an axe. The court agreed, but, as the earl's steward, Hervey of Boreham, admitted, no damages had been awarded, the excuse being that Eustace was a knight and more counsel was needed as to the appropriate amount. It was left to Bigod himself to tax the damages at 10 marks.[221] It says something for the authority and utility of the court at Clare that Grenville decided to litigate there although he claimed the assault breached the king's peace.

Just how intent Richard de Clare was to defend his liberties emerges in a case, outside the eyres, recorded by Tewkesbury abbey. It concerned the earl's hundred court at Cranborne in Dorset and his bailiffs' determination to try and hang there thieves caught red-handed in the adjoining Tewkesbury manor of Monkton Up Wimborne, this in defiance of the abbot's claim to try and hang them at Up Wimborne itself. The matter was so serious that the abbot thrice made his case in person to the earl, after all the abbey's patron, only to find him 'cruel' and concerned to stage a proper inquiry into the abbot's rights. Had the liberty claimed, the earl asked, ever been actually used? It was only when going abroad that Clare eventually, without prejudice to his rights, allowed the trial of the latest thief to go ahead at Up Wimborne. However, he stipulated that, if convicted, the thief must still be hanged on his gallows at Cranborne. The abbot assembled a large court and made a record of the pathetic sequel. The thief was called John Milksop of Cranborne. He was now accused of stealing at night, in the house of a certain widow, 31d from the purse of Walter Wymond of Bristol. With the hue and cry raised he had been caught red-handed in a nearby wood. On trial, Milksop was able to say 'nothing which might help him'. So he was convicted and sentenced to hang. The record failed to add where he was hanged, so almost certainly, in accordance with the earl's instructions, he was led to Cranborne, four miles away, for execution.[222]

## THE SITUATION IN SOUTH-EAST SUSSEX

I have left till last the evidence from the pleas heard in Sussex in December 1260 by Hugh Despenser, Hugh Bigod's successor.[223] They give a remarkable picture of magnate power in the south of the county between Pevensey and Chichester. Just how ready officials were to defend their

[221] *SERHB*, ii, no. 871. The assailant was one William fitzRichard.

[222] Tewkesbury, 142, 511–16.

[223] TNA JUST 1/911. There are both new cases and a continuation of ones found in TNA JUST 1/911 in TNA JUST 1/537, where the pleas were heard at the Tower of London early in 1261. Some of the cases are printed in Jacob, *Studies*, 353–65, and *SCWR*, 122–34. For an analysis, see Jacob, *Studies*, 109–15. He rightly comments on the remarkable nature of the evidence. I am grateful to Christopher Whittick for helping me in many ways with the Sussex material.

master's interests, sometimes against the mightiest in the land, is seen from the action of Hugh Bigod's own bailiff. Because three greyhounds, two of Simon de Montfort's, one of Henry of Almain's, were led on a leash through Hugh's warren at Bosham, his bailiff lamed each dog by cutting off nearly an entire foot. The limping hounds were brought before Despenser. Since by this time, in December 1260, Bigod and Montfort had fallen out in a big way (as we will see), the crime was perhaps politically motivated. It was certainly considered by a jury from the three Sussex rapes to be an 'enormous' breach of the king's peace, done to Montfort's and Almain's shame and dishonour. The bailiff was sentenced to gaol and ordered to pay damages (taxed by all the knights of the county) at 40 marks and one leash.[224]

Another bailiff sentenced to gaol for brutality was William de Briouze's in the honour of Bramber, though this time the victim was a human, William of Badgeworth. Arrested during a sweep for thieves, although no stolen property was found on him, William was allowed to go to Badgeworth (in Gloucestershire) and get letters from the court there testifying to his good conduct. But when he returned and entered the court at Bramber, the bailiff refused to accept the letters and imprisoned him in a tower. There he was placed in irons and made to sit naked during the day. At night, although given a tunic, a pit was excavated under him and filled with cold water. As a result, his limbs had putrified and his life was despaired of. His story was confirmed by a jury of seventy-six men, drawn from the rapes of Arundel, Chichester and Bramber.[225]

The Sussex pleas also show the power wielded by John de Warenne's bailiffs from their great bastion at Lewes castle.[226] John de Burgh, son of the old justiciar, thus complained of a whole series of seizures from his manor at Portslade and put his damages at £100.[227] Another complainant was a Lewes merchant, whose ship at Seaford had been seized. (It was ready to sail with its thirteen crew and 80 marks to make purchases, presumably of wine, in Gascony.) Warenne's bailiff at Lewes was acquitted on this count but was convicted of shutting up the merchant's house in Lewes (violently taking the keys from his wife) until he was given 12 marks.[228]

In neither of these Warenne cases was an appeal made to the sheriff for help. He could indeed be of limited use as Robert of Cliffe (probably

---

[224] *SCWR*, 122–4; *CChR 1226–57*, 375. The damages were awarded to the man leading the dogs.

[225] TNA JUST 1/911, m.8 (image 1936).

[226] There is a full analysis of John de Warenne's power in Sussex in Spencer, *Nobility and Kingship* 158–70.

[227] TNA JUST 1/911, m. 15d (image 1991); *BF*, ii, 690. After the battle of Evesham, John de Warenne seized Portslade from John de Burgh: *CIM*, no. 918.

[228] TNA JUST 1/911, m. 7 (images 1933–4). The merchant's name was John le Beure, the bailiff Thomas de Ponte. The dispute was a private one.

Cliffe outside Lewes) found to his cost. Cliffe complained of 200 sheep and 6 oxen being driven to Warenne's manor at Rodmell. The culprits were Warenne's steward, the knight John de la Ware and four others. Cliffe twice asked the sheriff, Gerard of Evington, to intervene and recover the animals according to the law of the land. But Evington confessed he could do nothing 'on account of the might and power of John and the others'. In the end the two went to the exchequer, where Evington was ordered (a well-known procedure) to seize Ware's cattle, until he delivered Cliffe's.[229] This time Evington did act. He took cattle from Ware's manor of Folkingham (south-east of Lewes), and Cliffe's animals were restored. Retribution soon followed. Cliffe was seized by Ware, beaten up and put in the stocks at Lewes castle. A horse worth 10 marks was stolen from him as were 40 shillings in money. Cliffe put his damages at 200 marks. These events took place in 1257. This time Cliffe sought no redress until Despenser's eyre at the end of 1260.[230]

And so to Peter of Savoy. We have already seen how he raised the peasants' rents at Witley in Surrey. The men of Lincoln were equally bitter at the way he jacked up the toll they paid at St Botolph's fair.[231] In Essex, the knight Richard de Rumilly complained of having his animals driven into Cambridgeshire and detained there. He was being made to attend the two tourns at Peter's court at Finchingfield, although he only had fifteen acres there and no house.[232] These cases, however, are but faint echoes of the trouble caused by Peter's officials running his honour of Pevensey. They are by far the most striking cases to come before Hugh Despenser, striking both because of the number of the complainants and their high social level.[233] The chief culprits were Peter's stewards, Geoffrey de Brayboeuf and John de la Rede, but behind them stood very much Peter himself. He appeared before Despenser in person and vouched for all the actions of his men.

Peter had been granted the castle and honour of Pevensey in 1246.[234] He had rebuilt the castle, providing it with the curtain walls and drum towers (like those at the Tower of London) surviving to this day.[235] Symbol and sanction of his power, no one, seeing the new walls, could doubt Peter's determination to stamp his authority on the surrounding area. That authority was great. As he explained to Despenser, three special

---

[229] Around this time the exchequer was informed that when the sheriff sent bailiffs to seize cattle to get Warenne to pay his debts, the cattle were seized back 'against the peace': TNA E 159/31, m. 8d (image 0100).

[230] *SCWR*, 126–7. There are still stocks at Lewes castle and students from my Special Subject groups sometimes tried them out, a painful exercise.

[231] TNA JUST 1/1197, image 1521.

[232] *SERHB*, ii, no. 821. Finchingfield was part of the honour of Richmond.

[233] It was usually called either the honour of Laigle or Mortain after previous holders.

[234] *CChR 1226–57*, 296, 342, 410–12.

[235] See Goodall, *Pevensey Castle*.

liberties belonged to the honour. The lord had the right to all the goods from wrecks washed up between Pevensey and Seaford. He had the right of warren in all the lands once of the count of Mortain, the original holder of the honour, no matter who now held them. This meant, in those areas, he enjoyed the exclusive right to hunt the hare, fox and cat.[236] And, finally, attached to the honour were nine and a half private hundreds. (These lay to the west of the jurisdictional area around Pevensey itself, 'the lowy of Pevensey', and stretched from the coast as far north as East Grinstead.) At the court held outside the gate of Pevensey castle, Peter added, he had the right to try all trespasses connected with wreck and warren. A corollary was that it was perfectly legitimate for his officials to carry out distraints outside his fees to compel attendance at the court.[237]

Small fry were very much at the mercy of Peter's officials. The vicar of Eastdean had two oxen seized outside Peter's fee and driven to Pevensey, this to make him attend the court outside the castle gate. When there, told to enter the castle, the vicar was accused of trying to spy out Peter's treasure and imprisoned in a tower. He was then summoned to attend the court outside the gate and amerced 40s for his absence, despite shouting out where he was. The bailiff's account was different. The 40s had been imposed by judgement of the court because the vicar had taken three casks of wreck wine. Although, moreover, Eastdean was outside Peter's fee it was within his warren.[238]

Disputes over rights of wreck lay at the heart of quarrels with altogether more significant opponents. They included the baron William Bardolph, distrained out of fee to attend the Pevensey court,[239] and the Bestnover family, both prosperous merchants and considerable landholders. In the latter case men from the ports of Hastings and Pevensey complained that the Bestnovers had suffered '*superfattuosa* distraint', with 1,300 sheep, eight sacks of wool and chattels worth £100 all being seized. It cost the Bestnovers 45 marks to get everything back, by which time the sheep had been sheared. Meanwhile, Robert of Bestnover, besieged in his house for fifteen days 'as though in a castle', was unable to take his merchandise to the fair at Lille. Twenty-four jurors from the rapes of Hastings and Pevensey, plus six knights, agreed with these charges. The bailiff, John de la Rede, was sentenced to gaol and ordered to pay damages of 100 marks.[240]

---

[236] For warren, see *SPF*, cxxiii–xxxiv, and for grants of rights of warren under Henry III, Crook, 'The "Petition of the Barons" and charters of free warren'. With typical attention to detail, Peter had got the area of the warren defined in 1252: *CChR 1226–57*, 410; *CPR 1247–58*, 161.

[237] Jacob, *Studies*, 363, and TNA JUST 1/537, m. 1 (image 3146).

[238] Jacob, *Studies*, 361–4. The case, like many others, was adjourned to Easter 1261 and almost certainly never proceeded as by then the country was on the brink of civil war.

[239] Jacob, *Studies*, 355–61. In defence of his rights of wreck in 1260, Peter had brought a case against John de Warenne: TNA KB 26/ 165, m. 20 (image 0243).

[240] Jacob, *Studies*, 355–66.

A further cause of conflict was Peter's warren, not surprisingly since local landholders had their own woods within it. Some indeed had secured their own charters of warren from the king, thus creating a jumble of conflicting and overlapping rights. The complainants included John de la Haye, a leading follower of Simon de Montfort, Ralph Harengod, one of four Hampshire knights appointed for the inquiry of 1258, and Amfrid of Ferring, sheriff of Sussex in 1254–5.[241]

Another knightly complainant, and later a leading rebel, was John de la Ware, whom we have already met as the exacting steward of John de Warenne. Ware's grievances were across the board. He was not allowed to hunt on his own land, and had his greyhounds confiscated and his nesting falcons seized. (They were within Peter's warren where all falcons were claimed as his.) Ware's men were distrained, to answer at Pevensey for taking clothes and other things from washed-up bodies, while two casks of his own wine, claimed as wreck, were seized from his cart. There was also a clash over jurisdiction. A villein's house at Chalvington, where thieves were imprisoned before judgement at Ware's manorial court, was broken into at night and the thieves taken for trial at Peter's hundred court at Eastbourne. Ware put the damages for this breach of a liberty enjoyed 'from time out of mind' at £100.[242] Another prominent knight, William Marmion, complained about the taking of the *beaupleder* fine in the hundred court of Longbridge, this, as he said, in breach of the new legislation, meaning the Provisions of Westminster.[243]

In all these cases Peter of Savoy's bailiffs appear violent and aggressive. Yet they were often doing no more than defending what they claimed were Peter's rights, as would the bailiffs, given proper backing, of any other great lord. In one *beaupleder* case, the jurors agreed that the payment had been enjoyed by Peter's predecessors. Jurors from the rapes of Pevensey, Hastings and Lewes likewise agreed that Ralph Harengod's hounds *had* been in Peter's wood. As for the cutting of Ralph's trees, they were unable to say in whose wood they were, so long had there been contention over the matter. As the majority of cases were unconcluded, the claims made for Pevensey's liberties were never tested. What is clear, however, is that Peter's arrival had caused turmoil in the area. When, in 1259, he arranged for the honour to pass on his death to Queen Eleanor, William Marmion, William Bardolph, John de la Haye, Ralph Harengod and John de Warenne all put in their own unspecified counter-claims.[244]

---

[241] TNA Just 1/537, m. 4 (image 3152); *CChR 1226–57*, 412; TNA JUST 1/537, m. 3 (image 3150); TNA JUST 1/911, m. 18d (image 1983).
[242] TNA JUST 1/537, mm. 1, 2, 3 (images 3146–51); TNA JUST 1/911, m. 18d (image 1983); Jacob, *Studies*, 364–5.
[243] Jacob, *Studies*, 354–5; Brand, *Kings, Barons and Justices*, 120–1.
[244] TNA CP 25/1/283/15/358.

## THE EYRE AND REFORM OF THE REALM

In light of the evidence from the eyres, much that happened between 1258 and 1259 becomes explicable. The sheer number of complaints, their ventilation through hundredal juries, the verdicts of the trial juries, the damages awarded by Hugh Bigod and the punishments he imposed on erring officials reflect the levels of local discontent. The eyre itself seems absolutely necessary as does the wider reform of the realm.

A key aspect of the reform was, of course, the expulsion from England of the king's Lusignan half-brothers. The tide of hostility engulfing them is very apparent from the eyres. The complainants included individual peasants and peasant communities, county knights and leading members of the regime. The labelling of the Lusignans and their officials as 'Poitevins' shows how hostility to foreigners gave an edge to the critique. Given the trouble Peter of Savoy created in Sussex, that the Savoyards survived in 1258 while the Lusignans departed was thanks to the politics of the court. There was not much difference to their activities on the ground.

The material equally illuminates the pressure to reform the sheriff's office. Those who suffered at shrieval hands included manorial lords like Ralph de Aundely, Bardolph of Chastleton, Thomas de Clinton and Robert Waundard, as well as numerous lesser fry. No wonder the office was completely overhauled, with the sheriff becoming a substantial county knight, bound by an oath, promised a salary and holding office only for a year. The way the oath obliged the sheriffs to reduce the number and regulate the conduct of their subordinates is equally understandable given the multitude of abusive bailiffs found working in hundreds like that of Milton Regis in Kent. In terms of detail, the *beaupleder* fine, abolished by the legislation of 1259, was complained about again and again on the eyres.[245] So were the exactions at the tourn, hence the legislation insisted it should be held in accordance with Magna Carta, and also exempted lords from having to attend unless they actually lived in the hundreds concerned.[246]

Likewise understandable are the attempts to bring the peasantry within the scope of reform. Lords in 1258 must have been very aware of manorial discontents. If they faced no general peasants' revolt, there were many individual pockets of protest and resistance. If the reaction of some lords was simply to batten down the hatches, for others the teaching of reformist bishops and friars gained all the more point and purchase. True, there was no question of the reforms altering the legal rules doing down the unfree. In one case before Hugh Bigod, a disseisin committed by Simon de

---

[245] Brand, *Kings, Barons and Justices*, 87–90, with 418–19, cap. 5, for the correct texts.
[246] *DBM*, 84–5, caps. 17–18; 140–3, cap. 4; Brand, *Kings, Barons, Justices*, 83–7.

Montfort was justified on the grounds the plaintiff was a villein.[247] There was also tension about how much to give the peasantry. The Provisions of Westminster swung to and fro over the obligation of village communities to attend the tourn. A limitation, present in an early draft, was omitted from the final text.[248] But the rhetoric of the period spoke of giving justice to the free and unfree alike and it was not just talk.[249] The Provisions of Westminster benefited peasant communities both in abolishing the *murdrum* fine in cases of misadventure and in exempting villages from amercements because all over the age of twelve had not come to coroners' and other inquests. There was also potential benefit in the stipulation that the tourn and view of frankpledge be held in accordance with Magna Carta.[250]

The complaints explain why the conduct of seigneurial officials and the running of private courts became such a big issue. The prominence of private courts and the abuses connected with them is indeed one of the most striking features of the eyres. In response, the Provisions of Westminster limited attendance to where it was required by a charter of enfeoffment or had customarily been performed before 1230.[251] It also provided remedies for those distrained to attend in breach of these rules: animals seized were to be immediately restored, with damages being awarded by judgement of the court.[252] Another chapter forbad distraint out of fee, a practice complained about constantly on the eyres.[253] The existing rule that tenants need not answer for their free tenements in a private court without a writ from the king was affirmed, thus responding precisely to the case in Richard de Clare's court at Thrapston.[254] The legislation on *beaupleder* and the tourn applied to private as much as royal courts. Indeed, the rule exempting non-residents from attending the tourn

---

[247] *SERHB*, i, no. 167.

[248] Brand, *Kings, Barons and Justices*, 86–7; Carpenter, *Reign of Henry III*, 346.

[249] See above, 45.

[250] *DBM*, 146–7, caps. 21–2; Brand, *Kings, Barons and Justices*, 77–82. The issue of attendance at inquests is discussed below. The *murdrum* fine was paid by peasant communities when they did not prove that someone who had been killed feloniously or had died through misadventure (including starvation) was English, meaning in practice of servile birth. It threatened to become a terrible burden in 1258 when large numbers of unidentifiable vagrants were dying in the famine. Hence the legislation limited the fine to deaths by felony.

[251] *DBM*, 138–9, cap. 1. Brand, *Kings, Barons and Justices*, 43–53, gives a full discussion of the legislation and the issue of suit. The legislation, however, applied to honourial courts but not private hundreds, although that was clearly a major issue.

[252] *DBM*, 138–41, cap. 3.

[253] *DBM*, 144–7, nos. 11, 17; Brand, *Kings, Barons and Justices*, 94–8.

[254] *SERHB*, i, no. 363; *DBM*, 146–7, cap. 18. The chapter also forbad free tenants being forced to take an oath without a writ of the king. See Brand, *King, Barons and Justices*, 99–103.

fitted precisely the case of the knight, Richard de Rumilly, made to attend Peter of Savoy's court at Finchingfield.[255] Likewise the extraordinary detail in which the Ordinances of the Magnates sought to regulate the conduct of subordinate bailiffs is readily explicable given what the eyres reveal about their numbers and excesses.

Quite probably, knights who brought to the eyres their grievances against great lords were members of 'the community of the bachelery of England' which pushed through the 1259 legislation. Certainly an impressive number of knights spoke out on the eyres, many of them later rebels: Ralph of Imworth (killed at Lewes), Gilbert of Elsfield (killed at Evesham), Sampson Foliot, Ralph de Aundely, Simon of Pattishall, William de Coleville, Hugh of Culworth, Thomas de St Andrew, Richard de Rumilly, Jordan of Whitacre and,[256] in Sussex, John de la Ware, John de la Haye, Amfrid of Ferring, Ralph Harengod (another killed at Lewes) and William Marmion. Marmion appealed to the legislation abolishing the *beaupleder* fine, 'recently made in the general parliament of the lord king by the counsel of the princes and magnates of the kingdom of England'.[257] It sounds as though he was there. Such men could, of course, be oppressors as well as oppressed: John de la Ware appears, on the one hand, as John de Warenne's abusive bailiff, on the other as abused by the bailiff of Peter of Savoy. Yet, as the cases on the eyre show, there was a clear divide between knights and greater lords when it came to suit of court. Most knights had nothing like the latter's courts of honour and hundred and had everything to gain from legislation restricting both the obligation to attend and the distraint out of fee compelling them to do so.

## HOW BAD WAS THE SITUATION DURING HENRY'S PERSONAL RULE?

While many of the grievances ventilated on the eyres had been festering for years, the record by itself does not make it easy to gauge how far matters were getting worse. Here there can be differences of view. In one of his essays, Sir Maurice Powicke developed the idea that in the thirteenth century, more perhaps than at any other time in the medieval period, 'England was able to cope with herself . . . I mean that the *tempo* is more even, that the measure of agreement was greater . . . that the response to fresh influences or new tasks was clearer, and, if I may use the word, happier'. Powicke accordingly found 'difficulty in visualizing' the bad government complained about in 1258. The evidence 'seems to me to testify, not to any peculiar enormity, but to the persistence with which

---

[255] The same issue arose in Kent at the Cobham's hundred of Shamwell; see above, 145.

[256] For Jordan of Whitacre complaining of distraint out of fee at the hands of Peter de Montfort, see below, 364.

[257] Brand, *Kings, Barons and Justices*, 120–1.

abuses were investigated'.[258] In other words, there was just more testing! There is obviously some truth in this view. If people are invited to complain, they complain and not always fairly, as the jurors sometimes said. And while the forms and framework may vary, was it not always thus? When, starting my doctorate, I met for the only time the distinguished historian Sir Goronwy Edwards (then in his eighties), he told me that the older and wiser he got the more he believed in the tyranny of local officials. He was talking about medieval officials in general, not just those in the time of Henry III.

In support of his view that, in Henry's reign, 'men of good will' were responding positively to new tasks, Powicke might have pointed to something else revealed by the eyres. For they surely reflect one of the great successes of Henry's reign, namely the gigantic expansion of litigation in the king's courts according to the forms of the common law.[259] On Hugh Bigod's eyres, whereas there were 319 *querelae*, there were 1,349 other items of business, most of it common law assizes.[260] Some of the latter were actions against royal and baronial officials, but the majority were much like the general run of cases found in the eyre rolls, namely cases arising from disputes between neighbours and within families about comparatively small amounts of land and money. When the judges visited Warwick, early in 1260, the first cases heard involved disputes over a 20d rent, a 3s 3d rent, one messuage, six acres of common pasture, two messuages and four tofts, three acres of meadow, ten acres of land and the diversion of water so it no longer fed a mill.[261] Under Henry, more than ever before, the common law was dealing for the most part fairly and expeditiously with the concerns of ordinary people, reducing the likelihood of a resort to violence and helping to maintain the peace.

In some ways, moreover, the financial pressures on the kingdom during Henry's personal rule were less than under his father. Between 1237 and 1258 no tax on movable property was levied on the country, so there was no equivalent to the great tax of 1207 which brought in around £60,000. Whereas Magna Carta in 1215 stipulated that such taxes in future needed the common consent of the kingdom, the reforms of 1258 were silent on the matter. There was no need to reiterate Magna Carta's stipulation, despite its omission after 1215. Henry always sought the consent of the kingdom and, as a result, after 1237 never got a tax. One consequence was that Henry's revenues in his personal rule never approached those generated by King John between 1207 and 1212.[262] There was also a dramatic

---

[258] Powicke, *Ways of Medieval Life and Thought*, 116–18.

[259] The expansion is especially marked from around 1250, see volume 1, 528. It is related to the development of the legal profession, for which see Brand, *Origins of the English Legal Profession*.

[260] *SERHB*, ii, 776.

[261] TNA JUST 1/953, m. 1 (images 7258–9).

[262] Henry's taxes in 1232 and 1237 also generated far less revenue than John's tax of 1207 or indeed Henry's of 1225: Mitchell, *Studies in Taxation*, 91, 169, 205, 218.

decline in the money offered every year for concessions and favours, as the fine rolls show. Under John the amounts involved averaged over £20,000. Under Henry, between 1235 and 1257 the average was £5,500.[263] Henry's kingship was very different from his father's.

## THE INCREASING BURDENS IMPOSED BY ROYAL OFFICIALS

These benign comparisons, however, cannot be pressed too far. The decline in fine roll income was thanks in part at least to the disappearance of the large sums offered by magnates to succeed to their lands or escape the king's anger. Here both Magna Carta and Henry's emollient personality did their work. But the change was perfectly compatible with the general run of the population suffering as before from the exactions of the sheriffs and the justices in eyre. Here indeed the situation may well have worsened. At any rate that was the accusation made in a great critique of Henry's rule drawn up early in 1264. It alleged that the sheriffs instead of being 'prudent and knowledgeable knights of the counties, as was old custom', were 'men coming from far away and utter strangers in the counties'.[264] There was some truth in this but far from the whole truth. Certainly the standard of 1236, when county knights were generally appointed to the sheriffdoms, was not maintained. Some of the sheriffs in the 1240s and 1250s were clerks with little stake in their counties; Hugh de Manneby in Northamptonshire is an example.[265] But, outside the few years after 1236, there were probably as many county knights in office in the 1240s and 1250s as in earlier periods. Some of them were just as unpopular as their clerical colleagues, including William de Lisle, Manneby's predecessor.[266]

A much more potent complaint, found in the 1264 critique, related to the rising sums ('increments') the sheriffs had been made to pay above the traditional farms of their counties. These, it was said, could not be raised without 'recourse to illicit extortions and rapine', reducing 'the whole land to an incredible state of poverty'. The statement echoed complaints in the 1258 'Petition of the Barons' and in Matthew Paris before that.[267] It had some truth. The sums demanded above the farms had increased from £750 in 1230 to £1,540 in 1242, and then to £2,500 in 1257. William de Lisle's and Hugh de Manneby's malpractices in Northamptonshire doubtless owed much to the increments rising from 130 marks in 1252 to

---

[263] Volume 1, 702–3.

[264] *DBM*, 274–7, cap. 6. The critique was drawn up for presentation to Louis IX prior to his arbitration at Amiens, see below, 292–3.

[265] Manneby was probably Manby in Lincolnshire.

[266] Carpenter, *Reign of Henry III*, 178–9. The sheriff of Oxfordshire–Berkshire, Richard of Hendred, against whom Ralph de Aundely complained, was a Berkshire knight.

[267] *DBM*, 274–5, cap. 6; 82–3, cap. 16; Paris, v, 576–7. The Petition of the Barons linked together the high farms and the imposition of exorbitant amercements.

180 marks in 1257.[268] Because such sheriffs were having to pass a higher proportion of the farm revenues to the king, they had correspondingly less for their own upkeep and reward.[269] They reacted by demanding hospitality on a new scale, hence the regulations on the subject in the sheriff's oath of 1258. They also had every incentive to make money in all the ways we have seen, since what they extracted, having paid the farm and the increment, they could keep. The point was made by Gerard of Evington when admitting he had taken 6s 8d to place someone on bail. He was, he said, 'a farmer of the county' and was thus perfectly entitled to keep the money.[270]

Alongside the sheriffs, local society also suffered from increasing burdens imposed by the justices in eyre. The king's judges, or the best of them, certainly believed in their duty to give justice, but they also knew they must raise money for the crown. The judge William of York early in his career (he later became bishop of Salisbury) reported back on the daily takings while on eyre in Cumberland. (He also complained about the climate in the north and the long journey involved to get there.)[271] This was in 1227. Twenty years later, during the eyres of 1246–9, the burdens increased as the judges started to devise new ways to penalize local communities. On a far greater scale than before, they punished tithings for failure to raise the hue and cry and arrest members accused of crime.[272] They also, in an entirely new way, penalized villages for failure to come 'fully' to coroner's inquests, insisting that all over the age of twelve must attend.[273] Since members of all four villages neighbouring a dead body were obliged to turn up, the result could be four amercements being levied for one body.[274] The spectacular contrast between the eyres of the 1220s and those later in the reign can be seen in Essex. On the eyre of 1227 there were 29 amercements imposed on hundreds, villages and tithings. On that of 1255 there were around 300. The amercements for the flight of criminals rose from 13 to 50, those for failing to attend inquests from nought to 170.[275] No wonder the revenue from the eyres

---

[268] Carpenter, *Reign of Henry* III, 172; Cassidy, 'Bad sheriffs, custodial sheriffs', 39, and see volume 1, 659.

[269] For the farm revenues, see above, 9.

[270] *SESK*, no. 154. That Gerard of Evington was entitled to keep the money was not said explicitly but it is the implication of the statement. The point was that had he been a custodian sheriff (see above, 29), he would have had to account for all his revenues.

[271] Meekings, *Studies in 13th-Century Justice*, v, 497–500.

[272] Duggan, 'The limits of strong government', 411–12, and see also his 'The hue and cry in thirteenth-century England'.

[273] Brand, *Kings, Barons and Justices*, 81–2; Maddicott, 'Magna Carta and the local community', 47–8.

[274] I owe this point to Henry Summerson.

[275] TNA JUST 1/229, mm. 20–1 (images 6635–9); TNA JUST 1/235, mm. 27–32 (images 7365–80). Henry Summerson suggested I compare these two eyres, the point being that the lists of amercements survive for both. For overall figures for the rising revenue from the eyres, see volume 1, 661.

increased dramatically in the 1240s.[276] The penalties for letting men escape had at least something to do with law and order, but the insistence on villages attending inquests 'fully' was simply a way of making money.[277] The Petition of the Barons complained directly about the issue and the practice was banned in the Provisions of Westminster.[278]

## THE INCREASING BURDENS IMPOSED BY SEIGNEURIAL OFFICIALS

In the absence of before-and-after surveys of manors and honours, it is impossible to prove in any detailed way that lords and their officials were becoming more oppressive in the reign of Henry III. Three suggestive points, however, stand out from the eyre material. The first is the prominence of officials who are clearly professional administrators, some of them just as notorious as any sheriff. The most senior appear again and again, often working for their masters across several counties: William de Bussey; Gerard la Grue; Peter of Ashridge; Hervey of Boreham; Roger de Scacarrio; John de la Rede; Geoffrey de Brayboeuf and so on.[279] Such men, knights and clerks, moved easily from one lord to another and from the service of lords to the service of the king. The clerk Hervey of Boreham was steward first of the abbot of Westminster, then of Richard de Clare. Later he was a justice of the bench and baron of the exchequer.[280] The prevalence of such officials was new to the thirteenth century.[281] They and their lords also had a new form of expertise, for, prompted by the needs of demesne farming, manuals were being written about how to run manors and hear accounts.[282] The legislation of 1259 itself introduced a legal action helping lords bring to court bailiffs who absconded without accounting. No doubt Richard de Clare argued for this given his experiences with officials like the reeve at Yalding.[283]

---

[276] The individual amercements were not, however, of a size to break the back of village communities and one amercement usually sufficed even if there was more than one offence: see Duggan, 'The limits of strong government', 411–12.

[277] A point made by Paul Brand, *Kings, Barons and Justices*, 91.

[278] *DBM*, 82–3, cap. 14; 146–7, cap. 21. The Provisions covered all inquests connected with pleas of the crown, not just coroner's inquests. The villages were just to send sufficient people to carry out the inquests. For the issue, see Brand, *Kings, Barons and Justices*, 81–2.

[279] For a wide-ranging discussion, chronologically and conceptually, of seigneurial officials, see ch. 2 of John Sabapathy's *Officers and Accountability*.

[280] For a biography, see Brand, 'Hervey of Boreham'.

[281] For their appearance in the service of the bishop of Ely, see Miller, *Abbey and Bishopric of Ely*, 196–7.

[282] Several are brought together in Dorothea Oschinsky's *Walter of Henley, and other Treatises on Estate Management and Accounting*. For demesne farming, see below, 642.

[283] *DBM*, 146–7, cap. 19, with the subsequent writ introduced in 1260 at *CR 1259–61*, 162. The action was concerned with bailiffs who possessed no lands or tenements by which they could be distrained. For discussion, see Brand, *Kings, Barons and Justices*, 65–6, 117–19; and

The essential purpose of this expertise was naturally to increase the lord's income. Richard de Clare was following the advice exactly when he had valued the services owed by those who held from him in villeinage. Since, according to the Tewkesbury annals, this was 'to the greatest harm of the possessors', it was clearly a prelude to increasing their services.[284] This brings us to the second fact to stand out from the eyre material, namely the insistence of lords that their peasant tenants were unfree. The point, of course, was that there was then no legal bar to imposing additional burdens both by raising rents and exacting tallages. Equally, if there was resistance, the lord could simply deprive the tenant of his property.[285] Grievances over tallage in particular appear continually in the eyre material. If the complaints can be believed, and sometimes they were believed by juries, these were certainly new burdens. In the Ralph Stipol case, a jury gave a long account, dating back to John's reign, of how his ancestors had held freely in return for a 6d rent and minimal labour services and how tallages had then been introduced. When Stipol refused to pay them he was ejected from his land.[286]

The third point to emerge is, of course, the effort made by lords to get men to attend their courts, although, so the complainants argued, and again juries often agreed, no suit had been owed before. This coincides exactly with the allegations made in the critique of Henry's rule drawn up in 1264.[287] It may be that lords were now arguing in a new way that suit to an honorial court was inherent in tenure from the honour, whether or not performed before.[288] The expertise shown in running the manor could transfer just as well to the honour. Nicholas Achard, as marshal of bishop-elect Aymer's fees, evidently concentrated on such work.

Pressure to attend private courts was linked to another new development, one of the most striking during Henry's personal rule. This was the way lords were withdrawing their men from attending the hundred courts of the sheriff, the implication being that for hundredal business they were now attending courts of their lords. At the same time lords were preventing their men from making customary payments to the sheriff, payments like 'sheriff's aid', 'wardpenny' and 'hidage'. For these developments, overwhelming evidence is provided by the answers given by hundredal jurors

Sabapathy, *Officers and Accountability*, 47–51. The chapter in the Provisions of Westminster can be seen as lords securing some compensation for accepting the legislation on suit of court and distraint. Sabapathy, however, suggests lords could have argued it was a contribution to the general reform of local government: *Officers and Accountability*, 51.

[284] Tewkesbury, 146.

[285] There was a parallel movement where lords were commuting labour services into money rents, sometimes conceding freedom at the same time. But this too could be a way of increasing burdens. See Carpenter, *Reign of Henry III*, 348 n. 136, 372–3.

[286] TNA Just 1/567, m. 29 (image 7888).

[287] *DBM*, 274–5, cap. 4.

[288] *DBM*, 274–5, cap. 4; Brand, *Kings, Barons, Justices*, 43–53, for the whole issue, with 48–9 for the belief of some lords that 'regular suit was simply an incident of tenure'.

to questions put to them at the eyres of the 1240s and 1250s.[289] One new question was specifically about the withdrawal of men from attending the hundred courts. In Essex, between 1242 and 1258, thirty-five individuals are found removing such suits or otherwise depriving the sheriff of customary dues.[290] In Norfolk, the eyre of 1257 named around fifty individuals as being involved.[291] The same pattern is found in county after county.

A wide spectrum of lords were engaged in this washing away the rights of the crown: abbots, priors, barons and knights. The chief culprits, however, were a group of magnates close to the king: Richard de Clare, Richard of Cornwall, Peter of Savoy, William de Valence, Valence's father-in-law, Warin de Munchesney, Simon de Montfort and, in Kent, Archbishop Boniface. The Kentish jurors reported that Boniface now had return of writs in all his fees within the seven Wealden hundreds and 'receives all the amercements the king's bailiffs were accustomed to receive'.[292] This could sometimes leave tenants in an impossible position. In Reigate hundred they were amerced by Boniface's bailiff if they did answer the sheriff's summons and were amerced by the sheriff if they did not.[293] The aim of great men was the same, namely to shut out the sheriff altogether from their demesne manors and their fees. In Berkshire, Simon de Montfort excluded the sheriff from his manor of Hungerford; in Kent, his men from Brabourne stopped attending the hundred court; in Leicestershire, where he was said to have return of writs, the jurors did not know by what warrant his bailiffs withdrew five villages from their customary payments to the sheriff.[294]

Given the wide extent of his lands and fees, the magnate most involved in this activity was Richard de Clare. The sheriff of Buckinghamshire between 1256 and 1258, the knight Robert of Tothall, sent the exchequer a list of twenty-one villages whose revenues, enjoyed by his predecessors, he no long 'dared' to collect, because of the 'power' of various magnates. The villages had all been withdrawn from the view of frankpledge or the tourn and the total losses amounted to some £19.[295] Of these villages one

[289] See Carpenter, *Reign of Henry III*, 86–8, 102–5.

[290] Moore, 'Government and locality in Essex', 212.

[291] TNA JUST 1/567, mm. 1d–36.

[292] *SESK*, no. 350, and see no. 294.

[293] *SESK*, no. 71.

[294] Clanchy, *Berkshire Eyre*, no. 756; *SESK*, no. 355; TNA JUST 1/456, mm. 13, 14 (images 4742–4); Carpenter, *Reign of Henry III*, 104. For Montfort's bailiffs doing nothing in response to orders from the king, see *CRR*, xix, nos. 852, 1158, 1537.

[295] TNA E 101/505/9; Maddicott, 'Magna Carta and the local community', 50. Tothall was a manor in Hanslope. For his holdings: *BF*, ii, 873, 896. Other sheriffs were putting in similar claims, including Nicholas of Hendred whose exactions we have seen: *CR 1256–9*, 188. See also TNA E 368/44, m. 17d (image 6753) (Oxfordshire and Berkshire), and TNA E 159/46, m. 3d (image 8154) (Norfolk and Suffolk).

was held by William de Valence, six by King Richard and his wife, two by Queen Eleanor and a round dozen by Richard de Clare.[296]

These encroachments on the sheriff's authority were facilitated by a change in the type of person who held the office. In Henry III's minority, and for a while thereafter, sheriffs had often been powerful ministers of the crown, men close to the king who were allowed to retain a large slice of the revenue raised above the farm both as a form of patronage and a bolster to their local might. In the decade after 1236 these curial sheriffs departed from the shires. By the 1250s hardly one was left in office. The sheriffs were now men of lesser stature, clerks and county knights, who, instead of keeping for themselves the revenue above the farm, paid it to the king, hence the rising increments and indeed the reason for the change. But while the new sheriffs were able to enforce their will against the general run of the population, they had neither the court connections nor local resources to do so against great men. Henry recognized as much. In 1261, when he returned curial sheriffs to the shires he explained that, unlike the sheriffs of lesser power in office before, they would be able to maintain the rights of the crown and protect people 'from the servitude and oppression inflicted on them by many magnates'. In talking of sheriffs of lesser power, Henry was referring here to the sheriffs appointed since 1258, but he might just as well have been referring to those of his personal rule.[297]

## HOW FAR WAS HENRY TO BLAME?

It is a remarkable fact that Henry himself emerges from the eyres of 1258 to 1260 with a comparatively clean bill of health. Out of all the cases, only two involved him personally. The first was John fitzGeoffrey's complaint

---

[296] TNA E 101/505/9; TNA JUST 1/58, mm. 24d, 27d, 28d; Maddicott, 'Magna Carta and the local community', 50.

[297] *F*, i, 408–9. For reasons of space, I am not discussing here how far magnates wished their men to be sheriffs or retained those who were. Given the limited evidence for magnate retinues and pay rolls, the question is difficult to resolve, but the very process of withdrawing men from the sheriff's jurisdiction was eased by some hold over those who held the office. With the crisis of 1258, influence over the sheriffs must have become more important. Anketil de Martival, the new sheriff of Warwickshire–Leicestershire, was Montfort's steward. The sheriff of Devon, William de Courtenay, was the steward of the local magnate John de Courtenay. The sheriff of Surrey and Sussex was the Clare tenant David de Jarpenville, as was that of Kent, Fulk Payforer. Later the Clare steward Roger de Loges was sheriff of Surrey and Sussex for much of the time between 1263 and 1270, while Fulk of Rycote, King Richard's steward and tenant, was sheriff of Oxfordshire and Berkshire from Michaelmas 1262 to June 1264. For such connections, see Ridgeway, 'Mid thirteenth-century reformers and the localities', 69–70. There is a full discussion of how far magnates retained the king's local officials in Spencer, *Nobility and Kingship*, ch. 6. For the accusation that magnates had power over Henry's judges, see *DBM*, 272–3, with discussion in Carpenter, *Reign of Henry III*, 83–5, and Maddicott, *Law and Lordship*, 4–13.

about bishop-elect Aymer's attack on Shere in Surrey. This certainly was very personal. 'The king refused to hear him and wholly denied him justice' ran the record. Yet was it quite as blatant as that? Matthew Paris's account has Henry persuading fitzGeoffrey not to pursue the case, although clearly that did little to remove the sense of grievance.[298] The second case involved Roger de Mortimer, who accused Richard of Cornwall and the king of depriving him unjustly of the manor of Lechlade in Gloucestershire. Hugh Bigod gave the case close attention and in 1259 went to Lechlade to hear it.[299] Yet the record has none of the emotive language found in fitzGeoffrey's complaint. The issue was complex and Henry, who appeared personally at one stage, had reasons for saying he had acted within his rights. The case dragged on from parliament to parliament and was still unresolved when the baronial regime collapsed in 1261.[300]

Outside the eyres, the regime redressed two acts of injustice where Henry was involved. It decided the rate of repayment for a debt Peter de Brus owed William de Valence (a rate agreed by the king) was 'grievous and unjust' and reduced it by half.[301] Then, in November 1259, the council pardoned the astronomical 100,000-mark amercement allegedly imposed by Henry on Robert de Ros. (Ros was accused of maltreating the young queen of Scotland, Henry's daughter Margaret.)[302] There were other cases where men may have felt they had been deprived of property unjustly by the king's will or connivance, but they were not redressed by the baronial regimes between 1258 and 1265.[303] All this was very different from '1215', when King John in the deluge after Magna Carta was forced into some fifty acts of restoration.[304] It was different too from '1234' when Henry, after the fall of Peter des Roches, was made to confess to numerous

<hr/>

[298] *SERHB*, i, no. 5; Paris, v, 708. For the case, see volume i, 688. For its later history: *SESK*, no. 197; *CPR 1258–66*, 2, 5; *CR 1261–4*, 235; Stewart, *1263 Surrey Eyre*, nos. 687–9, 691, and p. xxxiv.

[299] *SERHB*, ii, no. 402.

[300] On the death of Isabella, Roger de Mortimer's grandmother, in 1252, Henry had taken possession of Lechlade. He had then granted it in hereditary right to Richard of Cornwall. This was why the case was brought in the first instance against Richard. Henry's justification was that Isabella only held for life and anyway her heirs were in the allegiance of the king of France. On her death, therefore, Lechlade should escheat to the crown. Mortimer, however, argued that *he* was Isabella's heir and indeed had been put in possession a few weeks before her death. However, he was able to advance no proof of any hereditary tenure. For the whole story, see Carpenter, 'A noble in politics', 186–97.

[301] *CPR 1258–66*, 4. The reduction makes it sound as though the rate of repayment had been imposed by Valence, but see *CPR 1247–58*, 33.

[302] *CChR 1257–1300*, 25. See volume i, 623–5, where I question whether a 100,000-mark amercement was really imposed.

[303] There was Giles de Argentan's claim to Lilley and Willian and Robert fitzWalter of Daventry's claim to Bradenham. Both Giles and Robert seized hold of the properties in the civil war but do not seem to have sought legal redress. For these and other cases, see above, 22 n. 91; volume i, 556–7, 690; Carpenter, *Reign of Henry III*, 33–4.

[304] Holt, *Magna Carta*, 360–1.

injustices.[305] In a great manifesto issued in 1261, Henry claimed he had deprived no one of their rights 'by force or will – *per vim vel voluntatem nostram*'. In other words, he had not broken the cardinal chapter 39 of Magna Carta. On the whole, when it came to his personal rule, this was a fairish claim.[306] Henry was certainly intent on claiming back property belonging to the crown. His officials were constantly looking to seize into the king's hands advowsons, escheats and lands alienated from royal manors and sergeanties. Often they hoped to be the beneficiaries of such recoveries. But such claims were usually made by legal process in the court, *coram rege*, where the king lost cases as well as won them.[307]

If, however, Henry could, on the whole, claim he had not deprived subjects of property 'by force and will', he was on much shakier ground when it came to the stipulation in Magna Carta's chapter 40 that justice be not denied, delayed and sold. In his manifesto of 1261, Henry claimed that, under him, everyone had been able to prosecute their rights as justice allowed. That was true enough for the great bulk of litigation. Had it not been so, the common law would never have expanded as it did. Henry was also guiltless of the blatant sale of justice found under his father. But Henry's claim that everyone had been able to bring prosecutions as justice allowed was far more questionable when the targets were his favourites and their officials. Hence William de Bussey's notorious question, 'If I do you wrong, who will do you justice?'[308] The impossibility of obtaining justice in such circumstances, and the consequent breach of Magna Carta, was a charge made in 1258 and developed at length in the critique of 1264.[309] The conclusion was that 'justice was virtually shut out from the kingdom of England'.[310]

Some support for this picture of 'justice shut out' is given by two allegations made before Hugh Bigod. The Kentish knights Walter de St John and Fulk Payforer alleged in similar terms they could get no justice because their opponents, Roger of Leybourne and Guncelin of Badlesmere, were in William de Valence's service.[311] Payforer 'wholly despaired' of

[305] See volume 1, 155–8.

[306] *F*, i, 408–9. For further discussion, see volume 1, 539–44. This is chapter 39 of the 1215 Magna Carta.

[307] For the court, see Meekings and Crook, *King's Bench and Common Bench*, 3–30, and passim. Much new light on its procedures will be shed by Douglas Chapman's forthcoming doctoral thesis. From 1247 the king's claims were advanced by Laurence del Brok as 'the first professional lawyer to be retained by the king' (see Brand, 'Laurence del Brok'), but he lost as many cases as he won, for example: TNA KB 26/150, mm. 16, 17–17d, 18 [1], 18d.

[308] For how well-known this became, see below, 407.

[309] Burton, 458–9; *DBM*, 271–5, cap. 3.

[310] *DBM*, 260–1, cap. 7. For a similar picture in even more emotive terms, see Waverley, 349–50.

[311] For the St John case, see *SESK*, no. 316, and Carpenter, *Reign of Henry III*, 34 (where I wrongly wrote fitzJohn not St John); and for the Payforer case, *SERHB*, i, no. 87. And see Ridgeway, 'William de Valence and his *familiares*', 248.

prosecuting Badlesmere as 'he had so many favourers and supporters, namely William de Valence and others of the king's council'. We cannot be quite sure of this evidence. Both knights were explaining away agreements made perhaps willingly with their opponents.[312] But at the very least, St John's and Payforer's excuses reflected the mood of 1258 and keyed into the belief that justice was hard to get.

A Surrey knight who seems to have come to that conclusion was Ralph of Imworth. Having been harried over many years by his neighbour, the spiky Robert Aguillon, a knight in the service of William de Valence, he waited till Bigod's eyre to seek redress.[313] Other complaints before the eyres were sometimes years old. Gilbert of Elsfield's against William de Valence and Ralph de Aundely's against Richard of Cornwall's steward dated back to the mid-1250s. So did complaints made against Peter of Savoy's bailiffs in Sussex.[314] Despite some of the complainants being substantial knights, they evidently thought it pointless to seek justice earlier.[315] There is also something in the charge that, while protected themselves, those in Henry's favour found it easy to bring whatever legal actions they liked. Here litigation in the court *coram rege* is striking. From a low base in the 1230s, by the 1250s the rolls are full of actions brought by ministers and magnates, native and foreign, defending their local interests, actions against those breaking into their parks, raiding their fishponds, doing violence to their men and in other ways challenging their rights. Whether or not Henry formally prevented writs being issued against his favourites, as Matthew Paris believed, he had certainly created a situation where justice against them was thought hard to achieve.[316]

The king has ultimate responsibility too for the exactions of the sheriffs and justices in eyre. Denied general taxation by parliament, he had to get money in other ways, although these made the prospect of taxation all the less likely. Henry followed the progress of the eyres with beady eyes and sometimes assigned their revenues before they had even come in. He was constantly harrying the sheriffs for money, often getting it paid direct into the wardrobe. Henry had also sanctioned the decline of the curial sheriff.

---

[312] Payforer may in the end have colluded in the disinheritance of Badlesmere's niece, so that Badlesmere could be the heir. Under the agreement, Badlesmere married Payforer's daughter while Payforer himself married the widowed mother of the heiress: *SERHB*, i, no. 87; *CPR 1247–58*, 483; *CFR 1272–1307*, 89.

[313] For this feud, see *CChR 1226–57*, 329, 402; *SESK*, lvii–viii, nos. 183, 185; Stewart, *1263 Surrey Eyre*, xxxiv–v, and no. 70; *CFR 1260–1*, no. 216; Paris, vi, 223; Ridgeway, 'William de Valence and his *familiares*', 244, 247–8; TNA KB 26/146, m. 5d (image 0005d); *CFR 1252–3*, no. 78. For Aguillon's later career, see Spencer, *Nobility and Kingship*, 162–9.

[314] For other examples of delays, see *SESK*, no. 340; *SERHB*, ii, nos. 805, 807, 811, 813, 856, 868, 870, 885, 922.

[315] See also the cases of Giles de Argentan and Robert fitzWalter of Daventry mentioned above, n. 303.

[316] For further cases and discussion, see volume 1, 537–9, and Carpenter, *Reign of Henry III*, 30–7.

A tribute in some ways to the stability of his personal rule, he no longer needed them to maintain peace and ward off rebellion. He could appoint sheriffs at far less cost who would account for a much greater slice of the county's revenues. But the result was sheriffs unable to stand up to great men, as Henry recognized in his manifesto of 1261.

The spread of magnate power in the localities at the sheriffs' expense was likewise facilitated by the king. In some cases (as with Simon de Montfort), Henry had sanctioned such expansion to encourage or reward good service.[317] But many other lords took what they wanted without any permission or consequences. Very few actions in the court *coram rege* were brought against magnates for withdrawing their men from attending the hundred court. Two exceptions turn out to be cases begun by lords of private hundreds.[318] Occasionally, the justices in eyre acted in response to the hundred jurors' litany of encroachments, but the most normal reaction in the 1240s and 1250s was simply to minute 'it is to be discussed', presumably discussed with the king. The result of such discussions seems to have been precisely nothing. So at the very time when magnates and their officials were becoming more and more oppressive, they were less and less subject to monitoring by the crown. All this was totally different from the great '*quo warranto*' legal proceedings launched in the next reign, when King Edward forced all and sundry to show warrant for their local government liberties and indeed recovered some of those usurped by the Clares in Kent.[319]

The plight of the localities was made worse by the suspension of the justiciarship and chancellorship, so there seemed no responsible and visible ministers at the centre of government to field complaints. There was no wholesale dismissal of sheriffs after 1236 and no inquiry into local government with the power to give redress to those suffering abuse. And after the legislation of the mid-1230s there was nothing more on the same scale till 1259. While the judges touring the counties were given new questions to ask about shrieval abuse, and while some sheriffs and magnates were brought to book, nothing was done on any scale or with much impact.[320]

Two facts make Henry's failure all the more egregious. The first is that he was perfectly aware of the rising tide of discontent, as his speech to the sheriffs in 1250 shows.[321] The second fact is that no one doubted the king's authority to put matters right. Not the least remarkable feature of '1258'

---

[317] Carpenter, *Reign of Henry III*, 103–4.

[318] *CRR*, xvi, no. 1210; *CRR*, xviii, no. 656.

[319] Ward, 'The Kent hundred rolls', 63.

[320] For William de Lisle in Northamptonshire, see volume 1, 659–60; and for the sheriff of Nottinghamshire–Derbyshire, Robert le Vavasour, see Sabapathy, *Officers and Accountability*, 112.

[321] Clanchy, 'Did Henry III have a policy?', 216, and volume 1, 528–30. See also Paris, *HA*, ii, 338.

is the acceptance that eyres *could* deal with the malpractices of baronial officials and legislation *could* limit the jurisdiction of baronial courts. Here indeed Henry was in a stronger position than Louis IX for France's more decentralized structure meant that Louis's *enquêtes* and ordinances were concerned with the abuses of the king and his officials, not at all with those of magnates and their men.[322]

Why then did Henry not seize the opportunity and reform the realm himself? There were several reasons. Confident that his alms, masses and devotion to the Confessor assured his spiritual health, he quite lacked Louis IX's conviction that grievances must be redressed to save his soul. In his will drawn up in 1253, Henry wanted his debts paid but said nothing about injustices he might have committed.[323] The king also had so much else to think about. There was the defence of Gascony, the campaigns in Wales, the crusade and then the Sicilian project, all requiring money and political support. Needing money, Henry was not prepared to reduce the financial burdens shouldered by the sheriffs, however much he regretted their misbehaviour. Needing support, he shied away from reforms attacking the interests of his leading nobles, both foreign and native born, however much he was aware of their misconduct.[324] In his 'simplicity' Henry quite lacked the political grasp of his son, who realized that reform of the realm was the key to unlocking taxation from parliament.

So nothing was done. Had there been no revolution at court in 1258, Henry's government might have stumbled on for all its local unpopularity. When that revolution occurred, reform of local government was inevitable. The level of discontent revealed in the eyres explains why some of the baronial leaders saw the reforms – the eyres themselves, the proclamations and the legislation – as a righteous cause, just as others saw them as a political necessity.

---

[322] A point confirmed to me by Marie Dejoux. For the parallel measures introduced by Alphonse of Poitiers in Poitou, see Chenard, *L'Administration d'Alphonse de Poitiers*, 494–524.

[323] See below, 654–5.

[324] Paris, iv, 20–1; *Song of Lewes*, lines 493–510.

Chapter 6

# TRIUMPH: HENRY'S RECOVERY
# OF POWER
## 1260–1261

In 1258–9, Henry had been stripped of power and subjected to the rule of a baronial council. Throughout 1260, nominally at least, he still accepted the council's authority. But the situation was fluid. Like pack ice cracking apart and crunching together, the baronial leaders were at times divided, at times united. Their divisions gave Henry far more clear water than before. Next year he formally denounced the council and began the struggle to recover power. He was helped by a development as important to his personal happiness as it was to his political recovery. The terrible rift within the royal family, which had done so much to facilitate the revolution, had healed over. Queen Eleanor now stood full square with her husband. So did Peter of Savoy. King Richard too, having opted out of English politics in 1259, now returned on Henry's side. As for Lord Edward, at least Henry and Eleanor could be assured of his neutrality. For several months in 1261, as the struggle intensified, the country hovered on the brink of civil war without quite falling over the edge. By the end of the year Henry had won through and re-established his kingship. This was one of the great achievements of the reign.[1]

## THE DEATH OF MATTHEW PARIS

The year 1259 is the last to be lit up by Matthew Paris's magnificent chronicle. He described Walter of Scotney's trial and execution that summer with characteristic verve and (when it came to the date) accuracy. It was the last thing he wrote. He died soon afterwards. His continuator, 'unworthy to unlace his shoe', penned a poignant drawing of him on his deathbed.[2] One has the same sense of loss as when Samuel Pepys ends his diary, leaving so much now unrecorded and in the dark.

---

[1] For an analysis of the events of 1261 to which I owe much, see Ridgeway, 'What happened in 1261?'

[2] Paris, v, 747–8, and frontispiece. For Paris's last phase, see Carpenter, 'Chronology and truth: Matthew Paris and the *Chronica Majora*'.

To be sure the period from 1259 is still illuminated by some fine contemporary historians.[3] At St Albans, Paris's chronicle was continued into 1261 by an unnamed successor, more moderate in tone, less expansive in content, but still informative and perceptive. After he laid down his pen, the only surviving text of his work was continued into 1265 not at St Albans but at Pershore abbey. The Pershore chronicle supports the Montfortian movement but with significant reservations regarding the treatment of the king.[4] There were no reservations at Dunstable priory, a house close to the great earl, and giving, in its chronicle, the most committed account of his career.[5] Events in London, meanwhile, are recounted in the chronicle of the alderman Arnold fitzThedmar, a unique urban history made the more vivid by frequent references to the places where events occurred – the guild hall, London Bridge, the king's chamber in the Tower, the bishop's house and churchyard at St Paul's, and then at Westminster, the great hall, the exchequer and the Abbey.[6]

All these accounts were composed soon after the events they recorded, but others written later also have value. One is the chronicle in English verse by Robert of Gloucester, perhaps a monk of the Benedictine abbey of St Peter's there. Although writing in the late thirteenth century, Robert could remember the sky darkening over the land while the battle of Evesham was fought in 1265. He provides unique detail about events around Gloucester and also in Oxford, where he may have studied. Writing later still, in the early fourteenth century, was William Rishanger, a monk of St Albans abbey. He copied much of his narrative from the Pershore chronicle, but also had information from those close to Montfort and sometimes showed a shrewd understanding of his situation.[7] And then there is Thomas Wykes.[8] Wykes was born in 1222 and so directly experienced the period of reform and rebellion. He had property in London and Oxford and may well have been in the service of Richard of Cornwall. In 1282 he became a canon of Osney abbey just outside Oxford. Though very aware of Henry's failings, and accepting the need for reform, his royalist views and his hostility to Montfort makes his account unique. Wykes was distinguished by his humanity and was appalled by the Montfortian massacre of the London Jews in 1264.

The period of reform and rebellion has, therefore, no lack of historians. Indeed, many were clearly inspired to write, or write more, by the drama

---

[3] For an account of the historians of the reign of Henry III, see ch. 18 of Antonia Gransden's *Historical Writing*. For a perceptive discussion of writing in this period, see Kjær, 'Writing reform and rebellion'.

[4] For the Pershore chronicle, see Carpenter, 'The Pershore *Flores Historiarum*'.

[5] For a new English translation of the Dunstable chronicle, see *The Annals of Dunstable Priory*. For discussion, see Harriet Webster's 'The annals of Dunstable Priory'.

[6] For fitzThedmar, see below, 388–9.

[7] For Rishanger, see Maddicott, *Simon de Montfort*, 87–90.

[8] For Wykes, see Denholm-Young, 'Thomas de Wykes and his chronicle'.

of events. But none of them came anywhere near the volume and vibrancy, the colour and the combativeness of Matthew Paris's *Chronica Majora*. The narrative of the tumultuous and terrible events between 1260 and 1267 would have been far richer had he been their chronicler.

## A WEDDING AND A FUNERAL IN PARIS

After the week celebrating the peace with France, Henry stayed on in Paris. He did so with the full consent of his councillors for there was much work arising from the treaty. Just before Christmas, Reginald de Pons and his wife came before Louis and Henry seeking possession of the castle of Bergerac. Likewise, Alphonse count of Poitou complained about the damage suffered by his men in Gascony. In response, Henry and his council told Lord Edward, as Gascony's immediate ruler, to give them justice. If he did not, he was warned, they might appeal for justice to the king of France. The judicial consequences of Gascony's status as a French fief were already apparent.[9]

In another area, Henry had Louis to thank. On 10 December, 'on the prayers of the illustrious king of France', Henry took steps to pay to Fontevraud abbey the arrears of its annual pension, a pension conceded 'by the progenitors of the king for the celebration of their anniversaries each year'. The progenitors were, of course, Henry II, Eleanor of Aquitaine and Richard the Lionheart. Henry had seen their tombs on his visit to Fontevraud in 1254, but it was much harder for him to remember ancestors than it was Louis.[10] The bodies of Louis's Capetian forbears, stretching back now for centuries, had nearly all been buried at Saint-Denis where they merged seamlessly with those of their Carolingian and Merovingian predecessors.[11] Henry doubtless saw their tombs when he visited the monastery. The bodies of the much-broken line of English kings, by contrast, were scattered across France and England. No English king had been buried at Westminster since the Confessor in 1066. There, in creating a dynastic mausoleum to rival Saint-Denis, Henry must make a new start.[12] Throughout his time in France, the progress of the Abbey was never far from Henry's thoughts. He was astonished to find his order assigning the issues of the seal to the works had not been carried out.[13] Before leaving England, he had ascertained that the total cost of the work

[9] *CR 1256–9*, 232. The Bergerac affair is succinctly summarized in Labarge, *Gascony: England's First Colony*, 39.

[10] *CR 1259–61*, 225–6. Henry, before leaving England, had tried to establish the size of the arrears owed to Fontevraud, so he perhaps anticipated the issue might be raised: *CLR 1251–60*, 483.

[11] Louis did not, however, commission the tomb effigies of his predecessors until 1263–4: Le Goff, *Saint Louis*, 273–89; and Brown, *Saint-Denis: La Basilique*, 384–93.

[12] For comparisons between Westminster and Saint-Denis, see Jordan, *A Tale of Two Monasteries*.

[13] *CR 1259–61*, 241.

to date had been £28,127 15s 10½d.[14] It was a sum equivalent to a whole year's annual revenue and perhaps Henry intended to boast about it to King Louis, as he had earlier boasted to Matthew Paris about the cost of the shrine.[15]

Henry had, of course, more to discuss with Louis than the progress of the Abbey. Now at last, emotional and voluble, he could give his own version of events in England. The task was complicated for Louis also heard other voices. There was Queen Eleanor explaining how grievously her husband had been led astray by the Lusignans. There was Simon de Montfort saying how the Provisions of Oxford were justified by Henry's misrule. Fortunately, Henry could bring more than words to the argument. His whole conduct showed that here was a king, guided by the hand of God and acting as a good king should. How wrong for him to be stripped of power. The reality should once more match the outward show. Louis, when the time came, should help him recover power.

In the weeks after the treaty, Henry remained at Saint-Germain-des-Prés. He held no great feasts, but his household roll still shows expenditure (most of it on food and drink) running at a significant level: £36 a day in the week from 7 December, and £33 a day in the week from the fourteenth.[16] In England in 1255, an income of £15 *a year* had been sufficient qualification for knighthood. For Christmas itself, Henry made a bigger effort, the total for the vigil and the feast (joined together in the accounts) being £101 15s. Nearly all of it represented the costs of Christmas Day itself since the vigil was a fast day. Henry also burnt 170 pounds of wax, 75 of them in the chapel and the almonry, so enough for over 300 of the usual half-pound candles. The almonry too was busy feeding 450 paupers. The accounts only reveal half of the festivities for, according to Matthew Paris's continuator at St Albans, Henry celebrated the feast 'ceremonially' with Louis and his nobles. Fortunately, Louis had no eye for clothes, otherwise he would have seen that, while Henry's knights were decked out in new robes, his clerks and sergeants were making do with old ones, this because Henry was running short of money. On 22 December he wrote home asking urgently for funds.[17]

Henry's intention had been to return to England after Christmas. However, negotiations for the marriage of his daughter Beatrice to John, son and heir of the duke of Brittany, had now concluded and Henry, 'at

---

[14] *BA*, 198–9 (xxi). Henry asked whether the sum included the cost of buying lead and repairing his buildings at Westminster.

[15] Paris, *HA*, ii, 454–5 (not *FH*, as cited in volume 1).

[16] For the household roll for Henry III's forty-fourth regnal year (TNA E 101/349/27 (images 0126–75)), see above, 99 n. 66. Until the end of the year (27 October 1260), the information given about Henry's feeding of paupers, expenditure on food and drink and consumption of wax for candles comes from this source.

[17] Fortunately Henry had abolished as 'indecent' the custom of a man coming before the king on Christmas day to perform a leap, a whistle and a fart: TNA Just 1/ 833 m.11 (image 6689); a reference I owe to Henry Summerson.

the instance of the king and queen of France', agreed that the nuptials should be celebrated in the presence of the royal families at Compiègne on 14 January.[18] Henry, therefore, stayed on and, after Christmas, went for two days, 28–29 December, to Saint-Denis. He came, according to the monastery's own account, 'with great devotion and reverence', 'desiring to visit the blessed Denis'. He was received 'with great honour' by the convent, dressed in silk copes, his gifts including a gold chalice and a bowl of great weight.[19] But why had Henry come on this precise date? The answer reveals the same sensitivity of conduct he showed throughout this visit to France. For Henry had gone to Saint-Denis to celebrate the vigil and the feast of Thomas Becket's martyrdom. He did so with an abundance of candles for, across the two days, he burnt 179 pounds of wax, 90 of them in his chapel and almonry. Thus, surrounded by light, Henry cleansed his dynasty of its greatest crime by commemorating Becket before the monks of Saint-Denis, the great upholders and propagandists of the Capetian state.

After his days at Saint-Denis, Henry visited two royal palaces on the western side of Paris, first Saint-Germain-en-Laye and then, from 2 January, Pontoise. The latter was the favourite residence of Louis and Queen Margaret. Their chambers were one above the other linked by a spiral staircase where, in the early days of their marriage, they would meet out of sight of Queen Blanche, Louis's interfering and overbearing mother. If she approached, ushers would raise the alarm and they would scuttle back to their chambers so as not to be found together.[20] If Henry heard such stories, perhaps he reflected back to the happier days of his own marriage when he had constructed passages to link his chamber with Eleanor's. Did he also reflect on whether his own mother, had she been around, would have done something to hold Eleanor in check?

It was at Pontoise on 5 January that Henry celebrated a supreme day in his religious year – the anniversary of the death of Edward the Confessor. He did so by feeding 1,500 paupers, the highest number during his time in France. Surprisingly, the general costs of the household on the day were low, amounting to only £22. But one wonders whether Louis too was at Pontoise and had thrown the great feast himself. So just as Henry had honoured St Denis, Louis honoured the Confessor.

On 11 January, Henry left Pontoise and returned to Saint-Denis. Beatrice's wedding was scheduled for three days later but tragedy now supervened. Louis's fifteen-year-old son, Henry's nephew, had died. The heir to the throne, he was also called Louis. Thus, 14 January became the day not of a wedding but of a funeral. The body stayed the night at Saint-Denis and on the morrow was borne on the shoulders of King Henry

[18] *CR 1259–61*, 267–8 (*DBM*, 164–9).
[19] Nangis, *Gesta*, 410–13.
[20] Joinville, ch. 606.

and 'the most noble barons of France and England' for half a mile on its way to Royaumont, the great Cistercian monastery founded by Louis. Henry thus showed how unified were the royal families in their grief. Described in no English source, his conduct made a deep impression in France and was sculpted on the prince's tomb chest, where Henry can be seen to this day shouldering his doleful burden.[21]

The marriage between John and Beatrice now took place at Saint-Denis on Thursday 22 January. Henry played his part in the festivities for the household's expenses rose to £49, nearly double those of the day before and the day after.

It was not, of course, just hospitality which bonded together the royal families and their courts during these weeks in Paris. Equally important was the exchange of gifts. A high proportion of the 171 rings, 57 brooches, 50 belts and 50 cups that Henry gave away in the regnal year 1259–60 were probably given away in France.[22] Eleanor, meanwhile, bestowed rings on the countesses of Brittany, Gusines and Eu, on the queen of Navarre and on her sisters, Queen Margaret and Beatrice, countess of Provence, the wife of Charles of Anjou.[23] Just as the entertainment at the great feasts reached out from the high table to embrace the followers lower down the hall, so did the gifts. Indeed, Eleanor's rings went to Queen Margaret's knights and ladies and also to her cooks, her baker, wine buyer, doorkeeper and the 'valet' who 'cut' her meat, as well as to the master of the royal children.[24] Many of these rings cost 2s 6d, so rather different from a ruby ring that Eleanor gave King Louis in 1262 valued at £13 6s![25] In 1254, Louis had given Henry an elephant and Margaret a fantastic jewel shaped like a peacock. There was nothing quite like that this time, but Henry did receive from Louis two cloths of gold, a cup of gold weighing the equivalent of 622 silver pennies and a great silver incense boat weighing all of 22 pounds. Another cloth of gold was received from Alphonse of Poitiers while a samite came from his wife, a sign perhaps they accepted the fate of the Agenais and the Saintonge under the treaty.[26]

Vital to Henry's performance in Paris was money. To have run out and been rescued by Louis would have been too humiliating. Fortunately, by cash and credit, Henry kept going, although, as we have seen, it was some-

---

[21] Nangis, *Gesta*, 412–13; Saint-Denis, 119. The scene on the tomb is a nineteenth-century restoration but based on the original (see plate IV). See Wright, 'A royal tomb program in the reign of St Louis', 226 n. 7. I am grateful to Lindy Grant for this reference and discussion of the subject. See also Le Pogam and Vivet-Peclet, *Saint Louis*, 66–8, 223–4.

[22] Wild, *WA*, cxliii, 90–1. The gifts would also have included precious items from the stock left by Peter de Rivallis: Wild, *WA*, 93–7.

[23] TNA E 101/349/26 (images 0083–124). See Howell, *Eleanor of Provence*, 78–80, 165.

[24] TNA E 101/349/26. Eleanor gave a similar spread of rings to the staff of her other sister, the countess of Provence.

[25] TNA E 101/349/26.

[26] Wild, *WA*, 90–1, 98.

times a close-run thing. He never once allowed Louis to take over all the costs of his household as Archbishop Boniface had done at Canterbury before departure. It was one thing to accept 'total hospitality' from a subordinate, quite another from a superior. The money had come from £2,400 supplied by the exchequer before departure, from a loan of £640 contracted with the Paris Temple and from £2,181 raised by the sale of what was left of Henry's gold treasure. As a result, over 20,000 of Henry's gold pennies were sold in Paris, presumably disappearing into the melting pot.[27] If this was an inglorious end for the coins that depicted Henry sitting proudly on his throne, holding orb and sceptre (the latter modelled on the sceptre of the Confessor), it was money well spent. Henry's conduct in Paris had been absolutely right, right in his abundant hospitality, his exchange of gifts, his visits to Saint-Denis and his bearing of young Louis's coffin. Henry had achieved all his objectives. He had demonstrated the majesty of his kingship as it ought to be. He had explained to Louis how illegitimate were the restrictions placed upon him. He could return to England with his confidence restored, ready at the very least to act as head of his council, ready, when the time came, to overthrow the council's authority altogether.

## THE SICILIAN AFFAIR AND BISHOP-ELECT AYMER

The circumstances of the visit to France, with the division of the council, had made it easier for Henry to assert himself. It became easier still after Christmas. Montfort himself, with his offstage cries, was now gone. So were his allies on the council, Richard de Grey and Peter de Montfort.[28] Another councillor, William de Forz, earl of Aumale, last appears in February and was probably a sick man. (He died the following May without returning to England.) Chancellor Wingham also left court (in February he was consecrated bishop of London) and the seal remained in the hands of malleable chancery clerks. Meanwhile Henry got rid of Giles de Argentan, the steward imposed on him in 1258. He is not found at court after 21 February. That gave increasing prominence to his erstwhile colleague, the Savoyard, Imbert Pugeys.[29]

The men who really counted at court in this period were Richard de Clare and John Mansel. Both worked closely with Henry, many royal letters being authorized by the three together. Judicious and considerate,

---

[27] *CLR 1251–60*, 483–4; TNA E 403/18; *CPR 1258–66*, 122; *CR 1259–61*, 240; Wild, *WA*, 87, 95, 102. In February, Bigod sent another £1,000 followed by 400 marks at the start of March: *CLR 1251–60*, 494, 497; TNA E 403/18.

[28] Peter, as we have suggested, may have been in Montfort's company throughout, but Richard de Grey was with the king.

[29] However, Peter of Savoy had now left court. He is last found there on 16 January 1260 (*CR 1259–61*, 265).

seemingly a friend to all, Mansel, as a member of the council, had co-operated with the regime. Yet he remained a king's man, and gave Henry good and loyal advice, not all of it taken. Clare still believed in the council's control of the king, or at least if he was the dominant councillor. He was quite prepared to bypass the council if it was an obstacle to his plans. Before Christmas, out in Paris, he was conceded a wardship provided he paid for it. Hugh Bigod back home was to implement the concession 'by the counsel of our magnates who are of our council in England', so all very respectful of the council's authority and the idea that wardships should be sold. But that was only how the writ was first drafted. In the version actually sent the reference to the council was deleted. Clare did not want interference from that quarter. He aimed to lay low his enemies (Montfort of course and Edward) and restrict some of the local reforms. To these ends he was perfectly prepared to co-operate with the king.

In these favourable circumstances, or so he hoped, Henry decided to act in two areas close to his heart. The first, believe it or not, was Sicily. In mid-January, while awaiting Beatrice's marriage, Henry wrote to the archbishop of Messina. He would be able, he said, to attend to Sicily 'more freely and efficaciously' now there was peace with France. He hoped the archbishop would do all he could to help the project forward. There was a theoretical logic here, since the initial point of the peace had been to clear the way for Sicily. There was also a total impracticality. Henry himself acknowledged, in his letter, that the pope might not look favourably on the idea.[30] He also said nothing about the initiative being sanctioned by his councillors. If he had the support of the queen, Henry's second initiative was sure to offend her.

Since the end of December, Eleanor had been absent from court. Probably she had been staying with her sister Queen Margaret and offering consolation over the death of her son. Eleanor finally returned on 18 January and was appalled to discover what her husband was up to. For Henry had, yet again, been in secret communication with the pope over bringing bishop-elect Aymer back to England! Eleanor was not having that and she had plenty of support. The last thing Richard de Clare wanted was Aymer's return given the likely threat to his possession of Portland. John Mansel too had seen the unwisdom of the Lusignans' return and had persuaded Henry (back in November 1259) to prevent that happening through Bristol. Eleanor also had friends at home. Before his departure, at her instance, Hugh Bigod (and John Mansel) had promised a wardship to Matthias Bezill for his long service to the queen and king.[31]

Not surprisingly, Henry's plan was soon in tatters. In another of those extraordinary letters that run through the chancery rolls, this one issued the very day the queen returned, he begged the pope not to send Aymer,

[30] CR 1259–61, 265–6.
[31] CPR 1258–66, 63, 87.

'who acts as though he is bishop of Winchester', back to England. Alexander should not believe suggestions (doubtless emanating from Henry himself) that earlier letters had been issued against 'the royal will'. Henry then explained how Aymer had 'provoked him many times' against the queen and had divided him from Edward. His return would plunge the kingdom into chaos. Whereas Henry's letter seeking to revive the Sicilian affair made no reference to his councillors, this one was authorized by Richard de Clare, William de Forz, Peter of Savoy and John Mansel.[32]

## HENRY IN FRANCE, MONTFORT AND EDWARD IN ENGLAND

The setback over Aymer was not the only check Henry now encountered. On 25 January he at last began a slow journey back to England. Having reached St Omer on 15 February, he remained there all the way through to 15 April. It was only on 23 April that he finally crossed the channel.

In letters to the home government, Henry was quite open about remaining in France although disingenuous about the reasons. He needed, he said, the council's advice on who should arbitrate over the money due to him under the Treaty of Paris. In fact, the issues connected with the arbitration could perfectly well have been settled by the councillors with Henry in France or by the whole council after his return to England. The real reason for the delay, one Henry wished to conceal for fear of making matters worse, was the news of what Montfort and Edward were up to in England.

After the conclusion of the Treaty of Paris, Montfort had returned to England without taking leave of the king. He then, so Henry later alleged, set about gathering men and making alliances.[33] As early as 20 December, Henry and his councillors were trying to stop armed men getting into the kingdom.[34] By this time Montfort's alliance with Edward must have been well known. Edward indeed seemed completely out of control. In defiance of the king, Richard de Clare and John Mansel, he had dismissed Robert Walerand from the custody of Bristol and replaced him with Roger of Leybourne. He had then celebrated Christmas there himself.[35] The fact that Walerand was with Henry in Paris (where he authorized many letters), and was close to the queen, made this all the worse. To compound the offence, Edward also removed Mansel from the custody of Tickhill and the bailiff of Peter of Savoy from Hastings.[36] Eleanor must have felt she had lost her son completely.

---

[32] CR 1259–61, 264–5.

[33] DBM, 208–9, cap. 34.

[34] CR 1259–61, 228.

[35] Studd, 'Acts of Lord Edward', nos. 742–3, 745. At same time (on 7 December), Edward arranged for the purchase of thirty warhorses in Spain.

[36] Pershore, Chronicle, 243–4; Studd, 'Acts of Lord Edward', no. 715; Howell, Eleanor of Provence, 163–4.

Montfort was acting quickly because he expected Henry to be back in England at much the same time as himself. The aim was clear. He and Edward were gathering the power to dominate the king, the council and the future course of politics. Richard de Clare could be put in his place. Edward could resist attempts to restrict his freedom. Montfort could look for better success in a renewed arbitration over Eleanor's dower. (The process was starting up again in February).[37] He could also settle the question of Eleanor's landed endowment. Here, disappointingly, the exchequer's investigation of Domesday Book had shown that nearly all the manors granted back in 1259 were indeed ancient demesne of the crown and thus could not be given to Montfort outright. Henry, Clare and Mansel, moreover, believed that the manors had been undervalued and thus Montfort had received far too much. They therefore ordered Hugh Bigod to carry out a fresh valuation.[38]

The situation in England placed Henry and his councillors in considerable danger. If they returned unprepared they might find themselves at Montfort's mercy. And there was one particular event coming up with the potential to make that all the more the case. Under the Provisions of Oxford, parliament was to meet on 2 February. Back in November, Hugh Bigod had assumed that it would go ahead even if the king was still out of the country.[39] Probably Henry himself had taken that view. Now he had good reason to change his mind.

Montfort's long absence had not dulled his popularity. Matthew Paris's continuator opined that England had long been 'widowed' by his absence. In admiring terms he described Montfort's visit to the monastery (on 10 February) and his offering of a precious cloth at St Alban's shrine.[40] Montfort always behaved perfectly on such occasions. The parliament itself would meet at a high point in the movement of reform. The special eyres hearing everyone's complaints were under way in many counties.[41] On 6 December, the very day of Henry's great feast in Paris, Hugh Bigod had opened his session at Chelmsford in Essex and was soon hearing complaints against the officials of Richard de Clare.[42] In this kind of

[37] *CR 1259–61*, 269. The arbitrators were the same as before: the earls of Norfolk, Hereford and Philip Basset.

[38] TNA E 368/35, m. 3 (image 5585); *CR 1259–61*, 237–8. Another annoyance for Montfort was that where the manors were held on lease, all that he received was the rent. He would only get possession when the leases expired: TNA E 159/33, m. 2 (image 0005). And see TNA E 368/ 35, m. 9 (image 5596), a hit at Bishop Aigueblanche and a sign of Montfort's presence in England and influence at the exchequer.

[39] *CR 1259–61*, 15.

[40] Paris's Continuator, 443.

[41] Crook, *Records of the General Eyre*, 189–91.

[42] *SCWR*, 97; *SERHB*, nos. 802, 858–9; Jacob, *Studies*, 107–8. For Bigod himself following up over the damages awarded, see TNA KB 26/161, m. 23 (image 0093); TNA KB 26/167, m. 21 (image 0060).

atmosphere, Montfort had every chance of whipping up support from knights and free tenants in and out of the parliament. There was self-interest here. He thus strengthened his own position and undermined that of Richard de Clare. There was also righteousness, for Montfort had believed from the start in the cause of reform. Had he not bound Edward in their alliance to support 'the enterprise made by the barons of the land'? Montfort had missed the parliament of October 1259 but had doubtless heard about the protest made by the 'community of the bachelery of England'. He might now become their leader.

Fearful of what might happen at the parliament, Henry acted. On 24 January, just before leaving Saint-Denis, he authorized a letter ordering Walter of Merton, keeper of the seal in England, to issue no writs summoning a parliament until his return. Two days later Henry ordered Bigod himself to prevent any parliament being held. As in later letters, this defiance of the Provisions of Oxford was masked by exaggerated respect for the council's advice over the arbitration.[43] Here surely we detect John Mansel's subtle hand. In England, when 2 February came, Montfort arrived in London ready to attend the parliament. The king later alleged he came with horses and arms, something Montfort did not deny. Bigod had now to decide whether to respect the letter of the Provisions or obey the order of the king. He obeyed the king and forbad the holding of a parliament until Henry's return. Montfort (so Henry later alleged) went ahead and held a parliament anyway.

An open breach with the other councillors was, however, avoided. Twice in February, Montfort joined with them to urge Henry's return. The realm, Henry was told, was at peace. Edward too sent reassuring messages. At one moment Henry decided to set off, only immediately to change his mind, probably hearing more about what Montfort was up to. At council meetings he was now urging the removal of Peter of Savoy. That must have pleased Edward, given Peter's interference in his affairs. It must equally have infuriated the queen.[44] On 19 February, Henry sent another letter to the councillors, asking again for advice over the arbitration and reiterating it was not his 'will' that parliament be held in his absence: it would be 'unfitting' and 'not in accord with our honour'. Henry had not used language like that since the revolution, yet the letter was authorized by Richard de Clare as well as John Mansel. As for Edward, Henry promised to send someone to England to discover 'whether deeds match words'.[45]

[43] CR 1259–61, 235, 267–8 (DBM, 164–9).

[44] DBM, 206–7, cap. 33. Montfort alleged that Peter had informed him of his resignation. Almost certainly this was twisting the truth. Peter may well have told Montfort that he would not be back in England for some time (he did not return until December 1260), but it is inconceivable he would have resigned, thus gravely weakening the position of the queen.

[45] CR 1259–61, 270–3, 278 (DBM, 170–3, 174–7).

Henry was also worried about something else. He had come to realize that on each of his returns to England he ought to offer a mark of gold at the shrine of 'the blessed Edward'. But he had not done so, he now remembered, in 1230, 1243 or 1255. Hardly a good preparation for the Confessor's support this time round! So, from St Omer on 24 February, Henry ordered four marks of gold to be ready for his offerings, thus covering the present return and clearing off the shameful arrears.[46]

Yet still Henry did not set off. Instead, early in March, Richard de Clare went in his place. The situation was going from bad to worse. There were no more reassuring letters from the council. Rumours abounded that Edward intended to imprison his father and rule in his stead.[47] In a series of fraught meetings of the council, Montfort warned Bigod not to send money to the king. If he did, he would have to repay it himself. He should also tell the king not to bring foreign troops into the country. If they came, they would be given such a reception that no more would want to follow! This was virtually a threat of civil war. Bigod took no notice. He sent Henry several thousand pounds, and now counselled his return with a military force.[48]

Henry thus started to recruit a body of paid troops from the Pas de Calais and the Low Countries. Here, as in getting loans, he was helped by the connections Queen Eleanor enjoyed with the magnates and merchants of the area.[49] Henry was also raising forces in England. On 27 March he sent to Hugh Bigod a list of loyalist magnates who were to muster in arms in London on 25 April. So critical was the situation, and so keen were Bigod and Walter of Merton to prove their loyalty and efficiency, that they drew up a special memorandum recording when the order was received (on 1 April at table) and when the writs were drawn up and sent out. Henry, however, hardly deserved such diligence for he did not intend to be at the muster himself. It was Bigod, Richard de Clare and Philip Basset who were to give his orders to the assembled throng.[50]

Now, however, came an intervention from someone with a far better understanding of the duties of kingship than Henry himself. Who should visit him at St Omer between 27 March and 1 April but King Louis himself. Louis was thus able on Maundy Thursday (1 April) to witness Henry feeding 321 paupers. Perhaps the two kings joined together in washing the paupers' feet. They also conversed about the situation in England and Louis gave Henry some good advice. 'It is shameful to us and our whole kingdom that we should be away so long, as the king of France and other friends have told us,' Henry wrote on 1 April. This was surely an amazing confession: that a king of England had to be told by a king of

---

[46] *CR 1259–61*, 243.
[47] Wykes, 123–4; Dunstable, 214–15.
[48] *DBM*, 208–11, caps. 36–9; *CLR 1251–60*, 500; *CPR 1258–66*, 122–3; Wild, *WA*, 87, 102.
[49] Howell, *Eleanor of Provence*, 168–9.
[50] *CR 1259–61*, 157–9 (*DBM*, 180–3); *CPR 1258–66*, 123.

France that he really must go home and do his job![51] Since the confession came in a letter to Richard de Clare, one suspects Clare had been giving contrary advice. Go home, though, Henry at last prepared to do. Indeed, he soon announced that he would attend in person what he now called the parliament called for 25 April.[52] He was helped here not merely by Louis's words but also by Louis's money. In two instalments, one in March and one in April, Louis gave Henry £5,690 as an advance payment on the money due for the 500 knights. Another £3,320 may have followed a little later.[53]

Having been taught his duty by one king, Henry was saved from his previous dereliction by another, namely his brother Richard, King of Germany. There was no way the muster planned for 25 April could be kept secret. Soon both Montfort and Edward were mobilizing their own forces in and around London. Montfort was also bringing warhorses over from France: 'you can see from that how he behaves towards us these days', Henry wrote bitterly to Louis.[54] With the kingdom on the brink of war, King Richard intervened to keep the peace. During Easter week (4–11 April) he entered London, with Hugh Bigod, and banned Montfort, Edward and Clare from entering the city.[55] Henry himself, having recruited a large force of knights and sergeants, finally crossed the channel on 23 April. The orders about his oblations had been met and he received four marks of gold, thirty-six gold coins, a gold buckle, twenty of his new gold pennies and an embroidered cope for his offerings to the Confessor.[56]

Henry had not neglected more secular routes of success. Before leaving France, he had drawn up a great manifesto for home consumption, the precursor of several issued in the next few years.[57] He recalled how God, 'the creator of heaven and earth who disposes all things', had brought him to the throne as a minor in the middle of a general war and had then restored unity and peace. That happy situation had continued until now when, without reason, men were gathering in London with horses and arms, while troops were being recruited from abroad. It was Henry's intention, he said, to lay to rest these commotions through 'the exhibition of justice', bound as he was to keep his kingdom in due order under God. He was returning with knights not to harm 'the community of the realm', which he dearly loved, but to restore its tranquillity. All his subjects as 'famous men' should demonstrate in their deeds the strength of their devotion to him and their loyalty.

[51] Carpenter, 'Meetings of kings', 22; *CR 1259–61*, 282 (*DBM*, 178–81).
[52] *CR 1259–61*, 250–1.
[53] *CPR 1258–66*, 81, 121, 123; Wild, *WA*, 87.
[54] *CR 1259–61*, 285–6 (*DBM*, 188–91); *CPR 1258–66*, 121.
[55] FitzThedmar, 44–5 (Stone, FitzThedmar, no. 735); Paris's Continuator, 447.
[56] *CLR 1251–60*, 509.
[57] *CR 1259–61*, 253–4; Treharne, *Baronial Plan*, 231.

All this was impressive and surely owed much to John Mansel, who was the only member of the council still with the king. But the effect was rather spoilt by one other passage where Henry thought fit to explain his long absence from the kingdom. He had hoped, he said, to pass the reason over, but could not. On leaving England, he had known there were sparks of dissension abroad. But with the withdrawal of his person he had hoped they might be extinguished. Instead, they had flared up, and he could no longer be silent. This explanation can only have come from Henry himself. He stands forth as a king with so small an understanding of his duty and so little faith in his abilities that he thought the best way of achieving peace was to absent himself from his kingdom.

## THE DEFUSING OF THE CRISIS, APRIL–JUNE 1260

Having landed at Dover, Henry made his way to London, which he reached on 30 April. Over the first two days there, he announced his presence and won spiritual support by feeding 666 paupers, 344 on the first day, 322 on the second. The daily feed then dropped back to a still impressive 150, the standard when the queen was at court. Henry remained in London with Eleanor, living in the episcopal palace at St Paul's, for more than a fortnight. (On the first day Bishop Wingham supplied all the food and drink.) At least Henry was able to avoid the Tower, but that Westminster was out of bounds is a measure of the crisis. How grievous for Henry not to make his offerings at the shrine of the Confessor and not to view the progress at the Abbey. While waiting to cross the Channel, Henry had ordered Hugh Bigod to find money so that the work on the church and the shrine were not delayed.[58]

Troops now surrounded London.[59] So as not to exacerbate the situation, Henry wisely left the bulk of his foreign forces across the river. Controlling London Bridge, he could always bring them into the city if necessary. Meanwhile, Edward's and Montfort's men were at Clerkenwell and in all the houses between the city and Westminster. Together, judging from those the king later sought to punish, they had built up a formidable party.[60] Henry and Hugh Bigod had been rallying their own supporters. The summons to the muster on 25 April had gone out to seven earls and

---

[58] *CR 1259–61*, 257.

[59] FitzThedmar, Paris's Continuator and Dunstable are the main sources for what follows.

[60] TNA E 368/35, m. 13d (images 5675–6). On the list of those whose debts were to be paid were the Edwardians Warin of Bassingbourn and John de Verdun. Those close to Montfort were Bishop Cantilupe, Peter de Montfort, Richard de Grey and the young Nicholas of Seagrave. Humphrey de Bohun junior was there too, a first sign of his Montfortianism, as were his father, the earl of Hereford, and Richard de Grey's brothers, John and William. Included too were William Bardolph and the marcher barons John fitzAlan, Reginald fitzPeter and William de Briouze.

ninety-nine barons and knights. From the start, Henry could count on the support of Roger Bigod, earl of Norfolk. Fortunately, earlier in the year Hugh Bigod, as justiciar, had presided over a judgement affirming Roger's rights at the exchequer as marshal of England.[61] Henry and Hugh, by judicious promises, also won over John de Warenne and Henry of Almain, two of Edward's closest friends. As soon as he arrived at Dover, Henry allowed them to enter London along with Roger Bigod and Richard de Clare.[62]

## HENRY WINS THROUGH

As the stand-off continued, Montfort's and Edward's position began to weaken. If Montfort still wished to give the king's foreign troops such a welcome none would dare to follow, he found his men had no stomach for the fight. Edward, therefore, tried to make terms. At first Henry refused to see him. 'If he appears before me, I could not stop myself kissing him', the Dunstable annalist recorded him as saying, a telling glimpse at Henry's love for his son. In the end, however, thanks to the good offices of King Richard, Edward was able to clear himself of the worst charges. His quarrels with Richard de Clare were referred to Henry and Richard, the result being an anodyne injunction to observe previous agreements.[63] More significantly, Edward was forced to back down over Bristol. On 15 May, Philip Basset became keeper of the castle in place of Roger of Leybourne, this on terms effectively imposed by the king and the council. New castellans were also appointed to Montgomery and (replacing Roger of Clifford) the Three Castles, Grosmont, Skenfrith and Whitecastle.[64] Henry and Eleanor then gave Edward the kiss of peace and next day, 16 May, went joyfully to Westminster.

The Dunstable annalist blamed Eleanor for the quarrel with Edward. Certainly she had hated her son's rejection of his Savoyard councillors and his alliance with the Lusignans. She must have been delighted to see him, as she hoped, back in her camp. The root cause of the trouble, however, went wider. It lay in Edward's quarrel with Richard de Clare over Bristol and his general desire to be free from control, whether of his father, his mother or the council.

The great loser from the events was Simon de Montfort. He had hoped to become the dominant figure on the council. Instead, he was totally out. Between June and October 1260 there is no sign either of him or his allies Peter de Montfort and Richard de Grey at court.[65] Even worse, Henry, probably supported by Hugh Bigod, intended to bring charges against

---

[61] TNA E 368/35, m. 8/9 (image 5596).
[62] CR 1259–61, 287; CPR 1258–66, 79, 123; Prestwich, Edward I, 27–8.
[63] CPR 1258–66, 79.
[64] CR 1259–61, 42; Studd, 'Acts of Lord Edward', nos. 790–5.
[65] The bishop of Worcester, however, is found at court.

him. The great winner, by contrast, was Richard de Clare. Having effectively banished Montfort and his allies from the council, he was now
unchallenged at court. He was there for long periods in every month
between May and October 1260, and attests nearly every royal charter. He
was also involved in authorizing a large number of royal letters. If he
made little progress in his quest for Bristol, he secured one major gain.

In the early months of 1260, Clare must have learnt with increasing
irritation about the progress of the great eyres commissioned in November
1259. His officials were being had up both for oppression and for
encroaching on the rights of the crown. Clare's response came as soon as
he got back to England. On 18 March he secured an inquiry into the
money potentially lost to the crown if he was granted 'return of writs'
throughout his lands. Evidently this was Clare's ambition. If realized it
would have excluded the sheriff from his lands altogether.[66] When it came
to the eyres, King Richard, in much the same predicament as Clare, had
found his own solution. In January 1260 the judges were no longer to hear
complaints against his bailiffs. Instead, their abuses were to be corrected
by Richard himself.[67] Clare now managed to go one further. Early in June
the eyre was suspended altogether.[68]

Henry's record during the crisis of 1260 was mixed. Had he been a king
like William Rufus or Richard I, he would have hurried to England with
or without an army and scattered his enemies. But then had Henry been
like that, there would have been no crisis in the first place. Henry's inac-
tion had nonetheless served him well. He had avoided civil war and
emerged with his freedom enhanced.[69] Formally he was still subject to the
council's authority. He had not overthrown the Provisions of Oxford, or
indeed tried to do so. Some royal letters were still authorized by the
council: over forty of them are found in the chancery rolls between May
and July. What that meant in practice is hard to say. Eleven members of
the council are found at court between May and September. Robert
Walerand, who had replaced the earl of Aumale, doubtless to Henry and
Eleanor's delight, was often there. But of the councillors, only Richard de
Clare and John Mansel seem to have been active in day-to-day business.
Between May and July, Clare authorized around twenty royal letters and
Mansel around thirty. Frequently they acted together. Hugh Bigod shoul-
dered a much bigger burden. Acting alone he authorized over forty letters.
Even more striking is the role of the king. Between the revolution of 1258

---

[66] *CPR 1258–66*, 99.

[67] *CR 1259–61*, 26. If, however, Richard had not acted by Easter, the king and his judges
would do so.

[68] *CR 1259–61*, 172–3.

[69] I am sceptical of the view (found, for example, in Treharne, *Baronial Plan*, 219, 234,
242) that Henry cleverly remained in France precisely to foment divisions within the
council. He remained because of real fears as to what was happening in England.

and the autumn of 1259, as we have seen, he authorized hardly a single letter. He was totally in the background. Now between May and July 1260 he authorized roughly forty-five letters alone, twenty-five with Hugh Bigod, and fifteen with the council. At last he was once more a king.

## PUNISHMENT: THE 'TRIAL' OF SIMON DE MONTFORT

Henry celebrated Whitsun at Westminster on 23 May in fine style, feeding 464 paupers and throwing a feast costing in food and drink at least £141. Henry's foreign mercenaries began to leave England. The home forces were disbanded. In June, King Richard set off again for Germany, hoping he might go on from there to the papal court for his coronation as emperor.[70] Henry, meanwhile, ordered 'a great samite' to be made into two choral copes, each to be adorned with the widest orphreys that could be found in London. The copes were to be ready, 'as you love us', to celebrate the feasts of Peter and Paul at Westminster on 29 June.[71] But the appearance of normality was deceptive. The removal of Richard's stabilizing hand was itself a cause of anxiety.[72] When Henry convoked a parliament in July he ordered his supporters to come armed, before apparently changing his mind. One point of tension was Henry's determination to punish his opponents. An early victim was the abbot of Peterborough, John de Caux, who had lent money to Edward and then refused it to the king. Henry personally ordered his local officials to show the abbot no 'grace' and find some offence for which he could be prosecuted. As so often the king's anger cooled and the abbot, thanks to John Mansel's intervention, was soon saved from being treated 'unjustly'.[73]

Henry anyway had bigger fish to fry. On 19 May, soon after he arrived at Westminster, there was a major change in the custody of royal castles. Gilbert de Gant, William Bardolph, Peter de Montfort and John de Grey, Richard de Grey's brother, were all sacked. Here Henry was working with his allies on the council.[74] Next month he went on the attack alone. On his direct orders, the exchequer sent out writs instructing the sheriffs, as they loved all they had, to raise in double quick time the money (in some cases running to hundreds of pounds) that twenty magnates owed the king, the victims being those who had joined Montfort and Edward earlier in the year. In fact, there is no sign anything was done in response to the orders and Henry was wise to let the matter drop. Some of the magnates attacked

---

[70] *Layettes*, iii, no. 4471 (a litany of praise from the pope); Paris, v, 747; Paris's Continuator, 427–8; Denholm-Young, *Richard of Cornwall*, 99–100; Weiler, *Henry III of England and the Staufen Empire*, 182–3.

[71] *CR 1259–61*, 63. A few days earlier (p. 60) Henry looked after a poor widow with seven children whose husband had been hanged for felony.

[72] Paris's Continuator, 453.

[73] *CR 1259–61*, 51–2, 87.

[74] *CPR 1258–66*, 70–1.

were to stand loyally with him in the future.[75] When it came to Simon de
Montfort himself, Henry was far more enraged and determined. He drew
up a whole series of charges against the earl and intended to add more at
the parliament due to open on 8 July. There was, however, an agreement
over the process, a sign that relations had not totally broken down. A
group of bishops were to investigate the truth of the charges and give their
report to the king and the council. If the charges were found to be true,
the council, sitting with earls and barons who were Montfort's peers,
would judge what amends Montfort should make. According to one
account Montfort stipulated that five of his enemies should be excluded
from the court.[76]

Henry's charges and Montfort's replies survive in one of the most
remarkable documents of the thirteenth century. In a modern edition it
runs to eight printed pages with thirty-nine separate exchanges.[77] Never
have the fractured relations between a king and a nobleman been so
vividly displayed. Henry covered the whole gamut of Montfort's crimes
since 1258: the refusal to make the renunciations; the delay to the Treaty
of Paris; the extraction of the royal demesne manors; the obstruction of
the arbitration; the unlicensed return to England; the attempt to hold a
parliament; the making of alliances; and the threats to Hugh Bigod.
Montfort's replies, probably taken down verbatim, in their arrogance,
disdain, injured innocence, flat denials, manipulation of truth, haggling
over details and utter certainty in the rightness and righteousness of his
conduct, get to the heart of this formidable and frightening man. The ease
and contempt with which Henry's carefully mounted attack was swiped
aside must have been utterly infuriating. Infuriating too, indeed positively
alarming, were the political ideas revealed in Montfort's defence.

Again and again, in justification of his conduct, Montfort appealed to
what he now called evocatively 'the common enterprise' and its 'common
provisions'. In his mind, these had authority in the realm superior to that
of the king himself. It was to support 'the common enterprise' that he had
gathered men and made alliances. It was to keep his oath to the 'common
provisions' that he had tried to hold the February parliament. It was in
parliament too 'according to the law' that he would answer the charges
brought against him. At the heart of the Provisions, of course, was the
authority of the council and to that Montfort returned again and again:
the council needed to consent to any 'great gift' made by the king; 'all of
the council' with the king had granted him the demesne manors; before

[75] TNA E 368/35, m. 13d (images 5675–6). This was true of John and William de Grey
and the marcher barons John fitzAlan, Reginald fitzPeter and William de Briouze. For
those attacked see above, note 60.

[76] TNA KB 26/167, m. 26 (image 0073); Jacob, 'A proposal for arbitration', 80–1; Paris's
Continuator, 449.

[77] *DBM*, 194–211.

the council he had urged the replacement of Peter of Savoy and had issued his warnings to Hugh Bigod; and before the council he should answer for what he said. Montfort believed profoundly in all this. He also knew it would resonate in parliament and beyond. And with his sure political instinct, he picked up another popular issue. Henry's bringing in foreign troops, he said, 'harmed and dishonoured both king and land in common, for it seemed the king put his trust more in foreigners than in men of his own land'.[78] This was an issue on which Henry knew he was vulnerable. Montfort was to exploit it for all he was worth. Hostility to foreigners later became a central plank in his programme and appeal. In July 1260 there was one other indication of Montfort's political awareness. He conceded that the men of the archbishop of Rouen should only have to attend his hundred court at Odiham twice a year, this, as he said, being in accordance with Magna Carta.[79]

The hope was that the bishops would deliver the results of their investigation to the July parliament. They did not do so. In truth they had an impossible task. The quarrel, as Montfort framed it, turned on the validity of the reforms as much as his own conduct. And in that conduct there was no flaming torch to set alight all the rest. In the end, Montfort had not taken up arms against the king. Politically, moreover, he was down but not out. His alliance with Edward remained intact, despite the latter's submission. Montfort had also, in his replies, exploited his relations with King Louis. On several points he declared he would stand or fall on the recollection of the king of France. Indeed, during July, Louis's councillor Eudes Rigaud, archbishop of Rouen, came to England to give Montfort his support.[80]

## A CRISIS IN WALES

There was another reason why Henry made no progress in pressing his charges. The parliament was forced to shift focus by dramatic events in Wales. Since the revolution of 1258, Llywelyn ap Gruffudd had been offering money, much money, for a peace settlement with the king, one which would regularize the dominant position he had achieved in Wales. The council had put him off. With much else to do, it could decide neither to throw back his advances nor to make a peace accepting them. A complicating factor was that Edward, the chief sufferer from Llywelyn's conquests,

---

[78] *DBM*, 208–9, cap. 38.

[79] Hampshire County Record Office, Photocopy Accessions Ph. 62c, from an original in the Archives de Seine-Maritime at Rouen. I am grateful to Nicholas Vincent for sending me a copy of this document. See Maddicott, *Simon de Montfort*, 198–9. The relevant chapter is 35 in the 1225 Magna Carta.

[80] Maddicott, *Simon de Montfort*, 198; Powicke, 'The archbishop of Rouen, John de Harcourt and Simon de Montfort'. Hence the concession mentioned in note 79 above.

would be the gainer from the first and the loser from the second. The result was simply a series of truces accepting the situation as it had been in 1258 and thus Llywelyn's virtual conquest of the Four Cantrefs.

Eventually, Llywelyn lost patience with his peace policy. In January 1260, in an apparent breach of the current truce, he moved south and laid siege to Builth. The castle was one of Edward's, the castellan, Roger de Mortimer, a member of the council. When Henry heard the news out in France, he urged Hugh Bigod to co-ordinate measures for the castle's defence. Indeed, this was another reason for not holding a parliament.[81] In fact, the siege was soon abandoned, and attempts were made to patch up the truce. But then suddenly, in July, Builth fell to a surprise attack, Mortimer being away at the parliament. When the shocking news arrived, Mortimer's fellow councillors (including Richard de Clare, Roger Bigod and Humphrey de Bohun) rallied round and issued a letter saying he was blameless, only for Edward to protest against the let-off. The clash fore-shadowed the divisions about what to do next.[82]

On 1 August, Henry summoned two armies. One was to muster at Shrewsbury on 8 September, the other at Chester. Edward above all must have urged this martial response. Indeed, he journeyed to Chester to lead the northern expedition. He also secured the recall of none other than Simon de Montfort, for Montfort was one of those summoned to Chester. Matthew Paris's continuator described him as 'the commander of the army, *dux exercitus*'. There was, however, soon no army for him to lead for, alongside these military preparations, negotiations were in train for a prolongation of the truce. On 1 September, Henry announced their success and the musters were cancelled. The truce recognized Llywelyn's de facto hegemony over the other Welsh rulers and was due to last until June 1262.[83] Behind the truce were surely Edward's and Montfort's enemies. If the two led a victorious campaign in Wales, it would transform the political situation in England. Henry too seems to have favoured the truce. He later complained merely about the failure to get any money for it.[84]

## THE DURHAM ELECTION

On 17 August 1260, Henry left Windsor for Guildford and then went on to Winchester, Clarendon and Marlborough, residences he had not seen since his return from France. At Winchester he was greeted by a procession and announced his arrival by feeding 282 paupers.[85] During this

[81] *CR 1259–61*, 267–8 (*DBM*, 164–9).

[82] *F*, i, 398 (*CPR 1258–66*, 85). For what follows, I am indebted to the acute analysis in Smith, *Llywelyn ap Gruffudd*, 126–32.

[83] *CR 1259–61*, 191–4, 200–1; *AWR*, no. 342; Smith, *Llywelyn ap Gruffudd*, 131–2.

[84] Ridgeway, 'King Henry III's grievances against the council', 232, 241, cap. 28.

[85] Winchester, 98.

period he had with him only a small entourage: the costs of its food and drink were sometimes less than £5 a day. He was also separated from the queen, who had gone direct from Windsor to Marlborough. For some of the time no members of the council were present. This was the setting for a remarkable plot hatched by John Mansel, the queen and the king in defiance of the council. It was a plot to make Mansel bishop of Durham.[86]

The bishop of Durham, Walter of Kirkham, had died on 9 August 1260. On 17 August, now at Guildford, Henry placed the vacant bishopric in the keeping of John Mansel's son or nephew Master John Mansel. Matthew Paris's continuator claimed this was done by the king 'against the common provision', and such a major appointment should surely have been sanctioned by the council. The chancery rolls, as a cover note, recorded that 'this commitment was made by order of the king by mandate of John Mansel through John de St Denis, his clerk, coming to the king on his behalf at Guildford'. The aim of the appointment, of course, was to bring pressure on the monks through Mansel junior to elect Mansel senior as their new bishop.

When a few days later a couple of Durham monks arrived at Winchester seeking licence to elect, they had a friendly welcome from Henry and were entertained to dinner. Immediately afterwards, messengers arrived from the queen with letters urging Henry to press for John Mansel's election. Henry can have needed no urging and promptly did so. He also wrote a formal letter to the convent warning of the dangers if his 'honest petition' was 'repulsed' and praising Mansel's morality, probity, circumspection and long labour in the government of the kingdom. He followed this up by sending his almoner and the Savoyard household knight Imbert de Montferrand to explain his 'will' more fully. Eleanor wrote even more enthusiastically and mellifluously in Mansel's favour. It was to no avail. The two monks reported back on 'the state of the court as they perceived it', doubtless explaining that Henry was acting without conciliar consent. Meanwhile, Edward, in defiance of his parents, wrote separately urging the election of Hugh de Cantilupe, nephew of Montfort's great supporter Walter de Cantilupe, bishop of Worcester. He referred to Cantilupe's 'high birth' (Mansel's of course was low) and the pleasure the appointment would bring 'to the whole people', another indication of his awareness of the wider political community. In the circumstances the monks felt they could perfectly well do as they pleased and elected an old alumnus, Robert Stichill, now prior of Coldingham. Robert came to London at the time of the October parliament. At first Henry refused assent to his election, only then a few days later to agree to it. It was not the only defeat he suffered at the parliament.

---

[86] For what follows, see Paris's Continuator, 454–6; *CPR 1258–66*, 90, 98; Muniments of the Dean and Chapter of Durham, Loc. I. 60, m. 3d, and the full account in Howell, *Eleanor of Provence*, 172–4. In September, Hugh Bigod was on eyre in Yorkshire: Crook, *Records of the General Eyre*, 189.

## MONTFORT'S RETURN CENTRE STAGE: OCTOBER 1260

The feast of the translation of Edward the Confessor on 13 October was always the greatest day in Henry's religious year. In 1260 it had a special significance. Just as on 13 October 1247 he had knighted his brother William de Valence, so now on 13 October 1260 he intended to knight his son-in-law John of Brittany. In September, Henry personally authorized the expenditure of up to 2,200 marks on the preparations, including the robes of silk and cloth of gold to be worn by the participants. He also laid on water music in the Thames, telling the Cinque Ports to send boats adorned with banners and filled with trumpeters.[87] On the great day, Henry girded John and twenty-four others with the sword of knighthood and threw a gigantic feast costing well over £200. He also fed 5,016 paupers.[88]

Henry must have hoped that this joyful celebration would win him a reward at the parliament. He had already made preparations for his interventions. In September he had ordered the wrought-iron and gilded lectern, under manufacture since 1259, to be assembled and placed in the Abbey's chapter house ready for his arrival. He surely intended to speak from the lectern during parliament's meetings, supported and empowered on either side by the glittering tiles with his coat of arms which ran in two great bands across the floor.[89]

Alas, thanks in large part to Simon de Montfort, neither the knighting, the feast nor the parliament worked out as Henry wished. Edward himself muscled in on the first by knighting, on the same day, Montfort's two eldest sons, Henry and Simon, thus underlining his continuing alliance with the earl.[90] As for the feast, here, 'in shame of the king', Montfort performed his service as steward of England without being summoned by Henry to do so. The fact that he performed the service through a deputy did little to lessen the offence.[91] Even worse were the appointments made at the parliament. The new treasurer of the exchequer, in place of the recently deceased John of Crakehall, was none other than John de Caux, the very abbot of Peterborough who earlier in the year had lent money to Edward and refused it to Henry. The new chancellor in Henry of Wingham's place was Nicholas, archdeacon of Ely. Very much in the spirit of 1258, he was given by the council a salary of 400 marks a year to sustain himself and his clerks.[92] The new justiciar, in place of Hugh Bigod, was Hugh Despenser. In all three cases, Henry had put forward his own candidates

[87] *CLR 1251–60*, 528; *CR 1259–61*, 116, 126–8, 211.

[88] Paris's Continuator, 456; TNA E 101/349/27; Carpenter, 'Household rolls', 41, 43.

[89] *CR 1259–61*, 112; Carpenter, 'King Henry III and the chapter house', 36–7.

[90] Paris's Continuator, 456. On 20 October both Montfort and Henry of Almain witnessed a charter of Edward: TNA C 61/4, m. 1 (Studd, 'Acts of Lord Edward', no. 861).

[91] *F*, i, 402 (*CPR 1258–66*, 96); Ridgeway, 'King Henry III's grievances against the council', 241, cap. 29.

[92] *CLR 1260–7*, 9; Dibben, 'Chancellor and keeper of the seal', 48.

and been rebuffed. It was not till the following summer that he was able to make Wingham's deputy, Walter of Merton, chancellor and Philip Basset justiciar.[93]

Of the three changes, the most significant was Hugh Bigod's replacement as justiciar by Hugh Despenser. This was above all Montfort's doing. After their acrimonious exchanges early in the year, he must have regarded Bigod as an enemy, perhaps even a mortal one. After all, had he not broken his oath to uphold the Provisions? The hatred was mutual, judging from the way Bigod's forester (in December) insulted Montfort by arresting and laming his hounds.[94] Clare too, remembering how his officials had been punished on Bigod's eyres, was probably glad to see him gone.[95] Bigod's replacement, Despenser, was one of Montfort's most devoted followers.[96] Probably the initial link between the two men was one of neighbourhood, the great Despenser manor at Loughborough being only ten miles north of Leicester. Montfort's influence had got Despenser as the last man onto the baronial twelve in 1258. He failed to make the council of fifteen, but was one of the twelve representing the community at parliament and was soon regarded as a leading member of the regime.[97] At the start of 1259 he appears as an advisor to the executors of Montfort's will. Lord of many manors in Leicestershire, Yorkshire, Lincolnshire and Rutland, and married to an heiress (Alina, daughter of Philip Basset), he could give powerful support to Montfort's cause. He was to die with Montfort at Evesham.

Despenser's arrival was particularly unwelcome to the king for the two men were in no way close. The Despensers had been major tenants of the earls of Chester, holding the honorary position of 'despenser' in their household. In the 1220s, thanks to Earl Ranulf's influence, both Hugh's father, another Hugh, and his uncle, Geoffrey, had begun long careers at court. Hugh must surely have hoped to follow them. He made a good start. In 1245, Henry gave him wine to celebrate his knighting. For a few years there were more gifts.[98] Then nothing. Hugh seems to have been almost totally out of favour. Why is unknown. He went with Richard of Cornwall to Germany in 1257 but little seems to have come of that connection. It was with Montfort that he allied.

Montfort, therefore, had now placed his man at the very centre of English government, and there was more to come. On 13 October, Montfort had at least acted as steward through a deputy. Soon he was very much in Henry's face. Between 20 October and 2 December he witnessed nearly every royal charter and must have been pretty constantly at court,

---

[93] *DBM*, 222–3, cap. 4 [8].
[94] See above, 154.
[95] However, on Clare's death in 1262, Bigod is found as one of his executors.
[96] For a biography, see Knowles, 'Hugh Despenser'.
[97] See above, 34 n. 36.
[98] *CR 1242–7*, 283; *CR 1247–51*, 3, 134, 195.

the first time he had been there on any regular basis since February and March 1259.[99]

What then had brought about this extraordinary reversal in Montfort's fortunes? The answer is that he had made an alliance with his old enemy Richard de Clare. The first sign of that appears in another defeat for Henry. He had attempted, probably at the October parliament, to revive the charges against Montfort. To gain ammunition, he had ordered the exchequer to total up all the money Montfort had received from the crown since 1236. It amounted to an astonishing £21,160: £14,399 in direct cash payments from the exchequer and £6,761 from other sources.[100] But if Henry revealed this, speaking from his gilded lectern in the chapter house, it failed to cut through. Montfort and Clare, acting together, prevented any charges going forward. As Henry later complained, he had been denied common justice: 'such contempt and injury had never been suffered before either by rich or poor'.[101] Montfort and Clare appear equally standing shoulder to shoulder witnessing royal charters. They were now the dominant figures at court.

There is no record of the agreement between Montfort and Clare, but the advantages to both are clear enough. Montfort blocked any renewal of the king's charges and returned centre stage. In the process he reaffirmed the council's control over the king. Clare himself had a particular reason for wanting that maintained. In May 1260 the pope had finally consecrated Aymer de Lusignan as bishop of Winchester. Aymer was now on his way back to England, determined to resume his office. If allowed to do so, he would surely seek to recover the isle of Portland, thus threatening Clare's great gain from the revolution of 1258. Clare knew only too well how keen the king was to have Aymer back. With Montfort's backing he could stop it. That backing would be all the stronger given Montfort's continuing alliance with Lord Edward, an alliance so very publicly proclaimed in Edward's knighting of Montfort's sons. Montfort could also bring in Henry of Almain.[102] It was Henry who acted as Montfort's deputy on 13 October. Later in the year their greyhounds, led on the same leash, were arrested and mutilated together by Hugh Bigod's forester.

Montfort and Clare could thus agree on the council's control over the king. Next year they both resisted Henry's attempt to overthrow it. Where they had disagreed was over local reform, especially reform of how magnates ran their own estates. On this issue, Montfort now gave way.

[99] *RCWL*, ii, 130–2.

[100] *CLR 1260–7*, 272 n. 2. I am grateful to Richard Cassidy for bringing this memorandum to my attention. That Henry ordered the inquiry is my speculation.

[101] Ridgeway, 'King Henry III's grievances against the council', 231, 241–2, cap. 31. Clare was also one of the councillors who agreed to Montfort acting as steward through a deputy: *F*, i, 402 (*CPR 1258–66*, 96).

[102] Throughout the summer and autumn, Montfort and his party had continued to witness Edward's charters: Ridgeway, 'The politics of the English royal court', 364, 370.

During the summer the special Provisions of Westminster eyre with its hearing of everyone's complaints had been suspended, almost certainly at Clare's behest. The excuse given, the burden of the eyre in a time scarcity, at least implied it would be resumed. Instead, something else happened. An ordinance was promulgated by the whole council giving every magnate the power to hear the complaints made against their bailiffs. The idea that magnates themselves should correct the abuses of their officials was an old one. It had already been exploited both by King Richard and Richard de Clare. Now it seems to have been given official form and teeth.[103] The likelihood of magnate officials having to answer complainants before a revived Provisions of Westminster eyre was thus greatly reduced. In fact, the eyre never was revived. Instead, in November 1260, orders went out for the holding of ordinary general eyres with no special provision for the hearing of complaints.[104] The most striking feature of the local reforms of 1258–9, the one most objected to by Clare and other magnates, had thus been abandoned.[105]

Montfort, however, could think he had saved the most vital part of the Provisions, namely the council's control of the king. Without that all would be lost. He had also, up to a point, remained true to the cause of local reform, if in partisan fashion. It was surely with his encouragement that Hugh Despenser, in deliberate counterpoint to the new eyre, decided to hear complaints in just the same manner as had Hugh Bigod. In December 1260 he went to Sussex to do so, hearing many cases against the bailiffs of Peter of Savoy. No reference seems to have been made to the Ordinance allowing magnates to deal with such cases themselves.[106] For Montfort the eyre served two purposes. It attacked Peter of Savoy and it showed a continuing commitment to hearing complaints against the bailiffs of great men. If in 1259 Montfort's attachment to reform could be questioned, the same was hardly the case in 1260. He had been in England for nearly all the year. In seeking to hold the February parliament, in appealing to the council's authority during his 'trial', in seeing through the change of ministers in October, in encouraging Hugh Despenser's eyre, he had stood forth as the champion of the reforms. His commitment and leadership would become even clearer in the following year.

---

[103] *CPR 1258–66*, 97; *DBM*, 134–5, 162–3, caps. 7–8, 11.

[104] Crook, *Records of the General Eyre*, 126–8.

[105] Another watering-down affected the sheriffs. They were not changed at Michaelmas 1260, after their year in office, and nothing came of the scheme to make the office partly elective. Perhaps this was in the cause of administrative efficiency. Perhaps also the barons were content with the current sheriffs, having many connections with them, as Henry later alleged. For such connections see Ridgeway, 'Mid thirteenth-century reformers and the localities', 69–70, 73–4.

[106] For the cases see above, 155–7.

## THE KING'S BID FOR FREEDOM

For Henry, the events at the October parliament and the return of Montfort to court had dispelled any hope that the controls of 1258 would simply wither away. He soon found the council cancelling his appointment of a new bailiff to run the manors attached to Windsor castle. Henry also felt the council was irresponsibly spending his money. Indeed, he instructed the exchequer to make no payments until it had a 'special discussion' with him. At the end of the year, 'to his vexation', he found he lacked money to provide for the feast of Edward the Confessor on the coming 5 January.[107] Of course, Henry had been humiliated and frustrated before, but now at last he could act. This was above all because of the changing attitudes of King Richard, Peter of Savoy and Queen Eleanor.

After his return to England in January 1259, King Richard had done nothing to disrupt the council's authority. He was now of a different mind. Earlier in the year he had intervened to keep the peace and had then departed for Germany. He returned in October to find the disturber of that peace, Simon de Montfort, dominant at court and Montfort's man Hugh Despenser heading the government as justiciar. Even worse, at the end of 1260, he found his tenure of Lechlade being challenged by Despenser and the council, acting on behalf of Roger de Mortimer.[108] That Despenser had once been in his service made it all the worse. With his hopes of imperial coronation dashed, Richard had the time to put matters right in England.

The queen and Peter of Savoy had likewise changed their minds.[109] According to the Waverley abbey annalist, the provisions of 1258 had pleased the queen because they meant the expulsion of the Lusignans. But now, as the annalist noted, with her compatriots threatened, she looked at things very differently.[110] The person threatened above all, of course, was Peter of Savoy. In 1259, Montfort had opposed money from the Winchester bishopric being used to pay Savoyard pensions. Probably he had also opposed the deal with the duke of Brittany allowing Peter to keep Richmond. In 1260, in Peter's absence, Montfort had tried to remove him from the council. Peter was now back in England and from early December witnessing royal charters at court. There he linked up with other Savoyards: the steward Imbert Pugeys and the knights Ebulo de Montibus, Imbert de Montferrand and Peter de Champvent.

In all this, Eleanor knew there would be a price to pay for the overthrow of the baronial regime. Her husband would surely want back his Lusignan half-brothers. A lucky event, however, now made that prospect less repugnant. On 4 December 1260, Bishop Aymer died in Paris on his way to

---

[107] TNA E 159/35, mm. 3d, 4d (images 0187, 0190); *CLR 1260–7*, 13.

[108] *CR 1259–61*, 335; *CPR 1258–66*, 181; Carpenter, 'A noble in politics', 197.

[109] During Peter's absence the queen had acted as his representative in England. See TNA KB 26/165, m. 34 (image 0288); TNA KB 26/167, m. 8 (image 0021).

[110] Waverley, 355.

England. Henry was distraught and had had 30,000 paupers fed for the health of his brother's soul.[111] Eleanor, by contrast, was delighted for she disliked Aymer far more than the other brothers, or at least there is more evidence for her dislike. Over the return of the others she now made Henry accept her conditions. They were only to reappear having given security to the queen of France for their good behaviour.[112]

One other factor cleared the way for Henry's demarche. Edward was absent. The peacemaking of 1260 had seen Henry and Eleanor reconciled to their eldest son. They cannot, however, have welcomed his continued alliance with Simon de Montfort. Indeed, since the alliance bound Edward to sustain 'the enterprise made by the barons of the land', there was a real danger he would oppose his parents' bid for freedom. Recently, with Montfort back in the saddle, he had been favoured by the baronial regime. In October 1260 he received the lands of the earl of Aumale in wardship.[113] But soon afterwards, Edward left England taking with him Montfort's two eldest sons, John de Warenne and the rest of his entourage. His ultimate destination was Gascony. He did not return to England until March 1261. His parents could thus plot their moves without his potentially unreliable and disruptive presence.

It may be that some preliminary plotting had taken place back in October 1260. That month saw the arrival at court of King Alexander as well as King Richard. Alexander was soon followed by Queen Margaret so that three kings and three queens were together in London, just the kind of family reunion Henry and Eleanor loved, although Matthew Paris's continuator complained of the expense. Next month Alexander returned to Scotland, leaving his pregnant queen to stay with her mother until she gave birth, another glimpse of the tight bonds within the royal family. Those bonds had very clear political dimensions. It seems likely that Henry and Richard explained what might be afoot and secured at the least Alexander's promise of non-intervention. The last thing they wanted was for the baronial alliance with the Scottish magnates made back in 1258 to be invoked. In return, and in response to Alexander's demands, 500 marks were now given towards Margaret's still unpaid dowry.[114]

If the non-intervention of King Alexander facilitated the bid for freedom, the way was finally cleared through what seems a catastrophic mistake made

[111] *CLR 1260–7*, 12–14.
[112] Howell, *Eleanor of Provence*, 180. The queen's power is shown by the way the Hilary exchequer respited debts on her orders, for example TNA E 159/34, m. 5d (image 0194).
[113] This was all the more a concession if the wardship had initially been fingered by Richard de Clare: Paris's Continuator, 450.
[114] *F*, i, 402–3 (*CPR 1258–66*, 94–5, 105, 128); *CR 1259–61*, 124; Wild, *WA*, 87, 103. Paris's Continuator, 459–60; Reid, *Alexander III*, 154–7. For the importance of these family reunions, see Armstrong, 'The daughters of Henry III', 162–75. Alexander arrived at the end of October so missed John of Brittany's knighting: fitzThedmar, 45 (Stone, FitzThedmar, no. 741). The alliance between the English and Scottish magnates (see above, 39) is mentioned by Paris's continuator in connection with the visit.

by the ruling regime, explicable only in terms of over-confidence. Early in December, Hugh Despenser, Richard de Clare and Simon de Montfort all left court. Despenser set off for Sussex to hear those pleas against Peter of Savoy, Clare departed perhaps to celebrate Christmas on his estates. Montfort himself went to France in part to settle private disputes with the Lusignans. (The moment he left, Peter of Savoy reappeared at court, as though the two men could not bear each other's presence.)[115] Neither Clare nor Montfort is found at court again before the end of February, by which time the political situation had been transformed.[116]

Henry, Eleanor and King Richard celebrated the Christmas of 1260 together at Windsor in fine style.[117] Orders had gone out for over 5,000 loaves of the best bread to be baked and all the necessary furs to be acquired for the king's gifts to his queen, children and household. As for the paupers, 150 were to be clothed and shod for the 'maundy' of the king and queen, and another 21 for the maundy of the royal children. Henry also ordered 'a beautiful jewel', costing 15 or 20 marks, to be offered to the Confessor on 1 January, the feast of the Circumcision.[118] Counselled by King Richard, the queen, Peter of Savoy and John Mansel (their names come up again and again in the chronicle sources), Henry decided now was the time to act.

## THE THREE-PART STRATEGY

What emerged from the discussions at the Christmas court was a clever three-part strategy, just the kind of thing one might expect from the fertile brains of King Richard, John Mansel and Peter of Savoy. The first part was to secure, in secret, a papal annulment of the oath taken by Henry and everyone else to accept the work of reform. The second was to free the king from the rule of the council, *before* the arrival of the papal thunderbolt. And the third, as a smokescreen, was to pretend meanwhile that Henry's objections to the council related to its behaviour rather than its authority. Indeed, if it behaved better, Henry might still be prepared to accept its advice. This strategy was well co-ordinated. It was vital to have a measure of control when the envoy with the papal bulls arrived, otherwise he might be sent packing just like Velascus in 1259. And it was sensible to defuse opposition until the unveiling of the bulls by pretending the king might still be prepared to go along with the council after all.

[115] Montfort's last attestation is on 2 December, Peter's first on the next day: *RCWL*, ii, 132; Ridgeway, 'The politics of the English royal court', 377–8.

[116] Maddicott, *Simon de Montfort*, 204–5 (the issue was Eleanor's claims to a share of her mother's county of Angoulême). A letter dated 28 December is authorized by Clare and others but that is not certain proof he was at court.

[117] Paris's Continuator, 461. Queen Sanchia, however, remained at Berkhamsted, perhaps ill. She died a few months later: Jobson, 'A queen in the shadows', 766–7, 772.

[118] *CR 1259–61*, 311–12, 314, 316–17.

The central plank in this strategy was the easiest to put in place. It was probably sometime in January that Master John Mansel departed for the papal court.[119] The choice shows how deeply involved was John Mansel himself. He was displaying considerable courage. If the bid for freedom failed, King Richard and Peter of Savoy could depart for their continental dominions. Henry and Eleanor would simply be back to where they were before. Mansel, on the other hand, would be finished. After his betrayal, there would be no place for him in a new reform regime. Indeed, he might be treated as a mortal enemy and lose his possessions and even perhaps his life.

The second part of the strategy required Henry to recover control of his seal from the council and start issuing orders once again on his own authority. That was more tricky than simply sending an agent to the pope but it was achieved. The council sanctioned grants and orders on 28 December and 7–8 January. After that there is virtually no evidence of its activity. The chancellor, Nicholas of Ely, although appointed under the terms of the Provisions, was now taking his orders from the king. A struggle for the allegiance of Roger de Mortimer showed this very clearly. On 14 December, as part of a policy to win over members of the council, Henry had granted robes to Mortimer as a member of the king's household.[120] A fortnight later the council, in its own bid for Mortimer's loyalty, sanctioned an inquiry into his claims to Lechlade. But, remarkably, the writ in question was witnessed not by the king, as was usual, but by Hugh Despenser. Evidently the king was no longer co-operating with the regime. By 20 January 1261, Nicholas of Ely was not co-operating either. The terms of the 28 December inquiry were now altered 'because the king does not remember that the [original] inquiry proceeded by him or by his order'.[121] Although there were still members of the council of fifteen at court – Savoy, Mansel, Philip Basset and Robert Walerand – Henry now regarded them as king's councillors, as they regarded themselves, not as councillors appointed by the Provisions.[122]

## THE RIVAL PARLIAMENTS AND THE MOVE
## TO THE TOWER: FEBRUARY 1261

Having recovered control over his seal, Henry proceeded to a far more public and dangerous demonstration of his authority. Back in December 1260, Hugh Despenser had stated that parliament would meet on

---

[119] *CR 1259–61*, 340, 377; TNA E 159/34, mm. 9, 14 (0025, 0038).

[120] *CR 1259–61*, 317.

[121] *CPR 1258–66*, 181. At the new year of 1261, the queen had given rings to Ely, his clerk, and the four men in charge of sealing: TNA E 101/349/26.

[122] Basset too had been granted robes as a member of the king's household. The others whom Henry sought to retain, alongside Mortimer, were James of Audley, Hugh Bigod and Hugh Despenser; *CR 1259–61*, 317.

9 February, this being the meeting laid down by the Provisions. Henry, however, took a different view. On 3 February he announced that 'the parliament of the king', as he pointedly called it, would meet on 23 February.[123] Did Montfort, as in 1260, try to hold a parliament in defiance of the king? That there was trouble seems certain for on 8 February, the day before the parliament scheduled in the Provisions, Henry left Windsor and went straight to the Tower of London.[124] He was to remain there till 23 April. This was quite extraordinary. In the whole of his personal rule Henry had never lived at the Tower, apart from the few days in 1238 during the crisis over the Montfort marriage. Westminster, with its palace, Abbey and Confessor was far more congenial. That they were now out of bounds is the best measure of the threat facing the king. Henry wanted no repeat of the events of 1258 when the barons had marched into Westminster Hall and forced his submission.

How worthwhile, Henry could now think, was all his expenditure on the military and domestic architecture of the Tower. Starting in 1238, he had spent more than £5,000 on a new gateway and a curtain wall with round flanking towers, thus bringing the defences right up to date. With the move to the Tower in 1261, over £1,000 was assigned to complete the work. Given the fortress was well munitioned, Henry and the court could feel completely safe. Indeed, never in the whole of its history did the Tower play a more critical part in national politics than in 1261. Henry and Eleanor could also be comfortable for Henry had ordered the construction of new privies, wardrobes and kitchens, while Eleanor's chamber was wainscotted and painted with roses. In his own great chamber (in what is now the Wakefield tower), Henry could relax sitting in the window bays overlooking the Thames and pray privately in his chapel, separated from the rest of the chamber by a wooden screen. The chamber also spoke very much to his regal state for its wooden shutters were painted with the royal arms.[125]

In the fortnight before the meeting of the king's parliament on 23 February tensions rose. On 13 February, Henry went with King Richard, Archbishop Boniface and John Mansel to St Paul's cross where he extracted an oath of fealty from the Londoners and ordered all the gates of the city to be shut day and night, save for London Bridge gate, Ludgate and Aldgate which were heavily guarded.[126] Three days later Henry summoned a group of twenty-seven magnates to come to the parliament with horses and arms. On the same day Hugh Despenser was

[123] Sayles, *Functions of the Medieval Parliament*, 96; *CR 1259–61*, 309, 343.

[124] The queen remained behind with her daughter Queen Margaret, who gave birth in the following month.

[125] Colvin, *History of the King's Works*, ii, 711–15. The great chamber has been rearranged to look as it might have looked in Henry's day.

[126] FitzThedmar, 46 (Stone, FitzThedmar, no. 743).

at Westminster, where he issued a writ in his own name. He seems to have been setting up his own administration. Indeed, at some point before July, on his own authority, he removed the sheriff of Nottinghamshire– Derbyshire and put new keepers in his place.[127] Henry's summons to his parliament shows him counting on a powerful group of supporters, including the earl of Winchester, John de Balliol and Thomas Grelle (members of 1258's parliamentary twelve), William Bardolph (one of the original baronial twelve) and the marcher barons John fitzAlan, Reginald fitzPeter and Thomas Corbet. Reginald fitzPeter (with interests also in Sussex) had been amongst Henry's opponents in 1260, but from now on, granted a money fee, he remained in the royal camp. William Bardolph and John fitzAlan, on the other hand, are soon found again with the opposition. Its strength is clear from those omitted from Henry's summons: no Montfort, of course, and no Richard de Clare, Roger Bigod, Humphrey de Bohun or Roger de Mortimer.[128] Henry and Eleanor must have been particularly disappointed by Clare's conduct.[129] After all, Bishop Aymer was now dead so there was nothing to fear from that quarter. Perhaps Clare genuinely believed in conciliar control of the king. Perhaps he disliked the Savoyard-dominated court. For whatever reason, his alliance with Montfort held and they stood together in resisting the king. Faced with Henry's own military muster the opposition came armed themselves. Henry wished the parliament to meet in the Tower. The barons insisted it be at Westminster. So there was an armed stalemate. Civil war was very near.

In order to defuse the tension and play for time, Henry and his advisers now developed the third strand of their strategy. On the one hand, they argued that the behaviour of the council fully justified Henry's conduct. Yet, on the other, they held out the hope that if the council mended its ways, Henry might still co-operate with it. Henry had not after all formally denounced the Provisions and still accepted that Hugh Despenser was justiciar. Indeed, for all his base at Westminster, Despenser still played a part in Henry's government, entering the Tower to do so. He heard pleas there and, in the king's chamber with Henry, Philip Basset and John Mansel, settled a dispute between the citizens of London and Northampton.[130] Discussions were also in train with the baronial leaders. Indeed, at the end of February, Bishop Cantilupe, Clare and Montfort himself were in the Tower, where they attested a charter with King Richard, Peter of Savoy,

---

[127] TNA E 368/36, m. 3d (image 5814); and see also TNA JUST 1/ 82, m. 12 (image 0464); *CPR 1258–66*, 164.

[128] *CR 1259–61*, 457; Reginald fitzPeter, the son of Peter fitzHerbert, was lord of Blaen Llyfni.

[129] For Eleanor's closeness to Clare, see volume 1, 654, 692.

[130] TNA JUST 1/537 (Jacob, *Studies*, 352); FitzThedmar, 46–8 (Stone, FitzThedmar, nos. 744–6); and see TNA KB 26/156, m. 1 (image 0120).

John Mansel and Robert Walerand. Eventually, around 14 March, an agreement was reached to submit the dispute to six arbitrators, three chosen by the king and three by the barons. They were to examine all the actions since the oaths at Oxford. Whatever they found done contrary to the Provisions and to the detriment of the king and crown was to be remedied, while what was done well was to be maintained. Henry had certainly pulled the wool over some eyes. One writer ascribed the agreement to Henry's wish 'above everything' to preserve 'the pristine oath at Oxford about the governance of the kingdom'.[131] Henry followed up the agreement by sending a letter to all the sheriffs. They were to proclaim his 'sincere love for the magnates and the community of our realm' and arrest those spreading rumours that he intended to impose new taxes and customs. Unfortunately, this letter was accompanied by another ordering the sheriffs to send to the exchequer all the money they could raise.[132]

At the same time as this general arbitration, Henry agreed to another designed to deal, one way or another, with his most dangerous opponent. On 14 March, Henry on the one side, Simon and Eleanor de Montfort on the other, agreed to submit their disputes to the judgement of King Louis or, if he would not act, to that of his queen and one of his ministers, Peter the Chamberlain. Henry here had much to gain. If Montfort was condemned by the eventual verdict, as Henry hoped, then his political power would surely be weakened. If rewarded, then that might lessen his enthusiasm for the reforms.[133]

## HENRY'S COMPLAINTS AGAINST THE COUNCIL

In preparation for the arbitration, Henry drew up a long list of complaints about the conduct of the council. Very personal and probably direct from his mouth, they reveal the range and depth of his bitterness. In one version, he even rejected outright his initial agreement to accept the 'counsel' of the councillors: he was thereby 'deprived of all honour and pristine royal dignity'.[134] The councillors were also contravening their oath to uphold his 'earthly honour'. In the event, Henry was pulled back from this outright rejection of '1258'. In the final version of the complaints (the one replied to by the council), he stuck to his usual line and accepted the validity of the initial agreement. Indeed, 'even now', he wished to uphold whatever the council did for the good of the realm.[135]

---

[131] Ridgeway, 'King Henry III's grievances against the council', 235, 242.

[132] *CR 1259–61*, 461–2.

[133] *CPR 1258–66*, 135–6 (for an attempted arbitration in January), 145–6; BN Clairambault 1188, fo. 19. For Henry's 'hope', see his letter to Louis: *CR 1259–61*, 465.

[134] Ridgeway, 'King Henry III's grievances against the council', 241, cap. 27. As this important paper shows, there were three versions of Henry's complaints, one of them brought to light by Ridgeway himself.

[135] *DBM*, 236–7, cap. 26.

Despite this effort at conciliation, Henry still mounted what he doubt-less saw as a devastating indictment. There was the broken promise over Sicily, the failure in Wales, the mismanagement of royal finances, the resulting poverty of the king and the way his castles and palaces had been allowed to go to rack and ruin.[136] Instead of being the head of the council, he had been treated as a 'ward', excluded from its meetings, his wishes ignored, his seal used without his knowledge. He was no better than the 'humblest subject in the realm'. When he did issue orders they were 'disobeyed and despised' as though he was not a king. As for local govern-ment, here, so Henry alleged, the bailiffs appointed by the regime were in the pockets of the councillors and dared not enter their lands and liberties to give justice to the people and uphold the rights of the king. Henry's conclusion was that 'since this ordinance, nothing has been done for the good of the king or the realm'. Always sensitive to his name and fame, he felt acutely the shame of it all both at home and abroad. He had been 'stripped of all power and all earthly lordship to the great scandal of all loyal men'.[137]

While Henry was preparing his complaints, there was some easing of tension. On 9 April, in the Tower, Hugh Despenser even authorized a concession in favour of Simon de Montfort.[138] On 22–23 April, Henry felt able to leave the Tower for the bishop of London's house at St Paul's, where he celebrated Easter (on 24 April). The queen found the multitudes who had access to the house extremely disagreeable, indeed shameful, but Westminster, the usual location for Easter, was evidently still out of bounds.[139] If, as seems likely, it was around now that Henry saw the coun-cil's replies to his complaints, his fears are understandable. The council welcomed Henry's continued acceptance of its authority and promised to put right whatever he showed had gone amiss. But the only major area where it acknowledged some failure was over Wales. For the most part its replies oscillated between the unapologetic and the insulting. Over Sicily, it disclaimed all responsibility. As for the king's finances, well it had tried to reduce the costs of his household and set aside revenues from wardships to pay his debts, only to be obstructed by the king. As for local govern-ment, the sheriffs had been elected by the counties, not chosen by the council.[140]

The replies were at their most defiant and abrasive when it came to the authority of the council and its treatment of the king. The council had been set up by an agreement between the king and 'the community of England'

---

[136] In 1260 there had been a lot of writs ordering work only 'where absolutely necessary'.
[137] *DBM*, 236–7, cap. 27.
[138] *CR 1259–61*, 366–7.
[139] *CR 1259–61*, 472.
[140] Local elections had been planned (see above, 33) but there is no sign of them taking place.

and the king had granted that he would accept its advice. Its authority
included 'from the start' the right to appoint the justiciar, the chancellor
and the treasurer. It had done nothing with the king's seal which was
not for his profit and honour. True, the councillors had indeed held their
meetings apart from the king, and their debates about appointments were
secret, but Henry, 'whenever he talks well, *la ou il diarra bien*', was heard and
listened to as lord of them all, although 'nothing' was done 'on his sole
word'.[141] Phew! Here surely we hear the voice of Simon de Montfort. The
echoes of his replies to the king's charges the year before are unmistakable.
The idea that the king would only be heard when he talked well, apart from
being personally insulting, had constitutional implications quite beyond the
restrictions of 1258. Given the poor view held of Henry's wisdom, it might
mean he would rarely be listened to at all.[142]

## THE RETURN OF EDWARD AND WILLIAM DE VALENCE

Henry, therefore, when he saw the council's replies knew he was in for a
struggle. The regime of 1258 would not go quietly. It had indeed just
received an accession of strength. Around Easter 1261, Edward returned to
England. The distance between him and his father was apparent in Henry's
complaints against the council. It was blamed (very unfairly) for allowing
Edward to squander his possessions and make appointments (in particular
to the seneschalship of Gascony) contrary to Henry's will. Henry also
declared that 'by the counsel of a certain man', evidently Montfort, Edward
had been seduced 'from his father's friendship and obedience'. Henry was
right to be anxious. Edward on his return renewed his oath to the reforms
and formed an alliance with Montfort and Richard de Clare. They threatened war if the king's evil councillors, meaning evidently the Savoyards,
were not removed.[143]

There was another complicating factor. Edward's alliance with his
Lusignan uncles was still very much in place.[144] He now returned to
England with none other than William de Valence.[145] Henry had not seen
Valence since his expulsion from the country in 1258 and must have
welcomed his return. But he had to be careful given the feelings of the

---

[141] *DBM*, 222–5.

[142] For discussion, see Melve, 'Public debate during the baronial rebellion', 55.

[143] Paris's Continuator, 466–7; FitzThedmar, 49 (Stone, FitzThedmar, no. 748). Edward's
alliance with Montfort had been strengthened by their co-operation in the affairs of
Bigorre, for which see Maddicott, *Simon de Montfort*, 199–200.

[144] In August 1260, Valence and Guy and Geoffrey de Lusignan were appointed by
Edward as his commissioners to deal with the affairs of Bigorre: *RG Supp*, xcii–iii, nos.
20–3. In December 1260 a charter that Edward issued in Paris was witnessed by Bishop
Aymer, Guy, Geoffrey and William de Valence: TNA E 368/94, m. 47 (image 0094). A
reference I owe to Ridgeway, 'The Politics of the English Royal Court', 373 n. 3.

[145] Paris's Continuator, 466; Pershore, 474.

queen. Dutifully he sent letters to Valence and Edward stressing the former could not return until the agreed security was given to Queen Margaret. Evidently it was forthcoming because on 30 April Henry restored Valence to Hertford castle and all his other lands.[146] Eleanor, however, seems to have made a further condition, namely that Valence should not appear at court. He is hardly found there throughout the rest of 1261, a sharp contrast to his prominence before the revolution.[147] The same was true of Elyas de Rabayne, who also returned in April. There was nothing here, therefore, to challenge the dominance of the Savoyards.

At first sight, it seems extraordinary that the barons allowed Valence back. After all, the removal of the Lusignans had been a cornerstone of the 1258 revolution. But circumstances had changed. The Lusignans' great ally Lord Edward was now the friend rather than the foe of the regime. The brothers were also back on terms with Simon de Montfort.[148] Bishop Aymer's death, meanwhile, had removed the threat to Richard de Clare's possession of Portland. Valence was thus able to return 'with the assent of the barons', but they nonetheless made conditions just as the queen had done. According to Matthew Paris's continuator, Valence 'scarcely obtained entry' and had to take an oath to observe the baronial provisions and answer all complaints against him.[149]

## THE SECURING OF DOVER, MAY 1261

It was almost certainly at Dover that Valence had entered the country. Henry himself had told Hugh Bigod, as castellan, not to let him in without the king's licence.[150] It may well be that Bigod's dutiful reply, if such it was, encouraged what happened next. At any rate, Henry now embarked on a dramatic attempt to gain hold of the castle. The queen, King Richard, Peter of Savoy, John de Plessis and John Mansel were all at court and thus involved in the decision. Control of Dover carried with it control of the Cinque Ports and thus of the Channel. It was through Dover and the other ports that Henry and, so Henry feared, Simon de Montfort, were planning to bring in forces from abroad. And it was at Dover, if it could be secured, that John Mansel junior could land with his precious letters. His arrest was too disastrous to contemplate.[151]

[146] CR 1259–61, 467; CPR 1258–66, 150.

[147] In this period Valence only attests one royal charter during the rest of the year (on 18 June at Guildford): RCWL, ii, 134.

[148] For the arbitration going on in 1260 and 1262 to settle the rival claims of Eleanor de Montfort and the Lusignans to their mother's Angoulême: BN Clairambault 1188, fos. 16d–23; Maddicott, Simon de Montfort, 199–200, 204–5.

[149] Paris's Continuator, 466; FitzThedmar, 49 (Stone, FitzThedmar, no. 748).

[150] CR 1259–61, 467.

[151] For Henry trying to secure the coasts in 1261, see Jobson, 'The maritime theatre', 221–2.

Leaving the queen at St Paul's and John Mansel at the Tower, Henry left London on 29 April and by the evening was at Rochester. A memorandum on the patent rolls recorded what happened next. 'On 2 May the king came to Dover and on the morrow took into his hands the castle of Dover and the wardenship of the Cinque Ports, which Hugh Bigod had held before at the king's bail by the counsel of the magnates of the council, and he committed these during his pleasure to Robert Walerand.'

The phraseology here was deliberate and significant for it showed the authority of the council was at an end. In giving Dover to Bigod, Henry had acted 'by the counsel of the magnates of the council', but there was no suggestion he had done the same in transferring the castle to the trusty Robert Walerand. Walerand was to hold during the king's pleasure.

Bigod himself had been entrusted with Dover castle by the council after Richard de Grey's failure to keep out Velascus back in 1259. Presumably he had taken an oath not to surrender it without the council's consent. Yet now he did so simply on command of the king. Indeed, he witnessed a royal charter while the king was at Dover and seemed more concerned about an allowance for his use of the castle's wine than anything else.[152] Henry had certainly come to Dover in military array. He had with him John de Plessis, the Savoyards, a group of marcher barons (Reginald fitzPeter, Thomas Corbet and Maurice de Berkeley) and the knights Alan la Zouche, John de Grey and Robert Aguillon. In March and April, perhaps in preparation for this hour, he had strengthened the household forces by granting money fees to around thirty men, including Corbet, Berkeley, Aguillon, Zouche and Zouche's two brothers.[153] But there was no way he could have secured the castle so quickly had Bigod been minded to defend it. Bigod has left no explanation of his conduct. But his bruising confrontations with Montfort the year before and his subsequent dismissal as justiciar were presumably factors. In 1260 he had put obedience to the king above the strict letter of the Provisions. He had been granted robes in December 1260 as a member of the king's household and in February 1261 is found with Henry in the Tower.

Henry had, therefore, struck a mighty blow both materially, for Dover was 'the key to England', and morally, for here was Hugh Bigod, the conscientious justiciar of 1258, the chief minister of the reform regime, tamely abandoning the reforms. Yet in the localities the reforms were far from dead. On 2 May itself, the very day of the king's Dover triumph, there were protests about the justices hearing pleas at Hertford without baronial consent and against 'the common provision'.[154] Meanwhile there was less than full attendance when Henry summoned the knights and freemen of Kent to swear oaths of allegiance. A plan to advance into Sussex and take

[152] *RCWL*, ii, 133; *CR 1259–61*, 374.
[153] *RCWL*, ii, 133–4; *CPR 1258–66*, 147.
[154] Paris's Continuator, 468; Crook, *Records of the General Eyre*, 127.

similar oaths there was abandoned.[155] By 14 May, Henry was back in the Tower of London. He was building up his military forces and arranging for the count of St Pol, Gerard de Rodes and Alard de Seningham (all friends of the queen) with their knights, horses and harness to come to England.[156]

## THE NEUTRALIZATION OF EDWARD

The month of May did not only see the securing of Dover. The process began of prising Edward back from the baronial fold. Here Eleanor's role was probably vital. Matthew Paris's continuator specifically mentions how she won men back to the king's side around this time.[157] For Edward there was immediate reward. His sale of the Aumale wardship was sanctioned and another wardship was granted in its place, while a loan obtained from King Louis was repaid.[158] Around the same time, Peter of Savoy wrote to the king listing some of the men who remained faithful and had not deserted in his great necessity. They should be rewarded so that others were encouraged to follow their example. The list included Warin of Bassingbourn and others close to Edward. In July 1261, a major concession, Bassingbourn was appointed castellan of Bristol.[159] Perhaps there was one other factor. Did Edward reflect, not before time, on how the principles and practice of conciliar control might impinge on his own kingship? Significantly, the first sign that he was back on side (around 13 May) comes when, with John Mansel and Peter of Savoy, he appealed against the statutes of an ecclesiastical council held at Lambeth, this on the grounds they prejudiced the rights of the crown and the dignity of the king. The same could of course be said of the baronial reforms.[160]

Edward, however, a salve perhaps for his conscience, decided that if he would not fight with his former allies, at least he would not fight against them. In July, with the country on the brink of civil war, he returned to Gascony. That was good enough for Henry and Eleanor. It was not good enough for Montfort. Indeed, it was a betrayal. Edward had conspicuously broken his oath to stand with the earl in 'maintaining the enterprise made by the barons of the land'. Their alliance was at an end. Edward's reputation for treachery had begun.

## THE UNVEILING OF THE PAPAL LETTERS, JUNE 1261

Throughout May, Henry waited anxiously for news from Rome. He must have known that John Mansel junior was having difficulties. Almost

---

[155] *CR 1259–61*, 377; *CPR 1258–66*, 153.
[156] *CPR 1258–66*, 152.
[157] Paris's Continuator, 467; Howell, *Eleanor of Provence*, 180.
[158] *CPR 1258–66*, 156, 158, 161.
[159] TNA SC 1/5/26; *CAD*, iv, 51; Ridgeway, 'What happened in 1261?', 96.
[160] Canterbury/Dover, 212–13; *C&S*, ii, 668–9; *CPR 1258–66*, 155; *CR 1259–61*, 481–2. See Hoskin, 'Natural law', 86–7.

certainly the baronial opposition had its own men at the papal court, giving a very different picture of the situation. As a result, it was not till 13 April that Pope Alexander, exercising his 'plenitude of power', issued a letter absolving Henry from his oath to observe 'the statutes and ordinances' supposedly made for the reform of the realm. The pope did so because, so he said, they diminished Henry's power and 'depressed royal liberty'. What, however, of the oaths sworn by everyone else? Here it was not till 29 April that Alexander acted. This time he commanded Archbishop Boniface, the bishop of Norwich and John Mansel to absolve the prelates, magnates and others from their oaths. Any opposition they could punish with ecclesiastical censures. A final letter, issued on 7 May, empowered the trio to excommunicate all those who disobeyed the king.[161]

The first two of these letters were enough for Henry's purposes and they had probably arrived in England by the end of May. There was a problem, however, in the role assigned to Archbishop Boniface. His statutes promulgated at the Lambeth conference had offended the king. He was very rarely at court and cannot have been deep in Henry's counsels. Fortunately, the pope had said that any two of the trio could pronounce the absolution and both John Mansel and the bishop of Norwich (the former judge Simon of Walton) could be counted on. The question, then, was where to publish the explosive letters. A declamation at St Paul's cross was one possibility, but there was always the danger of trouble from the Londoners. To do it within the Tower would seem all too defensive. So Henry decided on something else. He would proclaim the letters at Winchester, where the bishopric was in his hands (thanks to Aymer's death), and where the great castle on the hill dominated the town beneath and gave complete security to its inmates.[162] The choice also made a useful point about Henry's Englishness, for Winchester was his birthplace, the ancient capital of the kingdom and home to the shrine of St Swithun, the Anglo-Saxon bishop of the city.[163]

Henry, therefore, left London on 26 May. At Guildford, 'out of compassion for his poverty', he took steps to see that a man had enough to live off (he was heavily in debt to the Jews) and was not 'forced to beg'. In the castle, he doubtless admired the image of the Virgin and the paintings of the Confessor and pilgrim commissioned earlier in the year. At Winchester, if the pattern of the previous August was repeated, he was greeted by a procession and fed 282 paupers. He was soon giving firewood to both orders of friars. Eleanor had travelled separately, joining

---

[161] *DBM*, 238–47.

[162] Just when the king recovered Winchester castle from Montfort's keepership is unknown but he evidently had.

[163] For Henry, Winchester and St Swithun, see Shacklock, 'Henry III and the native saints', 27–31. During his personal rule, however, Henry was only twice at Winchester for the feast day of St Swithun on 15 July.

up on the way with the count of St Pol and giving rings to him and his companions.[164]

Henry now had time for preparations, the date set for the unveiling of the letters being Whitsunday, 12 June.[165] Whitsun had been chosen as the first great feast in the ecclesiastical calendar after the arrival of the letters. It was also deeply appropriate. At Whitsun the Holy Spirit had rushed in upon the apostles. The office for the day began 'For the spirit of the Lord filleth the world'. The appointed psalm was sixty-eight: 'Let God arise and let his enemies be scattered: let them also that hate thee flee before him.' And this was the collect: 'God, who at this time didst teach the hearts of the faithful people, by the sending to them the light of thy holy spirit, grant us by the same spirit to have right judgement in all things, and evermore rejoice in his comfort.' Henry, of course, would not quite have equated the papal letters with the coming of the Holy Spirit, let alone have equated himself with Christ. But nonetheless the parallels were obvious. How Henry must have hoped the letters would re-establish 'right judgement' in his own people and make them once again respect him as their lord, rejoicing in his comfort and protection.

Just where and how the papal letters were proclaimed is unknown but clearly the rituals of the day enhanced their impact. After earlier masses in the castle there was presumably a great service in the cathedral. Henry certainly gave shoes to 171 paupers and robes to the hundred or so knights now attached to his household.[166]

## PHILIP BASSET BECOMES JUSTICIAR

Having proclaimed the letters, Henry acted at once to demonstrate his new freedom. Probably on Whitsunday itself, he dismissed Hugh Despenser as justiciar and replaced him with Philip Basset. There could be no clearer proof the revolutionary regime was over. At the same time the decision to continue with the office was clearly a concession, if one with limits. There was no intention of Basset going on eyre to hear everyone's *querelae* in the fashion of Hugh Bigod and Hugh Despenser. King Richard would have been horrified at the idea. Henry himself had his own objections. In his complaints earlier in the year, he had said that the justiciar's eyre took cases away from the court *coram rege*, thus inconveniencing litigants and reducing the revenue of the crown.[167] Later he was to say there was no need for the

[164] *CFR 1260–1*, no. 551; *CLR 1260–7*, 21; *CR 1259–61*, 388; Howell, *Eleanor of Provence*, 182.

[165] For events at Winchester, see Paris's Continuator, 469–70; and Wykes, 128.

[166] *CR 1259–61*, 389–94; *CLR 1260–7*, 45.

[167] *DBM*, 216–19, caps. 23 [10], 25 [11], 226–7, caps. 10 [23], 11 [25]. For the meaning of these chapters see Hogg, 'Henry III, the justiciarship and the court *coram rege* in 1261'.

office at all when the king was in England.[168] Nonetheless Basset's appointment was not just cosmetic. He presided over the court *coram rege* and acted
as the king's chief minister.[169] When Henry did go abroad in 1262, Basset
was left in charge.

There was also conciliation in the choice of Basset himself for he was
widely respected. In 1245, indeed, he had been one of the representatives
of 'the baronage of all England' at the council of Lyon. Basset was a
wealthy magnate having inherited the lands of the Bassets of High
Wycombe on the death of his brother Fulk, bishop of London, in 1259.
Before that, a good businessman, he had built up a considerable estate of
his own.[170] He had made a high-status marriage to Ela, the widow of the
earl of Warwick and daughter of William Longespee and Ela, countess of
Salisbury.[171] Back in 1233, Philip, as a young man, had joined his elder
brother Gilbert's rebellion, but this was the only blemish on his record of
loyalty. Thereafter he had served for many years as a senior household
knight of the king. He was also a close associate of Richard of Cornwall.
Yet Basset had been sufficiently 'in' with the revolutionary regime to be
appointed to the council of fifteen on John fitzGeoffrey's death. He had
been accepted by Simon de Montfort as one of the arbitrators deciding
the issue of the dower. His only child, Alina (by a first marriage), was the
wife of none other than Hugh Despenser. Over the next years this brave
and wise man would give tremendous service to both king and kingdom.

After proclaiming the papal letters, it is unclear what Henry intended
next. In the event, the decision was made for him. John Mansel had not
gone with Henry to Winchester. Now, fearing the king was in danger, he
hurried there and counselled an immediate return to the Tower. Henry
took the advice and slipped out of Winchester with a small following.[172]
By 22 June he was once more in the Tower. He was to stay there till the
end of July. It was a humiliating end to what had seemed triumphal
Whitsun celebrations.

## THE DISMISSAL OF THE SHERIFFS, JULY 1261

Henry, as we have seen, had strengthened his household forces, and these
would be a great prop in what was to come. They were supported with
money fees. They were also comforted and encouraged by gifts of wood

---

[168] *DBM*, 252–3, cap. 1.

[169] See Hogg, 'Philip Basset at the court *coram rege*, 1261–3', behind which is Malcolm
Hogg's doctoral thesis, 'The justiciarship during the Barons' War'.

[170] For Philip's career see Hogg, 'Philip Basset (d.1271)', and Stewart-Parker, 'The Bassets
of High Wycombe', chs. 4–6.

[171] For Ela, see below, 391–2.

[172] Paris's Continuator, 470. John Mansel attested a royal charter at Guildford on 29 May
on the road to Winchester, so he went part of the way there. He does not attest at
Winchester on 1 June, but does on 14 June, just before the king's departure: *RCWL*, ii, 134.

and deer from the royal forests. As the crisis deepened, these reached unprecedented levels.[173] There were twenty-five such gifts in June, forty in July, and thirty-four in August. The beneficiaries apart from the household knights were ministers and numerous magnates whom it was vital to keep onside.

Back in the Tower, Henry put a brave face on the situation. He explained in a letter to Llywelyn ap Gruffudd how he was absolved from his oath and had recovered the fullness of royal power. His situation was improving from 'moment to moment'. He had taken possession of Dover, the city of London and the Tower. He was ruling in peace with the assent of the community. The only trouble was coming from certain malevolent people whose machinations he hoped soon to stop with God's help and the pope's.[174] In the Tower, Henry took another step to demonstrate his control of government. On 12 July he removed the seal from Nicholas of Ely and gave it to Walter of Merton instead. Nicholas had proved a compliant chancellor and was thanked for his good service with a gift of game.[175] The change was thus largely symbolic but important for all that.

It was one thing for Henry to make changes at the centre. Quite another to control the localities. This too Henry now attempted. On 8–9 July he dismissed nearly all the sheriffs.[176] The new appointees were either loyalist magnates such as Reginald fitzPeter, John de Balliol and James of Audley (a member of the old council of fifteen) or household knights like Alan and William la Zouche and John and William de Grey, the two Greys having separated themselves decisively from their elder brother, Richard. Philip Basset was given control of Somerset, Dorset, Oxfordshire and Berkshire, together with Corfe, Sherborne and Oxford castles. Wisely, Henry appointed only two foreigners, John de Plessis, earl of Warwick, and Matthias Bezill, the latter adding the county of Gloucester to the castle where he had been left in place by the reformers of 1258. These were all powerful men who could meet any challenge to the king's authority. Clearly Henry expected there might be trouble. He was not mistaken.

## RESISTANCE IN THE SHIRES

During July the standoff with the baronial leaders continued. There were fresh and ultimately abortive attempts to set in train arbitrations over both Montfort's personal grievances and the quarrels in the realm. Civil war

---

[173] Between January and the end of September around 160 gifts were made.

[174] *CR 1259–61*, 481–2.

[175] *CPR 1258–66*, 165–6; *CR 1259–61*, 415. The abbot of Peterborough, however, remained in place as treasurer of the exchequer and, as several gifts show, had won the king's favour.

[176] *CPR 1258–66*, 163–4. Those dismissed were for the most part the sheriffs appointed back in 1259.

remained close. When the baronial leaders 'near London' (no wonder Henry stayed in the Tower) begged King Louis to take on the arbitration, they said if he did not, the realm would suffer 'desolation, destruction and irreparable harm'.[177] The letter was written in the names of Bishop Cantilupe, Simon de Montfort, Roger Bigod, Richard de Clare, John de Warenne and Hugh Bigod. Warenne had been on the king's side in 1258 but perhaps his quarrels with Peter of Savoy now brought him into the baronial camp. Even more remarkable was the appearance of Hugh Bigod. Despite his surrender of Dover, he had not thrown in his lot with the king. He was soon flatly contradicting his earlier conduct, to say he was under oath not to surrender Scarborough and Pickering castles without the council's consent. Had Montfort won him round, apologizing for his earlier abuse and recalling the movement's high ideals? Or had Roger Bigod? Hugh's wavering course certainly shows the strains that such men were under in 1261.[178]

The baronial leaders were far from relying on some negotiated settlement. They also took vigorous action on the ground. Reacting to Henry's grab for Dover, Montfort and Clare toured the Cinque Ports and secured a written undertaking from their men to stand with the barons 'for the honour of God, the faith of the king and the profit of the realm', precisely the terms used in the great oath of 1258. The portsmen were also to prevent foreigners entering to harm the realm. When he discovered what was happening, Henry wrote a desperate letter, crying out against Montfort's efforts to bring in horses and arms, and begging the Cinque Ports to remain loyal.[179]

The barons were also active on the diplomatic front. Bishop Cantilupe appealed against the papal letters, and efforts were made to persuade the pope to change his mind. Here there was some success for Pope Urban, elected in August 1261 following Alexander's death, refused at first to renew his predecessor's condemnation of the oaths, much to the dismay of Henry's envoys.[180] It was, however, the king's attempt to recover control in the shires that really gave the baronial leaders their chance. With Henry safely in the Tower, there was no way they could subject him once more to the baronial council. What they could do was to carry the fight into the localities by defying the authority of his new sheriffs.

This they did with a vengeance. Over the next months at least eleven of Henry's sheriffs, holding seventeen counties (so more than half the total), stretching from Yorkshire in the north to Sussex in the south, were defied by rival sheriffs appointed in many, perhaps in all, cases 'by letters

[177] Bémont, *Simon de Montfort*, 331–2; *CPR 1258–66*, 162, 169; *F*, i, 407.
[178] Bémont, *Simon de Montfort*, 331–2; Canterbury/Dover, 210–11; *F*, i, 408.
[179] Canterbury/Dover, 213; *F*, i, 406 (*CPR 1258–66*, 185).
[180] Canterbury/Dover, 210; *DD*, no. 331.

of the barons'.[181] In Gloucestershire, where Henry had made Matthias Bezill sheriff, 'the barons decreed it was not well done but against the provisions', the offence being aggravated by the fact Bezill was a Frenchman. So, in his place, 'by common council', they appointed 'a knight of the county, Sir William de Tracy', who 'clean put out Sir Macy'.[182] Other sheriffs too were in difficulties, although we do not know the names of their rivals. The baronial leaders did not restore the sheriffs appointed in 1259 and dismissed by Henry. The new sheriffs were generally men of greater power and higher status, usually closely connected to the regime. In Norfolk, there was William Bardolph; in Cambridgeshire and Huntingdonshire, Giles de Argentan; in Buckinghamshire, John fitzJohn, the son of John fitzGeoffrey. Several of the sheriffs were closely linked to the baronial leaders: William de Tracy (probably) to Richard de Clare, Bardolph and William de Boville (in Suffolk) to Roger Bigod. Most striking of all, John de la Haye (Sussex) and Ralph Basset of Sapcote and Thomas of Astley (Warwickshire and Leicestershire) were all followers of Simon de Montfort. One suspects that Montfort was central to what was going on.[183]

Soon letters full of woe from Henry's sheriffs were pouring in to him and his chancellor, Walter of Merton. James of Audley wrote of the 'contradiction' he faced in Shropshire and Staffordshire. John de Balliol told how he could collect no revenue in Nottinghamshire and was unable to buy ten cartloads of lead for the work at Westminster.[184] In Lincolnshire, William de Grey, commanded by the king to hold the county court, replied he could not (his son was dying at Rochester), but he was sending his knight Guy Gubaut in his place, 'whose ancestors have always served you faithfully'. Guy would make a careful inquiry into who were the rebels. But Guy (a Lincolnshire knight) was to rebel himself. Grey also asked for letters to be sent to Adam de Newmarch, appointed by the barons to run the county, telling him not to hold the county court. But later Grey wrote saying everyone was obeying Adam and not himself.[185]

There was not merely resistance to the king's sheriffs. As we have seen, the justices in eyre had met it at Hertford in May when they tried to hear

---

[181] TNA E 368/36, mm. 5, 7, 8–8d, 9d, 11d–12, 16, 17; TNA E 368/37, mm. 5d, 15d; *CR 1259–61*, 499–500, 503; *CPR 1258–66*, 178; *CR 1268–72*, 41, 342–3. The counties involved (hyphenated where joint sheriffdoms) were Yorkshire, Nottinghamshire–Derbyshire, Lincolnshire, Norfolk–Suffolk, Warwickshire–Leicestershire, Northamptonshire, Cambridgeshire–Huntingdonshire, Bedfordshire–Buckinghamshire, Surrey–Sussex, Kent and Gloucestershire. See Treharne, *Baronial Plan*, 268.

[182] This is as recalled later by Robert of Gloucester: Robert of Gloucester, ii, lines 11,060–67. Bezill was already castellan of the castle.

[183] Ridgeway, 'What happened in 1261?', 104–5; Morris, *Bigod Earls of Norfolk*, 85; Maddicott, *Simon de Montfort*, 61–2, 66–7.

[184] *CR 1259–61*, 488–9; TNA SC 1/7/32; *CLR 1260–7*, 55.

[185] TNA SC 1/3/157; SC 1/7/ 129; *CR 1261–4*, 346; *CIM*, no. 804; *CPR 1258–66*, 472. For Adam and the Newmarch family (not connected with Newmarket in Suffolk) see Cokayne, *Complete Peerage*, ix, 542–8.

pleas without the consent of the baronage and against 'the common provision'. They met resistance again at Worcester in July.[186] There were challenges to Philip Basset's position as justiciar. He was described by a jury as one 'who says he has taken the place of the chief justiciar'.[187] In all this the baronial leaders were drawing on a large well of popular support.[188] The Pershore abbey chronicler wrote of 'tumult and dissension in the people throughout the counties of England' as a result of the king's sheriffs replacing those appointed by the barons and 'the community of the land'. 'The inhabitants of the counties, animated by the help, supported by the counsel, and educated by the great wisdom of the best men of the kingdom, vigorously repulsed the new sheriff overlords and did not wish to obey them.'[189]

The education was partly the work of 'preachers', probably friars.[190] It was also intended to be the work of a baronial parliament. Such an assembly was summoned by Bishop Cantilupe, Simon de Montfort and Richard de Clare to St Albans on 21 September. With a brief to consider 'the common affairs of the kingdom', three knights were to attend from each county.[191] Whether the parliament ever met is unknown (the king, as will be seen, tried to stop it), but clearly this was an attempt to educate the knights in the 'common enterprise' and send them back to their counties all the more its partisans and propagandists.[192] It was a constituency Montfort was to appeal to again at the parliaments held during his personal rule.

It cannot have been difficult to stir up resistance. The sheriffs of the reform regime had not been given salaries, had not been elected by their counties and had not been changed in October 1259, but they were still local knights and shouldering lighter financial burdens than before 1258. They were very different from the curial sheriffs Henry was now appointing. Meanwhile, the legislation promulgated in October 1259 was becoming well known. The chapter abolishing the '*beaupleder*' fine was appealed to on the eyres of 1260 and 1261.[193] A writ had been quickly devised to enable

[186] Paris's Continuator, 468; *CR 1259–61*, 377; Pershore, *Flores*, 472; Crook, *Records of the General Eyre*, 126–7; Treharne, *Baronial Plan*, 248–9.

[187] TNA JUST 1/1194, m. 4 (image 1223). This was in 1264 but probably reflects views held in 1261 as well.

[188] Ridgeway, 'What happened in 1261?', is more sceptical about the degree of popular support than is Maddicott, *Simon de Montfort*, 210. Since in the end there was a settlement, there is no list of rebels, a point made in Moore, 'Government and locality in Essex', 223.

[189] Pershore, *Flores*, 473.

[190] *RL*, ii, 158. Where John Mansel observes it would be well for the king to have 'preachers' like the *pars contraria*.

[191] *DBM*, 246–9. Nothing was said about how they were to be chosen.

[192] For events at St Albans, we not only lack Matthew Paris, but also his continuator, who ceased work just after his account of the king's flight from Winchester: Paris's Continuator, 470–1. His chronicle was continued at Pershore abbey, see Carpenter, 'The Pershore *Flores Historiarum*'.

[193] Brand, *Kings, Barons and Justices*, 120–3.

litigation under the provisions on suit of court and numerous cases were commenced. The writ itself was propaganda for the regime. It described how the legislation had been promulgated by 'the counsel of the whole realm', the 'counsel' itself being sometimes described as that of 'the magnates of England'. It was therefore 'the king's subjects, and more especially his magnates, who had taken the initiative in promulgating the reforms, rather than the king or his officials'.[194] The men of Bloxham hundred in Oxfordshire appreciated as much. They described the legislation on the *beaupleder* fine as part of 'provisions made by the barons'.[195] There was even a belief that the provisions did more than they did. When the eyres were stopped on the grounds they were 'against the common provision' it was because seven years had not elapsed since the last eyre, but there was no provision on that point in 1258–9.[196]

Sensitivity to breaches in the provisions and attendant oath was widespread. Matthew Paris's continuator thought they had been contravened in 1260, both by committing the bishopric of Durham to John Mansel junior and the Aumale wardship to Richard de Clare.[197] There was an understanding of the reforms very much as the barons had conceived them. The Canterbury/Dover annalist thought how wrong it was for the oath to be overthrown for it had bound people to act in loyalty to the king as well as for the honour of God and the profit of the realm.[198] The oath indeed seemed central to the resistance. A poet in forty-seven verses of impassioned verse urged Richard de Clare, Simon de Montfort and Roger Bigod to stick to what they had sworn and save England from desolation.[199] Another poem written in French and English on the overthrow of the Provisions stigmatized the pope and mentioned the oath and the sentences of excommunication in support of the 'new law' set up by the king on the advice of his people.[200]

---

[194] Brand, *Kings, Barons and Justices*, 109–15, with the quotation at 112–13. Brand (in very fragmentary material) found seventeen actions under the legislation between 1259 and 1263. A writ was also devised to implement the legislation limiting the obligation of magnates and others to attend the sheriff's tourn: Brand, *King, Barons and Justices*, 115–17.

[195] *SCWR*, 105–6.

[196] There must also have been an awareness that the eyres of 1261 were very different from the *querela* eyres of 1258–60. Doubtless the baronial leaders kept quiet about the fact it was they who had closed the latter down.

[197] Paris's Continuator, 450, 455. In fact, the wardship (without any payment) went to Edward not Clare.

[198] Canterbury/Dover, 213; and likewise Osney, 128; Burton, 'Politics, propaganda and public opinion', 61–4.

[199] Rishanger, 18–20; *Political Songs*, 121–4. Rishanger places the poem in 1264 but, with Gloucester and Bigod as joint leaders, it fits 1261 much better.

[200] *ANPS*, 56–66. I am grateful to John Maddicott for bringing this song to my attention and pointing out that it belonged to the period of reform and rebellion. For discussion see Somerset, 'Complaining about the king in French'.

The resistance to the king gained strength from finding a way to describe the programme it was rallying behind. Since the reforms had all begun at Oxford, the key word in the description was Oxford itself. The reforms were thus called the ordinances, statutes, constitutions or, most often, the provisions of Oxford. The judge John de Wyvill thus described the eyre commissioned in November 1259 as hearing the wrongs and trespasses committed 'against the provisions of Oxford'.[201] The poem protesting about the king's breach of his oath in 1261 was headed 'Concerning the Provision of Oxford'. The Osney annals thought the king was seeking to overthrow 'the statutes and provisions provided in the general parliament at Oxford'.[202] The Pershore chronicler wrote out the text of what he called, more concisely, 'the provisions of Oxford'.[203] For some of the baronial leaders the key feature was the council's control of the king. For those in the shires it was the local reforms. 'The Provisions of Oxford' served all purposes for the term covered the totality of the reforms promulgated in 1258-9. The opposition now had a compelling way of describing what they were struggling for.

## THE KING'S RESPONSE: AUGUST, SEPTEMBER 1261

Faced with these challenges, Henry remained in the Tower till the end of July and then moved in a day (far from his usual leisurely pace) to Windsor where he stayed until 24 September. He had swapped one great fortress for another but at least at Windsor he could relax in the park (he took steps to repair its fencing) and enjoy the palatial apartments built for himself and his queen. He could also control traffic on the Thames, guard the approach to London from the west and give encouragement to the neighbouring sheriffs. Alexander of Hampden in Buckinghamshire and Bedfordshire was having a particularly hard time. (From August onwards he collected no revenue.)[204]

Queen Eleanor herself may have urged the move to Windsor, always her favourite residence. Peter of Savoy was there too, as were the other Savoyards.[205] While with 'certain magnates rebelling', efforts were made to bring in knights and sergeants from abroad,[206] the essential strategy was to remain on the defensive, win over hearts and minds and hope the opposition would collapse. Henry never led forces out of Windsor to help Alexander of Hampden or anyone else. Instead, he did everything possible

---

[201] TNA SC 1/5/85.

[202] Osney, 128.

[203] Pershore *Flores*, 473-4. The text does not survive.

[204] *CR 1268-72*, 41. He was not popular: Ridgeway, 'Mid thirteenth-century reformers and the localities', 72-3.

[205] *RCWL*, ii, 135.

[206] *CR 1259-61*, 487.

to publicize and exploit the papal annulment of the 1258 oath, helped here by a reconciliation with Archbishop Boniface. In June, Boniface was granted a market at his manor of Maidstone. In August he was with Henry at Windsor. Acting under the authority of the papal letters, he now joined with the bishop of Norwich and John Mansel in sending instructions to the bishops. They were to order everyone to obey the king in 'the untramelled fullness of his royal power'. The archbishop of York hastened to say he had done as bid.[207] Boniface, again on the authority of the papal letters, also went further. Working closely with John Mansel, he ordered, on pain of excommunication, the keepers appointed by the baronial regime to surrender their castles. This was the order Hugh Bigod refused to obey.[208]

Henry also strove to win over hearts and minds in a great proclamation issued on 16 August, the fullest and most eloquent of the reign.[209] The king had heard with bitterness, so he now said, about the attempts to wrest people from their fidelity by false and malicious suggestions. This was all the more painful because for the forty-five years of his reign he had not ceased to labour for the peace and tranquillity of everyone. Thanks to God 'through whom all kings reign', the kingdom had suffered neither interdict nor civil war as it had in the past, a reference of course to John's reign. Instead, everyone had enjoyed their possessions in peace and had retained and obtained their rights 'according to what is just'. Henry had dispossessed no one 'by force and will' and had exiled no one unjustly. Suggestions to the contrary should not be believed. Henry then countered rumours that he was bringing foreign soldiers into the country to the harm of his native subjects. He also defended the sheriffs he had just appointed. As men of power, they would be better able to preserve the rights of the king and defend the king's subjects from oppression than the outgoing sheriffs, pawns of the magnates as they were.[210] It was the baronial leaders who were seeking to oppress the people and the king who was seeking to protect them. The proclamation certainly had impact. The Pershore annalist thought it a persuasive call to show the reverence and fidelity due the king.[211]

Henry thus reached out to the shires. Another option was to bring the shires to him, by summoning knights from each county to a parliament. This, however, Henry did not think of doing. Only when he heard of the three knights from each county summoned by Bishop Cantilupe, Montfort

---

[207] I deduce this from TNA SC 1/7/154, and *DBM*, 242–7. In August, Bishop Cantilupe is found at court, presumably as part of ongoing negotiations: *RCWL*, ii, 135.

[208] *F*, i, 408; TNA SC 1/7/157.

[209] *F*, i, 408–9 (*CPR 1258–66*, 173). See also *F*, i, 407; *CPR 1258–66*, 170, 174. For discussion of the form and rhetoric of royal letters see Hennings, 'The language of kingship under Henry III', and Neal, *The Letters of Edward I*.

[210] For connections between the 1258–60 sheriffs and baronial leaders, see above, 167 n. 297.

[211] Pershore, 473–4. The translation of '*pietas*' as 'reverence' I owe to Daniel Hadas.

and Clare to St Albans for 21 September did he take action. He ordered the sheriffs to make sure the knights came to Windsor on that day instead. They would then understand, Henry explained, how he planned to do nothing save what was for 'the honour and good' of the realm. Probably Henry intended to make a speech much on the lines of the 16 August proclamation. How many knights actually turned up either at St Albans or Windsor is unknown, but that Henry merely reacted to the baronial summons suggests he was far less confident of local support than were the baronial leaders.

While Henry sat tight in Windsor castle, much depended on his agents in the localities. Here too the watchwords were 'don't provoke'. When the sheriff James of Audley asked what to do about the 'contradiction' he faced in Shropshire and Staffordshire, he was told to act 'with caution' and pass over simply verbal resistance.[212] Meanwhile, John Mansel was in Sussex inspecting the works at Sedgwick castle. There he 'confirmed the hearts' of neighbouring men in their allegiance and advised the king to have 'preachers' like those on the other side.[213] One suspects he was the author of the 16 August proclamation.

The proclamation itself was linked to putting Philip Basset's position as justiciar on a proper footing, another conciliatory move. On 13 August he was given a salary of 1,000 marks a year (the same as Hugh Bigod's), and everyone was informed of his appointment for 'the preservation of the king, the tranquillity of the realm and the showing of justice to all'.[214] This was not, however, the precursor to an eyre in Bigod's fashion. That would have been impossible in the circumstances. Instead, Basset set off on a tour with the aim of arresting disturbers of the peace and imprisoning them in the castles along his route. His conduct, however, seems to have been unprovocative. In Somerset and Dorset (a joint sheriffdom) he appointed a local man, Henry of Alton, as under-sheriff to run the county.[215] Basset was certainly well informed and quick to act. When he learnt that Roger de Somery was going to attend the baronial assembly at St Albans, he wrote at once to Walter of Merton with instructions to summon him to the Windsor parliament instead. He added the information that the letters should be sent to Somery at his Berkshire manor of Bradfield.[216] The one sheriff who did take violent action on the king's behalf was Matthias Bezill at Gloucester. When William de Tracy

[212] *CR 1259–61*, 488–9.

[213] *RL*, ii, 157–8; *RCWL*, ii, 135. In the letter Mansel said the moat at Sedgwick would soon be able to hold water. Part of it survives as do some earthworks. The castle has a magnificent site on high ground with panoramic views over the Sussex weald. For Mansel's acquisition of the manor, see Liu, 'John Mansel', 173.

[214] *CPR 1258–66*, 172.

[215] Ridgeway, 'Dorset in the period of baronial reform and rebellion', 29–30.

[216] TNA SC 1/7/33 (Sayles, *Functions of the Medieval Parliament*, 97–8).

sought to hold what was probably the Michaelmas session of the county court, Bezill broke in with an armed force, pulled Tracy from the dais, dragged him out into the street and trampled over him with horses in the mud. Tracy was then hauled off to imprisonment in the castle.[217] The foreign knights in Henry and Eleanor's service were the reverse of wilting courtiers.[218]

Between 24 and 26 September, Henry left Windsor and returned to London. According to the chronicler, Thomas Wykes, he entered the capital in secret, 'fearing sedition of the barons since they refused to hold a parliament with him'.[219] It looks as though Henry's parliament summoned to Windsor had been a failure. With rebel barons at large perhaps around Windsor itself, he felt safer within London's walls. With the exchequer probably installed in the bishop of London's house at St Paul's, where Henry now took up residence, he could also be around for the start of its Michaelmas session.

The picture at the start of the session, when sheriffs were supposed to come with money, was mixed. Little or nothing was received from eleven shires. On the other hand, all Henry's sheriffs turned up either in person or through deputies. There were some surprising successes. From Lincolnshire, for all the opposition of Adam de Newmarch, William de Grey was able to deliver 200 marks. Despite his difficulties in Shropshire–Staffordshire, James of Audley raised £60. From Warwickshire–Leicestershire came 100 marks, although this was the heart of Montfort country. The total amount brought from the counties, at £791, was down from the £918 of Michaelmas 1260 and the £1,246 of 1259 but not catastrophically so. The amount coming from the towns held up rather better.[220]

## VICTORY, NOVEMBER 1261

Installed at St Paul's, Henry was preoccupied with one question above all. Would he be able celebrate the feast of the Confessor's translation on 13 October at Westminster? In the event he did so, yet, for all the spiritual balm radiating from his patron saint, it was the most uncomfortable celebration of the reign. Probably the Abbey and palace had to be guarded to prevent an attack. Henry came just for the day and returned immediately afterwards not to St Paul's but to the greater security of the Tower. He was to be holed up there for almost the next two months. The Pershore

---

[217] Robert of Gloucester, ii, lines 11,060–83; *CPR 1258–66*, 220; *CR 1259–61*, 442.

[218] For William Marmion's action in Norwich see *CFR 1260–1*, no. 996; *CR 1268–72*, 342–3.

[219] Wykes, 129.

[220] TNA E 368/36, mm. 17, 35 (image 5760, 5804); Cassidy, 'Adventus vicecomitum', 616.

annalist wrote of the 'magnates of England' gathered in arms around London and thought the situation was getting daily worse.[221]

In this critical situation, Henry ordered over 130 tenants-in-chief to muster in London at the end of October with horses and arms. Thirty-seven abbots were also to send their service. At the same time Henry tried again to recruit forces from abroad (the count of St Pol was asked to come with sixty knights). King Richard wrote urging a careful check as to where these forces could land. If the Cinque Ports gave difficulty, not to worry, he could arrange for landings elsewhere. Anyway, he would soon be with the king to give advice on the subject.[222] Meanwhile Henry's sheriffs were encouraged to spend money on their castles and were equipped with letters promising the king would give justice to all and preserve everyone in their rights.[223] Fierce letters were also sent to the opposition sheriffs, threatening them with disinheritance if they did not cease their usurpations.[224]

Henry, therefore, prepared for war yet hoped for peace; hoped that a mixture of threats and assurances would restore order to the counties; hoped also for a negotiated settlement with the baronial leaders, although only one which would leave victory in his hands. The barons were indeed ready to parley. On 17 October a safe conduct was given to Richard de Clare and further letters of conduct for unspecified barons followed, lasting into November. The place assigned for the negotiations was Kingston in Surrey.[225]

Eventually on 21 November a 'certain form of peace' was agreed by the negotiators. The Dover annals mention Richard de Clare and King Richard as the two principals procuring the agreement.[226] When the baronial negotiators agreed Magna Carta with King John in 1215, it took four days for them to sell it to the assembled throng at Runnymede. This time the selling proved much more difficult. The 'form of peace' was regarded in some circles as a sell-out. It covered simply the question of the sheriffs, although that reflected how important the issue was for the localities.[227] Any county so wishing could elect four knights to come to court on

---

[221] Pershore, *Flores*, 474.

[222] *CR 1259–61*, 494–9; *RL*, ii, 193–4. Those at court in October included Humphrey de Bohun, earl of Hereford and Essex, who had remained loyal, unlike his eldest son; *RCWL*, ii, 135; *CR 1259–61*, 500. The young earl of Devon, Baldwin de Lisle, was also on Henry's side.

[223] *RL*, ii, 192–3; *CPR 1258–66*, 178–9.

[224] *CR 1259–61*, 499–500, 503. The letters went to John de la Haye (Surrey–Sussex); Giles de Erdington (sic) for Argentan (Cambridgeshire–Huntingdonshire); John fitzJohn (Buckinghamshire–Bedfordshire); William le Blund (Suffolk); William Bardolph (Norfolk); and William Marshal of Norton (Northamptonshire).

[225] *CPR 1258–66*, 178–9, 189; *RL*, ii, 194.

[226] Osney, 128–9; Treharne, *Baronial Plan*, 272, 279 n. 1; Canterbury/Dover, 213.

[227] *RL*, ii, 197–8; *F*, i, 411–12, 415.

6 January. Henry and King Richard with the counsel of the exchequer would then choose one of them as sheriff. The scheme to make the sheriffs partly elected harked back to proposals of October 1259, although they had never been implemented. It also meant the sheriffs would be local men, something, it was said, that would win the king the hearts of his people.

All this, however, was to be but a temporary arrangement. The method of appointment from Michaelmas 1262 was to be decided before Pentecost 1262 by a panel of six arbitrators, three chosen by the king and three by the barons.[228] The arbitration, however, only covered those counties where the opposition sheriffs had held the county court at or before Michaelmas 1261. So elsewhere the king was free to do what he liked. Since, moreover, if the arbitrators disagreed, the matter was to be referred to King Richard, Henry had little to fear from the results, as indeed proved the case.

If this was not bad enough for the opposition, the arbitration did not cover at all the heart of the Provisions, namely the council's control over the king. In effect that control was a dead letter. Henry was free. Not surprisingly, therefore, a powerful group of barons refused to accept the settlement. Led by Simon de Montfort and Roger Bigod, they included John de Warenne, Roger de Mortimer, Hugh Despenser, William Bardolph, John fitzAlan and a group of young men, later all key Montfortians, John fitzJohn, Henry de Hastings, William de Munchesney, Nicholas of Seagrave and Geoffrey de Lucy.[229] Probably the group had argued for the rather different scheme of arbitration described in the Osney annals. Here six arbitrators, three chosen by the king and three by the barons, were to ordain on the Provisions themselves. To be sure, King Richard was once again to decide any dispute, but at least here the Provisions had not been abandoned.[230]

In the end a sufficient number of barons came in behind the narrow settlement dealing just with the sheriffs. It was sealed on 5 December and two days later announced by King Henry alongside a pardon for all the evils committed by his opponents during the dispute. All the contemporary accounts agree that the crucial factor in bringing about the settlement was Richard de Clare's defection. In the words of the Dunstable annals, 'as though apostasizing, he deserted Simon de Montfort and the other magnates to whom he had sworn an oath of alliance to preserve the good

[228] The six were, for the king, Philip Basset, Walter of Merton and Robert Walerand and, for the barons, John de la Haye, Richard Foliot (both opposition sheriffs) and Richard de Middleton. It was the baronial arbitrators who made the point about the appointment of local men winning hearts and minds for the king.

[229] F, i, 411–12 (CPR 1258–66, 194–5); CR 1261–4, 95. Munchesney and Seagrave were there despite earlier submissions: CR 1259–61, 489, 491.

[230] Osney, 128–9. The baronial three were the dean of Lincoln, Roger Bigod and Peter de Montfort. The king's three were the bishops of Salisbury and Hereford and John Mansel.

laws of the land'. One chronicle ascribes Clare's decision to the influence of Queen Eleanor and the two had certainly once been close.[231]

Henry now appealed to Montfort, Roger Bigod and the rest to seal the settlement. If they were unwilling to come in person, they could just send their seals. If they did not, then they would be outside the pardon.[232] How many of the group formally agreed to the settlement is unknown, but with one exception they all in practice accepted the king's recovery of power. With that Henry wisely was content.

The exception was Simon de Montfort. Throughout 1261 he had been at the forefront of the opposition. Surely behind the council's contemptuous replies to the king, he had secured the oaths of allegiance from the Cinque Ports, placed his own men over counties, summoned (with Clare and Bishop Cantilupe) the knights to St Albans and brought horses and arms into the kingdom from abroad. Now, rather than bow down before the king and see the overthrow of the Provisions, he left for France. The Dunstable annalist catches what he probably said to all and sundry. He would rather 'die without land than be a perjurer and depart from the truth'.[233] This was the pivotal moment in Montfort's career. Montfort alone of the great English barons had refused to accept the king's recovery of power. He alone, he could now say, had remained true to the Provisions. He was leaving England because he believed in their cause and in the fidelity to his oath. This was a stand for the truth and the public good. The complaint that he was driven by his private interests could not be levelled at him. He would rather die landless than be perjured. And indeed, it is hard to see how in purely material terms Montfort had anything to gain from his departure.[234] When he did return it would be to resurrect the Provisions.

Richard de Clare seems to have received no immediate reward for his defection. Perhaps, in the last resort, he was simply unprepared to fight for the Provisions and was infuriated by Montfort's insistence that he should. As in 1259, he found himself traduced as an oath breaker by his self-righteous colleague. Perhaps Clare's knightly followers were equally unready for war. Yet there was no way, short of a victorious war, that Henry could be put back under conciliar control. What could be done was something about the sheriffs, perhaps anyway the issue of most appeal to Clare's men.

While the baronial leadership split apart, the royal family had come together. Without that, Henry could never have mounted his bid for freedom.[235] He owed much to the queen, Peter of Savoy and the Savoyard

[231] Osney, 128–9; Dunstable, 217; Canterbury/Dover, 213; Battle, 374; Howell, *Eleanor of Provence*, 184; volume 1, 654, 692.

[232] *F*, i, 411–12 (*CPR 1258–66*, 194–5); *CR 1261–4*, 95.

[233] Dunstable, 217.

[234] Maddicott, *Simon de Montfort*, 215, takes a different view here.

[235] There is a full analysis of Henry's strengths in Ridgeway, 'What happened in 1261?', 93–7.

knights, who were at court for much of the year. It was almost certainly as a reward for his labours and expenses that, in July 1261, Peter's executors were allowed to have the profits of Richmond for a full seven years after his death, an unprecedented concession.[236] Henry also owed much to King Richard. Next year he wrote feelingly of Richard's 'wearying labours', during 'the crisis . . . for the restoration of our state'.[237] Another whom Henry commended, very rightly, was John Mansel: 'in the restoration of our right and honour, according to his due fidelity, he has stood effectively and constantly, obstructing with all his strength those seeking to damage us'. This was said in a letter to the cardinals rebutting accusations that Mansel had sown discord between the king and his nobles. Clearly the opposition saw him as a key player in what had happened.[238]

Henry also profited from a lack of outside interference. There was no repeat of the baronial alliances with the king of Scotland and the Welsh rulers which had done so much to damage King John in 1215–16. The agreement made with King Alexander at the meetings back in October 1260 (if such it was) had held. To make assurance doubly sure, at the end of July 1261 Henry gave Alexander 1,000 marks out of the wardrobe as another contribution to Queen Margaret's dowry.[239] As for Llywelyn ap Gruffudd, in March 1261 the existing truce was renewed until June 1262. The barons had urged him to join them, but he had refused. After all they had done nothing to meet his demands for a permanent settlement. Perhaps he might do better with Henry, a belief the king did something to encourage. Next year Llywelyn was commended for his 'laudable' behaviour during the crisis.[240]

The neutrality of Alexander and Llywelyn, in Alexander's case sympathetic neutrality, was enough for Henry. From King Louis there was more positive help. Between June and December 1261 he sent Henry no less than £6,928 as an advance on the money owed for the 500 knights. Henry spoke of it being spent in the service of God and for the benefit of church and kingdom, as the treaty stipulated. He no longer mentioned the need for the consent of the upstanding men of the land.[241] Money was indeed the vital lubricant for Henry's victory. The new fees promised to knights in March and April 1261 committed him to payments of around £600 a

---

[236] *CPR 1258–66*, 161; and see also *CChR 1226–57*, 259; *CChR 1257–1300*, 41. On the face of it these arrangements disadvantaged the queen, who had been left all Peter's English lands in his will, but I doubt if in 1261 Peter was doing anything to antagonize her. For later arrangements see below, 336 and 532–3.

[237] *CR 1259–61*, 175–6.

[238] *F*, i, 414 (*CPR 1258–66*, 230).

[239] *CPR 1258–66*, 170; Wild, *WA*, 87, 103. For the only other payment I have noticed, see *CLR 1251–60*, 330.

[240] *F*, i, 404 (*CPR 1258–66*, 147); *CR 1261–4*, 100–1; Smith, *Llywelyn ap Gruffudd*, 134.

[241] Gavrilovitch, *Étude sur la traité de Paris*, 58, 119; *F*, i, 410, 412; *CPR 1258–66*, 151, 190, 194; Wild, *WA*, 107.

year. He was also spending large sums of money hiring knights, sergeants and crossbowmen.[242] Fortunately, revenue in the first half of the year had held up reasonably well. The receipt roll shows the exchequer received £6,177 during the Easter term.[243] Henry was lucky in that he still had in his hands the bishopric of Winchester, from which the wardrobe and exchequer received £6,216 between December 1260 and August 1262.[244]

Henry's recovery of power in 1261 was one of the great political triumphs of the reign. It was also the last achieved without help from his son Lord Edward. For the triumph Henry has a fair share of the credit. Without the good relations he had established with King Alexander and King Louis (his conduct in Paris in 1259–60 had been perfect), he might not have enjoyed the sympathetic neutrality of the one and the money of the other. Without his reputation as a pious and decent individual, Montfort would have found it much easier to rally support for a war in the Provisions' defence. As for the tactics employed in 1261, we can only speculate. Given the contrast with Henry's blundering attempt to defy the council in 1259, the clever moves at the start of 1261 probably owed much to King Richard, Peter of Savoy and John Mansel. They must also have agreed the underlying strategy throughout the year, namely, to do nothing militarily to provoke the opposition. The strategy chimed well with the temperament of both King Richard, a mediator rather than a man of war, and of Henry himself, sedentary and pacific as he was. Henry never once toured the country with the aim of reasserting his authority and taking on his critics. Apart from his dash to Dover to seize the castle and his journey to Winchester to unveil the papal letters, he spent the year locked down in Windsor castle and the Tower. The sheriffs too were told to remain on the defensive. Behind this quietude, there was judgement as well as disposition. Henry and his advisors calculated that if nothing was done to provoke a war, the baronial leaders would not begin one. Given they could not win without a war, they would ultimately back down. The calculation proved correct. England was spared a civil war in 1261. Unfortunately, it would prove but a temporary reprieve.

---

[242] Unfortunately, there is no breakdown of the £13,400 spent by the wardrobe on knights, sergeants and crossbowmen between 1258 and 1264: Wild, *WA*, 88, 103, 112, 114.

[243] Whitwell, 'Revenue and expenditure under Henry III', 710; Cassidy, 'The English exchequer',' 35.

[244] Howell, *Regalian Right*, 230.

## Chapter 7

# DISASTER: SIMON DE MONTFORT'S RETURN AND HENRY'S CAPITULATION
## 1262-1263

Henry's itinerary in the first half of 1262 was remarkably sluggish, even by his standards. He made no effort to demonstrate and affirm his recovery of power by touring the country. He did not even visit his favourite palaces and castles. He ordered 500 paupers to be fed on the day Bishop Aymer's heart was buried at Winchester but was not there himself.[1] Instead, Henry divided his time between Westminster and Windsor. He was at Westminster indeed, for the whole period from 23 December 1261 to 10 February 1262 and then again from 29 March through to 4 July, apart from a week in May at Windsor. Perhaps Henry imagined his presence in the provinces might be provocative or even dangerous. He also had another reason for hugging Westminster close. After almost a year away, apart from that hurried and fearful visit on 13 October 1261, Henry could at last inspect the progress of the new church. The crisis of 1261 had inevitably reduced the money available for the works, but they had continued.[2] Henry could now climb over the building, talk with his masons and craftsmen, and view the gradual rising of the four new bays of the choir. He could also pray again before the shrine of the Confessor, to whose intercession at God's right hand he surely owed his victory.

## A NEW SHRINE FOR THE CONFESSOR

Henry's debt to the Confessor now inspired, or so it may be suggested, a major decision about the Abbey, one of great imagination and also of great visual and spiritual significance. This was to commission a new shrine base to hold aloft the golden reliquary containing the Confessor's body. Henry had previously envisaged a base made of Purbeck marble. Indeed, it had partly been constructed. But now Henry decided on something quite different, for the new base was to be made not by English Purbeck marblers but by a family of mosaicists from Rome, the Cosmati. The structure the Cosmati created was dismantled at the Reformation but

---

[1] *CLR 1260–7*, 81.
[2] Colvin, *History of the King's Works*, i, 156.

reconstructed in clumsy fashion by Abbot Feckenham during the brief restoration of the Benedictine monastery under Queen Mary. Enough survives today to conjure up its original appearance, the mosaics of coloured glass and porphyry stones covering the surfaces and radiating a shimmering magnificence quite unlike anything seen before in England.[3]

Intelligence about the Cosmati almost certainly came from the new abbot of Westminster, Richard of Ware.[4] Later, Ware brought to England the stones to make the great Cosmati pavement before the Abbey's high altar, so his connection with their work is certain.[5] He had first seen it at Anagni in Italy where, in March 1259, he was made a papal chaplain.[6] He was probably back in England by the following August, when his temporalities were restored following his confirmation by the pope. Two further visits to the papal court, on the affairs of king and Abbey, followed in 1260 and 1261.[7] Fired by Ware's enthusiasm, Henry came to think he must have Cosmati work in the Abbey. In his expansive way, he had covered every surface of the church with diapered roses. He would now cover every surface of the shrine base with mosaics of glass and stone.

The porphyry stones promised by the Cosmati were not their first appearance in England. They were found in the great marble pavement laid out in Canterbury cathedral before Becket's shrine. With this, Henry must have been very familiar. Yet he had done nothing to bring something similar to Westminster, let alone introduce such marble work into the Confessor's shrine. Given Henry's ambivalent relationship with Becket, perhaps this was not surprising. The Confessor's light was not to be dimmed by any reminder of the saint murdered by his king.[8] The Cosmati gave Henry the chance to make a new start and with associations not with Canterbury but with Rome. With his interest in artistic detail, Henry was also intrigued and entranced by Cosmati methods.[9] The family cut some of their porphyry stones into sizable squares, rectangles and disks, usually of purple and green, and often about 20–25 centimetres across. But the heart of the technique was something different, something not found at all in the Canterbury pavement. This was the use of tesserae, tiny porphyry stones and pieces of glass of different colours (purple,

---

[3] Rodwell and Neal, *The Cosmatesque Mosaics*, with multiple and magnificent illustrations, now provides a comprehensive analysis of the structure and materials of the Cosmati works. Volume I covers the pavements and volume 2 the shrine and royal tombs. I discuss the chronology of the Cosmati work in Appendix 1.

[4] For a brief biography, see Carpenter, 'Richard of Ware'. He appears throughout in William Jordan's *A Tale of Two Monasteries*. He had been elected in December 1258.

[5] See below, 549.

[6] *CPReg*, 364; see Foster, *Patterns of Thought*, 16–17.

[7] *CPR 1258–66*, 7, 39, 117, 135; *CR 1256–9*, 351. Henry had given his assent to the election in December 1258.

[8] For Henry's ambivalent relationship with Becket, see volume 1, 316–17.

[9] For what follows, see Rodwell and Neal, *The Cosmatesque Mosaics*, ii, 594–5.

green, grey-black and white/cream) all cut into a multiplicity of shapes –
squares, rectangles, triangles and trapezia – the glass either opaque or
translucent and sometimes no more than 3 millimetres across. It was from
these tesserae, thousands and thousands of them, that the mosaics framing
the larger stones were made up. The method, as doubtless the Cosmati
assured Ware and Henry, could easily transfer from pavements (for which
the Cosmati were chiefly famous) to decorating the shrine base of the
Confessor; indeed it was ideal for such a purpose.

There were, therefore, clear aesthetic reasons for going with the
Cosmati, but their materials also had a deeper meaning.[10] All the purple
porphyry used in the medieval period had come originally from a single
mine, that at Gebel Dokhan in Egypt, some twenty miles inland from the
Red Sea. The mine, however, had closed in the fifth century and was only
rediscovered in the late nineteenth. The purple porphyry the Cosmati
used came, therefore, not direct from the mine but from the ruined buildings of ancient Rome. The same was true of the green porphyry, the
origins this time being the mines near Sparta in the south-eastern part of
the Grecian Peloponnese. Both purple and green porphyry were prized for
their colour and their rarity. Their hardness made them excellent building
stones, especially for pavements. Beyond that, purple porphyry also had a
very special status. In ancient Greece and Rome a rare and expensive dye
made from the mucus of sea snails was used to colour purple the robes of
kings, emperors, generals and high officials. The children of later Byzantine
emperors were described as 'born in the purple', the room in which the
empress gave birth having purple drapes. The stones of the Cosmati, in
their imperial colours, were thus of the highest possible status, and
brought from Italy they linked Henry, the Confessor and the whole Abbey
project to the papacy and to Rome. That Henry's own brother was king
of the Romans, and hoped one day to be emperor, made the connection
seem all the more right.

Just when the contract with the Cosmati was struck and they arrived in
England is unknown.[11] What is certain is that in the years from 1259 to
1267, the only time when England was at peace and Henry in full control
of government, was between December 1261 and the outbreak of civil war
in June 1263. Henry in the long days at Westminster early in 1262 had the
leisure to make the final decision about the shrine, the power to do something about it, and at least the hope the Cosmati would arrive in a time of
peace. And there was now an additional reason why Henry should wish to
honour the Confessor and the papacy. It was to them he owed his victory.

[10] For what follows, see Foster, *Patterns of Thought*, 35–6. Rodwell and Neal, *The
Cosmatesque Mosaics*, i, 262–73, has a full analysis (by Kevin Hayward) of all the stone used
by the Cosmati at the Abbey.
[11] One possibility is that the contract was fixed up by the proctors Henry was maintaining at the papal court in 1262. See *DD*, nos. 350–1, 364–5, 367.

The shrine base was thus Henry's thanks offering for his recovery of power in 1261.

## THE WESTMINSTER ABBEY SHIELDS

Henry's work at the Abbey around this time also said something else about his rule. It was something immensely reassuring and just right for the circumstances of 1262. For within the community of Christian Europe, Henry indicated he would rule very much in concert with his native barons. This takes us to the great heraldic shields carved and painted in the wall arcade of the Abbey's new choir.[12] Work had started on the choir, as we have seen, in 1259 when a further section of the Confessor's church had been thrown down. Given the time taken to dismantle the old structure and dig the foundations of the new one, it was probably not before 1262 that the wall arcade itself was ready for the shields.[13] Just when Henry conceived the scheme is impossible to know, but the presence of Montfort's shield makes it almost certain it was before the latter's rebellion in 1263.[14] If, as I think most likely, both the carving and the erection took place in 1262 itself, Henry was acting in a very conciliatory spirit, given the events of the previous year. For in the wall arcade of the north aisle, after the shields of France and the empire, were the shields of Richard de Clare, Roger Bigod and Montfort himself, followed by the shields of John de Warenne, Humphrey de Bohun and the earl of Aumale.[15] In the south aisle, in pride of place beside the monk's doorway from the cloister, were the shields of the Confessor and Henry himself, followed east to west by those of Scotland, Provence (for the queen of course) and then the earls of Winchester, Lincoln and Cornwall.[16]

When it came to the Confessor himself, Henry had acted decisively to put him into this heraldic company. He had given his patron saint a coat

---

[12] For a discussion of the shields, see Binski, *Westminster Abbey and the Plantagenets*, 76–86.

[13] As suggested by Robert Turner, drawing on Warwick Rodwell's estimate of the chronology: Turner, *Medieval Arms of Westminster Abbey*, 15. (I am grateful to Robert Turner for sending me a copy of this privately printed book.) The shields were probably carved not *in situ* but in the workshop.

[14] It is possible to suggest a variety of chronologies on the basis of the earls included and excluded, one suggestion being that the scheme may originally have been conceived before 1258. The shields seem to have been continued, presumably just painted, in the nave of the Confessor. When it was demolished in the fourteenth century, they were then repainted in the wall arcade of the new nave. Some of these survive. The nave shields are listed in Camden, *Reges, Reginae, Nobiles*, 79, and are discussed in Turner, *Medieval Arms of Westminster Abbey*, 34–51. The arms of the earls of Oxford and Derby appear there, as well as those of William de Valence.

[15] This is running east to west.

[16] The final shield in the sequence remains a puzzle. It bears the arms of the Scottish earl of Ross, but there seems no reason for his inclusion.

of arms. The shield in the wall arcade bearing a cross between five birds is its first known appearance.[17] The idea had come from one of the Confessor's pennies. Its obverse, showing the Confessor enthroned, had already prompted the design of Henry's gold penny. The reverse, bearing a cross with a bird in each of its four angles, now inspired the Confessor's coat of arms.[18] Henry would certainly have claimed that the kind of co-operative rule, evinced so powerfully in the shields, had been his vision all along. The arms of English barons had thus featured in the sword belt he gave to the count of Champagne, probably in 1254. In 1243 he had ordered a painting of a king and queen sitting with their baronage to be put up behind the dais in his new hall in Dublin castle.[19] And, of course, it was precisely for just, peaceable and consensual rule that the Confessor was famed.

## THE SITUATION IN THE COUNTIES

Henry was also thinking at this time about how to beautify the surroundings of the palace and the Abbey. In March 1262 he ordered ten pear trees to be planted in the little enclosed garden beside the penthouse leading from his chamber to the Abbey's south transept doorway.[20] This was the way into the Abbey he always took outside grand occasions. Once through the doorway, he could go up a staircase, cross over the end of the transept and enter the royal pew with its large painted heads of a king and queen and its dramatic bosses of centaurs fighting dragons.[21] From the pew Henry looked across, through the arches of his new church, to the place where the Cosmati shrine of the Confessor would be placed.

In early 1262, Henry needed very much the Confessor's support and all the Abbey's messaging for the situation remained tense. The Dover annalist reported that 'many great and small' did not consent to the king's recovery of power. Henry himself, writing to the pope (in March 1262), recalled his subjects' 'rebellion' and 'hoped' they were now reduced to obedience.[22] He was evidently not entirely sure. Late in 1261 the government had

---

[17] No arms are given to the Confessor in the thirteenth-century rolls of arms (including those by Matthew Paris) printed in *Rolls of Arms, Henry III*.

[18] Two of these coins were discovered at the Abbey in the last century. There is much discussion as to the identity of the birds in the coin and also in the Abbey shield. In later heraldry, they are depicted as 'martlets', described in the *Oxford English Dictionary* as 'an imaginary bird without feet'. But the birds in the wall arcade shield have very pronounced feet. For discussion, see Turner, 'Battle rages over whether Edward's birds are based on doves, eagles – or swallows', 34–7.

[19] *CR 1242–7*, 23 and volume 1, 605. I have now seen the sword belt.

[20] *CR 1261–4*, 29. The doorway is almost the only external part of the Abbey to retain its original masonry.

[21] When working late in what is the library in the 1960s and 1970s, I always went out across this south transept passage.

[22] Canterbury/Dover, 213; *CR 1261–4*, 111.

tried to restart the general eyres abandoned earlier in the year. But when, in January 1262, the judges came to High Wycombe to hear the pleas for Buckinghamshire, the knights and free tenants of the county refused to attend on the grounds they had received insufficient summons. Meanwhile in several counties (including Buckinghamshire) the king's sheriffs were still challenged by baronial keepers. Yet gradually the situation improved. The Dover annalist himself, having mentioned the discontent, added that no one was able to resist the king's recovery of power. Henry made a concession over the Buckinghamshire eyre and it went ahead, as did the eyres in Bedfordshire, Warwickshire, Leicestershire, Surrey and Sussex, all counties where there had been opposition to the sheriffs of the king.[23]

Gradually, too, the baronial sheriffs were reeled in. When the arbitrators appointed to decide how sheriffs should be appointed met at the end of January 1262, they failed to agree, not surprisingly. The king's side wanted complete freedom of appointment. The baronial side, in the disputed counties, wanted sheriffs to be local men. So the matter was referred to King Richard. That the baronial arbitrators accepted any limitations should end after ten years so as not to disinherit the king or prejudice his 'dominion' suggests their confidence was draining away. There had been no qualms of that kind in 1258 when the sheriffs were all to be vavasours of their counties. During February and March, in the disputed counties Henry went ahead and reappointed his 1261 sheriffs without waiting for Richard's verdict.[24] Meanwhile, seven of the baronial sheriffs, appearing obsequiously before Henry, the council and the exchequer, acknowledged they must account for their periods of rule.[25] When the exchequer opened for its Easter term, the money brought by the sheriffs was comparable to that produced in years of peace.[26] On 20 May, King Richard's 'dictum' was delivered to the king. It gave him complete freedom to appoint whatever sheriffs he wished.[27]

## THE NEW PAPAL LETTERS

A centrepiece of Henry's recovery of power in 1261 had been Pope Alexander's bulls quashing the oaths taken to obey the Provisions. Since Alexander's death, Henry's proctors had been working desperately to get the bulls renewed by the new pope, Urban IV. It was not easy, for, as they explained in long letters home, they were obstructed at every turn by

---

[23] *CPR 1258–66*, 198; *CR 1261–4*, 22–3; Crook, *Records of the General Eyre*, 126–8, 130–2.

[24] *F*, i, 415; *CPR 1258–66*, 202; *CFR 1261–2*, nos. 221–37.

[25] TNA E 368/36, m. 11d (image 5831). They included the Montfortian stalwarts Ralph Basset of Sapcote, Thomas of Astley and John de la Haye.

[26] Cassidy, 'Adventus vicecomitum', 616.

[27] *CR 1261–4*, 126; *F*, i, 415.

envoys and friends of the barons. But at last, on 25 February, Urban confirmed the fulminations of his predecessor. Henry had the new bull proclaimed in London at St Paul's Cross. In early May he followed up with an eloquent letter to all the sheriffs. It related the whole history of events since 1258: how Henry had agreed to the reform of the realm in return for promises that had not been kept; how the conduct of the barons had prejudiced royal power and damaged the king's subjects. Consequently, Henry felt no longer bound by the agreement and had been absolved from his oath by Popes Alexander and Urban. He now intended to exercise freely his royal power. All this the sheriffs were to proclaim throughout their counties, stressing, at the same time, the king's desire both to give justice to everyone and observe Magna Carta. Anyone 'preaching and trying to persuade the people' to resist the king and his sheriffs was to be arrested.[28] Evidently, Henry still feared opposition in the localities, but his letter was far more confident than those issued the year before. Words now as well as deeds were to be punished.

## THE REORDERING OF EDWARD

Henry had another reason for satisfaction in the first half of 1262. He was at last, or so he hoped, bringing order to the affairs of his eldest son and putting their relationship on a sound footing. Here Henry and Eleanor stood very much together. Edward was now twenty-two, addicted to tournaments and eager to display his prowess as a knight. There was much here his parents admired, Eleanor especially. But Edward also wanted to be free, free from the restraints of his parents, free to govern his appanage as he wished. Here there was much his parents found alarming. Edward seemed to be displaying all the irresponsibility of youth. No wonder he was always so short of money. He had squandered his possessions although, as Henry said, they were supposed to be inseparable from the crown of England.[29] He had made key appointments without consulting his parents. He had got in with absolutely the wrong crowd. Here Henry thought above all of the alliance with Simon de Montfort, Eleanor of how Edward had thrown over his Savoyard councillors and found a new crew of followers, several of them like his steward, the knight Roger of Leybourne, and John de Warenne, earl of Surrey, closely connected with the Lusignans. Edward simply could not be trusted. Promises came and went. In 1260, Henry had sent a special envoy to England to see, as he said, whether Edward's deeds matched his words. In 1262, Edward promised to be with his father at Easter 'little wishing that what proceeds from my lips be considered vain'.[30] Evidently, Henry suspected just that.

[28] *DBM*, 248–51; FitzThedmar, 49–50 (Stone, FitzThedmar, no. 754); *CR 1261–4*, 123.
[29] *DBM*, 216–17, cap. 20.
[30] *F*, i, 417.

It was in the Michaelmas term of 1261, before indeed his recovery of power was complete, that Henry moved to put his son's affairs in order, this by summoning Edward's bailiffs to come before the exchequer to render their accounts. Henry justified this action (in a letter to a perhaps doubtful exchequer) on the grounds that Edward was now overseas (he had left for Gascony in July) and held nothing save by concession of his father. Henry, as he explained, thus regarded Edward's welfare as his own and needed to attend to his affairs. On the face of it, the king was staging a takeover of his son's administration, something Edward would surely resent. Yet he was probably acting with Edward's agreement. Thus it was Edward's seneschal who supplied the exchequer with the list of those to be summoned and they were then to account before those Edward appointed.[31]

The particular target here was Roger of Leybourne. According to the Dover annals, Queen Eleanor had caused her son to fall out with his former steward. For former he was. Having been once so close, Edward had dismissed Leybourne sometime in 1261. We do not know why. Perhaps Leybourne objected to Edward abandoning Montfort. Perhaps Edward already suspected him of maladministration. That Eleanor wanted him out we may be sure.

When Leybourne did eventually come to account, his debts amounted to £382. At this point (in April 1262) Henry himself took action. He marched into the exchequer and made a declaration very much on the lines of his earlier writ. Considering, therefore, the money owed by Leybourne 'as his own', he ordered it to be raised by the sheriff of Kent from Leybourne's lands. A little later, Leybourne's situation deteriorated further for his debts, including sums he had received from Edward's wardrobe, were now put at a colossal £1,820.

Henry's intervention shows better than anything else his proprietary attitude to Edward's affairs. If he meant to keep the money raised for himself, he was being extremely stupid, for nothing was more likely to antagonize his son. Fortunately, wiser counsels prevailed and Henry later made clear the money was to be raised for Edward's use. Leybourne, meanwhile, to prevent their seizure, desperately removed his chattels from his manors in Kent, Essex and Sussex.[32] He was also attacked on another front. In April 1262, Henry commenced litigation to prize from him the valuable manor of Elham in Kent, given him by Edward in hereditary right back in December 1260.[33] Henry now said he had never consented to the gift of a manor which anyway should never have been separated from the crown.[34]

---

[31] TNA E 159/36, m. 4d (image 0098).

[32] TNA E 368/36, mm. 10, 15d (images 5743, 5843); *CR 1261–4*, 170–1; Canterbury/Dover, 220–1.

[33] For the grant, see TNA E 368/94, m. 47 (image 0094).

[34] Canterbury/Dover, 214.

This reordering of Edward's affairs was concluded by a new financial settlement after his return to England in February 1262. Edward, in the king's presence, gave up to Peter of Savoy the castle and honour of Hastings and received in return a collection of manors in Norfolk, Suffolk and elsewhere. At the same time (in early June 1262), all profits and issues from the Jews were given to Edward for three years. In return he gave to his father a long list of lands including those just received from Peter. Edward must have consented to this deal. It diminished his ability to reward his followers with land but also enabled him to raise from the Jews large amounts of ready cash.[35]

To their intense satisfaction, Henry and Eleanor had thus restored Edward's finances and punished his evil servants. But they were playing with fire. Roger of Leybourne was a dangerous man. He had first come to prominence in the 1250s by killing someone (accidently it was claimed) at a tournament. Now a virtual fugitive, he was far from friendless. During the course of 1261, Edward had broken not just with him but also with John de Warenne, earl of Surrey, and the marcher lords Hamo Lestrange and Roger of Clifford, the last dismissed as Edward's custodian of the Three Castles. (He too had been summoned to account.) Close to Edward for so long, none of these men, any more than Leybourne, accompanied him when he went to Gascony in July 1261. A party of ex-Edwardians was forming. It would be central to Henry and Eleanor's downfall.

## THE SAVOYARD COURT

Henry's court in the year after his triumph retained its Savoyard hue.[36] Alongside Robert Walerand, the two stewards of the household were Imbert Pugeys and Ebulo de Montibus, the latter probably appointed in February 1262.[37] One of the marshals was Imbert de Montferrand. When King Richard's *dictum* on the sheriffs was delivered to the king, those present apart from the chancellor, Walter of Merton, were all Savoyards: the steward Imbert Pugeys, the knights Aymon Thurbert and Peter de Champvent, and the keeper of the wardrobe, Henry de Ghent.

Above these lesser lights, until he left England in June 1262, stood Peter of Savoy.[38] Still very close to the queen, he probably brokered as he certainly profited from the settlement with Edward. In March 1262 he obtained a royal charter tightening his hold of Richmond and allowing

---

[35] *CPR 1258–66*, 233; *CChR 1257–1300*, 44–5; Howell, *Eleanor of Provence*, 189. Peter of Savoy coveted Hastings because it sat well with his honour of Pevensey.

[36] Howell, *Eleanor of Provence*, 186–7, 189–90.

[37] *CLR 1260–7*, 78–9. In volume 1, 672, I was wrong to say that Ebulo had been appointed in 1256.

[38] He attests royal charters in every month between January and May inclusive, save for April where no royal charters were enrolled.

him to dispose of it not merely to his brothers and kinsmen but to whoever he wished.[39] When Henry left for France later in the year he wrote an extraordinary letter showing just how much he depended on 'his dear uncle', as he called Peter. Everything else put aside, Peter, on his faith and love of the king, was told he must join Henry in Paris, his presence there being absolutely necessary. If he failed to come, either Henry would return immediately to England with his business unfinished or would personally seek Peter out wherever he was![40] Was this a joke or an example of the histrionic threats to which Henry was sometimes prone?

Secure in her position, the queen now made a major concession, very pleasing to her husband. She accepted William de Valence's return to court. From the start of 1262 he appears once again in the witness lists of royal charters, back indeed to his old place above Peter of Savoy.[41] At the same time Henry made gigantic efforts (not all of them successful) to compensate Valence for his losses during the baronial regime. If on a smaller scale, he also provided compensation and support for Guy and Geoffrey de Lusignan, Guy de Rochefort and William de Sancta Ermina, all exiled to much applause in 1258.[42] At the end of 1262, Eleanor gave Valence a ring as a new year present.[43] The great rift in the royal family which had done so much to cause the revolution of 1258 seemed really to be over. Henry had at last achieved the harmonious family circle he had always wanted.

There can be no doubt that Henry, at this time, was thinking far too much of how to reward his foreign relatives and far too little about how to conciliate his English magnates, many of whom had acquiesced so reluctantly in his recovery of power. Yet to say Henry's regime had an entirely foreign complexion would be incorrect. Close to its heart were John Mansel and Robert Walerand, both, of course, English. Equally important was the justiciar, Philip Basset, a fixture at court in the first half of 1262. Hugh Bigod was there too, now a member of the king's council. The charter securing Richmond for Peter of Savoy was witnessed by a whole group of Savoyards – Bishop Aigueblanche, Ebulo de Montibus, Imbert Pugeys, Peter de Champvent, Imbert de Montferrand and Ingram de Fiennes, an Anglo-Flemish knight close to the queen.[44] But also there were Philip Basset, the marcher baron Reginald fitzPeter, Hugh Bigod, John Mansel and Walter of Merton.[45] Alongside fitzPeter, Henry rewarded

[39] *CChR 1257–1300*, 41; and *CChR 1226–57*, 259.

[40] *CR 1261–4*, 131.

[41] *RCWL*, ii, 136–8. Valence attests in January, February and May.

[42] *CPR 1258–66*, 202, 2056, 209, 218, 223; *CR 1261–4*, 25, 33, 65, 74, 76, 150–3, 156–7, 169, 199; *CLR 1260–7*, 73, 93, 95, 105, 110 and *DD*, nos. 354–5, for Geoffrey de Lusignan lauding William de Sancta Ermina.

[43] Howell, *Eleanor of Provence*, 191.

[44] For Ingram, see Howell, *Eleanor of Provence*, 168.

[45] *RCWL*, ii, 137.

other magnates who had stood by him in 1261, notably Humphrey de Bohun, earl of Hereford, James of Audley and John de Balliol. In return for a promised marriage worth between £500 and £1,000 year, Balliol was given the heir of Thomas Grelle as the husband for his daughter.[46]

What, though, of Richard de Clare? Nothing had been more crucial in Henry's recovery of power than his volte-face. Clare appeared at court in February 1262 and received a pardon for a forest offence in July.[47] There was also a concession of more moment. The king did not, as Richard wanted, grant him the liberty of return of writs throughout his lands, but he did agree to its possession in various Suffolk manors, including Clare itself.[48] As for the men who were still standing out against the treaty of Kingston at the end of 1261, both Roger Bigod, earl of Norfolk, and Roger de Mortimer (with yet another promise over Lechlade) fell in with the king. Bigod was at court in June when Henry made him a present of deer and personally suspended the payment of his debts until further notice.[49] The three Montfortians on the old council of fifteen, Bishop Cantilupe, Peter de Montfort and Richard de Grey, all made their accommodation with the king.[50] The Dover annalist, writing of the period after Edward's return in February 1262, declared that all the magnates had come to the peace of the king save Simon de Montfort who was overseas.[51]

## SICILY AND THE CRUSADE

As his confidence grew, Henry began to revive old plans and contemplate wider horizons. In April 1262 his second son, Edmund, wrote to the pope.[52] He called himself 'king of Sicily' and begged Urban to consummate what Pope Innocent had so generously begun. To that end, Edmund explained he was appointing proctors to receive the kingdom from Urban and agree a date for his own arrival. Yes, Henry was reviving the Sicilian project! At the same time, Henry himself, explaining how the disturbances in the kingdom had hitherto thwarted his wishes, raised with Urban 'the business of the cross'. Yes, Henry was once again contemplating a crusade. That this was no mere ploy to please the pope is shown by his deal with Edward over the Jews. There Henry reserved revenues for himself should he go on crusade to Jerusalem.[53]

[46] *CPR 1258–66*, 200–2.
[47] *RCWL*, ii, 136; *CFR 1261–2*, no. 745.
[48] TNA JUST 1/1191, m. 17 (image 1039).
[49] *CPR 1258–66*, 215; *RCWL*, ii, 138; *CR 1261–4*, 61, 66; TNA E 368/36, m. 15 (image 5757); Morris, *Bigod Earls of Norfolk*, 87–8.
[50] *CR 1261–4*, 92–3, 118; and for Montfort, see below, 249. Cantilupe attested charters at court in January, February and June: *RCWL*, ii, 136, 138.
[51] Canterbury/Dover, 214.
[52] *CR 1261–4*, 111–14.
[53] *CPR 1258–66*, 233.

His return to them now shows how deeply Henry cared about the
crusade and the Sicilian project, yet of course, in current circumstances,
he was moving in a world of make-believe. He asked both King Louis and
Queen Margaret to intercede with the pope over Sicily. But it was to
Louis's brother Charles of Anjou that Pope Urban was to turn.[54]

## HENRY GOES TO FRANCE

Henry could not go on crusade, but he could and did go to France. It was
in April 1262 that Henry wrote to Louis requesting a meeting.[55] As he
explained, he hoped they could sort out the many issues connected with
the implementation of the Treaty of Paris. Henry could also be present
when Queen Margaret arbitrated on his differences with Simon de
Montfort.[56] Here Henry was torn between conciliation and confrontation.
If Montfort's private grievances were remedied, might that not weaken his
attachment to the Provisions? In that hope Henry was still prepared to
make concessions. In May he gave Montfort timber to repair his weir at
Rodley in Gloucestershire, although this was one of the manors extracted
from the royal demesne back in 1258. He also authorized personally the
writ making the usual payment for Eleanor de Montfort's dower.[57]
Montfort's place in the Westminster shields is thus not so surprising. The
Rubicon had not been crossed. Montfort, for all his threats, had not taken
up arms against the king, and the king, for all his anger, had not taken up
arms against Montfort. Montfort was still lord of Kenilworth castle, still in
possession of all his lands in England. With his own men accepting the
overthrow of the Provisions, might he not do so too, thus ceasing to be
a lurking menace across the channel? Yet Henry was also aware there
might be another outcome. Might not the arbitration go decisively against
Montfort, discrediting him at the French court, forcing him to make large
reparations for his conduct? To that end, Henry summoned to Paris
Gaillard de Solers so he could testify to all the evil Montfort had done in
Gascony. Henry also drew up an indictment of Montfort's conduct, begin-
ning with his own 'great good will' in accepting Montfort as his man in the
first place. It was here that Henry recalled Montfort's cutting words at
Saintes in 1242: 'it would be well if he was taken and kept apart like
Charles the Simple'.[58] Whatever the verdict, King Richard, in a letter of
May 1262, urged his brother to observe it 'in all things'.[59]

---

[54] For the sequel see below, 283.

[55] *CR 1261–4*, 120.

[56] *CR 1261–4*, 120; BN Clairambault 1188, fo. 19d; Maddicott, *Simon de Montfort*, 217.

[57] *CR 1261–4*, 48; *CLR 1260–7*, 77, 89.

[58] Maddicott, *Simon de Montfort*, 217–18; Bémont, *Simon de Montfort*, 332–43, and at 341.

[59] *RL*, ii, 174–5, where the year should be 1262.

In leaving for France at this juncture, Henry naturally assumed the kingdom was now at peace, just as did the Dover annalist.[60] He also had nothing to fear, or so he thought, from Llywelyn ap Gruffudd. After all, the Welsh prince had behaved well in 1261, ignoring pleas to cause trouble. In January 1262, Henry wrote to congratulate him on his conduct.[61] Yet Henry's departure caused unease at the time. The Dunstable annalist remarked that no one knew the reason for it, and many feared the king's absence would lead to trouble, as indeed it did.[62] The truth, moreover, was that neither the Montfort arbitration nor the treaty negotiations provided imperative reasons for Henry's going and indeed neither were advanced by his presence. Queen Margaret herself acknowledged that Henry might appear before her through proctors.[63] Almost certainly the main reason for Henry's trip was different. It was personal. As he said in his letters to Louis and Margaret, he wished 'from his heart' to see them. Queen Eleanor, who of course was going too, felt the same. In June, when Louis offered Henry either Poissy or Saint-Maur as his residences, Henry chose the latter 'so that with you at Vincennes we can more easily enjoy your conversation and presence'.[64]

Having placed Philip Basset in charge of the government, Henry bad farewell to the Londoners at St Paul's Cross on Sunday 2 July and next day set off with Eleanor for the coast.[65] On the night of 3 July they stayed in the Hospitallers' house at Sutton at Hone, where the chapel Henry used still survives. On 7 July they were at Canterbury to celebrate the feast of the translation of Thomas Becket, all their expenses, save those of their stables and almsgiving (they fed 187 paupers), being met by Archbishop Boniface. They finally crossed from Dover on the thirteenth. Edward and Edmund were already overseas, Edward with the aim of shining at various tournaments.[66]

## THE DEATH OF RICHARD DE CLARE

Soon after arriving at Boulogne, Henry heard of two deaths, both consequential. The first occurred on the day of the crossing. It was that of Henry

---

[60] For Henry's apparent neglect of maritime defences in 1262, see Jobson, 'The maritime theatre', 224.

[61] *CR 1261–4*, 100–1.

[62] Dunstable, 218.

[63] *DD*, no. 362.

[64] *CR 1261–4*, 120, 130.

[65] FitzThedmar, 50 (Stone, FitzThedmar, no. 756). Henry took the great seal with him while a 'substitute' great seal was used by Basset: Chaplais, *Piers Gaveston*, 38; Tout, *Chapters*, i, 304 n. 1.

[66] In what follows, information about Henry's itinerary and household expenses (his feeding of paupers, consumption of wax and the daily costs of food and drink) comes from a fragmentary household roll which covers the period from June to August 1262: TNA C 47/3/6.

of Wingham, bishop of London. In the great crisis of 1261, Wingham had
opened his house at St Paul's to Henry and doubtless did much to keep
London quiet. His successor was to be very different. The other death, on
15 July, was that of Richard de Clare. His entrails were buried at Canterbury
(where Archbishop Boniface sang mass), and his heart was buried at
Tonbridge, while his body was eventually entombed at the house monastery
of Tewkesbury in the presence of the bishop of Worcester, the bishop of
Llandaff and eight abbots. The Tewkesbury monks spoke of Richard as a
'noble man, worthy of all praise'. The Pershore annalist penned some
verses comparing his virtues to those of classical heroes: he had the modesty
of Hippolyta, the face of Paris, the sense of Ulysses, the piety of Aeneas
and the anger of Hector.[67] With his great power, Richard had certainly
played a critical part in the politics of the last few years. His joining the
baronial coalition in 1258 (when Henry hoped otherwise), his reservations
about the scope of local reform, his feud with Simon de Montfort and
subsequent reconciliation, his final desertion of Montfort and acceptance
of Henry's recovery of power all had critical consequences. If only he had
left some explanation of his divergent conduct.

Richard de Clare's heir was his nineteen-year-old son Gilbert.[68] Gilbert
crossed at once to Boulogne only to find Henry unwelcoming. Next day,
thanks to the intervention of William de Valence, the atmosphere was
better, but Gilbert still left without achieving his objective. This was to
secure, in return for a financial payment, immediate entry into his estates
rather than having to wait until the end of his minority on becoming
twenty-one. Gilbert was married to Alice, the count of La Marche's
daughter, the niece of both Henry and William de Valence, hence
William's intervention on Gilbert's behalf. Henry, however, was determined to exercise his rights of wardship and take the vast Clare estates
into his hands. He soon entrusted those in south Wales to Humphrey de
Bohun. The motive cannot have been financial. Indeed, Henry could
probably have made more money, more quickly, by accepting Gilbert's
offer.[69] Rather, Henry wanted to put this demanding and potentially over-
mighty young man in his place. At the same time he aimed to investigate
and reverse all the encroachments made by Earl Richard and his bailiffs
on the rights of the crown. In August the sheriffs were commissioned to
stage just such an inquiry.[70] Of course, Henry should never have allowed
such usurpations in the first place but it was better to do something about
them now than never.

---

[67] Tewkesbury, 169; Pershore, *Flores*, 475.
[68] There is a full account of Gilbert's career between 1263 and 1267 in Altschul, *A
Baronial Family*, 94–121. The *ONDB* entry is by Clive Knowles.
[69] Henry, however, immediately took 240 deer from Richard de Clare's parks: *CR
1259–61*, 145.
[70] *CR 1261–4*, 171–2.

From other points of view Henry was right to be masterful. Treating Gilbert as he did showed everyone he was back in control. And if the political situation was still uncertain, all the more reason to deprive Gilbert of the means of dabbling in it. Yet here again Henry was playing a dangerous game. Gilbert had all the anger of Hector and none of Hippolita's modesty. He had a considerable physical presence, being known later as the 'red earl since he was red headed and handsome in appearance'.[71] He had a very strong sense of the position due to him as the greatest magnate in the realm. He was enraged at not assuming that position at once. The consequences were to be unfortunate for the king.

## HENRY'S PIETY IN PARIS

Henry and Eleanor left Boulogne on 19 July and next day reached Amiens. On the twenty-fifth they were at Beauvais, where Henry must have marvelled at the extraordinary internal height of the cathedral, over 50 feet more than Westminster Abbey. On 31 July the royal party reached Paris to be welcomed by King Louis and the monks of Saint-Denis. After two days at Saint-Denis, Henry went, as arranged, to Saint-Maur-des-Fossés, before moving in mid-August to the spacious monastery of St-Germain-des-Prés to the west of the city walls. He was to remain there until October.

We have no Matthew Paris to light up this visit to France. A fragmentary roll, running into August, recording the costs of the household's daily food, drink, stables and almsgiving suggests this was a much quieter visit than that of 1259. Henry threw no feast comparable to that of 6 December 1259. But he still acted as befitted a king, shouldering his own costs throughout. Indeed, the daily costs in France averaged some £24 a day, as opposed to only £14 in England, although this was partly because less was coming from stock. On the last day at Saint-Denis and the first at St Maur, the costs rose to around £34. On 15 August, the feast of the Assumption, celebrated at St Germain, they were £61. Throughout Henry and Eleanor continued their practice of feeding at least 150 paupers a day. On the feast of Mary Magdalen at Amiens, a distribution of bread was made to thousands more. The household roll also illuminates the work behind the scenes while at St Maur: the casks, bowls, cauldrons, small dishes, great plates and chests obtained by the scullery; the carpenters busy repairing the windows of the hall and making tables, trestles and benches; and the eighteen more tables and twenty-eight benches obtained on hire.

If Henry did not impress with his alimentary largesse, he certainly did with his conduct in another area. To this visit to Paris belongs a remarkable story illustrating both Henry's devotion to the mass and his intimate

[71] Dugdale, *Monasticon*, ii, 61.

relations with King Louis. The story only survives as an extract made from a now lost historical work. Its details may be exaggerated but the whole has a ring of truth. The author was writing before 1297 for Louis is not yet a saint. He knew that Henry was staying at St-Germain-des-Prés and, as duke of Aquitaine, was attending Louis's 'parliament'.[72]

The author begins his account by introducing two 'Catholic kings'. One, Louis, delighted in hearing sermons between masses. The other, Henry, heard three or more masses a day. It was these masses that explained why Henry, on the first day of the parliament, arrived late at the 'royal palace', indeed so late that no business could be done. Henry had first heard numerous masses at St-Germain-des-Prés before setting off. He had then dismounted at all the churches along his route, remaining in each until mass was completed. On the next day, despite being urged by Louis to be on time, and dutifully getting up before dawn, exactly the same thing happened. Louis and his councillors, in desperation, now ordered all the churches to be shut until Henry had gone past. Next day this produced Henry on time only for him to declare he could not possibly attend the parliament because the closed churches showed Paris was under an inter-dict! At this, Louis confessed his ruse and asked a question: 'Beloved kinsman, why do you like hearing so many masses?' Henry responded with a question of his own: 'Why do you delight in so many sermons?' 'It seems to me exceedingly delightful and healthy to hear very often about my creator', replied Louis. 'And to me it appears even more delightful and healthy to see him frequently than to hear about him' came back the answer, Henry referring, of course, to seeing the body of Christ during the elevation of the host, the supreme moment of the mass when the bread and wine were transformed into the body and blood of Christ.

We cannot know whether the author of this account was English or French, although the latter, from the setting, seems more likely. The story certainly shows how highly Henry was regarded for he is put absolutely on a par with Louis. The account ends with the two kings, in order to be uninterrupted in their devotions, delegating their business to others so it could be carried on in their 'holy absence'.


## HENRY FALLS ILL

Henry's ability to ride from St-Germain-des-Prés to the palace in the Île de la Cité did not last for long. In late August illness swept through the court. The young Baldwin, earl of Devon, and the much-favoured house-hold knight Ingram de Percy both died. John Mansel and Edmund, who had joined his father, fell ill. So did Henry himself. On 12 September he wrote home to say he was stricken with double tertian malarian fever, but

---

[72] For the source of the story, see Carpenter, 'Meetings of kings', 26; Vincent, *Holy Blood*, 36 and n. 18.

was now on the mend. Next day, he sought spiritual help by having sent out from England all the chests with his relics and the ornaments of his chapel. (They had been stored before departure in Dover castle.) He also gave orders for the celebration of the Confessor's 13 October feast at Westminster. A total of 300 candles were to be placed around the shrine and seventy gold coins attached to it. The convent were to have the same food and drink on the day as when they feasted with the king.[73] But Henry made no swift recovery. At the end of the month he was only just getting out of bed, although he hoped soon to be able to travel. On 11 October a letter home still mentioned his illness though saying again he was improving.[74] The day before Henry had issued a charter giving Queen Eleanor a much-enhanced dower. Peter of Savoy headed the largely Savoyard witness list. Eleanor was evidently making quite sure of her position in the event of Henry's death. Around the same time Henry also took steps to pay the executors of Thomas of Savoy (what a dance he had led the king) the arrears of the pension owed their master, while one of Thomas's sons was promised the marriage of an heiress.[75]

As Henry said, his illness had necessarily impeded his business in Paris. There is no evidence that progress was made over the rights Louis was supposed to hand over in the Three Dioceses, the issue most immediately outstanding from the Treaty of Paris. The same was true with the case being brought in the parlement of Paris by Reginald de Pons and his wife for possession of the castles of Bergerac and Gensak, although at the end of August Henry appointed proctors (one was Robert Walerand) to represent him.[76]

## SIMON DE MONTFORT DESCENDS
## ON ENGLAND: OCTOBER 1262

One other affair, however, did come to a crashing conclusion. This was the Montfort arbitration before Queen Margaret. On 8 October, Henry wrote home to say he was now advised not to proceed any further 'by that way'. He then warned Philip Basset and Walter of Merton of Montfort's intention to enter the country and sow dissension amongst the people. They were to take steps to prevent the kingdom being disturbed by his 'machinations'. Henry's intelligence was all too correct. According to the Dover annalist, Montfort landed at Romney on 15 October and hurried to the parliament being held at Westminster by Philip Basset. There, for all Basset could do to stop him, he unveiled papal letters confirming in all things the Provisions of Oxford and revoking the letters of absolution

[73] CR 1261–4, 151.
[74] CR 1261–4, 174–6; DD, no. 370.
[75] CPR 1266–72, 732, 735–7; Howell, Eleanor of Provence, 189–90.
[76] CPR 1266–72, 730; DD, nos. 366A–B.

from the oath to observe them. He then left at once and was soon back in France. Whether Montfort had really obtained papal letters of this kind is doubtful. At most, perhaps, he had a draft of some kind, which his supporters at the curia had pressed on the pope. But the damage was done. According to the Dover annalist, Montfort left behind many accomplices and supporters ready to prosecute his cause. Once again, he had nailed his colours to the mast of the Provisions of Oxford.[77]

How are we to interpret this critical episode, foreshadowing so much of what was to come? Was it the failure to remedy his private grievances that brought Montfort storming back to England in support of the Provisions, just as it had arguably in 1260? The probity of his public stand is polluted by his private ambitions.[78] Or was it his very support for the Provisions that caused the arbitration's failure? There is much to be said for the second view. The issue of the Provisions must have come up because Henry's accusations now covered the whole course of Montfort's conduct, and Montfort's defence of his actions since 1258 necessarily turned on his adherence to the Provisions, just as it had in his replies to the charges levelled against him by the king in 1260. In terms of his private quarrels with the king, progress was actually made, for the Montforts, at some point, issued a charter promising to hand back the royal manors they had received in 1259, presumably in return for compensation.[79] The crux now was not private but public. It lay in Henry's demand that Montfort accept the overthrow of the Provisions and Montfort's refusal to do so. As Montfort had said at the end of 1261, he would not depart from the truth and be perjured.

## HENRY GOES ON PILGRIMAGE

By mid-October, Henry was able once again to travel. He would surely now hurry back to England to contain the disruption caused by Montfort's intervention. Other signs of trouble lay in the tournaments Philip Basset was striving vainly to prevent. One in August was planned by Peter de Montfort junior, son of Earl Simon's old associate, and by the ex-Edwardians Roger of Leybourne, Roger of Clifford and Hamo Lestrange.[80] A very ominous coalition. Yet Henry did not return. Instead, in a decision of outstanding irresponsibility, he decided to stay in France until February 1263, the date fixed by Louis for the resumption of their business.[81] Meanwhile he elected to go on a pilgrimage to 'various and remote parts of Burgundy', as John Mansel put it. Leaving Paris in mid-October, Henry

---

[77] *DD*, no. 369; Canterbury/Dover, 217.
[78] See Maddicott, *Simon de Montfort*, 219.
[79] *CPR 1258–66*, 241, and see also *CR 1261–4*, 152.
[80] *CR 1261–4*, 133.
[81] *CR 1261–4*, 177.

journeyed towards Reims, probably with the shrine of St Edmund at Pontigny as his ultimate destination. All he did for the security of England was to ban assemblies and send his son Edmund home to act as captain of the king's forces if war broke out. As Edmund was also going back because he was sick, this was hardly very reassuring. At least Henry took steps to secure 'a great and beautiful' cloth for his son to offer at the shrine of the Confessor.[82]

Henry's pilgrimage prompted John Mansel to write a despairing letter home 'to his dearest friend' Walter of Merton.[83] Ill himself, Mansel was returning to England through Flanders, the only place he could find money to pay off his creditors. The king, on the other hand, as Mansel explained, although still weak, was persevering with his pilgrimage 'which without doubt is wholly against our counsel. For we, when we were with him, did not cease to urge him to return to England, and afterwards by our letters have frequently done the same and continue to do so. He, however, does not agree and by letters and messengers ceaselessly urges us to join him, being now, as I understand, somewhere near Reims.' Faced with these entreaties, Mansel, as he told Merton, felt he must rejoin the king, the more especially as Henry was 'almost alone and has no one with him from his own land'.

This remarkable letter (how one wishes more of Mansel's had survived) illuminates perfectly Henry's relationship with his wisest and most faithful servant. Henry, very much with a will of his own, disregards Mansel's advice, yet Mansel, loyal councillor that he is, continues to give it. He has, moreover, the knack of doing so without giving offence, hence Henry wants him back at court. That was partly because Henry also appreciated he was 'almost alone'. He was, however, less worried about having men with him from his own land. (It is telling that Mansel was.) Apart from summoning Mansel, he also ordered out from England both William de Valence and Peter de Aigueblanche![84]

Henry reached Reims on 10 November and stayed there nearly a fortnight. For the first time he could see the great French coronation church on which so much of Westminster Abbey was based. It must have been a thrilling, unforgettable experience. Here were the models for the Abbey's flying buttresses, radiating chapels, rounded east end and double lancet windows with their roses above. Here too were angels on the west doorway, smiling down at Henry as he went in, so like in spirit to the censing angels framing the Confessor and the pilgrim high up in the facade of the Abbey's south transept. Henry must have appreciated Reims's superior

---

[82] CR 1261–4, 161–2.

[83] F, i, 422.

[84] CR 1261–4, 177. Mansel had been in charge of the seal in France and on his departure Henry summoned John of Chishall (then keeping the exchequer seal) over to France to take his place: CR 1261–4, 158, 164.

height, 118 feet inside against the abbey's 104, yet he could still feel the Abbey had an edge. It boasted a spacious galleried triforium where Reims had old fashioned single lancets in front of bare walls, and, whereas at Westminster the triforium design was carried triumphantly across the transept ends, at Reims it was interrupted altogether. Above all, in place of the bareness of the Reims masonry, the Abbey offered glinting Purbeck marble and a profusion of diapered roses.

Even before he arrived at Reims, Henry realized that news from England now compelled his return. Intending to be at Westminster for Christmas, he wanted the robes for his household knights, his 'bachelors', to be ready for distribution. There were also to be a large and precious brooch, worth 15 marks, for Becket's shrine, and a brooch worth 20 marks, together with a large and precious cloth of gold, for the shrine of the Confessor.[85] On the way home there was a last meeting of the two kings at Compiègne, whither Louis had come at Henry's request. Henry had asked Queen Margaret to be there too so that 'in mutual conversation' he could say goodbye to both of them.[86] Doubtless Eleanor, who had been with Henry all this time, also wished to see her sister.

At Compiègne, Henry realized 'the debility of his body' meant he could not after all be back at Westminster for Christmas, so he switched the celebrations to Canterbury instead.[87] In the event, it was not till 20 December that he landed with Eleanor and John Mansel at Dover. Fortunately, elaborate preparations had been made for Christmas at Canterbury with venison being obtained for the feasts and 165 pairs of shoes made for distribution to the poor. To decorate the tables, two chests with silver vessels along with the king's silver knights and horses were to be sent from Westminster. Henry also commissioned a new bed and three new robes, one of scarlet, one of green and one of camlet for riding. He was evidently determined to make a show, but the Dover annalist noted that while Philip Basset came to meet him, few others did. The new bishop of Chichester, Stephen of Bersted, sent a letter excusing himself on the grounds of his own illness, the shortness of the summons and certain affairs touching his church.[88] It was hardly a good return to England. Worse was to come.

## THE RISING IN WALES

Henry had been brought home by the situation in England. But on landing he was immediately confronted by a crisis in Wales. After two years of restraint, Llywelyn ap Gruffudd had acted and set the march in

[85] CR 1261–4, 180 (from Reims on 15 November).
[86] CR 1261–4, 163; DD, no. 372.
[87] CR 1261–4, 181.
[88] Canterbury/Dover, 218; CR 1261–4, 166–7; TNA SC 1/2/157.

flames. In the north, he was challenging what remained of Edward's hold
in the Four Cantrefs and threatening Chester. In the south rumours
abounded of an attack on the Clare lordship of Glamorgan. Worst of all
was the situation in Maelienydd. Here the Welsh, at the end of November,
had risen against the rule of Roger de Mortimer, Llywelyn himself laying
siege to Mortimer and Humphey de Bohun junior in the castle of Cefnllys.
Situated on a strategic ridge in the south-west portion of Maelienydd and
'the main symbol of the power of the Mortimer dynasty in the march of
Wales', its fall would open up the English lordships further south to
attack.[89] At Dover, Henry heard from Philip Basset that, having been
expelled from the castle, Mortimer and Bohun were now back in possession. But then at Canterbury over Christmas, letters from the pair arrived,
revealing they were once more under siege, could get no food and were in
great danger.

This intelligence was followed, early in January 1263, by a letter sent from
Gloucester by the bishop of Hereford, Peter de Aigueblanche. The 'whole
march' was disturbed as never before in his time. Many knights had simply
deserted their homes and fled. Llywelyn, 'prince of Wales', had entered the
lordship of Roger de Mortimer with 300 horse and 3,000 foot. Cefnllys
itself had surrendered, with Mortimer being allowed to depart with his
household, circumstances leading some to suspect collusion, although
Aigueblanche did not believe it. The Welsh were now burning and pillaging
both the vale of Wigmore and around Weobley only a few miles from
Hereford. Aigueblanche had, he said, fortified Hereford castle, urged loyalty
on the citizens and then set off to see the king. 'The petrified bishop', he has
been called, perhaps unfairly.[90] He was at least on the spot, not safely back
in Savoy. Indeed, when gout prevented him getting any further than
Gloucester, he offered to return to Hereford with the forty horse he urged
the king to send, 'as you love the march and wish to save it'.[91]

It is easy to see why Llywelyn had moved so decisively. He had stood
aside in 1261 hoping that Henry's recovery of power would lead to meaningful peace negotiations. At the start of 1262, Henry, thanking Llywelyn
for his conduct, had promised as much.[92] But nothing had happened.
Deeply frustrated, Llywelyn was also antagonized by Roger de Mortimer's
attacks on the lands of Gruffudd of Bromfield in northern Powys, this, he
felt, in clear breach of the truce.[93] Supporting, perhaps fomenting, the
rising against Mortimer in Maelienydd was his revenge. The moment was
ideal. The king and Edward were out of the country. Richard de Clare was
dead and his Welsh lordships were in the hands of the loyal but lacklustre

---

[89] *F*, i, 423; Smith, *Llywelyn ap Gruffudd*, 140–1.
[90] Smith, *Llywelyn ap Gruffudd*, 150.
[91] For Aigueblanche in this period, see Barrow, *EEA Hereford*, lxii–iii.
[92] *CR 1261–4*, 100–1. For what follows, see Smith, *Llywelyn ap Gruffudd*, 146–57.
[93] *CR 1261–4*, 133–7.

Humphrey de Bohun. Llywelyn's aim was thus to punish the marchers. It was also to pressurize Henry into recognizing both his territorial gains and his hegemony over the other Welsh rulers. To demonstrate the fact, in 1263 he began to style himself 'prince of Wales'. Indeed, he was given the title, as we have seen, in the bishop of Hereford's desperate letter. Llywelyn now wanted a peace which recognized what was fast becoming a reality.[94]

What Llywelyn had begun to suspect was that Henry would never concede such a peace save in utter extremis. There he was quite right. Henry had never lost hope of recovering his position in Wales. Out in France in July 1262, when he heard rumours of Lywelyn's death, he jumped into action. He summoned an army to go with him against his 'Welsh enemies' and urged the marcher barons to occupy Llywelyn's lands and prevent the succession of Dafydd, his younger brother.[95] Alas for such hopes. Llywelyn was not dead and there was now unrest in England.

The situation confronting Henry on his return came, therefore, as a terrible shock. What a contrast between the respect shown him everywhere in France and this maelstrom back in England. That he was still far from well made it all the worse. Not surprisingly, in a fast-changing situation, he dithered over what to do. He summoned forces to Hereford (he would be there himself if health permitted) only to cancel the muster when he learnt that Mortimer had surrendered Cefnllys. He placed Humphrey de Bohun in overall command only to replace him with John de Grey when Bohun said he was usually unwell during Lent (presumably because of the meatless diet)![96] Above all, Henry appealed to Edward in an emotional letter which reveals all too clearly both his conflicted attitude to his eldest son and his despair at his own situation.[97] Edward, Henry said, should put aside all idleness and childish games (a reference presumably to tournaments) and return from France at once, fulfilling his promise to be home soon after Christmas. It was disgraceful and shameful that Llywelyn was breaking the truces and threatening Edward's own people in Cheshire when Edward was in the flower of youth and Henry was old, sick and unable to campaign. Llywelyn was acting, moreover (this was Henry's final thrust), 'incited and counseled by certain people of our kingdom'. Already (the letter was written around 24 December), Henry suspected his English enemies were in alliance with the Welsh.

Despite these warlike preparations, and his distrust of Llywelyn, Henry still hoped the truce might be restored and the whole problem go away.[98] Even before his return, Philip Basset had urged the marchers, somewhat optimistically, to turn the other the cheek even if Llywelyn was the guilty

---

[94] CR 1261–4, 297.
[95] CR 1261–4, 143–4.
[96] CR 1261–4, 278.
[97] CR 1261–4, 272–3.
[98] CR 1261–4, 269; CPR 1258–66, 239.

party.[99] At the start of March 1263, Henry arranged a meeting with Llywelyn where amends might be made for the ways the truce had been broken. He took the precaution of making all this subject to Roger de Mortimer's consent, but Mortimer was so angry he imprisoned Henry's envoy for a while, or at least so Llywelyn alleged.[100] The fact was that under cover of fair words, Llywelyn had been making further advances. Early in March, when John de Grey arrived at Hereford to take command, he found that all the Welsh in the marcher lordships from Brecon running south to Abergavenny had done homage to Llywelyn and were devastating the lands of the king's men. They were supported by an army led by Llywelyn's steward and the Welsh rulers of Deheubarth now very clearly in Llywelyn's allegiance. In the event, Grey and Peter de Montfort (in command at Abergavenny), aided by Roger de Mortimer, Reginald fitzPeter and Humphrey de Bohun junior, put the Welsh to flight, but the situation remained threatening. Peter de Montfort prophesied that in another attack the Welsh would destroy the king's land as far as the Severn and seize hold of Gwent.[101]

Fortunately, Edward was now at hand. He had returned at last in February. In April he joined up with John de Grey at Hereford and set off for Chester. His aim was to advance into Gwynedd and destroy Llywelyn's power at its heart.[102]

## HENRY TRIES TO AFFIRM HIS AUTHORITY IN ENGLAND: JANUARY–MARCH 1263

Henry left Canterbury after Christmas and was back at Westminster in time to celebrate the feast of Edward the Confessor on 5 January. It was very cold. The Thames froze over for three weeks. Henry was still far from well and remained fixed at Westminster for the next four months. In an age before antibiotics, it was very hard to shake off illness. His depression was increased by a disastrous fire on 7 February. With a spark from the chimney, it began in the king's chamber (with its magnificent bed) and then swept into the adjoining chapel (where Simon de Montfort had been married), the small hall (where Henry so often fed paupers) and the room where the exchequer received its revenue. The fire was reported by all the chroniclers and considered a sinister portent.[103] Henry appealed for help to rebuild the palace only for the new bishop-elect of London, Henry of Sandwich, to refuse in an insulting letter. Sandwich hoped the fire would

---

[99] *CR 1261–4*, 135–7.

[100] *CR 1261–4*, 293–5, 297.

[101] *CACW*, 17–18; *RL*, ii, 219–21, 230–1; *F*, i, 340.

[102] *CACW*, 19; Gough, *Edward's Itinerary*, 66–7.

[103] FitzThedmar, 51 (Stone, FitzThedmar, nos. 764–5); Dunstable, 220; Pershore, *Flores*, 477; Burton, 500; Bury St Edmunds, 26–7.

not disturb the king and aggravate his illness, but, he went on to say, the
keepers of the bishopric during the recent vacancy had so wasted its
woods (to say nothing of its parks and fishponds) that there was likely to
be nothing left for the king.[104]

Henry's illness did not mean he was uninvolved in government affairs.
He personally authorized a series of writs in these months about a wide
variety of business. Philip Basset, having spoken to Henry about the affairs
of the abbot of Osney, then wrote to the chancellor, Walter of Merton,
explaining the king's decisions and telling him to make out the appropriate
writs.[105] Henry was still thinking of his crusade and even hoped through
the influence of King Louis and Queen Margaret to receive a subsidy
from the pope to make it possible![106]

More realistically, Henry was also trying to shore up his position in
England. To that end, in January 1263, with maximum publicity, he issued
a set of 'constitutions'.[107] Although the legislation was presented as new,
in fact it was not. In slightly revised form, it replicated the Provisions of
Westminster issued by the baronial regime at the parliament of October
1259. This then was the legislation which limited the jurisdiction of baronial courts and reined in the malpractices of the justices in eyre and the
sheriffs, the legislation whose publication had been pushed through by the
community of the bachelery of England. Henry was thus reaching out to
the knights, free tenants and peasants in the counties. In doing so, he
stressed both his sovereignty and his benevolence. It was, he said, of his
own free will, in the fullness of his power and on his own authority, that
he was issuing and commanding the enforcement of the legislation, doing
so 'for the reformation and improvement of his kingdom'. He was acting
'counseled by his faithful men', but this was very different from October
1259 when the provisions had been presented as a joint legislative act by
king and magnates acting together. The most significant change to the
legislation was also designed to promote its popularity in the shires. The
range of cases actionable through writs of entry was thus increased, a
change quite likely to reduce the amount of litigation going to baronial
courts. The change had been mooted in 1259 but only now reached the
statute book.

Henry should, of course, have issued his Ordinances in January 1262,
not 1263. He was a year too late. Still his constitutions did have an impact.
FitzThedmar in London and the Pershore and Osney chroniclers all noted
their issue. Indeed, the Pershore chronicler praised Henry for taking 'salu-
brious counsel' and acting for 'the peace of the magnates and the

---

[104] Hoskin, *EEA, London*, 109 (*F*, i, 424), despite *CR 1261–4*, 153.

[105] TNA SC 1/7/34; *CPR 1258–66*, 249.

[106] *CR 1261–4*, 281.

[107] For all of what follows, see Brand, *King, Barons, Justices*, 140–61 (with 145–6 on changes
to the preamble), 414–15, 430–1.

improvement of the kingdom'.[108] Henry was also helped in a way he had not intended. While his constitutions had cleverly appropriated the rhetoric of '1258' in saying they were for the kingdom's 'reformation', there was no suggestion they owed anything to the provisions of October 1259. Yet this fooled nobody. And since all the reforms of 1258–9 were now indelibly associated with Oxford, the chroniclers and indeed the exchequer wrote of Henry now ordering the observation of the 'provisions' 'statutes' or 'constitutions' of Oxford.[109] What was there left to argue about?

In March, Henry took another step to shore up his position, or so he hoped. He ordered everyone to swear they would adhere faithfully to him against all mortals. After his death, everyone was to adhere with equal fidelity to Edward and help him obtain his coronation. This did not quite work out as Henry planned. The oaths were certainly taken by the Londoners, but in the provinces they led to rumours that Henry had died. Indeed, the Tewkesbury annalist wrote Henry's obituary. While, moreover, many magnates came to Westminster to do homage and fealty to Edward, as Henry's heir, Gilbert de Clare refused to do so.[110] To the grievance over his inheritance, another had been added. Although not unprecedented it was unusual for a widow to be assigned a castle in dower. But, in February 1263, Henry gave Gilbert's mother, Maud de Lacy, the castles of both Clare and Usk. If this 'stuck', Gilbert would be deprived of two principal fortresses until his mother's death.[111]

If this was not ominous enough, Henry had reason to fear an intervention from an altogether more dangerous quarter: Simon de Montfort. In October 1262, Henry had abandoned the arbitration designed to sort out their fractured relations. For a while he seemed confident he could put Montfort in his place, just as he had done Gilbert de Clare. Over Christmas at Canterbury, the court *coram rege* under Philip Basset thus ordered the implementation of a verdict passed against Montfort in a Leicestershire lawsuit earlier in the year. The sequel, however, was not encouraging, for Montfort's steward, Anketil de Martival, prevented the judgement's enforcement.[112] Henry's confidence, if such it was, soon evaporated. In their last conversation at Compiègne, Louis had apparently

[108] Pershore, *Flores*, 477.

[109] Pershore, *Flores*, 477; FitzThedmar, 52–3 (Stone, FitzThedmar, no. 768); Osney, 130–1; TNA E 368/37, m. 9d/11d (image 6033); TNA JUST 1/1191, m. 15 (image 1036); Brand, *Kings, Barons, Justices*, 144 n. 21.

[110] *CPR 1258–66*, 285–6; *F*, i, 425; FitzThedmar, 53 (Stone, FitzThedmar, no. 769); Dunstable, 220; Carpenter, *Reign of Henry III*, 253–60.

[111] *CPR 1258–66*, 242–3, 588, 663; see Wilkinson, 'Reformers and royalists', 162–3, and for Maud below, 395–6. Gilbert must also have been irritated by the numerous cases brought by his mother in which she sought dower in lands alienated by her late husband, for example TNA KB 26/172, m. 3 (image 4085).

[112] TNA KB 26/173, m. 21 (image 0106). The case had been brought by Eudo la Zouche and his wife.

suggested a 'peace' with Montfort might still be possible. On 18 January, Henry urged Louis to find one, the more especially since the realm had sustained and was sustaining great damage from Montfort's activities.[113] Louis certainly tried. Henry was 'his dearest relation', but Montfort too, so eloquent, so pious, was 'his beloved earl of Leicester'. Perhaps Edward too was involved. This may explain why he remained in Paris until early February. But in the end, on 22 February, after detailed discussions both with Montfort and Henry's envoys, Louis sadly announced his failure. Montfort had told Louis, as Henry's envoys reported, that he knew Henry wished him well, but there were councillors who wanted the contrary. Consequently, it did not accord with his 'honour' to make peace at this time. The envoys would explain his further reasons by word of mouth on their return.

There are grounds for thinking these last negotiations were again about public as much as private matters.[114] Indeed, they apparently produced a scheme in which Montfort would be involved in planning further reforms. Thus Arnold fitzThedmar in London, when reporting the king's assent to 'the statutes of Oxford', adds he was also to observe the 'statutes' promulgated by Roger Bigod, Simon de Montfort, Philip Basset and Hugh Bigod.[115] The four were evenly balanced. Roger Bigod was likely to side with Montfort, Basset and Hugh Bigod with the king. But in the event nothing came of the idea. Montfort's 'honour' would allow him to make peace only if the conciliar control at the heart of the Provisions was restored. Henry would allow Montfort into his peace only when he accepted their overthrow, so no 'way of peace' could be found. This time, ominously, it was Montfort himself who asked Louis to labour no more in the matter.[116]

## THE MONTFORTIAN PROGRAMME:
### ENGLAND FOR THE ENGLISH

According to the later but well-informed historian at Merton abbey, Simon de Montfort was eventually 'recalled' to England by 'the vigorous knights' whom Edward had dismissed from his service.[117] That such an alliance was at the heart of the drama to come is certain, but to say Montfort was simply 'recalled' gives him far too little agency. He had been wishing and planning for this hour. It is highly likely that the initiative was his and that he showed the ex-Edwardians how they might make common cause together. The go-betweens in the negotiations were probably Henry

[113] *RL*, ii, 234 (*CPR 1258–66*, 240–1).
[114] For a different emphasis, see Maddicott, *Simon de Montfort*, 222–4.
[115] FitzThedmar, 52–3 (Stone, FitzThedmar, no. 768).
[116] *DD*, nos. 322 (where misdated), 377.
[117] Dunstable, 221; Merton, *Flores*, 256.

of Almain and the greatest of the ex-Edwardians, John de Warenne, earl of Surrey. Both landed at Dover together on 10 March with Henry de Montfort, Simon's eldest son.[118] The Edwardians had now additional reasons for their disaffection, for Edward himself had returned to England with a large group of foreign knights, intending apparently, as the Burton annalist put it, to subdue the Welsh 'without the help of the English'. The exclusion of his former friends could not have been plainer or more humiliating.[119]

Before those thus disaffected, Montfort spread out a compelling programme. The Provisions of Oxford must be restored in full, which meant the restoration of the council's control over the king, not just the legislative reforms. Montfort would thus achieve the objective for which he had stood out alone since the end of 1261. He would also draw in the ex-Edwardians. Unlike Montfort, they had no deep-rooted attachment to the Provisions, but the Provisions brilliantly served their turn. The new ruling council would both bring them back centre stage and punish their enemies. To make that punishment absolutely sure, Montfort also proposed an addition to the Provisions of Oxford. There should now be a 'statute' banning aliens from holding office and laying down that the realm was henceforth to be governed by native-born men. Many chroniclers came to believe that such a statute had been part of the Provisions of Oxford in 1258. The Petition of the Barons, drawn up at the Oxford parliament, had certainly called for castles to be held by, and heirs and heiresses to be married to, those who were native born. But there had been no actual legislation on these subjects, any more than there had been a blanket ban on foreigners holding office. The Lusignans had been expelled from England but the Savoyards had remained. It was the queen and her Savoyards who were now the targets. Dominating the court since 1261, they had been central both to the overthrow of the Provisions and to the persecution of Edward's former followers.

The proposed statute thus served the turn of Warenne, Leybourne, Clifford and the rest. With Warenne it had an additional edge given his quarrels with Peter of Savoy. As lord of Lewes, he resented the challenge to his local rule posed by Peter's lordship of Pevensey. He was equally angry at the way his estates had been pillaged while in Peter's hands during his minority. Perhaps he also blamed the queen and the Savoyards for the way, on coming of age, he had never succeeded to the rich manors of Stamford and Grantham, once held by his father.[120] These grievances

---

[118] Canterbury/Dover, 219.

[119] Burton, 500.

[120] Warenne's quarrels with Peter are fully discussed in Spencer, '"A vineyard without a wall"', 57–64, and see volume 1, 218, 480 n. 315, 561. Stamford and Grantham, worth a colossal £400 a year or thereabouts, had been given by King John to Warenne's father as compensation for his losses in Normandy. Since they had not been conceded in hereditary

had helped solidify his position on the king's side in 1258, when the Savoyards were with the reformers, only to sap it in 1263, when they were back with the king.

Montfort's anti-alien programme was important not just for the ex-Edwardians. It also, as he well knew, could bring him much wider support. It appealed to churchmen and laymen infuriated by the way the pope provided Italians to English livings; it appealed to the magnates in parliament who had seen a court filled with Savoyards and Lusignans; and it appealed to the knights, free tenants and peasants who had been oppressed by the local agents of the aliens or had heard stories of those who were. As the Bury chronicle put it, 'wherever they held dominion, [the aliens] behaved intolerably like kings and tyrants'.[121] And then there were more recent events: the role of the queen in the overthrow of the Provisions, and the way that Henry in 1260 and 1261, and now Edward in 1263, had brought foreign soldiery into the country. In 1261, Henry, in a proclamation, denied he had done so in order 'to trample upon the native-born of our realm'.[122] Clearly that was what many thought.

Montfort was thus seeking to make 'England for the English' central to what he was all about. In that, as we will see, he was brilliantly successful. Montfort had long grasped how Henry was vulnerable on the issue. In 1252, according to Matthew Paris, he had accused the king of wishing to disinherit him in order 'to enrich some Provencal or Poitevin with my earldom'. In 1260, according to his own testimony, he had complained that the king 'seemed to place his trust more in foreigners than in men of his own land'.[123]

Of course, there was here a paradox for Simon himself was not native born. Technically, he too should have been banned from office by the statute against aliens. In some quarters, the paradox was simply accepted, indeed celebrated. The Melrose chronicler described Montfort as 'the shield and defender of the English, the enemy and expeller of aliens, although he himself was one of them by nation'. In other quarters, Montfort was regarded as a kind of honorary Englishman. Matthew Paris indeed once described him as '*naturalis*', 'native-born'.[124] That was untrue but Montfort had at least inherited the earldom of Leicester. He was not like William de Valence brought landless to England and foisted on a rich heiress. Montfort's children, moreover, were native born as of course was

right, there was nothing 'illegal' in them not passing to Warenne. But, given their value, their recovery was a central ambition. In 1253, Stamford and Grantham formed part of the queen's dower. They then passed to Edward as part of his appanage. Warenne's early closeness to Edward may well have been inspired, at least in part, by the hope his good service would be rewarded by a grant of the two manors.

[121] Bury St Edmunds, 23.

[122] *F*, i, 408–9.

[123] Paris, v, 289, 338; *DBM*, 208–9, cap. 38.

[124] Melrose, 127.

his affinity of midlands knights. Through them he was in close touch with the grievances and aspirations of local society.[125]

## THE ROLE OF VIOLENCE

Montfort, therefore, produced a programme. He also masterminded the means of bringing it about. At its heart there was violence. The estates of the Savoyards and the king's ministers were to be ravaged. Sometimes their persons too were to be seized. The Montfortians would also take possession of towns and castles, win over the allegiance of local communities and, as in 1261, set up their own administration in the shires. The historian R.F. Treharne liked to think that the acts of violence and plunder had nothing to do with Montfort.[126] The reverse is true. They were central to his vision, central to punishing the regime, proving its powerlessness and forcing its surrender. That Montfort was behind the attack on Peter de Aigueblanche at Hereford, with which the violence began, is stated directly by the Merton chronicler.[127] Quite probably Montfort had wanted to take up arms in both 1260 and 1261. As the Pershore chronicler put it, he 'excelled in warlike things'. In terms of military experience, his time in Gascony put him head and shoulders above all the other magnates. It had also taught him about warfare as ravage. Montfort knew that if he could move matters to the military plane he was onto a winner. In 1260 and 1261 he had lacked the necessary support. Now his alliance with Roger of Leybourne, John de Warenne, Roger of Clifford, Hamo Lestrange and the rest gave him plenty of muscle.

In some eyes there was nothing illegitimate about the violence; it was the normal way of making war.[128] That the Montfortians *were* making war was shown by the way their armed bands moved round the country with banners unfurled.[129] And yet at the same time the Montfortians could still claim they were doing nothing illegal or rebellious. Again and again since 1258, Montfort had appealed to the oaths everyone had taken, at the king's command, to maintain the Provisions. In 1262 he had appeared at the October parliament and alleged that the pope had once more made them binding. A central feature of the oath was that those who contravened it should be treated 'as mortal enemies'. Their property and persons could thus be attacked. It was this stipulation Montfort now produced to justify

---

[125] For the 'political construction of ethnicity' and Montfort's own 'ethnic strategies' see Hennings, 'Simon de Montfort and the ambiguity of ethnicity', 137–52.

[126] Treharne, *Baronial Plan*, 301–2. For the view that the opposition (between 1258 and 1265) 'deliberately limited their use of force', see Valente, *Theory and Practice of Revolt*, 70–8.

[127] Merton, *Flores*, 256; and see *CPReg*, 411, and for Montfort's orders TNA JUST 1/58, m. 16 (image 1502); TNA JUST 1/42, m. 2d (image 1217).

[128] This point is well made in Jobson, *The First English Revolution*, 87.

[129] For the display of banners, see *CCR 1272–9*, 333; and for its significance, King, ' "War", "rebellion" or "perilous times" ', 113–14.

the violence.[130] But, making what happened all the more acceptable, the violence was only aimed at those who had broken their oath and overthrown the Provisions. The king's own possessions, moreover, were to be left untouched. This was a loyalist movement. As the oath to accept the Provisions said, they were made 'for the honour of God, *in the faith of the king*, and for the utility of the realm'.

## MONTFORT'S RETURN, HENRY'S CAPITULATION, MAY–JULY 1263

According to the Dunstable annals, Montfort finally returned to England around 25 April. The date can only be approximate and may in fact have been somewhat later.[131] During April itself, Henry seems unaware a blow was about to fall. He remained at Westminster and could take some comfort from the opening of the Easter exchequer. All the sheriffs turned up in person or through deputies and the money produced from the counties was actually more than at Easter the year before.[132] The Montfortians tried to give no clue as to what was afoot. When, during April and May, the king's judges visited Rutland they heard pleas involving Simon de Montfort, Hugh Despenser and Peter de Montfort as though everything was normal. Montfort's excuse for not appearing in person was recorded (he was overseas), as was the king's order that pleas involving Peter de Montfort should be transferred to the judges at Westminster during their Trinity term. (This was almost certainly because he was supposedly serving the king in Wales.)[133] During May, however, Henry gave increasing signs of alarm. He moved restlessly back and forth between Westminster and the greater safety of St Paul's. On 8 May he upbraided the keepers of numerous ports for allowing in, as he had heard, men with horses and arms.[134]

Henry's focus, however, remained on the situation in Wales. Edward had enjoyed some initial success, winning over to his side Dafydd, Llywelyn's younger brother. He had then entered the Four Cantrefs and munitioned his castles at Dyserth and Deganwy. But he achieved little else. By the last week of May he was back in London. It was Henry and Edward together,

---

[130] Dunstable, 221; FitzThedmar, 53–4 (Stone, FitzThedmar, no. 770); Wykes, 134.

[131] Dunstable, 221 (around the feast of St Mark).

[132] Cassidy, 'Adventus vicecomitum', 616. In 1263, Easter day fell on 1 April.

[133] TNA JUST 1/721, mm. 4, 7, 14 (images 0340–2, 0344, 0356, 0365, 0368). In late April 1263, Peter de Montfort's reason for not appearing before the judges at Winchester was his serving the king in Wales: TNA JUST 1/1195, m. 19d (image 1381). In the Easter term of 1263, Hugh Despenser appeared in a case before the bench: TNA KB 26/172, m. 8 (image 4097).

[134] *CR 1261–4*, 300. Henry was not helped in rallying support by the comparative paucity of gifts from the royal forests. Perhaps he was trying to help them recover from all the gifts made in 1261. For Windsor forest, see *CR 1261–4*, 68.

therefore, who took the next step. On 25 May they summoned to Worcester the tenants-in-chief for a campaign to put down Llywelyn and his fellow 'rebels'. Included in the summons (some with the encouragement of being knighted by Henry at Worcester) were many who were around now signing up with Montfort. Perhaps Henry was here testing loyalties and summoning an army to use against the English opposition as well as Llywelyn. But, if so, he did not think he faced any imminent threat. The army was not due to gather at Worcester till 1 August.[135] Had Henry known what was afoot, he would have realized this gave the Montfortians a clear run.

Once back in England, Montfort's first move, again according to the annals of Dunstable, was to hold a secret 'parliament' of his supporters at Oxford. The date is unknown but it was probably in May, around the time Henry summoned his Welsh army. Oxford as a place was deeply symbolic and it was there the decision was taken to treat all those who had contravened the 'statutes of Oxford' as mortal enemies. Probably agreed too was a document preserved by Arnold fitzThedmar, a formal 'Petition of the Barons' to the king. Here the barons asked Henry 'humbly and devotedly' to maintain the Provisions of Oxford, although if good men chosen for the purpose found anything in them prejudicial to the king and kingdom, it would be withdrawn. The barons also demanded that the kingdom henceforth be governed by native-born men, and not by others, which meant of course not by foreigners. Here then was the origin of the eventual 'statute' against the aliens.[136]

The Dunstable annalist also gives a list of those with Montfort 'in counsel and deed' around this time.[137] There were, of course, the ex-Edwardians John de Warenne, Henry of Almain,[138] Leybourne, Clifford, Hamo Lestrange and John de Vaux. Close to this group (they had planned tournaments together) was John Giffard.[139] Aged thirty-one in 1263, lord of Brimpsfield near Gloucester and many other manors in the county, a great huntsman and very much a '*miles strenuus*' (a veteran of campaigns in Wales), his addition added much to Montfort's military might.

Another group, identified by the Dunstable annalist, were the young men who had stood out to the last with Montfort against the king's recovery of power in 1261: John fitzJohn (the son of John fitzGeoffrey), William de Munchesney, Henry de Hastings, Geoffrey de Lucy, Nicholas

---

[135] *CR 1261–4*, 302–5. In early June, Henry also intended to go to Chester: *CPR 1258–66*, 262.

[136] FitzThedmar, 54 (Stone, FitzThedmar, no. 771); Carpenter, *Reign of Henry III*, 265–6, 279.

[137] Dunstable, 222.

[138] For Henry and Montfort in 1260, see above, 196.

[139] *CR 1261–4*, 133. For Giffard, see Crouch, 'John Giffard', and Birrell, 'A great thirteenth-century hunter'.

of Seagrave and the lord of Westmorland, Robert de Vipont.[140] Thomas
Wykes gives the same names and adds to them that of John de Vescy, the
still underage lord of the great Northumberland barony of Alnwick.
These were, he says, 'the young boys of England', mouldable as wax.[141]
Montfort was here tapping into wells of existing friendship and grievance.
Hastings, Seagrave, Munchesney and Vipont had all stood pledge for
Geoffrey de Lucy back in 1260 when accused of unlicensed hunting in the
king's forests.[142] The friendship between Lucy, Hastings and Seagrave
went back to the 1250s when they were wards together growing up in the
households of the king and queen. Later, John de Vescy was there too
alongside Edmund, the king's second son.[143] Several of these men were
also unified by the way their estates had been exploited when held in
wardship by the Lusignans or in Vescy's case by Peter of Savoy.[144] Through
Nicholas of Seagrave himself the group had a direct line to Montfort.
Seagrave the place is only eight miles north of Leicester, and Nicholas's
father had been a well-rewarded member of Montfort's affinity.[145]

The Dunstable annalist adds one further name to the list, that of
Gilbert de Clare. His presence was hardly surprising given his treatment
by the king. Excluded from his estates, his role in 1263 was limited, but
Henry's position would have been much the stronger had he attracted
rather than alienated this potentially powerful man.

Of the most prominent Montfortians before 1263, the Dunstable annals
only names Hugh Despenser, but both Peter de Montfort and Richard de
Grey were soon back in Simon's camp as was Bishop Cantilupe. So too
were Montfort's following of midlands knights headed by Thomas of
Astley and Ralph Basset of Sapcote.[146] Above all Montfort had himself.
All the contemporary accounts agree he was the absolute leader. In terms
of experience, prestige, power, intelligence and charisma, he towered
above everyone else in the movement. The only other earl in the company
was John de Warenne of Surrey, over twenty years Montfort's junior and
with nothing like his status. Montfort alone knew how to drive forward a
military campaign. He alone knew how to turn an assortment of material
grievances into a righteous cause.[147]

---

[140] *CR 1261–4*, 95.

[141] Wykes, 133–4; Maddicott, *Simon de Montfort*, 249.

[142] *CR 1259–61*, 79.

[143] Wild, *WA*, 81, 112.

[144] William de Munchesney's lands had been in the wardship of William de Valence,
who had married his half-sister. For a biography, see Ridgeway, 'William de Munchensi'.
Geoffrey de Lucy's lands had been in the wardship of Geoffrey de Lusignan: *SESK*, lix.

[145] Carpenter, *Reign of Henry III*, 228; Maddicott, *Simon de Montfort*, 66–73. For Nicholas,
see Jewell, 'Nicholas of Seagrave'.

[146] Dunstable, 221–2; Wykes, 133–4; *CR 1261–4*, 95.

[147] Powicke puts this beautifully. 'Then a great man reappears on the scene, a man of
enormous prestige and wide experience, an implacable man whose austere charm can rally

## THE VIOLENCE BEGINS: JUNE 1263

At the end of the Oxford parliament, the barons sent Henry a letter sealed by Roger of Clifford. It called on him to observe the 'ordinances and statutes made at Oxford' and then defied all those who contravened them, saving only the person of the king and queen. The letter was in effect a declaration of war and after its despatch the violence, as fitzThedmar noted, followed immediately.[148] The barons moved with a large army to Hereford and there on 7 June they struck the first blow. The target was Bishop Aigueblanche. He was seized and carried off, with several of his Savoyard canons, to imprisonment in Eardisley castle. The barons then went on to ravage his estates. The leader of the attack was Roger of Clifford, but Giffard, Leybourne, Lestrange, Vaux, Montfort's sons and indeed Montfort himself were all in some way implicated.[149] So was Humphrey de Bohun, the eldest son of the earl of Hereford, and from now on an important figure in Montfort's camp. He was lord through marriage of Hay, Brecon and Haverford, where his interests had clashed with those of William de Valence in Pembroke.[150]

Aigueblanche was a carefully chosen target. He was the most unpopular churchman in England thanks to his schemes to raise money for the Sicilian project. He and his Savoyard canons were also hated in Hereford itself, despite the beautiful new transept, influenced by Westminster Abbey, that he was adding to the cathedral.[151] After Hereford, the barons moved on to Gloucester where they demanded that Matthias Bezill surrender the castle. Here there was a history for Bezill, 'a foreign knight appointed against the Provisions', had two years before dragged the baronially appointed sheriff, the local knight, William de Tracy, off to imprisonment in Gloucester castle.[152] Now no threats would persuade him to break his

the young adventurers and the disappointed squires into a passionate, if temporary, unity of purpose': *King Henry III*, ii, 436.

[148] FitzThedmar, 53–4 (Stone, FitzThedmar, no. 770). FitzThedmar does not mention the Oxford parliament and that the letter was sent at its close is my suggestion. FitzThedmar does, however, say that the letter was sent before Pentecost (so before 20 May). Historians have accepted this date and assumed that the Oxford parliament itself must have been held before 20 May. My own view is that fitzThedmar is here mistaken. (I thank Adrian Jobson and Ian Stone for discussing the question.) Once Henry received Clifford's letter, he must have known he was in deadly danger. Yet there is no sign of any such realization until the second week of June. Meanwhile, Henry pushed on with preparations for a campaign in Wales. It seems, therefore, far more likely that the Oxford parliament took place after 20 May and that Clifford's letter was delivered in early June, just before the violence was about to begin.

[149] *CR 1264–8*, 512; *CPReg*, 411, 620; Canterbury/Dover, 221–3; Pershore, *Flores*, 479–81; Robert of Gloucester, ii, lines 11,110–26.

[150] *WAR*, 14–15.

[151] See below, 380.

[152] For the importance of Gloucester and the sieges of its castle between 1263 and 1265, see Oakes, 'The nature of war', 94–103.

oath to keep the castle for the king and his son. He had, however, but a small garrison and the barons were able to storm the castle after a four-day siege. They then took a carpenter, whose arrow had killed a squire of John Giffard, to the top of the keep and made him jump off. 'He was bruised and died speedily', wrote the local chronicler. Bezill, his gallantry admired on all sides, fared better and joined Aigueblanche in prison at Eardisley, while Giffard went off to pillage his manor at Sherston in Wiltshire.[153]

Worcester was next and here the citizens surrendered without difficulty. Those of Bridgnorth put up more of a fight until Welsh forces joined up with the barons, an indication that an alliance with Llywelyn was in place. After these successes, the barons left the Welsh marches and set out for the south of England. They had, so the Pershore chronicle tells us, taken Montfort 'as their leader by whom they were ruled'.[154]

The pillaging of the estates of Aigueblanche and Bezill did not stand alone. On the contrary, it was part of a co-ordinated attack on the properties of the queen, Peter of Savoy and other Savoyards.[155] Targeted too were many native ministers, the most conspicuous being John Mansel, Robert Walerand and Walter of Merton.[156] That the inoffensive Merton was a victim shows just how 'political' these attacks were. In later legal actions redress was sought by over forty men, including the Savoyards Ebulo de Montibus, Imbert de Montferrand, Aymon Thurbert and Ingram de Fiennes, the curial knights Nicholas de Molis and John and William de Grey, and the loyalist magnates James of Audley, John de Balliol, Henry de Percy and William de Briouze.[157] Another victim was Simon of Walton, the bishop of Norwich, who had published the papal bulls annulling the Provisions. Fearing the same treatment as Bishop Aigueblanche, he fled to the safety of Bury St Edmunds.[158] Something of the performance behind the attacks can be glimpsed in Dorset where, according to a later lawsuit, 'enemies of the king' from the retinues of Roger of Clifford and John Giffard 'went with banners flying through the country plundering loyal subjects'.[159] In Essex, the co-ordinator was Richard de Tany, sheriff of the county between 1259 and 1261. He had willing helpers for around a dozen knights took part in the plunder in a widespread uprising against the king's men.[160]

---

[153] Pershore, *Flores*, 480; Robert of Gloucester, ii, lines 11,060–11,109.

[154] Pershore, *Flores*, 480–1.

[155] For the ravage of Peter of Savoy's estates see Stewart, *RJS*, xxi–ii, xxvi, and nos. 26, 35, 39, 85, 90; *CR 1261–4*, 369–70.

[156] For the pillage suffered by Merton, see below, 334 n. 108.

[157] The attacks are often not dated, and some may have taken place later than 1263, especially in the period before Lewes.

[158] *CR 1261–4*, 243–54, 257, 265, 369–70; Bury St Edmunds, 27.

[159] Jacob, *Studies*, 206–7; Ridgeway, 'Dorset in the period of reform and rebellion', 33; and see Coss, 'Retinues, agents and garrisons', 189.

[160] Moore, 'Government and locality in Essex', 244–9, a valuable analysis.

The violence also spread to attacks on the persons and properties of foreign clerks provided to English livings. Archbishop Boniface later in the year wrote a stinging denunciation of the atrocities committed in the Canterbury province by 'the sons of iniquity'. They had even dared to appoint clerks in place of those they had driven from their livings. He named the usual suspects – Montfort's sons Henry and Simon, Humphrey de Bohun junior, Leybourne, Clifford, Giffard, Lestrange, Vaux, Hastings, Seagrave and Ralph Basset (of Drayton) – and then added it had all happened on Montfort's authority and with his assent.[161]

These catastrophic events took Henry almost completely by surprise. On 10 June 1263 he moved again from Westminster to St Paul's, at the same time taking measures for the defence of Dover against 'adversaries and rebels'. Two days later he appointed captains for the defence of the north and the south-east of the kingdom against 'certain rebels' who were plundering ecclesiastical property, imprisoning churchmen, and devastating with fire the lands of the king's faithful subjects.[162] But the sheriff of Yorkshire, Robert de Neville, soon wrote back asking for money and warning that those he had thought faithful had either been won over entirely 'by the preaching of the rebels' or were at least 'tepid' in their loyalty. The household knight Ralph Russel likewise appealed for money and warned there were very few ready to defend Old Sarum castle from attacks threatened by 'a great multitude of armed rebels'. In Lincolnshire the sheriff, William de Grey, and the justices in eyre were forced by Adam de Newmarch to flee the county.[163] Henry was terribly behind events. On 15 June he dispatched forces to garrison Gloucester although the castle, in all probability, had already fallen. Next day he still thought Hamo Lestrange was loyal although he was firmly in the rebel camp. Some of the desertions must have seemed terrible betrayals: the young boys who had been brought up in his household; Henry of Almain, whom Henry had treated as a leading councillor and given as late as 20 April a gift of deer; Peter de Montfort, placed in command at Abergavenny, who had only just assured Henry and Edward of his loyalty 'all his days' 'whatever others might say'; and indeed John de Warenne, who in April 1263 is actually found on the king's council.[164]

While Henry remained safe in London, Edward took action. In mid-June he went to Kent and with some difficulty extracted oaths of fealty from the men of the Cinque Ports. The chaos surrounding Henry himself

---

[161] Bodleian Library, Oxford, MS Bodley 91, fos. 136–136v (Denholm-Young, 'The Winchester-Hyde chronicle', no. 2); *CPR 1258–66*, 378. The letter is printed in Wilshire, *Boniface of Savoy*, 88–9. For armed action earlier in the year by Ralph Basset of Drayton: TNA KB 26/ 173, m. 5 (image 0011).

[162] *CPR 1258–66*, 262–4; Jobson, 'The maritime theatre', 224.

[163] *CR 1268–72*, 584–5.

[164] *CR 1261–4*, 226; *RL*, ii, 231; *F*, i, 427.

is reflected in the chancery rolls, where very few letters were enrolled after 15 June. We do not know therefore whether he attempted a last desperate summons of loyalist barons and household knights to London, although events were moving so fast they could hardly have arrived in time. He certainly never modified the summons for the Worcester muster on 1 August. One problem facing Henry was lack of cash. Much of his treasure as well as the issues of the Easter exchequer had gone to fund Edward's campaign in Wales. In May, Henry was forced to contract loans because the exchequer was empty.[165]

Even worse for Henry was the situation in London. In 1261 the aldermanic rulers of the city had accepted the overthrow of the Provisions of Oxford, however much they had welcomed them in 1258. Indeed, Henry, sometimes in the bishop's palace, sometimes in the Tower, had made London the base for his recovery of power. Here he was helped by the bishop of London, his old servant Henry of Wingham. The situation in 1263 was very different. Henry was again in the bishop's palace but Wingham's successor, Henry of Sandwich, was unsympathetic, if not downright hostile.

The problem of the bishop, however, paled before that posed by the Londoners themselves. Henry had done little to conciliate them. In March 1263 he ordered arrears of London's tallages to be levied without delay.[166] Perhaps he felt sure of London's rulers, but excited by the crisis in the kingdom, inspired by Montfortian promises of reform, a popular revolution now took place. The result was that the city, with the support of the mayor, Thomas fitzThomas, swung full square behind Montfort and his movement. With the houses of foreign merchants and prominent courtiers being pillaged, on 19 June Henry left the bishop's palace and hurried to the Tower.[167]

Montfort soon moved to formalize his alliance with the city. As he led his army from the Welsh marches to the south-east of the kingdom, he sent a letter (around 24 June) to the Londoners, sealed with his seal, asking if they wished to stand by the ordinances made at Oxford. At the same time he showed them the 'Petition of the Barons', referred to earlier, with its demand that the kingdom be henceforth governed by native-born men.[168] The citizens were allowed into the Tower to consult the king. Probably they saw Henry in the hall adjoining his chamber in the Wakefield tower. He was alone save for the queen, King Richard, Edward ck from Kent) and Robert Walerand. Henry was told that 'all the

1258–66, 253, 258; *CLR 1267–72*, nos. 2308, 2310.
262–3, no. 293.
dmar, 55 (Stone, FitzThedmar, no. 773); Stone, 'Book of Arnold fitz 8; Dunstable, 222–3. For a fuller discussion of London's place in the vement, see below, 385–90.

commune' wished to observe the Provisions. It also wanted to exclude from the city foreign knights and sergeants, they being 'the cause of all the discord between the king and the barons'. Henry seems to have made no reply to the citizens.[169] Instead, he hoped something might come from the intervention of King Richard.

## KING RICHARD'S INTERVENTION

Richard had returned to England in February 1263 and thereafter made several appearances at court.[170] Yet could he have done more to support his brother? That was Henry's view, if he was behind, as seems likely, a blistering letter of Pope Urban later in the year. This lambasted Richard for failing to act against the rebellion and reported rumours that he had actually condoned it.[171] Certainly, Richard did nothing in any military way to obstruct the Montfortian movement. His son Henry of Almain was part of it.[172] That Richard had returned to England hoping to become king if Henry died, as some believed, is surely incredible although it reflects the wild stories circulating at the time. More to the point is the fact he returned 'with few men'.[173] He thus lacked the military force to intervene, all the more so since he doubted the loyalty of his followers, a good proportion of whom now sided with the barons.[174] Richard was also worried about his German and imperial ambitions. In 1263, Pope Urban decided he should be styled not king of the Romans but only king-elect. This was because Urban was now adopting a neutral stance between Richard and his rival Alfonso of Castile.[175] With his chances of becoming king of the Romans, let alone emperor, in the balance, the last thing Richard wanted was to get bogged down in an English civil war. His abstention was encouraged by the conduct of the barons themselves, since they carefully avoided pillaging his estates.

If, however, Richard opted out of any military intervention, he was perfectly prepared to act as a peacemaker, and with this Henry went along. It seemed the only way to stop what was happening. Indeed, on 16 June, Henry himself had tried vainly to open conversations with Montfort,

[169] FitzThedmar, 56 (Stone, FitzThedmar, nos. 770–1).

[170] CPR 1258–66, 263. For a full discussion of Richard's role in 1263, to which I am indebted, see Jobson, 'Richard of Cornwall and the baronial opposition in 1263'.

[171] Reg. Urban IV, ii, no. 724 (CPReg, 402); Denholm-Young, Richard of Cornwall, 122.

[172] There is no hard evidence, on the other hand, that he supported Montfort. Dunstable, 221 (and see Wykes, 135), has him present at the initial baronial parliament at Oxford. If this is not a mistake (which I suspect it is), he was probably there as a mediator.

[173] Burton, 500; and see Canterbury/Dover, 219.

[174] This is a major theme in Jobson, 'Richard of Cornwall and the baronial opposition', 66–74.

[175] Weiler, Henry III of England and the Staufen Empire, 183–7; Jobson, 'Richard of Cornwall and the baronial opposition', 62.

giving him a safe conduct to come to court with Eleanor and his sons provided they came without arms.[176] Richard kept Henry closely informed about his own efforts. On the 28 June he wrote from Isleworth saying, after breakfast next day, he would set off for Wallingford where he expected to find the barons. Meanwhile, until the results of the meeting were known, Edward should refrain from warlike acts. (There was no reference to any being made by the king!) On the next day, a Friday, Richard reached his manor at Cippenham, just north of Windsor, and heard that Montfort and his followers were already at Reading. He immediately sent messengers inviting Montfort to a meeting on the Saturday where they could discuss a peace. But although, as Richard reported, the messenger had arrived at daybreak, Montfort had refused the invitation. 'He was not able at all to meet us nor alter his previous plans.' These, Richard understood, were to press on to Guildford for the night, and then head to Reigate (a castle of John de Warenne).[177]

This surely was an extraordinary moment. Here was Richard, king of the Romans '*semper Augustus*', a famous arbitrator and fixer, coming to meet Montfort with peace proposals, only to be utterly spurned. Nothing shows better the clearness of conscience, clarity of purpose and confidence in the conclusion with which Montfort drove forward the events of 1263. Others would now have paused, thought they had done enough and settled down to negotiate some kind of compromise. Not Montfort. He had a plan of campaign and would stick to it. His aim was to skirt London and head for the Cinque Ports. Having secured their allegiance, there would be no need to parley with King Richard or anyone else. Henry would be at his mercy.

## MONTFORT'S VICTORY, JULY 1263

On 30 June, therefore, Montfort moved from Reading to Guildford. On the way he and his companions took ten deer and hinds from the king's forests, good sport doubtless and also good food. Montfort had with him his sons Henry and Simon, as well as Leybourne, Clifford, Hastings, Vescy *and* Roger de Mortimer. This is the only evidence that the great marcher baron was on Montfort's side in 1263. It cannot, for various reasons, have been an easy alliance and it ended in appalling acrimony.[178]

There was one other reason why Montfort had no use for King Richard. He was already letting Henry know, direct, the non-negotiable terms for a settlement. On 29 June, the day King Richard was advancing towards him, the bishops of Lincoln, London and Coventry were on their way to Henry with a 'form of peace'. Bishop Cantilupe, in an anguished

[176] *CPR 1258–66*, 266.
[177] *RL*, ii, 247–8.
[178] Stewart, 'Simon de Montfort and his followers'.

letter, begged 'his dearest friend', Walter of Merton, to persuade Henry and Edward to accept it. Only thus could peace be secured and terrible danger be avoided. The 'form of peace' taken by the bishops was the same as the earlier 'Petition of the Barons', but with two additions. First, the king was to surrender control of his castles. Second, aliens were not merely to be excluded from office. They were also to leave the kingdom 'never to return', the only exceptions being those whose stay was unanimously accepted by the faithful men of the realm. The language here with its 'never to return' was deliberatively emotive. Far from tuning down the anti-alien rhetoric, Montfort was tuning it up. He was encouraging and exploiting the xenophobia sweeping the country in order to win wide support for his cause.[179]

While all this was happening, there was panic in the Tower. On 28 June, Edmund and John Mansel left the fortress by boat with the widowed countess of Devon (a daughter of Thomas of Savoy) and other foreign women. Next day they reached Dover. Edmund stayed in the castle, hoping to bolster its defences, but the rest of the party crossed over to Wissant on the northern French coast. Mansel, as all his career showed, was no coward, but he was now, as the Dover annalist put it, 'fearful for his skin'.[180] Having been central to the overthrow of the Provisions, he was a marked man. He never returned to England.

On 29 June, Edward himself took decisive action. With no one in the city willing to give him or his father a halfpence of credit, he went in the evening to the Temple and asked to see his mother's jewels. Once admitted (with Robert Walerand), he broke open the chests of many magnates and stole sums put either at £1,000 or £10,000. He then departed with his foreign soldiery to Windsor castle. From there he made a lightning dash to Bristol, in the hope of securing its loyalty, only for the citizens to rebel and lay siege to him in the castle. Rescued through a truce brokered by Bishop Cantilupe, by 20 July he was back at Windsor.[181]

Edward had, however, received help from Ireland, for Walter de Burgh, lord of Connacht (old Hubert's great-nephew), was now with him. On 15 July (the day of Henry's eventual surrender), Edward granted Walter the lordship of Ulster, both a reward for support at a critical moment and an attempt to strengthen this leading loyalist's position in Ireland.[182] The grant had important consequences both in the short and the long term. Short term, it provoked the conflict between Walter de Burgh and his

---

[179] F, i, 427; Carpenter, Reign of Henry III, 266, 272–3, 279.

[180] CPR 1258–66, 287; Canterbury/Dover, 222; Hui Liu, 'John Mansel', 128–9.

[181] Dunstable, 222–3; Canterbury/Dover, 222; Pershore, Flores, 482–3; Studd, Lord Edward's Itinerary, 70–1; CPR 1258–66, 279.

[182] BL Add MS 4790, fo. 104v, and BL Add MS 6041, fo. 100v; Frame, 'Ireland and the Barons' Wars', 164. Ulster had been in royal hands since the death of Hugh de Lacy in 1242.

great rivals amongst the settler families, the Geraldines of Offaly (later the earls of Kildare).[183] As a result, it was not till 1265 that Irish lords appeared again on the English political scene. In the longer term, Connacht and Ulster together brought the de Burghs a potential lordship of over 40 per cent of Ireland's landmass. During the time of Walter's son Earl Richard, 'Ireland came close to being a condominium, with authority shared between the earl in the north and west and the king's justiciar in Dublin'.[184] Whether Edward would ever have granted Ulster to Walter de Burgh outside the crisis of 1263 may be doubted, so the English civil war had a major impact on the political shape of Ireland. It would have looked very different had Ulster remained in royal hands.

But back to the events of July 1263. With King Richard, Edward, Edmund, John Mansel and Robert Walerand all gone, with the populace roaming through London's streets, with an insufficient garrison for its defence, the Tower, in early July, must have been, for Henry, a lonely and frightening place. One can imagine him gazing anxiously over the river from his chamber in the Wakefield Tower and praying in its small chapel fervently for help. What was he to do? The answer was to give up. On 4 July, with Montfort now securing the allegiance of the Kentish knights and the Cinque Ports, Henry asked the bishops of Lincoln, London and Coventry, his confessor John of Darlington and the judge William of Wilton to make peace with the barons 'touching the contentions over the constitutions made at Oxford'. Henry also sent to Dover some London citizens, who promptly confirmed their alliance with the barons and swore to 'live and die with them', just like the men of the Cinque Ports. The terms offered Henry were as before though now he had also to hand Dover castle over to the bishop of London and order the release of Henry of Almain. (Chasing after Mansel, Henry of Almain had been captured at Wissant by the queen's friend Ingram de Fiennes.)[185] On 10 July, Henry accepted these terms. Two days later Montfort came to Canterbury and heard the news from the bishops. Totally victorious, he set off for London.[186]

King Henry, then, had caved in. Queen Eleanor had not. Indeed, 'inflamed with womanly anguish' (as the Pershore chronicler put it), she opposed submission with all her might. Nothing, however, could stir her wilting husband into resistance. The most conspicuous thing he did in these last days was to assign William de Valence £1,000 from the lands of Gilbert de Clare, hardly something very sensible, practical or likely to

---

[183] There is no evidence, however, that the Geraldines were connected with Montfort.

[184] Frame, 'Ireland and the Barons' Wars', 166.

[185] Carpenter, *Reign of Henry III*, 266 n. 4; Howell, *Eleanor of Provence*, 195. King Richard wrote thanking Henry for his son's release and regretting there was no opportunity at the moment to show his gratitude (*F*, i, 427). I hope Henry harrumphed at that.

[186] Canterbury/Dover, 223; *CPR 1258–66*, 268–9.

please Eleanor.[187] She now refused to remain tamely with her husband in the Tower waiting for Montfort's arrival. Instead, on 13 July, she went out onto the jetty by the Wakefield tower and took a boat upriver intending to join Edward at Windsor. The news, however, of her intended escape had spread. At London bridge she was met with cries of 'harlot' and pelted with stones, mud and eggs. Forced to turn back to the Tower, she found Henry unwilling to let her in, either from anger at her desertion or from fear of admitting the mob. In the end Eleanor had to be rescued by the mayor and taken to the house of the bishop.[188] Next year at the battle of Lewes, Edward was to take bloody revenge for this assault on his mother.

Montfort arrived in London on 15 July to a rapturous welcome from the citizens.[189] He then went to see Henry in the Tower. How one wishes an artist of the Victorian age had captured the scene in the Wakefield tower. The light glinting through the stained-glass windows bearing the king's coat of arms, Montfort kneeling before Henry and asking whether he would now observe the Provisions, Henry raising Montfort and giving his assent. The form was respectful, the substance humiliating. Henry was abased, Montfort ascendant.

Next day, 16 July, now back at Westminster, Henry issued a proclamation explaining the terms of the settlement.[190] The Provisions of Oxford were to be inviolably observed although with the possibility of some revision. In addition (in what Louis IX later referred to as a 'statute'), office was to be confined to native-born men and all foreigners were to leave the country 'never to return', although with the possibility of some exceptions. Henry was once more in chains. That the proclamation was sealed by King Richard as well as the king showed how far the former was going along with the revolution.

The shock of all this for Henry must have been profound. One feels for him, yet he could surely have done more on his own behalf. He should have reissued the Provisions of Westminster a year or more before he did. He should have accepted John Mansel's advice and returned to England in the autumn of 1262 instead of going on a pilgrimage to remote Burgundian shrines. He should surely have put up more of a fight in 1263, as both Eleanor and Edward attempted to do. Even Edmund, with none of Edward's martial spark, was astonished at his father's capitulation. Speaking for all the garrison, he refused to surrender Dover at the first time of asking: it was 'indecent and absurd to give up such a great castle, and one so fortified and munitioned'.[191] Of course, in 1261 too Henry had sat still in the Tower and it had all worked out. But then his opponents had not unsheathed their swords. Now they had, and sitting still was no good.

---

[187] CPR 1258–66, 268–9. CFR 1262–3, no. 727, also has the date 8 July but it is, I think, later.
[188] Pershore, Flores, 481–2; Dunstable, 223.
[189] Dunstable, 224.
[190] Carpenter, Reign of Henry III, 280 (CPR 1258–66, 269–70).
[191] F, i, 427–8.

Having said that, before the sudden collapse, was Henry not entitled to think the kingdom was returning to normal? The justices on eyre and at the bench were holding their pleas in the accustomed fashion. All the sheriffs turned up in person or through deputies at the start of the Easter exchequer and brought in a revenue quite comparable with other years.[192] There was also some success in claiming ownership of the Provisions of Westminster. In one case before the bench in the Trinity term of 1263, they were described as published 'through all the realm' by the king on 'the common counsel of his faithful men', so there was no reference at all to the magnates having joint, let alone sole, responsibility.[193] Henry's own reputation in some quarters stood high. When, in March 1263, the monks of Tewkesbury thought he had died, they produced a wholly flattering obituary. The king was: 'A true lover and adorner of holy church; a protector and consoler of religious orders; a vigorous governor of the kingdom; a skilful restorer of peace and quiet; a generous giver of alms to the poor; of widows and orphans always a pious helper.'

The praise given to Henry's vigorous government might have been modified had the obituary been written a few months later, but it is perfectly understandable given the king's recovery of power in 1261 and his firm treatment of Tewkesbury's patron, Gilbert de Clare. The praise for the restoration of peace and quiet shows how valued had been the long years of Henrician peace, after the turmoil of John's reign, and how effective had been Henry's propaganda on the subject. Henry appears as a good and pious king, not one who in any way deserved to be stripped of power.[194]

Henry could also think he was not wholly to blame for what had happened. However much he and his queen had egged Edward on, it was Edward's failure to manage his followers that had caused the rebellion. Henry could think too he was being overthrown by a faction quite unrepresentative of the kingdom. The revolution of 1263 was very different from that of 1258, when most of the great nobles had been against him. Now Henry had an array of English magnates on his side: Philip Basset, Hugh Bigod, Humphrey de Bohun, earl of Hereford, William Mauduit, earl of Warwick,[195] the northerner John de Balliol and the marcher barons Reginald fitzPeter, James of Audley and William de Briouze (the last lord of Gower and Bramber in Sussex). Henry also enjoyed at least the neutrality of Roger Bigod, for all his role in 1258 and stand at the end of 1261. On 12 May 1263, at St Paul's, with his brother Hugh and Philip Basset, he witnessed a charter in John Mansel's favour. There is no sign he did anything in Montfort's support.

[192] Stewart, *1263 Surrey Eyre*, xxxvi; Cassidy, 'Adventus vicecomitum', 616.
[193] TNA KB 26/173, m. 18 (image 0102).
[194] Carpenter, *Reign of Henry III*, 253–60.
[195] Mauduit succeeded to the earldom (much depleted by dower portions) on the death of John de Plessis in February 1263.

## THE NEW BISHOPS

To be fair again to Henry, in some ways his situation was more difficult than in 1258 or 1261. There was the political revolution in London. There was also the transformation of the episcopal bench.[196] In 1258 the bishops had largely stood aside. Only Montfort's old friend Bishop Cantilupe of Worcester gave outright support to the revolution. Likewise, only Cantilupe of the bishops had resisted the king's recovery of power in 1261.[197] The year 1263 was quite different. Cantilupe was no longer alone. The 'form of peace', he urged on the king, was taken to Henry by the bishops of Lincoln and London, Richard of Gravesend and Henry of Sandwich.[198] Ostensibly they were acting as peacemakers. In reality they were partisans. Like Cantilupe they must have urged Henry to give way. Later it was to the bishop of London that Dover castle was to be surrendered. Cantilupe might maintain that 'the form of peace' was compatible with the king's honour, but this was nonsense. How could it be true of a document subjecting the king once more to conciliar control? Perhaps it was the bishops who persuaded Montfort to agree the Provisions might in some way be revised, but the 'form of peace' was still a revolutionary document, indeed more revolutionary, given its expulsion of foreigners, than the provisions of 1258. It is astonishing that bishops should have had anything to do with it.

Cantilupe, Gravesend and Sandwich were later suspended by the pope for supporting Simon de Montfort. So were two more bishops, Winchester's John Gervase and Chichester's Stephen of Bersted. All five of these prelates were together at Canterbury on 27 May 1263 (Trinity Sunday) for Sandwich's consecration as bishop of London.[199] Their conversation would have been instructive. The ceremony was performed by Gervase under licence from an absent Archbishop Boniface. The latter did not return to England until May 1266. There was no chance, therefore, of him influencing events either by taking Henry's side or by acting as peacemaker, the role played by Archbishop Edmund in 1234 and Langton in 1215.

All the suspended bishops, save Cantilupe, had reached the bench since the revolution of 1258 and none were king's men.[200] In terms of background they were academics not civil servants or royal kin. Gervase had

---

[196] For what follows, see Ambler, *Bishops in the Political Community*, ch. 6; Ambler, 'The Montfortian bishops'; and Hoskin, 'Natural law'.

[197] Canterbury/Dover, 210–11 (misdated to 1260).

[198] For 'the form of peace', see above, 264–5. The third bishop was Roger de Meuland, of Coventry-Lichfield; for him, see Carpenter, 'Roger de Meuland'.

[199] Canterbury/Dover, 220. For biographies of the new bishops, see Knowles, 'Stephen Bersted'; Kingsford and Vincent, 'John Gervase'; Haines, 'Richard of Gravesend'; Knowles, 'Henry of Sandwich'.

[200] Gravesend was elected to Lincoln in September 1258, Bersted to Chichester in May 1262 and Sandwich to London in November 1262 (while Henry was out of the country). Gervase was provided by the pope in June 1262.

taught at the University of Paris, the rest were Oxford masters.[201] Their
elevation shows how much Henry had lost control of episcopal appointments thanks to the revolution and also the actions of the pope. Having,
in the past, worked so hard to get his own man as bishop of Winchester,
the pope's provision of Gervase in June 1262 must have been particularly
galling.[202]

The new bishops had all belonged to the circle around Robert
Grosseteste and Bersted's predecessor at Chichester, Richard of Wich. It
was a circle given added lustre by Wich's canonization by the pope in
February 1262. All these men must have resented Henry's mistreatment of
the church. Wich, in his will, had said he would seek payment 'in the court
of the most high' for all the revenues taken so unjustly from the bishopric
during the dispute over his appointment.[203] Sandwich, as we have seen,
claimed that the pillage of his bishopric during the vacancy before his
appointment meant he could not help with the rebuilding of Westminster
palace. Gervase, meanwhile, had to offer over £2,000 to obtain the corn
and stock of his bishopric, £1,000 being received into the treasury early in
1263. Henry was arguably within his rights, but it was not a way to win
favour.[204] These bishops had good reason to agree with Grosseteste that
Henry's treatment of the church put him grievously at odds with 'natural
law', the law of God on which the universe was based and which earthly
law should follow.[205] This view had been given powerful expression in the
preamble to the statutes promulgated at the Lambeth council of 1261.[206]

The new bishops felt just as deeply about Henry's general misrule.
Indeed, in their minds, the grievances of church and state were inseparable. Gravesend, as dean of Lincoln, had taken remarkable steps to
promote Magna Carta, having Pope Innocent's confirmation of the 1253
sentences of excommunication circulated in English and in French. All
this, Gravesend hoped, with God's help, would bring 'honour to the
kingdom, tranquillity to churches and peace to peoples'.[207] Now in 1263
the hope was the restoration of the Provisions of Oxford would do the
same. That was all the more the case thanks to the character and conduct
of Montfort himself.

At the time of the 1258 revolution, only Cantilupe of the bishops had
any intimate connection with Montfort. Richard of Gravesend's election

---

[201] Gervase is often styled Master John of Exeter and needs to be distinguished from the
king's clerk of the same name who was not a master. For both of them together, see *CR
1261–4*, 174.

[202] Canterbury/Dover, 218–19; Harvey, *Episcopal Appointments*, 67, and see Appendix
under Winchester. The papal provision followed a split election.

[203] *Saint Richard of Chichester*, 6, 8, 69, 226, 244.

[204] *CR 1261–4*, 148–9, 174, 217; *CPR 1258–66*, 229, 242; Howell, *Regalian Right*, 91.

[205] See Hoskin, 'Natural law', 89–91.

[206] *C&S*, ii, 669; Hoskin, 'Natural law', 91–2.

[207] Burton, 321–2; Ambler, *Bishops in the Political Community*, 177.

as bishop of Lincoln later in the year added a second. 'My dear father Richard', he is styled when named in 1259 as an executor of Montfort's will.[208] Before their elevations, Bersted, Sandwich and Gervase probably knew Montfort only by reputation, but now they could see at first hand the intensity of his religious life and the breadth of his wider vision, one where the reform of the realm and the teachings of churchmen were intimately linked. Thus it was that before the battle of Lewes, in an offer conveyed to the king by Bishop Bersted, Montfort said he would accept whatever was decided about the government of the realm by 'the best men, whose faith is lively, who have read the decretals, or have taught well theology and sacred philosophy and know how to lecture in the Christian faith'.[209]

## MONTFORT'S WIDER SUPPORT

There were other factors undermining Henry's position. Outside the baronage, Montfort had won wide support for the insurgency. A good proportion of the knights in each county and many of lesser status were involved in the rebellion between 1263 and 1265.[210] And while clerical writers were uneasy about the attacks on church property, to a remarkable extent they sanitized the violence, stressing it was largely targeted against aliens and those who had overthrown the Provisions of Oxford. The argument that this was a loyal movement was widely accepted. FitzThedmar, in his account of 1263, described the Provisions on three occasions as made 'for the honour of God, in fealty to the king and for the utility of the kingdom'.[211] He even stated it was the king's banner the raiding parties carried before them. This was the easier to believe because the king's own properties were indeed largely unmolested. We hear nothing of attacks on the palaces at Woodstock and Clarendon although they must have been extremely vulnerable.[212]

Inherent in such acceptance was another extraordinary fact. Montfort had taken control of the agenda. The war was being fought entirely on his terms. All the contemporary narratives, from the Montfortian annals of Dunstable, the middle-of-the-road annals of Pershore, the royalist Thomas Wykes and fitzThedmar in London, accepted that, however mixed some of the participants' motives, the revolt had been caused by the overthrow

[208] Bémont, *Simon de Montfort*, 328–30.

[209] *Song of Lewes*, lines 198–206; Ambler, 'The Montfortian bishops', 139; Hoskin, 'Natural law', 93–4. For discussion of the *Song*, probably written by a friar in the entourage of Bishop Bersted, see below, 410–5. Maddicott, 'Who was Simon de Montfort?', 51, stresses the impact of Montfort's personal religiosity including his hair shirt and his praying late into the night. The appeal of his charisma is discussed in Ambler, *Bishops and the Political Community*, 128–36, and Hoskin, 'Natural law', 94–5.

[210] Montfort's support is discussed more fully in ch. 8.

[211] So Dunstable, 222; FitzThedmar, 53–4 (Stone, FitzThedmar, nos. 770–1).

[212] Jacob, *Studies*, 224–5.

of the Provisions.[213] Henry himself accepted as much. He later routinely issued pardons for what had been done 'by occasion of the non-observance of the provisions or statutes of Oxford'.[214] Evidently, Henry's reissue of the 1259 provisions had not been enough. They might be called the Provisions of Oxford, but, as the Lewes annalist said, they certainly were not all of them.[215] Key features of the Provisions had clearly been overthrown. Henry had got the pope to quash the oaths of 1258 and had announced he was now exercising the fullness of royal power. He had overthrown the baronial council and dismissed the knightly sheriffs. Montfort, moreover, had given the Provisions a new and sharper edge by linking them to the attack on foreigners. All the contemporary accounts made that attack central to the events of 1263.[216] The Pershore chronicler observed that anyone who could not speak English was 'despised and held in contempt by the vulgar masses (a vulgo)', a comment that shows just how far down the social scale the issue resonated.[217]

There was also a recognition that this could be a righteous, indeed a holy cause. Wykes himself admitted that some of Montfort's baronial supporters 'out of simplicity' thought they were engaged in a 'pious undertaking'.[218] Another chronicler has Montfort returning to England declaring that 'he had taken the cross [to crusade in the Holy Land] but was just as willing to die fighting against wicked Christians for the liberty of the land and the holy church as against pagans'.[219] One writer even imagined that Montfort had his noble followers tonsured before they set off to attack their enemies. The picture of Clifford, Leybourne and the rest solemnly sitting down to be tonsured has its comic side, but the story captures the spirit of the time.[220] Montfort surely believed his army was 'an army of God', just like that in 1215.

The enthusiasm for the Montfortian movement in 1263 stands out powerfully in a contemporary poem. It was written in French so was not for a mass audience but would certainly have appealed to barons, knights and churchmen. Here the violence was not merely accepted but celebrated. The attacks on the bishop of Norwich, John de Grey, Matthias

---

[213] Dunstable, 221–2; Wykes, 133–5; Pershore, *Flores*, 479; FitzThedmar, 44–5 (Stone, FitzThedmar, nos. 770–1). And see also Winchester/Worcester, 448; Furness, 540–1; St ·Werburgh, 82; Barlings, cxiv. The evidence is usefully brought together in Burton, 'Politics, propaganda and public opinion', 87–8.

[214] For example, *CPR 1266–72*, 201, 219, 222.

[215] BL Cotton MS Tiberius A X, fo. 170.

[216] Carpenter, *Reign of Henry III*, 273, 279.

[217] Pershore, *Flores*, 481.

[218] Wykes, 134. I owe what follows to Maddicott, *Simon de Montfort*, 232–3.

[219] St Benet at Hulme, 226. For further discussion of the crusading element in the Montfortian movement, see below, 408.

[220] Merton, *Flores*, 232. This is a royalist account of events, written in hindsight. The tonsure story is meant as ridicule.

Bezill and Bishop Aigueblanche ('he thought to eat up all the English') are described in joyful detail. The leading barons Warenne, Giffard, Peter de Montfort, Clifford, Leybourne and the northerner John de Eyville are lauded. And then the poem comes to Montfort himself. He is 'acknowledged and praised by the common folk of the land. He can be glad and joyous of this renown. He is strong, and has great chivalry. He loves right and hates wrong. And he will have the mastery.'[221] Montfort had become the first leader of a political movement in English history to seize power. He was also the first to reach out and generate widespread enthusiasm for a political cause.[222] He had indeed won the mastery. Could he keep it?

[221] *ANPS*, 12–23; *Political Songs*, 59–63. For discussion of this and related songs, see Somerset, 'Complaining about the king in French'.

[222] Maddicott, *Simon de Montfort*, 231–2. The only precedent would be Richard Marshal in 1233–4.

## Chapter 8

# THE COLLAPSE OF SIMON DE MONTFORT'S RULE AND THE CIVIL WAR

## JULY 1263–MAY 1264

Henry had given up in July 1263 without much of a fight. Perhaps it was almost a relief when, in the end, his sons submitted too. On the second time of asking, Edmund surrendered Dover without difficulty. Edward, holed up in Windsor castle with his foreign soldiers, was expected to cause more trouble. Accordingly, on 20 July, in an order showing the total change in the situation, the barons and knights whom Henry had summoned to Worcester for 1 August to campaign against Llywelyn were now told to join him as quickly as possible in order to expel the aliens from Windsor castle.[1] By the end of July the garrison had surrendered and was soon on its way out of the country. The queen showed her appreciation for its efforts and disgust at events by presenting rings to many of the foreign knights.[2]

What of Edward himself? Almost certainly Montfort wanted to reimpose the controls of 1258, perhaps even keep him in custody. With Bishop Cantilupe, he prevented Edward returning to Windsor following the negotiations at Fulham over the castle's surrender.[3] But, in a fragile situation, stripping Edward of his foreign soldiery had to be enough. Fortunately, there was also help from Llywelyn. Seizing the moment, in late July, as Edward was being prized from Windsor, the Welsh prince laid siege to Dyserth. Having taken the castle, he destroyed it so completely that, as a Welsh chronicler put it, not a stone remained.[4] Then at the end of September, Llywelyn starved the castle of Deganwy into submission, despite attempts to negotiate a truce in which it could be supplied by one boat with twelve oars. So the two great castles Henry had built to hold

---

[1] *CR 1261–4*, 308–9.

[2] *CPR 1258–66*, 272; Pershore, *Flores*, 482–3; FitzThedmar, 57 (Stone, FitzThedmar, no.777); Howell, *Eleanor of Provence*, 198.

[3] Pershore, *Flores*, 482–3; Studd, *Lord Edward's Itinerary*, 71.

[4] When I wandered over the hilltop on a dark misty day in 1979, I could find nothing of the castle despite what is said in Colvin, *History of the King's Works*, ii, 645. Today the remains are revealed in photographs by John Northall: http://www.castlewales.com/dyserth.html.

down the Four Cantrefs, costing more than £10,000, were no more.[5] Llywelyn was now master of the whole area between the Conwy and the Dee. In the summer he received the homage of Gruffudd ap Gwenwynwyn of southern Powys, the one ruler who had hitherto remained loyal to the English crown. Truly Llywelyn was now prince of Wales.[6]

All of this, however, only served to augment Edward's indignation and anger. He remained very much at large, a constant thorn in Montfort's side. He was soon doing all he could to break up the regime by recovering the allegiance of his old followers.

## HENRY'S SITUATION

Henry himself enjoyed no such freedom. Apart from going to Fulham in late July for the negotiations over Windsor, he remained stationary at Westminster from 16 July through to 18 September. Meanwhile all the Provisions of Oxford's controls were restored. Hugh Despenser returned as justiciar in place of Philip Basset. Nicholas of Ely returned as chancellor in place of Walter of Merton, receiving the seal on 19 July in the presence of Montfort and 'other magnates of the realm' but not apparently the king. At least Nicholas cannot have been personally objectionable to Henry, but he must have taken an oath to seal nothing save with the council's consent. Henry later complained that during this period the seal was out of his hands.[7] Just who was on the council we do not know. Only four members of the original council of fifteen were still alive and on Montfort's side: Montfort himself, Bishop Cantilupe, Richard de Grey and Peter de Montfort. The authority of the council is, however, very apparent. Between mid-July and mid-August it authorized some eighteen royal letters dealing with a wide variety of business. In the same period Henry, acting alone, authorized only two. Montfort himself was involved in authorizing seven letters; Hugh Despenser as justiciar many more.

Henry had also to put up with insulting changes to the personnel of the royal household. The stewards Robert Walerand and the Savoyard Ebulo de Montibus went out and were replaced by Montfort's knight John de la Haye and, believe it or not, Roger of Leybourne.[8] Few people can have been more objectionable to Henry and Eleanor. Almost as bad was the change at Windsor, Eleanor's main home, where the Savoyard Aymon Thurbert gave way as castellan to Giles de Argentan, the steward of the

---

[5] Colvin, *History of the King's Works*, i, 113; ii, 624–6, 644–5.

[6] *AC*, 101; St Werburgh, 84–5; Smith, *Llywelyn ap Gruffudd*, 157–60.

[7] *CR 1261–4*, 242; *CPR 1258–66*, 271, 381. Nicholas had been Henry's treasurer of the exchequer since at least May 1263. He was replaced as treasurer by Henry, prior of St Radegund's, Dover, a house with which Montfort had connections: Maddicott, *Simon de Montfort*, 239.

[8] Also, Alan la Zouche was appointed in early 1263 in place of Pugeys.

household imposed on Henry in 1258. It was on Argentan's orders that game was to be taken for the queen from the king's forests and parks.[9] Meanwhile Dover castle was placed under Richard de Grey and Winchester under Montfort himself, thus reaffirming the appointments made back in 1258.[10]

In all these ways the controls of the Provisions of Oxford were being restored, but there was also one ominous addition. It related to Montfort's own position. Describing the events of July 1263, the Canterbury/Dover annalist states that Montfort 'was made steward of England'. This is not exactly right because Montfort had inherited the stewardship with the honour of Leicester back in 1231. Indeed, in 1236, with characteristic ambition and acuity, he had defended its ceremonial rights at the queen's coronation. From July 1263, however, Montfort began to make much more of the position. He appears with the title in public documents in a way he had never done before. As steward, he may well have claimed he could appoint the subordinate stewards of the royal household. As steward, he could be the head of the council, not just an equal member.[11] Within the regime of the Provisions of Oxford, Montfort was beginning to think how he could entrench his personal power and demonstrate his supremacy. Not a pleasant prospect for Henry.

With little or no control over his seal, Henry also had to put up with the regime making free with gifts of deer and wood from the royal forests. Between July and September the beneficiaries included Bishop Cantilupe, Richard de Grey, Peter de Montfort, John de la Haye, Ralph Basset of Sapcote, Giles de Argentan, Humphrey de Bohun junior, Robert de Vipont, John de Warenne, Henry of Almain and John de Vaux.

## MONTFORT'S PROBLEMS

It was one thing for Montfort to seize control at the centre and pull the levers of patronage, quite another to get control in the localities. Henry's sheriffs and castellans, many of them appointed back in 1261, were still in place. There were also large numbers of loyalist magnates and ministers whose estates had been occupied and pillaged. Some (like Mansel and Geoffrey de Langley) had fled abroad but others remained at large and were demanding compensation and restoration. But that meant the magnates who had led the revolt would have to disgorge their gains. One sign of the disorder was that, in July and August, the usual flow of litigants coming to court to purchase writs virtually dried up. Indeed, with a dearth of litigants, the judicial bench at Westminster was suspended.[12]

[9] *CPR 1258–66*, 273.
[10] *DBM*, 264–5, cap. 14.
[11] Canterbury/Dover, 224; Maddicott, *Simon de Montfort*, 239–40.
[12] *CR 1261–4*, 372; Treharne, *Baronial Plan*, 336.

Another problem lay in Montfort's relations with potentially his greatest supporter amongst the magnates and also, if he was not careful, his deadliest enemy. This was Gilbert de Clare. The Dunstable annalist has Clare attending Montfort's Oxford parliament in 1263 and also lists him amongst Montfort's supporters. But apart from this, there seems no evidence of Gilbert's involvement in the uprising. He is conspicuously absent from those accused of ravaging royalist estates.[13] His edgy relations with Montfort may explain the way he now entered his inheritance. Back in July, before his submission, Henry was still determined to hold onto the estates until Clare came of age in September 1264.[14] But now, in August 1263, he was made to take Clare's homage and grant him full possession. The concession, however, came at a price. Clare was expected to pay the full value of the crops currently in his lands and give £1,000 for those of the following year (the last before he came of age). More remarkable still, Henry's concession of £1,000 to William de Valence from the Clare lands, made in the dying days before his surrender, was to stand. Henry must have welcomed these terms but, given the circumstances in August 1263, they were surely of Montfort's devising. If they reflected his rapprochement with William de Valence, their essential purpose was to deprive Clare of money and reduce his power. Here they failed. Clare was to hand over virtually none of the cash.[15] By the end of the year he was in neither Montfort's camp nor the king's.

Faced with these problems, Montfort sought to place key castles in the hands of his supporters. He secured the Tower, Windsor, Winchester and Dover, but other castles remained in the hands of Henry's partisans.[16] Montfort also sought to bypass Henry's sheriffs by appointing over their heads separate keepers of the peace: John de Eyville in Yorkshire, Adam de Newmarch in Lincolnshire, John fitzJohn in Befordshire, John de Vaux in Suffolk and so on. Although they were soon charged with taking over nearly all the sheriff's functions, the keepers' first task was to prevent any further plunder, especially of church property, and restore possessions to those despoiled unjustly. Between August and September they received orders to restore around fifty individuals to their lands and chattels. That Montfort was involved in authorizing some of the writs shows how important such restorations were. In the case of chattels, however, the orders often covered only those seized after the peace on 16 July or after the victims had come in and taken an oath to accept the Provisions.[17] John de

---

[13] The complaint of the bishop of London, on this score, relates, I think, to the events of 1264: Hoskin, *EEA London*, 102–3.

[14] So much is clear from *CPR 1258–66*, 268.

[15] *ERF*, ii, 402–3 (*CFR 1262–3*, nos. 727–9); *CPR 1258–66*, 268–9, 273, 350, 354, 553; Altschul, *A Baronial Family*, 99.

[16] *CPR 1258–66*, 278–9.

[17] *CPR 1258–66*, 271–3; *CR 1261–4*, 243–61; Treharne, *Baronial Plan*, 316–19.

Vaux was specifically allowed to keep all he had taken before then. This left large numbers of men feeling very aggrieved.[18]

Not surprisingly, a parliament summoned for 8 September met in an atmosphere of acrimony. One possible way forward might be through the 'good men' who were supposed to correct anything doubtful in the Provisions, but there is no evidence they were ever appointed. The problem of deciding their identity and terms of reference was insuperable. All that happened in the parliament, therefore, was the reading out of the 16 July settlement before the king, Edward and a large gathering at St Paul's. Nothing much was done by way of compensation for those whose estates had been ravaged, although the release of the bishop of Hereford and Mathias Bezill was agreed. Henry was allowed to give Bishop Peter fifty oaks for the fabric of his cathedral and Bezill a complete new set of clothes.[19] Not surprisingly the bishop soon escaped abroad.

## THE INTERVENTION OF LOUIS IX AND
## THE MEETING AT BOULOGNE

Henry attended the September parliament, according to Thomas Wykes, with virtually no military entourage.[20] Yet he must have sensed that the Montfortian regime was standing on shaky ground. With Eleanor he was already involved in a plot to weaken it further by appealing to King Louis.

The early stages of Louis's intervention have to be pieced together from contemporary chronicles.[21] According to the Canterbury/Dover annalist, both Louis and Queen Margaret were appalled at Queen Eleanor's treatment. So they invited Henry, Eleanor, Montfort and other barons to a meeting. Other chroniclers believed Louis and Margaret were acting here after an appeal from Henry and Eleanor, an appeal, so the Dunstable annalist says, they made in secret. Doubtless Henry and Eleanor hoped that Louis would examine the rights and wrongs of recent events and end up condemning the barons.[22]

When Montfort and the council heard of Louis's invitation they took control of the process. They were prepared to meet Louis, but would not let Henry go without guarantees. On 16 August, therefore, Henry was made to write two humiliating letters. The first acknowledged how Henry himself, the queen and their sons had been invited to see Louis so that he could give 'counsel and aid around the improvement of the king's state', quite probably how Henry and Eleanor had indeed put it. But, Henry

---

[18] *CR 1261–4*, 250.

[19] *CR 1261–4*, 256, 261.

[20] Wykes, 136.

[21] The main chronicle sources are Canterbury/Dover, 224–5; Dunstable, 225; Pershore, *Flores*, 484; and Tewkesbury, 176.

[22] *F*, i, 429 (*CPR 1258–66*, 275).

continued, the baronial council would not allow him to leave the kingdom unless Louis, by his letters patent, guaranteed his speedy return. The second letter went further and asked Louis to compel Henry's return if he broke his promise to come back within a week of Michaelmas.[23] There is no sign that Louis complied with these conditions. In the end the regime had to be content just with Henry's oath both to return, whatever his state of health, and to seek nothing from Louis detrimental to himself and the kingdom.[24]

The meeting with Louis eventually took place at Boulogne between 30 September and 7 October. The place itself was a concession to the barons since it enabled Henry's visit to be short. Crossing over with him were Eleanor, Edward, Edmund, Henry of Almain and John de Warenne. Montfort went separately under his own sail. Also present at Boulogne were Archbishop Boniface, Peter of Savoy and John Mansel, all effectively exiled from England, and a large group of French nobles including Louis's brother Charles of Anjou. Hugh Despenser and Nicholas of Ely were left with the great seal in charge of the home government.[25]

What happened at Boulogne? According to the Canterbury/Dover annals, to the charges brought against them the barons replied that they should answer for their deeds not in the court of the king of France but in the court of the king of England where they would be judged by their peers. Eventually this argument carried the day.[26] There is nothing unbelievable about this. Louis sympathized with Henry but was a stickler for correct procedure. Although Henry wrote of being summoned so that 'we might speak with you as lord', that overlordship related to Henry's French territories. It gave Louis no right to interfere in England.[27] Montfort, with his usual cleverness, was able to spin Louis's abstention as a victory. According to the friendly Dunstable annalist, he had answered to Louis's satisfaction the charges over seizures and despoliation and had returned 'with honour' to England.[28]

Montfort's success at Boulogne was linked to another, one which revealed the strength of his support amongst the episcopate. Archbishop Boniface, infuriated by the attacks on the church during the summer, had not waited till the end of the Boulogne meeting to take action. On

---

[23] F, i, 429 (CPR 1258–66, 275).

[24] F, i, 432 (CPR 1258–66, 280). The knight Geoffrey Gascelin swore to all this on Henry's behalf.

[25] CPR 1258–66, 280.

[26] Canterbury/Dover, 224–5.

[27] F, i, 429 (CPR 1258–66, 275).

[28] Dunstable, 225. The Tewkesbury annals have Louis saying that no king could rule without coadjutors and the realm should be governed by native-born men not aliens: Tewkesbury, 176; and also Robert of Boston, 114. This sounds like wishful thinking. Jobson, *The First English Revolution*, 101, is equally sceptical. See also Maddicott, *Simon de Montfort*, 243–4; Howell, *Eleanor of Provence*, 200.

3 October he ordered the bishops of the Canterbury province to publish sentences of excommunication against the culprits. He supplied a list of names including that of Montfort himself, the essential author, he indi- cated, of all that had happened.[29] The publication was to take place on Sundays and feast days, with burning of candles and ringing of bells. All association with those excommunicated was to be prohibited. If they remained unrepentant after a month, their lands were to be placed under an interdict. This for Montfort was a critical moment. If the bishops went ahead and published the sentences of excommunication, his regime would have been in peril. But they did not go ahead. Instead, in January 1264, they sent back to Boniface one of the most disobedient letters ever received by an archbishop of Canterbury from his own bishops. It point- edly ignored the excommunications Boniface had commanded and just said that all the bishops stood together in defending ecclesiastical rights and liberties in the Canterbury province. The letter was written in the names of the bishops of London, Winchester, Worcester, Lincoln and Chichester, all committed Montfortians, and also the other bishops of the province.[30] They were thus united in defying their primate and saving the Montfortian regime. Montfort's success at Boulogne proved short lived. Louis was soon to sing a very different tune. The support of bishops remained a stay until the end.

## THE KING'S ESCAPE, EDWARD TAKES COMMAND

Henry arrived back at Dover on 8 October. He had thus kept to the time- table for his return, a testimony both to the authority of the barons and to his desire to be at Westminster for the feast of the Confessor on the thir- teenth. He just made it, arriving the day before and indeed entering the exchequer and making a concession there 'of his special grace'.[31] Earlier, fearing he would miss the feast, he had ordered 100,000 paupers to be fed 'if they should come'![32] Later in the month, he sought desperately to provide money so the works at the Abbey could continue.[33]

Henry must have been disappointed with the results of the Boulogne meeting, however much Louis was sympathetic in private. The fact that Eleanor and Edmund stayed behind in France showed how dangerous the situation was thought to be. Montfort still controlled the seal. If the king's authority was recognized at the exchequer, so was his own.[34] He might

[29] These are the letters referred to above, 261.
[30] Bodleian Library, Oxford, MS Bodley 91, fo. 136v. I am grateful to Felicity Hill for advice as to the nature of the excommunication. For the efforts of the bishops to give the church some redress, see Ambler, *Bishops in the Political Community*, 142–3.
[31] TNA E 159/38, m. 1 (image 0004).
[32] *CPR 1258–66*, 282–3.
[33] *CPR 1258–66*, 293. The money was also for work on the palace.
[34] TNA E 159/38, m. 1d (image 0039). An order for the respite of two debts.

also hope the restoration of property would eventually reconcile royalists to the regime. Before the Boulogne meeting he had even reached out to John Mansel, taking the latter's castle at Sedgwick in Sussex from Peter de Montfort and giving it to John Mansel junior.[35] Philip Basset, moreover, was working alongside Hugh Despenser and Nicholas of Ely in charge of central government.[36]

Despite these attempts at compromise, when parliament met on 13 October the celebrations of the Confessor's translation did little to defuse the tension. The dispossessed demanded justice. Henry demanded the right to choose his own household officials. Nothing could be agreed. The good men who might decide about modifications to the Provisions were once again not appointed. There seemed to be stalemate. The disorder in the country is reflected in the sums brought in from the counties and boroughs at the start of the Michaelmas exchequer. They were over £1,000 less than the year before.[37]

Left to himself, Henry might well have meandered on, hoping Montfort's regime would just gradually disintegrate. Neither during his recovery of power in 1261 nor its loss in 1263 had he taken military action. Instead, he had remained safely in the Tower. But now something decisive happened. Edward took command of the king's cause. From now on, down to the battle of Lewes in May 1264, it was he, far more than his father, who called the shots, and shots they were, for Edward's essential strategy was to make war on the king's enemies.

Edward was now twenty-two, already considered by the Pershore annalist a man 'of great prowess'.[38] Up till now, he had never been centre stage in his father's cause. Indeed, his course had been tortuous. In 1259–60 he had been in alliance with Montfort and pledged to uphold the baronial enterprise. In 1261 he accepted his father's recovery of power but did nothing to bring it about. In the summer of 1263 events had moved too fast for him to do more than make a lone stand at Windsor. Now, however, Edward's blood was up. His mother had been attacked, he had been humiliated. He was also, as Wykes says, thinking of the future and realizing, not before time, that what was done to his father might have consequences for himself.[39]

Edward was thus determined to overthrow the Montfortian regime and saw how to do it. The first priority was to get out of Montfort's clutches and that meant getting out of London, where the citizens were up, and whither Montfort had summoned both Welsh foot-soldiers and his

---

[35] *CPR 1258–66*, 81, 279. The writ here was authorized by Bishop Cantilupe and Peter de Montfort. It was soon, however, in the hands of Simon de Montfort junior.

[36] *CPR 1258–66*, 281.

[37] Cassidy, 'Adventus vicecomitum', 616.

[38] Pershore, *Flores*, 484.

[39] Wykes, 137.

own supporters with horses and arms. Soon after the start of the October parliament, therefore, Edward, under cover of a private visit to his wife, left London for Windsor. Giles de Argentan, taken by surprise, was ejected from the castle. Next morning (probably that of 17 October), Henry himself escaped from Westminster and joined up with his son.[40] He had not brought the great seal, but was able to authenticate documents with the privy seal temporarily in the custody of none other than Hugh Bigod. The first move, using the privy seal, was to summon to Windsor those who had come with horses and arms to London. With the specious promise that nothing would be done to infringe the Provisions, Henry and Edward were here appealing largely to Montfort's supporters, in many cases to no effect. The names of Peter de Montfort and Robert de Vipont were crossed off the list of those to be summoned evidently as hopeless cases.[41] Many great men were, however, already gathered at Windsor including William de Valence, the earls of Norfolk, Hereford and Surrey, Philip Basset, the Anglo-Scottish lord Robert de Brus and the great marcher baron Roger de Mortimer. John de Warenne, earl of Surrey, and Roger de Mortimer (of whom both more later) were thus no longer on Montfort's side.[42]

## PEACE AND WAR: THE REFERRAL TO KING LOUIS AND THE START OF MILITARY ACTION

From this point in October, the king's side pursued what seem two contradictory paths. On the one hand, at the end of the month, it agreed to refer the quarrel to Louis IX. Yet, on the other, it began a military campaign. Quite possibly there were divided councils in the royal camp, Henry hoping Louis's arbitration might lead to a peaceful settlement without further action, Edward seeing it as no more than a cover for his campaign, a campaign which would leave him all the better placed to enforce the eventual verdict. Indeed, the verdict might do no more than set the seal on his victory.

The appeal to Louis owed something to King Richard. Having lain quiet since the summer, he now emerged, once again as a mediator. In this he was supported by several bishops. The result was that at the end of October both sides agreed to ask King Louis to decide the rights and wrongs both of the Provisions and everything else that had happened down to 1 November. Meanwhile there was to be a truce.[43]

---

[40] FitzThedmar, 58 (Stone, FitzThedmar, no. 784).

[41] *CPR 1258–66*, 290.

[42] *CPR 1258–66*, 291.

[43] *CPR 1258–66*, 292, 294, 296; *DBM*, 280–5. It was not till 13/16 December that the two sides made their formal submissions to Louis. But the fact that their letters empowered him to pronounce on everything that had happened down to 1 November, and there was then

In placing his trust in Louis, Henry had to get over one major disappointment. In May 1263, Louis had allowed Pope Urban to offer the kingdom of Sicily to one of his brothers.[44] Two months later Urban wrote expressing his astonishment that Henry had taken badly the news that he was looking elsewhere. He was now sending the archbishop of Cosenza both to receive back all the documents relating to Sicily and absolve Henry and Edmund from their promises and obligations. If, however, Henry believed he still had some rights, he was given four months for an appeal to Rome.[45] Given all that was happening in England, there was no way Henry could do that. It would have made no difference if he had. In 1264, Urban finally signed up Louis's brother the ruthless Charles of Anjou. So that was the end of a pointless project on which Henry had expended so much emotion and which had done so much to bring him down in 1258. With a far better deal than Henry had negotiated, and far better placed as count of Provence, Charles went on to defeat and kill Manfred, king of Sicily, and take over the kingdom. Henry and Edmund were a million miles away from ever doing that.[46]

But if Henry felt let down by Louis over Sicily, he was confident of his sympathy and support when it came to England. His appeal to Louis is readily understandable. Montfort's is more puzzling. One explanation is that he assumed Louis would work within the terms of the 16 July settlement and so would seek to alter details of the Provisions while leaving their substance in place.[47] That Henry was still saying he accepted the Provisions lends some credence to this idea. But it finds no support in the documentary evidence. In the formal documents both sides issued in December, they accepted whatever Louis decreed 'high or low' about the Provisions. Likewise, in the arguments made before Louis, the king asked for the Provisions to be condemned *in toto* and the barons defended them *in toto*.[48]

---

a separate agreement he should also look at events between 1 November and 13 December (*DBM*, 286–7, cap. 8), strongly suggests his arbitration was first agreed on at the end of October. This is confirmed by the Montfortian complaint that 'after the compromise was *first* made and fortified with seals and an oath', Henry seized Winchester castle and took the seal from Nicholas of Ely. These events took place in November. The Montfortian complaint then refers to further events 'after the publication of the compromise and the oath last made', referring here to events after the final submissions on 13/16 December: *DBM*, 264–7, caps. 14–18.

[44] *Layettes*, iv, no. 4853; Dunbabin, *Charles I of Anjou*, 131.

[45] *Reg. Urbain*, IV, no. 297; Weiler, *Henry III of England and the Staufen Empire*, 157. At least at the same time Urban wrote saying how shocked he was by the terrible news of Henry's illness and how delighted he was at Henry's recovery. He had a 'fervent love' for him beyond all other Catholic kings and princes: *Reg. Urbain*, IV, no. 302. Given the situation in England it is doubtful whether the archbishop of Cosenza ever came.

[46] *Layettes*, iv, no. 4853; Dunbabin, *Charles of Anjou*, 131–2.

[47] Treharne, *Baronial Plan*, 340–1; Powicke, *King Henry III*, ii, 452–3. I am unconvinced by Treharne's views about the legal framework of Louis's Mise advanced in his later 'The Mise of Amiens'.

[48] Stacey, 'Crusades, crusaders', 142.

Other explanations have stressed both the precariousness of Montfort's position and his confidence in Louis's verdict.[49] Both have elements of truth. If Montfort had the exchequer at Westminster in his power, it was virtually empty of money.[50] He had lost control of the king and a formidable coalition was forming against him. Yet, he too was close to Louis and also to Louis's brother Charles of Anjou. At Boulogne, Montfort had persuaded Louis to accept his jurisdictional arguments. Now he hoped for more. Montfort believed profoundly in the righteousness of his cause. In the case he later made to Louis, one statement stands out like a flash of lightning in a darkening sky. The Provisions were 'holy, *sancta*' and 'made for the honour of the lord king and the common utility of the kingdom, the king being bound to give justice to everyone'. Surely Louis of all people would appreciate that.[51]

The king's party reaped an immediate dividend from the referral to Louis. The Montfortians believed that the truce involved the maintenance of the status quo.[52] Montfort, therefore, thought it safe to leave London for Kenilworth, probably to rally his knightly supporters in the area.[53] His hold of the capital seemed secure for, in defiance of the king, 'the people' had once again elected Thomas fitzThomas as mayor. FitzThomas had immediately taken the oath of office without being admitted by the king.[54] Montfort's absence from the south, however, gave Edward all the freer rein to start his campaign. If what he planned breached the truce, he probably thought Montfort was not going to observe it either.

Thus it was that at the end of October, Edward and his father left Windsor and with 'a great army as if always ready to fight' marched to Oxford.[55] The immediate aim was to stamp the king's authority on the town where the revolution had begun both in 1258 and 1263 and where the clerks of the University, or at least some of them, were passionate supporters of Montfort's cause.[56] At Oxford, Henry's household was quartered in the castle and the town, but he stayed himself with the Dominican friars, thanking them for their hospitality with generous gifts of timber. This too was symbolic for the friary was the place where the barons had met in 1258 to draw up their reforms.[57] On arrival at Oxford, in defiance

[49] Stacey, 'Crusades, crusaders', 142–3; Maddicott, *Simon de Montfort*, 243–4.

[50] TNA E 159/38, m. 2d (image 0043).

[51] *DBM*, 264–5, cap. 13. In agreeing to Louis's arbitration both in October and December, Montfort was presumably unaware that Louis had asked the pope to send a legate to England empowered to quash the Provisions: *CPReg*, 396–7.

[52] *DBM*, 264–5, caps. 14–17.

[53] Dunstable, 225–6; Maddicott, *Simon de Montfort*, 247.

[54] FitzThedmar, 58–9 (Stone, FitzThedmar, no. 785); *CPR 1258–66*, 295, whence TNA E 159/38, m. 1d (image 0041).

[55] Abingdon, 15.

[56] I follow here Maddicott, *Simon de Montfort*, 255.

[57] *CR 1261–4*, 314, 316; Maddicott, *Simon de Montfort*, 255.

of the truce the Montfortians thought was in place, Nicholas of Ely was dismissed as chancellor and Henry recovered control of the great seal.[58]

## EDWARD WINS BACK HIS OLD FOLLOWERS

It was at Oxford that Edward's erstwhile followers formally returned to the king's camp and allegiance. As listed by the Abingdon chronicle they were John de Warenne, Henry of Almain, Clifford, Leybourne, Lestrange, Vaux and John Giffard.[59]

This was a grievous blow to Simon de Montfort. It had been the ex-Edwardians who had facilitated his return to England and supplied the muscle behind the attack on the aliens and the king's supporters. He had made efforts to keep them on side, placing several key castles in their custody.[60] Leybourne himself, quite apart from becoming steward of the royal household, had been granted the manor of Elham in Kent in hereditary right.[61] But now the group's firepower was available to the other side.

For some time Edward had been working to this end, here showing himself a flexible and forgiving politician. Indeed, he had already made his own peace with the group before they arrived at Oxford. On 18 August, Edward, on the one side, and Leybourne, Vaux, Lestrange and Giffard, on the other, had submitted their differences to the arbitration of John de Warenne and Henry of Almain, although this was still saving the oath to maintain the Provisions.[62] Evidently Warenne and Almain were already back on terms with Edward. In Warenne's case this was after a colossal tug of war. On 7 August the Montfortian government had granted him custody of Peter of Savoy's castle at Pevensey. It looked as though he was at last driving Peter out of Sussex. What made the grant all the more telling was that Warenne could never hope to keep Pevensey if he sided with Edward and the king. Edward, however, hit back at once with the one concession capable of outdoing Montfort's. On 10 August he granted Stamford and Grantham to Warenne in hereditary right, thus giving way to the ambition closest to Warenne's heart. Warenne, therefore, went over to Edward's side and accepted Pevensey's loss. Peter of Savoy soon entrusted it for safekeeping to Edward himself.[63]

The results of Warenne's and Henry of Almain's arbitration, if it took place, are unknown, but in October, as soon as he was back from France,

---

[58] Treharne, *Baronial Plan*, 325; *DBM*, 264–5, cap. 15. At the same time, Henry tried to assert control over the exchequer: *CR 1261–4*, 313; Treharne, *Baronial Plan*, 317–18 and n. 7: *CPR 1258–66*, 295; FitzThedmar, 58–9 (Stone, FitzThedmar, no. 785).

[59] Abingdon, 14–15; *CPR 1258–66*, 296.

[60] *CPR 1258–66*, 273–4; *CR 1261–4*, 242.

[61] TNA E 368/94, m. 47 (image 0094).

[62] *F*, i, 430.

[63] *PQW*, 429–30; *RH*, i, 288; *CPR 1258–66*, 274, 295; Spencer, '"A vineyard without a wall"', 63–4. For Stamford and Grantham, see above, 253.

Henry forgave the group all their actions in support of the Provisions. Just over a fortnight later, a formal settlement with Edward was reached. Clifford, Leybourne, Lestrange, Vaux and Giffard joined his retinue, swore to help him with all their power and did homage for the benefits he had given them.[64] The Abingdon chronicler believed these included grants of land worth £50 a year.[65] The stage was set for the group to come to Oxford whither they were summoned by the king.[66] Leybourne, now a king's man, and presumably profuse in his explanations and apologies, resumed his post as steward of the household. John de Vaux joined it as a marshal.[67]

It is easy to regard the Edwardians as materialistic and unprincipled men who deserted Montfort as soon as they had a better offer. They were certainly stigmatized as turncoats at the time.[68] Having embraced the Provisions simply to punish the queen for ruining their relationship with Edward, they abandoned them as soon as the relationship was restored, probably what they wanted in the first place. But perhaps it was more complex than that.[69] These men were all '*milites strenui*', shot through with chivalric ideas and ideals. Concepts of honour and loyalty were as important as the display of prowess and the rewards expected from a generous lord. If the Edwardians had been disloyal to Edward, it was because Edward had been disloyal to them. Now none of them can have found deserting Montfort and breaking their oath to the Provisions easy. The oath was explicitly protected in the arbitration with Edward arranged in August. After that it took over two months for the Edwardians to come in. Even then they could point to Henry's public protestations about observing the Provisions and making peace with the barons.[70]

The troubled consciences involved in the change of allegiance are revealed in the case of John Giffard. He had never been part of Edward's inner circle but had been included in the arbitration and been summoned to Oxford with the other Edwardians. According to the Abingdon chronicle he accepted Edward's charter granting him land and rode with the army to Winchester and then to Reading. But there he handed the charter back to Edward and returned to Montfort, adhering to him thereafter

[64] Larking, 'On the heart-shrine in Leybourne church', 168, 175–6; *CPR 1258–66*, 284.

[65] Abingdon, 14–15.

[66] *CPR 1258–66*, 296.

[67] For a grant of free warren to Vaux in December 1263, see *CChR 1257–1300*, 47.

[68] So Abingdon, 15; Rishanger, 17.

[69] The reverend Lambert Larking, a staunch believer in Leybourne's probity, felt that 'an unprejudiced reader . . . will hardly bring himself to believe [the group] were brought over by bribes' ('On the heart-shrine in Leybourne church', 181). According to his obituarist (T.D.H., 'The Rev. Lambert Blackwell Larking', 327), Larking's labours (including a dissertation on the Kent Domesday) were retarded by 'a desire to exhaust every source of information within his reach, a craving for perfection that can never be attained'. A salutary warning.

[70] *CPR 1258–66*, 296. The nearness of peace was especially mentioned in the letter summoning the Edwardians to come to the king.

'faithfully and vigorously'.[71] A story preserved by the St Albans monk William of Rishanger shows Henry of Almain equally troubled. Having been rewarded by Edward with the custody of Tickhill, he went to Montfort and sought licence for his departure, explaining that, while he could no longer fight for him against his uncle and father, he would not fight against him either. Montfort's reply captures the spirit that made him so inspiring a leader: 'Lord Henry, I had hopes for you not because of your arms but because of your special constancy. Go and return with your arms. I do not fear them.'[72]

## THE REBUFF AT DOVER

With his old followers back on side, Edward was determined to capitalize on his military might. Thus it was that the royal army left Oxford and headed for Winchester. When it passed through Abingdon on 7 November, its banners were displayed as in time of war.[73] At Winchester, Montfort's deputies were easily expelled and Henry now once more controlled his birthplace. This again, according to the Montfortians, was a clear breach of the truce.[74]

Henry may well have thought he had now done enough. At any rate, at Winchester on 10 November, he ordered the paintings in his chamber at Westminster and in the chapel behind his bed to be ready by Christmas. It sounds as though he intended to be there.[75] Instead, after a brief respite at Windsor, he was off again, this time to Dover, where he and Edward arrived on 3 December with what the local annalist described as a 'great army'.[76] The aim was, of course, to get control of Dover castle and the ports and thus make it easy to disembark troops from abroad. And here proceedings were co-ordinated with Queen Eleanor. How pleasurable for her to be working hand in glove with her eldest son.

Eleanor had remained in France after the Boulogne meeting not to take shelter but to take action. She did so with great vigour on three fronts.[77] First, she laboured to raise money both by pawning jewels and, with

---

[71] Abingdon, 15. The story may capture the spirit of Giffard's conduct but not the precise chronology. He appears on neither side in the submissions made to Louis in December 1263 and see CPR 1258–66, 358. He was certainly with Montfort in 1264, however. Another person who seems to have changed his mind is Ralph Basset of Drayton. See Ridgeway, 'Ralph Basset of Drayton'.

[72] Rishanger, 17. Rishanger was writing in the early fourteenth century and often simply copied the Pershore Flores. But he also has original material. See Maddicott, Simon de Montfort, 89–90, 245–6.

[73] Abingdon, 14.

[74] DBM, 264–5, cap. 14.

[75] CR 1261–4, 316.

[76] Canterbury/Dover, 229.

[77] For what follows, see Howell, Eleanor of Provence, 202–3.

Queen Margaret's help, by persuading Louis to pay some of the money still due under the Treaty of Paris. Second, she induced Louis and Margaret to intervene with Pope Urban and get a legate sent to England. Here there was immediate success. The day after hearing from the French king and queen, Urban appointed as legate the cardinal Guy Foulquois, giving him power to revoke the Provisions, restore Henry to his former state and confer on those resisting the rebels the same spiritual benefits as crusaders going to Jerusalem. Louis himself was urged to help the legate (an old servant) and stretch forth the hand of his royal power so that Henry could be restored to his due state.[78] And third, Eleanor busied herself raising troops to send to England. To that end, again with Queen Margaret's help, she begged Alphonse of Poitiers to send ships and galleys by the second week of December. There they could ferry across the Channel the forces Eleanor was gathering. It was to give the fleet safe passage that Henry and Edward were now attempting to secure Dover castle and the Cinque Ports.

At Dover, however, Henry met a check.[79] On 3 December he and his army approached the castle gate (the gate rebuilt by Hubert de Burgh after the Magna Carta civil war), only to be refused admission. Richard de Grey, Dover's castellan, was away with Montfort but he had left behind a substantial garrison commanded by Montfort's knight John de la Haye, so recently the steward of Henry's household. Haye and the rest now said there could be no admission in Grey's absence. For good measure, they added that, appointed by the council set up at Oxford, he was under oath not to surrender the castle without the council's consent: another indication of how '1258' was still thought to be valid. All the garrison would allow was for Henry to enter privately and unarmed. Naturally, this dangerous invitation was refused. Another attempt to gain entry on the following day having equally failed, Henry departed for Canterbury. With Dover castle unsecured, with the loyalty of the Cinque Ports uncertain, there was no way substantial forces could be brought across the channel. Still Henry had a large army already and felt able to tell Eleanor, Archbishop Boniface and Peter of Savoy to come over with just six knights. He affirmed with an oath that he had no need for more. Three days later he changed his mind and told them to stay put.[80]

The Henricians, however, remained confident, and they had one important new recruit. With Henry at Dover and Canterbury, perhaps indeed with him since the start of the campaign, was none other than King Richard. In October he had acted as a mediator between the sides, just as he had in the summer. Now he threw in his lot with his brother, indeed was

---

[78] *Reg. Urban IV*, i, nos. 581, 586–7, 5956. For Guy, from an aristocratic Italian family, and a nephew of Pope Innocent IV, see below, 329.

[79] For what follows, see Canterbury/Dover, 229–30.

[80] Canterbury/Dover, 230.

a member of his council.[81] The pope's attitude was important here. Richard must by now have received the papal letters, written in September, summoning him to Rome, no longer as 'king of the Romans' but only as 'king elect', this to answer his rival, equally 'king elect', Alfonso, king of Castile. Another papal letter, as we have seen, damned his neutrality or worse during the summer and demanded he now stand shoulder to shoulder with his brother. Despite a good number of his knights being drawn into the rebel camp, Richard knew that if he was to keep the kingship of the Romans, he needed to show his loyalty to the king of England.[82]

## THE CRISIS AT SOUTHWARK

When he heard of events at Dover, Montfort left Kenilworth and hurried south. He was behaving almost like a king. At Northampton, he received the fealty of the burgesses; at Dunstable, the prior hastening out to meet him, he was received into the confraternity of the house. No wonder the priory's annals were so staunchly Montfortian. By 8 December, by which time he was at Croydon, Henry knew that both Montfort and the young earl of Derby, Robert de Ferrers, were in London. In a letter he authorized with King Richard, he ordered the citizens to expel them. He also denied the allegations, 'more hurtful to us than any mortal war', that he had gone to Dover to bring in aliens, wishing to 'disinherit' his faithful subjects. The events proved such allegations untrue.[83]

Around this time with Henry, now at Kingston, and with Edward's forces spread out in the nearby fields around Merton, some secret intelligence reached the royal camp. Some of the aldermen said they could lock the gates of the city and thus prevent Montfort, in Southwark, from getting back in across London Bridge. Deprived of the support of the populace, denied the safety of London's walls and with an army much smaller than the king's, he would be trapped. Hearing this, Henry and Edward advanced on the city and called on Montfort to surrender. His first reaction was to cross back into London, only indeed to find the gates shut against him. Others might then have quailed. Not Montfort. Affirming, according to the Dunstable annals, that he would never surrender to perjurers and renegades, he armed his men and had them marked back and front with 'the sign of the holy cross'. The soldiers confessed their sins and took the sacrament 'ready to meet the onslaught of their enemies and struggle with them for the sake of truth'. The small army then prepared to march towards the fields at Lambeth there to do

---

[81] Canterbury/Dover, 224; *CPR 1258–66*, 300. At Christmas, Henry granted him the lucrative Mowbray wardship: *CPR 1258–66*, 304; see also *CR 1268–72*, 407.

[82] *F*, i, 430–2; *Reg. Urban IV*, no. 724 (*CPReg*, 402); Canterbury/Dover, 231–2; Jobson, 'Richard of Cornwall and the baronial opposition'.

[83] Dunstable, 225–6; *CR 1261–4*, 371.

battle. But there was nothing foolhardy and uncalculating about Montfort's leadership. So, when at the last moment the London populace, suddenly aware of the danger, broke down the gates, Montfort led his army over the bridge back into the safety of the city.[84] He would fight certainly in his righteous cause but on his own terms.

This episode marked a decisive moment in the history of Montfort's movement. From his return in 1263, there had been a belief that his was a 'pious undertaking', as Wykes acknowledged. Now, in the donning of crosses and the taking of the sacrament, that had been demonstrated in the most public way and in the most critical of circumstances. The movement and the cause had been elevated to an altogether new religious level, one very much akin to a crusade.[85]

## THE FORMAL AGREEMENT TO LOUIS'S ARBITRATION AND ROGER DE MORTIMER'S ACTION

These dramatic events took place on 11 December. Henry then went to Windsor and, with the military situation in stalemate, both sides returned to Louis's arbitration. His envoys were now in England and demanding cast-iron authorization for his intervention. Just as he had wanted the whole council of fifteen to agree the Treaty of Paris, now he wanted the leaders on both sides to issue letters recording their oaths to accept his award. On 13 December, in London, Montfort and twenty-three of his party issued the required letter. Three days later, at Windsor, Henry in one letter, Edward and thirty magnates in another, did the same.[86]

The king's side, however, were far from sitting back and quietly awaiting Louis's verdict. On 20 December, Henry sent out another of his great proclamations, one to be read out in all the county and hundred courts. Once again he sought to rebut the rumour that he had gone to Dover to bring in aliens. Evidently it had gained purchase. He also forbad the payment of a tax designed to support four or five men from each vill going to the coast to resist invasion. No one was to leave their county without permission. Evidently Montfort on his own authority was trying to raise a great army. Henry went on to explain he had no need of foreign support since nearly all the magnates, bar few or none, were on his side and soon with their help he would suppress all resistance. This sounded bullish yet Henry also said he would always keep to the oath sworn at Oxford. Evidently there were strong feelings in its favour throughout the realm.[87]

Henry and Edward were also conjuring up an action far more aggressive than a mere proclamation, one with devastating consequences. This

---

[84] Dunstable, 225–6; Canterbury/Dover, 230–1; Tyerman, *England and the Crusades*, 146.
[85] For further discussion, see below, 408.
[86] *RL*, ii, 302–3 (*CPR 1258–66*, 231–2); *DBM*, 280–7.
[87] *F*, i, 433 (*CPR 1258–66*, 357).

brings us to Roger de Mortimer.[88] The great feud between him and Simon de Montfort, the feud which did so much to bring Montfort down, was about to begin. Now in his thirties, and very much not a 'jeune', Mortimer was easily the most formidable of the marcher barons. In 1258 he had been placed on the council of fifteen. In the recent fighting in the march he had won 'eternal fame' (as the Pershore chronicler put it), slaughtering hundreds of Welshmen.[89] He had long harboured a grievance over his loss of Lechlade in Gloucestershire to Richard of Cornwall, yet the litigation he had launched in 1259 had got him nowhere.[90] In the summer of 1263 he had joined up with Montfort, but the two were unnatural allies. Mortimer cannot have welcomed Montfort's co-operation with Llywelyn. He also resented the way Montfort had prised the three Herefordshire manors of Lugwardine, Marden and Dilwyn from Henry III. These made Montfort a power right in the heart of Mortimer territory.

By October 1263, when Edward and Henry left Westminster for Windsor, Mortimer was back on their side. In December they took a decisive step to keep him there. Henry granted Mortimer and his heirs £100 a year from the royal manors of Norton and Bromsgrove in Worcestershire. In return, Mortimer surrendered his claims to Lechlade. The case was over. Appeased and supported in this way, Mortimer was ready for action. In mid-December he was granted in some form Lugwardine, Marden and Dilwyn by the king. There was no prospect of him peacefully taking possession. Rather, Roger's brief was to do exactly what he did do. He descended on the manors with a considerable force and devastated them, carrying off Montfort's chattels. He then attacked the nearby castle of Henry of Pembridge, one of his tenants who had taken Montfort's part. Naturally, Montfort complained bitterly to Louis about these breaches of the truce.[91] Without strategic purpose (like say securing Dover), they were a deliberate provocation, in effect a declaration of war at the very time Louis was trying to broker peace. Edward was confident in Louis's verdict, but he also calculated that even if the Montfortians accepted it, they would remain a danger until defeated in war. This was the moment to provoke one, rather than allow matters to drift on.

## THE MISE OF AMIENS, JANUARY 1264

With the meeting with Louis now scheduled to take place at Amiens, Henry crossed from Dover on 2 January with a small company, including

---

[88] For what follows, see Carpenter, 'A noble in politics', 198–201; Maddicott, *Simon de Montfort*, 257.

[89] Pershore, *Flores*, 476–7.

[90] See above, 168.

[91] *DBM*, 266–7, caps. 18–19; Dunstable, 226.

Hugh Bigod. The feast of the Confessor on 5 January was celebrated at Boulogne with the queen, John Mansel and Archbishop Boniface. Then, complaining of his health and labours by land and sea (this was after all January), Henry journeyed on to Amiens, which he finally reached on the twelfth. Edward, having launched the Mortimer missile, had set out earlier with Henry of Almain, being nearly lost in a great storm in the channel. King Richard remained in England in charge of the home government, another indication of his rapprochement with his brother.[92] Montfort himself had set out from Kenilworth, whither he had gone for Christmas, only for a fall from his horse and a broken leg to keep him in England. In the end, the baronial delegation was headed by Henry de Montfort and included Bishop Cantilupe's nephew Master Thomas de Cantilupe, who knew Louis well.[93]

Both sides made written submissions to Louis.[94] Henry's was almost perfunctory, reflecting his confidence in the outcome. It also bears signs of haste, perhaps being put together after Louis asked for just something in writing. If Henry dictated the document (as seems not unlikely), it does not say much for the coherence of his thought. He took his stand on custom. The baronial council had appointed the chief justiciar, chancellor, treasurer, sheriffs, judges, castellans and household stewards, whereas the king and his ancestors had always in the past chosen and removed such officials as they pleased. And anyway, a justiciar was unnecessary while the king was within the realm. Henry went on to demand compensation of both £300,000 and 200,000 marks for 'the injuries done him'. How these typically inflated figures were related or justified was unspecified, though presumably they covered all the damage suffered in the recent outrages. The conclusion was to ask Louis to quash the Provisions and restore Henry to his original 'state', the more especially since, Henry now remembered, the pope himself had condemned the Provisions and excommunicated their adherents. On the back of the document there was another afterthought. The king could not accept the Provisions because they contravened his coronation oath (presumably here referring to the obligation to preserve the rights of the crown.) Equally in agreeing to them his subjects were breaking their oath of fealty to the king.

The Montfortian case was totally different. It was embodied in a long, wide-ranging, coherent and compelling document, evidently the product of a great deal of thought, and one of the great political manifestos of the

---

[92] By this time Henry had placed the great seal in the custody of his clerk John of Chishall, who remained behind with Richard. In France, and briefly on his return, he used a substitute great seal, for which see Chaplais, *Piers Gaveston*, 37–9, and plate III.

[93] Canterbury/Dover, 232; Dunstable, 227; Wykes, 139; *CPR 1258–66*, 305, 376.

[94] The king's case is printed in *DBM*, 252–7. The Montfortian case is now in two documents, printed in the wrong order as *DBM*, nos. 37A and 37B. For the correct order, see Stacey, 'Crusades, crusaders', 137–9.

thirteenth century. It was probably the work of Thomas de Cantilupe, but Montfort too surely had a hand in it. He could not believe that Louis would condemn the Provisions, once he understood their rationale and righteousness. The first part of the case set out in detail the nature of Henry's misrule. Having freely conceded Magna Carta in return for taxation, he had then violated it in a whole variety of ways.[95] He had denied free elections to bishoprics and abbeys, had ruthlessly exploited both ecclesiastical vacancies and secular wardships, had refused justice to those complaining against his foreign relatives and other favourites, and had taken without payment far more than the customary prizes from foreign merchants, who consequently would no longer enter the country, to its great impoverishment.

The manifesto then listed other abuses where the connection with Magna Carta was implied but not stated. Sheriffs had been forced to pay impossibly high increments above their farms and were strangers in their counties where once they had been local knights. 'Aliens, courtiers, and nobles' had forced men to attend their courts and had extracted so much money and land from the king that he was impoverished and reduced to seizing what he needed for his daily bread. The final part of the indictment turned to the crusade and how Henry's vow had been 'unreasonably converted' to an attack on fellow Christians, with all the resulting financial burdens (set out in detail) placed on the church.

The second half of the case turned to the necessary remedies. Having explained how Henry had voluntary agreed to reform of the realm, it set out in detail how the individual reforms both to central and local government met exactly the problems posed by his personal rule. The conclusion was that the provisions were 'holy and honest and made for the honour of the lord king and the common utility of his kingdom'.

The baronial case was made with great ingenuity and some fairness. The summary of the reforms was accurate enough apart from claiming that contraveners of the Provisions had been excommunicated when in fact the sentence had only related to the legislative reforms of October 1259. The case played on Louis's known preoccupations and principles: his passion for the crusade, his desire to reform local government and above all his concern for justice. The section on Henry's denial and manipulation of justice was the longest in the case with its conclusion that 'justice was virtually shut out from England'. The reforms were for the honour of the king 'who is bound to give justice to everyone'. The case advanced no great political theory and, in some ways, was deliberately low key. Henry was neither described as a tyrant nor his rule denounced as tyranny. Indeed, a council was needed simply because the king 'no matter how wise he might be' could not alone deal with all the affairs of the kingdom.

---

[95] Stacey, 'Crusades, crusaders', analyses the baronial case and brings out the importance of Magna Carta and of the crusade.

None of this cut any ice with Louis. He had been given until 8 June to pronounce his award but, like a jury sure of its verdict, he came back almost at once. Perhaps he also thought the situation in England brooked no delay. The award was pronounced on 23 January and it was clear and uncompromising. Louis first set out in full the letters from both sides giving him power to pronounce 'high and low' on the Provisions of Oxford. Then, with his authority established, and having, as he said, heard the rival arguments, he declared that the Provisions had detracted from 'royal right and honour'. They had also led to disturbances and depredations in the kingdom and had been condemned by the pope. Accordingly he quashed them completely. So that there should be no doubt what this meant, he then went into details. No one should be regarded as a mortal enemy for contravening the Provisions; the king's castles should be restored to him; henceforth he should be able to appoint the chief justiciar, chancellor, treasurer, judges, sheriffs and household officials as he wished just as he had done before the time of the Provisions. Louis also quashed the 'statute' of July 1263 which had confined office to native-born men and expelled foreigners from the country. This was mentioned in neither of the cases, but Henry must have pushed it onto the table.[96]

The only qualification in the award was that the 'charters, liberties, statutes and laudable customs of the realm of England in force before the time of the Provisions' were still to be valid. So Magna Carta remained. Perhaps the legislative reforms of October 1259 did too since Henry in January 1263 had reissued them of his own volition. Unfortunately, he made no move to say so. It was easy to think Louis had condemned all the work of reform between 1258 and 1259.

Perhaps the outcome might have been different had Montfort been present to plead his own cause, but probably not. Louis might agree that Henry had ruled badly. He might acknowledge that the local reforms echoed his own in France. But none of that justified depriving the king of power. That Henry was a willing party he knew was specious. Louis had already secured from the pope a legate with authority to quash the Provisions. Later, referring to them, he declared that he would 'rather break clods behind the plough than have a rule of that kind'.[97]

Louis had also been empowered to pronounce on all the other disputes arising from the Provisions down to 13 December 1263.[98] He could thus take cognizance of Henry's claim for financial compensation and the Montfortian complaints about the breaches of the truce. Here, however, Louis, so decisive over the Provisions, was virtually silent. His award condemned the treatment of the royalists as mortal enemies and thus implicitly destroyed the justification for the attacks upon them. But

[96] An original text of Henry's 16 July 1263 proclamation, with the statute, is in the French Archives Nationales: *Layettes*, iv, no. 4860.

[97] 'Processus Legationis', 230.

[98] Rishanger, 120–1.

nothing was said about the destruction, let alone compensation for it. Instead, Louis simply told Henry and the barons to bury their enmity and do nothing to harm each other in the future.

The business at Amiens was not confined to Louis's award. The two kings at last agreed on the total sum due under the Treaty of Paris for the 500 knights, Henry not waiting for any formal arbitration on the matter. The total was some £30,500 of which Henry acknowledged he had received around £17,300.[99]

Louis and Henry also discussed the new crusade to the Holy Land launched by Pope Urban in 1263.[100] To this Louis was becoming increasingly committed, another reason for wanting peace in England. Henry himself had never ceased to worry about his own unfulfilled vow. It had, of course, been brought up against him in the baronial case. Was it, indeed, a cause of all his troubles? Henry, therefore, decided to make at least a start in putting matters right. At Amiens itself, in Louis presence, he assigned over £450 of the money due for the knights to John de Valenciennes. John was Louis's knight and lord of Haifa. He was to take the money to the Holy Land and expend it in God's service.[101]

Amidst the press of business at Amiens, Henry surely made time to inspect the progress of the great cathedral. Far more of the triforium and clerestory east of the crossing were in place than on his visit in 1260. With his expert eye he doubtless evaluated the changes to the design – external windows to the triforium instead of the previous bare wall (a great success), the gable heads placed over the internal triforium arches and the six light clerestory windows instead of the previous four (neither improvements in my view). Whether critical or not, Henry must again have been awed by the massive size of the church, standing above the river Somme and visible from afar (as for the First World War soldiers) across the surrounding plain. It might seem to reflect the massive decision Louis had to make and the massive authority he had to do so.

The meeting at Amiens was the last time Henry and Louis met. How Henry must have wished to go back with his kinsman, his friend and his lord to Paris, to see again Saint-Denis, the Sainte-Chapelle and Notre-Dame, and then proceed on pilgrimage to Reims and Pontigny. Instead, he had to return to all the turmoil of England. Of course, Henry hoped that Louis' verdict would bring that turmoil to an end. On 24 January he proclaimed his readiness to receive into his peace all those who swore to accept the award.[102]

[99] F, i, 434–5 (CPR 1258–66, 379). For payments CPR 1258–66, 81, 121, 123, 151, 194; Wild, WA, 87, 102, 107; Gavrilovitch, Étude sur le Traité de Paris, 58–61, 199; and above, 185, 225. The evidence for payments is not entirely clear, however.

[100] Tyerman, England and the Crusades, 145–6.

[101] CPR 1258–66, 317. For John de Valenciennes, see Powicke, King Henry III, 458–9.

[102] CPR 1258–66, 378.

## THE RIVAL CAMPS

Henry's hopes were not entirely fanciful. Louis' award became widely known and was copied in full by several chroniclers.[103] And then the royal party seemed far stronger than Montfort's. In making the submission to Louis, it included, William de Valence, Henry of Almain, Hugh Bigod, Philip Basset, the earls of Norfolk, Surrey and Hereford, the marcher lords Roger de Mortimer, John fitzAlan, Reginald fitzPeter, William de Briouze and James of Audley, the northerners Robert de Brus, John de Balliol, Henry de Percy, Adam of Jesmond and William Latimer, the midlanders Roger de Somery, Philip Marmion and Alan la Zouche, and the Edwardians Roger of Clifford, Hamo Lestrange (both marcher lords), John de Vaux, Roger of Leybourne and Warin of Bassingbourn.[104]

The Montfortian party making the submission began impressively with two bishops, Cantilupe of Worcester and Sandwich of London, but Montfort himself was the only earl. His list was bulked out by his two oldest sons, Henry and Simon, and by Humphrey de Bohun, son and heir of the earl of Hereford, already through marriage a powerful force in the Welsh marches. There were then Montfort's long-standing followers Hugh Despenser, Peter de Montfort, Richard de Grey and Ralph Basset of Sapcote, all with substantial interests in the midlands, like indeed another on the list, William Marshal (of whom more later). There too were '*les jeunes*' (though all major magnates) Henry de Hastings, John fitzJohn, Nicholas of Seagrave, Geoffrey de Lucy, John de Vescy and Robert de Vipont, the two last great northern barons. Another young man and northerner, appearing for the first time, was Baldwin Wake, lord of Bourne in Lincolnshire, this despite or perhaps because of the time he had spent as the ward of his father-in-law, Hugh Bigod. Other northerners were Robert de Ros, Walter de Coleville of Castle Bytham and Adam de Newmarch, who had acted as a baronial sheriff in Lincolnshire in 1261 and a keeper of the peace in 1263.[105] This was certainly a powerful group but hardly (especially when it came to earls and marcher barons) comparable with those on the king's side.

There were also signs of anxiety amongst Montfort's own supporters or potential supporters. The annals of Tewkesbury preserve a remarkable tract written by 'a certain faithful Englishman' early in 1264.[106] 'Fearing

---

[103] Canterbury/Dover, 233; FitzThedmar, 59–61 (Stone, FitzThedmar, nos. 987–8); Tewkesbury, 177–9.

[104] *DBM*, 282–3, cap. 4. The others on the list were John de Verdun and John de Grey.

[105] I suspect the Robert de Ros in Montfort's list was the Robert who was lord of Helmsley (he inherited probably in 1264) and through marriage lord of Belvoir, rather than Robert de Ros of Wark. The others on the list were William Bardolph, William le Blund and the Essex knight Richard de Tany.

[106] Tewkesbury, 179–80.

for our skin and your own', the author warned about a legate being sent to revoke the Provisions and punish all those disturbing the realm. If he was not admitted to England, sentences of excommunication and inter-dict would follow. So if the nobles did not think their cause was just, better to submit now to avoid disinheritance, all the more so because the king of France was himself ready to invade. The writer went on to give advice about how to resist such an invasion. Alliances with Ireland, Scotland and Wales would be vital and contingents should be raised from each village so as to form a great army.

The tract also revealed criticism of Montfort himself. The advice to think of a successor in case Montfort, 'already old', died was neutral enough, but hardly so the passage beginning 'Beware, Simon de Montfort'. If Montfort had ejected some aliens, the tract explained, he had protected others. Even worse, amongst other similar gifts, he had bestowed the lands of John Mansel on one of his sons.[107] 'If he laboured for the common good, his followers ought not to seek for spoils and gain.' Since the patron of Tewkesbury was Gilbert de Clare (very much not 'old'), the critique may well have come from someone in his circle. It perhaps reflects the reasons Clare gave for as yet refusing to join up with the great earl. In December 1263 his name is absent from both submissions to Louis.

## THE SLIDE TO WAR: FEBRUARY–MARCH 1264

If Henry hoped for peace, he was, however, far from confident about it, hence Eleanor, Edmund, John Mansel and Archbishop Boniface all remained abroad. The precaution soon seemed amply justified. Henry arrived at Wissant on the French coast on 8 February and sent over two household knights to inquire whether the garrison would let him into Dover castle. When the answer was a defiant 'no', Henry was reluctant to return at all, rather as in 1260 and 1262. In the end, Roger of Leybourne had to cross over and bring him back! At Dover on 15 February, Henry was 'honourably' received at the priory but again denied entry to the castle despite a public reading of the Mise of Amiens. This was the general pattern. In the short term, none of the baronial leaders submitting the case to Louis abandoned their oath to the Provisions and came over to Henry's side. FitzThedmar stated that Louis' award was wholly rejected by the Londoners, the Cinque Ports and 'nearly all the commune of the middle people of the kingdom of England'.

The baronial leaders had, of course, sworn to accept Louis' verdict whatever it was. Yet just as Montfort's belief in the righteousness of the Provisions had led him to trust in Louis' judgement in the first place, so now it justified the rejection of a verdict so obviously unrighteous. As the

---

[107] This was true. In August 1263, Mansel's lands had been committed to Simon de Montfort junior: *CPR 1258–66*, 273.

Dunstable annalist put it, Louis had acted 'having neither God nor the truth before his eyes'. From Montfort's supporters other reasons poured forth to explain the illegitimacy of the award: Louis had exceeded his powers; he had been corrupted 'by the serpentine wiles of a woman' (Queen Eleanor); his acceptance of Magna Carta justified the maintenance of the provisions 'since they were founded on the Charter'; and anyway the 'middling people' had never submitted to the award in the first place. Even the royalist Wykes thought that Louis had acted hastily and unwisely.[108]

After his humiliation before Dover castle, Henry moved to Canterbury and then on to Rochester and Windsor. Clearly London was completely out of bounds. Perhaps Henry hoped the situation would prove little worse than when he rejected the Provisions in 1261, so a struggle for control in the counties rather than outright insurrection. He was soon to be disabused. Control of events was passing to the men of war.

Edward's attitude was quite different from that of his father. He wanted war and, as we have seen, had sent Mortimer to ravage Montfort's Herefordshire manors in order to provoke it. The tactic worked to perfection. Montfort probably waited just long enough to know that Louis had quashed the Provisions and done nothing about the breaches of the truce. When he did know, his dogs were all ready to go. Private revenge now moulded perfectly with public policy. While the contemporary writers lamented the violence, they all accepted that the barons were fighting under the banner of the Provisions.[109] On 4 February, King Richard at Windsor knew that baronial forces were crossing the Severn, or planning to cross it, in order to attack Mortimer's lands. What is more they were collaborating with Llywelyn. Montfort had placed his sons Henry and Simon in charge of the expedition and with Llywelyn's help they ravaged the lands of Mortimer and Roger of Clifford and took the Mortimer castles of Wigmore and Radnor.[110]

Edward had anticipated something like this. Indeed, he had hurried back to England before his father without waiting for Louis' verdict.[111] At Windsor on 4 February he and Henry of Almain sought to stop the Montfortian forces getting over the Severn.[112] In company with King Richard, Edward then marched to Worcester and on to Hereford.[113] There he met up with Roger de Mortimer and the two headed west to attack Hay, Huntingdon and Brecon, possessions of Humphrey de Bohun junior.

---

[108] FitzThedmar, 61 (Stone, FitzThedmar, no. 790); Dunstable, 227; Tewkesbury, 177; Rishanger, 17; Worcester, 448; Wykes, 139.
[109] So, for example, Winchester/Worcester, 448–50.
[110] Smith, *Llywelyn ap Gruffudd*, 160–1.
[111] Bury St Edmunds, 28; Studd, *Lord Edward's Itinerary*, 75–6.
[112] *CR 1261–4*, 374.
[113] For what follows, see Abingdon, 15–16; Dunstable, 227–8; Pershore, *Flores*, 486–7; Robert of Gloucester, ii, lines 11,254–309; Winchester/Worcester, 448–9.

It was at this point that Robert de Ferrers, the young earl of Derby, entered the fray.[114] Around fifteen on his father's death in 1254, he had come of age and done homage to the king in 1260. In the intervening period his lands had been held in wardship first by Edward and then, in return for a payment of £4,000, by the queen and Peter of Savoy. It was probably the way the wardship was exploited that turned Ferrers against the court, despite his marriage to Mary de Lusignan. In 1262 he was ordered to pay up in quick time the large debts owed by his father.[115] If this was a demand he could resist, he was already in financial difficulties. With his mother's dower reducing his income by a third, he was selling off land to raise money.[116] As a result he was all the keener to make good the long-standing family claim to the castle and honour of the Peak in northern Derbyshire.[117] But that placed him directly at odds with Edward, who held the Peak as part of his appanage.

None of this, however, made Ferrers a devoted follower of Simon de Montfort. Just like Gilbert de Clare, he thought himself far too grand for that. Montfort loyalists tended always to come from his subordinates rather than his equals. Just like Gilbert de Clare, Ferrers was determined to play his own hand. But hot-headed and uncalculating, he did so with far less skill, ultimately with disastrous results. In December 1263, Ferrers had joined Montfort with horses and arms in London, but he was not one of the Montfortians submitting the dispute to King Louis. He does not appear again until the end of February, when with Henry, Montfort's eldest son and Peter de Montfort, he seized hold of Worcester, pillaging the town, killing the Jews and taking the chest with all their bonds back to his castle at Tutbury.[118]

Next to pile in was John Giffard. From his castle of Brimpsfield in the Cotswold hills, he could look down towards Gloucester only ten miles away.[119] One day, early in March, he and a fellow knight, disguised as merchants, rode up to Gloucester's west gate on horses loaded with woolpacks and gained admittance to the town. They then jumped to the

---

[114] For Robert de Ferrers, see Golob, 'The Ferrers earls of Derby', i, ch. 7. There is also a detailed discussion of his quarrel with Edward and his role in 1264 in Oakes, 'The nature of war', 244–51.

[115] TNA E 368/36, m. 17d (image 5847).

[116] Golob, 'The Ferrers earls of Derby', i, 314–19.

[117] For the claim, see Carpenter, 'The struggle to control the Peak', 39. The castle and honour of the Peak were the part of the inheritance forfeited to the king by William Peverel in 1155, a catastrophic event for the Ferrers since they were his heirs. In 1199, at the start of King John's reign, Robert's grandfather William de Ferrers recovered some of the inheritance but resigned his claim to the Peak. Its recovery became a major Ferrers ambition. The honour included valuable forests and lead mines, as well as the castle of Bolsover. While William de Ferrers was back in possession between 1216 and 1222, he took from the forests 2,000 deer and 10,000 oaks.

[118] Golob, 'The Ferrers earls of Derby', i, 323–4; CR 1264–8, 83.

[119] For what follows, see Robert of Gloucester, ii, lines 11,254–9; Dunstable, 227–8.

ground, pulled off their mantles and revealed they were armed 'from head to toe'. The porters fled, throwing them the keys, and the rest of the baronial force, led by Henry de Montfort, entered the town unopposed. It then began a fierce siege of the castle where Roger of Clifford (long at odds with Giffard) held out for the king. Hearing the news, Edward with Henry of Almain hastened to Gloucester, arriving on Ash Wednesday (5 March). With a daring matching Giffard's own, Edward commandeered a boat belonging to the abbot of Tewkesbury, got across the Severn and entered the castle.[120]

Edward's success was short lived. The sudden appearance of Robert de Ferrers with a substantial force (the man he feared more than anyone according to one account) meant he was likely to be trapped. So he went out of the castle unarmed and, thanks to the good offices yet again of Bishop Cantilupe, agreed a truce with the gullible Henry de Montfort.[121] Robert de Ferrers, not consulted, rode away in fury.

When Henry de Montfort later met up at Kenilworth with his father, he was upbraided for letting Edward go. It seemed all the more foolish once it was clear Edward was not abiding by the truce. Left in possession of the town, he punished the burgesses and then set off to join his father, dispatching William de Valence to ravage the lands of Robert de Ferrers and other enemies.[122] Edward's conduct enhanced his reputation for duplicity, but then he himself had been tricked into surrendering Windsor castle the year before.

## HENRY IN OXFORD

Henry was now in Oxford. He had arrived on 8 March and was to remain there until 5 April. Explaining that the town would soon be full of men whose 'savagery' he could not control, Henry ordered the University to disperse until tranquillity returned. He may also have distrusted some of the clerks' political opinions.[123] His own purity of conscience, in these fraught days, was displayed in a striking act, one far more in tune with his character than the warlike preparations all around. Oxford's saint was Frideswide, the virginal Anglo-Saxon princess enshrined in the Augustinian priory of St Frideswide's (now Oxford cathedral). According to the legend, King Algar, Frideswide's would-be seducer, was struck blind when he entered Oxford, since when no king had dared enter the city. Certainly the normal residence from the twelfth century was the king's 'hall' beyond the city's northern gate. It was there in 1275 that Edward, on his first visit

---

[120] For the castle, see Colvin, *History of the King's Works*, ii, 652–3. Nothing of it now remains.

[121] *RL*, ii, 244–5, presumably refers to this truce or a later one.

[122] Dunstable, 228; St Werburgh, 87.

[123] *F*, i, 435 (*CPR 1258–66*, 307); Rishanger, 22. See below, 399–400.

as king, 'terrified' by the old superstition, decided to stay, turning down at the last moment an elaborate welcome prepared for him in the town.

Henry was no match for his son in the business of war, but when it came to spiritual things he was made of sterner stuff. On this visit he stayed not in the king's hall but again in the Dominican friary. It was the friars, offering the support of their prayers and masses, who now persuaded him to enter the town. So, on foot, supported on either side by friars, and having fasted the day before, Henry processed in through Oxford's south gate and on to St Frideswide's, where he made his offering at the high altar. The day was well chosen for it was 25 March, the feast of the Annunciation of the Virgin Mary. For the souls of himself, his ancestors and successors, Henry granted the convent 10 marks a year both to sustain a chaplain celebrating daily service and to provide four candles burning day and night around Frideswide's shrine. He also promised even more benefits if God gave him victory over his enemies.[124]

On 6 March, before he left Windsor, Henry had summoned to Oxford with horses and arms over 150 barons and knights. A note in the close rolls stated that those who were against the king were not written to. All the bishops and abbots were also ordered to send their due service. At this point, Henry seems unaware of the full scale of the trouble. At any rate, the ostensible reason for the summons was the devastation being carried out by Llywelyn and his accomplices. By 18 March he was under no illusions. Writs summoning local knights to Oxford with all their power spoke of a 'grave disturbance in the kingdom' and threatened the forfeiture of all they had if they failed to turn up.[125]

## THE FAILURE OF PEACE NEGOTIATIONS

At the same time as he was summoning armies, Henry, from at least 13 March, under cover of some kind of truce, was involved in peace negotiations, proctors from both sides eventually meeting at Brackley in Northamptonshire. Montfort himself had come south from Kenilworth, staying a day or two in Northampton to secure the town, and then settling at Banbury. Royal letters spoke consistently of the negotiations being with Montfort and 'those adhering to him', another indication of his dominance. The initiative behind the talks was almost certainly Montfort's own. At the very least he wished to demonstrate how he and his followers were embarking on war with a clean conscience, having done all they could to avoid it. Doubtless Montfort was urged on by his episcopal

---

[124] Robert of Gloucester, ii, lines 11310–30; Osney, 142–3, 264; Wykes, 142–3, 264; *CPR 1258–66*, 308; *St Frideswide Cartulary*, 64–5. Henry must have been intrigued by the priory's idiosyncratic twelfth-century architecture with the triforium placed beneath the arches of the main arcade.

[125] *CR 1261–4*, 377–81.

supporters and there was another factor. The negotiations were attended by King Louis' knight John de Valenciennes. He had come to England to raise money for the crusade and also perhaps to find out for Louis what was going on. Faced with the rumours that Louis might invade, Montfort had every reason to masquerade as a peacemaker.

The climax of the negotiations came when Montfort sent his episcopal supporters – the bishops of Worcester, London, Winchester and Chichester – to Henry with what seemed a dramatic proposal. If only Henry would agree that aliens should be removed from England and the kingdom be governed through native-born men, then the Montfortians would accept everything else in King Louis' award. The proposal was rejected with contempt. The king would not depart one jot from the award. The statute against aliens Louis had specifically condemned. It threatened the position of the Savoyards and Lusignans and ended the king's right to give favour and office to whoever he liked. Why should Henry agree to this now when his son assured him he was about to embark on a victorious war? The bishops were told to leave court at once and not return for more peace talks unless summoned. Before departing, in the church of the Dominicans where presumably the meeting had taken place, they excommunicated all violators of 'ecclesiastical peace'. It was an attempt to protect the church in the civil war they knew now must come.[126]

Montfort's final position in the negotiations was brilliantly chosen and shows again his political skill. The statute against the aliens, in retaining some restrictions on the king, preserved only the bare minimum of the Provisions but a minimum which had become their most popular element: England for the English. If any slogan was going to galvanize support on the eve of war, this was it. Montfort cannot have thought his offer had any chance of success. He too wanted war, wanted the negotiations to fail. But he could not be sure. King Richard, after all, was a famous broker. Might he not drain away Montfort's momentum by miring him in long drawn-out talks. Aware of the danger Montfort took a brutal step designed to avoid it.

This takes us back to events in London. There the people had formed themselves into armed bands and appointed a constable and a marshal whose banners they were to follow in expeditions outside the city when summoned by the great bell of Saint Paul's. One early morning the bell rang and Hugh Despenser, the constable of the Tower, led the Londoners out to Isleworth where they destroyed the opulent manor of King Richard. On their return they pulled down his house near Westminster for good measure. This was a calculated act that must have been conceived by Montfort himself. The Londoners, fitzThedmar tells us, when they set out, knew not where they were going. Despenser would never have taken such

---

[126] *RS*, 196; Abingdon, 16; *F*, i, 436–7 (*CPR 1258–66*, 307–8); London, 61.

a step, fraught with consequences, on his own authority. The outrage was just as provocative as Mortimer's earlier attack on Montfort's Herefordshire manors. It took place either at the start or during the course of the peace negotiations, and was, fitzThedmar tells us, in breach of the truce 'while the parliament lasted'. It punished Richard, hitherto immune, for siding with the king. It also ensured that his support was given to a policy of war not peace. It was a war Montfort wanted. With God's help he was sure he could win it.[127]

## MONTFORT'S ALLIANCE WITH THE LONDONERS

The strategic considerations which governed the early phases of the war in 1264 are clear.[128] Geographically, Montfort had two great areas of strength. The first was in the south where he held London and Dover castle, 'the key to England'. The second was in the midlands. Here was his great castle of Kenilworth, on which he had lavished money on walls and waterworks, much to the admiration of contemporaries. Twenty-five miles to the north-east was Leicester itself and all around were the lands of some of Montfort's closest supporters. As a shield to the midlands base and as a point for advances south was Northampton, which Montfort had taken such pains to secure. He was right to do so for Northampton was the most important town in the midlands. It was wealthy with, it was later said, 300 cloth workers there in Henry's reign. It was strategically placed with roads heading south both to London and Oxford and north to Leicester and Nottingham. Widely regarded as 'in the middle of the kingdom', 'almost all traffic between London and the north passed through it'.[129] The royalist strategy was inspired by this division in Montfort's support. By raising his standard at Oxford, Henry drove a wedge between the Montfortian bases. From there he could move north or south and easily unite with Edward coming up from Gloucester.

After the failure of the negotiations, Montfort headed for London, probably anticipating that the royal army too would come south. It was thus in the city, probably on 31 March, that he sealed a formal alliance

---

[127] FitzThedmar, 61 (Stone, FitzThedmar, no. 791); Wykes, 140–1. For discussion of the date, see Denholm-Young, *Richard of Cornwall*, 126 n. 5. I suspect the devastation of King Richard's properties in Suffolk, with which Montfort was directly linked, took place around the same time: Jacob, *Studies*, 319.

[128] Much of what follows about the war comes, sometimes verbatim, from Carpenter and Whittick, 'The battle of Lewes', where full references may be found. This account supersedes that in my earlier *The Battles of Lewes & Evesham*.

[129] Treharne, 'The battle of Northampton', 303. This article (at times almost Powickian in its descriptions) gives a full account of Northampton's importance and the ensuing battle. Lawrence, 'The university of Oxford and the chronicle of the Barons' Wars', reveals the importance of a near contemporary account of the battle and subsequent events found in the later chronicle of Walter of Guisborough.

with the Londoners. Montfort himself, his baronial supporters, the mayor
of London, Thomas fitzThomas, and 'the commune of the same city of
London' took an oath to help each other against all who wished to harm
them and to make no peace without common consent. This was quite
different from the alliances of 1258 and 1263 which had bound the
Londoners to support the Provisions. Here they went unmentioned, taken
for granted. This was instead an alliance to make war together. It was
intended, moreover, to embrace all the Londoners for the aldermen were
to administer the oath to everyone over the age of twelve in their wards.
What is probably Arnold fitzThedmar's speech introducing the oath in his
ward survives. The city elite were thus co-operating with 'the steward of
England', as Montfort was described in the text of the oath.[130]

The followers sealing the agreement with Montfort show how well he
had kept his party together. Of those who had agreed to the referral to
Louis, nearly all were with him. There were also two new names right at
the head of the list. One was Robert de Ferrers, so he was now with
Montfort despite what had happened at Gloucester. The other, placed
next after Montfort himself, was Gilbert de Clare. At the time of the
submission to King Louis back in December 1263, Clare had been in
neither the royal nor Montfortian camp. This is the first documentary
proof that he had joined with Simon de Montfort. Just when he joined up
we do not know. If the Tewkesbury letter reflected his views, Clare was
already critical of Montfort's leadership. Yet, he had no reason to look
favourably on the king either. Henry had kept Clare out of his inheritance,
given his mother the castles of Clare and Usk in dower, and failed to invest
him with his comital titles. In the London agreement he still appears
without them. There were other provocations. Although Clare had been
restored to his lands, Henry continued to act as though he was lord of
Portland.[131] And he ordered the exchequer to raise by distraint 500 marks
from Clare's lands, 'astonished and angered' by Clare's failure to pay the
money to the keepers of the works at Westminster.[132] Henry was now to
pay the price for his ill-considered treatment of this dangerous young
man.

## THE BATTLE OF NORTHAMPTON, 5 APRIL 1264

Having made his alliance with London, Montfort had at once to alter his
dispositions, this on learning that Henry intended to move north on

---

[130] The text of the oath and the speech were discovered by Ian Stone. See his 'The rebel
barons of 1264 and the commune of London', where the texts are printed with full discussion.

[131] Ridgeway, 'Dorset in the period of baronial reform and rebellion', 30.

[132] This was in November 1263: TNA E 159/38, m. 2 (image 0006); *CPR 1258–66*, 354.
The money was due from the fine that Clare had made to enter his inheritance.

Northampton, not south on London. Accordingly, Montfort sent his son, Simon junior, Peter de Montfort and Baldwin Wake north at top speed to defend the town. The intelligence was right. On 3 April, Henry, Edward and King Richard marched out of Oxford with their army, its banners flying, the king's dragon standard with its flashing eyes and fiery tongue to the fore.[133] They had with them, amongst others, Clifford, Vaux, Leybourne, Philip Basset, Roger de Mortimer, William de Valence and a powerful Anglo-Scottish contingent led by John Comyn, John de Balliol and Robert de Brus, the two last lords of Galloway and Annandale as one contemporary account notes. Here was another reason for confidence for Henry had the complete support of his son-in-law, King Alexander. The date of the king's departure from Oxford was carefully chosen for it meant Henry arrived outside Northampton on 5 April, the Saturday before Passion Sunday and thus the day on which, as Wykes observed, 'the universal church throughout the world begins to sing the hymn "the banners of the king go forth"'.[134]

At first sight, Northampton was not going to be easy to take. The city was walled and had a large castle on its western side. The contingent sent from London had arrived in time and Simon junior and Peter de Montfort were in command. The walls were festooned with the banners of the defenders, including those of clerks expelled from Oxford and (with the keys of Saint Peter) knights of Peterborough abbey. William Marshal, lord of Norton hundred in the county, had pressurized and persuaded numerous local knights to join the garrison.[135] Marshal's methods were certainly forceful but he did not neglect hearts and minds. In Cow Meadow, outside Northampton's southern walls, he organized preaching to the people 'on behalf of the earl of Leicester'. Here Montfort himself had become the cause.[136]

The royalist forces, however, had a stratagem. While Henry approached Northampton's southern gateway and diverted the garrison by suggesting a parley, a contingent under Philip Basset created a large breach in the northern walls adjoining St Andrew's priory, alerted to this point of weakness (so the Montfortians believed) by the prior, who was a foreigner. Simon junior tried gallantly to restore the situation by charging repeatedly into the breach, but in the end he plunged with his horse into the town ditch and was captured. The town was soon in Henry's hands. Perhaps the

---

[133] For the dragon standard, see Ambler, *Song of Simon de Montfort*, 274.

[134] Wykes, 143. The full text of the hymn can be found by putting '*Vexilla regis prodeunt*' into a search engine on the internet. The king's army probably took the road through Brackley and Silverstone, now the A43. Much of it has been made into a dual carriageway and landscaped, but the bypassed section (now downgraded to the B430) between Weston-on-the Green, Middleton Stony and Ardley gives an impression of the original route.

[135] William was the great-nephew of the old regent, William Marshal, earl of Pembroke. For him and his branch of the family, see Cokayne, *Complete Peerage*, viii, 525–9.

[136] Guisborough, 190; *RS*, 120, 153, 194–5; Carpenter, *Reign of Henry III*, 338–9.

defence was not helped by William Marshal's methods, for some knights, coerced into coming, fled to churches as soon as they saw the standards of the king. One threw his hauberk down a latrine. Another slipped out of the town by a postern gate and swam with his horse across the moat to the king's side.[137]

The town lost, Peter de Montfort and others retreated to the castle but, without munitions, they surrendered on the following day.[138] Henry was able to make a triumphal entry into Northampton and celebrate Passion Sunday there. How appropriate he must have found the office for the day. It was Psalm 43 and began:

'Judge me O God, and defend my cause against the ungodly people. O deliver me from the deceitful and wicked man, for thou art the God of my strength'[139]

Unfortunately, Henry's cause was stained by his men looting the churches, robbing the burgesses of their last half a penny (according to the Dunstable annalist) and killing some of the common people. This time the Jews escaped as they had fled to the castle, where they remained out of fear for the next two months.[140]

Henry himself, incensed by the banners of the Peterborough knights (after all a royal foundation), had sworn to destroy the house completely. He was even crosser when some of the captured knights said (falsely according to the abbey's chronicler) that they were there on the abbot's orders. But he was soon appeased by the abbot offering him £200.[141] The scale of his triumph was underlined by the number of prisoners. One list has seventy names, including those of Peter de Montfort, his two sons, William Marshal, Simon of Pattishall, Simon fitzSimon, 'who first raised the standard against the king', and the northerners Adam de Newmarch,

---

[137] TNA JUST 1/59, m. 18 (image 1506); *RS*, 165; Jacob, *Studies*, 232–3. For those who had fled to a church, the Dictum of Kenilworth gave easier terms for the recovery of their land: *DBM*, 332–5, cap. 29.

[138] With its ring roads, railways and Carlsberg Brewery where Henry's army mustered outside the south gate, it is hard at first to envisage Northampton at the time of the battle. The last masonry of the castle was destroyed and the motte sliced in half to make way for the railway, while the grounds of St Andrew's priory are covered by nineteenth-century housing and a trade park. But Northampton has fine medieval churches, Cow Meadow survives (now Becket's Park) and from the remaining half of the motte one can appreciate the castle's strategic position above the river Nene, even if the view is now over railway sidings. There is still some open parkland between the Nene and the terraced houses where the breach in the wall probably took place. Henry would have loved the ornate thirteenth-century gothic of the Victorian town hall.

[139] *Sarum Missal*, 98.

[140] *CPR 1258–66*, 320.

[141] *Historiae coenobii Burgensis*, 134–5; Guisborough, 190; Lawrence, 'The university of Oxford', 100. The abbot of Peterborough was Robert of Sutton, the successor of John de Caux.

Baldwin Wake and Roger Bertram.[142] Henry and Edward had struck what seemed a devastating blow.

After their triumph at Northampton, the royalists must have debated what to do next. Go south towards London or attack the Montfortian bases in the midlands and the north? Given Montfort's presence in the south, the latter seemed easier, so Henry marched on Leicester, entering it without opposition (there was no castle) probably on 11 April. Next to fall was Nottingham. Here the blow to Montfort lay not only in the loss of its castle, a key to the north, but also the ominous defection of its castellan, William Bardolph. One of the baronial twelve in 1258, an opponent to the last of Henry's recovery of power in 1261, he had been amongst the Montfortians agreeing the submission to King Louis. But now having, as he said, received 'around the hour of prime' on 11 April Henry's order to surrender the castle, he promised to come to Leicester on the following day 'ready to obey you in all things as my liege lord'.[143] Henry was thus able to rest for a week at Nottingham, where he ordered the lands of the leading Montfortians to be seized into his hands.[144] Edward, meanwhile, carried on the war, seizing Ferrers' castle at Tutbury and ravaging his lands. In all this there was one consolation for Montfort. The royalists had conspicuously avoided Kenilworth and the long siege needed to reduce it. That left its commanders, Henry de Montfort and John Giffard, free to sally forth and capture Warwick castle from the new earl, William Mauduit.[145]

Montfort, on hearing of the king's march on Northampton, had set out at once from London, hoping to raise the siege. But he got no further than St Albans before hearing of the disaster. He had lost a town of great strategic importance and the shield to his bases further north. With so many of his supporters now in captivity, he had lost a good part of his military strength. Montfort's immediate reaction was to return to London, probably expecting once again that Henry would descend on the city. There he was responsible for an horrific massacre of the city's Jews.

## THE MASSACRE OF THE JEWS IN LONDON, APRIL 1264

Throughout this period Jewish communities in the towns were subject to attack, as we have seen at Worcester. Only in London, however, are there detailed accounts of what happened. One comes from an eyewitness, the alderman Arnold fitzThedmar.[146] He writes as follows:

---

[142] Rishanger, 124–5. The list printed here comes from an appendix of documents attached to the Hyde chronicle: Denholm-Young, 'The Winchester-Hyde chronicle', 244, no. 8.

[143] TNA SC 1/2/144; Wykes, 146.

[144] *CFR 1263–4*, nos. 101, 105–8.

[145] Mauduit had become earl on John de Plessis's death in 1263.

[146] FitzThedmar, 62 (Stone, FitzThedmar, no. 793). For what follows, I am indebted to a full analysis of all the sources for the massacre in Tolan, *England's Jews*. I am grateful to John Tolan for letting me see a draft of his book in advance of publication.

In the week before palm Sunday [13 April] the Jewry in London was destroyed, and all their goods taken away, and as many Jews as were found, naked and despoiled, were afterwards killed at night in a body, to the number of more than 500. Those who survived, were saved by the justiciar and the mayor, having been sent to the Tower before the killing.

What makes the account so chilling is the implication that the murders took place not in some hot-headed riot but in cold blood at night after the victims had been separated from those to be spared. Thomas Wykes captures the full horror of what happened, describing how, sparing neither sex nor age, old men and children at the breasts of their mothers were all killed together. Of those responsible for the outrages, Wykes named particularly John fitzJohn, who killed the wealthiest of the Jews, Cok, son of Aaron, with his own hands. He then shared part of the spoil with Montfort himself, 'so neither were immune from the crime of rapine and homicide'.[147] Wykes puts the numbers of Jews killed at nearly 400, fitz-Thedmar, as we have seen, at more than 500. If these numbers are anything like correct, this London pogrom was far worse than that suffered by the Jews of York in 1190.[148]

Wykes believed that the attack on the Jews had been motivated by the desire to seize their wealth, many of the Montfortians being short of cash. But that can scarcely account for the massacre, especially if committed in cold blood. The Dunstable annals have a different account.[149] Here Montfort, having returned to London (after the fall of Northampton), received intelligence that the Jews were planning a rebellion. They had acquired Greek fire and on the eve of Palm Sunday (12 April) intended to set the city alight. They also had forged keys to all the gates and indeed, 'so it was said', had made underground passages. Montfort, accordingly, 'caused the Jews to be killed, from the greatest to the least, save certain of the most senior from whom he wished to find out more, and those who were willing to receive baptism'. Gilbert de Clare, the annalist added, did the same to the Jews of Canterbury.

The account makes absolutely clear the massacre took place on Montfort's orders. Given his closeness to Dunstable priory, it may also reflect his explanation for what happened. That some such rumours (however baseless) were indeed circulating is not impossible given the

---

[147] For Cok (in fact son of Aaron son of Abraham), see Hillaby and Hillaby, *The Palgrave Dictionary of Medieval Anglo-Jewish History*, 237–8.

[148] Hillaby and Hillaby, *The Palgrave Dictionary of Medieval Anglo-Jewish History*, 228, 419–21. The annals of Winchester give the figure of Jews killed as up to 700: Winchester, 101, whence Winchester/Worcester, 450.

[149] Dunstable, 230.

fevered atmosphere in the city after the fall of Northampton.[150] Whether Montfort actually believed them is another matter. More probably they were just an excuse for filling the coffers of himself and his supporters while at the same time venting his hatred on the Jews as moneylenders and threats to Christianity. For both those reasons, Montfort had expelled the Jews from Leicester soon after inheriting the town. Henry too had stoked the fires of hostility. Alongside seeking to convert Jews to Christianity, he had promulgated anti-Jewish legislation and sanctioned the belief (after the events at Lincoln in 1255) that Jews ritually murdered Christian boys. Henry's anti-Jewish activities were universally applauded by contemporary chroniclers. It was not so with the Montfortian massacre. Thomas Wykes made no mention of a conspiracy and set out the long-sanctioned view that it was 'inhumane and impious' to kill the Jews 'without cause'. They were humankind, created in the image of God, and would be converted at the end of the world.

## THE SIEGE OF ROCHESTER AND ITS
## AFTERMATH, APRIL 1264

Montfort soon learnt the king's forces were not advancing on London but were on the loose in the north. Should he set out once again to combat them? He decided not to. Instead, in a brilliant strategic decision, shaping the whole course of the war, he moved not north but east. His aim was to take Rochester. He would thus eliminate the one royalist stronghold between London and Dover. He would also, he calculated, draw the royalists off from their attacks in the north and bring them south to raise the siege. They would come to him, not he to them.

The siege of the town began on 17 April.[151] Gilbert de Clare, coming from his castle of Tonbridge, attacked from the south, while Montfort, coming from London, established himself at Strood, where he was separated from the town by the Medway. The town was well defended. Roger of Leybourne, in overall command, had stuffed the castle full of provisions and increased its garrison. He was joined by John de Warenne, Henry of Almain, William de Briouze, John fitzAlan and Reginald fitzPeter. By mid-April

---

[150] Later in 1264, when England was threatened with invasion, there were rumours that disturbances would be caused in Oxford by a multitude of Jews seeking to enter the town: *CR 1261–4*, 363–4. For the Jews of Winchester massacred by Simon de Montfort junior, see below, 440.

[151] For the siege, I am indebted to Summerson, 'Civil war and society: the impact of the siege of Rochester in 1264', which draws on Roger of Leybourne's financial accounts submitted later to the exchequer: TNA E 101/3/2 and TNA E 101/3/3. Montfort was lucky in having the support of the young baron Robert de Crevecoeur, the lord of Leeds and Chatham (although his income was much diminished by dower portions). He inherited at the age of twenty-four in May 1263. Montfort made him 'keeper of the peace': *CIM*, no. 728.

provender was being provided for 164 horses. Montfort, moreover, could not get across the Medway because the townsmen had pulled down the bridge on his side of the river and then used what was left on their side as bulwark from which they repulsed two assaults.

Montfort solved the problem with that mixture of stratagem and daring which were his hallmarks.[152] Towards evening on 18 April (Good Friday) he sent a fireboat down to burn the remains the bridge and in the resulting panic and confusion managed to cross the Medway and fight his way into the town. With Gilbert de Clare breaking in at the same time (the attacks were clearly co-ordinated), Rochester was soon in Montfort's hands. The next day, Easter eve (19 April), Montfort was able to take the bailey of the castle, but the great keep, to which a wounded Leybourne and the rest had retreated, still defied him, just as it had defied King John in 1215. It still seems to dominate the Medway estuary and the Rochester scene. The garrison was in good heart and celebrated Easter Day and the end of the Lenten fast by consuming eight sides of bacon, four and a half oxen, eight sheep and 1,400 eggs, all lubricated with quantities of wine and ale. Throughout the next week Montfort prosecuted the siege until on the night of Friday 25 April he learnt that the king's army was approaching.

Henry had heard of Montfort's attack on Rochester while he celebrated Easter Day (20 April) at Nottingham. The reaction, dictated one suspects by Edward, was immediate. Henry moved later in the day to Grantham, probably to get astride the main London road, and then hurried south. By 26 April he was at Aylesbury, having covered eighty miles (as the crow flies) from Grantham in five days, an average of sixteen miles a day, no small pace for what was probably a large army with many foot-soldiers and a long baggage train. Wykes indeed, describing the march, mentions nights without sleep. Henry then seems to have pressed ahead with just the cavalry, for by the evening of 26 April he was forty-five miles further on at Croydon, hardly more than twenty-five miles from Rochester.

Montfort had been half successful. He had brought the royalists south but had failed to take Rochester castle. Faced now with the prospect of the king's army severing his communications with London (where there were fresh rumours of insurrection), he returned during the night of 25–26 April to the capital. Hearing of Montfort's withdrawal, Henry was able to doubleback on 27 April and receive the surrender of Clare's castle at Kingston. He then pushed on to Rochester and broke up the remnants of the siege. Once again the initiative was firmly with the royalists. Wisely, instead of immediately investing London, they decided to make sure of the south-east. On 30 April, therefore, Henry was at Tonbridge where Clare's wife, Alice de Lusignan, surrendered the castle. He then marched south with the aim of securing the wavering allegiance of the Cinque Ports.

[152] Canterbury/Dover, 235; Pershore, *Flores*, 490.

One wonders naturally how Henry was bearing up during these days of martial movement, so unlike his sluggish campaigns in the past, so unlike his general sedentary way of life. Was he still managing to feed 100 paupers every day? Was he hearing again and again (as we know he did in 1265) the special mass in honour of Edward the Confessor? How he must have longed to return to the comfort of his homes and the consolations of Westminster Abbey. The glimpses we have of him at this time, however, show his anger and, in a gruesome episode, his revenge, at least against those outside the knightly class.

The route from Tonbridge to the coast took Henry's army by narrow ways through the hilly, wooded Weald of Kent and Sussex, where it was constantly sniped at by local archers organized in some cases by the Montfortian captain John de la Haye. On 2 May as the army passed through Goudhurst, Thomas the king's cook, riding out in front (perhaps to get ahead and prepare Henry's meal) was killed 'by a certain pleb'. In response that evening, at Flimwell near Ticehurst, 315 enemy archers were beheaded, allegedly in Henry's presence. According to the most detailed account, they had been tricked by Kings Richard's offer of peace into coming in to the king. It is only fair to add that Wykes, so shocked by the murder of the Jews, considered this justified revenge. Next day, Henry reached Battle abbey and was received by the monks 'in a solemn procession'. He showed them 'a face of anger' and extracted 100 marks from the abbot, saying that the latter's men had been amongst those executed at Flimwell and indeed had been encouraged by him. The Battle chronicler admitted the truth of the first charge but not the second, for 'at that time it was not in the power of lords to restrain their men from doing such things'.[153]

From Battle, the royal army moved on to Winchelsea, where some of the troops got drunk on its wine – a welcome relief from the dearth of provisions in the Weald – and Henry received oaths of fealty (secured with hostages) from the men of the Cinque Ports. The portsmen were now ordered to prepare a fleet for the blockade of London.

Henry must have felt sanguine about the course of events, even if he had contributed little to them. If the art of war is to keep the initiative and make the enemy dance to your tune, he had apparently succeeded. Only once, by attacking Rochester, had Montfort caught the royalists off balance. For the rest it was he who had done the dancing. Quite apart from the early failure to capture Gloucester, he had lost Northampton, Leicester, Nottingham, Kingston and Tonbridge, had failed to take Rochester, twice ignominiously returned to London and now faced a blockade of the capital. Edward had out generalled him completely. The situation, however, was about to change. On 6 May, Montfort's army marched out of London. From now on it was the great earl who would call the tune.

---

[153] BL Cotton MS Nero A IX, fo. 71v (a Mendicant chronicle with the detailed account of the Flimwell incident); Battle, 375; Wykes, 147–8. For Thomas, see *CPR 1258–66*, 134.

## THE BATTLE OF LEWES: THE PRELIMINARIES

The fact was that by bringing the king's army south, Montfort had wrought a complete change in the strategic situation. However successful that army's progress, it had sacrificed its position between the two centres of Montfortian power. Montfort could unite his forces. One man failed him, Robert de Ferrers, earl of Derby. After being with Montfort in London at the end of March, he had gone north, quite reasonably, to defend his properties from Edward's assault. But, instead of returning to join in the wider struggle, he went off to ravage Edward's lands. The climax came when he managed to secure hold of the castle of the Peak, thus realizing that long-standing family ambition.[154] By contrast, both Henry de Montfort and John Giffard left Kenilworth and joined the main army in London.

In marching out of London, Montfort had only one aim. To bring the king to battle. This was a decision of equal confidence and courage. Great set-piece battles were rare events. Not a single person on either side in 1264 had ever been in one. The political consequences could be decisive, as Bouvines and Lincoln had shown. The personal consequences could also be traumatic. If nobles were rarely killed, they faced, if captured, imprisonment and heavy ransoms. Montfort's army, moreover, was, as all accounts agree, considerably smaller than the king's. A leader with less clarity of mind and confidence in his cause might well have remained in London, seeking to disrupt the blockade and show the king he could not win. There might then have been negotiations for a compromise peace. But Montfort was not like that. He wanted total victory and believed, with God's help, he could have it. The only route to that victory was to win a decisive battle. Montfort, therefore, marched out of London to find the king and fight him 'with all for all'.[155]

Henry heard the news of Montfort's advance at Battle abbey on 9 May, whither he had returned from Winchelsea. He was taken completely by surprise, having intended to be in Canterbury on 12 May to meet the royalist troops being raised in the Weald. Henry's reaction was to set off at once for Lewes. The Battle abbey chronicler, observing the army's departure, noted it now behaved 'more cautiously' than before with Henry and the rest wearing armour. The army spent one night at Herstmonceux, feeding off the game in the park, and arrived at Lewes on 10 or 11 May. Edward established himself in the castle while Henry, no doubt with a sigh of relief, settled down in the great Cluniac priory of St Pancras in Southover, just outside the town's walls. On 12 May, Henry was able to enjoy the ceremonies and celebrations marking the patronal feast. With

---

[154] Battle, 376; Gilson, 'An unpublished notice of the battle of Lewes', 522; Rishanger, 20; Dunstable, 224. Coss, 'Retinues, agents and garrisons', 185.

[155] Like Charles I at Naseby but with different results. Just before leaving London, Montfort knighted a group of nobles, including John fitzJohn: Canterbury/Dover, 236.

Montfort's army heading for him, his move to Lewes made every sense. With its town walls, castle and priory, and its loyalist lord, John de Warenne, earl of Surrey, it was the one place in the vicinity where he could be both comfortable and secure.

Montfort himself set up camp on 11 May at Fletching, eight miles north of Lewes, a village dominated by his adjoining demesne manor at Sheffield and protected from surprise attack by the surrounding forest.[156] The town of Lewes is situated in a cleft in the South Downs through which the river Ouse runs southwards to the sea at Newhaven. On 12 May, Montfort's army advanced close to the town and took up station west of the Ouse in the belt of arable and grassland between the foot of the Downs and the start of the forest. Montfort now sent the bishop of Chichester and a party of friars to Henry with the offer of a settlement. The Provisions of Oxford were to be reaffirmed but doubtful points in them could be submitted to a panel of learned ecclesiastics. At the same time the bishops of London and Worcester offered around £30,000 both as compensation for the damage suffered by the royalists in the war and as inducement to accept the proffered peace.

It is striking that the three bishops were by Montfort's side at this time and doubtless they pressed him to make these final offers. The promise of £30,000 dealt with grievances over the destruction of property, although it was far smaller than the amount Henry had demanded. Few can really have thought the negotiations would succeed. The king's party had rejected a compromise over the Provisions back in March. They were hardly likely to accept one now after what seemed a successful war.[157] As before, Montfort wished to show he had done all he could in the cause of peace. He and his men could fight with a clear conscience and be seen to be doing so. It is possible nonetheless that Henry, faced with the frightening prospect of a battle, now wavered. A newsletter written soon afterwards claimed that he wished to accept the compromise, but was persuaded otherwise by Edward and King Richard.[158] *The Song of Lewes*, the great poem written soon after the battle, pictures Edward demanding the Montfortians appear with halters round their necks ready for drawing and hanging. Wykes has King Richard rejecting the 'form of peace', 'realising that, in effect, it threatened to disinherit the king of England and his heirs and depress their power'. That certainly got to the heart of the matter.[159]

---

[156] Sheffield Park is now a station on the preserved steam railway, the Bluebell Line. Gibbon, who often stayed at Sheffield Park, is buried in Fletching church.

[157] For the hopes of defections in the days before the battle: *CPR 1258–66*, 316–17; *CR 1264–8*, 383–5; and below, 376.

[158] Burton, '1264: some new documents', 323; and later Furness, 542–3; and Rishanger, 30.

[159] Wykes, 148–9.

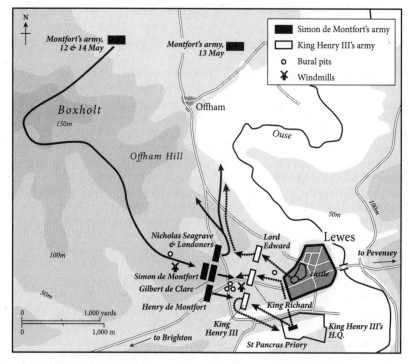

3. The Battle of Lewes

## THE BATTLE OF LEWES: THE ACTION, 14 MAY 1264

With parleys for peace ended, Montfort seized the initiative. On 13 May, from 'the wood by Lewes', 'the barons' sent a letter to Henry, authenticated with the seals of Montfort and Gilbert de Clare. It promised continuing fidelity to Henry himself but declared the intention of 'harming, as we are able, our enemies who are also yours and those of all your kingdom'. In his reply, Henry spurned these professions of loyalty, manifestly false, he said, given the general war being waged in the kingdom. Instead, he defied Montfort, Clare and their followers as his enemies. In an accompanying letter, one significantly angrier in tone, King Richard and Edward threw down their own gauntlets. They defied Montfort, Clare and their 'perfidious accomplices' as 'public enemies' and vowed to do all they could to injure their persons and properties. On receipt of these letters the Montfortians, like the rebels of 1215, withdrew their homage and fealty from the king.[160]

The royalists had reasons for confidence, for their army was much larger than that of the rebels. The size of the king's cavalry in contemporary

[160] For copies of the letters, see Maddicott, 'The Mise of Lewes', 589 and n. 2.

accounts is given variously as 1,200 knights (plus Edward's substantial force), 1,500 and 3,000; that of the Montfortians as only 200, or 500 properly armoured and more just with helmets. The newsletter mentioned above gives the royalists 10,000 men in all as against just 2,000 Montfortians. These figures need to be treated with caution coming as they do from Montfortian partisans. The greater the odds the more miraculous the victory. The Londoners on Montfort's side, as well as a contingent of Welshmen, must have evened out the number of foot-soldiers. Yet even the royalist Wykes thought Henry had far the larger army.[161]

Nor surprisingly given its numerical superiority, Henry's army had been far from simply sheltering in Lewes. It was eager for action but faced a problem set by Montfort's generalship. Since the Montfortian army was north of Lewes and west of the Ouse, the only way to attack it was through a marshy defile less than 500 yards wide between the river and the Downs at Offham. When Montfort, on 13 May, having issued his letter of defiance, moved nearer to Lewes, his aim was probably to lure the king's army into this treacherous terrain. Wisely it refused to be drawn, but that left the initiative in Montfort's hands. Again he seized it to purpose. During the night of 13–14 May he marched his army up an ancient droveway onto the top of the Downs. His destination was an area called Boxholt, some three miles northwest of Lewes and thus far enough away for the move to go undetected. Boxholt was also well suited for a rendezvous, being the customary meeting-place of the southern hundreds of the Rape of Lewes.[162]

At Boxholt, Montfort's army sorted itself out and had something to eat and drink. It then proceeded south-east until it reached its final station on the edge of the Downs immediately above the town, a spot marked by a great windmill. From here, as dawn broke (sunrise was around four a.m.), Montfort could see Lewes laid out before him, its houses dwarfed by the great priory and the castle with Edward's banner flying from the keep. The open downland, cropped by sheep, descended to the walls of the town.[163] The only significant buildings in the way, alongside the road running out of Lewes, were a leper house, another windmill (known as Snelling's mill) and St Anne's church. This was ideal terrain for a battle

---

[161] Wykes, 149.

[162] The location of Boxholt is known thanks to John Bleach and Christopher Whittick, who discovered it on a map of 1772. Whittick's research showed it was a hundredal meeting place. See Carpenter and Whittick, 'The battle of Lewes', 50–1, and ns. 57, 59. I have done the walk up onto the Downs many times and in all weathers (once when it was pouring down like stair rods) around the anniversary of the battle with the students from my Special Subject group on the reign of Henry III. There is no contemporary comment about the weather on the day.

[163] Houses have now encroached on the lower downland and, bar some bare walls, nothing is left of the priory, but the castle still rises above the town and early on a May morning, from the top of the Downs, it is easy to imagine what Montfort saw. Given the change in the calendar in the eighteenth century, 14 May in 1264 is more like 27 May today.

and all the advantage was with the Montfortians, who could charge down the hill while the royalists struggled up.

Montfort now prepared his men for the coming conflict. He knighted a group of nobles, including Gilbert de Clare, and addressed the troops. Their cause was just. They were fighting for the kingdom of England and the honour of God. The soldiers threw themselves to the ground with arms extended in the form of a cross and prayed for victory. They confessed their sins and received absolution from the bishops of Worcester and Chichester. White crosses were donned both as distinguishing marks and to signify the holy nature of the cause. 'In the history of the Provisions as a holy cause . . . this was perhaps the culminating moment.'[164]

Montfort's march up onto the Downs had worked to perfection. The Franciscan friar Richard of Durham liked to think that the royalists had spent much of the night enjoying wine, women and song before the very altars of the priory, although if so they would not have had Henry's approval. According to another story, all were asleep when roused by a returning foraging party with the news of Montfort's approach. Henry's shock when he saw the banners of the rebel army waving on the top of the Downs may be imagined. Without martial energy and expertise, he could hardly share his son's excitement at the thought of action. In the anxious period before the battle, Henry had sought to put himself right with God. On 13 May, reaffirming the assignment made at Amiens, he wrote to King Louis asking for the £450 promised for the Holy Land to be given to John de Valenciennes. This was all the more important, Henry explained, because circumstances might prevent him fulfilling his vow to go in person![165] On the morning of the battle, his mind turned to Queen Eleanor. If anything did go wrong, she and Edmund would have to sustain his cause. And so Henry tried to ensure that Eleanor received from Louis all the money still due under the Treaty of Paris. In the surrounding hubbub of men rushing to arms, there were no chancery staff present and so the resulting letter was written out in his own hand by the chancellor of King Richard. Present were Henry, Edward, King Richard, Henry of Almain and Roger of Leybourne.[166]

The main business of this meeting must have been to decide the royal line of battle. It was arranged into three divisions: Edward's was placed on the right beyond the castle, King Richard's in the centre in front of Snelling's mill, and Henry's on the left beyond the priory. These corresponded to Montfort's divisions up on the hill where on the left, opposite

---

[164] Maddicott, *Simon de Montfort*, 271, and for Powicke's evocative description of the mood, *The Thirteenth Century*, 188.

[165] *CPR 1258–66*, 317.

[166] *F*, i, 440 (*CPR 1258–66*, 317). For Eleanor's need for such a letter which acknowledged that Louis had paid all the money, see Gavrilovitch, *Étude sur la traité de Paris de 1259*, 120–1; Blaauw, *The Barons' War*, 358–9; Howell, *Eleanor of Provence*, 207.

Edward, were the Londoners with Nicholas of Seagrave, Henry de Hastings and Geoffrey de Lucy; in the centre were Gilbert de Clare, John fitzJohn and William de Munchesney; and on the right Montfort's sons Henry and Guy. There was also a fourth division under Montfort himself, presumably held in reserve. Until he charged, Montfort had far more command and control than Henry and Edward. Since the terrain outside the town is like a saddle, falling away sharply on either side of Richard's central position, neither Henry nor Edward could see what was happening to each other.

So the battle began. The royalists advanced up the hill and the Montfortians came down to meet them. On the right, Edward smashed into the Londoners and put them to flight. Some scattered across the Downs, others rushed north and were drowned trying to cross the Ouse. Three unfortunate citizens, imprisoned in a coach flying Montfort's standard for refusing to fight against the king, were butchered before they could make explanations.[167] Edward kept up the pursuit for some miles, slaughtering the lightly armed foot-soldiers of the city militia and taking ample revenge for the treatment of his mother. Quite probably the flower of the royal army was with him, and certainly, in his absence, disaster overtook the remaining royalist divisions. Montfort's centre, coming down the hill, collided with King Richard's division near the leper house and drove it back in disorder towards the town. Richard himself, king of the Romans, 'semper Augustus', was forced to take refuge in Snelling's mill. 'Come out, come out, you worst of millers', chanted the surrounding throng.

Montfort's right, meanwhile, attacked Henry's own division as it struggled in the difficult sloping ground beyond the priory. For Henry himself the clash of arms must have been terrifying. He was fifty-seven years old and not in the best of health. He had campaigned in Wales and France, he had witnessed the battle of Northampton, he had worn armour, but he had never personally been in a fight. There is no evidence he had even attended tournaments. Had he ever before drawn a sword other than to admire its craftsmanship? Had he ever before worn a helmet other than to try it briefly for size. Now he had to wear a helmet in earnest, enduring its heat, claustrophobia and limited vision. It was soon worse than that. For all his entourage could do to protect him, the fighting reached Henry himself. According to the chronicler of Lewes priory, he had two horses killed under him and was much beaten with swords and maces. The chronicler does not say that Henry did any beating back! Around him the judge William of Wilton was killed and the clerk William of Axmouth, paymaster to the king's knights and serjeants, badly wounded. (He died later of his injuries.) Philip Basset, fighting with great valour, refused to surrender so long as he could stand and was finally taken covered with wounds. Perhaps Montfort

---

[167] Wykes, 150. The episode is much elaborated in Melrose, 196. Wykes says the flying of the standard above the coach was a decoy, intending to give the impression that Montfort was within it, but I doubt if this was the case.

himself got near the king. Certainly his standard bearer, William le Blund, was amongst the fatalities. Eventually, however, Henry's attendants extricated him from the fray and got him back to the priory. The morning was hardly over. The Lewes chronicle states that the 'greater part' of the king's army was destroyed between sunrise and noon.

When Edward at last returned to Lewes from his pursuit of the Londoners, the Montfortians came out to meet him. Battle again was joined and John de Warenne, William de Valence, Guy de Lusignan and Hugh Bigod fled, taking the disastrous news to Queen Eleanor in France. Edward with his remaining force circled the town before managing to join his battered and bruised father in the priory.

The priory itself had its own wall and was defendable. The royalists still held the castle and an important prisoner in John Giffard. (Aspiring to strike the first blow he had been taken early in the fight.)[168] Meanwhile arrows from the castle had set a large part of the town alight, while the number of dead and wounded in the streets made it difficult for the Montfortians, careering about, to distinguish friend from foe. Montfort's first instinct was to attack the priory and indeed his arrows set fire to the church. But the flames were soon extinguished and the attack was abandoned. For reasons of conscience and reputation, Montfort shied away from storming a religious institution. But a siege, allowing time for royalist forces to rally from elsewhere in the country, was equally dangerous. Montfort needed to seal his victory with a quick settlement. To that end, he threatened to execute King Richard and Philip Basset if the king did not accept his terms, or at least so a later royalist account of the battle believed.[169] But he also offered concessions.

On the evening of the battle, therefore, and for much of the next day friars shuttled between the sides with Montfort's proposals. Initially Edward was defiant and wanted to go out again to fight, but Henry himself had had enough. So it was that on 15 May a settlement, known as the Mise of Lewes, was reached.[170] Henry and Edward both surrendered, Henry giving up his little-used sword to Gilbert de Clare and thus escaping the humiliation of surrendering it to Montfort. It was agreed that the Provisions of Oxford should stand unbroken and, to underline the point, Henry swore to remove all his evil councillors both foreign and native born. This looked like total victory, but Montfort made two concessions. The first concerned the marcher barons. Mortimer, Clifford, Lestrange

---

[168] For conflicting evidence about John Giffard at the battle, see Carpenter and Whittick, 'The battle of Lewes', 65 n. 92. Robert of Gloucester, ii, lines 11,470–2, also implies Giffard was taken early in the battle.

[169] Merton, *Flores*, 260.

[170] For its terms, which do not survive in any official copy, see Maddicott, 'The Mise of Lewes'. The summaries of the Mise he prints there may have derived from a newsletter, see Burton, '1264: some new documents', 318–20, 323–5.

and their ally Roger of Leybourne had been with Edward in the battle and had ended up with him in the priory. Now Montfort agreed they could all go free. Given that he and Mortimer were already deadly enemies, this seems an astonishing decision. Montfort must have made it realizing that otherwise there would be no settlement. He also insisted that in return for their release and as security more generally for maintaining the peace, both Edward and Henry of Almain should become hostages.[171] Doubtless, in the euphoria of victory, he thought this would be enough to keep the marchers quiet. He was wrong and they would come to play a major part in his downfall.

The second concession concerned the Provisions of Oxford and was little more than a sop to ease the surrender, although it may also have appealed to Montfort's episcopal allies. If anything in the Provisions needed 'correction' it was to be 'corrected' by four of the 'more noble' English bishops or magnates. If they disagreed, a decision was to be given by Louis IX's brother Charles of Anjou and the duke of Burgundy. Once Henry and Edward were safely out of the priory and in Montfort's hands, nothing more was heard of this proposal.

Alongside this scheme of arbitration, there was to be another. It was to begin with Louis IX convening a panel of three French prelates and three nobles. The purpose, apparently, was to set in train a process leading to the modification or nullification of the Mise of Amiens, thus putting Montfort's regime on a secure footing. Surely, after his great victory, Louis would recognize that the Provisions were indeed 'holy'. This scheme too came to nothing.

Finally, the Mise also dealt with some immediate issues. Henry pardoned those who had fought against him and restored their lands. The prisoners taken by the royalists at Northampton were to be released. Those taken by the Montfortians at Lewes were to be retained until ransomed by their captors. Underlining the extent of the victory, the prisoners included Humphrey de Bohun, earl of Hereford (his eldest son fighting on the other side), Roger de Somery, John fitzAlan, John Comyn, Robert de Brus, Henry de Percy and the turncoat William Bardolph.

Montfort now hoped that the kingdom would settle down in peace and one feature of the conflict did give some hope in that direction. Northampton and Lewes were the last of the chivalric battles. To be sure, the king's army had marched out of Oxford with banners flying. That symbolized that death and destruction awaited its enemies.[172] But while townsmen were slaughtered at Northampton, that was not the fate of the rebel knights. Young Simon, taken in arms against the king, was clearly a traitor. His life was forfeit as was that of the knights caught fighting in the town.[173] Henry himself, his blood

---

[171] *CPR 1258–66*, 374; Dunstable, 232.
[172] Ambler, *Song of Simon de Montfort*, 274–5.
[173] For the nature of treason, see below, 470 n. 73.

up, had sworn to hang the Oxford clerks fighting under their own banner. But nothing like this happened. Despite all the bitterness, chivalric conventions held. Edward himself, according to Wykes, protected young Simon. The Montfortians simply went off to captivity, Simon and Peter de Montfort to Windsor castle.[174] Nothing happened to the clerks either. It was pointed out to Henry that their many relations on the king's side would never permit their execution, and, characteristically, he was soon placated.[175]

Lewes was much the same. Before the battle, Edward had demanded the Montfortians appear with ropes round their necks, ready for execution. The dramatic (and widely copied) letters of defiance issued before the battle meant that both sides were freed from all rules and could attack and kill each other without let or hindrance.[176] Yet, in the event, at Lewes, the nobles did not kill each other. No more than a handful of knights are known to have perished. There was one suspicious death on Montfort's side, that of Ralph of Imworth. Perhaps his enemy Robert Aguillon made sure he was finished off.[177] But other deaths were probably due to falls from horses and unlucky thrusts through armour. In general, when knights could not fight on, they offered to surrender and their surrenders were accepted. Phillip Basset was badly wounded but not finished off. John Giffard was taken back to the castle. A variety of factors were at work here. There were many family connections between the sides. Philip Basset, according to one account, was rescued by his son-in-law, Hugh Despenser. The prospect of ransom gave every reason to take prisoners. And then there was simply the long tradition of not killing knightly opponents. At the decisive battle of Lincoln in 1217, the only great noble killed, and that accidentally by a chance thrust through his vizer, was the count of Perche and everyone was sorry about that. Of course, many people were killed at Lewes. In 1810 three pits were discovered near the leper house, each containing an estimated 500 bodies. At the time, a widely quoted figure for the fatalities, as counted by those who buried them, was 2,700 (or sometimes 2,070).[178] These, however, were almost certainly the bodies of lightly armoured foot-soldiers.[179] At Lewes, the heavily armoured knights had a wonderful time killing everyone else. At Evesham next year it was to be very different.

---

[174] Treharne, 'The battle of Northampton', 312–14.

[175] Guisborough, 190.

[176] For discussion, see Carpenter, 'From King John to the first English duke', 29–35.

[177] For their quarrel, see above, 170. For Aguillon receiving Imworth's lands: *CPR 1258–66*, 315; Stewart, *RJS*, no. 623; *CR Supp*, no. 336. Aguillon appropriately means a sharp point or a goad and so 'a nickname for an irritating person'. I wonder if the single fleur de lys on Robert's arms was meant to have a sharp point.

[178] Burton, '1264: some new documents', 318, 323; Blaauw, 'On the early history of Lewes priory', 29.

[179] Canterbury/Dover, 237, comments specifically on the number of foot-soldiers killed on the baronial side.

Chapter 9

# MONTFORT VICTORIOUS: FROM THE BATTLE OF LEWES TO THE PARLIAMENT OF 1265

'The Lord has many times brought over us the waves of his indignation, by his just judgment, for man suffers nothing unjustly.' So wrote the bishop of Lincoln to John Mansel in 1261.[1] Did Henry feel the same after the catastrophe of Lewes? On the eve of the battle he had worried about his failure to crusade. Was that the reason now why God had punished him? Or did it lie in the failures of his rule laid bare by the baronial case at Amiens? But perhaps Henry thought none of these things, preferring to place the disaster within an altogether more fundamental and universal setting. For was not Montfort an agent of the Devil in the last days before the end of time?

Adam Marsh had once explained how the Devil, 'by his breath, by his embrace, and his deadly lash, produces mortally dangerous division. At the present day, the last of the perilous times that are now upon us, he stirs up deadly discord . . . so as utterly to destroy the offspring of peace. With his lash inflicting violent injuries, with confusion seducing men with massive deception . . . he ceases not to harass the whole world with his monstrous insolence'.[2] For Marsh, therefore, the end of time was not some remote event, it was already in progress. Indeed, many believed that some of the portents described so mysteriously yet compellingly in St John's Book of Revelations had already come to pass. Were not, for example, the two witnesses who challenged the Antichrist, the two new mendicant orders? Marsh himself, in writing of deadly discord in the letter quoted above, was merely urging the prior of Christ Church Canterbury to settle a dispute with Robert Grosseteste. But clearly the idea that the Devil was loose could, on a grander scale, explain the turmoil and tragedy of 1264.

Henry himself was familiar with the terrible events of the last days for they were graphically portrayed in illustrated Apocalypses.[3] One of the most splendid, now known as the Trinity Apocalypse, was quite likely

[1] TNA SC 1/7/17. I thank Daniel Hadas for the translation.

[2] *Letters of Adam Marsh*, i, 230–1. See Power, 'The uncertainties of reformers', 6, 10. The Devil was frequently portrayed as a dragon as in St John's Book of the Apocalypse.

[3] Morgan, 'Illustrated apocalypses of mid thirteenth-century England', 3.

owned either by Eleanor of Provence or her daughter-in-law Eleanor of
Castile.[4] Here Henry would have seen Antichrist in the form of a seven-
headed beast, leading out his force of heavily armoured warriors, sitting
astride splendidly caparisoned horses. And one of those warriors carried
a shield depicting none other than the arms of Simon de Montfort – a
silver lion with a forked tail on a red background.[5] The Trinity Apocalypse
is usually dated to the mid-1250s, so whether the reference to Montfort was
intended (as opposed to these just being attractive arms) may be questioned, but a decade later the identification would have been irresistible.
Montfort was in the army of the Antichrist.[6]

If Henry did take an Apocalyptic view of Montfort's rule, he could also
draw some comfort from it. In the Trinity Apocalypse, the very next
image, after the army of the beast, showed an angel pushing the beast
down into the jaws of hell, while the bodies of his knights lie prostrate and
as food for birds.[7] The commentary to the final section of the Trinity
Apocalypse assured readers of the rewards of divine justice and ended
with a prayer begging for Christ's protection from enemies without and
vices within.[8] Henry, with all his works of piety, might feel sufficiently
purged of internal vice. As for the attacks of his enemies, ultimately they
would surely be defeated, however much Henry might sometimes cry out
'How long, Oh Lord, how long?' Henry had far from lost faith in the
Confessor. Indeed, during the period of Montfortian rule, he was, as we
will see, assiduously appealing to his patron saint for help.

## THE ORDINANCE FOR THE GOVERNMENT
## OF THE REALM, JUNE 1264

The most detailed account of the days immediately following the battle of
Lewes is found in the Canterbury/Dover chronicle.[9] Henry, with Edward,
King Richard and Henry of Almain were taken by Montfort first to

[4] McKitterick, *The Trinity Apocalypse*, 93, and plate 15(b). For a discussion of possible
ownership, see Morgan, 'Illustrated apocalypses of mid thirteenth-century England',
15–16, and Short, 'Introduction', 135.

[5] McKitterick, *The Trinity Apocalypse*, plate 15(b), and 93 from Revelations 19:17–19.
Images are available online if one puts into a search engine 'Wren Digital Library' and
goes from there. The beast leading his army is on fo. 23r.

[6] For the date, see Morgan, 'The Trinity Apocalypse', 27–30. The arms were differenced
from those of Montfort by having a green border. Slater, *Art and Political Thought*, 147–51,
believes that the warrior with Montfort's shield is the one in a red surcoat. In the next
image the latter is prominent amongst the slain in the army of the beast. She, therefore,
suggests the Trinity Apocalypse may date to after Evesham. However, to my mind, the
red warrior is not the one with the shield. His arm does not reach far enough across to
grasp it.

[7] McKitterick, *The Trinity Apocalypse*, plate 17 (fo. 23v).

[8] Morgan, 'Illustrated apocalypses of mid thirteenth-century England', 17.

[9] Canterbury/Dover, 238–9; Dunstable, 232–3.

Canterbury, where they all arrived on Tuesday 20 May, Gilbert de Clare was also in the party. The next four or five days were spent in continuous debate about 'public affairs', although whether Henry, Richard and Edward had much input may be doubted. Eventually, on Sunday 25 May, Montfort with Henry and King Richard departed for London while the two hostages, Edward and Henry of Almain, were taken by Henry de Montfort off to captivity in Dover castle. All the aliens expelled from Henry's and Edward's service now crossed the Channel under oath never to return 'to the land of England'. Meanwhile, the households of both Edward and Henry of Almain were purged by Henry de Montfort. The two princes were alone.

Montfort arrived in Rochester on Tuesday 26 May. Denied entry to the castle, he swore not to dine until it was surrendered. When the castellan refused to comply without an order from the king, Montfort began preparations for an assault. This did the trick. The garrison came across to the cathedral priory and entered the chapter house where they gave up the castle to Henry and Montfort together. Montfort then appointed Richard de Grey as its keeper. This scene in the chapter house of Rochester is one of the few placing Montfort and Henry together during the period of Montfortian rule. The two men spent little time in each other's company. At Rochester itself Henry was staying in the priory, Montfort, with King Richard, in the hospital at Strood across the Medway.[10] Henry must have hated the very sight of Montfort. Montfort must at the very least have found Henry's presence uncomfortable, having to go through the forms of obedience to a man he had cast down.

There is no description of Montfort's triumphal entry into London on 28 May with two captive kings in his train. What an extraordinary sight for the celebrating citizens! Montfort placed King Richard 'ignominiously' in the Tower.[11] He allowed Henry to spend a couple of days at Westminster before lodging him in the bishop's house at St Paul's.

Montfort's discussions at Canterbury must have included the precise structure for the new government. The Mise of Lewes had said that, apart from the revision of details, the Provisions of Oxford were to stand 'unbroken'. But what did that mean? After all, there was no possibility of reviving 1258's council of fifteen. The answer was provided by an 'Ordinance' issued in June 1264 at a parliament that Montfort convoked in London.[12] Under its terms, three 'electors' were to be chosen with power to appoint and remove (if they behaved badly) nine councillors of the king. Of the nine, at least three were always to be at court. On the advice of the nine, Henry was to dispose of the affairs of the kingdom and appoint his officials 'great and small'. The castellans, justiciar, chancellor and treasurer were

[10] For the hospital, see *VCH Kent*, ii, 228–9.
[11] Wykes, 153; FitzThedmar, 63 (Stone, FitzThedmar, no. 798).
[12] *DBM*, 294–9.

specifically mentioned The Ordinance itself did not give the names of the electors and the councillors but they too were settled at the parliament. The electors were Montfort himself, Gilbert de Clare and Stephen of Bersted, bishop of Chichester. The nine councillors were Henry of Sandwich, bishop of London, Humphrey de Bohun junior, Adam de Newmarch, Peter de Montfort, Roger de St John, Ralph de Camoys and Giles de Argentan, together with two clerks (unchosen at first), one of whom was supposed to be chancellor and the other the treasurer.[13] Initially, Hugh Despenser had been one of the nine, but he was soon replaced (by Humphrey de Bohun), probably because, as with Hugh Bigod in 1258, it was thought better for the justiciar to be outside the council, Hugh Despenser having returned to the justiciarship immediately after Lewes.[14]

The form for electing the council echoed that in 1258, when four electors had chosen the council of fifteen. The difference was that this time the electors were to remain permanently in being over and above the council. The whole constitution was Montfort's devising, designed to entrench and enhance his authority. Instead of having to share power with eight other councillors, he had to share it with only two, and since one was the devoted Stephen of Bersted, he would always come out on top. Montfort could also be sure of the council of nine. Bishop Sandwich of London was as committed to his cause as was Bersted. As for the lay members, given that Humphrey de Bohun had yet to succeed to the earldom of Hereford, none of them had anything like Montfort's power and status. At most they were magnates of middle rank. Bohun, Adam de Newmarch and Giles de Argentan had all proved their loyalty in the struggles since 1258. Peter de Montfort's connections with the great earl went back much longer.

Equally dependable was the new man, Roger de St John, who for the first time emerges as a major player at this level. He was certainly worth having for, lord of Great Barton and Stanton St John in Oxfordshire, Swallowfield in Berkshire and Godstone in Surrey, he was a knight with an income of baronial proportions. In his mid-forties he was also no 'jeune'. In 1262, St John had been allowed to fortify his house at Godstone, so, although never close, he was still on terms with the king.[15] Next year he is absent from the lists of Montfort's supporters. His emergence now was probably due to his relationship with Hugh Despenser for he was married to Hugh's sister.[16] A latecomer to Montfort's cause, he stood with him to

---

[13] The appointments of the treasurer and chancellor will be seen below.

[14] Denholm-Young, 'Documents of the Barons' Wars', 162–3; *DBM*, 295 n. 3; Burton, '1264: some new documents', 320–1, 325. The constitution is fully analysed in Maddicott, *Simon de Montfort*, 285–9.

[15] He had gone on the 1253 expedition to Gascony and received some reward. For his career, see *CR 1251–3*, 389; *CPR 1247–58*, 231, 263; *CPR 1258–66*, 199; *CChR 1257–1300*, 56. There is a history of the family in Cokayne, *Complete Peerage*, xi, 340–51, with Roger at 348.

[16] He had been the ward of Hugh's uncle, Geoffrey Despenser: *Patent Rolls 1225–32*, 323.

the end. The only man amongst the nine whom Montfort might doubt was Ralph de Camoys. Another newcomer at this level, he was in his forties and, if heavily in debt to the Jews, possessed of a considerable estate. But unlike St John, he had no Montfortian connections. Rather, he was a major tenant of Gilbert de Clare and almost certainly owed to Clare his place on the council. It says something for the balance of power that Camoys was the only man Clare had there.[17]

Montfort thus hardly needed the power of dismissal to keep the council in line but it was always there as a threat. The setup had another advantage. Montfort was not tied to court. He could safely leave much of the business there to the councillors, while he held his own court wherever he was. Throughout the period of his power he was issuing letters in his own name threatening enemies, encouraging friends and ordering about royal officials.[18] He had a considerable entourage. In July 1264 he was allowed to travel with horses and arms because of the hostages and prisoners he had with him.[19] Montfort's court, more than the king's, was now the centre of the realm.

None of this meant that the constitution was completely oligarchic and lacked any wider consent. The Ordinance laid down that 'the community of the prelates and barons' could, if it felt necessary, remove and replace any of the three electors. So the three were ultimately answerable to parliament. The Ordinance itself was made with the consent of the prelates, barons and 'community there present'.[20] It was sealed by the bishops of Lincoln and Ely, by Humphrey de Bohun junior, William de Munchesney, the mayor of London, Thomas fitzThomas, and, more surprisingly, by Roger Bigod, earl of Norfolk. So the old earl, on the king's side at the time of the Mise of Amiens, absent from the battle of Lewes, was now going along with the new regime. Another witness was a young earl, Robert de Vere, earl of Oxford. Robert's father, Hugh de Vere, of age in 1231, had played little part in public affairs before his death in 1263. To be sure the Veres were poor earls, but still, with their great castle at Hedingham, they could wield considerable power in Essex and Suffolk. Robert had actually done homage to the king for Hedingham and the rest of his estates in March 1264, but he had then, a young man in his early twenties, fought

---

[17] Camoys had manors in seven counties. For him, see *CIPM*, no. 443; *CChR 1257–1300*, 49; *CPR 1258–66*, 199; and *CIM*, nos. 639, 697, 699 (showing his connection to Clare), 715. For the family, see Cokayne, *Complete Peerage*, ii, 506–12. Clare's man Hervey of Boreham was also active in central government and became a justice of the bench as well as keeper of Hadleigh castle: Brand, 'Hervey of Boreham'; Moore, 'Government and locality in Essex', 251–2.

[18] For example, Stewart, *RJS*, no. 84; *Merton College Rolls*, 22.

[19] *CPR 1258–66*, 337.

[20] *DBM*, 296–9. Likewise, 'the bishops, earls, barons and clergy and people of England' gave their assent to Bishop Bersted, Montfort and Clare going ahead and electing the council: Gilson, 'The parliament of 1264', 500.

for Montfort at Lewes, being knighted by him before the battle. He was to become another devoted follower of the earl.[21]

Officially, the Ordinance of June 1264 was only to last until the process of arbitration agreed at Lewes had been completed. In fact, Montfort saw it as a constitution that was quite likely to continue throughout Henry's lifetime and into the reign of his son. Later, indeed, this was stated specifically. Montfort, therefore, made no discernible move to set in train the English arbitration with its brief to correct anything amiss in the Provisions. As the chronicler Nicholas Trevet later put it, once Montfort had got the kingdom's castles under his control, 'he became more difficult about treating for peace according to the promised form since he now had the king and all the kingdom in his power'.[22]

## THE SUMMONS OF KNIGHTS TO
## THE JUNE 1264 PARLIAMENT

The reference to the 'community' agreeing to the Ordinance of June 1264, as well as the prelates and barons, was no mere rhetoric, a point which introduces the most striking and original feature of the June parliament. For to it were summoned four knights from each county to 'treat of the affairs of king and kingdom'. They were to represent 'all of the county' and be elected by the county, presumably in the county court.[23]

Montfort had attempted such a step before during the crisis of 1261, for with Bishop Cantilupe and Richard de Clare he had summoned three knights from each county to the assembly at St Albans.[24] But now the summons was in the king's name to an 'official' parliament, not to some baronial assembly the king tried to prevent. Montfort was thus moving decisively beyond the parliament envisaged by the Provisions of Oxford where there had been no reference to knightly representatives. Instead, those who were to attend parliament and discuss 'the common business', 'on behalf of all the community of the land', were simply twelve magnates chosen 'by the community' or, in another version, rather giving the game away, chosen 'by the barons'.[25] Evidently, in 1258, 'the barons' still felt able to answer for the realm. In 1264 they were no longer expected to do so. This was an important moment in parliamentary history, creating, at least in embryo, a House of Commons.

---

[21] For Robert de Vere, see Cokayne, *Complete Peerage*, x, 216–17; and Maddicott, 'Follower, leader, pilgrim, saint', 216.

[22] Trevet, 261.

[23] *DBM*, 292–3. See Maddicott, *Origins of the English Parliament*, 254–6, for a full discussion of the parliament.

[24] See above, 216.

[25] *DBM*, 104–5, cap. 10; 110–11, cap. 22.

The only precedent for the summons of June 1264 was in February 1254 when two knights from each county were to come to parliament, in order to say how much taxation the counties were prepared to grant. They only came, however, because the king's tenants-in-chief were exempted from the tax, being about to campaign with the king in Gascony. Had they not been, the tenants-in-chief would probably have answered for the realm by themselves, as they had always done before. That was still Henry's expectation in 1258 when he demanded the Sicilian tax from the Westminster parliament. At the Oxford parliament, two months later, it was just a committee of twenty-four magnates, 'chosen by the community', who were to consider the tax promised by the king.[26]

Behind the summons lay hard political facts. With limited baronial support, Montfort looked to the shire knights to endorse his new constitution and provide a basis for the continuation of his rule. In all this Montfort felt he was on safe ground. He had organized the opposition in the shires to the king's recovery of power in 1261, felt the enthusiasm for the anti-alien programme in 1263, and seen all the knights fighting alongside him at Lewes. The knights would not let him down.

Montfort, then, had clear political reasons for summoning the knights. He may also have been influenced by ideas about representation and consent held by the churchmen so prominent in his movement.[27] Bishop Cantilupe indeed had joined with Montfort and Richard de Clare in the summons of 1261. The Fourth Lateran Council had laid down that taxation of the church for secular purposes needed the consent of the bishop and his clergy. In Henry's reign this was taken as meaning that consent had to be sought not merely from the bishops but also from the lower clergy, from deans and chapters and parish priests. In 1240, according to Matthew Paris, the bishops obstructed an attempt, this time by the pope, to tax the lower clergy with the declaration that 'this affair touches all: all therefore ought to be convoked; without them it is neither fitting nor expedient to reply.'[28] The Roman law tag 'quod omnes tangit ab omnibus approbetur' ('what touches all shall be approved by all') was familiar long before it was cited by Edward I when summoning his parliament of 1295. In 1254 itself the summons of the knights had probably been modelled on parallel ecclesiastical procedure. Just as the sheriffs were to explain the king's needs in the county courts, whereafter knights would come to parliament to say what tax they would grant, so the bishops were to speak to the assembled clergy of their diocese, whereafter delegates would appear on the same day as the knights with the reply from the lower clergy. At the parliament of 1264 (like that of 1265) taxation was not the issue, but the principle of consent could equally apply to the fundamental changes now being proposed in the governance of the realm.

---

[26] *DBM*, 104–7, cap. 11.

[27] For what follows, see Carpenter, *Reign of Henry III*, 400–2.

[28] Paris, iv, 37.

How many knights actually turned up to the June 1264 parliament is unknown. The timetable was short, reflecting the urgency of the situation: the writs went out on 4 June and the knights were to appear on the 22nd. As a result, one suspects they were often chosen informally rather than in any meeting of the county court. It was probably in anticipation of absentees that four knights were to come from each county, as opposed to three in 1261 and two in 1254. Montfort was determined to get his knights. Had they all appeared, they would have numbered 140, more probably than the prelates and magnates combined.[29]

To be more sure of knightly support, Montfort did something for the local reforms so important in the shires. There was a wholesale change of sheriffs, mostly carried through during the course of the parliament. In all, twenty-two new sheriffs were appointed covering thirty-two counties.[30] The appointments were made in the form 'provided by the king and the barons' and that form was in accord with the Provisions of Oxford. As in 1258, all the new men were appointed as custodians who were expected to account for all the issues of their shires. The implication (although not spelt out) was that, as proposed in 1258, they should receive allowances to cover their expenses. In 1258–9 the system had not worked and was soon abandoned.[31] Whether it would have worked better under Montfort there was never time to find out, but its revival was designed as a popular move. Nearly all the new sheriffs held property in the shires to which they were appointed and were 'solid local landholders', just as had been the case in 1258. It seems highly likely that they were either chosen by the county knights at the parliament or chosen from them, in which case the counties had a large say in the appointments, just as had been proposed in 1259. Nine of the sheriffs had been knights on the county panels appointed in 1258 to investigate local abuse; seven had acted as sheriffs for the reform regime between 1258 and 1260. At least one (Simon of Pattishall in Bedfordshire–Buckinghamshire) later regarded Montfort as a saint.

While Montfort reached out to the knights, at the parliament he also taught a sharp lesson to barons unreconciled to his rule. William de Briouze was lord of Gower in Wales and Bramber and Knepp in Sussex. Given a money fee by the king in 1261, his estates ravaged by the Montfortians in 1263, he was, not surprisingly, one of the king's party referring the dispute to Louis IX. In April 1264 he was with John de Warenne in the garrison of Rochester.[32] In Sussex itself Briouze was at odds with Simon de Montfort junior, who was busy building up his power

---

[29] Maddicott, *Origins of the English Parliament*, 256.

[30] For the detail which follows about the sheriffs, see Cassidy, 'Simon de Montfort's sheriffs', 6–10. See also Moore, 'Local administration during the period of reform and rebellion', 85.

[31] See above, 34.

[32] *CPR 1258–66*, 147; *CIM*, no. 731. For William, see Cokayne, *Complete Peerage*, ii, 302–3.

in the county. Simon junior now complained that, thanks to Briouze, his fishponds had been poisoned, his woods and parks destroyed, his men captured and tortured, and his castle at Sedgwick (once John Mansel's) pulled down.[33] Doubtless Simon junior had given as good as he got, but only his sufferings were considered. Henry de Montfort, Hugh Despenser and Henry de Hastings were appointed to do the job. They declared that Briouze, having agreed to accept their award over the compensation due to Simon (surely untrue), had then failed to turn up. Hardly surprising because Simon's losses were put at an absurd 10,000 marks. Under the award, he was now to hold Knepp castle, with its park, and have Briouze's eldest son as hostage, until Briouze gave sureties for paying the whole amount. The date of the award was 30 June and since the money was to be paid within a fortnight, clearly impossible, this was just a way of giving Knepp to young Simon and placing Briouze entirely in his power. The award was witnessed by some of the usual suspects – John Giffard, Nicholas of Seagrave, Robert de Ros, John de la Ware and John de Vescy. But, a striking indication of how they were going along with the regime, it was witnessed too by the professional judges Gilbert of Preston, Giles of Erdington and Nicholas de Turri.[34]

## THE DEFIANCE OF THE LEGATE

The June parliament did not merely confirm Montfort's constitution. It also in the most abrasive way tried to prevent any intervention by the papal legate, Guy Foulquois. Guy, archbishop of Narbonne between 1259 and 1261, had been in the service of Louis IX and acted as one of his *enquêteurs*, but this did not give him any sympathy with reforms reducing the king to a cipher.[35] Guy had been empowered by the pope to restore Henry to power, if necessary by employing the full range of ecclesiastical sanctions, even the proclamation of a crusade. He was now in Paris about to set off for England.[36] In a letter sent from the parliament, he was accordingly accused of lacking charity and told it was against the privileges of the kingdom for a legate to enter the country unless asked for. If he did want to talk, the letter went on, he should come to Boulogne. However, 'the will of all the community' was that the bishops should not cross over to join him, or at least not without guarantees against being ordered to publish sentences detrimental to kingdom and people.[37] One thing the legate was not told in the letter, though doubtless he heard about it. At the parliament the magnates had 'unanimously' decided that anyone bringing

---

[33] Briouze claimed to be overlord of Sedgwick: *AP*, 174–5.

[34] Bémont, *Simon de Montfort*, 353–5; Maddicott, *Simon de Montfort*, 325–6.

[35] There are many references to him in Dejoux, *Les Enquêtes de Saint Louis*.

[36] *CPReg*, 396–8. For his appointment, see above, 288.

[37] 'Processus Legationis', no. 14.

or publishing letters of excommunication and interdict should be beheaded![38] Not surprisingly, Guy decided against any immediate descent on England and instead sent his chaplain, Alan, to prepare the way.

Guy was right to be cautious. On Alan's arrival at Dover, he was arrested and taken to the castle. He was than searched (his upper tunic ripped off) and his letters seized. He was threatened with death if anything damaging to the kingdom was found. The realm, he was told, had been destroyed by aliens, who held the richest benefices and oppressed native-born men. As for admitting the legate, Henry de Montfort, in command at the castle, said he could do nothing without consulting his father.[39] Not surprisingly, Alan's advice was that the legate would do better not to come at all.

## THE CAPTIVE KING[40]

Where was Henry during the June 1264 parliament? Was he kept out of the way or paraded in humiliating compliance? We do not know. The chronicle of Bury St Edmunds opined that, after Lewes, the barons 'did not guard the king as a captive but courteously as their lord'.[41] This was true in the sense that Henry was not imprisoned in a castle like King Richard and Lord Edward. Doubtless some outward respect was shown him. But that he was in effect a prisoner and pawn of the regime is certain. The Ordinance's claim to have been made 'with the will, consent and on the order of the king' concealed the truth. The Ordinance itself spoke of the council simply advising the king. But in an earlier draft the council was to act '*vice*' the king, so 'on behalf of' or 'in his place'. The letter of the clergy and people, giving authority for its election, spoke of the affairs of the kingdom being 'ruled' by the council of nine without any mention of the king at all.[42]

When it came to issuing royal letters, Henry was, for the most part, deprived of independent initiative. His chancellor, John of Chishall, remained in post but seems to have been totally subservient to the regime. Indeed, Henry complained that when he was 'in the keeping' of Simon de Montfort, many things were sealed against his will.[43] Chishall did, however, take the precaution of often noting on whose authority letters were issued. Thus we know that between the battle of Lewes and the end of 1264, not a single letter was issued on Henry's sole authority. By contrast, around sixty letters were

[38] Gilson, 'The parliament of 1264', 501.

[39] 'Processus Legationis', no. 12; Maddicott, *Simon de Montfort*, 292–3.

[40] I take this heading from the title of Ben Wild's article 'A captive king'.

[41] Bury St Edmunds, 28.

[42] *DBM*, 298–9; Burton, '1264: some new documents', 321, 325–6; Gilson, 'The parliament of 1264', 500.

[43] *CPR 1258–66*, 436.

authorized 'by the council' or by 'the counsel of the barons (or magnates) of the council'. Other letters were issued by groups of named councillors (they very rarely acted alone). Hugh Despenser as justiciar took the lead here, being associated with over thirty letters. He was followed by Giles de Argentan with over twenty and by Peter de Montfort, Adam de Newmarch and Ralph de Camoys, who were all involved in authorizing around half a dozen. Between July 1264 and Easter 1265, Argentan and Newmarch both spent nearly 130 days at court and Peter de Montfort 178.[44]

As for the council of three, Gilbert de Clare was only associated with two letters and Bishop Bersted with one. Montfort, by contrast, was involved in authorizing around ten, usually ones of importance dealing with such matters as the custody of castles. Montfort 'and the whole council' thus authorized the letter commanding Robert de Neville to surrender York castle.[45] It sounded as though Montfort was the council's head, as in reality he was.

In one humiliating respect Henry seemed in a worse position now than in 1258-9. Then he had been more or less ignored by the council. Now he was forced to co-operate with it and lend his authority to some of its acts. Thus while he authorized no letters alone, he authorized over twenty-five with the council or with named councillors, once or twice with Simon de Montfort in addition. Some of these letters Henry would have been happy enough with, for example that restoring property to his old chancellor Walter of Merton. But he surely resented the way he had to do this in company with Peter de Montfort, Giles de Argentan, Ralph de Camoys and Roger de St John.[46] Other letters were far more objectionable. He had to join with Montfort, Despenser and the bishop of London in authorizing the appointment of John de Eyville as constable of Scarborough. He had to endorse the start of a new policy in which the regime pardoned debts owed to the Jews by its partisans. The first concession of this kind bene-fited Ralph de Camoys, who for his 'laudable service' (how ironic Henry must have found that) was pardoned all the debts he owed to Cok son of Aaron 'lately defunct', defunct of course because killed by John fitzJohn during the massacre of the London Jewry. The letter making the conces-sion was authorized by Henry together with Despenser, Peter de Montfort, Adam de Newmarch, Giles de Argentan and 'others of the council'. Most bitter of all, Henry had actually to authorize the letter (with Peter de Montfort and Giles de Argentan) transferring Bristol from Edward to Simon de Montfort.[47] It is conceivable that in these letters, Henry's name was being used without his knowledge, but, on the whole, I think there must have been some degree of compliance. In October 1264 he was

---

[44] *CLR 1260-7*, 170-1.
[45] *CPR 1258-66*, 373.
[46] *CR 1264-8*, 81.
[47] *CPR 1258-66*, 346; *CFR 1263-4*, no. 226; *CR 1264-8*, 395.

prepared to sit at the exchequer and receive the oath of office from the Montfortian mayor of London, Thomas fitzThomas, whose admission he had forbidden the year before.[48] The Bury St Edmunds chronicle declared that 'the king went wherever the barons went and what they decreed should be done, he did freely and diligently'.[49]

In all this, Henry cuts a very unimpressive figure. He seems virtually to have given up. Had he possessed more resolution and kingly spirit, would he not have defied the regime and refused his co-operation? Yet Henry was under terrible pressure. He was in captivity and very much alone. He remained at St Paul's for the whole period from 30 May to 11 August. To be exiled by Montfort from his palace at Westminster, from the Abbey, from the Confessor, must have been painful. At St Paul's he was doubtless monitored by the bishop's men and by the bishop himself, Henry of Sandwich being, of course, one of the council. It could have been worse, but only just. Henry might have been sent to the Tower.

The king's diminished and degraded state is reflected in the accounts of one of his buyers, Robert of Linton, covering the thirty-one weeks from 28 May 1264 to 1 January 1265. When averaged out, Linton's expenditure on cloths, furs, wax and spices was some 30 per cent down on the level reached in the previous 146 weeks. He acquired only six cloths of gold, an average of one every five weeks, as against two a week in the previous period.[50] The only consolation was that, for the moment, the keeper of the wardrobe, Henry de Ghent, remained in place. So probably did the staff of Henry's chapel and almonry. The one type of cloth which was acquired in greater abundance than before down to the end of the year was the coarse cloth for the king's alms to the poor. A roll from 1265 shows the services in Henry's chapel proceeding apparently as normal. The papal legate exempted from his anathemas the priests and clerks of the chapel. 'Although they converse with the barons we do not believe that in their minds they adhere to them.' But there were changes. FitzThedmar noted that while at St Paul's many of Henry's household were 'removed from him'.[51] The steward Robert Aguillon, still with Henry after Lewes, was dismissed. His colleague before the battle Roger of Leybourne was now a fugitive, rumoured to be hiding out with a widow called Feidina in the isle of Thanet.[52] In their stead as stewards came in Adam de Newmarch and the Essex knight Walter of Crepping. Both were strangers to Henry. So was the Kentish knight Stephen Soudan, handpicked by Montfort to be a marshal of the king's household.[53] Judging from their attestations of

[48] TNA E 368/39, m. 2d (image 6231); FitzThedmar, 70 (Stone, FitzThedmar, no. 821).
[49] Bury St Edmunds, 29.
[50] Wild, *WA*, 113–14. I am grateful to Richard Cassidy for his analysis of these figures.
[51] FitzThedmar, 63 (Stone, FitzThedmar, no. 796); 'Processus Legationis', 218.
[52] *CIM*, no. 1024 (p. 312). He soon joined the marchers.
[53] *CIM*, no. 1024 (p. 312).

royal charters, Newmarch and Crepping, together with Ralph de Camoys, Giles de Argentan and Soudan, formed a tight circle around the king.[54]

Henry had also to look on as the regime once again made free with deer and wood from his forests. During the eleven months between June 1264 and April 1265 around 110 such gifts were made. About 30 of them, mostly of wood, went to friaries and religious houses and probably were indeed from the king himself, doubtless with the hope the recipients would pray for his welfare. A few of the rest may likewise have come from Henry – so the gifts of wood to his chancery clerk, Adam of Chesterton, and his doctor, Thomas of Weasenham. Probably everyone agreed on the six deer given to the gallant Philip Basset, as he recovered from the wounds sustained at Lewes. But the most conspicuous gifts to laymen went to leading members of the regime and its key supporters.

In practice, had Henry not co-operated with the regime, probably nothing in the short term at least would have happened to him. Montfort would have just gone on without him, using the seal as he wished. But it was easy for Henry to think otherwise. The Merton abbey chronicler averred it was only threats of deposition that got him to accept the Ordinance of June 1264.[55] That his removal was spoken of is certain for in a letter he was made to write to King Louis, he mentioned the danger of the 'perpetual disinheritance of us and our heirs'.[56] Henry must also have feared for the fate of Edward and Henry of Almain being held as hostages. In another letter to Louis he referred darkly to the dangers to them under 'the law of nations'.[57] In these circumstances, Henry's compliance becomes understandable. Like the clerks of his chapel, he had to converse with the barons however much in mind he abhorred them.

## DISORDER IN THE COUNTRY

Simply framing a constitution was the easy part of Montfort's task. More difficult was restoring order to the country. The two sides were still at each other's throats and there was a great deal of freelance violence. William Marmion on his way home from the battle of Lewes burnt down the hall, chambers and granges at Myridale belonging to Edward's knight Nicholas of Cogenhoe.[58] There were many other similar attacks, doubtless often tit for tat. Montfort's response to such disorder was to repeat (on 4 June) the

---

[54] *RCWL*, ii, 143–5. Tout, *Chapters*, i, 310. For Crepping, see *CIM*, no. 667. He may have owed his promotion to the earl of Oxford. See *CFR 1263–4*, no. 48; Turner, *The English Judiciary*, 143–4.

[55] Merton, *Flores*, 262. At the same time Edward was, so the chronicler believed, threatened with perpetual imprisonment.

[56] *CR 1261–4*, 390.

[57] *CR 1261–4*, 389, 396–7.

[58] *RS*, 188; Jobson, *The First English Revolution*, 102. I suspect the manor of Myridale was at Cogenhoe.

expedient of 1263 and appoint keepers of the peace in every shire. They were again leading members of the regime and men of power in the counties concerned. Several had been baronial anti-sheriffs back in 1261 and keepers of the peace in 1263. Their brief now was to prevent anyone, on pain of disinheritance and peril of life and limb, from bearing arms and engaging in 'assaults, plunder, slaughters, arson, robbery, exactions and other outrages'. At the end of the month further measures were taken, the outrages mentioned this time including the seizure of men and the holding of them to ransom.[59]

Another problem was that many of the king's castles were still in royal hands. In June and July accordingly, Montfort appointed new constables to around twenty castles.[60] The problem now was to make such appointments a reality. By early July, Montfort had secured the surrender of Windsor and placed it under John fitzJohn. He had far less success in the north. There the castles of Carlisle, York, Scarborough, Newcastle and Bamburgh remained under loyalist castellans while John de Balliol, Peter de Brus, Robert de Neville, Adam of Jesmond and others refused to come south to make their submission to the regime. They claimed they were under attack from John de Eyville, John de Vescy and others. With Carlisle castle taken by Eyville and then apparently retaken by Eustace de Balliol (John's brother), the civil war in the north was still continuing.[61] Here, in one key respect, Montfort's situation was worse than that of the rebels in 1215. They had received powerful support from King Alexander II of Scotland. There was no way that would happen under Alexander III.[62] Indeed, a group of Anglo-Scottish barons – John de Balliol, Robert de Brus and John Comyn – had fought for Henry at Lewes, bringing with them (doubtless with Alexander's encouragement) many foot-soldiers, the latter slaughtered 'in great numbers'.[63]

The situation in the Welsh march was as bad as in the north. There the marcher barons let go after Lewes – Roger de Mortimer, Roger of Clifford, James of Audley, Hamo Lestrange and their ally Roger of Leybourne – refused to come to the June parliament and held onto the prisoners taken at Northampton. Edward and Henry of Almain, of course, were being held as security for the marcher's good behaviour, but here a weakness appeared in Montfort's position. He might threaten the hostages but would he really dare to execute them? The marchers far more than Henry were prepared to call his bluff. By mid-July, Montfort

[59] DBM, 290–3; F, i, 442; CPR 1258–66, 327, 362.

[60] Oakes, 'King's men without the king', 55–6. Oakes's paper has a full discussion of the way Montfort gradually gained control of the king's castles.

[61] The situation in the north is analysed in Oakes, 'The Barons' War in the north of England'.

[62] Reid, Alexander III, 197–201. Around Christmas 1264 the Pershore chronicler mentions John de Balliol holding out with help from the king of Scotland: Pershore, Flores, 504.

[63] Pershore, Flores, 496.

saw he must resort to other measures. He set off for the Welsh march, in company with Gilbert de Clare. In a lightning campaign, aided by Llywelyn, he devastated Mortimer's lands and gained control of Hereford, Hay, Richard's Castle and Ludlow. Under this pressure the marchers came to terms and gave hostages for their future good behaviour.[64] Montfort then hurried east. He was facing a terrible threat from abroad.

## THE QUEEN'S INVASION

Queen Eleanor had learnt about Lewes from Hugh Bigod and the others who had fled the battle. Already raising troops before the battle, she now sought to do so on a much grander scale. Nothing less than an invasion with a large army could rescue her son and husband and put matters right. Eleanor's first move was to hurry to King Louis in Paris. By 1 June, with the help of Peter of Savoy and John Mansel, she got him to hand over all the money (around £12,750) still due for the 500 knights under the Treaty of Paris, this instead of it being paid in instalments over two years. Probably Louis needed little persuading. He and Queen Margaret were appalled by events in England and eager to help.[65] In August, Louis gave Eleanor another £5,000 in return for recovering the rights in the Three Dioceses ceded under the Treaty of Paris. Agreeing the deal were Peter of Savoy, John de Warenne, Hugh Bigod and Mansel.[66] Helped by all this money, Eleanor's army mustered at the port of Damme in Flanders in early August. Wykes wrote of it being drawn from Flanders and Brabant (great areas for mercenaries), Germany and many parts of France.[67] The Worcester annals mention messengers sent to muster troops in Gascony and Ireland.[68] Great efforts were made to obtain shipping. For the next two months invasion seemed likely, even imminent.

In all this, Eleanor received considerable help from her uncle Peter of Savoy. In the summer of 1263 a great change had come over Peter's life. On the death of his young nephew he had become count of Savoy.[69] Peter had often in the past, or so it seemed, exploited English resources to further his Savoyard ambitions. Would he now devote himself entirely to Savoyard affairs, complex and time consuming as they were? But not a bit of it. If ever the patronage bestowed by Henry proved justified, it was now. Peter remained with Eleanor at Damme throughout September and with

[64] Pershore, *Flores*, 498–9; *CPR 1258–66*, 337, 363, 366–7.

[65] Gavrilovitch, *Étude sur le traité de Paris*, 120–1; *CPR 1258–66*, 381. For all of what follows, see Howell, *Eleanor of Provence*, 211–19.

[66] Gavrilovitch, *Étude sur le traité de Paris*, 121–3.

[67] Wykes, 154; Winchester/Worcester, 452–3.

[68] Winchester/Worcester, 452–3. For further evidence about Ireland, see Frame, 'Ireland and the Barons' Wars', 162; Howell, *Eleanor of Provence*, 223–4.

[69] Cox, *Eagles of Savoy*, 303.

her became commander of the growing army.[70] He took out loans, summoned forces from Savoy, and at the end of the month made payments to over seventy knights.[71] He also tried to raise money from Ireland and gave characteristically exact instructions about its transfer, although these did show the difficulties of the situation. Because of the dangers of the journey, Peter's agent was to come back via La Rochelle or Normandy. Only if there was peace would he return through England.[72]

Peter's reference to the possibility of peace shows there was some hope the Montfortians might just give in. But in case there was no peace, Peter gave thought to Eleanor's position. This involved a new will and new provisions for 'our dearest niece, illustrious lady and queen of England' as he called her. Eleanor, under the will of 1255, had been made the heir to all Peter's lands in England, but these had been overrun by rebels. So Peter now made Eleanor the heir to Savoy itself. His daughter, by contrast, was merely to have her due share of Peter's goods (the amount was not specified) from what might now be a worthless honour of Richmond. This remarkable arrangement, giving Eleanor essentially a safe haven in Savoy, reflected just how doubtful her future in England was.[73]

## MONTFORT'S ARMY ON BARHAM DOWN

Montfort knew Eleanor was raising an army as early as 6 July. It says much for his energy and confidence that he still made time for a campaign to put down the marchers. In resisting invasion, Montfort had one great strength. He controlled Dover castle and had the allegiance of the Cinque Ports. The portsmen and the Londoners were always linked together in the warnings and anathemas of the legate. There was every chance that the enemy fleet would be destroyed in the channel, just as Louis' had been in 1217.[74] But, of course, there was no certainty of that and so, before setting off for the Welsh march, Montfort summoned an army to muster in London on 3 August. Composed of four main elements, it was to be of vast size. All tenants-in-chief were to come not just with their due service but with all the horses, arms and foot-soldiers they could raise. All other knights and free tenants were to come too 'with all their power'. There was

[70] Pershore, *Flores*, 499.

[71] Von Wurstemberger, *Peter der Zweite*, iv, nos. 644, 649, 656.

[72] Von Wurstemberger, *Peter der Zweite*, iv, no. 648; Howell, *Eleanor of Provence*, 219, 222–3.

[73] Andenmatten, 'Contraintes lignagères et parcours individuel', 272, 281 (where the suggestion of a safe haven is made), and 284–92 for the wills, with provision for Eleanor at 284–5, 288. Her tenure of Savoy was not to pass to her sons, however, the heirs being Peter's brother, Philip, archbishop-elect of Lyon, and then his nephew, the eldest son of Thomas of Savoy. For Peter's last will, see below, 533.

[74] For Montfort's measures of maritime defence, see Jobson, 'The maritime theatre', 230–1. Good commander as he was, he also took precautions against a landing further north.

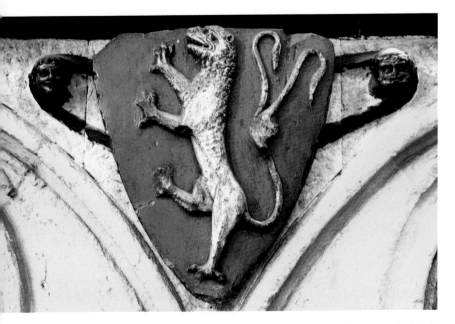

. Simon de Montfort was central to the revolution of 1258 and led the resistance to the king's ecovery of power in 1261. Henry was thus being conciliatory if, as is likely, it was in 1262 hat Montfort's shield, with those of other barons, was placed in Westminster Abbey's new hoir. The shield shown here would not have been erected after Montfort's rebellion in 1263.

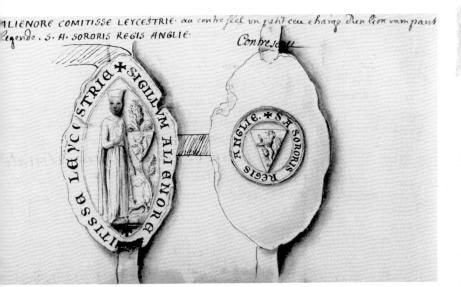

. Simon and Eleanor de Montfort made a formidable husband-and-wife team. Both the front nd the back of Eleanor's seal (shown here in an eighteenth-century drawing) display Montfort's rms. But whereas on the front she is 'countess of Leicester', on the back she is 'sister of the ing of England', thus stressing her royal status.

1258, Oct. 18, (42 Hen. III)
Proclamation of K. Henry III; the only English
one of Henry III, and one of two copies known;
very carefully edited by Prof. W. W. Skeat for
the Philological Society in 1882.   H. 29

**3.** In October 1258 Henry III was made to issue this proclamation ordering everyone to observ
on oath the ruling council's statutes and treat those who contravened them as mortal enemies
In order to be understood by the widest possible audience, the proclamation was issued i
English, the first government document in the native tongue since soon after the Norman
Conquest. This is the text sent to Oxfordshire.

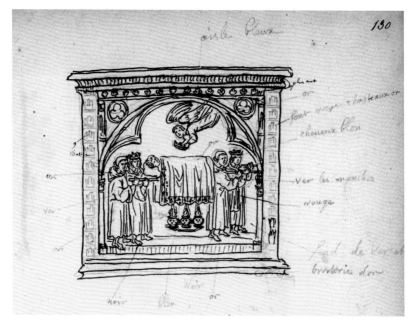

**4.** In 1259–60, Henry's behaviour in Paris was perfect and cemented his relationship wit
Louis IX. Here he is bearing Louis IX's eldest son to burial at Royaumont as depicted on th
prince's tomb. The scene on the reconstructed tomb (now at Saint-Denis) is based on this drawin
made around 1700 by Roger de Gaignières. The other king is Theobald, king of Navarre.

5. The ruling council's ratification in October 1259 of the peace with France is the most striking visual testimony to its authority. All the councillors' seals (plus Hugh Bigod's) are here save the earl of Aumale's. Montfort's and Richard de Clare's seals are third and fourth from the left. James of Audley's seal appears twice. The scribal hand is French, not English.

**6.** This photograph (*c.* 1869), taken from the castle, shows the battlefield of Lewes before the encroachment of later housing. The mill on the horizon marks where Montfort's army formed up. The mill where King Richard was captured was closer to St Anne's church (on the left) than the one shown here (beyond the prison).

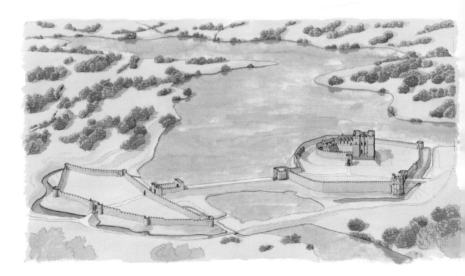

**7.** Kenilworth castle as it may have looked in Montfort's time. With water defences making it second only to Dover as the mightiest castle in England, Kenilworth gave Montfort great local power. In 1266 it resisted the king's army for over five months until starved into submission.

**8.** With his arms depicted in the tiled floor, and with a specially designed lectern, Henry envisaged Westminster Abbey's chapter house, shown here, as a place where he would address parliament in all his state. But in February 1265, during Montfort's parliament, it was here his humiliating submission to the Montfortian regime was proclaimed.

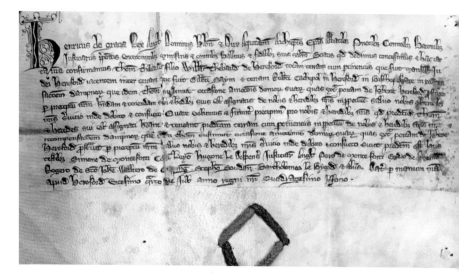

**9.** Henry, controlled by the Montfortian regime, issued this charter from Hereford on 24 July 1265. (It is in favour of a Hereford citizen.) Within ten days, most of the witnesses, headed by Simon de Montfort, were dead. Is the scribe, with his elaborate 'H' at the start, topped by what almost seems a crown, making a royalist point?

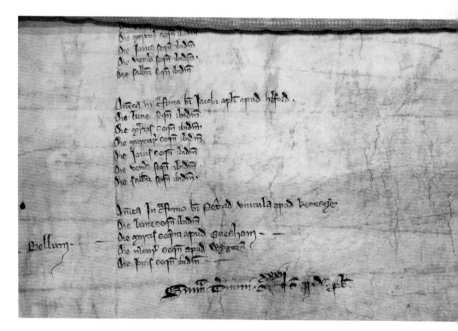

**10.** Henry's itinerary before the battle of Evesham, from a roll recording his daily offerings at mass. With the dates expressed with reference to saints' days, he is at 'He[re]ford' on 26 July, at 'Kemeseye' (Kempsey) on 2 August, and at 'Evesham' on Tuesday 4 August, the scribe writing 'Bellum' ('Battle') in the margin. The next day Henry is at Worcester.

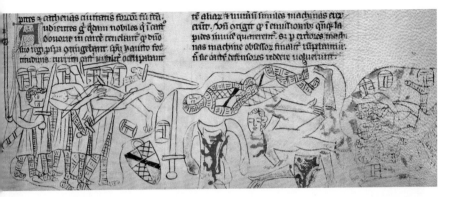

**1.** As shown in this drawing from an early fourteenth-century chronicle, after his death at Evesham, Montfort's body was cut up, thus proclaiming he was a felon and a traitor. The body in the centre, identified by the arms on the surcoat, is that of Hugh Despenser, while his shield is to the left.

**2.** This scene from an illuminated Apocalypse dating to after Evesham shows the destruction wrought by Satan's knights. The banner depicts in black the lion rampant with forked tail of Montfort's arms. If Henry commissioned the work, as is possible, here is his view of the Montfortian movement.

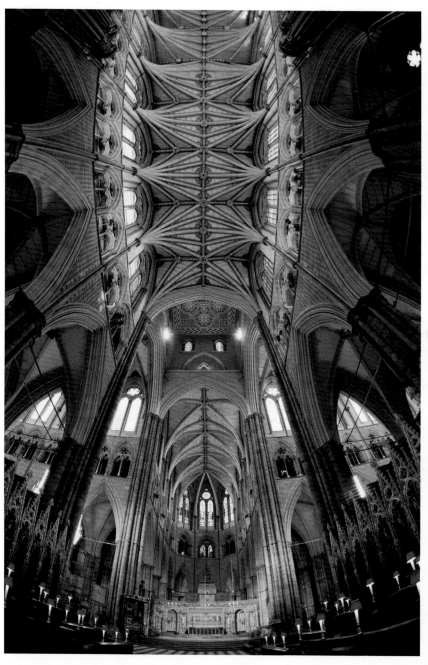

**13.** As this photograph shows, Henry's choir at Westminster Abbey, erected between 1259 and 1269, had a more elaborate vault than the earlier work to the east. Extra shafts were also added to the Purbeck marble columns of the main arcade. The fifteenth-century screen behind the high altar blocks the view onwards to the Confessor's shrine, thus cutting the Abbey off from its spiritual heart.

**14.** In 1268, the Cosmati family of mosaicists installed the great pavement before the Abbey's high altar, using stones brought from buildings of ancient Rome. Henry and Abbot Ware were central to procuring the pavement. Now cleaned and conserved it creates a magnificent setting for the coronation, as Henry intended.

**15.** The pavement represented the universe, an inscription giving the date of its end and thus of the Last Judgement. The stone in the centre, shown here, depicted the earth, the red veins symbolizing its angry strife. How necessary then to proceed to the shrine of the Confessor, there to seek his intercession for the peace of the kingdom and one's own salvation.

**16.** The paintings in Henry's great chamber at Westminster belong to the years after a disastrous fire in 1263 and were probably completed shortly before his death. The centre piece, at the head of Henry's bed, was the painting of Edward the Confessor's coronation, known now only from this copy made in 1819. The rod topped by a dove was adopted by Henry himself in his new seal made in 1259.

**17.** I discovered this sketch of Henry III's head on the cover of an exchequer record (its memoranda roll) for 1266–7. Underneath is written 'Rex Henricus tercius'. The drawing of Henry's right eye is intended to show (perhaps the point of the sketch) the drooping eyelid from which he suffered. This may be the earliest drawing of an identified king in a government record.

**8, 19.** These paintings of kings in Westminster Abbey's sedilia (dating to the early fourteenth century) are likely to represent Henry and Edward I. Henry is dignified but elderly and has none of the power and authority radiating from his son.

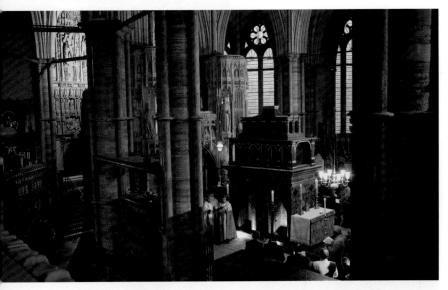

**0.** A view of the Confessor's chapel, showing the Cosmati shrine base (as reconstructed during Queen Mary's reign), its early sixteenth-century canopy, and to the left Henry III's Cosmati tomb with his effigy. Behind the shrine rises the chantry chapel of Henry V with a statue, on the extreme left, of the Confessor's nemesis, Saint George, slaying the dragon. It was to shut out the noise from the chantry that the screen was built behind the high altar. The service shown was commemorating the 800th anniversary of Henry's birth in 2007. Henry would have been disappointed by the small number of candles around the shrine.

**21.** Far tougher than her husband, Henry III's queen, Eleanor of Provence, played a major part in politics. Although not buried with Henry in Westminster Abbey, on the underside of the metal table supporting Henry's effigy there are these engravings of a queen and a young woman. They may represent Eleanor and one of her daughters praying for Henry's soul.

**22.** The profile of Henry's head from the gilt bronze effigy on his tomb made in the earl 1290s by the goldsmith William Torel.

also to be a *levée en masse*, for every village was to send, with their expenses for forty days, between four and eight of its best men armed with lances, bows, arrows, swords, crossbows and axes. And finally, the sheriffs and keepers of the peace were to raise suitable numbers of foot and horse from the boroughs.

In justifying this extraordinary summons, Montfort sent letters to the shires of tremendous eloquence and power. In London, they so impressed fitzThedmar that he copied out in full the one going to Essex. The letters were written in the king's name but everyone knew they came from Montfort. Indeed, they justified everything he had been saying since 1260 about the king bringing in foreign troops to oppress his native subjects. The letters thus conjured up a threat to the very lifeblood of the country. It was certain, the shires were told, that a great multitude of aliens, with shipping gathered from everywhere, were preparing to invade to the 'confusion and disinheritance' of everyone in the kingdom. No excuses for missing the muster (like the imminent harvest) could be tolerated, for it was better to endure some small damage now than to suffer 'the total loss of land and goods at the impious hands of those who, thirst for our blood, and will spare neither sex nor age a cruel death'. Those who failed to turn up would be punished as men who cared nothing for the 'perpetual disinheritance' of the kingdom.[75]

Walkers who follow the pilgrim's way eastwards from Patrixbourne in Kent head up through fields and woods until they come out onto the high ground above the village of Barham. This is Barham Down. Today much of it is divided by trees and hedgerows into fields put down to corn and rape, but there are still some areas of grassland (coloured in summer with dandelions, buttercups and daisies) to give an impression of the Down's ancient aspect. The Down stands immediately above the road, the old Watling Street, running between Canterbury and Dover, nine miles from the one, eleven from the other. Here an army was ideally placed to block an invader's route on to Canterbury and thence along Watling Street to London. It could equally advance down the road and do battle nearer Dover. It was on Barham Down that King John had mustered his army to repel invasion in 1213. It was also here that Montfort's army gathered in the summer of 1264.

The army was a triumph. According to fitzThedmar, 'innumerable people' mustered 'on horse and foot from every county of England'. The Winchester and Dunstable annalists say much the same. The numbers were so great that the demand drove up the price of food.[76] In the late summer days we can imagine Montfort riding through the ranks, the very sight of him riveting and inspiring, urging the troops to defend themselves,

[75] *F*, i, 444; *CPR 1258–66*, 362–3; FitzThedmar, 67–8 (Stone, FitzThedmar, no. 813).

[76] FitzThedmar, 69 (Stone, FitzThedmar, no. 814); Winchester, 453; Dunstable, 223; Jacob, *Studies*, 291–2, 410–11; *CR 1261–4*, 362, 364, 405–6.

their families and their land from this invasion by brutal and pitiless foreigners. Doubtless there were also numerous preachers eulogizing the great earl and proclaiming the God-given nature of the cause.[77] Doubtless too they had the skill to turn to advantage what might otherwise have been an ominous omen, for throughout August 'a comet of leaden colour with its tail pointing south appeared in the eastern sky before the dawn of the day'.[78]

Montfort hoped that the peasant contingents would be self-funded, but he was helped by his episcopal supporters. Normally so hostile to any form of taxation, the bishops agreed that the revenues from parish churches should either fund men in the army or provide money in lieu, the money soon being defined as a tenth of each church's income.[79] When £27 from the remains of the tax in the dioceses of Rochester and Chichester were received into the king's wardrobe, it was described as having been assessed by Montfort himself and 'certain bishops to preserve the coast from invasion by aliens'.[80] Dunstable priory, that seat of Montfortian enthusiasm, both paid the tenth *and* sent four men with horses and arms plus six foot-soldiers to the army. The total cost, leaving aside the purchase of horses and arms, was £20.[81]

## THE NEGOTIATIONS WITH KING LOUIS AND THE LEGATE: MONTFORT HOLDS THE LINE

Henry himself was now moved from London to Canterbury where he arrived on 12 August. He was to stay there until October, presumably living in the archbishop's palace. Montfort probably arrived at the same time. We see him in Canterbury on 24 August attesting royal charters with five bishops and the earls Gilbert de Clare and Robert de Vere.[82] To stamp his authority on the locality and show his power over the king, in Henry's presence he now heard pleas at the August and September sessions of the Kent county court.[83]

While the great army was being mustered and maintained, the Montfortian regime also sought to ward off the invasion by drawing King Louis and the legate into negotiations for some kind of peaceful

---

[77] For the atmosphere on Barham Downs and an evocative comparison between Montfort and Mr Churchill in 1940, see Maddicott, *Simon de Montfort*, 291. The preachers doubtless spoke in English. I suspect Montfort was able to do so too, but there is no proof.

[78] Bury, 29.

[79] The churches in question were those in the hands of rectors and religious houses.

[80] Wild, *WA*, 111, and see *Bronescombe Register*, 53.

[81] *CPR 1258–66*, 364–5; *CR 1261–4*, 403–5; Wild, *WA*, 111; Dunstable, 223.

[82] *RCWL*, ii, 143. Clare now has his comital titles and was presumably invested by Henry immediately after Lewes.

[83] This was the reason the sheriff gave for returning no revenues from the courts: TNA E 389/91. I owe this information to Richard Cassidy.

settlement.[84] Although the central question was the power to be allowed the king, there is not a single reference to Henry's own involvement. The same is true of Edward although he was also brought to Canterbury, and the conditions of his release were another major issue. In all this, the regime was far from united. Montfort himself was defiant. He saw the value of the negotiations in delaying the invasion, but was damned if he was going to water down the essence of his new constitution. If that meant the negotiations broke down and the invasion took place, he was ready for it. That was not, however, how his episcopal supporters saw it. Under intense pressure from the legate, they were prepared to reduce the restrictions on the king to a bare minimum. So were other baronial leaders. The whole episode was critical for Montfort's leadership and authority.

Montfort had made contact with King Louis within a fortnight of the battle of Lewes. Writing in Henry's name, he asked for the French side of the arbitration envisaged in the Mise of Lewes (the one designed to modify the Mise of Amiens) to be set in motion.[85] Yet, in all his confidence, he was completely frank. If a quicker and more suitable way of peace could be found, it would be adopted.[86] He was already anticipating his June constitution. The French arbitration might not be needed after all. Henry was made to write again to Louis in July, this time asking him to prevent the threatened invasion, and suggesting he come to Boulogne for discussions over a form of peace. Henry, of course, must have longed to pour out his woes to Louis in person, but this the regime would not permit. The letter explained that Henry and his council would come to Dover so that, with Louis at Boulogne, messengers could pass easily back and forth between them. So Henry was not to see Louis at all.[87] At least, when Louis accepted the Boulogne suggestion, Henry did try to make a stand. At the end of July, he wrote to Montfort and Gilbert de Clare, now campaigning in the Welsh marches, asking that the hostages, Edward and Henry of Almain, be allowed to come to Dover too. When later in the day he learnt they had been moved from Wallingford to Kenilworth, thus making their appearance at Dover all the more difficult, he stamped his feet and wrote again to say he would not leave London until Edward and Henry were sent to him.[88]

In the event, both the legate and Louis did come to Boulogne, the former arriving on 9 August, the latter on the tenth.[89] On 12 August the

---

[84] The course of these negotiations has been unravelled in Maddicott, *Simon de Montfort*, 295–301, through an analysis of the detailed account in the legate's own record: 'Processus Legationis', 194–248; and see also Ambler, *Bishops in the Political Community*, 162–9.

[85] See above, 319.

[86] *CR 1261–4*, 385–6.

[87] *CR 1261–4*, 389–91.

[88] *CR 1261–4*, 396, 399.

[89] There are full accounts of the Boulogne negotiations in Maddicott, *Simon de Montfort*, 295–301, and Ambler, *Bishops in the Political Community*, 162–9.

former ordered Montfort and his followers, on pain of excommunication, to admit him to England by 1 September. They were also to free the hostages, abjure the Provisions and restore Henry to power. Threatened by legatine anathemas and the invasion of a foreign army, surely the regime would now retreat and agree to water down the June Ordinance. But the reverse was the case. It was now decided that if the Mise of Lewes was not completed, the Ordinance was to last throughout Henry's lifetime and on into a period to be determined in the lifetime of his son. So for the first time, the prospect of the Ordinance enduring for many years was openly recognized. One other point was clarified. The three electors, the nine councillors, the castellans and all royal officials were always to be native born. So the statute against aliens was being reintroduced. The only modification was that its second clause under which all foreigners were to depart was abandoned. Instead, aliens, including of course merchants, could come and go freely. This was not much of a concession since the exclusion of all foreigners had never been practical politics. These additions to the Ordinance, together with the full text of the Ordinance itself, were embodied in a new 'form of peace', known as 'the Peace of Canterbury'. On 15 August it was sent to Louis and the legate with the request they approve it![90]

All this was surely Montfort's work and it is difficult to think of anything more defiant. The legate had already, on 12 August, condemned the Provisions of Oxford as a total usurpation of royal power.[91] Louis, in the Mise of Amiens, had specifically rejected restricting office to native-born men. The reaction in Boulogne was hardly surprising. The legate expressed his shock at the way the bishops had agreed to a peace which destroyed 'the liberty of royal power'. It deposed or buried the king and put three kings (the three electors) in his place. Later he quoted Louis IX as saying that 'he would rather break clods behind the plough than have a rule of that kind'.[92]

This rebuff for a moment rocked Montfort's position. On 11 September, acknowledging that Louis had rejected the Peace of Canterbury, a totally different proposal was drawn up.[93] The Peace was now to be emended by four arbitrators, the only restrictions on their award being that all royal officials were to be native born and that all the quarrels between Montfort and the king were to be resolved by King Louis before the peace was concluded. It was precisely because he might be personally vulnerable under such a settlement that Montfort insisted his grievances must be settled first.[94]

[90] *DBM*, 294–301; *CPR 1258–66*, 366; 'Processus Legationis', 21–3.
[91] 'Processus Legationis', 20 (a).
[92] 'Processus Legationis', nos. 22–3, 29 (c).
[93] *F*, i, 446 (*CPR 1258–66*, 369); *DD*, nos. 393–4.
[94] The four arbitrators were to be the bishop of London, Hugh Despenser, Charles of

It seems highly probable that it was the bishops who forced Montfort into this concession. Indeed, Bishop Sandwich of London was to be one of the arbitrators. As peacemakers they naturally wished to avoid the horrors of an invasion, all the more so given the church's sufferings during the last bout of strife. They were equally desperate to escape the legate's sentences of excommunication and prevent his arrival in the kingdom.[95] To that end, they argued they were doing their best to prevent the seizure of church property and secure restoration of the spoils. In July, Bishop Cantilupe had made a major speech at St Paul's along those lines.[96] But in their debate with the legate (carried on initially through letters), it was much harder to explain their support for the Montfortian regime. Here the legate's stand, like Louis', like Henry's, was based simply on the rights of kingship and the wrongs of any restrictions. The bishops themselves felt quite unable to tackle this head on. Instead, they argued that the June constitution, in appointing councillors to rule the kingdom, did not restrict Henry's freedom at all, here drawing on all kinds of biblical and other parallels. Thus God had placed the stars in heaven 'for the natural government of those below'. Moses, as ruler of Israel, 'had instructed that wise and noble men be appointed as princes, chosen by men of their tribe'. And the pope himself caused cardinals to sit with him 'as brothers and coadjutors in providing judgements'. The legate sliced through all this. God, Moses and the pope were not in any way forced to do what they did. Was the pope bound to accept the counsel of the cardinals? Of course not. The very idea was absurd. The three electors and the nine councillors left the barons with 'effective authority (*utile dominium*)' and made the king's authority ineffective '*inutile*', because only nominal.[97]

With their arguments thus dismissed, and faced with the persistent demand that they both appear personally before the legate and promulgate the sentences of excommunication, the bishops thus pushed Montfort into major concessions. But if Montfort was unable to prevent proposals for a new arbitration being drafted, he fought tooth and nail against them going forward. He was successful. The scheme was abandoned, and a very different proposal was drawn up.[98] This, in a concession to the legate,

---

Anjou, reputedly a friend of Montfort (although there was doubt over whether he would act), and the abbot of Bec.

[95] In September the bishops were involved in arranging for Henry of Almain's temporary release so he could go to France and, it was hoped, use his influence in the cause of peace. Nine bishops pledged he would return on pain of losing 20,000 marks: *F*, i, 446 (*CPR 1258–66*, 345).

[96] Canterbury/Dover, 239–42, summarized with other measures in Ambler, *Bishops in the Political Community*, 141–2.

[97] 'Processus Legationis', nos. 28–9, with the quotation on p. 230. I thank Daniel Hadas for the translation. The arguments on either side are fully discussed in Ambler, *Bishops in the Political Community*, 163–6.

[98] *CPR 1258–66*, 347–8, 370–1.

dispensed with the three electors (the legate's 'three kings'), but Henry was still not to choose his own councillors. Instead, they were to be chosen by five arbitrators. All the councillors, moreover, were to be native born and they were to have extensive powers. The king was to give credence to them in the giving of justice, the appointment of officials (all were to be native born), the management of his finances and the observance of the Charters and the Provisions of Westminster. The aim here, it was said, was to stop the king's 'immoderate expenses and immense liberality' so that he could live of his own, without burdening merchants and officials. Under the scheme, therefore, a council the king had not chosen would effectively govern the realm. Since it was inconceivable that Montfort would not be one of the councillors, he would effectively be the council's head. Montfort thus felt safe enough to withdraw the stipulation about the settlement of his private grievances.[99] A further safeguard was that only when the new constitution was firmly established would Edward and Henry of Almain be released and that on conditions. If the arbitration did not proceed, the Peace of Canterbury was to stand.

This proposal was taken out to Boulogne on 24 September by the bishops of London, Worcester and Winchester, Hugh Despenser and Peter de Montfort. So the bishops were at last exposed to the full force of the legate's incisive intelligence and deep disapproval. His first move was to read out to them the letters setting out the panoply of his legatine powers. A quavering Bishop Gervase of Winchester asked at once to be absolved by the legate in case he had already incurred the sentence of excommunication. Under this pressure, the English delegation made some modifications to the proposal but they were nowhere near enough.[100] The legate, as usual, got to the heart of the matter and skewered the bishops with one question: did they agree with the barons that the king should be made to have certain councillors and be bound to follow their counsel? To their credit, all three bishops answered 'yes'. At this point, Eleanor and Edmund weighed in through their proctor, Philip of Savoy, archbishop-elect of Lyon. They wished simply to stand by Louis' Mise. If any changes were necessary they should be made by Louis himself or by the legate.[101]

How Montfort and the barons back in England reacted to the modifications made by the bishops we do not know. Another proposal was sent back to Boulogne, but the letters were stolen by the sailors taking the

---

[99] Montfort was safeguarded from any challenge to his position on the council by the stipulation that after the councillors' election there should be no further question of their fitness. Two of the arbitrators were the legate himself and the French minister Peter the Chamberlain, but Montfort could expect a majority through his close friend Eudes Rigaud, archbishop of Rouen, Bishop Sandwich and Hugh Despenser. In one version of the scheme, the legate would only be called in if the four could not agree.

[100] Contrast *F*, i, 446 (*CPR 1258–66*, 370–1), with 'Processus Legationis', no. 42. See Maddicott, *Simon de Montfort*, 299.

[101] 'Processus Legationis', no. 43 (a); Howell, *Eleanor of Provence*, 215, 220.

envoys over, along with other things doubtless more valuable. Queen Eleanor learnt enough to express her dismay that nothing was being done for the hostages. The stalemate continued.[102] Early in October the legate made one final effort. He sent the bishops of Worcester and London back to England with a proposal that, subject to various qualifications and guarantees, everything should be placed in his hands. The bishops, like Gervase when he returned earlier, also had instructions to publish the sentences of excommunication and interdict. They were to do so if the barons were not reconciled to the legate within fourteen days.[103]

The end was now in sight. When the bishops arrived at Dover, they were frisked just like the legate's chaplain earlier and the letters containing all the papal anathemas, found in the baggage of Bishop Sandwich, were torn up and cast into the sea.[104] The official rejection of the legate's offer was equally contemptuous. The barons wrote a letter saying they 'did not wish to accept it at all' and would not depart from the June Ordinance and the Peace of Canterbury. The letter, with the texts of the Ordinance and the Peace, were placed in a box and on 11 October handed over at sea to the keeper of the port of Wissant for onward transport to the legate.[105]

So Montfort had triumphed. After some wavering, his party had stood fast behind the Ordinance and the Peace of Canterbury. Yet the negotiations had served their turn. They had lasted long enough to exhaust Eleanor's money. By mid-October, when the court left Canterbury, her army had dispersed. There would be no invasion.

There was one other alleviation. Montfort got away with his defiance scot-free. On 20 October at Hesdin the legate solemnly excommunicated the rebellious barons and their adherents and placed their lands under an interdict.[106] But the legate could do nothing to follow this up, thanks, for Montfort, to a stupendous piece of luck. On 2 October, Pope Urban died (was that what the comet foretold?) and the legate's commission thus came to an end. He had no authority to do anything when Gervase, Cantilupe and Sandwich ignored their solemn undertakings and failed to publish the sentences of excommunication in their dioceses. There was, however, a sting in the tail. Guy Foulquois returned to Rome where in February 1265 he was elected as Pope Clement IV.

Henry himself must have been torn throughout the summer by hopes and fears – hope that the invasion, or better still just the threat of invasion, would bring down the Montfortian regime, fear of what would happen to him and Edward if it was defeated. As for the queen, she must have been bitterly disappointed. Her husband and son were still captives, still indeed

---

[102] 'Processus Legationis', no. 43 (d).
[103] 'Processus Legationis', nos. 44, 46.
[104] Canterbury/Dover, 239; Pershore, *Flores*, 501; Wykes, 156–7.
[105] 'Processus Legationis', no. 45 (b).
[106] 'Processus Legationis', no. 50.

in danger.[107] She had nonetheless been magnificent and contemporaries recognized as much. The Pershore chronicler thanked God for dispersing the army but then added: 'this, however, ought to be recorded to the praise and magnificence of the noble lady of the English, Queen Eleanor, that she sweated so valiantly, strenuously and vigorously, like a most powerful virago, to rescue her lord king and Edward her son'.[108]

## THE SECOND CAMPAIGN AGAINST THE MARCHERS

By mid-September, in Canterbury, Henry was desperately hoping he could be back at Westminster for the feast of Edward the Confessor on 13 October. He issued an order (or was permitted to issue one) for the acquisition of gold so that the paintings in his chamber, 'in which we will stay', could be finished by then. In early October he was worried about the supply of wax for all the candles needed for the great service. He had none at the moment in his wardrobe and supplies were difficult to obtain because of the disturbances. So he ordered the exchequer (just now starting up again) to acquire 1,000 pounds of wax 'immediately, every-thing else put aside, as you love our honour'. In the event, Henry just made it, arriving in London on 11 October. The exchequer came up trumps, and judging from the cost, acquired well over 1,000 pounds' weight of wax for candles, as well as the usual twelve gold coins for Henry's offerings.[109] Thanks to the legate's anathemas being kept out of England, the service could go ahead as normal, although it must have been a pale reflection of the celebrations of former days. Henry, more-over, was only allowed to stay at Westminster till the end of the month. He was then moved back to his virtual captivity at St Paul's.

Montfort had little time to enjoy his victory over Louis and the legate before there was a fresh crisis. It was the marchers again. Mortimer, Audley, Clifford, Lestrange, Leybourne and the rest had refused to surrender their prisoners and failed to turn up to defend the Kent coast. Early in October they laid siege to Clare's castle at Hanley in Worcestershire,

[107] It was probably Eleanor's pressure that led the bishops of Worcester and London, just before they left, to engage in yet another scheme to bring about Edward's release. It too came to nothing: 'Processus Legationis', no. 48.

[108] Pershore, *Flores*, 221; Carpenter, 'Pershore *Flores*', 1363; See Howell, *Eleanor of Provence*, 221. It was while the crisis was at its height in September that Walter of Merton took deci-sive steps towards the foundation of his Oxford college: *Merton College Rolls*, ed. Highfield, 24–6. His aim was to prevent the properties with which it was to be endowed being ravaged in a fresh civil war. (For their previous sufferings, see Stewart, *RJS*, nos. 81, 84, 107–8.) As overlord of the properties, in charters issued from Wickhambreaux in Kent, Gilbert de Clare confirmed the gifts and gave them his protection: Merton College Muniments, nos. 597, 909. I am grateful to the librarian of Merton, Julia Walworth, for sending me images of the charters.

[109] *CR 1261–4*, 366; TNA SC 1/2/80; FitzThedmar, 69 (Stone, FitzThedmar, no. 819); *CLR 1260–7*, 143–4.

although, so they were told, Clare too was demanding the release of Edward and Henry of Almain. In November they attacked Hereford.[110] Meanwhile, Robert Walerand and Warin of Bassingbourn had occupied Bristol. From there, encouraged by the queen (or so it was thought), they made a daring dash to Wallingford in the hope of rescuing Edward from his captivity. They arrived at dawn and took the outer works of the castle only for Edward himself to appear on the walls and beg them to go, 'otherwise he would be dead', catapulted out to them by a mangonel! After this episode, Edward was moved, along with Henry of Almain and King Richard, to the greater security of Kenilworth.

By mid-November, Montfort had had enough. With Gilbert de Clare, he mustered his forces and set out again for the Welsh march. This time Henry was taken too. The Pershore annalist (who saw the court when it passed through Pershore in December) gives a picture of him at this time, so subservient that he could do nothing important without Montfort, yet also, 'it seemed', with a 'heart' inclined to the marchers who were fighting to free him 'from captivity' and rescue Edward.[111] Montfort's campaign was short and decisive. The marchers broke down the bridges over the River Severn but were pinioned between Montfort, 'a most sagacious warrior', as the Pershore annalist described him, and Llywelyn who attacked them in the rear. At Worcester in mid-December they came to terms.

## EDWARD LOSES CHESTER

The marchers achieved one main ambition, at least if promises were kept. Montfort now summoned a parliament to meet in January where arrangements were to be made for Edward's release. But the price was high. The marchers were to leave the country for a year and a day, surrender their lands and castles into Montfort's hands and give up their prisoners. The price was even higher for Edward himself, so much so that the marchers were allowed to go to Kenilworth to see if he would pay it. He was, as the only hope of getting out of prison. Under the agreement, Edward was to surrender Bristol to Montfort, although this was but a temporary transfer, reversible if Edward behaved himself. Much more devastating, because permanent, Edward had to grant Montfort in hereditary right the castle and county of Chester and the castle and honour of the Peak. Chester and Cheshire, the most solid and strategic of Edward's possessions, did indeed pass, in January 1265, without fuss into Montfort's hands.[112] Although Edward was supposed to receive from Montfort other lands in compensation, as it turned out they were as

---

[110] *CPR 1258–66*, 374; *CIM*, no. 291. For the narrative of what follows, see Pershore, *Flores*, 502–4; Dunstable, 234–5; and the accounts in Maddicott, *Simon de Montfort*, 306–8, and Jobson, *The First English Revolution*, 130–1.

[111] Pershore, *Flores*, 503.

[112] St Werburgh, 90–1.

nothing compared with what he was losing and included not a single castle. This was an awesome transference of power. How galling for Henry to have to authorize the relevant writs. Edward was trodden down, Montfort raised up. But only thus, Montfort insisted, could Edward be safely released.

## THE PROVISIONS OF WORCESTER, DECEMBER 1264

Montfort's treatment of Edward showed his belief in material power. Without it his regime had no future. Yet at the very same time, Montfort also showed his belief in the power of reform. Its popularity might also sustain the regime. It was while at Worcester in December 1264 that Montfort took ownership of the Provisions of Westminster, the Provisions Henry himself had tried to appropriate back in January 1263. Described evocatively as articles 'against the oppressions of justices, sheriffs and other bailiffs', both the June 1264 Constitution and the schemes offered to Louis IX and the legate had said they should be enforced.[113] Now at Worcester, Montfort went further. In the king's name, he sent the whole text of the Provisions round to all the counties with a new conclusion saying they were to be observed 'for the benefit of the whole community of England'. To make that all the more certain, they were to be published every month in the county, hundred *and* baronial courts, much of the legislation, of course, being directed against baronial malpractice. The sheriffs were to punish those contravening the Provisions or, if they could not, let the king know the names of the culprits so that he could punish them himself.[114] The measure showed Montfort at his most imaginative and populist, for there was no precedent for monthly proclamations of legislation, or indeed monthly proclamations of anything at all.[115] His success in taking ownership of the Provisions can be judged from a remark of Arnold fitzThedmar. In setting out Henry III's reissue of the Provisions in 1267, he noted that 'the greater part of them were ordained in the time of the earl of Leicester in the year 1264'.[116]

The new text of the Provisions was issued at exactly the same time in December 1264 as the writs of summons for the parliament Montfort planned to hold at Westminster in January 1265, a parliament to which knightly representatives were summoned from every shire. Nothing was more likely to send them to Westminster in a positive mood.[117]

---

[113] *CPR 1258–66*, 371.

[114] Brand, *Kings, Barons and Justices*, 163–4, 450–1.

[115] A point made in Maddicott, 'Politics and the people', 10.

[116] Stone, FitzThedmar, no. 1184. This does not appear in the printed version in FitzThedmar.

[117] For the link, see Maddicott, *Origins of the English Parliament*, 257–8.

Montfort's campaign against the marchers taught lessons elsewhere in the country.[118] During December the royalists in the north surrendered Newcastle-upon-Tyne, Scarborough, Nottingham and probably York and Carlisle too.[119] In the same month, Roger of Clifford vacated Gloucester castle, while Warin of Bassingbourn, Robert Walerand and the rest of the Edwardian garrison agreed to give up Bristol.[120] At Michaelmas 1264 both the exchequer and the bench reopened and litigants once more started to buy writs for judges to hear their cases in the localities.[121]

## THE TWO CHRISTMASES

Henry himself left Worcester on 19 December and spent Christmas at Woodstock, where he had not been since 1260. He found the wall of the park in disrepair and the chamber of his chaplains close to collapse. Apart from putting these defects right, he ordered 100 pear trees to be planted in his garden at Everswell.[122] Henry celebrated the feast 'solemnly', which was perhaps true in more ways than one. Certainly, the Pershore annalist, who makes this comment, was far more impressed by Montfort's own Christmas at Kenilworth.[123] 'The earl, with fortune shining on everything he conceived, celebrated the feast surrounded by many knights. It was said he had belonging to his own household at least 140 in pay . . . all devoted to him. The whole of England save the far north, was subject to him . . . and everything was ordained by him, all the castles of the king being in his power.' What made the celebrations at Kenilworth all the more remarkable was that Lord Edward and King Richard were both captives in the castle. One wonders whether they were put on show or confined to their cells.

The Pershore chronicler, however, mixed admiration with anxiety. Was all this really proper? 'The king, who had already reigned for fifty years, had but the shadow of a name, so that he was unable to traverse and travel through his land, and was completely subject to the lead and decision of another.'[124]

---

[118] But for violent disorder even in Leicestershire when Peter de Montfort sought to take possession of Garthorpe, now given him in place of Robert Walerand, see *CPR 1247–58*, 215; *CPR 1258–66*, 321, 389, 408–9, 479; *CChR 1257–1300*, 51, 56; *CR 1261–4*, 361; TNA JUST 1/1197, m. 17 (image 1520); Stewart, 'A year in the life of a royal justice', 160–1. I am grateful to Henry Summerson for pointing this case out to me.

[119] *CPR 1258–66*, 390–1, 395–6; Oakes, 'The Barons' War in the north of England', 212–13. For Carlisle in this period, see Summerson, *Medieval Carlisle*, i, 125–6.

[120] *CPR 1258–66*, 397; Oakes, 'King's men without the king', 59–60. For Gloucester, see *CLR 1260–7*, 208–9.

[121] See Stewart, 'A year in the life of a royal justice'.

[122] *CLR 1260–7*, 154.

[123] At least Henry was able to have some lampreys. Two were sent to him at Woodstock for Christmas: *CLR 1260–7*, 162.

[124] Pershore, *Flores*, 504–5; Carpenter, 'Pershore *Flores*', 1354–5, 1363; Wild, 'A captive king', 49.

## HENRY AT WESTMINSTER, 1265

After his Christmas at Woodstock, Henry returned to Windsor before continuing on to Westminster for the 5 January feast of the Confessor. The acquisition of seventy-two gold coins for his offerings had been sanctioned by Hugh Despenser, as had the adornment of two choir copes and the purchase of a large sauce boat and dishes. Less pleasant was the discovery that there was a shortage of new wine in London, leaving only old wine which Henry considered unpalatable. Doubtless the threat of invasion had disrupted the trade with Gascony, but at least London was able to supply forty oxen and other food for the feast.[125]

Henry remained at Westminster until 6 April, the parliament itself running from 20 January until at least 11 March. He was finding himself even more isolated and confined. On 1 January, Henry de Ghent, his appointee as keeper of the wardrobe (in office since July 1261), was replaced by Ralph of Sandwich, a Kentish knight, nephew of Bishop Sandwich of London, and a stranger to the king before entering the royal household after the battle of Lewes.[126] Sandwich's accounts survive for the period from 1 January down to 6 August 1265 and reveal Henry's diminished state.[127] The daily costs of the household (most of it going on food and drink) were running at £8 10s a day as against £15 15s a day for the period from July 1261 to December 1264.[128] There was also almost a complete end to Henry's gift-giving. From 1 January to 6 August, Henry gave away two rings, three brooches and no belts.[129] When Henry recovered power after Evesham, rings were bestowed at a rate of nearly five a week, brooches at over one a week and belts at one every ten days. One entry in Sandwich's accounts also refers to the payments to 'certain mounted sergeants staying with the king through the same time'. Were these there less to protect Henry than to watch him?[130]

A similar picture of emasculation emerges from the authorization notes to royal letters issued between January and April 1265. Here there was little change from the pattern seen in the months immediately after Lewes. Henry authorized alone no more than a handful of letters, including gifts to his chaplain at Kempton, the London Dominicans and the hermit of Cripplegate.[131] By contrast, over sixty letters were issued by the council, sometimes emphatically 'by the whole council'. Yet, as before, Henry was made to co-operate. He authorized around forty letters in the company of

---

[125] *CLR 1260–7*, 156, 158, 162.

[126] For Ralph, see Whittick, 'Sir Ralph Sandwich'.

[127] For what follows, see the analysis in Wild, *WA*, clxviii–ix, clxxii, clxxv.

[128] Carpenter, 'Household rolls', 35–6. To be fair, the low figure is partly because of the absence of the queen.

[129] Wild, *WA*, clxviii–ix, clxxv.

[130] As suggested in Wild, *WA*, clxxii, and see his 'A captive king', 45, 55–6.

[131] *CR 1264–8*, 18, 25–6, 29.

the justiciar, Hugh Despenser, the council or individual members of the council. Of the ministers, by far the most active was Despenser himself, followed by Giles de Argentan, Roger de St John, Adam de Newmarch and Ralph de Camoys. St John spent 108 days 'with the king' between the end of October 1264 and April 1265 and is sometimes styled his 'secretary'. Not surprisingly, Henry's one known attempt to assert his will ended in failure. In March 1265 he managed to issue a letter patent appointing Edward's chaplain to the deanery of Bridgnorth. Next month, this was cancelled since the appointment had been made without the council's consent.[132]

Henry's co-operation with the regime was largely in private, within the confines of the court and chancery. How far he appeared in public is less clear.[133] There is no evidence that he was allowed to speak at the parliament, very different from the old days when his oratory had been much in evidence. We do, however, glimpse him once again at the exchequer, this time sitting with his council, although the matter in hand was not of much importance.[134]

## MONTFORT'S GREAT PARLIAMENT, JANUARY–MARCH 1265

Montfort's parliament was due to meet on 20 January.[135] It has become rightly famous as the first to which representatives of both the counties and the towns were summoned. The writs of summons, issued around Christmas, had ordered the sheriffs to send two knights from each county. Given the timescale, there cannot have been formal elections, so presumably the sheriffs chose the knights themselves or picked them from the four chosen to attend the parliament of June 1264. Alongside the knights, Montfort also summoned representatives from the cities of York, Lincoln and 'the other boroughs of England'.[136] That this was something new is suggested by Arnold fitzThedmar. For the only time in his chronicle, he comments on the composition of a parliament. To this one, he says, there came men from 'the Cinque Ports and from each city and borough'.[137] Montfort had seen the contingents from the counties and the towns in the great army mustered on Barham Down.[138] Short of magnate support, it was natural now to reach out to this wider constituency. Wykes himself got close to what was going on.

---

[132] *CPR 1258–66*, 407, 410 (an episode I owe to Ian Bass).

[133] The point is made by Ambler, 'Magna Carta', 805, 829.

[134] TNA E 368/39, m. 8 (image 6189).

[135] For what follows, see Maddicott, *Simon de Montfort*, 314–18; Maddicott, *Origins of the English Parliament*, 257–60.

[136] *CR 1264–8*, 86–7, 89; *DBM*, 300–5.

[137] FitzThedmar, 71 (Stone, FitzThedmar, no. 825); Stone, 'Book of Arnold fitz Thedmar', 236.

[138] This link with the parliament is made by Powicke, *King Henry III*, ii, 483.

Montfort, he said, distrusted the magnates and wished to break their power so that he could more easily subject 'the vulgar people' to his rule.[139]

There is one indication that the representatives were far from a passive presence at the parliament. FitzThedmar states that on 14 February important proclamations were made in the chapter house of Westminster Abbey. Perhaps he was there himself as one of the London members. That the knights were there too, and vocal, is suggested by an order issued on the very next day. This increased the expenses enjoyed by the knights (they were having to stay longer than expected) while also showing concern for the burdens being born by their constituents, 'the communities of the counties' as they were called.[140] The issue of MPs' expenses has a long pedigree.

In terms of the magnates summoned, Montfort's parliament was indeed a narrow and partisan assembly. There were only four earls called besides Montfort himself: Gilbert de Clare, Robert de Vere and of more doubtful commitment Roger Bigod and Robert de Ferrers. The earls of Cornwall, Hereford and Warwick were prisoners of the regime while John de Warenne, earl of Surrey, was with the queen overseas, as were William de Valence and Peter of Savoy. The eighteen magnates summoned were all loyalists. They included the lay members of the council, the northerners John de Vescy, Gilbert de Gant and Roger Bertram of Mitford, and *les jeunes*, fitz John, Hastings, Seagrave and Lucy. Montfort, however, compensated for his paucity of magnate support not merely by summoning knights and townsmen. He also summoned 120 ecclesiastics, including 12 bishops and 102 heads of religious houses.

The stated reason for the summoning of the parliament was to make provision for Edward's release, but, as the writs explained, this was linked to securing the more general peace and tranquillity of the kingdom. A step in that direction was taken by the meeting in the chapter house on 14 February described by fitzThedmar. Henry had conceived the chapter house as a place where he would address the realm from his specially designed lectern, empowered by the glittering tiles bearing his coat of arms running on either side in great bands across the floor. But now the chapter house witnessed the nadir of his kingship. A proclamation was read out stating that neither he nor Edward would seek to harm Montfort, Gilbert de Clare, the Londoners and their adherents on account of events during the disturbances. In addition, Magna Carta, the Charter of the Forest and the Ordinance of June 1264 were all to be observed. Henry had no problem with the Charters. The 1264 Ordinance which had destroyed his kingship was quite another matter.

---

[139] Wykes, 160.
[140] FitzThedmar, 71 (Stone, FitzThedmar, no. 825); *DBM*, 304–7. The enrolled writ is directed to the sheriff of Yorkshire, but similar writs probably went to the other sheriffs.

On 8 March, near the end of the parliament, the proclamation about the June 1264 Constitution was fleshed out and placed on the charter rolls. It recited the Constitution in full with the statement that Henry and the barons had agreed it should be 'firmly kept'.[141] The addition made at Canterbury in August 1264, however, saying the Constitution should last for Henry's lifetime and into the reign of Edward, was not included. So the only indication that the Constitution might have an end remained the possibility of completing the Mise of Lewes. Since that was a dead letter, rule by the three and the nine was now effectively to be permanent.

## THOMAS DE CANTILUPE BECOMES CHANCELLOR

Montfort's wider constituency might welcome the restrictions on the wayward king but they were chiefly interested in the reform of law and local government. Here the position of chancellor was crucial. Before 1258, a major cause of justice being shut out from England, writs had been refused to plaintiffs wishing to bring actions against the king's favourites, while those favourites had got whatever writs they liked. So much, at least, had been alleged in the case prepared for Louis at Amiens, a case almost certainly written by Master Thomas de Cantilupe. It was none other than Cantilupe who now became chancellor. The change took place on 25 February 1265, during the course of the parliament, Cantilupe replacing Henry's pliant and pallid nominee (in office since 1263), John of Chishall.[142] More than anything else during his period of rule, Cantilupe's appointment shows Montfort's commitment to the cause of reform. There was nothing pliant about Thomas. He would stand up not just to the king, but also more generally for law and justice.

Now in his forties, Thomas de Cantilupe was physically vigorous being an enthusiastic huntsman. He gained status from his lineage and his family connections. The nephew of Bishop Cantilupe, he displayed the fleur-de-lys of the Cantilupe arms on both sides of his later episcopal seal. Thomas was also an academic of repute, learned in both canon and civil law. While at the University of Paris, where he lived in some comfort, he made friends with Louis IX. At Oxford, where Thomas became chancellor in 1261, he kept the unruly clerks in order and once indeed intervened physically to break up a fight. As the author of the case made to Louis, no one had thought more extensively and coherently about the evils of Henry's rule and the justification of the Provisions of Oxford. Plucked from academia, Thomas was determined, as chancellor, to act in their spirit. According to a later story, he threatened to resign when he

---

[141] F, i, 451–2 (CChR 1257–1300, 54).

[142] For what follows here and later about Thomas de Cantilupe, see Carpenter, Reign of Henry III, 293–307. This sketch also owes much to the picture of Thomas in Ambler, Bishops in the Political Community, 147–8.

disagreed with a letter Henry wanted him to seal. Like the chancellor envisaged in 1258, he would seal nothing important on the king's sole word. But equally he refused consent to at least one letter that the councillors wanted. He also greatly increased the notes in the chancery rolls indicating on whose authority letters were issued.[143] To enable him to run the chancery without the money from bribes and undercover payments, Thomas secured an increase in the chancellor's salary from 400 to 500 marks a year. In the presence of St John, Despenser, Newmarch and the steward Walter of Crepping, Henry witnessed the sealing of the letter fixing the new amount and folded it with his own hand.[144]

Here then was a chancellor who could be regarded, like Ralph de Neville, as a 'column of truth and faith' in public affairs. Those in the localities, for the first time since Neville's day, had a man of name and fame to whom they could address their complaints and petitions. In one area, indeed, Thomas de Cantilupe returned chancery practice to Neville's day. The case made to Louis IX had called for a responsible chancellor not merely to monitor the issue of writs, but also to prevent 'excessive and unreasonable grants' of the king.[145] During Neville's time all royal charters had ended with the statement that they had been 'given by the hand' of the chancellor, meaning the chancellor had authorized their issue. But after taking the great seal from Neville in 1238, Henry had replaced him as the 'giver'. Now Thomas de Cantilupe replaced Henry and 'gave' all the charters himself. He was thus directly responsible for their issue and could refuse consent to concessions he considered 'excessive and unreasonable'.

Thomas de Cantilupe's appointment linked with other measures showing Montfort's commitment to reform. During the parliament itself a writ was devised to help enforce the legislation forbidding the levying of the *beaupleder* fine in private courts. The exchequer, meanwhile, moved to enforce the chapter on attendance at the sheriff's tourn.[146] As we have seen, the order to obey Magna Carta and the Forest Charter had been proclaimed in the Westminster chapter house on 14 February. And then, at the end of the parliament, the king himself took an oath to observe the Charters and the Provisions of Westminster, the latter now referred to as 'the articles of Worcester'. Montfort really had taken ownership. Henry also enjoined all officials (so baronial ones as well) to take the same oath. If they failed to do so, another novel provision, they were not to be obeyed.

---

[143] TNA C 66/83, m. 21d (*CPR 1258–66*, 481–2); Carpenter, *Reign of Henry III*, 301.

[144] *CPR 1258–66*, 416; *CLR 1260–7*, 169; Dibben, 'Chancellor and keeper of the seal', 48.

[145] *DBM*, 260–3, cap. 9. The appointment to the deanery of Bridgnorth (above, 349), allowed under Chishall, was cancelled under Cantilupe.

[146] *CR 1261–4*, 100; Brand, *Kings, Barons and Justices*, 171, 173; Powicke, *King Henry III*, ii, 489 n. 2. However, rather puzzlingly (as Brand notes), the writ cites Magna Carta rather than the specific banning of the fine in the Provisions of Westminster: Brand, *Kings, Barons and Justices*, 418–19, cap. 5

The texts of the Charters and the articles of Worcester were again sent to the counties with instructions that they be read in the county courts.[147] The letter in which Henry circulated the full text of the 1225 version of Magna Carta was given by Cantilupe and witnessed by nine bishops, and then by Montfort and all his leading followers. The whole Montfortian coalition thus stood behind reform of the realm.[148]

## THE THREAT OF FORCE

Montfort believed profoundly in the reform of the realm. He also knew it would make his regime popular. Yet, as before, Montfort, the man of war, also saw the need to support his constitution with force or the threat of force. Both Henry and Edward were made to swear that, if they challenged the Constitution or did anything to disturb the peace of the realm (notably by acting against their past opponents), then everyone was permitted, indeed was obliged, to rise up against them. Only when matters were put right would the king be obeyed as before. These sanctions were modelled on the revolutionary security clause of the 1215 Magna Carta and since the clause had been omitted from the subsequent versions of the Charter, Montfort had done his homework.[149] His sanctions, however, went beyond those of 1215. Then, only the king had been threatened. Now, all those who might come to the aid of Henry and Edward would suffer perpetual disinheritance.

These frightening threats of retribution were given maximum publicity. Indeed, they were sent to all the counties in exactly the same letters in which Henry and Edward proclaimed their adherence to the Charters and the articles of Worcester.[150] The letters were to be kept in the county court in the custody of trustworthy men elected for the purpose 'as a constant reminder' of what had been agreed. The letters summed up perfectly the two sides of the Montfortian regime, and indeed of Montfort's approach to politics: a belief in reform and a belief in force.

## THE IMPRISONMENT OF ROBERT DE FERRERS

At the parliament itself, there were telling examples of how Montfort could punish his enemies. First, William la Zouche (Edward's erstwhile constable

---

[147] DBM, 312–13.

[148] Ambler, 'Magna Carta', 810–14. The witnesses included Hugh Despenser, Thomas de Clare (Gilbert's brother), John de Burgh, John fitzJohn, Peter de Montfort, Ralph de Camoys, Adam de Newmarch, Giles de Argentan, Roger de St John, Nicholas of Seagrave, William de Munchesney, John de Vescy, Walter of Crepping and Ralph of Sandwich.

[149] Carpenter, 'The secret revolution of 1258', 41–2; F, i, 451–2 (CChR 1257–1300, 54). For the way the 1215 Charter remained well-known, see my Magna Carta, 432–3.

[150] DBM, 308–15.

at Chester) was arrested for making threats against Montfort.[151] Then a much greater adversary was attacked.[152] This was Robert de Ferrers, earl of Derby. Ferrers had been forgiven for his absence from Lewes. He was in London on 8 June 1264 (the feast of Pentecost) when one of his charters was attested by Montfort himself as 'steward of England'.[153] But then Ferrers went absent without leave again, this time from the great army gathered in Kent to meet the threatened invasion. Instead, continuing his feud with Edward, he secured hold of the Peak and launched an attack on Cheshire. He also extracted 100 marks from the abbot of Buildwas and committed numerous disseisins in Derbyshire and further afield. Many of his victims were tenants whom he considered disobedient and disloyal.[154] After a long minority Ferrers was reasserting control over his men. Probably his violence was no worse than that of the marchers in 1263, the northerners or Gilbert de Clare, but it was committed on his own account with not even a tinge of allegiance to the Montfortian cause. Even worse, in the process, he came into conflict with Peter de Montfort and then, fatally, with Montfort himself. For, thanks to the agreement with Edward, the castle and honour of the Peak were now supposed to be in Montfort's hands.

At Christmas 1264, Ferrers was ordered both to surrender the Peak to Montfort and come south to the January parliament.[155] Back in the 1220s, Robert's grandfather, when ordered to vacate the Peak, had choked back his anger and complied.[156] Robert did the reverse. However, far too confident, he did come to the parliament. There his various excesses in supposedly a time of peace provided easy grounds for proceeding against him. Ferrers was also charged with being in alliance with the rebel marchers. And he faced the anger of the king himself thanks to his attacks on Edward's lands. In an impossible position, surrounded by enemies, Ferrers 'dared not await judgement' and 'submitted himself wholly, life, limbs and lands to the king's grace'. He was taken off to imprisonment in the Tower as a 'public enemy'.[157] This was the fate that awaited those who crossed Montfort.

## EDWARD'S 'RELEASE'.

Nowhere was Montfort's belief in force and the facts of power better seen than in the final arrangements for Edward's supposed release. Here

---

[151] *CR 1264–8*, 99.

[152] For what follows, I am indebted to the detailed analysis drawing on unpublished material in Golob, 'The Ferrers earls of Derby', i, 329–38.

[153] *Beauchamp Cartulary*, no. 352.

[154] For his attack in late June or early July 1264 on the Derbyshire lands of one of his major tenants, William of Montgomery, see TNA KB 26/174, m. 1d (*AP*, 156).

[155] *CPR 1258–66*, 397; *CR 1264–8*, 86.

[156] Carpenter, 'The struggle to control the Peak', 45–6.

[157] *CPR 1258–66*, 409; Robert of Gloucester, ii, lines 11456–63; Waverley, 358; Wykes, 160; St Werburgh, 90–1.

Montfort was determined to go through with the deal agreed at Worcester back in December 1264, one hugely increasing his power at Edward's expense. So, in March 1265, Edward formally returned the county and castle of Chester, the castle and honour of the Peak, and the castle of Newcastle-under-Lyme to the king, who granted them at once to Montfort in hereditary right. In return, Edward received just a scattering of lands, including the very manors Montfort had extracted from the king back in 1259.[158] Edward also confirmed his surrender of Bristol to Montfort. It was to be held for a year while all these transfers were put into place. Nor was this all. A set of new provisions were introduced, going way beyond what had been outlined in December. After the year was up, Edward was not to recover Bristol. Rather, with five other royal castles, it was to be handed over for five years to the council as 'hostage' for his good behaviour. During that time neither he nor Henry were to enter them. The castles were the mightiest in the land: Dover, Scarborough, Bamborough, Nottingham and Corfe. Since the council already controlled appointments to royal castles, this really was making assurance doubly sure.

Edward had also to accept a whole series of further restrictions. No wonder Wykes commented that he was in a worse condition free than when a captive.[159] His household and councillors were to be native born ('men of the land') and chosen with the agreement of the council. He was not to bring aliens into the land; for three years he was to be confined to where the king's writ ran in England, so he was excluded from Wales, as well as Ireland and Gascony. Most ominous, most extraordinary of all, were the sanctions if any of these restrictions were broken. All Edward's lands, lordships, dignities and honours would be confiscated, and he and his heirs would be disinherited 'for all their days'. This was to be final. It was stated explicitly that Edward would lose all right to challenge his disinheritance.

Edward's 'release' on these terms took place on Wednesday 11 March and was described by fitzThedmar, who was probably present.[160] In the great hall at Westminster before all the people, Edward and Henry of Almain were delivered to King Henry 'free and quit'. The king's letters explaining his adherence to the Montfortian constitution and the penalties for its breach were read out. Then nine bishops robed in pontificals and holding lighted candles excommunicated all who contravened the Charters, the constitution of June 1264 and the articles of Worcester. The king, as far as the account goes, was silent. It was a very different scene from that in the great hall in 1253 when, after the sentences of excommunication, Henry, with his own voice, had reserved the rights of the crown.[161]

---

[158] CChR 1257–1300, 52; F, i, 451–2; CR 1264–8, 109; Maddicott, Simon de Montfort, 321–2.
[159] Wykes, 161.
[160] FitzThedmar, 71 (Stone, FitzThedmar, no. 826); Stone, 'Book of Arnold fitz Thedmar', 236.
[161] F, i, 306.

The excommunications did not conclude the proceedings. 'As greater security' for Edward's obedience, Henry of Almain 'willingly' (?) surrendered himself to Henry de Montfort, to remain in custody till August, or till November, if an army of 'aliens' was threatening invasion.[162] So Henry of Almain was not to be released after all. One other announcement was made on this day. Whereas the king before the battle of Lewes had defied Montfort, Clare and their adherents, now all the freemen of England were to renew their oaths of homage and fealty to the king. This, however, was to be saving everything in the letters just read out, which included the right of resistance 'notwithstanding the fealty and homage' owed the king. Henry learnt the shaming impact of this provision a few days later when the mayor of London, Thomas fitzThomas, and the aldermen came before him in St Paul's to renew their oaths. FitzThomas told Henry to his face that 'as long as you wish to be a good king and lord to us, we will be faithful and devoted to you'.[163] The declaration just about summed up the debasement of Henry's kingship at the great parliament of 1265.

---

[162] FitzThedmar, 71–2 (Stone, FitzThedmar, nos. 826–31). Presumably by November the threat of invasion would be over for the year.

[163] FitzThedmar, 73 (Stone, FitzThedmar, no. 832 and note). FitzThedmar added this comment after the battle of Evesham: Stone, 'Book of Arnold fitz Thedmar', 236–7.

Chapter 10

# MONTFORT'S KINGDOM[1]

During his great parliament of 1265, Simon de Montfort seemed at the height of his power. He was surrounded by his redoubtable sons and a loyal core of leading magnates. He had support from the bishops and other churchmen, in some cases fervent support. The parliament was attended, for the first time in English history, by both burgesses from the towns and knights from the shires, there to applaud and affirm Montfort's measures. London was absolutely his, as probably were other towns. Modern research has shown just how many county knights, in some way or other, at one time or another, supported his insurgency and subsequent regime. It was not, moreover, just the knights. Beneath them large numbers of freemen and peasants were involved in the rebellion. There was at all levels a belief that Montfort and his men were fighting for the good of the country and 'the community of the realm'. In terms of participation and understanding, English politics resonated across society in a way never seen before.[2]

The supporters of the regime could feel energized and justified by its God-given success: the victory at Lewes, the repulse of the queen's invasion, the defeat of the marcher barons, the promulgation of reforms (including the statute against the aliens) and now this prodigious parliament at Westminster. As Montfortians awoke in the morning, as they passed through the day, they felt the balm of these miraculous events, rather as, flying in from a cold England, one feels at once on landing in the wonderful heat of a Mediterranean summer. Nowhere are such feelings better exemplified than in the poem *The Song of Lewes*, written in the months after the great victory. Its 968 mesmerizing lines of Latin verse show just how intense was belief in the man and his cause. Those who, during the parliament, saw the great earl in all his pietistic pomp progressing from Peter of Savoy's house on the Strand (where he stayed) to the halls and chambers at Westminster, saw him in the Abbey's chapter house, saw his great shield newly erected and painted in the Abbey's choir, must surely have believed he would always be victorious. No wonder

---

[1] This chapter heading echoes that of ch. 8 in Maddicott's *Simon de Montfort*.
[2] The involvement of 'not just nobles but the entire people of the realm' is the theme of Claire Valente's chapter on 1258–65, 'The Community of the Realm': Valente, *Theory and Practice of Revolt*, ch. 4.

people later spoke of 'the time of the earl' and 'the time of the king' as though they were equivalents.[3] Of course, in reality Montfort's regime was fractured and fragile. After the close of the great parliament it lasted for less than six months. That is the story of the next chapter. Here we look in more detail at the strengths of Montfort's kingdom.

## THE RESTORATION OF ORDER AND GOVERNMENT

Up to a point the confidence in the regime shown in *The Song of Lewes* was reflected in the situation on the ground. During March 1265 much of the resistance in the north ended. John de Balliol came to court and surrendered Castle Barnard as security for his good behaviour. Peter de Brus did likewise with his castle of Skelton.[4] By this time, all the king's castles throughout the country were in Montfortian hands save Bamburgh, Richmond and Pevensey, and they hardly threatened the lifeblood of the regime.[5]

There were other signs of a return to normal. Between 10 January and Henry's departure from Westminster in April, around 250 people came to court to buy writs to initiate or further common-law legal actions. At an average of fifteen a week this was three times the level achieved between June 1264 and January 1265. The professional judges were working for the regime and one of them, Gilbert of Preston, criss-crossed the country hearing cases.[6] He and his fellows were commissioned to hear assizes in nearly every county, the only conspicuous exception being Shropshire. In the grip of Hamo Lestrange, it also failed to send representatives to parliament.

The exchequer was getting into its stride.[7] At Easter 1265 the total brought from the counties and boroughs was £1,361 with all the sheriffs bar one (that for Cumberland) attending in person or through deputies. The figure was lower than that produced in most peacetime years (the average between the Easters of 1250 and 1258 was over £2,000), but it was a far better performance than at Michaelmas 1264. Then only £339 had been brought, with eight sheriffs not attending at all.[8] In some counties

---

[3] Jacob, *Studies*, 296 n. 1, comments on the significance of this.

[4] Oakes, 'The Barons' War in the north of England', 212–13.

[5] For further discussion on the three castles, see Oakes, 'King's men without the king', 61–7.

[6] The figures are from *CFR 1263–4* and *CFR 1264–5*. See Stewart, 'A year in the life of a royal justice'. For Shropshire and Lestrange, see *DBM*, 306–9; *CIM*, no. 291.

[7] William Marshal (of Northampton fame) joined as a baron of the exchequer: TNA E 368/39, m. 5 (images 6181). William, however, was dead by September 1265: *CIM*, no. 818 (where it is not said he died in any conflict). Much effort went into summoning Henrician sheriffs to account and getting in the money owed by the sheriffs for 1264 when nothing had been received because of the disturbances; see for example, TNA E 368/39, m. 9 (images 6191–2).

[8] TNA E 159/39, m. 27d (image 0163); Cassidy, 'Adventus vicecomitum', 616. The Easter 1265 figure was larger than that at Easter 1258.

local government was proceeding more or less as normal. In the first part of 1265, sheriffs were holding regular courts in Kent, Wiltshire, Norfolk, Suffolk, Nottinghamshire and Derbyshire. In Surrey, the sheriff was able to raise £186 of the £260 he was ordered to collect from the proceeds of the last eyre.[9] Montfort, moreover, was not dependent on the revenues of the crown. His wealth, a great stay of the regime, came from other sources: from the lands and ransoms of the prisoners taken at Lewes, from the pillage of the Jews in London, from the piracy of the Cinque Ports and from seizures of wool waiting to be exported. As well as Edward's Cheshire, Montfort held the lands of King Richard including Cornwall with its tin mines.[10] Henry later believed that after Evesham, Eleanor de Montfort took 11,000 marks out of the country.[11] The wealth was used to support Montfort's retinue of knights. According to the Pershore chronicler at Christmas 1264, he had 140 knights in his pay. In March 1265 he arrived at Odiham with 160 horses. When Henry de Montfort and Simon junior came to Dunstable for a tournament in the middle of the parliament, 'they abounded in money and had an innumerable company of paid knights'.[12]

## MONTFORT'S SONS

'Even if everyone universally deserts me, I, with my four sons, will stand steadfastly for the just cause which I have sworn to uphold, for the honour of God and the utility of the kingdom, nor will I fear battle.' Montfort's declaration, reported by Rishanger, reflects very well the importance of his sons.[13] This was a family affair. Henry, the eldest, was now coming up to twenty-seven. Simon junior was around twenty-five and Guy twenty-one. All three were able, ambitious, militaristic men very much in their father's mold. Henry and Guy had been with their father at Lewes. Simon junior had been the captain at Northampton. The sons were highly educated. Henry had written out in his own hand his father's will.[14]

The sons now reaped rich rewards. Guy de Montfort took over Cornwall and King Richard's lands in Devon. Simon junior added the Sussex lands of John de Warenne to those of John Mansel. He also sought to marry the wealthiest woman of the age, Isabella de Forz, countess of Devon in her

---

[9] Cassidy, 'Simon de Montfort's sheriffs', 14–17; Cassidy, 'Bad sheriffs, custodial sheriffs', 47. Regular courts were probably being held elsewhere but these are the counties for which there is evidence.

[10] For Montfort's wealth, see Maddicott, *Simon de Montfort*, 309–11; and for Cornwall, see Page, 'Cornwall, Earl Richard and the Barons' War', 21, 23, 31–2.

[11] *CR 1264–8*, 136; Wykes, 157–9.

[12] Maddicott, *Simon de Montfort*, 311; Wykes, 161–2.

[13] Rishanger, 17.

[14] The third son, Amaury, was already making his way in the church. The fifth son, Richard, was too young to play much part in events between 1263 and 1265.

own right and with a dower third of the lands of her late husband, the earl of Aumale. According to Isabella's later story, she was pursued round the country by young Simon and had to take refuge in Wales. Certainly she avoided coming to the king to do homage, which would have put her into Montfort's power.[15] Meanwhile, Henry de Montfort was placed in command of Corfe, Dover and (from January 1265) Cheshire. He was also given the £1,000 ransom of Robert de Stuteville.[16] Amaury, the clerical son, now in his mid-twenties, was promoted to the lucrative treasurership of York, vacant thanks to John Mansel's death.[17]

In the fullness of his power, Montfort also moved to increase the inheritance of his eldest son. In March 1265 he and Eleanor granted to Henry in hereditary right Luton and three Kentish manors, including Sutton with its castle. But this they had no right to do. The grant implied that the properties were part of Eleanor's inheritance but in fact she only held them in dower and on her death they should have passed to the numerous Marshal heirs.[18] Montfort here appears at his most unscrupulous and yet there was a justification. Was this not some compensation, however arbitrary, for all the profit the Marshal heirs had made at Eleanor's expense through the short change over her dower? Back in November 1264, Montfort had formally raised the question for the last time when the bishop of Worcester, Hugh Despenser and Peter de Montfort were appointed to inquire into Eleanor's losses and give her compensation. There is no evidence they acted, or at least that their actions had any result. Even for these Montfortian stalwarts the rights and wrongs of the matter were hard to unravel. Their commission implied that the king was wholly to blame but the gainers had been the Marshal heirs and any settlement was bound to touch them. The issue was impossible to resolve without lengthy inquiries and litigation. In getting permanent hold of Luton and the other manors, Montfort acted for himself.[19]

It is easy to think all of this shows the 'voracious quest for profit' which had marked and mired Montfort's career.[20] Yet the context was now very different. The private and the public had become inseparable. Montfort and his sons were the heart of the regime. Their strength was the necessary

---

[15] *AP*, 172; *CR 1264–8*, 112; *CFR 1262–3*, no. 713.

[16] St Werburgh, 90–1; TNA E 159/39, m. 1 (image 0003–4). A charter here of Stuteville granting two manors to Henry (if he failed to pay the ransom) was witnessed by Hugh Despenser and Giles de Argentan and 'given in the cloister of Westminster', an intriguing glimpse of business being carried on there.

[17] *CPR 1258–66*, 404, 436; Maddicott, *Simon de Montfort*, 324–5. The appointment fell to the king as the archbishopric of York was vacant.

[18] After Evesham, Sutton was granted to William de Valence as part of his wife's share of the Marshal inheritance – hence the name Sutton Valence: *CPR 1258–66*, 588.

[19] *CChR 1257–1300*, 54; *CChR 1226–57*, 102; *CPR 1258–66*, 388–9. The grant was witnessed by Edward: *RCWL*, ii, 148.

[20] Maddicott, *Simon de Montfort*, 309.

condition of its survival and the survival, Montfort would have said, of the Provisions of Oxford. As Rishanger put it, Montfort's control of the lands and castles of his captives was absolutely justified for, with many deserting, only thus could the 'statutes of Oxford' be secured.[21] His sons too were not idly living off the lands of captives. They were having to control areas of great strategic importance. Simon junior may or may not have chased Isabella de Forz across the country. He was certainly engaged in a long (and admittedly fruitless) siege to get Peter of Savoy's garrison out of Pevensey castle.

## MONTFORT'S CORE SUPPORT

Montfort's power was fully endorsed by his closest partisans. In that sense, the regime was solid. The crucial charter transferring Edward's possessions to Montfort was 'given' by Thomas de Cantilupe and witnessed by Hugh Despenser and five members of the council: the bishop of London, Peter de Montfort, Camoys, Newmarch and Humphrey de Bohun junior.[22] At the end of the parliament the king's confirmation of Magna Carta was again given by Cantilupe and witnessed by all these men together with John fitzJohn, John de Burgh, Giles de Argentan, Roger de St John, John de Vescy, Nicholas of Seagrave and William de Munchesney. Apart from Camoys and John de Burgh, all these men remained loyal to their leader. Wykes believed that both Despenser and fitzJohn felt short changed by Montfort's division of the spoils, but both were with him at Evesham, Despenser dying there. In fact, fitzJohn, besides being castellan of Windsor (from where he terrorized the surrounding population), was given custody of the lands of his late brother-in-law Robert de Vipont and so became ruler of Westmorland.[23] Despenser, besides his salary as justiciar and his custody of the Tower, held the castles of Devizes, Oxford, Orford and Nottingham and ransomed one prisoner taken at Lewes for 700 marks. Like other members of the regime, he was able to pass down favours to his own men, so his knight Gilbert of Elsfield was given a licence to hunt in the Oxfordshire forests.[24] A longish list could be made of other members of the regime who were given custody of lands, castles and London houses or received other concessions, including remission of debts to the Jews. Peter de Montfort at last saw the money fee he received from the king converted into land by the grant of Garthorpe manor in Leicestershire,

---

[21] Rishanger, 41–2; Maddicott, *Simon de Montfort*, 317–18, describes this as 'one of those telling comments by which he [Rishanger] reveals himself almost as the mirror of the earl's mind'.

[22] *RCWL*, ii, 148.

[23] *CPR 1258–66*, 322, 349.

[24] *CR 1264–8*, 105; *CPR 1258–66*, 352; and see *CFR 1264–5*, no. 387; TNA JUST 1/1197, m. 21 (image 1531). For Gilbert ravaging the Berkshire estates of Reginald fitzPeter, TNA Just 1/ 42, m.10d (image 1231).

thus setting aside the earlier grant to Robert Walerand.[25] Such rewards could attract and cement loyalty. At Worcester in December 1264 the king (meaning Montfort) gave the local landholder Richard of Spetchley two deer to stock his park. Later Richard died at Evesham.[26]

Many of those around Montfort at the Westminster parliament had signed up during the course of the struggle. That was true of Humphrey de Bohun junior, John fitzJohn, Roger de St John, William de Munchesney and others. But Montfort also had followers with whom he had longer and closer connections, connections going back well before the testing time between 1263 and 1265. Many of these men have already appeared in these pages: Peter de Montfort, Hugh Despenser, Richard de Grey, Ralph Basset of Sapcote, Thomas of Astley, Nicholas of Seagrave and John de la Haye. Peter de Montfort, Ralph Basset, Astley and de la Haye had all gone with Montfort to Gascony in 1248.[27] In 1259, Hugh Despenser was appointed in Montfort's will as an adviser to the executors and their connection by then must have been well established. The same was probably true of Richard de Grey, named by the king in 1260 (again with Peter de Montfort) as one of Montfort's friends on the ruling council. Richard of Havering, Montfort's steward (very often in his company), dated back to the 1230s, having been in Eleanor's service before her marriage.

The heartland of this inner group lay overwhelmingly in Warwickshire and Leicestershire, counties dominated by the great earl.[28] Here he was lord of Leicester and many manors besides. From 1244, by the king's concession, he held the castle of Kenilworth. The castle's impact on the surrounding 'pays' must have been profound. Protected by its lake and interplay of water defences (so the main gate could only be approached across a causeway), Kenilworth was arguably, after Dover, the most formidable castle in the kingdom. In 1266 it resisted the king's army from June through to December. The Pershore annalist wrote of how Montfort had strengthened the castle with 'wonderful' buildings and 'machines' hitherto unknown. Montfort himself boasted of the money he had spent on it.[29] At Kenilworth, he held his great Christmas court in 1264. At Kenilworth, after his death, the place where he sat, presumably in the great hall, radiated spiritual power. The rector of Sapcote, in the castle after Evesham, was cured there of a painful gout.[30] Kenilworth, dwarfing the manor houses and castles (if they had them) of the surrounding knights, showed Montfort in a different league of power.

---

[25] *CChR 1257–1300*, 51, 56; *CPR 1247–58*, 215; *CIM*, no. 769.

[26] *CR 1264–8*, 7; *CIM*, no. 936; *Worcestershire Eyre of 1275*, no. 847.

[27] *CPR 1247–58*, 31.

[28] There is a full discussion of Montfort's following in Maddicott, *Simon de Montfort*, 59–74. See also Carpenter, *Reign of Henry III*, 226–9; and Williams, 'Simon de Montfort and his adherents'.

[29] Paris, v, 697; Pershore, *Flores*, 489.

[30] 'Miracula', 87.

Many of Montfort's closest followers held lands in the Leicester, Kenilworth area. Richard de Grey's manor of Alvington was in the outskirts of Leicester; Sapcote, Seagrave, Hugh Depenser's Loughborough, Kibworth Harcourt of Montfort's knight Saer de Harcourt and Noseley of his steward Anketil de Martival were all within a dozen miles of the town. Astley and Peter de Montfort's Beaudesert were under twelve miles from Kenilworth. The tie of neighbourhood was strengthend in some cases by ties of tenure and its attendant act of homage. Richard de Grey, Ralph Basset, Thomas of Astley, Nicholas of Seagrave, John de la Haye, Anketil de Martival and another family in Montfort's service, the Trussels, all held at least some of their land from the earl.

Montfort was also highly successful in attracting to his service the tenants of other lords. Here he was lucky for the lack of rival earls in the area had cleared the field.[31] If the staunchly royalist Zouches of Ashby de la Zouche escaped Montfort's orbit, they were hardly competitors for service and support.[32] From the tenants of the earl of Winchester, Montfort thus recruited Saer de Harcourt; from those holding from the defunct earldom of Chester, Hugh Despenser and the Seagraves; and from those of the earl of Warwick, Peter de Montfort.

Just as they were tied to Montfort by neighbourhood, so Montfort's men were tied by neighbourhood to each other and to other rebels.[33] This often meant they were also connected by marriage. Both neighbourhood and intermarriage had created the axis between the Montforts of Beaudesert and the Cantilupes, as we have seen.[34] Here then Montfort could step into a ready-made alliance, one providing him with utterly committed spiritual and political support.[35]

Montfort solidified this inner circle by judicious acts of patronage. He granted the manor of Bagworth in Leicestershire to Gilbert of Seagrave, Nicolas's father, and Ilmington in Warwickshire to Peter de Montfort. (This was nice for Peter as Ilmington adjoined his manor at Whitchurch.)[36] Another knightly tenant of the earl of Winchester, Peter le Porter, was given a marriage and a wardship.[37] Had more evidence survived, it would almost certainly show gifts to his men of money, wine, rings, precious objects, deer and wood, replicating here the kind of gifts made by the king.

---

[31] See above, 113. The theme is developed in Williams, 'Simon de Montfort and his adherents', 174–6.

[32] For the Zouches, see Cokayne, *Complete Peerage*, xii, 930–3.

[33] The ties of neighbourhood binding together the rebels in Warwickshire is a major theme in Fernandes, 'The midlands knights and the Barons' War'.

[34] See above, 53. I am grateful for a detailed study of the Montforts of Beaudesert by David Crouch, compiled as part of his work on comital charters.

[35] For their closeness see TNA SC 1/7/20.

[36] Subsequently, however, Ilmington was given to John de Harcourt, presumably with Peter receiving compensation: Maddicott, *Simon de Montfort*, 198.

[37] *CIM*, no. 930.

Once Montfort gained power, of course, he could use the resources of the king to reward his followers.

Montfort's inner circle was comparatively small, no more perhaps than a dozen knights at any time, although it might well appear larger had more evidence survived.[38] It was, however, a following of considerable power. Peter de Montfort, Richard de Grey and Hugh Despenser in particular came from the top level of the knightly class and had incomes of baronial proportions. They are better thought of as 'magnates' rather than simple knights. They gave Montfort support at the highest level of national politics, as we have seen. They also boosted his local power for all three were major landholders across several counties. In Warwickshire, the extensive earthworks of Peter de Montfort's castle at Beaudesert, situated on a long low hill above Henley in Arden, remain impressive.[39] Peter was very ready to use force in local quarrels. On the 1260 eyre (the one commissioned by the Provisions of Westminster), the knight Jordan of Whitacre complained that on Peter's orders a band of ten men had broken into his house at Elmdon, wounded his man and taken assorted oxen and pigs back to Peter's manor at Hampton in Arden. He put his damages, for this action of distraint out of fee, at 100 marks. Peter denied the break-in but admitted the seizure. It had been done to enforce the payment of relief and the 1257 Welsh scutage.[40] Later, during the civil war, Peter de Montfort's men staged another attack on Jordan's manor at Elmdon.

Jordan of Whitacre, by his own account, adhered 'faithfully and constantly' to the king and Lord Edward, hardly a surprise given his quarrels with Peter. But Peter's activities were not always so counterproductive.[41] Between 1260 and 1262 six Warwickshire knights stood surety for him. All were to rebel. One, Robert Hastang, was his tenant for a manor close to Beaudesert.[42] Peter also consolidated the place of the Trussels in Montfort's following. Tenants of the earl in Northamptonshire, their

---

[38] The witness lists of charters provide key evidence for a noble's entourage but only twenty-four survive issued by Montfort himself. There are no account rolls to show how he was spending his money.

[39] Fernandes, 'The midlands knights and the Barons' War', 173, 175–7. Beaudesert has been subject to a three-day Time Team dig to unravel 'the mystery of Henley's missing castle': https://www.youtube.com/watch?v=mHg9i–Az8–k. Some foundations of a hall were found and some tiles, but on the whole the castle remained missing and a mystery. For the torture of a boy in the castle during Peter's minority, see TNA JUST 1/951A, mm. 1–1d (images 6961, 7008).

[40] TNA JUST 1/953, m. 7 (image 7270); TNA KB 26/167, m. 6d (image 0094); TNA KB 26/174, m. 3d (image 0052); CFR 1256–7, no. 128; CChR 1226–57, 453; Fernandes, 'The midlands knights and the Barons' War', 173; and see Coss, Lordship, Knighthood and Locality, 294 n. 108, 325. For other quarrels involving Peter, see TNA KB 26/160, image 0204 and TNA JUST 1/721, images 0365, 0368; TNA KB 26/161, m. 21 (image 0084); CIM, no. 875.

[41] TNA KB 26/174, m. 3d (image 0052).

[42] TNA JUST 1/953, m. 7 (image 7270); TNA JUST 1/954, m. 23d (image 7476); Fernandes, 'The midlands knights and the Barons' War', 175–6.

manor at Billesley was only six miles from Beaudesert. William Trussel, a justice of the bench, acted as Simon's attorney, while Richard Trussel would die at Evesham. Peter's power, as perceived by one Northamptonshire knight, is shown in a telling episode. When Simon de Montfort summoned William of Welton, to join him with horses and arms, Welton went to Kenilworth and gave the earl 10 marks 'for peace'. At the same time he gave Peter a horse worth £15.[43]

Montfort's leading followers did not merely recruit men into his service. They also held local office. Richard de Grey became castellan of Dover in 1258, and returned to the post in 1263. Peter le Porter was one of the four knights investigating abuses in Leicestershire in 1258, Anketil de Martival being one of those in Warwickshire. Anketil went on to be sheriff of the two counties in 1258–9. Thomas of Astley and Ralph Basset of Sapcote were baronial sheriffs in Warwickshire and Leicestershire in 1261 and then Montfortian keepers of the peace, as was John de la Haye in Sussex. In 1264, La Haye, as constable at Dover, recruited men for the siege of Rochester, while next year he was Eleanor de Montfort's commander in the castle. Meanwhile, Richard of Havering was in command at Wallingford and Berkhamsted. The loyalty of the inner circle survived until Evesham. Peter de Montfort, Hugh Despenser, Thomas of Astley and Richard Trussel were all killed there, as were other Warwickshire knights including William of Birmingham (Thomas of Astley's son-in-law) and Robert of Hartshill (just by Astley), while Thomas of Arden and Henry de Curzun (a Montfort tenant) were captured there.[44]

## THE COUNTY KNIGHTS

If Montfort's heartland lay in Warwickshire and Leicester, there was plenty of backing in other shires. The evidence for Suffolk, wrote E.F. Jacob, revealed 'the presence and support of a fairly numerous country gentry'.[45] Detailed studies of the knights in other shires have similar findings.[46] Here, the main criteria for inclusion on the side of the insurgency are the same: participation in the conflicts at Northampton, Lewes, Evesham and Kenilworth; holding office during the regime; participating in raids on the property of loyalists; having lands seized after Evesham for being against the king; and having to pay a fine to recover

---

[43] RS, 154–5.

[44] For the eight rebels in Warwickshire's Hemlingford hundred, including Birmingham, Astley and Hartshill, see CIM, no. 928; and Fernandes, 'The midlands knights and the Barons' War', 176.

[45] Jacob, Studies, 299–300.

[46] There is also a country-wide sample of involvement by Claire Valente, covering all classes and coming to much the same conclusions as to the knights. Valente, Theory and Practice of Revolt, 90–107 and 254–9.

lands thus confiscated.[47] Although the groups examined vary, and the evidence is uneven, the broad pattern is clear. While the largest number of knights give no clue to their allegiance one way or the other, a very significant proportion (often around a third or more in each shire) at one time or another supported the Montfortian movement, or were at least accused of doing so. The number of knights known to have sided with the king is always much smaller.

To give some details from these county studies, in Dorset, while the largest number of knights (as far as the evidence goes) 'kept their heads down', fourteen, at least a third of those in the shire, were involved in the rebellion, while only eight or nine supported the king.[48] In Kent, there were around eighty active knights in the years 1263 to 1265. The allegiance of thirty-one is unknown. Twenty-six (33 per cent) can be found on Montfort's side in 1264–5, while another five knights were in the allegiance of Gilbert de Clare. There were eighteen knights on the king's side including seven followers of Roger of Leybourne. In 1263 the king's side was weaker, Montfort's stronger, since Leybourne was then in the Montfortian camp.[49] Moving across the Thames, to Essex, nearly 150 members of Essex gentry families played some part in the hostilities on one side or the other, around a half of the whole. Of these the overwhelming majority supported Montfort, though they included some important knights in the following of Gilbert de Clare.[50]

In a range of other counties, historians have proceeded by examining the allegiance of the knights sitting on grand-assize juries in the years immediately before the rebellion. Such groups, sometimes quite small, do not include all the county knights and often exclude the most senior who were above such duties. They do, however, provide a fairly representative sample of knights active in their counties. In Buckinghamshire, of the twenty-eight knights surveyed, ten took some part in the rebellion, while there was only one conspicuous loyalist (King Richard's steward and

---

[47] The evidence itself is fairly abundant. Alongside that running through the chancery rolls, three sources are particularly important: the county-by-county survey, commissioned in September 1265, into the lands of those against the king 'in the late war and disturbance' (*CIM*, nos. 608–940, 1024); the rolls of the justices in eyre appointed in 1267 to enforce the terms of the Dictum of Kenilworth, under which former rebels were allowed to buy back their lands, and the records of the litigation brought by loyalists against those who had ravaged their estates (see below, 578–9).

[48] Ridgeway, 'Dorset in the period of baronial reform and rebellion', 36–40. See also his 'The exploits of two Dorset knights at the battle of Lewes'.

[49] These figures are from Jeremy Quick's thesis, 'Government and society in Kent', 264–72, with 242–62 for general discussion.

[50] Moore, 'Government and locality in Essex', 241, with a detailed list in Appendix 4, between pp. 304 and 312. As the size of these figures suggests, the group here is not confined to those who were knights.

tenant, Fulk of Rycote).[51] In Oxfordshire, of twenty-nine knights, eleven (38 per cent) were rebels and five were loyalists, leaving the rest (45 per cent) with their allegiance unrecorded.[52]

Moving north to Northamptonshire, of a larger group, this time of fifty-eight knights, as many as thirty-nine were rebels, so well over half. There were eight loyalists leaving only sixteen unrecorded. A much smaller group studied in Cambridgeshire has nineteen knights, with eight rebels and one loyalist. In Warwickshire, where the group does not include many of Montfort's chief supporters, of the twenty-nine knights, twelve were rebels and five loyalists.[53] Only one county seems to buck the general trend: Berkshire. Here, of twenty-five knights, while there were only two royalists, only five knights were accused of rebellion, and three of these, rightly or wrongly, were acquitted of the charge.[54]

These figures, of course, are subject to all kinds of qualifications. Contemporaries often spoke of those supporting one side or the other 'in thought word and deed' and these figures are derived only from deeds. They tell nothing about any wider groundswell of sympathy for one side or the other. They are also very likely to underestimate the support given to the king, the evidence for rebellion being far greater than that for loyalty. The king had by far the larger army at Lewes, and some of the knights who appear uncommitted may well have been there on his side. Unless they were rewarded, or held office during periods of Henrician rule or unless they brought lawsuits because their lands were attacked by rebels, we know nothing about them.

In terms of the rebels, how reliable is the evidence for their guilt? That of some brooked no denial, but others claimed they were unjustly accused and had always stood by the king. Sometimes juries agreed with these excuses, sometimes not. Sometimes they disagreed with each other. One jury said that Thomas of Higham (in Kent) had been against the king at

---

[51] I have studied Buckinghamshire myself although I cannot claim in the same detail as historians of the other counties. The knights are found on TNA JUST 1/58, mm. 1, 1d, 2d (images 1143, 1208–9). I have added in the knights appointed to investigate abuses in 1258 where they do not appear on the juries. For the county in this period, see Valente, *Theory and Practice of Revolt*, 256–9, and for the fortunes of knights more generally across the thirteenth century, see Polden, 'A crisis of the knightly class?'

[52] As studied by Adrian Jobson: Jobson '1261 Oxfordshire Eyre', ch. 6.

[53] Northamptonshire, Cambridgeshire and Warwickshire are studied in Mario Fernandes's doctoral thesis, 'The role of the midlands knights in the period of reform and rebellion'. For Staffordshire, see Hunt, 'Families at war', 4.

[54] Berkshire is another county where I have attempted my own study. For the jury, see TNA JUST 1/40, m. 1 (image 1034). I have included the county coroners at the time of the eyre and the knights of 1258 when they do not appear on the jury. Support for the insurrection in the north has yet to be studied at the level of the county knights, but for the involvement of magnates, see Oakes, 'The Barons' War in the north'. Leading rebels included John de Vescy, Robert de Vipont, John de Eyville and Gilbert de Gant, but the north was not the seat of the rebellion against King Henry as it was against King John.

the siege of Rochester and had maintained a crossbowman at his own cost for the attack on the castle all the time the earl of Leicester was there. Another averred that he had been forced to go to Rochester by the earl's bailiffs and on the way had given two tuns of wine to be allowed to go home.[55]

There is also the problem of the changing shape and size of Montfort's following, as we have already noted in Kent. The records often have land seized because an individual was 'against the king' without indicating how and when. That there was 'drop-out' is suggested by the knights present at Northampton who then, so juries agreed, took no further part in the hostilities. Many knights must have been taken in and out of Montfort's camp by Edward's erstwhile followers and later by Gilbert de Clare. Yet if such considerations serve to diminish the numbers on Montfort's side at any one time, others cut the other way. Some local juries seem to have closed ranks and kept silent, thus protecting rebels from having their lands seized. An inquiry of around 1275 into this happening in Kent revealed half a dozen knights who benefited in this way.[56] The rebellion was thus almost certainly larger than the surviving evidence suggests.

While then much is unknown and unknowable about the rebellion, the primary conclusion remains. A very significant number of knights from across the counties of England gave some support to Montfort's movement.

## FREE TENANTS AND PEASANTS

While it is possible to hazard an actual percentage of the knightly class involved in the rebellion, the same cannot be done lower down the social scale. The numbers involved were nonetheless large if only a tiny proportion of the whole. Peasants and free tenants are thus found garrisoning castles, fighting in armies and taking part in plundering raids.[57] The numbers who did so, moreover, were much larger than revealed by the evidence, for those of small estate were far more likely to avoid detection than those higher up the social scale. In the Kentish survey mentioned above, there were over thirty individuals below the level of the knights who had up till then escaped detection.

We have mentioned the role played in English society by the leading men from each hundred who gave evidence to the justices in eyre.[58] At the

[55] Summerson, 'Civil war and society', 27–9; Stewart's introduction to *RJS*, 159–60, and no. 50 for the plundering of his lands apparently as a royalist.

[56] *CIM*, no. 1024; TNA C 145/27. The problems of using the evidence from inquiries and legal proceedings are usefully discussed in Oakes, 'The nature of war', 197–203; and in King, 'The Friar Tuck syndrome'.

[57] Jacob describes those taking part in the raids as often being 'a motley collection of villagers': *Studies*, 224–5.

[58] See above, 119.

top of the scale, in each jury, there might be an occasional lord of a manor, even a knight; at the bottom, there were men with holdings of peasant proportions; the majority of the jurors coming somewhere in between. (The unfree were excluded although they occasionally appear.) Men from this 'hinge' group could be vigorous participants in the rebellion. On the Buckinghamshire eyre of 1262 twelve men represented the hundred of Mursley.[59] Of these, half were later involved in, or at least profited from, the rebellion. One, John le Franc (the free) of Great Horwood, was convicted of being in Kenilworth castle 'unjustly and against the peace'. His land, valued at an annual half a mark, consisted of a half virgate in Great Horwood held for a small rent.[60] Another peasant in the castle was Richard Borre of Stewkley (six miles from Great Horwood). He was not a juror, held no land and his chattels were worth only 10s, but a juror, William Champayne of Stewkley, went surety for his future good behaviour.[61] One of Champayne's colleagues, Ralph le Sage of Salden (a hamlet adjoining Mursley), was convicted, with nine other local men (he is first on the list so probably the leader), of pillaging the nearby property of Richard Grosset, a follower of the loyalist John de Grey.[62] The goods seized were worth over £14. Sage held just over a virgate of land for a 4d rent from the lord of Mursley and Salden, the rebel knight Robert fitzNigel, who perished at Evesham.[63]

Another picture of involvement below the level of the knights comes from the Kentish survey mentioned above. The lathe of Sutton at Hone (a Kentish version of Sussex rape) is the westernmost in the county, running south from Blackheath and Dartford down to the Sussex border. Here, of the twenty men who had 'taken the part of the earl of Leicester', three had been at the siege of Rochester and the battle of Lewes, two apiece had been either at Rochester or Lewes, and the rest had simply been 'plunderers, *depredatores*'. Only one of those identified was a substantial knight. (He had lands in Kent and Sussex worth £60 a year.) Another five had lands worth £10 a year, so below the £15 level set in 1256 as qualification for knighthood. One more had land worth an

---

[59] For the jury, see TNA JUST 1/58, m. 30 (image 1204). And for what follows, TNA JUST 1/59, mm. 11, 15–15d, 18d (images 1493, 1500–1, 1527–8, 1531–2), *RH*, ii, 334–7.

[60] He held from the prioress of Newton Longville.

[61] Champayne was one of the electors of the jury as well (as was usual) serving on it. Stewkley has one of the most complete and unaltered Norman parish churches in the country.

[62] The property (*RH*, ii, 341) was at Morton (Maid's Moreton). The village of Mursley tops a low hill amidst rolling Buckinghamshire countryside with Whaddon chase lying to the north. Hugh Trevor-Roper has left some descriptions of hunting in the area: Trevor-Roper, *The Wartime Journals*, 122–3.

[63] Carpenter, *Reign of Henry III*, 314–15. FitzNigel also seized Grosset's land: TNA JUST 1/1197, m. 20 (image 1477); Stewart, 'A year in the life of a royal justice', 161–2. For further analysis of the situation in Buckinghamshire, see Valente, *Theory and Practice of Revolt*, 256–9.

annual 10 marks, while the lands of the remaining thirteen were valued at between 2s and £3 a year.[64]

Some free tenants of modest estate played a very active part in Montfort's movement. In Buckinghamshire, William Capel held two virgates of land, worth 4 marks annually, and another ten acres worth 10s. These were in Hanslope, a manor of the great rebel John fitzJohn. Capel was convicted of carrying out a series of raids, including one against the property of the king's attorney, Laurence del Brok. In explanation, he confessed to having been a 'principal procurator' in the county drawing people into the party of the earl of Leicester. What he had received of the plunder had been a reward from his lord. If Capel thought this was an excuse he was disappointed. The jury agreed he had indeed been a 'procurator' attracting people to Montfort's side and he was sent to gaol.[65] Another activist on Montfort's behalf was Roger de Fonte. He had land worth a mere 5s a year in Westerham in Kent so was very much of peasant status. In 1263 he had wanted to go to Montfort and John de la Haye (then at Reigate) in order to betray Westerham to them. He was, however, caught by three villagers and dragged back. Next year, in the garrison of Tonbridge castle after its taking by the king, he gave 6d to go out and then betrayed its state to Haye and Simon de Montfort junior. He also armed the men of the countryside so they could recover by force goods seized by the loyalist lord of Westerham, John de Canville. 'It is openly said that he is the king's enemy', stated the inquiry of September 1265, not very surprisingly.[66]

Westerham was clearly far from united in its Montfortian sympathies, but that was not true of all vills, at least according to later allegations. In Worcestershire, the men of Norton and Bromsgrove were 'supporters of the earl of Leicester with all their forces', the one exception being a man who was at Evesham with Lord Edward.[67] In Buckinghamshire, the vills of Aylesbury (where John fitzJohn was lord), Dorton and Walton were charged with sending men against the king and generally preaching and working against him. The vill of Wendover (another fitzJohn property) was similarly charged with disloyalty and with plundering the land of the king's supporters.[68] The pattern of peasant involvement in the raids was repeated in other counties.[69] In Suffolk, around 300 men were involved in over a hundred acts of robbery. Some of the raids were directed by knights, but there were many instances of peasants acting for themselves.

---

[64] TNA C 145/27. The rest of the survey is in print as *CIM*, no. 1024. The figure of twenty omits some men in the household of one of the rebels. The surname of the knight '*dominus* Thomas' is lost. Perhaps he was Thomas de Bendinges.

[65] *CIM*, no. 447; TNA JUST 1/59, m. 9d (image 1520).

[66] *CIM*, no. 760; *RH*, i, 233. I speculate these events took place in 1263 and 1264.

[67] *CIM*, no. 936 (p. 282).

[68] Carpenter, *Reign of Henry III*, 314.

[69] For Cambridgeshire, see Carpenter, *Reign of Henry III*, 315–7.

Few did better than the villein Hervey Todding (his chattels were valued at 5s). He seized a man from Walberswick and held him in a neighbouring park till a fine of 100 marks was paid.[70]

The biggest collective gatherings of lower orders in Montfort's support came, of course, in the armies. Almost certainly the peasants and free tenants known to have been at Lewes are representatives of a much larger number. Before the battle, it was peasant archers from the Weald who harried Henry's army and killed his cook. As the Battle abbey chronicler said, it was not in the power of lords to restrain their men from doing such things. Probably it was peasants and townsmen (on both sides) whose bodies filled the three burial pits found in the nineteenth century, beside the Lewes–Brighton turnpike road, each supposedly containing around 500 corpses. After the battle the fleeing royalists, according again to the Battle abbey chronicler, 'were everywhere slaughtered by villeins of the neighbourhood'.[71] The biggest muster of all was for the great army assembled later in 1264 to resist the queen's invasion. As we have seen, it was designedly a *levée en masse* with each vill, according to size, sending four or eight 'footmen, well equipped with suitable arms, namely lances, bows, arrows, swords, crossbows and axes'. To this army the men of Aylesbury, Dorton and Walton acknowledged they sent contingents.[72] They said they were doing so on the king's orders, technically true but substantially false. No one can have doubted that this was Montfort's army summoned to resist the invasion of Henry's queen.

## MOTIVATIONS

In the 1260s the people of England were divided politically in a way unseen again until the 1640s and (over Brexit) the 2010s. The divisions cut across families. Humphrey de Bohun, earl of Hereford, was a royalist, Humphrey his son and heir, a Montfortian. In Essex, the other way round, Richard de Tany, the father was the Montfortian, his son, another Richard, the royalist. Daughters of leading loyalists were sometimes married to leading Montfortians, so Philip Basset's daughter was the wife of Hugh Despenser, and Roger de Somery's daughter was the wife of Ralph Basset of Drayton. Why then did people join the rebellion? Questions of ideology, the appeal of the cause and how it was justified, we leave to the chapter's final sections. Here, although of course there is overlap, we consider material grievances and the pressures exerted on lesser men by leading rebels.

Sometimes, of course, the violence of the war had little to do with national politics, however much the opposite was claimed. In 1264 the

---

[70] Jacob, *Studies*, 313–28 (an impressive analysis), with Todding on p. 321.
[71] Battle, 375–7.
[72] Carpenter, *Reign of Henry III*, 317–19.

Suffolk lord Hamo Chevre had his dykes near the castle of Clare in Suffolk destroyed on the grounds he was an enemy of 'the community of the realm'. Hamo, however, claimed this was false. Indeed, he had sent his esquire to Lewes and turned up himself to guard the coast against the queen's invasion. A jury agreed. Hamo's property had been attacked thanks to the slanderous allegations of an old enemy in the castle garrison.[73]

Some of the violence can seem robbery pure and simple without political overtones other than being let loose by the war. The increasing poverty experienced by sections of the peasantry may be part of the background here.[74] In Suffolk, William King, a peasant with six acres of land, was described as a 'principal robber lying in wait on the high road for loyal subjects'. One may doubt whether Hervey Todding's exploits in the same county had much political motivation. There was also piracy and not just by the Cinque Ports. A ship of Cologne was robbed at sea and goods worth 60 marks taken back to the port of Dunwich.[75]

Sometimes local disputes helped bring men into Montfort's camp, while equally having the opposite effect. It was surely his quarrels with the royalist Robert Aguillon that explain Ralph of Imworth's presence in Montfort's army at Lewes – with fatal consequences. The quarrel with his half-brother John brought Richard de Beauchamp into the king's army at Northampton, the reward being soldiers sent to eject John from his share of their father's inheritance. After the Montfortians had won the war, John was naturally restored.[76] In Staffordshire, Ralph Basset of Drayton and Philip Marmion of Tamworth were already at daggers drawn before the rebellion. In 1262, Marmion was charged with sending 'a great multitude of outlaws and Welshmen and other armed men' to attack Basset's property, doing damage to the tune of £100. Not surprisingly, they took opposite sides in the war, Basset a Montfortian, Marmion a royalist.[77] Competition for local power with Basset equally helps explain why the baron Roger de Somery of Dudley sided with the king. Somery's attempts to force two of his major tenants, William of Birmingham and William de Parles, to attend his court at Dudley every three weeks,

---

[73] TNA JUST 1/1191, m. 17 (images 1039–40). The case first came to my attention thanks to the reference in Valente, *Theory and Practice of Revolt*, 47. For Hamo, who purchased exemption from knighthood in 1256, see *CRS*, no. 173; *BF*, ii, 904, 920. The other reason for the destruction of the dykes was that they impeded the defence of the castle.

[74] For discussion, Carpenter, *Struggle for Mastery*, 54–9.

[75] Jacob, *Studies*, 314–15; *RS*, 228–9.

[76] TNA JUST 1/1194, mm. 1, 5 (images 1217, 1226). The soldiers were sent on Philip Basset's orders. The father was the Buckinghamshire coroner Miles de Beauchamp: *CR 1264–8*, 15.

[77] Though for Basset being tempted into Edward's camp, see above, 287 n. 71.

doubtless encouraged their rebellion.[78] 'The war', it has been said, 'was for some an opportunity to pursue their own objectives within local society, local disputes reflecting this, rather than, necessarily, support for de Montfort or the king.'[79] True, but this did not make the support generated for Montfort any the less real. Ralph Basset of Drayton was a leading ravager of royalist estates in 1263 and died with Montfort at Evesham.[80] So did William of Birmingham.[81]

The rebellion against King John, J.C. Holt has written, was a rebellion of the king's debtors. The same could not be said of the rebellion against Henry III.[82] Few of the leading Montfortians had been harried to pay money to the crown. The same is true of the knights examined in the various county studies. Montfort's own grievance was that Henry owed him money, not the other way round.[83] Some magnates who did pay substantial sums to the king, like John de Balliol and John fitzAlan, turned out to be royalists rather than rebels.[84] What about acts or perceived acts of injustice? These certainly existed, running down from Montfort himself with his thwarted claims over Eleanor's dower. Giles de Argentan, Robert fitzNicholas, Robert fitzWalter of Daventry and the Essex knight Hugh of Elmstead had all been deprived of property unjustly, or so they may have claimed.[85] Fulk Payforer (Montfort's sheriff of Kent in 1264) had spoken of his inability to obtain justice under Henry.[86] Others like Gilbert of Elsfield, Ralph of Imworth and all those knights in Sussex antagonized by Peter of Savoy had waited till the revolution to make their complaints, presumably because they despaired of getting justice earlier.[87]

Some of these grievances were linked to others about lack of royal favour. Hugh Despenser, Giles de Argentan and Robert fitzNicholas had all failed to follow their fathers in careers at court. Had Argentan done so, he would surely have secured the Hertfordshire manors of Lilley and Willian, to which he cherished a long-standing claim, instead of seeing them go to the king's steward Paulinus Peyvre. Another rebel who looked

---

[78] Birmingham was also married to Thomas of Astley's daughter.

[79] For all this see John Hunt's 'Families at war', 18, 25–8, with the quotation at 27.

[80] Basset was with Montfort in London soon after the battle of Lewes: *Beauchamp Cartulary*, no. 352.

[81] For other examples of pre-existing quarrels and different sides taken in the war, see Coss, 'Retinues, agents and garrisons', 197–8; Ridgeway, 'Dorset in the period of baronial reform and rebellion', 375; and TNA JUST 1/1197, m. 9d (image 1503); *CChR 1257–1300*, 46–7; *RS*, 227–8.

[82] See Carpenter, *Reign of Henry III*, 88–93.

[83] One is reminded of the aphorism of my old supervisor, John Prestwich: 'In the early Middle Ages (meaning the period from 1066), the barons owed money to the king, in the later Middle Ages the king owed money to the barons.'

[84] See volume 1, 623–5.

[85] For these cases, see volume 1, 537, 690; and above, 22 n. 91.

[86] How true the claim was is another matter.

[87] See above, 170.

enviously at Peyvre's ascent was Eustace de Grenville, for it was Peyvre, not Eustace, who received the lands of the Norman branch of the Grenville family.[88] At least Peyvre was native born and had risen from the ranks of the county knights. Those most in favour at court, of course, were the king's foreign relatives and many Montfortians had clashed directly with them, like Montfort himself. Geoffrey de Lucy had been a ward of Geoffrey de Lusignan and seen his lands wasted. William de Coleville had fallen foul of bishop-elect Aymer, as had John fitzGeoffrey, the father of John fitzJohn. The knights Gilbert of Elsfield, Thomas de St Andrew and Eustace de Grenville had all clashed with William de Valence. It was to Valence that Robert fitzNicholas had been pushed to sell his Nottinghamshire manor at Dunham. In Sussex, John de la Haye, John de la Ware, Ralph Harengod, William Marmion and others had quarrelled with Peter of Savoy.[89] In the north of England, Peter's wardship of John de Vescy's lands probably had much to do with Vescy's rebellion. Montfort's own antipathy to Peter, manifest from 1259, may well have been encouraged by his men. Hostility to the king's foreign kin was not confined to their baronial and knightly victims. Peter of Savoy's activities in Sussex had alienated the Cinque Ports.[90] Many peasant communities complained on the 1258–60 eyres about the oppressions of the king's relatives. Here were reasons why Montfort's Statute against the Aliens had such wide appeal.

## LORDS AND LOCALITY

How far did knights and others follow greater men into insurrection, how far did they make independent choices? Here much depended on the local political situation. A study of Essex has suggested a 'relatively independent gentry'.[91] A study of the midland counties, where Montfort wielded so much power, has suggested the reverse.[92] Gilbert de Clare could be equally powerful. A common excuse after the war was that of being with him at the siege of Rochester and the battle of Lewes and then converting to the king when he converted.[93] Yet the followings of even the greatest lords could be friable. Of the entourage King Richard took to Germany in 1257, eight, 20 per cent of the whole, joined the rebellion, including as we have seen, Hugh Despenser and Gilbert of Elsfield. Of seventeen Oxfordshire knights holding from the honours of Wallingford and St Valery, four

---

[88] *CChR 1226–57*, 328, 341; TNA JUST 1/1195, mm. 7, 2d (images 1317, 1349).

[89] See Stewart, *RJS*, xxii–iv; and above, 143–4, 156–7.

[90] For the portsmen's attacks on the property of Peter's agents, see Stewart, *RJS*, nos. 43 and n. 45, 105, 121.

[91] Moore, 'Government and locality in Essex', 242–3.

[92] Fernandes, 'The midlands knights and the Barons' War', 180–1, reiterating a theme throughout his doctoral thesis, 'The role of the midlands knights'.

[93] For example, TNA C 145/27; *RS*, 199.

rebelled, including John de St Valery.[94] John had been one of Richard's German party and was still close to him in 1261. But then, while Richard languished in prison after Lewes, he took service as the Montfortian sheriff of Oxfordshire and Berkshire.[95]

Beneath the level of the earls and greater barons, an important role in upholding Montfort's cause was played by a group of magnates, many of them senior knights. In the north there was John de Eyville, who 'was with horses and arms against the king, being at the capture and sack of castles and taking booty in diverse places'.[96] In the midlands, there was Peter de Montfort, Henry de Hastings and William Marshal, in Essex, Peter de Tany, and in the west country, Brian de Gouiz and Adam Gurdun.[97] Gouiz was said to have 'run through the county of Somerset on behalf of the earl of Leicester because he made him a knight'. Around fifty people were listed soon after Evesham as having been in Gurdun's following, including fellow knights, parish priests and peasants with incomes of only a few shillings a year.[98]

At the level of the hundred, a great deal of course depended on the allegiance of the local lords. The involvement of the Mursley jurors in the rising is hardly surprising given the manors held in the hundred by the rebels Robert fitzNigel, William of Birmingham, John Passelewe, John fitzJohn and his steward Richard de la Vache.[99] At the level of the manor, Montfort and his followers naturally expected a full turnout of their men and full obedience to their officials.[100] Three of fitzJohn's villeins said they had been forced by his bailiffs to carry out a robbery in Wiltshire, although they admitted they had each received a sheep in return.[101] One of Montfort's own bailiffs, twelve years in his service, told how, obeying a letter from the earl, he had taken the rent at Aylesbury belonging to one of the king's judges.[102]

---

[94] The sample is drawn from the knights who sat on grand-assize juries on the Oxfordshire eyre of 1261.

[95] On the other hand, as these figures show, the majority of Richard's Oxfordshire tenants did not join the rebellion. Fear of his reprisals may explain why the same is true of the Berkshire knights mentioned earlier.

[96] *CIM*, no. 940, and see nos. 851, 937, 939. For John, see De Ville, 'John Deyville'.

[97] *CIM*, no. 871, and, for Gouiz's following, nos. 647, 700, 871–2, 875, 877. Richard de Tany, as sheriff of Essex between 1259 and 1261, vigorously challenged the liberties claimed by King Richard: TNA KB 26/161, m. 23 (image 0092).

[98] Ridgeway, 'Dorset in the period of baronial reform and rebellion', 34–5.

[99] *CIM*, no. 633; *RH*, ii, 334. Passelewe's manor is now Drayton Parslow.

[100] The role of officials is stressed in Oakes, 'The nature of war', 204–8.

[101] TNA JUST 1/42, m. 1d (image 1212); Coss, 'Retinues, agents and garrisons', 194. The villeins (*nativi*) said they did not wish to trouble (*fatigare*) a jury, so placed themselves in mercy, very good of them!

[102] TNA JUST 1/59, m. 16 (image 1502); Jacob, *Studies*, 230–1. For a similar case from Berkshire, see TNA JUST 1/42, m. 2d (image 1216).

We have seen how loyalty in Warwickshire was consolidated by ties of neighbourhood.[103] The same pattern is found elsewhere. East of Oxford, Roger de St John's Stanton St John, Gilbert of Elsfield's Elsfield and Iffley of Gilbert's comrade-in-arms Robert fitzNigel (all three died at Evesham) were within a five-mile radius of each other. This must have helped them stand up to King Richard, whose manor at Beckley was in the same area. Sometimes the conflicting pressures made the choice of allegiance difficult. Just before the battle of Lewes, there were hopes that two Kentish barons, both at the siege of Rochester, would now come over to the king. They were William de Say of Swanscombe and Robert de Crevecoeur of Leeds and Chatham. In the event, Say did and Crevecoeur did not come over. One can see why the decision was problematic. Their neighbours included on the one hand, Richard de Grey, and on the other, Roger of Leybourne. Sometimes such pressures made neutrality by far the best policy as in the case of Thomas de Bréauté (Falkes's son), whose manors in Oxfordshire adjoined those of rebels and royalists alike.[104]

## COERCION

The pressures exerted by powerful men raises the question of coercion. Again and again in the inquiries and litigation after Evesham, men were said to have taken part in the insurrection because they were forced to do so: forced to participate in raids, go to sieges, join garrisons and sometimes just be 'with' Simon de Montfort.[105] In Kent, a jury from Chart hundred stated that Robert de Crevecoeur, acting as Montfort's 'keeper of the peace' (!), had 'ordered' around a dozen 'poor men', most with either 'nothing' or lands and goods worth a few pence, to go to the siege of Rochester.[106] The men of Hungerford, Holt and Kintbury in Berkshire, a jury agreed, were 'driven' by the Wallingford garrison to the siege of Marlborough by threats of death and arson.[107] In Buckinghamshire, the 'principal plunderer', William de Lay, threatened to hang one man at his door, kill the son of another and set fire to houses, if people did not join the raids.[108] A jury agreed that men from Windsor had been forced into the castle garrison by John fitzJohn and had stayed there 'for fear of their families', presumably anticipating reprisals if they tried to leave.[109] There

---

[103] In Warwickshire's Hemlingford hundred there were eight rebels, including Thomas of Astley, William of Birmingham, Nicholas of Seagrave and Henry de Hastings. *CIM*, no. 928, and Fernandes, 'The midlands knights and the barons' war', 176.

[104] Jobson, 'The rebels four dilemmas', 97; Jobson, '1261 Oxfordshire Eyre', i, 193.

[105] Many of the examples in what follows may be found in Jacob, *Studies*, 231–6, and Coss, 'Retinues, agents and garrisons', 190–8.

[106] *CIM*, no. 728.

[107] TNA JUST 1/42, m. 3 (image 1177).

[108] TNA JUST 1/59, mm. 18, 19d (images 1507, 1541). For William see *CIM*, no. 928.

[109] TNA JUST 1/42, m. 15 (image 1201).

certainly were reprisals. A man from Montfort's manor at Hungerford who stepped out of line had his lands seized and had to buy them back.[110] Thomas Burnel, having escaped from Windsor castle, was hunted down by fitzJohn's men, taken to London and imprisoned for four days and nights until he paid a ransom of 70s.[111]

Most of those thus dragooned into the war were small fry, but juries accepted the same excuses further up the social scale. Walter de Riparia was one of the four knights investigating abuses in Berkshire in 1258. He then became sheriff of the county. Yet he was taken by force on a raid to the park of the loyalist baron Reginald fitzPeter and was thrown three times from his palfrey when he tried to escape.[112] In Warwickshire itself, the returns from two hundreds to the inquiry after Evesham said that the knight Richard de Amundeville had been with Montfort unwillingly and by distraint.[113] Another knight, Robert de Mortimer, sent a man to the siege of Buckenham castle in Norfolk because otherwise Henry de Hastings would have burnt his manors.[114] A good number of knights, as we have seen, claimed they had been forced into Northampton by William Marshal. In the north, the 1265 inquiry stated that several knights were with John de Eyville under compulsion.[115]

Claims of compulsion were not only made by those seeking to excuse their conduct. The Canterbury/Dover annals have nearly all the knights of Kent flocking to Montfort in 1263, having seen the fate of his enemies.[116] Yet one should not exaggerate the extent of the coercion. Of all the Warwickshire and Leicestershire knights, only Richard de Amundeville was said to have been with Montfort by distraint. The juries themselves often discounted the excuse or allowed it only in part. A 'great jury of knights' said that, while Eustace de Grenville had gone unwillingly with William de Lay to a robbery at Stony Stratford (Lay had turned up at his house and taken him), he had plundered 'with a good will' the properties of the queen and John de Grey.[117] When John de Musson of Hungerford was accused of being in the garrison of Wallingford and despoiling the surrounding countryside, he said he was a man of Simon de Montfort and had acted under compulsion. The jury disagreed. He had acted 'willingly'. In Northamptonshire, thirteen men accused of being at the siege of Fotheringhay and robbing the properties of John de Balliol said they had

---

[110] TNA JUST 1/42, m. 10d (image 1231).

[111] TNA JUST 1/42, m. 16d (image 1240).

[112] TNA JUST 1/42, m. 12 (image 1196). His attacker was William of Berkeley (*CPR 1258–66*, 619).

[113] *CIM*, nos. 929–30. For Richard, see *BF*, ii, 938, 956; *CChR 1226–57*, 409; *CPR 1247–58*, 212, 439, 646. In 1266, however, he held out to the last in Kenilworth castle.

[114] *CIM*, no. 826.

[115] *CIM*, nos. 937–40.

[116] Canterbury/Dover, 223. Wykes, 134, also has people joining up out of fear.

[117] TNA JUST 1/59, m. 13 (image 1491).

been forced to go 'by the barons making transit through the manor of King's Cliffe'. Again, a jury begged to differ. The excuse worked for four of the men. The rest had gone 'with a good will'.[118]

There can be no doubt that a great deal of the support enjoyed by Simon de Montfort can be explained by material grievances, the ties of neighbourhood and the links and levers of lordship. But even when knights and others were following greater men that does not mean they were without influence. Doubts over the loyalty of his men were quite probably factors in King Richard's failure to support the king in the summer of 1263.[119] Key themes in Simon de Montfort's programme, the local reforms, the attack on aliens, surely owed much to what he learnt from his knightly followers. There was also, throughout society, a belief in the cause itself. To that we will turn, but first there follow sections on the role of the towns, women and clergy in this period.

## THE TOWNS

In 1265 representatives of the towns were summoned to Simon de Montfort's great parliament at Westminster. This suggests he was confident of their support. The support was certainly not total. Within Montfortian towns, there were those loyal to the king. Some towns remained loyal seemingly as a whole. Winchester refused to admit Simon de Montfort junior in 1265 and was sacked for its pains. Afterwards, 'in consideration of their losses sustained for the king', Henry pardoned the citizens their annual rent for a full six years.[120] Henry was also pleased with Rochester's conduct in resisting Montfort's attack in 1264. In 1266 he made concessions to the town in return for 'the faithful service which the citizens have done us and for the damages and injuries they sustained on our behalf in the time of the disturbances in our kingdom'.[121]

The loyalties of individual townsmen are not easy to discern beyond London. The inquiries and legal proceedings after the war did not seek out rebels within towns in the same way as they did rebels in the rest of the country. Instead, offending towns were punished by large block fines that everyone had to pay, much to the dismay of those who claimed the innocent were suffering with the guilty. Thomas Wykes did, however, offer an analysis of the internal dynamics swinging towns Montfort's way. Under the year 1263, having described with some contempt the political

[118] TNA JUST 1/42, m. 1d (image 1213); TNA JUST 1/618, m. 7 (image 1259).

[119] Jobson, 'Richard of Cornwall and the baronial opposition', 67–70.

[120] *CPR 1258–66*, 471; *CFR 1265–6*, no. 212. For Montfort's concession to the citizens, see *CPR 1258–66*, 391.

[121] Bartlett, *Rochester Charters*, 21. The two original charters (duplicates) are described in Nicholas Vincent's census of Henry III's original acta.

and social revolution that brought London onto Montfort's side, he then added that London's pernicious example spawned similar movements in other towns. 'Communes of low people (*ribaldi*) were formed in nearly every city and town. They publically proclaimed themselves "bachelors" and oppressed the greater men of the cities and boroughs with their violent deeds.'[122] Wykes, of course, was writing later (in the 1280s) but he had lived through the period of reform and rebellion and his observations command respect. There certainly was a great deal of tension within towns between the governors and the governed. If only in London can we see for certain the Montfortian consequences, that may be because elsewhere the evidence is so limited.[123] This does not mean, however, that the urban elites always sided with the king. Wykes himself named four leading Londoners who joined the popular movement. Nor were the divisions in towns always as Wykes describes them, for sometimes they were less within the citizen body than between the citizens and the religious houses that claimed a share in the town's government. At the end of the day, while historians have struggled, outside London, to offer much detail about the towns in this period, enough remains to suggest why Montfort was confident of their backing.[124]

## TENSIONS WITHIN TOWNS

By the reign of Henry III most major towns were in varying degrees self-governing. They answered directly to the exchequer for the annual rent owed the king. They controlled their own law courts and regulated trade. The governors were usually the richer citizens, who acted, so their critics believed, too often in their own interests. The division between the governors and governed differed and was often not clear cut, but it might be between a merchant elite and craftsmen, or between richer and poorer merchants. The grievances ranged from the rigging of markets to unfair apportionment of tallage and other financial burdens. Rigging the market was at the heart of two cases heard by Hugh Bigod, back in 1258 and 1260, the first concerning Grimsby, the second Scarborough.[125]

The most detailed account of the tensions between rulers and ruled comes from Oxford. Here in 1253 'the burgesses of the lesser commune', in a petition to the king, drew up twenty-nine separate articles of complaint against the 'burgesses magnates', who controlled the town's

---

[122] Wykes, 138. The use of 'bachelor' in this context is discussed below.

[123] Hence Powicke's cautious observations: *King Henry III*, ii, 448–9.

[124] Jacob's section, 'the support of the towns 1264–5' (*Studies*, 281–98), in fact deals with many other subjects as well. The role of the towns in the fighting is now covered in Oakes, 'The nature of war', ch. 4.

[125] For all this, see Hershey, 'Baronial reform, the justiciar's court and commercial legislation'; Jacob, *Studies*, 118–20.

government.[126] One group of complaints focused on discriminatory regulations about trade and manufacture. Another, the most numerous, were about the unfair apportionment of financial burdens.[127] Here the petition recorded a dramatic episode when the king's clerk William of Axmouth came to assess a tax. The king, Axmouth said, was very angry having heard that the greater burgesses took tallages and other payments entirely from the lesser commune and paid themselves not a penny. To this 'nearly all the people cried with one voice, "that is very true and we are ready to say so to our lord the king"'.[128] The petition was also designed to reveal the arrogance, tyranny and sheer childishness of the ruling elite. A man from the lesser commune and his wife were beaten up because the smoke from their chimney was getting into the house of the mayor, Adam Feteplace. During Feteplace's time, an ordinance was issued establishing punitive penalties for anyone speaking against the provisions issued by the mayor and council.[129] And yet it was these greater burgesses who had pulled each other's hair out in an argument over who had more of the wine taken from the lesser commune!

## TENSIONS RELEASED DURING THE PERIOD OF REFORM AND REBELLION

The loosening of authority during the period of reform and rebellion released some of the tensions in towns and led to acts of violence. An early example came at Hereford during the king's absence from England in 1259–60. 'The commune of the city' insulted the bishop, Peter de Aigueblanche, and trapped him in the town by closing the gates and ringing the common bell calling the townsmen to arms. In 1262, after the king's recovery of power, the commune had to give 200 marks for the bishop's forgiveness and accept a disadvantageous settlement of their jurisdictional quarrels.[130]

---

[126] *CIM*, no. 238. For full discussion, see Hammer, 'Complaints of the lesser commune'. The accusations were never tested in court, so what follows needs to be read with that proviso.

[127] One of these derived from the money demanded by Richard of Cornwall when a servant lost the sight of an eye having been hit by a snowball; another from the money owed Aymer de Lusignan (then studying in Oxford) after the killing of a man from his household. Here (perhaps to please the king), we have a favourable picture of Aymer. 'Moved to pity' at hearing the money had been taken from the lesser commune, he asked for it to be returned although in fact the mayor and bailiffs just kept it for themselves.

[128] *CIM*, no. 238 (81, cap. 10).

[129] *CIM*, no. 238 (81, cap. 13). I am reminded here of an episode my father witnessed at Westminster Abbey. At a great dinner for the Abbey community, the dean, by way of jollification, read out from an ancient statute something along the lines of 'if any minor canon or singing man doth speak disrespectfully of the dean and chapter, he shall be fined the sum of 6 shillings'. At this, one of the minor canons present jumped up and cried out 'Money well spent!'

[130] For all this, see *CPR 1258–66*, 232; TNA JUST 1/1191, m. 3 (images 1005–6, 1013).

In the anarchic period before the battle of Lewes in 1264, there were insurrections in other towns. On 4 May the loyalist citizens of Winchester rose up against the prior and convent of St Swithun's, burnt the gate of the priory, the gate (Kingsgate) with the church of St Swithun above and killed some of the convent's men within the precincts.[131] The immediate cause of the conflict is unknown, although since the townsmen were for the king and the convent for the barons, there were probably political overtones. At Bury St Edmunds, a little earlier in the year, the cause of the insurrection is very clear. It was control of the town's government by the abbot.[132] According to the abbey's own account, a 'multitude' from the town, 300 or more in number, calling themselves 'bachelors', set up a 'gild of youth'. They bound themselves together on oath to accept no alderman or bailiff save those they had chosen, this in defiance of previous custom where the choice had been the abbot's. Their own alderman and bailiffs were henceforth to judge disputes in the town and sound their own horn to gather the commune together, this in place of the abbot's horn which had previously done so. Those who opposed all this were to be treated as 'public enemies'. One day the conspirators had gone so far as to attack the abbey and fire arrows into its court.

The movement in Bury was apparently led by young townsmen who called themselves 'bachelors' probably to give a certain knightly frisson to their deeds. Wykes had written of the 'bachelors' rising against the town elites, but here the target was the abbot, not the richer townsmen. In the end nearly all the citizens, great and small, resisted the abbot's entry when he hurried to the town after the attack on the abbey. That the events at Bury were the product of the Montfortian movement seems clear. Treating opponents as 'public enemies' subject to attack has a very '1258' ring. The townsmen must have heard of events in London, where Montfort had profited from and sanctioned a revolution in the town's government. They felt they were safe to attempt the same. Significantly, while the insurrection was in progress, William le Blund, one of Montfort's principal lieutenants, was in the town. (He was to be killed a few weeks later bearing Montfort's standard at Lewes.) Blund attempted to mediate between the two sides. In other words he did *not* side with the abbot. His conduct was very different from that of John de Warenne and William de Valence in 1266. Their inquiry reaffirmed the right of the abbot to choose both the alderman and the porters guarding the city gates.[133]

## TOWNS IN MONTFORTIAN ACTION

The towns in general had good reasons for siding in the civil war against the king. They were divided from him by the issue of tallage (ten had been

---

[131] Winchester, 101.

[132] For what follows, see Davis, 'The commune of Bury St Edmunds, 1264'.

[133] *CR 1264–8*, 197; Bury St Edmunds, 34–5.

levied between 1234 and 1258), just as much as tallage, through its inequitable distribution, caused division amongst themselves.[134] Henry may have been angry about the way tallages and other impositions burdened the poor in Oxford more than the rich. In 1258 he launched an investigation after similar complaints in London. But nothing resulted. The London episode seems more a way of putting the aldermen in their place than helping the poor. The baronial regime in 1258 promised to reform the state of London and all other cities 'which have gone to poverty and ruin on account of tallages and other oppressions'.[135] If nothing seems to have resulted, only one tallage was levied during the period of baronial and Montfortian rule. That was in 1260 and some attempt was made to see it was assessed fairly.[136] There was also legislation (in August 1258) which, at least for a while, ensured the king's agents paid promptly for their purchases, failure to do so being another major grievance.[137]

How, if at all, such grievances translated into Montfortian support is too little known. The only towns mentioned by name in the summons to the 1265 parliament were York and Lincoln.. One wonders how far in February 1264 the mayor and citizens of York obeyed the king's order to get John de Eyville out of York castle – no easy task. They certainly received two letters of protection from the Montfortian government.[138] At Lincoln there was a particular grievance over the way Peter of Savoy was threatening the rights of the city at Boston fair. The town also displayed the familiar tensions between the governing elite and the rest of the citizens.[139] Did the latter give particular support when Adam de Newmarch took over the city from the king's sheriff, William de Grey? Not surprisingly, the Jews suffered once again. Later the citizens had to pay fines of 1,000 marks and £1,000 for their offences although some of these probably followed Evesham.

We are on firmer ground with the towns involved in the main course of the war. In June 1263 one can well imagine the citizens of Hereford applauding the seizure of Bishop Aigueblanche. Early in the following year they pulled down houses outside the walls and widened the ditches so as to defend the town from Roger de Mortimer's attack.[140] During the Montfortian occupation in 1265, one citizen was given compensation for his losses in such operations. After the king's return to power, Hereford had to pay 500 marks to recover his goodwill.[141] In 1263, a month after

---

[134] Mitchell, *Studies in Taxation*, 406.

[135] *DBM*, 110–11, cap. 19.

[136] *CPR 1258–66*, 75–6; Mitchell, *Studies in Taxation*, 289–90.

[137] FitzThedmar, 39 (Stone, FitzThedmar, no. 714); *DBM*, 274–5, cap. 5.

[138] *CPR 1258–66*, 341, 383, 392.

[139] *CPR 1266–72*, 270. For Lincoln in this period, see Hill, *Medieval Lincoln*, 208–13.

[140] *CIM*, no. 291.

[141] However, within days of Evesham, Henry took the burgesses into his grace subject to them making amends: *CPR 1258–66*, 436; *CR 1264–8*, 165.

Aigueblanche's seizure, Edward had descended on Bristol, aiming to reaffirm his lordship over the city. Instead, a quarrel arose between his knights and the townsmen with the result that, according to the Pershore annalist, the whole city withdrew from Edward's service and allegiance. Not surprisingly, the townsmen had later to give money to recover Edward's goodwill.[142] In 1264, it was Gloucester that was in Edward's firing line. Furious with the burgesses for letting the barons into the town, he enticed them into the castle with promises of forgiveness, only then to imprison them without food and drink 'as traitors'. They were eventually let go in return for a ransom put variously at 1,200 marks or £1,000. Edward also pillaged the town.[143]

These incidents at Bristol took place in March 1264 before Edward joined his father in Oxford for the campaign that started with the battle of Northampton. Occupied as the town was by the barons, the Northampton burgesses had little choice about joining the rebellion. One man, suspected of loyalty to the king, was imprisoned by Montfort's clerk in the house where the earl was staying (in February or March 1264) and had to give 6d a day not to be tied up.[144] Montfort had earlier passed through Northampton in December 1264 and, according to the Dunstable annalist, 'received [an oath of] fealty from the burgesses'. It does not sound as though there was much reluctance about it.[145] Certainly, when it came to it, the citizens fought vigorously to defend the town and suffered grievously in its subsequent sack.[146] This was not the end of their troubles. According to the Osney annals, they were disinherited after Evesham along with all the other rebels. It was not till 1268 that the town was pardoned and restored to its liberties.[147]

In Oxford the divisions within the town had political consequences, or so it can be suggested. In October 1264, so very much during Montfort's ascendancy, Nicholas of Stockwell was elected mayor 'by the bailiffs, good men and whole community of Oxford'. Since this is the first time 'the community' appears as part of the electoral body, it is possible that Stockwell was elected 'by revolutionary means' in order to bypass a royalist oligarchy.[148] When the king occupied Oxford in March 1264, the Montfortians in the town must have kept quiet. On other occasions they

---

[142] Pershore, *Flores*, 482; *CPR 1258–66*, 439; *CPR 1266–72*, 451.

[143] Robert of Gloucester, ii, lines 11,284–305; Abingdon, 16; Pershore, *Flores*, 487; *CR 1261–4*, 336–7.

[144] *RS*, 195–6, 199–200.

[145] Dunstable, 226.

[146] Rishanger, 23; *CPR 1258–66*, 311, 320 (for the escape of the Jews). For one incident during the sack, see TNA JUST 1/618, m. 18 (image 1282).

[147] Osney, 179; *CPR 1266–72*, 225.

[148] Hammer, 'Complaints of the lesser commune', 369. Stockwell was one of the greater burgesses complained about in the 1253 petition, but he may have joined the popular movement as Thomas fitzThomas did in London.

had more opportunity to express political views. When Edward with a large force arrived outside Oxford in February 1264, on his way to the Welsh march, the burgesses closed the gates against him. In the summer, they sent men at arms to the army mustered in Kent to repel the queen's invasion. The following year when Simon de Montfort junior arrived on his way to Kenilworth, he *was* allowed into the town. He stayed three days, and would have killed the Jews had he found any.[149] One person he did find was the former mayor Adam Feteplace, one of the principal targets of the 1253 petition, as we have seen. Feteplace was imprisoned and forced to grant a rent to Master Guy, Simon de Montfort senior's tailor.[150] After Evesham the Oxford burgesses had to offer Edward 500 marks as pardon for their conduct, although this was reduced to 200 marks in return for quick payment.[151]

The great majority of towns between 1263 and 1265 saw, of course, neither armies nor military action, yet they still had one major opportunity to show their Montfortian colours. That, of course, was in the army mustered during the summer of 1264 to resist the queen's invasion. To the army, 'cities, castles and boroughs', alongside every vill, were ordered to send, according to their size, footmen and horsemen.[152] In response, according to Arnold fitzThedmar, 'innumerable people' came 'on horse and foot from each county of England'.[153] There is one piece of evidence showing the organization behind the urban contingents. The 'communities' of the towns were supposed to raise money to pay, at different rates, their mounted men and footmen, the latter receiving three pence a day, later raised to four pence. Responding to the usual complaint about the unfair sharing of burdens, the money was to be faithfully assessed 'by the community' with no one being unduly burdened. Indeed, the government promised an inquiry to make sure that was so.[154]

Had the queen's invasion taken place, Montfort's forces, mustered on Barham Down, would doubtless have fought strenuously in his cause. But before the queen's army could even land it had to evade or defeat the men of the Cinque Ports.[155] Their support for Montfort was second in importance only to London's, which was why control of Dover castle and the

---

[149] Robert of Gloucester, ii, lines 11,638–41, 11871–91; *CR 1261–4*, 409. Earlier, during the queen's threatened invasion, the Montfort government had worried about disturbances in Oxford connected with a multitude of Jews entering the town: *CR 1261–4*, 363–4.

[150] *CIM*, no. 294; *CR 1264–8*, 190–1; *CPR 1258–66*, 442.

[151] *CPR 1258–66*, 576. Edward's exclusion and Simon junior's admission are open, however, to less political interpretations.

[152] *F*, i, 444.

[153] FitzThedmar, 69 (Stone, FitzThedmar, no. 814).

[154] *CR 1261–4*, 364. The writ here is addressed to the mayor and bailiffs of Bedford, but I suspect there were similar arrangements in Oxford (*CR 1261–4*, 409) and presumably other towns.

[155] For the Cinque Ports in this period, see Jobson, 'The maritime theatre', 230–2.

wardenship of the Cinque Ports was so vital. In 1261 both Montfort and Richard de Clare had toured the ports and secured a letter promising they would prevent aliens entering the country and stand by the barons in the terms of the 1258 oath.[156] In July 1263, Montfort visited the ports again, 'in order to animate them to resist aliens with all their might'. The result was that the portsmen, spurning an oath taken to Lord Edward earlier in the year, swore to 'live and die' with the barons.[157] During the threatened invasion of 1264, under the leadership of Henry de Montfort, castellan of Dover and warden of the ports, 'innumerable ships from the Cinque Ports . . . went to sea with armed men well equipped to resist the aliens with a strong hand'.[158] To win the portsmen's favour, Montfort turned a blind eye to their piracy so that, according to fitzThedmar, 'they sailed through the sea in galleys and other ships plundering all they found entering or leaving England, and cruelly throwing them into the sea, sparing no-one English or alien'. It was said, fitzThedmar added, that Montfort and his sons received a third part of the spoils.[159] Montfort also took the part of the Cinque Ports in their long-standing quarrel with Yarmouth. In October 1264, in return for their manifold labours in defending the sea and maritime parts 'against the invasion of aliens, not without great peril and expense', they were promised compensation for their losses at Yarmouth's hands.[160] Not surprisingly, against this background, whereas from the other towns only two men were to come to Montfort's 1265 parliament, from each of the Cinque Ports four men were summoned.[161]

## LONDON

Between his return to England in 1263 and his death at Evesham two years later, London was far and away Simon de Montfort's greatest urban base. The size of its population in the thirteenth century has been much debated. Had it reached 100,000 by around 1300 or was it less? Whatever the exact figure, London was many times larger and wealthier than Norwich, Bristol, York and Winchester, its nearest rivals.[162] That wealth

---

[156] Canterbury/Dover, 213.

[157] Canterbury/Dover, 223, 236.

[158] FitzThedmar, 73 (Stone, FitzThedmar, no. 814). For the efforts to equip and munition the ships, see Jobson, 'The maritime theatre', 230–1.

[159] FitzThedmar, 78 (Stone, FitzThedmar, no. 834).

[160] CPR 1258–66, 352. However, in March and May 1265, with as he hoped the return of peace, Montfort sought to prevent the piracy and the attacks on Yarmouth: CPR 1258–66, 482–3; CR 1264–8, 122–3.

[161] CR 1264–8, 89 (DBM, 304–5).

[162] For some comparative figures, see Carpenter, Struggle for Mastery, 43–4. For contrasting views on London's population, see Keene, 'London from the post-Roman period to 1300', 195, and for smaller figures, Nightingale, 'The growth of London in the medieval economy', 97–8. Barron, London in the Middle Ages, 45, suggests 80,000 for around 1300.

was Montfort's to tap into through loans, voluntary or not, from leading citizens and through the seizure of Jewish property and the property of foreign merchants. London provided a base that was absolutely secure. The extent of its walls, together with the frontage on the river, meant no army could mount a blockade and starve the city into submission. An assault on one of the gates, or a breach of the walls, was a possibility, but it would meet with fierce resistance from the Londoners, who, as a last resort, had chains kept ready to bar the streets. Montfort also, of course, from the king's surrender in July 1263, controlled the Tower of London.

The Londoners made their own contribution to the violence bringing Montfort to power in 1263. Within the city they plundered the house of John de Grey and seized thirty-two of his horses, John himself having to escape through a drain. In the same period, or later, they ravaged outside London the lands of William de Valence, Peter of Savoy, Philip Basset and Walter of Merton.[163] When the queen tried to escape from the Tower upriver to Windsor, she was driven back by the missiles pelted from London Bridge. Later the people broke down the gates to let Montfort back into the city over London Bridge when he was cornered in Southwark. Next year, having rejected Louis IX's Mise at Amiens, the Londoners made a formal alliance with Montfort for making war together.[164] By this time London's military forces were organized under a constable and marshal at whose summons (by the great bell of St Paul's), they were to march out of the city ready for action.[165] March out they did to ravage King Richard's manor at Isleworth, to join in the siege of Rochester and then, of course, to fight at Lewes. There they formed the left wing of Montfort's army and were slaughtered by Lord Edward in revenge for the insult to his mother. Since, however, Edward was thereby removed from the field, the Londoners made a major contribution to Montfort's victory.

How then to explain this Montfortian London? Its loyalties seem very different from 1261 when the city had been the king's base for his recovery of power. But the circumstances were now very different. The Tower was poorly munitioned and the bishop was no longer the king's man Henry of Wingham, but the Montfortian Henry of Sandwich. There had also, and above all, been a popular revolution in the city.

The government of London was in the hands of the mayor, two sheriffs and the twenty-four aldermen, each acting as a kind of magistrate in his ward. It was a government dominated by the richer merchants, trading in wine, cloth, spices and precious objects. Between them and those they ruled there were familiar tensions. One was over the unfair apportionment of tallage, something exploited by the king's attack on the aldermen in

[163] Dunstable, 223; *London Eyre of 1276*, nos. 146, 287–8; Williams, *Medieval London*, 224.
[164] Stone, 'Rebel barons of 1264 and the commune of London', 4–5, 17–18.
[165] FitzThedmar, 61 (Stone, FitzThedmar, no. 791).

1258. Another was over who should elect the mayor, the aldermen (as had been the custom) or the 'folkmoot', the assembly of all the citizens, whose vitality had been sapped by the aldermanic regime. And then there was the regime's refusal to allow fishmongers, cordwainers, skinners, girdlers and others to organize. It was these 'middle-class' citizens who lay at the heart of the popular movement. Indeed, they were prominent in the bands ravaging royalist estates around London, although much of the violence was also the work of what might be called the London mob.[166]

What happened in 1263 was that as news spread of Montfort's doings – the ravaging of royalist estates and his advance towards the south coast – the tensions in London exploded. In June and July the aldermen struggled to keep order as 'innumerable people on foot' roamed the streets day and night and broke into houses of foreign merchants. The mayor, Thomas fitzThomas, decided to go with the popular tide. In the words of the alderman Arnold fitzThedmar, he 'so nourished the people of the city, that calling themselves "the commune of the city" they had the first voice in the city'. The mayor would say 'do you wish it done', and if the commune said 'ya, ya', it was done, 'with the aldermen and the magnates of the city not consulted as though they did not exist'. It was thus 'all the commune' that now said it wished to support the Provisions of Oxford, as, next year, it was the mayor and commune making the alliance with Montfort. The reward for their support came in two constitutional victories. With Montfort's encouragement, those prevented from organizing before were allowed to promulgate their own statutes. And both in 1263 and 1264, Thomas fitzThomas was elected mayor 'by the people, with the aldermen and magnates of the city hardly consulted'.[167]

Described thus in fitzThedmar's terms, it sounds as though the aldermanic elite were totally hostile to what was going on. Certainly some of the city leaders tried to act for the king by closing the gates against Montfort in December 1263. But London would never have been the great Montfortian base without the acquiescence and sometimes the active involvement of leading men. Significantly, there was no purge of aldermen during Montfort's time.[168] One, Michael Tovy, was very involved in the violence, both inside the city and outside, bringing Montfort to power.[169] Wykes names him as one the citizens in 1263 who 'annexed' themselves to the ribald populace. Another Wykes named was Master Thomas of Puleston. This remarkable man was the only newcomer to join the city elite during the Montfortian period, and it was

---

[166] Williams, *Medieval London*, 228–9.

[167] FitzThedmar, 55–6, 58–9 (Stone, FitzThedmar, nos. 772–3, 776, 785, 821).

[168] For a valuable survey of the aldermen in this period, see McEwan, 'Civic government in troubled times', 130–8.

[169] *London Eyre of 1276*, no. 146; Williams, *Medieval London*, 226. In 1276, having made the mistake of appearing for trial, Tovy was convicted by a jury and hanged.

well for Montfort that he did.[170] A king's clerk, in the early 1260s he appears as a justice of the Jews and an envoy sent to Louis IX. He was also a London citizen, married to a kinswoman of Michael Tovy.[171] Puleston became constable of the London militia and led it on the raid to Isleworth. He doubtless also led the Londoners out to Lewes but during the battle he was actually with Montfort himself. 'The commander of the fourth division', wrote one chronicler, 'was the earl with lord Thomas of Puleston', a striking testimony to how prominent Puleston now was in Montfort's councils.[172] He must have given Montfort detailed knowledge of everything going on in the city.

Above all, of course, Montfort had the support of the mayor, Thomas fitzThomas. FitzThomas was a draper with considerable property in the city.[173] His family had been part of the aldermanic ruling class since at least the 1220s. As a sheriff of London, he escaped dismissal during the king's purge in 1258, and was mayor in 1261 and 1262 during the king's ascendancy. What motivated his change of stance thereafter is unclear. Perhaps he hoped for reward.[174] Perhaps he had imbibed some of the movement's radical ideas. In 1265, in swearing allegiance to the king, he told Henry to his face, 'before all the people', that he would be faithful and loyal 'so long as you wish to be a good king and lord to us'.[175] His popular credentials were not forgotten. In 1266 the '*fatui de vulgo*', as fitzThedmar called them, cried out loudly that they would have no mayor save fitz-Thomas and he should be released from prison.[176]

Alongside the aldermen at the forefront of the Montfortian regime were others who co-operated with it, despite their doubts. Of these, Arnold fitzThedmar is the conspicuous example. His grandparents had come from Cologne to visit Becket's shrine and then settled in London. FitzThedmar himself was born in 1201 and became the chief representative of German merchants in the city. Despite or perhaps because of his German connections he was fully embedded in city life. He was an alderman from the 1250s while a sister was married to the great wine merchant, mayor and sheriff John de Gisors, a loyalist credited with trying to shut Montfort out of the city in 1263. It is possible that fitzThedmar was officially charged with keeping city documents and perhaps this inspired him to write his chronicle. Full of vivid events, full too of fitzThedmar's own opinions, it is certainly one of the great urban histories.[177]

---

[170] McEwan, 'Civic government in troubled times', 132.

[171] FitzThedmar, 149 (Stone, FitzThedmar, no. 1074).

[172] Guisborough, 194. For his role, see *CPR 1258–66*, 416, 419–20.

[173] For a short biography, see Carpenter, 'Thomas fitzThomas'.

[174] In August 1264 he was granted a wardship: *CPR 1258–66*, 341, 353.

[175] FitzThedmar, 73 (Stone, FitzThedmar, no. 832 and note).

[176] FitzThedmar, 86 (Stone, FitzThedmar, no. 874).

[177] FitzThedmar's career and the writing of his history is fully discussed in Ian Stone's doctoral thesis, 'Book of Arnold fitz Thedmar'. See also his 'Arnold fitz Thedmar: identity, politics and the city of London in the thirteenth century'.

Although based on contemporary notes, the section of the chronicle between 1258 and 1264 was written up in fitzThedmar's own hand soon after Lewes and thus during the fullness of Montfort's power. That he was still highly critical of the popular movement[178] makes his more positive remarks all the more likely to be genuine. Coming from someone now in his sixties, they were far from those of some young hothead. He thus welcomed the Provisions of Oxford as abolishing the evil customs by which the realm had been oppressed both by the king and powerful men. It was only afterwards over an erasure that he described the Oxford parliament as 'insane'. Describing the crucial events of 1263, he contrasted the indiscriminate violence of the London mob with that of the barons themselves who only targeted the enemies of the Provisions of Oxford. He repeated again and again the baronial claim that the Provisions were conceived for 'the honour of God, in fealty to the king and for the utility of all the kingdom'. The outbreak of the war, he said, had been thanks to the failure to observe them. Next year, it was surely with a touch of approval that he recorded the total rejection of Louis IX's Mise of Amiens by the Londoners, the Cinque Ports and 'the middle people' of the kingdom' (so not *a vulgo*). Indeed, he justified their conduct by saying they had never agreed to King Louis' arbitration in the first place.[179] From later in 1264, fitzThedmar preserved the text of Montfort's alliance with the Londoners and wrote out with his own hand what was perhaps the speech he made explaining the consequent oath to be taken by all over the age of twelve in his ward,[180] In November he is found witnessing a property transaction with none other than Thomas fitzThomas and Thomas of Puleston.[181]

FitzThedmar's co-operation with the regime was probably much the same as that of other aldermen, despite the many commercial links they had with the court. There had after all been fierce quarrels with the king over London's status and its consequent liability to taxation. Were the Londoners freemen, barons even, with the right to consent to taxation, or were they serfs, as the king allegedly said, whom he could tallage at will? To this old argument there was also added a new one, for the Londoners absolutely refused to concede to Westminster Abbey the liberties Henry wished the Abbey to have in Middlesex.[182] As a result of these and other quarrels, the government of London was taken into the king's hands at

[178] FitzThedmar, 56, 114–15 (Stone, FitzThedmar, nos. 776, 992, and p. 250 n. a).

[179] FitzThedmar, 53–6 (Stone, FitzThedmar, nos. 710, 712, 770–3, 790).

[180] Stone, 'The rebel barons of 1264 and the commune of London', 4–7. Here, significantly, fitzThedmar describes the alliance as made with 'the mayor and barons of London' not 'the mayor and commune'.

[181] McEwan, 'Civic government in troubled times', 135.

[182] The liberties would have exempted the lands and men of the Abbey from the jurisdiction of the sheriff, and thus from the jurisdiction of London, since the sheriff of London (chosen by the citizens) was also sheriff of Middlesex.

least ten times between 1239 and 1257.[183] The climax came in 1258 when, in a move allegedly on behalf of the poor men of the city unfairly burdened by tallage, all the aldermen were deposed. While most quickly returned to office, seven did not. FitzThedmar himself, unjustly accused, or so he said, was not exonerated and reappointed until November 1259.

FitzThedmar then and other aldermen had no reason to look favourably on Henry III. With Montfort it was different. Indeed, in one respect his regime was better than that of 1258. FitzThedmar had been appalled at the way Hugh Bigod, on his eyres, had set aside London's liberties. Montfort was quite different. Far from trespassing on London's liberties, he protected them. In October 1263, as fitzThedmar tells us, the dispute between London and Westminster Abbey was terminated by a judgement at the exchequer. And it was terminated, after a verdict pronounced by twelve Middlesex knights, wholly in London's favour. A year later, to make assurance doubly sure, given all that had happened in the intervening period, the case was heard all over again, with exactly the same result. The abbot and convent even issued a charter admitting defeat.[184] Simon de Montfort, therefore, had handled London with some skill. To the old ruling elite he had given victory over Westminster Abbey. To the 'middle classes' he had given the right to organize. To the mob he had given the proceeds of their plunder. Indeed, one suspects that Londoners of all ranks profited from the attacks on the foreign merchants and the massacre of the Jews. If, as seems clear, Montfort had supporters in many English towns, London was the jewel, an ugly jewel, in his urban crown.

## WOMEN IN POLITICS

At first sight, it is difficult to give women much role in the politics of this period. Only one had a major influence on events, Henry III's queen, Eleanor of Provence. Only one stands out as giving major support to Simon de Montfort, his wife Eleanor. Women often appear as victims, fleeing to churches, sheltering in religious houses, beaten up when their homes are raided and forced by threats to reveal the whereabouts of their husband's chattels.[185] In the mid-thirteenth century the knightly family of Hotot still remembered their ancestress Dionisia: in the wars of King Stephen's time, she had charged a knight and unhorsed him with one blow from her lance. But no similar exploits by women are recorded in this period. The 700 prostitutes, fancifully thought to have followed the royal army on its way to Lewes, are the only women mentioned in connection with the battle.[186]

---

[183] Williams, *Medieval London*, 208.

[184] FitzThedmar, 57–8 (Stone, FitzThedmar, no. 782). For the full story, see Carpenter, 'Simon de Montfort, Henry III, London and Westminster Abbey'.

[185] For the last, see TNA JUST 1/618, m. 18 (image 1280).

[186] *Song of Lewes*, lines 151–3.

This negative picture is, however, misleading. There is plenty of evidence, slight in individual cases, cumulatively significant, to show that women understood the political issues, tried to influence the male actors, acted themselves and, if they took no direct part in the battles, were frequently in command of castles.[187] The majority of the women were, of course, noble, but there is also evidence for understanding and activity further down the social scale.[188]

The influence and power of noble women came from their landed wealth, wealth they brought in marriage to their husbands and controlled themselves as widows after their husband's death. In default of a brother, a woman inherited the estates of her parents. She also took into her marriage a marriage portion (a *maritagium*), usually in land. As a widow she was entitled as dower to a third of her late husband's estates. Magna Carta had laid down that widows should enter without payment their inheritances, marriage portions and dowers immediately after their husband's death. It also forbad widows being forced into remarriage. On the whole these provisions were respected under Henry III. One result was the numbers of women in Henry's reign who, often spurning pressures to remarry, remained widows for long periods of time. They included Isabella, countess of Arundel (1243–82), Margaret de Lacy, countess of Lincoln and Pembroke (1245–66), Alice, daughter of the marquis of Saluzzo, countess of Lincoln (1258–1304), Maud de Lacy, countess of Gloucester (1262–89),[189] and Isabella de Forz, countess of Aumale (1260–93) and (from 1262) countess of Devon and lady of the Isle of Wight.

Wealth and noble birth gave women like this high status. Philip Basset's wife, Ela, was the widow of the earl of Warwick and the daughter of William Longespée, an illegitimate son of Henry II. Her mother, Ela, was in her own right countess of Salisbury. On one side of her seal the Basset arms are in the centre. On the other, Ela stands between the arms of her first husband and her father.[190] Appended to one surviving deed, Ela's seal is far more impressive than Philip's. Whereas, moreover, in the text he is merely styled Philip Basset 'knight', she appears as Ela, countess of

---

[187] In what follows, I am greatly indebted to Louise Wilkinson's 'Reformers and royalists'.

[188] For a pioneering study of women across society see Louise Wilkinson's *Women in Thirteenth-Century Lincolnshire*. There are three valuable doctoral theses: Susanna Annesley's 'Countesses in the age of Magna Carta'; Polly Hanchett's 'Women in thirteenth-century Oxfordshire'; and Harriet Kersey's 'Aristocratic female inheritance and property holding in thirteenth-century England'.

[189] Alice of Saluzzo was Margaret de Lacy's daughter-in-law and Maud de Lacy was Margaret's daughter.

[190] Coss, *The Lady in Medieval England*, 42.

Warwick.[191] Another striking seal is that of Joan de Stuteville, the heiress who brought such wealth to Hugh Bigod. She appears riding side-saddle and holding up the arms not of her husband but her father.[192]

The friar Ralph Bocking imagined a widow who hastened to remarry 'because as a weak and feeble woman I do not know how to control my dower and my inheritance from my father and my other rights and properties'.[193] But churchmen knew full well that not all widows felt like that. When Margaret de Lacy was widowed in the 1240s, Robert Grosseteste gave detailed advice as to how she should run both her estates and her household. To uphold her honour she was to ensure her knights and gentlemen wore her liveries. And she was to sit in the middle of high table so that her presence was visible to all.[194] Margaret was to remain in command as a widow for some twenty years.[195]

It was accepted that the role of women was to give good counsel to men. Adam Marsh thus enjoined Eleanor de Montfort, through her 'prudence, meekness and kindness', to give her husband 'constant help in everything related to the worship of God, righteous living, and right judgement', a pretty wide agenda. In another letter, thinking of rash agreements that Simon de Montfort had made (probably in Gascony), Eleanor was 'to direct him with quiet advice to negotiate with more care in future'. Given that Marsh also rebuked Eleanor for her anger, one suspects her advice was not always 'quiet'.[196] The counsel and interventions of noble women are especially clear when it comes to the interests of their children and grandchildren. When the marriage of Margaret de Lacy's grandson Henry was being planned in 1257, she was part of the negotiating team along with Simon de Montfort and Hugh Despenser.[197] Later, in 1258, acting with her daughter-in-law Alice of Saluzzo, she secured the wardship of the Lacy lands until Henry, later earl of Lincoln and Salisbury, came of age.[198] The kind of advice a mother could give is seen in a letter Hawise de Neville wrote to her son Hugh in 1267. Away on crusade, having lost extensive lands in England through his rebellion, Hugh was urged to 'travel with all possible haste, and . . . go to the court

---

[191] In the profusion of alms and masses that Ela arranged for the good of her soul, she mentioned neither of her husbands. On her seal she is described as Ela Basset, countess of Warwick, but after Basset's death, she appears as Ela Longespée, countess of Warwick. For her, see Amt, 'Ela Longespée's roll of benefits'.

[192] Coss, *The Lady in Medieval England*, 46–7.

[193] *Saint Richard of Chichester*, 83, 161.

[194] 'Rules of Robert Grossesteste', 388–407, at 403.

[195] For a full study of her career, see Wilkinson, 'Pawn and political player'.

[196] *Letters of Adam Marsh*, ii, 379, 385.

[197] Wilkinson, 'Pawn and political player', 120.

[198] *CPR 1247–58*, 649. This was after the death of Margaret's son Edmund de Lacy in 1258, leaving Alice a widow. A similar joint effort brought the Aumale wardship in 1261 to Isabella de Forz and her mother-in-law, Amice, countess of Devon. They later fell out.

of Rome, and procure if you can the letter of the pope, express and stringent, to the king of England, that he should restore your lands'.[199]

In terms of political awareness, noble women obviously knew how Magna Carta guaranteed their property rights as widows and saved them from being forced into remarriage. Isabella, countess of Arundel, berated Henry to his face over his breaches of the Charter, this when he sought to deprive her unjustly of a wardship. Her remarks were so stinging that Henry asked her not to repeat them.[200] In 1258–9 noble women engaged directly with Hugh Bigod's eyres, both as plaintiffs, like Denise de Munchesney, and as defendants, like Ida de Beauchamp (another daughter of William Longespée and Ela, countess of Salisbury).[201] They were familiar with ideas about the community of the realm. It was while Clare castle was in the hands of Maud de Lacy, the widow of Richard de Clare, that a local landholder was targeted as 'an enemy of the community of the realm'.[202] Widows running their own estates must have understood the ideas leading the reformers in 1258–9 to tackle the malpractices of seigneurial officials as well as the officials of the king. Robert Grosseteste had warned the countess of Winchester that if she did not restrain the vices of her agents, 'those vices will be considered your sins'. He likewise told Margaret de Lacy to ensure her bailiffs did not oppress the poor in any way. If they did she was to establish the facts by a formal inquiry and give appropriate compensation.[203]

There was also political awareness further down the social scale. Some very poor women litigated before Hugh Bigod, both individually (like Juliana punched when gathering corn outside Oxford) and in company with male colleagues (like the women of Brill). At Peatling Magna in Leicestershire, where the inhabitants sought to attack royalists passing through the village in the days after Evesham on the grounds they were acting against the community of the realm and the barons, there was a dominant woman, the wife of Robert of Pillerton. When the royalists returned a few days later, it was she 'and some others of the village' who agreed to pay 20 marks to prevent the village being burnt. When the royalists demanded hostages as guarantee of payment, she picked them out.[204] Two years later, a widow, Desiderata, was very aware of the measures that the king was taking to restore law and order. Meeting a friend carrying a bow and arrow, she asked him if he was one of those going through the country on the king's orders to arrest robbers. Saying she

---

[199] Wilkinson, 'Reformers and royalists', 152. As Wilkinson says, the letter 'reflects the centrality of women to aristocratic families'.

[200] See Annesley, 'Isabella countess of Arundel'; and volume 1, 553–4.

[201] See above, 146, 150.

[202] TNA JUST 1/1191, m. 17 (image 1039); see above, 372.

[203] Robert Grosseteste, 70; 'Rules of Robert Grosseteste', 390–1.

[204] SCWR, 43–4. Peatling Magna remains a small village amidst undulating countryside. In 2022 my wife and I attended the queen's Platinum Jubilee fete there.

could overcome two or three like him, she seized him by the neck, crooked her leg and threw him to the ground. She sounds as though she could easily have taken part in the fighting during the war.[205]

Women, indeed, were far from always helpless victims of the violence. When, after Evesham, the agents of Gilbert de Clare came to arrest a man at Sittingbourne in Kent, the wife of Thomas of Higham told him not to surrender and drove him back into the manor house.[206] One woman in 1265 played a far more constructive part in the king's cause than did the prostitutes allegedly following the king's army to Lewes. The vital intelligence enabling Lord Edward's attack on Simon de Montfort junior's forces at Kenilworth was given him by a woman spy named Margoth, who 'although she was a woman went about in men's clothes as though she was a man'.[207]

The closest (as far as is known) that women came to the fighting was in their keeping of castles. At one time or another, between 1258 and 1267, Cockermouth, Pontefract, Clare, the Tower, Tonbridge, Winchester, Carisbrooke, Wigmore and Usk were all in female hands. So was Dover, commanded by Eleanor de Montfort in 1265 and the queen in 1267. Far from all noble women were on the rebel side. Joan de Munchesney gave sterling support to her husband, William de Valence, when he was exiled in 1258.[208] We glimpse their relationship in a letter that Valence sent her in 1267 when she was his deputy in charge of Winchester castle. Written in French and addressed to 'sa chere conpaigne et amie', he stressed that the knight being sent to help in keeping the castle was to be under her command 'in all things'.[209] Valence's niece Alice de Lusignan also acted for the king. She was married to Gilbert de Clare, although they were later divorced. In 1267, according to the well-informed Dunstable annalist, it was Alice who warned the king that Clare's allies were planning to attack him.[210] Both countesses of Lincoln, Margaret de Lacy and her daughter-in-law Alice of Saluzzo, acted for the king in a more aggressive way. In 1265 both seized the lands of rebels within their fees. No wonder the Montfortian government in May 1265 tried to get Alice out of Pontefract castle. It would have been no easy job. When, a few years later, the sheriff's bailiffs entered the liberty of Pontefract, they were assaulted by Alice's men and one of them was imprisoned in the castle.[211] Some noble women had good reason for siding against Montfort. Isabella de Forz had fled to Wales to

---

[205] *CIM*, no. 2133. The sequel was unfortunate. Falling on top of her victim, his arrow pierced her heart and she died on the spot.

[206] *CIM*, no. 747.

[207] For this story, see Guisborough, 199. For the attack, see below, 441.

[208] Wilkinson, 'Reformers and royalists', 157.

[209] *RL*, ii, 311.

[210] Dunstable, 245–6.

[211] *CIM*, nos. 366, 938; *CPR 1258–66*, 428.

escape the clutches of Simon junior.[212] Perhaps worse happened to Maud, the wife of Roger de Mortimer, another great heiress.[213] In 1265, after Lord Edward's escape from captivity, she welcomed him to Wigmore castle. After Montfort's death at the battle of Evesham, his head was sent to her at Wigmore. In the words of Robert of Gloucester, 'she foully abused it'.[214] It sounds as though Maud had some deep personal grievance against Simon, perhaps thanks to her maltreatment when the Montfortians seized Wigmore and ravaged the Mortimer lands early in 1264.[215]

Noble women, however, also acted against the king. In 1267, Ela, countess of Warwick, Philip Basset's wife, persuaded the papal legate not to place an immediate interdict on London.[216] This seems a highly political act, making it easier for Gilbert de Clare to establish himself in the city. (He had occupied London in the cause of securing better terms for the Montfortians disinherited after the battle of Evesham.)[217] It looks as though Ela shared her husband's sympathy with the disinherited's plight, loyalist though he was. During Montfort's own time, control of the Tower of London had been an important prop to his authority in London, and here too a woman played a part. When Hugh Despenser departed on the campaign that ended at Evesham, he left his wife, Alina, in command. One suspects she was in charge during other periods of Despenser's absence following his appointment in 1263.

Another noble woman, commanding a castle against the king, was Denise de Munchesney. She was accused of imprisoning loyalists in her castle of Anstey in Hertfordshire (part of her inheritance) and harbouring there those who went out to plunder the countryside. She escaped retribution after Evesham thanks to the protection of Gilbert de Clare.[218] Suggestive too is the case of Gilbert's mother, Maud de Lacy, the widow of Richard de Clare. According to Thomas Wykes, it was she who persuaded Gilbert, her son, to join up with Montfort in the early part of 1264.[219] At first sight this seems puzzling for Gilbert resented the extensive dower assigned his mother. Since this was an act of the Henrician government, it

---

[212] AP, 172; Powicke, King Henry III, ii, 708. The prior of Breamore alleged Isabella had been neutral during the war. For the Montfortian government in April and May 1265 swinging to and fro as to whether her lands should be confiscated, see CR 1264–8, 112, 118.

[213] For a study of her career, see Mitchell, Portraits of Medieval Women, ch. 4.

[214] Robert of Gloucester, ii, lines 11,732–3.

[215] See Cavell, 'Intelligence and intrigue in the march of Wales', 5–6, where Maud's role in the fall of Llywelyn ap Gruffudd is also explored.

[216] London, i, 77.

[217] See below, 505.

[218] TNA JUST 1/83, m. 10 (image 0611). The king himself testified that Denise was 'de amicitia' of Gilbert. Evidently her quarrel with Richard de Clare (or his steward) had been made up. See above, 150, and below, 583, for Gilbert's protection of his followers. Denise made strenuous efforts to save her son William from the consequences of his rebellion: CPR 1258–66, 635, 636, 640, 667.

[219] Wykes, 140.

may well have been an attempt to keep Maud on-side.[220] Yet there is other evidence of her contrary political sympathies. We have seen already the actions of the Clare garrison while the castle was under her control. Then, in February 1265, during Montfort's great parliament, she was given custody of a manor. In April she was visited by Eleanor de Montfort.[221] Most striking of all, after Montfort's death she went on a pilgrimage to Evesham. Returning from thence to Tewkesbury, her palfrey drank from the spring rising from the place where Montfort had died and was immediately cured of asthma. (Its head was also washed in the water.) The countess and all her household testified to the miracle.[222]

Perhaps the most evocative document to survive from 1265 is the household roll of Eleanor de Montfort, now preserved in the British Library.[223] Between 19 February and 29 August it records the daily costs of the household's food, drink and stables. It also records payments to messengers going with letters and other miscellaneous expenditure. During the period covered by the roll Eleanor and Simon were together only for a fortnight before Easter.[224] This makes the roll all the more interesting for it shows a noble woman in independent command.[225] The climax came during the final crisis of the regime when Eleanor, from 15 June, took over at Dover, a subject for the next chapter. Before that, Eleanor was based at Odiham in Hampshire, the castle given her by the king before her marriage to Simon, so very much her own home. Given she was there from 19 February, she must have missed the Westminster parliament, unless she was there for the opening stages, but she was far from politically inactive.[226] Indeed, her court at Odiham, alongside that held by her husband, meant there were twin bases of Montfortian power. The roll suggests around 200 people might be fed each day, with the daily consumption of herrings during Lent ranging between 400 and 1,700.[227] The number of

---

[220] For discussion, see Mitchell, *Portraits of Medieval Women*, 36, with ch. 3 a study of her career and that of Margaret de Lacy.

[221] *CPR 1258–66*, 409; Wilkinson, *HR*, cv, and no. 96.

[222] 'Miracula', 68–9. For Maud as the subject of a joke made by Margaret, queen of France, see below, 462. She was a benefactor of the Austin friars at Clare: *Clare Cartulary*, nos. 3–7, 9–12.

[223] The roll has now been splendidly edited (with full translation) for the Pipe Roll Society by Louise Wilkinson: *The Household Roll of Eleanor de Montfort*. Wilkinson's comprehensive introduction covers all the points mentioned below. Earlier the roll formed the basis for Margaret Wade Labarge's *A Baronial Household of the Thirteenth Century*. For what follows, see also Kjær, 'Food, drink and ritualised communication in the household of Eleanor de Montfort'.

[224] See below, 416.

[225] Indeed, as Montfort took over all the costs when with Eleanor, it is only for their times apart that we have information from Eleanor's roll.

[226] She arrived at Odiham on 22 February, having been at Wallingford on 19–20 February and Reading on the 21st.

[227] Wilkinson, *HR*, xxxviii, lxxxi–ii.

horses stabled was often in the thirties but there could be forty, fifty or sixty. The roll also reveals Eleanor feeding paupers; on 14 April no fewer than 800 of them had bread and cider.[228] Eleanor's clothes were striking if we may judge from the cloth of blood-coloured scarlet bought for her and her daughter from Luke of Lucca. The cost was over £8, so more than half the annual income making a man liable to take up knighthood.[229] Eleanor had been rebuked by Adam Marsh for her love of finery and it seems to have continued despite her husband's decision (if such it was) to wear plain clothes following his commitment to reform in 1258.

During this period at Odiham, Eleanor was constantly 'networking' both through those she entertained and through the letters she sent. Those entertained included her sons Amaury, Guy and Richard, such leading Montfortians as Thomas of Astley, Richard of Havering and Anketil de Martival, and, amongst the religious, the abbot of Waverley, the chaplain of Kemsing (a Montfort manor in Kent) and the prioress and nuns of Wintney. A visit from the prioress of Amesbury led to Eleanor writing to the chancellor and Peter de Montfort on her behalf.[230] Other letters were sent to the bishop of Lincoln, Lord Edward, Simon de Montfort junior and, on several occasions, Simon de Montfort himself. Eleanor, out of pity and perhaps also calculation, looked after her brother King Richard in his captivity. She sent him raisins, spices, a barrel of sturgeon and red scarlet cloth for his Pentecost robes. She also helped clothe Edmund, Richard's son, evidently a captive with his father.[231]

Throughout this period, Eleanor was in close contact with other noble women. She sent letters to the countesses of Lincoln, Devon, Gloucester and Gilbert de Clare's wife, Alice, who was at Cardiff. Apart from visiting Maud de Lacy, countess of Gloucester, she also entertained over Easter the countess of Devon, Isabella de Forz.[232] If, as seems likely, she pressed young Simon's suit, she had no success. It was after this that Isabella fled to Wales where she stayed till the end of the war. Perhaps she had felt the rough side of Eleanor's tongue. Eleanor's time at Odiham was during what was still the pomp of the regime. Her activity was to be even more vital in the crisis to come.

Detecting the role of women in this period is like looking at a landscape just before dawn when only the most prominent features are visible. If only the dawn could break it would reveal, I suspect, women from all sections of society very much engaged with politics and on both sides of the political divide. If, as seems the case, large numbers of men, in one way or another, took Montfort's part, that was probably true of women also.

---

[228] Wilkinson, *HR*, ci, no. 111.
[229] Wilkinson, *HR*, no. 144.
[230] Wilkinson, *HR*, no. 129.
[231] Ray, *Edward I's Regent*, 9.
[232] For these contacts, see Wilkinson, *HR*, civ–v, cxiv–v.

## THE CLERGY

Amongst churchmen there were divided views about Simon de Montfort, just as there were within other sections of society. Lively debates took place at Peterborough abbey with at least one monk blaming the earl for stirring up discord.[233] With the collapse of the regime, churchmen, like others, said they had given Montfort support only because they were coerced. The abbot of Abingdon claimed he had sent his knights to garrison Windsor castle when told his granges and cellars would otherwise be closed, thus depriving the convent of its food and drink.[234] Master Henry Sampson, accused of being Montfort's clerk and furthering his affairs, said he had been forced into his service and had left as soon as he could.[235] Others claimed they had just been falsely accused. A jury agreed that the abbot of Reading had not, as was rumoured, warned Montfort of the attempt to spring Edward from Wallingford castle.[236]

Yet it is very clear that churchmen gave very substantial moral and material support to the Montfort movement.[237] Indeed, the Furness abbey chronicler describing the events of 1263 believed that 'the major part of the clergy were with the barons'.[238] Such support had survived the attacks on church property, partly because the chief sufferers were alien clerics, partly because the regime had taken at least some steps to put matters right.[239]The support ran from top to bottom of the clerical order – from bishops down to parish priests and unbeneficed clerks. It was hardly surprising, given the way Henry had oppressed the church, despite his personal piety. Churchmen could also agree with everyone else about the more general defects of his rule. Montfort's religiosity was quite on a par with the king's and his closeness to leading churchmen promised a new dawn in relations with the church. Indeed, in one area, '1258' had already brought that about for Henry's manipulation of episcopal elections had ended, hence the number of Montfortian partisans reaching the bench.

The clergy, first and foremost, were the regime's propagandists. We have seen how John Mansel wanted the king to have 'preachers' like those on the other side. When 'the community of the county of Northampton'

---

[233] 'Miracula', 81–2. For differences of view at Pershore abbey, see Carpenter, 'The Pershore *Flores Historiarum*'.

[234] Jacob, *Studies*, 295–6.

[235] *RS*, 178–9; King, 'The Friar Tuck syndrome', 41, 47. Sampson had his lands seized by Montfortians and only went to Montfort, so he said, in the hope of recovering them. He was pardoned by the king in 1266 and presented to a living: *CPR 1258–66*, 562; *CPR 1266–72*, 18.

[236] Jacob, *Studies*, 295.

[237] For Jacob's survey, see his *Studies*, 293–7. James King's 'The Friar Tuck syndrome: clerical violence and the Barons' War' explores particularly the role of churchmen in the pillaging of estates.

[238] Furness, 540.

[239] See above, 341.

were gathered in Cow Meadow outside the town, it was Master Walter de Hyldeborw, rector of Little Billing, who 'preached to the people on behalf of the earl'.[240] In the same county, the chaplain of Hemington was accused of 'publicly preaching for Simon earl of Leicester against the king'.[241] In Nottinghamshire, the rector of Langford, Walter de Grey, and his reeve were said to have opposed the king and Lord Edward 'in word and deed'.[242] These were not isolated examples. After the war, investigations were launched to discover 'the men of religion' who promoted the business of the earl of Leicester 'and drew people to him by lies and falsehoods, lauding the earl and blaming the party of the king and his son'.[243]

Popular sermons, preached in English, doubtless focused on the righteousness of the great earl, his miraculous victories, his saving England from foreigners and his commitment to the Provisions of Oxford. Clergy also provided more sophisticated and learned justifications of the regime, the most notable, of course, being *The Song of Lewes*. Oxford University itself was the home to some very radical ideas. One of those who lectured to the Franciscans there was the friar John of Wales. He was also writing a great teaching aid for preachers called the *Communiloquium*. With obvious relevance to Henry's rule, this argued that the prince was subject to the law, must be advised by wise councillors, give justice to all and serve the interests of the whole community. Nothing very unusual here, but what was unusual, and dangerous, was John's view that it was no sin to kill a ruler who transgressed these norms. John of Salisbury had questioned whether a tyrant could be killed and equivocated over the answer. John of Wales had no doubt about it. 'The overall message is not of a kind that Henry III would have wanted to hear in the average English pulpit.'[244]

Within Oxford University, there were divided views like everywhere else.[245] At this very time the loyalist Walter of Merton was setting up the college that would bear his name. Yet some clerks when the war broke out in 1264 were very keen to translate their Montfortian ideas into action.[246] In March 1264, soon after his arrival in Oxford, Henry had ordered the University to go home. His stated reason was that the town was now filling

---

[240] *RS*, 194–5; Carpenter, *Reign of Henry III*, 338–9. Walter denied the charge of preaching for the earl and was acquitted by juries drawn from three hundreds, but a jury from another hundred told the story of the Cow Meadow episode.

[241] *RS*, 207. Here the chaplain, Roger Sparewe, declined to put himself on a jury and had to pay a fine of £5 to the king.

[242] *CIM*, no. 851.

[243] FitzThedmar, 96 (Stone, FitzThedmar, no. 914). The investigations were part of the business of the Dictum of Kenilworth eyre.

[244] Swanson, *John of Wales*, 68–101, with tyrannicide on 11 and 79–81, and the quotation at 81–2. For further discussion, see Slater, *Art and Political Thought*, 122–4; and below, 419–22.

[245] For the university generally in the thirteenth century, see Lawrence, 'The university in state and church'.

[246] Lawrence ('The university of Oxford and the chronicle of the Barons' Wars') and Powicke (*King Henry III*, ii, 784–7) may both underplay the degree of Montfortian support.

with violent men. The University could return once peace and tranquillity had been restored.[247] Rishanger, writing much later, but sometimes well informed, believed Henry also suspected the loyalty of the clerks and feared they would side with the barons if the latter arrived.[248] Such fears were certainly justified by the sequel. For the clerks, or some of them, did not go home. Instead, they went to Northampton. This had an academic rationale since a university was growing up in the town, populated by émigrés from Cambridge. But the move was also highly political for Northampton at this time was a great Montfortian base, as the clerks must have known. Once there, the Oxford men did more than give moral support to the Montfortians. To Henry's fury, they raised their own standard aloft and took part in the fighting, bombarding the royalists, as they entered the town, with missiles fired from bows, slings and catapults.[249] No wonder Montfort, during his parliament of 1265, rewarded the Oxford clerks by issuing a royal letter exempting them from sitting on juries.[250]

How far clerics fought in the other battles of the civil war is unknown, although some did. In Kent, Walter the parson of Croxfeld was said to have been present at Lewes.[251] He was also described as a '*depredator*', and evidence for clerical participation in the pillaging is abundant. Indeed, in cases before the court *coram rege* between 1265 and 1268, around 400 clerics were accused of taking part in depredations. They included abbots, priors, rectors, vicars, chaplains and a host of simple 'clerks'.[252] In Kent, Matthew, the clerk of Sutton (a Montfort manor), and his two sons raided the property at Bicknor of the king's falconer, John of Bicknor.[253] A whole range of churchmen – parsons, chaplains, vicars, clerks and even the abbot of Bury St Edmunds – were accused of pillaging the manors of the royalist baron Robert of Tattershall.[254]

Material support for Montfort certainly came from religious houses. Some were accused of having knights in the garrisons at Northampton

---

[247] *F*, i, 435 (*CPR 1258–66*, 307).

[248] Rishanger, 22. Robert of Gloucester, ii, lines 11,230–2, believed the clerks were told to go because of a 'town v gown' riot earlier in the year (of which he gives a long description), but this is discounted by the annals of Winchester: Winchester, 101.

[249] Guisborough, 190; Lawrence, 'The university of Oxford and the chronicle of the Barons' Wars', 100.

[250] *CPR 1313–17*, 288. This concession by a letter patent on 2 February 1265 was not enrolled and is only known from Edward II's confirmation. I am grateful to Adam Chambers for drawing it to my attention and to Paul Dryburgh for sending me an image.

[251] TNA C 145/27.

[252] King, 'The Friar Tuck syndrome', 34, 39, 43. King has a good discussion of the problems of interpreting the evidence. Few of the cases are dated, and many may have arisen from incidents after Evesham. Only a tiny proportion of those accused appeared to defend the charges.

[253] TNA KB 26/175, m. 7 (image 0016). Walter was said to have land worth a mark in Sussex.

[254] King, 'The Friar Tuck syndrome', 45–6.

and Kenilworth.[255] Many probably sent contingents to the army mustered to repel the queen's invasion.[256] Individual monks could take an active part in events. After Lewes, John de Belham, an inmate of St Augustine's Canterbury, with three others, sought out Roger of Leybourne in the house of the widow 'Feidina' in Thanet, 'because it was said in the country he was hidden there'. Belham also sent supplies from St Augustine's manor at Minster in Thanet, where he was warden, to the fleet mustering to resist the queen's invasion.[257] That within monastic communities there was a belief, sometimes a passionate belief, in the Montfortian cause, is clear from the accounts of the period in their chronicles. Only one house, Merton priory in Surrey, argued the king's part. By contrast, Bury St Edmunds, Waverley, Tewkesbury, Pershore, Furness, Battle, Christ Church Canterbury, St Martin's Dover, Dunstable and Osney were all to a greater or lesser extent favourable to Montfort.[258] Attitudes at St Albans can probably be deduced from Rishanger's later work, those at St Peter's Gloucester from Robert of Gloucester's chronicle, if he was indeed a monk of the house.[259] At Peterborough abbey the whole convent testified to the miraculous way the monk who had dared criticize Montfort was brought to repentance. Its chronicle, although in most places carefully neutral, recorded the view that at Evesham 'the just died for justice'.[260] At St Swithun's Winchester, the chronicler praised the Londoners for their conduct in 1263, and lambasted that of the citizens of Winchester. In 1266 the convent had to give the king 500 marks for a pardon.[261]

Above all, Montfort had support from the bishops. They agreed to the tax levied to defend the kingdom against the queen's invasion. With one possible exception (that of Bath and Wells), they failed to promulgate the sentences of excommunication commanded by the legate. Nine bishops at the end of the 1265 parliament witnessed the king's confirmation of Magna Carta. Presumably they were the same nine who a few days earlier had promulgated the sentence of excommunication in Westminster Hall against those who violated the Charters, the Provisions of Westminster *and* the Constitution of 1264. The nine also sealed the full version of the final agreement which had all the details of Edward's emasculation and the

---

[255] So Ramsey and Peterborough: *CIM*, nos. 840, 851; Peterborough, 18.

[256] So Bury St Edmunds, 31–2; Dunstable, 233. At the Winchester parliament after Evesham the abbot and convent of Bury were consequently fined 800 marks.

[257] *CIM*, nos. 1024 (p. 312), 1209; *CPR 1258–66*, 349, 584.

[258] The chronicles are given here in the order they are discussed in Gransden, *Historical Writing*, 401, 411–16, 419 (where the *Flores* in question was written at Pershore), 421–3, 428, 432.

[259] For the king in 1266 remitting his anger against St Albans, see *CPR 1258–66*, 559. For Robert of Gloucester, see Gransden, *Historical Writing*, 435–7.

[260] Peterborough, 17.

[261] Winchester, 101; *CPR 1258–66*, 558; *CPR 1266–72*, 339–40.

threats of his disinheritance.[262] They could not have lent their authority more brazenly to the extremities of Montfort's cause.[263] Four of the bishops were partisans: Chichester (one of the three electors of the council), London (one of the nine councillors), Worcester and Winchester. Three other bishops, Robert Stichill of Durham, Hugh of Balsham of Ely and Walter de la Wyle of Salisbury, were at least Montfortian sympathizers. All three were accused after Evesham, along with the other four, of acting against the king. Yet those sealing the agreement also included two bishops who escaped such censure, the king's kinsman Roger de Meuland of Coventry and Lichfield and Walter Giffard, recently elected as bishop of Bath and Wells. Giffard, indeed, was to became Henry's first chancellor on his recovery of power.[264]

Of the sixteen English bishops in post in 1265, nine then gave their support to the settlement at the end of Montfort's parliament. Another bishop, Gravesend of Lincoln, though absent, would certainly have done so.[265] Of the rest, Carlisle's Robert de Chaury and Exeter's Walter of Bronescombe both co-operated with the regime. So, ultimately, did the former judge Norwich's Simon of Walton.[266] Threatened during the parliament with the money being raised from his own goods, he began to collect the tax conceded to repel the queen's invasion.[267] That just left Archbishop Boniface, Aigueblanche of Hereford and Laurence de St Martin of Rochester. The first two, of course, were the regime's deadly enemies, but they were overseas, as probably was St Martin. With the episcopate, therefore, the Furness abbey statement that 'the major part of the clergy' were with Montfort rings absolutely true.

## JUSTIFICATIONS

For those closest to the great earl, those long in his service, much hinged on the loyalty they owed him as their lord and leader. It was a virtue Montfort much prized. He had, he said, valued Henry of Almain not for his arms but for his 'special constancy'.[268] After the war, the knight Richard de Vernon explained his conduct by saying 'in the whole time of the war I stood with my lord, Robert de Ferrers, earl of Derby, from whom I held

---

[262] *F*, i, 451–2; *DBM*, 314–15.

[263] See Wykes's comment: Wykes, 159–60.

[264] For an analysis of the bishops, see Ambler, 'Magna Carta', 814–16, 823–4.

[265] Gravesend was present at the parliament but, as Ambler suggests ('Magna Carta', 823), may have avoided witnessing the final instruments, having been suspended by the pope.

[266] *CPR 1258–66*, 269, 292, 324, 335, 477, 488.

[267] *CR 1264–8*, 82, 87–8, 91–2. He does not seem to have answered the summons to come to the parliament.

[268] Rishanger, 17, said when Henry of Almain deserted, see above 287.

my land to whom I had done homage'.[269] Many of Montfort's tenants would surely have said the same, said it unto their deaths. So, if in different terms, would those in Montfort's service who had no tenurial connection with him. 'My lord, my lord, let it be. Today we shall drink from one cup, just as we have in the past,' cried Hugh Despenser when rejecting Montfort's suggestion he should fly from Evesham and escape approaching death.[270] Of course, loyalty was two-way. In actual fact, Richard de Vernon did not follow Ferrers all through the war. Who would remain loyal to so foolish a lord? But Montfort's men had the honour of following a lord of gigantic prestige and supreme ability.

Loyalty marched with the other chivalric virtues. Many of Montfort's knights doubtless hoped to be like the legendary Fulk fitzWarin, who 'had such grace he never came into any place in which courage, chivalry, prowess or bounty were, but he was held as the best and without peer'.[271] Such ideals could inspire loyalty irrespective of the merits and religiosity of the cause, yet the two easily interlinked, for knighthood was a religious calling. Hence the purifying bath before the ceremony of knighting. There was thus nothing incongruous in the way Nicholas of Cogenhoe, like so many of his fellows, was depicted on his tomb not in the clothes of peace but those of war. The knightings before Lewes, the taking of communion and the donning of crosses were inseparable. 'It is not for the knight of Christ to fly but rather to suffer death at the sword of his enemy for the sake of truth,' proclaimed Montfort before Evesham, according to the Osney annalist.[272]

The 'truth' of the cause resonated from top to bottom of society. At the top, even the hostile Thomas Wykes acknowledged that nobles joined Montfort in 1263 believing his was a 'pious undertaking'.[273] At the bottom, the villagers of Peatling Magna understood the concept of the community of the realm and thought the barons were acting in its interests. Indeed, those acting against it were guilty of treason.[274] Much here was due to the nature of the conflict. Those of the twelfth century had been largely 'baronial', at their centre struggles for the throne between different noble

---

[269] Carpenter, 'The second century of English feudalism', 66; Golob, 'The Ferrers earls of Derby', i, 356.

[270] Laborderie, Maddicott and Carpenter, 'The last hours of Simon de Montfort', 410.

[271] Romance of Fulk fitzWarin, 367.

[272] Osney, 169. For comment by Paul Binski on 'the relationship between warfare and the spirit, so mutually informing yet so dichotomous to the modern mind', see his *Westminster Abbey and the Plantagenets*, 81. He comments that the shields in the Abbey's choir (above, 230–1) 'illustrate the continuum of the Christian/military ethos, rather than any religious/secular divide'.

[273] Wykes, 134. In discussing Montfortian ideology, I have been helped by Andrew Lomas's MA dissertation, 'Montfortian ideology and its understanding'.

[274] *SCWR*, 43; Carpenter, *Reign of Henry III*, 310–11, with references to the extensive comment on the episode.

factions. The conflicts of the thirteenth century, by contrast, were 'national', with at their heart broad-based attempts to reform the realm.[275] If '1215' was the first such movement, '1258' went far beyond it both in the reach of the reforms and the political role played by knights, free tenants, peasants, churchmen and townsmen. On a far greater scale than in 1215, the king's opponents needed to justify what they were doing to a broad political audience.[276]

One way of doing so was through the formal proclamation of reforms. Here the regime of 1258 got off to an innovative start with its proclamations in French and English as well as Latin. In December 1264, Montfort ordered his version of the Provisions of Westminster to be read monthly in the county courts. Next year, to preserve their 'memory', his ordinances for Edward's release and the future government of the realm were to be kept in the county court 'by trustworthy men elected for the purpose'.[277] So that no one could plead ignorance, precise instructions were given for their reading out, this time (more aware perhaps of the audience's patience) twice a year. As well as proclaiming the reforms, Montfort also issued letters (in the king's name) explaining his actions, none more eloquent than when summoning the army to resist the queen's invasion. There were also, of course, many informal channels of information. As one aphorism from the period put it, 'from mill and from market, from smith and anchorite's house, one hears the news'.[278] Montfort had summoned knights to the parliaments of 1264 and 1265 as also to a baronial assembly in 1261. They would lend weight to the decisions. They would also, when they got home, talk to all and sundry about what they had seen and heard.[279]

In some cases the lines of informal communication from the top to bottom of society are clear. In April 1265 a pardon was issued for the peasant Wodard of Kibworth. (He had killed a man in self defence.) Usually, such pardons just gave the name of the beneficiary. This one, by contrast, was issued at the instance of Saer de Harcourt, the lord of Kibworth. And Saer himself is described as the knight of Simon de Montfort, earl of Leicester and steward of England. The pardon is thus designed to proclaim Saer's Montfortianism and, by extension, Wodard's too. Montfort's mantle is thrown over them both and in a most public way, for the pardon was embodied in letter patent, addressed to everybody

[275] For the contrast, see Maddicott, 'Politics and the people', 9–10.

[276] For what was known and how news circulated, see Maddicott, 'Politics and the people'; Coss, 'How did thirteenth-century knights counter royal authority?'; and (for wider conceptual discussion) Melve, 'The public debate during the baronial rebellion'.

[277] Montfort's version of Magna Carta was included here: DBM, 313–15.

[278] From the 'Ancrene Rewle', a spiritual guidebook for anchoresses, cited in Maddicott, 'Politics and the people', 7.

[279] In 1261, Henry himself had summoned knights to Windsor so they could see and understand his good intentions: DBM, 248–9.

with the king's seal hanging beneath. Wodard could thus show his fellow villagers how the pardon joined him both to Saer and to Simon; the peasant, the knight and the earl who was ruling England together, the community of the realm encapsulated in a single document.[280]

In justifying their actions the Montfortians were, of course, in a more difficult position than their predecessors in 1258. The events of 1263 could hardly be portrayed as taking place with the king's consent.[281] Yet they could be justified, as we have seen, under the terms of the 1258 oath binding everyone to accept the reforms promulgated by the council and to treat their opponents as mortal enemies. The oath of fidelity to the reforms could seem just as binding as the oath of fidelity to the king. Indeed, the fate of mortal enemies might well be as bad as the fate of traitors. Just how many people actually took the oath is unknown, but it remained central to the discourse throughout the period of reform and rebellion.[282] When the pope sought to restore Henry to full power, it was the oath he quashed. 'Keep the oath', cried the poem calling on the earls to continue their resistance in 1261. For the author of *The Song of Lewes*, Montfort's fidelity to the oath was one of his defining characteristics.

Allegiance to the reforms was strengthened by how they were described: 'for the honour of God, in the faith of the king and the profit of the realm'. These words were used again and again from start to finish of the movement.[283] And then from 1260, as we have seen, the reforms got a name, one which stuck and became universal: the Provisions of Oxford. In 1263, therefore, the attacks bringing Montfort to power were against those who had broken their oaths, deserted the Provisions of Oxford and deserved to be treated as mortal enemies. Chronicler after chronicler saw the events in these terms.[284] So did knights on Montfort's side in the localities. In Leicestershire, in 1264, William of Swinford said, 'because of the oath of Oxford', he had seized the land of someone who was against 'the Provisions of Oxford'.[285] The oath and the authority of the council

---

[280] For this case, see Carpenter, 'A peasant in politics'. The commission leading to the pardon was issued when the king was at Canterbury in October 1264. Almost certainly, therefore, Wodard and Saer were in the army mustered to resist the queen's invasion.

[281] For justifications of revolt and resistance, see Ambler, *Bishops in the Political Community*, ch. 7 (on justifying the Montfortian regime), and Valente, *Theory and Practice of Revolt*, ch. 2 (on theories of resistance). The latter covers the period between 1215 and 1399. For a survey of the problems of restraining kings, short of deposition, in the long thirteenth century, see Spencer, 'Dealing with inadequate kingship'.

[282] One puzzle is why, in contrast to 1215, no mechanism was set up for the taking of the oath. For discussion see Hey, 'Two oaths of the community', 224–7. It may be the regime wished to avoid any suggestion of coercion in the taking of the oath.

[283] So, for example, 'Letter of Richard, earl of Gloucester', 69; Carpenter, *Reign of Henry III*, 251; Canterbury/Dover, 213; FitzThedmar, 53–4 (Stone, FitzThedmar, nos. 770–1); F, i, 433 (*CPR 1258–66*, 357); *DBM*, 314–15.

[284] See above, 255–6.

[285] TNA JUST 1/1194, m. 4d (image 1264). The victim was William de Maleshoures.

equally justified a refusal to surrender castles to the king. It was in those terms that Hugh Bigod refused to hand over Scarborough and Pickering in 1261 and John de la Haye, Dover in 1263.[286]

Alongside the appeal of the oath and the Provisions, the Montfortians had one other ideological strength. They stood for, indeed they were, 'the community of the realm'. What was, therefore, at best a faction within the kingdom, thus seemed to embrace everyone within it. The idea of 'the community of the realm' had been there from the start. In the proclamation announcing the oath and the council's authority in 1258, the king said the council had been chosen by himself and 'the community of our realm', 'la commune a nostre reaume'. (In the Latin it would have been by the 'communitas regni'.)[287] Henry thus seemed to indicate he stood on one side while everyone else stood bound together on the other. From this start in a widely circulated proclamation, the idea took flight. It was strengthened by the oath itself, for those who took it could feel they were part of a community of sworn brethren. Again and again, from top to bottom of the Montfortian movement, reprisals were justified by saying the victims were acting 'against the community of the realm'. The claim was made by Peter de Montfort on the ruling council,[288] by the young barons Norman de Arcy and John de Beauchamp of Bedford,[289] by the knight Peter Picot,[290] and by the villagers of Peatling Magna.[291] Some of those accused rebutted the charge in the same terms. The Suffolk lord Hamo Chevre, as we have seen, said he had always been faithful to the community of the realm.[292]

The oath, the Provisions of Oxford and the community of the realm became, therefore, a golden trinity around which Montfortians could rally. They were often linked together. William of Swinford said his enemies were acting against both the oath and the Provisions, Peter Picot that they were acting against the Provisions and the community of the realm.[293] Disloyalty to the oath and the Provisions meant, therefore, disloyalty to everyone in the kingdom. The Provisions, moreover, were more than a

---

[286] F, i, 408; Canterbury/Dover, 230.

[287] No Latin text survives. The French 'commune' was probably becoming part of spoken English, there being no English equivalent. It is true that when the clerk Robert of Fulham wrote out the English version of the 1258 proclamation, 'la commune de nostre reaume' became (in modern English) 'the people of the country of our kingdom', but this may be because he was instructed to write in English and so avoided 'loan' words. For discussion, see Carpenter, Reign of Henry III, 336–7 n. 97, and for loan words Ingham, 'Middle English borrowing from French'.

[288] CR 1264–8, 45–6.

[289] TNA JUST 1/1197, mm. 18d–19 (images 1476, 1522).

[290] TNA JUST 1/1191, m. 17d (image 1077). For Peter, who was a follower of Gilbert de Clare, see CFR 1254–5, no. 293; CChR 1226–57, 426; CIM, no. 771.

[291] SCWR, 43.

[292] TNA JUST 1/1191, m. 17 (images 1039–40).

[293] TNA JUST 1/1194, m. 4d (image 1264); TNA JUST 1/1191, m. 17d (image 1077).

mere slogan. They would never have had such an appeal if they had been. As we have seen, they seemed to meet exactly many of the well-publicized and widely felt defects of Henry's rule.[294]

How well that was understood is shown by a tract written soon after Evesham. The author was probably a monk from the Cistercian abbey of Rufford in Nottinghamshire, but he concentrated not on the grievances of the church but on the general sufferings of the realm.[295] Montfortian preachers may well have set out their stall in much the same way. There had, the tract explained, been magnates in England, some native born, some foreign (the latter the kinsmen of the king and queen), who oppressed the people and against whom it was impossible to get justice, although justice ought to be freely available. A steward of William de Valence had even said if his lord did anyone an injury no judge appointed by the king would dare pronounce against him. Clearly William de Bussey's remark, quoted by Matthew Paris, had gained wide currency. 'Meanwhile', the account continued, new suits of courts and many other abuses of custom had been introduced into England. The king himself, instead of being sustained by his own ample demesnes and rents, had been so profligate in his gifts to foreigners that he was forced to live off rapine and the tears of the poor. The violent exactions of his sheriffs and bailiffs included frequent tallaging of towns and the high and intolerable annual farms exacted from the counties and hundreds. The author was thus well aware of all the local grievances.

Faced with this misrule, the bishops, earls, barons, knights, clergy and people had met at Oxford and introduced 'new provisions' so that justice could be available to everyone.[296] The reforms were affirmed by corporal oaths and supported by sentences of excommunication. A chief justiciar was appointed and the foreigners expelled when they refused to accept justice. Sheriffs and their bailiffs were appointed 'according to the new provisions' and a new morning of justice dawned in England. But, the tract continued, certain courtiers, helped by the queen, then persuaded Henry to secure absolution from his oath by the pope. It is at this point that Simon de Montfort stepped forth. Under his leadership, supported by his sons, the barons insisted on maintaining the Provisions of Oxford. The result ultimately was the civil war. 'It seems to me,' the author writes, 'that the provisions were very necessary for the reform of law in England and it was by evil counsel that the king was persuaded to break his pact with his people.'

---

[294] See above, 158–60.

[295] Corpus Christi College Cambridge, MS 385, fos. 57–60; Powicke, *King Henry III*, ii, 470; Burton, 'Politics, propaganda and public opinion', 96. I thank the sub-librarian of the Parker library, Dr Alexander Devine, for helping me decipher some of the marginal annotations. The volume is now available online if one searches for 'Corpus Christi Cambridge MS 385'.

[296] The tract stresses the role of John fitzGeoffrey. The remark of Valence's steward was made to him.

To the original appeal of the Provisions, Montfort, when he returned to England in 1263, added two further elixirs. The first was the statute against the aliens promulgated that July alongside the Provisions' confirmation. Thenceforth, 'England for the English' became a central plank of the movement. Indeed, many came to think the general expulsion of foreigners had been part of the original Provisions in 1258.[297] The second elixir, building on the idea of '*reformatio*' and the claim the reforms were for 'the honour of God', was, of course, to transform a largely secular programme into a holy cause, something symbolized by the taking of communion and the donning of crosses at Southwark and Lewes. No wonder the author of the tract quoted above believed that those who laboured 'with charity' to sustain the Provisions of Oxford and 'correct' the laws of England would receive the blessings of the Lord and ultimately 'see the God of Gods in Syon'.[298] Technically, the Montfortian movement could not be a crusade, for only the pope could confer the same spiritual benefits on Christians fighting against Christians as enjoyed by Christians fighting against the infidels in the Holy Land. The legate Guy Foulquois had been empowered to do that for those fighting against Montfort, not for him. But there is no doubt many viewed Montfort's movement in crusading terms. Hence the way one chronicler imagined Montfort saying he had taken the cross (to crusade in the Holy Land) but was just as willing to die fighting against wicked Christians for the liberty of the land and the holy church.[299] And perhaps it was more than imagination. At Lewes (and presumably also at Southwark), the crosses the Montfortians wore were white and white crosses were the particular emblem of English crusaders.[300] In getting his men to wear them, Montfort was implying they too had crusading status. Since, moreover, Bishop Cantilupe, who absolved the army of its sins before Lewes, had been empowered by the pope in 1263 to preach the crusade and confer all the usual spiritual benefits on those who went, his blessing had very much a crusading aura.[301]

There was also one other crusading context, one giving confidence to Montfort himself as much as his men. This was the example of his heroic father. Before his great victory at Muret in 1213, conscious of his inferior forces, Simon senior had urged his men to fight as 'Christian knights', 'strengthened by the virtue of God more than of men'. All this is related at length in the annals of Waverley abbey, a Cistercian house Montfort knew well. On his visits there he may well have been told of the passage

[297] So Waverley, 349–50.

[298] Corpus Christi College Cambridge, MS 385, fos. 79–79v. This occurs in another tract by the same author, this one written in 1264.

[299] St Benet at Hulme, 226. For discussion stressing the crusading nature of the movement, see Jahner, *Literature and Law in the Era of Magna Carta*, ch. 5.

[300] Rishanger, 31.

[301] Tyerman, *England and the Crusade*, 59–60, 134, 139, 144–51.

about his father. He certainly behaved in exactly the same way at Southwark and at Lewes.[302]

If the Montfortians thought theirs was a holy cause before Lewes, how much more was that the case after the great victory. Some even believed that Saint George and Thomas Becket had miraculously appeared on the field to aid Montfort's troops.[303] The bishop of London, Henry of Sandwich, writing to Gilbert de Clare, described how 'the Lord, powerful in battle . . . by whose almighty command one man can rout a thousand and two men can rout ten thousand', had brought about the 'glorious triumph' and thus made possible 'the reform of his church and kingdom' before 'greatly corrupted'.[304] Villagers too were quite capable of putting the victory into a religious context. At Kibworth Harcourt, they turned their traditional Pentecost procession to the church at Market Harborough into a celebration.[305]

There was, at the village level, a great deal of sheer excitement at what had happened. At Tonge in Kent, little more than a fortnight after the battle, a playful fight after dinner between two boys, one taking the part of Montfort, the other Lord Edward, got out of hand and someone trying to break it up was killed.[306] That the poem about the capture of King Richard in the windmill was written in English shows it was designed for a popular audience. The hero is Montfort, who says what he would do with two escapees from the battle, John de Warenne and Hugh Bigod, had he them in his power:

Sir Simon de Montfort hath sworn by ys chyn,
Hevede he nou here the Erl of Waryn . . .

For all the joy in the outcome, the battle of Lewes posed fresh problems for the Montfortians in terms of justifying their conduct. When it came to taking up arms, the king himself had helped. He had defied the Montfortians before the battle, as had King Richard and Lord Edward.

---

[302] Waverley, 279–80, and for Montfort's connections with the house see Ambler, *Song of Simon de Montfort*, 101–3. The battle of Muret was fought against the king of Aragon and the count of Toulouse, who were seeking to recover the lands Montfort had conquered from 'the heretics'. In the event the odds were evened by the arrival of French forces.

[303] Canterbury/Dover, 237–8. Ambler, *Song of Simon de Montfort*, 277–8, discusses the significance of St George and Becket in this context. At Pershore abbey, a positive but comparatively restrained account of Montfort's victory was altered so as to stress its God-given nature: Carpenter, 'The Pershore *Flores Historiarum*', 1343–4, 1362–3.

[304] Hoskin, *EEA, London*, 102–3. I am grateful to Daniel Hadas for a translation of this passage. Sandwich was quoting Deuteronomy 32:30.

[305] When the route was barred by William King of Harborough (a royal manor), a fight started in which he was killed with an axe by Wodard of Kibworth, hence Wodard's need for a pardon. The episode featured in Michael Wood's BBC Four TV series, 'Story of England': http://www.bbc.co.uk/programmes/bootw231.

[306] Summerson, 'Repercussions from the Barons' Wars'.

The Montfortians, in their turn, had renounced their homages and with-drawn from the king's allegiance. This was a time-honoured procedure and one followed by the barons in 1215. Both sides in 1264 thus accepted the ritual of '*diffidatio*' and acknowledged there was a proper way of proceeding when beginning to fight against the king. Indeed, Henry had once complained that Llywelyn the Great (grandfather of Llywelyn ap Gruffudd) had made war on him without going through the procedure.

If, however, the *diffidatio*, solved the problem of making war on the king, it was no help with the situation following the Montfortian victory. The task now was to find a way to justify placing what might be permanent restraints on the king. This was all the harder given the oath of 1258 had twice been quashed by the pope and the Provisions as a whole condemned by King Louis. Something new was required. The problem was addressed by *The Song of Lewes*.

## THE SONG OF LEWES

In the British Library there is small vellum volume in a binding of the early eighteenth century. Catalogued as Harley 978, it is the work of several hands and miscellaneous content. It begins with various antiphons and a calendar which includes the obits of abbots of Reading, hence the probability that Reading abbey was once the owner. At the heart of the book a single hand has copied out in double columns thirty-three separate items. They include attacks on the papal court, tracts on the Trinity and the Incarnation, pieces about Thomas Becket and advice on falconry. One item takes up a full fifteen folios. It has no heading and lacks the coloured capitals and paragraph marks found in some of the earlier pieces. It does not look very exciting. But this is the only known copy of *The Song of Lewes*. (The name itself was that bestowed or at least popular-ized by C.L. Kingsford in his 1890 edition.)[307]

The *Song* was evidently written in the immediate aftermath of the battle of Lewes and certainly before Montfort's defeat and death the following year. The copy in Harley 978, judging from the hand, may well have been made in the same period.[308] Given the length (it is by far the longest piece copied), it testifies to the copyist's enthusiasm for Montfort's

---

[307] The edition, with text and English translation, is an impressive work of scholarship and fully describes the contents of the volume: *Song of Lewes*, xi–xviii. Digitized images are online: http://www.bl.uk/manuscripts/FullDisplay.aspx?ref=Harley_MS_978. They come up if one just searches for 'British Library Song of Lewes'. The name does not appear in the earlier 1839 edition where the heading given is just 'The Battle of Lewes': *Political Songs*, 72. For recent discussion of the *Song*, see Ambler, *Bishops in the Political Community*, 169–76; Slater, *Art and Political Thought*, 125–9; and Jahner, *Literature and Law in the Age of Magna Carta*, 205–12, which places the *Song* very much within a crusading context.

[308] A copy was also made of a piece written in or soon after 1262: *Song of Lewes*, xvi (no. 108), 154–8.

cause and thus also, if he was a monk of Reading, to enthusiasm within the great royal abbey where Henry III so often stayed. But the labour of copying was as nothing to that of composition. The rhyme running through the poem came not merely at the end of each line, but in the middle as well on the seventh of the thirteen syllables. So, for example:

*Comparati canibus angli viluerunt,*
*Set nunc victis hostibus caput extulerunt.*[309]

The English likened unto dogs were become vile,
But now have they raised their head over their vanquished foes.

To have sustained this form (often flowing with alliterations like '*comparati canibus*') over 968 lines required tremendous imagination, ingenuity and commitment. Equally impressive is the cleverness with which Montfort's cause is justified. Partly original, partly conventional, it drew on a deep knowledge of the bible and also on familiar ideas about the nature of the body politic and the ingredients of just rule. The result is a poetic and political masterpiece. Its author, alas, is unknown, but he was clearly an eyewitness to the events immediately before Lewes, perhaps being in the entourage of Stephen of Bersted, bishop of Chichester. (Bersted is referred to in the poem as hearing Montfort's offers to the royalists before the battle.) If he was a Franciscan friar, as is often suggested, that might explain how the *Song* came to Reading abbey, for the Franciscan house in the town had close connections with the monastery.[310]

*The Song of Lewes* is essentially in two parts. In the first, the author celebrates Montfort and his cause, vindicates his personal conduct and vilifies that of his opponents. In the second, he justifies the restrictions placed on the king.

In Part 1, Montfort appears as the utterly dominant leader. His sons are mentioned, a significant point, but they are unnamed. Indeed, the only person named on Montfort's side is Bishop Bersted. So, no Gilbert de Clare or anyone else. It is Montfort's faith and fidelity alone that has brought peace to all England.

*Fides et fidelitas Symonis solius*
*Fit pacis integritas anglie tocius.*[311]

A central theme in Part 1 is Montfort's fidelity to the oath taken at Oxford and the general holiness and utility of the Provisions themselves. The oath had been to support 'constitutions, catholic and canonical' for the

---

[309] *Song of Lewes*, lines 11–12.
[310] *Reading Cartulary*, ii, 207–10.
[311] *Song of Lewes*, lines 267–8.

'reformation of the royal honour' and 'the preservation of the peace of the realm'.[312] The only qualification showed Montfort's respect for learned churchmen. In the negotiations before the battle he had offered to accept whatever was decided by 'the best men whose faith is lively, who have read the decretals or have taught theology and sacred philosophy', an offer rejected with contempt by his unholy adversaries.[313]

The other major theme is that of Montfort the saviour of England and the English. 'For certain men had aimed to blot out the name of the English whom they had already begun to hold in hatred.'[314] There follows an attack on what are evidently Henry's foreign relatives and all the patronage they had received. Montfort is eager 'to obviate this evil'. 'Let foreigners come but quickly to withdraw, as though for a moment but not to remain', a reference quite probably to the statute against aliens. As a result of Montfort's labours, England can breathe again, hoping for liberty and prosperity.[315]

The *Song* then moves on to defend Montfort against the attacks of his enemies. It rebuts the accusations that he was seeking his own advancement and those of his sons. How could that be true when he was prepared to die, like Christ, for the cause? How could it be true, even more, when God himself had spoken. 'Neither fraud nor falsehood moved the earl but the divine grace which knows who to help.'[316] The proof of that was Lewes itself. Here the *Song* made nothing of Montfort's military skills. The victory of his small force against a much larger army was due to God alone. The God-given victory at Lewes is thus Montfort's ultimate justification.

Alongside justifying Montfort, the *Song* assaults his enemies. There is the outrageous conduct of the king's men – the sacking of Northampton, the despoiling of Battle abbey and the train of prostitutes following the army. And then there is Edward. Part I concludes with a fierce attack upon him. His valour is acknowledged, but all is marred by his treachery and his lawlessness. The *Song* thus compares him to a leopard, a lion in fierceness, but a pard in inconstancy and willfulness. Anxiety is betrayed about what will happen when he ascends the throne. He is urged to respect law and justice for only then will he be a worthy king enjoying the love of his subjects.

This concentration upon Edward confirms absolutely that he was now the driving force in the king's party. What of the king himself? Henry is never mentioned by name in the *Song*, even though the complaints clearly refer to the ills of his rule. Instead, reference is just made to an unnamed

---

[312] *Song of Lewes*, lines 227–38.
[313] *Song of Lewes*, lines 197–206, 238–42.
[314] *Song of Lewes*, lines 283–324.
[315] *Song of Lewes*, lines 9–12.
[316] *Song of Lewes*, lines 349–50.

'king'. This must be because Henry was not viewed, like his son (or his father), as a 'bad' man. Instead, 'the king' in the *Song* is often seen as going wrong through lack of intelligence and wisdom. He is seduced by flatterers without perceiving their trickery. He is unable to choose his councillors, being 'less wise than he ought to be'.[317] Henry's absence from the *Song* was not much of a compliment, indeed no compliment at all, but does help to explain how he survived the Montfortian revolution and lived to reign again.

In the second part of the *Song*, the author seeks to justify the restraints placed on the king. He does so at length, here not at all relying on the God-given victory at Lewes. The need to do so, he may well have felt, was urgent for the regime itself had advanced no convincing justification for its conduct. At Amiens the baronial case had still taken the line that everything had happened with the king's consent.[318] At Boulogne, later in the year, the bishops' attempt to compare the authority of the council to that of the cardinals was dismissed by the legate as both ignorant and absurd.[319] Old arguments and precedents for the magnates deposing a tyrannical ruler or correcting individual acts of injustice were hardly relevant to imposing a permanent council on the king. Although the picture of a king 'less wise than he ought to be' suggested parallels with the *rex inutilis*, who might remain as king, while others governed the kingdom, the *Song* did not develop the idea in any set-piece way. Perhaps, like the reformers in 1258, the author knew the pope had in the past been central to the process.[320] The pope is indeed conspicuously absent from the *Song*. The author did not want to complicate his case with arguments about papal authority.

In this difficult ground, the *Song* begins its defence by setting out very fairly the case of the king. He should be 'free', indeed his freedom is integral to the whole nature of kingship. Deprived of it, he ceases to be a king. This was not, however, as set out, an argument for freedom across the whole range of royal activity. Rather, the king's case concentrates on what was indeed the crucial issue between the sides, namely his right to choose his own ministers. It is only in this context that the Roman law tag 'the will of the prince has the force of law' is quoted.[321] In support of these claims, the king observes that every earl is thus his own master and can appoint whom he likes as his own officials, so why should the king himself be in a worse condition? He also points out that all previous kings had been free and had 'conferred their own at their own pleasure', being in no way subject to their men. The barons, therefore, wish to disinherit the

---

[317] *Song of Lewes*, lines 587–8, 759. I see the reference to the 'fury' of the king in line 78 as a reference to the 'fury' of the king's party, amply seen in the *Song*.

[318] *DBM*, 256–7.

[319] See above, 341.

[320] See above, 41.

[321] I well remember Barbara Harvey pointing this out to me.

king, and place him '*in custodiam et subiectionem*'. In all this, the author showed considerable knowledge of the king's arguments. The analogy with the position of earls and barons had been made by Henry himself at a parliament of 1248. The appeal to precedent had been central to the case at Amiens, while the claim that the baronial demands placed the king '*in custodiam*' was exactly what Henry had said in his complaints against the council in 1260.[322]

How then could the king's case be answered? At the heart of the *Song*'s reply is the elevation of 'the people', the '*universitas*', 'the community' or 'the community of the realm', the words are used interchangeably. 'We give the first place to the community,' the author writes. His justification is theological for the people are God's not the ruler's. Hence Solomon had not punished the Israelites 'because he knew it was God's people that he ruled'.[323] The king, therefore, must govern for the benefit of his people, in accordance with the law *and*, here now getting to the crux of the argument, counselled by native men not foreigners. Again, the proof is biblical for Moses, David and Samuel did not 'set strangers' over their people but ruled through their own men.[324] (Part 2 has another diatribe about all the evils flowing from the king doing the contrary.) From these theological and biblical foundations, the *Song* goes on to advance purely practical reasons as to why, if the king transgresses, the people (led by the native magnates) have the right and duty to impose ministers on him. They have every *need* to do so, for 'the governance of the realm is the safety or ruin of all . . . and, just as on the sea, all things are confounded if fools are in command'.[325] With so much at stake, the people have thus every interest in choosing ministers imbued with a 'motherly fear of the kingdom suffering harm'.[326] And they also have the *knowledge* to do so, for 'the men of the counties know better than anyone else their own realm's customs', handed down as they are by those who have gone before.[327]

The view that on the governance of the realm depended the safety or ruin of all leads into a short section in which the *Song* rebuts the king's argument that he leaves his barons quite free to do what they like with their own. He was quite wrong to do so. Since the realm is like a body in which the health of the whole depends on that of its parts, the king should restrain the folly of his subjects lest the realm as a whole be weakened.[328]

---

[322] *DBM*, 212–13, cap. 7 [5].

[323] *Song of Lewes*, lines, 848, 709, 621–4.

[324] *Song of Lewes*, lines 747–52.

[325] *Song of Lewes*, lines 809–15.

[326] The comparison is here made with the true mother's concern for her child in the judgement of Solomon.

[327] *Song of Lewes*, lines 765–802, and line 768 for '*cuncti provincie*', which I have loosely translated as 'the men of the counties'.

[328] *Song of Lewes*, lines 819–38. Less convincing is an attempt to show that constraints on the king did not impinge on his freedom: *Song of Lewes*, lines 668–86.

In fact, Henry *had* been concerned with the conduct of his magnates and their officials, hence his cry that everyone should obey Magna Carta. He had been foolish to suggest otherwise.

*The Song of Lewes*'s argument that the king should rule for the benefit of his people in conformity with the law was, of course, hardly original, any more than was its view of the body politic. What was original, and in its own terms convincing, was the combination of theological and practical arguments giving first place to the people and justifying their right to choose the king's ministers. That the community was far more likely to know than a wayward king who would govern best in its interests was hard to dispute.

While known perhaps at Reading abbey, the *Song*'s impact in the short period while the Montfortian regime had life must have been limited. Only one copy survives. Given its Latin, the audience can only have been churchmen. Indeed, it was the limited audience that gave the author the freedom to argue as he did. His position was quite different from that of the barons at Amiens confronted by a critical King Louis, or the bishops at Boulogne quavering before a hostile legate.[329] Yet if relevant but to a moment in time, the *Song* stands as eternal witness to the passionate support enjoyed by Montfort and his cause. It ends on a defiant note. If the king seeks to oppress his own men, his subjects would be mad to obey him. Unfortunately, many, by the time the *Song* was completed, were thinking it was mad to obey Simon de Montfort.

---

[329] This point is made in Ambler, *Bishops in the Political Community*, 169. I was reminded of it by John Hill in a King's College London MA dissertation on *The Song of Lewes*.

## Chapter 11

# MONTFORT'S DOWNFALL: FROM THE PARLIAMENT OF 1265 TO THE BATTLE OF EVESHAM

Simon de Montfort left London soon after the end of his great parliament and on 19 March arrived at Odiham where Eleanor de Montfort had been since the previous month. As he came with 160 horses, he brought a considerable entourage.[1] Montfort could surely hope that he had done enough, at least in the short term, to contain his enemies and stabilize his regime. Yet there were equally reasons for anxiety, reasons for thinking indeed the regime might have a very short life.

Many to the end thought the regime righteous and God-given. It is hard to think of the author of *The Song of Lewes* changing his mind. Yet his very efforts to justify the regime suggest the pressure it was under and how well known was the case of the king. We have seen the doubts about the king's treatment evinced by the Pershore annalist, although he admired Montfort and believed in reform of the realm. In London, FitzThedmar was appalled by the 'wretched' mayor's statement of conditional loyalty, although he too had seen good in the Provisions and even now kept his views to himself. Wykes, writing later, was far more outspoken. The regime was wholly illegitimate, a total reversal of the right order of things. It was sustained by a leader, glorying in his success and strength ('*virtus*'), and displaying an arrogance and pride worse than Lucifer's.[2] There were many who must have thought exactly that. Loyalty to the king was not confined to those of baronial and knightly status. When John fitzJohn's men, in command at Windsor castle, sought to bring back into the garrison one of its former sergeants-at-arms, Nicholas Tonney, 'having taken', as he later put it, 'an oath according to the fashion of the enemies of the king', Tonney refused. He would take no oath 'save for the benefit of the king and his sons'. The reply to this was brusque: 'matters of this kind have nothing to do with a sergeant'. But clearly Tonney took another view.[3]

Montfort had reached out to the shires, but the reaction to his proclamations was surely mixed. The sanctions set out suggested resistance was

---

[1] Wilkinson, *HR*, nos. 4–77; Wilkinson, *Eleanor de Montfort*, 110–11.
[2] Wykes, 153–4. For Wykes's use of 'virtus' in a pejorative sense, see Kjær, 'Writing reform and rebellion', 118.
[3] Carpenter, *Reign of Henry III*, 323.

expected and showed how far the regime was based on fear and threat. In a private agreement made by John of Chishall during the 1265 parliament, money owed him did not have to be paid if 'common war' broke out with the destruction of crops and barns.[4] There were both internal and external threats. The marchers had failed to fulfil the agreement made at Worcester and kept postponing the date of their departure for Ireland, something Montfort, occupied with the parliament, could do nothing about. There was also the prospect of another invasion by an 'alien' army. Indeed, Henry of Almain remained a hostage as security for Edward's conduct in case that happened.

In the localities, while some individuals had recovered their properties, others had obtained no redress. In July 1264, William of Swinford acknowledged he was still retaining lands he had seized during the disturbances from a man opposed to the Provisions of Oxford. He argued he should continue to do so until 'by the common counsel of the magnates of the land' it was decided whether such land should be restored.[5] But the magnates never made such a decision. When victims of seizures sought to recover their lands, often by actions of novel disseisin, they were still met by Swinford's defence.[6] Cases thus led nowhere, with adjournments sometimes continuing till the collapse of the regime. As it was stated in one such case, this was because 'no judgement has yet been made'.[7] The result was large numbers of people deprived of property and totally unreconciled to the regime.

Meanwhile, there was piracy in the channel where the Cinque Ports attacked foreign shipping as they liked.[8] The shortages Henry himself experienced were general. According to Wykes, the prices of wine and wax roughly tripled, while the seizures of wool by Henry de Montfort brought hardship to merchants. Montfort, ever the populist, declared that England could live off its own. Some of his followers, to please him, put on robes made of white native cloth rather than the coloured variety imported from abroad. But all this must have enhanced the sense of impending crisis.[9]

Two problems lay at the heart of the regime. The first was its narrow and narrowing base in terms of magnate support. The witnesses to the king's confirmation of Magna Carta at the end of the parliament included

<hr />

[4] TNA E 368/39, m. 13d (image 6255).

[5] TNA JUST 1/1195, m. 4d (image 1264). The victim was William de Maleshoures.

[6] For example, the cases on TNA JUST 1/1194, mm. 4, 5 (images 1224, 1226).

[7] TNA JUST 1/1194, m. 4d (image 1264); TNA JUST 1/1197, m. 19 (image 1476) and image 1522 (with the judgement not yet made, the case between Ralph the Falconer and Norman de Arcy). These cases found in assize rolls are probably a small proportion of the whole as the rolls of the bench and court *coram rege* for the Montfortian period are lost.

[8] Jacob, *Studies*, 287.

[9] Wykes, 157–8.

only one earl, Montfort himself.[10] The earl of Derby had joined Cornwall, and probably also Hereford and Warwick, in prison.[11] Roger Bigod, wielding great power in East Anglia, was summoned to the parliament but failed to turn up. He had been on the king's side when the quarrel was submitted to Louis at the end of 1263, but had then missed the battle of Lewes. After the battle, at the June 1264 parliament, he had endorsed Montfort's Constitution and indeed sealed the letter refusing entry to the legate. But thereafter he appears detached from the regime. During the invasion scare, he was replaced as castellan of Orford and keeper of the surrounding coast.[12] Meanwhile, in France, Hugh Bigod, heir to the earldom, John de Warenne, earl of Surrey, and William de Valence, backed by the queen and Edmund, were actively planning a fresh invasion. Montfort's paucity of comital support made the adherence of Gilbert de Clare all the more important. But here, as we will see, a terrible fissure was about to open up.

Montfort's second problem was even more fundamental. His regime depended on keeping Henry and Edward in captivity or at least under very tight control. Henry was not much of a problem. Edward was quite another matter. Montfort had been under intense pressure to arrange his release – from the bishops, the marchers, possibly from Gilbert de Clare. Indeed, his release was the quid pro quo for the marchers' submission at Worcester. Montfort insisted it could only take place if Edward was stripped of power. Yet even with that done, Edward remained a danger. Burning with resentment, full of youthful energy and with many supporters still at large, he would never be reconciled to the regime. Some kind of deal, some kind of soft landing, in which, either as prince or king, he was given his freedom in return for accepting Montfort's tenure of Chester, was surely inconceivable. Edward's only ambition now must be to destroy Simon de Montfort outright. He could never really be set free. So, in the end, Edward's release, in the great ceremony on 11 March, was, as we have seen, a sham. Henry of Almain became a hostage at once for his good behaviour. Edward in practice remained under the guard of Henry de Montfort.[13] He was released only in the sense that Henry now took him round the country instead of keeping him confined in a castle prison. After the parliament the two of them arrived together at Odiham a few days before Montfort got there, presumably surrounded by a posse of armed men.[14]

Montfort's own very personal precautions are revealed in a story belonging to this time. The abbot of Dryburgh had been sent on a mission

---

[10] It is a puzzle why the young earl of Oxford was not present since he was certainly a Montfortian enthusiast.

[11] But for Humphrey de Bohun, see TNA E 368/39, m. 1 (image 6171).

[12] Morris, *Bigod Earls of Norfolk*, 92–3.

[13] Merton, *Flores*, 263.

[14] Eleanor de Montfort's household roll: Wilkinson, *HR*, 13–14.

to Edward by King Alexander and Queen Margaret. Edward was being kept in a high chamber and Montfort insisted on preceding the abbot up the stairs and then watching over the conversation, so ensuring nothing dangerous was said and no letter was passed across. Montfort then followed the abbot out of the chamber, thus again preventing any contact.[15] There is some indication that even those closest to Montfort were thinking all this was unsustainable, or at least were hedging their bets. Later, after Evesham, the property of Montfort's right-hand man, Richard of Havering, was protected, in part because of his good service to Edward when the latter had been his prisoner at Wallingford.[16]

## KING SIMON?

With his clear-sighted vision, Montfort himself knew perfectly well his regime might not last in its current form. He also knew there was another solution, one more revolutionary still, yet also, if it could be achieved, far less complex than the array of restrictions so problematically being imposed on Henry and his son. The solution, of course, was the deposition of King Henry, the disinheritance of Edward and Edmund, and the elevation of King Simon and his sons in their place. In his own mind, perhaps in discussions with his most intimate followers, Montfort must have pondered the possibilities and pitfalls of bringing this about.

That this deposition and disinheritance were talked about in 1264–5 is clear from the threats made to Henry and Edward, as we have seen.[17] At the end of the 1265 parliament Henry had licensed rebellion and was only to be 'obeyed as before' when his transgressions were put right.[18] But did anyone think after a fresh war that this would really happen? The arrangements for Edward's 'release' were franker and more revealing. If he broke the agreement, he and his heirs were to be disinherited without hope of appeal. In May 1265, after Edward's escape, this was stated even more specifically. He had forfeited 'his right to the realm and all his demesnes'.[19] The next month, Henry himself seemed threatened. If he broke the agreements made during the 1265 parliament, the payments due under a treaty with Llywelyn (of which more later) were to be made to his 'heir or successor'.[20] So they were not simply to be suspended until Henry had put matters right and was being obeyed 'as before'. Rather they were

---

[15] This story, not to my mind unbelievable, is found in a eulogy of Simon de Montfort, known as the *Opusculum de nobili Simone de Monteforti*, written between 1286 and 1291 as part of the Melrose chronicle: Melrose, 215 (fos. 72r–v); (under Melrose *Chronica de Mailros*) Broun and Harrison, *Chronicle of Melrose*, 168–9.

[16] *CR 1264–8*, 257. For Richard, see Maddicott, *Simon de Montfort*, 67–8.

[17] See above, 333, 355.

[18] *DBM*, 310–11. This followed the security clause of the 1225 Charter.

[19] *CPR 1258–66*, 432.

[20] See below, 436.

to be made to a new king who would not necessarily be Henry's immediate heir.

Constitutionally, within England, there was no bar to the deposition of
a king. Montfort must have known about attempts to remove King John.
Indeed, the plotters in 1212 (according to the Dunstable annalist) had
intended to 'elect' in his place none other than Montfort's father, thus also
demonstrating it was not essential for a new king to have any kind of
hereditary claim.[21] In 1215 the baronial rebels had indeed gone ahead and
deposed John, offering the throne this time to Louis, eldest son of the king
of France. They had thus not merely deposed the father, they had also
disinherited his sons. The Crowland chronicler, who gives the most
detailed account of the procedure, saw nothing illegitimate about it. The
barons recognized that the business needed 'the common consent of all
the kingdom', so all the great men were summoned to a meeting. Not all
agreed to John's removal, but the majority went ahead and 'elected' Louis
anyway.[22] Louis' manifesto, issued on arrival in England the following
year, said much the same thing: the barons 'by common counsel and
approval of the kingdom, judging [John] unworthy of royal authority,
elected us as king and lord'.[23]

The barons here were exploiting the long-standing elective strand in
English kingship. Louis, in his manifesto, claimed that John had been
'elected', and John, in a proclamation, had indeed ascribed his succession to
'hereditary right, divine mercy, and the unanimous consent and favour of
clergy and people'.[24] Henry had made no parallel proclamation but clearly
the acclamations at his coronation could be seen as tantamount to election
by the people. And what the people had given the people could take away.

Montfort's claim to be king could be strengthened by certain strands of
academic thought. Thomas Docking, who lectured to the Oxford
Franciscans in the mid-1260s, wrote that, 'if some man who is prudent and
well fitted for the business of rule, seeing God's people endangered by
defect of government, should aspire to the dignity of ruling solely for the
love of God and the benefit of his subjects, his aim is good and he desires
to do a good work'. Whether Docking had Montfort in mind here is
uncertain. He may have been referring more to ecclesiastical than secular
governance. Docking also believed in obedience and thought nothing
justified deposing a superior.[25] Yet another Oxford Franciscan, John of
Wales, at this very time was justifying tyrannicide, as we have seen.[26]

---

[21] Dunstable, 33.
[22] Crowland, 224–5.
[23] *F*, i, 140.
[24] *F*, i, 75.
[25] Maddicott, *Simon de Montfort*, 254–5; Lachaud, 'The contribution of Thomas Docking',
62–3, 67.
[26] See above, 399.

Those hearing both teachers might easily conflate their thought and think that Henry's and Edward's collective failures fully justified their removal and replacement by a man who would indeed rule for 'the love of God and the benefit of his subjects'. Montfort would thus be the kind of king envisaged in *The Song of Lewes*, 'the great seer, who knows what may be needful for the ruling of the kingdom', one who governs naturally in concert with the magnates for his people's benefit.[27] In Montfort's hands, the practice and principles of the Provisions of Oxford would be completely safe.

In one respect Montfort might think his position was stronger than Louis' in 1216. Then, Louis and his supporters had all been excommunicated by the legate Guala. As a result, no senior churchmen would touch them. Louis could not be crowned for there was no bishop to crown him. But now the legate and his anathemas had been kept out of England and the bishops were pillars of the regime. Might they not be prepared to officiate at a Montfortian coronation? The circumstances in which deposition and or disinheritance would take place were clear from the threats made to Henry and Edward. It would be after some new uprising against the regime. If Edward's death or escape abroad removed him from the scene so much the better. If not, under the terms of his 'release', he had clearly forfeited his right to the succession.

If the problem of a coronation was nonetheless insuperable there was a lesser solution, one which would postpone the issue. Montfort must have known about the settlement of 1153. Then, King Stephen had disinherited his son and had accepted that Henry of Anjou, the future Henry II, should be his heir. Henry on his part had accepted that Stephen could remain king until his death. Might not a frail King Henry be persuaded to do something similar, all the more so if the throne was to pass not to Montfort himself, but to Henry de Montfort, Montfort's eldest son, the king's nephew and grandson of King John. The hereditary line was thus being adjusted but not entirely set aside. Certainly, Henry de Montfort's status as the king's nephew was very much up in lights for he was routinely described as such in the royal charters and letters patent issued by the Montfortian regime.[28] As for Montfort's own role while his son waited through the twilight years of Henry III, perhaps he had given thought to that too. In April 1265 he inquired of Loretta, widow of the last Beaumont earl of Leicester (now a recluse at Hackington in Kent), what rights and liberties pertained to the stewardship of England.[29] Might he not then as steward control the government until his son's succession?

Of course, if Montfort speculated about these possibilities, he also knew they presented terrible difficulties. Would the bishops really brave

---

[27] *Song of Lewes*, lines 921–8.
[28] Henry had also stepped into Edward's shoes as lord of Chester.
[29] *CR 1264–8*, 115–6.

the pope, from February 1265 none other than Guy Foulquois himself? Would the pope, would Louis IX, would the queen and Edmund (assuming the latter had not perished in a fresh invasion) ever be reconciled to a Montfortian monarchy? For the time being, as the great parliament of 1265 closed, Montfort had no alternative but to continue with the current constitutional arrangements. But if he had emerged victorious from a new war, he would, I think, have sought in one way or another a solution leading to a Montfortian king.

## KING HENRY

If Montfort thought like this, it was thought for the future, not for the present. And here, at last, Henry had himself to thank. As king he had been incompetent and profligate. But he was also a good and pious man who had brought many years of peace to the country. So much had been acknowledged by the Tewkesbury annalist, right at the start of the civil war, in that obituary penned on the false rumour of Henry's death[30] Even amongst supporters of the regime, like the Pershore chronicler, there were doubts about his treatment. The author of *The Song of Lewes* left Henry unnamed and mounted no kind of personal attack. Henry was also, in the period of Montfortian rule, doing much to help himself. He was assiduously attending mass. He was praying over and over again for help from the Confessor.

Between January and July 1265 we can follow something of the daily services in Henry's chapel through a roll recording his offerings at mass, one of only two to survive, the other being for 1239. The most striking difference with 1239 lies in the way some of masses are now described as 'solemn masses' belonging to either the Virgin Mary or a particular saint. This meant that the mass was sung rather than said and thus lasted longer and was 'more visually and acoustically impressive'.[31] Here, the Confessor's mass was dominant. Between January and July, Henry heard twenty-one in his honour, thirteen of them while he was at Westminster between January and March. Against that, he heard eleven masses for the Virgin Mary and three for Becket. No other saint had more than one.[32] In his horrendous situation, the Confessorial mass must have been an immense comfort and encouragement. The hymn, sung during the mass, went through the miracles and wonders performed by the Confessor, including the way 'the earl' (the nefarious Godwin) had choked to death on the

---

[30] See above, 268.

[31] Wild, 'A captive king', 52–3.

[32] TNA E 101/349/30. Wild, 'A captive king', 51–4, has an analysis of the two rolls, and see Vincent, *Holy Blood*, 36 n. 16, and Shacklock, 'Henry III and the native saints', 36–9. We cannot know when these 'solemn masses' were introduced. The difference with 1239 may just be one of record-keeping.

bread the Confessor had blessed. How Henry must have hoped that could happen to Montfort. The mass also included psalm 20:

> The king rejoices in thy might, O lord:
> Well may he exult in thy victory,
> For thou hast given him his heart's desire
> And has not refused him what he asked.

> Your hand shall reach all your enemies:
> Your right hand shall reach those that hate you.
> The lord in his anger will strike them down,
> And fire shall consume them.
> It will exterminate their offspring from the earth
> And rid mankind of their posterity.
> For they have aimed wicked blows at you,
> They have plotted mischief but could not prevail.[33]

No wonder Henry wanted to hear this again and again.

There is some reason to think Montfort tried to keep Henry's devotions from the public, knowing they would enhance his reputation.[34] On the 5 January feast of the Confessor in 1239, Henry had heard two masses, one in his chapel and one in the Abbey. But in 1265 there was no second mass in the Abbey, although Henry did offer a piece of gold at the high altar. The next day, the feast of epiphany, Henry heard just one mass in his chapel, whereas in 1239 there had been two masses, the second presumably in the Abbey, where Henry also made an offering to the relics. How far in 1265 Henry was allowed to feed thousands of paupers, as customary, on the feast of the Confessor is unknown, but the ritual in which he gave his ring to the Confessor and then made an offering to receive it back seems to have been suspended.[35]

Henry's desire to 'get out' and make his piety public was finally shown at Easter, when no longer perhaps under Montfort's eagle eye.[36] On Good Friday, having 'adored' the Holy Cross in the Abbey, and left beneath it one piece of gold and twelve gold coins, Henry went on a peregrination through the churches of London, distributing 49s 6d in alms. The day

---

[33] *Missale Westmonasteriensis*, ii, cols. 738–40, 975–6. The translation is from the New English Bible.

[34] See Wild, *WA*, clxix–xx.

[35] For this ritual, see Wild, *WA*, lxx, clxix.

[36] Montfort had arrived at Odiham on 19 March and stayed there till 1 April: Wilkinson, *HR*, nos. 77–81. It is possible he then went back to London to celebrate Easter. On 6 April (Easter Monday) he authorised a writ at Westminster: *CR 1261–4*, 44. However, this is no certain proof of his presence. He also authorized a writ at Westminster on 19 March, the day Eleanor's household roll shows him arriving at Odiham: *CR 1261–4*, 34. Evidently, he sometimes conveyed his instructions to the chancery and ministers with the king by letter or oral message.

before, Maundy Thursday, he had given shoes to 150 paupers and presumably washed their feet in the great silver bowl kept in the wardrobe for that purpose. On Easter day itself he heard two masses, one in the Abbey, and left gold pieces at the high altar and the shrine of the Confessor.[37] Sir Maurice Powicke described Henry at this time as 'the miserable king'.[38] That may be right, but Henry was surely confident that his alms, his masses and his devotion to the Confessor would ultimately save him. Perhaps some of the Londoners who saw him progressing through the streets distributing alms thought the same.

Henry might also hope the art and architecture at Westminster would make the case for his kingship. In 1265 the radiating chapels, apse, transepts and great north door of the Abbey were more or less complete, standing high-shouldered above the Westminster scene. Started in 1259, work was continuing on the four new bays of the choir. Since they were finished by 1269, they must now have been reaching triforium level. During the parliament of 1265, around a hundred stone-cutters, marblers, layers, carpenters, painters, smiths, plumbers, glaziers, polishers, sawyers and labourers were busy at the Abbey.[39] Of course, in allowing the work to continue Montfort was taking ownership of the Abbey, just as the council had sought to do back in 1259.[40] Indeed, between November 1264 and the summer of 1265, the exchequer gave £436 towards the works.[41] Presumably by this time Montfort's shield had been sculpted and painted in the wall arcade of the new choir: the silver rampant lion with its forked tail against the red background. Yet no one could take away from Henry that the Abbey was his. Was it now, the main arcades finished, that he decided in the choir to go for three round windows in the triforium gallery's external walls rather than the single large windows of the earlier work? The new galleries would afford even more space for the paupers and people attending the feasts of the Confessor. Henry was offering the Confessor to the realm as its national saint, just as the Abbey was also to be its national church. How could a king doing all this be treated as he was, let alone be deposed altogether?

## THE BREACH WITH GILBERT DE CLARE

If his regime was to continue, Montfort surely needed to keep on side his one great comital ally, Gilbert de Clare. But it was here he made his most fatal blunder.

---

[37] *CLR 1260–7*, 168; TNA E 101/349/30; TNA C 47/3/44. On Maundy Thursday 1239, Henry had given charity to 300 paupers and so had a lot more feet washing to do.

[38] Powicke, *King Henry III*, ii, 492.

[39] These figures come from a roll of wages paid from 26 July until 17 October but probably reflect the situation earlier in the year: *BA*, 388–99.

[40] See above, 69–71.

[41] *BA*, 416–17; *CLR 1260–7*, 159, 170, 172.

Montfort was now in his mid-fifties, Clare in his early twenties. The aura of Montfort's character and career had attracted many young men to his side. But it was one thing for the Montfort magic to work on youths of obviously inferior status like Nicholas of Seagrave, Henry de Hastings, John fitzJohn and John de Vescy, quite another for it to have the same effect on Gilbert de Clare, in terms of power every bit Montfort's equal and expecting to be treated as such. Montfort's problem was that whereas he inspired subordinates, he antagonized equals, not an uncommon characteristic with certain types of leader. In the period immediately after Lewes, Clare had certainly got his share of the spoils. He was given custody of William de Valence's Pembroke, the lands of John de Warenne (save Lewes and Reigate castles) and the lands of Peter of Savoy including Richmond castle. These gifts, however, brought Clare into conflict with Simon de Montfort junior, who held Warenne's Sussex lands and was soon besieging Peter's castle at Pevensey.[42] There were also rumours that Clare resented the way Dover, Portchester and Corfe had been given to Montfort's sons.[43]

Another point of conflict was over the numerous prisoners taken at Lewes and their lucrative ransoms. The precise rules in play here are unclear, but Montfort seems to have asserted rights over anyone taken by those in his following, perhaps indeed overall rights as commander-in-chief. This was doubtless how he acquired the numerous prisoners he dragged with him round the country.[44] Clare felt short-changed especially when brusquely refused the custody of King Richard, although it was to him Richard had surrendered.[45] He was, nonetheless, involved in the Canterbury negotiations with the legate and then went with Montfort on the expedition against the marchers. Perhaps this was the point when things really turned sour. The marchers had been told Clare was eager for Edward's release.[46] If true, that was surely because Clare expected a slice of the Edwardian cake in return, just as did Montfort. And the slice Clare wanted was obvious. It was Bristol to which he nourished a long-standing family claim. But when the preliminary terms were agreed with Edward at Worcester, Clare got nothing. Edward's possessions, including Bristol, were to go to Montfort, not at all to Clare. Admittedly, unlike Chester and the rest, there was no suggestion that Bristol should pass to Montfort in hereditary right. It was just a guarantee while the other transfers of property took place. But Clare's anger and astonishment can still be imagined.

Clare, as we have seen, was summoned to the January parliament. At its end, in the confirmation of the June 1264 Constitution, his name still

[42] *CPR 1258–66*, 322, 326, 333. Richmond castle proved hard to get hold of.
[43] Winchester/Worcester, 453.
[44] *CPR 1258–66*, 337.
[45] Guisborough, 197; Rishanger, 32; Winchester/Worcester, 453.
[46] *CPR 1258–66*, 374.

appears with Montfort's and Bishop Bersted's as one of the three electors. But there is no sign he played a part in the parliament's business. Unlike Montfort, he attested none of the royal charters issued during its course.[47] As for Bristol, in the final terms with Edward, all that Clare secured was a note saying that the arrangements were not to prejudice any rights he had to the castle. His feelings were well portrayed by Robert of Gloucester: 'For so great a man as he was [Montfort] regarded him too little, and it seemed to him that there was in Sir Simon too great pride.'[48]

In mid-March, soon after the parliament ended, there was a further irritant. One of the royal castles to be handed over to Edward, so he could then surrender it as a hostage for his good behaviour, was Bamburgh. But Bamburgh was still held by the great royalist captain in the north Robert de Neville.[49] Somehow, probably earlier in the year, Gilbert had agreed to get Neville to surrender the castle, but he now refused to do so. The result, on 19 March, was a letter authorized by Montfort and the council, telling him in sharp terms to secure the castle's delivery. Next month, there was an even sharper follow-up, this time authorized by Montfort, Despenser, Peter de Montfort, Roger de St John and 'others of the council'.[50]

During the parliament, the tensions between Clare and Montforts' sons might well have exploded in a tournament planned at Dunstable. In the event it was banned, to Clare's fury.[51] The episode was quickly followed by the arrest of Robert de Ferrers. According to Wykes, with accusations being made that he too was conniving with the marchers, Clare feared he would be next. He left the parliament and hurried to his Welsh lordships where he was by early April.[52]

It is easy to say that Montfort should have done more to keep Clare on-side. Would the course of events have been different had his claims to Bristol been recognized? But conciliation and concession were never Montfort's style. Having done so much, was he irritated by the claims to parity of a boy who had done so little? Did he also suspect that Clare was plotting not just with the marchers but with Edward too, hence his insistence on the latter's release? It would be folly indeed to increase Clare's power when the next moment he would be seeking to overthrow the regime. In any case, Montfort believed in his star and his cause. If it came to it, he would win another war.

Whatever Montfort's feelings and motives, Clare's defection was a body blow. The young earl had large numbers of local officials well placed to

[47] *RCWL*, ii, 146–8; Ambler, 'Magna Carta', 821.

[48] *F*, i, 452; Robert of Gloucester, ii, lines 11466–7.

[49] For Robert, see Young, *Making of the Neville Family*, 82–6; and Cokayne, *Complete Peerage*, ix, 495–7.

[50] *CR 1264–8*, 33–4, 43–4.

[51] Dunstable, 238; London, 65; Rishanger, 32; *CPR 1258–66*, 406.

[52] Wykes, 160; Waverley, 358; *CR 1264–8*, 43–4.

seize the lands of his enemies, as they now started to do. He went to Wales with a considerable body of knights and was joined by John Giffard of Brimpsfield, a man alienated by another dispute over ransoms. Back at Canterbury in the autumn of 1264, Giffard had demanded the custody of Alan la Zouche, taken during the battle by one of his knights. (Zouche had later escaped but was found hiding in the priory dressed as a monk.) Montfort had said no, perhaps claiming Zouche for himself since Giffard had been fighting as part of his household. Giffard was angry. Was it for this that he had spurned Edward's blandishments and remained loyal to Montfort? Hoping for better lordship he now joined Gilbert de Clare and soon become one of his intimates.[53] Thus Montfort lost a daring and resourceful warrior – he who had brought about the fall of Gloucester in 1263 by entering the town disguised as a wool merchant. Giffard soon turned around the allegiance of at least five knights, including Miles de Hastings, who had been for two years in the company of Simon de Montfort junior and in receipt of his robes.[54]

Gilbert de Clare posed one other danger. Far from being a young hothead, like Robert de Ferrers, he was a clever politician and saw how to turn a key Montfortian slogan, 'England for the English', back on Montfort's head. He thus claimed that Montfort was bringing aliens in to garrison castles. It was 'ridiculous' for him, a foreigner, to dominate the country.[55] The charge had all the more purchase given the way Montfort sometimes berated the English, or at least the English who had deserted the Provisions, for deceit and disloyalty.[56]

## THE MOVE TO THE WELSH MARCH

Henry finally left Westminster on 16 April and journeyed sixteen miles to Ruislip, not by the Piccadilly line.[57] Then, in daily stages, he moved on to St Albans (where he heard a mass of the Virgin), Dunstable, Hanslope and

[53] Robert of Gloucester, ii, lines 753–4; Wykes, 160–1; London, 65 (where the dispute is said to be about Alan's brother, William la Zouche). Clare's defection may also have affected the behaviour of Ralph de Camoys, a major tenant. He last appears at court with fellow Montfortians on 20 March: *RCWL*, ii, 148. Although he sent knights to Kenilworth and his lands were seized by the loyalist Robert de St John (another of his overlords), it was also said he did nothing against the king. The land seized was returned to him by Gilbert de Clare: *CIM*, nos. 639, 697, 699, 715; *CIPM*, no. 443; *CPR 1266–72*, 61. For Montfort and Despenser, in April 1265, sacking Clare's man Hervey of Boreham as a justice of the bench, see *CR 1264–8*, 51–2.

[54] *CPR 1258–66*, 500; *CIM*, nos. 627, 853, 936.

[55] Rishanger, 32; Waverley, 358; Robert of Gloucester, ii, lines 11,450–5. Waverley adds that as part of a reconciliation between the two earls at the 1265 parliament the aliens left the country, but there seems no evidence for the statement.

[56] Wykes, 160; Rishanger, 18.

[57] Until the battle of Evesham, Henry's itinerary can be followed day by day in his oblation roll: TNA E 101/349/30.

Northampton, arriving there on 20 April in time to celebrate the mass
of the Confessor. On each day of travel, as customary, he distributed
4s 2d (so 50d) in alms. At Northampton, Henry celebrated the feast of
St George and heard a mass in honour of Becket and yet another in
honour of the Confessor. He left on 24 April and on the twenty-sixth was
at Winchcombe abbey where he offered a piece of gold at the feretory of
Saint Kenelm, an Anglo-Saxon boy king, allegedly murdered by his sister:
that must have given Henry food for thought![58] He also heard a requiem
mass for the soul of his long dead sister Isabella, wife of Frederick II. Next
day he arrived at Gloucester where he was soon hearing further masses of
the Confessor, the Virgin and Thomas Becket.

It was Montfort who had brought both Henry and Edward to
Gloucester. He had gone there to deal with the defection of Gilbert de
Clare and the disobedience of the marchers. By having Henry and
Edward with him, he demonstrated his power. He also kept them under
his eye and showed that Henry at least was working with the regime.
There was now a major change in Montfort's own method of work, one
which for the first time reveals him in direct command. Previously,
although manifestly the regime's head, he had left the authorization of
royal letters to the councillors. Between January and March 1265 only four
bear his name. By contrast, between the arrival at Northampton and the
end of June (when records cease), he was involved in authorizing over
twenty-five letters, many of the greatest importance. He thus placed his
authority behind the king's orders and proclamations, for the authorization notes appeared on the letters themselves as well as on the rolls.
Montfort, however, made it clear he was no lonely autocrat. He never
authorized letters alone. He only did so in company with other councillors
and often also with the king. Many letters were still left to the councillors,
of whom the most prominent were Despenser, Giles de Argentan, Roger
de St John and Peter de Montfort.[59]

In all this time, Henry remained compliant. In company with one or
more councillors he authorized around forty letters. In fifteen of them
Montfort was there as an authorizer as well. The two men had never
before been in such close, uncomfortable collaboration. Henry's power of
independent action, however, was almost nil. At Northampton, he was
able, on his own authority, to make a gift of timber to his chaplain, but
another gift to the town's Franciscans was authorized by Roger de St John
and Peter de Montfort. At Gloucester, a gift of a red samite cloth to
Edward was authorized by Henry, Simon de Montfort and Hugh

---

[58] I owe the point to Antonia Shacklock's 'Henry III and the native saints', 39. Her
doctoral thesis 'Piety and politics in the kingship of Henry III' is forthcoming.

[59] Nearly always in company with other councillors Despenser authorizes around
45 letters, Argentan and St John about 30, and Peter de Montfort around 25.

Despenser.[60] Later, when the burgesses of Bristol wondered whether orders were being issued without Henry's knowledge, they were told to send twelve of their number to the king to learn his will.[61] Henry seemed safe. Edward too complied. With his father, Montfort and Hugh Despenser he authorized a writ dealing with the affairs of the Jews still nominally in his custody.[62]

## NEGOTIATIONS WITH GILBERT DE CLARE
## AND THE MOVE TO HEREFORD

When he arrived at Gloucester, Montfort exuded his usual confidence. He had dealt with the marchers before, if not conclusively. He expected to reach some kind of agreement with Gilbert de Clare. Although he had with him a large retinue of knights, and ordered local forces to join him at Gloucester, he had commanded as yet no general muster. Negotiations were indeed opened with Clare, who lay in the woods around Gloucester. John Giffard, on the hill at Brimpsfield, lit a great fire, eerily visible during the night from the town. Clare with his usual skill complained of breaches both to the Provisions of Oxford and the Mise of Lewes, but on 12 May agreed a settlement. He and Montfort submitted their disagreements to the arbitration of Bishop Cantilupe, Hugh Despenser, John fitzJohn and William de Munchesney.[63]

Given the Montfortian make-up of this panel, it is hard to think Clare was serious. He was playing for time while he solidified his alliance with the marchers and awaited events. One key event was already known by 10 May and must have made Montfort wonder about the agreement even before it was finalized. This was the landing at Pembroke of William de Valence, John de Warenne and Hugh Bigod. The queen had almost certainly played a large part in plotting this descent. In early 1265 she had gone to Gascony where she raised money for her 'dearest son' and gathered shipping. The expedition may well have sailed from Bordeaux or La Rochelle.[64] Certainly Eleanor and her party had learnt from the year before. With the men of the Cinque Ports sweeping the channel, an attempted landing on the south coast was full of hazard. So the destination was Valence's own lordship of Pembroke, now in the custody of Gilbert de Clare. Presumably Clare disclaimed all knowledge but he was surely complicit.

---

[60] *CR 1264–8*, 49–51.

[61] *CPR 1258–66*, 429–30.

[62] *CR 1264–8*, 52, 115–16.

[63] Waverley, 361–2; Robert of Gloucester, ii, lines 11526–34; FitzThedmar, 73 (Stone, FitzThedmar, no. 833).

[64] Howell, *Eleanor of Provence*, 225–7, 229. A charter she issued on 26 July from Bordeaux in favour of the inhabitants of Monségur survives (as a register copy) in the town archives, information I owe to Claire Gaskell and Marie-Claude Jean.

On hearing news of the landing, Montfort moved with Henry and Edward to Hereford, entering the city, Wykes thought, with pomp and circumstance, confident in his strength. Major work was begun on the defences and comforts of the castle, including new glass for the king's chapel.[65] Hereford was to remain the base until 25 June. Here Montfort was strategically placed. He could, or so he hoped, block Valence's advance from the west and threaten Mortimer's castle at Wigmore only twenty-two miles to the north. If he did not launch an immediate offensive, it was partly because he hoped that, with Henry and Edward as his prisoners, the crisis would evaporate. As late as 15 May he was planning to hold a parliament in early June either at Westminster or Winchester.[66] There were still signs of normality. During May over eighty litigants, from sixteen counties, came to Gloucester or Hereford to buy writs related to common-law legal actions.[67]

## EDWARD'S ESCAPE, 28 MAY

Before he could launch any major offensive, Montfort needed to reach an agreement with Llywelyn, thus making it possible to attack the marchers in the rear. Negotiations were probably ongoing in mid-May but Llywelyn's price was high. Meanwhile, with the marchers and Gilbert de Clare circling round, Montfort could not move.[68] He was active on the diplomatic front, however, trying to ward off interventions by King Alexander and King Louis. It was perhaps to help with France that on 7 May Thomas de Cantilupe (a friend of Louis) left court, having laid down strict regulations for the keeping of the seal (by Ralph of Sandwich) during his absence.[69]

So through much of May there was stalemate. It was eventually broken by one of the most famous individual exploits of the thirteenth century. On the evening of 28 May, Edward was allowed to take the air outside the walls of Hereford. One by one he tried out and exhausted the horses of his guards, until, with only one left, he galloped away on it:

---

[65] Wykes, 162; *CLR 1260–7*, 174–5. The castle stood above the River Wye east of the cathedral. Virtually nothing survives apart for a portion of the moat. The large bailey is now Castle Green with a monument to Nelson in the centre.

[66] *DBM*, 314–17; *CR 1264–8*, 117–18.

[67] *CFR 1264–5* nos. 416–503.

[68] *CR 1264–8*, 117–18; Merton, *Flores*, 264; Waverley, 362.

[69] *CPR 1258–66*, 423–5; *CR 1264–8*, 54–5, 120–1; Carpenter, *Reign of Henry III*, 304–5. As in 1264, during the negotiations at Boulogne, so now in May 1265, Henry of Almain was released from being a hostage and sent to Louis in the cause of peace. He had evidently reached an accommodation with the regime and was trusted to make its case: *F*, i, 446, 455 (*CPR 1258–66*, 345, 425).

'Lordings,' he said, 'have now good day,
And greet well my father the king; and I will, if may,
See him well betimes, and out of prison take him.'[70]

Edward met up with Roger de Mortimer in a nearby wood and then proceeded to Wigmore, where he received a rapturous welcome from Lady Mortimer.[71] There is nothing in Henry's alms roll for 28 and 29 May to reflect these dramatic events. He made his usual offering of 5s after the mass in his chapel. But a great surge of hope and fear must have filled his breast when he heard the news.

Edward's escape had been carefully planned with Clare and Mortimer. Clare's younger brother, Thomas de Clare, hitherto trusted by Montfort, was in on the plot and escaped with Edward. Madly, as it seems, on 23 May, Roger of Clifford and Roger of Leybourne had been give safe conducts to come and see Edward.[72] This was at Edward's request and presumably he promised to secure their surrender. The meeting must have been closely monitored, but perhaps some intelligence was slipped across either to Edward or, more likely perhaps, to Thomas. The Wigmore rendezvous was followed next day by a meeting with Gilbert de Clare at Ludlow. There Edward swore to observe the ancient laws of the kingdom, abolish evil customs, remove aliens from his council and exclude them from the custody of castles and any role in the government of the kingdom.[73] Clare had given up on Montfort, but not the Montfortian programme. Whether anything was said about Bristol, we do not know.

Edward's escape jolted Montfort into action. On 30 May, in the king's name, he at last summoned all loyal tenants-in-chief (those on the side of Gilbert de Clare were specifically excluded) to come day and night to Worcester with all their power. He also ordered the king's pavilions to be sent from London. His most loyal followers were with him already: Hugh Despenser, Peter de Montfort, Giles de Argentan, Roger de St John, John fitzJohn, William de Munchesney, Henry de Hastings, Robert de Ros (of Belvoir) and Nicholas of Seagrave, as well as Henry de Montfort.[74] Meanwhile Montfort ordered King Richard, in captivity at Kenilworth, to be loaded with chains (what an indignity for the king of the Romans), and instructed Eleanor to take command at Dover. So urgent was the situation, she left Odiham late in the day and covered the first leg to Portchester by night. Travelling via Winchelsea, where she entertained the burgesses to dinner, she reached Dover on 15 June. Once there, she consolidated the

---

[70] Robert of Gloucester, ii, lines 11,564–6.
[71] Robert of Gloucester, ii, lines 11,566–71; Wykes, 163–4; Pershore, *Flores*, 2; *CR 1264–8*, 124–5.
[72] *CPR 1258–66*, 427.
[73] Wykes, 164–5; Merton, *Flores*, 264.
[74] *CR 1264–8*, 63–4, 124–5; *CFR 1264–5*, nos. 495, 498.

loyalty of the Cinque Ports by entertaining the Winchelsea burgesses again and those of Sandwich twice over. She was equally active in wider Montfortian politics. She received envoys from the king of France and messengers from Thomas de Cantilupe and the countess of Lincoln. She sent knights to join Simon junior in London and dispatched messengers to John fitzAlan, the garrison at Kenilworth, Simon junior and of course, desperate for news, her husband.[75] Just like the queen the year before, she appears very much a *virago potentissima*.

## MONTFORT IS TRAPPED BEHIND THE SEVERN

Montfort's plans for a muster at Worcester were soon in ruins. He had failed to block the advance of William de Valence, John de Warenne and Hugh Bigod and they joined up with Edward. With Edward too were the knights led by Robert Walerand and Warin of Bassingbourn who had been in the garrison at Bristol. By 7 June, Worcester was in Edward's hands, forcing Montfort to move his muster to Gloucester. But by the end of the month Gloucester had fallen too, the town on 14 June, the castle on the 29th. The latter was surrendered by one of the leading Montfortian '*jeunes*', Geoffrey de Lucy, on condition he was not disinherited or punished in life or limb, an ominous crack in the regime.[76] At the same time, Edward and Clare broke down the bridges over the Severn, seized boats and hollowed out fords. Montfort was effectively trapped behind the river. No reinforcements could reach him, nor could money and victuals, of which he was running short. This made co-operation with Llywelyn all the more vital while at the same time raising its price. While men flocked to join Edward, Montfort's support, with the writing on the wall, began to slip. The Cinque Ports, London and the bases in the midlands remained firm, but at least nine sheriffs seem to have deserted.[77] On 7 June 1265, Montfort urged Roger Bigod to repress risings in Norfolk–Suffolk inspired by the news of Edward's escape.[78] There is no evidence that Bigod tried to do so.

Edward was also mustering support in Scotland and Ireland. His brother-in-law King Alexander, according to a Scottish chronicle, 'raised three men from every hide of land', which sounds as though a large army was being gathered to go south.[79] In Ireland, the quarrel between Walter

---

[75] For Eleanor at Dover, see Wilkinson, *HR*, cvi–xviii.

[76] *CR 1264–8*, 246–7. The same terms were granted to all the garrison.

[77] For desertions, see Cassidy, 'Simon de Montfort's sheriffs', 19–20; Maddicott, *Simon de Montfort*, 336–7; Knowles, 'The disinherited', pt. 1, 9–16, 81; Quick, 'Government and society in Kent', 247–52; Ridgeway, 'Dorset in the period of baronial reform and rebellion', 35. I have added Eustace of Watford (Northamptonshire) and Fulk Payforer (Kent) to the sheriffs as their lands seem not to have been confiscated.

[78] *CR 1264–8*, 125.

[79] Reid, *Alexander III*, 199–200.

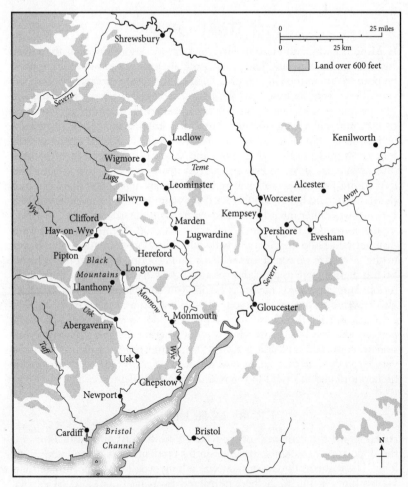

0     25 miles
0    25 km

Land over 600 feet

Shrewsbury

Ludlow

Kenilworth

Wigmore

*Teme*

Alcester

Leominster

*Lugg*

Worcester

*Avon*

Dilwyn

Kempsey

Clifford

Marden

Pershore

Evesham

Hay-on-Wye

Lugwardine

Pipton

Hereford

*Wye*

*Black
Mountains*

Longtown

Llanthony

*Severn*

*Monnow*

Monmouth

Gloucester

*Usk*

Abergavenny

*Wye*

Usk

*Taff*

Chepstow

Newport

Cardiff

*Bristol
Channel*

Bristol

N

4. The Campaigns between May and August 1265

de Burgh and the Geraldines had been settled, thus enabling a large Irish contingent to cross to England.[80] In fact, it arrived in time only to applaud Edward's victory.[81] The Scottish forces, hearing the news, never set out at all. But these events reflected how the walls were closing in on the Montfortian regime.

## MONTFORT'S APPEALS

If Montfort was stationary in Hereford, he was more eloquent than ever. Indeed, during May and June, to consolidate loyalty and mobilize support, he poured out, in the king's name, some of the most powerful letters of his rule. They were addressed to the regime's officials and through them to 'the people' whose 'hearts' were being moved and 'devotion' undermined by false and malevolent rumours. Montfort himself was adept in using facts or fake facts. The landing in Pembroke, he said, had been made by only four ships and 120 men; Montfort and Clare were agreed in everything (this as late as 20 May); Edward had escaped with only two knights and four squires; the rebels so far were few but quick action was needed to put them down. And here Montfort tried yet again to ring the alien alarm bell. Edward was either intending to flee overseas or would send others to bring in aliens through Pembroke. Their arrival would threaten everyone with disinheritance and the kingdom with ruin. Montfort also retained his belief in the attractive power of the reforms he had done so much to promote. So the sheriffs were to proclaim yet again the Charters and 'certain constitutions lately provided', meaning the provisions of Worcester. And Montfort also resorted to threats. Everyone should rise up and resist those helping Edward and Clare. Those who refused to do so would suffer in their persons and goods 'as those who care not whether the king's realm is given over to confusion and destruction'.[82] In a letter sent to Ireland, he made very clear the fate that might now await Edward. By his own agreement, he had forfeited 'his right to the realm and all his demesnes'.[83]

## HENRY IN HEREFORD

At Hereford the cathedral offered Henry both spiritual consolation and the opportunity to demonstrate again his credentials as a good and pious king. The cathedral's patron saint was a king even more unfortunate than Henry himself, the Aethelbert murdered by King Offa or, as St Albans abbey preferred to believe, by Offa's nefarious queen. Aethelbert's body

---

[80] Waverley, 365; Frame, 'Ireland and the Barons' Wars', 161, 163.

[81] However, Maurice fitzGerald took part in an (unsuccessful) action against Llywelyn.

[82] *CPR 1258–66*, 423–4, 429–30; *CR 1264–8*, 119–20, 124–5; *F*, i, 455 (*CPR 1258–66*, 426).

[83] *CPR 1258–66*, 432. For the unavailing efforts of the Montfortian government to get a grip on events in Ireland, see Frame, 'Ireland and the Barons' Wars', 161–2.

had been buried at Hereford, but his head was preserved at Westminster Abbey, so Henry already knew his story. Now on six occasions between 11 and 26 May he went into the cathedral to make offerings at Aethelbert's relics.[84] One of the occasions was the feast day of the saint, which fell on 20 May. Another was on the feast of Pentecost, when Henry also provided 100 paupers with new tunics. It looks as though he was still able to feed 100 paupers a day. But he did not feel well. On the day before Pentecost the king's wardrobe bought a medicine described as a 'stomach comforter' from an apothecary in Hereford.[85]

Henry had, however, something to celebrate. He had last been in Hereford nine years before on his tour of the Welsh marches in 1256.[86] He must then have seen the beginnings of the new north transept of the cathedral being constructed by Bishop Aigueblanche. The work was now complete. On 10 May, so two days after his arrival, Henry heard a 'solemn mass' for the transept's consecration and made an offering at the high altar.[87] How providential to have arrived in time to celebrate, perhaps to instigate, this great event in the cathedral's life. Henry would have been delighted by the transept's design for it paid graceful tribute to the Abbey, tribute in its round clerestory windows and the diapered spandrels of the triforium's elegant arcade. But, intriguingly, the transept was also far more than just an imitation. The round windows at the Abbey had been in the external walls of the triforium, not in the clerestory,[88] and while, at the Abbey, the dominant window form was that of two lancets supporting a sexafoil rose, at Hereford it was three narrow lancets supporting three quatrefoils. Along the west side of the transept, where there was no aisle, these windows soared to the height of the church, while on the transept end the design was doubled so the whole space, in spectacular fashion, was filled by six lancets with their quatrefoils, and then above a sexafoil rose.[89]

If Henry hoped that the consecration would make the regime think the better of Bishop Peter, he was disappointed. At the start of June, he had to issue a letter threatening the confiscation of Peter's temporalities if he did not return from abroad to take up his spiritual duties. As it was, the wardrobe had already received £133 as a 'loan' from the keeper of the bishopric, and another loan followed from the precentor of Hereford, the bishop's kinsman Aimery de Aigueblanche.[90]

---

[84] TNA E 101/349/30. The offerings were all of 5s, the usual amount found in the oblation roll. For Henry and Aethelbert, see Shacklock, 'Henry III and the native saints', 39.

[85] TNA E 101/350/1.

[86] Volume 1, 640.

[87] TNA E 101/349/30. The mass is described as *de dedicatione magne ecclesie*, but there seems little doubt the new north transept was meant.

[88] At Hereford they are sexafoils, at the Abbey octafoils.

[89] The three grouped lancets supporting three quadrefoils also appear in the internal triforium arcade, here the lancets being cusped.

[90] *CPR 1258–66*, 429; TNA E 101/350/3.

## THE AGREEMENT WITH LLYWELYN

By 19 June, Montfort and Llywelyn had reached an agreement.[91] It gave
the latter everything he wanted and completely destroyed the king's
hegemony in Wales. Llywelyn and the heirs of his body were thus to retain
all they currently held, so Henry and Edward were to lose Builth and,
more importantly, those cherished conquests of the 1240s, the Four
Cantrefs between the Conwy and the Dee. Llywelyn was also to be recognized as prince of Wales and enjoy 'dominion' over all the native
'magnates' of Wales. So the homages of the other Welsh rulers were now
due to him not the king, a complete reversal of everything Henry had
previously stood for. Llywelyn was also to have the two castles built during
the campaigns of 1223 and 1231: Montgomery (once it could be wrested
from the king's 'enemies'!) and Painscastle, which Llywelyn immediately
took and destroyed.

In return for all this, Montfort got what he wanted. Llywelyn now swore
that he would support 'with all his power' 'the magnates of the kingdom
of England' against all who sought to overthrow the 'Ordinance for
Edward's delivery'. In other words, he would join with all his might in the
struggle against Edward, Clare and the marchers. The alliance between
the two men was sealed by a matrimonial pact. It was almost certainly at
this point that Llywelyn agreed to marry Eleanor, Montfort's seven-year-
old daughter. This probably explains why the king's concessions were
made to Llywelyn and the heirs of his body, his heirs, that is, or so it was
hoped, by Eleanor de Montfort.[92]

Henry, on his part, must have been appalled by this settlement, and it
had one other chilling feature. Under the terms, Llywelyn was to pay the
king 30,000 marks at the rate of 3,000 marks a year starting at Michaelmas
1265.[93] But this was conditional, as we have seen, on Henry continuing to
abide by the Ordinance. If he did not, then payment was to be made to
the 'heir or successor' who was willing to accept it.

Montfort and Roger de St John had been empowered to negotiate with
Llywelyn on 12 June, so it took about a week for an agreement to be
reached.[94] During this time the two leaders must surely have met, perhaps
at some midway point between Hereford and Pipton (twenty-seven miles
away further up the Wye), where Llywelyn was encamped. It was a meeting
of the doomed. Both men were to die violently in combat, Montfort in a
few weeks, Llywelyn in 1282. Their deaths destroyed their visions for the

---

[91] The texts of the agreements are found in *AWR*, nos. 361–2, and *F*, i, 457 (*CPR 1258–
66*, 433–4). For full discussion, see Smith, *Llywelyn ap Gruffudd*, 165–70; Maddicott, *Simon de
Montfort*, 325, 337–8.

[92] A point made by Smith, *Llywelyn ap Gruffudd*, 167–8.

[93] No immediate cash-down payment was thus stipulated, but it is possible Montfort
himself received cash as part of the marriage agreement.

[94] *CPR 1258–66*, 432.

future governance of England and Wales. There was to be no Montfortian constitution, let alone King Simon. There was to be no principality of Wales held by Llywelyn and the heirs of his body. Eleanor died giving birth to her only child just before the final crash in 1282. The child, Gwenllian, lived out her long life in monastic seclusion. Edward was the victor over both men. Yet none of this was certain during the long June days of 1265 when the agreement was being negotiated. Of course, Llywelyn knew he was taking a risk. He might be next in the firing line if Edward won a comprehensive victory. Yet it was a risk worth taking. Only Montfort was prepared to give him the principality he craved. Only a Montfortian victory, the victory of his prospective father-in-law, would ensure its continuance. And was victory so unlikely? Montfort had won against the odds at Lewes. He might do so again. Llywelyn had every interest in bringing that about.

## THE MARCH TO THE SEVERN ESTUARY

Montfort's agreement with Llywelyn gave him power to act. He gained the immediate co-operation of the prince and a large contingent of Welsh foot-soldiers (around 5,000 according to the Pershore annalist were with him at Evesham).[95] The key to his strategy was for his son Simon junior to muster an army east of the Severn. They would then meet up and bring Edward and Clare to battle. On 22 June, when the final documents relating to the treaty were exchanged, Edward and Clare were still laying siege to Gloucester castle.[96] A letter written at the time suggested Montfort would advance on them from the Welsh side of the town while Simon junior advanced from the English side.[97] But events were moving too fast. In early June, young Simon had been with his mother at Odiham where they learnt together of Edward's escape. He had then moved with her to Portchester and thence to Dover. He left the castle on 17 June, already with a hundred horses in his train, his destination London where he could recruit from the citizenry.[98] Montfort must have calculated that his son could not possibly reach Gloucester, or reach it with sufficient force, in time to effect the pincer movement anticipated by the letter writer. So even before the fall of Gloucester castle on 29 June, Montfort decided on a different strategy. He would march southwards to the Severn estuary and ferry his army across to Bristol, still firmly in his hands. He could then

---

[95] Robert of Gloucester, ii, lines 11,618–21; Pershore, *Flores*, 5.

[96] The course of events from now on has chiefly to be followed in the chronicle sources. For full references, see Cox, *The Battle of Evesham: A New Account*, and Carpenter, *Battles of Lewes & Evesham*, 37–51.

[97] *RL*, ii, 288.

[98] Wilkinson, *Eleanor de Montfort*, 116; Wilkinson, *HR*, nos. 297–9; Wykes, 169; FitzThedmar, 74 (Stone, FitzThedmar, nos. 837–8).

unite with young Simon and fight the decisive battle. For the next month Henry was dragged around south-east Wales as Montfort tried and failed to put this strategy into effect. The king had seen the mountains and river valleys of the area once before – in 1233 during Peter des Roches's war against Richard Marshal. That had been bad enough. This was far worse.

On Thursday 25 June, Montfort with the prisoner king left Hereford and took the winding and undulating road due south.[99] By the evening they were nineteen miles further on above Monmouth, and could look down on the town nestling in its valley at the confluence of the rivers Wye and Monnow. The unpleasantness of Henry's situation is revealed in his oblation roll. Before leaving he was able to hear a special mass of the Confessor in his chapel, but his offering, instead of the customary 5s, was only 15d, a reflection of the wardrobe's lack of money. On the journey itself, instead of the customary 4s 2d distributed daily in alms when on the move, Henry distributed nothing at all. In this case, more than lack of money was to blame. Henry was on no ordinary perambulation. He was in the middle of a military campaign. Montfort's army was advancing into hostile territory, for Monmouth and Usk were both in Clare's hands. The former was defended by John Giffard and it was not till 1 July, after its capture, that Henry was able to make his offerings at the relics in 'the great church'.[100] This is the last entry on Henry's oblation roll. Thereafter it was reduced to a bare record of his itinerary. Entries on the chancery rolls cease around the same time.

Montfort's situation had worsened with the fall of Gloucester castle on 29 June, for then Edward and Clare had advanced westwards across the Severn. This explains why, instead of moving from Monmouth due south down the Wye to reach the Bristol channel at Chepstow, Montfort followed the course of the Usk and reached the channel at Newport instead, a longer journey by ten miles. Clearing the way by taking Usk castle, probably on 2 July, he entered Newport on the fourth. On the same day Henry himself made the twenty-nine-mile journey from Monmouth.[101] In all this, Llywelyn's help had been vital. The Pershore chronicler describes how he devastated the area round Montfort's route with fire and sword. Montfort himself extracted £15 from the men of Newport to save their town from being burnt.[102]

At Newport, Henry could pray at the shrine of Saint Gwynllyw, the legendary Welsh king, founder of the town, who had abandoned a life of

[99] This is now the A466 but it remains a single carriageway.

[100] TNA E 101/349/30. The 'great church' was presumably the priory, later the parish church. Little of its medieval structure survives.

[101] The oblation roll shows Henry still in Monmouth on 2 and 3 July and at Newport the following day. However, 'Oske' is written in the margin against the entry for 2 July. The roll records Henry's whereabouts, not necessarily that of Montfort and the army.

[102] Pershore, *Flores*, 3, and see also Evesham, 341; Waverley, 363; TNA E 101/350/3; Wild, *WA*, 123–4.

rapine to become a hermit. The hill with the saint's church and adjoining castle had panoramic views over the mouth of the Usk, the Bristol channel and the Somerset hills beyond.[103] But the whole basis of the march south had collapsed, for Edward and Clare had destroyed the shipping needed to ferry Montfort's army across to Bristol. Indeed, they now threatened to cross the bridge over the Usk at Newport and bring Montfort to battle. This was the last thing Montfort wanted. He would fight, certainly, but only when he had joined up with his son. So he burnt the bridge and fled during the night of 8 July. His immediate aim was to return to Hereford, but the way via Usk was now closed for Clare's forces had retaken the castle. Instead, with the great mass of the Glamorgan mountains looming to his left, Montfort marched seventeen miles northwards to Abergavenny. Henry must have remembered its situation, surrounded by great hills, from 1233. Then he had ridden on to Hereford but now Montfort found that Hereford itself was threatened. So, in another retreat, Montfort went not to Hereford but to Hay. Leaving Abergavenny on 11 July, Henry was there by the evening of the same day. With the Black Mountains in between, which of three possible routes the army took is unknown. If it went through the vale of Ewyas, 'about an arrow shot broad, encircled on all sides by lofty mountains' as Gerald of Wales put it, it could have received spiritual and alimentary succour at Llanthony priory, but it then faced a steep climb up to Hay bluff.[104]

Henry remained at Hay for a week and then, on 19 July, at last got back to Hereford, doubtless making what oblations he could at the shrine of Saint Aethelbert. He was to remain in the town until 1 August. At least the wardrobe reaped some benefit from all the surrounding violence, receiving £200 from the prior of Leominster to prevent his town and church being burnt.[105] Just one document from these final days survives, the last known produced by the regime. Now in the Herefordshire Record Office, having always been in the city archives, it is a charter issued by Henry on 24 July in favour of a Hereford citizen, Thomas Thebaud. To help with the defence of the town, he had pulled down his houses outside one of the gates. In compensation he was now granted the land once of Mansel 'a Jew of Hereford'. The charter was witnessed by Simon de Montfort, Hugh Despenser, Peter de Montfort, Giles de Argentan, Roger de St John, the steward Walter of Crepping and the marshals Stephen Soudan and

---

[103] The Anglicized form of Gwynllyw is Woolos. The church is now Newport or Woolos cathedral. It has a fine twelfth-century nave entered through a highly carved doorway. I am grateful to the dean of Newport, Ian Black, for showing me the church and the view from the adjoining deanery. Nothing now survives of the castle. The ruins down by the Usk are those of a second castle built in the early fourteenth century.

[104] As now at the Priory Hotel. When Hugh Trevor-Roper arrived at Llanthony in 1945 after a strenuous walk, he found to his disappointment only half a pint of beer left at the inn: Trevor-Roper, *The Wartime Journals*, 251.

[105] TNA E 101/350/3; Wild, *WA*, 123–4. See also Pershore, *Flores*, 3–4.

Bartholomew Bigod. Apart from Bigod, all these men were Henry's enemies. Within little more than a week most of them were dead. The charter is neatly written and preserves fragments of Henry's seal in green wax. It gives no indication of the fraught situation. But perhaps the clerk sought to make a point. He decorated the 'H' of Henry's name and drew across the top what looks quite like a crown![106]

## EDWARD'S TRIUMPH AT KENILWORTH; MONTFORT CROSSES THE SEVERN, 2 AUGUST 1265

So far the campaign had been a humiliation for Montfort: trapped behind the Severn, confined for weeks at Hereford, unable to relieve Gloucester, and beaten back from Newport. All along he had danced to Edward's tune. Now, at last, the tune was to change, if briefly. The reason was the army raised by Simon junior at last coming into play. To join up with his son had been the key to Montfort's strategy. Only then, with all his strength gathered in, would he bring Edward to battle. Yet co-ordinating the movements of the two armies, hundreds of miles apart, separated by the Severn and Edward's and Clare's ranging forces must have been fiend-ishly difficult. Day to day, neither Montfort nor his son can have known each other's location. They must have been equally ignorant about the location of the opposing forces. In the 1640s civil war, it is worth remem-bering, armies were sometimes marching less than twenty miles apart without knowing it.

Nonetheless, co-ordination was something Montfort ultimately achieved, a measure of his ability as a general even in extremis. Simon junior, as we have seen, had left his mother at Dover on 18 June (while Montfort was at Hereford) and gone to London.[107] Having mustered a large army, he moved first to Winchester, on 16 July sacking the town after the citizens resisted its entry and killing all the Jews.[108] Historians have been puzzled by this move, since Winchester is not on the direct route from London to Bristol, where Montfort, reaching Newport on 4 July, intended to land having made the Severn crossing.[109] But Winchester (by old roads) is only some eighty miles from Bristol and, in its great castle, Simon junior could be safe while he awaited events.[110] At Winchester,

---

[106] Herefordshire Record Office BG/11/15/6. I am grateful to Nicholas Vincent for the reference to this charter, part of his census of surviving Henry III originals. In 1271, Thebaud took the precaution of getting a new charter: Herefordshire Record Office BG/11/1/8. The 1265 charter is illustrated in plate 9.

[107] For Young Simon going to London, see Wykes, 169–70; FitzThedmar, 74 (Stone, FitzThedmar, no. 838); Wilkinson, *HR*, nos. 291–8, 340, 354.

[108] Wykes, 169–70; Robert of Gloucester, ii, lines 11629–35.

[109] As Maddicott, *Simon de Montfort*, 339, points out.

[110] For rumours that Edward was indeed approaching Winchester, see FitzThedmar, 74 (Stone, FitzThedmar, no. 837). In mid-May, Montfort had envisaged holding a parliament

however, Simon evidently heard of the Newport disaster and received fresh orders. He was to go north and establish himself at Kenilworth. From that great Montfortian stronghold he could threaten Edward's hold on the Severn (Worcester being thirty-five miles away) and facilitate in some fashion the union of the two armies. Simon junior fulfilled his brief. Having marched north to Oxford (where he could find no Jews to kill) and then made a diversion via Northampton, perhaps from fear of interception, he arrived at Kenilworth after sunset on the last day of July.[111]

The advance of Simon junior towards Kenilworth set Edward an acute problem, as it was meant to do. His aim, of course, had been to defeat the two Montfortian armies individually before they could join up. But Montfort had escaped from Newport and Simon junior was about to threaten the Edwardian hold of the Severn. In the end, Edward decided to withdraw from west of the river, and by the end of the month he was established at Worcester. The weakening of his presence had already permitted Montfort's return to Hereford on 19 July. Better was to come, or so it seemed.

During the mid-afternoon of Saturday 1 August, so the day after Simon junior's arrival at Kenilworth, Edward and Gilbert de Clare left Worcester. Montfort, some twenty-seven miles away at Hereford, probably learnt of the move early next day. Although Edward and Clare had made a feint towards Shrewsbury, Montfort must have guessed their destination was Kenilworth, as it indeed it was. Fine. Let them spend time there in a fruitless siege. Meanwhile Montfort had recovered his freedom of action. He moved at once. During the course of Sunday 2 August, he left Hereford with Henry in his train and, as night fell, was able to ford the Severn at Kempsey, a manor of the bishop of Worcester some four miles south of Worcester. By the next day the whole of his army was established there.

But Edward had not gone to Kenilworth to mount some fruitless siege. He was acting on priceless intelligence. His spies (one the woman Margoth, disguised as a man) had told him that much of Simon junior's army was staying in the priory, in the vill and in tents around the castle.[112] It was thus vulnerable to a surprise attack. Given the distance to be covered before daybreak, Edward's cavalry led the way and was thus confronting a much larger force. If anything went wrong, the results would be disastrous. Very aware of the risks (for Edward was no hothead), at one point he decided to turn back, only to be shamed by Roger of Clifford – 'forward

---

at Winchester (*CR 1264–8*, 52–3; *DBM*, 316–37), but the circumstances were very different a month later after Edward's escape.

[111] Robert of Gloucester, ii, lines 11,638–41. It is possible that Clare was meant to intercept young Simon. At any rate the Pershore chronicler speaks of him at this time making a 'tedious stay' in England: Pershore, *Flores*, 3.

[112] Guisborough, 198–200; Melrose, 198–9 (fo. 66v).

with the banners' – into continuing.[113] In the event all went as planned. At dawn on 2 August the Edwardians fell upon the sleeping soldiery and took Robert de Vere, Adam de Newmarch, William de Munchesney, Baldwin Wake, Gilbert de Gant and Richard de Grey prisoner. Others fled half naked including Simon junior, who escaped by boat across the lake to the castle. After dealing this shattering blow, Edward returned at once to Worcester. On Monday 3 August with the Montfortians still at Kempsey, the two armies were but four miles apart.

## MONTFORT'S MARCH TO EVESHAM

Montfort must have learnt of the Kenilworth disaster during the course of 3 August, but it did not change his strategy.[114] The disaster was far from total, for young Simon, in the words of Robert of Gloucester, 'had not lost all his power . . . but kept a great host'.[115] Montfort, therefore, still aimed to meet up with him. He probably remembered how the Lewes campaign had begun with the capture of his men at Northampton yet had ended in stupendous victory. As evening drew in on 3 August, Montfort's army thus slipped out of Kempsey. The immediate destination was Evesham, some sixteen miles to the south-east. Having given the Edwardian army a wide berth, Montfort could then march north towards Kenilworth some thirty miles away. Simon junior was told of the plans and ordered to rendezvous with his father on the Evesham–Kenilworth road.

I used to think that Montfort's route to Evesham took him south of the river Avon via Pershore. But what we now know to be the Pershore chronicle makes no mention of him passing through. It is more likely that he marched north of the Avon along what is now the A44.[116] If so, when he got within a couple of miles of Evesham, he had a crucial decision to make. Here the road forks and he could either march up onto the hill above Evesham and join the Kenilworth road or head down into Evesham itself. Montfort's decision was understandable. His army was exhausted having marched through the night. He thought he had given Edward the slip. So he went down into Evesham and with a tired and frightened king entered the great Benedictine abbey which dominated the town. According to the Evesham chronicle it was still before the first hour of the day at sunrise, so still before 5 a.m.[117]

[113] *PROME*, 675–6; Prestwich, *Edward I*, 50, 353–4. The gist of this story strikes me as quite believable.

[114] Evesham, 341, which I prefer to Guisborough, 200, and St Benet at Hulme, 207, which say he did not know.

[115] Robert of Gloucester, ii, lines 11,665–7.

[116] Pershore, *Flores*, 4–5. Pershore also says Edward followed Montfort and we know he came along the road north of the Avon. The southern route would also have involved crossing two bridges over the Avon, one at Pershore and one at Evesham itself.

[117] Evesham, 342 n. 30; Wykes, 172.

Arrived in the abbey, the first thing was for them to hear mass, then food. Wykes states that 'the king and the earl heard mass early in the morning and ate a little'. The Waverley abbey annalist, by contrast, has Henry eating and Montfort refusing food. In Robert of Gloucester's account, Henry refuses to continue until he has eaten.[118] Here and elsewhere one can only narrate the different accounts of this traumatic day. If Henry and Montfort heard mass together, then this was probably the last time, outside the battle, they were in each other's company. Certainly, Henry can have played no part in the tense discussions about what to do next. At least in the mass, he and Montfort could share a common devotion. The Montfortians remained undisturbed in Evesham between the time of their arrival and around the third hour of the day at 8.30 a.m. Then catastrophic news arrived. Edward was upon them.[119]

## EDWARD'S ARRIVAL

Montfort had been out-generalled. During the night of 3–4 August he had lost touch with Edward while Edward had kept touch with him. For the terrible truth was that Edward had followed him through the night and by the third hour was approaching Evesham along the road north of the Avon, the same road Montfort had probably used a few hours before. When a couple of miles distant, Edward could climb the small hill at Craycombe and confirm with his own eyes that the Montfortians had yet to move from the town. There was time, therefore, for the Edwardian army to pause and enter the great meadow of Mosham between the road and the Avon, something revealed by a newly discovered account of the battle, probably written by a monk of Evesham abbey soon after the event.[120]

In Mosham meadow, Edward and Clare knighted several men and then appointed twelve sergeants whose only task in the battle was to break through to Montfort and kill him.[121] Of that more later. Edward and Clare also decided the line of battle. Along with many historians, I once argued that this involved splitting the army into three divisions which were

---

[118] Wykes, 172; Waverley, 364; Robert of Gloucester, ii, lines 11,665–7.

[119] For these times, see Evesham, 342 n. 30.

[120] The account was discovered by Olivier de Laborderie. See Laborderie, Maddicott and Carpenter, 'The last hours of Simon de Montfort', where there is a full discussion. The text itself, both in original French and an English translation (by John Maddicott), is between pp. 406 and 412. I imagined the account, written on the back of a fourteenth-century genealogical roll of kings of England, had been found in some French archive. In fact, it was at the College of Arms less than a mile from King's College!

[121] Laborderie, Maddicott and Carpenter, 'The last hours of Simon de Montfort', 408, 411. I well remember exploring Mosham with John Maddicott where a hedged ditch mentioned on an Anglo-Saxon survey still survives.

to approach Evesham from different directions and close all possible routes out of the town. In particular, one division was sent to block the bridge over the Avon just to the south of the Abbey. This view had some warrant in the contemporary sources but also posited night manoeuvres of near impossible complexity, as a veteran of Dunkirk pointed out to me after one of my talks on the subject![122] It was also contradicted by the Evesham chronicle itself which seemed to indicate that all three divisions were stationed together on the hill above Evesham.[123] The new account of the battle both confirms the stationing of the divisions on the hill and also, as will be seen, shows the bridge out of Evesham was not blocked.[124]

From Mosham, therefore, the Edwardian army marched up onto the hill above Evesham, Green Hill as it is now called, with Clare's division probably on the left running down to the Avon, Edward's division in the centre astride the main road, and Roger de Mortimer's on the right. The way out of Evesham towards Kenilworth was thus decisively blocked. Montfort could no longer join up with his son.

All kinds of stories were told later about how Montfort learnt the fateful news of Edward's arrival. According to the Osney chronicler, he was in a chapel hearing a mass conducted by the bishop of Worcester. According to Wykes, he and the king were about to mount their horses and ride out of Evesham towards Kenilworth. In the account preserved in the chronicle of Walter of Guisborough, Nicholas, Montfort's barber, 'a man skilled in the recognition of heraldry', saw the enemy from afar but thought he recognized Montfortian banners. He had in fact seen the banners that Edward had captured at Kenilworth and was now carrying as a disguise. Montfort imagined that his son was at hand but sent Nicholas up the bell tower of the abbey to make sure. From there the barber recognized the divisions of Edward, Clare and Mortimer. 'We are all dead, for it is not your son as you believed,' he shouted. The Evesham sources themselves give a graphic picture of the clamour in the abbey and the town with men rushing to arms when the news arrived.[125]

Something of the anguished debates in the abbey are captured in the new Evesham account. They show Montfort at his most dominant, heroic and inspiring.[126] The debates were posited on one overwhelming fact. The

---

[122] For the argument, see Carpenter, *Battles of Lewes & Evesham*, 52–9, 69–70.

[123] Cox, 'The battle of Evesham in the Evesham chronicle', 342, 345, and his *Battle of Evesham*, 10–11.

[124] Laborderie, Maddicott and Carpenter, 'The last hours of Simon de Montfort', 398–402. The views of David Cox (see previous note) were thus proved completely correct and those of David Carpenter completely wrong!

[125] Osney, 168; Wykes, 172; Guisborough, 200; Laborderie, Maddicott and Carpenter, 'The last hours of Simon de Montfort', 390.

[126] Laborderie, Maddicott and Carpenter, 'The last hours of Simon de Montfort', 393–4. One needs, however, to remember that the account was probably produced for those coming to Evesham to venerate Montfort as a saint.

Montfortians were heavily outnumbered, far more so probably than they were at Lewes. Given that fact, one course urged on Montfort, the more especially given the exhausted state of his men and horses, was to hold out in the abbey until help arrived. Montfort would have none of that. 'No, fair friend, no. One ought to seek knights on the battlefield and chaplains in churches.' So the decision was made to go out and fight. In an illustrated Apocalypse of this period, Saint Mercurius is raised from the dead to fight against Julian Apostate. The Virgin herself, in a dazzling golden robe, hands him his hauberk while angels swoop down to deliver his shield, sword, helmet and banner.[127] The Montfortians had to be armed by their squires, but they too had spiritual succour for Bishop Cantilupe was at Evesham. To him Montfort confessed his sins and received communion 'with great devotion'.[128] Doubtless others too received the same consolations. The Montfortians, as at Lewes, donned white crosses on their breasts and backs both as distinguishing marks and as testimony to the holy nature of their cause.[129]

If Henry himself hoped somehow to be left behind in the abbey, he was disappointed. He was going too. According to the narrative in Walter of Guisborough's chronicle, he was kitted out in a suit of Montfort's own armour. He was also equipped, from his own wardrobe, with two silken belts worked with silver, weighing over a pound and a half. One may doubt whether a sword was hanging from them.[130]

When all was ready, Montfort rose and took leave of the bishop of Worcester, with whom he had been sitting in council, spiritual presumably as much as political. Cantilupe then left for his manor of Blockley, 'weeping hot tears'.

## THE BATTLE OF EVESHAM, 4 AUGUST 1265

As the army went out of the abbey, Guy de Balliol shattered to pieces the lance bearing Montfort's standard against the top of the gate. At the same time the sun disappeared and the day became dark, the wind howled and large drops of rain began to fall, only for the storm to pass as quickly as it had come, leaving the sky clear and the air mild. During the day, summer storms with thunder and lightning were experienced in many parts of the country. Years later, Robert of Gloucester still remembered the darkness which swept over his town. At Bury St Edmunds the darkness was so profound the monks could not see the food before them for dinner, while

---

[127] Slater, *Art and Political Thought*, 138 and plate VI. A splendid war horse is also depicted.
[128] Evesham, 341.
[129] Pershore, *Flores*, 6.
[130] Guisborough, 201; Wild, *WA*, 127. For the Guisborough narrative, see above, 304 n.129.

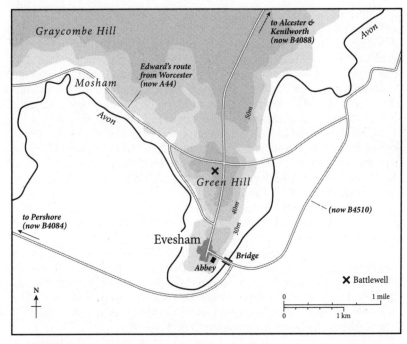

5. The Battle of Evesham, 1265

elsewhere monks in the choir could not read their service books.[131] The parallel with the darkness covering the land at time of the Crucifixion was of course obvious. If these were daunting omens, more invigorating was the great war whoop let out by the Welsh foot-soldiers, as they formed up in battle order under the command of Humphrey de Bohun. But here something went wrong and Montfort reprimanded Bohun for placing the foot-soldiers in the rear: 'Sir Humphrey, Sir Humphrey, that's no way to conduct a battle. I know well how this will turn out.' When the army leaving Evesham reached the town's washing place, Montfort addressed his men. He urged those with young families and also Hugh Despenser (the kingdom would need his wisdom) to flee across the bridge and avoid 'the great peril that is to come'.[132] To this Despenser replied, echoing the famous passage in Matthew (10:22, 23): 'My lord, my lord, let it be. Today we shall all drink of one cup, just as we have in the past.'[133]

[131] Robert of Gloucester, ii, lines 11,746–9; Bury St Edmunds, 31; Rishanger, 47.
[132] This is the evidence the bridge was not blocked.
[133] These details all come from Laborderie, Maddicott and Carpenter, 'The last hours of Simon de Montfort', 394, 408, 410 and 391–2 for Despenser's reply which is found in many sources. I can remember the surprise when I first read about the bridge in the new

All of this suggests that Montfort went out willingly to meet his death, having refused either to fly or take shelter in the abbey. The Osney abbey chronicler has him saying 'It is not for the knight of Christ to fly but rather to die for truth by the sword of the enemy.'[134] Another of his widely reported remarks, supposedly made when he saw the opposing forces, was 'Our bodies are theirs, our souls are God's.'[135] Perhaps, on this last morning, when he saw the forces ranged against him above Evesham, he felt he would now, like his father, die in a righteous cause.[136]

Yet one cannot be sure that we have here the totality of Montfort's mood and mind. All the accounts are, of course, shaped by knowledge of what actually happened. Even so, Robert of Gloucester gives a different picture when he writes that Montfort 'instructed his host right well and, through God's grace, hoped to win that day the mastery of the place'.[137] As the white crosses showed, Montfort's cause was as holy now as at Lewes, when he had won against all the odds. With God's help, might he not do so again? In refusing to remain in the abbey and in disdaining flight, he was arguably making rational calculations about the best route to victory. Edward would certainly have mopped up the foot-soldiers in the town and surrounded the abbey had the Montfortians remained there. It is doubtful whether Montfort could have held out for long or whether the arrival of Simon junior would have made much difference. Unless Montfort went out to fight, he risked being trapped in the abbey and forced into a humiliating surrender like Henry at Lewes.

Of course, there was still the possibility of flight. Montfort had no objections in principle to that if it served a strategic purpose. He had fled from Newport a few weeks earlier. He had fled from Southwark across London Bridge in December 1263. Since the bridge at Evesham remained open, he could have escaped across it just as he urged Hugh Despenser to do. But again, there was probably no way the bulk of the army could have been got away before Edward came down the hill and attacked it in the rear with shattering consequences. Montfort might save himself but after such a defeat and cowardly flight his reputation would be blasted and his

account discovered by Laborderie as it flatly contradicted what I had believed about the battle, a warning about being too sure of anything in history. For a recent account of the battle with much local knowledge, see Snowden, *1265: The Murder of Evesham*.

[134] Osney, 169.

[135] Laborderie, Maddicott and Carpenter, 'The last hours of Simon de Montfort', 391. Montfort was also widely quoted as blaming his sons for his predicament and as admiring the way his enemies advanced: 'they learnt that from me'. They may well have learnt how to march through the night, remembering Montfort's night march up onto the downs above Lewes, on which, of course, Clare had been present.

[136] See Ambler, *Song of Simon de Montfort*, 31, 325, where Montfort's acceptance of death is placed within a wider family tradition (embracing also his two elder brothers and his uncle) of dying in a holy war. Waverley, 290 has a Simon senior passing immediately to heaven, a reference I owe to Jenni Jolly, who is writing a doctoral thesis on the Waverley Chronicle.

[137] Robert of Gloucester, ii, lines 11,694–5.

political career over. There was also one cardinal reason for thinking death might not be the outcome. Young Simon's arrival might make limited difference with the Edwardians already in Evesham and Montfort bottled up in the abbey. It might make a great deal of difference if he crashed into the rear of the Edwardian army as it was struggling with Montfort himself. It was this that Montfort hoped would happen. Accordingly, on the morning of the battle he sent a message to his son urging him to come at once.[138] Wykes may capture his mood best as he left the abbey: 'Confident in the strength of his followers, he animated them to battle. And they, armed in warlike fashion, with standards erect and in line of battle, left the town and advanced manfully to meet the multitude of their enemies.'[139]

Montfort's line of battle was dictated both by his desire to join up with his son and his inferiority of numbers. He seems to have formed his cavalry into a single powerful wedge with the aim of breaking through the Edwardian lines strung out as they were in three divisions across Green Hill. There was help here from Edward's own tactics for Edward did not charge down the hill to meet the Montfortians. He had no desire to drive them back into the town and have all the bother of extracting them from the abbey. Rather he wanted them to come up the hill where they, or at least the leaders, could be surrounded and killed or captured.

Montfort, therefore, ascended the hill and charged into Edward's division.[140] Just for a moment, if Robert of Gloucester can be believed, he carried all before him and the Edwardians began to retreat, indeed to flee. But then they were rallied by Edward's trusty Warin of Bassingbourn and soon the weight of numbers told. The wings of the Edwardian army under Clare and Mortimer closed in and encircled the Montfortian force, squeezing it together into the dense mass described by many chroniclers. There was no help from the Montfortian foot who remained in the rear. Equally, there was no help from Simon junior. He did set out from Kenilworth but got no further than Alcester, nine miles from the field, before hearing of the disaster. If only, Robert of Gloucester lamented, he had not halted there for a meal. Evidently, his father's latest messages had not got through.

So 'within a small space of land' (as the Guisborough narrative puts it), the killing began. Montfort himself, his son Henry, Hugh Despenser, Peter de Montfort, Roger de St John, Guy de Balliol, Ralph Basset of Drayton, Thomas of Astley, Walter of Crepping and at least twenty other knights

---

[138] Evesham, 341. The Melrose chronicle states specifically that Montfort hoped his son would attack Edward's army in the rear: Melrose, 199–200 (fo. 67r).

[139] Wykes, 172. But for this passage, see Kjær, 'Writing reform and rebellion', 118.

[140] The long straight road northwards out of Evesham follows the same route as in 1265 although of course it now runs over the railway line and on past red-bricked tree-lined houses before reaching the flat summit of Green Hill. In recent years the Simon de Montfort Society (founded by the late Iris Pinkstone) has done much to raise public awareness about the battle.

of name were slain, including Despenser's knight Gilbert of Elsfield and Gilbert's comrade in arms Robert fitzNigel. Others were captured, including Guy de Montfort, Giles de Argentan, John de Vescy, John fitz-John, Henry de Hastings, Nicholas of Seagrave, Ralph of Sandwich and Humphrey de Bohun, who died later of his wounds. No one of note seems to have escaped. On the other side, the Pershore chronicler thought that only one knight and one man at arms were killed and they were the victims of 'friendly fire' having failed to wear the red crosses on their arms which distinguished the Edwardian forces.[141]

Henry himself was in the midst of this dark and fearful slaughter, glimpsing through the eyepiece of his helmet the raining down of blows, hearing the continuous roar produced by the clash of arms and the shouts and screams of angry and dying men. According to the Guisborough narrative, he cried out in a loud voice, 'I am Henry of Winchester, your king, do not kill me.' The Melrose chronicler has him shouting 'by God's head', and 'by the piety of God', 'I am Henry, the old king of England. For the love of God, do not hit me, for I am too old to fight.' If he was indeed in a suit of Montfort's armour, there was a real danger of being mistaken for Montfort himself. Both the belts he wore were lost in the battle, presumably wrenched from him in the melee. In the end, wounded in the shoulder, his helmet was pulled off, with many others the prelude to being stabbed to death. Instead, mercifully, he was recognized by Adam de Monte Alto and hurried to safety by Edward himself. It had been an appalling experience for this 'simple man, peaceable not warlike'.[142]

Many different stories were told about Montfort's end. He saw his son Henry fall first. His horse was killed, after which his enemies dismounted to surround him. He fought them on foot, wielding his sword against twelve men. At last, while Edward was taking his father to safety, he was seized from behind, his armour opened at the back and a dagger was plunged deep into his neck.[143] In the new Evesham account, it is Roger de Mortimer who deals the fatal blow, running Montfort through the neck with his lance, having recognized him from his armour and his shield.[144] Some accounts have Montfort refusing all quarter.[145] Guisborough, on the other hand, has him crying out 'Is there no mercy with you', the reply being 'What mercy can there be for a traitor?' According to the Osney chronicler, Montfort's foes rushed on him chanting 'Old traitor, old traitor,

[141] Pershore, *Flores*, 6.

[142] Guisborough, 201; Pershore, *Flores*, 5; Melrose, 201 (fo. 67v). The Melrose account of the battle was written between 1286 and 1291: see (under Melrose *Chronica de Mailros*) Broun and Harrison, *Chronicle of Melrose*, 168–9. Adam de Monte Alto had been appointed sheriff of Lancashire on Henry's recovery of power in 1261. He later went on crusade with Edward.

[143] Lanercost, 76; Cox, 'The tomb of Simon de Montfort', 159.

[144] Laborderie, Maddicott and Carpenter, 'The last hours of Simon de Montfort', 408, 411.

[145] Battle, 380; St Benet of Hulme, 208.

it is impossible for you any more to live.'[146] The death squad appointed by Edward and Clare in Mosham meadow did its work.

While the leading Montfortians were surrounded on Green Hill, the foot-soldiers in the rear were driven back towards Evesham where many were killed in the town and the surrounding fields and gardens. Others drowned in fruitless attempts to escape across the Avon. The new Evesham account gives a graphic picture of the massacre:

> Within the town, the abbey courtyard, the cemeteries and the monastery church, the dead bodies lay thick and dense on the ground like animals, and, what was horrendous to see and painful to speak of, the choir of the church and the inside walls and the cross and the statues and the altars were sprayed with the blood of the wounded and the dead, so that from the bodies that were around the high altar a stream of blood ran right down into the crypts. And this lasted from terce until mid afternoon.[147]

The scene on the top of Green hill was equally horrendous. There the bodies of the slain must have been stripped of their armour and laid out naked on the ground, for goulish inspection and celebratory identification, their death wounds raw and open. The men who had given such loyal support to Montfort over the last excruciating months, the men, some of them – Despenser, Peter de Montfort, Astley – who had been so close to him over so many years – now lay united with him and his eldest son in death. When it came to Montfort himself the scene evoked not compassion but contempt. His head, hands, feet and testicles were cut off, the testicles being hung either side of his nose and then stuffed in his mouth. The head was sent to Maud de Mortimer at Wigmore, 'who right sorely abused it', while other parts of the body were distributed round the country.[148]

'After the battle', the Osney chronicler relates, 'certain friends of the earl, weeping and lamenting . . . came into the field and collected on an old and shaky ladder, the remains of his body which lay abandoned under the sky. They covered it with an old and cheap cloth and brought it back to Evesham abbey, where wrapping it in a pure clean cloth, they placed it in a new grave where no one had yet lain.'[149] Other accounts say that Montfort's body was buried before the step below the high altar alongside

---

[146] Guisborough, 201; Osney, 169–70.

[147] Laborderie, Maddicott and Carpenter, 'The last hours of Simon de Montfort', 409, 411–12.

[148] Wykes, 174–5; FitzThedmar, 75–6 (Stone, FitzThedmar, nos. 842); London, 69; Furness, 548; Robert of Gloucester, ii, lines 11,728–9, where William Maltravers is blamed for the mutilation. For Maud de Mortimer, see above, 395.

[149] Osney, 174–5, but as David Cox points out ('The tomb of Simon de Montfort', 159–60), the account echoes that in the gospels of Christ's entombment.

his son Henry and Hugh Despenser.[150] This was done, so the Waverley annals say, with the king's licence, so perhaps Henry felt some compassion. Henry de Montfort, after all had been named after him, indeed had been raised by him from the font. Nicholas Trevet (writing in the early fourteenth century) has Edward himself ordering the monks of Evesham to bury the bodies of the great in decent fashion, and personally attending the obsequies of Henry de Montfort, his friend since childhood. The Evesham chronicler tells a somewhat different story. The monks buried the bodies of Montfort and the other nobles 'in less than honorable fashion out of fear'.[151]

Whatever the formalities, nothing could hide the unprecedented nature of the slaughter on Green Hill. 'The murder of Evesham for battle was it none,' wrote Robert of Gloucester and he was right.[152] There was nothing, of course, unprecedented in foot-soldiers being killed in battle. But for knights to be killed in such numbers was unheard of. In battle, armour usually protected the knight from serious injury. If he was surrounded and could not fight on, then he would offer to surrender and in the usual course of things his surrender was always accepted. This did not mean that those in rebellion against the crown were any the less traitors, deserving of death. Before the battle of Lewes, Edward had demanded that the Montfortians surrender with halters round their necks ready for hanging.[153] But in practice, as we have seen at Northampton and Lewes, the penalty was never exacted. At Kenilworth too, while many 'common people' perished, the knights were all taken prisoner on Edward's own instructions.[154] At Evesham itself, that it was sergeants who were appointed to kill Montfort, not knights, shows there was still thought to be something dishonourable about it.

What made the battle so bloody was not new theory but new practice, the key difference being that surrenders were not accepted. While it is possible, likely even, that Montfort and his closest friends refused to capitulate, that cannot have been true of all the others. In many cases, when surrounded and unable to fight on, pleas for mercy went unheard and men were deliberately done to death. Hence the 'murder' of Evesham. There was, however, no general injunction to kill, since many Montfortians were taken prisoner. In the heat of battle, much of the killing seems to have been indiscriminate and haphazard, hence those who perished from friendly fire, hence the lack, in some cases, of any clear distinction between

[150] Cox, 'The tomb of Simon de Montfort', 159–62, has a full discussion of the first burial place.

[151] Osney, 174–6; Waverley, 365; Trevet, 266; Evesham, 343.

[152] Robert of Gloucester, ii, line 11,736.

[153] But for the view that rebellion was not yet treasonable in this period, see Valente, *Theory and Practice of Revolt*, 32–41.

[154] Guisborough, 199–200; FitzThedmar, 75 (Stone, FitzThedmar, no. 839). The fact that the Montfortians were surprised asleep was doubtless a factor in this clemency.

those who lived and those who died. Why was Henry de Montfort killed and his brother Guy, a very dangerous man as events would show, wounded but not finished off? Amongst '*les jeunes*' why did both William de Mandeville and John de Beauchamp perish (to Wykes's sorrow), while John fitzJohn, Mandeville's elder brother, Henry de Hastings and Nicholas of Seagrave, men far more involved with Montfort, all lived?[155] In the case of fitzJohn, there is an answer for he was saved by his kinsman Roger of Clifford. At least sometimes ties of family and friendship acted across the political divide to save lives amidst the awful destruction of the battle.[156]

There were two reasons for the brutality at Evesham.[157] One was hotly emotional. Both Edward and Clare had been allies of Montfort. Now, with many others, they hated him. The desire for revenge after Montfort's contempt for Clare, humiliation of Edward and debasement of the king found its outlet in the gigantic hecatomb of Evesham. The other reason was coldly political. If Montfort and his closest associates survived the battle, how were they to be got rid off? In the fourteenth and fifteenth centuries they would have been executed out of hand with at most some show trial, but there was no precedent for that in the thirteenth century. King John executed none of the nobles he took in the Magna Carta civil war. None of those captured at Kenilworth or at Evesham were executed either. The last thing Edward wanted was for Montfort to survive in captivity, a potential source of trouble. He was far too dangerous to live. But Edward equally shied away from putting him on trial (what damage might still be done by that silver tongue), let alone executing this, in many eyes, heroic and righteous man. Getting rid of Montfort once and for all on the battlefield was a much better solution. The dismemberment of his body and its dispatch round the kingdom made absolutely clear he had indeed been a traitor.[158] Precisely the same treatment had been given to the body of the man executed for attempting Henry's assassination back in 1238.[159] But with Montfort it was far more personal. *His testicles were stuffed in his mouth.*[160] So the testicles which had generated Montfort's brood of sons now choked the mouth from which had flowed so many threats, so many insults, so many demands, so much self-righteous cant and so much

---

[155] John de Beauchamp's death brought to an end the Beauchamp barony of Bedford.

[156] Wykes, 174; Osney, 172.

[157] For the wider European context and the importance of the pope sanctioning holy war against Christians, see Ambler's discussion of 'the end of chivalry', in the *Song of Simon de Montfort*, 334–8.

[158] For the treatment of the body, see Weiler, 'Symbolism and politics', 29–30, and Cavell, 'Intelligence and intrigue in the march of Wales', 6–7.

[159] Tewkesbury, 113; Paris, iii, 497–8. The Furness chronicler thus says that Montfort's body was dismembered as 'he had been unfaithful and had stirred up all this sedition': Furness, 248.

[160] London, 69.

danger.[161] Montfort's two most vital organs were insulted and condemned together.

After being rescued, Henry was placed in the keeping of some of Edward's knights. Presumably he was taken somewhere other than the blood-spattered abbey. His wound was fairly superficial for next day he was able to move to Worcester. What might have happened if, by some miracle, the battle had gone the other way, we can only speculate. Would Montfort have seen to Edward's killing on the field? Would Henry himself have somehow perished? The Melrose chronicle preserved or concocted the sinister story that the Montfortians intended Henry to die with them, hence the way he was made unrecognizable by being kitted out in someone else's armour.[162] Clearly, Henry's anonymity could equally have facilitated his death, one way or another, in a Montfortian victory. As it was, the threat to Henry's kingship was over. There would be no ruling council. There would be no King Simon.

## SIMON DE MONTFORT

Even writing 750 years later, one has a sense of awe at the death of one of the most remarkable men ever to dignify and defile the English political scene. What an extraordinary career. Here was a younger son of a French noble, who became earl of Leicester, the king's brother-in-law, crusader in the Holy Land, regent in Gascony, friend of King Louis, leader of the 1258 revolution and then, having won the battle of Lewes, ruler of the kingdom. He was the first magnate to seize power and govern the country in the king's name. He was also the first populist leader in English history.[163]

The turning point in Montfort's career came in 1258. Although fore-shadowed by the zeal and ruthlessness of his time in Gascony, the way in which reform of the realm became central to his being could not have been predicted. In embracing 'the common enterprise', as he called it, Montfort was seeking to follow in the footsteps of a famous father who had fought and died in a holy cause. He was also swept along by the ideas of Robert Grosseteste, Adam Marsh and King Louis, who saw reform as necessary both for personal salvation and the creation of a well-ordered Christian community.

None of this initially meant Montfort was any the less attached to his material interests. In 1259 at times he placed them above any commitment to reform. But gradually 'the common enterprise' enveloped everything else. In 1260 he justified his conduct entirely in terms of his loyalty to its cause. In 1261, having led the resistance, he was the only noble who

---

[161] This sentence echoes a passage in a talk given by Andrew Spencer at Evesham in October 2021.

[162] Melrose, 200–1 (fo. 67v).

[163] Maddicott, *Simon de Montfort*, 231–2.

refused to accept the king's recovery of power. 'He would rather die land-less than depart from the truth and be perjured.' His adherence thereafter to the Provisions of Oxford prevented any settlement with the king. He only returned to England in 1263 when he could spearhead a movement dedicated to their restoration. After Lewes, Montfort was certainly intent on entrenching his own power and that of his family. But that power also guaranteed the survival of the Provisions. For Montfort, moreover, this meant more than just control of the king. He remained true to the legisla-tive and local reforms so that at the very time he was stripping Edward of Chester, he was taking ownership of the Provisions of Westminster. Had Montfort become king, I suspect he would have embarked on a reform of the realm, much like the one later driven forward by Edward I.

There were several factors explaining Montfort's rise to supreme lead-ership and supreme power. He had an income placing him amongst the richer earls. He had the great castle of Kenilworth and a loyal affinity of midlands knights.[164] He had the fame of his ancestry and the lustre of his own career. And then there was his piety and his intimacy with leading churchmen. But none of this would have counted without other charac-teristics. Montfort was a hard, flint-like man, very different from the malle-able king. He was rarely for turning. He would bend others to his will, not bend himself. Between 1258 and 1265 his only compromise was when, in 1260, he secured the alliance with Richard de Clare, and that he could claim was necessary for the survival of the Provisions. After 1261, he stood alone, the only great man to have remained true to their cause.

Montfort was hugely intelligent, with a quick wit and a sharp tongue, characteristics seen to perfection in his clever, sarcastic, sometimes disin-genuous replies to the charges brought by the Gascons in 1252 and the king in 1260. Would any other noble have had the spirit, let alone the historical knowledge, to tell Henry to his face he ought to be put away like Charles the Simple? This grasp and intelligence were not confined to the politics of the court. Helped by his knightly affinity, he understood the appeal of Magna Carta and the popularity of the Provisions of Westminster. He saw too the potency of 'England for the English' and thus, in 1263, joined to the Provisions of Oxford the 'statute' against the aliens.

To this programme, Montfort added something else, something abso-lutely central to his success, something far less present with Magna Carta in 1215. Helped by his personal piety, he turned what might have been a largely political and secular movement into something akin to a crusade.[165] The belief that God was on his side underpinned the final ingredient in his success, namely his confidence in the use of force and his knowledge of how to use it. He was a great general. Already in 1260 and 1261 he had

---

[164] Maddicott, *Simon de Montfort*, 47–76.

[165] Powicke, *King Henry III*, ii, 442, put this more cynically: Montfort 'could always turn an adventure into a crusade and dress politics in the trappings of a sacred cause'.

wanted to take up arms in support of the Provisions. In 1263 he had seen the way to reimpose them was through warfare – the ravaging of the estates of his enemies. Next year, rather than sit tight in London and nego-tiate some kind of compromise settlement, he seized the initiative and marched out of the capital to fight 'with all for all'. He then seized the initiative again with that daring night march onto the top of the Downs so that next day he could charge down and win the battle of Lewes. Later in the year he marshalled a great army on Barham Down and twice, in light-ning campaigns, defeated the marchers. Even in 1265 he had a strategy for victory, however much it was in the end a failure.

These then were the characteristics that won Montfort wide support as well as the devotion of an inner band of followers, many of whom died with him at Evesham. But, of course, none of the band had anything like Montfort's standing. They were middle-ranking magnates, often of young age, easily dazzled and dominated by the great earl. Montfort's problem, as we have seen, was that, while he inspired subordinates, he antagonized equals, or would-be equals. In the end, his failure to manage a man, very much his equal, Gilbert de Clare, brought about his downfall. Quite apart from doubts about the legitimacy of his regime, such men found his cutting criticisms and contempt for waverers insufferable. One glimpses what it was like to be under Montfort's lash in the threats to Hugh Bigod in 1260 – if Hugh, as justiciar, sent money out to the king in France, he would have to repay it from his own pocket![166] What made this worse was Montfort's apparent hypocrisy. No one expected him simply to abandon his material claims, but they came ill from someone who preached he would rather die landless than depart from the truth. As the tract preserved in the annals of Tewkesbury put it, having noted Montfort's gift of John Mansel's lands to his son, 'his followers ought not to thirst after spoils and gain, if he laboured for the common good'.[167] No wonder *The Song of Lewes* felt obliged to rebut at some length the charge that Montfort was out for himself.[168]

In 1258 the folly of the Sicilian affair, the king's free-flowing patronage of favourites and his failure to reform the realm had reduced the kingdom to an 'imbecilic state', amply justifying the revolution. The first phase of reform had positive achievements and a positive legacy. The procedures via '*querela*' in Hugh Bigod's eyres were adopted in the eyres of Edward I. The Provisions of Westminster, re-enacted by Henry in both 1263 and 1267, met real problems and helped inspire Edward's later legis-lation.[169] In driving forward the Lusignans' expulsion, insisting on conciliar control of the king and promulgating the Ordinances of the Magnates,

---

[166] *DBM*, 208–11, cap. 39.
[167] Tewkesbury, 180; and see above, 297.
[168] *Song of Lewes*, 40.
[169] See Maddicott, 'Edward I and the lessons of baronial reform'.

Montfort had played a key role, in part one for good. Yet his conduct had disrupted the regime and prevented the council, as some hoped, simply helping Henry be a king. If Montfort did much to create the Provisions, he also did much to destroy them.

If '1258' is easy to justify, '1263' seems quite another matter. It brought terrible destruction to the country for no tangible reward. '1258' would probably have taken place in some form without Montfort, '1263' never would have. Without his return to England and violent leadership, the ex-Edwardians would never have overthrown the king. Whatever Montfort believed, and persuaded others to believe, was it any longer a worthy cause? Was Montfort indeed not a deceiver and a false prophet? Henry had, after all, now accepted the Provisions of Westminster. Had he been left in peace down to his death, his distribution of patronage and pursuit of policy might still have been wayward, but hardly as dire as before 1258. Had Montfort wanted, he and his family could still have occupied a high place in English life.

In 1258–9, as justiciar, no one did more to uphold the cause of reform than Hugh Bigod. Yet by 1261, he was wavering, his loyalty to the Provisions shaken by the extremism of their leading proponent. From 1263 onwards he was on the king's side, fighting for him at both Lewes and Evesham. Hugh Bigod was a much lesser man than Simon de Montfort. But his political course between 1258 and 1265 seems much more right. In the last analysis, it was better to have King Henry and King Edward than King Simon.[170]

This account has, of course, left out one cardinal fact. Montfort's great parliament of 1265 was the first attended by knights from the counties and burgesses from the towns.[171] So Montfort can fairly claim to be 'the father of the House of Commons'. He had for some time been moving towards such an assembly, one strikingly different from that envisaged in the Provisions of Oxford. In September 1261 he was the driving force behind the summons of county knights to the baronial parliament at St Albans. He summoned knights again to the parliament held after the battle of Lewes. The summons of burgesses to the 1265 parliament was the logical next step. Montfort's parliament set a pattern for the future. Knights and probably burgesses too were summoned to the last parliaments of Henry III, as they were certainly to the parliaments of Edward I. At work here were ideas about consent and also long-term changes in the structure of society, both suggesting that an assembly of tenants-in-chief could no longer answer for the realm.[172] But without Montfort's parliament, and the more general politics of reform and rebellion, that awareness might have taken much longer to crystallize and produce constitutional results.

[170] Spencer, 'Dealing with inadequate kingship', 83.
[171] The *locus classicus* for the development of parliament is, of course, John Maddicott's *Origins of the English Parliament*.
[172] See above, 327.

The disaster at Evesham did nothing to blast Montfort's reputation. Indeed, he was soon regarded as a saint. Yet his career could also be viewed in a very different light. Saint John, in one of his apocalyptic visions, had seen the slaughter inflicted on the people by Satan's knights, their horses with heads of lions and tails like serpents.[173] In the scene as depicted in the Trinity Apocalypse of the 1250s, the faces of the knights are devilish indeed, but only one knight has a drawn sword and that is upright. The bodies of the victims, seven of them, lie separate with no apparent injuries, having been dispatched at a distance by streams of fire issuing from the lions' mouths.[174] The same scene as depicted in the so-called Douce Apocalypse, a work almost certainly dating to after Evesham and quite possibly commissioned by Henry himself, is totally different. Here there is a maelstrom of destruction. The warriors, brandishing scimitars, are depicted as Saracens (so the reverse of crusaders), while the victims are trodden down by hooves, bitten by serpents and sprayed with fire at close quarters from the open jaws of the lions. Altogether fifteen bodies are shown, most with blood streaming down their faces. Above this horrific scene there is a banner. It bears in black the lion rampant with forked tail of Simon de Montfort.[175]

Henry, however, had survived, but his experiences had been horrendous. He had been beaten by swords and maces in one battle, wounded in another, in between a virtual prisoner. He must often have felt like someone caught in a continuous mistral, the wind battering his body and howling in his ears, all around heaving trees and bushes, able only to pray again and again for it all to stop. Now it had stopped and the relief must have been intense. Henry owed his victory to his son. But he also owed it to himself. His reputation as a *rex Christianissimus* saved him from deposition, whatever Montfort's plans for the future. Unfortunately, neither Edward's aggression nor Henry's innocence were the qualities required in the aftermath of the war. The passage from Saint John's Revelations describing the slaughter of the people struck a warning note. The people had failed to repent.[176] More suffering, therefore, was to come. That was indeed to be the case in England.

---

[173] Revelations 9:17–21.

[174] McKitterick, *The Trinity Apocalypse*, 84 and plate 7 (fo. 10r).

[175] The lion is on a gold ground. This image from the Douce Apocalypse (see plate 12) is depicted on the front cover of Maddicott's biography and, as he says, may well represent a royalist view of Montfort. For the work, see Morgan, *The Douce Apocalypse*. There are images online if one puts into a search engine 'Douce Apocalypse'. The scene discussed here (on fo. 28r) is image no. 95. For the suggestion that Henry III was the original patron, see Binski, 'The illumination and patronage of the Douce Apocalypse', 132–3. The commentary explains how the horses represent 'the insane people', the riders 'the princes of the land', the armour 'their hardness of heart' and the fire 'the cruel mind of persecutors'. For the relevance more generally of apocalypses to the politics of this period, see Slater, *Art and Political Thought*, 131–54, with 152 for this scene from the Douce Apocalypse.

[176] Revelations 9:20–1.

## Chapter 12

# THE WAR OF THE DISINHERITED
## 1265-1267

After Evesham, Henry had no doubt who had caused the terrible disturbance in the kingdom. It was, of course, one man, Simon de Montfort.
The 'rebels' and 'enemies' of the king were thus described in royal letters
as those who, 'to our disinheritance and the destruction of our crown', had
'adhered to Simon de Montfort, once earl of Leicester, our enemy and
felon, in the time of war lately moved by him and his supporters'.[1] Here
the word 'felon' was especially damning for it indicated Montfort had been
guilty of the worst and most wicked of crimes, crimes for which the
penalty could only be the loss of life, limb and land.[2] With the root of this
evil dead, the Henricians must have thought their troubles were over. They
would restore peace to the kingdom very much on their own terms. Yet
nothing like that happened, largely because of one disastrous policy. This
was disinheritance. Under the wise terms concluding the 1217 civil war, all
the former rebels were restored to their estates. The reverse happened in
1265. The rebels were disinherited and their lands granted away in hereditary right to the victors. Naturally they stirred up fresh rebellion. It was to
be more than two years before peace would return to England.[3]

With the battle of Evesham, Henry was restored to the fullness of royal
power. Although there are occasional references to the council, Henry was
no longer subject to its direction. His will is once again apparent in acts of
piety, patronage and much else besides. And that will was easy to express
because the chancery and the seal continued to follow his person. If there
are signs he questioned the policy of disinheritance, he never stood out
against it in any determined way. He was appalled by the conduct of his
'enemies' and 'rebels'. He could now use their estates to reward the family
and friends who had suffered so much in the turmoil. These included, as

---

[1] For example, Nottingham University Library, Mi D 4681/1, TNA E 40/15184, and a
charter (sold at Sotheby's in 2015) dated 25 October 1265. I know of these from the census,
compiled by Nicholas Vincent, of the surviving original charters and letters of Henry III.

[2] Pollock and Maitland, *History of English Law*, ii, 464–8. For a new perspective and much
fuller discussion see Kamali, *Felony and the Guilty Mind* (a work brought to my attention by
Nicholas Vincent).

[3] For a clear and concise account of this period, see Jobson, *The First English Revolution*,
ch. 6.

before 1258, his foreign relatives and their connections. Here Henry was very determined to put the clock back.

Yet if Henry had some influence on events, it often paled before that of his eldest son. In 1265, at the time of Evesham, Henry was fifty-eight years old, coming up to fifty-nine. He had been seriously ill in 1262 and remained in uncertain health. Edward, by contrast, was now twenty-six, in the fullness of manly vigour. He had killed Montfort, rescued his father and restored the crown to all its rights. The pope had no doubt who was responsible. Elected in February 1265, as Clement IV, he was Guy Foulquois, so he was well informed about the English scene. In letters congratulating Henry and Edward on the outcome, he was clear that Henry, 'your innocence', owed it all to Edward, 'the most precious ornament of your family', a God-given prince divinely protected both in captivity and in battle, and now, with his mighty hand, his father's salvation.[4] From now on Edward as much as his father was the ruler of the kingdom. From August 1265 he was sending detailed instructions to the chancellor about the letters the king should be issuing, instructions which show him thinking round the angles in a way foreign to Henry and reminiscent of King John. Thus letters to the garrison of Kenilworth (described as 'his enemies', not the king's) were to be entrusted to no one save a man in religious orders. In giving his instructions Edward made no reference at all to Henry's own opinions. He seems to have taken for granted that his word would be obeyed, as indeed it was.[5] Sir Maurice Powicke described one of these early letters as Edward's 'first recorded act of state'. As such, he thought, it 'deserves a place of its own in our history'![6] The remark revealed Powicke's all too rosy view of Edward's reign ('our history' presumably did not include that of the Welsh, the Scots and the Jews), but still catches a truth. It was certainly Edward, not his father, who acted, again and again, to extinguish the flames of rebellion still burning between 1265 and 1267. He equally bears the largest measure of responsibility for fanning those flames through the policy of disinheritance in the first place

## HENRY AFTER EVESHAM

After the battle of Evesham, Henry spent two or three days at Worcester, and then moved south to Gloucester where he stayed until the end of August, perhaps recuperating from his wound. He was very aware of his debt to Edward. He was equally aware that behind Edward had been the

---

[4] *F*, i, 463–4.

[5] *RL*, ii, 289–91, 296; *CPR 1258–66*, 488–9; *CR 1264–8*, 131, 217–18, 228. For other letters, see *RL*, ii, 294–6; TNA SC 1/8/21–2. Note how in his letters to Chancellor Giffard, Edward initially put his name second and then swapped to putting it first: *RL*, ii, 291, 294, 296.

[6] Powicke, *King Henry III*, ii, 504.

hand of God. As Pope Clement explained in the same congratulatory letters, while God had permitted Henry for a time to fall into the hands of those thirsting for his blood and wishing to grind him up for food,[7] a just judge had now punished the impious authors of evil. God was thus continuing His ever-watchful care over Henry's affairs. Having rescued him at the start of the reign, and directed his acts during his long rule of peace, He had now restored him again to 'power and high estate'.[8] The psalm sung during the mass of the Confessor, the mass Henry had heard over and over again during the period of what the pope called his 'profound oppression', had come true. The lord in his anger had indeed struck down Henry's enemies.[9]

As he recovered, Henry must have appreciated most of all the total change in his entourage. Gone were the uncongenial Montfortian ministers. Of the stewards foisted on him by the regime, Walter of Crepping had died at Evesham while Adam de Newmarch was now in captivity. Their places were filled by the return of Roger of Leybourne and Robert Aguillon and by the appointment of the household knight William of Ayot, who had served before as Henry's butler.[10] The Montfortian keeper of the wardrobe, Ralph of Sandwich, likewise in captivity, was replaced by the clerk Nicholas of Lewknor. Sandwich had doubled up as keeper of the seal after the Montfortian chancellor, Thomas de Cantilupe, left court. The chancery was now entrusted to Walter Giffard, the bishop of Bath and Wells. Elected just after the battle of Lewes, he had co-operated with the Montfort regime, without damaging his loyalist credentials.[11]

Henry's new freedom was shown in the gifts of wood and deer he could make from his forests. No longer had he to do so at the behest of an obnoxious regime. Back at Hereford he had even presented oak trees to Montfort himself and Montfort's chaplain. Now all such gifts were cancelled, though Henry was careful to maintain the one made to the Dominican friars at Gloucester.[12] In the regnal year from October 1265 to October 1266, Henry made around 100 such gifts. How pleasant to reward once again William de Valence (and his cook), Elyas de Rabayne, Imbert de Montferrand and the veteran household knight Nicholas de Molis. Four oaks and three deer went to bishop-elect Aymer's old servant Peter de Sancto Mauro, whose attack on Shere had sparked the revolution of

---

[7] The precise translation here is difficult and the text may be corrupt. Daniel Hadas has helped me with the passage and points out that it is based on Sirach (Ecclesiasticus) 51: 4–5.

[8] *F*, i, 463.

[9] See above, 423.

[10] Aguillon had been appointed after Henry's recovery of power in 1263.

[11] Wykes, 164; Howell, *Eleanor of Provence*, 106–7, 221–2; and above, 402. See Dobson, 'Walter Giffard'. His mother, Sybil, had attended the queen at Edward's birth and been thereafter a firm favourite.

[12] *CR 1264–8*, 57, 69–70.

1258.[13] And naturally too gifts went to the 'heavies' who had won the war: to Roger de Mortimer, John Giffard, Roger de Somery, Roger of Leybourne, Robert Walerand, his nephew Alan Plugenet and Edward's men, Roger of Clifford, Warin of Bassingbourn and Nicholas of Cogenhoe. Two deer were given to William Maltravers, the man credited with dismembering Montfort's body.[14] Henry's return to action was also apparent in his gifts of rings, brooches and belts. These had almost dried up during Montfort's ascendancy. Now between August 1265 and March 1268 (the period covered by the account), he disbursed 646 rings, 187 brooches, 102 belts, 78 cups and 42 silver bowls.[15]

At the end of August, Henry finally left Gloucester and set out for his castle at Marlborough, where he had not been since September 1260, an example of how the unrest had disturbed his usual itinerary. On the way, staying at Malmesbury, he made gifts of timber to the abbot, the sick monks and the sacrist, the last for work on the church. At Marlborough itself, he commissioned repairs to the castle's houses, bridge and fishpond, arranged for a chaplain to celebrate mass daily and ordered the paintings in the chapel to be renewed and an image of St Nicholas to be placed there. Later in the year, his mind wandering back to Marlborough, Henry had his seat in the chapel painted and a screen placed around it. He was back in business.[16]

After a week at Marlborough, Henry moved to Winchester, preparing the way with a gift of timber to its Dominicans.[17] The city was in a sorry state after its sack by Simon de Montfort junior earlier in the year. In consideration of their losses and their loyalty, Henry remitted to the citizens the annual rent they owed for the next six years.[18] At Winchester, Henry held a parliament (of which more later), then moved to Windsor, where he ordered a new fence for the park. In October he arrived back at Westminster in time to celebrate the feast of the Confessor on the 13th. At least progress on the Abbey had continued during Montfort's rule. On his arrival Henry at once had another 50 marks delivered for the works.[19] The king did not have a second coronation, as did Richard the Lionheart after his return from captivity in 1194. But this feast of the Confessor was almost the equivalent. As described by Wykes, Henry 'having recovered his royal majesty, which for a long time he lacked, and with the ignominy of his captivity put to sleep, shone forth gloriously, adorned with the royal crown, before an innumerable multitude of the magnates of the kingdom'.[20]

[13] *CR 1264–8*, 208–9; Ridgeway, 'Ecclesiastical career of Aymer de Lusignan', 161, 163, 165–7, 173. Peter was archdeacon of Surrey.

[14] *CR 1264–8*, 197; Robert of Gloucester, ii, lines 11,727–32.

[15] Wild, *WA*, clxxv, 136–43.

[16] *CR 1264–8*, 57, 70–1; *CLR 1260–7*, 180, 183.

[17] *CLR 1260–7*, 179–80.

[18] *CPR 1258–66*, 470; and see *CFR 1265–6*, no. 212, for the loyalist mayor.

[19] *CLR 1260–7*, 181–2; *BA*, 388–99; Carpenter, 'Westminster Abbey in politics', 51.

[20] Wykes, 177.

For Henry, perhaps the most grievous feature of his captivity was the isolation from his family. We can glimpse the strength of familial ties from letters written to him around this time by his daughter Beatrice and her mother-in-law, Blanche, countess of Brittany.[21] Beatrice lamented how, since her departure, she had heard no certain news of her father through his messengers. She begged him 'in every way I am able' to let her know his state by the bearer of her letter, adding that though suffering from a fever, it was not giving her continuous grief. Countess Blanche likewise begged for news: 'Know my dear lord, I have such great joy every time I hear good news of you.' As for Beatrice's fever, there was every hope it would soon be gone. Her son Arthur, meanwhile (as yet Henry's only grandson), was beautiful and healthy. When Beatrice received letters from Henry giving what was probably the news of Evesham, she wrote back '*vehementer exultantes*' at his success. Her husband, for his part, promised to come with horses and arms, whenever required.[22]

Most of all, Henry wished to have back his queen. They had not seen each other since Henry's return to England in February 1264 after the Mise of Amiens. Henry thus urged Queen Margaret to hasten Eleanor's arrival. Margaret's letter in reply, perhaps more than any other single piece of evidence, illuminates the intimate friendship between the English and French courts, and shows how they shared the same light-hearted sense of humour. Margaret thus told Henry she wished very much she could keep Eleanor with her. Nonetheless, she was speeding her return lest, because of the long absence, Henry decided to marry the countess of Gloucester instead! 'I know she is in your neighbourhood'. Perhaps Henry's letter had been sent from Gloucester. In any case, the reference was to the widow of Richard de Clare, Maud de Lacy. It was, of course, a humorous flight of fancy on Margaret's part and one she must have known would cheer Henry up and make him laugh.[23]

In the event, Eleanor landed at Dover on 29 October, with Edmund and Ottobuono the papal legate (of whom much more later).[24] Henry had gone to meet her and next day they entered Canterbury with much rejoicing.[25] Fully aware of all he owed his queen, Henry gave her a garland of gold, studied with rubies, emeralds and pearls, worth 40 marks. Two months later, in December 1265, for the health of their joint souls, he

---

[21] The strength of these ties is a major theme of Abigail Armstrong's doctoral thesis, 'The daughters of Henry III', with 181–4 for an analysis of these letters.

[22] *F*, i, 464–5; *RL*, ii, 318–19.

[23] *DD*, no. 244. The date and nature of the letter was first appreciated by Margaret Howell. See her *Eleanor of Provence*, 231–2. For Maud, see above, 395–6. For Margaret, asking of news of Henry in the most fulsome terms, see *DD*, no. 430; Neal, *Letters of Edward I*, 100–1.

[24] Ottobuono, appointed legate by Pope Clement IV, belonged to the Fieschi family who were counts of Lavagna. His was a brilliant appointment, as we will see.

[25] Wykes, 179.

granted a royal manor to her nunnery at Tarrant in Dorset.[26] The court could now resume its full splendour. It is both Eleanor's presence and the more general recovery of royal state that explains the daily costs of the household's food, drink, stables and alms running at a little over £14 a day between Evesham and March 1268 against the £8 10s earlier in 1265.[27] The king's wardrobe accounts show £91 being spent between 1265 and 1268 on cutting the clothes of the queen and the ladies of her chamber. The same entry has the cost of ornamenting two robes of scarlet for Henry himself.[28] There was one person who did not return with the queen: John Mansel.[29] With Eleanor throughout her exile, he had died in January 1265. Courageous, wise and moderate, he was the best minister the king ever had. Henry could have done with him now.

## THE LIQUIDATION OF THE REBELLION?

As the news of Evesham's slaughter spread to manor houses and monasteries, to castles and cathedrals, to towns and villages, the shock for surviving Montfortians must have been profound. Just as after Lewes, they had bathed in the balm of victory, so now they drowned in the blood of defeat. For days and days it must have been hard to think of anything else. The monastic author of one tract, written soon afterwards, despaired. With Montfort and his 'most noble' followers killed, the party of the Provisions was wholly cast down. The worst customs of old were likely to be restored and new ones added. The author could only pray to God that those killed defending the Provisions had not died in vain. But he feared the current sufferings were God's punishment for the sins of the people, including indeed those of some Montfortians.[30]

In these circumstances, Henry must have felt his victory would soon be complete. Just before Eleanor's return, Thomas Wykes describes him as being 'full of inestimable joy' at his success.[31] On 26 October, at Canterbury, he granted Montfort's honour of Leicester to his second son

---

[26] Wild, *WA*, 135, 137; *CFR 1265–6*, no. 88; *CChR 1257–1300*, 228; Howell, *Eleanor of Provence*, 282.

[27] Carpenter, 'Household rolls', 35.

[28] *CLR 1260–7*, 180; Wild, *WA*, 136–7.

[29] There is a comprehensive account of Mansel's career in Hui Liu's doctoral thesis 'John Mansel', and an excellent summary by Robert Stacey, 'John Mansel', *The Oxford Dictionary of National Biography*. The hall of the Augustinian priory he founded at Bilsington in Kent survives. When I visited the site in the 1980s, the foundation charters were still in a neighbouring house.

[30] Corpus Christi College Cambridge, MS 385, fos. 57–9, 79–80. This is the tract, probably by a monk of Rufford, referred to above, 407. Likewise, a poet writing soon after Evesham declared that with Montfort gone the English had no one to defend them: Maitland, 'A song on the death of Simon de Montfort', 318.

[31] Wykes, 179.

Edmund in hereditary right, so the royal family was benefiting directly
from the victory.[32] In London a panicky plot by the mayor to arrest and
murder the leading loyalist citizens (fitzThedmar thought he was on the
list) was abandoned as soon as news of Evesham came in. Alina Despenser,
Hugh's widow, in command at the Tower, immediately released her prisoners, vacated the fortress and, sorrowing for the loss of her husband,
went off to shelter with her father, Philip Basset.[33]

In this favourable ground, Edward obtained at once the surrender of
King Richard's castles at Berkhamsted and Wallingford. That Richard of
Havering, in command, surrendered them without fuss shows this leading
and long-standing Montfortian servant thought all was over. After these
successes, Edward headed for Chester. There Montfort's castellan, Luke
de Tany, had withstood a siege throughout the summer. Now, on
13 August, he tamely resigned the castle into Edward's hands.[34] As for
Kenilworth, Simon junior (according to Wykes's story) having seen his
father's head go by on the top of a spear, had retired to the castle where
for several days he would neither eat nor drink.[35] Surely the lesson of
Evesham, 'where by divine clemency the king obtained victory', and the
dire penalties involved in trying to hold out, would now bring the castle to
its senses.[36] They had some effect. According to Rishanger's not unlikely
story, the garrison had wished to strangle King Richard in revenge for
Evesham but were prevented by Simon junior. On 6 September, Richard
was released promising, in return, to be a loyal friend to Eleanor 'our
sister', her children and all their people. Indeed, he would help them with
all his power to obtain their 'right' in England.[37]

More trouble was expected from London. It had after all been the great
seat of Montfortian power; its populace had attacked the queen at London
Bridge, rescued Montfort when he was trapped at Southwark, ravaged the
property of King Richard at Iselworth, and then fought against the king
at the battle of Lewes. Its mayor, Thomas fitzThomas, only a few months
before had told Henry his loyalty was conditional. Most of the aldermen,
if with misgivings, had co-operated with the regime, including Arnold
fitzThedmar. At Windsor, in late September, Henry and Edward mustered
a force to advance on the city. Some of the Londoners wished to resist, but
the leading citizens threw themselves at once on the king's mercy. In what
followed they never saw Henry or Edward personally (the go-betweens
were that deadly duo Roger of Leybourne and Robert Walerand), but the

---

[32] *CChR 1257–1300*, 58; *RCWL*, ii, 150. The first layman witnessing the charter was Hugh
Bigod.

[33] FitzThedmar, 114–15 (Stone, FitzThedmar, nos. 991–3); Wykes, 175–6.

[34] *RL*, ii, 291; *CR 1264–8*, 131, 228, 257; St Werburgh, 94–7.

[35] Wykes, 175.

[36] *RL*, ii, 289–90; *CPR 1258–66*, 488–9.

[37] Rishanger, 50–1; Blaauw, *The Barons' War*, 361–2; *Layettes*, v, no. 720.

anger of the king and his son, and their determination to punish the city, are very plain. On 4 October the mayor and forty of the more substantial citizens, including Arnold fitzThedmar, arrived at Windsor. On entering the castle they were immediately imprisoned in the keep despite their letters of safe conduct. Even Wykes thought this was disgraceful but then the conduct of the Londoners had been disgraceful too. FitzThedmar and the rest remained in lugubrious captivity through the night and on until the evening of the next day when they were allowed out into the castle's bailey, all, that is, except the five Montfortian ringleaders headed by fitzThomas and Master Thomas of Puleston. They remained heavily fettered in the keep. Puleston's offence was made the worse for having once been in Edward's service.

With Leybourne now in control of the Tower, with the chains across the city streets removed, with the leading Londoners, loyal and disloyal alike, detained at Windsor, and with the whole community of the city (or so it was said) having submitted to the king's will touching life, limbs, lands and goods, Henry was able to come up to Westminster, in time, as we have seen, for the feast of the Confessor. He gave to Edward the persons and the properties of fitzThomas and Puleston. Sixty houses of other Londoners deemed his 'enemies' (not always fairly) were likewise given away, and their families expelled from the city. Around 20 October most of those detained in the bailey at Windsor were released but there was no question of London recovering control of its government. Instead, the city was placed under Edward's knight Hugh fitzOtto, who took over at the Tower and appointed two bailiffs to replace the elected sheriffs and mayor. Henry made clear that the Londoners must offer a large sum of money to recover his goodwill, and large it was. The sum finally agreed in January 1266 was 20,000 marks and even that did not restore London to its liberties.[38] Not surprisingly, as a further corollary of the king's victory, the city's triumph over Westminster Abbey was reversed and the Abbey was restored to all the liberties it claimed in Middlesex.[39]

The king put some of London's money to good use in another repair to the damage done by the war. In her extremity in 1264, Queen Eleanor had sold back to King Louis for around £5,000 the rights in the Three Dioceses of Cahors, Limoges and Périgueux ceded under the Treaty of Paris. In 1266 Henry, doubtless with Edward's full support, used some of London's money to buy these rights back.[40]

By early October, therefore, Chester, the Tower and London itself were all in royal hands. What of Dover under Eleanor de Montfort? During the

[38] FitzThedmar, 79–82 (Stone, FitzThedmar, nos. 854–61); Wykes, 176–8; *CPR 1258–66*, 461–8, 519, 524, 530–1; *RL*, ii, 293–4, 369–70; Williams, *Medieval London*, 232–6.
[39] WAM 502; WAM 562; *CChR 1257–1300*, 238, 241; *CPR 1258–66*, 588; FitzThedmar, 85–6 (Stone, FitzThedmar, nos. 871–2).
[40] *CPR 1258–66*, 658–9, 662, 667–8.

summer she had tried desperately to keep in touch with her husband. As late as 1 August her messenger, the aptly named Slingaway, was despatched to him.[41] When news arrived of the disaster, Eleanor donned widow's weeds, withdrew to her chamber and gave up both meat and fish.[42] On 11 August the entire garrison dined in the hall, consuming large amounts of wine and ale, in what may have been a communal wake. On the same day, Eleanor sent the master of the Dover hospital to the king. She must have been asking anxiously about Guy's wounds and crying out about the treatment of her husband's body.[43] For all her grief and anxiety, Eleanor had no intention of following the path of Alina Despenser at the Tower. With a garrison commanded by the Montfortian stalwart John de la Haye, she held fast, perhaps hoping in some way to give comfort to Simon junior at Kenilworth.[44] Her plans to hold out were, however, disrupted when the captives in the castle revolted and managed to seize the keep. Again, it was Edward who acted. With a large force, he hurried 'without sleep' down to Dover and began to assail the castle. On 26 October, Eleanor gave up and agreed its surrender. In return, 'at the instance of our most dear aunt, the lady countess of Leicester', Edward admitted members of her household to his grace. He also told the chancellor to issue letters restoring them to their lands. Eleanor was leaving nothing to chance and supplied a list of twenty-six individuals, including John de la Haye, plus the names of the sheriffs to whom the letters should be sent.[45] Two days later she set sail for France.[46] It was on this day that Edmund was granted the honour of Leicester in hereditary right. Whatever the mercy shown to Eleanor's household, the Montforts seemed finished in England.

By this time, the structure of central government was coming back into place. During October both the bench and the exchequer were re-established at Westminster. At the same time a run of new sheriffs were appointed with several loyalists returning to the counties they had previously held for the king.[47] The arrival of the legate Ottobuono, meanwhile, helped solve the question of what to do with the Montfortian bishops. At first, Henry thought of dealing with them himself. During the Michaelmas

[41] Wilkinson, *HR*, nos. 398, 413. Domestic life continued in the castle. Eleanor's daughter Eleanor was given twenty-five gilded stars for her hood and the day before Evesham presented a gold brooch to the child of the garrison commander, John de la Haye (nos. 403, 405).

[42] Wykes, 179; Wilkinson, *Eleanor de Montfort*, 123–4; Wilkinson, *HR*, cxvii–xxiii, where there is a detailed study of the reaction to Evesham.

[43] Wilkinson, *HR*, no. 418. The questions asked were suggested by Louise Wilkinson in a talk at Evesham in October 2021.

[44] Eleanor was certainly in touch with young Simon: Wilkinson, *HR*, cxix, cxxii.

[45] *RL*, ii, 296. For the garrison, see Wilkinson, *HR*, cxxv–xxxiv.

[46] Wykes, 178–9; Canterbury/Dover, 243; *RL*, ii, 294–6; Wilkinson, *Eleanor de Montfort*, 124–5, where the contrast with Alina is made.

[47] *CFR 1265–6*, nos. 828–52.

term of 1265, in the court *coram rege*, he brought proceedings against eight bishops for their transgressions during the time of disturbance.[48] The pope, as the legate defied by the bishops in 1264, however, had other ideas.[49] In a long letter to Ottobuono he lambasted the bishops for their conduct and said they were to be sent to Rome for punishment.[50] Ottobuono accordingly convened a church council in London at the start of December 1265. There he accused four bishops, Sandwich of London, Gervais of Winchester, Gravesend of Lincoln and Bersted of Chichester, of being especial supporters of Montfort. All were suspended from office and went eventually to Rome.[51] Henry meanwhile abandoned the actions *coram rege* against the bishops, those of Winchester, Lincoln and Salisbury offering substantial sums of money to assuage his anger and recover his goodwill.[52]

One Montfortian bishop did not appear at the London council. This was Walter de Cantilupe of Worcester. Now in his seventies, he had celebrated mass for Montfort on the morning of Evesham and then departed sorrowing for his manor of Blockley. But his spirit was not crushed, his activity in the Montfortian cause not stilled. In September 1265 he was at Kenilworth, where he guaranteed the promises made to Simon junior by King Richard.[53] Later, while too ill to attend the London council, let alone go to Rome, he defiantly appealed against his suspension.[54] Yet on his deathbed, in February 1266, he regretted his support for Montfort and asked the legate for absolution, at least if the story in the Westminster chronicle can be believed. Wykes himself acknowledged the friendship and fortitude with which he had stood by the earl of Leicester. Had it not been for that, Wykes thought, his exceptional piety would have justified his canonization. It tells us a great deal about Montfort and his cause that he retained through thick and thin the loyalty of this great ecclesiastic.[55] In Cantilupe's place the king accepted at once Master Nicholas of Ely's election. On the face of it this seemed to indicate the divisions of the war were healing over. After all, Nicholas had been appointed chancellor at the parliament of October 1260, been dismissed when Henry recovered power in 1261, and then been reappointed by Montfort on his return in

---

[48] TNA KB 26/174, mm. 20d (*AP*, 159–159b), 24, 25d; Ambler, 'Magna Carta', 814.

[49] *F*, i, 463.

[50] Ambler, *Bishops in the Political Community*, 185–90.

[51] *C&S*, ii, 725–8.

[52] The amounts were respectively 1,000 marks, 500 marks and 100 marks: *CR 1264–8*, 176; *CFR 1265–6*, nos. 760, 772; Ambler, *Bishops in the Political Community*, 187. Money from the other bishops may be included in the general wardrobe receipts from fines for the king's goodwill.

[53] Blaauw, *The Barons' War*, 361–2; *Layettes*, v, 720.

[54] Canterbury/Dover, 243.

[55] Westminster, *Flores*, 9; Wykes, 180; Ambler, *Bishops in the Political Community*, 189–90, and for an assessment of his whole career, see Lawrence, 'Walter de Cantilupe'.

July 1263. Yet, a clever and prudent man, he had somehow managed to retain the favour of the king.[56]

## DISINHERITANCE

Unfortunately, Eleanor de Montfort's exile reflected far more the post-Evesham spirit than Nicholas of Ely's election. Henry's joy at the recovery of Dover was premature. With the queen by his side, he returned to the comfort of Westminster and the completion of the Abbey, but all around him, out in the shires, there was chaos. The success in securing Wallingford, Berkhamsted, Chester, Dover, London and the Tower had not ended hostilities at all. For that, most of the blame falls on the policy of disinheritance.

In any circumstances the restoration of peace and order would have been difficult. The victors had seen their lands seized and despoiled by the Montfortians.[57] They now wanted compensation and revenge. They acted at once to obtain it.[58] Within a few weeks of Evesham, more than a thousand estates had been seized or pillaged 'in an irresistible wave spreading outwards from the battlefield'.[59] Far from all the victims had been rebels. There was a good deal of robbery, settling of scores and attacks on those whom, juries agreed, had never been against the king.[60] Edward's own bailiffs, evidently on his orders, got hold of Leicester itself and Montfort's surrounding lands, but by and large royal officials played a limited part in the process[61] After all, until a new set of sheriffs were in place the king was without trustworthy local agents. Instead, the lead, alongside the military captains who had won the war (like Roger of Leybourne and John Giffard), was taken by Gilbert de Clare. He had land and local officials throughout much of England. In the month after Evesham his men seized more than 160 properties. Much of this was orchestrated by the earl himself. As early as 6 August from Worcester, he appointed two of his knights to seize the lands of 'our enemies' in Bedfordshire, Buckinghamshire and Huntingdonshire.[62] It almost seemed as though Clare was taking over the kingdom.[63]

---

[56] Wykes, 180. For Ely's career, see Jewell, 'Nicholas of Ely'. For an unflattering drawing of him on the memoranda rolls of the exchequer, see TNA E 159/42, m. 5 (image 0015).

[57] In the Michaelmas term of 1268, in the court *coram rege*, over 200 cases were ongoing about manorial spoliation during the rebellion: Jacob, *Studies*, 202 n. 3.

[58] The most detailed study of what follows is found in Clive Knowles's doctoral thesis, 'The disinherited', pt. 3, 1–8, from which much of the following detail is taken. There is a summary of the main themes in his article, 'The resettlement of England'.

[59] Knowles, 'The resettlement of England', 26, and see Moore, 'Government and locality in Essex', 266.

[60] For example, *CIM*, no. 855 (yet further sufferings of Ralph de Aundely).

[61] *CIM*, no. 772.

[62] Jacob, *Studies*, 406.

[63] In Essex, Clare and his followers were responsible for seventy-four seizures, two thirds of the whole: Moore, 'Government and locality in Essex', 267.

It was vital, if Henry and Edward were to have any authority, they now stopped this free-for-all and took possession of the rebel lands themselves. After all, the rebellion had been against them not Gilbert de Clare. At the parliament, held at Winchester in September 1265, they carried the point. On 17 September it decided that the lands of the rebels should be surrendered to the king by whomsoever had occupied them. To ease the process, the occupiers were allowed to keep whatever chattels they had taken.[64] A few days later, to put the decision into motion, two knights were appointed in each county to take possession of the lands and send a valuation of them to the king. Their surviving returns reveal both the scale of the rebellion and the subsequent seizures.[65]

In a less acrimonious atmosphere, all this might have prepared the way for the eventual rehabilitation of rebels and restoration to their lands. Instead, the parliament decided that all the rebels should be disinherited. The sentence, pronounced by Robert Walerand on 16 September, was reaffirmed when parliament reassembled at Westminster in October.[66]

There was no question of the king keeping for himself the properties now coming into his hands. Instead, he gave them away, and gave them in hereditary right. Among the beneficiaries were the leading loyalists who had brought Henry victory. Roger de Mortimer got the lands and the comital title of Robert de Vere, 'once' earl of Oxford; his wife, Maud, possessor of Montfort's head, was given all the lands of eleven rebels in the Wigmore area. Hugh de Neville's lands went to Robert Walerand, Roger de St John's to Roger of Leybourne, and Simon of Pattishall's to John Giffard, now a member of Clare's household. Clare himself gained the lands of John fitzJohn, in this case keeping the lands he had seized immediately after Evesham. Robert Aguillon naturally got the lands of his Surrey enemy Ralph of Imworth.[67]

Both the victims and the beneficiaries of the great transfer went far beyond the leaders of the two regimes. In one list of the grants, the lands of 316 rebels were distributed to 133 loyalists.[68] In another, over 110 loyalists received the lands of some 215 rebels in around 240 separate locations. The number of places affected was in fact much larger, for sometimes (as in the case of the earl of Oxford) the beneficiary just received all the victim's lands.[69] Many of those rewarded, like their victims, came from the lower sections of society, for loyalist ministers and magnates rewarded their own men from the lands of lesser rebels. Thus the constable of John

---

[64] *CPR 1258–66*, 493.

[65] *CPR 1258–66*, 512; *CIM*, nos. 608–940.

[66] St Andrews Northampton, 102; Winchester/Worcester, 455; Waverley, 367; Osney, 179; FitzThedmar, 76–7 (Stone, FitzThedmar, no. 844); Wykes, 183–4.

[67] *CR Supp*, nos. 336, 439, 443; *RS*, 129, 137, 250; *CFR 1267–8*, no. 479; Maddicott, 'Follower, leader, pilgrim, saint', 644.

[68] Knowles, 'The resettlement of England', 26, from *RS*, 247–58.

[69] *CR Supp*, nos. 316–462. The overlap between the lists is limited to about twenty entries.

Giffard's castle at Brimpsfield got all the land of one nearby rebel worth an annual 40s.[70]

Perhaps some of the beneficiaries always intended to strike deals enabling their victims to retain a portion of their lands. But they were under no obligation to do so. The grants specifically extinguished all rights and claims of the previous owners. One may be pretty sure that the likes of Roger de Mortimer intended to hold on to everything they had. What was threatened therefore was a tenurial revolution in which across the kingdom the lands of the vanquished were to pass for ever into the hands of the victors.

The policy of disinheritance was either too brutal or not brutal enough. The king's agents were instructed to seize the property of his 'adversaries and rebels' but nothing was said about placing those rebels under arrest. Equally, no effort was made to try them for treason, let alone put them to death. The result was that the king's policy alienated large numbers of men while leaving them very much at large. There was certainly no incentive here for Kenilworth to surrender. According to FitzThedmar, Simon junior came under safe conduct to the Winchester parliament. Presumably he hoped something might come from the promises of King Richard, whom he had just released. But when nothing acceptable materialized, he returned to the castle and filled it with knights and sergeants for fresh resistance.[71] Large numbers of men, as the legate Ottobuono appreciated, were thus afflicted by the loss of their temporal possessions and despaired of ever rising again.[72] They saw no way out but a renewal of the civil war.

## HENRY, EDWARD AND THE POLICY OF DISINHERITANCE

The policy of disinheritance thus turned out to be disastrous. Could it have been avoided? It had, to be sure, required no new theory. The idea that rebellion was treason and that the penalty for treason could be disinheritance was centuries old.[73] Yet there was still something very new in 1265, for now the penalty was being enforced not just in individual cases but across the board.[74] As we have said, nothing like that had happened in

[70] *RS*, 252.

[71] FitzThedmar, 76 (Stone, FitzThedmar, no. 844); Stone, 'Book of fitzThedmar', no. 844.

[72] Graham, 'Letters of Cardinal Ottoboni, 116–17.

[73] This was true whether treason was defined in 'feudal' terms as breach of faith to one's lord, or in Roman law terms as '*laesae maiestatis*'. For discussion, see Vincent, 'From rebellion and reconciliation to treason and disinheritance'; Vincent, 'Rank insubordination: disobedience and disinheritance amongst the Anglo-French nobility', 156–65; and Carpenter, 'From King John to the first English duke', 29–35. For the view that rebellion did not amount to treason, see Valente, *Theory and Practice of Revolt*, 32–41.

[74] The closest parallel was in 1204 when those who retained their Norman lands by doing homage to King Philip lost their lands in England.

1217, although the rebels acknowledged they would suffer perpetual disinheritance if they rebelled again.[75] In 1265 the disinherited themselves thought the policy had been opposed. Indeed, they alleged that King Richard, Roger Bigod, earl of Norfolk, and Philip Basset had left court rather than agree to it.[76] In one area, the policy was limited, for simply holding office during the Montfortian regime, whether centrally or locally, was not taken as a reason for disinheritance.[77] There was also a different spirit abroad when it came to the wives and widows of those captured and killed in the rebellion. They were summoned to the Winchester parliament where provision for them was to be discussed.[78] One who came was Juliana, widow of Hugh Despenser's knight Gilbert of Elsfield. She had spent the war sheltering with the nuns at Studley priory (four miles from Elsfield) and must have been as shocked as Eleanor de Montfort and Alina Despenser when she heard the news of Evesham. The lands of her husband were immediately seized by Thomas de Clare. Yet Juliana went to Winchester and recovered a portion for her support.[79] She was not alone. From 20 September onwards the king was making provision for wives and widows from the lands of their husbands or late husbands. Eventually, by a formal decision of the king and council, the women were to recover their own inheritances and marriage portions. Where widowed, they were also to have between a quarter and a third of their late husbands' lands in dower.[80]

Another factor making for moderation and mercy were ties of family. Of course, they were no guarantee of harmony as Montfort's relations with his brother-in-law showed all too well. But, on the other hand, Roger Bigod helped his nephew John fitzJohn as Roger, son of Hugh Bigod, helped his half-brother Baldwin Wake. It may have been to protect them that Hugh himself obtained Baldwin's lands, as John de Grey got some manors of his older brother Richard. Since Humphrey de Bohun, earl of Hereford, received the lands of Humphrey junior, his eldest son, the Bohuns escaped the consequences of the latter's death in rebellion.[81] Loyalists were particularly active on behalf of their female relations. James of Audley helped his sister, the widow of Peter de Montfort. The favour won by his 'laudable service' enabled Roger de Somery to improve the provision made for his daughter Margaret, the widow of Ralph Basset

[75] See the charters issued by returning rebels in TNA C 47/34/8/1–29, of which images were sent me by Nicholas Vincent.

[76] Rishanger, 65. There is no proof of them leaving court, but their opposition is also recorded in Waverley, 367, whence Robert of Gloucester, ii, lines 11,787–96.

[77] See below, 387–8.

[78] Waverley, 366.

[79] TNA JUST 1/42, m. 8d (image 1228); *CIM*, no. 625.

[80] *CR 1264–8*, 130, 199–200; *CPR 1258–66*, 130, and for the whole subject see Knowles, 'Provision for the families of the Montfortians'.

[81] *CR 1264–8*, 257; *CR 1268–72*, 244–5; *CPR 1258–66*, 504; *CR Supp*, nos. 444, 451.

of Drayton. Philip Basset likewise helped his daughter Alina, widow of Hugh Despenser.[82] Basset also obtained the Despenser lands and later bequeathed the fine for their recovery to Alina, who left it in turn to her son, another Hugh Despenser.[83] So the Despensers ended up owing the fine to themselves, thus escaping unscathed from Hugh the justiciar's long and loyal association with Simon de Montfort. A pity perhaps given all the trouble the family caused in the reign of Edward II.

But against these forces of conciliation, there were others far more powerful. After all, the Montfortians were only being repaid in their own coin, for Montfort himself had frequently threatened his opponents with disinheritance, indeed had threatened Edward himself. Rishanger was also right in thinking the policy was driven forward by magnates thirsting for gain. He names specifically Gilbert de Clare, Roger de Mortimer and John Giffard, all of whom certainly profited, as we have seen.[84] John de Warenne, for his part, had twice to be promised lands worth £100 a year and eventually received estates of Henry de Hastings and Walter de Coleville. Roger of Clifford demanded that the lands promised him should be in a solid block and he eventually swept up the holdings of several midlands rebels worth in total £400.[85] If these loyalists were not satisfied, there was the danger that they would simply keep what they had seized. Rishanger described them as behaving 'like kings' in their usurpation of royal power. In the end, even the opponents of the policy, if such they were, decided they could not be left out. King Richard was promised land worth 2,000 marks a year and received the estates of Adam de Newmarch in part payment. His son Henry of Almain obtained the lands of William Marshal and Gilbert de Gant.[86] Philip Basset too turned in a profit.[87] If Roger Bigod remained aloof or excluded, his brother and heir Hugh Bigod gained a package of nine manors belonging to four separate rebels, this over and beyond what he received from the lands of Baldwin Wake.[88]

All this was hardly surprising for the situation was very different from that in 1217. Then, Louis had refused to abandon his followers. Indeed, he insisted on their retaining their lands as the price for his resigning the throne. The regency government knew any other policy would mean the continuation of the civil war. There was no Louis now. The Montfortians seemed utterly defeated. It would have taken more prescience than the royalists in September 1265 possessed to see that was not the case.

---

[82] *CR 1264–8*, 228; *CPR 1258–66*, 459–60, 497–8. A true insider, Philip wrote to Chancellor Giffard asking for the charter in Alina's favour to be duplicated: 'we much desire it and you can certainly do that without danger': TNA SC 1/8/16.

[83] *CCR 1279–88*, 88; Knowles, 'The resettlement of England', 33–4.

[84] Rishanger, 48–9.

[85] *CPR 1258–66*, 536, 539; *CR Supp*, nos. 390, 410, 438, 452.

[86] *CR 1264–8*, 67, 407; *CR Supp*, no. 436; *CFR 1265–6*, no. 215.

[87] *CR 1264–8*, 439; and see also *RS*, 174, 177; *CChR 1226–57*, 116; *CR 1268–72*, 107.

[88] *CR Supp*, no. 451.

There are just a few signs that Henry himself was a force for moderation, however feeble. His orders making provision for wives and widows stressed he was acting out of 'grace and humanity'.[89] When, at Edward's behest, he urged the Kenilworth garrison to surrender, he spoke of his 'innate benevolence' and his wish to deal with them mercifully rather than judicially. Likewise, in a letter to the men of the Cinque Ports, he promised grace rather than vengeance if they submitted. Edward's own letters gave no hint his father should adopt this conciliatory tone.[90] Rishanger's account of the Winchester parliament has the king's anger sedated by the offerings of churchmen, only then for the running to be made by Clare, Mortimer, Giffard and others thirsting for rewards. In the most detailed account of the sentence, as pronounced by Robert Walerand, those who had adhered to the king ask for the rebels to be disinherited and the king simply 'agrees'.[91]

Henry can also be credited with the settlement reached with Robert de Ferrers, earl of Derby, one a good deal less harsh than Edward probably wanted. According to Wykes, Ferrers was the one prisoner Alina Despenser did not release when she vacated the Tower of London after Evesham. It was not long, however, before he was out and attacking the estates of his Montfortian enemies in Derbyshire.[92] If, however, Ferrers had quarrelled with Montfort, he was even more daggers drawn with Edward, having humiliated him at Gloucester, attacked Chester and seized the Peak. Henry, earlier in 1265, had been equally offended by Ferrers' conduct, but now, early in December 1265, he tried to arrange a settlement.[93] Apart from remitting his own 'rancour and indignation', he promised to 'acquit' Ferrers 'towards Edward' touching all their quarrels and all the trespasses Edward had suffered at Ferrers' hands. In effect this meant Henry had undertaken to preserve Ferrers from Edward's vengeance. A further promise to protect him from disinheritance indicates clearly enough what form that vengeance might have taken. In return for all this, Ferrers gave Henry a golden drinking cup weighing over 7 pounds and decorated with pearls and emeralds. This was just the kind of thing Henry loved and it was received directly into the wardrobe.[94] There was also money. Ferrers agreed to give £1,000, a substantial sum but less than the annual value of his lands, and much less than the penalties later imposed on the disinherited Montfortians. One wonders if Ferrers' marriage to the king's niece Mary de Lusignan was a factor in Henry's leniency. In any case, Ferrers had enjoyed a narrow escape. He was not to learn from it.

[89] Waverley, 366; *CPR 1258–66*, 540–1; Knowles, 'Provision for the families of the Montfortians', 127.

[90] *RL*, ii, 289–90; *CPR 1258–66*, 488–9.

[91] Rishanger, 48–9; St Andrews Northampton, 103.

[92] Wykes, 175; *CIM*, no. 646. For what follows, see Golob, 'The Ferrers earls of Derby', i, 342–6.

[93] *CPR 1258–66*, 518–19.

[94] *CPR 1258–66*, 518, 522; *CFR 1264–5*, no. 68; *CLR 1267–72*, no. 323; Wild, *WA*, 137.

Yet, for all Henry's benevolence to widows and his role in the settlement
with Ferrers, there is no sign that he actually resisted the policy of disinheritance. Having suffered so grievously under the Montfortians, Henry
must surely have felt they deserved punishment, all the more so if they
were indeed agents of the Antichrist. His writs complained bitterly of how
they had waged war to 'our disinheritance and the destruction of our
crown', even as far as taking part in 'battle' against him.[95] What is certain
is that he busily rewarded those closest to him. Edmund, as we have seen,
got the honour of Leicester. Queen Eleanor received lands worth more
than £300 a year, including those of John de Eyville. Equally rewarded
were the familiar group of Henry's foreign relatives and their connections
including Peter of Savoy, William de Valence, Geoffrey de Lusignan,
Matthias Bezill, Elyas de Rabayne and William de Sancta Ermina.[96]
Henry also looked after many lesser figures at court, giving small grants of
land to an assortment of esquires, cooks, saucerers, marshals, doorkeepers
and doctors.[97] Having had so little to give for so long, he must have been
overjoyed at this sudden bonanza.

If, then, Henry has some responsibility for the policy of disinheritance,
a far larger share goes to Edward himself. If anyone had the power to stop
or alter the policy, it was he. Significantly, Pope Clement was worried from
the start about Edward's likely conduct. Writing early in October, he asked
Henry to persuade Edward to show clemency. Nothing is said about
Edward persuading Henry to do the same. It is equally Edward, not
Henry, who is urged to put away 'cruelty', 'savagery' and 'inhumanity'.[98]
It is true that, in securing the surrender of Bristol before Evesham and
Berkhamsted, Wallingford and Dover afterwards, Edward promised to
preserve unharmed the persons and possessions of the garrisons.[99]
At Chester, his rage against the new abbot, whom Montfort had invested,
soon abated. Indeed, he sent him two casks of wine to make up for
those taken and consumed 'during the time of his anger'. Later, in
describing the submission of John de Vescy, Wykes commented on
Edward's generally merciful character. Yet he never claimed that Edward
opposed the policy of disinheritance, although, as an admirer of the
future king (he was writing in his reign) and a critic of the policy, he had
good reason to do so.[100]

In fact, no contemporary historian says that Edward was against what
happened. Glorying in his triumph, he was no more prescient than anyone

[95] Nottingham University Library, Mi D 4681/1, and TNA E 40/15184 (from Nicholas
Vincent's census of Henry III originals); Wild, 'Reasserting medieval kingship', 244. Wild
(p. 243) describes Henry as both 'peaceable and pugnacious'.

[96] RS, 200–1, 248–9, 251–4; CR Supp, nos. 392, 400; CR 1264–8, 506–7.

[97] For examples, see Jacob, Studies, 154–5.

[98] F, i, 463–4.

[99] Jacob, Studies, 407; RL, ii, 291; CR 1264–8, 131.

[100] St Werburgh, 94–6; CPR 1258–66, 638; Wykes, 198.

else. He could easily, he thought, put down any further resistance. The mercy he showed garrisons was simply designed to secure their quick surrender. Those who crossed him could expect the worst. His punishment of the leading Londoners we have already seen. His warnings to the garrison of Kenilworth on 24 August contain the first reference to the penalty of disinheritance. Edward also threatened them, if they did not surrender, with loss of life 'as they deserve'.[101] One is reminded of his demand before the battle of Lewes that the rebels surrender with ropes round the necks ready for hanging. Later, in 1266, according to the Waverley abbey annalist, he wished to hang Henry Pethun, one of the leaders of the Cinque Ports. It was Gilbert de Clare who advised that, left alive, Pethun would be able to secure the surrender of his fellows. Eventually, it was Clare not Edward who intervened to improve the terms offered to the disinherited. At Chester itself, back in August 1265, the castellan, Luke de Tany, despite his immediate submission, was imprisoned and waited till September 1266 for a royal pardon. It was then granted at the instance of Henry of Almain rather than Edward himself.[102]

Edward's centrality to the whole policy is finally suggested by the great gains made by those closest to him. His wife, Eleanor of Castile, amongst other things got Codnor and Chesterfield, principal manors respectively of Richard de Grey and Baldwin Wake.[103] His faithful knight Warin of Bassingbourn gained the lands of Thomas of Astley; another knight, Roger de Mortayn, the lands of Giles de Argentan. Roger of Clifford's haul from the holdings of several midlands rebels we have seen. Roger of Leybourne's package was granted quite specifically for his 'laudable service to Edward' and in return for the lands Edward had promised him.[104] John de Verdun was granted the lands of Ralph Basset of Sapcote, this in breach of an earlier agreement under which Edward had restored Basset to his lands.[105]

There was one other unfortunate feature of the policy of disinheritance, one which added to the grievances of the dispossessed: the resentments of those who felt inadequately rewarded. In October 1266 the king was urged to reward the many who had stood by him and had so far received nothing. Failure to do so might lead to further unrest.[106] Part of the trouble stemmed from the chaos of competing claims. After Evesham, Richard de Tany

---

[101] *RL*, ii, 289–90; *CPR 1258–66*, 488–9.

[102] Waverley, 369; St Werburgh, 94–6; *CPR 1258–66*, 638.

[103] Parsons, *Eleanor of Castile*, 126, 164.

[104] *RS*, 248–9; *CR Supp*, nos. 410, 430–2, 438, 443; *CPR 1258–66*, 464–6, 522. The package included the lands of the Kentish rebels Ralph of Sandwich, Stephen Soudan and Robert de Crevecoeur.

[105] *CR Supp*, no. 388; *CR 1264–8*, 385–6; *CPR 1258–66*, 167, 466; TNA SC 1/8/ 22, the last a letter of 14 October 1265 in which Edward releases Basset from prison, having been satisfied with a 'redemption', and restores him to his lands.

[106] *DBM*, 330–1, cap. 22.

seized Theydon Mount in Essex, the manor of the rebel Robert of Sutton.[107] Tany then went to court in order to secure a grant of the property from the king. It was, as he explained 'a fine manor and lies next to mine at Stapleford'. (The two villages are indeed adjoining.)[108] Loyalist son of a rebel father, he was not without influence.[109] But he was too late. The manor had already been granted away to the judge Robert de Brus, this in compensation for Brus having to resign other property to Robert Walerand. Tany, however, was not to be deterred. He somehow got a charter in his favour drawn up, sealed and recorded on the charter roll, a charter crucially bearing a date (26 October) three days before Brus's. On the strength of this, he ejected Brus from the manor. When the chancellor was later asked how this spurious charter had got through, he explained it was 'at a time when the king was granting out land to a great multitude of knights' and perhaps Tany's charter had been thrown in with the others and been sealed by mistake. This was an extreme case, but it sheds graphic light on the scramble for land and the king's failure to control it.

When he reflected on the policy of disinheritance, Thomas Wykes was scathing. The king and his accomplices, foolishly exalted by the triumph of Evesham, had given away the lands of the rebels to whatsoever petitioners came forward, foreigners as well as native born, without any consideration of merit and to the great damage of the kingdom.[110] This condemnation was absolutely justified. True, to have simply returned the lands to former rebels as in 1217, with no reward at all for loyalists, would have been impossible. But with the support of King Richard and others, the policy of allowing rebels to buy back their lands could surely have been introduced much earlier than it was. Henry's failure in this respect is a stain on his kingship. But really the blame lies with his son.

## THE NATURE OF THE WAR[111]

The war of the disinherited was significantly different from the wars of 1263, 1264 and 1265. In the first place it lasted much longer. Montfort's campaign in 1263 began with the attack on Bishop Aigueblanche on 11 June and was crowned with victory little more than a month later. The campaign of 1264 began with the king marching out of Oxford on 3 April and ended at Lewes on 14 May, so a period of some six weeks. The Evesham campaign started with Edward's escape on 28 May and was over

---

[107] For what follows, see Jacob, *Studies*, 199–201, 377–80; *CIM*, no. 657; *CChR 1257–1300*, 59; *RCWL*, ii, 150; *VCH Essex*, iv, 276–81.

[108] Now Stapleford Tawney after Richard's family.

[109] The king gave Tany possession of the land of his father: *CIM*, no. 706.

[110] Wykes, 183–4.

[111] I owe this section to the detailed analysis of the war in chs. 5 and 6 of Fergus Oakes's doctoral thesis, 'The nature of war and its impact on society during the Barons' War'.

two months and few days later. The war of the disinherited, by contrast, lasted all the way through from September 1265 to July 1267, so only a few months short of two years. The war was also very different from its predecessors in military terms. There were now no great battles. What is called 'the battle of Chesterfield' was no more than an ambush in which the king's men captured a group of rebels staying in the vill. At no time did the disinherited assemble an army to relieve the siege of Kenilworth or confront the royalists in open field. They did not possess London or (after the submission of the Cinque Ports in 1266) any other major town. Apart from Kenilworth they held no castle.

Yet for all these apparent weaknesses, the disinherited had two considerable strengths. The first was Kenilworth. In the end the king was forced to spend much of 1266 laying siege to the castle, the longest siege in English history. There had been castle sieges between 1263 and 1265, notably at Gloucester (on three occasions) and at Rochester, but they had lasted a few days, not many months. The second strength came from the way the rebels, as Robert of Gloucester put it, took 'to the woods and fields', from where they ravaged surrounding areas.[112] There had been attacks on property between 1263 and 1265 but they had hardly the duration and the scale of those between 1265 and 1267. This was partly because the disinherited were not merely punishing their enemies. Deprived of their own estates, they were plundering the goods they needed to carry on the struggle. In default of holding castles and towns, they had also found a base just as impregnable by occupying the Isle of Ely.

In sum, the disinherited, while unable to defeat the king, were quite able to make a mockery of his peace. If they could not achieve in toto their two major objectives – the revocation of the policy of disinheritance and the restoration of the Provisions of Oxford – the policy was eventually modified and at least the legislative side of the Provisions reaffirmed.

## THE MONTFORT CULT

The disinherited relied then on their strong right arms. But they were also inspired by something spiritual, something the king's party found as surprising as it was shocking. This was Simon de Montfort's posthumous cult and his widespread veneration as a saint and martyr. Nothing like it for a layman had ever happened before. The closest parallel was the cult of Becket to whom indeed Montfort was often compared. Clerical writers poured out their grief in passionate poems celebrating the great earl's life and deploring his appalling death.[113] Some religious houses drew up

---

[112] Robert of Gloucester, ii, line 11,885.

[113] For example, *ANPS*, 24–5; Maitland, 'A song on the death of Simon de Montfort'; Rishanger, 139–46 (which is also about the appalling condition of England after Evesham), 109–10, with the final line corrected in Lefferts, 'Two English motets', 223.

special liturgies complete with music to commemorate the anniversary of his death.[114] Stories about his personal life were collected by Franciscan friars and probably spread abroad in sermons. Most public of all, most embarrassing, most dangerous for the king were the miracles.[115] They started almost at once. In October 1266 the legate was asked to ban any talk of them, 'vain and fatuous' as they were. For the beneficiaries, suffering from dropsy, frenzy, loss of speech and loss of limbs (many could not walk without crutches or walk at all), there was nothing vain and fatuous about them at all. In a record made by the monks of Evesham in the 1270s no fewer than 196 miraculous cures were listed.[116]

The centre of the cult was Evesham itself. Indeed, a pilgrimage there was thought to be just as efficacious as one to Canterbury or even Jerusalem. At Evesham pilgrims could visit both the abbey, where Montfort's mutilated body was buried, and the spot on the hill above where he was killed. There indeed a spring with health-giving waters had miraculously appeared.[117] For those unable to make the journey there was another centre in the far north, for, thanks to John de Vescy, Montfort's foot, placed in a silver casket, and likewise with miraculous properties, was preserved at Alnwick priory. The mutilation of Montfort's body had thus spectacularly backfired. The severed limbs, far from showing he was a traitor, showed he was a saint. Indeed, when one of his hands was brought into a church, at the elevation of the host it emerged from the cloth into which it was sown and rose above the heads of the congregation.[118]

Montfort's power could be felt even when far from actual relics. Wherever one was, a prayer to the earl could result in a miraculous cure, sometimes with the additional bonus of his actual appearance in a dream or vision. In one vision, Christ himself appeared and announced 'whatever you seek in honour of my earl will be given to you'.[119] An appeal was usually linked to the ritual of being 'measured to the earl' just as one could be measured to other saints. This involved being measured with a string which then became the wick of a candle burnt in the saint's honour.[120]

[114] Lefferts, 'Two English motets'.

[115] These are discussed in Valente, 'Simon de Montfort'; Burton, 'Politics, propaganda and public opinion', 126–46; Finucane, *Miracles and Pilgrims*, 131–5.

[116] *DBM*, 322–3, cap. 8; Valente, 'Simon de Montfort', 30 n. 35.

[117] For the date of the discovery of what became known as the 'battle well', see Cox, *Battle of Evesham*, 23 and n. 172.

[118] These details about Montfort's members come from the tract about him, the *Opusculum de nobili Simone de Monteforti*, written between 1286 and 1291 as part of the Melrose chronicle. According to the *Opusculum*, another of Montfort's feet was preserved and venerated at Evesham: Melrose, 205 (fos. 67v–69r); Broun and Harrison, *Chronicle of Melrose*, 168–9. I owe much of what has been said here to a talk by Sophie Ambler at an Institute of Historical Research seminar in November 2021.

[119] 'Miracula', 83.

[120] Maddicott, 'Follower, leader, pilgrim, saint', 648.

The truth of a miracle was frequently vouched for by a village, parish or religious house. Although, in Evesham's own record, many of those cured were local to Evesham, over half came from forty miles away and a quarter from over a hundred miles. Only half a dozen counties, outside Durham, Cumberland and Westmorland, had no one cured at all.[121] After the miracle, it was usual to bring the candle (one of them measured the beneficiary's girth as well as height) to Evesham for burning by the body of the saint. Brought too were waxen images of the healed part – of a leg, arm, head, sometimes even of whole bodies. So from across England the pilgrims came, with their candles, images and supporters, seeking health from the earl or thanking him for the health he had already given.[122] They thus purified and sanctified the place of the great slaughter. The battle designed to kill off Montfort once and for all had only served to bring him back to life. The pilgrims and witnesses to the miracles were drawn from across English society. Nuns and monks, countesses and knights, tailors and millers, citizens of London and village constables all testified to Montfort's powers. A wife and a son from Brill in Buckinghamshire had their cures testified to by the whole village.[123] Robert de Vere, earl of Oxford, came to Evesham with twenty-five horses. Letitia Lamede, swollen with dropsy, came in a wheelbarrow, pushed from London by her heroic husband.[124] The knight Simon of Pattishall, one of the disinherited, restored to speech after being measured to the earl, came likewise with his offering. According to one calculation, 10 per cent of those featuring in the miracles were nobles, 25 per cent clergy and 5 per cent artisans, while most of the rest were probably peasants.[125] Around eighty of the miracles featured women as witnesses or beneficiaries. The breadth of Montfort's appeal across region, class and gender is very apparent.

Central to the cult was Montfort's reputation for personal piety – his hair shirt, his modest clothes, his praying through the night. One eulogist compared him at length to the apostle Simon Peter.[126] But equally important was the righteousness of his cause. Just as Becket had died for the rights of the church, so Simon had died for those of the kingdom. He was the 'protector of the people of England', 'the sustainer of the people of the land'.[127] The Provisions of Oxford were not forgotten, as we will see. The disinherited constantly demanded their reinstatement.[128]

---

[121] Valente, 'Simon de Montfort', 32–4; Maddicott, 'Follower, leader, pilgrim, saint', 647. The midlands and East Anglia were especially strongly represented.

[122] This sentence is but a pallid echo of Maddicott's evocative picture of the pilgrims: 'Follower, leader, pilgrim, saint', 649.

[123] A village which had brought its complaints before the reforming eyre of 1258 (see above, 130).

[124] Maddicott, 'Follower, leader, pilgrim, saint', 647, 652–3.

[125] Valente, 'Simon de Montfort', 30, 35.

[126] Melrose, 205–11 (fos. 68–70), from the *Opusculum de nobili Simone de Monteforti.*

[127] *ANPS*, 30, 33; 'Miracula', 109.

[128] Graham, 'Letters of Cardinal Ottoboni', 104; Rishanger, 60, 64.

If the king and his party found the cult of Montfort infuriating, for the disinherited it was consoling and inspiring. As Rishanger said, Christ had quickly turned sorrow to joy and shown in frequent miracles 'the insurmountable constancy of the unconquered man'. 'All the faithful in Christ' thus gained a certain hope that 'through the goodness of him who casts down the proud and exalts the meek', they would be rescued from 'the oppression of their malignant enemies'.[129] And some of the proud were indeed cast down. A man who spoke against Montfort was struck dumb, a monk of Alnwick who called him a traitor lost his sight and then his life, and the wretch who had cut off Montfort's testicles was drowned in the river Tay.[130] 'Be for us our intercessor with God, you who as our defender were so eminent in the world' ran one motet composed in Montfort's honour.[131] Surely he would not let his followers down.

## BYCARRS DYKE: THE ATTEMPTED SETTLEMENT, DECEMBER 1265, JANUARY 1266

The policy of disinheritance soon meant that parts of England descended into anarchy. At Michaelmas 1265 sixteen sheriffs failed to turn up, in person or through deputies, at the start of the exchequer session. The total revenue coming in from the counties and boroughs was a tiny £242.[132] At Kenilworth, as the Evesham chronicle put it, Simon de Montfort junior gathered a 'great army' from the followers of those slain, from those who had escaped and from those embittered by the death of their kinsmen. He 'subjugated the whole county of Warwickshire, appointing bailiffs as if he was the king of that county, and sending them now here and now there through the neighbourhood to prey upon the villages and manors of their adversaries'.[133] How intolerable in the very heart of the kingdom. In November, Henry began preparations for a siege by ordering his tenants-in-chief with all their forces to assemble at Northampton on 13 December. Masons with picks and axes were to be there too. On 10 December, however, Henry was still at Windsor and explaining he could not make the rendezvous 'without harm to our body', so was sending John de Balliol instead.[134] Hardly very inspiring. Henry was probably reluctant to go at

---

[129] Rishanger, 48–9.

[130] Valente, 'Simon de Montfort', 40; 'Miracula', 80, 89; Melrose, 212–13 (fo. 72), from the *Opusculum de nobili Simone de Monteforti*; Maddicott, *Simon de Montfort*, 346.

[131] Lefferts, 'Two English motets', 223.

[132] Cassidy, 'Adventus vicecomitum', 617; Jobson, 'Royal government', 184; Collingwood, 'Royal Finance', 264.

[133] Evesham, 344. The sheriff of Worcestershire said he could bring no revenue to the exchequer for fear of the rebels in the castle: Jobson, 'Royal government', 188.

[134] *CR 1264–8*, 150; *F*, i, 467 (*CPR 1258–66*, 520).

all. He must have known he would not be back at Westminster for the feast of Edward the Confessor on 5 January.

Of course, it was Edward who counted and in the event a large army was assembled including the count of St Pol from abroad and the knights of St Albans abbey with twenty horses. Simon junior, however, had not waited for the siege. The last thing he wanted was to be holed up in the castle and unable to influence events outside. He thus left Kenilworth and hurried to the Isle of Axholme, the area of forest, marshland and isolated villages in north Lincolnshire bounded by the rivers Trent, Don and Idle. There he was joined by John de Eyville and Baldwin Wake. Wake, captured at Kenilworth just before Evesham, had escaped from John Giffard's easy-going captivity at Brimpsfield. Eyville, a veritable '*miles strenuus*', had missed Evesham and been mainly active in the north.[135] He was the head of a major knightly family, tenants of the Mowbrays, with manors in Yorkshire, Nottinghamshire and Lincolnshire, including Adlingfleet in the isle of Axholme itself. What had turned Eyville into a rebel is unclear. He was no '*jeune*', having been active since the late 1240s. He was not out of favour for in 1257 the king had made him chief justice of the forest north of Trent. He was in debt to the Jews but his interests might have been served as well by loyalty as rebellion. As it was, Eyville was dismissed as keeper of the northern forests when Henry recovered power in 1261 and reappointed on Montfort's return in 1263. Throughout the 1261–5 period Eyville wielded power in Yorkshire, challenging the king's sheriffs and working as a Montfortian 'keeper of the peace'. With his lands given away to the queen, with a following of seven knights and nine esquires, he was now to act on a wider stage.[136]

Faced with this new threat, Edward moved at once. Leaving his father at Northampton, he advanced on Axholme with a substantial force including Henry of Almain. He blockaded the isle and constructed wooden bridges to penetrate within it. Simon junior had miscalculated. Instead of being secure he was trapped. So, as the king prepared to celebrate Christmas at Northampton with generous gifts of oak trees to the Dominican friars, Simon and 'his company' came to terms.[137] By an agreement reached on Christmas Day itself at Bycarrs Dyke, an ancient waterway (mentioned in Domesday Book) on the southern fringe of the Isle, they submitted themselves to the will and award of the king. This was to be pronounced between 6 and 13 January and Henry was to be counselled by Edward and those Edward wished to bring with him.[138] The only qualification was that the

---

[135] For what follows, see de Ville, 'John Deyville'.

[136] *CPR 1258–66*, 536; *RS*, 248; *CIM*, nos. 939–40. Eyville was named as one of Richard de Clare's 'friends and allies' in 1259, but he did not follow a particularly Clare path thereafter.

[137] Wykes, 181; *CR 1264–8*, 159–60.

[138] The text survives as a copy in Clairambault 1188, fo.26. The legate was involved and brother Oliver de Eyncurt swore to the agreement on his behalf.

award was to leave Simon and his company with their lives, limbs and liberty. As a guarantee they would accept the 'dictum' and indeed turn up before the king, six knights were given as hostages.[139]

On the face of it, only the last extremity could have brought Simon and his company to a deal as bad as this. But immediate appearances may be deceptive. The sparing of life, limb and liberty was clearly a bottom line. While it left the Montfortians open to disinheritance, the implication was that they would do better. The Dunstable and Winchester annalists, indeed, thought the Montfortians were to retain their lands and inheritances.[140] Edward, one may suspect, promised as much, and could remind Simon junior of how he had saved his life at Northampton. The situation also seemed very different from back in September when the sentence of disinheritance had been pronounced. By this time Henry and Edward had received passionate letters from the pope urging clemency. Henry (and this must have gone home) was reminded of how Christ on the cross had sought pardon for his crucifiers. Both Henry and Edward were told how counterproductive vengeance would be: '*clementia firmat imperium*' should be the watchword. The reverse would only stir up fresh discord and increase rather than reduce the number of enemies, just as cutting the branches of a tree created new growth.[141] And, of course, events had shown how right the pope was. His representative in England, the legate Ottobuono, was singing loudly from the same hymn sheet and had travelled with Henry and the queen to Northampton. Writing about those in Kenilworth, he too reminded Henry of Christ on the cross and declared that nothing illuminated a prince more (apart from a firm faith) than the mixing of justice with mercy.[142]

We do not know for certain the councillors Edward intended to bring with him to his father's award, but the legate, King Richard and Philip Basset are mentioned by the chroniclers as intended arbitrators.[143] If so, this was an indication of a conciliatory approach. According to Rishanger, Richard had not forgotten how Simon junior had saved his life when the Kenilworth garrison wished to kill him. He now worked with the legate to bring the parties 'amicably' together in a peace. Indeed, the two men asked Henry to delay his award so they had more time to act.[144]

At first everything seemed to go well. Simon and his company arrived at Northampton on 12 January under Edward's safe conduct, and reaffirmed the undertakings made at Bycarrs Dyke. Henry was now given till 21 January to pronounce his award, with Simon pledging he would then

---

[139] *CR Supp*, no. 438.

[140] Dunstable, 240; Winchester/Worcester, 456; see also Waverley, 368.

[141] *F*, i, 463–4.

[142] Graham, 'Letters of Cardinal Ottoboni', 103.

[143] Wykes, 181; Rishanger, 50.

[144] The role of Richard and the legate is set out in the confirmation of the 25 December agreement made on 12 January, after Simon junior's arrival at Northampton: Clairambault 1188, fo.28 (a copy).

go to Kenilworth and try to secure the castle's surrender.[145] What happened next has to be pieced together mostly from chronicle sources, the most detailed being Rishanger, who was writing much later, but, given the St Albans contingent at Northampton, was perhaps well informed about events. According to his story, with King Richard interceding, Henry gave Simon the kiss of peace. If so, this must have been a moment of great emotion, an apparent reconciliation across Evesham's bloody divide. The ceremony was preceded by the legate absolving Simon and his company from their sentences of excommunication.

The hard question, however, was what was to happen to the inheritances, now given away to the king's supporters, those of Simon himself to Edmund, the king's son. Rishanger actually believed that Simon would have obtained 'the fullness of the king's grace' had 'the savagery' of Gilbert de Clare and the marchers not prevented it. That Simon expected a substantial act of grace is suggested by his agreement to surrender Kenilworth. But in the event little grace was forthcoming. Under the terms of the award, Simon was to surrender Kenilworth and leave the kingdom until peace was secured and the magnates 'by common consent' allowed him back. Abroad, he was to do nothing to the kingdom's detriment. All he was to receive in return was a money payment from the king – either, depending on accounts, 500 marks a year from the exchequer or £500 a year from the lands of the earldom of Leicester.[146] The settlement was therefore harsh, amounting to exile and virtual disinheritance. Yet, in Rishanger's account, Simon accepted it and indeed went to Kenilworth under safe conduct to persuade the garrison to surrender. Now a virtual prisoner, perhaps he had little choice.[147]

Whether Edward had been dishonest in his promises or had simply changed his mind seems impossible to say. In the end, it is difficult to see there was much alternative to what happened. A settlement leaving Simon in the country with a landed estate would always have been problematic. It might reconcile him to the regime. It might, on the other hand, provide him with resources to plot revenge. Could Simon ever forget or forgive the murder of his father and brother and the outrageous dishonouring of his father's body. He might be a danger abroad. He would be a far greater one in England. Rishanger has Clare and the marchers insisting on young Simon's proscription, realizing he would pursue them 'with inexorable hatred' for the death of his father. That got to the heart of the matter.

The king's award had only dealt with Simon junior. When it came to his followers in the Isle, the matter was postponed till Easter. Remarkably,

---

[145] Clairambault 1188, fo.28 (a copy) and fo.27 where there is, as an original, Simon junior's half of an indenture (made on 15 January) recording the agreement. Edward's safe conduct was issued on 26 December at Misterton: BN Clairambault 1188, fo. 26d.

[146] Waverley, 368; Rishanger, 51; Wykes, 182.

[147] Waverley, 368, which also speaks of Simon being deceived.

Eyville, Wake, Hugh de Neville and others accepted this. Despite the treatment of Simon junior, these men must have thought the policy of disinheritance would be modified in their favour. In one case, that of Hugh de Neville, a modification did indeed take place. In June 1266, by a decision of the king, acting 'in the name of father, son and Holy Ghost' under the terms agreed at Bycarrs Dyke, Neville recovered land to the annual value of 400 marks, while leaving Robert Walerand in possession of his castle and manor of Stoke Curcy in Somerset. Walerand himself was far from pleased and extracted a promise of compensation for the 400 marks of revenue he had lost.[148]

### EARLY 1266: DISORDER THROUGH THE COUNTRY

The king's success in dealing with Simon and his company in the Isle weakened the resolve of some of the rebels. Between January 1266 and the end of March around eighty were given safe conducts to come to court. They usually undertook to stand trial if any wanted to proceed against them, but the implication was that they would now reach some kind of settlement with the king. Indeed, in the same period Henry remitted his rancour to around thirty individuals, including Giles de Argentan, John fitzJohn and Thomas de Cantilupe. Some of those regaining the king's grace were exempted from the threat of disinheritance. Others still faced the prospect, although they could keep any lands they subsequently acquired.[149] Probably all hoped to reach a settlement whereby they retrieved some of their lands from the current holders. Henry indeed was ratifying agreements along those lines, one of them between Andrew, son of Thomas of Astley, and Warin of Bassingbourn.[150] Recovery of the king's goodwill, however, did not come cheap. Between August 1265 and March 1268 over £3,700 was paid into the wardrobe from fines to obtain it.[151]

For all these hopeful signs, there was no peace; indeed, in some ways the situation went from bad to worse. Despite Simon junior's intervention, if such it was, the Kenilworth garrison did not surrender. They were alarmed by the treatment of their 'captain' and refused to resign the castle to anyone save Eleanor de Montfort herself.[152] After this rebuff, Henry and Edward shied away from an immediate siege. It was midwinter and the army at Northampton had been out long enough. Edward, anyway, wanted to deal with the Cinque Ports. Henry just wanted to get back to Westminster. He arrived there on or shortly before 26 January, travelling via Dunstable, St Albans and Waltham. The Kenilworth garrison, under

---

[148] *CPR 1258–66*, 577, 608–10, 654, 668; *CR Supp*, no. 437; *RS*, 249.
[149] For example, *CPR 1258–66*, 559.
[150] *CPR 1258–66*, 560, 615–16, 656–7, 670; *RS*, 177–8.
[151] Wild, *WA*, 131, 134.
[152] Rishanger, 51; Waverley, 369–70.

John de la Ware (Montfort's castellan at Bristol), was thus free to pillage the surrounding area and assemble stores against any future siege. They were also strengthened by the arrival of Henry de Hastings. Captured at Evesham, amidst the slaughter of his knights, he had now escaped from the prison of Thomas de Clare. It was Hastings who was held responsible when, early in March, in an act of contempt and defiance, the garrison cut off the hand of a royal messenger and then sent him thus mutilated back to the king.[153]

The garrison's determination was increased by Simon junior's escape to France, for that raised the prospect of him returning to England with an army. In what seems a clear breach of the award, Simon had not been allowed to depart the kingdom. Instead, he had been taken back to London and installed in Edward's 'court' at the Old Temple. There, he began to fear he would be sentenced to perpetual imprisonment. Just as Montfort had seen that Edward could never really be released, Edward had seen the same was true of Simon junior. On the night of 10 February, therefore, with his guards asleep, Simon slipped out of the Temple and escaped downriver, going first to Winchelsea and then on to France. Two months later he was joined there by Guy de Montfort, who had escaped from Dover.

Not surprisingly, in these circumstances, only Hugh de Neville of Simon's company seems to have made use of the terms agreed at Bycarrs Dyke. The fact that he failed to recover all his lands cannot have encouraged his colleagues. Both Baldwin Wake and John de Eyville cut loose and began to ravage the estates of their enemies. At some point they were joined with huge lack of foresight, given his narrow escape from disinheritance, by Robert de Ferrers, earl of Derby. Henry must have felt his troubles would never end. Over Christmas 1265 he worried about malefactors with horses and arms despoiling property and killing people in Middlesex, Hertfordshire and Buckinghamshire. A few days later, he learnt of disturbing rumours swirling through Kent and the West Country: Edward, it was said, had been fatally wounded; new quarrels had arisen between him and Gilbert de Clare; the lands of Roger Bigod had been given away to a foreigner, some said the count of St Pol. Henry ordered the sheriffs to arrest those spreading such stories, all the more dangerous since, so Henry opined, all the previous disturbances in the kingdom had been caused by false suggestions and pernicious preaching. The war, like a forest fire, seemed to be starting all over again. In Hampshire, the knight Adam Gurdun (whose lands had been given to Walerand's nephew Alan Plugenet) 'infested' the pass of Alton and blocked the road between Winchester and Farnham.[154] In Essex the sheriff was unable, from the end of March, to collect revenue and asked

---

[153] CR 1264–8, 240–1; DBM, 328–9, cap. 17; and CIM, nos. 610, 613, 632, 716, 718, 772, 806, 816, 833, 843, 846, 885–6, 895, 928–9, which offers a good panorama of his lands.

[154] Summerson, 'Adam Gurdun'; CR Supp, no. 322; Trevet, 269.

to be relieved. He had, he explained, taken the job at Michaelmas 1265 in a time of peace not thinking there would be another war. Now the situation was so changed, with malefactors roaming everywhere, he could not perform his office.[155] Further north, Baldwin Wake and John de Eyville sacked Lincoln, killing according to one story 160 people including women and children. Naturally the Jews were amongst the victims.[156] When the 1266 Easter exchequer opened, ten sheriffs did not attend at all and only £480 was handed in from the counties and boroughs.[157]

## HENRY AT WESTMINSTER: JANUARY–APRIL 1266

Having arrived back at Westminster on 26 January, Henry stayed there until 6 April. During this period, with Queen Eleanor constantly by his side, he lived in state. A surviving roll shows the daily costs of the household's food, drink, alms and stables averaging some £23 a day, the highest sum recorded for any appreciable length of time in the whole of the reign. By contrast, the overall average for the whole period from August 1265 to March 1268 was only £14.[158] Clearly hospitality was being dispensed on a large scale. The royal couple had also resumed their accustomed alms giving, for every day they fed 150 paupers. On Maundy Thursday they also clothed and shod them. Doubtless, before the paupers put on their new shoes, Henry washed their feet in the great silver bowl kept for that purpose in the wardrobe. Next day, Good Friday (26 March), there was a distribution of bread to thousands of paupers, for the pantry's expenditure of £18 3s was enough to supply over 8,500 half penny loaves, 17,000 farthing ones. And then on Easter Day itself the great feast cost around £150 while candles weighing 358 pounds were burnt, 278 of the pounds in the chapel and almonry.[159] (On ordinary days the wax consumed was 40 or 50 pounds.) It was a pity more sheriffs had not turned up, and turned up with money, to join in the festivities.

Henry was also hurrying on his works at Westminster – the paintings in his chamber, the shrine of the Confessor and the fabric of the Abbey. In March the exchequer was told to find 1,000 marks for the Westminster works. With the Abbey, the need was for timber and lead for the roofs, so evidently the new choir was up and standing. To help, Roger of Leybourne made a gift of forty oaks from his own woods. Meanwhile, Henry did not forget his buildings elsewhere and the impact they might make. In

---

[155] *CR 1264–8*, 265; *CR 1268–72*, 72, 176–7; TNA E 159/40, m. 11 (image 31). The sheriff was Richard of Southchurch.

[156] *CIM*, no. 313; Langtoft, ii, 150–1 (a reference I owe to Oakes, 'The nature of war', 185); Waverley, 370; *CPR 1258–66*, 617; *CPR 1266–72*, 95.

[157] *CPR 1258–66*, 663–4; Cassidy, 'Adventus vicecomitum', 617; Ridgeway, 'Dorset in the period of baronial reform and rebellion', 40.

[158] TNA E 101/667/50; Carpenter, 'Household rolls', 34–5.

[159] TNA E 101/667/50, m. 2.

February he ordered the doors and windows of his hall and chamber in Winchester castle to be adorned with the royal arms.[160] Nor did he forget all those religious institutions that needed timber for their own building. In this year he made gifts from the royal forests to, amongst others, the Dominicans in London, Yarm and Oxford, the Franciscans in Oxford, the penitential brethren of Christ in London and Bristol, the prioresses of Ankerwik and Catesby, and the hospitals at Oxford, Warwick and Ospring.

Henry thus sought to display his kingship in a cloud of majesty and piety. Perhaps the remaining rebels would now bow down and seek his forgiveness. There were certainly individuals who believed in the king's peace or coming peace. During this time at Westminster, around 130 people came to court to purchase writs furthering common-law legal actions. They came, moreover, from most of the counties of England, even from such centres of unrest as Warwickshire, Derbyshire, Essex and Hampshire.[161]

## THE CINQUE PORTS, ADAM GURDUN AND THE BATTLE OF CHESTERFIELD, MAY 1266

Unfortunately, while Henry's majesty burnt bright amidst the splendour of Westminster, elsewhere there was still turmoil as the settlement of Bycarrs Dyke collapsed and the 'pirates' of the Cinque Ports preyed on shipping in the Channel and further afield.[162] To put down the growing rebellion, Henry depended on the men of action, on Edward himself and the ubiquitous Roger of Leybourne, steward of the royal household, sheriff of Kent and warden of the Cinque Ports.[163] In mid-January, with a force of 80 horsemen, Leybourne attacked and took Sandwich with help from the men of Yarmouth and the eastern ports. In March, with nearly 600 archers briefly in his pay, he joined up with Edward and together they attacked Winchelsea. Some of the portsmen were killed, others drowned and the ringleader, Henry Pethun, was captured. The men of the Cinque Ports were then admitted to the king's peace, forgiven their trespasses and allowed to retain all their lands and liberties. In return they gave absolutely nothing, some contrast to the treatment of London, now labouring under its 20,000-mark fine. The treatment was prudential more than merciful: mercy to these ruthless men? The victory at Winchelsea had been far from total and the portsmen could still cause lots of trouble if not offered generous terms.[164]

---

[160] *CLR 1260–7*, 199, 203, 205–6, 223, 227, 230, 251, 253; *CR 1264–8*, 193.

[161] The Derbyshire and Hampshire fines were just after Henry left Westminster for Windsor.

[162] Jobson, 'The maritime theatre', 234. Back in October 1265 the men of the Cinque Ports had also sacked Portsmouth.

[163] For Leybourne and what follows, see Lewis, 'Roger Leyburn'.

[164] Waverley, 369; *CPR 1258–66*, 573–4, 579, 588, 653, 659, 661.

In May, Leybourne, with 500 archers and 32 knights in pay, took the fight to the insurgents in Essex.[165] Edward meanwhile drove the rebels out of Lincoln and forced the citizens to offer £1,000 for the king's goodwill.[166] He then headed south to Hampshire and ambushed Adam Gurdun in his forest lair. Their single combat became the stuff of legend. According to the stories, Edward, refusing help from his men, dealt mighty blows and forced Gurdun to surrender. Gurdun's companions were then hanged around on trees, but Gurdun himself had his wounds tended and was sent to the queen at Guildford to be looked after more 'like a guest than a prisoner'. Whatever the truth here (and other accounts have Gurdun loaded with heavy fetters), stories of this kind were never spread about Henry III![167]

There was one other victory. The task of subduing Baldwin Wake, John de Eyville and their company had been given to Henry of Almain, John de Balliol and Edward's knight Warin of Basingbourn. On the evening of 15 May they launched a surprise attack on Wake's manor of Chesterfield, the rebel base. John de Eyville, unhorsing a knight with a blow from his lance, managed to escape. Henry de Hastings, out hunting, was able to get back to Kenilworth. But Wake, although also hunting, soon came in and submitted. His rebellion was over. So was that of the great troublemaker Robert de Ferrers, earl of Derby. He too had been in Chesterfield, but, tortured by gout, was being let blood at the time of the attack. He was found hiding under a sack of wool and taken off to captivity at Windsor. Under the agreement of December 1266 all his estates were now forfeit to the crown.[168]

While the men of war acted, Henry was trying to win over hearts and minds. In May he sent round a proclamation to be read throughout the counties.[169] The theme was familiar. From the time of his accession he had, he said, laboured with all his heart and strength for the peace and tranquillity of his subjects. He was appalled that traducers of his 'majesty' were now saying that, instigated by certain councillors, he had disinherited men without the judgement of his court. In fact, to everyone in his kingdom, he was and wished always to be the 'debtor in justice' (meaning subject to and ruling in accordance with the law).[170] Anyone who had

[165] Lewis, 'Roger Leyburn', 203–4.

[166] Waverley, 370; CPR 1258–66, 594; CFR 1266–7, no. 626.

[167] Wykes, 189–90; Dunstable, 241; Westminster, Flores, 10; Trevet, 269; Prestwich, Edward I, 56; Morris, A Great and Terrible King, 76; Howell, Eleanor of Provence, 235.

[168] Wykes, 188–9; Dunstable, 41; Robert of Gloucester, ii, 11848–59; London, 63; FitzThedmar, 86–7 (Stone, FitzThedmar, no. 875); Hailes, 72; CPR 1258–66, 595, 610; Golob, 'The Ferrers earls of Derby', i, 347–52.

[169] CR 1264–8, 242–3. The enrolled copy is to the sheriff of Yorkshire, but it almost certainly went to other counties.

[170] See Wild, 'Reasserting medieval kingship', 247, citing Kantorowicz, The King's Two Bodies, 163–4.

suffered injury should now come to court and receive justice according to the law and custom of the realm. Henry did not quite say that the policy of disinheritance would be modified but he did admit some people might have been disinherited unjustly. Henry was also under pressure from Louis IX to make peace. In May he assured Louis (with I believe complete sincerity) that with peace secure he planned to fulfil his vow to go on crusade.[171]

## THE SIEGE OF KENILWORTH

But if there was to be peace, Kenilworth had to surrender, and for that more than proclamations were necessary. Having left the queen at Windsor and mustered a large army, Henry finally arrived outside the castle on 25 June. One person was not with him, namely Hugh Bigod. He had died the previous month. Montfort's extremism had transformed Hugh from the conscientious justiciar and committed reformer of 1258 to a loyal minister of the king. He had fought for Henry at Lewes and gone along with the policy of disinheritance. Others had made the same journey. Henry, sensible of Hugh's 'long and laudable service', made major concessions to his son the future earl of Norfolk.[172]

The mutilation of his messenger had given Henry a deeply personal reason for prosecuting the siege and punishing the garrison. In summoning the army he had told everyone of this 'atrocious injury to royal majesty'.[173] He certainly intended to look majestic for he had made a special 'gambeson', a type of padded jacket which offered less protection than armour but gave more freedom of movement. In Henry's case, it was much more than a utilitarian military tunic, for it was fringed with gold brocade, like many of his vestments, and decorated with dags, pointed pieces of cloth in different colours sewn onto the hems and shoulders.[174]

Having arrived, Henry took an oath that he would not leave Kenilworth until the castle was taken.[175] He thus sought to keep himself up to the mark (as so often with his oaths) and assure the army of his determination. He had a long time to wait. Against the whole might of the royal army, the siege lasted 172 days, from summer, through autumn to winter, and did not end till 14 December. For a moment Henry may have wavered. Was it with the intention of attending himself that he ordered twenty deer to be sent to Westminster for the feast of the Confessor on 13 October? But in the end he missed the feast and stuck it out to the end. There could be no more powerful indication of how vital victory was. Quite apart from his

---

[171] *RL*, ii, 304–5.
[172] *CR 1264–8*, 192, 209.
[173] *CR 1264–8*, 240–1.
[174] Wild, *WA*, 136; Wild, 'Siege of Kenilworth castle', 20.
[175] For a detailed account of the siege, see Wild, 'Siege of Kenilworth castle'.

personal animus against the garrison, Henry, as he explained when
summoning the army, knew that 'the peace and security' of the kingdom
depended on eradicating the 'rabies' of Kenilworth.[176]

Commanded by John de la Ware and Henry de Hastings, the garrison
of Kenilworth was very large: some 1,700 armed men, 120 women and
numerous servants, according to the Dunstable annalist. Spiritual support
came from Master Peter of Radnor, canon and penitentiary of Hereford
cathedral, 'the most valiant clerk in all England' according to Robert of
Gloucester.[177] The walls could therefore be manned at all points and large
posses sent on attacks out of the castle without endangering its defence. Of
course, that meant there were many mouths to feed, but then the garrison
had enjoyed plenty of time to stuff the castle full of provisions. At the heart
of the castle was the great square keep surrounded by a curtain wall. Then
there was another curtain wall defending the large bailey. And beyond that,
the feature which made Kenilworth unique, was the great lake which
rendered the castle impossible to attack from the south and west. To
approach the main gateway one had to penetrate a barbican, itself
protected by a walled bailey, and then run the gauntlet of a long causeway
with the lake on one side and a great pool of water on the other. King John
had spent over £1,000 on the castle's fabric. Montfort, according to the
Pershore *Flores*, had strengthened it with 'remarkable building and repair'.
He had also installed machines hitherto unseen in England for its defence.[178]
Dover perhaps aside, it was the most formidable castle in the kingdom.

According to the Dunstable annalist, Henry's army was divided into
four divisions commanded by Henry himself, Edward, Edmund and
Roger de Mortimer. Presumably the divisions were stationed opposite the
bailey leading to the causeway and then to the east and north of the castle
where the walls and a second gateway were only protected by a moat. The
mangonels and petraries of the king bombarded the castle night and day.
(Some of the great stone balls now decorate the castle's grounds.)
Edmund's division erected a wooden tower housing 200 crossbowmen and
got it up close to the walls. Another tower crammed with archers was
named 'the bear' because of its size. The army was supported by a vast
logistical effort: 60,000 crossbow bolts were ordered and some 2,000
wooden hurdles, the latter presumably to act as screens.[179]

For four weeks of the siege (between 18 July and 19 August) we have a
further section of the king's household roll.[180] This places the king 'outside
Kenilworth' and omits the customary daily entries for the costs of the

---

[176] *CR 1264–8*, 213, 240–1.
[177] Robert of Gloucester, ii, lines 11,887–95; *CPR 1258–66*, 324, 441; Barrow, *EEA
Hereford*, 194. Peter was archdeacon of Shrewsbury.
[178] Pershore, *Flores*, 489.
[179] The logistics of the siege are discussed in Oakes, 'The nature of war', 130–9.
[180] TNA E 101/667/50, m. 4.

chamber and the hall. The daily consumption of wax is roughly half what it had been at Westminster earlier in the year. All this suggests Henry and the household were living in tents outside the castle rather than in the greater comfort of the nearby priory. Henry needed to show he was with his troops. The daily costs of the household's food and drink were also smaller than at Westminster, but this was partly due to the absence of the queen, on the one hand, and the supplies delivered by sheriffs and other officials, on the other. The king's hospitality, contrasting with the increasing dearth within the castle, must have been important for the morale of his troops. The roll shows that, in the four and a half weeks it records, deliveries from sheriffs and others included 62 oxen, 176 muttons, 55 bacons, 94 lampreys, 20,055 herrings and 1,350 gallons of ale, all this over and above the amounts (costed but not described) procured by the food and drink departments themselves. On Tuesday 27 July, a not untypical day, 40 gallons of ale, 5 oxen, 10 muttons, 4 bacons and 1 lamprey (perhaps for the king himself) were served up from these outside supplies. The herrings, usually 2,000 to 3,000 a time, were consumed on Fridays and other fast days.

Throughout this period, Henry maintained his custom of feeding each day 100 paupers. On Sunday 15 August he celebrated the feast of the Virgin's Assumption in style. The cost to the departments (for once with no help from outside supplies apart from 200 gallons of ale from the bailiffs of Stratford) was £36 against a more usual £8 to £10. Had Henry's oblation roll survived, it would doubtless have shown him celebrating numerous masses of the Virgin and the Confessor, just as he had in the early part of 1265. He was praying very hard for victory.

During the siege Henry had one particular reason to rejoice. At Windsor on 14 July, Edward's wife, Eleanor of Castile, gave birth to a son. The Londoners showed their loyalty in parades and pageants and Henry promised £20 a year in land to the lucky messenger who brought the 'delightful' news.[181] The future of the dynasty seemed secure. The son was named John, less perhaps after King John than after John of Brittany, Edward's brother-in-law and favoured friend who was at this time in England. But if the news penetrated the castle, the garrison was bound to think of King John. It was not much encouragement to surrender.

As it was, neither the continuous bombardment nor the loss of their captain, John de la Ware (killed by a chance arrow), dulled the garrison's spirit or weakened its resolve.[182] It was buoyed up by the hope that Simon junior would soon be invading from abroad, something Henry himself was worried about.[183] Meanwhile, Montfort's machines maintained their own bombardment and destroyed the towers pushed up

---

[181] FitzThedmar, 87 (Stone, FitzThedmar, no. 879); *CR 1264–8*, 203; *CPR 1258–66*, 617.

[182] Hailes, 73–4, which says it was John de la Ware junior who was killed. For John senior, see *CPR 1258–66*, 649.

[183] *CPR 1258–66*, 664–5.

close to the walls. Henry granted a pension to sustain the widow and children of one of his slain crossbowmen.[184] Given the danger of attacks from the castle, Henry must sometimes have swapped his gambeson for his armour. In one raid the king's clerk and later bishop of Durham Anthony Bek was captured.[185] Since the main gate of the castle, in a wonderful show of bravado, was kept open night and day, one never knew when an attack might be coming. By contrast, the king's army (as far as is known) mounted no charge along the death trap of the causeway. An attempt to cross the lake in barges brought from Chester came to nothing. The Peterborough chronicler observed that, while the defenders frequently came out to attack the king, they 'never allowed the king with all his power and with all his warlike machines to acquire one foot of space within their bounds'.[186] The garrison flew Simon junior's banner from the keep and decorated the curtain walls with flags and pennants. It could be brutal, hanging from the walls a group, wishing to surrender, who had temporarily seized the keep. It could also be chivalrous. When a captured knight died of his wounds, his body was placed on a bier surrounded with candles and conducted out of the castle to his friends.

Failing any assault on the castle, the essential tactic became to starve it into surrender, but even by the autumn there seemed no immediate prospect of that happening. Meanwhile, the disinherited were causing mayhem in other parts of the country. John de Eyville with numerous followers had occupied the Isle of Ely and was plundering the surrounding area.

## OTTOBUONO'S INTERVENTION

This was the background to the efforts, led by Ottobuono, to reach a negotiated settlement. After the failure of the Bycarrs Dyke agreement, he was near to despair. He was placed, he said, amidst 'a people without law, without sense, a flock wandering without a leader, dispersed as though its pastors had been struck by an exterminating angel'.[187] At one point the pope thought he was close to giving up, something Ottobuono fiercely denied: 'Desertion is for the mercenary not the pastor'. When the king left London for Kenilworth, Ottobuono had remained behind in the Tower with the aim of keeping order in the city. (At the same time the bench and exchequer were installed at St Paul's, the bench in the bishop's hall, the exchequer in his chamber.)[188] Through envoys, Ottobuono contacted

---

[184] *CLR 1260–7*, 231, 258–9.
[185] *CPR 1258–66*, 649. He was swapped in return for setting free John de la Ware senior.
[186] Peterborough, 18.
[187] Graham, 'Letters of Cardinal Ottoboni', 100–1. I guess this letter to the cardinals belongs to this period.
[188] *CPReg*, 420; Graham, 'Letters of Cardinal Ottoboni', 96–8; FitzThedmar, 84 (Stone, FitzThedmar, no. 867).

groups of rebels. He deplored their insistence on standing by the Provisions of Oxford as though they knew better than the pope! Their refusal to submit until they had consulted all their 'accomplices' in England and overseas was, he added, simply impractical. Towards the end of May, he went to see Edward at Windsor and found him (as he hastened to tell the rebels) very much inclined to mercy. (This was clearly far more important than the attitude of the king.) The continued defiance of the Kenilworth garrison is unlikely to have changed Edward's mind. Its daring, *debonereté* and display was just the kind of thing he admired. These were the type of men he wanted in his service. After the meeting Ottobuono involved both Edward and John of Brittany in his efforts to bring about 'peace and reconciliation'.[189]

In early July, after the siege had been going a couple of weeks, Ottobuono decided he must go to Kenilworth himself. He took with him Boniface of Savoy, at last back in England, and a couple of other bishops. Having tried vainly for a fortnight to negotiate a settlement, he finally excommunicated the garrison. The response was typical of its élan and bravado. It dressed its surgeon, Master Philip Porpeis, up as mock legate and had him, standing on the wall, fulminate excommunications back. Ottobuono, however, despite this provocation, did not abandon the way of peace. Indeed, he now urged Henry to summon a parliament to Kenilworth where an authoritative offer could be made to the rebels.[190]

## THE DICTUM OF KENILWORTH: OCTOBER 1266

Henry proclaimed the result of the parliament at the end of August.[191] It had, he said, agreed that a committee of twelve should restore peace to the kingdom by ruling on the matter of the disinherited. Henry seems to have gone along with this solution readily enough. The Dunstable annals have both him and Ottobuono together wishing to avoid the spiritual and material damage to the kingdom involved in a continuation of the war.[192] Already in his May proclamation Henry had been striking a conciliatory note. Edward must have felt the same way and given his backing to the initiative. Yet the setting up of the committee was a reflection on Henry's kingship. The only reason for it was his failure to deal with the question of the disinherited himself. Can one imagine Louis IX, or any wise and masterful king, hiving off to others a decision of such fundamental importance for the future of the kingdom? But then had Henry been a wise and masterful king, he would never have been in this situation in the first place.

---

[189] Graham, 'Letters of Cardinal Ottoboni', 104–5, 107, 112–13; *CPR 1266–72*, 598, 669.
[190] Robert of Gloucester, ii, lines 11,924–30; Waverley, 371. Boniface had returned to England in June.
[191] *CPR 1258–66*, 671–2.
[192] Dunstable, 242.

He lacked the wisdom to judge what was necessary. He also lacked the authority to make any settlement stick.

The committee of twelve was chosen as follows. The parliament itself elected six men, namely the bishops of Exeter and Bath and the bishop-elect of Worcester, together with Alan la Zouche, Roger de Somery and Robert Walerand. These six were then to choose the other six, with any disagreement being decided by Ottobuono and Henry of Almain. In the event the other six were the bishop of St David's, Gilbert de Clare, Humphrey de Bohun, earl of Hereford, Philip Basset, John de Balliol and Warin of Bassingbourn. If the twelve, thus constituted, could not agree, then again Ottobuono and Henry of Almain were to decide the issue. If they did agree, nothing still was to be promulgated without Ottobuono's and Henry of Almain's consent, together with that of the king. The document setting out all this was issued at Kenilworth on 31 August and was sealed by the king, Ottobuono, Edward and Gilbert de Clare. The whole process, subject, as it was, to so many checks and balances, shows how contentious the issue was thought to be.

The task of the twelve (to which they swore on the gospels) was to come up with a solution bringing peace to the kingdom. The implication clearly was that the policy of disinheritance needed to be modified. That was not a universal view. Some of the twelve argued, on the contrary, that disinheritance should be enforced to the limit, and indeed that those disinherited should be exiled.[193] At least that solved the problem of large numbers of desperate men being left at large in the country. Most of the twelve, however, although they had profited from the lands of the disinherited, accepted that the policy needed to be changed. If the stories were correct, Philip Basset had opposed it in the first place, as had King Richard, Henry of Almain's father. Several of the committee, like Humphrey de Bohun and Roger de Somery, had family connections with former rebels. Both Gilbert de Clare and Henry of Almain had once been rebels themselves. The fact that Edward sealed the document setting out the terms of reference and was represented on the committee by his knight Warin of Bassingbourn showed his backing for the new policy. The bishops on the committee almost certainly backed it too. They had all co-operated with the Montfortian regime, none more so than Nicholas of Ely, now bishop-elect of Worcester.[194] Behind the committee, moreover, stood Ottobuono, without whose consent nothing could be done. His views about the need for conciliation were passionately held. He could now enforce them. Once the committee began work, he and Henry of Almain slapped down the

---

[193] *DBM*, 324 nn. h and 14; *SR*, 18.

[194] For the bishop of Exeter, Walter of Bronescombe, see Maddicott, *Simon de Montfort*, 195, 197, 285, 292, 302, 305. Jeffrey Denton describes him as a 'practical and conciliatory' man: Denton, 'Walter of Bronescombe'. The bishop of Bath, as we have seen, was the chancellor, Walter Giffard. He was soon to be archbishop of York.

attempts to continue with disinheritance and modified the award in other ways to make it less harsh.[195]

After long and tortuous debates, the Dictum of Kenilworth, as it was called, was finally published in the camp at Kenilworth on 31 October 1266.[196] Its key feature was to replace disinheritance with 'redemption', meaning that former rebels could now buy back their lands and had three years in which to do so. For the first time, and not before time, sensible distinctions were made between different levels of offence. At the top of the scale were Henry de Hastings and those in the Kenilworth garrison responsible for mutilating the messenger. They were to redeem their lands at seven times their annual value, thus reflecting how strongly Henry felt about the issue. A seven-year redemption fine was also inflicted on Robert de Ferrers, earl of Derby. The more general penalty, however, was a five-year fine. It was to be paid by those fighting against the king at the battles of Northampton, Lewes, Evesham and Chesterfield. It was to be paid too by those captured at Kenilworth just before Evesham, and by those still now in arms against the king. The last category thus included the Kenilworth garrison and those holding out in the Isle of Ely. A five-year fine was also to be paid both by those who had willingly sent military forces against the king and by the bailiffs of the earl of Leicester who had been involved in murder and depredation.

Below the five-year fines were those of two years' annual value. These were due from laymen (clerics were evidently left to ecclesiastical punishment) who had raised support for Montfort by spreading falsehoods. One-year fines were the lot of those who had been coerced into acts of violence and had gone home as soon as they could. Those at Northampton who had fled to the church as soon as they saw the arrival of the king did better and had only to redeem their lands at half their annual value. Thought was given to those unjustly accused. They were immediately to recover their lands and receive damages while their accusers were to be punished. An attempt was also made to protect the disinherited from further retribution. Those who had agreed to redeem their lands were not obliged to answer for the damage they had done to their opponents during the disturbances. Acts of revenge on both sides were to cease. Finally, thought was given to how this elaborate settlement could be implemented. This crucial question was referred to another committee. The legate, the king and Henry of Almain were to choose twelve men to put the Dictum into effect.

Only the Montforts and London were left outside the settlement. In respect of the former, Henry had already agreed to abide by an award of

[195] DBM, 324 n. 13; 325 n. 16; 326 nn. 18, 21; 328–9 n. 29; 333 nn.40, 43; 334 n. 45; SR, 18.

[196] DBM, 316–37, and SR, 18, for the decisions of Ottobuono and Henry of Almain on points of dispute.

King Louis.[197] The Dictum left it at that apart from asking the legate to put an end to Montfort's miraculous after life. As for London, the king was merely urged to provide for the immediate reform of its state and liberties, which rather implied those liberties would be restored.

The Dictum of Kenilworth was a statesmanlike settlement and probably as generous to the disinherited as circumstances permitted. It was more generous than Bycarrs Dyke, if the agreement between Robert Walerand and Hugh de Neville is any guide, since there Walerand held on to a major part of Neville's estate. Now, the disinherited had the opportunity of recovering all their lands. They had, of course to pay for the privilege, but without payment the loyalists would never have surrendered land they had hoped to hold in perpetuity. The five-year redemption payment was high but half the usual sale price of land, so the disinherited were not having to buy back their estates at the market value.

## THE DICTUM'S VIEW OF KINGSHIP

The hope then was that the Dictum of Kenilworth would be enough to bring the disinherited into the king's peace and end the rebellion. There was one other way in which it was designed to do that. The Dictum had a long preamble dealing with the prerogatives, principles and practices of Henry's kingship. It was well crafted, striking a balance between the reassertion of kingly power and the suggestion it would now be exercised in a just, lawful and responsible fashion. In that sense it was a critique both of Montfortian pretensions and of Henry's personal rule. Henry himself had often talked the talk, most recently in his May proclamation. How far he had walked the walk was more questionable.[198]

The Dictum, in its first chapter, began by declaring that 'the most serene prince, the illustrious king of England' was to exercise freely his 'dominion, authority and royal power without impediment or contradiction of anyone', previous restrictions having been against 'the approved rights and long established laws and customs of the kingdom'. So clearly all the controls imposed by the Provisions of Oxford were at an end. Indeed, the Dictum made no mention at all of Henry needing to rule with counsel and consent. Yet, on the other hand, in a preamble, the authors had explained how their authority had come both from the king and 'the barons, councillors of the kingdom and leading men of England'. And while chapter one stated that everyone, high and low, was fully and humbly to obey the king, such obedience was due to his 'lawful orders and precepts'.

This qualification prepared the way for a veritable lecture on good kingship. Henry was urged to appoint upright judges who would settle the

---

affairs of his subjects 'according to the praiseworthy laws and customs of the kingdom'. They would thus 'strengthen the throne and royal majesty with justice'. It is hard to imagine Louis IX being addressed in these terms, Louis whom Henry himself, in a letter sent from Kenilworth, had just praised for his 'far famed justice'?[199] Henry was also urged to observe Magna Carta, the Charter of the Forest and the concessions he had willingly made, presumably a reference to the Provisions of Westminster. The legate was to absolve him from any sentence of excommunication he might have incurred for failing to observe the Charters. Was Henry worried about this? The Dictum also addressed some of Henry's more recent failings. Those making false accusations were to be punished 'so that henceforth the king will not easily believe them', a telling reference to his credulity. Nor was the haphazard way he had distributed the spoils after Evesham forgotten. Since he had rewarded some above and some below their deserts, those who had received no land were to be compensated from the redemption fines. The Dictum, therefore, acknowledged Henry's failures and promised the disinherited that, if they submitted, things would be better in the future.

## THE AFTERMATH OF THE DICTUM

Ottobuono threw all his weight behind the Dictum and gave it the widest possible publicity. Explaining how he had laboured night and day in the cause of peace, he summoned the bishops, abbots, priors and cathedral chapters to witness with their own eyes the new 'health and glory of the whole English body'. Lay magnates were summoned too and so, before a great assembly of the realm at Coventry (six miles from Kenilworth), Otttobuono himself read out the Dictum.[200] He was its chief architect.

Would it work? With some it did. In November and December 1266 some 127 people were pardoned for their activities during the war, as opposed to 45 in the two previous months. There was also a marked increase in those receiving safe conducts to come to court to treat for peace.[201] But not everyone was impressed. The Dictum was rejected by John de Eyville and his company in the Isle of Ely. It was rejected too by the Kenilworth garrison. It had indeed one major flaw. Instead of recovering their lands as soon as they had agreed terms with the grantees, the disinherited were only to recover them if they paid all the money at once up front. If they could not do that, then they were to receive back a third of their lands when they had paid off a third of the fine and a half when a half. If by the end of the three years allowed, they had not paid off all the fine, then

---

[199] *CPR 1258–66*, 678.
[200] Graham, 'Letters of Cardinal Ottoboni', 109–10; *C&S*, ii, 729–32; Dunstable, 243. The sources differ as to whether the proclamation was on 31 October or 1 November.
[201] Wild, 'Reasserting medieval kingship', 246.

half of the remaining land was to stay with the grantees. Apart from being allowed to sell their woods and sell or lease their lands to the grantees, the disinherited were therefore prevented from using the revenues from those lands to pay off the fine. Some on the committee of twelve saw the dangers here but they faced determined opposition. It took the intervention of Ottobuono and Henry of Almain to secure a three- rather than a two-year period for the payment of the fine. They also prevented the loss of two-thirds rather than a half of the remaining land if the last instalment was not forthcoming.[202] They had done their best, but for many understandably it was not enough.

So the siege went on. Henry himself was hardly confident of the future. At the time the Dictum was proclaimed a wedding took place at Kenilworth. It was between Henry's kinsman Albert, duke of Brunswick, and the queen's 'niece' Alice of Montferrat.[203] Eleanor herself came from Windsor for the ceremony. But when Henry promised Albert an annual fee, he had to say its size would depend on the situation. It would be 'copious' 'if our state improves', smaller if it deteriorated. Where was the open-handed Henry of previous years? He soon reappeared. Three days later he gave the duke 1,000 marks out of the 20,000-mark fine owed by the Londoners![204]

The Dictum had been published at the end of October. The siege was still continuing a month later, but as autumn turned to winter the tactic of starving the garrison out, unheroic though it was, began to work. The defenders were having to eat horse flesh. They had burnt all their firewood and were freezing. They were suffering from dysentery. At last, a truce was arranged. The garrison agreed that if not relieved by Simon junior within forty days it would give up. In the event it did not hold out that long. On 14 December Henry de Hastings and the rest accepted the Dictum and surrendered to the king. When the royalists entered the castle, they were almost overcome by the stench. So Henry had stayed the course. He affirmed his triumph by two days later granting Kenilworth to Edmund in hereditary right.[205]

## THE SIEGE OF THE ISLE OF ELY: FEBRUARY–APRIL 1267

Henry celebrated the Christmas of 1266 'with all joy and jubilation' at Osney abbey just outside Oxford. On 5 January he was back at Westminster for the feast of Edward the Confessor surrounded, as 'befitted royal excel-

---

[202] *DBM*, 326 nn. 18, 21.

[203] Alice was the daughter of Boniface of Montferrat, who was married to one of Eleanor's cousins.

[204] *F*, i, 470 (*CPR 1258–66*, 3); *CR 1264–8*, 263–4; *CR 1268–72*, 49, 160–1, 372; London, 76; Howell, *Eleanor of Provence*, 135, 235; Williams, *Medieval London*, 241–2.

[205] *CChR 1257–1300*, 66–7; *RCWL*, ii, 153.

lence', with a great crowd of bishops and barons. Soon afterwards, he ordered 300 pounds of wax to be acquired for candles of his height to burn around the Confessor's shrine. There was, however, a sour note, as so often with Henry's celebrations. At the feast many in the hall objected to the way Henry placed Ottobuono in the royal seat and had him served first. There had been the same grumblings about Henry's treatment of the legate Otto back in 1240.[206] Ten days later, Henry took steps to improve his financial position. He entered the exchequer and said that no sheriff or bailiff coming to the exchequer was to depart until he had paid his debts in full. Like many in the past it was not a very sensible initiative, since many debts could only be paid in instalments. It was made worse by typical precautions against Henry breaking his own rules. If he did send a writ respiting the payment of a debt, the exchequer was not to obey it without consulting him first.[207]

By this time Henry must have been longing for peace and rest. It was still not to be. In the next months he faced disturbances in Hampshire, Surrey, Sussex, Essex, Hertfordshire, Nottinghamshire and the far north. Worst of all was the situation around Ely. Here the insurgents had occupied not the Isle itself (essentially an administrative district) but, much more dangerous, the islands within the Isle. There were half a dozen of these, the largest with the cathedral of Ely itself. They were true islands surrounded by 'immense marshes, now a black pool of water, now foul running streams'. This was the 'wild wilderness' occupied after the Norman Conquest by the legendary Hereward the Wake.[208] It was now occupied by John de Eyville and Nicholas of Seagrave, the lands of the one given to the queen, of the other to Edmund. They had with them a band of daring, desperate men, including the Peche brothers, Hugh, Robert and Thomas, knights '*potentes, prudentes et robustos*', as Barnwell priory described them.[209] The ranks were swollen by townsmen from Cambridge and peasants from the neighbouring villages. Armed bands from the islands ravaged the surrounding area and returned with supplies and prisoners who were held in fetters and threatened with decapitation unless they paid ransoms. There were also raids further afield, the most famous exploit, in mid-December 1266, being the sack of Norwich.[210] Cambridge itself, of course, was particularly vulnerable. The islanders extracted 200 marks from the citizens and seized 100 marks worth of corn and malt. They attacked the

---

[206] Osney, 197; Rishanger, 59–60; *CR 1264–8*, 275, 288.

[207] TNA E 159/41, m. 4 (image 0012).

[208] Miller, *Abbey and Bishopric of Ely*, 12–13, and the map between pp. 220 and 221. The quotations are from the *Life of Saint Guthlac*.

[209] *CIM*, no. 830; *CRSupp*, no. 378; *CPR 1266–72*, 390; Barnwell, 48. The Peches were the younger brothers of the baron Gilbert Peche of Bourn in Cambridgeshire, who seems to have remained loyal.

[210] Bury St Edmunds, 37; Wykes, 193.

Jewry, killed numerous Jews and took their goods off to the islands.[211] Just
outside the town, Barnwell priory had to endure daily visitations from the
'ministers of iniquity' who ate and drank as they wished and generally
wreaked destruction. The canons had no alternative but to put on a
cheerful face and eat and drink with them. At least this compliance paid
some dividends and an attempt to clear out the convent's stores (the prior
was woken in the middle of the night and asked for the keys) was stopped
by the prior's friends.

Henry, therefore, had no alternative but to act yet again. At the end of
January he left Westminster and journeyed to Bury St Edmunds (some
twenty-five miles from Ely) whither he had summoned a parliament.
Ottobuono, hoping both to pacify the realm and further the crusade (an
increasing preoccupation), summoned a church council to meet there at
the same time. In Henry's presence he sentenced the islanders to excommunication if they did not submit within a fortnight. He also begged
them, through envoys, to obey the pope, return to the faith of church and
king, accept the Dictum of Kenilworth and cease their depredations.[212]

The reply of the islanders, preserved by Rishanger, is one of the great
documents of the revolution.[213] It provides by far the most detailed insight
into how the disinherited justified their stand, showing once again they
were far more than mere men of violence. The islanders thus proclaimed
they would live and die by the faith of Saint Robert, Saint Edmund and
Saint Richard (Grosseteste, Archbishop Edmund and Richard of Wich,
bishop of Chichester). Their obedience to Rome did not mean they had
to accept its unjust exactions. Indeed, they were prepared to appeal
against the pope to a general council or to God himself. As for the legate,
he had 'irreverently' expelled the Montfortian bishops from the kingdom
and had taken the side of the king, thus negating his role as a peacemaker.
As for the sentence of disinheritance, this could hardly be pronounced
against those whose ancestors (in 1066) had conquered the land with the
sword. In any case, the sentence had been delivered not by their peers but
by a divided court with King Richard, Roger Bigod and Philip Basset
protesting against it. The Dictum of Kenilworth was no improvement for
the redemption payments amounted to disinheritance. Lands should be
recovered without charge. Meanwhile, how could the disinherited be
blamed for living off the goods of their enemies, who in any case were
responsible for much of the violence?

The injustice of their own treatment was thus made very clear, but
more was to come. The islanders also celebrated the righteousness of their

---

[211] Jacob, *Studies*, 265, 274, 395–406; Carpenter, *Reign of Henry III*, 315–17, 320; *RS*, 216,
220; *CPR 1266–72*, 31; Barnwell, 121.

[212] *C&S*, ii, 732–5; Graham, 'Letters of Cardinal Ottoboni', 102; Bury St Edmunds, 37;
Rishanger, 62–3, 65.

[213] Rishanger, 62–5; Powicke, *King Henry III*, ii, 539–41.

cause, the cause of reform of the realm. How profound had been Montfort's influence. Thus the oath of 1258, the oath Montfort appealed to again and again, had been taken 'for the utility of the kingdom and all the church'. It had also been supported by sentences of excommunication fulminated by the prelates. The Provisions of Oxford (whatever that meant) should now be observed and aliens removed from the king's council. The islands should be retained for five years as security for the king performing his undertakings. The defence ended with a final populist dig at pope and legate. Churches had been bestowed on aliens, 'enemies of the kingdom', who took money from the country and employed chaplains at the cheapest possible price to minister to parishioners. The preaching of the crusade would make matters worse by denuding the kingdom of people and leaving it open to attack.

It is hardly surprising, in view of this spirited response, that the islanders did not submit, so Henry had to mount yet another campaign. While the legate hurried back to London (scared by various rumours, according to the Bury annalist), Henry set off for Cambridge where he remained from 24 February till 24 April. King Richard came too and set up court in Barnwell priory. (Henry himself lived in the town.) Queen Eleanor meanwhile went to Dover castle where her presence might assure the loyalty of the Cinque Ports and her contacts help bring in foreign mercenaries.[214] Here she was doing for Henry what Henry's sister had done for Montfort.

At Cambridge, Henry's first aim was simply to protect the town and surrounding country from the assaults of the rebels. Here he had some success,[215] but no progress was made in actually dislodging the islanders, hence of course the length of Henry's stay. Henry's promise to go to King's Lynn to give 'help and succour' to the surrounding area remained unfulfilled. He sat tight in Cambridge. Wykes, perhaps a bit unfairly, judged the whole stay there 'frivolous and useless'.[216] One problem was that Edward himself, who might have driven operations forward with more vigour, was absent for much of the siege. This was because of a crisis in the far north. Five years younger than Edward, John de Vescy, lord of the great barony of Alnwick in Northumberland, had grown up in the royal household and been married to a kinswoman of the queen. Yet he had become a passionate Montfortian and been wounded and captured at Evesham. As we have seen, he later gave, as a holy relic, one of Montfort's severed feet to Alnwick priory. How he was released from captivity after Evesham is unknown, but in early 1267 he leagued together with other disinherited northerners and repossessed Alnwick castle and its adjacent lands. When he heard the news, Edward left Cambridge (probably in early March), headed north with a considerable force, and soon secured Vescy's

---

[214] Howell, *Eleanor of Provence*, 238–9.
[215] See Barnwell, 122–3.
[216] Wykes, 196–8; *CR 1264–8*, 369; *CPR 1266–72*, 44–5, 132–3.

submission. Wykes here praises Edward's mercy in pardoning rather than punishing Vescy. In fact, he was saddled with a 3,700-mark fine to recover his lands (the beneficiary was the count of St Pol), but he did later become one of Edward's closest friends. Doubtless his rapid submission helped here.[217]

Henry was also weakened on another front. He was running desperately short of money. In January 1267 the exchequer was told to make no payments save those to the king, queen, Edward and Edmund. Just to show this was not some Henrician whim, the instruction was authorized by Henry and his council, one of the few references to the council in this period. In practice, the king took little notice and continued to order payments for other purposes, but it made little difference since the exchequer had no money anyway.[218] According to Wykes, Henry was having to choose between supporting his household and paying his troops. During March the situation was so bad he began to sell his jewels and other precious objects. Here he was very hands-on and exempted 'by word of mouth' items belonging to the crown and regalia. The great silver bowl in which he washed his feet and those of paupers was also retained. But a silver alms dish weighing nearly 17 pounds was sold as were another £1,100 worth of silver, gold and jewels from the wardrobe treasure. Worse still, Henry was now forced to pawn the amazing array of jewels and precious objects he had collected over the years to adorn the new shrine of Edward the Confessor. If these were not returned to the Abbey by Michaelmas 1268, Henry asked pope and legate to place an interdict on his chapel. A full list was made of the treasure before it was taken from the Abbey to the Tower where the legate was in charge of the pawning process. This for Henry must have been one of the lowest points of his kingship.[219]

Yet more trouble was to come. That stalwart Philip Basset was present at the Bury parliament but not at Cambridge. Had he left in dudgeon, having argued unsuccessfully for further concessions to the disinherited? Whatever the reason, the king was soon desperate for his return and early in March sent him a very personal letter. As Henry promised to explain when they met, Basset's counsel was needed urgently on matters which, if delayed, would spell 'irreparable damage'. As he loved the king and as he wished to preserve him from 'supreme danger', he was to come at once with horses and arms and all his power.[220]

---

[217] Wykes, 197–8; Studd, *Lord Edward's Itinerary*, 100; *CLR 1260–7*, 271; *CPR 1266–72*, 260; TNA E 368/42, m. 13 (*CDS*, no. 2456); Knowles, 'The resettlement of England', 40–1; Knowles, 'The disinherited', pt. 4, 108. For Vescy's career, see Stringer, 'Nobility and identity'; Tout and Ridgeway, 'John de Vescy'.

[218] *CR 1264–8*, 287; *CLR 1260–7*, 260, 262.

[219] Wykes, 294 (commenting on the situation a little later); Westminster, *Flores*, 14–15; *CPR 1266–72*, 43, 50, 52, 61, 64–5, 69, 133, 135–40. For the precious objects, see below, 552.

[220] *CR 1264–8*, 367–8; *RCWL*, ii, 154–6.

## THE INTERVENTION OF GILBERT DE CLARE
## AND THE END OF THE WAR: APRIL–JULY 1267

The danger Henry feared so much stemmed from Gilbert de Clare. He had been one of the devisers of the Dictum of Kenilworth. He had been with the king at the end of the siege and attested the charter granting Kenilworth to Edmund.[221] But then he had refused to attend the feast of the Confessor on 5 January, the Bury parliament and the muster at Cambridge. He was rumoured to be gathering an army in Wales to attack his marcher enemies. He was indeed preparing to strike but his target, far more dangerous, was the very capital of the kingdom. In late March, Clare left Wales and marched eastwards across the country. On 8 April he arrived with a large force in Southwark.[222] Next day he was allowed across London Bridge into the city, this with the consent of Ottobuono, who believed, quite wrongly, that Clare was acting for the king. Two days later, on 11 April, who should arrive in Southwark but a contingent from the Isle of Ely led by John de Eyville and Nicholas of Seagrave. (Their followers had seized all the horses in Dunstable on the way.) Evidently, Clare was now allied with the disinherited.[223]

This was a decisive moment. The resistance at Kenilworth and the havoc wreaked elsewhere in the country had changed the policy of disinheritance into one of redemption. But if more was to be achieved, the remaining rebels needed outside help. It was Gilbert de Clare who was now to supply it. Clare has left no manifesto outlining his demands, but their gist is clear from the Dunstable annals: 'he was very angry that the king did not wish to give the grace to the disinherited which he sought'.[224] There is nothing to suggest that Clare had been opposed to the initial policy of disinheritance. Indeed, Rishanger indicates the reverse.[225] His close associate John Giffard benefited greatly from it. Clare himself received the lands of John fitzJohn. As a deviser of the Dictum, however, Clare presumably supported the replacement of disinheritance with redemption. Judging from the concession he later obtained, he also argued, or came to argue, that the disinherited should recover their lands as soon as they had made their redemption agreements, instead of having to wait until money had actually changed hands. This, at the very least, was the 'grace' he was demanding from the king.

One can understand why Clare sympathized with the disinherited. After all, he too until a late stage had been a rebel. After Evesham he

---

[221] *RCWL*, ii, 153.

[222] For the size of Clare's following, see Oakes, 'The nature of war', 56.

[223] Seagrave had been captured at Evesham and seems subsequently to have been released: *CPR 1258–66*, 642.

[224] Dunstable, 245.

[225] Rishanger, 49.

obtained letters for himself and his followers remitting the king's anger for
their trespasses during the time of disturbance and their adherence to
Montfort at the battle of Lewes. Doubtless to Clare's own anger, the letters
were not always successful in saving his followers from retribution.[226]
Despite deserting Montfort, he retained many connections with those who
had stuck it out to the end. Indeed, he recruited Montfort loyalists into his
retinue, including John fitzJohn himself, Simon of Pattishall and Brian de
Gouiz.[227]

Clare also took up the wider cause of reform of the realm, just as had
the disinherited in the Isle. He complained that the promises made to him
by Edward at Ludlow back in May 1265 had not been fulfilled, promises
that evil customs should be abolished and that aliens should be removed
from the king's council and be excluded from the custody of castles and
any kind of office. Rishanger adds that he also demanded the restoration
of the Provisions of Oxford.[228] That the promises about aliens had been
broken was very evident. Windsor castle had been placed under Ebulo de
Montibus, Dover under Matthias Bezill and Winchester under William de
Valence. William de Valence, Geoffrey de Lusignan, Peter of Savoy, Elyas
de Rabayne and William de Sancta Ermina, as well as Montibus and
Bezill, had all benefited from the lands of the disinherited. William de
Sancta Ermina was back at court and alongside Clare witnessed the
charter giving Kenilworth to Edmund.[229] The replies of the islanders to
the legate show how live the issue of the aliens remained. Clare here was
just as much a populist as Montfort.

Wykes believed that Clare's claim to be acting 'for the utility of the
republic and the cause of the community of the realm' was a 'ridiculous
fiction'.[230] That may be unfair. Clare's conduct was consistent with his
earlier Montfortianism and his agreement with Edward. Having said that,
he also had personal grievances. There was still argument over the extent
of his mother's dower. It led for a while in 1266 to Clare's Welsh lordships
being taken, nominally at least, into the king's hands.[231] There was also the
unresolved quarrel with Edward over Bristol and disputes with both Roger
of Leybourne and John de Warenne over lands seized after Evesham.
Most serious of all was the developing feud with Roger de Mortimer over
rival claims to the Bohun wardship.[232] An attempt to settle the quarrel

---

[226] *F*, i, 464 (*CPR 1258–66*, 460); Jacob, *Studies*, 215–17.

[227] Altschul, *A Baronial Family*, 122–3; *CPR 1266–72*, 145–7; 'Miracles', 106. Gilbert later
secured pardons for thirty bachelors (the list was headed by Simon of Pattishall) and
around twenty esquires.

[228] Wykes, 164–5, 199–200; Rishanger, 60.

[229] *RCWL*, ii, 153.

[230] Wykes, 199–200.

[231] *CPR 1258–66*, 588; Altschul, *A Baronial Family*, 117; Smith, *Llywelyn ap Gruffudd*, 340–1.

[232] This was the wardship of the lands of Humphrey de Bohun junior, who had died of
wounds sustained at Evesham.

over the Christmas of 1266 had come to nothing. Thereafter Clare claimed the threats of his enemies prevented him coming to court.[233] After Evesham, the pope had written letters to the king, Edward and Gilbert de Clare. The agreement leading to the Dictum of Kenilworth had been sealed by the king, the legate, Edward and Gilbert. On such occasions Clare seems at the very centre of affairs. But it was clearly not always like that. As with Montfort before, did Clare feel that 'for so great a man as he was' he was 'regarded too little'?[234]

Whatever the balance between personal grievances and public principle, Clare, just like Montfort, had been brilliant at putting his public case across. He was a man of vision and ambition. Both are seen in the gigantic castle he later built (rivalling anything built by Edward) at Caerphilly to guard his lordship of Glamorgan.[235] Both are equally seen in his occupation of London. What an extraordinary yet also a sensible thing to do, what courage yet also what calculation. A lesser man, a Robert de Ferrers for example, might simply have gone on the rampage. Clare saw this would lead nowhere other than to a new civil war. To avoid that, he sought to keep his followers in order. He also avoided the accusation of treason by proclaiming he would never bear arms against the king and Edward unless in self-defence.[236] With his clear eye, Clare saw that the occupation of London would force the king into a settlement. The enterprise was perfectly possible for the city, labouring under its 20,000 mark fine, was seething with discontent. The Dictum of Kenilworth's appeal for the restoration of London's liberties had fallen on deaf ears.[237] The occupation would also be hard to reverse for London was far too big to blockade or besiege. Once there, safe behind its walls, Clare's position would be impregnable. The cause of the disinherited had previously lacked any great town base. Now it had the greatest of all.

Henry's first reaction when he heard the news of London's fall was to attempt negotiations with Clare and the disinherited through King Richard and Philip Basset, a pair evidently chosen for their known moderation. Basset's sympathies may be deduced from the way his wife, Ela, countess of Warwick, managed to prevent Ottobuono (soon disabused of Clare's intentions) from placing an immediate interdict on the city.[238] When, however, attempts at negotiation came to nothing, Henry was left with the agonizing choice (as Wykes recognized) of either ignoring the outrage in London or marching south and leaving Cambridge to its fate. For though Eyville and Seagrave had joined up with Clare, a substantial

[233] Rishanger, 59–60; *CLR 1260–7*, 245; *CPR 1258–66*, 56; *CPR 1266–72*, 127.
[234] Robert of Gloucester, ii, lines 11,466–7.
[235] For a recent account, see Goodall, *The English Castle*, 192–4.
[236] Rishanger, 60.
[237] *DBM*, 322–5, cap. 11; Williams, *Medieval London*, 235–7.
[238] London, 77.

force remained in the islands. Indeed, a new commander had arrived in the shape – of none other than Henry de Hastings, despite his acceptance of the Dictum at the end of the Kenilworth siege.

In the end, bolstered by Edward's return, Henry went south. According to one story, he was spurred into action by the news, conveyed by Gilbert de Clare's wife, Alice de Lusignan, that John de Eyville was coming to attack him.[239] By the end of April, Henry was at Windsor castle. He had left a force behind to protect Cambridge, but it was insufficient. The islanders sallied forth and put the townsmen to flight, burning down the new gates Henry had built and the houses where he had stayed. Then, meeting in a windmill, they debated for two hours whether to burn down Barnwell priory, and in particular the hall, where King Richard had stayed. Fortunately, the Peche brothers declared they would rather die than see the bones of their ancestors, buried in the church, going up in flames, and so the priory was saved. The prior, however, fled and the monks continued to live in fear, hoping desperately for the return of peace.[240]

By the time Henry arrived at Windsor, Gilbert de Clare had strengthened his hold on the city. He bolstered the defences by extending the ditch round the walls. He imprisoned loyalists and released Montfortians. He took all the keys to the gates and allowed the disinherited in Southwark free entry over London bridge. The Jews were again attacked although some managed to flee to the Tower. Naturally the exchequer had to close down, weakening still further the king's financial position. Clare was supported by a popular revolution. The lesser people, 'calling themselves the commune of the city, as they had in the time of the earl of Leicester' (in the words of fitzThedmar), chose two bailiffs to run the city. Clare dismissed loyalist aldermen and put others in their place. He attempted to keep a kind of order and had malefactors bound hand and foot and thrown into the Thames. And he began to bombard the Tower. It had a substantial garrison commanded by Warin of Bassingbourn, but its catapults and engines were small and weak compared to Clare's. What made this worse that trapped in the Tower was none other than Ottobuono. What an appalling position for a papal legate to be in, frightening for him, humiliating for both king and kingdom.[241]

After a week at Windsor, Henry at last advanced on London. Early in the morning of what was probably 9 May, he and his army arrived, with banners flying, outside the eastern walls of the city adjoining the Tower. This created sufficient diversion for Ottobuono to escape from the postern gate by the river and join up with Henry. The two of them then set up home at the Cistercian abbey of Ham in Stratford, the legate turning the

---

[239] Dunstable, 245–6. For Alice, see Wilkinson, 'Reformers and royalists', 163–4.

[240] Barnwell, 123.

[241] London, 78. FitzThedmar, 91 (Stone, FitzThedmar, no. 891); Wykes, 201–2; TNA E 159/41, m. 6d (image 0064).

cloisters into a stables. (The site is now 'occupied by factories, railways and a sewage pumping station'.)[242] Henry was to remain there, at great cost to the abbey, all the way through from 9 May to 18 June. He had with him a largish army presumably commanded more by Edward than himself. The earls of Norfolk, Hereford and Surrey were all there at one time or another, as were King Richard, Henry of Almain, William de Valence, Philip Basset, John de Balliol and a contingent of marcher barons including Roger de Mortimer, Roger of Clifford and James of Audley. At the end of May, thanks to the efforts of Queen Eleanor and Roger of Leybourne, they were joined by the counts of St Pol and Boulogne with 100 or more knights. Thirty-two other foreign captains were in pay, each commanding a constabulary of around ten men.[243]

Despite this substantial force, the stalemate continued, hence Henry's long stay at Ham. Again, Wykes condemned this 'frivolous and useless' inactivity but it was understandable. Henry and Edward lacked the resources to blockade the city. There was also little chance of a solution by battle. Gilbert de Clare was not going to risk all by marching out to fight one. Here he was no Montfort. But the king's side too shied away from battle and for the same prudential reasons. There is no evidence they ever tried to force an entry in some repeat of the battle of Northampton. They would have had a warm welcome, given Clare's control over the city, even though he never took the Tower.

In this situation of stalemate, negotiations began for some kind of settlement. Henry's envoys were King Richard, Henry of Almain and Philip Basset, the usual emollient trio. One of Clare's delegations was led by John fitzJohn. Edward too was involved. Henry's own mood is best caught by a Westminster Abbey chronicler: 'an innocent man, God fearing, and desiring the end of the war'.[244] Ottobuono, despite his treatment, continued as an apostle of peace, partly for its own sake, partly to clear the way for the crusade. The negotiations were not easy but at last on 15 June a settlement was reached. Perhaps Clare was feeling pressure now that warships from Gascony had arrived in the Thames opposite the Tower.[245] He still, however, got off scot-free. Henry, on the advice of King Richard, the earls, barons and 'commune of the land', pardoned him and his 'household and company' all their trespasses since Clare's departure from Wales. The Londoners too were pardoned for all they had done. As for guarantees, King Richard and Philip Basset were to decide those to be given to Clare. They were also to decide whether the 10,000 marks Clare

---

[242] VCH Essex, vi, 112–14.

[243] RCWL, 156–8; Canterbury/Dover, 246; Howell, Eleanor of Provence, 240–1; CPR 1266–72, 147.

[244] FitzThedmar, 92 (Stone, FitzThedmar, no. 894); Wykes, 205–6; CPR 1266–72, 143; Westminster, Flores, 15.

[245] Westminster, Flores, 16.

himself offered as security for his future conduct was insufficient, as Henry (and doubtless Edward too) thought it was. Ultimately the pope, the final arbiter of the amount, did indeed double it to 20,000 marks. As for the tension between Clare and Edward, here the agreement simply stated that a peace should be made between them.[246] As for the disinherited, they were allowed to stay in Bermondsey for eleven days while they treated with the king for peace.[247] Already, almost certainly, there was an understanding that the terms of the Dictum of Kenilworth would be modified in their favour. Clare had not let them down.

After the settlement, on 18 June Clare crossed over London Bridge into Southwark and Henry made a joyful entry into the city.[248] He restored the aldermen Clare had dismissed, but, true to his promise, did not punish the Londoners, apart, that is, from securing 1,000 marks for King Richard as compensation for the attack on Isleworth back in 1264. As usual, Richard's magnanimity was mixed with money.[249] The settlement with the disinherited was finally announced on 1 July. Placing mercy before judgement, as Wykes put it, the king admitted John de Eyville, Nicholas of Seagrave and the rest of their party into his peace and forgave them their trespasses during the disturbances. The same admission and forgiveness was extended to all the other disinherited who submitted by 1 August. All had still to accept the Dictum of Kenilworth, but there was now a crucial modification. Henry promised to persuade all those who had received lands by his gift to return them to the disinherited as soon as agreement had been reached over payment of the redemption fine. In other words, the disinherited could now recover their lands *before* the payment of any money, and thus use the revenues from their lands to raise it.

There was also one further concession, one which highlights Ottobuono's sacrifices in the cause of peace, or at least the sacrifices he imposed on the church. The disinherited had told him there was no way they could pay their fines without ecclesiastical help. Ottobuono was well aware of the church's sufferings in the war but it was far better, he urged, to sustain some small further damage than for the war to continue. A legatine council, meeting in London soon after its liberation, agreed and consented to the levy of a twentieth on ecclesiastical revenues for the benefit of the disinherited, provided of course they now kept the peace and obeyed the king and legate.[250] In the settlement of 1 July, the king confirmed that the disinherited could indeed have the benefit of this subsidy.

[246] *CPR 1266–72*, 70–2, 144–5; FitzThedmar, 93 (Stone, FitzThedmar, no. 897); Wykes, 205–6.

[247] *CPR 1266–72*, 72–3.

[248] FitzThedmar, 92 (Stone, FitzThedmar, no. 893); London, 78.

[249] *CPR 1266–72*, 144. The king issued a parallel proclamation.

[250] *C&S*, ii, 735–7; Mitchell, *Studies in Taxation*, 294. The clergy were already paying a triennial tenth levied in 1266, for which see below, 522.

As a testimony to Henry's good faith, the two leaders of the disinherited in Southwark were immediately accorded these new terms. Nicholas of Seagrave recovered his lands from Edmund and was promised help from the ecclesiastical subsidy to pay the redemption fine. With John de Eyville it was more difficult because the queen, who held his lands, was absent in Dover castle. Henry went ahead anyway. The letter in which he explained himself is one of the few surviving between the royal couple and shows the sympathy and understanding which, at its best, characterized their relationship. Eleanor was told that Eyville, on the advice of Ottobuono, Edward and others of the council (so again this was not some Henrician whim), had been immediately restored to his lands. Relying on her 'spirituality', Henry had also (here going beyond the settlement) remitted one year of the five-year redemption fine. Henry and Ottobuono would stand surety for Eyville coming before the queen to agree terms for the payment of the rest. The letter concluded with Henry's 'loving request' that Eleanor accept all this for reasons he would explain more fully at their next talk. Henry knew that Eleanor would be disappointed but he also knew she would listen to reason, his reason. Here Henry seems the opposite of 'simplex'.[251]

By his stand, Clare had not reinstated the statute against aliens or the Provisions of Oxford, if those meant the imposition of a ruling council on the king. But he had significantly alleviated the lot of the disinherited. In a combination of power and cleverness, he achieved it by force yet without staging an open rebellion against the king. He had absolutely shown that, great man as he was, he could not be disregarded.

In his letter explaining the granting of the subsidy, Ottobuono opined that those in the Isle of Ely would soon be submitting as well.[252] In fact, it took one more blow to bring that about. It was Edward naturally who dealt it. On 11 July he managed to enter the islands guided by Nicholas of Seagrave or (according to one account) by Nicholas's mother. He was also helped by the summer heat drying out much of the marsh. He threatened the islanders with decapitation if they resisted but offered them the Dictum of Kenilworth, as modified by Gilbert de Clare, if they immediately surrendered and swore never again to bear arms against the king. On these terms on 13 July, Henry de Hastings, John de la Haye, Hugh Peche and others all submitted. The lesser fry made their way back to their towns and villages, not all of them to much of a welcome. One contingent from Dunstable, resuming its life of theft, drunkenness and debauchery, was forced out of the town and later (so it was believed) suffered death either by hanging or starvation.[253] Edward himself made a triumphal entry into

---

[251] *CPR 1266–72*, 74; and Howell, *Eleanor of Provence*, 241, for a perceptive commentary on the letter.

[252] *C&S*, ii, 738.

[253] Wykes, 207–10; Bury St Edmunds, 39; Dunstable, 246–7; *CPR 1266–72*, 152–3; *CR 1264–8*, 379.

Ely, where the citizens and the few remaining monks gave thanks to God for their rescue at his hands.[254]

The settlement with Gilbert de Clare and the fall of the Isle encouraged the remaining rebels to come in and make their peace. At the end of June twenty-five of them submitted to the Dictum, all finding sureties for their future good conduct. Those of Peter de Montfort junior included Henry of Almain. Towards the end of July, another thirty came in, including Simon de Montfort's knight Saer de Harcourt.[255]

The surrender of the islanders brought an end to the war. At last, at last. How the canons of Barnwell must have been relieved. How relieved Henry and everyone else. Wykes celebrated the return of peace in a long passage adorned with appropriate quotations from Isaiah, Exodus, Psalms, Judges and Proverbs. It was peace after five years of 'depredations, rapine, theft, sacrilege, perjury, and a multiplicity of losses and other vices', a period when 'law languished through the impotence of the king and everyone did as they wished'. What made the peace all the better was a bountiful harvest ushering in a period of great plenty so that 'the people ate bread to the full' (Exodus 16:2). There was also an abundance of wine from Gascony, which prompted Wykes to reflect on how wine brought joy to the heart of God and man.[256] Fittingly, he concluded his homily with an introit from one of the responses sung at Matins: 'Remember your covenant, O Lord, and tell the smiting angel to stay his hand that the land is not desolated and you do not lose all living things'. The lord had indeed remembered.[257]

Wykes was writing with hindsight. In fact, the future was still uncertain. All kinds of tortuous and troublesome questions remained about the Dictum's implementation, all with the potential to spark fresh conflict. Yet there was a real sense that, with care and consideration, the war would be over. All the major rebels after all had surrendered. Henry now dismissed his mercenaries and the queen returned from Dover. Legal procedures were soon in place to put the Dictum into effect.

Meanwhile, Ottobuono made one further contribution to the cause of peace. It was one which took him and King Henry to the march of Wales.

## THE TREATY OF MONTGOMERY, SEPTEMBER 1267

After Henry's entry into London on 18 June, he stayed a few days in the bishop's house at St Paul's and then on 23 June went to Westminster,

---

[254] Wykes, 210.

[255] *CPR 1266–72*, 148–50.

[256] Wykes, 210–12.

[257] I am indebted to John Reuben Davies for identifying this piece of liturgy. See http://cantusindex.org/id/007510.

doubtless to celebrate the feast of John the Baptist there on the 24th.[258] He then returned to St Paul's, remaining there throughout July. If this was partly because Westminster palace was a mess after its sack while Henry was at Ham, it was also to stamp his authority on London. Henry finally left the city at the start of August and, after a day or so at Windsor, set off on that familiar journey to the Welsh march, the last time he was to make it: Reading, Wallingford, Oxford, Woodstock, the archbishop of York's manor at Oddington in the Evenlode valley (where the first blows had been struck against Hubert de Burgh in 1232) and then Evesham. What memories that must have brought. Was Montfort's mutilated corpse still there in the abbey? Was this the occasion when it was removed to some obscure place?[259] By 18 August, Henry was at Worcester where for the last time he saw the tomb of his father. Then he moved north through Bridgnorth and Wenlock to Shrewsbury, arriving on 24 August.

Henry had Queen Eleanor with him and at Bridgnorth ordered a new oriel to be made at the door to her chamber in the castle.[260] Throughout the journey he made gifts to religious institutions along his route. In Oxford, the beneficiaries were the Carmelites, the prior of St Frideswide's, the hermits of the order of Saint Augustine and the prioress of nearby Littlemore. At Woodstock, inspired 'by charity', Henry pardoned a peasant his abjuration of the realm (for cutting off someone's hand) and allowed him to recover his messuage and virgate in the manor, although at double the previous rent.[261]

Henry remained at Shrewsbury for over a month. There too were Edward, Edmund, Walter Giffard, now archbishop of York, William de Valence, Henry of Almain, Roger de Mortimer and, of course, Ottobuono. The latter was given three cartloads of firewood every day for the duration of his stay.[262] Henry and his advisers were engaged in intense negotiations with Llywelyn. The result was a peace, a peace after more than ten years of warfare and intermittent truce. It was announced by Ottobuono on 25 September at Shrewsbury in a document sealed by King Henry, Edward, Llywelyn's representatives and Ottobuono himself. Four days

---

[258] The exchequer itself was based at St Paul's. On 2 July, Henry attended a session there and (a routine concession) gave religious houses a delay in answering for their liberties till Michaelmas: TNA E 159/41, m. 6d (image 0066).

[259] Osney, 177. David Cox suggests that a tomb with 'part of a skeleton' discovered during excavations in the crypt of Evesham abbey in 1815 may perhaps be Montfort's. The site is currently under grass in a public park and awaits further investigation: Cox, 'The tomb of Simon de Montfort', 165–9. He writes (p. 169) that 'ultimate proof would depend on extracting mitochondrial DNA from the bones and then matching it with a sample taken from someone who could be proved to have descended in a continuous female line from Earl Simon's mother Alice de Montmorency, or from one of her female ancestors'. He notes, of course, the success in identifying the bones of Richard III in Leicester.

[260] *CLR 1260–7*, 285, 287.

[261] *CR 1264–8*, 326, 329, 331; *CLR 1260–7*, 285.

[262] *RCWL*, ii, 160–1; *CR 1264–8*, 331.

later, Llywelyn ratified the peace and did homage to Henry.[263] The place almost certainly was the ford at Montgomery where so often English and Welsh envoys met.[264] The train from Shrewsbury to Aberystwyth today rattles past the fields on the English side of the ford where the homage probably took place: Henry enthroned, clasping the hands of a kneeling Llywelyn, while Ottobuono, Eleanor, Edward, Edmund and a throng of English and Welsh magnates and ministers looked on.

The appearance of submission was illusory. Llywelyn had got almost all he wanted. V.H. Galbraith once described Magna Carta as 'the most fantastic surrender' any king ever made to his subjects. When it comes to 'fantastic surrenders', the Treaty of Montgomery is in the same league. Against all previous royal policy, Henry now conceded Llywelyn and his heirs 'the principality of Wales', with the title 'prince of Wales' and the homages of the 'Welsh barons of Wales'. A completely new political structure was thus recognized, one where the native Welsh rulers did homage to the prince of Wales and only the prince did homage to the king of England.

Henry also made major territorial concessions. He granted Llywelyn and his heirs the Four Cantrefs between the Conwy and the Dee, so there was to be no attempt to recover these conquests and rebuild the great castles of Deganwy and Dyserth. Further south, in the middle march, Llywelyn was allowed to keep, on various terms, Builth, Brecon, Gwerthrynion and Cydewain and Ceri, this at the expense of the king and marcher barons alike. Finally, all previous agreements made between the king and Llywelyn were nullified, so that was the end of the 1247 Treaty of Woodstock with its cession to Henry of the Four Cantrefs and the homage of the Welsh rulers.

In return for all this, Henry did manage to achieve something. Llywelyn's hold on Brecon and Gwerthrynion could be subject to legal challenge. His brother Dafydd, in Edward's service, was to be restored to his lands. Robert of Mold was to be released from prison and his lordship of Hawarden restored, though no castle was to be built there for sixty years. Roger de Mortimer was left in possession of Maelienydd, subject to Llywelyn's claims, and could build a castle. The homage of one Welsh ruler, the loyalist Maredudd ap Rhys, was to remain with the king. Llywelyn also agreed to give 25,000 marks in return for all the concessions, 1,000 marks within a month, 4,000 marks by Christmas and the balance then being paid off at 3,000 marks a year. Another 5,000 marks were to be forthcoming if the king ever conceded him the homage of Maredudd ap Rhys.

In its fundamentals, the Treaty of Montgomery replicated Montfort's treaty with Llywelyn two years before. Henry had done a little better for,

---

[263] For the documents, see *AWR*, no. 363. The fullest discussion is in Smith, *Llywelyn ap Gruffudd*, 177–86.

[264] Smith, *Llywelyn ap Gruffudd*, 179 n. 152.

not surprisingly, the Montfort treaty did nothing for Roger de Mortimer (or for Dafydd and Maredudd ap Rhys). It had also conceded Llywelyn Painscastle, Hawarden, Ellesmere and (if it could be obtained) Montgomery. But when it came to the principality of Wales, the homage of the Welsh rulers and Llywelyn's major territorial gains, the treaties were the same. Henry had conceded the 1265 Treaty under duress when he was Montfort's captive. He must have regarded it as utterly illegitimate. Why was he conceding it again now? Why, even more, was Edward doing so?

After Montfort's death at Evesham, Llywelyn must have feared he would be next. Indeed, he had been sent one of Montfort's feet as a grisly warning.[265] In September 1265, Henry had nullified everything done by the Montfortian regime, so the treaty of June 1265 was no more. It was doubtless to bolster his defences against a coming assault that Llywelyn, in the same month, seized and destroyed Hawarden castle. He then scattered the forces under Hamo Lestrange sent against him.[266] But then nothing happened. For two years, Llywelyn was left alone, relations governed by a series of truces.[267] The reason, of course, was the civil war in England. But with that over, might not Henry and Edward seek to restore their authority in Wales? In 1266, after all, Henry had spent heavily, doubtless with Edward's support, in recovering his rights in the Three Dioceses due to him under the Treaty of Paris, rights the queen in her extremity had sold back to King Louis. Although Edward had transferred his lordships in south Wales to Edmund, he was still the great loser by the Treaty.[268] As lord of Chester, he no longer ruled the Four Cantrefs to the west. As future king, he would no longer have the homages of all the Welsh rulers. Instead, Llywelyn, mighty with the title prince of Wales, had both.

A key factor explaining what happened was, of course, Llywelyn himself. He had a tight hold of the Four Cantrefs and other lands further south. He was already de facto prince of Wales. There was no way he would surrender his position short of defeat in a major campaign, perhaps many campaigns. In other circumstances, Henry and Edward might have been up for that. They certainly were not with peace far from assured after a terrible civil war. There was also one particular danger. Llywelyn could no longer ally with the Montforts but he might with Gilbert de Clare. After vacating London, Clare had not reappeared at court. He played no discernible part in negotiating the Treaty of Montgomery. Although he and Llywelyn were competing for the allegiances of the Welsh lords in upper Glamorgan, early in 1267, before his march on London, they had

---

[265] Melrose, 205 (fo. 68r).

[266] Waverley, 366; *CPR 1258–66*, 489.

[267] Davies, *Conquest, Coexistence and Change*, 314: 'Montfort's death could be expected to lead to a sharp reversal of his fortunes. It did not do so.'

[268] He ceded Cardigan and Carmarthen to Edmund in December 1265 and the Three Castles and Monmouth to him in June 1267.

formed some kind of 'pact'.[269] Might they not co-operate again, if Llywelyn was now attacked? Certainly Clare had no interest in building up royal power in Wales. He also felt quite able to defend himself against Llywelyn either by diplomacy, as in the pact, or by military might, as in the castle at Caerphilly.

But if an all-out war against Llywelyn seemed impossible, why not avoid fundamental concessions and wait for better days by simply continuing with the truces? After all, these had more or less kept the peace since 1258. Early in 1267, Henry and Edward had indeed empowered their envoys to agree a truce to last for three years from that Easter.[270] Why the change of mind? One reason was certainly money. Llywelyn was offering 25,000 marks for a peace recognizing his position. He would give nothing for a mere truce. Admittedly, much of the money was in the future, to be paid at the rate of 3,000 marks a year, but a substantial sum was immediately available. By March 1268, 4,000 marks had been paid into the king's wardrobe.[271]

The other crucial ingredient was the role of Ottobuono. Montgomery was his treaty. Ottobuono's authority as legate ran in Wales just as much as in England. He had come to England as a peacemaker and saw peace between England and Wales as the final consummation of his work. As he explained to the pope, in a letter written after the eventual treaty, 'After these things [the establishment of peace in England], the most important issue remaining was Llywelyn prince of Wales, a great and powerful limb of the kingdom of England, who for a long time was segregated apart in discord, with great damage as a result. So I went to the march of Wales to try to bring about peace and reconciliation.' The result had been a peace bringing joy and exaltation to all the faithful. All this had been the work of God, 'who beyond measure of sin and merit, adds mercy and glory in these days, so disturbed, and has now opened the face of his piety and kindness and dissipated the remaining counsels of malignity, replacing them with the counsels of his eternal mercy. The treasure of divine will has descended to console men thanks to the prayers of the saints.'[272] When Ottobuono announced the final peace he did so again in religious terms. Here, moreover, he saw the peace not as one between rulers but in much wider terms as a peace between peoples. God, he proclaimed, 'looking upon the people of the English and the Welsh, for so long in discord and afflicted by many wars, with the eye of his mercy has banished evil and brought all things into concord'.[273]

---

[269] Smith, *Llywelyn ap Gruffudd*, 340–1; *Brut*, 256–7.

[270] *CPR 1266–72*, 40.

[271] Wild, *WA*, 133. This was presumably the 4,000 marks due at Christmas 1267. The 1,000 marks due cash down may have gone to Edward.

[272] Graham, 'Letters of Cardinal Ottoboni', 118–19.

[273] *AWR*, 538–9.

We have in these sentiments, I suspect, precisely the terms in which Ottobuono urged the peace upon Henry. The effect on this 'innocent and God-fearing man' was profound. He embraced the idea of peace, peace between princes and between peoples, with all his heart. Surely now the words of the sermon on the Mount would become true in his case, 'blessed are the peacemakers for they shall be called the sons of God'. In the end he placed everything in Ottobuono's hands. On 21 September, 'embracing the ways of peace' after so much 'contention and discord', he gave Ottobuono full power to reach a settlement with Llywelyn and agreed to accept whatever he decided.[274]

Ottobuono wanted peace for its own sake. He also wanted peace to clear the way for the crusade.[275] Back in October 1266, Pope Clement had urged him to preach the crusade 'more fervently'. Thereafter its promotion was as central to his mission as was the ending of the civil war. The two agendas marched perfectly together. The same was true when it came to peace with Wales. A final peace between the English and Welsh peoples would free men and resources for the crusade in a way a fragile truce would not. These considerations too were important for Henry. He was worried by his failure to crusade, all the more so after Louis IX, seven years his junior, took the cross for a second time in March 1267. Over the next few years, Henry spoke repeatedly of fulfilling his vow. Where Henry spoke, Edward acted. By the end of 1267 he was in touch with Louis IX and suggesting they should crusade together. There were no spiritual benefits from a war in Wales. But from a crusade they were overwhelming. A war in Wales offered a mere local triumph. A crusade promised prestige on an international scale. The cause of the crusade was a major reason why both Edward and Henry were prepared to make peace in Wales.[276]

None of this altered the fact that Henry and Edward were having to make major concessions. Henry, back in June, had said he wanted peace but one that 'cedes to our honour and advantage and that of our kingdom'.[277] Not the least of Ottobuono's achievements was to show how that was the case. In so doing he set out a new vision of Llywelyn's place in the English polity. In his letter to the pope, he thus described Llywelyn as a 'great and powerful limb of the kingdom of England', but one hitherto 'segregated' apart in discord. Now, however, after the composition of peace there had been 'a due exhibition of reverence with an oath made by the prince himself to the king'. In other words, the act of homage at Montgomery had restored this powerful limb to the English body. The peace, as Ottobuono put it,

---

[274] A sign of their closeness, Ottobuono arranged in his will for masses to be said for Henry's soul: Binski and Bolgia, 'The Cosmati mosaics at Westminster', 33; *F*, i, 473 (*CPR 1266–72*, 111).

[275] For what follows, see Lloyd, *English Society and the Crusade*, 41, 50 n. 32, 113–14; Tyerman, *England and the Crusades*, 124; *CPReg*, 422.

[276] See Tout, 'Wales and the march during the Barons' War', 88–97.

[277] *CR 1264–8*, 374–5.

conformed to the 'honour' of both sides. All this helps to explain the remark-able explanation offered in the treaty itself for Llywelyn's creation as 'prince of Wales': the king wished to 'magnify the person of Llywelyn and honour those who followed him in hereditary right'. Why should Henry wish to do that? Because, of course, by magnifying Llywelyn, he magnified himself. Under the Treaty of Paris, King Louis had received Henry's homage. Henry too had received the homage of a king, that of King Alexander of Scotland. Now he had received the homage of a prince as well.

Edward too shared something of Ottobuono's vision. He later described Llywelyn as 'one of the greatest of the magnates of our kingdom'.[278] Of course, we know that within little more than a decade it all went disas-trously wrong. It is easy to think there was always a fundamental divide between the view of Llywelyn as limb of the English kingdom and Llywelyn's view of his own status as prince of Wales. But there was nothing inevitable about that. There was plenty of room to negotiate a path reconciling these two views. Henry had made peace between peoples. The act of homage in the field by the ford was not some false show concealing both his humiliation and Llywelyn's triumph. It inaugurated, or at least had the potential to inaugurate, a new relationship between England and Wales, one which might indeed do honour to both sides. Henry had made peace with King Alexander and with King Louis. He might think the peace with Llywelyn was an equal achievement.

## THE STATUTE OF MARLBOROUGH, NOVEMBER 1267

Henry arrived back at Westminster just in time for the feast of the Confessor on 13 October. Two days later he paid for more candles of his height to stand around the shrine, the cost £7 10s for 300 pounds of wax. In early November, Henry was at Winchester, where he was greeted by a solemn procession. He had already ordered the chapel in the castle to be whitewashed against the stay of himself and his queen.[279] After two weeks at Winchester, Henry moved on to Marlborough, where he remained from 16 to 22 November.

It was at Marlborough that Henry promulgated a great act of legisla-tion, his first on any scale, outside the period of reform and rebellion, since the 1230s. (That alas tells us something about his kingship.) The legislation was soon known as the Statute of Marlborough.[280] Its general intention is very clear. Henry was seeking to win the favour of his subjects and bring the discord in the kingdom to an end. In a different way, the

---

[278] *TR*, no. 134 (p. 54).

[279] *CLR 1260–7*, 289, 291–2; Waverley, 67.

[280] The Statute is the subject of masterly analysis by Paul Brand in his *Kings, Barons and Justices*, ch. 7, with chs 8–16 about its enforcement and interpretation down to 1307. The text and translation are found between pp. 453 and 483.

statute was as integral to the peacemaking process as was the Dictum of Kenilworth.

The statute was promulgated in the presence of Henry, King Richard, Edward and Ottobuono. John de Warenne, Philip Basset, Roger de Mortimer, Robert Walerand, Walter of Merton and other ministers were in attendance.[281] A preamble placed the legislation firmly in the context of the recent troubles.[282] 'The kingdom of England' had been 'brought low by many tribulations and dissensions'. It now required 'a reform of laws and rights by which the peace and tranquillity of the inhabitants might be preserved'. Henry, therefore, was 'making provision for the amelioration of his kingdom and the better administration of justice as the king's office requires'. He appeared, therefore, as the king envisaged by the Dictum of Kenilworth, a king whose 'throne and royal majesty' were 'strengthened with justice'.[283] The preamble also stressed that Henry was acting with counsel and consent, and the counsel and consent not simply of the magnates but of a wider body. He had called together 'the wiser men of the kingdom from both the great men and the lesser men'. The legislation had been 'provided, decreed and ordained by common agreement . . . by the king and his faithful subjects'. Whether knights and burgesses were present at Marlborough, as they had been at Montfort's last parliament, is unknown, but Henry's language implied they were.[284]

In the preamble, Henry, therefore, was seeking to heal the wounds of the war and setting his kingship on a just and consensual path. Here the nature of the legislation was equally important. Henry now accepted in final and definitive form the greatest achievement of the period of reform and rebellion. With some revisions, the Statute of Marlborough was none other than the legislation promulgated at the great parliament of October 1259, legislation called by historians the Provisions of Westminster. Far too late, Henry had accepted the Provisions back in January 1263 but it was vital that he now reasserted his ownership. Montfort had issued his own version of the Provisions in December 1264 ('the articles of Worcester') and had confirmed them during his great parliament of 1265. In the death throes of the regime, he had ordered the sheriffs to obey them. Henry needed to wrest back control. He did so by making no reference at all to the legislation's provenance and Montfortian connections. As far as he was concerned, it was entirely new.

Of course, anyone in the political community reading or hearing the statute (and it was given wide publicity) would know this was not the case.

[281] *RCWL*, ii, 163. Walter of Merton and the judge Martin of Littlebury influenced the detail of the legislation: Brand, *King, Barons, Justices*, 196–9. Gilbert de Clare was not present.

[282] Brand, *Kings, Barons and Justices*, 454–5.

[283] *DBM*, 320–1, cap. 2.

[284] Maddicott, *Origins of the English Parliament*, 263–5.

They would recognize at once that, in essence, it was the legislation promulgated at the October 1259 parliament and affirmed later by Simon de Montfort. In London, Arnold fitzThedmar wrote out the 'new provisions' in full but noted that 'the greater part were ordained in the time of the earl of Leicester in the year of our lord 1264'.[285] But, in truth, this was no bad thing. Former rebels could think they had won after all. They had secured the principal achievement of 1258–9, just as the rebels of 1215–17 had secured Magna Carta.

The sense of achievement was enhanced by terminology. Montfort had fought for the Provisions of Oxford. The rebels in Kenilworth and the Isle of Ely had demanded their restoration. So had Gilbert de Clare. But the 'Provisions of Oxford' was a term used to cover all the reforms of 1258–9. The legislation of 1259 was just as much part of the Provisions of Oxford as were the conciliar reforms of 1258. Indeed, when Henry reissued them in January 1263, it was said he had reissued the Provisions of Oxford. The same perception was there in 1267. The Norwich cathedral chronicler, Bartholomew Cotton, remarked that Henry had conceded that the 'statutes of Oxford be observed, except a few of them'.[286]

What is striking here is how easily Cotton dismissed the elements in the Provisions Henry had ignored – the conciliar control and the ban on aliens holding office. His remark shows how central to the Provisions the legislation of October 1259 was thought to be. That was of course because they appealed across society to knights, free tenants and peasants, free and unfree. They protected lesser men from both the abuses of magnates and those of the king. This was, after all, the legislation that 'the community of the bachelery of England' had pushed through at the October 1259 parliament, with the protest that hitherto the barons had merely looked after their own interests and done nothing 'for the utility of the republic'.

The legislation, as revised in the Statute of Marlborough, did lose one feature of benefit to the lowest sections of society. While there was no question of watering down the chapter of most value to great men (that which limited their obligation to attend the sheriff's tourn), it was a different matter with the chapter preventing the justices in eyre amercing villages because not everyone over the age of twelve had attended the inquests of the sheriffs and coroners. The clause was now redrafted so as to make it virtually valueless, probably at the behest of the king's judges anxious to preserve his rights and revenues.[287] This, however, was the only significant change in that direction. The abolition of the *murdrum* fine in cases of death by misadventure remained. So did the abolition of the '*beaupleder*' fine in the courts of the eyre, the county and the honour.

[285] Stone, FitzThedmar, no. 1184.
[286] Cotton, 143; Maddicott, *Origins of the English Parliament*, 264.
[287] Brand, *Kings, Barons and Justices*, 190–1.

There were also additions to the legislation very much to the benefit of lesser men. These came in new chapters at the start explicitly designed to offer protection from oppression by the powerful.[288] Here again, Henry was trying to deal with the conditions prevailing during the civil war. Thus the statute stated that, during 'the recent disturbances', 'magnates' had refused to bow to the king's justice and had levied 'heavy distraints' on their neighbours until they received 'ransoms'. Henceforth anyone making distraints without the sanction of the king's court was to be punished by a 'ransom', meaning here a financial penalty heavier than an amercement and enforceable by imprisonment.[289] Another chapter expanded the earlier legislation on suit of court. Thus 'ransom' now became the penalty for those who were distrained to attend a lord's court when not belonging to his honour or not coming under his jurisdiction by virtue of a hundred. It was not merely the ransom here that was new. The legislation in the Provisions of Westminster had only been about suit to honorial courts. Now for the first time attendance at the hundred too was included, just as much a grievance as numerous cases on the 1258–60 eyres had shown.[290]

There was also a new chapter on Magna Carta.[291] Here too, of course, Henry was stealing Montfort's clothes. The parliament of 1265 had confirmed the Charter in a great ceremony at its end. Now Henry laid down it was to be obeyed in every article, 'both in those relating to the king and those relating to others'. Here, of course, Henry was singing an old royal song but now, for the first time, concrete steps were taken to enforce the Charter. Writs against those breaching the Charter were to be freely available for hearings before the king, the bench and the justices in eyre.

Writing of Henry's stay in London after Gilbert de Clare's submission, Wykes complained that Henry had engaged in protracted discussions ('as was his custom') and had produced nothing 'memorable or famous for the advantage of the kingdom'.[292] Well, Henry had done something 'memorable and famous' now, although Wykes curiously does not mention it, perhaps not wanting to overshadow the later legislation of Edward I. Henry in fact took great pains to publicize his provisions. Thirty copies were prepared for distribution to the justices in eyre and the sheriffs. (Each cost a shilling to write out with just under two shillings for parchment.)[293] The statute did become famous for it was copied out again and again in statute books, the unofficial collections of legislation made by lawyers. Henry had certainly won the battle for ownership, for the 1259 and

<hr />

[288] Brand, *Kings, Barons and Justices*, 456–65.
[289] I am grateful to Paul Brand and Henry Summerson for help with the meaning here of 'ransom'.
[290] Brand, *Kings, Barons and Justices*, 114, 193, 458–9, cap. 2, and see also 189–90.
[291] Brand, *Kings, Barons and Justices*, 460–1, cap. 5.
[292] Wykes, 207.
[293] *CLR 1267–72*, no. 228.

Montfortian versions were hardly ever referred to. In the statute books the Marlborough legislation usually comes after the 1236 statute of Merton and the sentence of excommunication promulgated against violators of the charter in 1253.

In the Dictum of Kenilworth, Henry had been urged to protect Magna Carta, observe the grants he had freely made (so the 1263 Provisions) and 'establish firmly other necessary measures' for the good of the kingdom. In the Statute of Marlborough he could claim to have done all three. The tragedy was that he had not done it ten years earlier, in 1257 not 1267. Then he might well have bound the hearts of his people to him in 'inestimable love', as Wykes has Edward I doing with his 1275 Statute of Westminster.[294]

## THE KING'S VICTORY

Henry had at last emerged victorious from troubles partly of his own making. After Evesham he wanted revenge. He endorsed the disastrous policy of disinheritance and profited from it. Yet Henry could also be merciful especially when it came to the treatment of baronial wives and widows. Under the influence of Ottobuono, at Christmas 1265, if Rishanger can be believed, he came close to a reconciliation with Simon de Montfort junior. Although moved to anger by the mutilation of his messenger, he accepted the procedures leading to the Dictum of Kenilworth. By the end, the Westminster chronicler is surely right in thinking the king just wanted the return of peace. That desire, under the urging of Ottobuono, helped him accept the Treaty of Montgomery. At no point, however, does Henry seem to have had a decisive influence on events. The fact that he delegated the framing of the Dictum of Kenilworth to a committee was a confession of his own failure, as was the lecture on kingship he received in the Dictum itself.

Both for good and ill, Henry's role in this period pales before that of Edward. He was surely a driving force behind the policy of disinheritance, just as he was the one person who could have stopped it. But if he caused the trouble, he also put it down. Henry did at least stick the siege of Kenilworth out to the end, but it was Edward who secured the surrender of Simon junior, the Cinque Ports, John de Vescy and the disinherited in the Isle of Ely. A realist, he was always ready to make exceptions when it came to disinheritance, notably when it secured a quick surrender. He too came to see the policy needed to be modified. Henry appreciated the role of his son and was reluctant to act without his 'counsel and consent'.[295] Whether without him Henry would ever have muddled through on his own may be doubted.

[294] Wykes, 263.
[295] *CPR 1266–72*, 133.

There were two underlying factors which supported Henry's survival. The first was something reflected in the Statute of Marlborough: royal justice was in demand. Throughout the disturbances, as the fine rolls show, people had still come to court to buy the writs furthering the common-law legal actions. The flow only dried up during the periods of open warfare. Between the Octobers of 1265 and 1266, around 680 purchases were made; between October 1266 and October 1267 the number was around 720. The litigants came, moreover, from nearly every county, even those most affected by the disturbances.[296]

The other factor in Henry's survival was money.[297] In terms of the sheriffs bringing in to the exchequer the king's ordinary revenues, this was a catastrophic period, reflecting the disorder throughout the country. Whereas in times of peace the sheriffs and town officials, at each Easter and Michaelmas 'adventus', would bring in thousands of pounds, in this period they never brought in more than hundreds.[298] Not surprisingly, Henry endured periods of financial crisis, none more so than when he had to pawn his jewels. Yet the overall position was sounder than all this suggests. One innovation boosted the finances of Lord Edward. In 1266 the king decided that all overseas merchants trading in England needed Edward's licence. In return for that licence and protection, Edward took a 'reasonable portion' of the goods the merchants exported or imported.[299] The 'new aid' as it was called ran into difficulties and when a customs duty was successfully introduced in 1275, it was on different lines. Nonetheless the aid probably brought Edward several thousand pounds a year.

The relative strength of Henry's own position emerges from his wardrobe accounts.[300] These show that between August 1265 and March 1268 (the period of the account) wardrobe receipts totalled some £28,081, so on average some £210 a day. This was considerably better than the £190 a day averaged between 1245 and 1252.[301] Henry's money financed some vital expenditure for winning the war: £3,994 went on gifts and payments to knights, clerks and sergeants, and another £2,948 on the wages of

[296] Many more writs 'of course', probably costing 6d, were sought but of these there is no record.

[297] For the struggle to restore finance and government after Evesham, see Jobson, 'Royal government and administration in post-Evesham England', and Collingwood, 'Royal finance', chs 6 and 7.

[298] Cassidy, 'Adventus vicecomitum', 617; Collingwood, 'Royal finance', 264.

[299] CPR 1258–66, 551; F, i, 468 (CPR 1258–66, 575–6). The whole story is told in Kaeuper, Bankers to the Crown, 135–7, 141–4.

[300] As analysed by Ben Wild in WA, clxxiii–ix, 130–7. For James Collingwood's analysis of the figures from the pipe rolls, see below 575 n. 25.

[301] These figures are subject to all kinds of qualifications. So, the low figure for 1245 to 1252 may just reflect that the king was paying more of his way through money out of the exchequer.

crossbowmen, archers (they were Welsh), engineers and masons at the siege of Kenilworth and during Henry's stay at Bury, Cambridge and Stratford.

So where did the money come from? Not surprisingly only 9 per cent was supplied by the exchequer, the smallest proportion in the whole of the reign.[302] But this deficit was offset by monies arising from the war. So £3,693 came from (unspecified) fines to recover the king's grace and another £673 from London's. There was also £685 from the money of foreign merchants arrested in the city. Another £1,352 came from fines to be exempt from serving in the armies, £1,517 from loans, £1,143 from the sales of plate and jewels, and £2,666 (4,000 marks) from Llywelyn.

There was one other source of revenue which brings us back finally to Pope Clement and Ottobuono. The wardrobe accounts recorded £1,607 and then another £1,520 received 'from the tenth conceded to the king by the Roman court'.[303] Henry had appealed to the pope for financial aid back in March 1266. In June, Clement had granted the king a tenth of ecclesiastical revenues for three years. The pope had some ulterior motive here for the 7,000 marks owed as arrears of the papal tribute (it had not been paid at all during the disturbances) was to come from the first proceeds of the tax. There would, however, be still plenty left for the king – and the queen.

It was left to Ottobuono to carry through the tax in England. He announced it at Kenilworth in August 1266 and instructed the collectors to undertake a fresh valuation of church property. The previous valuation for the Sicilian taxation was thought to be a gross understatement. Not surprisingly, the church protested at this new imposition, after all its losses in the war, but the collection went ahead. In the end the total yield seems to have been between £44,000 and £49,000, so more than from any other tax in Henry's reign. To the £3,127 received into the wardrobe down to 1268, another £8,000 was added before the end of the reign.[304] The money, with Ottobuono's consent, was also used to pay off debts to merchants and others. In July 1267 alone £2,240 was assigned to Italian merchants, while £324 went to pay off the count of St Pol. As for Queen Eleanor, she 'elicited' from the pope a promise of around £15,000 from the tax to pay off the debts incurred during her French exile. She showed her usual vigour in actually getting hold of the money.[305]

Ottobuono, therefore, had not merely brought peace to England and Wales. He had also refinanced the monarchy. Without him, one wonders what would have become of Henry and the kingdom. Nor was this all. Next year Ottobuono was to summon a great ecclesiastical council and promulgate influential statutes for the reform of the English church.

[302] Wild, *WA*, cxv, cxxix, cxliv, clviii, clxxvii.
[303] For a comprehensive account of the tax, see Lunt, *Financial Relations*, 155–6, 291–310.
[304] Wild, *WA*, clxxx, 147–8.
[305] *CPR 1266–72*, 88, 92; Howell, *Eleanor of Provence*, 236–7.

## Chapter 13

# PARLIAMENT, WESTMINSTER ABBEY AND THE CRUSADE
## 1268–1270

When the Statute of Marlborough was promulgated in November 1267, Henry III had just passed his sixtieth birthday. He had reigned for fifty-one years, fifteen longer than any previous English king. Five more years remained. They were for Henry comfortably sedentary. He was able to live almost exclusively at his favourite and familiar palaces and palace castles in the south: Westminster, Windsor, Marlborough, Clarendon, Winchester and Woodstock.[1] The only expedition further afield, apart from one to Norwich at the end of the reign, was to York in August 1268. He did not visit the Welsh marches. He did not go on pilgrimage either to Becket at Canterbury or the East Anglian holy sites.[2] Above all, his itinerary was dominated by Westminster. Now he could always be there for the 13 October and 5 January feasts of the Confessor. In between the two feasts he usually visited Marlborough and Clarendon, before celebrating Christmas at Winchester. Guildford was the usual stopping place on the midwinter journey back to Westminster for the 5 January feast. All this, of course, was an old pattern. But there was also a new one. In the past, Henry's stays at Westminster had been interleaved with visits to Windsor and elsewhere. Now that was much less the case. Having arrived in January, year after year he remained at Westminster for long periods: five months in 1268 interrupted only by a spring break at Windsor;[3] nearly three months in 1269; five months in 1270; a whole eight months in 1271, apart from ten days at Merton in July; and four months in his last year, 1272.[4]

In terms of travel, Henry's kingship had almost stopped. The reason was that, in this last period, he was frequently laid low by illness. Yet it would be quite wrong to think that his kingship had stopped too. Henry was sick and sedentary, but he was far from silent. Emerging from the shadows of reform and rebellion, his spirit shines forth in building works, almsgiving, commitment to the crusade, assertion of his rights, distribution

---

[1] In 1270 and 1272.
[2] He visited them in 1272 but the reason for the trip was the situation in Norwich.
[3] This was preceded by a period at Windsor after the 5 January feast.
[4] There were also some long stays at Winchester, especially in 1269.

of patronage and interest in money. He was even able to look back over the war with a certain humour, while at the same time revealing his knowledge of the classics. When, in March 1268, he gave Roger of Clifford permission to spend a month in Hereford, he assured the doubtful citizens that Clifford would defend the town 'in the fashion of the siege of Troy'! He would not, in other words, be repeating his violent assault on Hereford made back in 1264.[5] If the gifts given Henry by his subjects were now fewer than in periods of his personal rule, he still received, between March 1268 and the end of the reign, in combinations of gold, silver and silver gilt, 129 cups, 24 bowls, 55 rings, 10 brooches and a sapphire in a gold case.[6] These years also saw what for Henry was the greatest achievement of his reign. On 13 October 1269 his new Abbey at Westminster was consecrated and the body of Edward the Confessor translated to its new shrine.

It would be good to think that age and experience had brought Henry wisdom. Yet in this period he often appears, as of old, open-handed, impulsive, ill-advised and, when things went wrong, uncertain and apologetic. Fortunately, the damage he could do was limited. Little of importance happened without Edward's consent or, after his departure on crusade, without the consent of those he left behind to mind his and the kingdom's affairs. King Richard too, outside his last visit to Germany between the Augusts of 1268 and 1269, played a major part in the king's councils. Henry's court, with the queen back by his side, was also a far more unified, less factionalized place, than before 1258.

The period 1268–72 falls into two halves, divided by Edward's departure on crusade in August 1270. This chapter, covering the years 1268 to 1270, celebrates Henry's achievement at the Abbey. It also describes the struggle to secure a grant of taxation to finance Edward's crusade. As a result, the years between 1268 and 1270 became a period of parliamentary activity and constitutional significance. Parliament's control over taxation was confirmed. A place for knights and burgesses was consolidated. Parliament, in a new form, was seen to be central to national life.

## HENRY AS OF OLD

Henry in the last years of his reign sometimes authorized writs 'with his council' or 'with all the council'. The council, however, had no precise powers and imposed no precise restrictions on the king. Its members had to be summoned to meet together as a body.[7] The chancellors, Godfrey Giffard, John of Chishall and then (from July 1269) the former judge

---

[5] HRO BG/11/1/3; *CIM*, no. 291. I am grateful to Adam Chambers for drawing this letter to my attention, having spotted it in Nicholas Vincent's census of Henry III originals.

[6] Wild, *WA*, clxxxi, 149–53 (from the wardrobe account covering the period).

[7] See Sayles, 'Representation of cities', 583–4.

Richard of Middleton, had no authority to refuse Henry's orders.[8] Such orders were particularly abundant when it came to the refurbishment of the king's major residences. Here there was much to do. As early as 1261, Henry had criticized the ruling council for allowing his castles and houses to go to ruin.[9] So now, amongst other commissions, a carved and painted image of the Confessor was to be placed at the entrance to the hall at Winchester; at Woodstock, the chapel near the king's bed was to be painted and paved; at Marlborough, four stained-glass windows were to be made for his chamber; and at Northampton (which Henry visited on his way north in 1268), the king's seat in the hall was to be painted. At Clarendon too the king's seat was painted while saplings were planted in the garden and new rooms, with outer chambers and fireplaces, were made for both the Franciscan and Dominican friars. Henry gave many of the orders by word of mouth. He had lost neither his voice nor his love for building and decoration.[10]

Henry was equally active when it came to his alms and offerings. When the queen was at court, he continued to clothe 150 paupers on the great church festivals and almost certainly he was still feeding that number every day. Between March 1268 and the end of the reign, 339 precious cloths, and a great array of gold in foil, bezants, money of Murcia and the ill-fated pennies of 1257 went out of the wardrobe 'in the oblations of the king'.[11]

In these last years, as death came nearer, and as he prepared for the crusade, did Henry's conscience prick him over transgressions in the past, both his own and those of his father? The now-sainted Bishop Richard of Chichester had threatened to seek compensation 'in the court of the most high' if Henry did not restore all he had taken from the bishopric during the controversy over Richard's appointment. Now in August 1269, Henry made a pilgrimage to Richard's shrine at Chichester, and later offered some reparation to this bishop 'of happy memory'.[12] Equally striking was the grant of the royal demesne manor of Melksham to the nuns of Amesbury 'for the souls of Arthur of Brittany and Eleanor his sister', Arthur whom King John had murdered, Eleanor whom Henry had held prisoner all her life. The nuns were to celebrate their obituaries and those of Henry and his queen.[13] Henry also hoped his father and mother might, through his own efforts, share in the indulgence conferred on all who helped the Holy Land.[14] When in 1268, Henry agreed to Ottobuono

---

[8] Godfrey Giffard was the younger brother of Walter Giffard and became chancellor in 1266 on the latter's elevation to the archbishopric of York. He resigned two years later on his own elevation to the bishopric of Worcester. For him, see Davies, 'Godfrey Giffard'.

[9] *DBM*, 228–9, cap. 16 [18].

[10] *CLR 1267–72*, nos. 67, 121, 372, 549, 784, 891, 894, ?947, 952, 1192, 1212, 1304, 1321.

[11] Wild, *WA*, clxxxi, 151–2, 154.

[12] *Saint Richard of Chichester*, 69; *CLR 1267–72*, no. 1386.

[13] *CChR 1257–1300*, 100; *RCWL*, ii, 168. The charter was also witnessed by King Richard.

[14] See below, 566–7.

holding his legatine council, Wykes (for all his other criticisms) described him as a '*rex Christianissimus*'.[15]

Henry's activity was far from confined to alms and architecture. He was equally concerned with matters of revenue and expenditure. In May 1268 he entered the exchequer and ordered the barons to observe inviolably all its laws and customs as they had been best observed in the time of King John and his ancestors. In the exchequer memoranda rolls a large crown was drawn to mark the entry.[16] In 1270, Henry wanted to know at once what monies the sheriffs had brought in at the start of the Michaelmas term. His desire for exact information about his revenues was as strong as ever.[17] He was just as hands-on in other areas. It was by word of mouth he gave instructions both to the men collecting the clerical tenth in the Canterbury diocese and to those appointed to register debts owed to the Jews.[18] In January 1268 he personally authorized the writ assigning £326 to pay for cloth taken from various merchants.[19]

Henry wanted money but he was quite prepared to moderate his demands for those in his favour. When the exchequer imprisoned Robert de Percy for debt, Henry had him brought to Windsor to talk the matter over. The result was a generous settlement made 'of the king's special grace' in return for the loyal service of Robert's father, Peter de Percy, as sheriff of Northumberland during the war.[20] But Henry could also act with force and decision when defending the rights of the crown, though he was equally, of course, quite capable of acting in ways clean contrary to them. When John fitzJohn, having recovered his lands from Gilbert de Clare, did homage for them to Gilbert, in 'contempt' of the king, Henry ordered all the lands to be seized. This soon brought John in to court to do homage to Henry himself.[21]

If Henry appears impressive, there were other occasions when his ill-advised actions got him into trouble. In 1269 he admitted acting 'without deliberation and consideration' when dealing with the interminable quarrels between Isabella de Forz and her mother Amice, countess of Devon. Here he was persuaded to change his mind by Edward, Henry of Almain and Philip Basset.[22] Rather more serious, or at least potentially so, was

---

[15] Wykes, 215. Henry also made great efforts to pay the arrears of the pension owed to Fontevraud: see, for example, TNA E 159/43, m. 2d (image 0086).

[16] TNA E 159/42, m. 17 (image 0042).

[17] TNA E 159/45, m. 1 (image 0003); see also *CR 1268–72*, 226–7 and TNA E 159/42, m. 6 (image 0017).

[18] *CR 1268–72*, 54, 212.

[19] *CLR 1267–72*, no. 84.

[20] TNA E 159/43, m. 10d (image 0105); *CFR 1268–9*, nos. 299–300.

[21] *CFR 1267–8*, no. 479; *CR 1264–8*, 468.

[22] The issue was whether the quarrel should be settled by an award of the king or by a lawsuit: *CR 1268–72*, 24–5, 54, 242–3 (where Henry changes his mind again); *CR 1264–8*, 501.

Henry's quarrel with his brother King Richard. Richard had been at Marlborough when the statute was promulgated in November 1267 but had then left court in anger. This produced from Henry an extraordinary letter of apology. It listed the various promises made to his brother and admitted there were some he had failed to keep. In particular, he had made peace with the Londoners without Richard's counsel, 'on which we confess we did less than well'. So that matters could now be settled, he asked Richard to attend the Christmas court at Winchester where the chancery rolls containing the promises would be produced. (They were presently at the New Temple in London.) Richard was to come 'as you love us and our honour and your honour and as we trust you more than all mortals'.[23] At least the production of the rolls suggests Henry wanted chapter and verse on Richard's claims, but he hardly emerges from the episode in a very kingly light.[24]

Thomas Wykes was critical of Henry in these years on another familiar front, that of his prodigality. Thus the ecclesiastical tenth, granted by the pope brought, he said, no increase to the king's coffers since 'with accustomed prodigality, through the king's incompetence ('*imperitiam*'), it was lavished on unworthy people'.[25] Henry certainly used the tenth to pay money owed his foreign kin and connections. Assignments included over 600 marks to Guy de Lusignan (at court for a while from August 1269); 1,625 marks to the executors of Thomas of Savoy; 500 marks to the duke of Brunswick, married to the queen's kinswoman; 900 marks to the Savoyard archbishop of Tarentaise; 196 marks to Peter de Aigueblanche, bishop of Hereford (now back in England); and 2,100 marks to the count of Bigorre.[26] A writ Henry personally authorized also sought 200 marks from the exchequer for one of the count's followers who was about to be knighted.[27] Sometimes the king commanded these payments in the most urgent terms, even overriding previous arrangements to reserve money for the expenses of the household. The collector of the Salisbury tenth was to give the count of Bigorre 300 marks, 'notwithstanding any mandate to the contrary, as he loves the king's honour and his own'.[28] Clearly Henry felt his honour and prestige was bound up in these payments, but one can see why Wykes complained as he did.

Henry was equally under pressure to provide patronage of other kinds for family and loyal servants, sometimes as compensation for their expenditure during the war: Roger of Leybourne's claim was for over

---

[23] *CR 1264–8*, 407; Denholm-Young, *Richard of Cornwall*, 139. The promises included 1,000 marks worth of wardships and 2,000 marks from the lands of the disinherited.

[24] For the sequel, see below, 529–30.

[25] Wykes, 220.

[26] *CPR 1266–72*, 190, 197, 207–8, 210, 215, 223, 227, 232, 304, 327, 335, 340, 348, 350, 367, 391.

[27] *CLR 1267–72*, no. 229.

[28] *CPR 1266–72*, 210.

£3,000.[29] Just as before 1258, Henry was soon forming queues for those promised wardships and escheats. At the top were King Richard and John of Brittany. (The latter was owed 4,000 marks.)[30] Beneath them came Peter de Champvent, William de Sancta Ermina, William de Say, Master Richard of Ewell (the buyer of the wardrobe) and the treasurer of the exchequer, Master Thomas of Wymondham.[31] The pressure on patronage was exemplified by the scramble for the spoils after the death of that great Montfortian captain Henry de Hastings in 1269. The idea of selling the marriage of the heir so as to redeem the king's jewels in France was abandoned. Instead, the marriage went to William de Valence and the wardship of the lands to King Richard.[32] The favours given to Valence seem to bulk just as large as before 1258. His annual fee was resumed when the lands of William de Munchesney had to be resigned under the terms of the Dictum of Kenilworth. Steps were also taken to clear off £1,468 worth of arrears.[33]

In all this, Henry can appear a soft touch. In one discreditable episode he issued letters patent granting Walter Giffard, archbishop of York, the right to exclude the sheriff altogether from his episcopal manors in Yorkshire, Nottinghamshire and Gloucestershire. As an ex-chancellor, was Giffard concerned to protect the rights of the crown and save Henry from himself? No! His aim, like so many ministers, going back to Hubert de Burgh, was to escape the burdens of royal government while imposing them on everyone else. In this case there was a rebellion at court against the archbishop. A memorandum on the patent rolls stated that, in the presence of the king and council, Giffard had surrendered his letters 'and they were cancelled and broken and wholly annulled, and it was granted on both sides that they should have no place in future times'.[34] One wonders if Edward, in view of his later record, had a hand in this.

## HENRY AND HIS FAMILY

In these last years, Henry was made happy by the presence at court of those expelled so unjustly, as he thought, in 1258. William de Valence was a frequent attender before his departure on crusade in August 1270. Guy de Lusignan was there for periods in 1269 and 1270. Back too were both Elyas de Rabayne and William de Sancta Ermina. The Savoyard knight Peter de Champvent was another at court, although he at least had escaped proscription in 1258.

---

[29] *CPR 1266–72*, 251.

[30] This was the arrears of the compensation owed in place of the honour of Richmond.

[31] *CPR 1258–66*, 668, 677; *CPR 1266–72*, 167–8, 171, 182–3, 218, 250–1, 257–8, 262, 299, 338.

[32] *CPR 1266–72*, 323, 360, 546.

[33] *CPR 1266–72*, 193–4, 449; *CLR 1267–72*, nos. 1179, 1443–4; *CChR 1257–1300*, 84.

[34] *CPR 1266–72*, 59–60, 160–1.

Matthew Paris would have been appalled at the sight of these aliens. What had the revolution of 1258 been for if not to expel them? Was there not also here material for Gilbert de Clare to exploit? But in truth Henry's court had a far less alien hue than before 1258. Guy de Lusignan was absent after February 1270. Geoffrey did not appear at all. Peter of Savoy had left England in June 1262 and a year later became count of Savoy. He never returned to England, although presumably he would have commanded the queen's invasion army of 1264. Archbishop Boniface, never anyway a courtier, left England for the last time in October 1268. The stewards of Henry's household, Robert Walerand, Robert Aguillon, William of Wintershall and William of Ayot, were all English.[35] We have no formal list of the council but its leading members between 1268 and 1270 are fairly clear. Apart from William de Valence, they too were all English: Walter Giffard, archbishop of York, his brother Godfrey, bishop of Worcester, King Richard (when in England), Edward, Henry of Almain, Philip Basset, Roger de Mortimer, Roger de Somery and Roger of Leybourne, together with Godfrey Giffard's successors as chancellor and the stewards headed by Robert Walerand.[36]

Another important difference from the situation before 1258 was the absence of faction. While there was competition over patronage, there was no repetition of the old conflicts between the Lusignans and the Savoyards, the king's party and the queen's party. William de Valence, older, wiser and tested in the war, appears a far less divisive character than in the 1250s. The patronage Henry now gave him was authorized by Edward and 'all the council' and was bestowed for his services to the king and his son.[37] He was on his way to that placid effigy covering his tomb in Westminster Abbey.

Fundamental to the stability of this period were Henry's relations with his brother, his son and his queen. King Richard did not answer Henry's plea to attend the Christmas court of 1267, but he did appear at the end of January. He drove a characteristically hard bargain. He never came cheap. With or without proof from the chancery rolls (for they seem to have no record), Henry accepted that his initial promise had been worth £1,000 a year, not 1,000 marks. He also agreed both to put Richard at the top of the wardship queue and to consider his claim that the Mowbray wardship had never been part of the £1,000 deal and so the money was still owed in full. Next year, Richard was granted the Hastings wardship,

[35] For them all witnessing together as stewards, see *CChR 1257–1300*, 113. Wintershall is in Bramley (Surrey), just south of Guildford. William had been a steward of the bishop of Winchester. For him, see Stewart, *1263 Surrey Eyre*, no. 166. Another household steward, also English (a point confirmed to me by Huw Ridgeway), was John de la Linde.

[36] For lists of councillors, see *F*, i, 475–6, 483; Sayles, 'Representation of cities', 583–4.

[37] *CPR 1266–72*, 193–4, 323. His close relationship with Edward went back, of course, to before 1258.

and two more wardships followed in 1271.[38] Henry also made valiant efforts to repay Richard's loans. He evidently did enough for Richard continued to sustain Henry's kingship both with his counsel and his money.

Even more important, before his departure on crusade, was the role of Edward. He had not taken over government. He authorized no writs in this period simply on his own authority. But he often appears alongside his father. Thus either in the body of a writ or in the authorization note appended to it, a decision is said to be made by the king and Edward, by the king, Edward and 'all the council' or by the king, Edward and 'the rest of the council'.[39] The identity of the councillors is rarely given. It was Edward's name that counted and gave authority to the measures in question. These covered a whole range of topics including legislation on the Jews, patronage given to William de Valence and John de Warenne, and the precise location in Oxford for a magnificent marble and gilded cross, with images of the Crucifixion on one side and the Virgin and Child on the other.[40] Occasionally, one glimpses Henry and Edward in discussion. It was after a '*tractatum*' with his son that Henry allowed the earl of Norfolk to appoint a deputy marshal at the exchequer.[41] Edward was quite capable of getting his father to change course, as in the quarrel between the countesses of Devon and Aumale, and in a dispute involving the sister of John Mansel.[42]

None of this means Henry was unable to stand up to his son. The way Edward was running his appanage could still be a bone of contention. In November 1269, Henry learnt that Edward was preparing to hand back the castle of Belin in Gascony to Gaillard de Solers. Since, so Henry said, this was before Gaillard had shown any right to the castle, the concession involved the 'dismemberment of Gascony' and contravened the conditions on which the duchy had been given to Edward in the first place. The result was a stiff letter instructing Edward to retain the castle until Gaillard proved his right. Whether Edward took any notice may be another matter.[43] Henry loved and admired his son. He wrote to him with his 'paternal benediction'.[44] The knowledge that Edward's hand was ultimately on the tiller added greatly to the authority of the government.

Henry was also supported by his closeness to the queen, 'our dearest consort' as he described her. Tensions remained between Eleanor and

---

[38] *RCWL*, ii, 164; *CPR 1266–72*, 187, 360, 533, 546; but see *CR 1268–72*, 500.

[39] *CPR 1266–72*, 302, 323, 376; *CR 1264–8*, 440–1, 443–4, 516; *CR 1268–72*, 22–3, 40, 44, 69, 102, 264.

[40] *CPR 1266–72*, 302, 323; *CR 1268–72*, 22–3. This replaced a cross desecrated, it was said, by the Jews.

[41] *CR 1268–72*, 264.

[42] For this case, see *CChR 1257–1300*, 114, 166; *CR 1268–72*, 39–40.

[43] *CPR 1266–72*, 396; Trabut-Cussac, *L'administration anglaise*, 344; Studd, 'The Lord Edward and King Henry III', 11; Prestwich, *Edward I*, 62–3.

[44] *CLR 1267–72*, no. 1120.

Edward, but there were none, as far as can be seen, between Eleanor and her husband. In 1268, in a letter to Louis IX, Henry expressed 'his earnest desire' that Eleanor might accompany him to a proposed meeting at Boulogne, 'so that we may be cheered by the sight of her and by talking with her'.[45] Henry made concessions at Eleanor's instance, sought to find £500 for her expenses (this in July 1269), and attended to her physical comfort.[46] Much of the building work he commanded was for her benefit: at Woodstock her chamber was heightened and enlarged; at the Tower it was panelled; at Havering it was given stained-glass windows with forty shields; at Winchester it was paved and plastered and a privy chamber was constructed alongside it in the form of a turret; at Brill it got an adjoining oratory; at Clarendon a new chamber was made for her Franciscan friars.[47]

Just how Eleanor divided her time between the royal homes and how often she was with Henry, we do not know. Their almsgiving shows they were certainly together at the great ecclesiastical festivals. Eleanor's main residence remained Windsor where, of course, a whole new suit of apartments had been fashioned for her. Here the next generation of the royal family was growing up. It was at Windsor that Eleanor looked after Eleanor of Castile during the birth of her first son, John, in 1266. Another son was born in May 1268 and named Henry, surely after Henry himself. Henry was at Windsor at the time of the birth and gave 20 marks to the messenger bringing the news. His two grandsons were joined at Windsor by another grandson, namely the son of John of Brittany and Henry's daughter Beatrice, 'the beautiful Beatrice' of all those years ago. He too was named Henry. All three boys were looked after by the same staff.[48] For the Christmas of 1268, Henry decked out the two Eleanors, their knights and ladies in the same robes, thus giving visual expression to the unity of the royal family.[49] Nor did Henry forget his daughter Katherine, now lying under her silver effigy in Westminster Abbey. He saw personally to the wages of the chaplain in the hermitage of Charing who was saying masses for her soul.[50]

## PETER OF SAVOY'S DEATH

One episode helped solve a problem within the royal family, though it also revealed tension between Eleanor and Edward.[51] The trigger was the

[45] *CR 1264–8*, 552; Howell, *Eleanor of Provence*, 241.
[46] *CR 1268–72*, 49; *CLR 1267–72*, no. 761, where the £500 were paid through the assignment of tallies.
[47] *CLR 1267–72*, nos. 67, 109, 163, 339, 372, 409, 784, 829, 894.
[48] *CLR 1267–72*, nos. 272, 377, 556, 761, 896, 1315, 1320.
[49] *CR 1268–72*, 6–7.
[50] *CLR 1267–72*, no. 157.
[51] For what follows, see Howell, *Eleanor of Provence*, 242–4; Cox, *Eagles of Savoy*, 367–70.

death of Peter of Savoy, at Pierre-Châtel near Grenoble on 16 or 17 May 1268. What an amazing career! Peter had become a major English baron, a pre-eminent councillor of the king and also, through legislation and administrative reform, 'the real architect of the medieval Savoyard state'.[52] Henry had been entranced and entrapped by this great international statesman, much his age, but so much more intelligent and knowledgeable than himself. At times, Eleanor's own position had been immeasurably strengthened by her brilliant uncle. His prestige and political alliances had ensured she was on the winning side in 1258. Together they had then played a major part in the king's recovery of power in 1261. After Lewes they had laboured together to muster an army for the invasion of England. Yet, on the other hand, Peter's ruthless exploitation of his rights in Sussex had made him many enemies, including John de Warenne, earl of Surrey.[53] If he helped the king's recovery of power in 1261, his unpopularity was a factor in its loss two years later.

There was also an ambiguity about Peter's conduct in England. Was he always acting in the best interests of Henry and his family or serving himself and the house of Savoy? Certainly, in the early days, he had worked hard to protect the interests of Edward, but he had also used Henry's patronage for what seem purely Savoyard purposes.[54] He had entangled Henry in the Sicilian affair, even if he was not responsible for its disastrous second phase. Given all he had received from the king, well might Peter describe Henry as 'my most dear lord, the most illustrious king of England, in whom is all my hope and faith, in death and in life'.[55] But whether it was really money well spent, I wonder. Peter's final will certainly showed how little his heart was in England. There was not a single gift to an English religious institution while there were numerous continental beneficiaries. Peter's house on the Strand was to go to the famous hospice of Mont-Joux on the Grand-Saint-Bernard pass across the Alps.[56]

Nowhere was the ambiguity in Peter's conduct more apparent than over the future of his English honours, those of Richmond, Pevensey and Hastings, the last acquired by an exchange with Edward in 1262.[57] With his customary attention to detail, Peter had obtained the honours in hereditary right and with the extra proviso that he could grant them hereditarily to whoever he wished.[58] In fact, under his will of 1255, Peter left all his English possessions to the queen, thus excluding both his only child, his daughter Beatrice, married to the Dauphin of Viennois, and his

---

[52] Cox, *Eagles of Savoy*, 371.

[53] His quarrels with John de Warenne are a major theme in Andrew Spencer's ' "A vineyard without a wall" '.

[54] See volume 1, 214, 564, and above, 79–80.

[55] Andenmatten, 'Contraintes lignagères et parcours individuel', 286.

[56] Von Wurstemberger, *Peter der Zweite*, iv, no. 749.

[57] Peter had held it before as Edward's bailiff.

[58] This is a theme of Ridgeway, 'An English cartulary roll of Peter of Savoy'.

nearest male heir, his older brother, Thomas of Savoy.[59] In 1259, as part of a fresh agreement, Eleanor's title to Pevensey was strengthened and its constituent parts listed. She was also allowed to dispose of it freely.[60]

After this, however, Peter's intentions became more obscure and less reassuring.[61] Under his final will, made 'sound in mind but sick in body' in May 1268, the queen was indeed to get Richmond, but, in flat contradiction to the arrangements in 1259, Pevensey and the lands in Sussex (so Hastings as well) were to go to the sons of Thomas of Savoy.[62] In a codicil to the will, making this all the clearer, Peter begged Henry, Eleanor, Edward and Edmund to receive the brothers kindly and give them seisin.[63] Some hope! Perhaps Henry, left to himself, would have complied. There was no way Edward and Eleanor were going to. Eleanor herself must have felt let down, given Peter's earlier promises over Pevensey. Edward was determined not to let the vast estate pass from the crown. His first reaction to Peter's death (on 3 June) was to take all Peter's lands into his hands.[64]

On Pevensey, Henry, Edward and the council took their stand on Peter's concession to Eleanor back in 1259, but with a reservation almost certainly due to Edward. Instead of being able to assign the honour to whom she pleased, it was now, on her death, to revert to the crown, and so ultimately to Edward himself. After a while Edward went further still. With Eleanor's consent, he arranged to hold the honour himself directly from the king and then granted it back to her for life. It was the kind of attention to title worthy of Peter of Savoy himself.

When it came to Richmond, Edward was determined it should go to his brother-in-law John of Brittany, now one of his closest friends. This would also mean the Agenais eventually passing to the English crown.[65] Already in 1266, Edward had tried to get Peter out and John in.[66] Now he could have his way. In July 1268, with Eleanor's consent, Henry granted Richmond to John in hereditary right. In return Eleanor was to have the 1,200-mark rent that John received from King Louis until the Agenais was acquired, plus the annual 800 marks he was owed, over and above that, by the king. But here a fascinating division opened up between the pliant king and his far from pliant son. Whereas Henry granted Eleanor the 800 marks right away, Edward said he would only agree the deal if his mother proved

---

[59] Andenmatten, 'Contraintes lignagères et parcours individuel', 284–6.

[60] TNA CP 25/1/283/15/358. See above, 103 n. 74.

[61] See above, 225, 235–6, 336.

[62] Von Wurstemberger, *Peter der Zweite*, iv, no. 749. For Peter always regarding Thomas's sons as his ultimate heirs, see Ripart, 'Non est consuetum in comitatu Sabaudie', 316–21.

[63] Von Wurstemberger, *Peter der Zweite*, iv, no. 751.

[64] *CFR 1267–8*, nos. 476–8.

[65] For Breton claims to Richmond and the arrangements made over the Agenais under the terms of John's marriage agreement, see above, 97, 103.

[66] *CPR 1258–66*, 591, 666.

her title to Richmond under the terms of Peter's final will, although that in other respects was being set aside![67] Fortunately, Eleanor succeeded in doing so and thus in the end got the full 2,000 marks. Henry also, with overflowing generosity said that her executors could have 10,000 marks from the 2,000-marks annual payment, which meant in effect it would continue for another five years after her death.[68]

Only Hastings, therefore, remained, to be disposed of and here there was division between Edward and John of Brittany with Edward keeping the town and the castle and John receiving the rest of the honour. What finally of the sons of Thomas of Savoy?[69] Far from being welcomed to England and given Pevensey, they were fobbed off with the promise of a 100-mark annual pension.[70] So of all the great estate Peter had built up in England, for all his insistence that he could dispose of it freely, nothing remained to the Savoyards. The travellers across the Saint Bernard pass did not benefit either. The house on the Strand passed not to the hospice of Mont-Joux but to Edmund and thence to the earls and dukes of Lancaster. As the London residence of the hated John of Gaunt it was sacked during the Peasants' Revolt. At least the connection with Savoy was never forgotten and the Savoy hotel is now, of course, on the site.[71]

John of Brittany, therefore, had replaced Peter of Savoy as a great English magnate, the king's son-in-law in place of the queen's uncle. John was to serve Edward well, arguably better than Peter had served Henry. Although getting less than she might have hoped, Peter's death had left the queen with the honour of Pevensey and a pension of 2,000 marks a year. As Margaret Howell has remarked, she had shown a wise and realistic combination of 'determination and restraint'.[72] She had made good her claim to compensation in the face of Edward's challenge, yet had avoided any breach with her masterful son. She had learnt from past events how damaging that could be. Strictly speaking, the overriding of Peter's will was a lawless act. To my mind it was absolutely justified.


## PROVISION FOR EDMUND

The royal family was also strengthened in 1269 by a more than doubling of Edmund's landed estate. After Evesham, he had been given the lands of Simon de Montfort and thereafter styled himself earl of Leicester. In 1267

---

[67] Edward would be liable for the payment after his succession to the throne.

[68] *F*, i, 475–6; *CPR 1266–72*, 246, 301, 310–11, 362, 383, 433–4; Howell, *Eleanor of Provence*, 302.

[69] *CPR 1266–72*, 304, 313.

[70] *CPR 1266–72*, 487, 547; *CLR 1267–72*, no. 1679.

[71] A small plaque near the entrance records how Montfort stayed in the house during his parliament of 1265.

[72] Howell, *Eleanor of Provence*, 243–4.

the honour and county of Lancaster had followed.[73] But all this hardly seemed enough for a king's son, who had once paraded in robes as king of Sicily. A great marriage was one obvious way forward and the royal family had someone in mind: Isabella de Forz.[74] The marriage would bring Edmund, during Isabella's lifetime, the Isle of Wight and the lands of the earldom of Devon (both of which she held in her own right), together with her dower third (including Holderness) of the lands of her late husband, the earl of Aumale. No wonder Simon de Montfort junior, in 1264–5, had chased Isabella all over the country trying to capture her as his bride.[75] Unfortunately Isabella, protected by Magna Carta, was no readier to marry Edmund than she had been young Simon. So all Edmund in practice could be granted was any fine she might make either for the king's permission to marry someone else or for having married someone without the king's permission, neither event being very likely. Isabella was enjoying life as a wealthy and independent widow. Then suddenly the situation was transformed by the death, early in 1269, of Isabella's only surviving son by the earl of Aumale. This left her daughter, Aveline, aged ten, the sole heir to both the earldoms of Devon and Aumale. The daughter was thus an even greater prize than the mother and the royal family determined that Edmund should have her.[76] This required the consent of Isabella and her own mother, Amice, countess of Devon, to whom the rights over the marriage jointly belonged. In the negotiations with the two countesses, the queen took the lead, and it was she who found the money to pay them £1,000 apiece.[77]

The marriage took place on 9 April 1269 in Westminster Abbey before the king, the queen, Edward and all the people assembled for a parliament. Afterwards Henry held, in fitzThedmar's words, 'a great and noble court'. He had ordered 19,200 farthing loaves to be ready for the day ('wishing the marriage to be celebrated with due solemnity'), so there was surely enough both for the feasting in the hall and for a mass distribution of bread to the poor.[78]

## THE DISINHERITANCE OF ROBERT DE FERRERS

Edmund's marriage was quickly followed by another coup, for he soon obtained the lands of Robert de Ferrers, earl of Derby. Indeed, the marriage was probably the spur for moving forward on that front. It was

---

[73] *CChR 1257–1300*, 78; *CPR 1266–72*, 100; *RCWL*, ii, 159.

[74] *CPR 1258–66*, 275; *CPR 1266–72*, 303.

[75] Jacob, *Studies*, 210 n. 3; Powicke, *King Henry III*, ii, 708.

[76] Aveline would have the Aumale lands at once (less her mother's dower third) but would have to wait for the Devon lands until her mother's death.

[77] *CPR 1258–66*, 97, 161; *CChR 1257–1300*, 121–2; *CPR 1266–72*, 358; Howell, *Eleanor of Provence*, 244–5.

[78] FitzThedmar, 108–9 (Stone, FitzThedmar, no. 980); Wykes, 221–2; *CLR 1267–72*, no. 646.

not straightforward. Edmund had been given Ferrers' lands after the latter's capture at the battle of Chesterfield. Since then, Ferrers had remained a prisoner at Windsor castle. Yet the Dictum of Kenilworth had stipulated that all prisoners should be released, provided they found guarantors for their good conduct. It also stated that Ferrers should be allowed to redeem his lands at seven years their annual value. This was two years more than anyone else other than Henry de Hastings and the mutilators of the Kenilworth messenger, but was not an impossible burden. The royal family, however, was absolutely determined to get round the provisions of the Dictum and allow Edmund to retain the Ferrers' estate. Here keeping Ferrers in prison was the easy part. Indeed, since it prevented him getting the necessary guarantors for his release, it was technically not even in breach of the Dictum, though clearly a breach of its spirit. How, though, to get round the seven-year redemption fine was more difficult.

The process started at Windsor towards the end of April 1269.[79] Ferrers appeared before the king and the whole council and acknowledged that he was bound to pay Edmund an astonishing £50,000 for the redemption of his estates.[80] He was, moreover, to make the payment by 8 July, something clearly impossible. Why had Ferrers agreed to this terrible bargain when under the Dictum of Kenilworth the fine should have been at most around £10,000?[81] There were two reasons. The first was that, having been imprisoned now for three years, this seemed the only way to get out. The second was the stipulation in the agreement that, if he failed to make the payment in due time, the money was to be raised from his lands. This at least gave some hope that eventually the debt could be paid off. Indeed, if Ferrers could benefit from the concession obtained by Gilbert de Clare, then he could have possession of the lands while the sum was paid.

If, however, Ferrers hoped he would be immediately released he was disappointed. Instead, he was moved to King Richard's manor house at Cippenham some five miles from Windsor.[82] There he was placed, as he later complained, 'in a chamber under strict custody'.[83] King Richard himself was absent in Germany and had nothing to do with what followed, although he might well have approved of it, as certainly did Henry of Almain. It seems unlikely that the king himself was opposed to what was happening, however much back in 1265 he had tried to save Ferrers from

---

[79] The main documents connected with the process are transcribed as Appendix 2 in Golob, 'The Ferrers earls of Derby', ii; and see *CR 1268–72*, 122–6; Jacob, *Studies*, 388–94. Golob, 'The Ferrers earls of Derby', i, 367–79 gives a full analysis of what happened. For recent discussion, see Spencer, *Nobility and Kingship*, 182–4.

[80] *CR 1268–72*, 126. This memorandum is undated.

[81] For various valuations of the Ferrers estates, see Golob, 'The Ferrers earls of Derby', i, 319.

[82] The site now adjoins the M4 motorway.

[83] Jacob, *Studies*, 392–3.

Edward's clutches.[84] He was in at the start when Ferrers agreed to the monstrous £50,000 fine. He was in too at the end when the Ferrers' estates were finally consigned to Edmund. Probably the whole procedure was agreed by the royal family and the council, with Edward, Ferrers' personal enemy, in the lead. The reason for allowing Ferrers to think the £50,000 might be repaid from his lands was to get him to agree to the £50,000 in the first place. The reason for taking him to Cippenham was to scare him into conceding much more. Removed from the king's peace at Windsor, surrounded by a group of threatening knights, he must have felt very isolated and vulnerable. There is every reason to believe his later statement that his final concessions were made 'while a prisoner in custody, fearing danger to his body'.

Thus it was that on 1 May 1269, at Cippenham, Ferrers set his seal to a fatal document. He explained that he had found eleven guarantors who would pay the £50,000 if he could not. In order to preserve them from loss, he would immediately hand over to them all his lands and if he did not come up with the money by 8 July, they were permitted to grant those lands to Edmund until the money was paid. To make that all the more impossible there were two further stipulations. First, the £50,000 had to be paid in one go, not in instalments. Second, the issues of the lands were *not* to contribute to the payment. So this was a total reversal of the Windsor agreement where the money could be raised from the lands.[85] To make quite sure that Ferrers' concession was watertight, one final step was taken on 1 May. The chancellor, John of Chishall, entered the chamber where Ferrers lay and produced the document he had just sealed. Did he accept it and did he wish it to be registered on the chancery rolls? Fearing further imprisonment and danger to his body, Ferrers said 'yes'.[86] There was just one compensation. The £50,000, it was conceded, was for Ferrers' release from prison as well as the redemption of his lands. He could hope at last to be set free.[87]

But Ferrers was not freed, or not immediately. Instead, he was taken in a cart, with guards inside and out, to King Richard's castle at Wallingford.[88] There he remained for three weeks until Edward finally released him. Doubtless the delay was to make sure he caused no trouble. There was, of course, no prospect of raising the money, so the final denouement was inevitable. At Westminster on 9 July, the day after the deadline expired, the guarantors, headed by Henry of Almain, William de Valence and John

---

[84] See above, 473.

[85] TNA DL 25/2227 (Golob, 'The Ferrers earls of Derby', ii, Appendix 2, no. 2); *CR 1268–72*, 124–5; Jacob, *Studies*, 390–1, from where the place of issue and date comes.

[86] Jacob, *Studies*, 393.

[87] This was in a letter issued by the guarantors on 2 May: TNA DL 42/2, fo. 15, no. 55 (Golob, 'The Ferrers earls of Derby', ii, Appendix 2, no. 6).

[88] Jacob, *Studies*, 392–3.

de Warenne, in the presence of the king and council, handed the Ferrers lands over to Edmund.[89]

Ferrers was not entirely penniless or friendless. He could have recourse to his mother, Mary, who still held a dower third of the Ferrers lands. He could also inherit the estates she held in her own right as the daughter and co-heir of Roger de Quincy, earl of Winchester.[90] Ferrers was also quick to forge a new alliance. On 26 June 1269, so hardly a month after his release from prison, he married Eleanor, granddaughter of the aged Humphrey de Bohun, earl of Hereford, and daughter of the Montfortian Humphrey de Bohun, fatally wounded at Evesham.[91] She was no heiress but must have brought something to the marriage. Yet when Ferrers had needed help most, during his captivity at Windsor and then in those decisive days at Cippenham, none had been forthcoming. Gilbert de Clare was not involved in what happened but did nothing to stop it. Two years before, when he seized London in aid of the disinherited, the case of Robert de Ferrers featured nowhere on his agenda. In the event it was not till 1273 that he took up Ferrers' cause and then in return for a substantial bribe.[92] There seems to have been limited sympathy for the fallen earl. A powerful group of magnates, including three framers of the Dictum of Kenilworth (Henry of Almain, Roger de Somery and Robert Walerand), were prepared to act as his spurious 'guarantors', while a fourth, that upstanding man Philip Basset, headed the witnesses of the eventual transfer to Edmund. There was one other factor in Ferrers' fall. He was no longer family. His first wife, daughter of Hugh de Lusignan and so niece of the king, had died childless while he was in prison.

Up to a point, Ferrers had been unlucky. If he had not been captured at Chesterfield, his fate might have been different. Yet, after such a narrow escape in December 1265, when Edward had wanted his disinheritance and Henry had saved him, it was folly to tempt fate again. Ferrers was the only magnate to be imprisoned by both sides in the civil war. There was surely something exceptionally reckless and irresponsible about him.

In overriding the Dictum in Edmund's favour, the king and his council had resorted to sharp practice and intimidation. They had in effect acted in a lawless fashion. Yet in a way the whole procedure showed a respect for the Dictum. It could not simply be ignored, it had to be manoeuvred around. Ferrers had agreed the fine of £50,000 and had not been disinherited. However impossible, if he came up with the money he would still recover his lands. The procedure was strong enough to withstand the legal

---

[89] TNA DL 25/2219 (Golob, 'The Ferrers earls of Derby', ii, Appendix 2, no. 10); illustrated in *Christopher Hatton's Book*, no. 411.

[90] See Cokayne, *Complete Peerage*, v, 306 n. (a).

[91] TNA CP 40/31, m. 49, a reference I owe to Golob, 'The Ferrers earls of Derby', i, 366 n. 219.

[92] Golob, 'The Ferrers earls of Derby', i, 374–8, sets out the agreements in detail.

challenge made by Ferrers in the reign of Edward I. Here the crucial consideration was that Ferrers had acknowledged his concession before the king's own chancellor and had asked for it to be recorded on the chancery rolls. He could not have been a prisoner when he did that!

In territorial terms, the great gainer from the civil war was Edmund for he added the earldoms of Leicester and Derby to his honour of Lancaster. In the long term here there was danger to the crown. It was on the strength of this great endowment that Edmund's son Thomas of Lancaster challenged Edward II and Henry of Bolingbroke deposed Richard II.[93] Lancaster saw himself as a reincarnation of Montfort but quite lacked his courage, religiosity and charisma. He died not gallantly on the battlefield but at the stroke of an executioner's axe, having tamely fallen into the hands of his enemies.[94] In his own day, however, the royal family was strengthened by Edmund's elevation. Like John of Brittany, he gave long and loyal service to Edward. After his death in Gascony in 1296, his body was brought back for burial in Westminster Abbey, where it still lies beneath a high canopied tomb. In the centre of the canopy Edmund sits quietly on a horse, dressed in armour, his hands joined in prayer. It is a peaceful image of this prince who quite lacked the drive and martial ardour of his older brother. Edmund's first wife, Aveline, was already in the Abbey. She had died childless in 1274 so here the best-laid plans came to naught. Edmund did not get the earldoms of Devon and Aumale, although Edward made quite sure of securing for himself the Isle of Wight. Edmund mourned Aveline, so Wykes thought, as much for the loss of a loved one as for the loss of her possessions. Perhaps this explains her beautiful tomb in the Abbey with its graceful effigy lying beneath a trefoiled canopy.[95]

## THE LAUNCH OF THE CRUSADE AND THE DEPARTURE OF OTTOBUONO

After the end of the civil war Ottobuono had two main preoccupations. The first was reform of the church. In April 1268, the spiritual climax of his legation, he held a great church council at St Paul's in London. Its legislation affirmed and supplemented the canons promulgated at the council held by the legate Otto back in 1237. Divided into fifty-three separate chapters, in a modern printed edition, it runs to some forty-five pages. The whole gamut of church life was covered including baptism and

---

[93] Maddicott, *Thomas of Lancaster*, 8–39; Given-Wilson, *Henry IV*, 11–23. Thomas of Lancaster also inherited the earldoms of Lincoln and Salisbury.

[94] For Lancaster and Montfort, see Maddicott, *Thomas of Lancaster*, 119, 224, 292, 314, 321–2.

[95] Wykes, 260; Powicke, *King Henry III*, ii, 708–9. Powicke describes the tomb as 'a gracious and touching thing'.

confession, clerical dress and concubines, non-residence and pluralism, and the conduct of monks and nuns. Archbishops and bishops were urged to be present in their dioceses, especially during Lent and Advent. Was this, one wonders, a hit at Archbishop Boniface? He was currently in England, though whether at the council seems unknown. There were objections to some of the regulations, but Ottobuono defused them in one-to-one conversations. The statutes 'became the most important single collection of local law for the English Church'.[96]

Ottobuono's second preoccupation was the crusade.[97] This he had been preaching with increasing vigour since 1267. At Lincoln, that autumn, he ordered the city clergy, dressed in their 'sacred vestments', to process to the cathedral behind their crosses and banners. His ensuing sermon, translated by two friars, persuaded many clerics and laymen to take the cross.[98] Under his statutes of April 1268 there were to be 'public and solemn' processions every year after Pentecost with the faithful praying to God for peace and concord and the restoration of the Holy Land to Christianity.[99] The crusade was also promoted by the example of Louis IX. He had been preparing a crusade since 1266 and formally took the cross on 25 March 1267, fittingly the feast of the Annunciation. Henry and Edward's concern for the crusade had been a factor in their agreeing the treaty of Montgomery. By the end of the year, Edward had contacted Louis IX about joining his expedition.

Henry was very torn. In 1266 he had assured Louis in writing that once there was peace in England, he would carry through his crusading vow.[100] Down to 1271, he several times reiterated his intention of going. Louis's example remained both an inspiration and a reproof. Yet Henry also had doubts about both his crusade and Edward's. In January 1268, the pope, quite probably responding to his fears, wrote to Louis IX, setting out all the disadvantages of Edward going: peace in England was still fragile, the king was old and the church, given all its burdens, could provide no money. Later, in April, Clement gave Ottobuono authority to absolve Henry from his own vow provided Edmund went in his place. The implication was that Edward, far less expendable than his brother, would be staying at home too.[101]

Pope Clement's suggestion that Edmund replace Henry and Edward fell on deaf ears. Henry was unwilling to abandon all thought of his own crusade. Edward was determined to go himself and had Ottobuono's

[96] C&S, ii, 738–92.

[97] For Henry's and Edward's crusade, see Lloyd, *English Society and the Crusade*, and Tyerman, *England and the Crusades*, ch. 5.

[98] Barlings, cxv–vi.

[99] C&S, ii, 781–2.

[100] RL, ii, 304–5.

[101] CPReg, 422, 435; Lloyd, *English Society and the Crusade*, 123.

backing. The latter begged the pope to support the devout intentions of the king's son, famous, as he was, for his 'good will, pious actions, noble strength, and devoted faith'.[102] The climax of all Ottobuono's work for the crusade came at Northampton on 24 June 1268.

The place was deliberately chosen, for the round church in Northampton was modelled on the church of the Holy Sepulchre in Jerusalem.[103] The date was carefully chosen too, for it was the feast of that herald of Christ, John the Baptist, one of the great festivals of the church year. The psalm for the day, ninety-two, itself encouraged and comforted those about to undertake a perilous expedition in God's name. 'While thou, Lord, dost reign on high eternally, thy foes will surely perish, and all evil doers will be scattered'.[104] Ottobuono's words were given urgency by the situation: earlier in the year Antioch had fallen to the Saracens. Accordingly, Edward, Edmund, Henry of Almain, Gilbert de Clare, John de Warenne, William de Valence and numerous knights and lesser folk (of both sexes) now took the cross.[105]

After the ceremonies at Northampton, Ottobuono's work was done and he set off back to Rome. 'His patience and sagacity brought peace; his constitutions and his daily intercourse with every party and every interest in the Church breathed a new life into the ecclesiastical body. In contemporary eyes the mission was not an invasion but a work of healing. It was the noblest expression in English history in the later middle ages of the unity of the two powers, the lay and the spiritual, in a joint recognition of the underlying unity of western Christendom.'[106] Sir Maurice Powicke's encomium, lifting one's eyes beyond the narrow vistas of English politics, tells us more perhaps about the world as he wished to see it than the world as it really was. The Osney chronicler, in bidding his own farewell, described Ottobuono as charming and affable but added, remembering all the financial exactions, that he had the voice of Jacob but the hands of Esau.[107] England, however, had been healed by his labours. The papacy never played a more crucial and constructive role in English affairs than in the reign of Henry III with the four great legates Guala, Pandulf, Otto and Ottobuono.[108]

---

[102] Graham, 'Letters of Cardinal Ottoboni', 112; Lloyd, *English Society and the Crusade*, 147.

[103] This point is made in Morris, *A Great and Terrible King*, 83.

[104] Verse 9 in the New English Bible translation.

[105] Wykes, 217–18; St Andrews Northampton, 104.

[106] Sir Maurice Powicke's *King Henry III*, ii, 527–8.

[107] Osney, 218, quoting Genesis 27:22. And see also Wykes, 219. Powicke himself acknowledged the unpopularity: *King Henry III*, ii, 560.

[108] In July 1276, Ottobuono became Pope Adrian V, only to die the following month.

## PARLIAMENT AND THE STRUGGLE
## FOR CRUSADE TAXATION

Henry seems to have left Woodstock in order to attend the Northampton ceremony, for him surely a deeply moving occasion.[109] He then went back to Woodstock before, in mid-July, setting off on a slow journey to York, his last to the north. On the way he made a diversion to Lincoln, perhaps to impress his authority on a former rebel town, certainly to offer prayers to Saint Hugh, Little Saint Hugh and Grosseteste. Henry had not seen Lincoln since his brief visit in September 1258. Far more now of the new Angel choir must have been in place. To see it may well have been another reason for the visit. Henry could now gaze up to the angels set in the spandrels of the triforium, from which the choir derived its name. He must have been pleased to see the influence of Westminster where angels were similarly placed at the transepts' ends. If he regretted not using angels more extensively at the Abbey, he could still think Westminster's soaring height dwarfed what Lincoln had to offer.[110]

Henry was at York from 10 to 26 August. It was partly for reasons of family. Queen Eleanor, Edward, Edmund and Edward's wife and children had all come too, for a meeting with Henry's daughter and son-in-law Queen Margaret and King Alexander of Scotland. Henry must have been overjoyed. He had not seen Margaret and Alexander since 1260-1. That the letters of conduct spoke of them coming for 'recreation and relaxation' underlined the personal nature of the visit.[111]

York, however, was far more than just a family affair. A parliament met there and the main item on the agenda was the crusade. Edward had taken the cross but neither he nor the king had the cash to fund his expedition. The pope had already said the church could not help. So the only solution was to levy a tax on the whole kingdom. That might take several forms, but by far the most lucrative tax would be a fractional levy on the value of everyone's movable property, chiefly farm animals and agricultural produce. The taxes of 1225, 1232 and 1237 in that form were ruefully remembered. They had all brought in tens of thousands of pounds. General taxation, however, it was universally agreed, needed the kingdom's consent. That had been laid down in the 1215 Magna Carta and the relevant chapter, although omitted from the Charter's later versions, remained well known. Henry had always accepted the need for consent and had sought it again and again from parliaments during his

---

[109] Henry attests at Woodstock on 22 and 27 June and so could have been at Northampton in between.

[110] On the way to Lincoln, Henry celebrated the feast of Saint Oswald at Peterborough abbey where Oswald's right hand was preserved. The stay cost the monastery £600: *Historiae coenobii Burgensis*, 140. I owe this information to Nicholas Vincent.

[111] *CPR 1266-72*, 250; *CLR 1267-70*, nos. 374, 378; TNA E E72/ 114, m.12 (image 0774); Furness, 554; Bower, *Scoticronicon*, v, 370-1; Reid, *Alexander III*, 215-16.

personal rule. After 1237, the answer had always been 'No' save in return for concessions Henry deemed unacceptable. The securing of a tax was thus a real test of the government's status and prestige in this post-war, post-reform world. Would it do any better than before 1258?

If the need for consent to taxation had long been accepted, there was also now something new. This was the appreciation that a baronial parliament (as envisaged in Magna Carta) could no longer speak for the kingdom in the granting of taxation.[112] Consent had to be given as well by knights representing the counties and burgesses the towns. Both knights and burgesses had come to the great Montfortian parliament of 1265 to discuss the affairs of the kingdom. They needed now to come to agree taxation. That at any rate seems to have been the conclusion of Henry, Edward and their ministers, for there is every likelihood that knights and burgesses were indeed summoned to the crucial tax parliaments of the years 1268 to 1270.[113]

At the York parliament, in August 1268, no progress was made towards securing a tax and the business was postponed to a parliament due to meet at Westminster in October. Unfortunately, this clashed with a meeting at Boulogne proposed by King Louis to discuss the crusade. So Henry, while praising Louis's plans and expressing a desire to discuss them, asked for the meeting to be postponed. (This was when he asked if Queen Eleanor could come too.)[114] In fact, no meeting took place and Henry never saw Louis again. The parliament, however, went ahead and there is good evidence it was indeed 'full', as Henry told Louis it would be, with representatives present. Some kind of consent seems to have been given to a tax, perhaps one to be levied on land rather than movables, and county representatives chose panels of magnates to 'ordain' how it might be collected in their shires.[115] Yet in the end it all came to nothing, it is not clear why.[116]

---

[112] For the precedent of 1254, see above, 327.

[113] What follows is very dependent on Maddicott, 'The crusade taxation', where the case for the attendance of representatives is made through sifting a variety of chronicle and record sources. No writs of summons to these parliaments survive. The desire to get consent from townsmen is shown in a scheme from March 1268 under which representatives of twenty-seven towns were to come to Westminster almost certainly to discuss the levying of a tallage, although tallage was a tax the king could take from his towns and manors as of right, with no need for consent at all: Sayles, 'Representation of cities'; and for commentary see Powicke, *King Henry III*, ii, 563 n. 4, and Maddicott, *Origins of the English Parliament*, 265–6.

[114] *CR 1264–8*, 552.

[115] Furness, 554–5; *CR 1264–8*, 557–9.

[116] Proceedings at the parliament were disrupted by a revival of the old jurisdictional quarrel between Canterbury and York, caused by Walter Giffard of York having his cross born before him in Archbishop Boniface's very presence: Canterbury/Dover, 247–8; FitzThedmar, 108 (Stone, FitzThedmar, no. 976); *Giffard Register*, 140–2; *CPR 1266–72*, 265. Soon afterwards, Boniface left England. He did not return.

After Christmas at Winchester, another parliament met at Westminster in the January of 1269. Here Edward took the lead and secured the drafting of legislation designed, as it said, 'to relieve Christians of the grievances they have by reason of the Jewry of England'. The legislation banned Jews from drawing rent from land given them as a way of repaying a debt and forbad both the creation of such rents in the future and their selling on to Christians. (The grievance was partly how wealthy Christians bought up such rents and then acquired the land.) The legislation also banned, unless the king gave permission, any future sale of Jewish debts to Christians, a practice about which there had been protest at the Oxford parliament of 1258.[117] Edward, in Montfortian fashion, was seeking to conciliate knights and free tenants. Their representatives, he hoped, would thus be the more ready to grant a tax.

Another parliament met at Westminster in April 1269 and here the Jewish legislation was publicly proclaimed. Wykes was impressed and gave the credit to Edward and Henry of Almain.[118] Shortly afterwards, in a further act of conciliation, the king and council suspended the proposed Lincolnshire eyre. It would breach 'the custom used in the kingdom' of a seven-year interval between eyres. This was, of course, to revisit an issue over which there had been protests both in 1261 and 1263.[119] Edward, meanwhile, had been taking other measures to secure his authority and assure the peace in his absence. He had a friendly meeting with Llywelyn and, with the support of the council and King Richard, he arranged to give back to London most of its liberties.[120]

The next Westminster parliament was scheduled for Midsummer 1269 and here there is a first indication of Henry's uncertain health. On 21 June he wrote from Winchester saying he would not make the opening session having been detained by a tertian fever. He had indeed been stationary at Winchester since the end of May. However, Henry added, he was now better and would set off on the morrow so could everyone please wait for him. Meanwhile, he was sending the abbot of Westminster and Philip Basset to explain things. He would, he said, have sent the bishop of Winchester as well (Nicholas of Ely), but was reluctant to lose the 'recreation' he gained from his presence.[121] Doubtless Nicholas's role as a baronial chancellor was not one of the subjects of conversation.

In fact, Henry did not set off next day, but he still reached Westminster (on 1 July) in time for the parliament. Just what happened there is obscure.

---

[117] *DBM*, 86–7, no.25; *CPR 1266–72*, 359–60, 376; *CR 1268–72*, 268; Maddicott, 'The crusade taxation', 101–2; Richardson, *English Jewry*, 71–3, 104–5.

[118] Wykes, 221.

[119] *CR 1268–72*, 37–9; Crook, *Records of the General Eyre*, 134.

[120] *CPR 1266–72*, 344; *CR 1268–72*, 71; FitzThedmar, 108–9 (Stone, FitzThedmar, nos.979, 981; *CFR 1268–9*, no.169.

[121] *CPR 1266–72*, 384.

Henry, writing a month later, thought a tax had been granted – a twentieth on movable property – and certainly panels of knights were appointed in each county in order to collect it.[122] Yet there is no sign the knights actually started work and a parliament in October had to make a grant of the tax all over again. Perhaps Henry, in his impetuous way, was charging ahead on his own, assuming agreement when there had been none. Significantly, he issued the letter about the collection while on his pilgrimage to Chichester, so quite probably when few councillors were with him. He had some reason for impatience since, at this very time, Edward was on his way to Paris to see King Louis about the crusade.

On 28 August, in Paris, Edward and Louis IX reached an agreement. Edward was to join Louis at Aigues Mortes by 15 August 1270. On the crusade he was to obey Louis 'in doing the service of the Lord' like other barons of the realm of France. To make this possible, Louis lent Edward around £17,500, repayable from the Bordeaux customs. Of this sum, £6,250 were to go to Gaston de Béarn, who was to be in Edward's company. (Gaston had come out to Paris with Edward as had Henry of Almain.) As security for all this, Edward was to hand over one of his sons as hostage. In the event, Henry the younger was chosen, but Louis at once returned him.[123]

Louis thus secured for his crusade 'a man of great stature, great probity and bravery, and strong beyond measure', as Rishanger put it. There was nothing the least demeaning in Edward serving under Louis's banner. He was not yet king and very much Louis's junior in terms of age and prestige. He was also, as his father's deputy in Gascony, in effect a baron of France. Both Louis and Edward gained honour from their agreement. Rishanger adds that when Edward returned home and sought Henry's permission to go, his aged father was moved to pious tears and gave his blessing to everyone who wished to join the expedition.[124] It was now beginning to look like a reality.

## THE COSMATI WORK AT WESTMINSTER ABBEY

In all these years in the 1260s, the consecration of his new Abbey at Westminster and the translation of Saint Edward the Confessor to his new

[122] Wilkins, *Concilia Magnae*, ii, 20–1 (from Bishop Giffard's register). I owe knowledge of this letter to Maddicott, 'The crusade taxation', 103.

[123] *F*, i, 481; FitzThedmar, 111–14 (Stone, FitzThedmar, nos. 990, 994); Bury St Edmunds, 46. In May 1269, something Edward and his mother had been working for since 1266, Henry of Almain married the daughter of Gaston de Béarn. Since Gaston had no son, Henry thus became the heir to Béarn. Given all the trouble Gaston had caused in the past, the English hold on Gascony seemed all the more secure. See Studd, 'The marriage of Henry of Almain', with a calendar of documents from the Archives Départementales des Pyrénées Atlantiques.

[124] Rishanger, 60–1.

shrine had never been far from Henry's thoughts. That was even more the case after 1267 when he was freer to urge on the work and could see his target date looming closer. That date, as we have seen, was almost certainly the feast of the Confessor's translation on 13 October 1269, this because the year 1269, by a beautiful symmetry, had the same date for Easter and thus exactly the same ecclesiastical calendar as 1163, the year of the Confessor's first translation. In both years, therefore, 13 October fell on a Tuesday.

For the great event to be celebrated in appropriate fashion, two things were necessary. First, Henry needed to have finished, or finished enough to be usable, the four bays of the new choir started in 1259. Second, he needed to have ready the shrine of the Confessor. His goldsmiths had been labouring since the 1240s on the reliquary to contain the Confessor's body. It was a hugely elaborate structure, adorned with crosses, crockets, columns and images, and with new ornaments constantly being added, as new gifts came in, mostly from Henry himself. The work seems to have taken place in a specially constructed chapel somewhere in the precincts, its walls decorated with the Confesssor's history.[125] As for the base to hold the reliquary aloft and allow pilgrims to pray beneath the Confessor's body, here, as we have seen, Henry, daring and imaginative as always in artistic matters, had made a new start.[126] In the early 1260s he had engaged the Cosmati family of Italian mosaicists to work on the structure. Their leader was Peter 'the Roman citizen', named as responsible for the base in an inscription on the base itself. This was the beginning of the long Cosmati association with the Abbey. They went on to make the pavement around the shrine, the great sanctuary pavement before the high altar and after his death the tomb of Henry himself.[127]

## THE SHRINE BASE

The engagement of the Cosmati was one of the best decisions of Henry's life, for their work gave a new dimension to the Abbey's splendour.[128] The

[125] *CR 1251-3*, 290. I follow the interpretation in Colvin, *History of the King's Works*, i, 148 and n. 3.

[126] See above, 227–8.

[127] The precise chronology of the Cosmati work at the Abbey has been much debated by historians and mine is only one possible view. For discussion, see Appendix 1 at the end of this volume.

[128] For the following descriptions of the shrine base, surrounding pavement and sanctuary pavement I am indebted again to the comprehensive analysis and magnificent illustrations in Warwick Rodwell and David Neal's two-volume *The Cosmatesque Mosaics of Westminster Abbey*. Chapter 10 of volume 2 covers the base and chs. 4 and 7 the pavements. There is a brief summary of the conclusions in volume 1, between pp. xxiii and xxviii, and a full summary with consideration of the dating and process of construction in ch. 15 of volume 2.

magnificent pavement before the high altar survives, as does Henry's tomb. Even in its battered state, as reconstructed by Abbot Feckenham during the Marian restoration of the Abbey in the 1550s, enough remains of the shrine base to suggest its former glory. To English eyes it must have seemed marvellously, miraculously new, for Cosmati work was unknown in the country. The base would have been equally remarkable in Italy, for instead of being an entirely classical monument, it retained 'gothic' features and was made, in part, of English materials.

The base's core material was Purbeck marble. The massive stone slab running east–west down the centre, the slabs inserted to form the three niches either side where pilgrims could kneel and pray and the slabs for the end walls were all of Purbeck. So were the blocks of marble forming a band above the niches. And so too were both the row of stones for an inscription course and, at the top, the plinth to support the golden reliquary. All these materials must have been cut and prepared by English marblers. There were also some familiar 'gothic' motifs. The niches, dominating the sides of the base, were all given trefoiled heads, while at their backs the marble, in each niche, was fashioned into two lancets with sexafoil roses, thus precisely imitating the design of the Abbey's windows. With these Purbeck marble slabs roughed out, they were then clothed by the Cosmati with porphyry stones and tesserated mosaics. It has been calculated that in all 158,446 tesserae of glass and stone were employed. At the backs of the niches themselves, the imagination of the designers ran riot, for each one had a different combination of tesserated loops and circles within and (on the north side) across the lancets.

The base had another novel and eye-catching feature. At each corner descending from the overhanging inscription course were slender colonettes, free standing and thus visible in the round. They were made of Purbeck, but carved in a series of spiralling and fluted twists and then studded with glittering tesserae. The Purbeck marblers, used to their solid circular columns, must have looked at these strange creations with equal astonishment and admiration.[129] The altar standing in front of the shrine is lost but its retable survives now fixed to the west end of the base. Here too the Purbeck marble was covered with decoration: large lozenges of porphyry between loops and roundels with at their centres little crosses, the two surviving lozenges being made from the highest-status purple 'imperial' porphyry.[130]

The point of the base was to hold aloft the golden reliquary containing the Confessor's body and here height was important for the reliquary needed

---

[129] Rodwell and Neal, *The Cosmatesque Mosaics*, ii, 373–4. The surviving fragments of the colonettes have lost their tesserae, but their appearance can be judged from two further colonettes, now supporting the retable to the shrine's altar, though once perhaps supporting a canopy over Henry III's tomb: Rodwell and Neal, *The Cosmatesque Mosaics*, ii, 371–6.

[130] Rodwell and Neal, *The Cosmatesque Mosaics*, ii, 352–6.

to be seen above the high altar and its retable. (Now unfortunately it is hidden altogether by the fifteenth-century altar screen, thus cutting the rest of the Abbey off from its spiritual heart.) The height was achieved in two ways. First, the base was placed on a four-stepped podium. (Today there is only one.) Second, an extra 37 centimetres of height were gained by the band above the niches. Decorated with mosaics and rectangles and lozenges of porphyry, this frames a space where the body of the Confessor now lies. But it is inconceivable that in 1269 the Confessor was placed there out of sight rather than in the reliquary above. Originally the space was empty. The only purpose of this level was to make the shrine base higher and more imposing.

How then had this extraordinary structure come about? One plausible suggestion is that the Cosmati simply took over and refashioned the slabs already prepared for what was originally intended as a purely Purbeck marble base.[131] There is evidence such a base was under construction and it must have been relatively advanced by 1254 when Henry wanted the Abbey consecrated in October 1255.[132] Providing as it did the niches for the praying pilgrims, the Purbeck structure served the base's purpose well. Yet convenience and utility cannot be the only explanation for taking over the existing slabs. Set beside the gigantic work on the Abbey itself, the task of making a new base was hardly great. The Cosmati could easily have started from scratch and created an entirely classical monument as they did later for Henry's tomb. That they did not must have been an artistic decision and King Henry's decision above all. The inscription credits Peter 'Roman citizen' with producing the base, but its 'cause' is stated to be 'King Henry'. One can imagine him discussing the design with Peter, just as intently as he discussed the Abbey's design with Henry de Reyns. Henry liked the Purbeck structure with its trefoiled niches yet saw how it could be transformed by the stones and mosaics of the Cosmati. He, as much as Peter, was the begetter of the shrine base.[133]

## THE COSMATI PAVEMENTS

Having erected the shrine base in the Confessor's chapel, the Cosmati turned their attention to the surrounding pavement. This has always been the least known and least regarded of their works. It is in poor condition and (other than for inspection) permanently covered. Recent study, however, has explained its design and vindicated its quality. The Cosmati had a difficult task for the sides of the chapel were canted inwards with the turn of the apse, while the space itself was divided into three sections by the shrine.

---

[131] This is the suggestion in Rodwell and Neal, *The Cosmatesque Mosaics*, ii, 390, 564–5.

[132] Rodwell and Neal, *The Cosmatesque Mosaics*, ii, 604, 609 (from a calendar of writs about the shrine compiled by Matthew Payne), and see my volume 1, 588.

[133] For Henry's eye for architectural detail and involvement in design, see volume 1, 334, 344–5.

There was, therefore, no possibility of a pavement with any kind of formal and rectilinear pattern. The solution was a fluid 'carpet' design 'that would not visually fragment the area into three separate compartments, but would unite them and flow seamlessly around the sides of the shrine and altar'.[134] This was achieved by laying down a Purbeck marble floor and then sweeping across it a repeating pattern of tesserated medallions and roundels interlinked by curving bands.[135] Over fifty different designs of medallion have been identified, many extremely complex.[136] One, for example, was composed of twelve white equilateral triangles, each triangle then subdivided into a further twelve triangles of reducing size, the latter, each made from a single tessura.[137] Framed within the polished grey of the Purbeck marble, the pavement, in terms of both the ingenuity of design and the use of materials, formed a fitting setting for the shrine itself.

If the Cosmati arrived at Westminster in the early to mid-1260s, there was plenty of time to complete the base and its pavement before October 1269. In the case of the great pavement laid out in the sanctuary before the high altar, there was just time enough. The pavement is the one part of the Cosmati *oeuvre* securely dated, for an inscription states it was installed in 1268. In this case too the role of Abbot Ware is certain. In May 1269 the king acknowledged he owed Ware £50, amongst other things, 'for a pavement which he brought with him from the court of Rome for the king's use to be put in the church of Westminster before the great altar there'.[138] Ware's role was also celebrated in the pavement's inscription. It was King Henry '*tercius*', the city (Rome), Odoricus (the craftsman) and the abbot who had brought together 'these porphyry stones'. Ware decided he should be buried beneath the pavement and his tomb was integral to the design. An inscription declared this was the resting place of Abbot Ware, 'who bore the stones, which here he bears, from the city'. John Flete, whose fifteenth-century history of the Abbey preserves the inscription, added that he had bought the stones at his own cost.[139]

Quite probably Ware returned with the pavement from his visit to Rome in 1267. The Cosmati could thus arrive in a time of peace, the pavement being a thanks-offering to the papacy for Henry's victory, just as the shrine base was conceived as celebrating the victory of 1261.[140] That Ware shouldered much of the cost is likely since his £50 pardon can

---

[134] Rodwell and Neal, *The Cosmatesque Mosaics*, ii, 560.

[135] This time the chasing of the marble to create the matrices for the design was probably done with the Purbeck already *in situ* in the chapel.

[136] Rodwell and Neal, *The Cosmatesque Mosaics*, i, 243–4.

[137] Rodwell and Neal, *The Cosmatesque Mosaics*, i, 226, 228 (17b).

[138] TNA C 66/87, m. 17 (*CPR 1266–72*, 338).

[139] Flete, 113, 115. Flete also has Ware bringing the workmen.

[140] *CPR 1258–66*, 681, an earlier visit during the war; *CR 1264–8*, 332. Flete believed Ware brought back the pavement after his visit to Rome for his confirmation in 1259, but this seems unlikely given the pavement was only installed in 1268.

scarcely have covered it all, the more especially as it was also compensation for other expenditure.[141] But that Ware was a self-starter when it came to the pavement is inconceivable. The pavement's commission at such a late stage has all the hallmarks of Henry's enthusiasm.[142]

The large open space in the sanctuary before the high altar permitted a totally different pavement from that in the Confessor's chapel. It was regular in design and set out as a gigantic square. The base into which the matrices for the mosaics were chased was once against of Purbeck, while Purbeck too provided the strips, straight and circular, within which the mosaics were framed. Recent cleaning and conservation has revealed the sanctuary pavement once again in all its glory. No longer covered by a carpet, once again it enriches the Abbey's services. The large open space before the high altar permitted a totally different pavement from that in the Confessor's chapel. Set and framed in Purbeck marble, it was regular in design and formed a gigantic square. In the centre of the pavement, placed within a poised square (a square standing on its point), were four roundels set around a larger roundel, the roundels being composed of bands of mosaic framing disks of marble. All this was placed within a great square, in the corners of which were roundels, surrounded by two borders of mosaic, with their centres filled not with disks this time but with complex tesserated mosaic. Finally, around the great square, as the outer frame of the pavement, was a border made up of twenty roundels and, at the centre of the northern and southern sides, rectangular panels, that on the north covering Abbot Ware's tomb.

The sanctuary floor was regular in its overall design yet hugely varied in its detail for all the roundels had different designs. The pavement also had a deeper meaning. There was firstly a link with the coronation, for it was on the pavement that its rituals would be played out. Indeed the model for the design may well have been the pavement in the chapel of Saint Maurice in Saint Peter's Rome, on which the anointing of the emperor took place.[143] There was also a link with the Last Judgement. An inscription on the pavement, now lost but preserved by Flete,[144] indicated that the pavement depicted the universe, the whole cosmos of God's creation.[145] The roundels were so many stars, that in the very centre, with the largest and most exotic stone in the pavement, being the earth. Made of very rare alabaster possibly from Piedmont in Italy,

---

[141] There were the service given by the abbot at the siege of Kenilworth and money paid into the wardrobe.

[142] A major theme in Binski and Bolgia, 'The Cosmati mosaics at Westminster' is the involvement of Ottobuono. This seems very likely in September 1267 when he was at court crafting the Treaty of Montgomery. See the references to him at the time of Ware's mission in *CR 1264-8*, 331–2.

[143] As argued by Claudia Bolgia in Binski and Bolgia, 'The Cosmati mosaics at Westminister', 15–25. The article also has new ideas about the careers of Peter, the Roman citizen of the shrine base and Odericus of the pavement.

[144] Flete, 113; Rodwell and Neal, *The Cosmatesque Mosaics*, i, 118–19.

[145] See the discussion in Foster, *Patterns of Thought*, with the conclusion at 108–10. Foster offers as a free translation 'Here is the perfectly rounded sphere which reveals the eternal pattern of the universe'.

it was in different shades of yellow and orange, streaked by veins of red, like a tide of blood washed up on a jagged shore.[146]

The central inscription was designed to be read with another around the central roundels, one again preserved by Flete.[147] This set out a riddle which, when deciphered would give the end of the 'primum mobile', meaning essentially the end of the moving force behind the universe. In Christian terms that meant the end of the temporal world and the Last Judgement.[148] The date in question, if the calculations were done correctly, turned out to be 19,683. No countenance was thus given to the idea that the end of time was imminent, but the prospect still remained awesome, however long the wait.

The pavement before the Abbey's high altar, in its origins and originality, colours and complexity, messages and meanings, was utterly unique. Unique too was the decoration of the high altar itself. Four women worked for three and half years embroidering its frontal, the gold, pearls, enamels and garnets costing over £200. As for the altar's retable, here painters and carpenters came from Paris (perhaps commissioned during Henry's visit in 1262), the paintings, works of equal refinement and beauty.[149] How the whole ensemble, pavement, altar and shrine worked together to encapsulate the Abbey's meaning, we will see shortly.

## THE TRANSLATION OF THE CONFESSOR, 13 OCTOBER 1269

As October 1269 drew nearer, Henry bent every sinew to make sure everything was ready for the great day. There could be no question of postponement. The next year enjoying the same symmetry with 1163 was 1353! Mercifully, throughout the years of turmoil, money had continued to flow in for the works. Receipts totalled £2,974 between January 1264 and Christmas 1266; £1,303 between Christmas 1266 and September 1267; and, in the final phase, £2,422 between September 1267 and Christmas 1269. One staple here was the £355 a year assigned by the council in 1259 from the money owed by Alice of Saluzzo, countess of Lincoln, for the lands of her underage son. Another was the money from the issues of the great seal, assigned by Henry himself, in a moment of independence, later the same year. Revenue from the exchequer fluctuated wildly, not surprisingly given it was often empty. It contributed a paltry £140 between December 1266 and September 1267 and £1,097 in the final period down to Christmas 1269, a rise reflecting both the recovery of the king's revenues and his determination to get the works done.[150]

---

[146] The Westminster monk Richard Sporley interpreted the colours in the stone as representing the four elements of the world: fire, air, water and land: Flete, 114.

[147] Flete, 113. For what follows, see Foster, *Patterns of Thought*, 94–8, and for Sporley's interpretation, Flete, 114.

[148] Sporley thus thought the date meant 'the end of the world': Flete, 114.

[149] Scott, *Gleanings*, 113–14; Binski and Massing, *The Westminster Retable*.

[150] *BA*, 416–17, 420–1, 424–5.

In 1269 itself Henry could be excited and exalted by the thought he was living through 1163 all over again, with Easter and all the other movable feasts on the same date and day of the week. By this time, William of Gloucester, preparing the reliquary, had five men working with him.[151] They had much to do since all the treasures assigned to the shrine were only recovered from pawn in February 1269. So they had now to adorn it with twenty-eight rings, sixty cameos, a 'most beautiful' sapphire worth 100 marks, a great head with a golden crown, a golden majesty adorned with emeralds, an assortment of pearls and sapphires (worth £200) and the bejewelled and golden images of the Virgin Mary, Saint Peter trampling Nero and assorted kings and angels. One of the kings (valued at £103) held a shrine and was no doubt Henry himself.[152] When William of Gloucester died, twelve goldsmiths were elected (on 7 May) to carry on the work, two of whom were immediately sent to Henry at Windsor, doubtless for a motivational talk.[153] In August, Henry told the constable of the Tower to find by all possible means 20 marks for the completion of the reliquary, 'as we trust you and you love us and our honour.'[154] On 7 October, with less than a week to go, another 6 marks of gold were assigned to the work.[155] Meanwhile, the wooden coffin for the Confessor's body was painted and adorned with emeralds.[156]

As for the reliquary's Cosmati base and its surrounding pavement, there is some record evidence for their progress. The accounts from December 1266 to September 1267, and then again from September 1267 to December 1269, have payments for the wages of the masons and paviors working 'before the feretory of Saint Edward'.[157] The implication is that with the base in place the paviors were now installing the pavement around it. Since there are no entries for their work after December 1269, it seems to have been complete. The completion of the great pavement before the high altar is even more certain for, as we have seen, it is dated by its inscription to 1268 so it was just finished in time. The great church too was nearing completion or at least sufficiently near to make its consecration possible. Gold leaf and paint were being applied to the vaults, the tower over the transept crossing was being covered with tiles and straw, the windows were being glassed or filled in with canvas, and white stone was being broken and fashioned for the pavements. Lead for the roofs was another concern and the sheriff of Nottingham was told if he failed to send sixty cartloads by water he would have to make good the damage to

---

[151] There are also payments for the wages of four goldsmiths: *BA*, 426–7.

[152] *CPR 1266–72*, 135–40; WAM 9465; Colvin, *History of the King's Works*, i, 148.

[153] TNA E 368/ 43, m. 11d (image 6639).

[154] TNA SC 1/2/88. He did find the money: TNA E 372/114, m. 18 (image 0765).

[155] *CLR 1267–72*, no. 846.

[156] *BA*, 428–9.

[157] *BA*, 422–3, 426–7.

the works out of his own goods.[158] The join between the new choir and the old nave of the Confessor was difficult, given the differences in height, so the last new bay stopped short at clerestory level and was roofed with boards.[159]

To make the necessary purchases for the celebrations on 13 October, Henry ordered the exchequer to pay out over £500 and borrowed at least 800 marks from Jews and merchants. The 165 bucks to be supplied by the king's huntsmen provide just a glimpse of the mountains of food being brought together. Some 150 shoes were acquired as usual for Henry and Eleanor's alms for the poor, but the intention must have been to feed many thousands more.[160]

Henry had also made a decision about the nature of the ceremony.[161] He had long wanted to link the translation in some way to his kingship. Back in 1251, his idea was to knight Edward on the same day.[162] Nothing had come of that. Edward had been knighted by King Alfonso in Burgos and not on the feast day of the Confessor as Henry had hoped. But now Henry had a grander idea. He and Queen Eleanor would both 'wear their crowns'. Here Henry seems to have envisaged something like the great ceremony of 1194 when Richard, crowned and vested as though for a coronation, had processed into Winchester cathedral, beneath a canopy supported by the men of the Cinque Ports and behind nobles holding the three swords from the coronation regalia. In the cathedral the archbishop celebrated mass and gave Richard his blessing. Afterwards there was a great banquet with the Londoners providing, as for a coronation, the service of the butlery and men of Winchester that of the kitchen. In 1269 likewise Henry summoned them both to provide their due service.

The point of the crown wearing in 1194 had been to rededicate Richard's kingship after the stains of his captivity. The idea in 1269 was to do the same for Henry after the horrors and humiliations of the civil war. But, of course, the two ceremonies were very different for Henry planned to mould together the revivification of his kingship and the translation of his patron saint.[163] But in the end the idea of the crown wearing was abandoned. On 12 October, so with only a day to go, Henry had it proclaimed in Cheapside and Westminster Hall that he was 'not advised' to wear his crown 'for it ought to suffice for him to wear his crown but once'. That it

---

[158] TNA E 159/42, m. 3d (image 0114). '*Plumbum*' is written in large letters against this entry.

[159] *CLR 1267–72*, no. 1259. Hence the clerestory lancet and vault of the last new bay is the work of the fourteenth-century.

[160] *CLR 1267–72*, nos. 810, 815, 819, 822, 833, 841, 857, 1136, 1259; *CR 1268–72*, 227; TNA SC 1/2/89.

[161] For discussion of the ritual on the day, see Weiler, 'Symbolism and politics', 34–8.

[162] WAM Book II (Westminster Domesday), fo. 406v.

[163] The crown wearing would itself have been linked to the Confessor since the coronation crown was described as the crown of the Confessor. See below, 619.

was impossible to wear the crown twice (the coronation crown, that is) was not of course true, for Richard had done so. It is also unlikely that the quarrels between London and Winchester over their respective roles (present too in 1194) were the reason for cancelling the ceremony. Perhaps it was just thought logistically impossible to combine the crown wearing and the translation. Perhaps in the end Henry just wanted to make this great day the Confessor's own.

And a great day it was. All accounts agree there was a large gathering of lay and ecclesiastical magnates (including thirteen bishops), together with knights and townsmen. The new Abbey was consecrated by the arch-bishop of York in Boniface's absence, and the monks sang the mass of the Confessor in their new choir for the first time. The Confessor's body was taken from its old resting place and born round the outside of the church in its newly decorated coffin on the shoulders of Henry, King Richard, Edward, Edmund, John de Warenne and Philip Basset, with a crowd of other nobles all trying to lend a hand. Coming back into the Abbey the procession proceeded up the steps before the high altar, across the great Cosmati pavement and on into the chapel of the Confessor, where the coffin was hoisted up onto the Cosmati base and placed reverently into its golden and jewelled reliquary.[164]

There is alas no household roll to reveal the great feast in the palace which followed the service in the Abbey. Wykes says all present were struck with wonder and amazement.[165] The feast must surely have exceeded in every way that on 13 October 1260, where the costs approached £180 and Henry fed 5,016 paupers. Whether the paintings in his great chamber were entirely ready is uncertain, but Henry had done much, visually, to re-establish his kingship at the palace.[166] Between September 1266 and December 1267 money was spent on 'gilding two small lions, two turrets, two plates [and] three cups of copper for the king's throne in the great hall at Westminster'. Probably the throne now looked much like the ostenta-tious high-backed chair shown on Henry's second seal made in 1259. Henry was also concerned with sanitation and comfort. The £34 spent on the throne also covered the cost of five copper taps for the lavatory in the small hall and a spout of copper for a cistern near the king's chamber. No less than £50 was spent on repairing a building in which wood was kept for the chamber's fire.[167]

The day of 13 October 1269 must have been the happiest in Henry's life. It was an apotheosis. True, he had not replaced the Confessor's nave

---

[164] Henry offered 4 marks of gold on the day costing over £29; TNA C 47/3/7/12; *CLR 1267–72*, no. 899; TNA E 372/114, m. 38 (image 0808) – 40s were spent repairing Henry's crown.

[165] Wykes, 227.

[166] For the possibility the paintings were not finished till 1272, see below, 609.

[167] *BA*, 422–3; *CLR 1267–72*, no. 1259.

and given the Abbey its western towers, but he had translated the Confessor's body to a uniquely magnificent shrine in a uniquely magnificent church. In terms of initiative, it was all his own doing. Nothing would have happened without him.

## THE IMPACT OF THE ABBEY

Henry's aim, first and foremost, in all his works at the Abbey was to win the Confessor's favour and thus secure, through his intercession, success in this life and a safe passage to the next. He also hoped to harvest the prayers of all the pilgrims who came to the Abbey. Surely they would intercede for the temporal and spiritual welfare of the great king who had created all around them. To that end, Henry's name appeared on the chapter house floor, the high altar pavement and, as its 'cause', on the shrine itself.[168]

If, however, Henry wished to harvest prayers for himself, he also wished to harvest them for the realm. Those coming to the shrine were to 'pour out devout prayers for the state of the lord king and the peace of the kingdom', as the bishop of St David's put it in an indulgence issued when he was with Henry at Windsor in May 1269. However much God might at times have permitted the kingdom to suffer, the Confessor had always been there interceding for its return to health. Henry also, naturally, expected pilgrims to come seeking their own welfare, seeking it from a saint genuinely at God's right hand, not, as at Evesham, from some servant of the Antichrist. In encouraging pilgrimages, the indulgences made their own contribution. That of the bishop of St David's conceded forty days remission of penance for those who prayed at the shrine with their sins truly confessed.[169] Henry was doing the reverse of keeping the Confessor for himself. He was trying to ensure Edward became England's patron saint.

The radiating chapels, the flying buttresses, the galleried triforium, the great north portal with its gabled doorways and rose window made the Abbey a church without parallel in England. Indeed, the galleried triforium and the length of the transepts equally made it without parallel in France. If those entering the church through the north portal were awed by the scenes of the Last Judgement (almost certainly the theme of the central doorway), then once within they were comforted, uplifted and inspired by one of the most beautiful vistas of any church in Christendom. For the eyes swept up at once to the great height of the patterned and painted vault laid out across the eight bays of the two transepts either side of the central crossing. And at the end of the south transept, the eyes rested on the great rose window above two tiers of trefoiled lancets, a shimmering

---

[168] See below, 645.
[169] WAM 6668*.

cascade of stained glass framed in Purbeck marble, stone and sculpture. Set beneath the rose window, in the most prominent possible position, and perfumed with incense by smiling angels swinging their censers with easy grace, were the large painted statues of the Confessor holding up the ring and the pilgrim stretching out his appealing arm to receive it, the episode which prefigured Saint John conducting the Confessor up to heaven.

Thus assured that the Confessor was indeed a saint of mighty power, one could advance to the shrine, and here the relationship between the choir, sanctuary and Confessor's chapel was arranged as a gradual ascent past a hierarchy of altars. The choir was raised three steps above the transepts with its own altar under the central crossing. Two steps followed up to the high altar pavement. There were then four steps up to the Confessor's chapel, while another four supported the shrine itself. Since the height of the high altar's retable was kept deliberately low, the golden reliquary with the Confessor's body was visible to all standing on the Cosmati pavement and in the crossing and choir below. Henry had thus, in the words of Thomas Wykes, elevated the Confessor's body 'so that a light so radiant, now raised high above the candles, might shine its spiritual light the more copiously on those entering and departing'.[170]

Approaching the shrine across the high altar pavement there was a warning, much as there was entering the Abbey through the north door. In the centre of the pavement, as we have seen, was the great alabaster globe depicting the world, the red veins in the stone suggesting all its angry strife. The pavement itself, as the inscription indicated, was meant to prompt thoughts of the Last Judgement. But again there was hope, for painted in the centre of the high altar's retable, a few feet away, was the earth again but this time a verdant earth with plants, birds and animals, held in Christ's caring hand.[171] This was Christ neither of the Last Judgement nor the cross, but Christ the saviour of the world. The panels either side, framed by coloured glass, gems, cameos and enamels, continued in the same spirit. They depicted a smiling Virgin Mary and the miracles of Christ, including, of special moment for Henry, reminding him of his daughter Katherine, Christ raising up the centurion Jairus's daughter from the dead. Thus inspired, the pilgrims could finally advance into the Confessor's chapel and, with the whole scene lit by Henry's numerous candles, walk across the Cosmati floor, mount the steps to the shrine and make their offerings at the altar, before kneeling in the niches within the glittering base and praying for the state of the king, the peace of the kingdom and the health and salvation of themselves.

---

[170] Wykes, 226. See Matthew v, 15. The choir's floor was lowered to the transept level in 1848.

[171] Binski and Massing, *The Westminster Retable*, 63. This volume, with its remarkable illustrations, provides a comprehensive history and analysis of the retable. Between 1606 and 1827 it formed part of a succession of cupboards in which the Abbey stored the funeral effigies of kings and queens, hence its survival but also its battered state.

As those attending the great services left the Abbey by the north door, there was a final reminder of the royal dynasty. For if they looked up they would see above the door the head of a prince, clearly Edward himself. He had not in the end been knighted in the Abbey, as Henry had once hoped, but here, gazing out over the transepts, towards the scene of his future coronation, he was linked umbilically to the Abbey and the Confessor, the Confessor after whom he himself had been named. Henry had designed the Abbey from the start as a Coronation church. The spacious triforium galleries enabled thousands to gaze down on the great ceremony, while thousands more could be accommodated in the uniquely long transepts which framed the central crossing.[172] The high altar pavement, echoing quite probably the pavement in St Peter's where emperors were anointed, provided the perfect setting for the ceremony itself.[173] This was all the more the case because from the pavement the king, prelates and nobles would see rising up above them, behind the high altar, the shrine of the Confessor, the king saint watching over the whole ceremony, shielding and supporting the monarchy with his protective power.

While Henry thus linked the beginning of each reign to the Abbey and the Confessor, he also linked the end. For Henry, of course, wanted the Abbey to be the dynasty's mausoleum, and for that the Confessor's chapel, with spaces for tombs between the surrounding columns, was perfect. Yet if all this makes the Abbey a very kingly church its decoration also showed it was indeed a church for all the kingdom. Hence, the comital and baronial shields, including Montfort's own, sculpted in the wall arcades of the choir, and continuing in paint down the Confessor's nave. They reflected the Confessor's vision, Henry's vision (not always achieved) of a king ruling in concert with his nobles for the good of the community of the realm.[174] There was also a broader setting. The Abbey testified eloquently to the community of Europe. Much of its stone came from Caen in Normandy, the painters of the retable came from Paris. The whole design was heavily indebted to the great French cathedrals, notably Reims and Amiens. The shields in the choir included those of France and the Empire. And then, more important than anything else, was the connection with Rome and the papacy.[175] The Abbey, so it was believed,

---

[172] At the 1953 Coronation, I sat high up in the north transept.

[173] For the coronation, see volume 1, 45–6.

[174] It seems likely that baronial shields also appeared in the stained glass, although only the arms of the king, Richard of Cornwall and Provence now survive. The keepers of the Westminster works were ordered to supply forty stained-glass shields for the queen's chamber at Havering: *CLR 1267–72*, no. 109.

[175] The Abbey's 'Romanitas' is a major theme in Binski's *Westminster Abbey and the Plantagenets*, see, for example, 93–107.

had been miraculously founded by Saint Peter. In 1222 it had been freed from the bishop of London's jurisdiction and been made subject to Rome alone. The pope had been with Henry throughout his Abbey journey. He had issued indulgences for those helping the work and attending the eventual translation. Doubtless at Henry's prompting, he described the new church as being of 'wonderful beauty, *mire pulchritudinis*'. In March 1267 he gave permission for the translation to take place.[176] The papacy had saved Henry at the start of his reign, freed him from baronial control in 1261, and then, through the legate Ottobuono, restored peace to England after the civil war. The Sicilian debacle could be forgotten. The Cosmati work at the heart of the Abbey celebrated and proclaimed a relationship with the pope itself 'of wonderful beauty'. In characteristic fashion, Henry used the inscriptions to make the point. Those on the shrine base thus linked him with Peter the Roman citizen, that on the high altar pavement with 'the city', the city of Rome.

Henry hoped that the Abbey would have a profound impact on his subjects. But were his hopes fulfilled? Many, for a start, would have taken a totally different view of the papacy. There were also some disappointments and distractions on the day itself. Gilbert de Clare failed to turn up, as did Llywelyn despite a pressing invitation. Henry was confident that King Alexander and Queen Margaret were coming to enjoy more 'recreation and solace' in his company. But there is no evidence of their presence.[177] Although fitzThedmar avers that some bishops came from abroad, this was not a great international event like Becket's translation back in 1220. Disruption on the day was caused by the activities of Walter Giffard, archbishop of York. In Archbishop Boniface's absence he presided over the ceremonies but without the help of the other bishops. Because he insisted on having his cross born before him they remained sullenly in their stalls in deference to the rights of Canterbury. As a result, Giffard alone swung his censer in the procession taking the Confessor's body round the church and then up to its new shrine. Some of the Londoners too resented the way the king at the last moment cancelled their service at the banquet. Rather than attend, they just went home. At least this meant the men of Winchester enjoyed themselves all the more! One London annalist also observed that the golden reliquary itself was not completely finished, intelligence perhaps obtained from the goldsmiths, who had still to attach some of the once pawned jewels and images.[178]

In general, however, the contemporary writers described the translation very much as Henry would have wished. They marvelled at the reliquary

---

[176] WAM Book II (Westminster Domesday), fos. 386, 406v (*CPReg*, 262).

[177] *CR 1268–72*, 71; *CPR 1266–72*, 365, and 488 for the continuing question of Margaret's dowry.

[178] In 1270 the Londoners gave 100 marks to buy gold for work on the casket ('*basilica*'): FitzThedmar, 124 (Stone, FitzThedmar, no. 1013).

and said nothing about it being incomplete. The Abbey's own chronicler spoke of miracles – two men possessed of demons (Benedict the clerk of Winchester and John a layman from Ireland) were both cured on the day 'by the merits of the saint'. Thomas Wykes, by far the most intelligent commentator on these years, and often a critic of the king, absolutely appreciated Henry's achievement. Having praised, as we have seen, the pious devotion that had caused Henry to raise up the Confessor's body to a higher place, he described the hosts of people attending the ceremony and the procession with the body, the proceedings culminating in the stupendous feast. 'All these things were done in the conventual church of the monks of Westminster which the king had constructed in the most sumptuous fashion at his own expense. Both in expense and beauty it was seen to surpass all other churches in the world and have no peer.'

## THE CRUSADE, TAXATION AND PARLIAMENT, OCTOBER 1269–MAY 1270

The translation of the Confessor was followed immediately by the opening of parliament. In Henry's mind, the two events were intimately linked. The attraction of the translation would ensure a full attendance at the parliament and the rejoicing on the day would secure consent at last to the long-sought tax. It did not work out like that. Thomas Wykes lauded Henry's piety when it came to the translation but still condemned his extortion of the tax. He was not alone in making the distinction. The laity at the parliament did now agree to the assessment of the twentieth but not its actual collection. With churchmen, even less progress was made. The bishops were reasonably compliant, but when the abbots, priors and representatives of cathedral chapters and lower clergy met at the New Temple on 14 October, the day after the translation, they refused point blank to grant any tax at all! Instead, they drew up a schedule of complaint outlining all they had suffered from past and current taxation. The priesthood, they concluded, was in a worse condition than in the days of Pharaoh.[179] Certainly they had been more heavily taxed in recent years than the laity, hence their even stronger objection to the king's demands.

So yet another parliament was necessary. It was summoned at the end of March 1270 to meet on 27 April. Henry, however, with typical impetuosity decided not to wait. Early in April he gave verbal orders for the collection of the tax, with what effect is unknown.[180] The parliament's discussions were long and some of the churchmen departed before they were over. But in the end, with the date of Edward's departure fast approaching, the laity agreed to the collection of the tax, the clergy to its assessment and collection. Representatives from the lower clergy seem this

[179] *C&S*, ii, 797–800.
[180] *CPR 1266–72*, 418.

time to have been absent, perhaps by design, but they were subsequently brought into line in a series of provincial synods.[181]

The concession of the tax was facilitated by a reaffirmation of Magna Carta. On 13 May, a day or so after the tax was granted, nine bishops appeared at St Paul's Cross in full pontificals and read out the famous sentence of excommunication pronounced by the bishops in 1253 against all who violated the Charters. They also read out the bull of Pope Innocent IV confirming the sentence and then fulminated their own excommunications against all who breached the Charters and seized clerical property.[182] In the parishes of the Worcester diocese, the sentences were to be read out during mass every Sunday until Pentecost and expounded in the vernacular.[183] The day after the bishops appeared at St Paul's cross, Henry ordered the exchequer to enforce the legislation against Jewish loans secured on rents. Indeed, all such rents in the hands of Jews at Hilary 1269 were to be cancelled.[184] There were, to be sure, some qualifications, but still this promised a very considerable alleviation of the burden of Jewish debt. The knights present at the parliament must have pressed for the legislation's implementation, just as they probably joined with churchmen in pressing for the enforcement of Magna Carta.

The securing of the crusading tax had, therefore, taken the best part of two years, running through at least seven parliaments from York in August 1268 to Westminster in May 1270. Given that many nobles were committed to Edward's crusade and the bishops (led by Walter Giffard of York) were supportive, the opposition probably came rather from the knights in parliament and the lower clergy. In the end the opposition had secured legislation on the Jews and the excommunication of violators of the Charters. The central place of parliament in the kingdom's life and its control over taxation had been affirmed. The view that knights and burgesses must be summoned at least to tax-raising parliaments had been solidified. The whole process, culminating in the new excommunications, 'are likely to have told a large public . . . that royal authority was limited, taxes could be bargained for, and redress of grievances set against supply'.[185]

Yet in the end the strength of the regime had been affirmed. A tax had been granted, the first on movables since 1237. The concessions obtained by parliament were small compared with those demanded at the assemblies

---

[181] *LNR*, 38–9. For various descriptions of the clerical property on which the twentieth was levied, see *LNR*, 23–6, 38–9, and for discussion (necessarily inconclusive) Mitchell, *Studies in Taxation*, 296 n. 21.

[182] FitzThedmar, 122–3 (Stone, FitzThedmar, no. 1010).

[183] Maddicott, 'The crusade taxation', 110, citing Wilkins, *Concilia Magnae*, ii, 22–3.

[184] *CR 1268–72*, 268; Maddicott, 'The crusade taxation', 109–10.

[185] Maddicott, 'The crusade taxation', 111. I have omitted Maddicott's qualification: 'if only in a dimly comprehended way'.

of the 1240s and 1250s. We hear no more of parliament choosing the king's ministers, let alone setting up a ruling council. The revolutionary reforms of 1258 seem dead. The tax itself was a success and made Edward's crusade possible. By October 1272 it had yielded £31,500, of which £10,896 were paid directly to Edward before his departure and another £15,000 went in recruiting his knights.[186] It had been worth fighting for.

## KING HENRY'S CRUSADE TOO?

The writ of summons for the April parliament was issued on 28 March 1270. It revealed something unexpected. This was not merely to be Edward's crusade, it was to be Henry's too. Henry had never abandoned his crusading ambitions. In May 1269 the Jews were exempted from being tallaged (in return for £1,000) only so long as neither Henry nor Edward went on crusade.[187] In 1270 itself there was once again the example of King Louis. On 15 March, in Paris, he had processed barefoot from the royal palace to Notre-Dame and then set out on his crusade. His three sons were coming too.[188] The example was irresistible. Henry too would crusade with his sons. He would join his brother-in-law in the great enterprise. Thus it was that, in his writ of summons on 28 March, Henry announced that he and his sons (so Edmund as well as Edward) would be setting out on the feast of John the Baptist (24 June). He was summoning the parliament to make arrangements for the peace and security of the kingdom in his absence. Anther writ on 13 April reveals that Henry intended to travel with Edward to Gascony, and then go on from there to Aigues Mortes and the rendezvous with King Louis. The parliament itself went along with Henry's plans. The grant of the twentieth was made by the prelates in recognition of the pious intention of Henry and his sons to go on crusade. The tax was to be received by Henry or Edward, whoever departed first. Henry's intention remained that they should go together. Indeed, both on 12 and 20 May he reaffirmed his intention to set out with his sons, this time on the day after the feast of John the Baptist, so on 25 June. Accordingly, another parliament was summoned for the feast day itself so that Henry could bid farewell and decide to whom the guardianship of the kingdom should be entrusted.[189] With typical lack of realism, this left only a day to decide the matter if Henry really did depart on the morrow.

---

[186] For the accounts for the total receipts and expenditure of the tax, see TNA E 372/117, m. 6d (image 6413), partly printed in *Lancashire Lay Subsidies*, 100–5; and see Mitchell, *Studies in Taxation*, 298–9; Lloyd, *English Society and the Crusade*, 118–19, 126–7.

[187] *CR 1268–72*, 54.

[188] Le Goff, *Saint Louis*, 294–5.

[189] Sayles, *Functions of the Medieval Parliament*, 126–7; *CLR 1267–72*, no. 1069; *LNR*, 23–4; *F*, i, 483.

Edward cannot have welcomed the prospect of his father coming too. The king's councillors must have been equally discouraging. In late March, Archbishop Giffard was writing about the danger of a new war and the anxious nights he was spending without sleep. Admittedly, he was excusing himself from visiting Rome, but he was not alone in expressing such fears. This was hardly the time for Henry and his sons to leave the kingdom at the same time. That Henry overrode such opposition is testimony to his determination. But he was also being humoured. Probably no one believed that, in the event, he would actually go.

## EDWARD AND GILBERT DE CLARE

Henry's decision to crusade had little or no impact on Edward's preparations. The attitude of someone else did. Indeed, it threatened to derail the whole enterprise. The someone was Gilbert de Clare.[190]

Clare had taken the cross with Edward at Northampton on 24 June 1268 and for a while thereafter their relations were amicable. It was at Edward's instance that Clare was allowed to keep Tonbridge castle rather than surrender it as security for keeping the peace, as the pope had decided.[191] During 1268, Clare made several appearances at court. Indeed, on 28 December he witnessed the charter giving Edward Pevensey.[192] After that, however, he was absent for more than a year and a half. He next attests a royal charter in August 1270. He failed to turn up for the translation of Edward the Confessor on 13 October, a terrible snub to the king, and two days later had to be given a safe conduct to come to court.[193]

There were several reasons for this breakdown in relations. Clare felt he was owed money by the king, in part for his expenses during the Evesham campaign. He resented the challenge to his possession of Portland, which his father had obtained in dubious circumstances back in 1259. In the Michaelmas term of 1269, so at the very time of the Confessor's translation, the king, doubtless with Edward's encouragement, was seeking its recovery through a legal action in the court *coram rege*. In response, Clare showed his dangerous ability to link private interests to public principle. He argued that the action against him was unlawful. It had been begun by a special writ 'out of course', this when the king and magnates of the kingdom had ordained that all seeking right in the king's courts should proceed by writs common, that is, available to all.[194] Added to all this, there

---

[190] Much of what follows is dependent on Lloyd, 'Gilbert de Clare, Richard of Cornwall and the Lord Edward's crusade', where key documents are analysed and printed.

[191] *F*, i, 476 (*CPR 1266–72*, 246).

[192] *RCWL*, ii, 165–71; *CPR 1266–72*, 312.

[193] *CPR 1266–72*, 369.

[194] TNA KB 26/191, mm. 1, 3 (images 0749, 0751). The case seems to have been dropped.

remained the dispute with Edward over the possession of Bristol. And then there was tension arising from Edward seeming to condone Llywelyn's encroachments on Clare's south Wales lordships.[195] Wild rumours started to fly around: that Edward was over familiar with Clare's wife; that there had been a plot to poison Clare at Cardiff.[196] During the course of 1269–70 relations between the two broke down completely. Both accused the other of wanting to make war. Clare refused to come to court or attend parliament, fearing he might be attacked or arrested. Hence his need for a safe conduct. The treatment of Robert de Ferrers here cast a long shadow. What made this all the more serious was that Clare, as the events of 1267 had shown, was the one person capable of making a war to shake the kingdom.

Had Clare been prepared to crusade with Edward, much of the problem would have been resolved. Removed from the scene, he could not cause trouble. But here was the final crux of the dispute. By the end of 1269, Gilbert was refusing point blank to go with Edward. Indeed, there were serious doubts over whether he intended to go at all. His reasons were clear. The concord with Llywelyn that had permitted the march on London in 1267 was over. Clare now feared, if he went, his lands might be attacked by the Welsh prince as well as by Edward's men. In April 1268, in order to protect Glamorgan from the former, he began constructing his great castle at Caerphilly. He had every reason for staying behind to supervise its progress.

Clare's refusal to join Edward's crusade thus seemed to pose terrible dangers. Early in 1270, King Louis himself intervened. He called Clare out to Paris and, getting to the heart of the matter, told him bluntly that if he did not go Edward could not go either. But Clare was unmoved by the pleas even of the saintly king.[197]

When the April 1270 parliament opened at Westminster, therefore, the quarrel between Edward and Clare was as much on the agenda as was securing the crusading tax. In the end it was left to King Richard to decide the matter. He was evidently trusted far more than was the king. Richard eventually pronounced his award on 27 May.[198] It acknowledged that Clare would not accompany Edward. Evidently on that Clare was immovable. But Clare was to go in the first passage after Edward's. So, assuming Edward sailed in September 1270, Clare was to go in March 1271.[199] Clare was also urged, once in the Holy Land, to 'attend and aid' Edward, which probably meant campaigning under his banner. He was to receive 8,000 marks if he did, only 2,000 marks if he did not. Both his eventual departure

---

[195] For this, see *CPR 1266–72*, 385; Altschul, *A Baronial Family*, 126–7.
[196] Bury St Edmunds, 45.
[197] Canterbury/Dover, 540–1.
[198] The text is in *LNR*, 27–30.
[199] The passages here were those from the Mediterranean not the Channel.

and his keeping the peace in the meantime were to be guaranteed, amongst other things, by the surrender of Tonbridge and Hanley castles to King Richard. If Clare gave good reasons for not departing, then the castles were to remain in Richard's hands until Clare gave other security not to make war in England. On his side, all Edward had to do was to take an oath that, on pain of spiritual penalties, neither he nor his men would make war on Clare in Clare's absence.

The award was lopsided and Clare demanded modifications. The detailed arguments that followed show the forensic power of both men. Henry would have been quite out of his depth. In the end King Richard (and Wykes lauds his wisdom here) made some concessions, the most important meeting Clare's fears of never recovering Tonbridge and Hanley.[200] With these and other modifications, Clare accepted the award and reappeared at court. Edward clearly felt the guarantees were sufficient. His crusade could go ahead.

## EDWARD'S DEPARTURE

Back in May, Henry had announced that he and his sons would depart on 25 June 1270. That did not happen. Neither Edward not Edmund were ready. Henry was beginning to accept he would not go at all. The 20 May letter summoning everyone to say goodbye is the last we hear of his impending departure. Meanwhile Edward's own preparations were disrupted by a violent quarrel at court.

At Westminster on 28 June 1270 both John de Warenne, earl of Surrey, and Alan la Zouche attested a royal charter.[201] Two days later, in Westminster Hall, Zouche was assaulted and badly wounded by Warenne and his men. Zouche, a former steward of the royal household, had given stalwart service during the civil war and recently been constable of the Tower. Years before, as justice of Chester, he had boasted to Matthew Paris about how Wales was now subject to the king. Warenne had fought at Lewes, Evesham and Chesterfield, and taken the cross with Edward. He had helped with the disinheritance of Robert de Ferrers, and was frequently at court.[202] The quarrel between the two men centred on rival claims to the inheritance of David of Ashby, and was bound up with trafficking in wardships, dealings in debts owed to the Jews and the question of whether Ashby's lands should be redeemed under the terms of the Dictum of Kenilworth.[203] On 1 July, Warenne and Zouche appeared in person before the justices of the bench sitting in Westminster Hall. After an angry exchange of words, Zouche, unaware that Warenne's men had come armed (presumably their swords

---

[200] Wykes, 228–33.
[201] *RCWL*, ii, 181.
[202] Powicke, *King Henry III*, ii, 584.
[203] *RS*, 150–1, 156–7, 184–5; *CR 1264–8*, 428, 516.

were concealed beneath their robes), suddenly found himself under physical attack. He fled towards the king's chamber but was caught and badly wounded. Alan's son Roger was also assaulted but, perhaps more fleet of foot than his father, came off more lightly. After perpetrating this outrage, Warenne and his men escaped across the Thames.[204]

The attack was made all the more disgraceful by its setting: in the royal palace with both the king and queen in residence, with the justices of the bench in session and with the chancellor himself present in Westminster Hall. Even the revolutionaries who marched on the palace in 1258 had left their swords at the hall's entrance. There could be no more blatant breach of the king's peace. Edward and Archbishop Giffard went after Warenne to demand his submission. They were helped by the mediation of Henry of Almain and Gilbert de Clare, early evidence of the latter's reappearance. On 8 July, Warenne, having first hesitated, agreed to come to court in Edward's company, there to answer for his actions 'according to the law and custom of the realm'.[205] In fact, once there he simply threw himself on the king's mercy. In an act of public penance he was made to walk on foot with his knights from the New Temple to Westminster where they all swore they had acted in sudden anger without malice aforethought. At Winchester in early August twenty-four knights took an oath to the same effect and Warenne was allowed to purchase the king's pardon for a fine of 10,000 marks, mostly left unpaid.[206] It was perhaps the scandal and disruption which prevented Warenne accompanying Edward on crusade. As for the Zouches, they abandoned their legal action in return for a promise of 2,500 marks to be paid at the rate of 500 marks a year.[207] Alan, however, did not see the money. He had launched an appeal before the king, but his wounds festered and he died on 10 August.

It is tempting to see this episode as a product of the civil war and a symptom of the kingdom's continued instability. But that may be a mistake. It was a one-off event with no parallel in the rest of Henry's reign. Its most striking feature is the speed with which the court closed ranks and brought the 'tempest', as Wykes called it, to an end, although at the same time making very clear the unacceptability of Warenne's conduct. In general, the peace of the king's court was respected. It was not a violent place. The thousands of occasions when its members came together to witness royal charters typify its nature and processes far more than this one bloody incident.[208]

---

[204] The fullest account is in Wykes, 233–5, but for the correct date see Bury St Edmunds, 47.

[205] *CR 1268–72*, 282–3; *CPR 1266–72*, 418.

[206] Wykes, 235; Winchester, 108–9; *F*, i, 485 (*CPR 1266–72*, 451); *CPR 1272–81*, 146; *CPR 1301–7*, 496–7. Henry himself allowed the sum to be paid off at 200 marks a year.

[207] TNA E 159/44, m. 14d (image 0086). As the first payment was not due until Christmas, an initial payment may here be omitted.

[208] For discussion, see Powicke, *King Henry III*, ii, 584; Hyams, 'What did Henry III think in bed?', 121–2, and Hyams, *Rancor and Reconciliation*, 251–2.

Meanwhile Edward was taking steps to muster the force he would take with him. At the New Temple on 26 July he paid out £6,866 from the twentieth to fifteen lords who had contracted to come with some 100 knights. The largest contingent, one of 14 knights, was to be led by Henry of Almain. Other contractors were William de Valence, Roger of Clifford, Adam of Jesmond, Thomas de Clare and Adam de Monte Alto, the Adam who had rescued Henry at Evesham. Later, 10,000 marks were paid to Edmund and 1,200 marks to Hamo Lestrange when they prepared to join Edward in the following year.[209]

Edward also sought to secure the kingdom's peace and stability. In return for a 500 marks gift from the Londoners, he obtained at last a full restoration of their liberties so they now could elect once more their own mayors and sheriffs.[210] He also made sure he controlled local government. On 28 May, Henry committed to his custody a string of counties and castles across the kingdom. The commission was to last for three years but it was soon advanced to five. During that time, the sheriffs were to account as normal at the exchequer, but Edward or his councillors in England were to decide who they were and the financial terms on which they held office. It was thus Edward's wish, so the councillors told the exchequer, that Archbishop Giffard have custody of Nottinghamshire and Derbyshire, answering for a £100 increment and no more. This massive transfer of power was made by Henry on the advice of the council 'for the conservation of the peace and tranquility of our kingdom' and 'for the preservation and security of ourselves and our dearest Edward'.[211] That put it exactly. In Wales, on the other hand, Edward followed a different policy. In order to make money for the crusade and appease Llywelyn, he conceded to the prince the homage of Maredudd ap Rhys in return for the 5,000 marks stipulated in the Treaty of Montgomery. Here, without question, Edward placed the crusade above any future hegemony in Wales.[212]

The final arrangements for Edward's departure were made at a parliament meeting at Winchester in early August. Edward first did something to

---

[209] See the references in the note 186 above, 561. One of the contracts is printed in Richardson and Sayles, *Governance of Mediaeval England*, 464–5. The ratio was 100 marks for each knight. Leybourne, however, did not go on crusade and in 1269–70 was Edward's seneschal in Gascony.

[210] FitzThedmar, 124 (Stone, FitzThedmar, nos. 1012–13). This was on 1 June.

[211] *CFR 1269–70*, nos. 710–24; Wait, 'Household and resources', 136–53, where the extent of the transfer was first appreciated. For further appointments, see *CFR 1269–70*, nos. 1124, 1136–7, 1143–4, 1153–5, 1212, 1606, 1608. For the letter from Roger de Mortimer and Robert Burnell informing the exchequer of the archbishop's terms, see TNA E 159/46, m. 2d (image 8153).

[212] *CPR 1266–72*, 457. Whether, however, Llywelyn ever paid the money is unclear. See Huscroft, 'Robert Burnell and the government of England', 62 n. 18; Smith, *Llywelyn ap Gruffudd*, 349 n. 39. The map opposite p.1 shows Wales after the concession's implementation.

secure God's support for the enterprise. On a perilous Channel crossing, he had promised to found a monastery if he survived. On 2 August he fulfilled the vow and established a Cistercian house at Darnhall in Cheshire. The witnesses to the foundation charter, amongst a galaxy of the great and the good, included both Clare and Warenne.[213] On the same day, Edward entrusted the guardianship of his children, his castles and his lands to King Richard and a council composed of Archbishop Giffard, Philip Basset, Roger de Mortimer and Robert Walerand. They were to control the castles and counties recently conceded to him by the king as well as his own possessions.[214] They were also to pay his debts from the issues of his lands, especially those owed to the poor. There was no role in the arrangements for Edward's wife, Eleanor of Castile, because she was going too, indeed she had already left the country. There was also no role for Edward's father and mother, although Edward's children had been living with the queen at Windsor. In Henry's case it was because Edward thought too little of his father's grasp, in Eleanor's because he thought too much of it. He did not want her interfering.[215]

On 4 August, Henry issued a proclamation finally accepting he would not crusade himself. Although, he said, his whole desire was to cross with Edward in support of the Holy Land, he was now persuaded by the prelates, magnates and the community of the realm that it was neither safe nor prudent to do so. He and his son could not be absent at the same time. There was, however, a solution. Wishing to fulfil his vow while remaining behind to govern the kingdom, Henry committed 'the sign of our cross' to Edward who would crusade in his place. Quite probably in some physical ceremony, deeply moving for both father and son, Henry had taken off the cross he was wearing and handed it to Edward to wear instead.[216]

Henry thus hoped, through Edward, to obtain the same spiritual benefits as if he had crusaded himself. To that end, Henry asked his son to get a written declaration from the church of Jerusalem saying that was indeed the case. The letter, eventually issued by brother Bernard, the 'penitentiary' of the church, explained how 'the most serene prince, Lord Henry, illustrious king of England, having assumed the sign of the holy cross for his sins', had visited the Holy Land through his eldest son, the famous Lord Edward, 'to whom he had handed his cross to be born devoutly to the Holy Land for the completion of his vow'. Accordingly, Bernard now absolved Henry from 'all the sins and faults' of which he was truly penitent and confessed. The letter was issued from Acre on

[213] Dugdale, *Monasticon*, v, 709.

[214] *F*, i, 484; *DD*, no. 423. For the relationship between these two texts, see Huscroft, 'Should I stay or should I go?'

[215] For discussion of Eleanor's omission, see Howell, *Eleanor of Provence*, 250.

[216] *F*, i, 485 (*CPR 1266–72*, 452); FitzThedmar, 125 (Stone, FitzThedmar, no. 1015). Edward was also now to have all the money from the twentieth.

21 September 1272, so would not have reached Henry before his death two months later. But still it had been issued just in time.[217]

On 5 August 1270, Edward, having sought a final licence to depart from his father, came down from Winchester castle to the cathedral chapter house, where he begged for the prayers of the monks. He then set off for Portsmouth in the company of William de Valence, Roger of Clifford and Thomas de Clare. Henry stayed on at Winchester for a few days and then moved to Clarendon. Perhaps he felt a farewell at Portsmouth itself would be too upsetting. He must have known he was unlikely to see his son again.

In the event, thanks to the death of Archbishop Boniface and Edward's unavailing attempt to get his chancellor, Robert Burnell, elected in his place, Edward did not sail till 19 August.[218] In leaving for the crusade, he has been criticized by modern historians for foolhardiness and ill judgement. As papal warnings show, the critique was also made at the time. The dangers were reflected in the very arrangements Edward made at Winchester for his absence. The outbreak of war and the deaths of King Henry, King Richard, Henry of Almain and Edward himself were all raised as possibilities. Edward laid down that his sons were to come of age at twenty, and since John was four and Henry two, there was bound to be a very long minority in the event of his death. What would happen if the sons themselves died, as John did the next year and Henry in 1274, was not revealed at all. Would the throne then pass, assuming she was still alive, to Edward's only other offspring, his daughter Eleanor, born in 1264? Or would his brother Edmund, not mentioned at all in the arrangements, make a claim?[219]

Edward, then, was certainly taking a risk, yet it was not uncalculated. After all, young and strong, he was likely to return. Richard the Lionheart, Richard of Cornwall, Simon de Montfort and King Louis had all done so. For all the tensions in England, it was reasonable to think his councillors, dug in as they were to the castles and sheriffdoms, would be able to maintain the peace. Gilbert de Clare was likely to have his hands full in Wales, even if he did not in the end crusade. Edward was proved right. He did return surviving even an assassination attempt. His councillors kept the peace, despite the deaths of King Henry, King Richard, Henry of Almain and Edward's eldest son.

Edward, in any case, had quite a different perspective on what he was doing. The crusade, the greatest of all enterprises, would win him the

---

[217] TNA E 36/274, fo. 250. I owe knowledge and a full transcription of this letter to Nicholas Vincent. Bernard also made Henry's father and mother participants in the indulgence that the general council had conferred on all who helped the Holy Land.

[218] There is a full account of Burnell's career in Richard Huscroft's 'The political and personal life of Robert Burnell'. See also his 'Robert Burnell and the government of England'.

[219] Edmund, of course, was going on crusade but so was Henry of Almain, who was to replace King Richard in the event of the latter's death.

favour of both God and man. God had protected him through all the tribulations of the civil war and brought him victory. Henry's thank-offering was Westminster Abbey, Edward's was the crusade. If God wished to bring him safely home, He would do so. It was in God's hands. If some carped and criticized, many others shared this perspective. We get closest to how Edward hoped his crusade would be viewed and how he viewed it himself in a laudatory poem written after his accession but before his return.

Edward's valorous deeds, the poet sang, had made him as famous as Richard the Lionheart. He had defeated Simon de Montfort and subdued the disinherited. Then 'flying from idleness', he had 'taken up the sign of the cross, desirous of performing a worthy service to Christ, who had delivered him from this whirlwind of wars'.[220] Exactly. Edward had every hope he would be delivered again.

[220] *Political Songs*, 128–32.

## Chapter 14

# RECOVERY AND RESETTLEMENT

Edward's crusade was made possible both by the tax voted by the kingdom and the settlement with Gilbert de Clare. It was made possible too by the general recovery of royal government after its collapse in the civil war. And beyond all these was one other factor, more crucial to the peace and stability of the kingdom than anything else. This was the gradual process of reconciliation with the disinherited. In terms of their 'cause', the Statute of Marlborough had preserved the Provisions of Oxford's main legislative achievement and might seem to redeem the Dictum of Kenilworth's promise that the king would henceforth govern 'with justice'. While, moreover, there was no question of reviving the justiciarship, the office of chancellor had continued as established during the period of reform. On his appointment in August 1265, Walter Giffard was immediately conceded the same 500-mark annual fee as that enjoyed by Thomas de Cantilupe. But none of this would have counted unless the Dictum of Kenilworth was actually implemented and the disinherited restored to their lands. Here much depended on a whole series of private settlements between grantees and grantors. It depended too on the special judges touring the country to enforce the Dictum's terms. In the years between 1267 and 1272, while Henry lay at Westminster and Edward departed on crusade, the peace of the kingdom depended very much on this judicial work out in the shires.

## THE RESTORATION OF GOVERNMENT:
### FINANCIAL REFORM

At first sight any reference to the strength of the king's finances in these years might seem ludicrous, especially if viewed from the vantage point of the exchequer. On several occasions Henry acknowledged it was empty and he would have to borrow to pay his bills.[1] Many writs of *liberate* ordering the exchequer to shell out money were either left unpaid, paid in dribs and drabs or paid by handing over tallies, leaving debtors to collect the money themselves.[2]

---

[1] *CLR 1267–72*, nos. 827, 916, 1002, 1288.
[2] *CLR 1267–72*, viii, and nos. 237, 247, 259, 264, 735, 758–9, 761. See also *CR 1264–8*, 195–6.

How frustrating the situation could be is revealed in a letter the exchequer sent to Henry sometime in September 1270. On his orders, as so often in the past, it had scrutinized the receipt rolls to see the money coming in and also the writs commanding payments out. The news was not good. The king owed the merchants of Ypres £1,090 of which they had received only £60. As for paying for the works at Westminster, the purchases of the wardrobe and the expenses of envoys going overseas, the exchequer was powerless since, on the king's last departure, the keepers of the wardrobe had cleared out the treasury. Since then, 'not one ounce' had been received save money assigned to the queen, which was entirely controlled by her own clerks. As for loans, well, for the 1269 translation of the Confessor the exchequer had borrowed 800 marks from merchants and Jews. Since this had not been repaid no one was prepared to lend any money. So, the exchequer concluded, 'we can do nothing. It is most distressing to us. May the lord preserve you.'[3]

Up to a point the exchequer's plight is misleading. The performance would have been better a month or so later once the Michaelmas revenue was in. Throughout this period the exchequer officials, under a succession of treasurers (Thomas of Wymondham, John of Chishall and Philip of Eye), were making tremendous efforts to get control of the king's finances.[4] There was a double task. They had both to exact and audit the current revenue and also, as far as possible, get in the arrears and hear accounts for the period of the civil war. Probably the officials had never worked harder in the exchequer's history. On one occasion, the treasurer and barons recorded how, against all custom, they were still sitting on the Friday before Pentecost.[5] Perhaps it was pressure of work that aggravated a quarrel between the clerks of the 'great exchequer', as they called themselves, and the ushers over who was entitled to the bread and ale supplied daily by the Abbey's cellarer. (The ushers lost and were to have just the leftovers when the barons and their clerks shut up shop at the ninth hour.)[6] The clerk who made the record of this dispute in the exchequer memoranda rolls sketched in the margin a flagon for the ale and a plate for the bread. The rolls for this period have many marginal drawings. Hereford castle, the spire of St Paul's, the exchequer cloth and (rather unflatteringly) Nicolas of Ely, bishop of Worcester, all feature. The esprit de corps of the clerks seems high.

Pressure of work prompted reform. In 1268–9 there was a radical reordering of the memoranda rolls.[7] Then, in February 1270, soon after

---

[3] *CR 1268–72*, 226–7; Powicke, *King Henry III*, ii, 559.

[4] For Wymondham, see Jobson, "Royal government', 183–4.

[5] TNA E 159/42, m. 17d (image 0150).

[6] TNA E 159/46, m. 8 (image 8119).

[7] Now, grouped in separate sections, were, on the one hand, the writs issued by the exchequer summoning sheriffs and bailiffs to account, and, on the other, the acknowledgements by such

John of Chishall took over as treasurer, he and his colleagues suggested a new form for drawing up the pipe rolls, the great rolls recording the annual audit of the money owed the crown. The avowed aim was to free up time for the hearing of accounts by reducing the time taken in copying out the rolls. The reduction was to be achieved by removing from the rolls numerous old 'desperate' debts where there seemed little hope of recovery. That this new form was examined and accepted by King Richard, Archbishop Giffard, Edward and seven other named councillors shows its importance. Henry himself is not mentioned as being present.[8]

While labouring to exact money from the sheriffs, the exchequer had to be careful given all the controversy over the office during the period of reform and rebellion.[9] It was not helped in either direction by the fact that many of the sheriffs were leading members of the regime. Thanks to their status, they were sometimes hard for the exchequer to control. They were also, of course, not the county knights desired by the shires. In 1267–8 an important decision was made clarifying the financial obligations of the sheriffs, while at the same time offering to the shires a measure of reassurance. This was to establish the scale of the increments above the county farms for which the sheriffs should answer. Most of the sums were actually the same as those assessed by the reform regime in 1259 and were thus below the exorbitant levels reached before 1258.[10] Not all the gains of 1258–9 had thus been lost. Nonetheless the exchequer was still pressing the sheriffs hard for money. Again and again, in the most threatening terms, citing the king's 'great needs', it ordered them to search out and pay in specified sums at times outside the normal deliveries at Easter and Michaelmas.[11] The task was not helped by the dearth which followed the abundance of 1267.[12]

The cause of the exchequer's lack of liquidity prompted two decisions of the king and council. One was that henceforth all fees paid out of the exchequer should cease.[13] Those owed to the king's stewards and marshals were henceforth to be paid by the wardrobe. This was linked to an effort to buy out the fees granted to some individuals, including those owed to

men that they would come or that they owed money. There was also a separate section for the appointment of attorneys. The new order appears in the memoranda roll of the king's remembrancer: TNA E 159/43.

[8] *F*, i, 483; Jobson, 'Royal government', 194–5. For the whole story, see Meekings, *Studies in 13th-Century Justice*, ch. xx.

[9] For some of what follows, see Maddicott, 'Edward I and the lessons of baronial reform', 5–8.

[10] Compare *CFR 1259–60*, nos. 754–74; *CFR 1267–8*, 833–51.

[11] TNA E 159/42, m. 16 (image 0040); TNA E 159/43, mm. 10, 17 (images 0027, 0043); TNA E 159/44, m. 3d (image 0060); TNA E 159/45, m. 13d (image 0094). One of the orders, as recorded in the memoranda rolls, has a good drawing of a silver penny beside it.

[12] *LNR*, 39 (*Giffard Register*, 124–5).

[13] A 'fee' in this context means an annual money payment.

Geoffrey de Lusignan and the count of Bigorre.[14] The other decision, made before June 1268, was that henceforth all the money from the sheriffs and bailiffs was to be paid into the exchequer, with the king thus ceasing to draw directly on their revenues.[15] This, of course, was to return to the attempted reform of 1258-9. Henry claimed at one point he was obeying the new ordinance and for a while that seems to have been the case.[16] If ultimately the temptation to draw on local revenues proved too much,[17] the exchequer's cash flow did improve and it was able to make a far larger contribution to the wardrobe's funding than before. Whereas between August 1265 and March 1268 it had only sent the wardrobe £2,543, between March 1268 and the end of reign in November 1272 the figure was £12,109. In the first period it had contributed 9 per cent to wardrobe receipts, in the second 32 per cent.[18]

In several of these reforms, especially that on fees, one senses Edward's tight fist closing Henry's open hand. Perhaps that was also the case in another measure taken to restore the king's material position. This was the ban for three years on gifts of deer and wood from the royal forests. In November and December 1267, Henry had made no fewer than forty-two such gifts both to laymen and religious institutions. But then such gifts almost stopped. There were only six more before the end of May. After that, Henry, as so often, began to wriggle free and gifts were made explicitly setting aside the restrictions, first to religious institutions, then also to laymen.[19] In the next years the ban was increasingly honoured in the breach, but at least Henry had made an effort to obey his own rules.[20]

Despite the occasional emptiness of the exchequer and Henry's frequent expressions of need, his financial position in these last years was stronger than might appear,[21] in part thanks to continuing revenue from the papally sanctioned tenth. It helped pay all manner of bills and contributed, between March 1268 and the end of the reign, nearly £8,000 to

[14] *CPR 1266-72*, 326, 408; *CLR 1267-72*, nos. 587, 713a, 729, 735, 921, 1024, 1054, 1113, 1288, 2059. For discussion see Collingwood, 'Royal finance', 338-40. The measure had probably been introduced in October 1267: *CLR 1260-7*, 298.

[15] *CR 1264-8*, 465; *CPR 1266-72*, 300.

[16] There is a partial gap in writs ordering significant expenditure between March and November 1268: *CLR 1267-72*, nos. 221, 490.

[17] From drawings from the eyres Farr, Elrington and Summerson, *1268 Wiltshire Eyre*, lxxxix-xc; *CLR 1267-72*, nos. 587, 808, 1035, 1868; TNA E 159/45, m. 9d (image 0080).

[18] Wild, *WA*, clxxiii, clxxx. The sum produced at the Easter and Michaelmas *adventi* between 1269 and 1271 (when the sheriffs and town bailiffs came with their money) averaged over £1,000, a sum unseen since Montfort's Easter *adventus* of 1265. The average between Michaelmas 1265 and Michaelmas 1268 had been £363: Cassidy, 'Adventus vicecomitum', 617.

[19] *CR 1264-8*, 465, 471, 473-4.

[20] See below, 600.

[21] But see Barratt, 'Finance on a shoestring', 74-6.

wardrobe receipts, over 20 per cent of the whole.[22] Henry was still, it is true, running up a deficit on the wardrobe account. At the end of the reign, no less that £5,000 was owed to merchants and other creditors, including those in London, for cloth and other things obtained for the household.[23] This troubled Henry's conscience but also showed how successful his officials were in obtaining goods on credit. Wardrobe receipts, if averaged weekly between 1268 and 1272, were actually down 27 per cent compared with the period 1265 to 1268, but that was largely because money was no longer being spent on war. The costs of food, drink, alms and the stables, running at over £13 a day, were much the same as they had been between 1265 and 1268 and were higher than in several periods of Henry's personal rule.[24] Old and sick though he was, Henry was still living in state. His financial resources were an important factor in the stability of the realm.[25]

## THE RESTORATION OF GOVERNMENT: THE GENERAL EYRE OF 1267–70

A major step in the restoration of government came with the commissioning in December 1267 of a general eyre, a visitation, that is, of the king's judges throughout the country. To be sure, its jurisdiction was limited. It had nothing to do with the Dictum of Kenilworth's implementation. That was the work of a separate eyre. It was the Dictum eyre too, together with the court *coram rege*, that heard, for the most part, the cases of violence and pillage committed during the disorders. The visitation commissioned in December 1267, by contrast, was a traditional eyre, hearing both civil pleas and pleas of the crown. It was thus an important step in a return to normality. The kingdom was divided into three circuits, each under a senior judge, 'the most comprehensive programme of the reign'. By Henry's death, thirty-two counties had been visited, a great achievement and a testimony to the recovery of royal authority.[26] This was

---

[22] Wild, *WA*, clxxx, clxxxii.

[23] Wild, *WA*, clxxxvi, 150.

[24] Carpenter, 'Household rolls', 35.

[25] As James Collingwood shows, it is very difficult to use the pipe rolls in the period after Evesham to get any clear idea of the king's total revenue. Large sums of money were being written off as compensation for expenditure or losses during the war. In terms of the actual cash paid into the exchequer and wardrobe, after making adjustments for missing accounts and other factors, figures for annual revenue between 1265 and 1269 remain fairly steady at around £13,000 to £14,000. The figure is lower by £2,000 to £3,000 than the cash figure for 1258/9, but not catastrophically so. It also does not reveal the king's total cash income since it excludes much of the revenue from the ecclesiastical tenth. For Collingwood's figures, see his 'Royal finance', 145–6, 200–1, 269–70, 280–1, 317–18 and 300–1 for the tax.

[26] Crook, *Records of the General Eyre*, 133–42. The visitations were suspended in 1270 probably to reduce tension on Edward's departure on crusade.

all the more the case because eyres were unpopular. While their civil plea jurisdiction, with its cheap and speedy litigation, was welcomed, the amercements imposed on individuals and communities in the course of the crown pleas were deeply resented. This was why the counties jealously guarded the rule that there should be a seven-year interval between eyres. In 1269, perhaps after protests from knights in parliament, the Lincolnshire eyre had been postponed so the rule was not breached. The government, however, made no effort to encourage the hearing of complaints on the eyres on the lines of '1258'. It was not going to open that can of worms. It took Edward I, firmly in the saddle, to do so and also to appoint local knights as sheriffs.

We can see the actions of the judges on the crown pleas side in Wiltshire (a relatively quiescent county in the civil war).[27] Twelve jurors from each of the county's fifty districts, including its thirty-seven hundreds and seven boroughs, came before the justices headed by Nicholas de Turri. They answered all the usual questions about the rights of the king, official malpractice and crime committed since the last eyre (in 1257), crime, that is, unconnected with the war. Under the first two heads the jurors revealed the usurpations of Richard de Clare and the extortions of Amice, countess of Devon, and her bailiffs.[28] The judges took cognizance of 248 homicides, 67 cases of death by misadventure and 115 thefts. As usual, large numbers of those accused were acquitted and very few were convicted and hanged. The greatest number of all, having escaped, were outlawed and thus lived to offend again. But if this seemed a failure of the criminal justice system, the judges were very successful in imposing penalties on the local communities for their various misdemeanours. Over 100 amercements were slapped on tithings, mostly because a member had been outlawed or had abjured the realm. Some 260 amercements were imposed on villages for such things as failure to arrest criminals or follow up the hue and cry. While the *murdrum* fine was not imposed in cases of misadventure, villages were amerced for failing to come to inquests 'fully', thus exploiting the way the Statute of Marlborough had emasculated the 1259 legislation on the subject. Here the clock really was being put back. All this made money for the king. The issues of the Wiltshire eyre were £673. It also ensured the tithing groups and villages played their accustomed role in the maintenance of the peace. 'Standing at the apex of the existing system of law enforcement, the weight of the eyre . . . was largely responsible for keeping the parts below in place.'[29] This was never more needed than in the aftermath of the 1263–7 civil war.

---

[27] For what follows see Farr, Elrington and Summerson, *1268 Wiltshire Eyre* with an extensive introduction by Henry Summerson.

[28] Farr, Elrington and Summerson, *1268 Wiltshire Eyre*, nos. 249, 285.

[29] Farr, Elrington and Summerson, *1268 Wiltshire Eyre*, xliii.

## DEALING WITH THE DISORDERS

The great eyre commissioned at the end of 1267 was not, as we have said, concerned with the acts of ravage and pillage committed during the disturbances. Just how extensive these had been is impossible to gauge with any exactitude. There was no 'Domesday Book' survey made of England in 1267 to reveal the areas now reduced to 'waste'. While much light could be shed on the subject by analysing in comprehensive fashion the cases that came before the eyres and the court *coram rege* after 1265, this has yet to be done. The task would be both colossal and fraught with the usual difficulties over determining the veracity of the evidence.[30] No part of England, it seems certain, suffered the systematic destruction involved in William the Conqueror's harrying of the North. On the other hand, the violence was almost certainly on a totally different scale from that witnessed in peacetime. There was no equivalent then to castle garrisons, marauders from the Isle of Ely and the disinherited in the woods and fields pillaging surrounding areas and sacking towns in the search for supplies and money.[31] There was equally no peacetime equivalent to the widespread burning of property. By 1267 gutted barns and houses must have scarred the landscape just as did city bombsites after the Second World War. The amount of disorder revealed in the legal records in the years following 1265 thus goes way beyond anything seen in the years of peace. In Suffolk on the Dictum eyre around 300 individuals were accused of involvement in acts of violence and plunder.[32] Some of this activity was political, between participants in the war, some of it personal involving the settling of old quarrels, although often there was no distinction between the two, the quarrels determining political allegiance. Some of it again, under cover of the war, was simply robbery pure and simple.

Contemporary writers were quite clear that what had occurred was exceptional. The Furness abbey chronicler wrote feelingly of the 'outrages' committed. In one, a knight on the side of the barons, having returned home to find his manor sacked and park broken into, seized seven of the malefactors, shut them into a house and burnt them to death.

'Such horrible things happened in many parts of England, with old discords between neighbours being renewed, and with the powerful despoiling and oppressing the weak without fear of punishment, so common was the war through all the country. Whence, through the machination of the Devil, father rose up against son, son against father, brother against brother, and neighbour against neighbour.'[33]

---

[30] Problems of interpretation are discussed in King, 'The Friar Tuck syndrome'.

[31] I owe these points to Oakes, 'The nature of war', 222–3, 230. For the pillaging of castle garrisons, see Coss, 'Retinues, agents and garrisons', 191–6.

[32] Jacob, *Studies*, 313–28.

[33] Furness, 545, cited in Valente, *Theory and Practice of Revolt*, 75.

Another perspective on the troubles is offered by Peterborough abbey's account of its sufferings in the war.[34] The abbey's travails began when some of its knights, instead of answering the summons to muster for the king, joined the barons in Northampton and then, provocatively, raised the abbey's banner, with the keys of Saint Peter, on the walls. Henry, infuriated, swore he would destroy the abbey completely, but then was appeased by an offer of £200. Although this secured letters of protection, the royalists took no notice of them and separate payments had to be made to the bailiffs of John de Warenne, the castellan of Fotheringhay and Warin of Bassingbourn. (They were all despoiling the abbey's manors.) The abbot had now learnt his lesson and, in the period down to Lewes, he gave supplies worth £114 to Henry, King Richard and Lord Edward, while Henry and Roger of Leybourne both received palfreys worth 14 marks. All this secured further letters from Henry and Edward, these ones ordering property taken from the abbey to be restored. But again no notice was taken of them. Another £240 given to Edward for protection proved equally wasted.

After Lewes, it was the turn of the barons to take revenge on the abbot for having sided with the king. Montfort and Clare each received £20 while Henry de Montfort, Simon junior, John fitzJohn and Henry de Hastings had 10 marks apiece. After Evesham, it was the other way round again, with punishment for having sided with the barons! At the Winchester parliament, the abbot had to give 500 marks to the king, £200 to Edward, and 200 marks to Gilbert de Clare, with another £100 going to John de Warenne. (This was so he vacated the manors he had occupied.) There was further damage in 1266 and 1267, including the loss of seventeen horses and ten hauberks at the siege of Kenilworth, and a payment of 50 marks for having the king's 'perfect' love. In the end, the chronicler put the expenses incurred during the war at a stupendous £4,324. It would have been worse, he observed, had the abbey not kept open house, supplying both sides with food and drink, although this sometimes meant the monks went hungry. If a great monastery like Peterborough could suffer like this, one can imagine the fate of lesser fry.

Against this background, the government after the war had a twofold task. It needed to give loyalists some means of seeking redress for their losses. Yet at the same time it needed to prevent that redress going too far and provoking fresh disturbances, all the more so given that the Montfortians received no compensation for their own losses. In seeking to appease former rebels, the Dictum of Kenilworth laid down that those who had been 'redeemed' (meaning those who had agreed a redemption fine) were not bound to answer for the damage they had done to their enemies 'in

---

[34] *Historiae coenobii Burgensis*, 134–40. I thank Henry Summerson and Nicholas Vincent for bringing this chronicle to my attention.

the time of the disturbance'.[35] The Statute of Marlborough added that no one should lose life or limb for robberies, homicides and breaches of the peace committed by either side during the civil war, here treating rebels and loyalists just the same. The time of war was defined as from 4 April 1264, when the king marched out of Oxford, to 16 September 1265, when peace was proclaimed at Winchester. But, in addition, those who had committed homicides and robberies 'under the guise of war' between 4 June 1263 (when Bishop Aigueblanche was seized in Hereford) and 4 April 1264 were also covered, as were those who had participated with Gilbert de Clare in his seizure of London.[36]

These limitations, however, did not prevent loyalists bringing legal actions against those who had plundered their estates after 16 September. Many of the cases which do not mention the '*turbacio*' and simply complain of actions 'against the peace' were probably of that kind.[37] Other cases, where the offence had occurred '*occasione turbacionis*' or '*tempore turbacionis*', were probably ones where the defendants had not been 'redeemed', not very surprising given they were often of low social status. The cases were heard either in the court *coram rege* or in the special Dictum of Kenilworth eyre. E.F. Jacob calculated that the *coram rege* roll for Michaelmas 1268 had over 200 of such actions (out of 378). This seems remarkable but my count is much the same.[38] Most of the depredations are undated but when they are (as in those suffered by Walter of Merton), there was evidently a first wave on Montfort's return in 1263, a second in the skirmishing before the battle of Lewes, and then a third in all the disorder after Evesham.[39] Since, as we have said, there was no scope for the rebels to complain of their own sufferings, the cases reveal only half of the disorder.[40] Everything needs to be doubled or more than doubled to appreciate the gigantic orgy of destruction.

Some of the plaintiffs were innocent individuals, who, as Alice de Audeham said of herself, had taken no part in the conflict. Alice de Scales said the same. As a 'lady widow', she had simply 'stayed in peace in her house' until her manor was sacked.[41] The majority of the cases, however, were brought by leading members of the regime, including Edward

---

[35] *DBM*, 334–7, cap. 35.

[36] Farr, Elrington and Summerson, *1268 Wiltshire Eyre*, xliii–iv, and no. 600; and *CCR 1272–9*, 333.

[37] There are many cases of this kind, a point missed by Jacob. King, 'The Friar Tuck syndrome', 34–7, also notices them and has found examples where '*in tempore turbacionis*' is omitted at one stage of proceedings, while reappearing at another. It may be, therefore, that the omission, in some cases, is just due to the vagaries of the clerks.

[38] Jacob, *Studies*, 202 n. 3. James King counted more than 750 cases in the *coram rege* rolls between 1265 and 1268: King, 'The Friar Tuck syndrome', 34.

[39] Stewart, *RJS*, nos. 64, 81, 84, 97–8, 101–3, 107–8, and see above, 344 n. 108.

[40] Thus, Robert de Tyndale had letters patent from Edward empowering him 'to run against and destroy all the enemies of the king': *RS*, 180–1.

[41] TNA KB 26/174, m. 5 (image 0011); TNA KB 26/186, m. 7 (*AP*, 168, but with this part omitted).

himself, King Richard, Robert Walerand, Roger of Leybourne, Philip Basset, John de Grey, Walter of Merton and the executors of John Mansel. They were brought too both by Edward's men – Robert Burnell, Warin of Bassingbourn, Nicholas of Cogenhoe and Nicholas of Haversham – and by a whole raft of courtiers and officials, including the stewards of the household Robert Aguillon, William of Wintershall, William of Ayot and John de La Linde, the marshal of the household, William Belet, the wardrobe official Richard of Ewell, the falconer John of Bicknor, the chancery clerk Wibert of Kent and the judges Nicholas of Yattendon and William de St Omer. Naturally, William de Valence was a complainant, as were the queen and such Savoyards as Peter de Champvent, Imbert de Montferrand, Robert Pugeys (Imbert's son) and (in absentia) Peter of Savoy himself. The baronial complainants included Roger de Mortimer, John de Balliol, John Giffard, Thomas Corbet, John de Burgh and Robert of Tattershal. Gilbert de Clare's clerk, Hervey of Boreham, also featured. No cases were brought by Gilbert de Clare himself. He could look after himself.

Some of the victims had property pillaged in many counties. Some had individual properties pillaged many times.[42] The pattern everywhere was much the same. Corn, animals and valuables were seized (including in one case nine books of medicine).[43] Manor houses were sacked, fishponds broken open, buildings set on fire. There are occasional trivialities. In one case, John de Burgh, Hubert's son, won an action against a man who had robbed his boy of three lampreys being taken to Eleanor de Montfort, a case which might have raised further questions about John's loyalty.[44]

One feature of the cases was the large size of the raiding bands: twenty, thirty, forty, fifty, sixty individuals were often named, sometimes over a hundred. Many of those involved were peasants and artisans.[45] The bands were sometimes led by prominent rebels, but often not. The eighty-five men who ravaged King Richard's properties in Norfolk and Suffolk were headed by Alexander the sergeant of Tunstead.[46]

Another feature of the cases *coram rege* was the failure to bring the bands to justice. The sheriffs were ordered to produce the defendants and nearly always failed to do so. Some of those accused lived in other counties, others within liberties. When they could be attached they still failed to appear. The sheriff might then be ordered to attach them with better sureties with the result that double or triple the number of original defendants were caught up in the case. The plaintiffs nonetheless saw some point in

---

[42] For example, Robert of Tattershall and Nicholas of Haversham: *AP*, 160, 162–3, 165, 174–5, 177–8.

[43] TNA KB 26/174, m. 4 (image 0010).

[44] TNA JUST 1/83, m. 13 (image 0616). John seems to have deserted Montfort during the course of 1265 and thus avoided disinheritance.

[45] See above, 370–1.

[46] TNA KB 26/175, m. 15 (image 0032).

the litigation, presumably because at the very least it created difficulties for the defendants, who found themselves chased up by the sheriffs. Such litigation could, of course, go alongside violent action on the ground, but at least it was better than a total reliance on self-help and private revenge. It meant that 'the civil war which had racked the country since 1264 was in one sense transferred into the royal courts'.[47] So much the better for that!

## REDEMPTION AND REHABILITATION: THE ENFORCEMENT OF THE DICTUM OF KENILWORTH

The bitterness over the ravaging of estates created a dangerous situation. It made the loyalist victims all the keener to profit from the lands of the disinherited. It made the disinherited, deprived of legal redress for their own sufferings, all the more likely to make war if they did not recover their estates. Fortunately, the Dictum of Kenilworth was cleverly balanced and promised an advantage to both sides. By far the most pivotal feature of Henry III's last years is that, as modified by Gilbert de Clare, by and large it worked.[48] The bulk of the rebels recovered the bulk of their lands. By the end of the reign some were once more in the king's favour and working for his government.

Before looking at the process of recovery, two other cardinal factors making for the peace of the realm must be appreciated. The first, as we will see, is that just holding office during the Montfortian regime was not by itself a reason for disinheritance. The second is that many rebels had never had their lands seized in the first place. So much is clear from a survey of the rebellion in Kent made around 1275. Here over forty rebels were revealed as having escaped the confiscations.[49] The great majority were freemen holding land valued at less, often much less, than the £15 minimum set for knighthood in 1256.[50] It seems as though previous inquiries had been like a tide washing the larger flotsam up onto the beach but pulling much of the smaller back into the anonymity of the sea. But

---

[47] Knowles, 'The disinherited', pt. 4, 54.

[48] E.F. Jacob first unravelled and analysed the records of the Dictum eyre and the court *coram rege*, a remarkable work of pioneering and painstaking scholarship. See Jacob, *Studies*, pt. 2, and Appendixes 7–11. C.H. Knowles studied the same and related material in detail for his thesis on the disinherited, a thesis which should never have been left unpublished. See Knowles, 'The disinherited', pts. 3–4. There are, however, two printed articles by him: 'The resettlement of England' and 'Provision for the families of the Montfortians'. I did once ask Knowles why the thesis remained unpublished and he said his supervisor, R.F. Treharne (who disliked the criticisms of Simon de Montfort), had never suggested it should be, a warning against taking too much notice of one's supervisor, however distinguished. After Treharne's death, Knowles did publish an Historical Association pamphlet highly critical of Simon: Knowles, *Simon de Montfort*.

[49] *CIM*, no. 1024, and (for the last of Sutton) TNA C 145/27/50.

[50] For the last of Sutton, see above, 369.

some knights too were able to escape. Half a dozen were fingered in the Kentish inquiry, apparently for the first time, including Bertram de Criel, grandson of Henry's steward. There had also been escapes in other counties. Indeed, in Dorset half the knights involved at some point in the rebellion seem to have gone unpunished.[51] Some individuals were probably protected by changing sides, either under the auspices of the earl of Gloucester or on their own account. Others perhaps owed their immunity to friendly local juries. Just what lay behind the Kentish inquiry of 1275 is unknown. At any rate nothing seems to have come of it.

For those whose lands were seized, there were two ways of recovering them under the terms of the Dictum. One was by making a private agreement with the sitting tenant, sometimes after the king himself had commissioned a valuation of the lands in question. The agreement would be sanctioned by the king and recorded on the rolls of the chancery, exchequer or court *coram rege*. The other way was by a formal process before the Dictum eyre. Many of the greatest rebels made such private agreements. Their guilt was notorious. Their liability to a five fold redemption obvious. There was no point trying to challenge this by going before the eyre. Here are some examples of such agreements recorded on the rolls of the exchequer, chancery and court *coram rege* between 1267 and 1270:

| Former rebel | Grantee | Amount |
|---|---|---|
| Robert de Vere, earl of Oxford | Roger de Mortimer | 4,000 marks |
| Nicholas of Seagave | Edmund | 2,000 marks |
| Henry de Hastings | John de Warenne | £1,000 |
| Ralph Basset of Sapcote | John de Verdun | 1,000 marks |
| Giles de Argentan | Roger de Mortain[52] | 900 marks |
| John de Eyville | Queen Eleanor | 900 marks |
| Simon of Pattishall | John Giffard | 900 marks.[53] |

As for the eyre, it was commissioned in September 1267 when the king was at Shrewsbury negotiating with Llywelyn. The kingdom was divided into four circuits covering the north, the east, the midlands and the west.[54] The eyre lasted into 1272. Its plea rolls survive for seven counties: Northamptonshire, Cambridgeshire, Suffolk, Essex, Buckinghamshire, Berkshire and Surrey.[55]

[51] Ridgeway, 'Dorset in the period of baronial reform and rebellion', 35–6.

[52] Roger was one of Edward's knights.

[53] The figures are extracted from a larger table in Knowles, 'The disinherited', pt. 4, 108–9, and from the references in the notes to p. 110 and (for Ralph Basset) *CR 1264–8*, 385–6.

[54] *CPR 1266–72*, 160. For the eyre and its records, see Knowles, 'The disinherited', pt. 4, 20–31; Jacob, *Studies*, 162–3, 179–80.

[55] Jacob, *Studies*, 162–3. There is also one membrane from Norfolk. The roll of the Surrey eyre (which has some pleas from Kent and Sussex) is printed with a translation in

The eyre's most striking feature is the way the disinherited showed confidence in its procedures. They *did* come before it to seek the recovery of their lands. They could do that by proving their innocence or by accepting whatever redemption fine the judges imposed. As one plaintiff put it, 'the king has conceded in the Dictum of Kenilworth that no one who stood against the king in the disturbance should be disinherited'.[56] The Dictum eyre ensured that was the case. On the Northamptonshire eyre, the '*miles strenuus*', Simon fitzSimon, thus appeared before the judges and acknowledged 'by word of mouth', doubtless proudly, his presence 'against the king' at Northampton, Chesterfield and the Isle of Ely. The judges then ordered his lands to be valued and sentenced him to a redemption fine of five years their annual value.[57] Other rebels, however, disputed their guilt, or the degree of their guilt, in the hope of gaining a lesser fine, or escaping one altogether. The case would then go to the verdict of a jury, after which the judges fixed the redemption fine according to the scale of the offence.[58] Altogether on the Northamptonshire eyre, some twenty former rebels, many of them prominent knights, appeared, and there were around the same number of redemption agreements. The eyres also reviewed agreements already reached. A few of these it cancelled, as made without the consent of the king, but most it just accepted.[59]

One reason for the confidence of the disinherited was that their fate rested in the hands of juries. On numerous occasions these acquitted those accused, in whole or part, of the charges brought against them. When the Northamptonshire knight Simon of Lindon came before the eyre and offered to stand by the Dictum, a jury stated he had 'never been against the king, in thought, word or deed, in armies, vills or elsewhere'.[60] Juries also agreed that men had been coerced into going to Northampton (usually by William Marshal) or had gone there peacefully without evil intent. Both Richard of Floore and Nicholas of Dean were thus acquitted of all charges and recovered their lands from William de Sancta Ermina and Matthias Bezill. Sancta Ermina appealed against the verdict, but a second jury agreed with the first. He had to pay Richard of Floore twelve marks in damages. It

---

Stewart, *RJS*. All of the Essex roll, a large part of the Northamptonshire roll and portions of the rolls from Cambridgeshire and Suffolk are printed in *RS*, 106–246. The pleas for Cambridge itself and some of those for Buckinghamshire are printed in Jacob, *Studies*, 395–413. Jacob (*Studies*, 313–28) also provides a calendar of the presentations made by the Suffolk jurors at the eyre.

[56] TNA KB 26/205, m. 11d, as cited by Knowles, 'The disinherited', pt. 4, 55.

[57] *RS*, 167; For Simon, 'who first raised the standard against the king' at Northampton, see Rishanger, 125. His lands had been given to John de Vaux (see Vincent's census of Henry III's originals under 25 October 1265).

[58] For the procedure, see Jacob, *Studies*, 185–8.

[59] For examples in Essex: *RS*, 117–18, 128–9, 134, 136–7, 140–1.

[60] *RS*, 195.

was not just the king's foreign servants who lost out. Edward's knight Nicholas of Cogenhoe (by the end of the reign a marshal of the king's household) was convicted of falsely accusing Giles of Ashby of pillaging his manor at Myridale. In fact, the jurors said, Giles had fought for the king at Lewes and been captured by William Marmion. It was Marmion who had pillaged the manor. Giles was just his prisoner.[61] The juries frequently discriminated between the charges saying some were true and some were false.[62] In Surrey, for example, they agreed that Walter of Moseley had pillaged the lands of Walter of Merton at Malden, but denied he had been at Lewes. He had set off with Simon de Montfort for the battle but had fallen ill and gone home.[63] Just how 'truthful' the juries were when making these acquittals or partial acquittals is hardly the point. If they were doing favours to former rebels, that helped all the more the cause of peace.[64]

Another factor in making the eyres a success was the moderation and flexibility of the judges.[65] They imposed comparatively few fines at five times the annual value of the lands to be redeemed.[66] They also upheld the rule in the Dictum preserving those who had redeemed their lands from being sued for damages by their opponents in the war. The Surrey judges did so even against Nicholas of Yattendon, one of the judges on the midlands Dictum eyre.[67] From the poor and landless the judges often simply extracted oaths for future good behaviour. They demanded that one chaplain accused of receiving stolen goods should sing sixty masses for the king, the queen and their children.[68] They accepted the plea of two Berkshire mothers that they had received their sons not as rebels but as sons.[69]

The eyre was careful to respect the position of Gilbert de Clare. His followers were generally let off when they produced his letters testifying to their being in his service.[70] When, in a case *coram rege*, the exemption produced by William de Tracy (of Gloucester fame) was disputed, the judges declared the king wished the charter he had given to Gilbert (protecting also his followers) to be upheld in all things.[71]

---

[61] *RS*, 154–5, 171, 188. For other acquittals in Northamptonshire, see *RS*, 169, 181–2, 193, 195, 201, 206–7. Myridale was perhaps a name for the manor at Cogenhoe.

[62] See Jacob, *Studies*, 404–5.

[63] Stewart, *RJS*, no. 81.

[64] For a valuable study showing jurors themselves involved in the rebellion, see Asaji, *Angevin Empire*, 229–30, and Asaji, 'The Barons' War and the hundred jurors', 1263.

[65] Jacob, *Studies*, 186, 196–8; Knowles, 'The resettlement of England', 32–3; Knowles, 'The disinherited', pt. 4, 117–18.

[66] Knowles, 'The disinherited', pt. 4, 60–1.

[67] Stewart, *RJS*, no. 48; *RS*, 118; Knowles, 'The disinherited', pt. 4, 114.

[68] *RS*, 222.

[69] TNA JUST 1/42, m. 5, cited by Knowles, 'The disinherited', pt. 4, 118 n. 1. But I cannot find the case on m. 5.

[70] *RS*, 199; TNA JUST 1/59, m. 5 (image 1483); TNA JUST 1/83, mm. 10, 11d (images 0611, 0686).

[71] *AP*, 170; Jacob, *Studies*, 216 n. 1.

The eyre, therefore, was a triumphant success.[72] 'The English machinery of justice was never seen to better advantage than in the way [the terms of the Dictum] were carried out.'[73] Yet for all that the judges might order valuations of lands and fix redemption fines, there was still much that could go wrong. The former rebel William de Munchesney complained that William de Valence was keeping him out of his lands by challenging their valuation and demanding a fresh one. (The first valuation, Valence said, had been carried out by former rebels and men in Munchesney's homage.) Here the king ordered a new valuation only if it was clear the first was flawed, and in the event Munchesney soon recovered his lands. That he had won out against the king's brother must have reassured former rebels.[74]

In general, the disinherited seem to have recovered their lands as soon as they agreed the redemption fine. They did not have to wait until they had actually paid the fine as envisaged under the Dictum's original terms. So the concession won by Gilbert de Clare had effect.[75] Of course, the money had still to be found. In most agreements the payments were staggered, but there could be severe penalties for failure to keep the terms. If Walter of Moseley did not keep his for the recovery of houses in Southwark, he was to return the houses and lose all he had paid.[76] In his redemption agreement with Roger de Somery, the Warwickshire knight William de Wavers was to lose possession for ever of his manor of Marston Wavers if he failed to keep the terms. He also conceded all the revenues of Marston to Somery during the two years he had for payment. Since those revenues were not to contribute to the fine, it was in effect larger than the stated 200 marks.[77]

The money was raised in various ways.[78] It could be borrowed or it could come from the sale or lease of land, either to the grantee or to

---

[72] In addition to the actions brought by the disinherited, juries from each hundred appeared before the judges to answer a whole series of questions: FitzThedmar, 96 (Stone, FitzThedmar, nos. 910–29); Jacob, *Studies*, 182–3. One half of these related to the fate of rebel lands after Evesham. The other half concerned participation in the disturbances. In Cambridgeshire, around 130 men (including 50 individuals from Cambridge itself) were said to have joined the depredators from the Isle. There was evidently a danger here of stirring up fresh discord. The eyre was digging down beyond the principal Montfortians and casting a much wider punitive net. Yet, as the Kentish inquiry shows, many still escaped. Those who did not were often peasants and artisans who could be punished without repercussions. The judge leading the Cambridgeshire eyre, William de St Omer, based himself at Barnwell priory and stayed there for over a year. The prior, having entertained the rebels from the isle, now had to cater for St Omer's extensive retinue, including his wife and twenty-two ladies. Nonetheless St Omer concluded the business by imposing on the prior a fine of 40s: Barnwell, 124–5; Jacob, *Studies*, 181.

[73] Jacob, *Studies*, 173; Knowles, 'The disinherited', pt. 4, 117.

[74] *CPR 1266–72*, 32, 161, 181, 271–2; Knowles, 'The disinherited', pt. 4, 104–6.

[75] Knowles, 'The disinherited', pt. 3, 62–3.

[76] Stewart, *RJS*, no. 68.

[77] *CR 1264–8*, 389; Knowles, 'The disinherited', pt. 4, 106–7.

[78] Knowles, 'The disinherited', pt. 3, 58–62.

someone else. The 1,000 marks Ralph Basset of Sapcote owed John de Verdun was paid off in part by giving him possession of two manors, one being Sapcote itself.[79] In one major agreement, that between Roger de Mortimer and Robert de Vere, earl of Oxford, a different method was applied. Vere was to enjoy all the 'comfort' of his possessions – his houses, parks and fish-ponds – but all the revenues were to go to Mortimer to pay off the fine. At least the amount was reduced from 4,000 marks to 3,000 marks by Vere's agreement to marry his son to Mortimer's daughter.[80] In 1273, Vere went on a pilgrimage to Evesham yet, in this marriage agreement, he was joining his family to the man, in one account, directly responsible for Montfort's death.

By far the most important conclusion from the most detailed study of the disinherited is that by the time Edward returned from his crusade in 1274 'the process of pacification and resettlement . . . had been largely completed'. 'The greater part of the disinherited had successfully recovered all, or virtually all, of their lands from loyalist grantees.' The former rebels were also 'being re-assimilated into the political community'. If there were often financial strains, and a legacy of debt, 'surprisingly few families suffered financial shipwreck'.[81]

The heaviest losses were experienced by those forced into settlements outside the Dictum, not that this made it any better. That was true of Robert de Ferrers, Hugh de Neville and Henry of Pembridge. (Henry granted Pembridge itself to Roger de Mortimer to get out of Roger's prison.)[82] Still, the Nevilles and Pembridges remained major families based respectively in Essex and Herefordshire. The Ferrers descended from wealthy earls to middle-ranking magnates, but at least they survived at that level. Indeed, here they were helped by a decision of the king. In 1275 Ferrers, under the terms of the Dictum, recovered Chartley in Staffordshire from Roger Lestrange. The king and council decided that he need not pay a redemption fine having been kept out of possession for so long.[83] Here Edward showed praiseworthy magnanimity towards his fallen enemy.

No other major family was declassed in the same way as the Ferrers. Take the five lay members of Montfort's council of nine.[84] The Bohuns suffered nothing from the rebellion of Humphrey de Bohun junior thanks

---

[79] *CR 1264–8*, 385–6. There was also a threat that if Basset could not make the payments (to which the manors only contributed part), then the manors would pass to Verdun in hereditary right.

[80] *CChR 1257–1300*, 89–90; Knowles, 'The disinherited', pt. 3, 61–2.

[81] Knowles, 'The disinherited', pt. 3, 100; Knowles, 'The resettlement of England', 25.

[82] For the Pembridge case, see Knowles, 'The disinherited', pt. 4, 99–100.

[83] Golob, 'The Ferrers earls of Derby', i, 408–10; Knowles, 'The disinherited', pt. 3, 72–4. Chartley had been held by Robert's brother Thomas de Ferrers and had thus not been caught up in the confiscation of Robert's estates.

[84] For what follows, see Knowles, 'The disinherited', pt. 3, 65–73; Knowles, 'The resettlement of England', 32–4.

to the protection of his father, the old earl of Hereford. Giles de Argentan recovered all his lands, as did the family of Roger de St John.[85] Peter de Montfort's son, Peter junior (who survived Evesham), lost three manors but recovered his chief holdings, including the castle of Beaudesert.[86] The member of the council who did worst, heavily in debt and selling property, was paradoxically Ralph de Camoys, who changed sides in 1265, or at least hedged his bets, and was never disinherited. Still, it was far from a complete disaster for his grandson was summoned as a peer to parliament.[87] The pattern is much the same with a wider group, namely the seventeen lords summoned to Montfort's last parliament. Fifteen of them or their descendants recovered their lands and lost nothing in social status. The group included such Montfortian stalwarts as Hugh Despenser, John de Vescy, John fitzJohn, Henry de Hastings, Nicholas of Seagrave, William de Munchesney, Ralph Basset of Sapcote, Ralph Basset of Drayton and John de Eyville, though John was left with a heavy trail of debt.[88]

The Bassets, like Peter de Montfort, were very much part of Montfort's midlands affinity. What of his knights below the level of those summoned to parliament? Here there were certainly some losses. Saer de Harcourt managed to redeem his lands but was heavily in debt to the Jews. In 1270 he sold his chief manor of Kibworth Harcourt to Walter of Merton, from whom it ultimately passed to Merton College. He was allowed to live on in the manor house and was left 10 marks in Merton's will.[89] A sad end for one of Montfort's principal knights, although his childless marriage was perhaps a reason for surrendering his property. Harcourt's fate, however, was untypical for most of Montfort's affinity recovered their properties. A note on the chancery rolls indicated that William de Wavers had paid off his debt to Roger de Somery, so he did not lose Marston Wavers.[90] Andrew of Astley, son of the Thomas killed at Evesham, recovered Astley itself from Warin of Bassingbourn, although Warin had got permission to crenellate the house there and clearly intended to keep it. In this instance a private agreement made outside the Dictum was overturned in Astley's favour.[91] A similar pattern of recovery is found amongst the knights in Oxfordshire. Here the son of the Robert fitzNigel killed at Evesham benefited from the protection of his kinsman Walter of

[85] For Giles recovering his lands after an initial payment of 200 marks, leaving 700 marks to be paid at stated terms: TNA E 159/ 41, m. 14 (image 0043).

[86] For his grant to Walter of Merton, see *Merton College Rolls*, 28.

[87] For Camoys, see *CPR 1258–66*, 671; *CPR 1266–72*, 53, 61; *CIM*, nos. 631, 697, 699, 715. For the family, Cokayne, *Complete Peerage*, ii, 506–10.

[88] For de Eyville, see de Ville, 'John Deyville', 33–40.

[89] The story is told in detail from the Merton College archives in Knowles, 'The disinherited', pt. 3, 95–7; and see *Merton College Rolls*, 28, 42, 46, 49, 82, 108.

[90] *CR 1264–8*, 389–90.

[91] *CPR 1258–66*, 615, 648; *RS*, 177–8, 198; *VCH Warwickshire*, vi, 14–22; and see BL Cotton Charter XXVII 70, a reference I owe to Nicholas Vincent.

Merton.[92] The descendants of his neighbour, Gilbert of Elsfield, likewise killed in the battle, recovered Elsfield and his other manors. As late as 1295, thirty years after Evesham, Gilbert's son described himself as 'John of Elsfield, son of lord Gilbert of Elsfield'.[93] It sounds as though Gilbert's memory was much honoured.

In Kent there was one major casualty: the baron Robert de Crevecoeur. Robert de Grey's son, by contrast, had recovered all the family properties by death in 1272. His own son was summoned as a peer to parliament.[94] In the survey of c. 1275, referred to above, fifteen individuals or their descendants had recovered their lands while only two had suffered permanent losses.[95] Around twenty-five individuals, as we have seen, had never been dispossessed at all. 'These findings, reflecting the circumstances of a wide cross section of ordinary knights and lesser men, complement and confirm the picture which emerges from the study of the fate of the higher social ranks summoned to parliament.'[96]

Gradually, former rebels began to play a part in affairs. Thirteen former rebels including John de Vescy and Nicholas of Seagrave took part in Edward's crusade.[97] Both John of Havering, son of Montfort's steward Richard of Havering, and Ralph of Sandwich, keeper of the wardrobe in 1265, went on to long careers in his service. Thomas de Cantilupe, chancellor in 1265, joined Edward I's council and became bishop of Hereford. Robert de Vere, Ralph Basset of Sapcote, John de Eyville, William de Munchesney and Seagrave joined Edward's campaigns in Wales. In the end, half of the magnates summoned to Montfort's 1265 parliament (including three who deserted later in the year) re-emerged in public life.[98]

This process of reconciliation was helped by one major qualification to the policy of disinheritance already mentioned. Merely holding office during the Montfortian regime was not in itself a reason either for punishment or proscription. The Dictum of Kenilworth had thus nothing to say about such people. As it was, no fewer than eleven of Montfort's sheriffs

---

[92] Knowles, 'The disinherited', pt. 3, 73–5; Meekings, *Studies in 13th-Century Justice*, ch. ix, lxxiii.

[93] *St Frideswide Cartulary*, ii, 83.

[94] *CIPM*, no. 810; Cokayne, *Complete Peerage*, vi, 123–4. Crevecoeur's lands were given to his neighbour, the inevitable Roger of Leybourne, and later passed to Eleanor of Castile: TNA E 40/15184 (knowledge of which I owe to Nicholas Vincent's census of Henry III originals); Parsons, *Eleanor of Castile*, 176, 202. Without children, he lived out a long life pensioned off on other properties.

[95] *CIM*, no. 1024; Quick, 'Government and society in Kent', 321–2.

[96] *CIM*, no. 1024; Knowles, 'The resettlement of England', 34.

[97] Lloyd, *English Society and the Crusade*, 126–32. Lloyd here critiques the explanations offered in Beebe, 'The English baronage and the crusade of 1270', for the low level of participation by former Montfortians.

[98] Knowles, 'The disinherited', pt. 3, 109–11.

either continued in office after Evesham or quickly returned to it.[99] Fulk
Payforer, sheriff of Kent in 1267, had even treated as a legitimate expense
the money, when sheriff in 1264–5, he gave Henry de Montfort to fortify
Dover castle, although this was fortifying it against the king.[100] One might
have thought that the king himself, egged on by Abbot Ware, would have
punished those who had given judgement for the Londoners in their lawsuit
with the Abbey.[101] Yet Gilbert of Preston and Nicholas de Turri continued
as the senior judges at respectively the bench and the court *coram rege*. Of the
others sitting on the case, Roger de la Leye continued at the exchequer, while
Nicholas of Ely was elevated in quick succession to the sees of Worcester and
Winchester. John of Chishall did spells as both Henry's chancellor and treasurer before, under Edward I, becoming bishop of London. The policy of
disinheriting Montfort's supporters was disastrous for the kingdom, but at
least it did not touch office-holders of this kind. That moderation made no
small contribution to the return of peace to the kingdom.

Royal patronage also played a part. Henry issued charters granting
markets and fairs to John fitzJohn and Andrew of Astley. FitzJohn received
a licence to hunt in various counties and was allowed to pay off his debts
at the rate of £10 a year. He also appeared at court witnessing royal charters. In the last year of his life, Henry made gifts of wood and deer to
fitzJohn, Peter de Montfort junior and Adam Gurdun, now warden of
Aliceholt forest in Hampshire. In September 1272 who should be appointed
keeper of Norwich after disturbances there than that leader of the rebels
in the isle, Hugh Peche. Henry's anger had now been appeased. Between
March 1268 and the end of the reign there was only one more fine
received into the wardrobe for the recovery of his benevolence, that of
Brian de Gouiz.[102] It was by Henry's 'special grace' that Ralph Basset of
Sapcote was allowed to pay off his debts at £5 a year, the terms he had
enjoyed before 'the time of disturbance'. So for this great Montfortian
knight, it was as though the disturbance had never been.[103] When John
fitzJohn died in 1275, the Dover annals record the sorrow of Edward and
'all the court'.[104]

Just as former Montfortians continued in or returned to the king's
service, so they also entered the service of great lords.[105] By 1267, Gilbert

[99] Cassidy, 'Simon de Montfort's sheriffs', 19. In some cases this was probably helped by
a last-minute change of sides.

[100] TNA E 159/44, m. 1d (image 0050).

[101] See above, 390.

[102] *CChR 1257–1300*, 92, 157, 183; *CPR 1266–72*, 608; *RCWL*, ii, 180, 197; *CFR 1268–9*,
no. 158; Wild, *WA*, 146; *CR 1268–72*, 478, 518, 526.

[103] *CFR 1269–70*, no. 997.

[104] Canterbury/Dover, 281–2.

[105] This is a major theme in Adrian Jobson's 'Lordship, reconciliation and the recovery
process in post-Evesham England'. Some loyalists were also active in interceding with the
king for former rebels, Philip Basset being particularly active in this area as shown in

de Clare's 'bachelors' included Simon of Pattishall and Brian de Gouiz. No fewer than seven former rebels are found in King Richard's service in the years immediately after Evesham, including Montfort's steward Anketil de Martival, and that member of the council of nine Adam de Newmarch. Both also served the king.[106] Richard was even ready to re-employ those, like John de St Valery, who had deserted his service and held office during the Montfortian regime. So the kingdom benefited from Richard's cool temper and perhaps also his love of money, if as seems likely men like St Valery paid for his forgiveness.

Underlying this process of reconciliation were the many connections between loyalists and Montfortians. The executors of the great Montfortian bishop Walter de Cantilupe of Worcester included on the one side Thomas de Cantilupe and on the other Walter Giffard, bishop of Bath, and Warin of Bassingbourn. The executors of the exchequer clerk John le Francis were the treasurer of the exchequer, Thomas of Wymondham, and that military clerk Master Peter of Radnor, chaplain to the Kenilworth garrison.[107] Families torn apart by the war, like the Bohuns, Bassets and Greys, could now come back together. To this, however, there was one great exception.

## REVENGE: THE FATE OF THE MONTFORTS

If the great majority of rebel families survived the civil war, there was no survival, at least in English terms, for the greatest rebel family of all. Of course, the Montforts. Not that they went quietly. Their claims for restoration were constant, their vengeance in the end horrifying.

Having surrendered Dover in October 1265, Eleanor had withdrawn to France. Eventually she took up residence at the Dominican nunnery of Montargis, founded by Montfort's sister. If she shared in the life of the sisters, one centring on contemplation, prayer and psalmody, she had far from given up her material ambitions.[108] Indeed, at Montargis, south of Paris and east of Orleans, she was more centrally placed and better able to pursue them than had she gone to live at say Fontevraud. In England, Eleanor was intent upon recovering her dower as the widow of William Marshal.[109] In France, she was still pursuing her claims against her Lusignan half-brothers for her share of their mother's county of Angoulême. Her claims and grievances merged with those of her sons. In 1266, after their

---

Stewart-Parker, 'The Bassets of High Wycombe', 103. Between 1265 and 1270 he intervened in favour of up to twenty-seven former rebels or alleged rebels.

[106] Jobson, 'Lordship, reconciliation and the recovery process'.

[107] TNA E 159/42, mm. 6, 12d (images 0017, 0137) and m. 7d (image 0124) for the plunder of John's lands in five counties with damage claimed at over £600.

[108] For Montargis, see Wilkinson, *Eleanor de Montfort*, 130–1.

[109] She does not seem to have sought any dower as Montfort's widow.

escapes from England, both Simon junior and Guy de Montfort joined Eleanor in France. All three are found together in December 1266.[110] Also very much at large and close to his mother was the fourth son of the great earl, the learned and litigious clerk Amaury. He was determined to recover his lost benefices, including the lucrative treasurership of York.

This then was a formidable family grouping – and it was far from penniless. Eleanor had probably sent large sums of money out of the country, indeed as much as 11,000 marks, so Henry claimed.[111] The family also raised money by liquidating assets. The reason for the gathering in December 1266 was to exchange Montfort's pension from Louis IX for a down-payment of around £850.[112] Presumably cash also came from surrendering to the king of Navarre the family rights over Bigorre.[113] While, moreover, Amaury had lost his benefices in England, he retained those he held in France, including a canonry at Evreux and a prebend at Rouen.

The Montforts were also far from friendless.[114] King Louis agreed to swap his annual payment for a lump sum, as we have seen. He allowed Eleanor to pursue her claims to Angoulême at the parlement of Paris. Indeed, in 1269, she was awarded £400 a year in land 'in the money of the country' together with £800 worth of arrears.[115] Here Louis was doing no more than what he thought was just. There was no reason why Montfortian delinquencies in England should prejudice Eleanor's rights in France. But Louis also took up the Montforts' cause in England, despite the fact that Montfort himself had brazenly rejected his Mise of Amiens and brought so much destruction to the country.

Louis explained his reasons in a letter of May 1266, by which time the anarchy in England was all too apparent.[116] He had, he told Henry, already stopped the king's 'enemies' coming into England while, at the same time, facilitating the arrival of the king's friends. His attitude to the 'malevolent rebels', as he called them, was thus quite clear. But Louis then went on to give Henry a lecture, one doubtless reflecting the not infrequent course of their conversations. So Louis begged Henry to turn his mind in generous and kindly fashion to procuring 'peace and friendship' with Montfort's children and their mother, the countess of Leicester, 'and

[110] BN Clairambault 1188, fo. 25d (the transaction in question is referred to below). The Montforts' daughter Eleanor (betrothed to Llywelyn) was also present on this occasion and presumably living with her mother. By this time the youngest son, Richard, had probably died in Bigorre: Wilkinson, *HR*, cxx, and nos. 487–9, 491; Wilkinson, *Eleanor de Montfort*, 125, 133, and 181–2 n. 40; Blaauw, *The Barons War*, 362–3.

[111] *CR 1264–8*, 136.

[112] BN Clairambault 1188, fo. 25d.

[113] Blaauw, *The Barons' War*, 363; Wilkinson, *Eleanor de Montfort*, 181–2 n. 40.

[114] The pope supported the confiscation of their English lands, but refused to accept Amaury's loss of his livings, not that he ever recovered them: *CPReg*, 434.

[115] BN Clairambault 1188, fos. 29, 31; Wilkinson, *Eleanor de Montfort*, 132.

[116] *RL*, ii, 304–5.

with others of your land'. 'It seems to us,' he continued, that 'peace and concord will be most fruitful to you and all your kingdom', for 'with peace and concord established between you and them, you will be able, as you have written to us, to fulfil your vow of crusading in support of the Holy Land'.

Here then was Louis's motive. It was not primarily because of some sympathy for the sufferings of the Montforts. Rather, he was making a hard-headed calculation that without a settlement with them and their supporters there would be no peace in England, and without peace there would be no English contribution to the crusade. It was in that wider crusading cause he now intervened.

Henry's reaction was equally remarkable. He could very well, and with some justification, have told Louis to get lost. Indeed, he might have turned round the question Louis had asked him back in 1242 about the rebellion of the Lusignans: what has it to do with the king of France if the king of England punishes traitors? Simon's branch of the Montforts was now an English family or wished to be one. Indeed, Simon had refused (or so he said) to accept the regency of France during Louis's crusade precisely because he would not serve two masters. Louis might be Henry's lord, but the lordship was for lands in France not England and it was in England that the Montfort treason had been committed.

But Henry did not tell Louis to get lost. Quite the reverse. He asked him to become involved. When Louis's envoys arrived at Kenilworth in September 1266, during the height of the siege, Henry received them with 'reverence and honour'.[117] The envoys had come on the business of the Montforts and doubtless pleaded for a settlement, much as Louis had done in his letter that May. Henry himself acknowledged that what they said could make for 'the peace and tranquillity of the realm'. His reaction was to place everything in Louis's hands. He was ready, he said, to accept Louis's award 'high and low' on all his quarrels with the Montforts. The award could be enforced by action against the fiefs he held in France.[118] When the Dictum of Kenilworth was finally published at the end of October 1266, the situation remained the same. The Dictum said nothing about the Montforts 'as the lord king has placed their case in the hands of the king of France'.[119]

Henry's decision reflected his deep respect for Louis, and also, in all probability, an acceptance of his arguments about the crusade. Yet he also hoped an award would go his way. While Louis was to consider the wrongs the Montforts had suffered (there were none Henry said he was aware of), he was equally, Henry insisted, to consider all the damage done by the Montforts during the war, a war indeed 'not yet ended'. Henry wrote of

---

[117] For what follows, see *CPR 1258–66*, 641, 678.
[118] Henry also submitted himself to coercion by the pope.
[119] *DBM*, 334–5, cap. 34.

Louis's 'far famed justice and goodness, already so fruitful in our affairs'. He had not forgotten the Mise of Amiens and doubtless hoped for a favourable award again.

Louis was supposed to declare his award by Easter (17 April) 1267 but there were delays. In February 1267, when at Bury St Edmunds before moving on to besiege the Isle of Ely, Henry extended the deadline to Whitsun (5 June).[120] This time Louis did act. His envoys reached England in May, finding Henry at Stratford outside London. (This was during Gilbert de Clare's occupation of the capital.) The envoys came not with any final award but with suggestions as to the shape a settlement might take. Their words, and the connection with the crusade, were given all the greater weight by the head of the delegation, none other than John of Acre, Butler of France and son of John de Brienne, sometime king of Jerusalem and emperor of Constantinople.[121] On 24 May, after discussion with the envoys and his councillors, Henry wrote to Louis outlining the grant he was prepared to make. It was as follows.

Simon de Montfort junior could recover the lands of his father but through a proctor rather than in person. The lands would then be valued by two men, one chosen by the king, one by Simon. If they disagreed the matter would be decided by King Richard. With their value established, Simon was bound to sell the lands to the king or his children 'whenever required'. The price was left to Louis, but he was reminded that ten times the annual value was the usual rate of sale in England. He should also bear in mind all the trouble caused by the two Simons, Simon junior 'following in the footsteps of his father with all his might for which he deserves disinheritance'. The money was to be paid within three years provided Simon junior and his brothers did not enter the king's realms without the king's special licence. Henry's concession also covered Eleanor de Montfort's claims for dower. These were to be settled by a grant of £500 a year receivable by her proctor. If that was unacceptable, her proctor could sue for the dower before the king. Given the involvement of his envoys, Henry's offer cannot have been so far removed from Louis's own suggestions. Indeed, Henry later said it was made in response to Louis's prayers and out of reverence for him.[122] Yet he still accepted it might be modified by Louis's award. Within little more than a week, he promised yet again to abide by whatever Louis decided, this time the deadline being 15 August.

In the event, Henry's offer proved unacceptable to the Montforts, not surprisingly. If, as seems likely, the lands to be valued were simply the core Leicester inheritance, then Simon junior could expect at most some

---

[120] *CPR 1258–66*, 130.
[121] Powicke, 'Guy de Montfort', 6/74.
[122] *CR 1264–8*, 387.

£5,000, less if Louis took into account the damage Henry had suffered.[123] This was not much compensation for the permanent disinheritance clearly envisaged. As for Eleanor, £500 a year was far below the £930 a year she had previously enjoyed (£400 as a money fee, the rest in land), a sum itself much less than her entitlement, or so the Montforts had always said.[124] Faced with the Montforts' rejection, Louis shied away from simply pronouncing an award of his own. Instead, he made one more effort on their behalf. Henry's reply came in a letter of 6 September 1267, issued at Shrewsbury, where he was engaged in the negotiations with Llywelyn.[125] With the civil war now over, the reply (doubtless Edward's too) was uncompromising. If Simon junior did not accept the previous offer, it would not be renewed. Alternatively, he could come to England under safe conduct and answer for his 'excesses' according to the law and custom of the kingdom. He need not answer for his father's offences too, although by right they deprived him of any kind of 'hereditary succession'. As for Eleanor, if she did not like Henry's previous offer, she too could come under safe conduct and seek what she could according to the law and custom of the kingdom.

The offer, not surprisingly, was rejected by Eleanor, and she now sent a petition outlining her grievances to the pope. In February 1268, Clement sent this on to Henry and asked why he should not appear at the papal court to answer it.[126] Perhaps this inspired one last effort to find a solution through King Louis. At any rate, in April 1268, Henry, with the backing of 'the whole council', yet again promised to accept whatever he decided about the Montforts. The time limit now was Michaelmas.[127]

As far as the records go, this was the end of the matter. The Montforts remained empty handed. Henry had no desire to do more for his sister or her sons than he had offered and that under pressure from King Louis. If King Richard felt differently, there is no sign he intervened on their behalf. If he did, it had no effect. Robert of Gloucester saw the sadness in the treatment of their sister:

They banished her out of England, without returning.
Alas, her two brethren, each of whom was king.
And had but that one sister, and would exile her so.
Alas, where was the love then, such doom to decree?[128]

---

[123] This is assuming a ten-year valuation was given. For the Leicester inheritance being worth roughly £500 a year, see Maddicott, *Simon de Montfort*, 47–9. The offer was not that much different from the one made at Bycarrs Dyke, see above, 483.

[124] For these figures, see Maddicott, *Simon de Montfort*, 47–51.

[125] *CR 1264–8*, 386–8.

[126] *CPReg*, 422.

[127] *CPR 1258–66*, 216–17.

[128] Robert of Gloucester, ii, lines 11,804–7; Stevenson, 'Robert of Gloucester', lines 1244–7.

Henry's love had indeed evaporated. Probably he felt a deep sense of betrayal over Eleanor's behaviour. Louis himself had tried to play on the family relationship. In his letter to Henry in May 1266 he pointedly described Eleanor as 'your sister' while the Montfort children were 'your nephews'. But this struck no chord. In all Henry's many letters, Eleanor is only once described as his sister and that in special circumstances.[129] In referring the quarrel to Louis, Henry styled her 'sometime countess of Leicester' and wanted her offences to be considered alongside those of the other Montforts.[130]

When he escaped from England in 1266, Simon de Montfort junior took with him a good portion of his father's archive.[131] The documents eventually passed, presumably after Eleanor's death, to the French branch of the Montforts and in the early eighteenth century were in the hands of the duke de Chevreuse. (He then held the lordship of Montfort and had entered 'as a matter of course into possession of its archives'.) In 1708 the duke allowed the archive to be copied by the historian Pierre Clairambault. Clairambault also obtained some of the originals. Both copies and originals were bound into a large volume which now resides in the Bibliothèque Nationale in Paris: Clairambault 1188.[132] I well remember looking through it in 1981 as the sunlight filtered in through the high windows of the Bibliothèque's Salle des Manuscrits. Here then is the original letter patent in which the king made Montfort his regent in Gascony in 1248 and also (as a copy) the terms of his later resignation. Here from 1258 is the only known text of the baronial confederation formed at the Westminster parliament, a copy but with fine drawings of the seals of Richard de Clare, Roger Bigod, Simon himself, Peter of Savoy, John fitzGeoffrey and Peter de Montfort.[133] And then from 1259 there is the original of Simon's will, written in the hand of his eldest son, the will showing his concern for the poor people of his lands.[134] From the crisis of 1261 there is Montfort's defence to the charges of the king, and from 1265 the original charter, issued during his great parliament, giving him Edward's Chester and the Peak in hereditary right.[135] From this height of power to downfall there follow the only known texts of the agreements between Edward and Simon junior at Bycarrs Dyke, agreements leading to Simon's disinheri-

[129] CR 1264–8, 306; RL, ii, 294–6.

[130] CPR 1258–66, 641, 678.

[131] The archive is far more likely to have been with Simon junior at Kenilworth than with Eleanor at Dover. Some of the documents, moreover, relate to Simon junior, not his father, including the agreement with Edward at Bycarrs Dyke.

[132] Carpenter, Reign of Henry III, 242–3, and the references given there.

[133] Illustrated in Maddicott, Simon de Montfort, 153. The seal of Hugh Bigod is missing. How one wishes the original would come to light.

[134] Maddicott, Simon de Montfort, 175.

[135] BN Clairambault 1188, fo. 79.

tance and his flight from the kingdom.[136] The documents in Clairambault 1188 thus radiate the high hopes, gigantic ambition and ultimate disaster of Montfort's career. The final document in the sequence shows the family out of England altogether. It is the letter issued at the end of 1266, probably in Paris, in which Eleanor, Simon junior, Guy and their sister Eleanor exchange the annual pension from Louis IX for that lump sum. By this time Guy and Simon were making plans for new lives in Italy and it was there they would wreak their vengeance.

## THE MURDER AT VITERBO[137]

The piazza del Gesu in Viterbo is a small square, near the cathedral, surrounded by low houses, some of ancient aspect.[138] There is a fountain, a tower and cafés, their tables spilling out onto the piazza and sheltering from the summer sun under large umbrellas. On one side of the piazza stands the church of San Silvestro, its stone front undecorated, inside no more than a small aisle-less hall, its overall structure much the same as in the thirteenth century. The scene is peaceful now, but in 1271, lying on the ground before the church's door, lay the mutilated body of Henry of Almain, cut to pieces by Montfortian swords. For a murder so notorious and violent, Dante placed Guy de Montfort in the seventh circle of hell up to his throat in a river of boiling blood.[139]

The murder had taken place on 13 March 1271. Henry of Almain, from his lodgings in the piazza, had walked across to San Silvestro for morning mass.[140] At its close, he remained in prayer.[141] At that point, Guy and his brother Simon, swords drawn, burst into the church with a posse of armed men, Guy shouting in '*voce terribile*', 'you traitor, Henry you will not escape'. There was indeed no escape for Henry was unarmed and alone, apart, that is, from the clerks who had celebrated mass. The best he could do was flee to the altar. There the Montforts rained down on him blow after blow, wounding his side, thigh, face and limbs, and cutting off four fingers of the hand with which he clung to the altar. Even when he was dead they did not stop. They dragged him out of the church and continued their attack. Of the surrounding clerks, one was killed and others injured.

---

[136] BN Clairambault 1188, fos. 26d, 28, 75.

[137] For what follows, see Powicke, 'Guy de Montfort', and Powicke, *King Henry III*, ii, 608–12.

[138] I visited the piazza in the 1990s. There are several pictures of it online.

[139] Dante, Inferno, canto 12, lines 120–30. Still, Guy, as a mere murderer, was better off than murderers who were also tyrants. They were submerged in blood up to their eyebrows. On the front of the church of San Silvestro there is a plaque recalling the murder and quoting Dante. There are many images of the church online.

[140] The detail about Henry's '*hospitium*' comes from King Philip's letter about the event: FitzThedmar, 133–4 (Stone, FitzThedmar, no. 1036).

[141] Wykes, 241.

This narrative comes from the earliest detailed account of the murder, that issued by the pope in 1273.[142] The Florentine historian Giovanni Villani, writing at least thirty years later, adds some further details. Here, with the body left in the church, Guy comes out and is asked by a knight what he has done. He replies, 'I have had my revenge.' Although writing in the vernacular Italian, Villani gives this in French, as it would have been spoken: '*J'ai fait ma vangeance*'. The knight, however, was not satisfied. 'How? Your father was drawn' – '*Comment? Votre père fût trainé*', referring here to the way (in Villani's account) Lord Edward at Evesham had seized Simon's scalp and dragged him along the ground, before having him hanged. Hearing this reproof, Guy went back into the church, seized Henry by the hair and dragged him out. The story may be apocryphal, but its spirit is absolutely right.[143] Henry of Almain's bloodied body lying outside the church at Viterbo was indeed revenge for the butchering of Montfort's corpse on the Green Hill above Evesham. That had happened while Guy lay wounded perhaps only a few yards away; doubtless he still bore the scars on his body. Viterbo is some 1,200 miles from Evesham. How was it there that revenge was exacted?

Guy de Montfort almost certainly came to Italy in the wake of his second cousin Philip de Montfort, Charles of Anjou's vicar in the Sicilian kingdom.[144] His father's friendship with Charles himself must have helped his advancement. In August 1268, shouting his father's old battle cry, Guy struck mighty blows at the battle of Tagliacozzo, thus helping to win the victory that finally secured Charles the throne.[145] Possessed of all his father's military genius, gifts of leadership and personal address, magnificent rewards followed. Guy received large estates between Naples and Benevento, became Charles's vicar general in Tuscany, and married a great heiress – Margarita Aldobrandesca, only child of Ildebrandino of Pitigliano, known to all as 'the red count'.[146] Given that he was a younger

---

[142] *F*, ii, 501–2.

[143] For a translation of this chapter, see http://www.gutenberg.org/files/33022/33022–h/33022–h.htm#Page_235. It should be said it provides an utterly fanciful account of Edward's escape in 1265 and makes Henry of Almain out to be his brother.

[144] Philip was the grandson of Simon de Montfort's uncle Guy de Montfort, his father's younger brother. The family held La Ferté Alais, south of Paris, and (thanks to the Albigensian crusade) Castres in the Languedoc. Philip was close to Montfort and in 1259 became his lieutenant in Bigorre: *Layettes*, iii, no. 4476.

[145] John de Vignay, 662; Nangis, *Gesta*, 434, 436; Powicke, 'Guy de Montfort', 11/78.

[146] For Guy's Italian lands, see Powicke, 'Guy de Montfort', 12–15, 21–3/79–81, 87–8 (though without the map). His description of the Aldobrandine lands (14/81) shows him at his most mellifluous: 'They were extensive and they were safe. Stretching irregularly across southern Tuscany, where numerous rivers run their brief course to the sea on the one side, and the streams which form the Tiber have their source on the other, they came to a head in the difficult country north of Lake Bolsena.' For an equally lyrical description of the Vale of Pickering in Yorkshire, see Powicke, *Medieval England*, 25–7. When questioned about this by Menna Prestwich (at least according to her story), Powicke admitted he had not been there and had written up the account from a guidebook!

son, with no claim to the Montfort inheritance (as he was once reminded by the pope), he was now far more powerful than he might ever have been in England. At some point he was joined by his older brother Simon, and Simon too was granted rich estates.

Henry of Almain had accompanied Edward on his crusade and wintered with him in Sicily. It was then decided that, instead of continuing to the Holy Land, he should return to look after Edward's affairs, first in Gascony and then in England.[147] In March 1271, travelling up through Italy, he reached Viterbo. The city was full of cardinals vainly trying to decide on a successor to Pope Clement IV, who had died in November 1268. There too, hoping to secure the election of a French-leaning pope, were the new king of France, Philip III, and his uncle Charles of Anjou. Henry of Almain may well have arrived in their train. Philip and Charles were bringing back to France the body of Louis IX. (His flesh had been boiled away and separated from the bones, the coffin being borne on bars on the back of two horses.) The funeral cortege also included the bodies of Louis's son John Tristan, Philip's wife, Isabella of Aragon, and Theobald of Champagne, king of Navarre.[148] The party formed 'a body of mourners in a travelling necropolis. And Guy de Montfort must needs break in to add yet another corpse.'[149]

Guy, Simon and Guy's father-in-law, the red count, arrived in Viterbo on 12 March, the day before the outrage.[150] It was quite natural for them to meet up with their master, Charles of Anjou. They may also have heard that Henry of Almain, on Edward's behalf, was seeking a reconciliation.[151] And why not? Guy's Italian career commanded respect, he had no claims to land in England, and had not been involved in the resistance after Evesham. Simon's case was more difficult, and it was accordingly with 'Simon the eldest' that a discussion took place. It went far enough for Simon, in the presence of both kings, to guarantee Henry's safety.[152] Hence Henry had no fear entering church on the morrow. But either Simon was being disingenuous or the Montforts changed their mind during the night. Perhaps indeed the proffered reconciliation was a final

---

[147] Wykes, 239–40. For a biography, see Vincent, 'Henry of Almain'.

[148] Geoffroi de Beaulieu, caps. 46–47 *bis*; Le Goff, *Saint Louis*, 300–1.

[149] Powicke, 'Guy de Montfort', 20/86.

[150] Powicke, 'Guy de Montfort', 17/83–4, quoting the account of Guido de Corvaria who, he suggests, was present in Viterbo.

[151] Such a claim is made in Pope Gregory's account of the murder issued in 1273 (*F*, ii, 501–2) and may have come from Edward himself. The two had met earlier in the year.

[152] As Powicke ('Guy de Montfort', 18 n. 3) says, this account comes from Norman jottings added to a fifteenth-century fragment of the twelfth-century chronicle of Robert of Torigni: 'Annalibus Normannicis', 517. It is accurate on details, knowing Henry had not been at Evesham and Simon was the elder son. It also has Henry labouring for Simon's and Guy's restoration. Powicke acknowledged the writer's 'authority must have been contemporary', but doubted the truth of the story, wrongly in my view.

provocation. How could there be reconciliation with Edward, who had murdered and mutilated their father? There was no better way of rejecting the offer than by murdering and mutilating the envoy. On the day itself the murder was completely premeditated. It did not arise from a sudden argument, let alone from a fair fight. Henry was sought out in the church because he would be alone and defenceless.

It is sometimes suggested there was a degree of personal animus against Henry, hence the way he was accused of treachery.[153] There may be something in this for Henry had deserted Montfort and broken his oath to the Provisions. Yet, during his captivity after Lewes, he was on terms with the regime and was twice released to explain matters to King Louis.[154] He was not present at Evesham and had nothing to do with Montfort's death. Earlier in 1265, Eleanor de Montfort's household rolls, in poignant entries, show the hounds of Henry and Guy being looked after together, and presumably the two men hunted in each other's company.[155] In explaining the decision to send Henry back from the crusade, Wykes says 'he exceeded everyone else in wisdom'. His record suggests he was indeed a man of sense and moderation.[156] When Guy described him as a traitor, it was partly to justify the mutilation of his body, as Montfort's own had been mutilated. That dishonour, as much as his actual death, was what the Montforts found so unforgivable and so necessary to avenge. In 1267, Amaury de Montfort had complained to the pope about the way the body lacked a church burial.[157] Henry of Almain was not the obvious target. Roger de Mortimer, Gilbert de Clare, above all Edward himself would have been better. But Henry was Edward's envoy and cousin, so he would do.

With news of the murder reverberating through Viterbo, Charles of Anjou immediately confiscated the Montforts' lands and sent men to hunt them down.[158] But they had escaped with the red count (complicit in the crime) to the Aldobrandine hills. Their satisfaction must have been intense. Simon junior died later in the year. Guy still had a long career before him.[159]

---

[153] It is unlikely Henry's marriage in 1269 to the daughter and heiress of Gaston de Béarn added to the Montfortian antipathy. Gaston had designs on Bigorre, but by this time the Montforts had resigned their interests in the county.

[154] See above, 341 n. 95, 430 n. 69.

[155] Wilkinson, *HR*, nos. 75–6, 81, 199, 240, 267.

[156] As early as 1259, with Hugh Bigod, he was to be the ultimate arbitrator in any dispute arising from the agreement between Lord Edward and Richard de Clare.

[157] *CPReg*, 434.

[158] *F*, i, 489; and for King Philip's letter to King Richard, FitzThedmar, 133–4 (Stone, FitzThedmar, no. 1036).

[159] In 1273, Guy submitted to the pope. For his penance see Eubel, 'Der Registerband', 55–56, a reference I owe to David d'Avray. He was imprisoned, but by the early 1280s he was back in Charles of Anjou's service and was soon as powerful as ever. In 1287 he was captured in a sea battle during the Angevin attempt to recover Sicily from the king of

   The Montforts were not the only family to harbour resentments over what had happened at Evesham. In the reign of Edward II, Hugh Despenser promised to take revenge on the Mortimers for the death of his grandfather.[160] One noble family, around the same time, had an account of the battle, with gruesome descriptions of the slaughter, written on the back of a genealogical roll recording the descent of the English kings.[161] Evidently they wished to preserve the memory of what had happened. Yet whatever the feelings beneath the surface, on the whole they remained there. The murder at Viterbo had no parallel in England. The wounds of the civil war did heal over.

Aragon. Attempts to arrange a ransom failed, perhaps due to Edward's influence, and Guy died in a Sicilian prison in 1291 or 1292. There is a succinct summary of his later career in Maddicott, 'Guy de Montfort'. Edward, however, was reconciled to Eleanor de Montfort in 1273 (they may have met near Paris), and before her death in 1275 she had recovered some of her Marshal dower lands in England: Wilkinson, *Eleanor de Montfort*, 134–5.

   [160] *Vita Edwardi Secundi*, 109.

   [161] As discovered by Olivier de Laborderie: Laborderie, Maddicott and Carpenter, 'The last hours of Simon de Montfort', 378–85. This is the new account cited above, 443.

Chapter 15

# THE LAST TWO YEARS
## 1270-1272

Before his departure on crusade, Edward had put King Richard, Archbishop Giffard, Roger de Mortimer, Philip Basset and his able clerk Robert Burnell (a man much like John Mansel) in charge of his children and affairs.[1] These men could control the localities through the counties and castles placed in Edward's keeping. They could also get a grip of central government since they were all councillors of the king.

Westminster Abbey's chronicle portrays Henry at this time leading his life 'in innocence and fear of the lord', but he was still far from inactive.[2] At the start of the Michaelmas term of 1270 he again demanded exact information from the exchequer about the receipts from the sheriffs. At the Westminster parliament in October he enjoined Gilbert de Clare by word of mouth not to attack Llywelyn. At Clarendon in November, he ordered extensive work on the palace by word of mouth, including the painting of his seat in the hall. He continued to go to Winchester with the queen for Christmas. There in 1270 he worried about the wine needed for the forthcoming feast of the Confessor at Westminster, whither most of the magnates had been summoned. Without wine, Henry opined, the feast could not be celebrated. So the men of Southampton were to provide £100 to buy it 'as you love us and our honour and as you wish to preserve us from opprobrium and shame and wish to avoid our perpetual indignation'.[3] Henry was also free to make gifts of wood and deer from the royal forests. The three-year ban on such gifts, introduced at the start of 1268, was increasingly ignored and anyway expired at the end of 1270.[4] In 1268/9, Henry made 40 such gifts; in 1269/70 he made 120; in 1270/1, the number exceeded 200; in 1271/2 he made 180, of which 35 were of a charitable nature.[5] And Henry was still enjoying falconry.

---

[1] Edward had intended Burnell to crusade with him but changed his mind at the last moment: Huscroft, 'Should I stay or should I go?' There is a full study of Burnell's career in Richard Huscroft's 'The political and personal life of Robert Burnell'.

[2] Westminster, *Flores*, 19.

[3] *CR 1268–72*, 236; TNA E 159/ 45, m. 1 (image 0003); *CLR 1267–72*, nos. 1304, 1317, 1321, 1341.

[4] *CR 1268–72*, 218, for a last reference to it in August 1270.

[5] These are regnal years running from 28 October to the following 27 October. The figures are approximate.

In 1272 he gave John of Bicknor 5 marks 'because the king's goshawk, which is in John's keeping, took a duck in its first flight from the king's hand last season' – so in the autumn of 1271 when the falconry season began.[6]

Henry's health, however, remained precarious. In November 1270, Archbishop Giffard said it necessitated his presence at court.[7] Soon after arriving at Westminster for the 5 January feast of 1271, Henry did indeed fall seriously ill. Apart from a week at Merton in July, he was to remain at Westminster till the end of August, almost eight months. Back in June 1269, Henry had said he was suffering from a tertian fever. That was the reason he could not come up from Winchester for the parliament at Westminster.[8] Probably a fluctuating fever, very hard to shake off in an age without antibiotics, was the trouble in 1271 and again in 1272. That Henry was able to recover and enjoy periods of comparative health suggests there was nothing organically wrong with him. A fever might lay him completely low at one moment, yet permit some activity the next. Throughout his illnesses there were days when Henry was able to make his customary gifts of deer, wood and wine, as well as issue charters. But he was living more quietly than before. In the regnal year October 1270 to October 1271 the costs of his household averaged out at £11 10s a day as opposed to £13 10s a day for the whole period 1268 to 1272.[9]

## HENRY'S APPEAL TO EDWARD

On 6 February 1271, in the depth of his illness, Henry wrote to Edward.[10] He had, he said, received Edward's own letters and rejoiced at his success. The letters had certainly much to tell. Edward had arrived at Aigues Mortes to find the French army already in Tunis. He had then sailed for Tunis himself only to discover Louis IX had died there on 25 August 1270. The new king of France, Philip III, had accordingly postponed the crusade for three years so he could return home with his father's body. Edward had come back with the French party to Sicily and spent the winter there, but, as he must have told his father, he was still minded to go to the Holy Land. Henry was alarmed at the prospect. He was, he told Edward, suffering from a grievous illness. His life was despaired of both by his doctors and everyone else. If he should die, Edward would need to come home to assume the government of the kingdom, all the more so

---

[6] *CLR 1267–72*, no. 1847.

[7] *LNR*, 39 (*Giffard Register*, 144–5). This was part of a letter setting out a catalogue of woes excusing the paucity of his gifts to the papal court: Huscroft, 'Robert Burnell and the government of England', 60.

[8] *CPR 1266–72*, 384.

[9] Carpenter, 'Household rolls', 33–5.

[10] *CR 1268–72*, 397–8.

since King Richard might be summoned to Rome by a new pope and thus be unable to repress certain malevolent people of whom Edward well knew.[11] Edward should not, therefore, set off for 'remoter parts' until he had certain news of his father's state. Indeed, he could perfectly properly now return with King Philip. Henry, however, knew better than to give orders to his masterful son. He asked Edward, under his 'paternal blessing', to ponder these things and do what was best for his honour and the peace and tranquillity of the kingdom.

Remarkably, at the very time of this heartfelt appeal, Henry's second son, Edmund, was leaving on the crusade, just as he had promised Edward he would do. He went with his mother's blessing or at least (far more dutiful and compliant than his elder brother) she was entrusted with looking after his affairs.[12] Perhaps the attitude of King Richard and other councillors did not exactly tally with Henry's own. They may well have thought that, if Henry died, they could hold the fort, all the more so, being relieved of his erratic interventions.

In the event, Edward took no heed of his father's anxious letter. Having sent back Henry of Almain to look after his affairs (with the fatal results we have seen), he was determined to continue himself. He felt God was with him for, though a great storm had destroyed the French fleet, his had been preserved. According to one story he swore by God's blood to go to the Holy Land even if followed only by his groom Fowyn. He would return if there was war in England, but there was not. He sailed from Trapani in Sicily early in May 1271.[13]

On 7 March 1271, Henry issued a proclamation. In view of his illness, he commanded everyone to obey King Richard and the council in the maintenance of the peace and the chastisement of rebellion. In effect, Richard was being made regent. A few days later it was on the authority of Richard and the council that everyone was ordered to repress those forming congregations against the peace. During what turned out to be a brief regency, Richard was certainly active. In a jurisdictional dispute between Canterbury cathedral and Dover priory he summoned the contending parties to Wallingford and lectured them on the importance of keeping the peace.[14] Richard also helped the government financially. In June 1271 he loaned 3,000 marks and provided another 2,000 marks to help Edward's crusade. He was not always promptly repaid. An account at the exchequer in the spring of 1271 showed 1,000 marks were still outstanding from earlier loans. Repayments came in frustrating dribs and drabs from the eyres, the sheriffs and the exchequer. At least, in June 1271,

---

[11] Clement IV had died in November 1268. Gregory X was elected in September 1271.
[12] *CPR 1266–72*, 514, 588–9, 668–9; Howell, *Eleanor of Provence*, 251; Lloyd, *English Society and the Crusade*, 169.
[13] Rishanger, 68.
[14] Canterbury/Dover, 256–7.

Richard received the Mauduit, Huntercombe and Hastings wardships in part-payment of the £1,000 a year promised him in wards and escheats.[15]

## HENRY TAKES THE CROSS AGAIN

By the time he made these concessions to Richard, Henry had returned to health.[16] The monks of Westminster ascribed this to their own efforts. Fearing to lose their great patron, they had processed barefoot in the rain to the New Temple and there celebrated the mass of the Virgin for the king. Returning likewise barefoot they received the news that the king was better. Henry, ascribing his recovery to their prayers, then ordered the monks to chant the '*Gaudent in caelis*': 'The souls of the saints rejoice in heaven, who have followed in the footsteps of Christ, and since, for love of him, they have shed their blood, so they exult with Christ for ever more.'[17]

Henry's own explanation of his recovery was different and it was linked to an extraordinary decision. This was announced on 16 April in a letter patent. Henry explained that, having been seized by a grievous malady, he had put his trust in God not man and had again assumed the cross. Almost at once his condition had improved and 'by a marvelous miracle' he was now quite better. Henry then set out some reforms designed, so he said, to secure the necessary money for his crusade as also to pay his debts. He would now retain in his own hands all the revenues of the kingdom both to pay the debts and to maintain himself, his queen and his household. If wardships were sold, they were to be sold at the full price on the advice of the council. There were only two exceptions to these rules. Something was to be done for members of the household who had received little for their service. And Henry was to be allowed £120 in cash ('in pennies') to distribute in parcels as he wished. These restrictions, announced in a letter to King Richard, Archbishop Giffard and others of his council, were to last for a year.[18]

Henry's decision showed how much he was still troubled by his failure to crusade. It showed his power for he was surely acting against the advice of his council. And it showed his naivete for no one, outside Henry himself, can have thought the new financial controls were really designed to further his crusade. More likely, Richard and the council, with the lapse of Richard's formal powers, were using the excuse of Henry's crusade to push through a self-denying ordinance. The focus seems to have been

---

[15] TNA E 159/45, m. 9d (image 0080); *CPR 1266–72*, 533, 543–7; Wild, *WA*, 144; and see above, n. 40, and Denholm-Young, *Richard of Cornwall*, 160–1.

[16] He gave his doctors £40 for their expenses and later presented one of them, Master Nigel de Miriden, to a rich living: *CLR 1267–72*, no. 1537; *CPR 1266–72*, 647.

[17] Westminster, *Flores*, 22–3. Henry knew the chant well as it was sung on All Saints Day: *Missale Westmonasteriensis*, iii, 1362.

[18] *CPR 1266–72*, 531. The council was given the power to reform the king's household.

particularly on the king's open-handed gifts of cash, now limited to a yearly £120. The target was probably less Henry's orders for payments out of the exchequer than his gifts out of the wardrobe. Between 1268 and 1272 its accounts record gifts to knights, clerks, servants, valets and unspecified others totalling some £2,497.[19] King Richard himself was probably central in placing these restrictions on his brother, and there was here a degree of self-interest. He doubtless hoped to profit from Henry's repayment of his debts. For all the new rule about selling at full price, Richard paid nothing for the Mauduit, Huntercombe and Hastings wardships.

In the event, Henry's crusading plans seem to have been quietly forgotten. The letter of April 1271 is the first and last heard about them. In September the financial reforms were said to be in aid of Edward's crusade not Henry's.[20] Henry's health, however, remained better, or intermittently so. In July 1271 he gave orders by word of mouth about preparations for the Confessor's feast on 13 October.[21] However, the fact that he remained stationary at Westminster till the end of August suggests he had still not regained his full health.

## THE RAPROCHEMENT WITH GILBERT DE CLARE

During these uncertain times, one factor helped the stability of the realm. This was the rapprochement with Gilbert de Clare.[22] In 1270 he had been urged to join Edward's crusade. If he remained in the country, what trouble he might cause. In the event, he did not go and it did not matter. Clare had bade farewell to Edward at Winchester in August 1270 and was pledged to follow him early next year. In September he was reprimanded for fortifying the isle of Portland and told to stop. All the more reason to see him gone. For a while, it seemed he would go on crusade. At the end of October he received 1,000 marks from the twentieth in aid of his passage.[23] But then something happened. This was Llywelyn's attack on Glamorgan and the great castle that Clare was building at Caerphilly.

Under the terms of his arbitration settling the differences between Edward and Gilbert de Clare, King Richard himself was to determine whether Clare had a valid reason for abandoning his crusade. Although there is no direct evidence on the point, he almost certainly accepted that Llywelyn's attack was one. Probably he also decided that Clare no longer needed to give security for keeping the peace. At any rate, there is no evidence that Tonbridge and Hanley castles remained in Richard's hands, if they ever went there in the first place. Clare's predicament also brought

---

[19] Wild, *WA*, 149.
[20] *CPR 1266–72*, 574.
[21] *CR 1268–72*, 362.
[22] As noted by Powicke, *King Henry III*, ii, 587.
[23] *CR 1268–72*, 292; TNA E 372/117, m. 6d (image 6413).

him closer to the court. He did not look for military help, but he was keen to stop the government siding with Llywelyn. To that end, he came to court and parliament to make his case in October 1270, October 1271 and February 1272. He did not get all he wanted, but the government was on the whole supportive.[24] Clare also reappeared at court attesting royal charters in September 1270 and June and July 1271. By February 1272 he was a member of the king's council.[25] Later in the year, Hervey of Boreham, a long-time Clare servant, was appointed a baron of the exchequer.[26] In February 1272, Clare asked the king to correct the trespasses of his bailiffs and see that competent amends were made to complainants. A judge was appointed to do the job. Clare was thus acting very much in the spirit of the Provisions of Oxford.[27] Clever and perhaps as principled as he was mighty, it was just as well he was now on-side. The intelligence conveyed to Edward about his good behaviour doubtless eased the decision to continue with the crusade.

Underpinning the government in these years were frequent parliaments. No fewer than six met between October 1270 and November 1272 with regular sessions at Hilary, Easter and October. The central part played by parliament between 1268 and 1270 was no false dawn. Taxation and the crusade were no longer on the agenda, but parliament was summoned just as frequently. One issue was what to do about Llywelyn. Another was the trade war with Flanders. In September 1270, Margaret, countess of Flanders, had seized all the goods of English merchants to enforce payment of both her pension and all the debts owed to Flemish merchants. The English government retaliated by placing an embargo on the export of the English wool on which the Flemish cloth industry depended. It also seized all the property of Flemish merchants in England. With Margaret's envoys making 'impossible' demands, the dispute was still ongoing at the time of Henry's death.[28]

## HENRY'S GENERATION PASSES

In these last years Henry's generation was passing away. It is a shame we have no record of the alms and masses he doubtless offered up for their souls.[29] Roger of Leybourne died in November 1271, Philip Basset a few days earlier. Philip thoroughly deserved the encomium in the Osney annals: 'A noble man of great wisdom, faithful above all things, strenuous

[24] CR 1268–72, 234–6, 546–7; CPR 1266–72, 521, 581, 583.

[25] RCWL, ii, 185, 192–3; CR 1268–72, 462.

[26] TNA E 159/47, m. 2d (image 9046).

[27] CPR 1266–72, 693.

[28] It is best followed in FitzThedmar, 126–7, 135–41 (Stone, FitzThedmar, nos. 1041–50, 1058–60).

[29] No oblation, food and drink rolls survive for this period. If Henry tried to pay for the feeding of paupers through writs of liberate, they were not enrolled.

in arms, and with much love for the English and the community of the land, and promoting the affairs of the religious above all.' Wykes, writing in similar terms, added he was a great giver of alms to the poor.[30] No one gave such praise to Leybourne.[31]

July 1270 saw the deaths of both Roger Bigod and Archbishop Boniface. Bigod's last letter to Henry was dutiful enough. Asking admittedly for a favour, it was addressed 'to the famous prince, his lord, the most reverend Henry' and promised 'due service according to my strength'. Do we have a clue here as to why he could never bring himself to rebel?[32] On Roger's death, Henry hoped to make some money from the earl's debts, but he was on good terms with Roger's heir, Hugh Bigod's son Roger Bigod. The latter appeared at court, received gifts of deer and paid a £100 relief in accordance with Magna Carta.[33]

Boniface's appointment as archbishop had been a triumph for Henry but one that was short-lived. Boniface remained semi-detached from the court and was quite ready to brave royal displeasure. At the Lambeth council in 1261 he issued important statutes for the reform of the church, but it is hard to think well of an archbishop of Canterbury who was so often absent from England.[34] The range of Boniface's activities was revealed in his decision to be buried at Canterbury, Pontigny, Hautecombe or St Michael de Clusa, depending on where he died.[35] In the end, dying in Savoy, he was buried like his brother Thomas at Hautecombe, the family monastery on that promontory jutting out into the blue waters of the Lac du Bourget.[36]

A death that must have grieved Henry greatly was that of King Louis at Tunis in August 1270: Louis, his brother-in-law, friend, lord, supporter and guide. To Louis he owed much, the Mise of Amiens, of course, and also the Treaty of Paris with the security it brought to English Gascony. A more aggressive French king might well have expelled the English altogether from their continental possessions, thus completing Henry's humiliation. Instead, Louis added to those possessions in order to bring

[30] Osney, 247; Wykes, 247.

[31] Wykes, 247, mentions Leybourne's death without comment. His embalmed heart reposes in Leybourne church in Kent within a graceful niche formed of two trefoiled lancets with a quatrefoil above: Larking, 'On the heart-shrine in Leybourne church', with the dramatic discovery of the heart itself between pp. 136 and 137.

[32] *CR 1268–72*, 264: '*Salutem et debitum pro viribus famulatum*'.

[33] *CR 1268–72*, 212, 264, 357–8; *RCWL*, ii, 187–8, 192, 200; *CFR 1271–2*, nos. 144, 148.

[34] Boniface was beatified by the pope in 1839 (Cox, *Eagles of Savoy*, 392), something he certainly did not deserve. There is a statue of him on the west front of Westminster cathedral.

[35] His will is printed in Von Wurstemberger, *Peter der Zweite*, iv, 342–4. Unlike that of Peter of Savoy, there were many English benefactions.

[36] At Hautecombe the nineteenth-century effigies provided for Boniface and his mother, Beatrice, show them lying in peaceful repose, eyes closed. They are thus very different from Thomas's exotic effigy where, wearing a plumed helmet, he sits up holding a scroll and resting an arm on a sleepy lion.

the Treaty of Paris about. With the death of Alphonse of Poitiers and his wife in 1272, Henry was able to set in train the process that would eventually secure both the Saintonge and the Agenais for the English crown. Louis was also responsible, in their public meetings and private conversations, for some of the happiest moments in Henry's life.

A death closer to home in 1271 certainly hit Henry hard, namely that of his grandson John, Edward's eldest son, whose birth had been greeted with such joy back in 1266. He died at Wallingford, in the care of King Richard, around 1 August to the great grief, Wykes tells us, of Richard, Henry and the queen. John's features and character had made him beloved by all. He was laid to rest in Henry's and Richard's presence in Westminster Abbey.[37]

Earlier in the year Henry of Almain's battered body had returned to England and been buried (in May 1271) at Hailes, while his heart was placed in a casket near the Confessor's shrine in the Abbey.[38] King Richard, however, was no broken man. In June 1271 he made the substantial loans to Henry and Edward, referred to above. In October his own treasurer, Philip of Eye, became treasurer of the exchequer, so in effect Richard had control of Henry's finances. Richard was also comforted by the return to England of Edmund, his second son, who had left the crusade on hearing of his brother's death. But near the end of 1271 disaster struck. On 12 December, while staying at Berkhamsted, Richard had himself bled. The following night a stroke paralysed the left side of his body and deprived him of speech. He died on 2 April 1272 and was buried beside Henry of Almain and Sanchia at Hailes.

King Richard's reputation was mixed.[39] Some writers condemned his love of money, oppression of the poor and seduction of women. He fathered several bastards, quite unlike his brother.[40] Thomas Wykes, on the other hand, gave fulsome praise to Richard's wisdom and judgement.[41] That both Edward and Gilbert de Clare turned to him as an arbitrator shows he was not alone in that. Henry was very lucky in his brother. Their quarrel over the Montfort marriage in 1238 was their last of any substance. Thereafter, despite many exasperations, Richard supported Henry both with his money and his counsel. Had he been a fractious brother, Henry's personal rule might have ended much sooner than it did. Richard appreciated the folly of the Sicilian enterprise. (Germany was another matter, for becoming king of the Romans was practical politics.) His brief period as regent in 1253-4, when he summoned

---

[37] Wykes, 246.
[38] For its possible site, see Rodwell and Neal, *The Cosmatesque Mosaics*, ii, 329.
[39] See Vincent, 'Richard of Cornwall'.
[40] Jobson, 'Lordship, illegitimacy and the forging of a Familial Network'.
[41] For Wykes and the earl, see Denholm-Young, 'Thomas de Wykes and his chronicle', 247-8.

knights to parliament and urged Henry to keep Magna Carta, suggests he saw the need to conciliate local society and reform the realm. In 1265 he may well have resisted the policy of disinheritance, however much he profited from it. With the end of the war, he took former rebels into his service. There would have been no Westminster Abbey, but Richard would have made a better king than his brother. Recognizing that fact, as he must have done, his loyalty and restraint seem all the more admirable. Perhaps, like Henry, he could never forget the disasters of John's reign, hence his reluctance to rebel and his preference for peace-making over war-making.[42] But his conduct also owed much to the respect and generosity with which he was treated by his brother. Here Henry got something absolutely right. Matthew Paris was correct in observing that Henry loved his brother and wished to enrich and conciliate him before anyone else.[43]

## THE COMPLETION OF THE GREAT CHAMBER AT WESTMINSTER

In November 1271, Henry left Westminster for his usual winter visit to Marlborough and Clarendon before spending Christmas at Winchester. This was the last time the king would visit these favourite residences, the last time he would walk on the tiled floors at Clarendon (now in the Victoria and Albert Museum), the last time he would dine in the great hall at Winchester with the painting of fortune's wheel behind the dais. Queen Eleanor was with him and the 150 shoes for their Christmas offerings to the poor were made by the Winchester shoemaker, Geoffrey of Shaftesbury. (Half cost 5d a pair and half 4½d.)[44] The wheel of fortune, however, was about to swing Henry down, for at Winchester, as the local annals noted, his health again gave way.[45] For the first and only time in his life he was unable to leave his birthplace in time to celebrate the feast of Edward the Confessor at Westminster on 5 January. It was not till 13 January that he arrived back in London. Then something else unprecedented happened. Henry never lived at the Tower, save in moments of crisis, yet now, instead of going to Westminster, he went there, staying until 7 February. Nothing seems to have been wrong with Henry's health at this time. While at the Tower, he took someone's homage, remitted a debt for the good of his soul, held a meeting with his council and witnessed oaths (their hands on the gospel) taken by a large group of merchants.[46] He was as profuse as ever in his gifts of wood and deer from the royal forests. Indeed, in his three weeks at the Tower he made around sixteen such gifts.[47]

---

[42] I owe this thought to Adrian Jobson.
[43] Paris, *HA*, ii, 296–7.
[44] *CLR 1267–72*, no. 1786. He was also to be paid for the previous two years.
[45] Winchester, 111.
[46] *CFR 1271–2*, no. 288; *CR 1268–72*, 545; *CPR 1266–72*, 618, 685–6.
[47] *CR 1268–72*, 454–9.

What then was going on? The answer, it may be suggested, is that Henry was waiting for the paintings in his great chamber at Westminster to be completed, the paintings, redolent of his attitudes to kingship, commissioned after the conflagration that swept through the chamber in January 1263. These paintings no longer exist, having been consumed by the fire that destroyed the old palace of Westminster in 1834, but fortunately their appearance is preserved in fine watercolour copies made in the early nineteenth century. Although the subject matter of the paintings may well have replicated the earlier scheme, their style dates them to the years immediately after the fire of 1263.[48]

Work had begun on the paintings in 1263 itself. Henry indeed wanted the work finished by Christmas. Next year, saying he intended to stay in the chamber during the feast of the Confessor on 13 October, he described the chamber as 'already painted', although gold was needed for its completion. The small cost of all this work, however, suggests that it simply involved the repair of the old paintings damaged by the fire.[49] Later, by contrast, much larger sums were devoted to the work. Indeed, between December 1266 and September 1267 no less than £53 went exclusively on gold leaf and other necessaries for the paintings around the king's bed.[50] All this suggests that, with his recovery of power after Evesham, Henry made a new start and commissioned the entirely new paintings seen in the nineteenth-century watercolours. That they were finally ready in the early part of 1272 is suggested by one key piece of evidence. It was at this time that Henry granted £5 a year, convertible as soon as possible into land, to Walter of Durham, the master in charge of the paintings, this 'for his labour done, *pro labore suo facto*'.[51]

[48] For full discussion of the documentary evidence, style and dating, see Binski, *Painted Chamber*, 15–16, 45–69. For the debate about the dating and significance of the Old Testament scenes, which led to the chamber being called 'the painted chamber', see volume 1, 371 n. 103; Wilson, 'A monument to St Edward the Confessor', and now Binski, 'The painted chamber at Westminster and its documentation', where the accounts of the 1290s referring to the painting are printed.

[49] The work commissioned in November 1263 only cost £7 10s: *CR 1261–4*, 316; *CLR 1260–7*, 156. The cost of the gold needed in September 1264 was 20s: *CR 1261–4*, 366; *CLR 1267–72*, no. 80.

[50] Between September 1267 and December 1269 another £69 was spent on gold leaf, enamels and various colours, both for painting the chamber and the high vaults of the Abbey. Between December 1269 and February 1271 there was a further £50 for the chamber and Abbey paintings: *BA*, 426–35. And for a further £23 assigned to the chamber's paintings in December 1266 and January 1267, see *CLR 1260–7*, 251, 253. The expenditure between December 1269 and February 1271 also included the painting of the Confessor's reliquary. I suspect that the great bulk of the £588 spent between January 1264 and December 1266 on both the chamber's paintings and a large amount of material for the palace and the Abbey was incurred post-Evesham: *BA*, 418–9. Another £508 went generally on the wages of masons, carpenters, painters, plumbers, glaziers, labourers, works put out to task and messengers sent on business about the works.

[51] The king made his concession in a letter patent, but because it was not enrolled on the patent roll it seems to have gone unnoticed. However, the barons of the exchequer were

Putting all this together, what happened may be this. Towards the end of 1271, Henry said he wanted everything finally ready for his next arrival at Westminster, that is, for the feast of the Confessor on 5 January 1272. But even with the delay occasioned by his illness at Winchester, the paintings were not ready. The chamber, especially if work was still continuing around his bed, thus remained uninhabitable. Of course, Henry could have stayed elsewhere in the palace or the Abbey precincts as he must often have done after the fire. But, instead, Henry now said he would only return once the paintings were finished. He would then make a triumphal entry into his chamber. The totally unprecedented sojourn at the Tower was thus the result. In the end, Henry arrived back at Westminster on 8 February, celebrating his *adventus* with an offering of thirty gold coins.[52] His grant to Master Walter shows how delighted he was by what he saw.

The paintings spoke to Henry's kingship at its best. In the window splays were standing figures of the virtues, personified as queens in armour, trampling down their attendant vices, so 'LARGESCE' (so named) appeared triumphing over 'COVOITISE', and 'DEBONERETE' over 'IRA'.[53] In the splays of the window opposite the king's bed were the figures of the Confessor and the pilgrim. And then, on the opposite wall, behind the bedhead, was a painting of the Confessor's coronation. 'CEST LE CORONEMENT SEINT EDEWARD' ran an inscription in gold leaf just so everyone was quite sure. Amidst a throng of mitred ecclesiastics, holding aloft their golden crosses and croziers, the king was depicted enthroned with two bishops placing the crown on his head. So Henry had, behind his head, the glorious ceremony marking the start of the Confessor's reign and, before his eyes, the numinous meeting between the Confessor and the pilgrim that foreshadowed the reign's end and the Confessor's ascent into heaven. Nor was this Henry's only protection, for on either side of the bed were painted figures of knights, evidently the guardians of King Solomon's bed, a subject Henry also had painted beside his bed at Winchester.[54]

The impact of the paintings owed much to their size. Edward's coronation extended the whole width of Henry's bed, measuring some 3.23 metres

informed of the grant and instructed to have the letters patent read before them and enrolled. In fact, they enrolled (on the memoranda rolls) the letter telling them to do so: TNA E 159/56, m. 3 (image 8110); TNA E 368/45, m. 4 (image 6769). The copy of the letter did not include the date, but as it appears in the Hilary term it was later than 13 January. The first payment of the pension did indeed take place at the Easter term of 1272: *CLR 1267–72*, no. 1905. The paintings may not have been completely finished because between February and November 1272 nearly £8 were spent on them: *BA*, 434–5. However, it is quite possible this expenditure was retrospective.

[52] *CLR 1267–72*, no. 1825.

[53] These were the only complete pairings surviving in the early nineteenth century, but there were also the top halves of the virtue 'VERITE' and of another unnamed virtue, perhaps 'Fortitude': Binski, *Painted Chamber*, plates 7 and 8.

[54] *CLR 1245–51*, 325.

in length by 1.7 metres in height. The Virtues and Vices occupied architectural settings some 3.05 metres high and 1.12 metres wide.[55] The impact also derived from the sheer quality of the work, quite breathtaking in its richness and refinement.[56] The figures were tall and elegant, the faces long with fine straight noses. In the coronation tableau, the heads of the ecclesiastics appear both in profile and in full and quarter face, thus enhancing the sense of their involvement in the crowning. The power of the Virtues is increased by the delicacy of their chastizing hands and the stern impassivity of their faces. The dark reds, blues and greens of the robes and vestments (arranged in broad folds) are set off by their golden cuffs, embroidered fringes and, in the case of the Virtues, their high, floriated golden and jewelled crowns.[57] The style here, especially in the drapery, was very different from that of the earlier censing angels in the Abbey's south transept, brilliant though these are. Rather it derived from the wall paintings, manuscript illuminations and figure sculpture emerging in northern France in the mid-thirteenth century.[58] Henry himself would have seen magnificent examples in the great statues on the west front of Reims when he was there in 1262. The 'king's painter' in overall charge of the work was, as we have seen, Master Walter of Durham.[59] If he was the actual creator of the paintings, he was evidently steeped in the new style. He may equally have worked with artists recruited directly from France. The latter have certainly been thought responsible for the closely related high altar retable in the Abbey.[60] Their recruitment shows just how determined Henry was to get the best.

If the subject matter of the paintings in the chamber replicated what was there before the fire of 1263, their means of expression was thus stunningly new. Henry's taste had moved on, if not the preoccupations of his heart. The new style was not unique to Westminster. It was at this time influencing the sculptures in Lincoln's angel choir. But those who saw the paintings at close quarters in the great chamber at Westminster must have thought them as dramatically original as the Abbey itself.

Henry then was demonstrating in no uncertain terms that his kingship was back. He was also showing his kingship as he always intended it to be:

---

[55] Binski, *Painted Chamber*, 114–15.

[56] What follows draws on the description in Binski, *Painted Chamber*, 49.

[57] Some of these details, however, may have been touched up in later restorations: Binski, *Painted Chamber*, 47, 67–8.

[58] For this 'broad fold' style, as it is called, see Binski, *Painted Chamber*, 52; Liversidge and Binski, 'Two ceiling fragments from the painted chamber', 165; Binski, 'Function, date, imagery, style and context of the Westminster retable', 165; Morgan, *The Douce Apocalypse*, 24.

[59] For him, see *CLR 1260–7*, 109, 251, 253, 266; *CLR 1267–72*, nos. 82, 1063(b), 1905; *BA*, 390–1, 398–9, 422–3.

[60] For discussion of this issue, see Binski, 'Function, date, imagery, style and context of the Westminster retable', 32–40. The Douce Apocalypse is another closely related work. See Morgan, *The Douce Apocalypse*, 21–9, and Binski, 'The illumination and patronage of the Douce Apocalypse'.

wise, generous, courteous, consensual and above all supported by the
intercessions of his patron saint. Details in the paintings reinforced his
personal connection with the images and their message. Thus the figure
of Debonereté held a shield bearing the three leopards of the king's arms,
splendidly virile beasts much like those on the tiled floor of the Abbey's
chapter house. Then in the border around Largesse were again England's
arms, matched with the eagle of the empire, a nice tribute to King
Richard. The border around Debonereté combined the arms of England
with those of the Confessor and Saint Edmund. In the Coronation scene,
the crowd of ecclesiastics (there was not a single layman) stressed the
divinely ordained nature of kingship. It also reproved those bishops who
had so thoughtlessly supported Simon de Montfort.[61]

## HENRY'S DESCENT ON NORWICH

Having arrived at Westminster in February 1272, Henry remained there
for the next four months. On 18 May he gave instructions to the new
seneschal of Gascony by word of mouth. But his health was still not right.
On 20 May and again on 5 June he could not, he said, 'without peril of
death' travel to France to do homage to King Philip. Perhaps, although
with difficulty, he might get as far as Boulogne or Saint-Omer.[62] Then, as
before, the fever (if such it was) abated and Henry felt much better.

---

[61] There is a puzzle about the ceiling of the great chamber. As depicted in a painting by
William Capon in 1799, it consisted of a planked surface to which were fixed at regular
intervals a series of large and small wooden panels, quatrefoil in design. These ran the
whole length of the chamber, the larger ones four abreast. This was not, however, the
original form of the ceiling because a letter of 1820 reveals that in one half (it is not said
which), underneath the larger panels, were the painted heads of saints. Two of these heads
survive and are on display in the British Museum. Painted on oak boards, one is a stern-
looking Old Testament prophet, the other a smiling seraph. The style and quality of the
paintings make it fairly certain they were part of the work undertaken in the period after
the fire. Henry's aim seems to have been to place the paintings behind his bed and in the
window splays – the Coronation of the Confessor, the Confessor and the Pilgrim and the
Virtues and Vices – into a wider biblical context. The natural assumption is that it was only
in some later period that the paintings were covered by the panels. But this appears not to
have been the case. *Even before the paint was dry*, guide lines seem to have been scored across
the surface of the two surviving paintings so as to help with the alignment of the panels.
(One of the panels survives in Sir John Soane's Museum in London.) The paintings were,
therefore, covered up absolutely at once. Henry's change of mind, if such it was, seems
hard to explain. The detail of the heads cannot have been very visible from the floor, but
the same was true of many roof bosses and much stained glass in windows. The bosses and
planks were doubtless highly painted and the effect would have been striking, but, as
altered, the ceiling no longer made any biblical references. I still wonder whether the
panels are later. For all this see Liversidge and Binski, 'Two ceiling fragments from the
Painted Chamber at Westminster'. I thank both the Soane Museum for permitting examination of the panel and Martin Bridge for investigating the possibility of subjecting it to
dendrochronological dating.

[62] *CPR 1266–72*, 651, 697; *F*, i, 494–5.

Pentecost on 12 June he celebrated in his usual style. Some £550 was to be spent on the necessary purchases and another £100 on the fine linen for the robes of the king's servants, much of the money coming from the eyres. There were the usual 150 shoes for the poor and two embroidered copes (costing 110 marks) for offerings to the Confessor.[63]

Immediately after Pentecost, Henry set off on a tour. It took him first to Windsor, as it turned out for the last time, and then on to Reading, Wallingford and Oxford. The destination was Woodstock, where Henry stayed from 28 June to 17 July. For the last time he was able to take the summer sun in the cloisters around the pools at Everswell. Then it was back to Westminster via, as so often, St Albans and Waltham abbey. We have no Matthew Paris to describe this last visit to St Albans but no doubt it witnessed the customary offerings and rituals. The tour certainly saw characteristic Henrician behaviour: gifts to the Carmelites beginning their general chapter in Oxford, and to Oxford's Austin friars so they could buy a plot of land; new glass and wooden shutters for the windows in the king's house at Oxford; new surplices for the three chaplains at Woodstock and a gift to the fishermen there towards mending their broken nets.[64] Henry now felt so much better that he began preparations for his journey to France for his homage to King Philip. In August he took out a large loan from merchants for the purpose. It was to be repaid inevitably from the issues of various eyres, and Henry promised that if, through forgetfulness, he assigned the money elsewhere, the order was to have no effect![65]

Then all at once, Henry's plans were disrupted by a terrible event. It was at Norwich where the old tensions between the town and the cathedral priory suddenly exploded.[66] On 11 August, the day after Henry took out his loan, men and women of the town, provoked beyond endurance, stormed the priory. They forced an entry through one of the gates and set fire to the belfry from where archers were firing into the town. They then plundered the priory, and, in the ensuing struggle, killed some of its men. Meanwhile fire had engulfed the church with its towers. The dormitory, refectory, infirmary, sacristy, almonry and hall, as well as vestments, books and ornaments, all went up in flames. Only one chapel, the cloister and the bishop's house remained intact. Henry was appalled. 'Certain sons of blasphemy unmindful of their salvation', he wrote, had offended God, subverted ecclesiastical liberty, dishonoured the king and disrupted the peace. His 'anguish and grief' was all the greater since such 'detestable

---

[63] *CLR 1267–72*, nos. 1958–9, 1966, 1968, 1970; TNA E 159/46, m. 7d (image 8162).

[64] *CLR 1267–72*, nos. 1993, 2001, 2007, 2018, 2026.

[65] *F*, i, 495 (*CPR 1266–72*, 672); *CLR 1267–72*, no. 2051.

[66] There are accounts in Bury St Edmunds, 50–2; FitzThedmar, 145–6 (Stone, FitzThedmar, no. 1067); and (most detailed) Westminster, *Flores*, 24–7, here with an account from the Norfolk monastery of St Benet at Hulme.

crimes' had never been heard of before.[67] Ill though he had been earlier
in the year, Henry decided he would go to Norwich to put matters to
rights.

Leaving Westminster on 19 August, Henry went first to the royal manor
of Havering in Essex, where he remained for ten days. Havering had
never been in the premier league of Henry's residences, but he often
stayed there on his pilgrimages to and from East Anglia and also sometimes on tours which took in St Albans and Waltham abbey.[68] Havering
was also favoured by the queen. In 1268 she personally gave the orders for
making twenty stained-glass windows with forty shields in them to adorn
her chamber.[69] Nothing now survives of Havering's medieval buildings,
but the site's charm remains. It crowns the top of a hill with splendid views
over the Essex plain towards the Thames estuary and the hills of Kent
beyond. (Today one can see the upper supports of the Queen Elizabeth
bridge at Dartford.) Eleanor was always worried about air quality and
Havering's was excellent. This was the ideal place for Henry to rest and
recuperate before the journey to come.[70]

Henry left Havering at the end of August and by 2 September had
reached Bury St Edmunds, where for the last time he made offerings at St
Edmund's shrine. Then, accompanied by Gilbert de Clare and Roger
Bigod, earl of Norfolk (who entertained the court at his manor of
Lopham), he descended on Norwich.[71] He was there for seventeen days
until 26 September, staying in the bishop's house. The chief culprits were
seized and imprisoned in the castle. Convicted by a jury of local knights,
over thirty men and one woman were executed.[72]

Arnold fitzThedmar, sympathetic to the townsmen, opined that the
king showed them no mercy. But Henry, to the disappointment of the
Bury annalist, had not punished the whole town and indeed, from the first,
had tried to distinguish the innocent from the guilty. He also thought there
were faults on both sides and later accepted that the prior himself was
partly to blame. He had placed archers in the belfry and had installed
smiths making projectiles in the tower. When they had seen the belfry
alight, they had fled without extinguishing their fire and it had spread to

---

[67] *CPR 1266–72*, 675–6.

[68] For the works at Havering (now Havering-atte-Bower), see Colvin, *History of the Kings'
Works*, ii, 956–9. After a visit in 1251, Henry commissioned work costing some £900, despite
saving hard at the time for his crusade.

[69] *CLR 1267–72*, nos. 109, 1640 (for the queen at Havering); Howell, *Eleanor of Provence*,
72–4, 289, 294.

[70] The manorial complex was surrounded by an extensive park. Perhaps its situation and
air were the reasons why two queens in bad health took up residence at Havering, though
in the event both died there: Joan, queen of Scotland, Henry's sister, and Joan of Kent,
widow of Henry IV.

[71] *RCWL*, ii, 200; TNA E 101/684/10/1.

[72] The citizens also had to pay for the rebuilding of the church: Rishanger, 73.

the rest of the church. The prior, therefore, was made to resign. As he did sometimes at his best, Henry had steered a middle way.[73]

Having finished his business in Norwich, Henry did not set off for home. Instead, he headed north on a pilgrimage to Bromholm and Walsingham, where he had not been since 1256.[74] Then it was back to Westminster in time for the feast of the Confessor on 13 October. While at Norwich, Henry had sent out orders to procure the cloths of gold, wax and other necessaries for the ceremony. At the feast he knighted both Edmund, son of King Richard, and Henry de Lacy. He also invested them with the earldoms respectively of Cornwall and Lincoln.[75]

Henry had reasons for satisfaction. His good relations with Gilbert de Clare and Roger Bigod seemed to guarantee the peace of the realm. Gilbert was drawn all the nearer to the royal family by the marriage early in October of his sister to Edmund of Cornwall.[76] Henry was as close as ever to Queen Eleanor, 'his dearest consort'. In 1271 he presented silver-gilt images of a king and queen to the shrine of the Confessor. Eleanor was with him at all the major feasts and she received a generous gift of deer while Henry was at Bury. Just after the 13 October feast, Henry gave her two valuable wardships and promised others so that she could have £1,000 a year for the maintenance of her household. Around the same time she was given the custody of Windsor castle.[77] Although Henry no longer had his Savoyard and Lusignan relations with him, their satellites, Elyas de Rabayne, William de Sancta Ermina and Peter de Champvent, were prominent at court. Henry managed, after a good deal of effort, to endow the last two with land from wardships and escheats. In the process he seems to have converted the permission to give £120 in cash to permission to give it in land.[78]

Through all this time, Henry must have been worried about what was happening to Edward, all the more so if he heard of his attempted assassination at Acre on 17 June 1272. Edward was wounded but managed to throw his assailant to the ground, seize his dagger and stab him to death, a deed (on his thirty-third birthday) greatly adding to his legend. Next day Edward made his will, so his condition was serious. His recovery owed nothing to his wife sucking out the poison. That is a later story. According

[73] CPR 1266–72, 707; CR 1268–72, 526–7.

[74] TNA E 101/684/10/1.

[75] Wykes, 251; FitzThedmar, 154 (Stone, FitzThedmar, no. 1093); CR 1268–72, 525; CLR 1267–72, nos. 2058, 2124.

[76] Wykes, 251; FitzThedmar, 154 (Stone, FitzThedmar, no. 1092); Bury St Edmunds, 52; Ray, Edward I's Regent, 52–3. For gifts to Gilbert at Norwich, see CR 1268–72, 526.

[77] CLR 1267–72, no. 1524; CR 1268–72, 517–18, 521; CPR 1266–72, 682; CFR 1271–2, no. 1851; Howell, Eleanor of Provence, 252. Early in 1272, Eleanor had been given the custody of the lands of John de Grey, the eldest son of the Montfortian Richard, during the minority of his heir: CPR 1266–72, 617.

[78] CPR 1266–72, 568, 574, 610–11, 650.

to a contemporary ballad, it was Christ who healed the wound with sacred medicine, 'knowing his servant was worthy'.[79]

## THE DEATH OF THE KING

On 1 October 1272, Henry III passed his sixty-fifth birthday. Only Henry I of previous English kings had lived longer. None had reigned anywhere near as long. At the end of the month he would enter his fifty-seventh regnal year. As the descent on Norwich showed, Henry's health seemed restored and that remained the case well into October.[80] On the twenty-third he took the homage of a widow. On the twentieth and twenty-fifth he authorized writs, one showing his 'special grace' towards the abbey of Bec in Normandy. Looking to the future, a dispute in which Henry wished to do 'full justice' was to come before him and his council at Hilary 1273.[81] One issue troubling Henry was that of the debts run up by his household, especially those owed to the poor who had supplied it with provisions. Earlier in 1272 he had tried to set aside a tallage on the Jews for the necessary payments, only for the council to decide the money (or at least 1,000 marks of it) should go to Edward instead.[82] Now men from Norfolk and Suffolk complained that they had never been compensated for the money and victuals taken from them back in 1267. In response, 'having compassion on them and wishing to provide a remedy', Henry ordered the exchequer to mount an inquiry and send him the results. It is fitting that this writ, almost the last of Henry's enrolled on the memoranda rolls of the exchequer, should show his concern for the poor.[83]

Henry's return to health did not last. By 28 October he was seriously ill. On that day, when Westminster Hall filled with the London populace and the aldermen quarrelling over who should be the new mayor, their clamour, fitzThedmar tells us, 'reached the king in bed laboring under a grave infirmity'. Having suffered so much from the Londoners, they might at least have left him alone now. Over the next weeks the council tried desperately to settle the dispute, not wishing 'to disturb the king who was

---

[79] Wykes, 258–61; *Political Songs*, 132; *F*, i, 495; Prestwich, *Edward I*, 78; Morris, *A Great and Terrible King*, 100–1.

[80] Rishanger, 74 (written in the early fourteenth century), has Henry becoming ill at Bury St Edmunds, but this is belied by his ability to go on to Norwich, his subsequent pilgrimage and return to Westminster.

[81] *CR 1268–72*, 535–6; *CPR 1266–72*, 683–4; TNA E 159/47, m. 2 (image 8998).

[82] *CLR 1267–72*, no. 1987; *CR 1268–72*, 493–4, 498–9; TNA E 159/146, m. 10 (image 8123). For examples of such debts, see *CLR 1267–72*, no. 2088. The last royal charter was issued on 25 October: *CChR 1257–1300*, 184; *RCWL*, ii, 200. It simply had a household witness list headed by Robert Aguillon, Elyas de Rabayne and William of Wintershall.

[83] TNA E 159/47, m. 2 (image 8999). The writ as enrolled here (it is not on the chancery rolls) is undated but, judging from its place, was later than 18 October.

in a weak state'.[84] Presumably the fever plaguing Henry intermittently over the last few years had returned. But he had recovered before and might again. On or around 4 November, a statement was made in his presence, preparations began for Christmas at Winchester and Henry gave a vestment and altar frontal to the hermitage at Charing, where masses were sung for the soul of his daughter Katherine.[85] It was perhaps as much anticipating the king's recovery as his demise that the council on 10 November made yet another attempt to have all the revenues of the kingdom paid into the exchequer.[86] As late as 13 November the steward of Boston fair was summoned to come before the king at Hilary 1273 to answer for his behaviour.[87]

Desperate to live until Edward's and Edmund's return from their crusade, Henry put up a long fight for life. Edmund indeed, as perhaps Henry knew, was already on his way home. (He eventually arrived in London on 10 December and went at once to see his mother at Windsor.)[88] But Henry did not live. His final day was 16 November, the feast day of Edmund of Abingdon, to whose shrine at Pontigny he had gone on pilgrimage back in 1254. Henry survived until late in the day, so the scene must have been lit by candles, the queen perhaps praying by his bedside, the archbishop of York administering the last rites.[89] Towards the end, with the king 'labouring in extremis', Gilbert de Clare came before him and swore to preserve the peace of the kingdom and to keep it safe for Edward's use.[90] The final moments were peaceful or at least so Edward was informed. His father had died 'suaviter et sanctissime'.[91]

In the painting of the Confessor's deathbed, from the life by Matthew Paris, the Confessor lies with his arms folded across his breast, while from his open mouth a small figure of a king emerges. It is his soul which two angels swoop down to carry off to heaven. In the adjoining image, Saint John, with Peter standing by with his keys, ushers the Confessor, with a delicately helping hand, into Christ's presence. How Henry must have prayed that the Confessor and Saint John, their images looking on him from the window splays opposite his bed, would do the same for him.[92]

---

[84] FitzThedmar, 150 (Stone, FitzThedmar, nos. 1075–6).

[85] *CR 1268–72*, 582–3, 585–6.

[86] *CR 1268–72*, 585; TNA E 159/47, m. 2d (image 9047), whence the date.

[87] *CR 1268–72*, 586–7.

[88] FitzThedmar, 156 (Stone, FitzThedmar, no. 1101); Wykes, 253; Winchester, 112.

[89] *CR 1268–72*, 588.

[90] FitzThedmar, 155 (Stone, FitzThedmar, no. 1096). A St Albans chronicle written later than 1290 and attributed to Rishanger gives a formulaic picture of Henry's death: Rishanger, 74.

[91] *F*, ii, 497: 'gently and in a saintly fashion'.

[92] The image is the frontispiece to Paris, *La Estoire*, and is no. 63 in the online images. Queen Edith threads one arm through the Confessor's and raises the other in an anguished gesture.

Thomas Wykes at least was confident of the king's destination. He wrote of 'Henry the most serene king of the English, of pious record' changing 'the momentary glory of the world for the celestial palace, there to reign for ever in heaven with the king of kings'.[93]

## HENRY'S BURIAL

During his last years, beset by illness, Henry must have thought deeply about the form and function of his burial. Almost certainly he marked out the place for his eventual tomb beside the shrine of the Confessor. One suspects too that Henry gave instructions about the robes and insignia which should adorn his body, meaningful as these were. Here fortunately there is documentary evidence. Since 1261 the keepers of the wardrobe had accounted at the exchequer for an array of vestments and insignia they had permanently in their custody: rods, mantles, dalmatics, brooches, belts, swords, shoes, gloves and so on. Many of these were described as 'royal, *regalis*' and they were all clearly associated with the majesty of kingship.[94] As such, they were quite distinct from the precious objects which the king gave and received throughout the year. In the last wardrobe account of the reign, instead of the customary statement after the list of regalia that everything remains, we come, with a sudden shock to a very different conclusion:

> . . . from which [store of objects], one royal rod, one dalmatic of red samite with orphreys and stones, one mantle of red samite most splendidly adorned with orphreys and precious stones, a gold brooch, one pair of stockings of red samite with orphreys, one pair of shoes of red samite are handed over for the burial of the king. And all the other things remain.[95]

Henry's body, therefore, was adorned with regalia and what made the rod, dalmatic and mantle especially royal was their association with the coronation. Here after the king, stripped to his shirt, had been anointed, he was clothed in 'royal vestments', first a tunic and dalmatic, then a mantle. After the actual crowning a rod and sceptre were placed in his hands.[96] Henry with his dalmatic, his mantle[97] and his royal rod was thus

---

[93] Wykes, 252.

[94] Wild, *WA*, 92–3, 141, 152. For what follows, see ch. 21 of my *Reign of Henry III* (on the burial of Henry III, the *regalia* and royal ideology), where full references may be found.

[95] Wild, *WA*, 155; Carpenter, *Reign of Henry III*, 429.

[96] There are no detailed descriptions of Henry's coronations in 1216 and 1220 and these details come from Roger of Howden's account of Richard's coronation in 1189: Howden, iii, 9–12; Carpenter, *Reign of Henry III*, 430.

[97] The gold brooch was presumably used to fasten the mantle like the brooch on Henry's eventual effigy.

clothed in death as for his coronation, the great ceremony at the start of the reign setting him apart and above all his subjects.[98]

The appearance of Henry's body linked him in another way with the coronation and also with the Confessor, for Henry was buried not with a sword, like his father, but simply with a rod. Almost certainly this was a dove-topped rod like that on the Confessor's seal, a rod that had already replaced the sword on Henry's second seal made in 1259. It was also with such a rod that the king was invested at his coronation. Hence the Confessor is shown holding one in the coronation picture behind Henry's bed at Westminster. Since, unlike his son, Henry was only buried with a rod, not also with a sceptre, it probably lay vertically along the centre of his body. Henry could thus clasp the dove-topped rod of the Confessor with both hands to his heart.

In the arrangement of the rod, perhaps Henry was influenced by the effigies of Henry II and Richard he had seen at Fontevraud in 1254, for there too a sceptre is placed along the centre of the body. But if graceful reference was thus made to the dynastic past, in one final respect, the arrangements for Henry's burial showed care for the dynastic future, a future with which the Confessor was again intertwined. Thomas Wykes, probably present, described Henry as being borne to his tomb wearing a 'royal diadem', yet no crown appears amongst the items of regalia handed over for the burial. Evidently the crown used was kept outside the wardrobe, like, for example, the one Henry purchased for 500 marks in 1253.[99] The crown that *was* kept in the wardrobe, Henry did not take to his tomb. This is described in the accounts as 'the great royal crown with most precious rubies and other precious stones'. After Henry's death it was handed to John of London, clerk of King Edward, with all the other precious objects kept in the wardrobe.[100] The crown in question was almost certainly the coronation crown. Since 1220 it had been known as 'the diadem of the most saintly King Edward'.[101] It was being preserved for the coronation of all future kings.

Henry's burial took place on Sunday 20 November, the feast day of Saint Edmund, king and martyr, an appropriate date since Henry had revered Edmund second only to the Confessor and had given Edmund's name to his second son. Arnold fitzThedmar, probably present, described how Henry's body 'nobly adorned as was befitting a king, was given for burial in the conventual church of the monks at Westminster, before the

---

[98] For dalmatics, worn during officiating at the mass, see Browne, Davies, Michael and Zöschg, *English Medieval Embroidery*, 25–6, 33–4, 277.

[99] *CLR 1251–60*, 105.

[100] Wild, *WA*, 156. This crown appears amongst the *regalia* in the wardrobe account for 1258 to 1261 (Wild, *WA*, 92), but then does not appear again until recorded as being handed over to Edward's clerk.

[101] Crowland, 244.

great altar'.[102] Thomas Wykes gave his own version. 'The king was buried
with fitting honour in the most noble church at Westminster, which he had
constructed with sumptuous and incomparable work from its foundations.
His body, adorned as fitting with most precious garments and a royal
diadem . . . was born to the tomb on a bier by the chosen nobles of the
kingdom.' As Henry's own tomb had yet to be constructed, his body was
placed in the old tomb of the Confessor, evidently situated before the new
high altar, the tomb that had housed his body before its translation of 1163.
As Thomas Wykes commented, it was 'wonderful' that Henry should lie
thus in the tomb of one 'who, while he lived, he loved above all saints and
venerated with such great devotion'.[103]

Henry's burial was not quite his 'final blazon'. That came with the tomb
and effigy constructed under his son. But the burial still told much about
his view of kingship. The dalmatic and mantle proclaimed the spirituality
conferred by the coronation.[104] The abandonment of the sword and the
embracing of the dove-topped rod reflected his love of peace and his devotion to the Confessor, as did his resting in the Confessor's ancient tomb.
Saint Edward's crown, passed on for future coronations, told all succeeding
kings how they would rule guarded and guided by their sainted predecessor.

---

[102] FitzThedmar, 153–4 (Stone, FitzThedmar, no. 1087).
[103] Wykes, 252–3. The question of Henry's tomb is discussed in Appendix 1.
[104] For discussion of the spiritual gifts bestowed by the coronation, see volume 1, 45–7.

## Chapter 16

# EPILOGUE AND CONCLUSION

On 23 November, three days after Henry's burial, a letter was drawn up informing Edward of what had happened. Written in the names of the archbishop of York, five bishops, five earls and five magnates, it was addressed to 'the magnificent prince and their lord, Edward, king of England, lord of Ireland and duke of Aquitaine'. Edward was informed of his father's death '*suaviter et sanctissime*' late on Wednesday 16 November.[1] He was then told how, the following morning, his own 'peace' had been proclaimed in Westminster's great hall; and how on the twentieth, the feast day of Saint Edmund, king and martyr, Henry's body had been handed for burial in Westminster Abbey 'before the great altar'. The letter then described how, before Henry's tomb was closed, the writers had all sworn fealty to Edward as their king and had once again caused his peace to be proclaimed.[2] The Westminster Abbey chronicle pictures the earls of Gloucester and Warenne, with clergy and people, hastening to the high altar to swear the oath, so there must have been a great throng on the Cosmati pavement.[3] The letter of 23 November was issued from the New Temple, whither the magnates had gone for further debate. There Henry's seal was broken and Edward's seal, the same as his father's save for the alteration of their names, introduced.[4] The first letter it sealed, also on 23 November, was sent to all the sheriffs. Written in Edward's name with his full titles, it declared he had assumed the government of the kingdom 'by hereditary succession and the will of the magnates of the kingdom'. He now promised justice to everyone and commanded the sheriffs once again to proclaim his peace.[5]

Edward had left the Holy Land at the end of September 1272 and was at Trapani in Sicily when he learnt that both his son John and his father had died.[6] According to the chronicler Nicholas Trevet's story he brushed

---

[1] Called the feast day of St Edmund the Confessor (Edmund of Abingdon).

[2] *F*, ii, 497.

[3] Westminster, *Flores*, 28, and also FitzThedmar 153–4 (Stone, FitzThedmar, no. 1087).

[4] On the morning after Henry's death John of Kirkby had handed Henry's seal, under his seal and the seal of Peter of Winchester, keeper of the wardrobe, to the archbishop of York, in the presence of Robert Aguillon and other councillors: *CR 1268–72*, 588. Kirkby had kept the seal since Richard of Middleton's death in August 1272.

[5] *F*, ii, 497 (*CCR 1272–9*, 1); FitzThedmar, 154–6 (Stone, FitzThedmar, nos. 1089, 1099–1100).

[6] For Edward's activities between his father's death and his return to England, see Prestwich, *Edward I*, 79–85, and Morris, *A Great and Terrible King*, 103–10.

aside the first news but lamented the second. As he explained to his wondering host, King Charles, he had the power to sire more sons, but a father was irreplaceable.[7] On 19 January, in southern Italy, still King Charles's guest (indeed the letter was sealed with Charles's seal), Edward wrote home.[8] He was as well as could be expected given the bitter news of his father's demise. He urged everyone to keep the peace till his return. The letter of 23 November had begged Edward to come back as soon as possible, given the imminent dangers posed by his absence. Edward now said he was indeed hastening his return. Had he done so, he could easily have reached England by the spring of 1273. But in fact Edward changed his mind. The decision was helped by a key piece of information in the November 1272 letter, although not one referred to directly. Against all precedent, Edward had become king not on the day of his coronation but on the day of his father's burial. The home government, therefore, enjoyed at once regal authority. The letter also showed that Gilbert de Clare was behaving himself for he was one of its writers, as were two former Montfortians, John fitzJohn and William de Munchesney. Quite probably more reassurance arrived from Robert Burnell, now the effective head of the English government.

Edward, therefore, made a leisurely journey up through Italy, feted on his way as a famous crusader. He saw the pope and at last secured Guy de Montfort's excommunication, although abandoning plans to hunt Guy down himself. Across the Alps, he visited Savoy and then attended a tournament at Chalons, stories soon spreading about his deeds of derring-do. By July he was in Paris, where he did homage to King Philip as duke of Aquitaine and set in train the process of eventually securing the Agenais and the Saintonge. In Paris, Edward was made 'wonderfully content', as a letter home put it, by news about 'the state of his land and the actions of his magnates'.[9] And so he decided to go not to England but to Gascony, there to put down a revolt led by that old troublemaker Gaston de Béarn. It was not till August 1274 that Edward finally landed back at Dover. On Sunday 19 August he was crowned in Westminster Abbey. So for the first time the coronation rituals were played out in the setting Henry had created for the purpose, played out on the Cosmati pavement before the high altar and in the great theatre of space between the north and south transepts.[10] Historians have long debated how stable England was between Henry's death and Edward's return. What seems certain is that the home

---

[7] Trevet, 284, whence Rishanger, 78.

[8] FitzThedmar, 158–9 (Stone, FitzThedmar, no. 1110). The letter was probably widely distributed although the copy here was addressed to the Londoners.

[9] Trabut-Cussac, L'administration anglaise, 41–2, n. 3.

[10] For the pavement and the coronation, see Binski, 'The Cosmati at Westminster', 31–2, and for the coronation more generally, Binski, Westminster Abbey and the Plantagenets, 126–40.

government assured Edward it could cope, as indeed it did.[11] That is the best testimony to England's political condition at the end of Henry's reign. The civil war really was over.

## HENRY'S TOMB

When he arrived at Westminster for his coronation, Edward must have immediately entered the Abbey to offer prayers at his father's tomb. Situated before the high altar, in the old 'place' of the Confessor, it was conspicuous during the coronation itself. Yet Henry, quite certainly, had wished to lie not before the high altar but in the Confessor's chapel, beside the Confessor's shrine. It behoved Edward, accordingly, to construct a fitting tomb there for his father. The same obligation rested on Richard of Ware, the abbot of Westminster.

Edward, however, had much else to do. There was the introduction of customs revenues, the securing of taxation, the promulgation of legislation and the growing tensions with the prince of Wales, the latter culminating in the war of 1277 and the building of the great castles designed to affirm the victory. It was not then till 1279 that Edward returned from France with the Cosmati stones and presumably too the Cosmati workmen to make his father's tomb.[12] Abbot Ware was with him and probably Ware, on his visits to Italy, had made the contact with the Cosmati, building on his earlier role in bringing the high altar pavement to England. That king and abbot were able in 1279 to meet up with the workmen on their way to England was perhaps designed, perhaps fortuitous.[13]

Edward's desire to give his father a Cosmati tomb was hardly surprising, after the stupendous shrine they had created for the Confessor. He may also have seen more of their work on his passage through Italy. The Cosmati did not disappoint. The tomb they designed, surviving to this day, was just as magnificent as the shrine, but more coherent for it was largely classical and lacked the shrine's conspicuously gothic features. The tomb was also quite up to speed with the latest Cosmati work in Italy, indeed in some respects perhaps an advance upon it.[14]

Looked at from the Confessor's chapel, the tomb stands on a stepped podium.[15] It is then given height and grandeur by its two stages, a great

---

[11] For the debate, see Huscroft, 'Robert Burnell and the government of England', 59–60. Huscroft stresses the achievements of the home government.

[12] For fuller discussion of the date of Henry's tomb, see Appendix I below. Edward had gone to Amiens to see Philip III and had now secured the Agenais and the Saintonge under the terms of the Treaty of Paris. He also obtained the county of Ponthieu as the inheritance of his wife, Eleanor of Castile. See Prestwich, *Edward I*, 316.

[13] See Appendix 1.

[14] For the parallel works in Italy, see Binski, 'The Cosmati at Westminster', 23–5, and Binski, *Westminster Abbey and the Plantagenets*, 102.

[15] The tomb is described in magnificent detail in Rodwell and Neal, *The Cosmatesque Mosaics*, 435–79, from which much of what follows comes.

lower chest supporting a smaller chest above where the king's body lies. Looked at from the ambulatory, where the floor level is below that of the chapel, the impression of height is even more striking, the tomb seeming to consist of three stages not just two. On the chapel side, the lower chest is divided into three chambers, 31 centimetres deep, the central one having the appearance of a classical colonnaded temple with a pediment above. Since the chambers were originally barred, they were probably designed to house relics. On the ambulatory side, there are no chambers and instead the chest is divided into three panels, each containing slabs of green porphyry, circular in the centre, poised squares at either side. The porphyry here, however, pales before that adorning the chest above, housing Henry's body, for on both the ambulatory and chapel sides are gigantic panels of the highest-status purple, imperial, porphyry. Measuring 1.22/1.27 metres by 43 centimetres, these are easily the largest slabs of porphyry found in the Abbey and must have been brought specially for Henry's tomb. Setting off this porphyry, at the corners of the upper chest were spiralling colonettes, while fluted columns standing on the edges of the lower chest probably supported a now lost canopy above.[16] The whole structure, around the slabs of porphyry, was studded with the familiar Cosmati tesserae – white triangles, red tilted squares, chequered gold and blue lozenges and so on and so on, all told perhaps some 160,000 of them.[17] (They are now mostly seen on the ambulatory side where they are too high to be picked off.).[18] This was a sumptuous tomb very different from anything seen before in England.

The tomb first and foremost celebrated Henry himself. That he had in life been so often derided made that all the more imperative. The tomb also spoke more generally to the majesty of English kingship, a kingship the reverse of parochial given the connections now displayed with the papacy and with Rome.[19] In all this Edward was doubtless emulating the magnificent tomb King Philip was making for his father at Saint-Denis, probably well under way by the late 1270s.[20] Like all tombs, Henry's also had another function, namely to encourage prayers for the incumbent's soul. In the 1270s and 1280s several bishops issued indulgences for those who went to Henry's tomb and prayed accordingly.[21] The tomb in question must have been the one before the high altar, but prayers would surely

[16] The current canopy is late medieval.

[17] Rodwell and Neal, *The Cosmatesque Mosaics*, ii, 635–9.

[18] I well remember Laurence Tanner, long-time Keeper of the Muniments at the Abbey, reaching up beside the tomb and pointing this out to me.

[19] The wider significance of Henry's tomb and the Cosmati work more generally is explored in Binski, *Westminster Abbey and the Plantagenets*, 105–7, and his 'The Cosmati at Westminster', 28–33.

[20] For the date, see below, 650 n. 25.

[21] WAM Book II (Westminster Domesday), fos. 398–398v, 404v–405 or 398r–v, 404v–405r.

be all the more forthcoming once Henry was moved to his own elevated structure in the Confessor's chapel.

Was there more to it than that? If pilgrims came to pray at Henry's tomb, were they not hoping for something in return, hoping that the king would intercede for their restoration to spiritual and bodily health? Perhaps the tomb of the holy king at Westminster would witness miracles far outstripping those supposedly performed by the evil earl at Evesham. Perhaps they would even rival those now being performed at Louis IX's tomb at Saint-Denis? In that case Henry too might be on the way to canonization with the high-standing tomb already suitable as a shrine.

For a while, there were perhaps hopes along these lines. Edward was informed that his father had died '*sanctissime*, in saintly fashion'. Thomas Wykes wrote of Henry, on his death, 'passing to the glory of the heavenly palace to reign in heaven with the king of kings for ever'.[22] Evidently he was now in the company of the saints very able to intercede with them at God's right hand. The Westminster Abbey chronicle declared that Henry's merits in life were indeed revealed in miracles after his death.[23] When Henry's grandson young Henry was on his deathbed in October 1274, 'measures', candles of his height, were offered at both the Confessor's shrine and Henry's tomb, as though Henry's intercession as much as the Confessor's might have thaumaturgical power.[24] The Furness abbey chronicle, under the year 1275, reported that 'in these days frequent miracles were said to have occurred at the tomb of the blessed King Henry'.[25] But after this good start there seems to have been scant continuation. Neither the Westminster nor Furness chronicles give details of the miracles, and their bare statements contrast starkly with the forty pages of Montfortian miracles (in a later printed edition) collected by the monks of Evesham. There was equally no parallel at Westminster to what was happening at Saint-Denis. Admittedly an English leather worker, resident at Saint-Denis, mocked those going to Louis's tomb and declared Henry was the better man, but retribution soon followed and he was crippled until he acknowledged Louis's power.[26] Edward may have hoped for miracles but he wanted them to be the real thing. According to a story in Trevet's chronicle, when his mother believed a man had been cured of blindness at Henry's tomb, he scoffed at the idea. The individual was a notorious rogue. Henry would have torn his eyes out rather than given them sight.[27] The indulgences connected with the tomb were themselves

---

[22] Wykes, 252.

[23] Westminster, *Flores*, 28.

[24] Johnstone, 'Wardrobe and household of Henry, son of Edward I', 409. Earlier (p. 420), in the Abbey, Henry had offered 9d at the Confessor's shrine, Henry's tomb and the celebration of mass.

[25] Furness, 571.

[26] Carpenter, 'Meetings of kings', 28.

[27] Trevet, 302–3; Howell, *Eleanor of Provence*, 298.

not entirely reassuring. They solicited prayers for Henry's soul, so he was in purgatory after all. No one was asked to pray for the soul of the Confessor. That would have been ridiculous. One prayed for his intercession, not for his spiritual health.

Edward's argument with his mother occurred in 1282 and by that time the tomb, if begun in 1279, was probably well on its way to completion.[28] But Edward no longer saw it as a means of unblocking stagnant waters and reviving his father's faltering claims to sainthood. If he had, he would surely have moved Henry's body there at once so that tomb and body could join together their appeal and their power. Nothing like that happened, in part because Edward had other priorities. In 1283 and 1284 he was arranging for the government of Wales after the 1282 war of conquest. Between 1286 and 1289 he was absent in Gascony. On his return to England in August 1289, Edward waited until he could make the best possible use of his father's translation. In 1290 the moment came. 'On the night of the feast of the Ascension' (11 May), Edward had his father's body moved and 'put in a higher place next to the tomb of Saint Edward'. The annalist of Bury St Edmunds, here quoted, says all this happened 'suddenly and unexpectedly', but clearly there was publicity for the move was also noted in the London annals.[29] In fact, quite apart from the obvious appropriateness of Ascension day itself, Edward was 'stage-managing' his father's translation so as to impress one of the great parliaments of his reign. This was the parliament, opening at the end of April, that granted a gigantic tax in return for the expulsion of the Jews from England.[30] It was just the kind of accommodation with parliament that Henry had failed to achieve during his personal rule, though his treatment of the Jews had certainly prepared the baleful way. During his translation in 1290, Henry's body was uncovered, for the London annals say it had a long beard and was 'intact, *integrum*'. If the body was inspected in the hope its wholesome state would enhance Henry's claims to sanctity, nothing came of it. No more is heard of miracles despite the move to the new tomb.

In 1290, Henry's tomb still lacked an effigy.[31] Edward had seen that of King John at Worcester, those of Henry II and Richard at Fontevraud and the line of Capetian kings at Saint-Denis, but it was only the death of his wife that prompted him to do something for his father. Eleanor of Castile

---

[28] Trevet places the episode after Easter at Devizes (as it was in 1282) and while Edward was visiting his mother at Amesbury prior to leaving for the campaign in Wales. His known itinerary makes such a visit possible though it is unrecorded. Edward related what had happened to Hugh of Manchester, prior provincial of the Dominican order, so he was probably the source.

[29] Bury St Edmunds, 94; London, 98.

[30] Stacey, 'Parliamentary negotiation and the expulsion of the Jews from England', 86.

[31] For the suggestion that the effigy replaced a kneeling figure of Henry, see Rodwell and Neal, *The Cosmatesque Mosaics*, ii, 446, 583, 591. An upright figure of Louis has also been posited for his tomb, but this has been questioned. See below, 650 n. 25.

had died in November 1290 and was buried in the Confessor's chapel at Henry's feet.[32] Edward and her executors then commissioned tombs for her at Westminster and also at Lincoln where her entrails were buried. The tombs were of Purbeck marble so the Cosmati phase at Westminster was over. Alongside the tombs, effigies of Eleanor were commissioned from the London goldsmith William Torel. And Torel was also commissioned to make an effigy of King Henry. In May 1291 orders were issued to supply him with the necessary metal and materials for the work.[33]

Torel's gilt bronze effigy survives to provide what has always been the most famous image of the king. It rests on a metal table 7 feet 6 inches long and 2 feet 9 inches wide, studded with the leopards of England. Around the edge, there is an epitaph in French: 'Here lies Henry, once king of England, lord of Ireland, duke of Aquitaine, the son of King John, once king of England, to whom God give mercy. Amen.' This underwhelming inscription (anyway, too high to read), thus said nothing about Henry's kingship. All that needed to be said was in the effigy itself. Henry has lost the rod and sceptre once in his hands, the jewels have been picked from his crown and robe, but he lies there still in golden majesty. The crowned head, framed by curling locks, has a long finely shaped nose, small mouth, short neat beard, narrow yet speaking eyes and a slightly furrowed brow. If Henry looked like this he was handsome indeed, although probably Torel was simply giving an idealized portrait of what a noble and caring king should look like.[34] In that he succeeded brilliantly. If tomb and effigy could not speed Henry towards canonization, they might at least help banish doubts about his kingship.

In the years after Henry's translation, the bays around the Confessor's chapel were filled with the tombs of his family, just as he must have hoped. His daughter-in-law lay at his feet, his eldest son at his head, while beyond, only just outside the chapel, was the high canopied tomb of his second son, Edmund, once, how long ago it seems, the hoped-for king of Sicily. Over the other side of the chapel, before being moved in the next century, was probably the tomb of Henry's half-brother William de Valence, while the chapel also housed the tomb of his daughter Katherine. But in all this one person was conspicuously missing, Henry's queen, Eleanor of Provence.

In 1246, when Henry III elected to be buried in the Abbey, Eleanor had issued a charter saying she wished to be buried there too.[35] Yet when she died in June 1291, she was buried at the nunnery of Amesbury in Wiltshire. During her widowhood, Eleanor had often stayed at the monastery, a

---

[32] For further discussion see below, 649 n. 23.

[33] *CCR 1288–96*, 171. For the effigies of Henry and Eleanor, see Binski, *Westminster Abbey and the Plantagenets*, 107–10. There is a fine cast of Henry's effigy in London's Temple Church.

[34] However, see the sketch of Henry illustrated in plate 17.

[35] WAM Book 11 (Westminster Domesday), fo. 62v.

daughter house of Fontevraud, and she finally took the veil there in July 1286. Now in her sixties, living comfortably in her own quarters, lapped by the love and liturgy of the nuns, and consoled by the company of two granddaughters, who had also taken the veil, Eleanor had changed her mind. It is surely inconceivable that Edward would have overridden her wishes had she been determined to lie at Westminster. Yet Edward almost certainly approved the change and did nothing to challenge it. At Westminster he wished to celebrate the complaisant queenship of his wife not the combative variety of his mother.[36]

Eleanor of Provence had been a remarkable queen. When she arrived in 1236, no queen had played a part in English political affairs since Eleanor of Aquitaine (as a widow) in the 1190s. Eleanor was aged around twelve on her arrival and, if with high connections, brought no inheritance. Yet, intelligent, courageous and far tougher than her husband, she became a central figure in English politics. Her promotion of the Savoyards, her quarrels with the Lusignans, her struggles to control her eldest son, her support for the revolution of 1258, her role in the king's recovery of power in 1261, her defiance of her husband when he wished to surrender in 1263 and her raising an army to rescue him after his capture at Lewes fully justified the admiring tones in which, on her death, she was described by the Westminster chronicler. She was a 'noble *virago*'.[37]

Of course, Eleanor would never have played the part she did without the space afforded by her indulgent husband. She knew as much. In a poem written by her chaplain, John of Howden, after Henry's death, he appears in a list of great men. He is not credited, like them, with famous deeds. He is remembered rather for 'overflowing in giving like a living fountain'.[38] Eleanor may have changed her mind about her burial, but she had acted to hasten Henry's passage through purgatory. At Havering in 1274, her chaplain was told to mention Henry's soul in every mass.[39] Eleanor also came to believe in Henry's potential sanctity. In Trevet's story, when Edward expressed doubts about the miraculous cure for blindness, she angrily told him to leave the room. It may also be that till her death Eleanor cherished a precious relic of her husband. This brings us to the story of Henry's heart.[40]

---

[36] Howell, *Eleanor of Provence*, 309–10, has a judicious discussion of why Eleanor was buried at Amesbury. Her heart went to the Franciscans in London with whom her daughter Beatrice (the wife of John of Brittany) was buried.

[37] Westminster, *Flores*, 72, echoing here Margaret Howell's moving conclusion to her biography: *Eleanor of Provence*, 312. The chronicler also describes her as 'religiosa'.

[38] John of Howden, 510, lines 4003–4. I am grateful to Alice Rio for help with the translation.

[39] *CPR 1281–92*, 378.

[40] It is possible that Eleanor is remembered on Henry's tomb. When the underside of the brass platform bearing the effigy was examined in 1871, an engraving of a queen was found together with a young nun, both praying towards an unfinished figure, perhaps the Virgin. Is this meant to be Eleanor and one of the grandchildren with

In 1291, braving death by shipwreck, as the abbey's cartulary put it, the abbess of Fontevraud came to England. She returned with 'a most excellent treasure, namely the heart of the illustrious king of England of famous record'.[41] The handing over of Henry's heart was recorded in a letter issued by his son on 11 December. Edward explained how he had learnt that, when at Fontevraud (in 1254), Henry had left his heart to the monastery. The abbess had now come to England to redeem the promise. Accordingly, on 10 December the heart had been handed over to her in the Abbey in the presence of the abbot of Westminster, two bishops, Edmund and William de Valence.[42] The precise sequence of events here is unknown. Given Henry's body was uncovered in 1290, was his heart removed then? Or, as I think more likely, was it removed on his death in 1272?[43] But if so, why so long before going to Fontevraud? Was it because Eleanor kept her husband's heart by her side until her own death in June 1291?[44]

Although subject to some despoliation, as we have mentioned, Henry's tomb remained largely intact and undisturbed until 1871. In that year, the then dean of Westminster, A.P. Stanley, decided to examine the tombs in the Confessor's chapel of both Henry and Richard II.[45] In Richard's case the aim was to establish whether there was indeed a body in the tomb, in Henry's the opportunity arose from a desire to give the effigy a clean. Thus it was that on 24 October 1871, Henry's effigy and its 'table-bed' were carefully removed from the tomb and (it must have been an extraordinary sight) hoisted up to the triforium where the work of 'cleansing' could be carried on without interruption.[46] One point immediately emerged, namely the remarkable thickness of the metal, 1 inch on the bed, 3 to 4 inches on the effigy, testimony to Torel's concern

---

her at Amesbury praying for Henry's soul? For discussion, see Howell, *Eleanor of Provence*, 311–12. The engraving is illustrated in plate 21.

[41] BN MS Latin 5480, fo. 4. For what follows, see Howell, *Eleanor of Provence*, 304, 306–7, 310. The abbess was also seeking Eleanor's own body for burial at Fontevraud, so at the mother house rather than the daughter.

[42] WAM 6318B, with *CPR 1281–92*, 463, for the enrolment.

[43] For Henry's efforts in 1268 to establish and pay the arrears of the money owed to Fontevraud, see TNA E 159/43, m. 2d (image 0086). The debt amounted to £1,022.

[44] As suggested by Margaret Howell. This was not the end of the heart's travels, at least by repute. A heart, claimed as Henry's, escaped the destruction of the tombs at Fontevraud during the French Revolution and, through a tortuous process, by 1980 was in the possession of a convent of Ursuline nuns in Edinburgh. When I saw it then (with Michael Clanchy and Robert Bartlett) it was encased in a lead, heart-shaped container and appeared, through a hole in the container's side, to be like a small lump of pumice or desiccated wood. For the heart's escape and travels, see Pommier, *Observations sur une Relique*.

[45] For what follows, see Stanley, 'On an examination of the tombs of Richard II and Henry III', 317–22. And for recent discussion, Rodwell and Neal, *The Cosmatesque Mosaics*, ii, 476–9.

[46] The bed and effigy were not fixed in any way and were simply held in place by their weight.

for their durability. The effigy weighed 12 cwt and the bed 8 or 9 cwt. 'The united strength of nine men, with the help of pulley blocks, was required' to raise them to the triforium. With the bronze table thus removed, the tomb chest was found to be covered by three slabs of Purbeck marble, one on the north side nearly 8 feet long running the whole length of the chest.

The next steps took place on 14 November, 'the Dean having returned to London'. Stanley now directed the two smaller slabs of marble covering the south side of the tomb chest to be removed and this at last exposed the coffin, the chains for lowering it into the chest being still in place. It was of wood and was 6 feet 1 ½ inches long, 1 foot 10 ½ inches wide at the head, and 1 foot 9 inches at the foot. Under a thin coating of black dust, it was covered by a cloth of gold, 'woven in two alternating patterns of great beauty, consisting of striped stars and eight foils'. On a subsequent examination two days later on 16 November, part of the cloth was turned back and the coffin lid was shown to be 'a beautiful slab of hard oak, smoothly wrought to almost a polish'. The lid was not nailed down and was held in place simply by its weight. If it was the original coffin, this would have facilitated the inspection of the body in 1290. Henry, 581 years later, was now in danger of another inspection. Stanley tells us that, after the examination on 16 November, 'it was determined to reassemble on Monday 28 inst.,[47] that the coffin-lid might be removed and the contents seen and carefully investigated'. Had this occurred, Henry's body would quickly have disintegrated through the action of the air, much as happened to Edward I's body when his tomb was opened in 1774.[48] But Henry was spared. 'The meeting', Stanley continues, 'took place on the 28th as arranged, and the slabs were again removed, when a feeling was found to prevail that there did not seem, upon historical grounds, to be sufficient motive to warrant the opening of the coffin. The project was therefore abandoned, the whole of the tomb finally closed in, and the effigy and bed replaced in their position over it.'[49] I find this rather moving. Had I been there, I hope I would have raised my voice in favour of allowing Henry to rest in peace.[50]

---

[47] No doubt after the dean had inspected his diary.

[48] The cloth of gold on Henry's tomb, Stanley tells us (p. 319), soon lost much of its strength 'through action of the air'. Two fragments of silk, preserved at the Abbey, have been thought to come from the cloth of gold covering the tomb, but this is now discounted: Rodwell and Neal, *The Cosmatesque Mosaics*, ii, 478.

[49] Stanley, 'On an examination of the tombs of Richard II and Henry III', 322. For stories connected with both this episode and Stanley's exploration of royal tombs in general, see volume 1, 57, and nn. 202–3.

[50] The effigy and base were removed for safety during the 1939–45 war, but the tomb chest was not disturbed. This was when the photograph was taken of the praying queen engraved on the underside of the base, as illustrated in Howell, *Eleanor of Provence*, plate 9.

## THE OBITUARIES

The obituaries written of Henry show how contemporaries perceived both good and bad in his character and rule. The earliest, composed at Tewkesbury, on that false rumour of his death in 1263, was wholly favourable. Henry was a lover and adorner of the holy church and a generous giver of alms to the poor. He was also a restorer of 'peace and quiet' and even (here reflecting his recovery of power in 1261) a 'vigorous governor of the kingdom'.[51] Osney abbey's verdict, after Henry's actual death in 1272, was more nuanced. He had reigned for fifty-six years and twenty days and had done many 'wonderful things *mirabilia*'.[52] Unfortunately these are unspecified. Earlier in the chronicle Henry had been described, like the prophet Job, as '*simplex* and God fearing' (*vir simplex erat et timens Deum*).[53] He had founded a house for Jews converted to Christianity. He was also 'the father of the poor'. At one feast of All Souls he had ordered his servants to go out and gather 10,000 paupers to feed and been astonished when told it was impossible to find so many.[54] In the obituary itself, the chronicler did not mention the poor, but he did say that Henry 'above all kings before him loved the beauty (*decor*) of the house of God and divine service'. He then added, more depressingly, 'he loved aliens above all English men and enriched them with innumerable gifts and possessions'.[55] In his final remarks, Thomas Wykes also entered a qualification. As we have seen, he thought of Henry migrating at once to the heavenly mansions. He was full of praise for Westminster Abbey. Yet he also observed that when Henry's body, royally dressed, was carried to its grave it 'shone forth with greater splendour dead than appeared before while he was living'![56] Not surprisingly, the Westminster Abbey chronicle had no such reservations but it did hint at Henry's tribulations and even his lack of worldly wisdom. God and those who adhered faithfully to him would know how great was Henry's 'innocence, patience and devotion in the service of the Saviour'.[57] An *epithalium*, perhaps written by a monk of Westminster, concluded a rather anodyne set of verses by saying Henry was 'just, pacific, merciful and chaste'.[58] The chastity, a result both of

[51] Carpenter, *Reign of Henry III*, 260, and above, 268.

[52] Osney, 253–4.

[53] This is the subtitle of Stephen Church's biography of Henry in the Penguin Monarchs series: *Henry III: A Simple and God-Fearing King*. At 144 pages, it is a good antidote to these two volumes. The word *simplex* could either be a compliment as with many holy men, meaning honest and straightforward, or it could be a criticism meaning foolish, or it could be something in between; see volume 1, 166.

[54] Osney, 77, and volume 1, 166, 297.

[55] Osney, 253–4.

[56] Wykes, 252.

[57] Westminster, *Flores*, 28.

[58] Preserved in the annals of Hailes abbey: BL Cotton MS Cleopatra D III, fo. 47 (Hailes, 81).

Henry's piety and devotion to his queen, was indeed worth stressing. The absence of mistresses and bastards marked him out as very different from his father and grandfather.

One might have thought Henry's reputation as a peacemaker would hardly survive the civil war, but it did. The Furness abbey chronicler, writing probably in the 1290s, was able to forget the war altogether. Having praised Henry's piety in the usual terms, and described him as a 'lover and executor of peace and equity', he added that 'in all the days of his life there was an abundance of peace and happiness'.[59] Walter of Guisborough, writing a little later, was more measured. He praised Henry's generous almsgiving to the poor, the building of Westminster Abbey and his 'great devotion in God', but added he was '*simplex* in the administration of temporal affairs'.

The final obituary based on any knowledge was by Nicholas Trevet. He was writing in the 1320s but, born around 1258, the son of one of Henry III's judges, he was well informed. Trevet provides the only physical description we have of the king. Henry was of medium height, compact of body and with the lid of one eye dropping down over the pupil.[60] In terms of Henry's character, Trevet echoed Guisborough's balance between simplicity and piety. 'This king was considered to be as little prudent in secular affairs as he was great in devotion to God.' Having then said that Henry heard three sung masses a day and attended more privately, Trevet told the story of the meeting with King Louis where the two kings discussed the rival merits of masses and sermons.[61] Trevet's conclusion was that Henry was 'physically sturdy but reckless in his actions'. However, since he had a happy ending many thought he was like the lynx in Merlin's prophecies who penetrated all things. Whether Henry would have been altogether happy with the analogy one wonders.[62] He would certainly have been disappointed with his place in Dante's *Divine Comedy*, a work completed at much the same time as Trevet was writing. For here Henry was indeed in purgatory, though at least he was with other failed rather than downright evil rulers and just 'sitting apart' rather than being actually punished. The description of him as being 'of simple life' was also better than being called plain stupid.[63] But with Dante too there was a sting in the tail. He went on to say that from Henry came 'better issue', a clear reference to Edward I.

After his obituary of Henry, Trevet himself went straight on to the character of Edward. The contrast was marked. Edward 'was a man of

---

[59] Furness, 563.

[60] In Matthew Paris's drawing of Henry it is his left eye. In the sketch in plate 17, it is his right. See Volume 1, 56–7, where the condition is discussed.

[61] Trevet, 279–80; Gransden, *Historical Writing*, 501–7.

[62] Matthew Paris also compared Henry to a lynx, one penetrating every purse: Paris, iv, 511, a reference I owe to Richard Cassidy.

[63] Dante's *Purgatorio*, lines 1301–2: 'vedete il re de la semplice vita seder là solo, Arrigo d'inghilterra'.

tried prudence in the handling of affairs'.[64] According to another chronicler, Edward offered his own criticism of his father. On the day of his coronation, he removed the crown from his head and said he would wear it no more until he had recovered the lands given away by Henry to earls, barons, English knights and aliens.[65] Edward certainly tried to build up the landed estate of the crown and was judicious in his distribution of patronage.[66] There was an immediate contrast in the gifts of deer and wood from the royal forests. In his last full regnal year, Henry had made around 180 of them. In his first full year back in England, Edward's total was just 20.[67] Edward also began a reform of the realm, his model, an implicit criticism of his father's rule, being the inquiries, legislation and other measures of the years 1258–9.[68] No wonder, looking back, Wykes felt the contrast between the decision of Edward's parliaments and the dither and delay of Henry's.

This contrast between father and son was given visual expression in their full-length portraits dating from about 1300 in the sedilia of Westminster Abbey.[69] Here Henry is dignified certainly, he raises his hand to make a point or give a blessing, but he is old, his hair and beard (longer than in the effigy) are grey. He has nothing like the authority and latent power of Edward's adjoining portrait. Instead of looking down like Henry, Edward stares ahead, his locks still golden, his big chin given life by sprouting hairs, his gloves, unlike his father's, beautifully embroidered and behind him, framing his image, the lions of England. Of course, Henry was not always old, but even in youth he had been lethargic, hence the way he stayed so long under the tutelage of Hubert de Burgh.

Looking at what was said about him in the obituaries and at the critique inherent in Edward's rule, it becomes easier to understand why the stream of miracles dwindled and dried up. In terms of his personal religiosity, Henry's claims to sanctity were just as good as Louis IX's. Yet whereas Louis's religion made him a king committed to good government and reform of the realm, with Henry there was a much more limited connection. The obituaries thus contrasted the strength of Henry's religion, on the one hand, with his temporal failings, on the other, rather than thinking that the 'good' in the one fostered 'good' in the other. The knowledge of such failings must have discouraged any miraculous afterlife.

[64] Trevet, 281.

[65] Stubbs, *Constitutional History*, ii, 109 n. 2; Prestwich, *Edward I*, 91; Morris, *A Great and Terrible King*, 115 and n. 30.

[66] For Edward's patronage, see Prestwich, 'Royal patronage under Edward I'; Spencer, 'Royal patronage and the earls', and his *Nobility and Kingship*, 87–93.

[67] These are my figures. For a broader contrast, see Spencer, 'Royal patronage and the earls', 26–31.

[68] This is a major theme in Maddicott, 'Edward I and the lessons of baronial reform'.

[69] There are many images online. I think the paintings are of Henry and Edward but that has been questioned.

Perhaps it might have been different had Henry been martyred at
Evesham, but, as it was, his conduct in his last years did little to enhance
his reputation for secular wisdom.

One wonders too whether Edward himself was altogether supportive.
He had given his father a magnificent tomb, but he had taken his time
about it. He may also have left Abbot Ware to shoulder the cost. Edward
equally took his time over the actual translation of his father's body. Did
he really want Henry with all his failings canonized? He was sceptical
about one miracle, as we have seen. He also lost interest in the Confessor
and the Abbey. He rarely attended the feast of the Confessor's birth on
5 January, although Henry was always there. Edward never completed the
great church despite the injunction in Henry's will back in 1253. Instead,
his money was spent on the castles in Wales.[70]


## AN ASSESSMENT

The picture given of Henry in the obituaries was, therefore, mixed.
The same had been true earlier with Matthew Paris, on the one hand
impressed by Henry's piety, on the other infuriated by his rewards to
foreigners. Henry did not fit into either model of kingship advanced by
Paris at the start of his Life of Edward the Confessor. He was not one of
the kings who were mighty and very bold, like Arthur, Edmund Ironside
and Cnut. But his alleged lack of wisdom meant he was neither amongst
the kings, like the Confessor, who were 'more wise, peaceable and
moderate', although clearly he came nearer to the second model than
the first. This difficulty of categorization helps to explain why Henry has
left little stamp on the public mind, indeed become almost a forgotten
king.[71] At Westminster, while the 700th anniversary of Montfort's parliament and the 900th anniversary of the Confessor's Abbey were
both celebrated, the anniversaries of Henry's Abbey in 1969 and his
death in 1272 passed unnoticed.[72] He was not a warrior king like Richard
the Lionheart. He was not a 'bad' king like King John. He was not a
'great' king like Edward I. He was not a hopeless and hapless king, like
Edward II. He was not a canonized king like Louis IX. Over the years,
I have often had this kind of conversation: 'What are you working on?'
'Well, I am trying to write a biography of King Henry III.' 'Oh, which
one is that?'

---

[70] Rather than spend it on the Abbey, Edward's money also went on the abbey of Vale
Royal he had founded in Cheshire: Colvin, *History of the King's Works*, i, 248–53.

[71] Hence the subtitle of Darren Baker's biography, with its vigorous defence of the king:
*Henry III: The Great King England Never Knew It Had.*

[72] However, Westminster Abbey did celebrate both the 800th anniversary of Henry's
birth in 2007 and the 750th anniversary of the dedication of his church in 2019. The anniversary of his birth was also marked by a conference at King's College London.

If this biography has done anything, I hope it has shown how utterly wrong is this Henrician obscurity. The wonderful source material for the reign, and especially the flow of letters on the chancery rolls, means we can come closer to Henry than to any other medieval king. That does not, of course, make his record any the more impressive. He failed to recover the continental possessions of his predecessors. Within England, his rule led directly to the revolution of 1258. In 1258–9 he made only one attempt to break free from baronial control (in trying to bring back Bishop-elect Aymer to England) and that was singularly ill-judged. In 1260 he had to be told by Louis IX it was his duty to return to England. In 1262, with storm clouds gathering back home, he went on pilgrimage to Burgundian shrines. In 1263, to the queen's indignation, he surrendered to Montfort without a fight. In the subsequent warfare between 1263 and 1267 the fighting was done and victory ultimately secured by his son, not himself. Following the end of war in 1267, his performance was sometimes just as wayward as in the years of his personal rule.

And yet, for all this, much can be said in Henry's defence. By the time he assumed full power in 1227, the loss of Poitou had been added to the loss of Normandy and Anjou, making the recovery of the continental empire all the more difficult. In domestic politics Henry had far less freedom of action than earlier kings. The definitive version of Magna Carta was now in place making arbitrary rule less easy and stopping up some sources of revenue. With a far smaller income from land as well, Henry was much less wealthy than his twelfth-century predecessors and needed grants of general taxation in a way they had not. Since such taxation required the consent of parliament, Henry was the first king who had to deal with parliamentary power.

Henry's difficulties were also increased by the politics of the minority. They spawned the view that parliaments, if need be, should choose the king's chief ministers. They also laid the foundations for all the hostility generated by Henry's patronage of foreigners, for in the minority and again between 1232 and 1234 it was lawless foreigners who seemed to disturb the peace of the kingdom. The end of the Anglo-Norman realm, meanwhile, meant that, with a few exceptions, the English nobles were without continental possessions and thus native born.[73] They could thus feel as English as everyone else.

The minority had one other unfortunate consequence. Growing up as king, surrounded by ministers eager to retain and exploit his favour, was a difficult environment in which to hone political skills. Much of Henry's 'simplicity' must have been innate (as was his passivity), but it was reinforced by these conditions. Henry, nine when his father, King John, died, eleven when his mother left England, can also have learnt little from his

---

[73] But for exceptions and the 'gradual uncoupling of aristocratic ties', see Power, 'The Treaty of Paris (1259) and the aristocracy of England'.

parents. John, at the very least, could have taught his son not to trust everything he was told.

Against this background did Henry do so badly? To the charge, so often made, of wasting his resources, he could point to the county of Chester's acquisition for the crown. To the charge he had failed to recover the lost provinces in France, he could say at least that his expedition of 1253–4, by a mixture of campaign and conciliation, had saved Gascony after Montfort's harsh rule had threatened its loss. Both the Lusignans and Peter of Savoy played a large part in the Gascon success, so here was some justification for the patronage they received. Peter, apart from safeguarding the interests of Lord Edward, played a large part in the king's recovery of power in 1261 and would have commanded the army mustered to rescue Henry after Lewes, had it ever invaded.

In defending his domestic policies, Henry himself rightly stressed the peace of his reign, a peace, he said, for which he had laboured ceaselessly. There was here both calculation and personality. Henry wished to avoid 'the wars and hostilities' suffered by the kingdom before his time, referring here, of course, to all the strife under his father. Henry was also, as contemporaries said, a *rex pacificus*. Outside moments of petulant temper, he was affable and (save in things closest to his heart) pliable. He also coveted an easy and comfortable life. The resulting style of kingship, ideal in some ways for the post-Magna Carta age, made a large contribution to the domestic peace. Henry did not, in the fashion of his father, harry magnates to pay their debts, seize their property without lawful process, take hostages to ensure their good behaviour and demand money to escape his rancour and recover his goodwill. Likewise, he did not, in the fashion of his son, challenge his magnates to show 'by what warrant' they held their liberties in the field of local government. Indeed, he allowed magnates to expand their local power at the crown's expense. If the oppressions of both royal and baronial officials, and the protections offered to favourites, meant Henry's peace could be portrayed as peace with injustice, at least the absence of civil war (essentially for the whole period from 1217 through to 1263) created the conditions for a fast-expanding network of markets and fairs, an explosion of the money supply, the building and rebuilding of great churches and a rise in the population, although that may have left an increasing section of the peas-antry living on the edge of subsistence and starving in years of bad harvest.[74] However difficult it was to get justice against the king's favour-ites, the reign saw a gigantic increase in cases brought into the king's courts by ordinary people litigating against each other according to the forms of the common law. In the fine roll of 1221/2 over forty people purchased

---

[74] For markets and fairs, see Samantha Letters, *Gazetteer*, and her 'Markets and fairs in medieval England: a new resource'. For the money supply, see Bolton, *Money in the Medieval English Economy*, 151–4.

writs to further such common-law actions. Fifty years later, in the last full year of the reign, the number was over 1,770.[75]

Domestic peace was linked to an absence of foreign war. As a result, the reign saw a beneficial reshaping of England's relations with its neighbours. This would have been impossible without Henry's pacific character. A more aggressive and martial king might well have reasserted John's overlordship over Scotland, intervened in Ireland, completed the conquest of Wales and made a much greater effort to recover the lost territories in France. Instead, there was a long period of Anglo-Scottish peace, while Henry's campaigns in Wales were very much last resorts. In 1267 his desire for peace between Christian peoples played a part in the recognition of Gwynedd's ruler, Llywelyn ap Gruffudd, as prince of Wales. Meanwhile, the Treaty of Paris ushered in thirty-five years of Anglo-French peace. Without the family friendship he established with Louis IX, the peace would have been impossible. Henry's conduct on his visits to Paris in 1254 and 1259 had been perfect.

Even after 1258, something can be said in Henry's favour. His relationship with Louis ensured the latter's support in the struggle to recover power in 1260–1, with the money sent under the terms of the Treaty of Paris making a vital contribution. Also important in assuring a benevolent neutrality was Henry's relationship with his son-in-law Alexander III of Scotland. The tactics that secured 1261's triumph – the standing on the defensive and waiting for the baronial coalition to fall apart – owed much to Henry's pacific disposition and perhaps also something to his judgement. If such tactics had no place in the fighting to come, Henry might at least think the disaster of 1263 was the result less of his own failings than of Edward's quarrels with his old followers. Henry himself had done his best to reach a settlement with Simon de Montfort and had failed only because Montfort demanded the Provisions of Oxford's total restoration. In the war after Evesham, Henry lasted out the siege of Kenilworth and, if he accepted and profited from the policy of disinheritance, became also a voice for peace and reconciliation.

Throughout the period Henry had one great strength. No one doubted, as all the obituaries show, that he was a most Christian king, a *rex Christianissimus*. Here the contrast with King John was mercifully stark and probably owed much to Henry's desire to avoid his father's misfortunes in this life and fate in the next. True, in some ways Henry's religiosity played him false. Confident that his alms, his masses and the Confessor's intercession would see him right with God, he sometimes thought he could

---

[75] For this increase see volume 1, 528; Moore, 'Fine rolls as evidence for the expansion of royal justice', 66–71, and Hartland and Dryburgh, 'Development of the fine rolls', 198–9; Brand, *Origins of the English Legal Profession*, 24. The writs purchased on the fine rolls are but a small proportion of the whole, no records surviving of the ordinary writs 'of course' which initiated most litigation.

achieve the impossible, notably over Sicily. The same confidence meant he never thought, like Louis IX, that reform of the realm and redress of grievances were necessary to save his soul. Yet if Henry's piety sometimes hindered the business of kingship, it greatly strengthened his position as king.

Of this Henry was very aware, for he did all he could to make his piety public. When he travelled Henry announced his arrival in towns with large distributions of alms, made gifts to the neighbouring friaries, hospitals and religious houses, and lit up shrines and services with numerous candles. No previous king had given so many precious cloths to St Albans abbey and yes (in answer to his question) they had all, as doubtless elsewhere, been marked with his name. Not surprisingly, stories about Henry's almsgiving and masses spread far and wide, as did admiration for all he was doing at Westminster Abbey. If his reverses showed the limits of 'soft power', without his reputation, so genuine yet also so calculated, as a *rex Christianissimus*, it is doubtful whether he would have survived the years after 1258. King John had been deposed by the rebels in 1215. In the next century both Edward II and Richard II would be deposed and murdered. Simon de Montfort, ruthless and extreme, must have yearned to depose Henry. Yet he made no formal move to do so.[76] Henry's character and reputation made it impossible. They shielded Henry, as his arms could never do, from Montfort's might. Henry owed his victory to the valour of his son, but he also owed it to himself.

What of the reign's legacy? In terms of England and its neighbours, there was none. The new relationships with Wales, Scotland and France did not survive the century. Equally, while attempts to impose councils on the king, with some echoes of the Montfortian period, were attempted under Edward II and Richard II, they were just as unsuccessful. The solution to bad kingship became deposition, the one thing Montfort had not attempted. In other areas, for good or ill, the legacy was considerable. Henry's treatment of the Jews prepared the way for their expulsion from England in 1290. His rewards to Lusignans and Savoyards did much to tinge and taint English national feeling with hostility to foreigners, as did Montfort's exploitation of the issue. The massacre at Evesham and Montfort's gruesome death anticipated the violence of late medieval politics. More positively, the common law went from strength to strength. The tax-based parliamentary state, foreshadowed under Henry, achieved by his son, formed the basis for England's late-medieval and post-medieval polity.

So we leave Henry in his various guises as though dappled in different colours through a stained-glass window: being crowned, the anxious boy in Matthew Paris's drawing, by archbishop Langton in 1220; feeding paupers

---

[76] What would have happened after a Montfortian victory at Evesham may be another matter.

and kissing the feet of lepers before setting out on his 1230 expedition to Brittany; taking the shameful oaths at Burgh in the days before Hubert's fall; insulted by Simon de Montfort at Saintes in 1242 – 'you should be kept apart like Charles the Simple'; deciding the lions beneath the throne at Westminster would be more 'sumptuous' in bronze rather than marble; giving 'like a living fountain' to his queen and his Savoyard and Lusignan kin; processing with the Holy Blood to Westminster in 1247; making his speech to the assembled sheriffs at the exchequer in 1250; ordering his jester to be thrown into the bath at Bath; listing in friendly conversations with Matthew Paris all the baronies he could remember; behaving with such *debonereté* in his meetings with Louis IX; quailing in 1258 before the barons when they marched into Westminster Hall; surrendering tamely to Montfort in 1263; battered with swords and maces at Lewes; rescued, wounded, at Evesham; and, finally, surely the apotheosis, translating the Confessor's body to his new shrine in the new Abbey.

Henry was warm-hearted, emotional, courteous, accessible, humorous, profligate, angry sometimes but easily appeased, ambitious sometimes but pacific and physically lazy, in defeat quiescent rather than defiant, interested in detail but, in the secular sphere, lacking the intelligence to use it effectively, a king with a high sense of regality's outward show, but sometimes a low sense of its actual practice, a connoisseur of art and architecture, a lover of beautiful things and of the people closest to his heart, a king *simplex* in the sense of being pious and innocent but *simplex* too in being naive and foolish.

In the profusion of its decoration, its homage to the Confessor, its celebration of kingship, its welcome to all people, its connections with France and Rome, and even in the uncertainties of the design (so it quite lacks the confident precision of its French models), Westminster Abbey breathes Henry's spirit. There were failures. The Holy Blood never became a popular relic.[77] The Confessor never became England's national saint. Between Henry's favourite image of the Confessor giving his ring to the pilgrim and that of George slaying the dragon, there was ultimately no contest. Yet the coronation still takes place in the church Henry created. The Abbey remains his great achievement.

---

[77] For a full discussion, see Nicholas Vincent's 'Epilogue' to his *Holy Blood*, 186–201. The Abbey itself, however, despite Edward's failure, was finished, the nave in the fourteenth century, the western towers in the eighteenth. Henry would have been delighted at the way the nave paid tribute to his own work by following its design.

# GLOSSARY

**amercement**    What would now be called a fine.

**assize of**    The most popular of all the common-law assizes,
**novel**    assize just meaning legal action. With decision by a
**disseisin**    jury before the king's judges, and commenced by a
writ often only costing 6d, it provided a quick remedy
for those who believed they had been disseised
(dispossessed) of land they held freely (so not in
villeinage), 'unjustly and without judgement'. See below
**writ**.

*beaupleder*    A fine levied at the start of a court session to escape
penalization for mistakes in giving evidence.

**chancery**    The office travelling with the king responsible for writing
and sealing the charters, letters and writs through which
he governed the country. See also **letters patent**,
**letters close** and **writs**.

**common law**    At the heart of the common law were 'common
pleas', legal actions, that is (like novel disseisin),
coming before the king's judges and following the same
procedures throughout the kingdom, hence their being
'common'.

**Courts**
*the court coram*    The court travelling with the king presided over by a
*rege*    professional judge, later called the court of king's bench.
In the period of reform and rebellion the president was
sometimes the chief justiciar. The court heard cases
about the rights of the king and offences (like attacks on
their property) committed against magnates and ministers. Litigants could pay standard sums to have their
cases transferred to the court.

*the court of*    The court, usually fixed at Westminster, presided over by
*common pleas /*    professional judges, hearing civil litigation according to
*the bench*    the forms of the common law.

| | |
|---|---|
| *itinerant justices / justices in eyre / the general eyre* | Eyre just means a visitation. A general eyre was when, divided into circuits, the whole country was visited by the itinerant justices. It could take years to complete. The judges heard both common-law civil pleas and crown pleas, the latter involving cases of serious crime and investigations into the rights of the crown. Writs to bring civil pleas before the eyre only cost 6d. |
| *justices of assize* | In the intervals between general eyres, litigants could purchase writs to have their cases heard in the localities by justices who just heard common-law assizes. |
| *county court* | Presided over by the sheriff, it usually met once a month. It dealt with the preliminary stages of crown pleas before they went up to the justices in eyre. It could hear pleas of trespass, debt, detention of chattels and land, though most land pleas were heard by the justices of assize, eyre and bench. |
| *hundred court* | It met every three weeks and was presided over either by the sheriff or the lord or lord's bailiff. (For the many hundreds in private hands, see above, 134). It heard cases of minor disorder which did not breach the king's peace and were not thus pleas of the crown. Its jurisdiction was much the same as the county court above. See also **tourn**. |
| *honourial court* | Name given by historians with some contemporary warrant to the court held by a lord, usually a baron, for his 'feudal' tenants, the tenants, that is, who held from him by knight service (see above, 111 n. 9). It could meet once a month. It heard disputes over the tenure of the land held from the lord and between the lord and the tenants over the services owed. Lords forcing attendance at these courts and also at private hundred courts became a major issue under Henry III. |
| *manorial court* | Held by the lord of the manor for the peasants living within the manor. Dealt with disputes over customs and services and the tenure of land. Might try minor cases of disorder against the lord's peace. See also **infangenthief**. |
| *church courts* | These had jurisdiction over criminous clerks, property held in free alms, the moral offences of the laity (including disputes over wills) and matters concerning the order and discipline of the clergy. The clergy constantly complained of encroachments by the king on the jurisdiction of their courts. |

**demesne farming / demesne manor**   In the twelfth century, lords often leased out manors. In the thirteenth they took them in hand (in demesne) and sought to increase the area (the demesne of demesne manors) they directly exploited as opposed to it being held by tenants, hence demesne farming. The aim in part was to exploit the rising market for agricultural produce.

**disseisin**   Dispossession. See **assize of novel disseisin** above.

**distraint**   Action to force someone to do something, usually by seizing crops and farm animals. 'Distraint out of fee' by a lord was when the person distrained did not hold his land from the lords's fee or honour. See **honour**.

**escheat**   Land that has come into the king's hands by forfeiture or failure of heirs.

**exchequer**   Great office fixed at Westminster responsible for exacting the king's annual revenue and auditing each year all the debts owed him. The results of the annual audit were recorded on documents called pipe rolls. A great deal of material about the exchequer's business was recorded on the exchequer's memoranda rolls. There were also receipt and issue rolls recording the money coming in and going out.

**eyre**   See *itinerant justices* under **Courts**.

**farm**   A fixed annual payment owed for a county, hundred, town, manor or some other bailiwick. The county farm, owed by the sheriff, was derived from the profits of pleas in the county and hundred courts and various traditional payments. Royal manors had once made a major contribution but by 1258 most of these were run separately. See **increment**.

**fee**   See **honour**.

**honour**   The entity composed of the baron's demesne manors and the land held from him by tenants holding by knight service (see above, 111 n.9). Also described as the baron's fee.

**increment**   A fixed sum charged above a farm.

**infangenthief**   A liberty or privilege held by many lords and attached both to manors and private hundreds. It entitled them to hang thieves caught red-handed within the boundaries of the manor or hundred.

**letter close**   A letter issued by the king's chancery closed or sealed up. The usual form of the king's orders with thousands issued each year.

| | |
|---|---|
| **letter patent** | A letter issued by the king's chancery with the king's seal hanging beneath and so open or patent as opposed to being sealed up. Much used for proclamations. |
| **liberty** | A privilege held from the king, often involving some jurisdictional right. |
| **return of writs** | A liberty entitling a lord to exclude the sheriff from his hundreds and sometimes also the lands in his fee or honour. |
| **suit of court** | Attendance at court. Lords compelling attendance at their courts – raising new suits – was much complained about under Henry III. |
| **tallage** | A tax the king could impose at will on his manors and towns. |
| **tourn** | The Easter and Michaelmas sessions of the hundred court which far more people were expected to attend than the ordinary three-weekly sessions. See **view of frankpledge**. |
| **view of frankpledge** | Held at the Michaelmas session of the hundred court. It was a check to see that unfree peasants were in tithings, the groups of ten or twelve adult males sworn to keep the peace and bring a criminal within their ranks to justice. The amercements arising from the view were a considerable source of revenue. |
| **wardrobe** | The chief financial office travelling with the king. It received, stored and spent the money for his day-to-day expenses, drawing for funds both on the exchequer and sheriffs and other local officials. |
| **wardship** | The right of a king or lord to control the estate of an underage heir who held from him by knight service. |
| **writ** | In Latin '*brevis*'. Writs took the form of letters close (see above) and the terms were sometimes used interchangeably. However, writ was the common usage in legal contexts and it was through the purchase of writs, usually so called, that the common legal actions were initiated. See **assize of novel disseisin**. |

Appendix 1

# THE CHRONOLOGY OF THE COSMATI WORK AT WESTMINSTER ABBEY

There has long been debate about the chronology of the Cosmati work at Westminster Abbey. While everyone agrees that the great sanctuary pavement before the high altar was laid down in 1268 (it is securely dated by its inscription), very different views have been expressed about the rest of the work. One hypothesis is that the shrine base (with its surrounding pavement) was finished in time for the translation in 1269. Henry III's tomb was also a work of this phase and was thus made in his own lifetime.[1] A contrary hypothesis is that the base, if begun before 1269, was incomplete at the time of the translation and was finished ten years later in the reign of Edward I. Work on Henry's tomb began at the same time.[2] It is always possible that some new documentary or archaeological evidence will emerge in favour of one or other of these hypotheses, but for the moment, my own view sits somewhere between the two. On balance, I believe that the shrine base and surrounding pavement were finished for the great ceremony in 1269. Henry's tomb, on the other hand, I believe, was constructed after his death.

## THE DATE OF THE SHRINE BASE

The strongest argument that the shrine base was incomplete at the time of the translation lies in the inscription, which seems to give a date in the late 1270s. Apart from a surviving portion on the east end of the base, the inscription is now only known from a copy made by the fifteenth-century Westminster monk, Richard Sporley. He sets it out in five verses as follows:

*Anno milleno domini cum septuageno*
*Et bis Centeno cum completo quasi deno*
*hoc opus est factum quod Petrus duxit in actum*

---

[1] This is argued in Rodwell and Neal, *The Cosmatesque Mosaics*, with a preliminary summary of their views in volume 1, xxiii-xxviii and their conclusion as to chronology in volume 2, 596–600.

[2] For this view, with different shades of emphasis, see Carpenter, 'King Henry III and the Cosmati work', 189–90 (reprinted as chapter 20 in my *Reign of Henry III*) and Binski and Bolgia, 'The Cosmati mosaics at Westminster', especially 36–7, 54–8. For an earlier discussion, see Binski, 'The Cosmati at Westminster', 6–34 with, for the dating, especially 13–19 and 21–2.

*Romanus civis homo causam noscere si vis*
*Rex fuit henricus sancti presentis Amicus.*[3]

In the thousandth year of the Lord, with seventy
and twice a hundred with ten nearly complete,
this work was made which Peter brought into being,
a Roman citizen. O man if you wish to know the cause
the king was Henry, friend of the present saint.[4]

Just how these verses were arranged around the base's inscription course
can be debated, but their most obvious reading is that the date indicated is
1279 – a thousand plus seventy and two hundred, plus ten nearly complete.
This would fit neatly with the other evidence (discussed below) that the
Cosmati did indeed return to England in June 1279 to make Henry III's
tomb. That does not mean they had to make the shrine base from scratch,
for 'made, *factum*', in the inscription most probably indicated the date of
completion. How much completion was necessary, on this hypothesis, is
impossible to say. But that Henry is described as the 'cause' of the work,
suggests it was begun in his reign and presumably enough was there in 1269
to make the translation possible. Whatever the Cosmati did to the base on
their return in June 1279, they finished it (while presumably working too on
Henry's tomb) within nine months, assuming the year 1279 in the inscription
followed papal and English chancery practice, and thus started with the
feast of the Annunciation on 25 March and finished on 24 March following.

The hypothesis that the base was unfinished in 1269 and was completed
ten years later is thus strong and may be right. Yet a contrary view can still
be canvassed, a view positing that the base was there complete for the 1269
translation. A key piece of evidence here is provided by the references in the
building accounts to paviors working 'before the shrine of Saint Edward, *ante
pheretrum Sancti Edwardi*' in a period between December 1266 and December
1269.[5] A natural reading of this evidence is that the Cosmati base was
finished and the pavement was being laid around it.[6] The pavement would
hardly have been laid if work on the base was still continuing.[7] If, as I have
suggested, the Cosmati first came to England between 1261 and 1263, the
only period between 1258 and 1267 when the kingdom was at peace and

[3] Rodwell and Neal, *The Cosmatesque Mosaics*, ii, 385 where there is a photograph of the
original manuscript. The transcription above expands Sporley's abbreviations but retains his
capitalization. He inserts 'iii' above '*henricus*' but that would not have been there in the original inscription. In the last line Sporley places an oblique stroke between '*henricus*' and '*sancti*'.
[4] There are various translations but the gist is usually the same.
[5] *BAH*, 422–3, 426–7.
[6] The term 'feretory' could be applied to the base as well as the golden reliquary. For an
example see TNA C 66/ 50 m.4 (*CLR 1240–5*, 134), repeated in TNA E 403/ 1205, m.1d.
Referred to here is the marble base of the Confessor's shrine which was later replaced or
completely remodeled by the Cosmati version.
[7] That there are no further references to the paviors in the accounts after December
1269 suggests their work too was finished.

Henry in full control of government, then they had plenty of time to complete their work.[8] The Cosmati were thus unlike the goldsmiths labouring on the reliquary who had at the last moment to attach all the jewels recovered from pawn and not surprisingly did not finish in time.[9] Even if the Cosmati had other pressing commissions in Italy, it is hard to believe they would have wanted or been permitted to depart before their work was over.

So we come back to the inscription.

*Anno milleno domini cum septuageno*
*Et bis Centeno cum completo quasi deno*
*hoc opus est factum quod Petrus duxit in actum*
*Romanus civis homo causam noscere si vis*
*Rex fuit henricus sancti presentis Amicus.*

In the thousandth year of the Lord, with seventy
and twice a hundred with ten nearly complete,
this work was made which Peter brought into being,
a Roman citizen. O man if you wish to know the cause
the king was Henry, friend of the present saint.

Is the 1279 apparently given here really watertight? Could the inscription indicate 1269 after all? Some historians have argued just that by suggesting that Sporley made a mistake in his transcription. Instead of '*septuageno*, seventy', he should have written '*sexageno*, sixty'.[10] Sixty, plus ten nearly complete, thus takes us to 1269. I myself, however, believe there is a different solution.[11] Sporley's transcription is perfectly correct (always the most likely hypothesis) but it was nonetheless meant to indicate 1269 not 1279. This is because the '*cum completo quasi deno*, with ten nearly complete' meant that what was nearly complete was a ten *within* the 1270. Hence the date is 1269. In the past, along with others, I have discounted this idea. It requires '*cum*' to be used in a sense different from the first '*cum*' in the inscription, which plainly indicates an addition. But this may be to demand too high a standard of conformity and consistency. An inscription of this type was 'sui generis', with the author having to juggle meaning, rhyme and meter in a confined space. Here the author, having taken 1270 as the year from which the deduction was to be made, had then to work out how to get to 1269. He found it difficult to fit into the rhyme a subtraction of a single year. Only numbers in tens (ten, twenty, thirty etc) will give endings in 'eno' to rhyme with 'septuageno'. Equally, of course, he could not indicate that the '*completo quasi deno*', should itself be

---

[8] See above, 227–30.

[9] See above, 552, 558.

[10] See most recently Payne and Rodwell, 'Edward the Confessor's shrine in Westminster Abbey: its date of construction reconsidered', and with a modification of the hypothesis in their 'Edward the Confessor's shrine in Westminster Abbey: the question of metre'.

[11] I am grateful to Daniel Hadas for discussing this possibility with me.

subtracted from 1270 because that would have given him 1261. The solution, as we have said, was to use *'cum completo quasi deno,* with ten nearly complete' to mean that a ten was nearly complete within the 1270. Thus the date is 1269. The repetition of *'cum'* gave the inscription a certain symmetry while the *'deno'* preserved the rhyme.[12] In all this, the author was not bothered by the inconsistency in the use of *'cum'*. Everyone knew, especially with the reference to King Henry, that 1269 was meant. Unlike 1279, it was a famous date, the date of Abbey's consecration and the Confessor's translation. 1279 had no significance at all.

The solution suggested here gains strength from the parallel inscription on the sanctuary pavement for there too the date (1268) is reached by establishing an initial date and then deducting from it, in this case deducting four from 1272.

*Christi milleno bis centeno duodeno*
*cum sexageno, subductis quatuor, anno*[13]

In the year of Christ one thousand twice one hundred twelve with sixty, four having been subtracted.

The two inscriptions thus work in exactly the same way. Both begin by establishing an initial date:

Base: *Anno milleno domini cum septuageno et bis Centeno*
Pavement: *Christi milleno bis centeno duodeno cum sexageno . . . anno*

Both then subtract from it

Base: *cum completo quasi deno*
Pavement: *subductis quatuor*

The parallel with the sanctuary pavement helps explain one final point, namely why the author chose to work with the date 1270 in the first place. It was partly because he shared with the author of the sanctuary inscription a delight in reaching a date by a subtraction. It was also because the year in both cases was probably the year in which the inscription was inserted.[14]

[12] In Rodwell and Neal's suggested plan of how the inscription was laid out around the base, one can see how the 'cum' (apart from keeping the metre), fits neatly into the space: *The Cosmatesque Mosaics*, 386.

[13] This is the transcription in Flete, 113. Four letters from this part of the inscription survive in the pavement and much of the rest is recoverable from indents: Rodwell and Neal, *The Cosmatesque Mosaics*, i, 121.

[14] The suggestion has been made that the sanctuary inscription was put up after Henry's death, the 1272 referring to its year. But the inscription is so typical of Henry, I rather think he had it inserted during the long months he spent at Westminster in 1272. The fifty-six achieved by deducting the four from the sixty made a nice allusion to the fact this was now his fifty-sixth regnal year.

A conclusion. If the inscription does indicate 1279, then clearly the base was finished in that year. However, for the reasons I have suggested, I now incline to the view that the inscription means 1269 after all. In that case, the base was present in all its splendour for the Confessor's translation, just as Henry would have wished it to be. Next year, with a fitting sense of achievement, the inscription was put up recording the date of completion, naming the craftsman, and telling everyone that King Henry, 'friend of the present saint', was the 'cause'.


## HENRY'S INITIAL BURIAL PLACE

The idea that Henry's tomb was constructed in his lifetime is argued in Warwick Rodwell's and David Neal's book on the Cosmati work at the Abbey. It is closely related to a further hypothesis, namely that Henry was buried initially not in the tomb, although it was ready, but in a chamber beneath the floor of the Confessor's chapel, a chamber just to the west of the shrine. In rebuilding the Confessor's church, Henry, it is suggested, had carefully preserved this space because it was where the Confessor had lain before his translation in 1163. Henry wished to lie there too while he awaited his own canonization. He would then be translated to his Cosmati tomb, having conceived it from the first as a shrine.[15]

These are intriguing ideas but they confront many difficulties. The evidence for a chamber beneath the floor in the Confessor's chapel comes from examinations of the area by ground-penetrating radar.[16] These may suggest some kind of arched structure beneath the shrine's altar step, but only a full-scale excavation (clearly impossible) would reveal whether this was indeed the roof to some formal chamber.[17] In any case, whatever was there, it was not the place of Henry's burial in 1272.

The key pieces of evidence for the site of Henry's initial burial are twofold. First, there is the official letter sent to King Edward telling him of his father's death. This states that Henry's 'body . . . was handed for burial before the

[15] Rodwell and Neal, *The Cosmatesque Mosaics*, i, xxvii–viii, 254–7; ii, 554–5, 575–6, 588–91.

[16] Rodwell and Neal, *The Cosmatesque Mosaics*, i, 252–7. This section is by Erica Utsi, who carried out the GPR survey. I am most grateful to her for email correspondence about the results.

[17] Sometime between 1237 and 1267 (the date of his episcopate) Richard, bishop of Bangor, issued an indulgence for those who prayed, made offerings and attended mass in the chapel constructed under the chapel of the blessed Edward: WAM Book II (Westminster Domesday), fo. 405. Whether the space underneath Edward's shrine (thought to be two metres wide) was large enough for a chapel as well as a tomb chamber may be questioned. Another more likely candidate for the chapel of St Edward referred to here (as Paul Binski has pointed out to me) is the chapel constructed to house the work on the new reliquary. This had paintings of 'the history of Saint Edward' and was almost certainly known as St Edward's chapel. The chapel had a lower chamber adorned with religious paintings and may well have become known as the chapel beneath the Confessor's chapel. See *CR 1251–3*, 290, and Colvin, *History of the King's Works*, i, 148.

great altar, *corpus suum . . . ante magnum altare traditum fuerat sepulturae*'.[18] Second, there is Thomas Wykes, who states that Henry's body rested 'in the same place where [the Confessor] was buried for many years before his translation, *in eodem loco quo* [the Confessor] *sepultus extiterat et annis plurimis priusquam ipsius reliquiae translatae fuissent in scrinium*'.[19] Putting the two pieces of evidence together, it would seem that Henry was buried, yes, in the place where the Confessor's body had rested, but this place was in front of the great or high altar of the Abbey, not beneath the pavement in the Confessor's chapel.

In discussing this evidence, Rodwell and Neal suggest that all the official proclamation meant was that the body 'lay in state before the high altar'. It was then buried in the Confessor's original tomb beneath the chapel pavement, this being the place to which Wykes refers.[20] Yet those writing at the time clearly thought Henry's body *was* buried before the high altar, not simply displayed there. The annals of Winchester, copied by those at Waverley and Worcester, thus say Henry '*sepultus est . . . ante magnum altare*'.[21] The annals of Osney say much the same: '*sepultus est . . . ante altare autenticum*' ('high' is the usual translation of '*autenticum*' in this context).[22] The London alderman, Arnold fitzThedmar, on the spot, writing soon after the event, and probably a witness, was equally clear: 'his body was given for burial before the great altar. Having been buried, the archbishop of York celebrated mass, '*corpus suum . . . datum est sepulture . . . ante magnum altare. Ipso vero sepulto . . .*'.[23]

As for Wykes (perhaps also present), he says that Henry was buried in the place where the Confessor had lain but gives no indication as to where that was. There is no evidence at all it was beneath the pavement in front of the new shrine.

Rodwell and Neal also suggest an alternative explanation. They observe that in Westminster Abbey's own chronicle Henry is said to be buried not '*ante*' but '*coram*' the high altar. Translating '*coram*' as 'in the vicinity of', they suggest this is compatible with burial *behind* the high altar and thus in the chamber beneath the floor of the Confessor's chapel.[24] This seems to stretch the meaning of '*coram*' much too far, the usual translation being 'in the presence of' or 'in the face of'. In any case, there is good evidence that at this time '*coram*' and '*ante*', in the context of the altar, were synonymous. In 1268, as we have seen, Henry gave Abbot Ware some compensation for the costs of bringing from Rome 'the pavement to be put in the church of Westminster *coram* the king's great altar there'. As the place of the pavement itself shows, '*coram*' here meant 'before' the high altar, not behind it.[25]

---

[18] *F*, ii, 497.

[19] Wykes, 252–3.

[20] Rodwell and Neal, *The Cosmatesque Mosaics*, ii, 575–6.

[21] Winchester, 112; Waverley, 378; Winchester/Worcester, 461.

[22] Osney, 253.

[23] FitzThedmar, 153–4 (Stone, FitzThedmar, no. 1087).

[24] Westminster, *Flores*, 27–8; Rodwell and Neal, *The Cosmatesque Mosaics*, ii, 576.

[25] TNA C 66/87, m. 17 (*CPR 1266–72*, 338).

Rodwell and Neal also canvas a third explanation. According to their reconstruction of the layout, the chamber beneath the pavement in the Confessor's chapel would have been before the high altar of the old church pulled down by Henry III. They suggest this has caused 'confusion' in the minds of medieval and modern historians.[26] The implication seems to be that Henry was buried before the high altar, but the altar in question was not the existing high altar but the altar of the long-gone previous church. I find this highly unlikely.

The evidence that Henry's resting place was somewhere before the new high altar is thus pretty well conclusive. Putting that together with Wykes's statement, it follows that the 'place *locum*' where the Confessor had lain before his translation was also situated there. Since, as Rodwell and Neal point out, there is no archaeological evidence for a Confessorial tomb beneath the current Cosmati floor, the '*locum*' referred to by Wykes was either elsewhere before the high altar or a tomb chest above the ground like that illustrated in Matthew Paris's *Life of St Edward the Confessor*.[27] If the Confessor's body had lain in a tomb chest, it could, of course, have been moved around during the rebuilding of the Abbey. Whether its place in 1272 before the high altar was anywhere near its place in the old church seems impossible to say, as does whether the chest dated from 1066 or from later. Whatever the case here, Wykes's statement, as we have said, provides no grounds for believing that the Confessor had once lain in a place beneath his new shrine.[28]

None of this disproves the idea that Henry's tomb was finished in his lifetime. But, and here we come to the crux, if that was the case, why was he not buried there? The Confessor's old tomb may have been venerated but it was separated from his shrine by the high altar and could hardly compare with the place of honour enjoyed by Henry's new tomb at the Confessor's side. Much here depends on how one views Henry's outlook and the wider culture of the age. I, at least, find it impossible to believe that Henry would have planned his tomb as a shrine and laid down he was

[26] Rodwell and Neal, *The Cosmatesque Mosaics*, ii, 576.

[27] This is no. 75 of the images of Paris's *La Estoire de Seint Aedward* put online by Cambridge University Library, and see also nos. 64 and 71: https://cudl.lib.cam.ac.uk/view/MS-EE-00003-00059/64, 71, 75

[28] The Dunstable annals (Dunstable, 362) state that Eleanor of Castile was buried 'in the tomb of King Henry, *in sepulcro Henrici regis*'. This has led to the suggestion that she was buried in the old tomb of the Confessor and indeed lay in the supposed chamber beneath the Confessor's new shrine: Badham, 'Edward the Confessor's chapel', 200; Rodwell and Neal, *The Cosmatesque Mosaics*, i, 257, ii, 383. However, both the Abbey's own chronicle and the London annals state specifically that Eleanor was buried at Henry's feet, indeed the London annals 'at the feet of the monument of the lord King Henry': Westminster *Flores*, 71–2; London, 99. This was, of course, the site of Eleanor's eventual tomb, but both chronicles, in detailed accounts, are clearly referring to her burial there on the day of the funeral. I suspect the Dunstable annals meant to say no more than that Eleanor was buried close to Henry's tomb.

to be moved there once canonized, as Rodwell and Neal suggest. Such presumption would have seemed utterly scandalous. Nor was there any parallel in France. Louis IX, while deciding to be buried at Saint-Denis, had no tomb constructed for himself at all, let alone a shrine.[29] The magnificent gilded structure, topped with an effigy, was made under his son, King Philip III.[30]

In developing their argument, Rodwell and Neal give considerable weight to questions of style, yet these seem inconclusive. There are certainly parallels, in terms of detail, between the shrine base and Henry's tomb (for example in the design of capitals and colonettes),[31] but these hardly prove the two were made at the same time. The very different overall appearance of the two structures, the tomb quite lacking the base's 'gothic' features, seem more compatible with the tomb having been constructed later.[32]

## THE DATE OF CONSTRUCTION FOR HENRY'S TOMB

My own belief is that the work on Henry's tomb started in 1279. The evidence here comes from the chronicler Nicholas Trevet. He states that Edward, 'having returned from France, made his father's tomb *reparari* with the stones of jasper, which he had brought with him'. In fact, Trevet places this visit in 1280 but Edward did not go to France in that year.[33] The visit to which Trevet refers was evidently that between May and June 1279 when Edward went to Amiens for business connected with the Treaty of Paris. Rodwell and Neal discount this evidence on two grounds, neither

---

[29] By contrast, Louis IX had made for his children splendid tombs at Royaumont. With the abbot, Matthew of Vendôme, he was responsible for the lines of effigies at Saint-Denis commemorating his Carolingian and Capetian forbears. See Wright, 'A royal tomb program in the reign of St. Louis'. Wright argues, however, that the initiative for the Saint-Denis tombs came chiefly from the abbot and was designed to bind the dynasty more closely to the monastery and increase the likelihood that Louis would decide to be buried there himself.

[30] For Louis's tomb, see Geoffroi de Beaulieu, 78, 125; Wright, 'The tomb of Saint Louis', and for a different view of the effigy (recumbent, it is argued, rather than standing), see Brown, 'The chapels and cult of Saint Louis', 292–9. Wright (p. 74) suggests the tomb was most likely commissioned between 1274 and 1280. It was in place by 1282. See also Brown, *Saint-Denis: La Basilique*, 393–8. I am grateful to Cecilia Gaposchkin for drawing my attention to the articles by Wright and Brown. For discussion of the monuments at Westminster and Saint-Denis, see Jordan, *A Tale of Two Monasteries*, ch. 5.

[31] For example, Rodwell and Neal, *The Cosmatesque Mosaics*, ii, 323.

[32] Rodwell and Neal, *The Cosmatesque Mosaics*, ii, 440, say that 'the neat abutment' of the mosaics with the steps to Henry's tomb show that the steps were in place when the matrices for the mosaics were cut. I am not entirely convinced the abutment is that neat and in any case the matrices could have been fashioned up to a line marking the place where Henry's tomb was to be.

[33] Trevet, 301. Trevet also places in 1280 an ecclesiastical council at Lambeth which took place in 1281.

conclusive.[34] First they translate '*reparari*' as 'to be repaired' and suggest Edward was doing no more than applying additional ornamentation to the already existing tomb. But while the verb *reparare* can mean 'repair', there are also contexts where its meaning is clearly that of 'make' or 'construct'. That, I believe, is its meaning here.[35]

Rodwell and Neal secondly focus on the description of the stones as 'jasper'. This, they say, 'is a brecciated limestone occurring in a wide range of colours'. *But*, jasper like this, they continue, does not appear at all in the Cosmati work at Westminster. Trevet cannot, therefore, be referring to the stones brought for the substantive work on Henry's tomb. Instead, Rodwell and Neal argue that what the king brought back was simply a bag of jasper stones which were then used as tiny decorations on the already existing structure. The decorations are now lost but Rodwell and Neal suggest where they might have been placed.[36] The problem with this hypothesis is that the monks of Westminster themselves did not view 'jasper' in Rodwell's and Neal's terms. Instead, they saw it as integral to the Cosmati work at the Abbey. So much is clear from the history of the Abbey by the monk John Flete, who narrates how Abbot Ware brought back to England the stones '*porphyriticos, jaspides, et marmora de Thaso*', which formed the pavement before the high altar.[37] To my mind, Trevet likewise saw jasper as integral to the Cosmati work and was using the term as a shorthand for all the stones used to make Henry's tomb.

This view is strengthened if we consider the matter from the point of view of Trevet and his chronicle. He was writing in the 1320s, over forty years after events. Hence no doubt his mistake over the exact year. But he remains a good source and must have been using information recorded earlier. Trevet was born around 1258 and so was about twenty in 1279.[38] What is more, his father was employed by Edward I as a judge. In November 1278 he was commissioned to hear a case in Dorset.[39] Trevet was, therefore, well placed to know what Edward brought back to England. But that bringing would never have been worthy of record had it merely involved stones for some fairly minuscule surface decoration. No! Trevet is recording the arrival of the main materials for the construction of Henry's tomb.

A further context is provided to the events of 1279 if we go back to Abbot Ware. His connection with Italy and, we may suggest, the Cosmati

---

[34] Rodwell and Neal, *The Cosmatesque Mosaics*, ii, 577–8.

[35] Wilson, 'A monument to St Edward the Confessor', 165: 'The verb *reparare* ... was thoroughly ambiguous, for it could relate either to repair or totally new work.' For a good example, in a tomb context, where 'reparacio' seems synonymous with 'make', see TNA C 62/51, m. 12 (about the construction of the tomb for Edward's son Henry).

[36] So they formed 'cabochons' attached to the tesserae on the east end of the lower tomb chest.

[37] Flete, 113.

[38] For Trevet, see Gransden, *Historical Writing*, 501–7.

[39] *CPR 1272–81*, 294.

did not end with the pavement placed before the high altar in 1268. In the mid-1270s he was once more at the papal court on the king's affairs.[40] In 1279 itself he was one of those accompanying Edward to France.[41] Perhaps, therefore, Ware once again fixed up the contract with the Cosmati and then, with the king, met up with them on their way to England. He thus returned with the materials and the workers just as he had for the pavement.

The year 1279, as the starting date for Henry's tomb, helps resolve another puzzle. If the tomb was finished by 1272 it took some eighteen years before Henry's body was moved there in 1290. A start in 1279 makes the interval far more explicable. Rodwell and Neal suggest the tomb would have taken three to four years to complete.[42] In that case, it was not finished, quite probably, until 1283. But in 1283 and for the next few years, Edward was preoccupied with the affairs of Wales, following its conquest in the campaign of 1282. Between 1286 and 1289 he was in Gascony. The translation, as we have seen, took place at an appropriate time soon after Edward's return.[43]

A final note on payment. No evidence has yet come to light to show that Edward himself paid for Henry's tomb, although the money spent on the tombs of his sons John and Henry is recorded. Later, Edward certainly commissioned the effigy placed in the 1290s on top of the Cosmati structure. This is not conclusive proof that Edward did not pay. In the 1270s the workings of royal finance became labyrinthine and the cost could easily have been met, in ways now unknown, by Italian bankers.[44] I wonder, however, whether it was Abbot Ware who raised the money, just as, according to Keepe, he paid for the stones for the high altar pavement.[45] The motives of the abbot and the king in giving Henry so splendid a tomb we have already seen.

A conclusion. Henry had surely marked out where his tomb was to be in the Confessor's chapel but, on current evidence, there are no strong grounds for thinking it was constructed before his death. Rather the evidence points to construction having started in 1279.

---

[40] For Ware's missions overseas, not all necessarily to Rome, see *CPR 1272–81*, 3, 46, 128, 159, 162, 171, 231; *CCR 1272–9*, 117, 349 (a letter home from the papal court in 1276 where he had hoped to meet Charles of Anjou, now king of Sicily), 417; TNA C 62/52, m. 11 (100 marks expenses); TNA C 62/55, m. 7. For suggestions about the role of Charles of Anjou, see Binski, *Westminster Abbey and the Plantagenets*, 103–4.

[41] *CPR 1272–81*, 308.

[42] Rodwell and Neal, *The Cosmatesque Mosaics*, ii, 591.

[43] For the circumstances, see above, 626.

[44] For something of the labyrinth, see Carpenter, 'The English royal chancery', 58–62, pages I now find hard to follow myself!

[45] On his going to Rome, he did receive money from the king for his expenses so perhaps that made some contribution: *CPR 1272–81*, 231; TNA C 62/52, m. 7; TNA C 62/55, m. 11.

# Appendix 2

# HENRY'S WILL

Henry III drew up a will shortly before his departure for Gascony in 1253.[1] No text of any subsequent will survives and there appears no reference to one. Whether he made a second will is thus uncertain. Some of the provisions of the 1253 will could still have been valid in 1272, notably those concerning the Confessor and the Abbey. In 1253, Henry left his soul to God, the Virgin Mary and all the saints and then asked for his body to be buried in 'the church of the blessed Edward at Westminster', 'notwithstanding' his earlier decision to lie in the Temple church. He also offered to the Confessor the white vestments from his chapel, a silver image of the Virgin within a tabernacle and a cross given him by the countess of Kent (Hubert de Burgh's widow). As for the fabric of the Abbey, Henry 'left and committed' it to Edward for completion.[2]

Other provisions in 1253 had been superseded, in part thanks to Henry's achievements. There was no need any longer for 500 marks to be raised from the king's jewels for the completion of the Confessor's shrine. It was now essentially complete. Accordingly, Peter of Winchester, the last keeper of Henry's wardrobe, wished to sell the jewels, not to raise money for the shrine, but to support poor members of the late king's household.[3] As for the crusade, the 1253 will had stated that both Henry's gold treasure and his cross should be taken out to the Holy Land. The treasure, of course, by 1272 was long gone, mostly spent in Gascony, but at least Edward had taken Henry's cross on his crusade and had secured his father's absolution from sins truly confessed from the church of Jerusalem.[4]

If Henry did make a fresh will, he would have needed a new set of

---

[1] The will only survives as a fifteenth-century copy in a volume of miscellaneous historical material put together by the historian and antiquary William of Worcester. The volume is now at the College or Arms: Arundel 48, with the will on fo. 139. It is printed from there in *Foedera* (*F*, i, 496). I am grateful to the archivist of the College of Arms, James Lloyd, for locating the volume for me from the old reference in *Foedera*. An original of John's will does survive. See Church, 'King John's testament'. The preceding documents copied in Arundel 48 are texts of the Provisions of Oxford and Henry's 1261 complaints against the council and the council's replies. I have not collated them word for word but they seem coterminous with the texts printed in *DBM*, 96–113 and 219–39.

[2] Edward was left other vestments and ornaments from the chapel.

[3] Carpenter, 'King Henry III and the Cosmati work', 190.

[4] See above, 567–8.

executors for only one of those chosen in 1253 was still alive. That one was the queen. In 1253 she had very much pride of place for she was to have custody of the realm until Edward came of age. There would have been no equivalent role in 1272. Edward had made his own arrangements and they pointedly excluded his mother.

In the 1253 will Henry asked the queen and Edward to reward his knights and servants 'according to the merits of their service', an attention to merit not always present in Henry's distribution of patronage. When it came to paying his debts, the queen was to do this from the king's lands, although saving the interests of the heirs. The latter were to pay off any residue when they came of age. The will showed no concern for acts of injustice Henry might have committed and thus reflected one of the problems of his rule. The implication was that the Virgin Mary, the Confessor and the Abbey would look after his spiritual health. Another problem with Henry's rule was reflected in the personnel of the ten executors in 1253. They included only one great English baron, although this one was important – Henry's brother, Richard of Cornwall. Half the executors were foreigners, the queen herself, her uncles Archbishop Boniface and Peter of Savoy, the king's half-brother Aymer, bishop-elect of Winchester, and the keeper of the wardrobe, Peter Chaceporc. The remaining four executors were John Mansel, John, prior of Newburgh (Henry's chaplain), the steward, John de Grey, and the keeper of the seal, Henry of Wingham.

# BIBLIOGRAPHY

## UNPRINTED PRIMARY SOURCES

Full references to unprinted primary sources are given in the footnotes, where BL stands for the British Library, BN for the Bibliothèque Nationale in Paris, TNA for The National Archives at Kew and WAM for Westminster Abbey Muniments. The images cited with the TNA references are those on the University of Houston's Anglo-American Legal Tradition website (http://aalt.law.uh.edu/) where, thanks to the initiative and enterprise of Robert Palmer, images of a large proportion of the unprinted thirteenth-century government records preserved in The National Archives appear. (The website also has the records of later centuries.)

The following are the classes of unprinted documents cited from The National Archives.[1]

C 47 (Chancery: Miscellanea)
C 62 (Chancery: Liberate Rolls)
C 66 (Chancery: Patent Rolls)
C 145 (Chancery: Inquisitions Miscellaneous)
CP 25/1 (Court of Common Pleas, General Eyres and Court of King's Bench: Feet of Fines Files)
CP 40 (Court of Common Pleas: Plea Rolls)
DL 25 (Duchy of Lancaster: Deeds, Series L)
DL 42 (Duchy of Lancaster: Cartularies, Enrolments, Surveys and Other Miscellaneous Books)
E 36 (Exchequer: Treasury of the Receipt, Miscellaneous Books)
E 40 (Exchequer: Treasury of Receipt, Ancient Deeds, Series A)
E 101 (Exchequer: King's Remembrancer, Accounts Various)
E 159 (Exchequer: King's Remembrancer, Memoranda Rolls)
E 199 (Exchequer: King's Remembrancer and Lord Treasurer's Remembrancer, Sheriffs' Accounts, Petitions etc.)
E 352 (Exchequer: Pipe Office, Chancellor's Rolls)
E 368 (Exchequer: Lord Treasurer's Remembrancer, Memoranda Rolls)
E 370 (Exchequer: Lord Treasurer's Remembrancer and Pipe Office, Miscellaneous Rolls)
E 372 (Exchequer: Pipe Office, Pipe Rolls)
E 389 (Exchequer: Lord's Remembrancer and Pipe Office: Miscellanea, New Series)
E 401 (Exchequer of Receipt: Receipt Rolls and Registers)
E 403 (Exchequer of Receipt: Issue Rolls)
JUST 1 (Justices in Eyre and Assize: Plea Rolls)
KB 26 (Court of Common Pleas, King's Bench and Justices Itinerant: Early Plea and Essoin Rolls)
KB 27 (Court of King's Bench: Coram Rege Plea Rolls)

---

[1] Some of these classes are in print, either in full Latin or English calendar, and have been consulted simply to verify points.

SC 1 (Special Collections: Ancient Correspondence)
SC 5 (Special Collections: Hundred Rolls and Eyre Veredicta)

# PRINTED PRIMARY SOURCES

*Abingdon The Chronicle of the Monastery of Abingdon, from 1218 to 1304*, ed. J.O. Halliwell (Berkshire Ashmolean Society, 1844).

*AC Annales Cambriae*, ed. J. Williams ab Ithel (Rolls Series, 20, 1860).

'Annalibus Normannicis' 'Ex annalibus Normannicis', ed. O. Holder-Egger, in *Monumenta Germaniae Historica*, Scriptores Rerum Germanicum in Folio 26, ed. G. Waitz (Hannover, 1882), 512–17.

*ANPS Anglo-Norman Political Songs*, ed. I.S.T. Aspin (Anglo-Norman Text Society, 11, 1953).

*AP Placitorum in Domo Capitulari Westmonasteriensi asservatorum Abbreviatio*, ed. W. Illingworth (Record Commission, London, 1811).

*AWR The Acts of the Welsh Rulers, 1120–1283*, ed. H. Pryce with the assistance of C. Insley (Cardiff, 2005).

*BA Building Accounts of King Henry III*, ed. H.M. Colvin (Oxford, 1971).

Barlings, 'Extracts from the Barlings chronicle', in *Chronicles of the Reigns of Edward I and Edward II*, ed. W. Stubbs, 2 vols. (Rolls Series, 76, 1882–3). The Barlings chronicle is found in volume 2 between cxiv and cxvii.

Barnwell, *Liber Memorandorum Ecclesie de Bernewelle*, eds. J.W. Clark and F.W. Maitland (Cambridge, 1907).

Barrow, *EEA Hereford English Episcopal Acta 35: Hereford, 1234–1275*, ed. J. Barrow (Oxford, 2009).

Bartlett, *Rochester Charters The City of Rochester Charters*, ed. P.H. Bartlett (Rochester, 1961).

Battle, *The Chronicle of Battle Abbey*, ed. E. Searle (Oxford, 1980).

*Beauchamp Cartulary The Beauchamp Cartulary Charters, 1100–1268*, ed. E. Mason (Pipe Roll Society, new series, 43, 1980).

*BF Liber Feodorum: The Book of Fees commonly called Testa de Nevill*, 3 vols., with continuous pagination (London, 1920–31).

Boatwright, *1286 Buckinghamshire Eyre, The Buckinghamshire Eyre of 1286*, ed. L. Boatwright (Buckinghamshire Record Society, 34, 2006).

Bower, Walter, *Scotichronicon: Volume 5*, eds. D.E.R. Watt, S. Taylor and B. Scott (Aberdeen, 1990).

*Bracton Bracton de Legibus et Consuetudinibus Angliae: Bracton on the Laws and Customs of England*, ed. G.E. Woodbine, translated with revisions and notes by S.E. Thorne, 4 vols. (Cambridge, MA, 1968–77).

*Bronescombe Register The Registers of Walter Bronescombe (A.D. 1257–1280), and Peter Quivil (A.D. 1280–1291), Bishops of Exeter*, ed. F.C. Hingeston-Randolph (London, 1889).

*Brut Brut Y Tywysogyon or The Chronicle of the Princes: Red Book of Hergest Version*, ed. T. Jones (Cardiff, 1955).

Burton, 'Annales de Burton, AD 1004–1263', in *Annales Monastici*, ed. H.R. Luard, 5 vols. (Rolls Series, 36, 1864–9), vol. 1.

Bury St Edmunds, *The Chronicle of Bury St Edmunds, 1212–1301*, ed. A. Gransden (London, 1964).

*CACW Calendar of Ancient Correspondence concerning Wales*, ed. J.G. Edwards (Cardiff, 1935).

*CAD A Descriptive Catalogue of Ancient Deeds in the Public Record Office*, 6 vols. (London, 1890–1915).

Canterbury/Dover, *The Historical Works of Gervase of Canterbury: Volume 2*, ed. W. Stubbs (Rolls Series, 73, 1879–80), 106–272. This is the overlapping chronicle of Canterbury Cathedral priory and Dover priory but with portions original to each.

*Cartae Baronum Cartae Baronum*, ed. N. Stacy (Pipe Roll Society, new series, 62, 2019).

Cassidy, '1259 pipe roll' R. Cassidy, 'The 1259 pipe roll', 2 vols. (University of London, doctoral thesis, 2012).

CChR *Calendar of Charter Rolls preserved in the Public Record Office, 1226–1300*, 2 vols. (London, 1903–6).

CCR *Calendar of the Close Rolls preserved in the Public Record Office: Edward I, 1272–1307*, 5 vols. (London, 1900–08).

CDS *Calendar of Documents relating to Scotland preserved in Her Majesty's Public Record Office, London: Volume 1, A.D. 1108–1272*, ed. J. Bain (Edinburgh, 1881).

CFR *Calendar of the Fine Rolls of the Reign of Henry III*, available both on the Henry III Fine Rolls Project's website (https://finerollshenry3.org.uk/home.html) and within the *Calendar of the Fine Rolls of the Reign of Henry III, 1216–1242*, 3 vols., ed. P. Dryburgh and B. Hartland, technical directors A. Ciula, J.M. Vieira and T. Lopez (Woodbridge, 2007–9).

*Christopher Hatton's Book Sir Christopher Hatton's Book of Seals, to which is appended a Select List of the Works of Frank Merry Stenton*, eds. L.C. Loyd and D.M. Stenton (Oxford, 1950).

CIM *Calendar of Inquisitions Miscellaneous (Chancery) preserved in the Public Record Office: Volume 1, 1216–1307* (London, 1916).

CIPM *Calendar of Inquisitions Post Mortem and other analogous Documents, 1236–1307*, 4 vols. (London, 1904–13). Unless stated, all references are to volume 1.

Clanchy, *Berkshire Eyre The Roll and Writ File of the Berkshire Eyre of 1248*, ed. M.T. Clanchy (Selden Society, 90, 1973).

*Clare Cartulary, The Cartulary of the Augustinian Friars of Clare*, ed. C. Harper-Bill (Suffolk Record Society, 11, 1991).

CLR *Calendar of the Liberate Rolls preserved in the Public Record Office: Henry III, 1226–1272*, 6 vols. (London, 1916–64).

Cooper, *1241 Oxfordshire Eyre The Oxfordshire Eyre, 1241*, ed. J. Cooper (Oxfordshire Record Society, 56, 1989).

Cotton, *Bartholomaei de Cotton, Monachi Norwicensis, Historia Anglicana (A.D. 449–1298)*, ed. H.R. Luard (Rolls Series, 16, 1859).

*Court Baron, The Court Baron: Precedents of Pleading in Manorial and Other Local Courts*, eds. F.W. Maitland and W. Paley Baildon (Selden Society, 4, 1890)

CPR *Calendar of Patent Rolls preserved in the Public Record Office: Henry III, Edward I and Edward II, 1232–1327*, 13 vols. (London, 1893–1913).

CPReg *Calendar of Papal Registers relating to Great Britain and Ireland: Volume 1, 1198–1304*, ed. W.H. Bliss (London, 1893).

CR *Close Rolls of the Reign of Henry III preserved in the Public Record Office, 1227–1272*, 14 vols. (London, 1902–38).

CRR *Curia Regis Rolls of the Reigns of Richard I, John and Henry III preserved in the Public Record Office*, 20 vols. (London, 1922–2006).

Crowland, *Memoriale Fratris Walteri de Coventria*, ed. W. Stubbs, 2 vols. (Rolls Series, 58, 1872–3). All references are to volume 2.

CR Supp *Close Rolls (Supplementary) of the Reign of Henry III preserved in the Public Record Office, 1244–1266*, ed. A. Morton (London, 1975).

C&S *Councils & Synods with other documents relating to the English Church. Volume II: 1205–1313*, eds. F.M. Powicke and C.R. Cheney, 2 vols. with continuous pagination (Oxford, 1964).

DBM *Documents of the Baronial Movement of Reform and Rebellion, 1258–1267*, eds. R.F. Treharne and I.J. Sanders (Oxford, 1973).

DD *Diplomatic Documents preserved in the Public Record Office, Volume I: 1101–1272*, ed. P. Chaplais (London, 1964).

Dugdale, *Monasticon* William Dudgale, *Monasticon Anglicanum: A History of the Abbies and Other Monasteries, Hospitals, Frieries, and Cathedral and Collegiate Churches, with their Dependencies, in England and Wales*, eds. J. Caley, H. Ellis and B. Bandinel, 6 vols. (London, 1817–30).

Dunstable, 'Annales Prioratus de Dunstaplia, AD 1–1297', in *Annales Monastici*, ed. H.R. Luard, 5 vols. (Rolls Series, 36, 1864–9), vol. 3. There is now an English translation: *The Annals of Dunstable Abbey*, trans. D. Preest, ed. H.R. Webster (Woodbridge, 2018).

*EHD English Historical Documents: Volume III, 1189–1327*, ed. H. Rothwell (London, 1975).

*ERF Excerpta Rotulis Finium in Turri Londinensi asservatis Henrico Tertio Rege, A.D. 1216–72*, ed. C. Roberts, 2 vols. (Record Commission, London, 1835–6).

*ERW Early Registers of Writs*, eds. E. de Haas and C.D.G. Hall (Selden Society, 87, 1970).

Eubel, 'Der Registerband', K. Eubel, 'Der Registerband', Archiv f. katholisches Kirchenrecht 64 (1890), 1–70.

Evesham, 'The chronicle of Evesham', in D.C. Cox, 'The battle of Evesham in the Evesham chronicle', *Historical Research*, 62 (1989), 337–45. The chronicle is found between 340 and 344.

*F Foedera, Conventiones, Litterae et cujuscumque generis Acta Publica*, ed. T. Rymer, new edition, vol. I, pts. i and ii, eds. A. Clark and F. Holbrooke (Record Commission, London, 1816).

*FA, Inquisitions and Assessments relating to Feudal Aids; with other analogous documents preserved in the Public Record Office, A.D. 1284–1431*, 6 vols. (London, 1899–1920).

Farr, Elrington and Summerson, *1268 Wiltshire Eyre Crown Pleas of the Wiltshire Eyre 1268*, eds. B. Farr and C. Elrington, and H.R.T. Summerson (Wiltshire Record Society, 65, 2012).

FitzThedmar Arnold fitzThedmar, *De Antiquis Legibus Liber: Cronica Maiorum et Vicecomitum Londoniarum*, ed. T. Stapleton (Camden Society, 34, 1846). There is also a forthcoming Oxford Medieval Texts edition, see below under Stone, FitzThedmar.

Flete John Flete, *The History of Westminster Abbey*, ed. J. Armitage Robinson (Cambridge, 1909).

Furness, 'The chronicle of Furness abbey', in *Chronicles of the Reigns of Stephen, Henry II and Richard I*, ed. R. Howlett, 4 vols. (Rolls Series, 82, 1884–90). The chronicle is found in volume 2, 503–83.

Geoffroi de Beaulieu, *The Sanctity of Louis IX: Early Lives by Geoffrey of Beaulieu and William of Chartres*, trans. L.F. Field and eds. M.C. Gaposchkin and S.L. Field (Ithaca, NY, and London, 2015).

*Giffard Register The Register of Walter Giffard, Lord Archbishop of York, 1266–1279*, ed. W. Brown (Surtees Society, 109, 1904).

Gough, *Edward's Itinerary, Itinerary of King Edward the First throughout his Reign, A.D. 1272–1307, exhibiting his movements from time to time, so far as they are recorded*, ed. H. Gough (Paisley, 1900).

Graham, 'Letters of Cardinal Ottoboni' R. Graham, 'Letters of Cardinal Ottoboni', *English Historical Review*, 15 (1900), 87–120.

Grosseteste, '*Statuta*' Walter of Henley, *and Other Treatises on Estate Management and Accounting*, ed. D. Oschinsky (Oxford, 1971). This volume contains Grosseteste's '*Statuta*' between pp. 408 and 415.

Grosseteste, *Templum Dei* Robert Grosseteste, *Templum Dei*, eds. J. Goering and F.A.C. Mantello (Toronto, 1984).

Guisborough *The Chronicle of Walter of Guisborough*, ed. H. Rothwell (Camden Society, 89, 1957).

Hailes M.N. Blount, 'A critical edition of the annals of Hailes (MS Cotton Cleopatra D iii, ff. 33–59v) with an examination of their sources' (University of Manchester, master's thesis, 1974).

Hershey, *Drawings, Drawings and Sketches in the Plea Rolls of the Royal English Courts c.1200–1300*, ed. A.H. Hershey (List & Index Society, special series, 31, 2002).

*Historiae coenobii Burgensis* Walter of Whittlesey, 'Historiae coenobii Burgensis scriptores varii. E codicibus manuscriptis nunc primum editi', in *Historiae Anglicanae Scriptores Varii. E Codicibus Manuscriptis nunc primum editi*, ed. J. Sparke, 3 vols. in 1 (London, 1723). The *Historiae* will be found in volume 2, part 3, between 125 and 216. This is a fourteenth-century continuation of Hugh Candidus and Robert of Swaffham's chronicles of Peterborough abbey.

Hoskin, *EEA, London English Episcopal Acta 38: London, 1229–1280*, ed. P.M. Hoskin (Oxford, 2011).

Jobson, '1261 Oxfordshire Eyre', A. Jobson, 'The Oxfordshire eyre roll of 1261', 3 vols. (University of London, doctoral thesis, 2006).

John de Vignay, 'Ex primati chronicis per Iohannem de Vignay translatis', ed. H. Brosien, in *Monumenta Germaniae Historia*, Scriptores Rerum Germanicum in Folio 26, ed. G. Waitz (Hannover, 1882), 639–71.

John of Howden, L.W. Stone, 'Jean de Howden: poète Anglo-Normand de XIIIᵉ siècle', *Romania*, 69 (1946–7), 496–519.

John of Salisbury, John of Salisbury, *Policraticus of the Frivolities of Courtiers and the Footprints of Philosophers*, ed. and trans. C.J. Nedermann (Cambridge, 1990).

Joinville Jean de Joinville, *Vie de Saint Louis*, ed. J. Monfrin (Paris, 2010), and for an English translation, John of Joinville, 'The Life of St Louis', in *Joinville and Villehardouin. Chronicles of the Crusades*, ed. C. Smith (London, 2008). The chapter numbers are the same.

*Lancashire Lay Subsidies, Lancashire Lay Subsidies . . . from Henry III to Charles II: Volume 1, Henry III to Edward I (1216–1307)*, ed. J.A.C. Vincent (Lancashire and Cheshire Record Society, 27, 1893).

Lanercost *Chronicon de Lanercost, MCCI–MCCCXLVI. E Codice Cottoniano nunc primum typis mandatum*, ed. J. Stevenson (Maitland Club, 1839).

Langtoft *The Chronicle of Pierre de Langtoft, in French Verse, from the Earliest Period to the Death of King Edward I*, ed. T. Wright, 2 vols. (Rolls Series, 47, 1866–8).

Layettes *Layettes du Trésor des Chartes*, eds. A. Teulet, H.-F. Delaborde and E. Berger, 5 vols. (Paris, 1863–1909).

'Letter of Richard, earl of Gloucester', 'Letter of Richard, earl of Gloucester', in *Report of the Manuscripts of Lord Middleton preserved at Wollaton Hall, Nottinghamshire*, ed. W.H. Stevenson (Royal Commission on Historical Manuscripts, 69, 1911), 67–9.

Letters, *Gazetteer Gazetteer of Markets and Fairs in England and Wales to 1516*, ed. S. Letters, 2 vols. (List & Index Society, special series, 32–3, 2003).

*Letters of Adam Marsh The Letters of Adam Marsh*, ed. C.H. Lawrence, 2 vols. (Oxford, 2006).

*Letters of Grosseteste The Letters of Robert Grosseteste, Bishop of Lincoln*, eds. F.A.C. Mantello and J. Goering (Toronto, 2010).

*Life of Saint Guthlac Felix's Life of Saint Guthlac*, ed. B. Colgrave (Cambridge, 1956).

*LNR Historical Papers and Letters from the Northern Registers*, ed. J. Raine (Rolls Series, 61, 1873).

London 'Annales Londonienses', in *Chronicles of the Reigns of Edward I and Edward II*, ed. W. Stubbs, 2 vols. (Rolls Series, 76, 1882–3). The 'Annales Londonienses' are found in volume 1.

*London Eyre of 1244 The London Eyre of 1244*, eds. H.M. Chew and M. Weinbaum (London Record Society, 6, 1970).

*London Eyre of 1276 The London Eyre of 1276*, ed. M. Weinbaum (London Record Society, 12, 1976).

Meekings and Crook, *Surrey Eyre The 1235 Surrey Eyre*, eds. C.A.F. Meekings and D. Crook, 2 vols. (Surrey Record Society, 31–2, 1979–83).

Melrose *Chronica de* Mailros, ed. J. Stevenson (Edinburgh, 1835). The page numbers here are cited with the folio numbers in the facsimile edition: *The Chronicle of Melrose from the Cottonian Manuscript Faustina B IX in the British Museum*, eds. A.O. Anderson and M.O. Anderson (London, 1936). For an analysis of the stages in which the text was constructed, see D. Broun and J. Harrison, *The Chronicle of Melrose. A Stratigraphic Edition. Volume I: Introduction and Facsimile Edition* (Scottish History Society, 2007). There is also a forthcoming new edition of the chronicle edited by J. Reuben Davies.

*Merton College Rolls The Early Rolls of Merton College Oxford*, ed. J.R.L. Highfield (Oxford Historical Society, new series, 18, 1964).

Merton, *Flores Flores Historiarum. Volume 3*, ed. H.R. Luard (Rolls Series, 95, 1890), 239–327.

'Miracula' 'Miracula Simonis de Montfort', in *The Chronicle of William de Rishanger, of the Barons' Wars. The Miracles of Simon de Montfort*, ed. J.O. Halliwell (Camden Society, 15, 1840), 67–110.

*Missale Westmonasteriensis Missale ad usum Ecclesie Westmonasteriensis*, ed. J. Wickham Legg, 3 vols. (Henry Bradshaw Society, 1, 5, 12, 1891–7).

Nangis, *Gesta* 'Gesta sanctae memoriae Ludovici regis Franciae', in *Recueil des Historiens des Gaules et de la France: Tome vingtième*, eds. P.C.F. Daunou and J. Naudet (Paris, 1840), 309–465.

*Opusculum de nobili Simone de Monteforti* 'Opusculum de nobili Simone de Monteforti', in the *Chronica de Mailros*, ed. J. Stevenson (Edinburgh, 1835), 201–16, and *The Chronicle of Melrose from the Cottonian Manuscript Faustina B IX in the British Museum*, eds. A.O. Anderson and M.O. Anderson (London, 1936), fos. 67v–73v.

Osney 'Annales Monasterii de Oseneia, AD 1016–1347', in *Annales Monastici*, ed. H.R. Luard, 5 vols. (Rolls Series, 36, 1864–9), vol. 4.

Paris, *Matthaei Parisiensis, Monachi Sancti Albani Chronica Majora*, ed. H.R. Luard, 7 vols. (Rolls Series, 57, 1872–83).

Paris, *GA Gesta Abbatum Monasterii Sancti Albani*, ed. H.T. Riley, 3 vols. (Rolls Series, 28, 1867–9).

Paris, *HA Matthaei Parisiensis, Monachi Sancti Albani Historia Anglorum*, ed. F. Madden, 3 vols. (Rolls Series, 44, 1866–9).

Paris, *La Estoire Lives of the Confessor*, ed. H.R. Luard (Rolls Series, 3, 1858). Both text and translation of Matthew Paris's *La Estoire de Seint Aedward le Rei* can be found at 1–358 in this volume. For a new translation see *The History of Saint Edward the King by Matthew Paris*, ed. T. Fenster and J. Wogan-Browne (Tempe, AZ, 2008).

Paris's Continuator *Flores Historiarum. Volume 2*, ed. H.R. Luard (Rolls Series, 95, 1890), 426–71. This is the text of the chronicle composed by Matthew Paris's successor at St Albans.

*Patent Rolls 1225–32 Patent Rolls of Henry III preserved in the Public Record Office, 1225–1232* (London, 1903).

Pershore, *Chronicle* 'The Pershore Chronicle', in *Joannis Lelandi Antiquarii de rebus Britannicis Collectanea*, ed. T. Hearne, 2nd edition, 6 vols. (London, 1770), ii, 240–53.

Pershore, *Flores Flores Historiarum. Volume 2*, ed. H.R. Luard (Rolls Series, 95, 1890), 471–505, continuing into Volume 3, 1–6.

Peterborough *Chronicon Petroburgense*, ed. T. Stapleton (Camden Society, 47, 1849).

*Political Songs The Political Songs of England, from the Reign of John to that of Edward II*, ed. T. Wright (Camden Society, 6, 1839), with a new edition edited by P.R. Coss (Camden Society Classic reprints, 1996).

*PQW Placita de Quo Warranto, temporibus Edwardorum I, II et III*, ed. W. Illingworth (Record Commission, London, 1818).

*PR Pipe Roll* Citations to pipe rolls are to volumes published by the Pipe Roll Society. The year in the citation is that which appears on the cover of each volume.

*PROME The Parliament Rolls of Medieval England, 1275–1504*, eds. C. Given-Wilson, P. Brand, S. Phillips, W.M. Ormrod, G. Martin, A. Curry and R. Horrox, 16 vols. (Woodbridge, 2005).

'Processus Legationis' 'Processus legationis in Angliam Guidonis episcopi Sabinensis post-modum Clementis papae IV', in *Papst Clemens IV. Eine Monographie, 1 Teil: Das Vorleben des Papstes und sein Legationregister*, ed. J. Heidemann (Munster, 1903).

*RCWL The Royal Charter Witness Lists of Henry III*, ed. M. Morris, 2 vols. (List & Index Society, 291–2, 2001).

*Reading Cartulary Reading Abbey Cartularies. British Library Manuscripts: Egerton 3031, Harley 1708 and Cotton Vespasian E xxv*, ed. B.R. Kemp, 2 vols. (Camden Society, 5th series, 31, 1986–7).

*Reg. Urban IV Les Registres d'Urbain IV (1261–1264). Recueil des Bulles de ce Pape, publiées ou analysées d'après les manuscrits originaux du Vatican*, ed. J. Guiraud, 4 vols. (Paris, 1892–1958).

*RG Rôles Gascon*, eds. F. Michel and C. Bémont, 4 vols. (Paris, 1885–1906).

*RG Supp Rôles Gascons: Supplément au Tome Premier, 1254–1255*, ed. C. Bémont (Paris, 1896).

*RH Rotuli Hundredorum. Temp. Hen. III et Edw. I, in Turr' Lond' et in Curia Receptae Scaccarij Westm.*, eds. W. Illingworth and J. Caley, 2 vols. (Record Commission, London, 1812–18).

Rishanger *Willelmi Rishanger Chronica et Annales*, ed. H.T. Riley (Rolls Series, 28, 186.

*RL Royal and Other Historical Letters Illustrative of the Reign of Henry III*, ed. W.W. Shirley, 2 vols. (Rolls Series, 27, 1862–6).

*RLC Rotuli Litterarum Clausarum in Turri Londinensi asservati, 1204–27*, ed. T.D. Hardy, 2 vols. (Record Commission, London, 1833–4).

*RLP Rotuli Litterarum Patentium in Turri Londinensi asservati, 1201–16*, ed. T.D. Hardy (Record Commission, London, 1835).

Robert of Boston 'Robert of Boston', in *Historiae Anglicanae Scriptores Varii. E Codicibus Manuscriptis nunc primum editi*, ed. J. Sparke, 3 vols. in 1 (London, 1723). Robert of Boston will be found between 114 and 137 in volume 1.

Robert of Gloucester *Metrical Chronicle of Robert of Gloucester*, ed. W.A. Wright, 2 vols. (Rolls Series, 86, 1887). There is a rendering into modern English in *The Church Historians of England: Volume 5, Pt. 1*, ed. J. Stevenson (London, 1858), 349–81.

*Rolls of Arms, Henry III Rolls of Arms, Henry III: The Matthew Paris Shields c.1244–59; Glover's Roll, c.1253–8 and Walford's Roll c.1273*, eds. T.D. Tremlett and H. Stanford, with additions by A. Wagner (Harleian Society, 113–14, 1967).

Romance of Fulk fitzWarin 'Gesta Fulconis filii Warini', in *Radulphi de Coggeshall Chronicon Anglicanum*, ed. J. Stevenson (Rolls Series, 66, 1875), 277–41.

*RS Rotuli Selecti ad Res Anglicas et Hibernicas Spectantes*, ed. J. Hunter (Record Commission, London, 1834).

'Rules of Robert Grosseteste' *Walter of Henley, and Other Treatises on Estate Management and Accounting*, ed. D. Oschinsky (Oxford, 1971), 386–416.

St Andrews Northampton 'The chronicle of St Andrew's priory, Northampton', in H.M. Cam and E.F. Jacob, 'Notes on an English cluniac chronicle', *English Historical Review*, 44 (1929), 94–104.

St Benet at Hulme *Chronica Johannis de Oxenedes*, ed. H. Ellis (London, 1859).

Saint-Denis 'Extraits des chroniques de Saint-Denis', in *Recueil des Historiens des Gaules et de la France: Tome vingt-et-unième*, eds. J.-D. Guigniaut and J.N. de Wailly (Paris, 1855), 103–23.

*St Frideswide Cartulary The Cartulary of the Monastery of St Frideswide at Oxford*, ed. S.R. Wigram, 2 vols. (Oxford Historical Society, 28, 31, 1895–6).

*Saint Richard of Chichester Saint Richard of Chichester: The Sources for his Life*, ed. D. Jones (Sussex Record Society, 79, 1995).

St Werburgh *Annales Cestrienses or Chronicle of the Abbey of S. Werburg Chester*, ed. R.C. Christie (Lancashire and Cheshire Record Society, 14, 1886).

*Sarum Missal The Sarum Missal in English*, trans. A.H. Pearson (London, 1868).

*SCEP Select Cases in the Exchequer of Pleas*, eds. H Jenkinson and B. Fermoy (Selden Society, 48, 1931).

*SCWR Select Cases of Procedure without Writ under Henry III*, eds. H.G. Richardson and G.O. Sayles (Selden Society, 60, 1941).

*SERHB Special Eyre Rolls of Hugh Bigod 1258–1260*, ed. A.H. Hershey, 2 vols. (Selden Society, 131, 133, 2021).

*SESK The 1258–9 Special Eyre of Surrey and Kent*, ed. A.H. Hershey (Surrey Record Society, 38, 2004).

*Song of Lewes The Song of Lewes*, ed. C.L. Kingsford (Oxford, 1890).

*SPF Select Pleas of the Forest*, ed. G.J. Turner (Selden Society, 13, 1899).

*SPMC Select Pleas in Manorial and Other Seignorial Courts: Volume 1, Henry III and Edward I*, ed. F.W. Maitland (Selden Society, 2, 1888).

*SR Statutes of the Realm, Printed by Command of His Majesty King George Third in pursuance of an Address of the House of Commons of Great Britain; Volume the First* (Record Commission, London, 1810).

Stevenson, 'Robert of Gloucester' *The Church Historians of England: Volume 5*, Pt. I, ed. J. Stevenson (London, 1858), 349–81 (a rendering of Robert of Gloucester's chronicle into modern English).

Stewart, *RJS Royal Justice in Surrey, 1258–1269*, ed. S. Stewart (Surrey Record Society, 45, 2013).

Stewart, *1263 Surrey Eyre The 1263 Surrey Eyre*, ed. S. Stewart (Surrey Record Society, 40, 2006).

Stone, FitzThedmar I.W. Stone, 'The Book of Arnold fitz Thedmar: Appendices' (King's College London, University of London, doctoral thesis, 2016). This contains the text of the forthcoming Oxford Medieval Texts edition of FitzThedmar's book.

Studd, 'Acts of Lord Edward' J.R. Studd, 'A catalogue of the acts of the Lord Edward, 1254–1272' (University of Leeds, doctoral thesis, 1971).

Studd, *Lord Edward's Itinerary Itinerary of Lord Edward*, ed. J.R. Studd (List & Index Society, 284, 1999).

*Swinfield Register The Register of Richard de Swinfield, Bishop of Hereford (A.D. 1283–1317)*, ed. W.W. Capes (Cantilupe Society, 1909).

Tewkesbury 'Annales Monasterii de Theokesberia, AD 1066–1263', in *Annales Monastici*, ed. H.R. Luard, 5 vols. (Rolls Series, 36, 1864–9), vol. 1.

*Three Yorkshire Assize Rolls Three Yorkshire Assize Rolls for the Reigns of King John and King Henry III*, ed. C.T. Clay (Yorkshire Archaeological Society, 44, 1911).

*TR Treaty Rolls. Volume I: 1234–1325*, ed. P. Chaplais (London, 1955).

Trevet Nicholas Trevet, *Annales Sex Regum Angliae*, ed. T. Hog (London, 1845).

Villard, 'Autour de Charles d'Anjou' 'Autour de Charles d'Anjou. Angleterre et Sicile', ed. A. Villard, *Mémoires de l'Institut historique de Provence*, 20 (1945), 25–35.

*Vita Edwardi Secundi Vita Edwardi Secundi: The Life of Edward II*, ed. N. Denholm-Young (Edinburgh, 1957).

Walter of Henley *Walter of Henley, and Other Treatises on Estate Management and Accounting*, ed. D. Oschinsky (Oxford, 1971), 307–85.

*WAR The Welsh Assize Roll, 1277–1284*, ed. J.C. Davies (Cardiff, 1940).

Waverley, 'Annales Monasterii de Waverleia, AD 1–1291', in *Annales Monastici*, ed. H.R. Luard, 5 vols. (Rolls Series, 36, 1864–9), vol. 2.

Westminster, *Flores Flores Historiarum. Volume 3*, ed. H.R. Luard (Rolls Series, 95, 1890), 6–235. This is the continuation at Westminster of the *Flores* composed at Pershore abbey.

Wild, *WA The Wardrobe Accounts of Henry III*, ed. B.L. Wild (Pipe Roll Society, new series, 58, 2012).

Wilkins, *Concilia Magnae* David Wilkins, *Concilia Magnae Britanniae et Hiberniae, Britanniae et Hiberniae Synodo Verolamiensi, A.D. CCCCXLVI ad Londinensem A.D. MDCCXVII*, 4 vols. (London, 1737).

Wilkinson, *HR The Household Roll of Eleanor de Montfort, Countess of Leicester and Pembroke, 1265. British Library, Additional Manuscript MS 8877*, ed. and trans. L.J. Wilkinson (Pipe Roll Society, new series, 63, 2020).

Winchester 'Annales de Monasterii de Wintonia, AD 519–1277', in *Annales Monastici*, ed. H.R. Luard, 5 vols. (Rolls Series, 36, 1864–9), vol. 1.

Winchester/Worcester 'Annales Prioratus de Wigornia, AD 1–1377', in *Annales Monastici*, ed. H.R. Luard, 5 vols. (Rolls Series, 36, 1864–9), vol. 4. The Worcester annals as printed in *Annales Monastici* are from BL Vespasian E IV, which was copied at Worcester from a now lost Winchester chronicle but with Worcester sections inserted.

*Worcestershire Eyre of 1275 The Worcester Eyre of 1275*, ed. J. Röhrkasten (Worcestershire Historical Society, new series, 22, 2008).

Wykes 'Chronicon vulgo dictum Chronicon Thomae Wykes, AD 1066–1289', in *Annales Monastici*, ed. H.R. Luard, 5 vols. (Rolls Series, 36, 1864–9), vol. 4.

## SECONDARY SOURCES

Altschul, M., *A Baronial Family in Medieval England: The Clares, 1217–1314* (Baltimore, 1965).

Ambler, S.T., *Bishops in the Political Community of England, 1213–1272* (Oxford, 2017).

Ambler, S.T., 'Magna Carta: its confirmation at Simon de Montfort's parliament of 1265', *English Historical Review*, 130 (2015), 801–30.

Ambler, S.T., 'The Montfortian bishops and the justification of conciliar government in 1264', *Historical Research*, 85 (2012), 193–209.

Ambler, S.T., 'On kingship and tyranny: Grosseteste's memorandum and its place in the baronial reform movement', in *Thirteenth Century England*, 14 (Woodbridge, 2013), 115–28.

Ambler, S.T., *The Song of Simon de Montfort: England's First Revolutionary and the Death of Chivalry* (London, 2019).

Amt, E., 'Ela Longspée's roll of benefits: piety and reciprocity in the thirteenth century', *Traditio*, 64 (2009), 1–56.

Andenmatten, B., 'Contraintes lignagères et parcours individuel: les testaments de Pierre II de Savoie', in *Pierre II de Savoie 'Le petit Charlemagne' (†1268). Colloque international Lausanne, 30–31 mai 1997*, eds. B. Andenmatten, A. Paravicini Bagliani and E. Pibiri (Lausanne, 2000), 265–93.

Annesley, S., 'Countesses in the age of Magna Carta' (King's College London, University of London, doctoral thesis, 2011).

Annesley, S., 'Isabella countess of Arundel's confrontation with King Henry III', Henry III Fine Rolls Project, Fine of the Month for August 2009: https://finerollshenry3.org.uk/content/month/fm-08-2009.html.

Armstrong, A.S., 'The daughters of Henry III' (Canterbury Christ Church University, doctoral thesis, 2018).

Armstrong, A.S., 'Sisters in cahoots: female agency in the marriage of Beatrice of England and John of Brittany', *Journal of Medieval History*, 44 (2018), 439–56.

Arnold, J.H., *Inquisition and Power: Catharism and the Confessing Subject in Medieval Languedoc* (Philadelphia, 2001).

Asaji, K., *The Angevin Empire and the Community of the Realm* (Osaka, 2010).

Asaji, K., 'The Barons' War and the hundred jurors in Cambridgeshire', *Journal of Medieval History*, 21 (1995), 153–65.

Badham, S., 'Edward the Confessor's chapel, Westminster Abbey: the origins of the royal mausoleum and its Cosmatesque pavement', *The Antiquaries Journal*, 87 (2007), 197–219.

Badham, S., and Oosterwijk, S., 'The tomb monument of Katherine, daughter of Henry III and Eleanor of Provence (1253–7)', *The Antiquaries Journal*, 92 (2012), 169–96.

Baker, D., *Henry III: The Great King England Never Knew It Had* (Stroud, 2017).

Baker, D., *Simon de Montfort and the Rise of the English Nation: The Life of Simon de Montfort* (Stroud, 2018).

Barratt, N., 'Crisis management: baronial reform at the exchequer', in *Baronial Reform and Revolution in England, 1258–1267*, ed. A. Jobson (Woodbridge, 2016), 56–70.

Barratt, N., 'Finance on a shoestring: the exchequer in the thirteenth century', in *English Government in the Thirteenth Century*, ed. A. Jobson (Woodbridge, 2004), 71–86.

Barron, C.M., *London in the Later Middle Ages: Government and People, 1200–1500* (Oxford, 2004).

Barrow, J., 'The ideas and application of reform', in *The Cambridge History of Christianity: Volume III, Early Medieval Christianities c.600–c.1100*, eds. T.F.X. Noble and J.M.H. Smith (Cambridge, 2008), 345–62.

Bartlett, R.J., *England under the Norman and Angevin Kings, 1075–1225* (Oxford, 2000).

Beam, A., *The Balliol Dynasty, 1210–1364* (Edinburgh, 2008).

Beebe, B., 'The English baronage and the crusade of 1270', *Bulletin of the Institute of Historical Research*, 48 (1975), 127–48.

Bémont, C., *Simon de Montfort, Comte de Leicester* (Paris, 1884).

Billaud, R., 'The Lord Edward and the administration of justice across his apanage, 1254–72', in *Edward I: New Interpretations*, eds. A. King and A.M. Spencer (Woodbridge, 2020), 9–23.

Billaud, R., 'Similarities and differences: the Lord Edward's lordship of Gascony, 1254–1272', in *Thirteenth Century England*, 17 (Woodbridge, 2021), 89–109.

Binski, P., 'The Cosmati at Westminster and the English court style', *The Art Bulletin*, 72 (1990), 6–34.

Binski, P., 'Function, date, imagery, style and context of the Westminster retable', in *The Westminster Retable: History, Technique, Conservation*, eds. P. Binski and A. Massing (Cambridge and Turnhout, 2009), 16–44.

Binski, P., 'The illumination and patronage of the Douce Apocalypse', *The Antiquaries Journal*, 94 (2014), 127–34.

Binski, P., *The Painted Chamber at Westminster* (London, 1986).

Binski, P., 'The painted chamber at Westminster and its documentation', *The Walpole Society Journal*, 83 (2021), 1–68.

Binski, P., *Westminster Abbey and the Plantagenets: Kingship and Representation of Power, 1200–1400* (New Haven, CT, and London, 1995).

Binski, P., and Bolgia, C., 'The Cosmati mosaics at Westminster: art, politics and exchanges with Rome in the age of Gothic', *Römisches Jahrbuch der Bibliotheca Hertziana*, 45 (2021–2), 7–76.

Binski, P., and Massing, A., eds., *The Westminster Retable: History, Technique, Conservation* (Cambridge and Turnhout, 2009).

Birrell, J., 'A great thirteenth-century hunter: John Giffard of Brimpsfield', *Medieval Prosopography*, 15, no. 2 (1994), 37–66.

Blaauw, W.H., *The Barons' War, including the Battles of Lewes and Evesham*, 2nd edition (London, 1871).

Blaauw, W.H., 'On the early history of Lewes priory, and its seals, with extracts from a ms. chronicle', *Sussex Archaeological Collections*, 2 (1849), 7–37.

Bolton, J.L., *Money in the Medieval English Economy, 973–1489* (Manchester, 2012).

Brand, P.A., 'Hervey of Boreham (d.1277), administrator and justice', *Oxford Dictionary of National Biography* (2008), https://doi.org/10.1093/ref:odnb/37540.

Brand, P.A., 'Hugh Bigod (d.1266), baron and justiciar', *Oxford Dictionary of National Biography* (2008), https://doi.org/10.1093/ref:odnb/2377.

Brand, P.A., *Kings, Barons and Justices: The Making and Enforcement of Legislation in Thirteenth-Century England* (Cambridge, 2003).

Brand, P.A., 'The languages of law in later medieval England', in *Multilingualism in Later Medieval Britain*, ed. D.A. Trotter (Woodbridge, 2000), 63–76.

Brand, P.A., 'Laurence del Brok (d.1274), lawyer and justice', *Oxford Dictionary of National Biography* (2008), https://doi.org/10.1093/ref:odnb/37660.

Brand, P.A., 'Oldcotes v d'Arcy', in *Medieval Legal Records. In Memory of C.A.F. Meekings*, eds. R.F. Hunnisett and J.B. Post (London, 1978), 64–115.

Brand, P.A., *The Origins of the English Legal Profession* (Oxford, 1992).

Brand, P.A., 'Simon of Pattishall (d.1274), soldier and administrator', *Oxford Dictionary of National Biography* (2004), https:// doi.org/10.1093/ref:odnb/21545.

Brown, E.A.R., 'The chapels and cult of Saint Louis at Saint-Denis', *Mediaevalia*, 10 (1984), 279–331.

Brown, E.A.R., *Saint-Denis. La Basilique* (Saint-Léger-Vauban, 2001).

Brown, R.A., *Castles from the Air* (Cambridge, 1989).

Browne, C., Davies, G., Michael, M.A., and Zöschg, M., eds., *English Medieval Embroidery: Opus Anglicanum*, exhibition catalogue (New Haven, CT, and London, 2016).

Burt, C., 'A "bastard feudal" affinity in the making? the followings of William and Guy Beauchamp, earls of Warwick, 1268–1315', *Midland History*, 34 (2009), 156–80.

Burt, C., *Edward I and the Governance of England, 1272–1307* (Cambridge, 2013).

Burton, D.W., '1264: some new documents', *Historical Research*, 66 (1993), 317–28.

Burton, D.W., 'Politics, propaganda and public opinion in the reigns of Henry III and Edward I' (University of Oxford, doctoral thesis, 1985).

Cam, H.M., *The Hundred and the Hundred Rolls: An Outline of Local Government in Medieval England* (London, 1963).

Cam, H.M., *Liberties & Communities in Medieval England: Collected Studies in Local Administration and Topography* (London, 1963).

Camden, W., *Reges, Reginae, Nobiles, et alii in Ecclesia Collegiata Beati Petri Westmonasterii Sepulti* (London, 1606).

Carpenter, D.A., 'Aspects of the revolution of 1258', Henry III Fine Rolls Project, Fine of the Month for September 2012': www.finerollshenry3.org.uk/redist/pdf/fm-09-2012.pdf.

Carpenter, D.A., *The Battles of Lewes & Evesham 1264/65* (Keele, 1987).

Carpenter, D.A., 'Chronology and truth: Matthew Paris and the *Chronica Majora*', a 'related paper' placed on the website of the Henry III Fine Rolls Project (2013), https://finerollshenry3.org.uk/redist/pdf/Chronologyandtruth3.pdf.

Carpenter, D.A., 'The English royal chancery in the thirteenth century', in *English Government in the Thirteenth Century*, ed. A. Jobson (Woodbridge, 2004), 49–70.

Carpenter, D.A., 'From King John to the first English duke, 1215–1337', in *The House of Lords: A Thousand Years of Tradition*, eds. R. Smith and J.S. Moore (London, 1994), 28–43.

Carpenter, D.A., *Henry III: The Rise to Power and Personal Rule, 1207–1258* (London, 2020).

Carpenter, D.A., 'The household rolls of King Henry III of England (1216–72)', *Historical Research*, 80 (2007), 22–46.

Carpenter, D.A., 'King Henry III and the chapter house of Westminster Abbey', in *Westminster Abbey Chapter House: The History, Art and Architecture of 'A Chapter House beyond Compare'*, eds. W.J. Rodwell and R. Mortimer (London, 2010), 32–9.

Carpenter, D.A., 'King Henry III and the Cosmati work at Westminster Abbey', in *The Cloister and the World: Essays in Medieval History in Honour of Barbara Harvey*, eds. J. Blair and B. Golding (Oxford, 1996), 178–95.

Carpenter, D.A., *Magna Carta* (London, 2015).

Carpenter, D.A., 'The meetings of kings Henry III and Louis IX', in *Thirteenth Century England*, 10 (Woodbridge, 2005), 1–30.

Carpenter, D.A., 'A noble in politics: Roger Mortimer in the period of baronial reform and rebellion, 1258–1265', in *Nobles and Nobility in Medieval Europe: Concepts, Origins, Transformations*, ed. A.J. Duggan (Woodbridge, 2000), 183–203.

Carpenter, D.A., 'A peasant in politics during the Montfortian regime of 1264–1265: the Wodard of Kibworth case', Henry III Fine Rolls Project, Fine of the Month for September 2010: https://finerollshenry3.org.uk/content/month/fm-09-2010.html.

Carpenter, D.A., 'The Pershore *Flores Historiarum*: an unrecognised chronicle from the period of reform and rebellion in England, 1258–65', *English Historical Review*, 127 (2012), 1343–66.

Carpenter, D.A., 'Peter de Montfort (d.1265), magnate', *Oxford Dictionary of National Biography* (2008), https://doi.org/10.1093/ref:odnb/37845.

Carpenter, D.A., *The Reign of Henry III* (London, 1996).

Carpenter, D.A., 'Richard of Ware (d.1283), abbot', *Oxford Dictionary of National Biography* (2006), https://doi.org/10.1093/ref:odnb/94165.

Carpenter, D.A, 'Roger de Meuland (c.1215–1295), bishop of Coventry and Lichfield, *Oxford Dictionary of National Biography* (2008), https://doi.org/10.1093/ref:odnb/37908

Carpenter, D.A., 'The second century of English feudalism', *Past & Present*, 168 (2000), 30–71.

Carpenter, D.A., 'The secret revolution of 1258', in *Baronial Reform and Revolution in England, 1258–1267*, ed. A. Jobson (Woodbridge, 2016), 30–42.

Carpenter, D.A., 'Simon de Montfort, Henry III, London and Westminster Abbey', in *English Medieval Government and Administration: Essays in Honour of J.R. Maddicott*, eds. N. Saul and N. Vincent (Pipe Roll Society), forthcoming.

Carpenter, D.A., *The Struggle for Mastery: Britain 1066–1284*, paperback edition (London, 2004).

Carpenter, D.A., 'The struggle to control the Peak: an unknown letter patent from January 1217', in *Foundations of Medieval Scholarship: Records Edited in Honour of David Crook*, eds. P.A. Brand and S. Cunningham (York, 2008), 35–50.

Carpenter, D.A., 'Thomas fitzThomas (d. in or before 1276), mayor', *Oxford Dictionary of National Biography* (2004), https://doi.org/10.1093/ref:odnb/37419.

Carpenter, D.A., 'Was there a crisis of the knightly class in the thirteenth century? the Oxfordshire evidence', in *The Reign of Henry III* (London, 1996), 349–80.

Carpenter, D.A., 'Westminster Abbey in politics, 1258–1269', in *Thirteenth Century England*, 8 (Woodbridge, 2001), 49–58.

Carpenter, D.A., and Whittick, C., 'The battle of Lewes, 1264', *Sussex Archaeological Collections*, 152 (2014), 39–65.

Cassidy, R., 'Adventus vicecomitum and the financial crisis of Henry III's reign, 1250–1272', *English Historical Review*, 126 (2011), 614–27.

Cassidy, R., 'Bad sheriffs, custodial sheriffs and control of the counties', in *Thirteenth Century England*, 15 (Woodbridge, 2015), 35–50.

Cassidy, R., 'The English exchequer, the king, and the counties from reform to civil war, 1258–1264', in *Accounts and Accountability in Late Medieval Europe: Records, Procedures, and Socio–Political Impact*, Utrecht Studies in Medieval Literacy, 50, ed. I. Epurescu-Pascovici (Turnhout, 2020), 23–46.

Cassidy, R., 'Fulk Peyforer's wages', Henry III Fine Rolls Project, Fine of the Month for October 2012: https://finerollshenry3.org.uk/redist/pdf/fm-10-2012.pdf.

Cassidy, R., 'Simon de Montfort's sheriffs, 1264–5', *Historical Research*, 91 (2018), 3–21.

Cassidy, R., 'William Heron, "hammer of the poor, persecutor of the religious", sheriff of Northumberland, 1246–58', *Northern History*, 50 (2013), 9–19.

Cavell, E., 'Intelligence and intrigue in the march of Wales: noblewomen and the fall of Llywelyn ap Gruffudd, 1274–82', *Historical Research*, 88 (2015), 1–19.

Chambers, A., 'Aspects of chancery procedure in the chancery rolls of Henry III of England' (King's College London, University of London, doctoral thesis, 2022).

Chaplais, P., 'The making of the treaty of Paris (1259) and the royal style', in *Essays in Medieval Diplomacy and Administration* (London, 1981), 235–53.

Chaplais, P., *Piers Gaveston: Edward II's Adoptive Brother* (Oxford, 1994).

Chapman, D., 'The formative years of the central common law courts, 1234–1250' (University of Cambridge, doctoral thesis), forthcoming.

Chenard, G., *L'Administration d'Alphonse de Poitiers (1241–1271)* (Paris, 2017).

Church, S.D., *Henry III: A Simple and God-Fearing King* (London, 2017).

Church, S.D., 'King John's testament and the last days of his reign', *English Historical Review*, 125 (2010), 505–28.

Clanchy, M.T., 'Did Henry III have a policy?', *History*, 53 (1968), 203–16.

Clanchy, M.T., 'The franchise of return of writs', *Transactions of the Royal Historical Society*, 5th series, 17 (1967), 59–82.

Clanchy, M.T., *From Memory to Written Record: England 1066–1307*, 2nd edition (Oxford, 2009); 3rd edition (Oxford, 2012). All references are to the second edition.

Clementi, D.R., 'The documentary evidence for the crisis of government in England in 1258', *Parliaments, Estates and Representation*, 1 (1981), 99–108.

Cokayne, G.E., *The Complete Peerage of England, Scotland, Ireland, Great Britain and the United Kingdom*, eds. G.E. Cockayne, H.A. Doubleday, Lord Howard de Walden and G.H. White, 12 vols. in 13 (1910–59).

Cole, D., *The Tonbridge Knights Walk in 14 circular walks through the Weald of Kent* (King's Lynn, 2021).

Collingwood, J.A., 'Royal finance in the period of baronial reform and rebellion, 1255–1270' (King's College London, University of London, doctoral thesis, 1996).

Colvin, H.M., ed., *The History of the King's Works: The Middle Ages*, 2 vols. (London, 1963).

Coss, P.R., 'Bastard feudalism revised', *Past & Present*, 125 (1989), 27–64.

Coss, P.R., 'How did thirteenth-century knights counter royal authority?', in *Thirteenth Century England*, 15 (Woodbridge, 2015), 3–16.

Coss, P.R., *The Knight in Medieval England, 1000–1400* (Stroud, 1993).

Coss, P.R., 'Knighthood, heraldry and social exclusion in Edwardian England', in *Heraldry, Pageantry and Social Display in Edwardian England*, eds. P.R. Coss and M. Keen (Woodbridge, 2002), 39–68.

Coss, P.R., *The Lady in Medieval England, 1000–1500* (Stroud, 1998).

Coss, P.R., *Lordship, Knighthood and Locality: A Study in English Society c.1180–c.1280* (Cambridge, 1991).

Coss, P.R., *The Origins of the English Gentry* (Cambridge, 2003).

Coss, P.R., 'Retinues, agents and garrisons during the Barons' Wars', in *Baronial Reform and Revolution in England, 1258–1267*, ed. A. Jobson (Woodbridge, 2016), 183–98.

Coss, P.R., 'Sir Geoffrey de Langley and the crisis of the knightly class in thirteenth-century England', *Past & Present*, 68 (1975), 3–37.

Cox, D.C., *The Battle of Evesham: A New Account*, 2nd edition (Vale of Evesham Historical Society, 2019).

Cox, D.C., 'The battle of Evesham in the Evesham chronicle', *Historical Research*, 62 (1989), 337–45.

Cox, D.C., 'The tomb of Simon de Montfort', *Transactions of the Worcestershire Archaeological Society*, 3rd series, 26 (2018), 159–71.

Cox, E.L., *The Eagles of Savoy: The House of Savoy in Thirteenth-Century Europe* (Princeton, NJ, 1974).

Crane, S., 'Social aspects of bilingualism in the thirteenth century', in *Thirteenth Century England*, 6 (Woodbridge, 1997), 103–15.

Crook, D., 'The "Petition of the Barons" and charters of free warren, 1227–1258', in *Thirteenth Century England*, 8 (Woodbridge, 2001), 33–48.

Crook, D., *Records of the General Eyre* (London, 1982).

Crouch, D., *The English Aristocracy, 1070–1272: A Social Transformation* (New Haven, CT, and London, 2011).

Crouch, D., 'From Stenton to McFarlane: models of societies of the twelfth and thirteenth centuries', *Transactions of the Royal Historical Society*, 6th series, 5 (1995), 179–200.

Crouch, D., 'John Giffard (d.1299), baron', *Oxford Dictionary of National Biography* (2008), https://doi.org/10.1093/ref:odnb/10651.

Crouch, D., 'The local influence of the earls of Warwick, 1088–1242: a study in decline and resourcefulness', *Midland History*, 21 (1996), 1–22.

Crouch, D., Carpenter, D.A., and Coss, P.R., 'Debate: bastard feudalism revised', *Past & Present*, 131 (1991), 165–203.

Davies, R.R., *Conquest, Coexistence and Change: Wales 1063–1415* (Oxford, 1987).

Davies, S.J., 'Godfrey Giffard (d.1302), administrator and bishop', *Oxford Dictionary of National Biography* (2004), https://doi.org/10.1093/ref:odnb/10649.

Davis, H.W.C., 'The commune of Bury St Edmunds, 1264', *English Historical Review*, 24 (1909), 313–17.

Dejoux, M., 'À la recherche de la *reformatio regni* dans les royaumes de France et d'Angleterre au XIIIᵉ siècle', in *Reformatio? Les mots pour dire la réforme à la fin du Moyen Âge* (Paris, Éditions de la Sorbonne), forthcoming.

Dejoux, M., 'Des juges au travail: les enquêteurs réparateurs de Louis IX dans la sénéchaussée de Beaucaire', in *1216. Le Siège de Beaucaire. Pouvoir, société et culture dans le Midi rhodanien (Seconde moitié du XIIᵉ – première moitié du XIIIᵉ siècle)*, ed. M. Bourin (Société d'Histoire et d'Archéologie de Beaucaire, 2019), 227–55.

Dejoux, M., *Les Enquêtes de Saint Louis: Gouverner et Sauver son Âme* (Paris, 2014).

Dejoux, M., 'Valeur des choses et inscription de l'expertise dans les enquêtes de réparation de Louis IX (1247–1270)', in *Expertise et valeur des choses au Moyen Âge II: Savoirs, écritures, pratiques*, Collection de la casa de Velázquez, 156, eds. L. Fellent and A. Rodríguez (Madrid, 2016), 185–202.

Delaborde, H.-F., 'Instructions d'un ambassadeur envoyé par saint Louis à Alexandre IV à l'occasion du traité de Paris (1258)', *Bibliothèque de l'École des Chartes*, 49 (1888), 630–4.

Denholm-Young, N., 'Documents of the Barons' Wars', in *Collected Papers: Cultural, Textual and Biographical Essays on Medieval Topics* (Cardiff, 1969), 155–72.

Denholm-Young, N., 'Feudal society in the thirteenth century: the knights', in his *Collected Papers: Cultural, Textual and Biographical Essays on Medieval Topics* (Cardiff, 1969), 83–94.

Denholm-Young, N., *Richard of Cornwall* (Oxford, 1947).

Denholm-Young, N., 'Thomas de Wykes and his chronicle', in his *Collected Papers: Cultural, Textual and Biographical Essays on Medieval Topics* (Cardiff, 1969), 245–66.

Denholm-Young, N., 'The Winchester-Hyde chronicle', in his *Collected Papers: Cultural, Textual and Biographical Essays on Medieval Topics* (Cardiff, 1969), 236–44.

Denton, J.H., 'Walter of Bronescombe [Walter de Exonia] (d.1280), bishop', *Oxford Dictionary of National Biography* (2004), https://doi.org/10.1093/ref:odnb/37225.

De Ville, O., 'John Deyville: a neglected rebel', *Northern History*, 34 (1998), 17–40.

De Ville, O., 'Sir John Daiville (d.1290/1), rebel', *Oxford Dictionary of National Biography* (2008), https://doi.org/10.1093/ref:odnb/50769.

Dibben, L.B., 'Chancellor and keeper of the seal under Henry III', *English Historical Review*, 27 (1912), 39–51.

Dixon-Smith, S.A., 'Feeding the poor to commemorate the dead: the *pro anima* almsgiving of Henry III of England, 1227–1272' (University College, University of London, doctoral thesis, 2003).

Dobson, R.B., 'Walter Giffard (d.1279), archbishop', *Oxford Dictionary of National Biography* (2008), https://doi.org/10.1093/ref:odnb/10654.

Du Boulay, F.R.H., *The Lordship of Canterbury. An Essay on Medieval Society* (London, 1966).

Duggan, K.F., 'The hue and cry in thirteenth-century England', in *Thirteenth Century England*, 16 (Woodbridge, 2017), 153–72.

Duggan, K.F., 'The limits of strong government: attempts to control criminality in thirteenth-century England', *Historical Research*, 93 (2020), 399–419.

Dunbabin, J., *Charles I of Anjou: Power, Kingship and State-Making in Thirteenth-Century Europe* (London, 1998).

Dyer, C., *Standards of Living in the Later Middle Ages: Social Change in England, c.1200–1520*, Cambridge Medieval Textbooks (Cambridge, 1989).

English, B., *The Lords of Holderness, 1086–1260* (Oxford, 1979).

Faulkner, K., 'The transformation of knighthood in early thirteenth-century England', *English Historical Review*, 111 (1996), 1–23.

Fenster, T. and Collete, C.P., eds., *The French of Medieval England; Essays in Honour of Jocelyn Wogan-Browne* (Woodbridge, 2017).

Fernandes, M.J., 'The midlands knights and the Barons' War: the Warwickshire evidence', in *Baronial Reform and Revolution in England, 1258–1267*, ed. A. Jobson (Woodbridge, 2016), 167–82.

Fernandes, M.J., 'The role of the midlands knights in the period of reform and rebellion, 1258–67' (King's College London, University of London, doctoral thesis, 2000).

Finucane, R.C., *Miracles and Pilgrims: Popular Beliefs in Medieval England* (Basingstoke, 1995).

Forrest, I., 'Power and the people in thirteenth-century England', in *Thirteenth Century England*, 15 (Woodbridge, 2015), 17–34.

Forrest, I., 'The transformation of visitation in thirteenth-century England', *Past & Present*, 221 (2013), 3–37.

Foster, R., *Patterns of Thought: The Hidden Meaning of the Great Pavement of Westminster Abbey* (London, 1991).

Frame, R., 'Ireland and the Barons' Wars', in *Thirteenth Century England*, 1 (1986), 158–67.

Gavrilovitch, M., *Étude sur le traité de Paris de 1259 entre Louis IX, roi de France, et Henri III, roi de Angleterre* (Paris, 1899).

Gieben, S., 'Robert Grosseteste at the papal curia, Lyons, 1250: edition of the documents', *Collectanea Franciscana*, 41 (1971), 340–93.

Gilson, J.P., 'The parliament of 1264', *English Historical Review*, 16 (1901), 499–501.

Gilson, J.P., 'An unpublished notice of the battle of Lewes', *English Historical Review*, 11 (1896), 520–2.

Given-Wilson, C., *Henry IV* (New Haven, CT, and London, 2014).

Goering, J., and Taylor, D.S., 'The "summulae" of bishops Walter de Cantilupe (1240) and Peter Quinel (1287)', *Speculum*, 67 (1992), 576–94.

Golob, P.E., 'The Ferrers earls of Derby: a study of the honour of Tutbury, 1066–1279', 2 vols. (University of Cambridge, doctoral thesis, 1985).

Goodall, J., *The English Castle: 1066–1650* (New Haven, CT, and London, 2011).

Goodall, J., *Pevensey Castle* (London, 1999).

Gransden, A., *Historical Writing in England, c.550–1307* (London, 1974).

Gray, H., 'Money lending in twelfth-century England' (King's College London, University of London, doctoral thesis, 2007).

Giuseppi, M.S., 'On the testament of Sir Hugh de Nevill, written at Acre, 1267', *Archaeologia*, 56 pt. 2 (1899), 351–70.

H., T.D., 'The Rev. Lambert Blackwell Larking (in memoriam)', *Archaeologia Cantiana*, 7 (1868), 323–8.

Haines, R.M., 'Richard of Gravesend (d.1279), bishop', *Oxford Dictionary of National Biography* (2004), https://doi.org/10.1093/ref:odnb/11321.

Hammer, C.I., 'Complaints of the lesser commune, oligarchic rule and baronial reform in thirteenth-century Oxford', *Historical Research*, 85 (2012), 353–71.

Hanchett, P., 'Women in thirteenth-century Oxfordshire' (King's College London, University of London, doctoral thesis, 2007).

Harding, A., *England in the Thirteenth Century* (Cambridge, 1993).

Harding, A., 'Robert Walerand (d.1273), administrator', *Oxford Dictionary of National Biography* (2004), https://doi.org/10.1093/ref:odnb/28455.

Harmer, F.E., *Anglo-Saxon Writs*, 2nd edition (Stamford, 1989).

Hartland, B., and Dryburgh, P., 'The development of the fine rolls', in *Thirteenth Century England*, 12 (Woodbridge, 2009), 193–4.

Harvey, K., *Episcopal Appointments in England, c.1214–1344: From Episcopal Election to Papal Provision* (London, 2014).

Harvey, P.D.A., *A Medieval Oxfordshire Village: Cuxham 1240–1400* (Oxford, 1965).

Hasted, E., *The History and Topographical Survey of the County of Kent*, 2nd edition, 12 vols. (Canterbury, 1797–1801).

Hennings, L., 'The language of kingship under Henry III: civilian, canonical and dictaminal ideas in practice c.1230–c.1252' (University of Oxford, doctoral thesis, 2017).

Hennings, L., 'Simon de Montfort and the ambiguity of ethnicity in thirteenth-century politics', in *Thirteenth Century England*, 16 (2017), 137–52.

Hennings, M.A., *England under Henry III: Illustrated from Contemporary Sources*, University of London Intermediate Source-Books of History, 5, 1st edition (London, 1924).

Hershey, A.H., 'Baronial reform, the justiciar's court and commercial legislation: the case of Grimsby', in *Baronial Reform and Revolution in England, 1258–1267*, ed. A. Jobson (Woodbridge, 2016), 43–55.

Hershey, A.H., 'The earliest bill in eyre: 1259', *Historical Research*, 71 (1998), 228–32.

Hershey, A.H., 'Justice and bureaucracy: the English royal writ and "1258"', *English Historical Review*, 113 (1998), 829–51.

Hershey, A.H., 'The rise and fall of William de Bussey: a mid-thirteenth century steward', *Nottinghamshire Medieval Studies*, 44 (2000), 104–22.

Hershey, A.H., 'Success or failure? Hugh Bigod and judicial reform during the baronial movement, June 1258–February 1259', in *Thirteenth Century England*, 5 (Woodbridge, 1995), 65–87.

Hey, J., 'Two oaths of the community in 1258', *Historical Research*, 88 (2015), 213–29.

Hill, F.G., '*Damnatio eternae mortis* or *medicinalis non mortalis*: the ambiguities of excommunication in thirteenth-century England', in *Thirteenth Century England*, 16 (Woodbridge, 2017), 37–53.

Hill, F.G., *Excommunication in Thirteenth-Century England: Communities, Politics and Publicity* (Oxford, 2022).

Hill, J.W.F., *Medieval Lincoln* (Stamford, 1990).

Hillaby, J., and Hillaby, C., *The Palgrave Dictionary of Medieval Anglo-Jewish History* (Basingstoke, 2013).

Hogg, R.M., 'Henry III, the justiciarship, and the court *coram rege* in 1261', *The American Journal of Legal History*, 30 (1986), 59–78.

Hogg, R.M., 'The justiciarship during the Barons' War, 1258–65: the royalist justiciarship of Philip Basset, 1261–63' (University of Wales, doctoral thesis, 1981).

Hogg, R.M., 'Philip Basset at the court *coram rege, 1261–63*', *Irish Jurist*, new series, 21 (1986), 59–78.

Hogg, R.M., 'Philip Basset (d.1271), justiciar and royalist nobleman', *Oxford Dictionary of National Biography* (2008), https://doi.org/10.1093/ref:odnb/1643.

Holt, J.C., *Magna Carta* (Cambridge, 1965); 2nd edition (Cambridge, 1992); 3rd edition (Cambridge, 2015). Unless stated, all references are to the second edition.

Hoskin, P.M., 'Cantilupe's crusade? Walter de Cantilupe, bishop of Worcester and the baronial rebellion', *Transactions of the Worcestershire Archaeological Society*, 3rd series, 23 (2012), 91–102.

Hoskin, P.M., 'Natural law, protest and the English episcopate 1257–1265', in *Thirteenth Century England*, 15 (Woodbridge, 2015), 83–97.

Howell, M., *Eleanor of Provence: Queenship in Thirteenth-Century England* (Oxford, 1998).

Howell, M., *Regalian Right in Medieval England* (London, 1962).

Hunt, J., 'Families at war: royalists and Montfortians in the West Midlands', *Midland History*, 22 (1997), 1–34.

Huscroft, R., *Expulsion: England's Jewish Solution* (Stroud, 2006).

Huscroft, R., 'The political and personal life of Robert Burnell, chancellor of Edward I' (King's College London, University of London, doctoral thesis, 2001).

Huscroft, R., 'Robert Burnell and the government of England, 1270–1274', in *Thirteenth Century England*, 8 (Woodbridge, 2001), 59–70.

Huscroft, R., 'Should I stay or should I go? Robert Burnell, the Lord Edward's crusade and the Canterbury vacancy of 1270–3', *Nottingham Medieval Studies*, 45 (2001), 97–109.

Hyams, P.R., *King, Lords and Peasants in Medieval England: The Common Law of Villeinage in the Twelfth and Thirteenth Centuries* (Oxford, 1980).

Hyams, P.R., *Rancor and Reconciliation in Medieval England* (Ithaca, 2003).

Hyams, P.R., 'What did Henry III of England think in bed and in French about kingship and anger?', in *Anger's Past: The Social Uses of an Emotion in the Middle Ages*, ed. B.H. Rosenwein (Ithaca, NY, and London, 1998), 92–124.

Ingham, R., 'Middle English borrowing from French: nouns and verbs of interpersonal cognition in the *Early South English Legendary*', in *The French of Medieval England; Essays in Honour of Jocelyn Wogan-Browne*, ed. T. Fenster and C.P. Collette (Woodbridge, 2017), 128–39.

Irwin, D.A., 'Acknowledging debt in medieval England. A study of the records of medieval Anglo-Jewish money lending activities, 1194–1276' (Canterbury Christ Church University, doctoral thesis, 2020).

Jacob, E.F., 'A proposal for arbitration between Simon de Montfort and Henry III in 1260', *English Historical Review*, 37 (1922), 80–2, 320.

Jacob, E.F., *Studies in the Period of Baronial Reform and Rebellion, 1258–1267* (Oxford, 1925).

Jahner, J., *Literature and Law in the Era of Magna Carta*, Oxford Studies in Medieval Literature and Culture (Oxford, 2019).

Jahner, J., 'The poetry of the second Barons' War: some manuscripts contexts', *English Manuscript Studies 1100–1700*, 17 (2013), 200–22.

Jewell, H.M., 'Nicholas of Ely (d.1280), administrator and bishop', *Oxford Dictionary of National Biography* (2004), https://doi.org/10.1093/ref:odnb/8779.

Jewell, H.M., 'Nicholas of Seagrave (d.1295), baron', *Oxford Dictionary of National Biography* (2004), https://doi.org/10.1093/ref:odnb/25039.

Jobson, A., *The First English Revolution: Simon de Montfort, Henry III and the Barons' War* (London, 2012).

Jobson, A., 'John of Crakehall: the "forgotten" baronial treasurer, 1258–60', in *Thirteenth Century England*, 13 (Woodbridge, 2011), 83–100.

Jobson, A., 'Lordship, illegitimacy and the forging of a familial network', forthcoming.

Jobson, A., 'Lordship, reconciliation and the recovery process in post-Evesham England', in *Thirteenth Century England*, 19 (Woodbridge), forthcoming.

Jobson, A., 'The maritime theatre, 1258–1267', in *Baronial Reform and Revolution in England, 1258–1267*, ed. A. Jobson (Woodbridge, 2016), 218–36.

Jobson, A., 'The Morton incident: lordship, rebellion and divided loyalties during the first English revolution', in *English Medieval Government and Administration: Essays in Honour of J.R. Maddicott*, eds. N. Saul and N. Vincent (Pipe Roll Society), forthcoming.

Jobson, A., 'A queen in the shadows: Sanchia of Provence, Richard of Cornwall and a royal life unveiled', *Women's History Review*, 30 (2020), 766–89.

Jobson, A., 'The rebel's four dilemmas in the long thirteenth century', in *Thirteenth Century England*, 16 (Woodbridge, 2017), 89–111.

Jobson, A., 'Richard of Cornwall and the baronial opposition in 1263', in *Thirteenth Century England*, 12 (Woodbridge, 2009), 61–74.

Jobson, A., 'Royal government and administration in post-Evesham England, 1265–70', in *The Growth of Royal Government under Henry III*, eds. D. Crook and L.J. Wilkinson (Woodbridge, 2015), 179–95.

Johnstone, H., 'The wardrobe and household of Henry, son of Edward I', *Bulletin of the John Rylands Library*, 7 (1923), 384–420.

Jordan, W.C., *Men at the Center: Redemptive Governance under Louis IX* (Budapest and New York, 2012).

Jordan, W.C., *A Tale of Two Monasteries: Westminster and Saint-Denis in the Thirteenth Century* (Princeton, NJ, and Oxford, 2009).

Kaeuper, R.W., *Bankers to the Crown. The Riccardi of Lucca and Edward I* (Princeton, NJ, 1973).

Kamali, E.P., *Felony and the Guilty Mind in Medieval England* (Cambridge, 2019).

Kantorowicz, E.H., *The King's Two Bodies: A Study in Medieval Political Thought* (Princeton, NJ, 1957).

Keene, D., 'London from the post-Roman period to 1300', in *The Cambridge Urban History of Britain*, ed. D.M. Palliser, 3 vols. (Cambridge, 2000), i, 187–216.

Kersey, H., 'Aristocratic female inheritance and property holding in thirteenth-century England' (Canterbury Christ Church University, doctoral thesis, 2017).

King, A., '"War", "rebellion" or "perilous times"? political taxonomy and the conflict in England, 1321–2', in *Ruling Fourteenth-Century England: Essays in Honour of Christopher Given-Wilson*, eds. R. Ambühl, J.S. Bothwell and L. Tompkins (Woodbridge, 2019), 113–32.

King, E., 'Large and small landowners in thirteenth-century England: the case of Peterborough abbey', *Past & Present*, 47 (1970), 26–50.

King, J.R., 'The Friar Tuck syndrome: clerical violence and the Barons' War', in *The Final Argument: The Imprint of Violence on Society in Medieval and Early Modern Europe*, eds. D.J. Kagay and J.J.A. Villalon (Woodbridge, 1998), 27–52.

Kingsford, C.L., revised Vincent, N., 'John Gervase (d.1268), bishop', *Oxford Dictionary of National Biography* (2004), https://doi.org/10.1093/ref:odnb/14854.

Kjær, L., 'Food, drink and ritualised communication in the household of Eleanor de Montfort, February-August 1265', *Journal of Medieval History*, 37 (2011), 75–89.

Kjær, L., *The Medieval Gift and the Classical Tradition: Ideals and the Performance of Generosity in Medieval England, 1100–1300* (Cambridge, 2019).

Kjær, L., 'Writing reform and rebellion', in *Baronial Reform and Revolution in England, 1258–1267*, ed. A. Jobson (Woodbridge, 2016), 109–24.

Knowles, C.H., 'The disinherited, 1265–1280: a political and social study of the supporters of Simon de Montfort and the resettlement after the Barons' War' (University of Wales, doctoral thesis, 1959).

Knowles, C.H., 'Henry of Sandwich (d.1273), bishop', *Oxford Dictionary of National Biography* (2004), https://doi.org/10.1093/ref:odnb/24645.

Knowles, C.H., 'The justiciarship in England, 1258–1265', in *British Government and Administration: Studies Presented to S.B. Chrimes*, eds. H. Hearder and H.R. Loyn (Cardiff, 1974), 16–26.

Knowles, C.H., 'Provision for the families of the Montfortians disinherited after the battle of Evesham', in *Thirteenth Century England*, 1 (Woodbridge, 1986), 124–7.

Knowles, C.H., 'The resettlement of England after the Barons' War, 1264–67', *Transactions of the Royal Historical Society*, 5th series, 32 (1982), 25–41.

Knowles, C.H., *Simon de Montfort, 1265–1965* (Historical Association, 60, 1965).

Knowles, C.H., 'Sir Hugh Despenser (d.1265), justiciar', *Oxford Dictionary of National Biography* (2004), https://doi.org/10.1093/ref:odnb/7552.

Knowles, C.H., 'Stephen Bersted (d.1287), bishop', *Oxford Dictionary of National Biography* (2004), https://doi.org/10.1093/ref:odnb/2228.

Kosminsky, E.A., *Studies in the Agrarian History of England in the Thirteenth Century*, trans. R. Kisch and ed. R.H. Hilton (Oxford, 1956).

Kourris, A., 'The chancery of King Henry III: from charisma to the late medieval state' (University of East Anglia, doctoral thesis), forthcoming.

Labarge, M.W., *A Baronial Household of the Thirteenth Century* (London, 1965).

Labarge, M.W., *Gascony: England's First Colony, 1204–1453* (London, 1980).

Laborderie, O. de, Maddicott, J.R., and Carpenter, D.A., 'The last hours of Simon de Montfort: a new account', *English Historical Review*, 115 (2000), 378–412.

Lachaud, F., 'The contribution of Thomas Docking to the history of political thought', in *Thirteenth Century England*, 16 (2017), 55–69.

Lachaud, F., *L'éthique du pouvoir au Moyen Âge: L'office dans la culture politique (Angleterre, vers 1150–1330)* (Paris, 2010).

Larking, L.B., 'On the heart-shrine in Leybourne church', *Archaeologia Cantiana*, 5 (1863), 133–93.

Lawrence, C.H., *The English Church in the Thirteenth Century: Collected Papers of C.H. Lawrence*, ed. C.M. Barron and C.G. Daunton with contributions by Michael Robson and Claire Hatcher (Donnington, 2020).

Lawrence, C.H., 'The university in state and church', in *The History of the University of Oxford, Volume 1: The Early Oxford Schools*, ed. J.I. Catto (Oxford, 1984), 97–150.

Lawrence, C.H., 'The university of Oxford and the chronicle of the Barons' Wars', *English Historical Review*, 95 (1980), 99–113.

Lawrence, C.H., 'Walter de Cantilupe (d.1266), bishop', *Oxford Dictionary of National Biography* (2004), https://doi.org/10.1093/ref:odnb/4571.

Lefferts, P.M., 'Two English motets on Simon de Montfort', *Early English Music*, 1 (1981), 203–25.

Le Goff, J., *Saint Louis* (Paris, 1996).

Le Pogam, P.-Y., and Vivet-Peclet, C., *Saint Louis*, exhibition catalogue (Paris, 2014).

Letters, S., 'Markets and fairs in medieval England: a new resource', in *Thirteenth Century England*, 9 (2003), 209–23.

Lewis, A., 'Roger Leyburn and the pacification of England, 1265–7', *English Historical Review*, 54 (1939), 193–214.

Liu, H., 'John Mansel, councillor of Henry III: his life and career' (King's College London, University of London, doctoral thesis, 2004).

Liversidge, M., and Binski, P., 'Two ceiling fragments from the painted chamber at Westminster palace', *Burlington Magazine*, 137 (1995), 491–501.

Lloyd, S.D., *English Society and the Crusade, 1216–1307* (Oxford, 1988).

Lloyd, S.D., 'Gilbert de Clare, Richard of Cornwall and the Lord Edward's crusade', *Nottinghamshire Medieval Studies*, 30 (1986), 46–66.

Lloyd, S.D., 'James Audley (d.1272), magnate', *Oxford Dictionary of National Biography* (2004), https://doi.org/10.1093/ref:odnb/894.

Lomas, A., 'Montfortian ideology and its understanding 1263–1320' (King's College London, MA dissertation, 2018).

Lunt, W.E., *Financial Relations of the Papacy with England to 1327* (Cambridge, MA, 1939).

McEwan, J.A., 'Civic government in troubled times: London c.1263–1270', in *Baronial Reform and Revolution in England, 1258–1267*, ed. A. Jobson (Woodbridge, 2016), 125–38.

McKitterick, D., ed., *The Trinity Apocalypse* (London, 2005).

McSweeney, T.J., *Priests of the Law: Roman Law and the Making of the Common Law's First Professionals* (Oxford, 2019).

Maddicott, J.R., 'The crusade taxation of 1268–1270 and the development of parliament', in *Thirteenth Century England*, 2 (1988), 93–117.

Maddicott, J.R., 'Edward I and the lessons of baronial reform: local government, 1258–80', in *Thirteenth Century England*, 1 (1986), 1–30.

Maddicott, J.R., 'Follower, leader, pilgrim, saint: Robert de Vere, earl of Oxford, at the shrine of Simon de Montfort, 1273', *English Historical Review*, 109 (1994), 641–53.

Maddicott, J.R., 'Guy de Montfort (*c.* 1244–1291/2), soldier and administrator', *Oxford Dictionary of National Biography* (2006), https://doi.org/10.1093/ref:odnb/19047.

Maddicott, J.R., '"An infinite multitude of nobles": quality, quantity and politics in the pre-reform parliaments of Henry III', in *Thirteenth Century England*, 7 (Woodbridge, 1999), 17–46.

Maddicott, J.R., *Law and Lordship: Royal Justices as Retainers in Thirteenth- and Fourteenth-Century England*, in *Past & Present*, suppl. 4 (1978).

Maddicott, J.R., 'Magna Carta and the local community, 1215–1259', *Past & Present*, 102 (1984), 25–65.

Maddicott, J.R., 'The Mise of Lewes, 1264', *English Historical Review*, 98 (1983), 588–603.

Maddicott, J.R., *The Origins of the English Parliament, 924–1327* (Oxford, 2010).

Maddicott, J.R., 'Politics and the people in thirteenth-century England', in *Thirteenth Century England*, 14 (2013), 1–13.

Maddicott, J.R., *Simon de Montfort* (Cambridge, 1994).

Maddicott, J.R., *Thomas of Lancaster, 1307–1322: A Study in the Reign of Edward II* (Oxford, 1970).

Maddicott, J.R., 'Who was Simon de Montfort, earl of Leicester?', *Transactions of the Royal Historical Society*, 6th series, 26 (2016), 43–58.

Maitland, F.W., 'A song on the death of Simon de Montfort', *English Historical Review*, 11 (1896), 314–18.

Martin, G.H., 'Walter of Merton (d.1277), administrator and bishop', *Oxford Dictionary of National Biography* (2004), https://doi.org/10.1093/ref:odnb/18612.

Masschaele, J., *Jury, State and Society in Medieval England* (Basingstoke, 2008).

Meekings, C.A.F., *Studies in 13th-Century Justice and Administration* (London, 1981).

Meekings, C.A.F., and Crook, D., *King's Bench and Common Bench in the Reign of Henry III* (Selden Society, supplementary series, 17, 2010).

Melve, L., 'The public debate during the baronial rebellion', *Thirteenth Century England*, 12 (Woodbridge, 2009), 45–60.

Miller, E., *The Abbey and Bishopric of Ely: The Social History of an Ecclesiastical Estate from the Tenth Century to the Early Fourteenth Century*, Cambridge Studies in Medieval Life and Thought, 1 (Cambridge, 1951).

Mitchell, L.E., *Portraits of Medieval Women: Family, Marriage and Politics in England, 1225–1350* (New York and Basingstoke, 2003).

Mitchell, S.K., *Studies in Taxation under John and Henry III* (New Haven, CT, 1914).

Moore, T.K., 'The fine rolls as evidence for the expansion of royal justice during the reign of Henry III', in *The Growth of Royal Government under Henry III*, eds. D. Crook and L.J. Wilkinson (Woodbridge, 2015), 55–71.

Moore, T.K., 'Government and locality in Essex in the reign of Henry III, 1216–1272' (University of Cambridge, doctoral thesis, 2006).

Moore, T.K., 'Local administration during the period of reform and rebellion', in *Baronial Reform and Revolution in England, 1258–1267*, ed. A. Jobson (Woodbridge, 2016), 71–88.

Morgan, N.J., *The Douce Apocalypse: Picturing the End of the World in the Middle Ages*, Treasures from the Bodleian Library (Oxford, 2006).

Morgan, N.J., 'Illustrated apocalypses of mid thirteenth-century England: historical context, patronage and readership', in *The Trinity Apocalypse*, ed. D. McKitterick (London, 2005), 3–22.

Morgan, N.J., 'The Trinity Apocalypse: style, dating and place of production', in *The Trinity Apocalypse*, ed. D. McKitterick (London, 2005), 23–33.

Morris, M., *The Bigod Earls of Norfolk in the Thirteenth Century* (Woodbridge, 2005).

Morris, M., *A Great and Terrible King: Edward I and the Forging of Britain* (London, 2008).

Mundill, R.R., *England's Jewish Solution: Experiment and Expulsion, 1262–1290* (Cambridge, 1998).

Musson, A., *Medieval Law in Context: The Growth of Legal Consciousness from Magna Carta to the Peasants' Revolt* (Manchester, 2020).

Neal, K.B., *The Letters of Edward I: Political Communication in the Thirteenth Century* (Woodbridge, 2021).

Nightingale, P., 'The growth of London in the medieval English economy', in *Progress and Problems in Medieval England: Essays in Honour of Edward Miller*, eds. R.H. Britnell and J. Hatcher (Cambridge, 1996), 89–106.

Oakes, F., 'The Barons' War in the north of England, 1264–1265', in *Baronial Reform and Revolution in England, 1258–1267*, ed. A. Jobson (Woodbridge, 2016), 199–217.

Oakes, F., 'King's men without the king: royalist castle garrison resistance between the battles of Lewes and Evesham', in *Thirteenth Century England*, 15 (Woodbridge, 2015), 51–68.

Oakes, F., 'The nature of war and its impact on society during the Barons' War, 1264–67' (University of Glasgow, doctoral thesis, 2014).

*The Oxford Dictionary of National Biography*, eds. H.C.G. Matthew and B. Harrison, 60 vols. (Oxford, 2004), with the online edition at https://www.oxforddnb.com/ has biographies of all the leading actors appearing in this book.

Page, M., 'Cornwall, Earl Richard and the Barons' War', *English Historical Review*, 115 (2000), 21–38.

Palmer, R.C., *The County Courts of Medieval England 1150–1350* (Princeton, NJ, 1982).

Parsons, J.C., *Eleanor of Castile: Queen and Society in Thirteenth-Century England* (Basingstoke, 1994).

Payne, M., and Rodwell, W.J., 'Edward the Confessor's shrine in Westminster Abbey: its date of construction reconsidered', *The Antiquaries Journal*, 97 (2017), 187–204.

Payne, M., and Rodwell, W.J., 'Edward the Confessor's shrine in Westminster Abbey: the question of metre', *The Antiquaries Journal*, 98 (2018), 145–8.

Pélissié du Rausas, A., 'De guerre, de trêve, de paix: les relations franco-anglaises de la bataille de Taillebourg au traité de Paris (années 1240–années 1260)' (University of Poitiers, doctoral thesis, 2020).

Peters, E.M., *The Shadow King: Rex Inutilis in Medieval Law and Literature, 741–1327* (New Haven, CT, and London, 1970).

Polden, A., 'A crisis of the knightly class? Inheritance and office among the gentry of thirteenth-century Buckinghamshire', in *Regionalism and Revision: The Crown and its Provinces in England, 1200–1650*, eds. P. Fleming, A.J. Gross and J.R. Lander (London and Rio Grande, 1998), 29–57.

Pollock, F., and Maitland, F.W., *The History of English Law Before the Time of Edward I*, 2nd edition, 2 vols. (Cambridge, 1968).

Pommier, A., *Observations sur une Relique Possédée autrefois par Le Musée d'Orléans sous le Nom de cœur de Henry II (Plantagenet)* (Orléans, 1917).

Power, A., 'The uncertainties of reformers: collective anxieties and strategic discourses', in *Thirteenth Century England*, 16 (Woodbridge, 2017), 1–19.

Power, D., 'The treaty of Paris (1259) and the aristocracy of England and Normandy', in *Thirteenth Century England*, 13 (Woodbridge, 2011), 141–58.

Powicke, F.M., 'The archbishop of Rouen, John de Harcourt and Simon de Montfort in 1260', *English Historical Review*, 51 (1936), 108–13.

Powicke, F.M., 'Guy de Montfort, 1265–1271', *Transactions of the Royal Historical Society*, 4th series, 18 (1935), 1–23, reprinted in his *Ways of Medieval Life and Thought*, 69–88. Both versions are cited together in the text.

Powicke, F.M., *King Henry III and the Lord Edward: The Community of the Realm in the Thirteenth Century*, 2 vols. (Oxford, 1947).

Powicke, F.M., *Medieval England, 1066–1485* (London, 1950).

Powicke, F.M., *The Thirteenth Century, 1216–1307* (Oxford, 1953).

Powicke, F.M., *Ways of Medieval Life and Thought: Essays and Addresses* (London, 1950).

Prestwich, M.C., *Armies and Warfare in the Middle Ages: The English Experience* (New Haven, CT, and London, 1996).

Prestwich, M.C., *Edward I* (London, 1988).

Prestwich, M.C., 'Royal patronage under Edward I', in *Thirteenth Century England*, 1 (Woodbridge, 1986), 41–52.

Quick, J.A., 'Government and society in Kent, 1232–80' (University of Oxford, doctoral thesis, 1986).

Quick, J.A., 'The number and distribution of knights in thirteenth-century England: the evidence of the grand assize lists', in *Thirteenth Century England*, 1 (Woodbridge, 1986), 114–23.

Ray, M., 'Alien courtiers of thirteenth-century England and their assimilation' (Kings College London, University of London, doctoral thesis, 2003).

Ray, M., *Edward I's Regent. Edmund of Cornwall: The Man Behind England's Greatest King* (Barnsley, 2022).

Ray, M., 'Three alien royal stewards in thirteenth-century England: the careers and legacy of Matthias Bezill, Imbert Pugeys and Peter de Champvent', *Thirteenth Century England*, 10 (Woodbridge, 2005), 50–70.

Reid, N.H., *Alexander III, 1249–1286: First Among Equals* (Edinburgh, 2019).

Richardson, H.G., *The English Jewry under the Angevin Kings* (London, 1960).

Richardson, H.G., and Sayles, G.O., *The Governance of Mediaeval England from the Conquest to Magna Carta* (Edinburgh, 1963).

Richardson, H.G., and Sayles, G.O., 'The Provisions of Oxford, 1258', in *The English Parliament in the Middle Ages* (London, 1981), 3–33.

Ridgeway, H.W., 'Adam Gurdun at Dunster (c.1263–1265): an unknown rebellion of the community of the realm in Somerset', *Proceedings of the Somerset Archaeological and Natural History Society*, 159 (2015), 39–47.

Ridgeway, H.W., 'Dorset in the period of baronial reform and rebellion, 1258–1267', *Historical Research*, 87 (2014), 18–42.

Ridgeway, H.W., 'An English cartulary roll of Peter of Savoy', in *English Medieval Government and Administration: Essays in Honour of J.R. Maddicott*, eds. N. Saul and N. Vincent (Pipe Roll Society), forthcoming.

Ridgeway, H.W., 'The ecclesiastical career of Aymer de Lusignan, bishop elect of Winchester, 1250–1260', in *The Cloister and the World: Essays in Medieval History in Honour of Barbara Harvey*, eds. J. Blair and B.J. Golding (Oxford, 1996), 148–77.

Ridgeway, H.W., 'The exploits of two Dorset knights at the battle of Lewes', Henry III Fine Rolls Project, Fine of the Month for January 2012: https://finerollshenry3.org.uk/redist/pdf/fm-01-2012.pdf.

Ridgeway, H.W., 'Henry III, king of England 1207–1272', *Oxford Dictionary of National Biography* (2004), https://doi.org/10.1093/ref:odnb/12950.

Ridgeway, H.W., 'King Henry III's grievances against the council in 1261: a new version and a letter describing political events', *Historical Research*, 61 (1988), 227–42.

Ridgeway, H.W., 'The Lord Edward and the Provisions of Oxford (1258): a study in faction', in *Thirteenth Century England*, 1 (Woodbridge, 1986), 89–99.

Ridgeway, H.W., 'Mid thirteenth-century reformers and the localities: the sheriffs of the baronial regime, 1258–1261', in *Regionalism and Revision: The Crown and its Provinces in England, 1200–1650*, eds. P. Fleming, A.J. Gross and J.R. Lander (London, 1998), 59–86.

Ridgeway, H.W., 'The politics of the English royal court, 1247–1265, with special reference to the role of the aliens' (University of Oxford, doctoral thesis, 1983).

Ridgeway, H.W., 'Sir Giles d'Argentine (d.1282), baronial leader', *Oxford Dictionary of National Biography* (2008), https://doi.org/10.1093/ref:odnb/641.

Ridgeway, H.W., 'Sir Ralph Basset of Drayton (d.1265), baronial leader', *Oxford Dictionary of National Biography* (2004), https://doi.org/10.1093/ref:odnb/1645.

Ridgeway, H.W., 'Sir Ralph Basset of Sapcote (d.1279?), baronial leader,' *Oxford Dictionary of National Biography* (2004), https://doi.org/10.1093/ref:odnb/1646

Ridgeway, H.W., 'Warin of Bassingbourn', forthcoming.

Ridgeway, H.W., 'What happened in 1261?', in *Baronial Reform and Revolution in England, 1258–1267*, ed. A. Jobson (Woodbridge, 2016), 89–108.

Ridgeway, H.W., 'William de Munchensi (d.1287), baronial leader', *Oxford Dictionary of National Biography* (2004), https://doi.org/10.1093/ref:odnb/19530.

Ridgeway, H.W., 'William de Valence and his *familiares*, 1247–72', *Historical Research*, 65 (1992), 239–57.

Ripart, L., '"Non est consuetum in comitatu Sabaudie quod filia succedit parti in comitatu et possessione comitatus". Genèse de la coutume savoyarde de l'exclusion des filles', in *Pierre II de Savoie 'Le petit Charlemagne' (†1268). Colloque international, Lausanne, 30–31 mai 1997*, eds. B. Andenmatten, A. Paravicini Bagliani and E. Pibiri (Lausanne, 2000), 295–331.

Rodwell, W.J., and Neal, D.S., *The Cosmatesque Mosaics of Westminster Abbey. The Pavements and Royal Tombs: History, Archaeology, Architecture and Conservation*, 2 vols. (Oxford, 2019).

Sabapathy, J., *Officers and Accountability in Medieval England, 1170–1300* (Oxford, 2014).

Sanders, I.J., *English Baronies: A Study of their Origin and Descent* (Oxford, 1960).

Sanders, I.J., *Feudal Military Service in England: A Study of the Constitutional and Military Powers of the Barons in Medieval England* (London, 1956).

Sayles, G.O., *The Functions of the Medieval Parliament of England* (London, 1988).

Sayles, G.O., 'Representation of cities and boroughs in 1268', *English Historical Review*, 40 (1925), 580–5.

Scales, L.E., 'The Cambridgeshire ragman rolls', *English Historical Review*, 113 (1998), 553–79.

Scott, G.G., *Gleanings from Westminster Abbey* (Oxford and London, 1861).

Searby, R., 'Rethinking the royal prosecution of c.1234: England's Jewish Community and the "Poitevin" regime' (forthcoming).

Shacklock, A., 'Henry III and the native saints', in *Thirteenth Century England*, 17 (Woodbridge, 2021), 23–40.

Shacklock, A., 'Piety and politics in the kingship of Henry III' (University of Cambridge, doctoral thesis, forthcoming).

Short, I., 'Introduction', in *The Trinity Apocalypse*, ed. D. McKitterick (London, 2005), 123–38.

Short, I., 'On bilingualism in Anglo-Norman England', *Romance Philology*, 33 (1980), 467–79.

Simpson, G.G., 'The *familia* of Roger de Quincy, earl of Winchester and constable of Scotland', in *Essays on the Nobility of Medieval Scotland*, ed. K.J. Stringer (Edinburgh, 1985), 102–30.

Slater, L., *Art and Political Thought in Medieval England, c.1150–1350* (Woodbridge, 2018).

Smith, J.B., *Llywelyn ap Gruffudd: Prince of Wales* (Cardiff, 2014).

Snowden, D., *1265: The Murder of Evesham* (Simon de Montfort Society, 2020).

Somerset, F., 'Complaining about the king in French in Thomas Wright's *Political Songs of England*', in *The French of Medieval England: Essays in Honour of Jocelyn Wogan-Browne*, ed. T. Fenster and C.P. Collete (Woodbridge, 2017), 82–99.

Southern, R.W., *Robert Grosseteste: The Growth of an English Mind in Medieval Europe* (Oxford, 1986).

Southern, R.W., 'Robert Grosseteste (d.1253), scientist, theologian and bishop', *Oxford Dictionary of National Biography* (2010), https://doi.org/10.1093/ref:odnb/11665.

Spencer, A.M., 'Dealing with inadequate kingship: uncertain responses from Magna Carta to deposition, 1199–1327', in *Thirteenth Century England*, 16 (Woodbridge, 2017), 71–88.

Spencer, A.M., *Nobility and Kingship in Medieval England: The Earls and Edward I, 1272–1307* (Cambridge, 2014).

Spencer, A.M., 'Royal patronage and the earls in the reign of Edward I', *History*, 93 (2008), 20–46.

Spencer, A.M., '"A vineyard without a wall": the Savoyards, John de Warenne and the failure of Henry III's kingship', in *Thirteenth Century England*, 17 (Woodbridge, 2021), 41–64.

Stacey, R.C., '1240–60: a watershed in Anglo-Jewish relations?', *Historical Research*, 61 (1988), 135–50.

Stacey, R.C., 'Crusades, crusaders and the baronial *gravamina* of 1263–1264', in *Thirteenth Century England*, 3 (Woodbridge, 1991), 137–50.

Stacey, R.C., 'John Mansel (d.1265), administrator and royal councillor', *Oxford Dictionary of National Biography* (2008), https://doi.org/10.1093/ref:odnb/17989.

Stacey, R.C., 'Parliamentary negotiation and the expulsion of the Jews from England', in *Thirteenth Century England*, 6 (Woodbridge, 1997), 77–101.

Stacey, R.C., 'Richard de Grey (d. before 1272), baron', *Oxford Dictionary of National Biography* (2005), https://doi.org/10.1093/ref:odnb/11554.

Stanley, A.P., 'On an examination of the tombs of Richard II and Henry III in Westminster Abbey', *Archaeologia*, 45 (1880), 309–27.

Stevenson, A.L., 'From Domesday Book to the hundred rolls: lordship, landholding and local society in three English hundreds, 1066–1280' (King's College London, University of London, doctoral thesis, 2014).

Stewart, S., 'Simon de Montfort and his followers, June 1263', *English Historical Review*, 119 (2004), 965–9.

Stewart, S., 'A year in the life of a royal justice. Gilbert de Preston's itinerary, July 1264–June 1265', in *Thirteenth Century England*, 12 (2009), 155–66.

Stewart-Parker, W.J., 'The Bassets of High Wycombe: politics, lordship, locality and culture in the thirteenth century' (King's College London, University of London, doctoral thesis, 2015).

Stone, I., 'Arnold fitz Thedmar: identity, politics and the city of London in the thirteenth century', *The London Journal*, 40 (2015), 106–22.

Stone, I., 'The book of Arnold fitz Thedmar' (King's College London, University of London, doctoral thesis, 2016).

Stone, I., 'The rebel barons of 1264 and the commune of London: an oath of mutual aid', *English Historical Review*, 129 (2014), 1–18.

Stringer, K.J., 'Nobility and identity in medieval Britain and Ireland: the de Vescy family, c.1120–1314', in *Britain and Ireland 900–1300. Insular Responses to Medieval European Change*, ed. B. Smith (Cambridge, 1999), 199–239.

Stubbs, W., *Studies in the Constitutional History in its Origin and Development*, 4th edition, 2 vols. (Oxford, 1906).

Studd, J.R., 'The Lord Edward and King Henry III', *Bulletin of the Institute of Historical Research*, 50 (1977), 4–19.

Studd, J.R., 'The marriage of Henry of Almain and Constance of Béarn', in *Thirteenth Century England*, 3 (1991), 161–79.

Summerson, H.R.T., 'Civil war and society: the impact of the siege of Rochester in 1264', *Southern History*, 41 (2019), 16–38.

Summerson, H.R.T., *Medieval Carlisle: The City and the Borders from the Late Eleventh to the Mid-Sixteenth Century*, 2 vols. (Cumberland and Westmorland Antiquarian and Archaeological Society, extra series, 25, 1993).

Summerson, H.R.T., 'Repercussions from the Barons' Wars: a Kentish inquest of 1264', *Historical Research*, 91 (2018), 573–8.

Summerson, H.R.T., 'Sir Adam Gurdun (d.1305), soldier and rebel', *Oxford Dictionary of National Biography* (2004), https://doi.org/10.1093/ref:odnb/11754.

Sutherland, D.W., *Quo Warranto Proceedings in the Reign of Edward I, 1278–1294* (Oxford, 1963).

Swanson, J., *John of Wales: A Study of the Works and Ideas of a 13th-Century Friar*, Cambridge Studies in Medieval Life and Thought, 4th series, 10 (Cambridge, 1989).

Taylor, A, *The Shape of the State in Medieval Scotland 1124–1290* (Oxford, 2016).

Taylor, A.J.P., *A Personal History* (London, 1983).

Tilley, C., 'The honour of Wallingford, 1066–1300' (King's College London, University of London, doctoral thesis, 2011).

Tolan, J., *England's Jews: Finance, Violence and the Crown in the Thirteenth Century* (Philadelphia, PA, 2023).

Tout, T.F., *Chapters in the Administrative History of Mediaeval England: The Wardrobe, the Chamber and the Small Seals*, 6 vols. (Manchester, 1920–33).

Tout, T.F., 'Wales and the march during the Barons' War, 1258–67', in *The Collected Papers of Thomas Frederick Tout*, 3 vols. (Manchester, 1932–4), ii, 47–100.

Tout, T.F., and Ridgeway, H.W., 'John de Vescy (d.1289), baron', *Oxford Dictionary of National Biography* (2005), https://doi.org/10.1093/ref:odnb/28254.

Trabut-Cussac, J.-P., *L'administration anglaise en Gascogne sous Henry III et Édouard I de 1254 à 1307* (Geneva, 1972).

Treharne, R.F., *The Baronial Plan of Reform, 1258–1263* (Manchester, 1971).

Treharne, R.F., 'The battle of Northampton, 5th April 1264', in *Simon de Montfort and Baronial Reform: Thirteenth-Century Essays*, ed. E.B. Fryde (London, 1986), 299–316.

Treharne, R.F., 'The knights in the period of reform and rebellion, 1258–67: a critical phase in the rise of a new class', *Bulletin of the Institute of Historical Research*, 21 (1946), 1–12.

Treharne, R.F., 'The Mise of Amiens, 23 January 1264', in *Studies in Medieval History Presented to Frederick Maurice Powicke*, eds. R.W. Hunt, W.A. Pantin and R.W. Southern (Oxford, 1948), 223–9.

Treharne, R.F., 'An unauthorized use of the great seal under the provisional government in 1259', *English Historical Review*, 40 (1925), 403–11.

Trevor-Roper, H., *The Wartime Journals*, ed. R. Davenport-Hines (London and New York, 2012).

Turner, R., *An Account of the Medieval Arms of Westminster Abbey to be found in the Quire and the Nave* (privately printed, 2018).

Turner, R., 'Battle rages over whether Edward's birds are based on doves, eagles - or swallows', *The Westminster Abbey Chorister Magazine*, winter (2008/9), 34-7.

Turner, R.V., *The English Judiciary in the Age of Glanvill and Bracton, c.1176–1239* (Cambridge, 1985).

Tyerman, C., *England and the Crusades, 1095–1588* (Chicago, IL, and London, 1988).

Valente, C., *The Theory and Practice of Revolt in Medieval England* (Farnham, 2003).

Valente, C., 'Simon de Montfort, earl of Leicester, and the utility of sanctity in thirteenth-century England', *Journal of Medieval History*, 21 (1995), 27–49.

Valente, C., 'The Provisions of Oxford: assessing/assigning authority in time of unrest', in *The Experience of Power in Medieval Europe, 950–1350*, eds. R.F. Berkhofer, A. Cooper and A.J. Kosto (London, 2005), 25–41.

*The Victoria History of the Counties of England [VCH]*, eds. W. Page, L.F. Salzman, R. Pugh et al., 244 vols. (London, 1899–).

Vincent, N., 'From rebellion and reconciliation to treason and disinheritance: why, when, and how in the Anglo-French world', forthcoming.

Vincent, N., 'Henry of Almain [Henry of Cornwall] (d.1271), courtier', *Oxford Dictionary of National Biography* (2009), https://doi.org/10.1093/ref:odnb/12958.

Vincent, N., *The Holy Blood: King Henry III and the Westminster Blood Relic* (Cambridge, 2001).

Vincent, N., 'King John's lost language of cranes: micromanagement, meat-eating and mockery at court', The Magna Carta Project, Feature of the Month for March 2015, http://magnacartaresearch.org/read/feature_of_the_month/Mar_2015_3.

Vincent, N., 'Peter of Savoy, count of Savoy and *de facto* earl of Richmond (d.1268), magnate', *Oxford Dictionary of National Biography* (2008), https://doi.org/10.1093/ref:odnb/22016.

Vincent, N., 'Philip Lovel (d.1258), administrator and royal councillor', *Oxford Dictionary of National Biography* (2006), https://doi.org/10.1093/ref:odnb/17052.

Vincent, N., 'Rank insubordination: disobedience and disinheritance amongst the Anglo-French nobility, 1050–1250', in *Rank and Order: The Formation of Aristocratic Elites in Western and Central Europe, 500–1500*, ed. J. Peltzer (Stuttgart, 2015), 131–70.

Vincent, N., 'Richard, first earl of Cornwall and king of Germany (d.1272)', *Oxford Dictionary of National Biography* (2008), https://doi.org/10.1093/ref:odnb/23501.

Von Wurstemberger, L., *Peter der Zweite, Graf von Savoyen, Markgraf in Italien: Sein Haus und seine Lande; ein Charakterbild des Dreizehnten Jahrhunderts*, 4 vols. (Bern, 1856–8).

Wait, H.A., 'The household and resources of the Lord Edward, 1239–72' (University of Oxford, doctoral thesis, 1988).

Walker, R.F., 'The Anglo-Welsh wars, 1217–67' (University of Oxford, doctoral thesis, 1954).

Ward, J., 'The Kent hundred rolls: local government and corruption in the thirteenth century', *Archaeologia Cantiana*, 127 (2007), 57–72.

Waugh, S.L., 'John de Warenne (d.1304), 6th earl of Surrey, magnate', *Oxford Dictionary of National Biography* (2004), https://doi.org/10.1093/ref:odnb/28734.

Waugh, S.L., *The Lordship of England: Royal Wardships and Marriages in English Society and Politics, 1217–1327* (Princeton, NJ, 1988).

Waugh, S.L., 'Reluctant knights and jurors: respites, exemptions and public obligations in the reign of Henry III', *Speculum*, 58 (1983), 937–86.

Waugh, S.L., 'Tenure to contract: lordship and clientage in thirteenth-century England', *English Historical Review*, 101 (1986), 811–39.

Webster, H., 'The annals of Dunstable priory: from living memory to written record in a thirteenth-century textual community', *Journal of Medieval Monastic Studies*, 9 (2020), 147–73.

Weiler, B., *Henry III of England and the Staufen Empire, 1216–1272* (Woodbridge, 2006).

Weiler, B., 'Symbolism and politics in the reign of Henry III', in *Thirteenth Century England*, 9 (Woodbridge, 2003), 15–41.

Whittick, C., 'Sir Ralph Sandwich (d.1308), justice and administrator', *Oxford Dictionary of National Biography* (2008), https://doi.org/10.1093/ref:odnb/24646.

Whitwell, R.J., 'The revenue and expenditure of England under Henry III', *English Historical Review*, 18 (1903), 710–11.

Wild, B.L., 'A captive king: Henry III between the battles of Lewes and Evesham, 1264–5', in *Thirteenth Century England*, 13 (Woodbridge, 2011), 41–56.

Wild, B.L., 'Reasserting medieval kingship: King Henry III and the Dictum of Kenilworth', in *Baronial Reform and Revolution in England, 1258–1267*, ed. A. Jobson (Woodbridge, 2016), 237–58.

Wild, B.L., 'The siege of Kenilworth castle, 1266', *English Heritage Historical Review*, 5 (2010), 12–23.

Wilkinson, L.J., *Eleanor de Montfort: A Rebel Countess in Medieval England* (London, 2012).

Wilkinson, L.J., 'Pawn and political player: observations on the life of a thirteenth-century countess', *Historical Research*, 73 (2000), 105–23.

Wilkinson, L.J., 'Reformers and royalists: aristocratic women in politics, 1258–1267', in *Baronial Reform and Revolution in England, 1258–1267*, ed. A. Jobson (Woodbridge, 2016), 152–66.

Wilkinson, L.J., *Women in Thirteenth-Century Lincolnshire* (Woodbridge, 2007).

Williams, D.T., 'Simon de Montfort and his adherents', in *England in the Thirteenth Century*, ed. W.M. Ormrod (Stamford, 1985), 166–77.

Williams, G.A., *Medieval London: From Commune to Capital* (London, 1963).

Wilshire, L.E., *Boniface of Savoy, Carthusian and Archbishop of Canterbury, 1207–1270* (Salzburg, 1977).

Wilson, C., 'A monument to St Edward the Confessor: Henry III's great chamber at Westminster and its paintings', in *Westminster: The Art, Architecture and Archaeology of the Royal Palace and Abbey, part 2*, eds. W.J. Rodwell and T.W.T. Tatton-Brown, *British Archaeological Association Conference Transactions*, 39 (2015), 40–65.

Wogan-Browne, J., Collette, C.P., Kowaleski, M., Mooney, L., Putter, A. and Trotter, D.A., eds., *Language and Culture in Medieval Britain: The French of England, c.1100–1500* (York, 2009).

Wright, G.S., 'A royal tomb program in the reign of St. Louis', *The Art Bulletin*, 56 (1974), 224–43.

Wright, G.S., 'The tomb of Saint Louis', *Journal of the Warburg and Courtauld Institutes*, 34 (1971), 65–82.

Young, C.R., *The Making of the Neville Family in England, 1166–1400* (Woodbridge, 1996).

# INDEX

Achard, Nicholas, 144–5, 165
Agatha, widow, punched below ear, 127, 132, 133
Agenais, Fr, 99, 101, 107
  promised to Henry, 83
  duke of Brittany to hold, 103
  settled on John of Brittany, 104
  passes to English crown, 533, 607, 622
Aguillon, Robert, steward, 170, 208, 320, 372, 469, 529, 579
  dismissed, 332
  returns as steward, 460
Aigueblanche, Peter de, bishop of Hereford (1240–68), 245, 247, 255, 402, 435, 527, 578
  insulted by town, 380
  seized by barons 1263, 259
  released, 278
Alexander III, king of Scots (1249–86), 38–9, 419, 516, 542, 558, 637
  and king's recovery of power 1261, 199, 225
  support 1264, 305,
  raises army to support Edward, 432
Alexander IV, pope (1254–61), 180–1
  refuses to send legate, 38–9
  abandons Sicilian project, 73, 74
  absolves Henry from oath, 210
Alfonso, king of Castile, 263, 289, 553
aliens, 501, 638
  Henry's favouritism, generosity, 1, 527, 631, 633
  at court, 504, 528–9
  populist issue, 17, 254, 272, 504
  Montfort and aliens, 191, 265, 302, 427
  statute banning aliens, 253, 267, 294, 374, 408, 454
  threat of invasion, 337
  councillors and officials to be natives, 340
  attacked in *Song of Lewes*, 412
  Edward promises to exclude, 431

*See also* castles; Lusignans; Poitevins; Savoyards
Almain, Henry of, son of Richard of Cornwall, 154, 187, 196, 253, 257, 261, 263, 266, 285, 292, 296, 298, 300, 309, 345, 355, 402, 472, 475, 481, 488, 494, 498, 507, 510, 511, 526, 529, 536–8, 541, 545, 565, 568, 602
  one of king's twelve 1258, 11
  break with Montfort, 287
  held hostage, 323, 334, 339, 356, 417, 418
  and crusade, 566, 597
  murder at Viterbo, 595–9
  burial, 607
  character, record, 598
Amesbury, Wilts, nunnery, 397, 525, 627–9
Amiens, Somme, Fr, 100, 292
  Henry and the cathedral, 295
  *See also* Mise of Amiens
Anjou, Charles of, 238, 283, 319, 596–8, 652 n.35
Arcy, Norman de, 406
Arcy, Philip de, 146
Arden, Thomas of, 365
Argentan, Giles de, 215, 282, 324, 331, 333, 349, 361, 373, 428, 431, 439, 475, 484, 581, 586
  appointed steward, 22
  grievances, 22, n.91
  removed as steward, 179
  castellan of Windsor, 275
  captured at Evesham, 449
Ashby, Giles of, 583
Ashridge, Peter of, bailiff, 131, 133, 164
  evil reputation, 147–9
Astley, Andrew son of Thomas of, 484, 586, 588
Astley, Thomas of, 215, 258, 362, 363, 397, 475
  sheriff, keeper of the peace, 365
  killed at Evesham, 448

**Also in the Yale English Monarchs Series**

* Available in the U.S. from University of California Press